WORD
BIBLICAL
COMMENTARY

WORD

BIBLICAL

COMMENTARY

VOLUME 38A

Romans 1-8

JAMES D. G. DUNN

WORD BOOKS, PUBLISHER • DALLAS, TEXAS

Word Biblical Commentary
ROMANS 1–8
Copyright © 1988 by Word, Incorporated

Library of Congress Cataloging-in-Publication Data
Main entry under title:

Word biblical commentary.

  Includes bibliographies.
  1. Bible—Commentaries—Collected Works.
BS491.2.W67   220.7'7   81–71768
ISBN 0–8499–0237–1 (vol. 38A)   AACR2

Printed in the United States of America

The author's own translation of the Scripture text appears in italic type under the heading *Translation*.

89801239   AGF   987654321

To
Kingsley Barrett
and
Charles Cranfield
in whose steps it has been
my privilege to follow

EDITOR'S NOTE

For the convenience of the reader, page numbers for both volumes of this commentary on Romans (38A and 38B) are included in the Contents. Page numbers for the volume in hand are printed in boldface type, while those for the other volume are in lightface.

In addition, all of the front matter from Vol. 38A but the *Introduction* has been repeated in Vol. 38B so that the reader may have abbreviations, bibliography, and other pertinent information readily at hand.

Contents

Editorial Preface

The launching of the *Word Biblical Commentary* brings to fulfillment an enterprise of several years' planning. The publishers and the members of the editorial board met in 1977 to explore the possibility of a new commentary on the books of the Bible that would incorporate several distinctive features. Prospective readers of these volumes are entitled to know what such features were intended to be; whether the aims of the commentary have been fully achieved time alone will tell.

First, we have tried to cast a wide net to include as contributors a number of scholars from around the world who not only share our aims, but are in the main engaged in the ministry of teaching in university, college, and seminary. They represent a rich diversity of denominational allegiance. The broad stance of our contributors can rightly be called evangelical, and this term is to be understood in its positive, historic sense of a commitment to Scripture as divine revelation, and to the truth and power of the Christian gospel.

Then, the commentaries in our series are all commissioned and written for the purpose of inclusion in the *Word Biblical Commentary*. Unlike several of our distinguished counterparts in the field of commentary writing, there are no translated works, originally written in a non-English language. Also, our commentators were asked to prepare their own rendering of the original biblical text and to use those languages as the basis of their own comments and exegesis. What may be claimed as distinctive with this series is that it is based on the biblical languages, yet it seeks to make the technical and scholarly approach to a theological understanding of Scripture understandable by—and useful to—the fledgling student, the working minister, and colleagues in the guild of professional scholars and teachers as well.

Finally, a word must be said about the format of the series. The layout, in clearly defined sections, has been consciously devised to assist readers at different levels. Those wishing to learn about the textual witnesses on which the translation is offered are invited to consult the section headed *Notes*. If the readers' concern is with the state of modern scholarship on any given portion of Scripture, they should turn to the sections on *Bibliography* and *Form and Structure*. For a clear exposition of the passage's meaning and its relevance to the ongoing biblical revelation, the *Comment* and concluding *Explanation* are designed expressly to meet that need. There is therefore something for everyone who may pick up and use these volumes.

If these aims come anywhere near realization, the intention of the editors will have been met, and the labor of our team of contributors rewarded.

General Editors: *David A. Hubbard*
Glenn Barker †
Old Testament: *John D. W. Watts*
New Testament: *Ralph P. Martin*

Author's Preface

To write a commentary on the apostle Paul's letter to the Christians in Rome is a daunting undertaking. Paul's letters are such a dominant element in the New Testament, and so form a central part of the Christian scriptures, the constitutional documents of the Christian faith, which have exercised an influence quite literally beyond measure on Christian faith and life and on Western culture for more than nineteen centuries. And of all Paul's letters the one to Rome is the fullest and most carefully constructed statement of the Christian gospel and of the faith it called for during the foundation period of Christianity. To grapple with Romans is to engage in dialogue with one of the most creative theological minds of all time from the most creative period of Christian thought. Its influence on seminal theologians like Augustine, Luther and Barth has often been noted. And certainly it seems to have attracted more commentaries of note than any other NT or biblical writing. On not a few occasions during the writing of this commentary I have felt that even to attempt to follow in the train of commentators of the stature of Calvin, Godet, Sanday & Headlam, Lagrange, Michel, Kuss, Käsemann, Cranfield, Schlier and Wilckens is an act of foolhardiness at times bordering on impiety.

When the possibility of contributing Romans to the Word Biblical Commentary was put to me ten years ago I almost declined the invitation. I had of course worked with Romans frequently in the past, had indeed learnt the AV/KJV translation by heart as a young Christian, and relished the possibility of a sustained inquiry into this most systematic contribution of one whom I personally regard as the greatest theologian of all time. But with so many commentaries of high merit already on the shelves, why inflict another on fellow students of the NT? "Not another commentary on Romans!" was a frequent response when I described my research project in the early '80s. A sentiment that echoed my own first reaction. After such a wealth of scholarship has been expended on Romans over the years, is there anything fresh or original to be said? Would I not simply fall into one of the worst errors of the commentary genre—that of simply repeating the thoughts (in a different "mix") of those who had gone before?

On further reflection, however, I came to the conclusion that there were probably two areas where a further contribution would be possible and indeed desirable, two deficiencies which affected most previous work on Romans in greater or less degree. One was that in many large commentaries readers were frequently prevented from seeing the wood for the trees. With the commentator immersed in meticulously detailed word study, or complex debate regarding alternative renderings, or lengthy analyses of previous interpretations, the movement of Paul's thought was often lost sight of, and readers could find themselves very easily lost in a maze of detail. A letter written to be read out as a live exposition, and to be heard (and understood) at one or two sittings, had too often become as it were an antique corpse to be dissected over and over again in the mortuary of Christian curiosities so that its individual parts and limbs could be held up to mawkish display. Of course there had been several attempts to provide brief overview commentaries, some of them singularly successful on the whole, but mostly they had either skimmed the surface without penetrating into the depth of the argument, or they had succumbed to the second deficiency. This second weakness was the failure of most commentators to penetrate more fully into the historical context within which the letter was written and to which the letter was addressed, the life-setting in which it was first heard to speak as the word of God. The blinkers which for centuries have narrowed and distorted Christian appreciation of first-century Judaism also affected the view of Paul in relation to his ancestral faith, a relationship so very much at the heart of this letter in particular. But with the perspective-shifting work of E. P. Sanders fresh in mind it quickly became clear to me that a major attempt to set Paul's letter to Rome within "the new perspective on Paul" could and should be undertaken.

My first objective therefore was to grasp the movement of Paul's thought, the logic which led him from verse to verse and chapter to chapter. The format of the Word Commentary series lent itself to the endeavor in that I decided to use the final part of each section (*Explanation*) to write a running commentary on the letter as a whole. The first part of the commentary to be written therefore was the *Explanation* of chaps. 1–11, written over a period of two years with the aim of grasping the inner coherence of the text, the flow of Paul's argument and its theological logic within its historical context. I deliberately restricted my use of technical aids to concordances, lexica and the Kittel-Friedrich *Wörterbuch* (ET: *TDNT*), following up all cross-references and possible parallels of language and thought in other sources of the period, but allowing only a minimal reference to one or two recent commentaries, in the hope that the resultant exposition would be determined more by the questions arising from the text itself than by the history of its interpretation and the debates which have marked that history. All the while I tried to remember that the letter was written to be heard as it was read out in a congregation in Rome in the mid-first century A.D. All the while I was asking, What would this have meant to them? What understanding could Paul expect his readers to have of what he wrote? One of the immediate corollaries was an increased readiness to let ambiguities in the language stand as ambiguities, recognizing that Paul may have intended to be deliberately ambiguous, or at least that occasionally he so formulated his thought as to allow his readers/ hearers some freedom to hear it with different nuances. I hope that by such frequent reminders of original context I may enable the modern reader to experience again something of what the first readers experienced and to recover something at least of the freshness of the original text, or at least to share something of the excitement I experienced as the text became alive for me and I became aware of hidden currents and interconnections in arguments which had previously seemed obscure or confused.

A further corollary is that the *Explanation* sections can be read through as a continuous, nontechnical, indeed almost independent commentary. The nearest parallels would be the excellent commentaries of Schlatter and Barrett; and if I have achieved only part of the insight they have derived from the text I will be well pleased. It also means that the more extensive, detailed and technical treatments in the *Comment* sections may be regarded as equivalent to footnotes to the *Explanation*. It was a matter of some encouragement (and relief) to find that when I came to engage in the detailed interaction with other commentaries for the *Comment* sections it was only occasionally necessary to make a major revision of the *Explanation* section (3:9 in particular). For the most part the "feel" I had gained for the argument in that initial "running commentary" exercise I found to be sustained or sustainable in the face of other interpretations.

In consequence readers of this commentary who want to do more than consult specific verses or issues are advised to read first the *Explanation*, and only then to consult the *Comment*. The *Explanation* is not a mere summary of the main line of exposition, or of the findings of the *Comment* section. It is a full exposition of the argument in which I have attempted so far as possible to get inside the thought, to fill out the allusions and sentiments which Paul's words would have prompted in the minds of those who heard the letter first being read to them in Rome. Where the argument is tightly packed or the logic less clear to modern ears I have not hesitated to develop and explain it. Anyone reading lengthy sections of the commentary at a single sitting will inevitably find a degree of repetition—something which cannot be avoided since the more normal episodic use of a commentary requires that each section be sufficiently self-contained to be meaningful for such usage. Repetition of key points of Paul's argument, not always appreciated in their historical context and force, may be no bad thing anyway. But I am not sure that the balance between exposition in the *Explanation* and detailed analyses in the *Comment* has always been successful, though I have at least attempted to maintain a full cross-referencing in the *Comment* section, so that consultation of any verse in which a word or theme occurs should find a clear reference to where that word or theme is more fully treated. For briefer treatments and overviews the *Introductions* to lengthier passages and *Form and Structure* sections will usually be sufficient. I hope readers will find the format valuable and will welcome comments on the success or otherwise of my endeavors at this point.

With regard to my second objective, it should already be clear that for me the first task of exegesis is to penetrate as far as possible inside the historical context(s) of the author and of those for whom he wrote. So much of this involves the taken-for-granteds of both author and addressees. Where a modern reader is unaware of (or unsympathetic to) these shared assumptions and concerns it will be impossible to hear the text as the author intended it to be heard (and assumed it would be heard). In this case, a major part of that context is the self-understanding of Jews and Judaism in the first century and of Gentiles sympathetic to Judaism. Since most of Christian history and scholarship, regrettably, has been unsympathetic to that self-understanding, if not often downright hostile to it, a proper appreciation of Paul in his interaction with that self-understanding has been virtually impossible. But with the new perspective on Paul it has become possible to gain a more sensitively historical and theological appreciation of Paul's interaction with his own past, with his ancestral faith and with his fellow Jewish believers in

Messiah Jesus. It has been my second major objective to understand Romans within this new perspective. What this means in terms of the principal themes of Romans I begin to spell out in more detail in §5 of the *Introduction*. But perhaps I can convey here something of the excitement that the resulting insight brought to me as I began to work with the text both in its continuity of thought and in its detail, an excitement frequently renewed as fresh overtones and undertones came again and again from long-familiar passages.

The conviction began to grow in me that the reasons why Romans is such a powerful piece of writing, and why it has been so influential in Christian history, are one and the same. Because in it we see the emergence of Christianity from Judaism actually taking place; we see Paul the Pharisee, Paul the apostle, caught in the tension between his Jewishness and the impact of the risen Christ, between his inability to escape from the Jewish conviction of God's special choice of and revelation to Israel and the impact of a gospel that came to him independently of his Jewishness and despite his Pharisaic zeal for the law. We see Paul the Jew wrestling with the implications of his own and his converts' experience of grace and Paul the Christian wrestling with the implications of his Jewish heritage. We see in Romans Paul operating at the interface between Pharisaic Judaism and Christianity, and the transition from the one to the other in process of being worked out.

That, I would suggest, is why the letter has always struck a chord in those of subsequent generations conscious of a similar tension, caught at a similar point in time when long established traditions came under question from their own insight and experience, when well entrenched institutions and ideologies ceased to provide an answer to the sharpest of the new questions. That is probably why it exerted such a powerful influence on such as Augustine, Luther and Barth. Not for its literary or aesthetic appeal; not because they saw it as some dogmatic treatise; but because they too were at similar transition points in history (the disintegration of the western Roman Empire, the breakdown of medieval Christendom, the profound shock of the 1914–18 war on the old European empires and on the hitherto dominant liberal optimism). And in the Paul of Romans they recognized a kindred spirit whose wrestling with the tensions between his tradition and his experience spoke with word-of-God power to their own situation.

This also points up the importance of maintaining the right hermeneutical balance, why the attempt to get back into the historical context of the letter is so important. Because it is when Paul is most clearly seen within his own times and context, when the function of Romans is most clearly understood as Paul's thinking out the questions which deeply disturbed and profoundly affected him as a Jew who believed in Messiah Jesus as Lord, it is then that we come closest to Paul. And it is as we learn to hear him speaking to the reality of his own situation (not compiling an abstract treatise) that we begin to recognize that such periods of transition and tension are not new within the purposes of God, we begin to hear him speaking to our own situations of transition and of confusion in personal and national identity.

One of the most challenging lessons about Romans then is this: the more we see it as a dogmatic treatise which speaks the same message to every age, the less able are we to hear it in the way it was intended to be heard;

whereas when we hear it in all its historical relativity, then we may begin to appreciate the full power of its message to the great moments of crisis in world and ecclesiastical (as well as personal) history. To rediscover Romans as a statement sketched out on the interface between diverse traditions and visions and cultures is to liberate it to speak with fresh force to those concerned at the interface between Christianity and modern cultures, at the interface not least between Judaism and Christianity. To appreciate something of its power as word of God to the Christians in first-century Rome may be a vital first step to hearing it as God's word to equivalent situations today.

If there is anything in this, another volume would be required to work it out. I had envisaged a brief *Conclusion* at the end of the volume to develop these ideas, but that I fear would be inadequate since the temptation to read it without reference to the commentary itself would be unavoidable; and a lengthier treatment would extend still further an already too long manuscript. On reflection it seemed better to send forth the commentary as it is, as the indispensable exegetical foundation for such a theological endeavor. As part of an ongoing dialogue (I would never presume that anything I wrote was the last word on a subject) it would be better to let the commentary draw out the necessary and desired response of comment and criticism. If the foundation proves solid enough in the light of inspection by others, then would be the time to see what could be built on it; and if not, better to refrain from building on unsure foundations. It would be my hope, then, God willing, to return to the subject in a few years time, to attempt, in the light of any comment and criticism received in the interval, a fuller and integrated description of Paul's theology at the time he wrote Romans, and if possible to reflect on its continuing significance for today.

It should now be clear that, for all its length, the objectives of this commentary are limited. I have not attempted, for example, to provide a full-scale text critical analysis in the *Notes*. That is a task for others more proficient than I in the art, though of course I have not hesitated to make decisions regarding various disputed readings when that was necessary. Nor have I given full lists of witnesses for variants: the textual apparatus of Aland[26] and UBS will provide sufficient detail for almost all readers. In the *Notes* I have been content to provide brief explanations for the choice of readings where it is important, and sometimes to point out the significance of the fact that there are particular variants.

Nor have I attempted to provide a history of interpretation of the letter or of particular passages and themes. Here too I have had to leave that to others more proficient than I in the Fathers or medieval and reformation periods. The resulting deficiencies will be obvious to many, and I cannot but envy the depth of familiarity with the scholarship of previous centuries shown by commentators like Lagrange and Cranfield and acknowledge my indebtedness to the history of interpretation excurses particularly of Kuss and Wilckens. Many of the hermeneutical issues have remained little changed over the centuries, of course, but the issues thrown up by modern scholarship are complex and demanding enough, and to extend the hermeneutical dialogue back to earlier centuries would have lengthened to unmanageable proportions the commentary itself and the time needed to write it.

I cannot even claim to have engaged fully in dialogue with all the more recent scholarship on Romans. In fact my main discussion partners have come from the last hundred years, and I have sought out particularly those who have illuminated the historical context through their familiarity particularly with Jewish and Greco-Roman life and thought. But no doubt I have missed not a few contributions even from this more limited period which would have given me further insight into the text and its thought. And such is the flood of publications now on Romans itself that it has been almost impossible to keep up with everything which has been written. I do not therefore pretend to have scoured all periodicals and symposia, particularly of the more popular type, to ensure that the bibliographies are comprehensive. With the explosion of publishing made possible by modern techniques, scholarship will simply have to become more selective anyway or else drown in a flood of words. So too on disputed issues in the text I have attempted simply to be illustrative in the bibliographical references; anything more would merely have produced wearisome strings of names. No doubt here too there are many individual hypotheses and arguments to which I have done insufficient justice. And for that I can only beg indulgence in view of an already-too-well-packed manuscript.

May an author hope therefore that the value of his commentary will be judged in relation to the objectives he set in writing it, and not in terms of what he refrained from attempting.

Finally it is my pleasure and privilege to say thank you to all who have contributed to these volumes in various ways. First of all, there are those who have responded to lectures and papers which emerged as offshoots or "firstfruits," or who sent me offprints of their own contributions. The sequence of seminars on Paul at the annual meeting of the Society for New Testament Studies was particularly valuable. And my most helpful critics include the members of the postgraduate NT seminar here in Durham. I am particularly grateful to my own postgraduates, many of whose own work has overlapped or interacted with my own most fruitfully. The theses of Don Garlington and Paul Trebilco appear in the *Bibliography*. Others *in via* who have given me valuable help with bibliography (especially in periods when I was under great pressure from other university responsibilities) are David Goh, Dennis Stamps, Lung Kwong Lo, Ellen Christiansen, John Chow and Bruce Longenecker. The Inter-Library Loan service was indispensable and I am grateful to the Libraries of Cambridge and Tübingen, and particularly of Durham, of course, for their ready and efficient help. Above all, my wife Meta has had to bear an increasing burden of backup and support, particularly during the last year when the completion of the commentary seemed to consume more and more of my time. How can I thank her enough?

Two years after starting work on the commentary I had the honor of being appointed to the Chair of Divinity at Durham. The appropriateness of my project quickly became apparent to me. My predecessor, Kingsley Barrett, was appointed to his chair in 1957, the year in which his Black commentary on Romans was published. And his colleague, Charles Cranfield, was awarded his chair in between the publication of the two volumes of his International Critical Commentary on Romans. Clearly then a commentary on Romans is a kind of initiation test for Professors of New Testament at Durham. It is no little relief to have completed the task at last—only five years late! But have I passed?

January, 1988   JAMES D. G. DUNN
University of Durham

Note on bibliographical references and cross-references within the text:

(a) Commentaries as such have usually been cited by name alone and without page reference, the location of the reference being given by the verse commented on. Full details of the commentaries can be found in the *Commentary Bibliography* (p. xxxviii).

(b) In the case of other references, full details will be found either in the *Bibliography* section at the beginning of the passage; in the *General Bibliography*; or, in the case of chaps. 9–11, in the *Bibliography* at the beginning of chaps. 9–11.

(c) Cross-references usually take the form *see on 7:8, see on 14:2*, etc. Unless otherwise stated the reference is to the *Comment* on the passage indicated.

Abbreviations

A. General Abbreviations

Apoc.	Apocrypha	MT	Masoretic text (of the Old Testament)
c.	*circa*, about		
cent.	century	n.d.	no date
cf.	*confer*, compare	N.F.	*Neue Folge*, new series
chap(s).	chapter(s)	NS	New Series
DSS	Dead Sea Scrolls	NT	New Testament
ed.	edited by, editor(s)	OT	Old Testament
e.g	*exempli gratia*, for example	p., pp.	page, pages
et al.	*et alii*, and others	*pace*	with due respect to, but differing from
ET	English translation		
EV	English Versions of the Bible	par(s).	parallel(s)
		passim	elsewhere
f., ff.	following (verse or verses, pages, etc.)	q.v.	*quod vide*, which see
		sic	an unusual form exactly reproduced from the original
frag.	fragments		
FS	Festschrift, volume written in honor of		
		t.t.	technical term
hap. leg.	*hapax legomenon*, sole occurrence	*v.l.*	*varia lectio*, alternative reading
ibid.	*ibidem*, in the same place	viz.	*videlicet*, namely
i.e.	*id est*, that is	vol.	volume
LXX	Septuagint	v, vv	verse, verses
MS(S)	manuscript(s)		

For abbreviations of Greek MSS used in *Notes*, see Aland[26].

B. Abbreviations for Translations and Paraphrases

AV	Authorized Version = KJV	NIV	New International Version (1978)
GNB	Good News Bible = Today's English Version	NJB	New Jerusalem Bible (1985)
KJV	King James Version (1611) = AV	RSV	Revised Standard Version (NT 1946, OT 1952, Apoc. 1957)
Moffatt	*A New Translation of the Bible* (NT 1913)		
		RV	Revised Version (1881)
NEB	New English Bible (NT 1961; OT and Apoc. 1970)		

C. Abbreviations of Commonly Used Periodicals, Reference Works, and Serials

AB	Anchor Bible	AnBib	Analecta Biblica
ABR	*Australian Biblical Review*	*ANRW*	*Aufstieg und Niedergang des römische Welt*
Aland[26]	Nestle-Aland 26th ed. of NT Greek text (see under C.)		
		Aquila	Aquila's Greek translation of the Old Testament
ALBO	Analecta lovaniensia biblica et orientalia	ATANT	Abhandlungen zur Theologie des Alten und Neuen Testaments
ALW	*Archiv für Liturgiewissenschaft*		

BASOR	*Bulletin of the American Schools of Oriental Research*	ConB	Coniectanea biblica
BDB	E. Brown, S. R. Driver, and C. A. Briggs, *Hebrew and English Lexicon of the Old Testament* (Oxford: Clarendon, 1907)	ConNT	*Coniectanea neotestamentica*
		DBSup	*Dictionnaire de la Bible, Supplément*
		Dit., *Syll.*	W. Dittenberger, *Sylloge Inscriptionum Graecarum*, 4 vols. (1915–24)
BDF	F. Blass, A. Debrunner, and R. W. Funk, *A Greek Grammar of the New Testament* (University of Chicago/University of Cambridge, 1961)	DJD	Discoveries in the Judean Desert
BETL	Bibliotheca ephemeridum theologicarum lovaniensium	EB	Études bibliques
		EGT	The Expositor's Greek Testament
BEvT	Beiträge zur evangelischen Theologie	EKK	Evangelisch-katholischer Kommentar zum Neuen Testament
BGD	W. Bauer, *A Greek-English Lexicon of the New Testament and Other Early Christian Literature*, ET, ed. W. F. Arndt and F. W. Gingrich; 2d ed. rev. F. W. Gingrich and F. W. Danker (University of Chicago, 1979)	ER	*Epworth Review*
		ETL	*Ephemerides theologicae lovanienses*
		ETR	*Études théologiques et religieuses*
		EvQ	*Evangelical Quarterly*
		EvT	*Evangelische Theologie*
		EWNT	*Exegetisches Wörterbuch zum Neuen Testament*, ed. H. Balz and G. Schneider, 3 vols. (Stuttgart: Kohlhammer, 1980–83)
Bib	*Biblica*		
BJRL	*Bulletin of the John Rylands University Library of Manchester*		
		ExpT	*The Expository Times*
BJS	Brown Judaic Studies	FBBS	Facet Books, Biblical Series
BR	*Biblical Research*	FRLANT	Forschungen zur Religion und Literatur des Alten und Neuen Testaments
BTB	*Biblical Theology Bulletin*		
BWANT	Beiträge zur Wissenschaft vom Alten und Neuen Testament		
BZ	*Biblische Zeitschrift*	GLAJJ	M. Stern, *Greek and Latin Authors on Jews and Judaism*, 3 vols. (Jerusalem: Israel Academy of Sciences and Humanities, 1976, 1980, 1984)
BZNW	Beihefte zur ZNW		
CB	Clarendon Bible		
CBQ	*Catholic Biblical Quarterly*		
CBQMS	CBQ Monograph Series	HBT	*Horizons in Biblical Theology*
CIG	*Corpus inscriptionum graecarum* (1828–77)	HeyJ	*Heythrop Journal*
		HKNT	Handkommentar zum Neuen Testament
CIJ	*Corpus inscriptionum iudaicarum* (I, 1936; II, 1952)	HNT	Handbuch zum Neuen Testament
CIL	*Corpus inscriptionum latinarum* (1863–1909)	HR	E. Hatch and H. A. Redpath, *A Concordance to the Septuagint* 2 vols. (Oxford: Clarendon, 1897)
CJT	*Canadian Journal of Theology*		
CNT	Commentaire du Nouveau Testament		

HTKNT	Herders theologischer Kommentar zum Neuen Testament	LCL	Loeb Classical Library
		LD	Lectio divina
HTR	*Harvard Theological Review*	LPGL	G. W. H. Lampe, *Patristic Greek Lexicon* (Oxford: Clarendon, 1961)
HUCA	*Hebrew Union College Annual*		
		LR	*Lutheranische Rundschau*
IB	*Interpreter's Bible*	LSJ	H. G. Liddell and R. Scott, *A Greek-English Lexicon*, rev. H. S. Jones (Oxford: Clarendon, ⁹1940; with supplement, 1968)
ICC	International Critical Commentary		
IDB	G. A. Buttrick, ed., *Interpreter's Dictionary of the Bible* 4 vols. (Nashville: Abingdon, 1962)		
		LTK	*Lexikon für Theologie und Kirche*
		LumVie	*Lumière et Vie*
IDBSup	Supplementary volume to *IDB*		
IKZ	*Internationale Kirchliche Zeitschrift*	MAMA	*Monumenta Asiae Minoris Antiqua, 6 vols. (1928–39)*
Int	*Interpretation*	MM	J. H. Moulton and G. Milligan, *The Vocabulary of the Greek Testament* (London: Hodder, 1930)
ITQ	*Irish Theological Quarterly*		
JAAR	*Journal of the American Academy of Religion*		
		MNTC	Moffatt NT Commentary
JAC	Jahrbuch für Antike und Christentum	MThS	Münchener Theologische Studien
JBC	R. E. Brown, et al. eds., *The Jerome Biblical Commentary*	MTZ	*Münchener theologische Zeitschrift*
JBL	*Journal of Biblical Literature*		
JBR	*Journal of Bible and Religion*	NCB	New Century Bible (new ed.)
JES	*Journal of Ecumenical Studies*		
JETS	*Journal of the Evangelical Theological Society*	NDIEC	G. H. R. Horsley, *New Documents Illustrating Early Christianity* (North Ryde, Australia, 1981–)
JJS	*Journal of Jewish Studies*		
JLW	*Jahrbuch für Liturgiewissenschaft*		
		Neot	*Neotestamentica*
JR	*Journal of Religion*	NICNT	New International Commentary on the New Testament
JSJ	*Journal for the Study of Judaism in the Persian, Hellenistic and Roman Period*		
		NIDNTT	C. Brown, ed., *The New International Dictionary of New Testament Theology*, 3 vols. (Exeter: Paternoster, 1975–78)
JSNT	*Journal for the Study of the New Testament*		
JSNTSup	*JSNT Supplement Series*		
JSOT	*Journal for the Study of the Old Testament*	NovT	*Novum Testamentum*
		NovTSup	Supplement to *NovT*
JSS	*Journal of Semitic Studies*	NRT	*La nouvelle revue théologique*
JTC	*Journal for Theology and the Church*	NTAbh	Neutestamentliche Abhandlungen
JTS	*Journal of Theological Studies*	NTD	Das Neue Testament Deutsch
Jud	*Judaica*		
		NTF	Neutestamentliche Forschungen
KD	*Kerygma und Dogma*	NTS	*New Testament Studies*
KEK	H. A. W. Meyer, *Kritisch-exegetischer Kommentar über das Neue Testament*	NTTS	New Testament Tools and Studies

OBO	Orbis Bilicus et Orientalis
OCD	N. G. L. Hammond and H. H. Scullard, *Oxford Classical Dictionary* (Oxford: Clarendon, 1970)
OGI	W. Dittenberger, ed., *Orientis Graeci Inscriptiones Selectae* (Leipzig, 1903–5)
PCB	M. Black and H. H. Rowley, eds., *Peake's Commentary on the Bible* (London: Nelson, 1962)
PGM	K. Preisendanz, ed., *Papyri graecae magicae*, 2 vols. (Leipzig/Berlin, 1928, 1931)
PIBA	*Proceedings of the Irish Biblical Association*
P. Oxy.	Oxyrhynchus Papyri
RAC	*Reallexikon für Antike und Christentum*
RB	*Revue biblique*
RBén	*Revue bénédictine*
RelSRev	*Religious Studies Review*
RevScRel	*Revue des sciences religeuses*
RGG	*Religion in Geschichte und Gegenwart*
RHPR	*Revue d'histoire et de philosophie religieuses*
RHR	*Revue de l'histoire des religions*
RNT	Regensburger Neues Testament
RQ	*Revue de Qumrân*
RSPT	*Revue des sciences philosophiques et théologiques*
RSR	*Recherches de science religieuse*
RTL	*Revue théologique de Louvain*
RTR	*The Reformed Theological Review*
SANT	Studien zum Alten und Neuen Testament
SBL	Society of Biblical Literature
SBLASP	SBL Abstracts and Seminar Papers
SBLDS	SBL Dissertation Series
SBLMS	SBL Monograph Series
SBLSBS	SBL Sources for Biblical Study
SBLSCS	SBL Septuagint and Cognate Studies

SBLTT	SBL Texts and Translations
SBM	Stuttgarter biblische Monographien
SBS	Stuttgarter Bibelstudien
SBT	Studies in Biblical Theology
ScEc	*Sciences Ecclesiastiques*
SE	*Studia Evangelica I, II, III* (= TU 73 [1959], 87 [1964], 88 [1964], etc.)
SEÅ	*Svensk exegetisk årsbok*
SH	W. Sanday and A. C. Headlam, *Romans*, ICC (1895; ⁵1902)
SJT	*Scottish Journal of Theology*
SJTOP	*SJT Occasional Papers*
SNT	Studien zum Neuen Testament
SNTSMS	Society for New Testament Studies Monograph Series
SPCIC	*Studiorum Paulinorum Congressus Internationalis Catholicus 1961*. AnBib 17–18 (Rome: Pontifical Institute, 1963)
Spicq	C. Spicq, *Notes de Lexicographie Néo-testamentaire*, OBO 22, Editions Universitaires Fribourg Suisse (1978)
SR	*Studies in Religion/Sciences religieuses*
ST	*Studia theologica*
Str-B	H. Strack and P. Billerbeck, *Kommentar zum Neuen Testament*, 4 vols. (Munich: Beck'sche, 1926–28)
SUNT	Studien zur Umwelt des Neuen Testaments
SVM	E. Schürer, *The History of the Jewish People in the Age of Jesus Christ*, rev. and ed. G. Vermes and F. Millar, vol. 1 (Edinburgh: T. & T. Clark, 1973)
SVMB	Vol. 2 of the same, with M. Black (1979)
SVMG	Vol. 3 of the same, with M. Goodman (1986, 1987)
SymBU	Symbolae Biblicae Upsalienses
Symm.	Symmachus' Greek translation of the Old Testament

TDNT	G. Kittel and G. Friedrich, eds., *Theological Dictionary of the New Testament*, 10 vols., ET (Grand Rapids: Eerdmans, 1964–76)	UBS	The United Bible Societies Greek Text (1966)
		UNT	Untersuchungen zum Neuen Testament
TDOT	G. J. Botterweck and H. Ringgren, eds., *Theological Dictionary of the Old Testament*, ET (Grand Rapids: Eerdmans, 1974–)	*USQR*	*Union Seminary Quarterly Review*
		VC	*Vigiliae christianae*
		VD	*Verbum domini*
		VF	*Verkündigung und Forschung*
Th	*Theology*	*VT*	*Vetus Testamentum*
ThBeit	*Theologische Beiträge*		
ThBl	*Theologische Blätter*	WBC	Word Biblical Commentary
Theod.	Theodotion's Greek translation of the Old Testament	WH	Westcott and Hort, *The New Testament in the Original Greek* (1881)
THKNT	Theologischer Handkommentar zum Neuen Testament	WMANT	Wissenschaftliche Monographien zum Alten und Neuen Testament
ThViat	*Theologia Viatorum*	*WTJ*	*Westminster Theological Journal*
TJT	*Toronto Journal of Theology*		
TLZ	*Theologische Literaturzeitung*	WUNT	Wissenschaftliche Untersuchungen zum Neuen Testament
TNTC	Tyndale New Testament Commentary		
TP	*Theologie und Philosophie*	ZAW	*Zeitschrift für die alttestamentliche Wissenschaft*
TQ	*Theologische Quartalschrift*		
TR	Textus Receptus (Oxford, 1873)	ZKT	*Zeitschrift für katholische Theologie*
TR	*Theologische Rundschau*	ZNW	*Zeitschrift für die neutestamentliche Wissenschaft*
TS	*Theological Studies*		
TSK	*Theologische Studien und Kritiken*	ZRGG	*Zeitschrift für Religions- und Geistesgeschichte*
TTZ	*Trierer theologische Zeitschrift*	ZTK	*Zeitschrift für Theologie und Kirche*
TU	Texte und Untersuchungen		
TynB	*Tyndale Bulletin*		
TZ	*Theologische Zeitschrift*		

D. Abbreviations for Books of the Bible with Apocrypha

OLD TESTAMENT

Gen	2 Chron	Dan
Exod	Ezra	Hos
Lev	Neh	Joel
Num	Esth	Amos
Deut	Job	Obad
Josh	Ps (Pss)	Jonah
Judg	Prov	Mic
Ruth	Eccl	Nah
*1 Sam	Cant	Hab
*2 Sam	Isa	Zeph
*1 Kgs	Jer	Hag
*2 Kgs	Lam	Zech
1 Chron	Ezek	Mal

NEW TESTAMENT

Matt	1 Tim
Mark	2 Tim
Luke	Titus
John	Philem
Acts	Heb
Rom	James
1 Cor	1 Pet
2 Cor	2 Pet
Gal	1 John
Eph	2 John
Phil	3 John
Col	Jude
1 Thess	Rev
2 Thess	

APOCRYPHA

Add Esth	Additions to Esther	2 Macc	2 Maccabees
Bar	Baruch	Pr Man	Prayer of Manasseh
Bel	Bel and the Dragon	Sir	Ecclesiasticus (Wisdom of
Ep Jer	Epistle of Jeremy		Jesus the son of Sirach)
1 Esdr	1 Esdras	S Th Ch	Song of the Three Children
2 Esdr	2 Esdras	Sus	Susanna
Jud	Judith	Tob	Tobit
1 Macc	1 Maccabees	Wisd Sol	Wisdom of Solomon

Texts used:

Biblia Hebraica Stuttgartensia. Ed. K. Elliger and W. Rudolph. Stuttgart: Deutsche Bibelgesellschaft, 1967/77, 1984.

Septuaginta. Ed. A. Rahlfs. 2 vols. Stuttgart: Württembergische Bibelanstalt, ^{7}1962.

Novum Testamentum Graece. Ed. E. Nestle, K. Aland et al. Stuttgart: Deutsche Bibelgesellschaft, ^{26}1979 = Aland^{26}

*Note: to avoid unnecessary repetition and possible confusion I have almost always cited 1 Sam, 2 Sam, 1 Kgs and 2 Kgs as above, rather than using the LXX titles, 1–4 Kingdoms, when referring to the Greek text.

E. Abbreviations of Other Early Jewish Literature (usually called OT Pseudepigrapha)

Adam and Eve	Life of Adam and Eve	*4 Ezra*	4 Ezra (late 1st cent. A.D.)
Apoc. Abr.	Apocalypse of Abraham (1st to 2nd cent. A.D.)	*Gk Ap. Ezra*	Greek Apocalypse of Ezra (2nd to 9th cent. A.D.)
Apoc. Adam	Apocalypse of Adam (1st to 4th cent. A.D.)	*Jos. As.*	Joseph and Asenath
2 Apoc. Bar.	Syriac Apocalypse of Baruch (early 2nd cent. A.D.)	*Jub.*	Jubilees
		LAB	*Liber Antiquitatum Biblicarum* = Ps. Philo
3 Apoc. Bar.	Greek Apocalypse of Baruch (1st to 3rd cent. A.D.)	*3 Macc.*	3 Maccabees
		4 Macc.	4 Maccabees
Apoc. Mos.	Apocalypse of Moses	*Mart. Isa.*	Martyrdom of Isaiah
Apoc. Elij.	Apocalypse of Elijah (1st to 4th cent. A.D.)	*Odes Sol.*	Odes of Solomon
		Pr. Jos.	Prayer of Joseph
Asc. Isa.	Ascension of Isaiah	Ps. Philo	Pseudo-Philo = *LAB*
As. Mos.	*Assumption of Moses* (see *T. Mos.*)	Ps. Phoc.	Pseudo-Phocylides
		Pss. Sol.	Psalms of Solomon
1 Enoch	Ethiopic Enoch (2nd cent. B.C. to 1st cent. A.D.)	*Sib. Or.*	Sibylline Oracles
		Sim. Enoch	Similitudes of Enoch (= *1 Enoch* 37–71)
2 Enoch	Slavonic Enoch (late 1st cent. A.D.)	*T. Abr.*	Testament of Abraham (1st to 2nd cent. A.D.)
3 Enoch	Hebrew Enoch (5th to 6th cent. A.D.)	*T. Adam*	Testament of Adam (2nd to 5th cent. A.D.)
Ep. Arist.	Epistle of Aristeas	*T. Ash.*	Testament of Asher (in *T. 12 Patr.*)

T. Ben.	Testament of Benjamin (in *T. 12 Patr.*)	*T. Levi*	Testament of Levi (in *T. 12 Patr.*)
T. Dan	Testament of Dan (in *T. 12 Patr.*)	*T. Mos.*	Testament of Moses (1st cent. A.D.) (= As. Mos.)
T. Gad	Testament of Gad (in *T. 12 Patr.*)	*T. Naph.*	Testament of Naphtali (in *T. 12 Patr.*)
T. Isaac	Testament of Isaac (2nd cent. A.D.)	*T. Reub.*	Testament of Reuben (in *T. 12 Patr.*)
T. Iss.	Testament of Issachar (in *T. 12 Patr.*)	*T. Sol.*	Testament of Solomon (1st to 3rd cent. A.D.)
T. Job	Testament of Job (1st cent. B.C. to 1st cent. A.D.)	*T. 12 Patr.*	Testaments of the Twelve Patriarchs
T. Jos.	Testament of Joseph (in *T. 12 Patr.*)	*T. Zeb.*	Testament of Zebulun (in *T. 12 Patr.*)
T. Jud.	Testament of Judah (in *T. 12 Patr.*)		

Texts used:

Apocalypsis Henochi Graece. Ed. M. Black. Leiden: Brill, 1970.

Fragmenta Pseudepigraphorum Quae Supersunt Graeca. Ed. A.-M. Denis. Leiden: Brill, 1970.

Septuaginta. Ed. A. Rahlfs (as APOCRYPHA). For *Pss. Sol.* and *3–4 Macc.*

The Testaments of the Twelve Patriarchs. Ed. M. de Jonge. Leiden: Brill, 1978.

The Apocrypha and Pseudepigrapha of the Old Testament. Ed. R. H. Charles. 2 vols. Oxford: Clarendon, 1913.

The Apocryphal Old Testament. Ed. H. F. D. Sparks. Oxford: Clarendon, 1984.

The Old Testament Pseudepigrapha. Ed. J. H. Charlesworth. 2 vols. London: Darton, 1983, 1985.

F. Abbreviations of Dead Sea Scrolls, Philo, and Josephus

DEAD SEA SCROLLS

CD	Cairo (Genizeh text of the) Damascus (Document)	1QIsa[a,b]	First, second copy of Isaiah from Qumran Cave 1
p	Pesher = interpretation, commentary	1QpHab	*Pesher on Habakkuk* from Qumran Cave 1
Q	Qumran	1QM	*Milḥāmāh* (*War Scroll*) from Qumran Cave 1
1Q, 2Q, 3Q, etc.	Numbered caves of Qumran yielding written material; followed by abbreviation of the book	1QS	*Serek hayyaḥad* (*Community Rule, Manual of Discipline*) from Qumran Cave 1
1QapGen	*Genesis Apocryphon* from Qumran cave 1	1QSa	Appendix A (*Rule of the Congregation*) to 1QS
1QH	*Hôdayôt* (*Thanksgiving Hymns*) from Qumran Cave 1	1QSb	Appendix B (*Blessings*) to 1QS

4QFlor	*Florilegium* (or	4QPrNab	Prayer of Nabonidus
	Eschatological Midrashim)		from Qumran Cave 4
	from Qumran Cave 4	4QTestim	*Testimonia* text from
4QMess^{ar}	Aramaic "Messianic" text		Qumran Cave 4
	from Qumran Cave 4	11QMelch	*Melchizedek* text from
4QPat	*Patriarchal Blessings* from		Qumran Cave 11
	Qumran Cave 4	11QTemple	*Temple Scroll*, probably
4QpNah	*Pesher on Nahum* from		from Qumran Cave 11
	Qumran Cave 4	11QtgJob	*Targum of Job* from
4QpPs37	*Pesher on Psalm 37* from		Qumran Cave 11
	Qumran Cave 4		

PHILO

Abr.	De Abrahamo	Mos.	De Vita Mosis
Agr.	De Agricultura	Mut.	De Mutatione Nominum
Cher.	De Cherubim	Opif.	De Opificio Mundi
Conf.	De Confusione Linguarum	Plant.	De Plantatione
Cong.	De Congressu quaerendae	Post.	De Posteritate Caini
	Eruditionis gratia	Praem.	De Praemiis et Poenis
Decal.	De Decalogo	Prob.	Quod Omnis Probus Liber
Det.	Quod Deterius Potiori		sit
	Insidiari Soleat	Qu. Ex.	Quaestiones et Solutiones in
Ebr.	De Ebrietate		Exodum
Fuga	De Fuga et Inventione	Qu. Gen.	Quaestiones et Solutiones in
Gig.	De Gigantibus		Genesin
Heres	Quis Rerum Divinarum	Sac.	De Sacrificiis Abelis et
	Heres sit		Caini
Immut.	Quod Deus Immutabilis sit	Sobr.	De Sobrietate
Jos.	De Josepho	Som.	De Somniis
Leg. All.	Legum Allegoriae	Spec. Leg.	De Specialibus Legibus
Legat.	De Legatione ad Gaium	Virt.	De Virtutibus
Migr.	De Migratione Abrahami	Vit. Cont.	De Vita Contemplativa

JOSEPHUS

| Ant. | Jewish Antiquities | Life | Life |
| Ap. | Contra Apionem | War | The Jewish War |

Texts used:
Die Texte aus Qumran. Ed. E. Lohse. Darmstadt: Wissenschaftliche Buchgesell-
schaft, 1964, 1971.
The Temple Scroll. J. Maier. JSOTSupp 34. Sheffield: JSOT, 1985.
The Dead Sea Scrolls in English. Tr. G. Vermes. Harmondsworth: Penguin,
²1975.
The Essene Writings from Qumran. A. Dupont-Sommer. Oxford: Blackwell,
1961.
Josephus. Ed. H. St.J. Thackeray et al. LCL. 9 vols. London: Heinemann,
1926–65.
Philo. Ed. F. H. Colson et al. LCL. 12 vols. London: Heinemann, 1929–53.

G. Abbreviations of Early Christian Writings

Ap. Const.	Apostolic Constitutions	*Ign. Philad.*	Ignatius, *Letter to the Philadelphians*
Barn.	Barnabas		
1–2 Clem.	1–2 Clement	*Ign. Pol.*	Ignatius, *Letter to Polycarp*
Clement, *Strom.*	Clement of Alexandria, *Stromata*	*Ign. Rom.*	Ignatius, *Letter to the Romans*
Did.	Didache		
Diogn.	Diognetus	*Ign. Smyrn.*	Ignatius, *Letter to the Smyrneans*
Epiphanius,			
Haer.	Epiphanius, *Panarion seu adversus LXXX haereses*	*Ign. Trall.*	Ignatius, *Letter to the Trallians*
		Justin, *Apol.*	Justin Martyr, *Apology*
Eusebius, *HE*	Eusebius, *Historia Ecclesiastica*	Justin, *Dial.*	Justin Martyr, *Dialogue with Trypho*
Eusebius, *Praep. Evang.*	Eusebius, *Praeparatio Evangelica*	*Mart. Pol.*	Martyrdom of Polycarp
Herm. Man.	Hermas, *Mandates*	Origen, *Cont. Cels.*	Origen, *Contra Celsum*
Herm. Sim.	Hermas, *Similitudes*	Origen, *In Matth.*	Origen, *Commentary on Matthew*
Herm. Vis.	Hermas, *Visions*		
Ign. Eph.	Ignatius, *Letter to the Ephesians*	Pol. Phil.	Polycarp, *Letter to the Philippians*
Ign. Magn.	Ignatius, *Letter to the Magnesians*		

Texts used:

The Apostolic Fathers. K. Lake. LCL. 2 vols. London: Heinemann, 1912–13.
Patristic Evidence for Jewish-Christian Sects. NovTSupp 36. Leiden: Brill, 1973.
Eusebius: Ecclesiastical History. K. Lake and J. E. L. Oulton. LCL. 2 vols. London: Heinemann, 1926, 1932.
The Apocryphal New Testament. M. R. James. Oxford University, 1924.
New Testament Apocrypha. E. Hennecke. Ed. W. Schneemelcher. ET ed. R. M. Wilson. 2 vols. London: Lutterworth, 1963, 1965
For Gnostic and Nag Hammadi texts:
Gnosis. W. Foerster. ET ed. R. M. Wilson. 2 vols. Oxford: Clarendon, 1972, 1974.
The Nag Hammadi Library. Ed. J. M. Robinson. San Francisco: Harper and Row, 1977.

H. Rabbinic writings

b.	before a tractate indicates Babylonian Talmud	*Sipra*	Sipra
		Sipre	Sipre
Frg. Tg.	Fragmentary Targum	*Tg. Isa.*	Targum of Isaiah
m.	before a tractate indicates Mishnah	*Tg. Neof.*	Targum Neofiti
		Tg. Onq.	Targum Onqelos
Rab.	Rabbah, as in Gen. Rab. = Genesis Rabbah	*Tg. Ps.-J.*	Targum Pseudo-Jonathan
		Tg. Yer.	Targum Yerusalmi

Tractates

ᵓAbot	Pirqe ᵓAbot	Nazir	Nazir
ᶜArak.	ᶜArakin	Ned.	Nedarim
ᶜAbod. Zar.	ᶜAboda Zara	Neg.	Negaᶜim
B. Bat.	Baba Batra	Nez.	Neziqin
Bek.	Bekorot	Nid.	Niddah
Ber.	Berakot	Ohol.	Oholot
Beṣa	Beṣa (= Yom Ṭob)	ᶜOr.	ᶜOrla
Bik.	Bikkurim	Para	Para
B. Meṣ.	Baba Meṣᶜia	Peᵓa	Peᵓa
B. Qam.	Baba Qamma	Pesaḥ.	Pesaḥim
Dem.	Demai	Qinnim	Qinnim
ᶜEd.	ᶜEduyyot	Qidd.	Qiddušin
ᶜErub.	ᶜErubin	Qod.	Qodašin
Giṭ	Giṭṭin	Roš Haš.	Roš Haššana
Ḥag.	Ḥagiga	Sanh.	Sanhedrin
Ḥal.	Ḥalla	Šabb.	Šabbat
Hor.	Horayot	Šeb.	Šebiᶜit
Ḥul.	Ḥullin	Šebu.	Šebuᶜot
Kelim	Kelim	Šeqal.	Šeqalim
Ker.	Keritot	Soṭa	Soṭa
Ketub.	Ketubot	Sukk.	Sukka
Kil.	Kilᵓayim	Taᶜan.	Taᶜanit
Maᶜaś.	Maᶜaśerot	Tamid	Tamid
Mak.	Makkot	Tem.	Temura
Makš.	Makširin (= Mašqin)	Ter.	Terumot
Maᶜas Š.	Maᶜaser Šeni	Ṭohar	Ṭoharot
Meg.	Megilla	T. Yom.	Tebul Yom
Meᶜil.	Meᶜila	ᶜUq.	ᶜUqṣin
Menaḥ.	Menaḥot	Yad.	Yadayim
Mid.	Middot	Yebam.	Yebamot
Miqw.	Miqwaᵓot	Yoma	Yoma (= Kippurim)
Moᶜed	Moᶜed	Zabim	Zabim
Moᶜed Qa.	Moᶜed Qa	Zebaḥ	Zebaḥim
Našim	Našim	Zer.	Zeraᶜim

Texts used:

The Mishnah. H. Danby. Oxford: Clarendon, 1933.

The Babylonian Talmud. I. Epstein. 34 vols. Soncino, 1935–52.

Midrash Rabbah. H. Freedman and M. Simon. 10 vols. Soncino, [2]1951.

The Targums of Onkelos and Jonathan ben Uzziel on the Pentateuch with the Fragments of the Jerusalem Targums I–II. J. W. Etheridge. London: Longmans, 1862–65.

Neophyti I: Targum Palestinense MS de la Bibliotheca Vaticana. A. Diez Macho. 5 vols. Madrid, 1968–78.

For other ancient classical texts such as Epictetus, Juvenal, Seneca, LCL was used; *GLAJJ* also includes many relevant excerpts.

General Bibliography

Alexander, P. S. "Rabbinic Judaism and the New Testament." *ZNW* 74 (1983) 237–46. **Allison, D. C.** "The Pauline Epistles and the Synoptic Gospels: The Pattern of the Parallels." *NTS* 28 (1982) 1–32. **Amir, Y.** "The Term Ἰουδαϊσμός: A Study in Jewish-Hellenistic Self-Identification." *Immanuel* 14 (1982) 34–41. **Aune, D.** *The New Testament in Its Literary Environment.* Philadelphia: Westminster, 1987. Chap. 6. **Aus, R. D.** "Paul's Travel Plans to Spain and the 'Full Number of the Gentiles' of Rom 11:25." *NovT* 21 (1979) 232–62. **Baeck, L.** "The Faith of Paul." *Judaism and Christianity.* New York: Harper, 1966. 139–68. **Baird, W.** "On Reading Romans Today." *Int* 34 (1980) 45–58. **Banks, R.** *Paul's Idea of Community.* Exeter: Paternoster, 1980. **Barrett, C. K.** *From First Adam to Last.* London: Black, 1962. **Barth, M.** "Was Paul an Anti-Semite?" *JES* 5 (1968) 78–104. ———. *Justification: Pauline Texts Interpreted in the Light of the Old and New Testaments.* Grand Rapids: Eerdmans, 1971. **Bartsch, H.-W.** "Die antisemitischen Gegner des Paulus im Römerbrief." In *Antijudaismus im Neuen Testament.* Ed. W. Eckert, et al. Munich: Kaiser, 1967. 27–43. ———. "The Concept of Faith in Paul's Letter to the Romans." *BR* 13 (1968) 41–53. ———. "Die Empfänger des Römerbriefes." *ST* 25 (1971) 81–89. **Bassler, J. M.** *Divine Impartiality: Paul and a Theological Axiom.* SBLDS 59. Chico: Scholars Press, 1982. **Baumgarten, J.** *Paulus und die Apokalyptik.* WMANT 44. Neukirchen: Neukirchener Verlag, 1975. **Baur, F. C.** *Paul.* 2 vols. London: Williams & Norgate, 1873, 1875. **Beare, F. W.** *St Paul and His Letters.* Nashville: Abingdon, 1962. **Beck, N. A.** *Mature Christianity: The Recognition and Repudiation of the Anti-Jewish Polemic of the New Testament.* London: Associated University Presses, 1985. 59–72. **Beker, J. C.** *Paul the Apostle.* Philadelphia: Fortress, 1980. ———. "The Faithfulness of God and the Priority of Israel in Paul's Letter to the Romans." *HTR* 79 (1986) = *Christians Among Jews and Greeks.* FS K. Stendahl, ed. G. W. E. Nickelsburg and G. W. MacRae. Philadelphia: Fortress, 1986. 10–16. **Benoit, P.** *Jesus and the Gospel.* Vol. 2. London: Darton, 1974. **Berger, K.** "Zum traditionsgeschichtlichen Hintergrund christologischer Hoheitstitel." *NTS* 17 (1970–71) 391–425. **Betz, H. D.**, ed. *Plutarch's Theological Writings and Early Christian Literature.* Leiden: Brill, 1975. ———, ed. *Plutarch's Ethical Writings and Early Christian Literature.* Leiden: Brill, 1978. ———. *Galatians.* Hermeneia. Philadelphia: Fortress, 1979. **Bindemann, W.** *Die Hoffnung der Schöpfung: Römer 8:18–27 und die Frage einer Theologie der Befreiung von Mensch und Natur.* Neukirchen: Neukirchener Verlag, 1983. **Bjerkelund, C. J.** ΠΑΡΑΚΑΛΩ: *Form, Funktion und Sinn der parakalo-Sätze in den paulinischen Briefen.* Oslo: Universitetsforlaget, 1967. **Blank, J.** *Paulus: Von Jesus zum Urchristentum.* Munich: Kösel, 1982. **Bloch, R.** "Midrash." In *Approaches to Ancient Judaism: Theory and Practice,* ed. W. S. Green. BJS 1. Missoula: Scholars Press, 1978. 29–50. **Boers, H.** "The Problem of Jews and Gentiles in the Macro-structure of Romans." *Neot* 15 (1981) 1–11. **Bornkamm, G.** *Early Christian Experience.* London: SCM, 1969. ———. *Paul.* London: Hodder & Stoughton, 1971. ———. "Paulinische Anakoluthe." *Das Ende des Gesetzes.* Munich: Kaiser, 1952. 76–92. ———. "The Revelation of God's Wrath (Romans 1–3)." *Experience,* 47–70. ———. "The Letter to the Romans as Paul's Last Will and Testament." In Donfried, *Debate.* 17–31. **Bousset, W.** and **Gressmann, H.** *Die Religion des Judentums im späthellenistischen Zeitalter.* Tübingen: Mohr, [4]1966. **Brown, R. E.** and **Meier, J. P.** *Antioch and Rome.* London: Chapman, 1983. **Bruce, F. F.** *Paul: Apostle of the Free Spirit.* Exeter: Paternoster, 1977. **Bultmann, R.** *Der Stil der paulinischen Predigt und die kynisch-stoische Diatribe.* Göttingen: Vandenhoeck & Ruprecht, 1910, 1984. ———. *Theology of the New Testament.* 2 vols. London: SCM, 1952, 1955. ———. "Glossen im Römerbrief." *Exegetica.* Tübingen: Mohr, 1967. 278–84. **Buren, P. M. van.** *A Theology* *of the Jewish Christian Reality.* 2 vols. New York: Harper & Row, 1980, 1983. **Byrne, B.** *"Sons of God"—"Seed of Abraham."* AnBib 83. Rome: Biblical Institute, 1979. **Cambier, J.** "Romans." In *Introduction to the New Testament,* ed. A. Robert, et al. New York: Desclee, 1965. 447–470. ———. *L'Évangile de Dieu selon l'épître aux Romains.* Bruges: Brouwer, 1967. **Campbell, W. S.** "The Romans Debate." *JSNT* 10 (1981) 19–28. — ———. "Romans 3 as a Key to the Structure and Thought of the Letter." *NovT* 23 (1981) 22–40. ———. "The Freedom and Faithfulness of God in Relation to Israel." *JSNT* 13 (1981) 27–45. **Carcopino, J.** *Daily Life in Ancient Rome.* Yale University, 1940. **Cerfaux, L.** *Christ in the Theology of St Paul.* Freiburg: Herder, 1959. ———. *The Church in the Theology of St Paul.* Freiburg: Herder, 1959. ———. *The Christian in the Theology of St Paul.* London: Chapman, 1967. **Childs, B. S.** *The New Testament as Canon: An Introduction.* Philadelphia: Fortress, 1985. 243–63. **Collins, J. J.** *Between Athens and Jerusalem: Jewish Identity in the Hellenistic Diaspora.* New York: Crossroad, 1983. ———. "A Symbol of Otherness: Circumcision and Salvation in the First Century." In *"To See Ourselves As Others See Us": Christians, Jews, "Others" in Late Antiquity,* ed. J. Neusner and E. S. Frerichs. Chico: Scholars Press, 1985. 163–86. **Conzelmann, H.** *An Outline of the Theology of the New Testament.* London: SCM, 1969. ———. "Die Rechtfertigungslehre des Paulus: Theologie oder Anthropologie?" *Theologie als Schriftauslegung.* Munich: Kaiser, 1974. 191–206. **Cosgrove, C. H.** "Justification in Paul: A Linguistic and Theological Reflection." *JBL* 106 (1987) 653–70. **Cranfield, C. E. B.** *A Commentary on Romans 12–13.* SJTOP 12. Edinburgh: Oliver & Boyd, 1965. ———. *The Bible and Christian Life.* Edinburgh: T. & T. Clark, 1985. ———. "Some Comments on Professor J. D. G. Dunn's *Christology in the Making* with Special Reference to the Evidence of the Epistle to the Romans." In *The Glory of Christ in the New Testament: Studies in Memory of G. B. Caird,* ed. L. D. Hurst and N. T. Wright. Oxford: Clarendon, 1987. 267–80. **Cullmann, O.** *Christ and Time.* London: SCM, ³1962. ———. *The Christology of the New Testament.* London: SCM, 1959. **Cunningham, P. A.** *Jewish Apostle to the Gentiles: Paul As He Saw Himself.* Mystic: Twenty-third, 1986. **Dabelstein, R.** *Die Beurteilung der "Heiden" bei Paulus.* Frankfurt/Bern: Lang, 1981. **Dahl, N. A.** "The Missionary Theology in the Epistle to the Romans." *Studies.* 70–94. ———. "The Doctrine of Justification: Its Social Function and Implications." *Studies.* 95–120. ———. *Studies in Paul.* Minneapolis: Augsburg, 1977. **Dalman, G.** *The Words of Jesus.* Edinburgh: T. & T. Clark, 1902. **Daube, D.** *Paul and Rabbinic Judaism.* London: Athlone, 1956. **Davies, W. D.** *Paul and Rabbinic Judaism.* London: SPCK/Philadelphia: Fortress, 1948; ²1955, ⁴1981. ———. "Paul and the People of Israel." *NTS* 16 (1969–70) 4–39. ———. *The Gospel and the Land: Early Christianity and Jewish Territorial Doctrine.* Los Angeles: University of California, 1974. ———. *Jewish and Pauline Studies.* London: SPCK; Philadelphia: Fortress, 1984. **Daxer, H.** *Römer 1.18–2.10 im Verhältnis zu spätjüdischen Lehrauffassung.* Naumburg: Pätz'sche, 1914. **Deidun, T. J.** *New Covenant Morality in Paul.* AnBib 89. Rome: Biblical Institute, 1981. **Deichgräber, R.** *Gotteshymnus und Christushymnus in der frühen Christenheit.* SUNT 5. Göttingen: Vandenhoeck & Ruprecht, 1967. 61–64. **Deissmann, A.** *Bible Studies.* Edinburgh: T. & T. Clark, 1901. ———. *Light from the Ancient East.* Grand Rapids: Baker, 1965. **Delling, G.** "Partizipiale Gottesprädikationen in den Briefen des Neuen Testaments." *ST* 17 (1963) 1–59. **Dibelius, M.** *From Tradition to Gospel.* London: Ivor Nicholson & Watson, 1934. ———. "Vier Worte des Römerbriefs, 5:5, 5:12, 8:10 and 11:30f." *SymBU* 3 (1944) 3–17. **Dodd, C. H.** *The Bible and the Greeks.* London: Hodder & Stoughton, 1935. ———. "The Law." *Bible.* 25–41. ———. *According to the Scriptures.* London: Nisbet, 1952. **Donfried, K. P.** "Justification and Last Judgment in Paul." *ZNW* 67 (1976) 90–110. ———, ed. *The Romans Debate.* Minneapolis: Augsburg, 1977. **Doty, W. G.** *Letters in Primitive Christianity.* Philadelphia: Fortress, 1973. **Dülmen, A. van.** *Die Theologie des Gesetzes bei Paulus.* SBM 5. Stuttgart: KBW, 1968. **Dunn, J. D. G.** "Paul's Understanding of the Death of Jesus." In *Reconciliation and Hope,* FS L. L. Morris, ed. R. J. Banks. Exeter: Paternoster, 1974. 125–41. Rev. as "Paul's

Understanding of the Death of Jesus as Sacrifice." In *Sacrifice and Redemption: Durham Essays in Theology*, ed. S. W. Sykes. Cambridge University, 1989. ———. *Jesus and the Spirit*. London: SCM, 1975. ———. *Unity and Diversity in the New Testament*. London: SCM, 1977. ———. *Christology in the Making*. London: SCM, 1980. ———. "The Incident at Antioch." *JSNT* 18 (1983) 3–57. ———. "The New Perspective on Paul." *BJRL* 65 (1983) 95–122. ———. "Works of the Law and the Curse of the Law (Galatians 3:10–14)." *NTS* 31 (1985) 523–42. ———. "Pharisees, Sinners and Jesus." In *The Social World of Formative Christianity and Judaism*. FS H. C. Kee, ed. P. Borgen, J. Neusner, et al. Philadelphia: Fortress, 1988. **Dupont, J.** *Gnosis: La connaissance religieuse dans les épîtres de Saint Paul*. Louvain: Nauwelaerts/Paris: Gabalda, 1949. ———. "Le problème de la structure littéraire de l'Épître aux Romains." *RB* 62 (1955) 365-97. **Eckstein, H.-J.** *Der Begriff Syneidesis bei Paulus*. WUNT 2.10. Tübingen: Mohr, 1983. **Eichholz, G.** *Die Theologie des Paulus im Umriss*. Neukirchen: Neukirchener Verlag, 1972. **Ellis, E. E.** *Paul's Use of the Old Testament*. Grand Rapids: Eerdmans, 1957. ———. "Exegetical Patterns in 1 Corinthians and Romans." *Prophecy and Hermeneutic in Early Christianity*. WUNT 18. Tübingen: Mohr/Grand Rapids: Eerdmans, 1978. 213–20. **Feuillet, A.** "Le plan salvifique de Dieu d'après l'Épître aux Romains." *RB* 57 (1950) 336–87, 489–529. **Fitzmyer, J. A.** "The Use of Explicit Old Testament Quotations in Qumran Literature and in the New Testament." *Essays on the Semitic Background of the New Testament*. London: Chapman, 1971. 3–58. ———. "'4Q Testimonia' and the New Testament." *Essays*. 59–89. **Friedrich, G.** *Die Verkündigung des Todes Jesu im Neuen Testament*. Neukirchen: Neukirchener Verlag, 1982. **Funk, R. W.** "The Apostolic Parousia: Form and Significance." In *Christian History and Interpretation*. FS. J. Knox Ed. W. R. Farmer et al. Cambridge University, 1967. 249–68. **Furnish, V. P.** *Theology and Ethics in Paul*. Nashville: Abingdon, 1968. ———. *The Love Command in the New Testament*. Nashville: Abingdon/London: SCM, 1973. ———. *The Moral Teaching of Paul*. Nashville: Abingdon, 1979. **Gager, J. G.** *The Origins of Anti-Semitism*. Oxford University, 1985. **Gale, H. M.** *The Use of Analogy in the Letters of Paul*. Philadelphia: Westminster, 1964. **Garlington, D.** *"The Obedience of Faith": A Pauline Phrase in Historical Context*. Ph.D. Diss., Durham University, 1987. **Gaston, L.** "Paul and the Torah." In *Antisemitism and the Foundations of Christianity*, ed. A. T. Davies. New York: Paulist Press, 1979. 48–71. = *Paul*. 15–34. ———. "Paul and the Law in Galatians 2–3." In *Anti-Judaism in Early Christianity*. Vol 1, *Paul and the Gospels*, ed. P. Richardson and D. Granskou. Wilfrid Laurier University, 1986. 37–57. = *Paul*. 64–79. ———. *Paul and the Torah*. Vancouver: University of British Columbia, 1987. ———. "For *All* the Believers: The Inclusion of Gentiles as the Ultimate Goal of Torah in Romans." *Paul*. 116–34. **Georgi, D.** *Die Geschichte der Kollekte des Paulus für Jerusalem*. Hamburg: Herbert Reich, 1965. **Goppelt, L.** *Jesus, Paul and Judaism*. New York: Harper, 1964. ———. *Theology of the New Testament*. Vol. 2. Grand Rapids: Eerdmans, 1982. **Grayston, K.** "'I Am Not Ashamed of the Gospel': Romans 1.16a and the Structure of the Epistle." *SE* 2:569–73. **Gundry, R. H.** *Sōma in Biblical Theology*. SNTSMS 29. Cambridge University, 1976. **Haacker, K.** "Exegetische Probleme des Römerbriefs." *NovT* 20 (1978) 1–21. **Haenchen, E.** *The Acts of the Apostles*. Oxford: Blackwell, 1971. **Hahn, F.** *Mission in the New Testament*. London: SCM, 1965. ———. *The Titles of Jesus in Christology* (1963). London: Lutterworth, 1969. ———. "Das Gesetzesverständnis im Römer- und Galaterbrief." *ZNW* 67 (1976) 29–63. ———. "The Confession of the One God in the New Testament." *HBT* 2 (1980) 69–84. **Hainz, J.** *Ekklesia, Strukturen paulinischer Gemeinde-Theologie und Gemeinde-Ordnung*. Regensburg: Pustet, 1972. **Halter, H.** *Taufe und Ethos: Paulinische Kriterien für das Proprium christlicher Moral*. Freiburg: Herder, 1977. **Hanson, A. T.** *The Wrath of the Lamb*. London: SPCK, 1957. ———. *Studies in Paul's Technique and Theology*. London: SPCK, 1974. ———. *The New Testament Interpretation of Scripture*. London: SPCK, 1980. ———. *The Image of the Invisible God*. London: SCM, 1982.

Hebert, G. "'Faithfulness' and 'Faith.'" *Th* 58 (1955) 373–79. **J. P. Heil.** *Romans—Paul's Letter of Hope.* AnBib 112. Rome: Biblical Institute Press, 1987. **Heilegenthal, R.** *Werke als Zeichen.* WUNT 2.9. Tübingen: Mohr, 1983. **Hengel, M.** *Die Zeloten.* Leiden: Brill, 1961. ———. *Judaism and Hellenism.* London: SCM, 1974. ———. *The Son of God.* London: SCM, 1976. **Herold, G.** *Zorn und Gerechtigkeit bei Paulus: Eine Untersuchung zu Röm 1:16–18.* Frankfurt/Bern: Lang, 1973. **Hill, D.** *Greek Words and Hebrew Meanings.* SNTSMS 5. Cambridge University, 1967. **Hock, R. F.** *The Social Context of Paul's Ministry: Tentmaking and Apostleship.* Philadelphia: Fortress, 1980. **Hofius, O.** "Das Gesetz des Mose und das Gesetz Christi." *ZTK* 80 (1983) 262–86. **Hort, F. J. A.** *Prolegomena to St Paul's Epistles to the Romans and the Ephesians.* London: Macmillan, 1895. **Hübner, H.** "Existentiale Interpretation der paulinischen 'Gerechtigkeit Gottes.'" *NTS* 21 (1974–75) 462–88. ———. *Law in Paul's Thought.* Edinburgh: T. & T. Clark, 1984. ———. "Paulusforschung seit 1945: Ein kritischer Literaturbericht." *ANRW* II. 25.4 (1987) 2699–2840. **Hultgren, A. J.** *Paul's Gospel and Mission.* Philadelphia: Fortress, 1985. **Jeremias, J.** *The Central Message of the New Testament.* London: SCM, 1965. ———. "Zur Gedankenführung in den paulinischen Briefen." *Abba.* Göttingen: Vandenhoeck & Ruprecht, 1966. 269–72. ———. "Chiasmus in den Paulusbriefen." *Abba.* 276–90. ———. *Jerusalem in the Time of Jesus.* London: SCM, 1969. ———. *New Testament Theology. I. The Proclamation of Jesus.* London: SCM, 1971. **Jewett, R.** *Paul's Anthropological Terms.* Leiden: Brill, 1971. ———. *Dating Paul's Life.* London: SCM, 1979. ———. "Major Impulses in the Theological Interpretation of Romans since Barth." *Int* 34 (1980) 17–31. ———. "Romans as an Ambassadorial Letter." *Int* 36 (1982) 5–20. ———. *Christian Tolerance: Paul's Message to the Modern Church.* Philadelphia: Westminster, 1982. ———. "The Law and the Coexistence of Jews and Gentiles in Romans." *Int* 39 (1985) 341–56. **Jones, F. S.** *"Freiheit" in den Briefen des Apostels Paulus.* Göttingen: Vandenhoeck & Ruprecht, 1987. **Judge, E. A.** "St Paul and Classical Society." *JAC* 15 (1972) 19–36. **Jüngel, R.** *Paulus und Jesus.* Tübingen: Mohr, ³1967. **Käsemann, E.** "'The Righteousness of God' in Paul." *New Testament Questions of Today.* London: SCM, 1969. 168–82. ———. "Paul and Israel." *New Testament Questions.* 183–87. ———. *Perspectives on Paul.* London: SCM, 1971. **Karris, R. J.** "Romans 14:1–15:13 and the Occasion of Romans." *CBQ* 25 (1973). Repr. in Donfried, *Romans Debate,* 75–99. **Kaye, B. N.** *The Thought Structure of Romans with Special Reference to Chapter 6.* Austen: Schola, 1979. **Keck, L. E.** *Paul and His Letters.* Phildelphia: Fortress, 1979. **Kennedy, G. A.** *New Testament Interpretation through Rhetorical Criticism.* University of North Carolina, 1984. **Kertelge, K.** *"Rechtfertigung" bei Paulus.* Münster: Aschendorff, 1967; ²1971. **Kettunen, M.** *Der Abfassungszweck des Römerbriefes.* Helsinki, 1979. **Kim, S.** *The Origin of Paul's Gospel.* WUNT 2.4. Tübingen: Mohr, 1981. **Klaiber, W.** *Rechtfertigung und Gemeinde: Eine Untersuchung zum paulinische Kirchenverständnis.* FRLANT 127. Göttingen: Vandenhoeck & Ruprecht, 1982. **Klein, G.** "Paul's Purpose in Writing the Epistle to the Romans" (1969). ET in Donfried, *Romans Debate,* 32–49. ———. "Romans, Letter to the." *IDBS,* 752–54. **Kleinknecht, K. T.** *Der leidende Gerechtfertigte.* WUNT 2.13. Tübingen: Mohr, 1984. **Knox, J.** *Chapters in a Life of Paul.* London: Black, 1954. **Knox, W. L.** *St Paul and the Church of Jerusalem.* Cambridge University, 1925. ———. *St Paul and the Church of the Gentiles.* Cambridge University, 1939. **Koester, H.** *Introduction to the New Testament.* Vol. 2. Philadelphia: Fortress, 1982. 138–42. **Kramer, W.** *Christ, Lord, Son of God* (1963). ET. London: SCM, 1966. **Kümmel, W. G.** *The Theology of the New Testament.* London: SCM, 1974. ———. *Introduction to the New Testament.* Rev. ed. London: SCM, 1975. 305–20. ———. "Die Botschaft des Römerbriefes." *TLZ* 99 (1974) 481–88. **Kuss, O.** *Auslegung und Verkündigung* 1. Regensburg: Pustet, 1963. ———. *Paulus: Die Rolle des Apostels in der theologischen Entwicklung der Urkirche.* Regensburg: Pustet, 1971. **Ladd, G. E.** "Paul and the Law." In *Soli Deo Gloria,* FS W. C. Robinson, ed. J. M. Richards. Richmond: John Knox, 1968. 50–67. = chap. 35 of Ladd, *A Theology of the New Testament.* London: Lutterworth,

1975. **Lampe, P.** *Die stadtrömischen Christen in den ersten beiden Jahrhunderten.* WUNT 2.18. Tübingen: Mohr, 1987. **Lapide, P.** and **Stuhlmacher, P.** *Paul: Rabbi and Apostle.* Minneapolis: Augsburg, 1984. **Leon, H. J.** *The Jews of Ancient Rome.* Philadelphia: Jewish Publication Society of America, 1960. **Leon-Dufour, X.** "Situation littéraire de Rom 5." *RSR* 51 (1963) 83–95. **Lightfoot, J. B.** "The Structure and Destination of the Epistle to the Romans." In *Biblical Essays.* London: Macmillan, 1893. 285–374. **Lindars, B.** *New Testament Apologetic.* London: SCM, 1961. **Ljungman, H.** *Pistis: A Study of Its Presuppositions and Its Meaning in Pauline Use.* Lund: Gleerup, 1964. **Lohmeyer, E.** *Probleme paulinischer Theologie.* Stuttgart, n.d. 33–74. **Lohse, E.** *Die Einheit des Neuen Testaments.* Göttingen: Vandenhoeck & Ruprecht, 1973. ———. *Die Vielfalt des Neuen Testaments.* Göttingen: Vandenhoeck & Ruprecht, 1982. **Longenecker, R. N.** *Paul: Apostle of Liberty.* New York: Harper & Row, 1964. **Lorenzi, L. de,** ed. *Battesimo e giustizia in Rom 6 e 8.* Rome: Abbayia S. Paolo, 1974. ———, ed. *The Law of the Spirit in Rom 7 and 8.* Rome: St Paul's Abbey, 1976. ———, ed. *Dimensions de la vie chrétienne.* Rome: Abbaye de S. Paul, 1979. **Luedemann, G.** *Paul, Apostle to the Gentiles: Studies in Chronology.* Philadelphia: Fortress, 1984. **Lührmann, D.** *Das Offenbarungsverständnis bei Paulus und in paulinischen Gemeinden.* WMANT 16. Neukirchen: Neukirchener Verlag, 1965. ———. *Glaube im frühen Christentum.* Gütersloh: Gütersloher Verlag, 1976. **Lütgert, W.** *Der Römerbrief als historisches Problem.* Gütersloh: Bertelsmann, 1913. **Luz, U.** *Das Geschichtsverständnis des Paulus.* Munich: Kaiser Verlag, 1968. ———. "Zum Aufbau von Röm 1–8." *TZ* 25 (1969) 161–81. ———, with **Smend, R.** *Gesetz.* Stuttgart: Kohlhammer, 1981. **Lyonnet, S.** "Note sur le plan de l'Épître aux Romains." *RSR* 39 (1951/52) 301–316. ———. *Quaestiones in Epistulam ad Romanos.* 2 vols. Roma: Pontificio Instituto Biblico, 1962, 1975. **Maccoby, H.** *The Mythmaker: Paul and the Invention of Christianity.* London: Weidenfeld & Nicolson, 1986. **MacMullen, R.** *Roman Social Relations 50 B.C. to A.D. 284.* Yale University, 1974. ———. *Paganism in the Roman Empire.* Yale University, 1981. **Manson, T. W.** "St Paul's Letter to the Romans—and Others." *Studies in the Gospels and Epistles.* Manchester University, 1962. Repr. in Donfried, *Romans Debate,* 1–16. **Manson, W.** "Notes on the Argument of Romans (chapters 1–8)." In *New Testament Essays in Memory of T. W. Manson,* ed. A. J. B. Higgins. Manchester University, 1959. 150–64. **Marquardt, F.-W.** *Die Juden im Römerbrief.* Theologische Studien 107. Zürich: TVZ, 1971. **Marxsen, W.** *Introduction to the New Testament.* Oxford: Blackwell, 1968. 92–109. **Mattern, L.** *Das Verständnis des Gerichtes bei Paulus.* Zürich/Stuttgart: Zwingli, 1966. **Meeks, W. A.** "Towards a Social Description of Pauline Christianity." In *Approaches to Ancient Judaism,* vol. 2, ed. W. S. Green. BJS 9. Chico: Scholars Press, 1980. 27–41. ———. *The First Urban Christians: The Social World of the Apostle Paul.* Yale University, 1983. ———. "Breaking Away: Three New Testament Pictures of Christianity's Separation from the Jewish Communities." In *"To See Ourselves As Others See Us": Christians, Jews, "Others" in Late Antiquity,* ed. J. Neusner and E. S. Frerichs. Chico: Scholars Press, 1985. 93–115. **Merk, O.** *Handeln aus Glauben: Die Motivierungen der paulinischen Ethik.* Marburg: Elwert, 1968. **Minde, H.-J. van der.** *Schrift und Tradition bei Paulus.* Munich/Paderborn/Wien: Schöningh, 1976. **Minear, P. S.** *The Obedience of Faith: The Purpose of Paul in the Epistle to the Romans.* London: SCM, 1971. **Mohrlang, R.** *Matthew and Paul: A Comparison of Ethical Perspectives.* SNTSMS 48. Cambridge University, 1984. **Montefiore, C.-G.** "The Genesis of the Religion of St. Paul." *Judaism and St Paul* (1914). Repr. New York: Arno, 1973. 1–129. **Moore, G. F.** *Judaism in the First Centuries of the Christian Era.* 3 vols. Harvard, 1927–30. **Morris, L.** "The Theme of Romans." In *Apostolic History and the Gospel,* FS F. F. Bruce, ed. W. W. Gasque et al. Exeter: Paternoster, 1970. 249–63. **Moule, C. F. D.** *An Idiom-Book of New Testament Greek.* Cambridge University, ²1959. ———. *The Origin of Christology.* Cambridge University, 1977. **Moulton, J. H.** *Grammar of New Testament Greek,* vols. 1, 2. Edinburgh: T. & T. Clark, 1906, 1929. **Moxnes, H.** "Honour and Righteousness in Romans." *JSNT* 32 (1988)

61–77. **Müller, C.** *Gottes Gerechtigkeit und Gottes Volk: Eine Untersuchung zu Römer 9–11.* FRLANT 86. Göttingen: Vandenhoeck & Ruprecht, 1964. **Müller, K.** *Anstoss und Gericht: Eine Studie zum jüdischen Hintergrund des paulinischen Skandalon-Begriffs.* SANT 19. Munich: Kösel, 1969. **Müller, U. B.** *Prophetie und Predigt im Neuen Testament.* SNT 10. Gütersloh: Gütersloher, 1975. **Munck, J.** *Paul and the Salvation of Mankind.* London: SCM, 1959. 196–209. **Mundle, W.** *Der Glaubensbegriff des Paulus.* Leipzig: Heinsius, 1932. **Murphy-O'Connor, J.**, ed. *Paul and Qumran.* London: Chapman, 1968. **Mussies, G.** *Dio Chrysostom and the New Testament.* London: Brill, 1972. **Mussner, F.** "Heil für Alle: Der Grundgedanke des Römerbriefes." *Kairos* 23 (1981) 207–214. ———. *Tractate on the Jews: The Significance of Judaism for Christian Faith.* London: SPCK; Philadelphia: Fortress, 1984. **Neirynck, F.** "Paul and the Sayings of Jesus." *L'Apôtre Paul: Personnalité, style et conception du ministère.* Ed. A. Vanhoye. Leuven University, 1986. 265–321. **Neusner, J.** *From Politics to Piety.* Englewood Cliffs, NJ: Prentice-Hall, 1973. ———. *Judaism: The Evidence of the Mishnah.* University of Chicago, 1981. **Newton, M.** *The Concept of Purity at Qumran and in the Letters of Paul.* SNTSMS 53. Cambridge University, 1985. **Nilsson, M. P.** *Geschichte der griechischen Religion.* Munich, 1950. **Noack, B.** "Current and Backwater in the Epistle to the Romans." *ST* 19 (1965) 155–66. **Norden, E.** *Agnostos Theos* (1913). Darmstadt, [4]1956. **O'Brien, P. T.** *Introductory Thanksgivings in the Letters of Paul.* NovTSup 49. Leiden: Brill, 1977. **Ortkemper, F. J.** *Leben aus dem Glauben: Christliche Grundhaltungen nach Römer 12–13.* Münster: Aschendorff, 1980. **Osten-Sacken, P. von der.** *Römer 8 als Beispiel paulinischer Soteriologie.* FRLANT 112. Göttingen: Vandenhoeck & Ruprecht, 1975. **Patte, D.** *Paul's Faith and the Power of the Gospel: A Structural Introduction to the Pauline Letters.* Philadelphia: Fortress, 1983. 232–96. **Paulsen, H.** *Überlieferung und Auslegung in Röm 8.* WMANT 43. Neukirchen: Neukirchener Verlag, 1974. **Penna, R.** "L'évolution de l'attitude de Paul envers les Juifs." *L'Apôtre Paul: Personnalité, style et conception du ministère.* Ed. A. Vanhoye. Leuven University, 1986. 390–421. **Perkins, P.** *Love Commands in the New Testament.* New York: Paulist Press, 1982. **Perrin, N.** *The New Testament: An Introduction.* New York: Harcourt, 1974. 106–114. **Piper, J.** *The Justification of God: An Exegetical and Theological Study of Romans 9:1–23.* Grand Rapids: Baker, 1983. **Pohlenz, M.** "Paulus und die Stoa." *ZNW* 42 (1949) 69–104. Repr. in *Das Paulusbild in der neueren deutschen Forschung,* ed. K. H. Rengstorf. Darmstadt: Wissenschaftliche Buchgesellschaft, 1969. 522–64. **Poland, F.** *Geschichte des griechischen Vereinswesens* (1909). Repr. Leipzig, 1967. **Porter, C. L.** "A New Paradigm for Reading Romans: Dialogue Between Christians and Jews." *Encounter* 39 (1978) 257–72. **Prat, F.** *The Theology of Saint Paul.* 2 vols. London: Burns & Oates, 1927. **Prümm, K.** "Zur Struktur des Römerbriefes." *ZKT* 72 (1950) 333-49. **Räisänen, H.** *Paul and the Law.* WUNT 29. Tübingen: Mohr, 1983. ———. *The Torah and Christ.* Helsinki: Finnish Exegetical Society, 1986. **Reicke, B.** "Paulus über das Gesetz." *TZ* 41 (1985) 237–57. **Reitzenstein, R.** *Hellenistic Mystery-Religions* (1910; [3]1927). Pittsburgh: Pickwick, 1978. **Rengstorf, K. H.** "Paulus und die älteste römische Christenheit." *SE* 2 (1964) 447–64. **Reumann, J.**, et al. *Righteousness in the New Testament.* Philadelphia: Fortress/New York: Paulist Press, 1982. **Reynolds, J.**, and **Tannenbaum, R.** *Jews and Godfearers at Aphrodisias.* Cambridge Philological Society Supp. 12. Cambridge, 1987. **Rhyne, C. T.** *Faith Establishes the Law.* SBLDS 55. Chico: Scholars Press, 1981. **Richardson, P.** *Israel in the Apostolic Church.* SNTSMS 10. Cambridge University, 1969. **Ridderbos, H.** *Paul: An Outline of his Theology.* Grand Rapids: Eerdmans, 1975. **Robinson, D. W. B.** "The Priesthood of Paul in the Gospel of Hope." In *Reconciliation and Hope,* FS L. L. Morris, ed. R. J. Banks. Exeter: Paternoster, 1974. 231–45. **Robinson, H. W.** *The Christian Doctrine of Man.* Edinburgh: T. & T. Clark, [3]1926. 104–136. **Robinson, J. A. T.** *The Body.* London: SCM, 1952. **Roller, O.** *Das Formular der paulinischen Briefe.* Stuttgart, 1933. **Rowland, C.** *The Open Heaven.* London: SPCK, 1982. **Russell, D. S.** *The Method and Message of Jewish Apocalyptic.* London: SCM, 1964. **Sahlin, H.** "Einige Textemendationen zum Römerbrief." *TZ*

9 (1953) 92–100. **Sanders, E. P.** *Paul and Palestinian Judaism.* London: SCM, 1977. ———. "On the Question of Fulfilling the Law in Paul and Rabbinic Judaism." In *Donum Gentilicium,* FS D. Daube, ed. C. K. Barrett et al. Oxford: Clarendon, 1978. 103–126. ———. "Paul's Attitude toward the Jewish People." *USQR* 33 (1978) 175– 87. (With "A Response" by K. Stendahl, 189–91.) ———. "Jesus, Paul, and Judaism." *ANRW* II.25.1 (1982) 390–450. ———. *Paul, the Law, and the Jewish People.* Philadelphia: Fortress, 1983. ———. *Jesus and Judaism.* London: SCM, 1985. **Sandmel, S.** *The Genius of Paul* (1958). Philadelphia: Fortress, 1979. **Schechter, S.** *Aspects of Rabbinic Theology* (1909). New York: Schocken, 1961. **Schelkle, K. H.** *Paulus.* Darmstadt: Wissenschaftliche Buchgesellschaft, 1981. **Schenke, H. M.** "Aporien im Römerbrief." *TLZ* 92 (1967) 882–88. **Schlier, H.** *Die Zeit der Kirche.* Freiburg: Herder, 1955, ⁵1972. ———. "Von den Juden. Röm 2:1–29." *Zeit.* 38–47. ———. *Grundzüge einer paulinischen Theologie.* Freiburg: Herder, 1978. **Schmithals, W.** *Der Römerbrief als historisches Problem.* Gütersloh: Gütersloher, 1975. ———. *Die theologische Anthropologie des Paulus: Auslegung von Röm 7.17–8.39.* Stuttgart: Kohlhammer, 1980. **Schnabel, E. J.** *Law and Wisdom from Ben Sira to Paul.* WUNT 2.16. Tübingen: Mohr, 1985. **Schoeps, H. J.** *Paul: The Theology of the Apostle in the Light of Jewish Religious History.* London: Lutterworth, 1961. **Schrage, W.** *Die konkreten Einzelgebote in der paulinischen Paränese.* Gütersloh: Gütersloher, 1961. **Schweitzer, A.** *The Mysticism of Paul the Apostle.* London: Black, ²1953. **Scroggs, R.** *The Last Adam: A Study in Pauline Anthropology.* Oxford: Blackwell, 1966. ———. "Paul as Rhetorician: Two Homilies in Romans 1–11." In *Jews, Greeks and Christians,* FS W. D. Davies, ed. R. Hamerton-Kelly et al. Leiden: Brill, 1976. 271–98. **Segundo, J. L.** *The Humanist Christology of Paul.* New York: Orbis; London: Sheed & Ward, 1986. **Selwyn, E. G.** *The First Epistle of St Peter.* London: Macmillan, 1947. 365–466. **Snodgrass, K.** "Spheres of Influence: A Possible Solution to the Problem of Paul and the Law." *JSNT* 32 (1988) 93–113. **Stanley, D. M.** *Christ's Resurrection in Pauline Soteriology.* AnBib 13. Rome: Pontifical Biblical Institute, 1961. 160–99. **Stendahl, K.** "The Apostle Paul and the Introspective Conscience of the West." *HTR* 56 (1963) 199–215. Repr. in *Paul,* 78–96. ———. *Paul among Jews and Gentiles.* London: SCM, 1977. **Stowers, S. K.** *The Diatribe and Paul's Letter to the Romans.* SBLDS 57. Chico: Scholars Press, 1981. **Strecker, G.** "Befreiung und Rechtfertigung: Zur Stellung der Rechtfertigungslehre in der Theologie des Paulus." *Eschaton und Historie.* Göttingen: Vandenhoeck & Ruprecht, 1979. 229–59. **Stuhlmacher, P.** *Gerechtigkeit Gottes bei Paulus.* FRLANT 87. Göttingen: Vandenhoeck & Ruprecht, 1966. ———. *Das paulinische Evangelium.* FRLANT 95. Göttingen: Vandenhoeck & Ruprecht, 1968. ———. *Versöhnung, Gesetz und Gerechtigkeit: Aufsätze zur biblischen Theologie.* Göttingen: Vandenhoeck & Ruprecht, 1981. ———. "Das Gesetz als Thema biblischer Theologie." *Versöhnung.* 136–65. ———. "Sühne oder Versöhnung?" In *Die Mitte des Neuen Testaments,* FS E. Schweizer, ed. U. Luz and H. Weder. Göttingen: Vandenhoeck & Ruprecht, 1983. 291–316. ———. "Jesustradition im Römerbrief?" *ThBeit* 14 (1983) 240– 50. ———. "Paul's Understanding of the Law in the Letter to the Romans." *SEÅ* 50 (1985) 87–104. **Suhl, A.** *Paulus und seine Briefe.* SNT 11. Gütersloh: Gütersloher, 1975. **Synofzik, E.** *Die Gerichts- und Vergeltungsaussagen bei Paulus.* Göttingen: Vandenhoeck & Ruprecht, 1977. **Theissen, G.** *The Social Setting of Pauline Christianity.* Edinburgh: T. & T. Clark, 1982. **Theobald, M.** *Die überströmende Gnade: Studien zu einem paulinischen Motivfeld.* Würzburg: Echter, 1982. **Thüsing, W.** *Per Christum in Deum: Das Verhältnis der Christozentrik zur Theozentrik.* Münster: Aschendorff, 1965; ³1986. **Thyen, H.** *Studien zur Sündenvergebung im Neuen Testament und seinem alttestamentlichen und jüdischen Voraussetzungen.* FRLANT 96. Göttingen: Vandenhoeck & Ruprecht, 1970. **Travis, S. H.** *Christ and the Judgment of God: Divine Retribution in the New Testament.* Basingstoke: Marshall, 1986. **Trebilco, P.** *Studies on Jewish Communities in Asia Minor.* Ph.D. Diss., Durham University, 1987. **Trench, R. C.** *Synonyms of the New Testament* (⁹1880). Repr. Grand Rapids: Eerdmans, 1953. **Trocmé, E.** "The Jews As Seen by

Paul and Luke." In *"To See Ourselves As Others See Us": Christians, Jews, "Others" in Late Antiquity,* ed. J. Neusner and E. S. Frerichs. Chico: Scholars Press, 1985. 145–61.**Vielhauer, P.** *Geschichte der urchristlichen Literatur.* Berlin: de Gruyter, 1975. 174–190. ———. "Paulus und das Alte Testament." *Oikodome: Aufsätze zum Neuen Testament* 2. Munich: Kaiser, 1979. 196–228. **Watson, F.** *Paul, Judaism and the Gentiles.* SNTSMS 56. Cambridge University, 1986. **Watson, N. M.** "Simplifying the Righteousness of God: A Critique of J. C. O'Neill's *Romans.*" *SJT* 30 (1977) 453–69.**Wegenast, K.** *Das Verständnis der Tradition bei Paulus und in den Deuteropaulinen.* WMANT 8. Neukirchen: Neukirchener Verlag, 1962. **Wengst, K.** *Christlogische Formeln und Lieder des Urchristentums.* Gütersloh: Gütersloher, 1972. **White, J. L.** *Studies in Ancient Letter Writing.* Semeia 22. Chico: Scholars Press, 1981. ———. "Saint Paul and the Apostolic Letter Tradition." *CBQ* 45 (1983) 433–44. **Whiteley, D. E. H.** *The Theology of St Paul.* Oxford: Blackwell, 1964. **Wiefel, W.** "The Jewish Community in Ancient Rome and the Origins of Roman Christianity." *Judaica* 26 (1970). ET in Donfried, *Romans Debate,* 100–119. **Wikenhauser, A.** *New Testament Introduction.* Freiburg: Herder, 1958. 398–411. **Wilckens, U.** *Rechtfertigung als Freiheit.* Paulusstudien. Neukirchen: Neukirchener Verlag, 1974. ———. "Über Abfassungszweck und Aufbau des Römerbriefes." *Rechtfertigung.* 110–70. ———. "Christologie und Anthropologie im Zusammenhang der paulinischen Rechtfertigungslehre." *ZNW* 67 (1976) 64–82. **Williams, S. K.** "The 'Righteousness of God' in Romans." *JBL* 99 (1980) 241–90. **Wright, N. T.** *The Messiah and the People of God.* D.Phil. Diss., Oxford University, 1980. **Wuellner, W.** "Paul's Rhetoric of Argumentation in Romans." *CBQ* 38 (1976). Repr. in Donfried, *Romans Debate,* 152–74. **Zahn, T.** *Introduction to the New Testament.* Edinburgh: T. & T. Clark, 1909. 1:352–438. **Zeller, D.** *Juden und Heiden in der Mission des Paulus: Studien zum Römerbrief.* Stuttgart: KBW, 1973. ———. "Der Zusammenhang von Gesetz und Sünde in Römerbrief: Kritischer Nachvollzug der Auslegung von Ulrich Wilckens." *TZ* 38 (1982) 193–212. **Ziesler, J. A.** *The Meaning of Righteousness in Paul.* SNTSMS 20. Cambridge University, 1972. ———. "Some Recent Works on the Letter to the Romans." *ER* 12 (1985) 96–101.

Commentary Bibliography

M. Luther. Lectures (1515–16). ET, ed. W. Pauck. London: SCM, 1961. **J. Calvin** (1540). ET Edinburgh: Oliver & Boyd, 1961. **J. A. Bengel** (1742). ET Edinburgh: T. & T. Clark, 1866. **J. J. Wettstein.** Ἡ Καινὴ Διαθήκη. Amsterdam, 1752. **F. Godet.** (1879). ET 2 vols. Edinburgh: T. & T. Clark, 1880–81. **E. H. Gifford.** London: Murray, 1886. **J. B. Lightfoot.** *Notes on the Epistles of St Paul.* London: Macmillan, 1895. **W. Sanday** and **A. C. Headlam.** ICC. Edinburgh: T. & T. Clark, 1895; [5] 1902. **J. Denney.** EGT. Vol. 2. London: Hodder & Stoughton, 1900. **H. Lietzmann.** HNT. Tübingen: Mohr, 1906; [4] 1933. **A. Jülicher.** In *Die Schriften des Neuen Testaments,* vol. 2. Göttingen: Vandenhoeck & Ruprecht, 1910; [3] 1917. **T. Zahn.** Leipzig, 1910; [3] 1925. **E. Kühl.** Leipzig: Quelle & Meyer, 1913. **K. Barth.** (1919; [6] 1929). ET Oxford University, 1933. **M.-J. Lagrange.** EB. Paris: Gabalda, [2] 1922; [6] 1950. **C. H. Dodd.** Moffatt. London: Hodder & Stoughton, 1932. **P. Althaus.** NTD 6. Göttingen: Vandenhoeck & Ruprecht, 1932; [10] 1966. **A. Schlatter.** *Gottes Gerechtigkeit.* Stuttgart: Calwer, 1935. **K. E. Kirk.** CB. Oxford: Clarendon, 1937. **E. Brunner.** (1938, 1956). ET London: Lutterworth, 1959. **E. Gaugler.** 2 vols. Zürich: Zwingli, 1945, [2] 1958; 1952. **E. F. Scott.** London: SCM, 1947. **A. Nygren.** (1951). ET London: SCM, 1952. **J. Knox.** IB 9 (1954). **W. Barclay.** Edinburgh: St Andrew, 1955. **V. Taylor.** London: Epworth, 1956. **K. Barth.** *A Shorter Commentary on Romans* (1956). ET London: SCM, 1959. **C. K. Barrett.** London: Black, 1957. **F. J. Leenhardt.** CNT (1957). ET London: Lutterworth, 1961. **O. Michel.** KEK. Göttingen: Vandenhoeck & Ruprecht, [11] 1957; [14] 1978. **O. Kuss.** 3 vols. Regensburg: Pustet, 1957, 1959, 1978. **J. Murray.** NICNT. 2 vols. Grand Rapids: Eerdmans, 1959, 1965. **T. W. Manson.** In *PCB* (1962) 940–53. **F. F. Bruce.** TNTC. London: Tyndale, 1963. **H. W. Schmidt.** THKNT. Berlin: Evangelische, 1963. **J. A. Fitzmyer.** In *JBC* (1968) 291–331. **B. M. Metzger.** *A Textual Commentary on the Greek New Testament.* London: UBS, 1971; corr. 1975. **M. Black.** NCB. London: Oliphants, 1973. **E. Käsemann.** HNT (1973). ET London: SCM, 1980. **J. C. O'Neill.** Harmondsworth: Penguin, 1975. **C. E. B. Cranfield.** ICC. 2 vols. Edinburgh: T. & T. Clark, 1975, 1979. **H. Schlier.** HTKNT. Freiburg: Herder, 1977. **U. Wilckens.** EKK. 3 vols. Zürich: Benziger/Neukirchen: Neukirchener Verlag, 1978, 1980, 1982. **J. A. T. Robinson.** *Wrestling with Romans.* London: SCM, 1979. **R. A. Harrisville.** Minneapolis: Augsburg, 1980. **W. Hendriksen.** 2 vols. Edinburgh: Banner of Truth, 1980, 1981. **R. Pesch.** Würzburg: Echter, 1983. **A. Maillot.** Paris: Le Centurion, 1984. **P. Achtemeier.** *Interpretation.* Atlanta: John Knox, 1985. **D. Zeller.** RNT. Regensburg: Pustet, 1985. **B. Byrne.** *Reckoning with Romans.* Wilmington: Glazier, 1986. **J. P. Heil.** *Paul's Letter to the Romans: A Reader-Response Commentary.* New York: Paulist Press, 1987.

Introduction

§1. THE AUTHOR:
Romans within the Context of His Life and Work
(including date and place of origin)

Bibliography

Bornkamm, G. *Paul.* Part One. **Bruce, F. F.** *Paul.* **Dibelius, M.** *Paul.* Rev. W. G. Kümmel. London: Longmans, 1953. **Dietzfelbinger, C.** *Die Berufung des Paulus als Ursprung seiner Theologie.* WMANT 58. Neukirchen: Neukirchener Verlag, 1985. **Dunn, J. D. G.** "The Relationship between Paul and Jerusalem According to Galatians 1 and 2." *NTS* 28 (1982) 461–78. ———. "'A Light to the Gentiles': The Significance of the Damascus Road Christophany for Paul." In *The Glory of Christ in the New Testament: Studies in Memory of G. B. Caird,* ed. L. D. Hurst and N. T. Wright. Oxford: Clarendon, 1987. 251–66. ———. "Pharisees." **Gaston, L.** "Paul and Jerusalem." In *From Jesus to Paul,* FS F. W. Beare, ed. P. Richardson and J. C. Hurd. Waterloo, Ontario: Wilfrid Laurier University, 1984. 61–72. **Hemer, C. J.** "Observations on Pauline Chronology." In *Pauline Studies,* FS F. F. Bruce, ed. D. A. Hagner and M. J. Harris. Exeter: Paternoster, 1980. 3–18. **Hübner, H.** "Paulusforschung." 2658–67. **Jewett, R.** *Dating.* **Knox, J.** *Life.* **Kraabel, A. T.** "The Roman Diaspora: Six Questionable Assumptions." *Essays in Honor of Yigael Yadin,* ed. G. Vermes and J. Neusner. *JJS* 33 (1982) 445–64. **Luck, U.** "Die Bekehrung des Paulus und das paulinische Evangelium." *ZNW* 76 (1985) 187–208. **Luedemann, G.** *Paul.* **Maccoby, H.** *Mythmaker.* **Nock, A. D.** *St. Paul.* Oxford: University Press, [2]1946. **Räisänen, H.** "Paul's Conversion and the Development of His View of the Law." *NTS* 33 (1987) 404–19. **Segal, A. F.** *Rebecca's Children: Judaism and Christianity in the Roman World.* Harvard University, 1986. 96–116. **Suhl, A.** *Paulus.*

No doubt is today entertained regarding the author of this letter (see, e.g., Cranfield, 1–2). He identifies himself with his first word, "Paul," and is clearly the one known more or less from the beginnings of Christianity simply as "the apostle Paul." As we shall see, there is some dispute about the date on which he wrote the letter, though not much about its place of origin. More important than statistics of date and place for our understanding of the letter, however, are the background to the letter within the life and life-work of Paul and the point in his life and life-work at which he wrote. Three elements are of particular importance, without which much within the letter will remain at best obscure, at worst inexplicable.

§1.1 Paul was *a Jew.* He was born and brought up a Jew. He never ceased to be a Jew. The point is sometimes disputed (most recently by Maccoby), but only by willfully ignoring or discounting the main bulk of the evidence. Paul's own self-testimony (11:1—"an Israelite, of the seed of Abraham, of the tribe of Benjamin"; also Phil 3:5) cannot be set aside without very good reason; and no such reasons have been forthcoming. There is also no reason to doubt the information provided by Acts that Paul had been born at Tarsus in Cilicia (Acts 22:3). But if so, we can draw out two implications from other data: (1) Paul calls himself a "Hebrew of the Hebrews" (Phil 3:5). Within the context of diaspora Judaism that must mean that Paul was brought up to be strongly conscious of and proud of his heritage as a member of the Jewish nation. (2) He was highly competent in Greek, even if his style is not the most elegant (see Cranfield, 26), and he makes effective use both of the diatribe style much used in the philosophical schools (see below §4.2.2) and of Stoic ideas (see, e.g., 1:28). So he must have been given a substantial Greek education in Tarsus (we cannot be more specific), though we should note Josephus' self-testimony that his (spoken) Greek was deficient, "for our people do not favour those persons who have mastered the speech of many nations, or who adorn their style with smoothness of diction . . . but they give credit for wisdom to those alone who have an exact knowledge of the law and who are capable of interpreting the meaning of the Holy Scriptures" (*Ant.* 20.264).

We should not assume that these two elements in Paul's make-up (Hebrew and Greek) were in fundamental conflict. Diaspora Jews were often held in high regard within the cities where they had settled (see, e.g., Kraabel and below §2.2.2), and the strength of their desire to maintain their ethnic identity was respected (with special arrangements permitted, very unusually, for the temple tax to be collected and transported to Jerusalem each year) (see, e.g., SVMG 3:118–19). So it was quite possible for a diaspora Jew to be a Roman citizen (as was the case with Paul, according to Acts 22:25), without ceasing to be proud of his nationality and heritage, since the former (Roman citizenship) was more a matter of convenience than of self-identity. Nevertheless, these two elements in his upbringing (Greek-speaking Jew) must be borne in mind when we read of Paul's sense of indebtedness to "both Greek and barbarian" and of his sense of mission "to Jew first and also to Greek" (1:14,16).

Still more to the point is the fact that Paul was trained as *a Pharisee* (Phil 3:5; also Acts 23:6 and 26:5), which must have meant a period of study under a Pharisaic teacher—almost certainly in Jerusalem, since Pharisees were not widely dispersed beyond Judea (so Acts 22:3). The Pharisees were not an undifferentiated group at that time, but a common characteristic seems to have been their concern for "exactness or precision or strictness" (ἀκρίβεια) in interpretation and observance of the law; on this both Josephus (*War* 1.110; 2.162; *Ant.* 17.41; *Life* 191) and Acts (22:3; 26:5) agree, and the evidence from the synoptic Gospels coheres (Mark 2:23–3:5; 7:1–13; see further Dunn, "Pharisees"). Another word which evidently describes characteristic (though not exclusively) Pharisaic concern and dedication to maintain the law is "zeal," which Paul claimed both for himself, before his conversion (Phil 3:6; also Acts 22:3), and for his fellow Jews (see further on 10:2). Among his fellow (younger) Pharisees, Paul seems to have been particularly "zealous for the ancestral traditions" (Gal 1:14), and evidently he saw the persecution of the infant Christian church as the inevitable outworking of that zeal (Phil 3:6). From his Pharisaic training no doubt came Paul's tremendous grasp of the Scriptures, not only the Torah, but also the prophets and the writings, which is put to such extensive use in this letter. He also shows knowledge of Jewish writings which circulated in the diaspora without attaining the status of "scripture" (particularly Wisd Sol). From his Pharisaic training too no doubt came his skill as an exegete, with not a few hermeneutical "tricks of the trade" evident in such passages as chaps. 4 and 5.

The basic point for our understanding of the letter, however, is that his Jewish and Pharisaic background became and remained an integral part of Paul. His self-identity as a Jew and his concern with the heritage of his people provide one side of the dialogue which continues throughout the whole letter, the warp which runs back and forward throughout the whole pattern.

§1.2 The other side of the dialogue began with Paul's *conversion,* sometime probably in the early 30s (Acts 9, 22, 26). Fundamental here for the self-perception which informs his writing is Paul's conviction that in his encounter with the risen Christ he had been summoned and appointed by God to take the gospel of God's Son to the Gentiles (1:1, 5; Gal 1:15–16). In fact, as is now often noted, Paul never speaks of his encounter with Christ as a conversion, only as a calling and commissioning (so, e.g., Knox, *Life,* 117; Munck, *Paul,* 11–35; Stendahl, *Paul,* 7–12; though Gager, *Origins,* 209, with some justification warns against posing an unnecessary dichotomy). How soon this conviction captured him is not entirely clear (see further Dunn, "Light," in critique of Kim, *Origin,* and also Dietzfelbinger, vol. 3; cf. Beker, *Paul,* 15–16; Räisänen, "Conversion"), but certainly at least from the council of Jerusalem onwards his ministry to the Gentiles was widely recognized (Gal 2:9) and he himself had no hesitation in calling himself "apostle to the Gentiles" (11:13). The point of importance is that this apostolic commissioning clearly became the all-important factor which dominated the whole of his evangelistic activity during the last 10–15 years of his life. The all-consuming nature of this evangelistic drive is sufficiently clear from such passages as 15:17–20 and 1 Cor 9:16, 19–27, and must have been a determinative factor in the framing and shaping of this letter. The point may be put thus: from his own perspective Paul was first an evangelist and missionary, and only secondarily a theologian. Or, to be more precise, his theology was not independent of but rather servant to his "grand passion"—to preach Christ to and among the Gentiles (1:13–15; Gal 1:16).

The dialogue, of course, arises out of the fact that this apostle to the Gentiles is precisely Paul the "Hebrew of the Hebrews" and zealous Pharisee—now converted, but still sharing many of his earlier concerns. The suggestion that in his conversion Paul totally abandoned all that constituted his previous identity and made a quantum leap into a wholly different pattern of religion (Sanders, *Paul*) is unnecessary and unjustified. More serious still, it cuts itself off from the possibility of reaching a proper exegesis of Romans and condemns its interpretation of Paul to confusion and contradiction. For as will soon become apparent in the exegesis, Paul is debating not with an alien system but with himself and his own past: the weft of his faith in Christ interweaves with the warp of his Jewishness. Only so can we understand the anguish of such passages as 7:21–24; 9:1–3; 10:1; and 11:1–2. "In accepting the Jew, Jesus, as the Messiah, Paul did not think in terms of moving into a new religion but of having found the final expression and intent of the Jewish tradition within which he himself had been born. . . . he would not have conceived of himself as having ceased to be a Jew (Rom 9:3–11:1) or having inaugurated a new religion" (W. D. Davies, "Paul and the People of Israel," NTS 24 [1977–78] 20).

§1.3 The third element in Paul's own history which is of importance for our treatment of the letter is the fact that Paul's missionary work roused opposition from fellow Jews, including, not least, fellow Jewish Christians. When this opposition began and the course it ran are matters we need not pursue here. Suffice it to say that we can divide Paul's missionary work into two phases in terms of his *relationship with Jerusalem* and the mother church there. The first was a period when, probably as a missionary of the church in Antioch, Paul looked to Jerusalem as the primary authority for his own missionary work. This period is marked by the degree (and I mean "degree") of submissiveness which Paul indicates in Gal 1–2 (particularly the language used in 1:16; 2:2, 3, 6, 10—see Dunn, "Relationship"). The climax of this period was the council at Jerusalem where he succeeded in winning the support of the "pillar apostles" in Jerusalem for his offer of the gospel to Gentiles without requiring circumcision (Gal 2:3, 6–9). But it would appear that soon after, this positive working relationship broke down over the incident at Antioch (Gal 2:11–14). There the issue was not over gentile Christians being circumcised, but over Jewish Christians retaining their Jewish identity by continuing to observe the laws laid upon the covenant people, particularly the food laws which were such a distinguishing mark of the Jews as a whole (see below §5.3 and on 14:2). For Peter and Barnabas and the other Jewish Christians this maintenance of Jewish identity and covenant faithfulness was perceived as a matter of principle; such "works of the law" were not at odds with faith in Christ (Gal 2:16; see Dunn, "New Perspective" and "Works of the Law"; and further on 3:20). But for Paul the principle of faith in Christ had to be taken more radically as relativizing and sidelining such distinctively Jewish practices as well; not only circumcision, but other such "works of the law" *were* at odds with faith in Christ, since they effectively added a further requirement as part of the "package" in gentile acceptance of the gospel.

We need not go into further detail, though it is worth drawing attention to the importance of understanding Galatians aright if Romans is to be properly understood in turn (cf. particularly Zeller, 12–13). Suffice it to note that Paul probably lost the argument at Antioch (as most now agree), and that in consequence he had to loosen his older ties with Antioch (and Barnabas) and Jerusalem, to become a good deal more independent as a missionary, making his bases in Corinth and Ephesus in turn (Acts 18:11; 19:8–10; see further Dunn, "Incident"). The change in attitude and relationship with Jerusalem in particular is clearly indicated by the more distancing language which he uses with regard to Jerusalem by the time he actually wrote Galatians (particularly 2:6—"those reputed to be pillars—what they once were is [now] a matter of indifference to me"; see again Dunn, "Relationship"; Gaston, "Jerusalem," tries to sketch out other points of difference between Paul and Jerusalem). In fact the relationship between Paul and the mother church seems to have become very strained. The polemic in such passages as Gal 1:6–9; 5:2–12; 2 Cor 11:4; 12–15; and Phil 3:2 was certainly against other preachers and "apostles of Christ," who were almost certainly Jewish-Christian missionaries from Palestine anxious to ensure that new believers in Messiah Jesus went the whole way in becoming full members of the people of God (by receiving circumcision and undertaking other such "works of the law"). And these polemical passages are among the fiercest ever written in inter-Christian dispute. Paul for his part insisted that the agreement of Gal 2:9 should be observed and that each apostle should stick to his own commission and sphere of work (2 Cor 10:13–16); hence the fierce resistance to encroachment on his territory. But he was also desperately keen to maintain a positive relation with Jerusalem, or at least a positive relation between the churches he had established and the mother church in Jerusalem. Consequently his second great priority in the period before he wrote Romans was to make a collection from the churches he had founded and take it to Jerusalem as a mark of gentile solidarity with Jew in the blessings of Messiah Jesus and in material things too (see further on 15:25).

An appreciation of this background is essential for an understanding of Paul's letter to Rome. The letter comes at what Paul clearly regards as the end of a major phase of his work (15:19, 23), a phase greatly marked and marred by that hostility between Paul and an important strand of Jewish Christianity stemming from Jerusalem. The trip to Jerusalem to deliver the collection would be for Paul the fruit and seal of his success both in winning so many Gentiles to faith but also in maintaining the unity of the whole Christian movement. Paul's hopes and fears on the matter are lucidly portrayed in the language of chap. 15: that his ministry in winning so many Gentiles would be acceptable to God (v 16) and that their token of fellowship would be acceptable to the saints in Jerusalem (v 31); but evidently he is more fearful regarding the latter than about the former. It is in this spirit of hope and fear that Paul writes his letter to Rome.

So the tensions in which Paul was caught become successively more complex—the Hellenized but devout Jew, the dedicated Pharisee converted to become the dedicated Christian apostle, the leader of a mission to Gentiles which caused sharp strains and disagreements with those who saw the movement in more traditional Jewish terms. A letter written at the time he did write and on the subject he chose to write about could not help but express these tensions in greater rather than less degree. And so we will find.

§1.4 Besides this question of the setting of the letter within the life and work of Paul, the more detailed questions of precise *date* and place of *origin* are of comparatively less importance, since little hangs on them for purposes of exegesis, except insofar as they illuminate the background of certain passages, particularly 13:6–7 and 14:1 ff. Suffice it to say that the letter must have been written sometime in the 50s A.D., probably in the middle 50s, and most probably late 55/early 56, or late 56/early 57 (so, e.g., Georgi, *Geschichte*, 95–96; Bornkamm, *Paul*, xii; Cranfield, 12–16; J. A. T. Robinson, *Redating the New Testament* [London: SCM, 1976] 55; Bruce, *Paul*, 324; Jewett, *Dating*; Koester, *Introduction*, 138; Zeller, 15; see also Hemer, 9–12). Others prefer early 58 (including SH, xiii, xxxvii; Michel, 27–28; Black, 20); others again, early 55 (including Barrett, 5, Haenchen, *Acts*, 67; Suhl, 249). The one major challenge to this consensus is that of Luedemann, *Paul*, who argues for 51/52 (or 54/55; Luedemann acknowledges his debt to Knox, who dated Romans in 53–54, *Life,* 86). The former dating, however, seems improbably early: (1) it assumes that the collection must have dominated Paul's epistolary concern from Gal 2:10 onwards, despite the evidence of Galatians itself (not to mention Rom 1:5 and 15:15–20); (2) it compresses the period of Paul's earlier missionary work and leaves a long period following a journey to Jerusalem in A.D. 52 unexplained—when did Paul reach Rome? and when was he put to death on this dating?; whereas (3) a date early in Nero's reign (54–68) makes good sense of the circumstances in Rome which seem to be reflected in the letter itself (so particularly 13:6–7; and see below §2.2.3).

As to place of origin, the key factor is the information provided by Paul himself to the effect that he was about to journey to Jerusalem (15:25). This matches with the report of Acts 20:3 that Paul spent three months in Greece; that would almost certainly mean Corinth, where his mission had had most success in Greece (Acts 18:1–18; 1–2 Cor). And it fits well with the other snippets of information available to us: Phoebe, deacon of the church at Cenchreae (16:1–2), eastern seaport of Corinth, would pass through Corinth to take ship for Rome from Corinth's western port; and Gaius and Erastus probably lived in Corinth (see on 16:23; on the issue of whether chap. 16 belonged originally to the letter, see chap. 16 *Introduction*). So Paul most probably wrote from Corinth; on this there is scarcely any dispute.

§2. THE RECIPIENTS:
The Origin and Character of the Christian Community in Rome

Bibliography

Benko, S. "Pagan Criticism of Christianity during the First Two Centuries AD." *ANRW* II.23.2 (1980) 1055–1118. **Brown, R. E.** *Rome.* 92–127. **Bruce, F. F.** "Christianity under Claudius." *BJRL* 44 (1962) 309–26. ———. *New Testament History.* New York: Doubleday, 1972. 295–99, 393–97. ———. *Paul.* 379–92. **Carcopino, J.** *Daily Life.* **Cohen, S. J. D.** "Conversion to Judaism in Historical Perspective: From Biblical Israel to Postbiblical Judaism." *Conservative Judaism* 36 (1983) 31–45. **Collins, J. J.** *Athens,* particularly 162–68. ———. "A Symbol of Otherness." **Daniel, J. L.** "Anti-Semitism in the Hellenistic Roman Period." *JBL* 98 (1979) 45–65. **Edmundson, G.** *The Church in Rome in the First Century.* London: Longmans, 1913. **Fahy, T.** "St Paul's Romans Were Jewish Converts." *ITQ* 26 (1959) 182–91. **Finn, T. M.** "The God-fearers Reconsidered." *CBQ* 47 (1985) 75–84. **Georgi, D.** *The Opponents of Paul in Second Corinthians* (1964). Philadelphia: Fortress, 1986. Chap. 2. **Harvey, A. E.** "Forty Strokes Save One: Social Aspects of Judaizing and Apostasy." In *Alternative Approaches to New Testament Study,* ed. A. E. Harvey. London: SPCK, 1985. 79–96. **Judge, E. A.,** and **G. S. R. Thomas.** "The Origin of the Church at Rome: A New Solution?" *RTR* 25 (1966) 81–93. **Knox, W. L.** *Jerusalem.* 252–61. **Kraabel, A. T.** "The Disappearance of the 'God-fearers.'" *Numen* 28 (1981) 113–26. **Lampe, P.** *Die stadtrömischen Christen.* **Leon, H. J.** *Jews.* **Momigliano, A.** *Claudius: The Emperor and His Achievement.* Oxford: Clarendon, 1934. **Nolland, J.** "Proselytism or Politics in Horace, Satires 1.4.138–43." *VC* 33 (1979) 347–55. **Overman, J. A.** "The God-Fearers: Some Neglected Features." *JSNT* 32 (1988) 17–26. **Penna, R.** "Les Juifs à Rome au temps de l'apôtre Paul."

NTS 28 (1982) 321–47. **Reynolds, J.,** and **R. Tannenbaum.** *Jews and Godfearers at Aphrodisias.* Cambridge Philological Society Supp. 12 (1987). **Schiffman, L. H.** "At the Crossroads: Tannaitic Perspectives on the Jewish-Christian Schism." In *Jewish and Christian Self-Definition.* Vol. 2. *Aspects of Judaism in the Graeco-Roman Period,* ed. E. P. Sanders et al. London: SCM, 1981. 115–56. **Schmithals, W.** *Römerbrief.* 69–91. **Siegert, F.** "Gottesfürchtige und Sympathisanten." *JSJ* 4 (1973) 109–64. **Smallwood, E. M.** *The Jews under Roman Rule.* Leiden: Brill, 1981. **Trebilco, P.** *Studies.* Chap. 7. **Wiefel, W.** "Jewish Community." 101–8.

If it is self-evidently necessary to set the letter to Rome within the context of its author's life, it is less clearly necessary on a priori grounds to set the letter to Rome against the background of the history of its recipients, the Christian community in Rome. Paul could, after all, have been writing without any thought whatsoever of the circumstances of the Christian groups in Rome, in which case exegesis could proceed without going into such matters. However, there are various indications within the letter itself that Paul had a fair idea of the character and composition of the Christian groups in Rome. For example, the personal notes such as we find in 6:17 and 7:1, and the assumption that the calumny against Paul would be well known (3:8). And if chap. 16 is accepted as part of the original letter (see chap. 16 *Introduction*), that would mean that Paul had a number of personal contacts in Rome; through these, as well as through other Christians traveling from Rome by way of Corinth, he must have had at least some idea of the situation in which the Roman Christians lived out their faith.

Moreover, two basic features of the letter provide a strong prima facie case for further clarification of the historical context of the recipients in Rome. One is the fact that Paul is clearly writing to Gentiles (contra Fahy's recent restatement of an older view). This is obvious from 11:13–32 and 15:7–12 and strongly implied in 1:6, 13 and 15:15–16. The other is the fact that the letter seems to be so dominated by the issue of Jew/Gentile relationships ("to Jew first and also to Greek"—see on 1:16), by questions of identity (who is a "Jew"?—2:25–29; who are the "elect" of God?—1:7; 8:33; 9:6–13; 11:5–7, 28–32), and by an understanding of the gospel as no longer limited to Jews as such (chaps. 2–5), but still with the Jews wholly in view (chaps. 9–11), in the hope that both Jew and Gentile can praise God together (15:8–12). The implication, at least, is that Paul was aware of the ethnic composition of the Christian groups in Rome and thought it necessary, through his letter, to provide counsel on these matters—not just practical questions like disagreements over dietary practices (14:1–15:6), but precisely in the matter of how gentile and Jewish Christians should perceive their relationship to each other (so particularly 11:17–24).

We have little hard evidence regarding the earliest Christian groups in Rome, but the little evidence we have and the wider circumstantial evidence greatly strengthens this preliminary conclusion.

§2.1 A strong Jewish community had become established in Rome, particularly as a result of the many Jewish captives brought back to Rome by Pompey in 62 B.C., most of whom were subsequently freed. Already in 59

B.C. Cicero's reference to the large crowd (of Jews) at the trial of Flaccus indicates their strength in numbers and possible influence (*Pro Flacco* 28.66; *GLAJJ* 1:196–97; a similar picture is probably given by Horace, *Sat.* 1.4.142–43—see Nolland, "Proselytism"). In the first half of the 40s they were granted exemption from Julius Caesar's decree to dissolve the *collegia* and permitted to retain various ancestral rights including the right of assembly (Josephus, *Ant.* 14.214–15; Suetonius, *Julius Caesar* 42.3), rights which seem to have been ratified by Augustus (Philo, *Legat.* 156–57, 313; Suetonius, *Augustus* 32.1; see Smallwood, 134–36). Augustus also made the concession that Jews would not be deprived if the monthly distribution of food fell on a sabbath (Philo, *Legat.* 158), indicating a sufficient number of poor Jews who were also Roman citizens (who alone were eligible for the dole; Smallwood, 136–37; see also Leon, 11). The numerical strength of the Jews in Rome during this period is also indicated by Josephus' report that more than 8,000 Roman Jews supported the embassy from Judea in 4 B.C., to petition against Archelaus (*War* 2.80–83; *Ant.* 17.299–303). In A.D. 19, under Tiberius, there was a large-scale expulsion of Jews from Rome, at least partly, it would appear, because Jewish customs were becoming too attractive to many including highborn Romans (Smallwood, 202–10; interpreting the reports of Josephus, *Ant.* 18.81–84; Tacitus, *Ann.* 2.85.4; Suetonius, *Tiberius* 36; Cassius Dio 57.18.5a; texts with commentary in *GLAJJ* 2:68–72, 112–13, 365). But Philo indicates that after the fall of Sejanus, in A.D. 31, Tiberius became much more favorably disposed towards the Jews, reaffirming their established rights (*Legat.* 159–61), and presumably allowing them to return to Rome in large numbers. Whatever the precise facts, Philo, writing after the disturbances in Alexandria in A.D. 38, was able to report that "the great section of Rome on the other side of the Tiber is occupied and inhabited by Jews, most of whom were Roman citizens emancipated" (*Legat.* 155). Finally at this point, we may note the report of Cassius Dio that by 41 the Jews of Rome had multiplied to such an extent that Claudius thought it necessary to withdraw their right of assembly (60.6.6—*GLAJJ* 2:367). Added to all this is the inscriptional evidence, chiefly from the Jewish catacombs in Rome, with their many thousands of tombs, which give us names of some ten to thirteen synagogues, all of which may have existed in the first century A.D. (Leon, 135–66; Wiefel, 105–6; Penna, 327–28; SVMG 3:95–98; on the evidence for the organization of the synagogues see further Penna, 328–30, and below §2.3.3). Reckoning all the data together, the best estimate of the number of Jews in Rome in the middle of the first century A.D. is about 40,000–50,000 (see particularly Leon, 135–36), most of them slaves and freedmen.

§2.2 Christianity in Rome probably emerged first within the Jewish community there. This is what we might have expected anyway in the case of a movement which began as a sect within the spectrum of first-century Judaism and whose first missionaries were all Jews. And this a priori plausibility is confirmed by such evidence as we have.

§2.2.1 There were strong links between Jerusalem and Rome, exemplified in the warm relationship between Herod Agrippa I and the imperial family, particularly Caligula and Claudius; the business travel of people like Prisca and Aquila (see on 16:3); the implication of Acts 28:21 that the Roman

Jews looked to maintain a correspondence link with the mother country; the movement of temple tax and pilgrim traffic; and the later testimony of regular visits by leading rabbis to Rome (Leon, 35–38; Brown, 96—though the evidence requires careful scrutiny). This fits well with the report of Acts 2:10 that Jews from Rome were among the first audience for the proclamation of Jesus' resurrection, and with the information that the Christian "Hellenists" in Jerusalem belonged to a "synagogue of the *libertini*" (Acts 6:9), which can hardly refer to other than Roman freedmen (the Jews enslaved under Pompey) and their descendants (SVMG 3:133; despite the doubts of Leon, 156–57). It is quite likely then that among the first Greek-speaking Jews to embrace faith in Messiah Jesus were Jews from Rome or having strong connections with Rome. Through such contacts and the normal travel of merchants and others to the imperial capital, the new faith would almost certainly be talked of in the synagogues of Rome within a few years of the beginnings in Jerusalem, and groups would have emerged within these synagogues who professed allegiance to this form of eschatological Judaism. Since Pompey's conquest of the East, the movement of oriental religions to the capital of the Empire was a feature quite often remarked upon by Roman writers. As Juvenal was to put it: "the Syrian Orontes has long since poured into the Tiber, bringing with it its language and customs . . ." (3.62–63; cf. Tacitus, *Ann.* 15.44.3). Paul, who began his missionary work from Antioch on the Orontes, would not have been the first (Jewish) Christian who saw Rome as an obvious goal and desirable field for preaching.

§**2.2.2** The pattern of early Christian evangelism was most probably focused, at least initially, within the synagogues (as most agree; see, e.g., those cited by Hultgren, *Gospel*, 149 n.47; those who question the Acts evidence on this point include Georgi, *Opponents*, 178 n.15; Hahn, *Mission*, 105 n.2; Sanders, *Law*, 186). This again is what we would expect in a movement which saw itself as a form of Judaism; where else should they share their beliefs? The evidence of Acts coheres completely (Acts 11:19–21; 13:5, 14; 14:1; 17:1, 10, 17; 18:4, 19, 26; 19:8). And the strong implication of 2 Cor 11:24 is that Paul maintained a practice of evangelizing (as apostle to the Gentiles) within a context of Jewish jurisdiction (synagogues), despite being subjected no less than five times to one of the severest punishments permitted to diaspora Jewish communities ("this most disgraceful penalty"—Josephus, *Ant.* 4.238; see further Harvey, "Forty Strokes Save One"). Equally important, such a strategy would be an excellent way of reaching out to Gentiles as well, since most synagogues seem to have had a number of interested or sympathetic Gentiles who linked themselves with the synagogue. The debate here is easily sidetracked into the issue of whether such Gentiles, who had taken on the observance of Jewish custom but stopped short of circumcision, were known by a particular name, "God-fearers" (in recent years disputed particularly by Kraabel). But there can be no disputing the fact that many Gentiles were attracted to Judaism and attached themselves to synagogue congregations with varying degrees of adherence. Josephus and Philo both speak in undoubtedly exaggerated terms of the considerable attractiveness of Jewish customs, including sabbath and food laws (Josephus, *Ap.* 2.123, 209–10, 280, 282; Philo, *Mos.* 2.17–20; see also on 14:2 and 14:5). Josephus indicates that in Syria substantial numbers of Gentiles had "judaized" and become "mixed up" with the Jews during the first century (*War* 2.462–63; 7.45). Archeological and inscriptional evidence from Asia Minor confirms that Jewish communities were often held in high regard within the cities where they had settled (see particularly Trebilco). And a string of Roman sources confirms that Judaism proved a considerable attraction to many non-Jews within Rome itself (e.g., Plutarch, *Cicero* 7.6; Juvenal 14.96–106; Cassius Dio 67.14.1–3; Suetonius, *Domitian* 12.2; though the extent to which we should envisage an active policy of proselytizing, as Horace, *Sat.* 1.4.142–43, is often assumed to indicate, is another question—see again Nolland, "Proselytism"; I remain almost wholly unpersuaded by Georgi's talk of a "Jewish mission" [*Opponents*, 83–151], but the subject requires fuller treatment than can be given here). Whether they were known as "God-fearers," or as we prefer, "God-worship-ers" (following Trebilco), matters little (Kraabel's opposition has been undermined by the discovery of the Aphrodisias inscription—see Reynolds and Tannenbaum, 48–66; see further particularly Siegert; Finn; *GLAJJ* 2:103–6; Collins, "Symbol," 179–85; *SVMG* 3:160–71). What does matter is that there were many God-worshiping Gentiles who attached themselves to Jewish synagogues. Already open to a new and different religion, but unwilling to go the whole way and become proselytes (the typical Greek would regard circumcision as disfiguring), they would be all the more open to a form of Judaism which did not require circumcision and which was less tied to Jewish ethnic identity.

Something of this in Rome itself is suggested by the comment of Ambro-siaster (fourth century) that Christian Jews passed on the gospel to the Romans in a Jewish context, including observance of the law (text in SH, xxv–xxvi, and Cranfield, 20), though Cranfield justifiably questions whether Ambrosiaster has any substantive historical information to the effect. Brown, however, cites the passage in support of his thesis that "the dominant Christianity at Rome had been shaped by the Jerusalem Christianity associated with James and Peter, and hence was a Christianity appreciative of Judaism and loyal to its customs" (110–11)—an interesting attempt to give some substance to the otherwise unsubstantiated claim that the churches in Rome were founded by Peter. Whether the evidence will sustain such a developed thesis or not, in the light of the other evidence available the most attractive hypothesis must be that the Christian groups in Rome emerged from within the Jewish community itself, made up, at least initially, of Jews and God-worshiping Gentiles (see also Schmithals) who found themselves attracted to faith in Messiah Jesus, and whose meetings in each others' homes would probably not, in the first instance, be thought of as opposed to the life and worship of the wider Jewish community. (The older, more extreme thesis of Baur in his ground-breaking work, that Paul wrote to the Roman Christians as *opponents* [*Paul*, 369], can certainly not be sustained.)

§2.2.3 The famous report of Suetonius, that Claudius "expelled Jews from Rome because of their constant disturbances at the instigation of Chrestus" (*Claudius* 25.4), also provides important confirmation. It is generally agreed that "Chrestus" must mean "Christ," and that the reference is therefore probably to disturbances among Jews concerning Jesus, that is, to disagreements between Jews who had accepted Jesus as Messiah (Jewish Christians) and Jews who rejected the Christian claims (e.g., Momigliano, 33; *GLAJJ* 2:114–16; Smallwood, 211; Brown, 100–101; Lampe, 6–7; for an alternative view see Benko, 1057–62). This almost certainly indicates a significant presence of Christian beliefs in Rome before the late 40s, and precisely within the Jewish synagogues, so that onlookers saw the dispute simply as an internal Jewish squabble (cf. Acts 18:15). Indeed, it would appear that the new beliefs had become sufficiently established within the Jewish community (and its penumbra of God-worshipers) to constitute something of a threat, so that by the time of Claudius' expulsion of the Jews from Rome any "honeymoon period" for the new movement was over, and considerable strains had emerged between, on the one hand, the Jews and gentile God-worshipers who professed faith in Messiah Jesus, and, on the other, the Jews (and gentile God-worshipers) who disputed the new movement's claim to be a legitimate expression of Jewish belief and praxis (cf. Acts 28:22).

When the expulsion actually took place is a matter of some dispute. Some relate it to the note of Cassius Dio 60.6.6, to which reference has already been made—that is, A.D. 41 (so Leon, 23–27; *GLAJJ* 2:116; Luedemann, *Paul*, 6–7). But Dio explicitly says that Claudius was unable to expel the Jews because of their numbers, and says nothing about disturbances within the Jewish community or caused by Jews. The later date of A.D. 49 is more likely in view of the otherwise dubious report by Orosius, *Adversus paganos* 7.6.15, of an expulsion in that year, which is perhaps supported by Suetonius, since his brief note seems to refer to an action taken by Claudius in the course of his reign (he succeeded Caligula in 41 itself), and by Acts 18:2 (the date 49 fits better with a recent [προσφάτως] arrival in Corinth "from Italy on account of Claudius' command that all Jews should leave Rome"; see further on 16:3). The best solution is probably to see two actions by Claudius, in 41 and 49: the first an early palliative ruling, short–lived and limited in effect; the second more deliberate and drastic after his patience had worn out (presumably the suspected treachery, and subsequent death, of his erstwhile friend Agrippa in the early 40s did not help—Josephus, *Ant.* 19.326–27, 338–50; Acts 12:21–23) and when he was more sure of himself (so Momigliano, 31–37; Bruce, "Claudius," 315; also *History*, 295–99; Jewett, *Dating*, 36–38; Smallwood, 210–16; Watson, *Paul*, 91–93). Though whether the latter action was as drastic as Luke suggests (the typically Lukan "all" of Acts 18:2) is a question posed by the silence of Josephus on the subject, leaving the possibility of an expulsion which aimed primarily to root out the troublemakers (cf. Lampe, 6–7).

§2.2.4 Without going into detail we can simply mention the other evidence which strengthens the conclusion that Christianity in Rome emerged from within the Jewish community in Rome. Prisca and Aquila are first introduced to us as Jews who had to leave Rome because of Claudius' expulsion (Acts 18:2). Since their conversion is not reported in Acts 18, as it surely would have been if Paul had converted them, we can assume they were already Christians before they left Rome—that is, Jewish Christians in Rome, believers in Messiah Jesus, but functioning within the Jewish community (see further on 16:3).

Again, Paul in writing to the Christian groups in Rome can evidently assume that knowledge of the OT in its Greek version would be well enough known. But knowledge of the OT within the ancient world was confined almost wholly to Jewish and Jewish-derived communities: the LXX is not known in Greco-Roman literary circles (cf. Collins, *Athens*, 4). Consequently to be able to assume such a knowledge of the scriptures as Paul does in Romans he would have to assume that his readership by and large had enjoyed a substantial link with the synagogues in Rome. We may compare *1 Clement* to similar effect (Lampe, 59–60).

A final point to note is that only in the latter years of Nero's reign (A.D. 64) can we detect an awareness that Christians had become a distinct entity (Tacitus, *Ann.* 15.44.2–5—*GLAJJ* 2:88–89; Suetonius, *Nero* 16.2); though Tacitus' language may well imply that he thought of the *Christiani* as a sect of the hateful Jews (Benko, 1064). The implication is that prior to that time the movement had been neither strong enough nor distinct enough to be marked out from a larger group of which they had previously been counted part. That larger group would, of course, have been the Jews. The inference gains some further weight from Epictetus 2.9.20–21, which, well into the latter half of the first century A.D., still seems to think of Christians (distinguished by baptism) as "acting the part" of Jews.

In short, it must be judged highly probable that the synagogues of Rome were the natural matrix for emerging Christianity in Rome, and that Paul either knew for a fact or could take it for granted that most of his gentile listeners in Rome had been either proselytes or God-worshipers. Christian groups may initially have emerged and functioned within the context of the broader life of the Jewish community without causing too much controversy. But by the late 40s the claims made by these groups, and presumably their evangelistic activity, were provoking considerable tension, so that we may envisage a growing tendency for the Christian groups with their increasing numbers of baptized Gentiles to function quite separately from the synagogues, though not yet so as to be clearly distinct from the synagogues in the eyes of the authorities (against Watson, *Paul*; I doubt whether Meeks's claim that "socially . . . the Pauline groups were never a sect of Judaism" ["Breaking Away," 106] can be stated as quite so general a truth, but it applies even less to the situation in Rome).

§2.3 An important feature of the historical context of the recipients of Paul's letter was *the ambiguous and vulnerable status* of the Jewish community and so also of those still identified with it.

§2.3.1 We have already noted the attractiveness which Judaism evidently exercised on quite a wide social range within Rome (§§2.1 and 2.2.2), something we should bear in mind since it is often overlooked (e.g., Smallwood, 123–24; SVMG 3:150). Nevertheless we do find considerable hostility towards the Jews in the Greco-Roman literature of the period—in part at least an expression of the deep suspicion of all foreign cults which we find among the Roman intelligentsia, and partly fueled, no doubt, by that same success of such cults in attracting adherents and converts. So, for example, Cicero speaks of this "barbaric superstition" inimical to all that is Roman (*Pro Flacco* 28.66–69); according to Seneca, "the customs of this accursed race have gained such influence that they are now received throughout the world. The vanquished have given laws to their victors" (*De Superstitione—GLAJJ* 1:431); Pliny the Elder designates the Jews as "a race remarkable for their contempt for the divine powers" (*Nat. Hist.* 13.46—*GLAJJ* 1:491, 493); Martial speaks of "the lecheries of circumcised Jews" (*Epigrammata* 7.30—*GLAJJ* 1:525); and Tacitus, of course, is well known for the savagery of his anti-Semitism—"The Jews regard as profane all that we hold sacred . . . (and) permit all that we abhor"—and much more in the same vein (*Hist.* 5.4.1—*GLAJJ* 2:18, 25); see also Smallwood, 123–24. Against such hostility and ill will, exacerbated no doubt by the special protection and degree of preferential treatment given them by earlier rulers (Smallwood, 139), the Jewish community in Rome must have felt itself to be seriously under threat.

§2.3.2 This hostility had expressed itself in several official rulings directed against the Jews—three times that we know of within the lifetime of Paul: the expulsion of Jews under Tiberius in A.D. 19; the withdrawal of the rights of assembly by Claudius in A.D. 41; and the expulsion by Claudius in A.D. 49 (see above §2.2.3). In each case the ruling or edict became a dead letter with the passing of time, and particularly in consequence of the change of ruler (the fall of Sejanus in A.D. 31, and the death of Claudius in A.D. 54—Bruce, *History*, 295, 299). But the shifts and swings in the exercise of Roman *imperium* were sufficient to drive home the constant danger in which Jew and Christian stood during this period, and within ten years of Paul's writing his letter to Rome the Christians would feel the full and savage impact of Nero's power.

§2.3.3 A third factor to be noted is that in terms of organization the Jewish community in Rome appears to have been very weak. Each of the synagogues seems to have been regarded as an independent unit, the equivalent, for the purposes of the laws governing rights of assembly, of an individual *collegium* or club. Unlike the larger Jewish minority in Alexandria, there seems to have been no single controlling organization which could act on behalf of the Jewish community as a whole, no ethnarch to represent his people before the authorities (see Leon, 168–70; Wiefel, 105–8, with further details). This would naturally leave them in a more exposed position politically, since without the special protection which Julius Caesar and Augustus had accorded them, they would always be vulnerable to preventative or prohibitive measures taken against sects and *collegia*, even if not directed specifically against them. Insofar as the Christian groups were still identified with or seen as an offshoot of the Jewish community, they would be in a similarly vulnerable position. But equally, insofar as they were becoming distinct from the synagogues and seen to be such, they were in danger of being identified as yet another new sect from the east ("a sect professing a new and mischievous religious belief"—Suetonius, *Nero* 16.2) and treated accordingly.

§2.4 We are now in a position to sketch out more fully the probable situation of the Christian groups in Rome to which Paul wrote, drawing both on the context outlined above and on further details from and related to the letter itself.

§2.4.1 The Christians must have been well established and fairly numerous by the middle of the 50s. Paul had wanted to visit them "for many years"

(1:10;15:23). They had been sufficiently strong (or provocative) by A.D. 49 to provide the occasion for the "constant disturbances" within the Jewish community which resulted in the expulsion of (most? many of?) the Jews. And in 64 they could be described as a new "sect" (Suetonius, *Nero* 16.2), with "a great multitude" (πολὺ πλῆθος—*1 Clem.* 6.1), "vast numbers" (*multitudo ingens*) indicted by confessed Christians to provide many hours of "entertainment" by the varied deaths they suffered (Tacitus, *Ann.* 15.44.2–4) (see also Brown, 99). The widespread use of such punishments suggests that few of the Christians had citizens' rights.

§2.4.2 From Rom 16, assuming that it was written to Rome (see chap. 16 *Introduction*), we can deduce that a large proportion of the Christians in Rome were slaves or freedmen/women (at least 14 of the 24 personally greeted have commonly used slave names; cf. the discussion in Lampe, 141–53). A minority, perhaps as many as 8 of the 14, may have been fairly well-to-do, though since Paul was on balance likely to know more of the well-to-do than those located exclusively in Rome itself, the fact that he is unable to greet more may be significant. The relatively small proportion of specifically Roman names in the same list is also striking in view of the fact that more than half of all the names recovered from the Jewish catacombs in Rome are Latin (Leon, 107–8). Both observations suggest that Paul knew very few of the purely local Christians in Rome, and also that the Christians he actually does greet were only a relatively small proportion of the overall Christian community. The same chapter of Romans confirms that the Christians must have met in a number of house churches: the house church of Prisca and Aquila (16:5), and the two groups greeted in vv 14–15; and quite likely those belonging to the households of Aristobulus and Narcissus (vv 10–11) met as a group (of slaves and freedmen/women) within these great houses (cf. Bruce, *History*, 394). If the above deductions are correct, there must have been at least several other house churches unknown personally to Paul.

§2.4.3 The Christians were not yet clearly distinguished from the wider Jewish community (Paul speaks without awkwardness of "Abraham, our forefather," "our father" [4:1, 12], and assumes a good knowledge of the law [7:1]), and probably therefore shared their ambiguous and vulnerable position. Insofar as they had any legal status, they would meet presumably as a *collegium* or under the auspices of a synagogue. Here the fact that Paul never speaks of the Christians in Rome as a church ("the church in Rome") may well be significant, especially since it is so out of keeping with Paul's usual practice (1 Cor 1:2; 2 Cor 1:1; Phil 4:15; Col 4:16; 1 Thess 1:1; 2 Thess 1:1; cf. Gal 1:2). For one thing, it confirms that the Christians in Rome were too numerous to meet in a single house, but it may also indicate that a more public gathering (ἐκκλησίαν = "assembly"; see further on 16:1) was too hazardous to contemplate. And for another, it strongly suggests that the Christian house congregations shared the same sort of fragmented existence as the wider Jewish community. The Christians functioned as several "churches" in Rome but were not seen as a single entity—and if not by Paul, still less by others. Without a strong and unified political status, and less than ten years since the Jews had been last expelled from Rome, Paul's readership would certainly need to keep in mind the political realities within which they had to live.

§2.4.4 Following the expulsion of (many of?) the Jews in 49 most of the house churches would have become largely Gentile in composition (e.g., Kümmel, *Introduction,* 309–11; Brown, 109, despite his own qualification, 102; and those cited by them); and in their continuing growth they would have drawn in other Gentiles who had not previously been attracted to or been familiar with Judaism. With the death of Claudius (A.D. 54) and the lapse of his edict, Jews must have begun to return to Rome in significant numbers (as they had in the 30s following the lapse of Tiberius' action against them). With these Jews would have come Jewish Christians, like Prisca and Aquila, Andronicus and Junia, and the other Jews mentioned in chap. 16. The fact that Prisca and Aquila had established a (new?) church (16:5) may simply be indicative of the continuing expansion of the Christian movement. But it may also suggest some difficulty for returned Jewish Christians in regaining leadership roles they had previously been accorded within the house churches, now predominantly Gentile. On the other hand, Paul clearly expects his letter to be circulated by the various house churches, so we should not exaggerate differences within the Christian community.

Even so, it is likely that the return of a significant number of Jewish Christians caused at least some friction between Gentile and Jew within (and among) the Christian house churches (so particularly Wiefel, 111–13). The relatively greater vulnerability of the returning Jews would at least partly explain why Paul felt it necessary to warn his gentile readers against any feelings of superiority over their Jewish fellows (11:17–21). And the growing self-confidence of the gentile Christians in their sense of increasing independence from the synagogue and over against the returning Jewish Christians makes perfect sense as the background and context for Paul's counsel in 14:1 and in the following paragraphs (14:1–15:6; see particularly on 14:2 and 14:5).

In any case, at the time Paul wrote the letter, the gentile Christians in Rome were probably in a large majority (a suggestion consistent with the large majority of non-Jews among those greeted in chap. 16), and the Jewish Christians probably felt themselves doubly vulnerable as Jews, for they now had to identify themselves more fully with the largely gentile house churches in increasing distinction and separation from the synagogues. The fact that the Christian readers could be expected to think of Abraham as "our (fore)father" (4:1, 12) and to be thoroughly familiar with the law (e.g., 7:1), and yet at the same time were evidently not under pressure regarding circumcision (2:25), suggests that Paul is able to envisage a community well into the process of developing its own distinct identity over against the Jewish community from which it had emerged. This seems to make better sense of all the available data than the alternative suggestion of Judge and Thomas that "the church" in Rome was not founded till after Paul's arrival in Rome resulted in the Christians setting themselves up "in opposition to the synagogues" (cf. Bartsch, "Faith," 42–45). But Watson's thesis of three more or less clearly distinct and opposed groups—Jews, Jewish Christians, and gentile Christians—is much too clear-cut (see further below §3.3).

§2.4.5 The final piece of background information which can hardly be ignored is given us by Tacitus. In *Annals* 13 he reports that the year 58 was marked by persistent public complaints regarding indirect taxes. Nero's initial response was to propose the abolition of all indirect taxes. But the senators warned strenuously about the likely consequences—fall in revenue, and demands to abolish direct taxes as well. Nero relented, but it was generally agreed that tax collectors' acquisitiveness must be restrained. This report of Tacitus is sufficient to suggest the strong likelihood that in the years prior to 58 the collection of taxes was a sensitive matter within the public domain. Jews, by virtue of their special privileges regarding the temple tax, would be all the more open to charges of tax evasion. And Christians, identified with Jews, would be equally vulnerable in situations where tax collectors were levying additional duties, for example, on shipments and property. Should they refuse or complain and so leave themselves exposed to legal action, even if the tax collector had demanded more than his right? Or should they pay up and say nothing to avoid drawing hostile attention to themselves? It was, after all, only about seven or eight years until Christians were to be hounded as scapegoats for the fire of Rome. Christians might well be advised to "keep a low profile" on such a politically sensitive matter as public taxation. It is not surprising, then, that Paul's exhortation on Christians' responsibility vis-à-vis the state should end with firm advice about the payment of taxes (13:6–7; see *Comment* on 13:6–7).

In short, it must be judged highly likely that Paul knew quite a bit, at least in general terms, about the situation of the new movement in Rome. In particular, he was aware of its political context and the tensions between Jew and Gentile created by its emergence within the Jewish synagogues and by the steady recruitment of gentile converts which left the latter in a sizable majority.

Against this background the reasons why Paul wrote his letter to Rome become clearer.

§3. THE PURPOSE OF THE LETTER:
Stated Objectives and Structure of the Letter

Bibliography

Aus, R. D. "Travel Plans." **Bartsch, H. W.** "Die historische Situation des Römerbriefes." *SE* 4.1 (1968) 281–91. **Boman, T.** "Die dreifache Würde des Völkerapostels." *ST* 29 (1975) 63–69. **Bornkamm, G.** "The Letter to the Romans as Paul's Last Will and Testament" (1971). ET in Donfried, *Romans Debate*, 17–31. **Bruce, F. F.** "The Romans Debate—Continued." *BJRL* 64 (1981–82) 334–59. **Campbell, W. S.** "Why Did Paul Write Romans?" *ExpT* 85 (1973–74) 264–69. **Donfried, K. P.** "False Presuppositions in the Study of Romans." *CBQ* 36 (1974). Repr. in Donfried, *Romans Debate*, 120–48. **Drane, J. W.** "Why Did Paul Write Romans?" In *Pauline Studies*, FS F. F. Bruce, ed. D. A. Hagner et al. Exeter: Paternoster, 1980. 208–27. **Harder, G.** "Der konkrete Anlass des Römerbriefes." *ThViat* 6 (1959) 13–24. **Jervell, J.** "The Letter to Jerusalem." *ST* 25 (1971). ET in Donfried, *Romans Debate*, 61–74. **Karris, R. J.** "Romans 14:1–15:13." **Kaye, B. N.** "'To the Romans and Others' Revisited." *NovT* 18 (1976) 37–77. **Kettunen, M.** *Abfassungszweck des Römerbriefes.* **Klein, G.** "Paul's Purpose." **Minear, P.** *Obedience.* **Munck, J.** *Paul.* 196–209. **Preisker, H.** "Das historische Problem des Römerbriefes." *Wissenschaftliche Zeitschrift der Friedrich-Schiller-Universität Jena* 2 (1952–53) 25–32. **Rengstorf, K. H.** "Paulus und die älteste römische Christenheit." *SE* 2 (1964) 447–64. **Schrenk, G.** "Der Römerbrief als Missionsdokument." *Studien zu Paulus.* Zürich: Zwingli, 1954. 81–106. **Stuhlmacher, P.** "Der Abfassungszweck des Römerbriefes." *ZNW* 77 (1986) 180–93. **Suhl, A.** "Der konkrete Anlass des Römerbriefes." *Kairos* 13 (1971) 119–30. **Wedderburn, A. J. M.** "The Purpose and Occasion of Romans Again." *ExpT* 90 (1978–79) 137–41. **Wilckens, U.** "Abfassungszweck." 127–39.

On this subject there is a long and seemingly unending debate. The debate arises from two features in the letter: (1) the different reasons Paul indicates for his writing the letter in 1:8–15 and 15:14–33, and (2) the problem of how to relate these reasons to the body of the letter (1:16–15:13), since the rationale for providing such a lengthy and involved discussion to a largely unknown congregation is not immediately obvious. In fact, however, it is likely that Paul had several reasons for writing the letter (there is, of course, absolutely no reason why he should have had only one purpose in view), and most of the disagreements are a matter of different emphases between these several reasons. We can characterize them briefly and indicate something of the range of support for particular emphases.

§3.1 *A missionary purpose.* This emphasis is sufficiently clear from 15:18–24, 28. Paul sees himself as "apostle to the Gentiles" with a crucial role to play in bringing in "the full number of the Gentiles," with all which that meant (11:13–15, 25–26). He has completed one phase of his foundation-laying work (in the northeastern quadrant of the Mediterranean—15:19, 23) and he sees the next main phase as focusing in the northwestern quadrant of the Mediterranean (Spain—15:24, 28). For that he will need a base and good support, and where else to look other than Rome (ὑφ' ὑμῶν προπεμφθῆναι; see on 15:24)? So, e.g., Vielhauer, *Geschichte*, 181–84; Aus; Kettunen. It would also be consistent with this more specific purpose that Paul should use the opportunity to set out a more general statement of his missionary purpose as apostle of the universal gospel (Schrenk; Dahl, "Missionary Theology," 78—"It is not the problems of a local church but the universal gospel and Paul's own mission which in this letter provide the point of departure for the theological discussion"; Zeller, *Juden*, chap. 1, particularly p. 75; also *Römer*, 17).

Klein has argued on the basis of 15:20 that Paul thought the Christian community in Rome lacked an apostolic foundation ("Purpose," 44; also *IDBS*, 753–54) and therefore intended to evangelize Rome itself. This is far-fetched: (1) the desire to share his understanding of the gospel with the Roman Christians was wholly understandable—nothing more than that need be read out of 1:11–15; (2) the lavish congratulations of 1:8 and 15:14 would be deceitful on Klein's view, whereas the slight embarrassment evident in 1:12 and the careful language of 15:24 ("passing through") and 15:28 ("by way of you to Spain") is just what we would expect from Paul writing to a church in whose founding he had played no part (15:20; cf. 2 Cor 10:13–16); (3) the likely reason for Paul's avoidance of the word "church" in referring to the Roman community has already been explained above (§2.4.3), but it should also be

noted that Paul does not refrain from using the even more significant description, "one body in Christ" (12:5), in a first person plural reference which
clearly includes the Roman addressees; (4) in contrast to Klein, and in accordance with Paul's theology of apostleship (particularly 1 Cor 9:1–2; 12:28),
the existence of Christian groups in Rome was itself evidence of an "apostolic
foundation."

§3.2 *An apologetic purpose.* In setting out such a full statement of his understanding of the gospel (1:16–17 as a thematic statement for what follows),
Paul surely wished to gain acceptance for that understanding among the
believers in what, after all, was the capital of the Empire—and so potentially
the most influential of all the Christian churches (as events were to prove).
This is certainly consistent with the careful expansions made to his normal
opening paragraph (1:1–6). So, e.g., Koester—"a letter of recommendation
which Paul has written on his own behalf. . . . The topic of the letter
is . . . this gospel, and not the person of the apostle" (*Introduction* 2:140).
And 3:8 in particular certainly denotes a sensitivity on Paul's part to the
need for some sort of self-defense against actual misunderstandings of his
gospel. Bound up with all this and equally important is the evident desire
to gain the backing of the Roman congregations for his hazardous but crucial
trip to Jerusalem (15:25, 31); so, e.g., Wilckens, "Abfassungszweck," particularly 127–39, 167; Wedderburn; Bruce; Brown, 110–11. We need not take
this to mean that Paul hoped for actual physical or political support from
Rome while in Jerusalem (his intention may have been for a fairly quick
trip to be completed before any such support could reach Jerusalem)—although he clearly anticipated the possibility of his plans going badly wrong
(15:31) and may have hoped for support from Rome in such an event. Given,
however, Paul's belief in the importance and efficacy of prayer, his solemn
appeal for their support in the strenuous discipline of prayer (συναγωνίσασθαί
μοι, 15:30) suggests that he would regard this as help enough. The weight
of the preceding letter need not be regarded as out of keeping with such a
briefly stated request (15:30); rather, Paul would want to ensure that their
potentially powerful prayers were as well informed on behalf of himself and
his gospel as possible.

It is not inconsistent with this more specific purpose that Paul should
also see and seize the opportunity, given by his three month stay in Corinth
(Acts 20:3), at the end of a major phase of his life's work (Rom 15:19, 23),
to set out for the Roman (and other?) believers a careful statement of his
gospel and faith (one of the most obvious and popular views—e.g., Dodd
xxv; T. W. Manson, 2; Wikenhauser, 406–8; Munck, *Paul*, 199; Cambier,
"Romans," 465; Bornkamm, "Romans"; Kümmel, *Introduction*, 312–14; Michel, 30–33; Kaye, "Revisited"; Perrin, *Introduction*, 106–7; Cranfield, 815–
18; Wilckens, 1:41–48; Schlier, 6–9; Drane, 223; Stuhlmacher, "Abfassungszweck"); and not least with a view to the self-defense he would probably have
to offer in Jerusalem—hence Jervell's provocative title, as earlier Fuchs' assertion, that the Jerusalem church is "the secret addressee of Romans" (cited
by Jervell, 67; so also Suggs, 295).

§3.3 *A pastoral purpose.* Assuming that chap. 16 was part of the original
letter (see chap. 16 *Introduction*), another stated purpose is to introduce Phoebe

(16:1–2), and the following list of greetings (16:3–16) is intended as much to name individuals for Phoebe to call on as to ensure the letter a favorable response within the different Christian churches.

An increasingly popular view in the second half of the twentieth century is that Paul wrote to counter (potential) divisions within Rome among the Christian house churches, particularly the danger of gentile believers despising less liberated Jewish believers (11:17–25; 12:3, 16; 14:3; strongly maintained in the last few decades by, e.g., Preisker; Harder; Marxsen, *Introduction*, 95–104; Bartsch; Wiefel, "Jewish Community," 106–19; Donfried, "False Presuppositions"; Campbell; Beker, *Paul*, 69–74, as part of a larger "dialogue with Judaism" [77–89]). In the light of the historical context sketched out above (§2), this hypothesis must be regarded as possessing considerable strength. Minear's attempt to identify a number of factions, however, goes too far beyond the evidence. In particular 16:17–20 should probably not be related to the earlier discussion (14:1–15:6) but be seen rather as an expression of general foreboding by Paul in a personal postscript using traditional language calling for spiritual alertness in the face of perennial threats to community cohesion and faith's obedience (see on 16:18).

Watson's attempt also to argue from 14:1–15:13 (*Paul*, 94–98) in support of the specific thesis that Paul's objective was "to persuade members of the Roman Jewish Christian congregation to separate themselves from the Jewish community and to recognize and unite with the Pauline gentile Christian congregation" (141–42) has a better grasp on the social realities of the addressees, but is misdirected. (1) Given the size of typical house churches (see on 16:23), there must have been a fair number of Christian congregations in Rome, so that analysis in terms of opposition between a Jewish Christian congregation and a gentile Christian congregation is too simplistic. (2) Paul is arguing to maintain the bond between covenant people and Christian congregation (e.g., 3:25–26; 4:16; 11:11–32; 15:27), not for a divorce. (3) The call to acceptance in 14:1 is better understood of Gentile-Christian majority congregations welcoming individual Jewish Christians into their fellowship (see above §2.4.4), and as a call for mutual acceptance (15:7) among those who continue to hold strongly to their views on food and days, *not* as an attempt to convert "weak" into "strong" (see also on 15:7; also Jewett, *Tolerance*, 41, 68–91; against Watson, 100). (4) In 16:3–16 the intermingling of Jewish and gentile names is more obviously understood to reflect mixed Jewish/gentile Christian groups than two groups precisely distinguished as one Jewish and the other Gentile (see also on 16:3 and 7). Had Watson argued that the likely *effect* of Paul's advocacy was a polarization of synagogue and church, as Jewish Christians found it increasingly difficult to maintain the twin loyalties to law and faith, he would have been on stronger ground. But to see such separation between a gentile Christian church and the Jewish community as Paul's "sole aim" (22; "he wishes to turn a failed reform-movement into a sect"—106) is an astonishing assessment of Paul's objective in writing the letter.

The alternative view that no detailed knowledge on Paul's part of the situation in Rome need be assumed, and that 12:1–15:6 simply provides a general parenesis in which Paul sums up the teaching and lessons he had learned elsewhere, particularly Corinth (so especially Karris), can hardly command much support, in view of the background outlined above. As already noted, Rom 16 indicates well enough that Paul had many contacts in the Roman congregations, and it would be altogether surprising if some news of events and developments in Rome had not reached Paul. The congratulatory language of 1:8 and 15:14 is no doubt exaggerated, but must at least have some basis in fact, otherwise it would be read as sarcasm—which is hardly what Paul would want. And not least, on the basis of 13:6–7, it is hard to doubt that Paul was fairly well tuned in to the political and social gossip stemming from Rome (see above §2.4.5; and on 13:6). It is not necessary to assume a detailed knowledge on Paul's part of all the different Christian groups (as noted above, 16:3–16 probably alludes to only five of them). It is enough that he would know the general situation in broad terms, with some specific details. That would be sufficient to enable him to couch a parenesis in terms which he would know were relevant to most, at least, of the Christian groups in Rome.

§3.4 A point which has not been sufficiently drawn out, and which the discussion so far seems to support strongly, is that all three of these main emphases and purposes hang together and indeed reinforce each other when taken as a whole. This leads us into another major area of Romans research under which the point is best developed.

§4. THE FORMAL AND THEOLOGICAL COHERENCE OF THE LETTER

Bibliography

Aune, D. E. *Literary Environment.* 219–21. **Bultmann, R.** "Glossen." **Campbell, W. S.** "Romans 3." ———. "Freedom and Faithfulness." 38–41. **Dibelius, M.** *Tradition.* 238–43. **Doty, W. G.** *Letters.* **Dunn, J. D. G.** "Paul's Epistle to the Romans: An Analysis of Structure and Argument." *ANRW* II.25.4 (1987). **Dupont, J.** "Le problème de la structure littéraire de l'Épître aux Romains." *RB* 62 (1955) 365–97. **Feuillet, A.** "Le plan salvifique de Dieu d'après l'Épître aux Romains." *RB* 57 (1950) 336–87, 489–506. **Fraikin, D.** "The Rhetorical Function of the Jews in Romans." In *Anti-Judaism in Early Christianity,* ed. P. Richardson and D. Granskou. Waterloo, Ontario: Wilfrid Laurier University, 1986. 91–105. **Grayston, K.** "'I Am Not Ashamed of the Gospel': Romans 1:16a and the Structure of the Epistle." *SE* 2 (1964) 569–73. **Jewett, R.** "Ambassadorial Letter." ———. "Following the Argument of Romans." *Word and World* 6 (1986) 382–89. **Kennedy, G. A.** *New Testament Interpretation.* Esp. 152–56. **Kinoshita, J.** "Romans—Two Writings Combined." *NovT* 7 (1964) 258–77. **Lamarche, P.,** and **Dû, C. le.** *Epître aux Romains 5–8: Structure littéraire et sens.* Paris: Centre National de la Recherche Scientifique, 1980. **Louw, J. P.** *A Semantic Discourse Analysis of Romans.* University of Pretoria, 1979. **Luz, U.** "Zum Aufbau von Röm 1–8." *TZ* 25 (1969) 161–81. **Lyonnet, S.** "Note sur le plan de l'Épître aux Romains." *RSR* 39 (1951–52) 301–16. **Morris, L.** "Theme." **Mussner, F.** "Heil." **Noack, B.** "Current." **Prümm, K.** "Struktur." **Roland, P.** *Epître aux Romains: Texte grec structure.* Rome: Pontifical Biblical Institute, 1980. **Schenke, H. M.** "Aporien." 882–84. **Schmithals, W.** *Römerbrief.* **Schnider, F.,** and **Stenger, W.** *Studien zum Neutestamentlichen Briefformular.* NTTS 11. Leiden: Brill, 1987. **Scroggs, R.** "Paul as Rhetorician: Two Homilies in Romans 1–11." In *Jews, Greeks and Christians,* FS W. D. Davies, ed. R. Hamerton-Kelly and R. Scroggs. Leiden: Brill, 1976. 271–98. **Stirewalt, M. L.** "The Form and Function of

the Greek Letter-Essay." In Donfried, *Romans Debate,* 175–206. **Stowers, S. K.** *Diatribe.*
———. *Letter Writing in Greco-Roman Antiquity.* Philadelphia: Westminster, 1986. **White, J. L.** *Body.* ———, ed. *Studies in Ancient Letter Writing. Semeia* 22. Chico: Scholars Press, 1982. ———. *Light from Ancient Letters.* Philadelphia: Fortress, 1986. **Wilckens, U.** "Abfassungszweck." 139–67. **Wuellner, W.** "Paul's Rhetoric." 152–74.

The increasing emphasis of the last two decades on the importance of the historical situation addressed for an understanding of Romans has been matched by an increasing interest in its literary structure and rhetorical features (Donfried, *Romans Debate;* cf. Beker, *Paul,* 61–63).

§4.1 *The literary form of Romans.* The key issue here is the relation of the epistolary framework of the letter (1:1–15; 15:14–16:23) to the main body of the letter (1:16–15:13). On the one hand, it is generally recognized that the introduction and conclusion are essentially variations on the familiar pattern of letter writing in the ancient world (Doty, 13–14); this greatly strengthens the impression that however else Romans may be categorized, it was intended at least in part as a personal letter to a particular group of people in Rome in the middle of the first century A.D. On the other hand, the body of the letter is highly distinctive in content and character. It seems to share little if anything of the personal letter form and would more accurately be described as a "treatise" or "literary dialogue" or "letter essay" (Stirewalt). The tension between these two different literary forms in Romans has never been resolved with complete satisfaction—which simply underlines the distinctiveness of the form Paul created. Certainly any attempt to determine the letter's character solely in terms of literary parallels to introduction and conclusion is self-evidently defective; just as it is self-evidently essential that the character of the document be seen in the relation of the body of the letter to its introduction and conclusion.

The key fact here is that the distinctiveness of the letter far outweighs the significance of its conformity with current literary or rhetorical custom. Parallels show chiefly how others wrote at that period; they provide no prescription for Paul's practice and no clear criterion by which to assess Paul; and the fact that no particular suggestion has commanded widespread assent in the current discussion suggests that Paul's style was as much or more eclectic and instinctive than conventional and conformist. Thus to label Romans as "epideictic" (demonstrative; Wuellner, Fraikin) or "deliberative" or "protreptic" (persuasive; Stowers, *Letter Writing,* 114) does not actually advance understanding of the letter very far (Aune, 219), since the chief force of the letter lies in its *distinctive* Pauline art and content. At most we can speak comfortably of formal features which were part of the idiom of the age (what every well educated schoolboy learned as part of his basic equipment for social intercourse) and through which Paul naturally expressed himself in an unselfconscious way. This is probably true even of the most impressive suggestion, that Romans was written on the model of an "ambassadorial" letter (Jewett), which sheds occasional light on specific features of the introduction and conclusion. Similarly we may assume that the letter's familiar forms and idioms made it more readily hearable and assimilable for the recipients.

But the reason they retained the letter and recognized its authority was the distinctively Pauline use made of these, including the myriad idiosyncratic variations and embellishments, and above all, of course, the fact that they heard the word of God addressing them through both the more familiar and the less familiar content of Paul's words and sentences (cf. Barth, *Preface*[2]).

In terms of the document's coherence as between framework and body, however, the most important feature is the way in which the body of the letter (1:16–15:13) has been neatly sandwiched between two statements of Paul's future plans which are strikingly parallel (see 15:14–33 *Form and Structure*). The second statement, however, is markedly fuller and more explicit, particularly about Paul's purpose in coming to Rome. The most obvious deduction to draw from this is that Paul thought it necessary to elaborate his understanding of the gospel at length before he made his specific requests to the Roman Christians, on the assumption that they needed to have this fuller insight before they could be expected to give him the support he sought. This deduction seems to gain strength from the care with which Paul has meshed introduction and peroration into the body of the letter: 1:16–17 serves both as the climax to what has preceded and as the thematic statement for what follows (see 1:16–17 *Form and Structure*), with the overarching Christology already carefully embedded in the introduction (1:2–6); and 15:14–15 is a polite way of saying that the whole of the preceding treatise was an expression of Paul's grace as apostle, that is, an example of the charism to strengthen faith and of the gospel he had been given to preach (1:11, 15), with which he would hope to repay their support for his future missionary work (cf. 1:12 with 15:24, 27–29).

The other main problem regarding literary framework is whether chap. 16 was part of the original letter. The arguments have been reviewed repeatedly and most recent commentators accept that Rom 16 was part of the letter to Rome, even though the suggestion that it was originally directed to Ephesus continues to command a surprising amount of support. The case for its being part of the original letter is briefly outlined in the *Introduction* to 16:1–23. The textual history is complex (see *Notes* on 16:25–27), but it requires no detailed analysis to argue the greater likelihood of Paul's letter to Rome being copied in an abbreviated form (to omit the more explicitly personal references, perhaps including the specific mention of "Rome" in 1:7 and 15, as in some texts), than of Paul himself writing more than one version with chap. 16 appended to the version to Ephesus. A collector and distributor of Paul's letters would see no difficulty in circulating the letter with its introduction and conclusion largely intact; whereas Paul himself would be less likely to leave the introduction and peroration unchanged when they were so much less fitted to churches of his own foundation. The fact that the letter was not subjected to greater abbreviation (apart from the Marcionite elimination of all of chap. 15 as well as of chap. 16) is some indication that the coherence of framework and body was recognized by most copyists.

For other matters regarding language and style of the letter, reference may be made to SH, lii–lxiii, and Cranfield, 24–27.

§4.2 *The theological coherence of Romans.* In a review of Romans research one impression which could easily be given is that Romans *lacks* coherence.

Sanders, *Law,* 123–35, and Räisänen, *Law,* 101–9, find key points in chap. 2 at odds with what Paul says elsewhere. The function of chap. 5 within the development of the overall argument is greatly disputed (see 5:1–21 *Introduction*). Kinoshita suggests that Romans is a combination of two separate letters; Scroggs likewise argues that the letter is an amalgamation of two distinct homilies (chaps. 5–8, and chaps. 1–4, 9–11); and Noack, 164, describes chaps. 5–8 as a "backwater." Chaps. 9–11 are sometimes regarded as an excursus or appendix to the main argument, or indeed a completely preformed unit incorporated as it stood (Dodd). And several have found chaps. 12–15 completely unrelated to what has gone before, an application simply of standard parenetic tradition (e.g., Dibelius, 238–39).

Most radical in such denials of the integration and coherence of the letter as a whole have been Schmithals, arguing for two separate letters (A—1:1– 4:25 + 5:12–11:36 + 15:8–13; B—12:1–21 + 13:8–10 + 14:1–15 + 15:14– 32 + 16:21–23 + 15:33), and O'Neill, arguing for a much redacted and expanded original with major interpolations (consisting of 1:18–2:29; 5:12– 21; 7:14–25; 9:11–24; 10:7–15:13). Less radical have been the suggestions of Bultmann, of a number of glosses added to the letter at some stage subsequent to its composition by Paul (2:1, 16; 5:6–7; 6:17b; 7:25b; 8:1; 10:17; 13:5), and of Schenke that 14:1–15:13 + 16:3–20 were originally addressed to Ephesus.

A close study of the text, however, shows that all of these and similar suggestions are in greater or less degree unjustified. As for Schmithals in particular: since his letter A lacks a conclusion, and his letter B an introduction, and since the two fit together quite coherently, his surgery is unnecessary (on Schmithals and Schenke see also Wilckens, 1:27–29). O'Neill's reconstruction proceeds on the wholly unrealistic assumption that Paul was a paragon of literary and theological consistency, and by taking only one aspect of his complex treatment of such key motifs as "law" and "flesh" as genuine, he leaves a mutilated and monochrome Paul far less impressive than the author of Romans. Other individual claims will be dealt with in more detail chiefly in the introduction to each main section. For the rest we may confine ourselves here to more general observations.

§4.2.1 In the first place, we can illustrate the coherence of the letter from the integration of the various purposes Paul evidently had in writing the letter (see above §3). Paul's missionary purpose (§3.1) is hardly to be held quite apart from his apologetic purpose (§3.2). On the contrary, it was precisely his theological conviction regarding the eschatological fulfillment of the purpose of God in Christ for Gentile as well as Jew which provided Paul's motivation as a missionary. The Christological emphasis throughout ties together not only the main body of the letter (e.g., 3:21–26; 5:14–21; 8:1–4; 9:32–10:13; 12:5; 14:8–9; 15:1–9), but also the introduction and conclusion in which Paul attests that his commissioning for this gospel came from this Jesus (1:1–6, 9; 15:16–20). So also the personal note interjected at 11:13–14 is in no way erratic or out of character, but confirms that Paul saw the theological exposition climaxing in chaps. 9–11 as a necessary or essential explanation if his readers were to understand and sympathize with his powerful compulsion to take the gospel to Spain. Likewise, it is by recognizing the mixed (Jew/Gentile) character of the congregations in Rome (above

§2) that the tie-in between apologetic and pastoral (§3.3) purposes becomes clear: the Roman congregations were something of a test case for Paul's apostolic vision of the body of Christ consisting in each place of Jewish and gentile believers functioning in harmony (15:7–13). Paul's theological exposition of chaps. 1–11 is the ideological foundation for the particular parenesis of chaps. 12–15 (so also Wilckens, 1:39–42; cf. Wuellner, 171–72).

Not least do we need to recall the integration provided by Paul's own personal and spiritual pilgrimage and by his commission as Jewish apostle to Gentiles, taking to the non-Jewish world the message of God's promises to Abraham as fulfilled in and through Messiah Jesus. It is precisely the tension between "Jew first but also Greek" (1:16), which Paul experienced in his own person and faith and mission (above §1), which also provides an integrating motif for the whole letter. First he argues that Jew as much as Greek is in need of God's eschatological grace (1:18–3:20). Then he spells out the means by which Jew as well as Gentile, the "many," the "all," are brought within the experience of that grace (3:21–5:21), and explains how these blessings, characteristically understood as belonging to Israel, work out in the present for each of the "many," the "all" (chaps. 6–8). The question which has long pressed, "If Israel's blessings are freely open to Gentiles, what then of the promises to Israel itself?," at last commands center stage in the climax of the theological exposition (chaps. 9–11). Finally, with the character of the people of promise thus redefined (Jew *and* Gentile), traditional Jewish ethnic and social mores can no longer simply be assumed as the obvious ethical outworking for the people of the promise. Consequently, Paul spells out a fresh set of guidelines, inspired by a new model (the body of Christ), and made up of a discreet mix of older Jewish wisdom which still applies and the newer guidelines of the love of neighbor commended and lived out all the way to the cross by Jesus himself (12:1–15:6).

This is no doubt the fullest exposition Paul had attempted of a theological, apologetic, missionary, pastoral explanation for his work. That he had used and rehearsed elements of it in previous discussions and expositions to Jews, Jewish Christians, God-worshiping Gentiles and gentile Christians, need not be doubted. It is very likely, too, that he had an eye to the defense he would almost certainly have to offer in Judea and Jerusalem (if he had the chance to do so—15:31). But in the event, the exposition transcends the immediacy of its several purposes and provides a coherent and integrated vision of the eschatological people of God (Gentile *and* Jew) which is of lasting value.

§4.2.2 The importance of "Jew first but also Greek" as the integrating motif is also demonstrated by other features in Romans.

One feature of the treatise section is the repeated use of diatribe style (dialogue with an imagined interlocutor)—particularly 2:1–5, 17–29; 3:27–4:2; 9:19–21; 11:17–24. Here Paul certainly shows familiarity with this contemporary style of philosophic discourse. Characteristic of the diatribe is the attempt to criticize and correct pretension and arrogance. Stowers, *Diatribe*, 75–78, has also made the important observation that the typical function of diatribe was not as polemic against an opponent but, in a school context, as a critical questioning of a fellow student designed to lead him to the truth (so also Aune, 200–201, 219). Consequently, in Romans Paul's use of diatribe, particularly in chaps. 2 and 3, should not be seen as outright opposition to "the Jew" or to Judaism as such, but rather as a critical dialogue which Paul conducts with his fellow pupils within the school of Judaism, in which the aim is to understand aright the Jewish heritage common to both. This helps us to recognize, moreover, that a consistent concern of Paul's throughout the letter is to puncture presumption, wherever he finds it, and to prevent arrogance from raising its head. Thus we can see that the warning of 11:17–25 against gentile boasting is an attempt to prevent gentile believers from falling into the trap which had caught his fellow Jews (2:17, 23; 3:27; 4:2); and at the same time it ties the concern of the treatise section into that of the parenesis (particularly 12:3, 16 and 14:3).

Intertwined with the theme of "Jew first and also Greek" is the integrated thematic emphasis on the righteousness of God, on righteousness through faith, and on the faithfulness of God (1:17). Here it is important to give full weight to the insight of Stendahl ("Conscience" and *Paul*, 2–3) that Paul's treatment of the righteousness of God is primarily an exposition of the same Jew/Gentile theme, Paul's way of arguing that Gentiles are full recipients of the righteousness (= saving grace) of God, fully heirs of the promises to Abraham and Jacob as much as Jews are. The repeated emphasis on "all"— "all who believe" (1:16; 3:22; 4:11; 10:4, 11–13), "all injustice" (1:18, 29), "all who judge" (2:1), all who bring about evil/good (2:9–10), all under sin (3:9, 12, 19–20, 23; 5:12), "all the seed" (4:11, 16), "all Israel" (11:26), and so on—means primarily all Jews as well as Greeks, all Gentiles as well as Jews. So, too, the emphasis on God's faithfulness as an integral part of the same exposition comes to expression not just in key assertions like 3:3, 9:6, and 11:29, but also in the stress on "the truth" (= faithfulness) of God, which has the effect of setting the concept of God's covenant faithfulness within the larger consideration of God's faithfulness as Creator and Judge (1:18, 25; 2:2, 8, 20; 3:7). Not least of significance is the way in which Paul uses 15:7–13 both to integrate the parenetic section more fully into the overall theme and to underscore his claim that God's truth and faithfulness to the promises made to the fathers had in view all nations and all peoples united in a praise to the one God. The importance of this stress on God's faithfulness *as part of* the theme enunciated in 1:16–17 has not been given sufficient recognition in exposition of Romans.

Equally important is it to recognize the significance of the law as the chief secondary theme running through the letter. This has probably caused more confusion than any other aspect of the whole letter and to deal with it adequately we will have to step back a little to gain a fuller view of the issues.

§5. THE NEW PERSPECTIVE ON PAUL:
Paul and the Law

Bibliography

Barclay, J. M. G. "Paul and the Law: Observations on Some Recent Debates." *Themelios* 12.1 (1986) 5–15. **Barth, M.** "Die Stellung des Paulus zu Gesetz und Ordnung." In L. de Lorenzi, *Die Israelfrage nach Röm 9–11*. Rome: Abtei von St Paul, 1977. 245–87. **Bruce, F. F.** "Paul and the Law of Moses." *BJRL* 57 (1974–75) 259–79. **Bultmann,**

R. "Christ the End of the Law." *Essays Philosophical and Theological.* London: SCM, 1955. 36–66. **Cranfield, C. E. B.** "St Paul and the Law." *SJT* 17 (1964) 43–68. ———. *Romans.* 845–62. **Davies, W. D.** *Paul,* Preface to the Fourth Edition. xxi–xxxviii. ———. "Paul and the Law: Reflections on Pitfalls in Interpretation." In *Paul and Paulinism,* FS C. K. Barrett, ed. M. D. Hooker and S. G. Wilson. London: SPCK, 1982. 4–16. **Dodd, C. H.** "Law." **Dülmen, A. van.** *Theologie.* **Dunn, J. D. G.** "New Perspective." ———. "Works of Law." **Feuillet, A.** "Loi de Dieu, Loi du Christ e Loi de l'Esprit. D'après les epîtres pauliniennes: Le rapport de ces trois lois avec loi mosaïque." *NovT* 22 (1980) 29–65. **Fitzmyer, J.** "Paul and the Law." *To Advance the Gospel.* New York: Crossroad, 1981. 186–201. **Garlington, D.** *Obedience.* **Gaston, L.** "Torah." **Gundry, R. H.** "Grace, Works, and Staying Saved in Paul." *Bib* 66 (1985) 1–38. **Hahn, F.** "Gesetzesverständnis." **Hartman, L.** "Bundesideologie in und hinter einigen paulinischen Texten." In *Die Paulinische Literatur und Theologie,* ed. S. Pedersen. Aarhus: Aros/Göttingen: Vandenhoeck und Ruprecht, 1980. 103–18. **Haufe, C.** "Die Stellung des Paulus zum Gesetz." *TLZ* 91 (1966) 171–78. **Hofius, O.** "Gesetz." **Hooker, M. D.** "Paul and 'Covenantal Nomism.'" In *Paul and Paulinism,* FS C. K. Barrett, ed. M. D. Hooker and S. G. Wilson. London: SPCK, 1982. 47–56. **Hübner, H.** *Law.* ———. "Paulusforschung." 2668–91. **Jaubert, A.** *La notion d'alliance dans le Judaïsme.* Éditions du Seuil, 1963. Esp. 39–66. **Jewett, R.** "The Law and the Coexistence of Jews and Gentiles in Romans." *Int* 39 (1985) 341–56. **Klein, C.** *Anti-Judaism in Christian Theology.* Philadelphia: Fortress, 1978. **Kuss, O.** "Nomos bei Paulus." *MTZ* 17 (1966) 173–226. **Ladd, G. E.** "Law." **Lambrecht, J.** "Gesetzesverständnis bei Paulus." In *Das Gesetz im Neuen Testament,* ed. K. Kertelge. Freiburg: Herder, 1986. 88–127. **Lang, F.** "Gesetz und Bund bei Paulus." In *Rechtfertigung,* FS E. Käsemann, ed. J. Friedrich et al. Tübingen: Mohr, 1976. 305–20. **Limbeck, M.** *Die Ordnung des Heils: Untersuchungen zum Gesetzesverständnis des Frühjudentums.* Düsseldorf: Patmos, 1971. **Luz, U.** *Gesetz.* 89–112. **Moo, D. J.** "'Law,' 'Works of the Law,' and Legalism in Paul." *WTJ* 45 (1983) 73–100. **Montefiore, C. G.** "Genesis." **Nicholson, E. W.** *God and His People: Covenant and Theology in the Old Testament.* Oxford: Clarendon, 1986. **Osten-Sacken, P. von der.** "Das paulinische Verständnis des Gesetzes im Spannungsfeld von Eschatologie und Geschichte: Erläuterungen zum Evangelium als Faktor von theologischen Antijudaismus." *EvT* 37 (1977) 549–87. **Porter, C. L.** "New Paradigm." **Räisänen, H.** "Legalism and Salvation by the Law: Paul's Portrayal of the Jewish Religion as a Historical and Theological Problem." In *Die Paulinische Literatur und Theologie,* ed. S. Pedersen. Aarhus: Aros/Göttingen: Vandenhoeck und Ruprecht, 1980. 63–83. Repr. in *Torah,* 25–54. ———. "Paul's Theological Difficulties with the Law." In *Studia Biblica 1978,* ed. E. A. Livingstone. Vol. III. JSNTSup 3. Sheffield: JSOT, 1980. 301–20. Repr. in *Torah,* 3–24. ———. *Law.* ———. "Paul's Conversion and the Development of His View of the Law." *NTS* 33 (1987) 404–19. **Reicke, B.** "Gesetz." **Sanders, E. P.** "The Covenant as a Soteriological Category and the Nature of Salvation in Palestinian and Hellenistic Judaism." In *Jews, Greeks and Christians,* FS W. D. Davies, ed. R. Hamerton-Kelly and R. Scroggs. Leiden: Brill, 1976. 11–44. ———. *Paul.* ———. *Law.* **Sanders, J. A.** "Torah and Paul." In *God's Christ and His People,* FS N. A. Dahl, ed. J. Jervell and W. A. Meeks. Oslo: Universitetsforlaget, 1977. 132–40. **Sandmel, S.** *Paul.* 36–60. **Schechter, S.** "The 'Law.'" *Aspects.* 116–26. **Schoeps, H. J.** *Paul,* chap. 5. **Snodgrass, K.** "Spheres of Influence." **Stendahl, K.** *Paul.* **Stuhlmacher, P.** "Law." **Watson, F.** *Paul.* **Wedderburn, A. J. M.** "Paul and the Law." *SJT* 38 (1985) 613–22. **Westerholm, S.** "*Torah, Nomos,* and *Law* : A Question of 'Meaning.'" *SR* 15 (1986) 327–36. **Wilckens, U.** "Zur Entwicklung des paulinischen Gesetzesverständnis." *NTS* 28 (1982) 154–90. **Wright, N. T.** *Messiah,* chap. 2.

§5.1   A fresh assessment of Paul and of Romans in particular has been made possible and necessary by the new perspective on Paul provided by

E. P. Sanders, *Paul,* 1–12 and pt. 1 (though Limbeck's earlier critique of the negative depiction of the law in OT and "intertestamental" scholarship should also be mentioned; see also particularly Gaston, "Torah," 48–54, and Watson, *Paul,* 2–18; for examples of discussion in terms of older categories see Kuss, "Nomos," with review of earlier literature; Lang; and Hübner). Sanders has been successful in getting across a point which others had made before him (e.g., Stendahl, "Introspective Conscience," and Dahl, "Justification," particularly 110–11, 117–18), but which had been too little "heard" within the community of NT scholarship. The point is that Protestant exegesis has for too long allowed a typically Lutheran emphasis on justification by faith to impose a hermeneutical grid on the text of Romans (see, e.g., the way in which Bornkamm, *Paul,* 137, sets up his discussion of the subject). The emphasis is important, that God is the one who justifies the ungodly (4:5), and understandably this insight has become an integrating focus in Lutheran theology with tremendous power. The problem, however, lay in what that emphasis was set in opposition to. The antithesis to "justification by faith"—what Paul speaks of as "justification by works"—was understood in terms of a system whereby salvation is *earned* through the *merit* of *good works.* This was based partly on the comparison suggested in the same passage (4:4–5), and partly on the Reformation rejection of a system where indulgences could be bought and merits accumulated. The latter protest was certainly necessary and justified, and of lasting importance, but the hermeneutical mistake was made of reading this antithesis back into the NT period, of assuming that Paul was protesting against in Pharisaic Judaism precisely what Luther protested against in the pre-Reformation church—the mistake, in other words, of assuming that the Judaism of Paul's day was coldly legalistic, teaching a system of earning salvation by the merit of good works, with little or no room for the free forgiveness and grace of God ("the imaginary Rabbinic Judaism, created by Christian scholars, in order to form a suitably lurid background for the Epistles of St. Paul"—Montefiore, 65; in addition to the examples cited by Sanders and Watson, see, e.g., Leenhardt, passim, and Ridderbos, *Paul,* 130–35).

It was this depiction of first-century Judaism which Sanders showed up for what it was—a gross caricature, which, regrettably, has played its part in feeding an evil strain of Christian antisemitism. On the contrary, however, as Sanders demonstrated clearly enough, Judaism's whole religious self-understanding was based on the premise of grace—that God had freely chosen Israel and made his covenant with Israel, to be their God and they his people. This covenant relationship was regulated by the law, not as a way of entering the covenant, or of gaining merit, but as the way of living *within* the covenant; and that included the provision of sacrifice and atonement for those who confessed their sins and thus repented. Paul himself indicates the attitude clearly by his citation of Lev 18:5 in Rom 10:5—"the person who does these things [what the law requires] shall live by them." This attitude Sanders characterized by the now well known phrase "covenantal nomism"—that is, "the maintenance of status" among the chosen people of God by observing the law given by God as part of that covenant relationship (e.g., *Paul,* 544; see further Dunn, "New Perspective"; similarly Limbeck, 29–35; cf. Ziesler's earlier phrase "covenant-keeping righteousness"—*Righteousness,* 95). Sanders's review had not encompassed all the available Jewish literature of the period, but it has been confirmed by the work of one of my own postgraduates, D. Garlington, who has demonstrated the consistency of the "covenantal nomism" pattern throughout the Jewish writings contained in "the Apocrypha." See also Collins, *Athens*, who notes, however, that the pattern is not so consistent through all diaspora literature (14–15, 29, 48, 77, 141, 167, 178–81, 236–37). For the importance of the covenant in Judaism leading up to and at the time of Paul, see also particularly Jaubert.

Unfortunately Sanders did not follow through this insight far enough or with sufficient consistency. Instead of setting Paul more fully against and within this context of Judaism so understood, he advanced the thesis that Paul had jumped in arbitrary fashion (as a result of his Damascus road encounter) from one system (covenantal nomism) into another (Christianity; *Paul*, 550–52), leaving his theology, particularly in reference to the law, incoherent and contradictory (*Law*). On this last point he has been given strong support by Räisänen (*Law*), who also argues that Paul "intended to portray Judaism as a religion of merit and achievement" ("Conversion," 411) and that he thus "gives a totally distorted picture of the Jewish religion" ("Legalism," 72 [in agreement with Schoeps, 200]; though with an important concession in "Galatians 2:16 and Paul's Break with Judaism," NTS 31 [1985] 550 = *Torah*, 183). Just as puzzling from a different angle is the fact that the "covenantal nomism" of Palestinian Judaism as described by Sanders bears a striking similarity to what has been commonly understood as the religion of Paul himself (good works as the fruit of God's prior acceptance by grace; Hooker, "Covenantal Nomism")! What, then, can it be to which Paul is objecting?

§5.2   The exegetical questions exposed here focus very largely on the issue of Paul and the law (hence, not surprisingly, the titles of the books by Sanders and Räisänen, as also by Hübner). This is important since the law actually forms a major secondary theme of the letter, to an extent not usually appreciated ("an indispensable accompanying motif"—Hahn, 30). Rather striking is the way in which Paul regularly in Romans develops part of his discussion before bringing in the law (2:12 ff.; 3:27 ff.; 4:13 ff.; 5:20; chap. 7), while in other key sections it is the role of the law which provides a crucial hinge in the argument (3:19–21; 8:2–4; 9:31–10:5). Since these references taken together span the complete argument of chaps. 1–11 in all its stages, there can be little doubt that the tension between his gospel and the law and his concern to resolve that tension provide one of Paul's chief motivations in penning the letter.

Moreover, it is hardly a coincidence that several of the most recalcitrant exegetical problems in Romans are bound up with this central secondary theme of the letter. Thus it is significant once again that Sanders and Räisänen are unable to integrate Paul's treatment of the law in chap. 2 into the rest of his theology (Sanders, *Law*, 147—"true self-contradiction"; Räisänen, "Difficulties," 307—"contradictory lines of thought"; also *Law*). The use of νόμος in 3:27–31 has caused unending puzzlement: should we take νόμος in v 27 as a reference to the law or translate "principle"? And how can Paul claim in v 31 to be "establishing the law"? The centrality of the law in chap. 7 has been recognized, but how and whether that insight facilitates the exegesis of 7:14–25 in particular is a matter of unresolved controversy, with the meaning of νόμος in 7:23 and 8:2 disputed in the same way as in 3:27. In the obviously crucial resumptive section, 9:30–10:4, there is equal controversy over the meaning of νόμος δικαιοσύνης, "law of righteousness" (9:31), and τέλος νόμου, "end of the law" (10:4). And in the parenetic section the claim that love of neighbor is a fulfillment of the law (13:8–10) causes further puzzlement to those who think that Paul has turned his back on Judaism and its law. As Räisänen's withering critique has underlined (*Law*, 23–28, 42–83), the problem of holding together in an integrated whole both the positive and the negative statements regarding the law in Romans has not reached a satisfactory solution; though Räisänen's own atomistic treatment of the texts is itself a critical hindrance to an integrated and coherent overview of the theme.

Clearly, then, this major secondary motif in the letter presents problems of central importance for our understanding of the letter. It may be, indeed, that they all hang together, and a correct resolution of one may carry with it resolution of the others. At all events it will be necessary to gain a clearer view of the role of the law in first-century Judaism before we venture into the letter itself. Only when we can take for granted what Paul and his readers took for granted with regard to the law and its function will we be able to hear the allusions he was making and understand the argument he was offering. The confusion and disagreement still remaining with regard to the passages listed above strongly suggest that the role of the law, both within the Judaism against which Paul was reacting and within the new perspective on Paul, has not as yet been properly perceived. In what follows I will therefore attempt briefly to "set the scene" for an understanding of this important integrating strand of the letter.

§5.3 First of all, we should clarify a point that has occasioned some misunderstanding and confusion, namely, the appropriateness of νόμος/law as the translation equivalent or "meaning" of תּוֹרָה/Torah. Since Schechter and Dodd, "Law," it has frequently been claimed that *torah* does not mean νόμος or "law"; rather, *torah* means simply "instruction" or "teaching," and *the* Torah (the Pentateuch, or indeed the whole of the Scriptures) includes more than law. According to an influential body of opinion, this equation of torah/Torah with (the) law as given by the LXX translation of תּוֹרָה using the narrower word νόμος, subsequently contributed to Paul's "distorted" understanding of his ancestral faith, and lies at the root of the modern characterization of Judaism as "legalistic" (e.g., Dodd, "Law," 34; Schoeps, *Paul*, 29; Sandmel, *Paul*, 47–48; cited by Westerholm, 330–31; also Lapide, 39). However, Westerholm has now shown clearly (1) that νόμος can be an appropriate rendering of תּוֹרָה (e.g., Gen 26:5; Exod 12:49; Lev 26:46); (2) that the technical use of "*torah* to refer to a collection which spells out Israel's covenantal obligations" goes back to Deuteronomy, which provides the basis for Torah = νόμος = law as an appropriate title for the Pentateuch (e.g., Deut 4:8; 30:10; 32:46); and (3) that Paul's use of νόμος to sum up Israel's obligations as set out by Moses is "fully in line with Hebrew usage of *torah*" (cf., e.g., Rom 2:12, 17–18; 7:12; and 10:5 with 1 Kings 2:3; Ezra 7:6, 10, 12, 14, 26; Neh 8:14; 9:14, 34; and Jer 32:23).

In particular, the basic understanding of "covenantal nomism" is more or less self-evident in the central foundation act of Israel as a nation—the exodus from Egypt and the giving of the law at Sinai. As quintessentially expressed in Exod 20 and Deut 5, the law (here the ten commandments—cf. Deut 4:8 with 5:1) follows upon the prior act of divine initiative ("I am the Lord your God, who brought you out of the land of Egypt . . ."); obedience to this law is Israel's response to divine grace, not an attempt to gain God's favor conceived as grudgingly given and calculatingly dispensed. As already implied, the fullest and most sustained expression of this basic Jewish theologoumenon is Deuteronomy, the classic statement of Israel's covenant theology: the statutes and ordinances of the law (chaps. 5–28) set out explicitly as God's covenant made with Israel (5:2–3; 29:1); the promise (and warning) repeatedly reaffirmed in numerous variations, "This do and live" (e.g., 4:1, 10, 40; 5:29–33; 6:1–2, 18, 24; 7:12–13; etc.; see also on 2:13 and 10:5). Not surprisingly, in Romans Paul interacts more frequently with Deuteronomy than with any other section of the Pentateuch; and his exposition of Deut 30:12–14 is at the center of his attempt to expound the continuing and wider significance of the law in a way which retrieves the law from a too narrowly defined understanding of "This do and live" (10:5–13).

It is unnecessary to enter the debate about how deeply rooted this understanding of covenant and law was in pre-Exilic Israelite religion (see, e.g., Nicholson). Whatever the actual facts in that case, the attitude of covenantal nomism was certainly given determinative shape by Ezra's reforms in the post-Exilic period, with their deliberate policy of national and cultic segregation as dictated by the law (Ezra 9–10). This trend was massively reinforced by the Maccabean crisis, where it was precisely Israel's identity as the covenant people, the people of the law, which was at stake (1 Macc 1:57; 2:27, 50; 2 Macc 1:2–4; 2:21–22; 5:15; 13:14), and where "zeal for the law" became the watchword of national resistance (1 Macc 2:26–27, 50, 58; 2 Macc 4:2; 7:2, 9, 11, 37; 8:21; 13:14; see further on 10:2). So, too, in the period following the Maccabean crisis the tie-in between election, covenant, and law remains a fundamental and persistent theme of Jewish self-understanding, as illustrated by ben Sira (Sir 17:11–17; 24:23; 28:7; 39:8; 42:2; 44:19–20; 45:5, 7, 15, 17, 24–25), *Jubilees* (1:4–5, 9–10, 12, 14, 29; 2:21; 6:4–16; 14:17–20; 15:4–16, 19–21, 25–29, 34; 16:14; 19:29; 20:3; etc.), the Damascus document (CD 1:4–5, 15–18, 20; 3:2–4, 10–16; 4:7–10; 6:2–5; etc.) and Pseudo-Philo (*LAB* 4.5, 11; 7.4; 8.3; 9.3–4, 7–8, 13, 15; 10.2; 11.1–5; etc.). In particular we may note the outworking of all this in two of the main groups in Palestinian Judaism at the time of Jesus and Paul. The Qumran community defined membership of the covenant of grace in terms of observing God's precepts and clinging to God's commandments (1QS 1.7–8; 5.1–3), and commitment to the law had to be total and to be examined every year, with any breach severely punished (1QS 5.24; 8.16–9.2). And the Pharisees were known for their ἀκρίβεια, "strictness," in observing the law (see above §1.1), and evidently also for their concern to maintain a level of purity in their daily lives which the law required only for the temple cult itself (see also on 14:14). For rabbinic traditions on Israel's special relationship with the law see Str-B, 3:126–33. We may confine ourselves to two quotations provided by Schoeps, *Paul*, 195 and 216: *Sipre Deut* 53b–75b—God addresses Israel in the words "Let it be clear from the keeping of the commandments that you are a people holy to me"; and *Mek. Exod* 20:6—"By covenant is meant nothing other than the Torah."

§5.3.1 The law thus became a basic expression of Israel's *distinctiveness* as the people specially chosen by (the one) God to be his people. In sociological terms the law functioned as an "identity marker" and "boundary," reinforcing Israel's sense of distinctiveness and distinguishing Israel from the surrounding nations (Neusner, *Judaism*, 72–75; Meeks, *Urban Christians*, 97; Dunn, "Works of Law," 524–27). This sense of separateness was deeply rooted in Israel's national consciousness (e.g., Lev 20:24–26; Ezra 10:11; Neh 13:3; *Pss. Sol.* 17.28; *3 Macc* 3.4) and comes to powerful expression in *Jub.* 22.16:

> Separate yourself from the Gentiles,
>   and do not eat with them,
>   and do not perform deeds like theirs.
> And do not become associates of theirs.
> Because their deeds are defiled,
>   and all of their ways are contaminated,
>   and despicable, and abominable.

The letter of Aristeas expresses the same conviction in terms which reinforce the sociological insight.

> In his wisdom the legislator . . . surrounded us with unbroken palisades and iron walls to prevent our mixing with any of the other peoples in any matter. . . . So, to prevent our being perverted by contact with others or by mixing with bad influences, he hedged us in on all sides with strict observances connected with meat and drink and touch and hearing and sight, after the manner of the Law (*Ep. Arist.* 139, 142).

Similarly Philo, *Mos.* 1.278—a people "which shall dwell alone, not reckoned among other nations . . . because in virtue of the distinction of their peculiar customs they do not mix with others to depart from the ways of their fathers." And a funerary inscription from Italy praises a woman "who lived a gracious life inside Judaism [καλῶς βιώσασα ἐν τῷ Ἰουδαϊσμῷ]"—Judaism understood as "a sort of fenced off area in which Jewish lives are led" (Amir, 35–36, 39–40).

Consistent with this is the characterization of Gentiles as ἄνομος and their works as ἀνομία: by definition they were "without the law, outside the law," that is, outside the area (Israel) coterminous with the law, marked out by the law; so already in the Psalms (28:3; 37:28; 55:3; 73:3; 92:7; 104:35; 125:3), in 1 Maccabees (Gentiles and apostates—3:5–6; 7:5; 9:23, 58, 69; 11:25; 14:14), and in the self-evident equation, Gentile = "sinner" (as in Tob 13:6 [LXX 8]; *Jub.* 23:23–24; *Pss. Sol.* 1:1; 2:1–2; 17:22–25; Matt 5:47 with Luke 6:33; Gal 2:15). Not surprisingly this desire to live within the law and be marked off from the lawless and sinner became a dominant concern in the factionalism which was a feature of Judaism in the period from the Maccabeans to the emergence of rabbinic Judaism as the most powerful faction within post-c.e. 70 Judaism. It was expressed in the frequent complaints of "the righteous" and "devout" over against those (within Israel) whom they characterized as "sinners" (as in Wisd Sol 2–5; *Jub.* 6.32–35; 23.16, 26; *1 Enoch* 1.1, 7–9; 5.6–7; 82.4–7; 1QS 2.4–5; 1QH 2.8–19; CD 1.13–21; *Pss. Sol.* 3.3–12; 4.8; 13.5–12; 15.1–13; Pharisees probably = "separated ones"); see also on 3:7; 4:5, 7–8; and 9:6.

§5.3.2 A natural and more or less inevitable converse of this sense of distinctiveness was the sense of *privilege,* precisely in being the nation specially chosen by the one God and favored by gift of covenant and law. This comes out particularly clearly in writings which could not simply ignore and dismiss Gentiles as sinners, but which had to attempt some sort of apologetic for the claims of Israel in the face of a much more powerful gentile world. Thus both Philo and Josephus speak with understandable if exaggerated pride of the widespread desire among Greek and barbarian to adopt Jewish customs and laws (Philo, *Mos.* 2.17–25—"they attract and win the attention of all . . . the sanctity of our legislation has been a source of wonder not only to Jews and to all others also"; Josephus, *Ap.* 2.277–86—"The masses have long since shown a keen desire to adopt our religious observances. . . . Were we not ourselves aware of the excellence of our laws, assuredly we should have been impelled to pride [μέγα φρονεῖν] ourselves upon them by the multitude of their admirers"). Expressive of the same pride in the law of Moses is what seems to have been a fairly sustained attempt in Jewish apologetic to present Moses as "the first wise man," who was teacher of Orpheus and from whose writings Plato and Pythagoras learned much of their wisdom (Eupolemus, frag. 1; Artapanus, frag. 3; Aristobulus, frag. 3–4; from Eusebius, *Praep. Evang.* 9.26.1; 9.27.3–6; and 13.12.1–4; texts in Charlesworth).

Pride in the law as the mark of God's special favor to Israel is also well illustrated in the identification of divine Wisdom with the law, the assertion that the universally desirable Wisdom, immanent within creation but hidden from human eyes, was embodied within "the book of the covenant of the Most High God, the law which Moses commanded us as an inheritance for the congregations of Jacob" (Sir 24:23). The same claim is expressed more forcefully in Bar 3:36–4:4:

> [36] . . . (He) gave her to Jacob his servant
> and to Israel whom he loved
> . . . .
> [1] She is the book of the commandments of God,
> and the law which endures for ever.
> All who hold her fast will live,
> but those who forsake her will die.
> [2] Turn, O Jacob, and take her;
> walk towards the shining of her light.
> [3] Do not give your glory [τὴν δόξαν σου] to another,
> or your advantages [τὰ συμφέροντα] to an alien people.
> [4] Blessed are we, O Israel,
> for what is pleasing to God is known [γνωστά] to us.

For those confronted by the crushing power of Rome within Palestine this sense of privilege was difficult to maintain. *Psalms of Solomon* found a solution in pressing the older distinction between discipline and punishment (particularly *Pss. Sol.* 3, 10, and 13)—thus 13:6–11:

> The destruction of the sinner is terrible
> but nothing shall harm the righteous, of all these things,
> For the discipline of the righteous (for things done) in ignorance
> is not the same as the destruction of the sinners
> . . . .
> For the Lord will spare his devout,
> and he will wipe away their mistakes with discipline.
> For the life of the righteous (goes on) for ever,
> but sinners shall be taken away to destruction . . . .

Less easy to satisfy was the writer of *4 Ezra*, who in common with his fellow Jews saw the law given to Israel as a mark of divine favor (3:19; 9:31), but who could not understand how God could spare the sinful nations and yet allow his law-keeping people to be so harshly treated (3:28–36; 4:23–24; 5:23–30; 6:55–59).

§5.3.3 A sociological perspective also helps us to see how the conviction of privileged election and the practice of covenantal nomism almost inevitably comes to expression in focal points of distinctiveness, particular laws and especially ritual practices which reinforced the sense of distinctive identity and marked Israel off most clearly from the other nations. In this case three of Israel's laws gained particular prominence as being especially distinctive—circumcision, food laws, and sabbath (cf. Limbeck, 34; Meeks, *Urban Christians*, 36–37, 97; Sanders, *Law*, 102). These were not the only beliefs and practices which marked out Jews, but from the Maccabean period onward they gained increasing significance for their boundary-defining character, and were widely recognized both within and without Judaism as particularly and distinctively characteristic of Jews. Not that they were intrinsically more important than other laws, simply that they had become points of particular sensitivity in Jewish national understanding and were test cases of covenant loyalty. Since I will provide sufficiently full documentation later, I need say no more here (see on 2:25 and 14:2, 5).

§5.4 This, then, is the context within which and against which we must set Paul's treatment of the law in Romans. The Jews, proselytes, and God-worshiping Gentiles among his readership would read what Paul says about the law in the light of this close interconnection in Jewish theology of Israel's election, covenant, and law. They would, I believe, recognize that what Paul was concerned about was the fact that covenant promise and law had become too inextricably identified with ethnic Israel as such, with the Jewish people marked out in their national distinctiveness by the practices of circumcision, food laws, and sabbath in particular (Wright appropriately coins the phrase "national righteousness"). They would recognize that what Paul was endeavoring to do was to free both promise and law for a wider range of recipients, freed from the ethnic constraints which he saw to be narrowing the grace of God and diverting the saving purpose of God out of its main channel—Christ.

Not least in importance, by setting Paul's treatment of the law into this matrix we are enabled to offer a solution to the sequence of exegetical problems and disputes outlined earlier (§5.2). Thus it should occasion no surprise that chap. 2 turns out to be a developing critique of precisely these features of Jewish covenant theology which were sketched out above (§5.3)—the law as dividing Jew from non-Jew, the haves from the have-nots, those within from those without (2:12–14); the law as a source of ethnic pride for the typical devout Jew (2:17–23); and circumcision as the focal point for this sense of privileged distinctiveness (2:25–29; Hartman draws attention to the consistent strand of "covenant ideology" in and behind these chapters). Paul regularly warns against "the works of the law," not as "good works" in general or as any attempt by the individual to amass merit for himself, but rather as that pattern of obedience by which "the righteous" maintain their status within the people of the covenant, as evidenced not least by their dedication on such sensitive "test" issues as sabbath and food laws (see on 3:20 and 14:2, 5).

Likewise I will be arguing that an important hermeneutical key to such crucial passages as 3:27–31, 7:14–25, and 9:30–10:4 is precisely the recognition that Paul's negative thrust against the law is against the law taken over too completely by Israel, the law misunderstood by a misplaced emphasis on boundary-marking ritual, the law become a tool of sin in its too close identification with matters of the flesh, the law sidetracked into a focus for nationalistic zeal. Freed from that too narrowly Jewish perspective, the law still has an important part to play in "the obedience of faith." And the parenetic section (12:1–15:6) can then be seen as Paul's attempt to provide a basic guideline for social living, the law redefined for the eschatological people of God in place of the law misunderstood in too distinctively Jewish terms, with the climax understandably focused on a treatment of the two older test-cases, food laws and sabbath. It is my contention that only with such an understanding can we do adequate justice to both the positive and the negative thrusts of Paul's treatment of the law in Romans, and that failure to appreciate "the social function" of the law (as outlined above) is a fatal weakness both of alternative attempts (e.g., Cranfield, Hahn and Hübner) and of Räisänen's critique.

In short, properly understood, Paul's treatment of the law, which has seemed so confused and incoherent to many commentators, actually becomes one of the chief integrating strands which binds the whole letter into a cohesive and powerful restatement of Jewish covenant theology in the light of Christ.

With the letter thus situated within the contexts of its author, of those for whom he wrote, and of the issues with which he engaged, we can now turn to the task of exegesis.

WORD BIBLICAL COMMENTARY

Romans 1-8

I. Introduction   (1:1–17)

The letter falls into the three self-evident sections of almost all communications: beginning (1:1–17), middle (1:18–15:13) and end (15:14–16:27). The introduction consists of three paragraphs: 1:1–7, where Paul introduces himself with an unusual degree of elaboration and greets his readers in typical fashion; 1:8–15, where Paul makes a preliminary statement of his hopes to visit the Christians in Rome; and 1:16–17, where Paul sets out the main theme of the unusually lengthy exposition following thereafter.

A. Introductory Statement and Greetings (1:1–7)

Bibliography

Allen, L. C. "The Old Testament Background of (ΠΡΟ)ΟΡΙΖΕΙΝ in the New Testament." *NTS* 17 (1970–71) 104–8. **Becker, J.** *Auferstehung der Toten im Urchristentum*. SBS 82. Stuttgart: KBW, 1976. 18–31. **Boismard, M. E.** "Constitué fils de Dieu (Rom. 1:4)." *RB* 60 (1953) 5–17. **Bornkamm, G.** *Paul*. 248–49. **Brown, R. E.** *The Birth of the Messiah*. London: Chapman, 1977. Esp. 133–43. **Burger, C.** *Jesus als Davidssohn*. Göttingen: Vandenhoeck, 1970. 25–41. **Dahl, N. A.** "Missionary Theology." 74–78. ———. "The Messiahship of Jesus in Paul" (1953). In *The Crucified Messiah and Other Essays*. Minneapolis: Augsburg, 1974. 37–47. **Deidun, T. J.** *New Covenant Morality*. 3–10. **Dunn, J. D. G.** "Jesus—Flesh and Spirit: An Exposition of Romans 1:3–4." *JTS* 24 (1973) 40–68. **Eichholz, E.** *Theologie*. 123–32. **Friedrich, G.** "Lohmeyers These über das paulinische Briefpräskript kritisch beleuchtet." *TLZ* 81 (1956) 343–46. ———. "Muss ὑπακοὴ πίστεως Röm 1:5 mit 'Glaubensgehorsam' übersetzt werden?" *ZNW* 72 (1981) 118–23. **Gaffin, R. B.** *The Centrality of the Resurrection*. Grand Rapids: Baker, 1978. 98–113. **Garlington, D. B.** *Obedience of Faith*. **Haacker, K.** "Probleme." 12–14. **Hahn, F.** *Titles*. 246–51. **Harrer, G. A.** "Saul Who Is Also Called Paul." *HTR* 33 (1940) 19–33. **Hemer, C. J.** "The Name of Paul." *TynB* 36 (1985) 179–83. **Hengel, M.** *The Son of God*. London: SCM (1976). **Jewett, R.** "Ambassadorial Letter." 12–15. ———. "The Redaction and Use of an Early Christian Confession in Romans 1:3–4." In *The Living Text*, FS E. W. Saunders, ed. D. E. Groh and R. Jewett. Lanham/ New York: University Press of America, 1985. 99–122. **Kramer, W.** *Christ*. 108–11. **Linnemann, E.** "Tradition und Interpretation in Röm. 1:3f." *EvT* 31 (1971) 264–75. **Lips, H. von.** "Der Apostolat des Paulus—ein Charisma?" *Bib* 66 (1985) 305–43. **Lohmeyer, E.** "Probleme paulinischer Theologie I. Briefliche Grussüberschriften." *ZNW* 26 (1927) 158–73. **McCasland, S. V.** "Christ Jesus." *JBL* 56 (1946) 377–83. **Minde, H. J. van der.** *Schrift*. 38–47. **Nolland, J.** "Grace as Power." *NovT* 28 (1986) 26–31. **O'Brien, P. T.** *Introductory Thanksgivings*. 197–230. **Poythress, V. S.** "Is Romans 1:3–4 a *Pauline* Confession?" *ExpT* 87 (1975–76) 180–83. **Roller, O.** *Das Formular der paulinischen Briefe*. Stuttgart: Kohlhammer, 1933. 55–62. **Satake, A.** "Apostolat und Gnade bei Paulus." *NTS* 15 (1968–69) 96–107. **Schlier, H.** "Eine christologische Credo-Formel der römischen Gemeinde. Zu Röm. 1:3f." In *Neues Testament und Geschichte*, FS O. Cullmann, ed. H. Baltensweiler and B. Reicke. Zürich: Theologischer,

1972. 207–18 = *Der Geist und die Kirche: Exegetische Aufsätze und Vorträge.* Freiburg: Herder, 1980. 56–69. ——. "Εὐαγγέλιον im Römerbrief." In *Wort Gottes in der Zeit,* FS K. H. Schelkle, ed. H. Feld and J. Nolte. Düsseldorf: Patmos, 1973. 127–42 = *Geist und Kirche.* 70–87. **Schneider, B.** "Κατὰ Πνεῦμα ʿΑγιωσύνης (Romans 1:4)." *Bib* 48 (1967) 359–87. **Schweizer, E.** "Röm. 1:3f. und der Gegensatz von Fleisch und Geist vor und bei Paulus." *EvT* 15 (1955) 563–71 = *Neotestamentica.* Zürich/Stuttgart: Zwingli, 1963. 180–89. **Stanley, D. M.** *Resurrection.* 161–66. **Strecker, G.** "Das Evangelium Jesu Christi" (1975). In *Eschaton und Historie: Aufsätze.* Göttingen: Vandenhoeck, 1979. 183–228. **Stuhlmacher, P.** "Theologische Probleme des Römerbriefpräskripts." *EvT* 27 (1967) 374–89. ——. *Das paulinische Evangelium.* Göttingen: Vandenhoeck, 1968. ——. "Das paulinische Evangelium." In *Das Evangelium und die Evangelien,* ed. P. Stuhlmacher. WUNT 28. Tübingen: J. C. B. Mohr, 1983. 157–82. **Theobald, M.** "'Dem Juden zuerst und auch dem Heiden.' Die paulinische Auslegung der Glaubensformel Röm 1:3f." In *Kontinuität und Einheit,* FS F. Mussner, ed. P. G. Müller and W. Stenger. Freiburg: Herder, 1981. 376–92. **Wegenast, K.** *Tradition.* 70–76. **Wengst, K.** *Christologische Formeln.* 112–17. **Wiefel, W.** "Glaubensgehorsam? Erwägungen zu Röm. 1:5." In *Wort und Gemeinde,* FS E. Schott. Berlin: Evangelische, 1967. 137–44. **Wischmeyer, O.** "Das Adjectiv ΑΓΑΠΗΤΟΣ in den paulinischen Briefen. Eine traditionsgeschichtliche Miszelle." *NTS* 32 (1986) 476–80. **Zeller, D.** *Juden.* 46–49.

Translation

[1] *Paul, slave of Christ Jesus,*[a] *called to be an apostle, set apart*[b] *for the gospel of God,* [2] *which was promised beforehand through his prophets in the holy scriptures.* [3] *It concerns his Son*
 who was descended[c] *from the seed of David in terms of the flesh,*
  [4] *and who was appointed*[d] *Son of God in power in terms of the*
 spirit of holiness as from the resurrection of the dead,
Jesus Christ our Lord. [5] *Through him we received grace and apostleship with a view to the obedience of faith among all the nations for the sake of his name,* [6] *among whom you also are called to be Jesus Christ's.* [7] *To all those in Rome*[e] *who are beloved*[f] *by God, called to be saints: grace to you and peace, from God our Father and the Lord Jesus Christ.*

Notes

[a] Some manuscripts read "Jesus Christ," presumably altered to the more familiar form as in vv 4, 6, 7, and 8. See also SH.

[b] Perfect passive participle, denoting a past event whose effects are still in force.

[c] An attempt to represent the relative imprecision of γενομένου, "came into being, born." Some textual traditions removed the ambiguity by reading γεννωμένου, "born."

[d] The Old Latin textual tradition prefixes προ- to ὁρισθέντος, "predetermined, predestined."

[e] The absence of ἐν Ῥώμῃ in several witnesses (including G and Origen), if deliberate, raises questions about the form and function of the letter either originally or in subsequent recensions (see Lietzmann; and further *Introduction* §4.1).

[f] G and some other witnesses read ἐν ἀγάπῃ θεοῦ, "in the love of God," a modification perhaps connected with *Note* e. The support for αγαπητοῖς θεοῦ, "loved by God," however, is overwhelming.

Form and Structure

The opening paragraph is framed by the typical and long-established form for the beginning of a Greek letter: A to B χαίρειν, "Greeting" (within the

NT cf. Acts 15:23; 23:26; James 1:1; see further Roller, 55–56). Paul elaborates each of the three elements with characteristic features: his own self-identification as "servant of Christ Jesus" and "apostle . . ." (v 1) is more extensive than usual (presumably because he was writing to largely unknown congregations—though Rengstorf, "Paulus," justifiably warns against overemphasis on this point); the description of his addressees is elaborate (v 7a), but not unduly so (cf. 1 Cor 1:2; contrast Gal 1:2); and he concludes with his regular Christianized greeting, "Grace (χάρις) to you and peace from God our Father and the Lord Jesus Christ" (v 7b; cf. 2 Macc 1:1; *2 Apoc. Bar.* 78.2).

Unusually, however, Paul inserts a lengthy parenthesis about his gospel and apostleship between the first two elements of the standard opening (vv 2–6), presumably as a deliberate tactic to demonstrate his "good faith" and to deflect any suspicion or criticism from the start. This would explain, in particular, his incorporation of an older credal or evangelistic formulation (vv 3–4)—a clear indication to his Roman readers that he shares with them, as with those who were believers before him, a common faith and gospel.

Recognition of these distinctively Pauline features at the very beginning of the letter provides a first clear indication of Paul's concerns in writing: he writes preeminently as one "set apart for the gospel," whose apostleship is directed to the Gentiles (vv 1, 5); but each assertion is carefully formulated in characteristic Jewish terms—the gospel of God which he "promised beforehand through his prophets in the holy scriptures" (vv 1–2), Gentile converts "beloved of God, called to be saints" (v 7). Immediately therefore a theological dynamic is set up (out of which the structural tensions arise in large part): a Jewish gospel for Gentiles; what does this mean for the Gentiles?—and for the Jews as a whole? The thematic importance of what is thus signaled in the prescript is indicated by the subsequent frequency of the key words "faith" and "Gentiles," and also "obedience" (see on 1:5) ("the prescript has programmatic character for the whole epistle"—van der Minde, 38; see also O'Brien, 226–29, and Wright, *Messiah,* chap. 1).

That a pre-Pauline formulation is involved in vv 3–4 (and not just pre-Pauline phrases, as argued by Poythress) is indicated particularly by: (1) the two relative clauses in antithetic parallelism, (2) with the parallel verbs as aorist participles, and (3) two sets of parallel phrases attached (ἐκ σπέρματος Δαυίδ // υἱοῦ θεοῦ ἐν δυνάμει· κατὰ σάρκα // κατὰ πνεῦμα ἁγιωσύνης); (4) the untypical Pauline language (ὁρίζειν), (5) the Semitism πνεῦμα ἁγιωσύνης, (6) and the primitive description of Christ's resurrection as "the resurrection of the dead"; and (7) the evidence of similar primitive balanced formulations (son of David, son of God) in 2 Tim 2:8, Ign. *Smyrn.* 1.1 and in the common tradition lying behind the birth narratives (Matt 1:18–25; Luke 1:32–35; see Brown, *Birth,* 133–43, 309–16). That the lines are not exactly balanced says nothing to the contrary: theological adequacy would be regarded as more important than stichometric consistency; and the more redaction argued for, the less fitted would the formula be to serve its most obvious function of assuring the Roman addressees that Paul fully shared their common faith (*pace* Jewett, "Redaction").

That Paul framed the earlier material with the two Christological affirmations, "concerning his Son" and "Jesus Christ our Lord" is generally accepted.

The still popular view that ἐν δυνάμει is an insertion (by Paul or earlier) which disrupts the parallelism (so, e.g., Schlier and Wilckens; but see Hahn, *Titles,* 247, and Käsemann with further literature), depends too much on the older view that the Davidic Messiah was not thought of as God's son (as in Wegenast, 73–74—so that "son of David" and "son of God" could stand in abrupt antithesis), now overthrown by the evidence of the Dead Sea Scrolls (see on 1:4). The older view that the κατὰ σάρκα // κατὰ πνεῦμα antithesis is also a Pauline insertion has now been largely abandoned (e.g., Michel[5] against earlier editions, Wilckens; otherwise Wengst, 113; variation in Linnemann, 274–75, and Theobald, 382–83): the use of the κατὰ σάρκα // κατὰ πνεῦμα antithesis is not typical of Paul's use elsewhere, though the *meaning* of each phrase is not so different from Paul as Schweizer, "Röm 1:3f.," argued—κατὰ σάρκα, cf. 4:1, 9:3, 5; κατὰ πνεῦμα, cf. 6:4, 2 Cor 13:4; cf. Wengst, 113. Jewett argues that the two κατὰ phrases belong to a second, redacted, but still pre-Pauline level; but continues to depend on the unlikely suggestion that Paul added the unusual ἁγιωσύνης ("Redaction").

As examples of the quality of Paul's style we may note the wordplay in vv 1–2 (. . . εὐαγγέλιον . . . προεπηγγείλατο . . .), the neatly balanced sequence of prepositional phrases in v 5: εἰς . . . , ἐν . . . , ὑπὲρ . . . , and the balance between the phrases which he applies to himself in v 1 and those he applies to his readers in v 7:

δοῦλος Χριστοῦ Ἰησοῦ   κλητὸς ἀπόστολος
ἀγαπητοῖς θεοῦ   κλητοῖς ἁγίοις.

The naming of "Jesus Christ" four times in seven verses indicates the centrality of Christ to Paul's whole thought and endeavor.

Comment

1 Παῦλος, "Paul." The name by which Paul evidently wished to be known in all his letters. He never uses the name "Saul," though according to Acts that was how he was known at the time of his conversion and during the early part of his ministry and as a missionary of the church at Antioch (Acts 9:1, 4, etc., 13:1–2, 7). It would appear, however, from Acts 13:9 that at that time he already had the double name, "Saul, Paul," the latter which he presumably had used in the past in Greek circles (MM, 499; *NDIEC* 1:89–96). As a Roman citizen (a status enjoyed by many Jews of the period—see SVMG, 3:132–34) "Paul" was probably part of the formal name (e.g., C. Julius Paulus) by which he was registered according to law (Harrer, Hemer). "Saul" would then have been his familiar name, which persisted well into adulthood. In Acts the transition from "Saul" to "Paul" as his regular self-designation more or less coincides with the beginning of his active (recorded) outreach to Gentiles beyond the eastern seaboard of the Mediterranean. Since "Saul" was an unfamiliar name outside Jewish circles the transition to the more easily recognized name was a natural step. Yet, the completeness of the change strongly suggests a transition in Paul's self-perception, at least in terms of the social context within which he had his identity, perhaps a certain freeing of himself from the person he had been perceived to be as "Saul," or a willingness to engage in new relationships other than those enjoyed by "Saul." That "Paul" thus reflects his increasing commitment as "apostle to the Gentiles" is therefore quite likely. And since this commitment comes to the fore more or less clearly in all his letters, the consistent self-designation "Paul" in all his letters can also be seen as an expression of that commitment— and not least in Romans (cf. 1:5–7). Such an implication would obviously be lost on his Roman readers, unless they were familiar with his older persona.

Paul does not associate anyone else with his greetings, in contrast to his usual practice (though cf. Gal 1:1). This is not to be explained simply by the fact that he and his associates had had no hand in the founding of the Roman congregations (cf. 1 Cor 1:1). And, assuming chap. 16 is part of the original letter (see 16:1–23 *Form and Structure*), Timothy, his closest fellow worker, was beside him here too (16:21; cf. 2 Cor 1:1; Phil 1:1; Col 1:1; 1 Thess 1:1; 2 Thess 1:1). In this instance we may assume therefore that Paul wanted to present himself in his own person to these largely unknown congregations, as (the) apostle to the Gentiles (cf. 11:13), and with the subsequent exposition of the gospel understood very much as his (cf. 2:16; 16:25; Achtemeier). It was on their reaction to this very personal statement that the success or failure of this letter would hang (see also on 16:21).

δοῦλος Χριστοῦ Ἰησοῦ, "slave of Christ Jesus"—elsewhere among his introductory formulae only in Phil 1:1. Paul here clearly draws on his Jewish heritage. The Jewish worshiper quite naturally thought of himself as God's slave (Neh 1:6, 11; Ps 19:11, 13; 27:9; 31:16; etc.; 1QH 7.16; 9.10–11; etc.). The noun is used both in the plural and in the singular for Israel as a whole (Deut 32:36; Jer 46 [LXX 26]:27; Ezek 28:25). And great figures from the past are quite often referred to as Yahweh's slave, particularly Moses (e.g., 2 Kgs 18:12; Neh 9:14; Ps 105:26; Dan 9:11; Mal 4:4; Josephus, *Ant.* 5.39), and the prophets (Ezra 9:11; Jer 7:25; 25:4; 35 [LXX 42]:15; Ezek 38:17; Dan 9:6; Amos 3:7; Zech 1:6). As such the idea draws its force from Israel's conviction that it had been chosen by the one God to be peculiarly and particularly his—Israel as belonging exclusively to Yahweh and none other, Israel's great heroes honored by the title precisely because of the unconditional quality of their commitment to Israel's God and of their part in maintaining the covenant between God and his people. The idea itself does not necessarily imply that Paul placed himself in the line of such great figures. But in using it of himself Paul certainly wanted to indicate the same exclusiveness and unconditional character of his belonging and dependence. The phrase is not so much honorific as indicative of dedication. Hence also its wider use in early Christian vocabulary, not just of apostolic figures (Phil 1:1; 2 Tim 2:24; James 1:1; 2 Pet 1:1; Jude 1:1), but also of Christians generally (Acts 4:29; 1 Cor 7:22; Eph 6:6; Col 4:12; Rev 22:3; see further BGD, δοῦλος 4; and later *NDIEC* 2:54).

Paul's adaptation of the familiar Jewish language is distinctive in three ways. (1) He calls himself a slave "of Christ Jesus." This is the corollary of hailing Jesus as "Lord," but the degree to which the pious Jew's exclusive devotion to the one God has now become or come to include the same sort of devotion to Jesus as risen from the dead and exalted to God's right hand is highly significant as an indicator of how far developed the self-understanding of the Jesus movement already was (cf. Titus 1:1, "slave of God"). The degree of intended continuity with traditional Jewish faith would be heightened if Χριστός retained anything of its titular significance as the Greek translation of "Messiah." And this may be implied in the fact that Χριστός can stand first (an odd inversion if "Jesus Christ" had become solely a proper name— McCasland, 382). But the idea of Jesus as fulfillment of Israel's Messianic hope (and therefore worthy of the devotion previously restricted to the Lord, Yahweh) is clearly drawn in only in vv 2–4, and can only be recognized in v 1 as a reflection of the immediately following emphasis (see particularly Dahl, "Messiahship," 37–47; Kramer, 203–14).

(2) Paul very likely had in mind a particular OT passage—Isa 49:1–7 or 8. (a) It certainly played a role in shaping his own understanding of his call as apostle to the Gentiles, along with other "Servant" passages in Isaiah: Gal 1:15—Isa 49:1 (note also the self-reference as "Christ's slave" in Gal 1:10); 2 Cor 6:1–2—Isa 49:8; Rom 15:21—Isa 52:15; Phil 2:16—Isa 49:4; note also Acts 13:47—Isa 49:6; Acts 26:18—Isa 42:7. (b) The theme of God *calling* his *servant/slave* for ministry to the *Gentiles* (and the diaspora as part of his covenant purpose) is certainly prominent in both Isa 49:1–8 (LXX) and Paul's opening statement here (vv 1–7), in which case it is presumably implied that Paul saw his ministry to the Gentiles both as fulfilling Israel's covenanted role (according to Isaiah), and as bringing to full effect Jesus' own role as the Servant of Yahweh (cf. Dunn, *Jesus*, 112–13); see further on 15:21.

(3) The idea of the individual being slave of a deity was familiar enough in the East, and in the West through the spreading mystery cults. Otherwise it would have been at odds with cultured Greek thought, where the sense of the dignity of the free man made it virtually impossible for slavery to serve as an ideal or commendable type of relationship (*TDNT* 2:261–65; Lagrange). This sense of a fundamental distinction between slave and free was deeply rooted in Roman society (cf. Meeks, *Urban Christians*, 20–21), so that Paul must have been aware of it, and of the conflicting images the phrase would provoke in the minds of his Roman readers—not least the designation of himself as "slave" of the one who had suffered the "slaves' punishment" (see M. Hengel, *Crucifixion* [London: SCM, 1977] 51–63).

κλητὸς ἀπόστολος, "called to be an apostle"—the complete phrase only here and in 1 Cor 1:1. κλητός in common parlance would denote one who had been invited to a meal (e.g., 1 Kgs 1:41, 49; 3 Macc 5.14; Matt 22:14). This sense is derived from the verb καλέω, "invite," which also has the stronger force of "summon" (BGD, καλέω 1b, d, e), and which presumably had something of that stronger sense when the invitation to the banquet was given by a king or by a god (as in Matt 22:3, 9 and *NDIEC* 1:5–6). Even stronger is its Christian usage (cf. particularly Rom 4:17; 9:11–12)—Paul's readers defined precisely as "the called," those whose lives had been determined by God's summons, who had been drawn into God's ongoing purpose by the power of that call (1:6–7; 8:28, 30; 1 Cor 1:2, 9, 24; 7:15, 17–24; Gal 1:6; 5:8, 13; etc.—see *TDNT* 3:488–89, 494). Within that calling, which is one of the distinguishing features of all those belonging to Christ, Paul thinks of a

calling to a specific task (1:1; 1 Cor 1:1), though in both cases he takes care
to ensure that the idea of a specific calling cannot be separated from the
calling of all (1:6–7; 1 Cor 1:2; cf. Str-B, 3:1–2). The prominence of the
theme of God's summons both here (vv 1, 6–7) and in the context of the
Isaiah servant passages (Isa 41:9; 42:6; 43:1; 45:3–4; 48:12, 15; 49:1; 51:2)
strengthens the probability that Paul had the Isaianic theme very much in
mind.

ἀπόστολος has the basic force of "messenger, delegate, one sent on behalf
of" (MM, BGD; in Paul, 2 Cor 8:23; Phil 2:25). Hence the specialized sense
of "messenger, apostle of Christ," which had already become established as
a technical term in Christian vocabulary, even though it did not swallow up
the less specific sense for some time (*Did.* 11.4, 6). In calling himself an "apostle" Paul clearly presupposes a special commissioning by the risen Christ to
a limited group within a limited time period following his resurrection (1
Cor 15:8—"last of all"), and asserts an authority exercised particularly in
mission, in the establishing of churches (1 Cor 9:1–2). Here he announces
his title without making any great point of it, though he will shortly emphasize
its (for him) two main characteristics—an apostleship given through the exalted
Christ and an apostleship to the Gentiles (1:5; contrast the more vigorous
defense called forth in Galatians and 1 and 2 Corinthians). In each case he
acts on his conviction that his authority as apostle was circumscribed by his
sphere of mission and was to be exercised only in relation to the churches
founded by him (1 Cor 12:28; 2 Cor 10:13–16—see NEB; Rom 15:20). Paul
claimed a special apostleship to the Gentiles (see further on 11:13), but not
in an exclusive sense, since he also reckoned as apostles a wider circle than
the twelve, including several who were associated in one way or another
with him in the Gentile mission (1:5; 16:7; 1 Cor 4:9; 15:7; 1 Thess 2:6).
That "apostle" as a t.t. was not yet so limited as Acts 1:26 implies, helps
explain why Paul's claim to an apostolic commissioning was accepted by the
Jerusalem leadership (to the extent that they did so) despite the uncomfortable-
ness of his understanding of the gospel which belonged to his apostleship
to the Gentiles (Gal 2:1–10). The tendency already in Acts to confine the
title to "the twelve" anticipates later trends (cf. *LPGL*) not yet evident at the
time of Paul. For further discussion and bibliography see J. A. Kirk, "Apostleship since Rengstorf: Towards a Synthesis," *NTS* 21 (1974–75) 249–64; Dunn,
Jesus, 271–80; *NIDNTT* 1:136–37.

ἀφωρισμένος εἰς εὐαγγέλιον θεοῦ, "separated for the gospel of God," that is,
in his conversion = commissioning, on the road to Damascus (see also below)
or earlier (cf. Gal 1:15). ἀφορίζειν, "set apart," overlaps in meaning with ἅγιος,
"holy," and ἁγιάζειν, "sanctify, consecrate" (note particularly Ezek 45:4—
Cranfield). So it is possible that Paul had in mind Lev 20:26, where the two
ideas are stressed: the turn of the ages effected by Christ meant that the
ideal of separation *from* the Gentiles now became for Paul separation *for the
sake of* the Gentiles (but cf. 2 Cor 6:17 = Isa 52:11). Michel in his fifth
edition has retreated from his earlier strong support for the suggestion that
Paul intended a wordplay on "Pharisee" (separated one) (as advocated, e.g.,
in Zahn; *TDNT* 5:454; Nygren; Fitzmyer; Black); such a pun would almost
certainly have been lost on his readers.

εὐαγγέλιον, "gospel," is already clearly a t.t. in Christian vocabulary as "the gospel" (1:16; 10:16; 11:28; 1 Cor 4:15; etc.) = the good news of Jesus Christ. As such it is almost certainly to be understood as a Christian formulation, a very early outcome of Jewish believers preaching to their Greek-speaking (diaspora) kinsfolk. The unfamiliarity of the singular form in Greek texts of the period makes it very unlikely that Paul's Greek-speaking Jewish Christian predecessors adapted it from the more familiar plural form "good tidings," particularly as used within the context of the Caesar cult (references in LSJ; cf. *NDIEC* 3:12–15; against Strecker, *Eschaton*, 183–228; also *EWNT* 2:176–86). It must be considered much more probable that the Christian term was derived from earliest recollection of Jesus' own ministry in which the verb form was already firmly established in direct dependence on Isa 61:1–2 (Matt 11:5 // Luke 7:22; Acts 10:36). Its prominence in the second half of Isaiah (40:9; 52:7; 60:6; 61:1) was certainly influential in Jewish thinking in the period leading up to Jesus (*Pss. Sol.* 11.1; 1QH 18.14; 11QMelch 18). And the strong influence of this section of Isaiah on earliest Christian thought (as evidenced not least in Rom 1:1–7, and note also 10:15–16) makes it very likely that the singular noun εὐαγγέλιον was quickly formed in the Greek-speaking mission to serve as a convenient and appropriate referent to express the strong conviction that they had something to proclaim, "the good news of God" (see Stuhlmacher, *Evangelium*; also *Evangelien*, 157–82; Wilckens, 74–75).

εἰς εὐαγγέλιον, "for the gospel"—that is, for the purpose of preaching the gospel (cf. 2 Cor 2:12; Acts 13:2). Paul probably does not intend the noun to denote the act of preaching itself (cf. κήρυγμα—16:25; 1 Cor 1:21; 2:4; 15:14). His language rather reflects the fact that since his conversion the gospel had been the dominant and determinative focus of his whole life (cf. again Gal 1:16; see further *Introduction* §1.2 and on 1:16).

εὐαγγέλιον θεοῦ, "the gospel of God"—so 15:16; 2 Cor 11:7; 1 Thess 2:2, 8, 9; also Mark 1:14; 1 Pet 4:17. "Of God" is the source and authority behind the message (cf. 1:9). Paul departs from his more usual opening formula ("apostle of Jesus Christ," "by the will of God"—1 Cor 1:1; 2 Cor 1:1; Col 1:1; so Eph 1:1; 2 Tim 1:1; cf. Gal 1:1; 1 Tim 1:1; Titus 1:1), but still contrives a balanced statement in which Christ Jesus is named with God as the legitimating authority which validates his whole mission.

2 προεπηγγείλατο, "promised beforehand"—elsewhere in the NT only 2 Cor 9:5. The force of the middle voice may be to emphasize the subject of the promise—"which God promised," "which he promised on his own behalf" (cf. Moule, *Idiom Book*, 24). On "the dialectic of promise and gospel" see Käsemann. Cf. also van der Minde, 45.

διὰ τῶν προφητῶν αὐτοῦ, "through his prophets." "*His* prophets" (unusual in the NT) may also reflect Paul's concern to emphasize God's personal involvement in and authority behind the prophetic hope, though it may also be a continuing echo of the familiar OT phrase, "his/my (God's) servants (δοῦλοι) the prophets," which lies in part behind Paul's opening self-designation (see on 1:1). Paul avoids saying "the law and the prophets," though he uses the fuller phrase later in 3:21 to make a similar point, perhaps because it is precisely the role of the law within the divine purpose which he seeks to clarify in this letter, and almost certainly because he wants to strike the note of promise and fulfillment, of God's promise and his faithfulness to that promise, right from the beginning, as clearly as possible. The apologetic concern is already evident and prepares for the central role Paul gives to God's "promise" in chap. 4. The prophets and prophecies in question would have been established as Christian proof texts as one of the earliest apologetic requirements of the new movement (cf. 1 Cor 15:3–4). They would already include at least some of the texts cited or alluded to later on (see, e.g., on 4:25) and in the sermons in Acts, and here particularly 2 Sam 7:12–16 and Ps 2:7 (see on 1:3).

ἐν γραφαῖς ἁγίαις, "in [the] holy scriptures"—the only time this phrase ("holy scriptures") as such occurs in the NT. It refers to an established body of writings, already recognized as Scripture and sacred, that is, as having the status of divinely authorized statements or indeed of divine oracles in writing (cf. Philo, *Fuga* 4; *Spec. Leg.* 1.214; *Heres* 106, 159). The lack of the definite article makes no difference, as those same references show (cf. also 15:4 with 16:26; 2 Pet 1:20 with 3:16; see also BDF, §255). Nor does the plural mark a significant difference from the singular, which was already in use for the collectivity of the Scriptures (Philo, *Mos.* 2.84; *Ep. Arist.* 155, 168). The Scriptures in view would be more or less the books contained in our OT (cf. Sir prologue; Josephus, *Ap.* 1.37–42; *4 Ezra* 14:37–48), though the concept of a fixed and closed canon of Scripture was not yet clearly evident, as the larger scope of the LXX indicates.

3 περὶ τοῦ υἱοῦ αὐτοῦ, "concerning his Son," further defines "the gospel of God" (v 1)—another example of Paul contriving to make an opening statement in which God and Christ are balancing elements—perhaps prompted in part by the thought of God as Father with which he always begins his letters (see on 1:7). The title is not particularly prominent in Paul's thought but occurs quite naturally when Paul wants to speak of the relation between God and Jesus (1:4, 9; 1 Cor 15:28), or of God's concern for people expressed through or in relation to Jesus (8:29; 1 Cor 1:9; 2 Cor 1:19), particularly in its decisive moments (5:10; 8:3, 32; Gal 1:16; 2:20; 4:4; Col 1:13; 1 Thess 1:10; see further on 5:10). It is clear enough that already Jesus was understood as God's Son in a quite distinctive way—"his Son," where even before Paul embarks on the confessional elaboration (vv 3–4), it is obvious that a sonship is envisaged different from that affirmed of believers in the regular opening greeting (v 7). This is significant since as a title or description at the time of Paul it had a much wider potential reference—being used of oriental rulers, including occasionally the king of Israel (2 Sam 7:14; Pss 2:7; 89:26–27), of great philosophers or in Jewish circles of a famous rabbi (*m. Ta'an.* 3.8), and indeed of mankind as a whole (Stoic thought) or in Judaism of Israel as a whole (Exod 4:22–23; Jer 31:9; Hos 11:1; Wisd Sol 9:7; 18:13; *Jub.* 1.24–25; *Pss. Sol.* 17.30; 18.4; *T. Mos.* 10.3; *Sib. Or.* 3.702) or of the righteous in particular (Wisd Sol 2:13, 16, 18; 5:5; Sir 4:10; 51:10; 2 Macc 7:34; *Pss. Sol.* 13.8; the Qumran covenanters thought of themselves as God's "sons of truth"—1QM 17.8; 1QH 7.29–30; 9.35; 10.27; 11.11). See further on 8:14 and 9:4; Str-B, 3:15–22; *TDNT* 8:335–62; Hengel, *Son*; Dunn, *Christology*, 14–15.

Just how it came about that the earliest Christians acknowledged or recognized Jesus as uniquely God's Son is not entirely clear. (1) The simplest reading of the evidence is that it was rooted in the well-remembered fact of Jesus' own sense of sonship as expressed particularly in prayer (to which 8:15–17 and Gal 4:6–7 bear ample testimony), a sonship which the resurrection of Jesus rendered unique in the eyes of the first followers of Jesus (so the force of the following formula—see on 1:4). (2) An alternative possibility is that the recognition of Jesus as Messiah carried the implication of a unique sonship with it, since Messiah, Son of David, was also called God's Son in a quite distinctive sense (see below). However, the more an identification between Messiahship and Sonship is asserted, the more difficult it is to give weight to the second clause of the following formula, unless we allow that it implies Son of David = Son of God in weakness—but then the formula loses its sharpness and its antithetical parallelism becomes confused. (3) A third possibility is that the assertion of Jesus' uniqueness as God's Son stems from a recognition that he came from heaven (cf. the usual interpretation of 8:3 and Gal 4:4). This is less likely (despite its common assertion today—as, e.g., Stuhlmacher, "Probleme," 382–83; Murray; Eichholz, *Theologie*, 126; Ridderbos, *Paul*, 68–69; Hengel, *Son*, 60; Becker 19–20; Goppelt, *Theology*, 2:67, 69). The title itself would not be seen to carry that implication of itself. A reference to Jesus as an angelic being would not be sufficiently distinctive, since angels as a whole were called "sons of God" (Gen 6:2, 4; Deut 32:8; Job 1:6–12; etc.; Pss 29:1; 89:6). We would have to presuppose an identification of Jesus with the Logos, called "God's first-born Son" by Philo (*Conf.* 146; *Som.* 1.215), though we have no evidence of such an identification prior to the prologue of the Fourth Gospel (John 1:1–18). That an identification of Jesus as Wisdom (cf. 1 Cor 1:24, 30; 8:6; Col 1:15–20) would be recognized under the summary title "Son" is unlikely since "Wisdom" is a female figure (σοφία). As the identification of the Man of Dan 7's vision as "my Son" seems to have been fairly late in Jewish circles (*4 Ezra* 13.32, 37, 52), so the explicit assertion of Christ's preexistence as God's Son from eternity seems to be post-Pauline in Christian circles (John; cf. Heb 1:3). See also on 8:3 and further Dunn, *Christology*.

γενομένου, "came into being, born." Since γίνεσθαι ("become, come to be") merges into εἶναι ("to be"), the participle phrase has in view more the state of man (= "born of woman"—Job 14:1; 15:14; 1QS 11.20–21; 1QH 13.14; 18.12–13, 16) than the event of giving birth itself, for which γεννάω would be the more appropriate word (see *Notes*).

ἐκ σπέρματος Δαυίδ, "from the seed of David"—a clear assertion that Jesus was the anointed Son of David, the royal Messiah, the fulfillment of prophetic hopes long cherished among the people of Israel for the age to come (Isa 11; Jer 23:5–6; 33:14–18; Ezek 34:23–31; 37:24–28; *Pss. Sol.* 17.23–51; 4QFlor 1.10–13; 4QpGen 49; 4QpIsaᵃ 2.21–28; *Shemoneh Esreh* 14–15). That Jesus was descended from David's line is a common assertion in the NT, including the tradition lying behind the different birth narratives of Matthew and Luke (Matt 1:1–16, 20; Luke 1:27, 32, 69; 2:4; 3:23–31) and the older formulations quoted here and in 2 Tim 2:8 (see also Acts 2:30; Rev 5:5; 22:16 and regularly in Matt—1:1; 9:27; 12:23; 15:22; 20:30–31; 21:9, 15). The degree to which Jesus' Davidic pedigree was simply taken for granted is striking; there was evidently no consciousness of a need to argue for Jesus' Messiahship despite his not being of David's line (contrast Hebrews' special pleading for Jesus' priesthood). If anything there is rather a suggestion of some embarrassment over the title, reflected in Mark 12:35–37a, possibly in John 7:42, and here in the κατὰ σάρκα qualification (cf. *Barn.* 12.10)—if so, presumably because of its strongly this-worldly character (κατὰ σάρκα) and its nationalistic and political overtones (Dunn, "Jesus," 49–51). At all events Jesus' Davidic descent seems to have been a secure point in earliest Christian apologetic claims that Jesus was Messiah. Cf. on both points Eusebius, *HE* 3.12, 19–20. See further Brown, *Birth,* 505–12, with bibliography.

κατὰ σάρκα, "in terms of the flesh," that is, probably, insofar as he and his role were determined by the flesh or are to be understood in terms of the flesh (see on 1:4—κατὰ πνεῦμα). Σάρξ in Paul denotes man as characterized and conditioned by his mortality—its weakness, relationships, needs, and desires. In the Pauline letters its range of meaning extends from a more or less neutral usage, denoting the physical body, or physical relationship/kinship at the one end (particularly 11:14; 1 Cor 6:16; 15:39; Col 2:1), to a much more negative usage where man's fleshliness is understood as itself a source of corruption and hostility to God at the other end (8:5, 7, 12; 13:14; Gal 5:13, 24; 6:8; Col 2:11, 13, 18, 23); though see on 11:14. The negative side is particularly clear when σάρξ is set in antithesis with πνεῦμα, "Spirit" (2:28; 8:6, 9; Gal 3:3; 5:16, 17, 19; Phil 3:3, 4), not least when the antithesis has the form κατὰ σάρκα/κατὰ πνεῦμα (8:4–5; Gal 4:29) as here. It is very probable therefore that Paul read the formula he quotes here with at least some negative connotation attaching to the κατὰ σάρκα: that so far as Jesus' role in God's saving purpose through the gospel was concerned, Jesus' physical descent, however integral to that role, was not so decisive as his status κατὰ πνεῦμα. This would match the slightly negative overtone of κατὰ σάρκα later in the letter (4:1; 9:3, 5) where on both occasions Paul immediately goes on to stress that κατὰ σάρκα relationships are not the determinative factor in God's eyes (4:11–12, 16–17; 9:8). And it would fit well with Paul's opening emphasis: the gospel, which transcends the boundaries of Judaism (vv 5–7), concerns a Christ who transcends the role of a merely Jewish Messiah (vv 3–4; cf. particularly Theobald, 386–89, who draws attention to the answering emphasis in 15:8–9). Whether the original formula had such a negative overtone is disputed, but it seems to be implicit in the σάρξ/πνεῦμα antithesis (cf. Isa 31:3; Mark 14:38; John 3:6), and Paul presumably would not want to jeopardize the reception of his letter at Rome by imposing a different sense on a common creedal form. See further Dunn, "Jesus," esp. 43–49, with its qualification of earlier literature; and on 7:5 and 7:18.

4 ὁρισθέντος υἱοῦ θεοῦ ἐν δυνάμει, "appointed Son of God in power." ὁρισθέντος (only here in Paul) is quite frequently taken in the sense "designated" (RSV), "declared to be" (BGD, NEB, NIV). This would be acceptable so long as it is recognized that the verb denotes an act of God which brought Jesus to his designated status ("Son of God in power")—a sense which "appointed" conveys more accurately (see the evidence cited in MM and *TDNT* 5:450–51; and the strong statements, e.g., of Lagrange, Barrett, Murray, Michel, Käsemann, and Cranfield). The occasion of the "appointment" is clearly the resurrection ("as from the resurrection of the dead"); no doubt it was in recognition of this clear implication that the Old Latin textual tradition prefixed προ- to the verb (see *Notes*), to predate to eternity the decision to appoint ("predestined"). But here the act of appointment itself is described (in parallel with γενομένου), without raising the question as to whether it had been foreordained (for which the perfect ὡρισμένος would have been more appropriate; cf. Acts 2:23; 10:42) (despite Allen). According to the creedal formula, then, Jesus became something he was not before, or took on a role which was not previously his before (cf. Michel).

That status or role is described as "Son of God in power"; that ἐν δυνάμει should be taken with the noun rather than the verb is generally accepted to be the most obvious reading of the phrase (see, e.g., Lagrange, Gaugler, Fitzmyer, Cranfield; against NEB—"by a mighty act," NIV—"declared with power," Boismard). "In power" was presumably important to Paul. It indicated that Jesus' divine sonship (v 3) had been "upgraded" or "enhanced" by the resurrection, so that he shared more fully in the very power of God, not simply in status (at God's right hand—see below κύριος), but in "executive authority," able to act on and through people in the way Paul implies elsewhere (e.g., 8:10; 1 Cor 15:45; Gal 2:20; Col 2:6–7). For Paul this would be a further way of saying that the gospel was not about Jesus simply as Messiah; that role was inadequate for the full sweep of God's purpose; the full extent of God's purpose could only be realized through Jesus as Messiah (of Israel) risen from the dead to become the Son of God in power (for all); cf. Schmidt, 17–19, and again Theobald, 386–89.

For those aware that the royal Messiah was also called God's Son (2 Sam 7:14; Ps 2:7; 1QSa 2.11–12; 4QFlor 1.10–*fin.*; 4QpsDan A[a]) the phrase "in power" would be a natural qualification: Jesus did not first become God's Son at the resurrection; but he entered upon a still higher rank of sonship at resurrection. Certainly this has to be designated a "two-stage Christology" (the first line is not simply preparatory to the second, as the parallelism shows—against Wengst, 114–16), though what precisely is being affirmed of each stage in relation to the other is not clear. To describe the Christology as "adoptionist" (as Knox; Gaston, *Paul*, 113) is anachronistic since there is no indication that this "two-stage Christology" was being put forward in opposition to some already formulated "three-stage Christology" (as in later Adoptionism); cf. Maillot. And Paul would certainly see the earlier formula as congruent with his own Christology; as already noted under *Form and Structure*, it is hardly likely that Paul would both use the formula as an indication of common faith with his readers *and* attempt to correct it at the same time (Eichholz, *Theologie*, 130–31). 1:4 together with the similar very early Christological formulation in Acts 2:36 and early use of Ps 2:7 in reference to the resurrection (Acts 13:33; Heb 1:5; 5:5) should be seen more as evidence of the tremendous impact made by the resurrection of Jesus on the first Christians than as a carefully thought-out theological statement. That being said, it remains significant that these early formulations and Paul saw in the resurrection of Jesus a "becoming" of Jesus in status and role, not simply a ratification of a status and role already enjoyed on earth or from the beginning of time (see further Dunn, *Christology*, 33–36).

κατὰ πνεῦμα ἁγιωσύνης, "in terms of the spirit of holiness"; (NJB's "in terms of the Spirit and of holiness" is inadmissible). The term is clearly Semitic in character, modeled on the Hebraic form (not the LXX) of Ps 51:11 and Isa 63:10–11 (see also *T. Levi* 18.11; 1QS 4.21; 8.16; 9.3; 1QH 7.6–7; 9.32; 12.12; etc.); cf. the phrases used in Rom 8:15; Gal 6:1; Eph 1:17; and 2 Tim 1:7. It would almost certainly be understood by Paul and the first Christians as denoting the Holy Spirit, the Spirit which is characterized by holiness, partaker of God's holiness (see on 1:7); but these looser phrases remind us that the conceptuality of God's power active upon humankind and creation was not yet so sharply defined as in later Christian thought (cf. 11:8). Still important for the Pauline (and early Christian) conception of the Spirit as heavenly power is H. Gunkel, *Die Wirkungen des heiligen Geistes* (Göttingen: Vandenhoeck, 1888; ET *The Influence of the Holy Spirit*, tr. R. A. Harrisville and P. A. Quanbeck II [Philadelphia: Fortress, 1979]); further literature in Dunn, *Jesus*. See further on 5:5.

The κατά is probably deliberately vague; elsewhere Paul for one seems to go out of his way to avoid attributing Jesus' resurrection to the Spirit (6:4; 8:11; and further Dunn, *Christology*, 144). All he says here is that the new phase of Christ's existence and role was characterized by holy Spirit, just as the previous phase was characterized by flesh. The sense of πνεῦμα = "heavenly sphere or its substance," argued for by Schweizer in his influential article ("Röm 1:3f."; also *TDNT* 6:416–17) is too cosmological and static; with both σάρξ and πνεῦμα what is envisaged is a "condition" and power which determine the kind of existence actually lived out (so also the resurrection body as σῶμα πνευματικόν, "spiritual body"); cf. Käsemann, Theobald, 379, and *Form and Structure*. This helps us to see that the antithesis of the two lines once again need not be unnaturally exclusive. As the assertion of Jesus as Son of God "from the resurrection" need not exclude the idea of the royal Messiah as God's son, so the description of Jesus' resurrection sonship as κατὰ πνεῦμα need not exclude the idea that Jesus on earth was determined in some degree at least by the Spirit (as is testified in early traditions about Jesus—e.g., Matt 12:28 // Luke 11:20; Acts 10:38). Paul would certainly not be averse to seeing "flesh" and "Spirit" as competing forces in Jesus' life as much as in the believer's (Gal 5:16–17; Rom 8:12–14; cf. Althaus), or to the idea that Jesus provided a pattern for living "in terms of the Spirit" (see on 6:17 and 15:3). So he may well have seen Jesus' resurrection appointment κατὰ πνεῦμα as in some important sense an outworking of his life on earth lived κατὰ πνεῦμα (cf. 2 Cor 4:16–5:5). See Dunn, "Jesus." For the older view see Kuss, 6–8; and cf. Haacker and the still valuable treatment of Godet. Unconcerned by his use of anachronistic categories, Cranfield continues to argue that Paul "intended to limit the application of τοῦ γενομένου ἐκ σπέρματος Δαυίδ to the *human nature* which the One (God's Son, v 3) *assumed*" ("Comments," 270—my italics; similarly 278).

ἐξ ἀναστάσεως νεκρῶν, "as from the resurrection of the dead"—not "as from *his* resurrection *from* the dead" (see particularly Nygren). The phrase presumably reflects the earliest Christian belief that Jesus' resurrection was not simply a "one-off" event, but actually part of the beginning of the general resurrection prior to the last judgment; cf. Acts 4:2, 23:6, the metaphor of Christ's resurrection as the "first fruits" of the final resurrection (1 Cor 15:20,

23), and the obviously ancient tradition of Jesus' resurrection being accompanied by a more general resurrection in Matt 27:52–53—a clear indication of the impact made by Jesus' resurrection on the first disciples and of the enthusiasm engendered by it. Whatever the precise force of the ὁρισθέντος it is clear enough that in the formula Christ's divine sonship in power is thought of as beginning or as operative from the resurrection (see further above). On the question of whether the ἐκ is temporal or causal, see Wengst, 114–15.

Ἰησοῦ Χριστοῦ τοῦ κυρίου ἡμῶν, "Jesus Christ our Lord"—in apposition to "concerning his Son" (v 3) and with that phrase probably forming the bracket with which Paul framed the earlier formula (see *Form and Structure*), and by means of which he underlined the centrality of Christology in the common faith of the first Christians (Bornkamm, *Paul*, 249). One of Paul's regular phrases in speaking of Jesus, in which the word order was very flexible (usually ὁ κύριος ἡμῶν Ἰησοῦς Χριστός); as here in 5:21; 7:25; 1 Cor 1:9; Jude 25 (see BGD, κύριος 2cγ). κύριος is Paul's favorite title for Christ (about 230 times in the Pauline corpus); and its close link here to ἐξ ἀναστάσεως νεκρῶν reflects the degree to which, for Paul and the first Christians generally, the Lordship of Christ was a result of his resurrection—another element in his "becoming" (see on ὁρισθέντος κτλ. above, and further on 10:9; but also on 4:24). "Christ Jesus our Lord" is the other side of Paul's self-consciousness as "slave of Christ Jesus" (v 1), and its regularity in Paul's letters shows how much it had become second nature for Paul to think of himself and Christians at large as bound to Jesus as slave to master, their lives to be spent at the behest of the risen one.

5 δι' οὗ, "through whom." Not δι' ὅν, "on account of whom," that is, for the sake of a great servant of God now dead. Nor ἀφ' οὗ, "from whom," that is, from Christ as source of divine power (though cf. v 7). But δι' οὗ, "through Christ," that is, through the risen Christ as an active agent and participant in the process of salvation (cf. 5:9, 17–18, 21; 8:37; etc.). Already the sense of the exalted Jesus as mediator between heaven and earth (cf. also 1:8; 7:25; 2 Cor 1:20; Col 3:17) is clearly established and assumed and is certainly fundamental for Paul. See further on 1:8 and 2:16.

ἐλάβομεν, "we have received." Somewhat unexpectedly (in view of v 1) Paul links others with himself—*we* received. He does not regard himself as the sole apostle to the Gentiles, which would in any case have been a difficult position to maintain in writing to a largely Gentile church which he had not founded. The sensitivity shown here, among other things, confirms that for Paul church founding was integral to the role of an apostle (see on 1:1). That we have here, alternatively, simply an "epistolary plural" (Cranfield; Schlier with bibliog.) is unlikely, since on matters of apostleship Paul is usually careful in what he says (the plurals in 1 Cor 9:11–12; 2 Cor 1:12–14; and 1 Thess 3:1–2 are appropriate since in each case others are associated with him—Barnabas, Silvanus, and Timothy). See also on 3:8–9.

χάριν καὶ ἀποστολήν, "grace and apostleship." "Grace" is one of the great words which Christian vocabulary owes particularly to Paul, taken over by him from wider circulation (see LSJ; *TDNT* 9:373–76; Spicq, 960–66) and used especially to express God's free and unstinting concern in its outreach to humankind, in a way for which the LXX provided only partial precedent. In the LXX χάρις usually translates חֵן, which mostly appears in the formulation "find favor before/in the eyes of," though a more dynamic sense is evident in Exod 3:21, 11:3, 12:36, Ps 84:11 [LXX 83:12], Dan 1:9, and Bar 2:14 (see Nolland's important qualification of *TDNT* 9:379–81, 389). And the nearer equivalent, חֶסֶד ("loving kindness"), is translated in the LXX by ἔλεος (*TDNT* 9:381–87). In Paul, however, χάρις is never merely an attitude or disposition of God (God's character as gracious); consistently it denotes something much more dynamic—the wholly generous *act* of God. Like "Spirit," with which it overlaps in meaning (cf., e.g., 6:14 and Gal 5:18), it denotes effective divine power in the experience of men and women. See the still valuable G. P. Wetter, *Charis* (Leipzig: Brandstetter, 1913); Dunn, *Jesus*, 202–5. So here χάρις denotes something "received." What Paul has in mind in particular here is indicated by the accompanying noun ("apostleship"—elsewhere in Paul only 1 Cor 9:2 and Gal 2:8), with which "grace" almost forms a hendiadys (grace embodied, manifested in apostleship). It is the same experience of commissioning at the hands of the exalted Christ on the Damascus road of which he writes in Gal 1:12, 15–16. And though he would presumably not exclude the sense of the gracious power of conversion (as in 3:24; 5:15, 17, 20; 1 Cor 1:4–5; etc.), here as elsewhere the encounter with the risen Christ focuses on his commissioning (Gal 1:15–16; 1 Cor 9:1–2), and as in 1 Cor 15:10 on the gracious power which made his commissioning effective (cf. Gal 2:7, 9). Whether he deliberately avoided the word χάρισμα (spiritual gift, concrete manifestation of power—see on 1:11) here in order to distinguish apostleship from other χαρίσματα (charisms) is not clear; Satake would say Yes, but see von Lips—ἡ χάρις ἡ δοθεῖσα = χάρισμα. See also on 12:3.

εἰς ὑπακοὴν πίστεως, "with a view to the obedience of faith." ὑπακοή was a little known word at this time (see LSJ; MM), but seems to have become established in Christian terminology, probably as yet another word we owe to Paul's having given it some prominence in his own teaching (1:5; 5:19; 6:16; 15:18; 16:19, 26; 2 Cor 7:15; 10:5–6; Philem 21; Heb 5:8; 1 Pet 1:2, 14, 22). The verb ὑπακούω still displays its derivation from ἀκούω, "hear" (see LSJ, ὑπακούω—range of meaning includes "give ear to, answer, heed"; LXX uses ὑπακούω to translate שָׁמַע, "hear"); so what is envisaged primarily is response to a spoken word. The overlap in meaning with Gal 3:2, 5, ἀκοὴ πίστεως, "hearing of faith" (self-evident in the Greek) would be clearer if we translated our phrase here as "response of faith" (cf. 10:16–17); but Friedrich pushes this aspect too hard in suggesting that the phrase be translated "preaching of faith" ("Röm 1:5"); see also on 10:18.

To clarify what faith is and its importance to his gospel is one of Paul's chief objectives in this letter (πίστις and πιστεύω occur 40 and 21 times respectively in Romans; see particularly 1:17 and chap. 4). The genitive construction is probably to be taken as embracing both the sense "response which is faith" and "obedience which stems from faith"—"interchangeable ideas" (Ridderbos, *Paul*, 237); for alternative grammatical possibilities see Cranfield (there is a general consensus that "obedience to the faith" is not what Paul intended; "obedience to [God's] faithfulness" [Gaston, *Paul*, 169] does not seem to make much sense as a phrase). That "the obedience of faith" is a crucial and central theme, structurally important in understanding the thrust of the letter is indicated by its reappearance in the (albeit later added) concluding sentence (16:26), as well as by the prominence of ὑπακοή in the letter as a whole (7

times—see above; ὑπακούω—6:12, 16–17; 10:16; see further on 6:12 and
11:30–31). For the moment it would have been enough simply to allude to
what his readers well understood—their belief in the message about Jesus,
their commitment in baptism and the consequent lifestyle determined by
that faith (see also on 3:31; 4:12; 6:16; 8:4; 13:8–10).

ἐν πᾶσιν τοῖς ἔθνεσιν, "among all the nations." (τὰ) ἔθνη certainly means
"the Gentiles" (and not "the nations" including Jews); it is used in the LXX
to translate גוים, usually = other/foreign nations; and in Greek usage it
also usually denotes foreigners (see BGD). Once again this is no casual phrase,
inserted merely to provide a transition back to the greeting proper. That
his apostleship was to the Gentiles was absolutely fundamental in Paul's self-
understanding (cf. particularly 11:13; 15:16, 18; Gal 1:16; 2:2, 8–9), and that
the saving purpose of God always had the Gentiles in view is a central theme
of this letter (ἔθνος appears 29 times in Romans—9 of them in direct quotations
from the OT; see also on 15:9). The πᾶσιν is also significant, not only because
it confirms the truly universal scope of God's gospel ("all the nations"), but
also because it reminds us that Paul seriously contemplated this outreach
being achieved within his own lifetime, as the last act before the end and
the necessary preliminary to the salvation of Israel (1 Cor 4:9; Rom 11:13–
27). The ἐν ("among") probably also indicates Paul's recognition that "the
obedience of faith" would be patchy so far as Gentile response was concerned.

In linking the thought of "obedience" to "the nations" Paul's train of thought
may still show the influence of Ps 2 (v 8—God's son given the nations as his
inheritance and the ends of the earth as his possession; cf. 1:3–4) and Isa
49 (vv 6–7—God's slave/servant given as a light to the nations . . . princes
prostrating themselves; cf. 1:1). More probable still is the likelihood that
Paul had in mind the importance of obedience within Jewish self-understanding—obedience as Israel's proper response to God's covenant grace (as particularly in Deut 26:17; 30:2; the Shema of course begins שְׁמַע יִשְׂרָאֵל, "Hear,
O Israel" [Deut 6:4], though the LXX translates שְׁמַע here as ἄκουε). The
point would then be that Paul intends his readers to understand the faith
response of the Gentiles to the gospel as the fulfillment of God's covenant
purpose through Israel, the eschatological equivalent of Israel's obligation
under the covenant. As such, the phrase "the obedience of faith among the
Gentiles" provides a very neat and fitting summary of his complete apologetic
in Romans (Garlington, 329–55).

ὑπὲρ τοῦ ὀνόματος αὐτοῦ, "for the sake of his name." The "name" is one of
the ways in which a person can be known, through which one manifests
something of oneself, a means by which one can (as we may say) "gain a
handle" on another—all the more so in the ancient world (see TDNT 5:243,
250–51, 253–54). Hence "for the benefit of his reputation," that Christ may
be known as the one who fulfills God's covenant purpose in bringing the
Gentiles to the obedience of faith (cf. 2:24; 9:17; 10:13; 15:9). Indeed, there
may be a deliberate contrast with 2:24: for the Gentiles to fulfill God's covenant
purpose in the obedience of faith will enhance God's "public image," whereas
Jewish failure to fulfill the covenant, through pride and disobedience, reduces
God in the eyes of the nations.

6 ἐν οἷς ἐστε καὶ ὑμεῖς, "among whom you also"—ἐν οἷς rather than ἐξ ὧν because they are both part of and as a group still very much set within the context of the gentile world. The phrase therefore is probably one of the clearest indications that the Roman congregations were largely gentile, and probably mostly gentile (see also 1:13, 14–15; 11:13, 17–21; and further *Introduction* §2; Schlier with bibliography). But καί: they are by no means the only Gentiles who have responded positively to the gospel of God. In this delicate way Paul slides neatly round the problem that though he is apostle to the Gentiles (11:13) the Christians at Rome are not the fruit of *his* apostleship (see also 1:15; 15:15, 20, 24).

κλητοὶ Ἰησοῦ Χριστοῦ, "called to be Jesus Christ's"—not "by Jesus Christ," since elsewhere in Paul it is God who issues the invitation/summons (cf., e.g., 8:30; 11:29; 1 Cor 1:9; see further on 1:1). The Roman believers could be defined as the guests or dependents of Jesus Christ. As a description it marks them off from other cults and groups dependent on named patrons (such groups were a common feature in imperial Rome—see on 16:2), and not least from the Jews who did not share their beliefs regarding Jesus (see on 1:7).

7 πᾶσιν τοῖς οὖσιν ἐν Ῥώμῃ, "to all who are in Rome." At last the second part of the standard form of address. As usual the whole community is greeted and not just particular figures seen as representative of the whole. πᾶσιν is given a place of emphasis, possibly suggesting a degree of factionalism (cf. 16:17–20), or at least that there was some tension among the different Christian groups in Rome (see *Introduction* §3.3 and particularly 14:1–5). That he does not call them "the church in Rome," in contrast to his normal practice in his earlier letters (but contrast also Phil and Col), may also indicate that the numbers of believers in Rome were too large for them to meet together all at once, that is, to meet *as* "the church in Rome" (contrast the church in Corinth—Rom 16:23); see also *Introduction* §2.4.3 and on 16:1.

ἀγαπητοῖς θεοῦ, "beloved by God." The idea of being loved by the gods or by one god in particular was quite familiar outside the Judeo-Christian tradition (cf. Dio Chrys. 3.60—ἀγαπώμενος ὑπὸ θεῶν; other examples in BGD, ἀγαπάω 1.b, d). But the sense of a more established relation given by the adjective (ἀγαπητός) is more characteristically Jewish (cf. 11:28), though the nearest parallel in LXX would be Pss 60:5 [LXX 59:7] and 108:6 [LXX 107:7]. Other references in Schlier, Wischmeyer, and Str-B, 3:24. In Paul cf. 9:25; Col 3:12; 1 Thess 1:4; 2 Thess 2:13.

κλητοῖς ἁγίοις, "called to be saints" (so 1 Cor 1:2); "saints by virtue of having been called" (Hendriksen). For κλητοί see 1:1. The closest parallel to Christians as a group believing themselves distinguished from others as "summoned" to a particular cause is the Qumran community (1QM 3.2; 4.10–11; cf. 2.7; 14.5; 1QSa 1.27; 2.2, 11; CD 2.11; 4.3–4). ἅγιοι is used regularly in Paul for believers as a whole (8:27; 12:13; 15:25; 1 Cor 6:1–2; etc.; also Acts 9:13, 32; Heb 6:10; *Did.* 4.2; 16.7; *1 Clem.* 46.2; 56.1; Ign. *Smyrn.* 1.2; etc.). ἅγιος derives its sense of "set apart from everyday use, dedicated to God" principally from the cult. In this sense it was known and used in Hellenistic religious terminology (LSJ). But otherwise it is characteristically and overwhelmingly a Jewish term—as indicated not least in Jewish preference for the more dynamic concept of "holiness" over the elsewhere more popular

near equivalents ἱερός, ὅσιος, σεμνός, and ἁγνός, and in its use to describe a
whole community or nation as set apart to God—"the saints" (Pss 16 [LXX
15]:3; 34:9 [LXX 33:10]; 74 [LXX 73]:3; 83:3 [LXX 82:4]; Isa 4:3; Dan 7:18,
21, 22, 25, 27; 8:24; Tob 8:15; Wisd Sol 18:9; *T. Levi* 18.11, 14; *T. Iss.* 5.4;
T. Dan 5.12; cf., e.g., Lev 19:2; 20:7, 26; Num 15:40; Deut 7:6; 14:2; 26:19);
see further Lietzmann on 15:25. As such it expressed Israel's very powerful
sense of their having been specially chosen and set apart to God. Paul's drawing
together these two words (cf. 8:27–28) to describe a group in Rome predominantly Gentile in make-up is hardly accidental. Particularly significant is the
fact that such "holiness" in terms of faithful law keeping was meant to set
Israel apart from the nations (Lev 20:22–26) and that it functioned as a
self-description for various factions within Israel at the time of Paul, who
saw themselves as "holy" by virtue of their self-perceived greater loyalty to
the law (cf. *Pss. Sol.* 17.26; 1QS 5.13; 8.17, 20, 23; 9.8; *1 Enoch* 38.4–5; 43.4;
48.1; 50.1; etc.; see again Lietzmann on 15:25; and see on 15:25). To describe
nonproselyte (= non-law-keeping) Gentiles as "saints" is indicative of the
boldness of Paul's argument in the letter over against those more characteristically Jewish views. In more general terms the fact that Gentiles should count
themselves ἅγιοι when they offered no sacrifices, called no man "priest," practiced no rite of circumcision, must have been puzzling to most pagans and
offensive to most Jews (see also on 15:16).

χάρις ὑμῖν, "grace to you." The third and final part of the normal greeting,
with the usual χαίρειν replaced by the already characteristic Christian word
χάρις (see on 1:5). If we should rather speak of Paul's adapting an older
Jewish formula, "Mercy and peace be with you" (Gal 6:16; Jude 2; *2 Apoc.
Bar.* 78.2; Pol. *Phil.* inscrip.; Lohmeyer, 159–61; Käsemann with bibliog.;
cf. 2 Macc 1:1), the significance still lies in Paul's use of χάρις rather than
ἔλεος (see on 1:5); nor can the similarity in sound to the Greek χαίρειν have
been unintentional. We might paraphrase: "May you know the generous
power of God undergirding and coming to expression in your daily life."

εἰρήνη, "peace"—the typical Jewish greeting (as in Judg 19:20; 1 Sam 25:5–
6; Dan 10:19 Theod.; Tob 12:17; 2 Macc 1:1; James 2:16). The Hebrew
concept of peace (שָׁלוֹם) is very positive. The basic idea is something like
"well-being": for the ancient Israelite שָׁלוֹם was all that makes for wholeness
and prosperity (e.g., Deut 23:6; Pss 72:3, 7; 147:14; Isa 48:18; 55:12; Zech
8:12)—not just "spiritual" but also "material" well-being (e.g., Ps 85), and
not so much individual as social (as in 1 Kgs 5:12; Zech 6:13); peace as
something visible, including the idea of a productively harmonious relationship
between people. See *TDNT* 2:400–420; and see further on 5:1.

The richness of this new and distinctively Christian greeting, made up of
the transformed Greek and the typically Jewish greetings, can hardly be exaggerated. This is something Christianity probably owes to Paul also, since he
uses it in all his letters—elsewhere in this form only in 1 Pet 1:2; 2 Pet 1:2;
Rev 1:4; *1 Clem.* inscrip.

ἀπὸ θεοῦ πατρὸς ἡμῶν, "from God our Father." The concept of God as
Father was familiar in the ancient world, "Father" both as maker and as
ruler of the world and Father of humankind (Zeus was regularly described
as "Father of both men and gods"), not least in Stoic thought, with the idea

of a god as father of a particular group also evident in the mysteries (BGD, πατήρ 3a–c; *TDNT* 5:952–56). The understanding of God as Father of the nation is characteristically Jewish, the word implying a loving concern for and authority over, or (in a word) responsibility for his people by virtue of his choice of them (see particularly Deut 32:6; Isa 63:16; Jer 3:4, 19; 31:9; Mal 1:6; Tob 13:4; *3 Macc* 5.7), with the thought of God as father of the pious individual emerging clearly later, particularly in the wisdom literature (Sir 23:1, 4; Wisd Sol 2:16; 14:3). In appropriating the title as applicable to their relationship with God ("our Father") the first Christians were almost certainly influenced by Jesus, especially, of course, by the way he taught his disciples to address God in prayer (Luke 11:2; cf. Rom 8:15; Gal 4:6). That it is already set in a fixed formula in Paul at least (1 Cor 1:3; 2 Cor 1:2; Gal 1:3–4; Eph 1:2; Phil 1:2; Col 1:2; 1 Thess 1:1, 3; 2 Thess 1:1–2; Philem 3) shows how well established it already was in Christian self-understanding.

καὶ κυρίου Ἰησοῦ Χριστοῦ, "and the Lord Jesus Christ." See on 1:4. This phrase is equally firmly fixed in Paul's formula of greeting (as the same texts just cited show). It provides a further qualification in the concept of God's Fatherhood: both that God has chosen to share (some of) his authority with Jesus exalted (cf. Ps 110:1; 1 Cor 15:24–28), and that the special relationship which previously embraced Israel as a whole is now delimited more precisely by reference to those who acknowledge Jesus Christ as Lord. The appropriation of cherished elements of Jewish self-understanding is complete (see also on 10:9).

Explanation

1 Paul begins by introducing himself to his fellow believers at Rome, most of whom would not have known him personally. However much the form of his self-introduction was determined by convention, his choice of epithet tells us what he regarded as most important about himself, or at least as most relevant to his readers.

It is significant then that he describes himself first as a "slave of Christ Jesus," which is not part of his regular introductory formula. Those of his readers who were familiar with the LXX and the new movement's Jewish heritage would easily recognize the quite typical language of Jewish devotion transposed into devotion to Christ Jesus. They would be unlikely to read the phrase as an abandoning of the older piety (there is no hint anywhere in early Christian literature of any sense of contrast between the ideas "slave of God" and "slave of Christ"), but would see it rather, as Paul probably intended, as an appropriate expression of the older devotion in the circumstances set in train by Christ. As will become increasingly evident, Paul, who would previously have delighted to call himself simply "God's slave," is keen now to designate himself "Christ's slave," both because (vv 3–4) Jesus is the Christ, the one who has fulfilled Israel's hope of a Messiah and is now exalted as Lord, and because (vv 5–7) the "revelation of Jesus Christ" signals now for Paul the fulfillment of the Isaianic servant's/slave's role as "light to the Gentiles" and "for salvation to the end of the earth" (Isa 49:6).

But Paul, and his readers, would also be conscious of the more common usage of the word in the Greco-Roman world in reference to the lowest economic class of society—"bondsman." Paul, with deliberate emphasis, introduces himself to the capital of the empire not as a citizen proud of his freedom but as the slave of a crucified Jewish messiah.

His second self-description is the one he used most frequently in his epistolary greetings—"apostle." However the word would have been understood by others, Paul's usage is plain. He was an apostle by virtue of his summons on the Damascus road, his commission to take the "gospel of God" to "all the Gentiles" (v 5). The word is held for him in a firm tension between that beginning and that end.

What this meant for Paul is further elaborated in a third phrase—"set apart for the gospel of God." The thought is clearly the same as that spelled out in a previous letter—"set apart from my mother's womb . . . called through his grace . . . that I might preach him among the Gentiles . . ." (Gal 1:15–16), with its echo of Jer 1:5 conjoined to that of Isa 49:1. The conviction was evidently fundamental for Paul, and the commitment unreserved. His whole mission, indeed his whole life, was nothing more, but nothing less than a being committed to the gospel, a dedication to the task of offering to the Gentiles, in contrast to the good tidings of human triumph with which they were more familiar, the good news of the one God focused in a single person and message (vv 3–4).

2 He continues to introduce himself by appending a brief summary of this gospel. Why he should interrupt the flow of his normal greeting by this insertion is not immediately obvious. The most likely inference however is that he felt the need to define the terms of his apostolic commissioning in order to defuse any suspicion or criticism which might cause the reader or hearer to "turn off" too soon. That there was at least some confusion concerning and even hostility toward his understanding of the gospel, particularly among Jewish believers, is sufficiently obvious from Galatians. And the terms in which he here summarizes the "gospel of God" confirm that the issue at stake was the continuity between the revelation embodied in the Jewish Scriptures and Paul's concern for a universal outreach.

Paul's assertion is emphatic. The gospel to which he was set apart is in complete continuity with God's earlier revelation to Israel. The emphasis is threefold: it was promised beforehand, through his prophets, in the holy scriptures. That is to say, it was not something foisted upon the new movement by Paul, nor even something which began with Jesus himself. Even if vv 3–4 are an earlier formulation taken over by Paul, and even if the phrases used in v 2 echo already established Christian apologetic, v 2 is wholly his own. The force with which he makes the point is a signal to the listener and reader that this is something fundamental for Paul. And the prominence which it has within the opening greetings (when attention might be expected to be as yet undulled) implies that it is a central thesis for the argument which follows. The modern reader therefore will be well advised to bear in mind this firm assertion of the continuity between the Old Testament and Paul's gospel when trying to make sense of Paul's subsequent argument.

3–4 Paul develops his introductory description of the gospel by defining it in terms of Jesus Christ. If indeed he took up an earlier evangelistic or creedal formulation, as seems most likely, the reason why he did so may be twofold. One is that it was quite a well-known formulation or at least typical in its double affirmation (son of David, Son of God), and so would probably strike a familiar chord for many of the believers in Rome. The other is that it continued the thrust of the first line of the parenthesis—it emphasized the continuity between the gospel proclaimed by Paul and Israel: the one proclaimed by Paul was of David's royal line (the royal messiah)—a fundamental assertion of Jewish Christian faith and apologetic. Probably we should also see the Semitism ("spirit of holiness") and the primitive description of Christ's resurrection ("the resurrection of the dead") in v 4 as indications that Paul had taken pains to quote a formulation first coined by the Palestinian churches.

Most would agree that Paul has framed the earlier formula by the introductory phrase "concerning his Son" and the concluding phrase "Jesus Christ our Lord"; and if the formula was well enough known Paul would presumably expect his handiwork to be noticed. But we should not read too much significance into these phrases, as though Paul intended them to qualify or alter the emphasis of the earlier form. To engender such a suspicion among his readers would run counter to the more obvious purpose of the formula (that is, to defuse suspicion and to provide a common ground on which the Roman listeners and Paul could meet).

Neither of the main titles used seem to be given particular weight by Paul, and should probably be seen simply as convenient or familiar referents at this point. "Son" is not one of his regular titles for Christ, but may have been prompted by the formula he was about to cite. It certainly presupposes that a uniqueness of divine Sonship was already taken for granted in reference to Jesus ("his Son"). But how that sonship was different from the divine sonship attributed to Israel or the righteous, or indeed to the Messiah, is not clear: the formula itself indicates that the resurrection was a decisive moment in Christ's Sonship. And "Lord" is used simply as an established title in an established phrase.

We should certainly beware of interpreting the formula itself in a rigidly antithetical way—Son of David in respect of his human birth, but Son of God in respect of his resurrection—not least because the idea of the royal messiah as also God's Son was not unfamiliar to Jewish thinking. To that extent the formula remains within Jewish thought and hope and so reinforces Paul's emphasis on the continuity between Israel's hope and his gospel. Yet, at the same time, we should not ignore the force of the phrase "appointed . . . as from the resurrection of the dead." It is clear from this phrase that for Paul the resurrection marked a decisive stage in Christ's divine Sonship— not as marking its beginning (the possibility that this was implied in the earlier formulation is not strong and depends on reading "in power" as a Pauline addition), but certainly as marking a significant "heightening" or enlarging of its scope. Perhaps that heightening or enlarging is simply to be thought of in terms of the risen Christ's exaltation to the right hand of God— so that Paul's thought naturally runs on with the words, "Jesus Christ our Lord." But the phrase "from the resurrection of the dead" (rather than "from his resurrection from the dead") suggests that Paul also saw here a reference

to the universal aspect of the gospel. And it is quite possible that he read
the contrast between "according to the flesh" and "in power according to
the Holy Spirit" in a similar way. That is to say, Paul may well have read
this earlier formulation as implying that in and by the resurrection the purely
Jewish gospel of the royal messiah had been enlarged to embrace the full
scope of the Holy Spirit's outreach and of the final resurrection of the dead;
the Son of David of Jewish hope had through the resurrection become the
Son of God for all.

5–6 V 5 begins the transition back from the parenthesis of vv 2–4 to
the more usual form of greeting, with a return to his self-introductory assertion
of apostleship (v 1). This repetition of his claim to apostleship and the unexpected switch to the plural ("we received"—unexpected since he had not
associated anyone else with him in his opening greeting) probably indicates
a sensitivity on Paul's part that his claim to apostleship and/or his understanding of that apostleship had been (and still was) the subject of some dispute
(Galatians), in which case he will have chosen his words with care.

It is probably significant that his separation as an apostle "for the gospel
of God" is now defined explicitly as "apostleship for the obedience of faith
among all the Gentiles." On the one hand, his claim for the universal outreach
of his apostleship is now expressed explicitly—"all the Gentiles." Since the
believers in Rome evidently fall largely into this category (v 6), the addressees
themselves provide living proof of the gospel's outreach to all the nations.
But, on the other hand, the immediate object of his apostleship and means
of achieving its outreach is expressed in terms of the phrase "obedience of
the faith," that is, most probably, "obedience which consists in or springs
from faith." Here we may well be advised to recognize another signal for
what lies ahead—viz., that the faith which Paul's apostleship seeks to bring
about is not something different from obedience, from the response God
expected from his covenant people, but is rather the way in which that obedience must be expressed or the (only) effective source of that obedience. Only
so will God and his Christ be known in their true character ("name") and
accorded their appropriate honor. Once again we sense Paul attempting to
maintain the continuity between God's purposes for Israel (as expressed not
least in their covenantal obligations), and Paul's vision of the gospel's offer
and challenge to the whole world.

Not least of importance is the way in which Paul frames this basic assertion
of his apostleship with a double reference to Christ—"through whom . . . for
the sake of his name." This double emphasis strengthens the impression
that the chief function of the formula just quoted (vv 3–4) was to present
Christ as the linchpin holding together the earlier promise "through the
prophets in the holy scriptures" and Paul's claim to an apostleship with universal outreach. It was through this Jesus Christ, who stood foursquare within
the stream of Jewish inheritance and hope ("of the seed of David according
to the flesh"), that Paul and the others received their apostolic commissioning
and enabling to take the gospel to all the Gentiles. It was for the sake of
this Jesus Christ, whose divine sonship in power is correlated with the (universal) resurrection of the dead, Lord over all (Ps 110:1), that Paul and the
others sought to call the Gentiles (as well as the Jews) to obedience, the

obedience of faith. Of the effectiveness of this commission the Roman believers are themselves proof, even though it was not Paul himself (but presumably "the others") who had been instrumental in their conversion. They are (or include) Gentiles who had responded to the summons of Jesus Christ, Jesus Messiah of Jewish expectation.

7 With v 7 the transition back to the normal form of greeting has been completed. The addressees are specified, although already acknowledged in the final clause of the parenthesis (v 6)—all those in Rome who would recognize themselves as "the beloved of God, called to be saints." The first phrase has an Old Testament ring, though no specific parallel. The Jewish or proselyte listener, familiar with the LXX, could well be expected to take the implication that he was being numbered with Israel (cf. 11:28). The Gentile less familiar with the LXX might nevertheless recognize that in the phrase he was being embraced within a specially cherished relationship with the God of Israel whose gospel he had responded to (vv 1–2). Similarly the second phrase, though using terms familiar in the wider socioreligious context of the Hellenistic world, would by their conjunction again tend to evoke the more typically and specifically Jewish claims. Both words in effect reinforce each other in asserting the claim to have been specially chosen—called to be set apart, summoned and consecrated to the service of God. The continuity between ancient Jewish promise in the scriptures and new realization in Christ is underlined once again.

The opening sentence of the letter concludes with Paul's regular salutation— "grace and peace from God our Father and the Lord Jesus Christ." In Paul the more typical greetings of Jew and Greek have become a blessing which combines the strength of the word which perhaps more than any other characterizes his gospel ("grace") with the richness of the Semitic greeting ("peace")— a prayer for the unbounded and wholly generous outreaching power of God which makes for humankind's best well-being.

The source of this blessing is specified as conjointly "God our Father and the Lord Jesus Christ." In terms of our understanding of developing Christology this assertion of the role of Christ alongside God the Father cannot be without significance. On the other hand, too much should not be read into it. Nothing more than the thought of Christ's exaltation to God's right hand (Ps 110:1) is probably in mind—a coordinate, but subordinate regency. The possibility that the assertion might raise problems for Jewish monotheism seems not yet to be a factor in Christian thinking.

More significant is the fact that the two phrases (familiar to us but not necessarily to his Roman listeners) provide an effective conclusion to the underlying thrust of Paul's opening statement. By speaking of God as "our Father" rather than using the more Stoic idea of God as Father of the world or of all humanity, he implies that his thought is the more restricted Jewish one of God as the Father of Israel or of the righteous: Christians are now embraced within God's fatherly care hitherto most fully expressed in reference to Israel. And this has come about through Jesus (the Jewish) Christ in consequence of his exaltation as Lord. The grace of Christ (toward Gentile) and the peace of God (upon Jew) are not two separate, far less opposed factors. Each is bound up with the other. The gospel is about the grace-and-peace of the God whom the Jews have proclaimed and their Jesus whom God exalted to his right hand—old promise and new gospel are one.

In short, in this opening address Paul reveals something of himself and his supreme passion, as well as some strong hints about what is to follow—a life characterized in terms of service and apostleship, an apostleship defined and determined by the gospel it proclaimed, a gospel whose outline in its focus on Jesus Christ and fulfillment of Jewish expectations was not in dispute but whose interpretation in reference to the Gentiles was more controversial, an interpretation holding together Jewish heritage and Gentile outreach already beginning to emerge as a strong theme of the letter itself.

B. Personal Explanations (1:8–15)

Bibliography

Eichholz, G. "Der ökumenische und missionarische Horizont der Kirche. Eine exegetische Studie zu Röm 1:8–15." *EvT* 21 (1961) 15–27 = *Tradition und Interpretation*. Theologische Bücherei 29. Munich: Kaiser, 1965. 85–98. **Funk, R. W.** "Apostolic Parousia." **Jervell, J.** "Letter to Jerusalem." **Jewett, R.** "Ambassadorial Letter." **Klein, G.** "Purpose." **Knox, J.** "A Note on the Text of Romans." *NTS* 2 (1955–56) 191–93. **Lyonnet, S.** "'Deus cui servio in spiritu meo' (Rom 1:9)." *VD* 41 (1967) 52–59. **Minear, P.** "Gratitude and Mission in the Epistle to the Romans." In *Basileia*, FS W. Freytag, ed. J. Hermelink et al. Stuttgart: Evang. Missionsverlag, 1959. 42–48. Reprinted in *Obedience*, 102–10. **Mullins, T. Y.** "Disclosure: A Literary Form in the New Testament." *NovT* 7 (1964) 44–50. **O'Brien, P. T.** *Introductory Thanksgivings.* **Sanders, J. T.** "The Transition from Opening Epistolary Thanksgiving to Body in the Letters of the Pauline Corpus." *JBL* 81 (1962) 348–62. **Schelkle, K. H.** "Römische Kirche im Römerbrief." *ZKT* 81 (1959) 393–404. **Schubert, P.** *Form and Function of the Pauline Thanksgivings.* BZNW 20. Berlin: Töpelmann, 1939. **Sundberg, A. C.** "Enabling Language in Paul." In *Christians among Jews and Gentiles*, FS K. Stendahl, ed. G. W. E. Nickelsburg and G. W. MacRae. Philadelphia: Fortress, 1986. 270–77. **Thüsing, W.** *Per Christum.* 174–83. **Trocmé, E.** "L'Épître aux Romains et la méthode missionaire de l'apôtre Paul." *NTS* 7 (1960–61) 148–53. **White, J. L.** "Introductory Formulae in the Body of the Pauline Letter." *JBL* 90 (1971) 91–97. **Wiles, G. P.** *Paul's Intercessory Prayers.* SNTSMS 24. Cambridge: Cambridge UP, 1974. 186–94. **Zeller, D.** *Juden.* 50–60.

Translation

[8]*First of all I thank my God through Jesus Christ for*[a] *you all, because your faith is being spoken of all over the world.* [9]*For God is my*[a] *witness, whom I serve with my spirit in the gospel of his Son, how constantly I mention you,* [10]*in my prayers, always asking that I might somehow now at last succeed by God's will to come to you.* [11]*For I long to see you, that I may share with you some spiritual gift so that you may be strengthened;* [12]*or rather, so that there may be mutual encouragement among*[a] *you through each other's faith, both yours and mine.* [13]*I do not want*[a] *you to be unaware of the fact, my brothers, that I often made plans to come*

*to you, though I have been prevented hitherto, in order that I might have some
fruit among you as well, just as among the rest of the Gentiles.* [14] *I am debtor to
both Greeks and barbarians, to both wise and foolish.* [15] *Hence my eagerness to
preach the gospel to*[a] *you who are in Rome*[b] *as well.*

Notes

[a] Minor modifications have been made at these points at some time in the history of the
text's transmission to improve Paul's thought and/or its expression in writing.

[b] G and the Latin translation of Origen omit τοῖς ἐν Ῥώμῃ, as in 1:7 (see *Notes* on 1:7).

Form and Structure

Following the conventions of his day (Doty, 31–33), Paul includes a thanksgiving and prayer on behalf of his readers, though once again mirroring his
own characteristic and distinctive concerns—his main concern being their
faith (vv 8, 12). In terms of "rhetorical analysis" this section is part of the
"exordium" (Wuellner), one of whose functions, according to *Rhetorica ad
Herennium* 1.4.7–8, was to make the hearers more attentive and receptive
by, among other things, discussing one's own person (Betz, *Galatians*, 44).
The rather striking combination of fulsome praise, assurance of deep personal
concern, somewhat lame-sounding excuses, and eagerness to visit are certainly
designed to win a sympathetic hearing, though the style seems to owe more
to Paul's sincerity and awkwardness than to conscious rhetorical art. The
awkwardness, particularly at vv 10 and 12, so untypical of "the even flow
and calm dignity which usually characterize the style of Paul's thanksgivings"
(Schubert, 5), presumably arises from the difficulty of pitching his address
at the right level to unknown congregations. Funk, however, does note some
characteristic features of Paul's self-explanations in such passages (cf., e.g.,
1 Cor 16:1–11; 1 Thess 2:17–3:11; Philem 21–22). More detailed analyses
probably become overrefined, including the classification of vv 13–15 as "body-
opening" (White) or as *narratio* comparable to Gal 1:12–2:14 (Jewett). On
the other hand, it is clear that in extending the thanksgiving Paul continues
to underline his chief concerns (faith, Gentiles, evangelize) and to lead into
the letter's thematic statement (vv 16–17). Nor is it accidental that once Paul
has completed the main body of the letter (1:18–15:13) he returns at once
to the same concerns as here (15:14–33; for structural comparison see 15:14–
16:27 *Form and Structure*). These structural features are sufficient confirmation
that the personal reasons for writing outlined in these passages cannot be
isolated from the argument which they bracket.

Comment

8 πρῶτον, "first" (of a sequence), but without continuing the series—nicely
conveyed by NEB, "Let me begin by . . . ." Cf. 3:2; 1 Cor 11:18. See BGD,
πρῶτος 2b. Thanksgiving is Paul's first priority.

εὐχαριστῶ τῷ θεῷ μου . . . περὶ πάντων ὑμῶν, "I give thanks to my God
for you all," is Paul's version of the regular thanksgiving in private correspon-

dence (*TDNT* 9:408; cf., e.g., 2 Macc 1:11) and a regular feature of Paul's
opening remarks (1 Cor 1:4; Eph 1:16; Phil 1:3; Col 1:3; 1 Thess 1:2; 2
Thess 1:3; Philem 4; cf. 2 Cor 1:11). MM gives parallel occurrences in the
papyri, and *NDIEC* 4:127–28 in inscriptions. The μου ("my God") does not,
of course, signify "mine and not yours"; it is simply a way of stressing the
fervor of his devotion, his deep personal commitment (so Phil 1:3; Philem
4; used regularly in the Pss—3:7; 5:2; 7:1, 3, 6; 13:3; 18:2, 6, 21, 28–29; 22:1–
2, 10; etc.). "This phrase, 'my God,' expresses . . . the whole of true religion"
(Bengel).

διὰ Ἰησοῦ Χριστοῦ, "through Jesus Christ." As is Paul's normal style, he
gives thanks to God *through* Jesus Christ (5:11; 7:25; 1 Cor 15:57; Col 3:17;
cf. Rom 16:27; 2 Cor 1:20; 3:4; so also Heb 13:15; 1 Pet 2:5; 4:11; Jude
25); cf. also 10:1. The exalted Christ is understood here as filling the role
elsewhere in Judaism already attributed to archangels (Tob 12:12, 15; *1 Enoch*
9.3; 99.3; 104.1; *T. Levi* 3.5; 5.6–7; *T. Dan* 6.2), and already to the patriarchs
by Philo (*Praem.* 166; cf. *2 Enoch* 7; 53.1), though in these cases it is their
role as heavenly intercessors which is primarily in mind (cf. Rom 8:34). That
Paul puts Christ's mediatorial role in terms of thanksgiving probably says as
much about his confidence in what has already been done (by God through
Christ) on behalf of humankind's salvation, as about the extent of Christ's
absorption and supersession of all other heavenly intermediary functions as
then conceived. Certainly the presentation of him who had so recently been
Jesus of Nazareth as a two-way channel of χάρις within a few verses (vv
5, 8) is a striking testimony to early Christian understanding of the exalted
Christ's role as heavenly mediator. For all that Paul emphasizes Christ's Lordship (vv 4, 7), he never forgets that God is over all, so that thanksgiving is
rendered not *to* Christ but through Christ, just as the call to be Christ's comes
from God, not from Christ (see on 1:6); "Christ's lordship does not annul
Paul's monotheism" (Althaus on 1:7); see further Thüsing, 174–83. This
theological reserve has to be borne in mind when assessing the significance
of passages like 10:13, 1 Cor 16:22, and 2 Cor 12:8. See further on 2:16;
4:24; 5:1, 10; 6:13; 8:34, and 10:9.

ὅτι ἡ πίστις ὑμῶν καταγγέλλεται ἐν ὅλῳ τῷ κόσμῳ, "because your faith is
spoken of in all the world." That it is their faith in particular for which
Paul gives thanks is again typical (Eph 1:15–16; Col 1:3–4; 1 Thess 1:2–3;
2 Thess 1:3–4); as also the laudatory terms in which he describes it (Col
1:5–7; 1 Thess 1:7–8; 2 Thess 1:3–4; Philem 5; cf. 1 Cor 1:5–7, tailored to
the situation in the church at Corinth). For πίστις see on 1:17. The use of
the somewhat formal word καταγγέλλω, "proclaim, announce" (BGD, MM)
indicates that Paul is consciously striving for effect.

9 μάρτυς γὰρ μού ἐστιν ὁ θεός, "For God is my witness," is a familiar appeal
in both Greek and Jewish literature (e.g., 1 Sam 12:5–6; *T. Levi* 19.3; Josephus,
War 1.595; Polybius 11.6.4). So elsewhere in Paul—2 Cor 1:23; Phil 1:8; 1
Thess 2:5, 10; cf. 2 Cor 11:31; Gal 1:20. For Paul to use such a solemn
formula underlines his concern lest he be misunderstood and not given a
sympathetic hearing. If he knew Jesus' teaching on oaths (Matt 5:33–37; cf.
James 5:12) he presumably did not regard it as necessarily relevant to such
conversational conventions.

ᾧ λατρεύω ἐν τῷ πνεύματί μου ἐν τῷ εὐαγγελίῳ τοῦ υἱοῦ αὐτοῦ, "whom I serve
with my spirit in the gospel of his Son." Particularly against the background
of Judaism the cultic overtones of λατρεύω are clear (Luke 2:37; Heb 8:5;
9:1, 6, 9; 13:10; Rev 7:15; cf. BGD); see also on 12:1 and 15:16. This is one
of the relatively few instances where Paul uses πνεῦμα for the human spirit
(see also particularly 8:16; 1 Cor 5:3–5; 16:18; 2 Cor 2:13; Gal 6:18; Phil
4:23; 1 Thess 5:23; Philem 25), referring to that part, or better, dimension
of the person by which he/she is related to God (cf. particularly 8:16; 1 Cor
2:10–13). That it is thus through the human spirit that the Spirit of God
acts upon and communicates with the human being results in some experiential
ambiguity (1 Cor 14:14, 32; 2 Cor 4:13; and cf. Rom 1:9 with Phil 3:3; elsewhere, e.g., Mark 14:38; James 4:5); but it does not follow that Paul means
God's Spirit at this point (against Kümmel, *Römer 7*, 33; Schweizer, *TDNT*
6:435). The phrasing here clearly implies that Paul is deliberately contrasting
the worship appropriate in relation to the gospel with the typically cult-oriented
worship of his fellow Jews (cf. 2:28–29; 12:1; 15:16; Phil 3:3). Whereas Paul's
Pharisaic contemporaries sought to enhance the holiness of the cult by extending its purity requirements to everyday life (see particularly J. Neusner, *Politics
to Piety*, and elsewhere), Paul abandoned the cultic distinctiveness of Judaism
by "spiritualizing" the cultic language and applying it to all activity which
expressed commitment to Christ and his gospel. For εὐαγγέλιον see on 1:1;
for "his Son" see on 1:3. To speak of "the gospel of his Son" so soon after
speaking of "the gospel of God" is striking (similarly 15:16 and 15:19); and
while the genitive construction here should perhaps be taken in the sense
"the gospel concerning his Son" (objective genitive—so 1:3), the fact that
both phrases are of precisely the same form and are inevitably ambiguous
should not be ignored.

9–10 ὡς ἀδιαλείπτως . . . δεόμενος, "how constantly I mention you, in
my prayers, always asking." This is once again the characteristic assurance
of personal concern, as in 1 Cor 1:4; Eph 1:16; Phil 1:3–4; Col 1:3; 1 Thess
1:2–3 (in very similar terms); 2:13; 2 Thess 1:3, 11; 2:13; Philem 4. That
the language is somewhat fulsome does not mean that it is insincere—especially
in view of the oath just taken (v 9); cf. particularly 9:2.

ἐπὶ τῶν προσευχῶν μου, "at my prayers." Paul presumably maintained regular
times of prayer: perhaps three times a day, as already established in Jewish
practice (cf. Dan 6:11; Acts 3:1; 10:3), and taken over by Christianity (*Did.*
8.3) (see J. Jeremias, *The Prayers of Jesus* [London: SCM, 1967], 67–72); or
perhaps following Jesus' practice of extensive prayer (Mark 1:35; 6:46; 14:32–
42), or prayer as occasion prompted (cf. Acts 10:9), or prayer as he traveled
("unceasingly"?). For ἀδιαλείπτως see Spicq, 41–43; through Paul's usage it
became a characteristic way of describing the concern shown in prayer (1
Thess 5:17; Ign. *Eph.* 10.1; *Herm. Sim.* 9.11.7; Pol. *Phil.* 4.3). δέομαι is a strong
word in Paul—"ask earnestly, beg" (2 Cor 5:20; 8:4; 10:2; Gal 4:12; 1 Thess
3:10).

10 εἰ πως ἤδη ποτέ, "whether somehow now at last." The piling up of
adverbs indicates his concern not to be misunderstood. The more he stresses
that his desire to visit the Roman congregations is of long standing, the more
he is open to criticism for not coming sooner. Hence the equal stress on

divine initiative; the slave cannot order his life in accordance with his own wishes (so also v 13). See BGD, εἰ VI.12; ἤδη 1c.

εὐοδωθήσομαι, "succeed." Literally, "be led along a good road" (cf. Tob 5:16), so "prosper, succeed" (cf. 2 Chron 32:30; Sir 41:1; 1 Cor 16:2); but in view of the context Paul may have the original meaning in mind (Lightfoot)— cf. 1 Thess 3:11.

ἐν τῷ θελήματι τοῦ θεοῦ, "by the will of God." τὸ θέλημα τοῦ θεοῦ is an established phrase in Paul—12:2; 15:32; 1 Cor 1:1; 2 Cor 1:1; 8:5; Gal 1:4; (Eph 1:1; 6:6); Col 1:1; 4:12; 1 Thess 4:3; 5:18. For the widespread use of the pious qualification "God willing," see Deissmann, *Bible Studies*, 252; BGD, θέλω 2. That a certain degree of anxiety as well as uncertainty is involved here (not least in view of his intervening trip to Jerusalem) is indicated more clearly in 15:30–32.

11 ἐπιποθῶ, "I long." Paul does not hesitate to use emotive language in describing the mutual relations of his readers and his team (cf. 2 Cor 9:14; Phil 1:8; 2:26; 1 Thess 3:6).

ἵνα τι μεταδῶ χάρισμα ὑμῖν πνευματικὸν εἰς τὸ στηριχθῆναι ὑμᾶς, "in order that I may share some truly spiritual gift with you through which you will be strengthened." μεταδῶ, "share": a characteristic of a spiritual gift for Paul is that it is not for oneself, but for sharing (cf. 1 Thess 2:8), for the common good (1 Cor 12:7); the very act of sharing (one's means) is itself a charism (Rom 12:8). χάρισμα, *charisma*, "charism, spiritual gift," is another word Christian (and sociological!) vocabulary owes almost entirely to Paul; prior to his taking it over and giving it significance it had only a minimal currency. As the form of the word implies, χάρισμα denotes an embodiment of grace (χάρις), the concrete expression of God's generous and powerful concern for his human creation, so that it can be used of any act or utterance which is a means of divine grace, a medium through which God's graciousness is experienced, whether the thought is of the totality of what God has given by means of Christ (5:15–16; 6:23; cf. 11:29; 2 Cor 1:11), or more often of particular ministries, occasional or regular (12:6; 1 Cor 1:7; 7:7; 12:4, 9, 28, 30–31; cf. 1 Pet 4:10). See further on 12:6 and Dunn, *Jesus*, esp. 205–7. What Paul has in mind here is not specified, nor could he be sure how God would bring his grace to expression through him. But clearly he has sufficient confidence in God's grace working in and through him (1:5) that he can hold out the firm promise that God will use him in some way for their benefit (not necessarily in a specifically "apostolic" way; and the "gift" is not necessarily "the gospel"—against Barth, *Shorter*); cf. Schlatter, Leenhardt.

The use of πνευματικόν, "spiritual" (that is, belonging to the Spirit, embodying or manifesting Spirit) is striking, since in 1 Cor 12:1 and 14:1 πνευματικά = χαρίσματα. Here it must be regarded as adding emphasis—"a truly spiritual gift," some act of ministry which is both of the Spirit and a means of grace (see further on 7:14). Käsemann's restriction of the thought to "the blessing which comes with preaching" is unjustified. So too is Michel's distinction between apostolic ἐξουσία ("authority") and pneumatic χάρισμα (Paul would not accept such a sharp distinction between χάρις [1:5] and χάρισμα), and his assumption that πνευματικόν must imply the presence of "Pneumatiker" in the Roman congregations before whom Paul seeks to legitimate himself as a Spirit-bearer. On the question of why Paul is not more specific in his reasons for wishing to come to Rome see *Introduction* and 15:14–33.

στηρίζω, "confirm, strengthen, establish"—again a typical expression of his concern and hopes for the congregations to which he writes (16:25; 1 Thess 3:2, 13; 2 Thess 2:17; 3:3; here the divine passive, "strengthened by God"). Paul's assurance, that God would work through him for the benefit of his audience in Rome, should not be regarded as a sign of arrogance on the part of Paul or as an attempt to overawe his readers: Paul assumes that all believers have been given God's grace (see on 1:5) and that God's grace will naturally express itself through them in particular acts and utterances and ministries (charisms), which, almost by definition, will be for the benefit of their fellow believers (see further on 12:6).

12 τοῦτο δέ ἐστιν συμπαρακληθῆναι ἐν ὑμῖν διὰ τῆς ἐν ἀλλήλοις πίστεως ὑμῶν τε καὶ ἐμοῦ, "that is, that there may be mutual encouragement among you through each other's faith, both yours and mine." Paul catches himself ("I would rather say"—Lightfoot), perhaps suddenly realizing that his understanding of spiritual gifts might not be familiar to his readers, particularly the degree of mutual interdependence fundamental in the exercise of such charisms (12:4–5; 1 Cor 12:14–26). This verse then is not so much a correction as an elaboration or clarification of what charismatic ministry and community involve, not least the experience of *mutual* encouragement (συμπαρακληθῆναι, the first of the characteristically Pauline συμ- compounds in the letter; see on 6:4) and the sharing of the faith they hold in common (cf. Philem 6)—that is, presumably, talking together about what they believed, their understanding (and lack of understanding) of it, their convictions and questions, and how their faith worked out in daily life. See also 15:24, 32. Gaston, *Paul,* 169, as usual translates "faithfulness."

13 οὐ θέλω δὲ ὑμᾶς ἀγνοεῖν, ἀδελφοί, "I do not want you to be unaware, brothers." The phrase carries a certain solemnity—Paul's way of giving extra weight to the words which follow (11:25; 1 Cor 10:1; 12:1; 2 Cor 1:8; 1 Thess 4:13). The technique would not be unfamiliar (see BGD, ἀγνοέω 1), but the actual form is characteristically Pauline. The addition of ἀδελφοί, "brothers," makes the appeal all the more personal and affective, as quite often in this letter (7:1, 4; 8:12; 10:1; 11:25; 12:1; 15:14, 30; 16:17), as indeed in all his letters. The use of ἀδελφός for members of a religious association was familiar at the time (Lietzmann; MM; BGD; Meeks, *Urban Christians,* 87 and nn. 73, 77; *NDIEC* 2:29–50); so also among the Qumran covenanters (1QS 6.10, 22; 1QM 13.1; 15.4, 7; 1QSa 1.18; CD 6.20–7.2; 20.18). But Paul was probably even more mindful of its traditional Jewish use, as in 9:3 (e.g., Exod 2:11; Lev 19:17; Deut 3:18; 15:12; Neh 5:1, 5, 8; Isa 66:20; Tob 1:3; 1 Macc 2:40–41; 2 Macc 1:1; Philo, *Spec. Leg.* 2.79–80). So Paul's regular usage would not be particularly remarkable, as also when he uses the word in a sense approaching "colleague" (16:23; 1 Cor 1:1; 16:12; 2 Cor 1:1; etc.)—though his usage never becomes merely formal and often expresses deep regard for and personal commitment to those so named (e.g., 1 Cor 8:13; 15:58; Phil 2:25–30; 4:1; Col 4:7, 9; Philem 7). What would be more distinctive is the assertion that Christ, the central figure to whom the Christian association was devoted, is the eldest of the brothers (8:29; Col 1:18; cf.

Rom 8:17; Gal 4:6–7). For possible sexist overtones see on 16:1 and 17. See
also on 9:3.

ὅτι πολλάκις προεθέμην ἐλθεῖν πρὸς ὑμᾶς, καὶ ἐκωλύθην ἄχρι τοῦ δεῦρο, "that I
often intended to come to you, and have so far been prevented." Once again
it would be unduly critical to assume that Paul was exaggerating. Rome, the
capital of such a mighty empire, Rome, to which all roads led, would naturally
be a magnet for Paul. In his strategy for the universal outreach of the gospel
(1:5—"all the nations"), he must often have considered the importance of a
strong Christian grouping there and the desirability of his linking up personally
with it. What it was which "prevented" him, he does not say, nor when he
repeats the claim in 15:22. It is certainly possible that he thought the repeated
hindrances were of demonic/Satanic origin (as in 1 Thess 2:18); and the
expulsion of Jews from Rome by Claudius in 49 (see *Introduction* §2.2.3) would
certainly have provided a strong disincentive. But with someone like Paul,
who threw himself so unreservedly into his work, it might simply be that
ever fresh opportunities and the particular problems of his already established
churches, not to mention the organization of the collection (15:22–29), made
unceasing demands on his time which he could not easily ignore—so ἐκωλύθην,
divine (?) passive: "I was hindered (by God?)." "Paul is not master of his
plans" (Eichholz, "Horizont," 92).

ἵνα τινὰ καρπὸν σχῶ, "that I might have some fruit"—καρπός in the sense
of "appropriate result or return," here of "beneficial outcome." The imagery
is obvious and would be familiar particularly from Stoic and Jewish thought
(*TDNT* 3:614; see, e.g., Amos 6:12; Philo, *Fuga* 176; Josephus, *Ant.* 20.48;
elsewhere in NT Matt 3:8; Heb 12:11; 13:15; James 3:17–18; in Paul Rom
6:21–22; 7:4; 15:28; Gal 5:22; Phil 1:11, 22; 4:17; Col 1:6, 10; also Eph
5:9); see also on 6:22. It can obviously be used in a missionary context (cf.
Phil 1:22; Col 1:6), but cannot be described simply as "a phrase of missionary
language" (against Klein, "Purpose," 38). See also 15:29.

καὶ ἐν ὑμῖν καθὼς καὶ ἐν τοῖς λοιποῖς ἔθνεσιν, "among you also just as among
the rest of the Gentiles." By "the rest of the Gentiles" Paul would have in
mind particularly the congregations established by him in Asia, Macedonia,
and Greece. Again the thrusting dynamism of Paul's call to the Gentiles asserts
itself. However much he recognizes the two-way nature of ministry within
the Christian community (v 12), what drives him on personally is his overpowering conviction that God has chosen to use him for special ministry among
the Gentiles. So even if he is not the founder of the Roman congregations
he would hardly be true to his calling if he did not expect some fruitful
outcome of his visit to Rome. Here again the strongly Gentile composition
of the Roman congregation is clearly implied; see also 11:13, 17–24; 15:7–
12, 15–16.

14 Ἕλλησίν τε καὶ βαρβάροις, "to both Greeks and barbarians." From its
first appearance this was not merely a contrast between Greeks and other
nations, or Greek speakers and non-Greek speakers. The very word βάρβαρος
carried derogatory significance. It referred to a speaker of a strange, unintelligible language (cf., e.g., Ovid, *Tristia* 5.10.37; 1 Cor 14:11); and from its early
use in reference particularly to the Medes and Persians, the historic foes of
Greece, it gained a clear note of contempt—hence Roman unwillingness to

be classified as βάρβαροι (see BGD; also MM). Thus the phrase came to be used by cultured Greeks conscious of their sophistication over against the rest, and since Greek culture had indeed captured the main centers of population in the eastern Empire it could be used by all who aspired to being "Greeks" over against the rest as uncultured—an international "set" with whom Paul would often have rubbed shoulders on his travels and with whom indeed he could identify to a significant extent. In using the phrase here, however, Paul is not necessarily accepting the viewpoint of the "Greeks" or designating particular groups as "barbarians." By now it had simply become a standard phrase to include all races and classes within the Gentile world. See further *TDNT* 1:546–53; Lagrange; Michel; Hengel, *Judaism*, 1:38, 65, 300.

σοφοῖς τε καὶ ἀνοήτοις, "to both wise and foolish." This is a similar way of classifying humankind as a whole, which the "Greek" would consider synonymous with the preceding contrast. The same derogatory note is implied: all who do not share my insight are fools! ("the educated as well as the ignorant"— NJB). For the contrast cf. Prov 17:28; Plato, *Timaeus* 30b. In ἀνόητος the high hellenistic regard for the νοῦς (mind) is reflected; whereas in Jewish wisdom literature ἄφρων (foolish, ignorant) is preferred (cf. particularly 2:20). That Paul should be thus prepared to designate the Gentile world in categories of culture and rationality (rather than of races or geographical areas) is striking; it indicates his confidence in the power of his message even in the face of hellenistic sophistication (cf. 1:16); see also Schlatter. For his view of human wisdom see especially 1 Cor 1:17–2:13; 3:18–20.

ὀφειλέτης, "one who is obliged to do something." This is not a very common word (in Paul only 8:12; 15:27; Gal 5:3). Paul presumably means "obligated" by virtue of his call (see further Minear, "Gratitude," esp. 43–45). Hence, as apostle to the Gentiles, he looks at the world as Gentiles see it. Since he was also a truly cosmopolitan man of his age (Jew, Hellenist, Roman citizen), who had already traveled widely through the northeastern quadrant of the Mediterranean countries (15:19), it is possible that he also includes the sense of how much he owed to all sorts and conditions of people, uncultured as well as sophisticated (cf. 1 Cor 1:26–28).

15 τὸ κατ᾽ ἐμὲ πρόθυμον, "my eagerness." For syntax see Cranfield. For πρόθυμος (elsewhere in the NT only in the Gethsemane scene of Mark 14:38 // Matt 26:41) see LSJ, MM, BGD. Paul sustains the insistence on his desire to visit the congregations in Rome throughout this section.

εὐαγγελίσασθαι, "to preach the gospel." The word is well enough known in Greek, but its meaning is almost entirely Jewish and Christian (see on 1:1). (1) To preach the gospel, (2) to the Gentiles, sums up the heart of Paul's understanding of his calling. The conviction of what he personally had been called to do dominates vv 13–15, without diminishing the force of the clarification in v 12. He does not, of course, imply that his readers need to be evangelized (the Western addition of ἐν, "among you," rather than "to you" is an attempt to reduce the possibility of misunderstanding here), though the openness of the Christian gatherings to outsiders and inquirers (cf. 1 Cor 14:23–25) makes that sense not altogether inappropriate. It is simply that if any one verb sums up his lifelong obligation it is this one—"to preach the gospel"—so that its use can embrace the whole range of his ministry, including his explication of the gospel, as in this very letter. Certainly it is the case that Paul elsewhere uses εὐαγγελίζεσθαι in the sense of "evangelize," a preaching which aims for conversion (10:15; 15:20; 1 Cor 1:17; 9:16, 18; 15:1, 2; 2 Cor 10:16; 11:7; Gal 1:8, 9, 11, 16, 23; 4:13; so also Eph 2:17; 3:8; 1 Pet 1:12, 25; and regularly in Acts). But Paul did not confine his apostolic "set-apartness to the gospel" (1:1) or "service in the gospel" (1:9) to "first time" preaching of the gospel, or restrict the gospel simply to the initial impulse on the way to salvation (1:16), and 1 Thess 3:6 is sufficient evidence that his use of εὐαγγελίζεσθαι was not narrowly fixed (against Zeller, *Juden*, 55–58). Klein in particular makes too much of the conflict between this verse and 15:20: "the founding of a church was at stake" ("Purpose," 47), which is an unlikely explanation, despite the lack of ἐκκλησία (see *Introduction* §3.1), since Paul otherwise addresses his Roman readers in precisely the same terms as he addresses the churches of his own foundation (see on 1:8– 10; cf. 15:14; 16:19).

Explanation

Following his usual practice, Paul's first act after the formal greeting is to give God thanks for his readers, particularly for their faith. The element of exaggeration at this point is not untypical either ("in all the world," "unceasingly," "always"), though with the amount of movement to and from Rome news of the churches established in the empire's capital city would be more widely dispersed than in most other cases. Paul's language however should not be taken as necessarily implying that the Christians in Rome had been particularly courageous or that their numbers included members of particular significance.

As elsewhere in Paul, the thanksgiving is offered *through* Jesus Christ, not *to* Christ, nor to God *and* Christ. That this phrasing follows immediately on v 7 confirms the need for caution in interpreting the association of God as Father and the Lord Christ in v 7. If in v 7 both are named as conjointly the source of grace and peace, in v 8 it is equally noticeable that Christ is assumed to have a more intermediary (and subordinate) role.

The oath of v 9 may be merely formal, especially if it refers only to Paul's assurance of unceasing prayer as part of the formal hyperbole. But the movement of the sentence is clearly towards the object of his prayer (that he might come to them), and this suggests that the oath serves a more apologetic function, that is, to assure his Roman hearers of his integrity and good intentions. That is to say, Paul's language reads rather as though he had expressed his desire to visit Rome on more than one occasion, but had never carried the intention through, and consequently had exposed himself to some criticism for his lack of good faith or lack of resolute purpose (cf. 2 Cor 1–2). Hence not only the oath, but also the awkwardness of the phrasing in v 10, the repeated assurance of his earnest desire to see them at the beginning of v 11, the yet further and somewhat labored reassurance of v 13 with its explanation of his having been prevented despite his best and often reaffirmed intention, and the final assurance of v 15. This continued consciousness of vulnerability to criticism and sensitivity to (likely) actual criticism, in a letter to unfamiliar congregations, is a reminder of how exposed Paul's position must have been within the earliest expansion of Christianity.

The relative clause which interrupts the opening of this piece of self-apologia, "whom I serve with my spirit in the gospel of his Son" (v 9), seems designed in part at least to maintain the thrust already expressed in the opening paragraph. Paul describes his apostleship to the Gentiles as a cultic ministry, not however in terms of particular cultic acts, but as a spiritual act, as the work of (preaching) the gospel motivated and enabled from the level of the spirit. Here again those familiar with Paul's thought would probably recognize the outline of a characteristic emphasis (cf. particularly 2:28–29; Phil 3:3): the requirements of the law fulfilled from within, because God's Son had transformed the whole level of obedience and covenant loyalty to a new plane, which was continuous with the old and still able to be described in terms drawn from the old, but which nonetheless was transformed in meaning and outworking.

The two purpose clauses which link together this piece of self-apologia (vv 11, 13) reflect Paul's burning drive as apostle to the Gentiles, particularly his consciousness of the success of his ministry, and of how much he had been used by the Spirit to establish and strengthen his churches. The last clause of v 13 confirms not only the predominantly Gentile character of the Roman churches—which makes the repeated emphasis on Jewish issues thereafter all the more striking—but also Paul's self-understanding as above all else an apostle to the Gentiles. At the same time, the way Paul checks or corrects himself in v 12 should not go unnoticed. Perhaps it signifies Paul's sensitivity to the ground rules governing apostolic mission about which he obviously felt strongly—that is, the obligation not to interfere with other apostles' missionary territory and churches (15:20; 2 Cor 10:13–16). But probably more significant here is Paul's desire to recognize the charismatic and spiritual stature of the churches of the Gentile mission, including his own (e.g., 1 Thess 5:12–22). This would explain why he backs away from any hint that he sees himself as a preeminent source of spiritual gifts, and hastens to underscore the mutual interdependence of each group of believers in the sharing of their common faith for their mutual benefit, and moreover numbers himself with them in this. Even as apostle to the Gentiles he is as dependent as each of them on the mutual ministry of the caring, sharing community of faith. It should not escape notice that this is the first subordinate theme to which he returns (chap. 12) after the exposition of the primary theme is complete with chap. 11.

That being said, it is all the more striking that his conviction of being the specially chosen instrument of God's purpose and blessing for the Gentiles reasserts itself at the end of v 13 as he begins to wind up to the thematic statement of his letter's main argument (vv 16–17). Equally striking are the categories he names in v 14, "Greeks and barbarians, wise and foolish," rather than the perhaps more expected contrast of Jew and Greek. For these are the categories of self-conscious Hellenism rather than the words most natural to a Jew. For the Hellenist, conscious of rich cultural and intellectual heritage, the world could be categorized into Greeks and all the rest as uncultured barbarians, and society could be divided into those who use their minds and those who do not, intellectuals and nonintellectuals. The significance then is that Paul, in elaborating his sense of call to evangelize the Gentiles, deliberately looks at the world through the eyes of a Gentile, from the perspective of sophisticated Hellenism. His commission as apostle to the Gentiles embraces all races, both those whom Hellenism owns and those it despises, and all levels of society, both those highly regarded within Hellenism and those disregarded. The obligation laid upon him in his commissioning by the risen Christ was to take the gospel to all Gentiles without regard to Gentile distinctions of race and status.

It is this sense of obligation which explains his eagerness to come to Rome. We should not press the continuity of thought between vv 14 and 15 to produce the inference that the churches in Rome were necessarily comprehensive in membership (mixed in race and social class). At the same time it is just as likely that the terms used in v 14 were deliberately general so that no one would take offense, even if any did not recognize themselves as "Greek" or "wise." The final word ("to preach the gospel") is slightly surprising, but only if we confine the sense to preaching the gospel for the first time. And even so we should not take it that Paul thought his Roman readers still needed to be evangelized, since he clearly chose the word to provide a lead into the central statement of the whole letter.

C. Summary Statement of the Letter's Theme (1:16–17)

Bibliography

Achtemeier, E. R. and **Achtemeier, P. J.** "Righteousness." *IDB* 4:80–85, 91–99. **Barrett, C. K.** "I Am Not Ashamed of the Gospel." In *Foi et salut selon S. Paul*, ed. M. Barth et al. AnBib 42. Rome: Biblical Institute, 1970. 19–41. Repr. in *New Testament Essays*. London: SPCK, 1972. 116–43. **Barth, M.** "Jews and Gentiles: The Social Character of Justification in Paul." *JES* 5 (1968) 241–67. **Berger, K.** "Neues Material zur 'Gerechtigkeit Gottes.'" *ZNW* 68 (1977) 266–75. **Brauch, M. T.** "Perspectives on 'God's Righteousness' in Recent German Discussion." In Sanders, *Paul*, 523–42. **Bultmann, R.** "ΔΙΚΑΙΟΣΥΝΗ ΘΕΟΥ." *JBL* 83 (1964) 12–16. Repr. in *Exegetica*. Tübingen: Mohr, 1967. 470–75. **Cavallin, H. C. C.** "'The Righteous Shall Live by Faith.'" *ST* 32 (1978) 33–43. **Cremer, H.** *Die paulinische Rechtfertigungslehre im Zusammenhange ihrer geschichtlichen Voraussetzungen.* 2d ed. Gütersloh: Bertelsmann, 1900. **Dahl, N. A.** "Justification." **Eichrodt, W.** *Theology of the Old Testament.* London: SCM, 1961. 239–49. **Feuillet, A.** "La citation d'Habacuc 2:4 et les huit premiers chapitres de l'Epître aux Romains." *NTS* 6 (1959–60) 52–80. **Fitzmyer, J. A.** "Habakkuk 2:3–4 and the New Testament." In *To Advance the Gospel: New Testament Studies.* New York: Crossroad, 1981. 236–46. **Fridrichsen, A.** "Aus Glauben zu Glauben, Röm 1:17." *ConNT* 12 (1948) 54. **Glombitza, O.** "Von der Scham des Gläubigen. Erwägungen zu Röm 1:14–17." *NovT* 4 (1960) 74–80. **Gyllenberg, R.** "Die paulinische Rechtfertigungslehre und das Alte Testament." *ST* 1 (1935) 35–52. **Herold, G.** *Zorn.* **Hill, D.** *Greek Words.* 82–162. **Hübner, H.** *Law.*

124–36. ———. "Paulusforschung." 2694–2709. **Hultgren, A. J.** *Gospel.* 12–46. **Käsemann, E.** "The Righteousness of God in Paul" (1961). In *New Testament Questions of Today.* London: SCM, 1969. 168–82. **Kertelge, K.** *Rechtfertigung.* **Klein, G.** "Gottes Gerechtigkeit als Thema der neuesten Paulus-Forschung." In *Rekonstruktion und Interpretation.* Munich: Kaiser, 1969. 225–36. **Koch, D.-A.** "Der Text von Hab 2:4b in der Septuaginta und im Neuen Testament." *ZNW* 76 (1985) 68–85. **Lohse, E.** "Die Gerechtigkeit Gottes in der paulinischen Theologie" (1971). In *Einheit.* 209–27. **Michel, O.** "Zum Sprachgebrauch von ἐπαισχύνομαι in Röm 1:16." In *Glaube und Ethos,* FS G. Wehrung, ed. R. Paulus. Stuttgart: Kohlhammer, 1940. 36–53. **Moody, R. M.** "The Habakkuk Quotation in Romans 1:17." *ExpT* 92 (1980–81) 205–8. **Müller, C.** *Gerechtigkeit.* **Piper, J.** *Justification.* 81–101. **Rad, G. von.** *Old Testament Theology.* Vol. 1. Edinburgh: Oliver & Boyd, 1962. 370–76. **Reumann, J.** *Righteousness.* **Ridderbos, N.** *Paul.* 159–81. **Schmid, H. H.** "Rechtfertigung als Schöpfungsgeschehen." In *Rechtfertigung,* FS E. Käsemann, ed. J. Friedrich et al. Tübingen: Mohr, 1976. 403–14. **Smith, D. M.** "Ο ΔΕ ΔΙΚΑΙΟΣ ΕΚ ΠΙΣΤΕΩΣ ΖΗΣΕΤΑΙ." In *Studies in the History and Text of the New Testament,* FS K. W. Clark, ed. B. L. Daniels and M. J. Suggs. Salt Lake City: University of Utah, 1967. 13–25. **Stuhlmacher, P.** *Gerechtigkeit.* **Taylor, V.** *Forgiveness and Reconciliation.* 2d ed. London: Macmillan, 1946. 29–69. **Williams, S. K.** "Righteousness." **Zeller, D.** *Juden.* 60–64, 141–49. **Ziesler, J. A.** *Righteousness.*

Translation

[16] *For I am not ashamed of the gospel, since it is the power of God for salvation, to all who believe, Jew first[a] but also Gentile.* [17] *For the righteousness of God is being revealed in it from faith to faith—as it is written, "He who is righteous by faith shall live."*

Notes

[a] The omission of πρῶτον (first) by some witnesses, including B G and the Sahidic version, may be due to Marcion, for whom the idea of Jewish priority would have been unacceptable (Metzger).

Form and Structure

Vv 16–17 is clearly the thematic statement for the entire letter. As such it is the climax of the introduction: note the deliberate buildup in the talk of εὐαγγέλιον/εὐαγγελίζεσθαι (vv 1, 9, 15, 16) and of πίστις/πιστεύειν (vv 5, 8, 12, 16, 17). Attention should not be focused exclusively on v 17: the principal emphasis is actually on the saving power of the gospel (v 16b), with v 17 functioning as the chief justification ("for") for the assertion (Zeller, *Juden,* 62). V 16b in fact ties the whole letter together (chaps. 1–15); though it is also true that v 17 in effect provides the text for the main didactic section (chaps. 1–11):

God's righteousness to faith:
   "the righteous by faith . . .   —1:18–5:21
   . . . shall live"   —chaps. 6–8
God's righteousness from faith:
   "the righteous by God's faithfulness"—chaps. 9–11

(Feuillet, "Hab 2:4," argues for a division after 5:11; but see on 5:1–21 *Introduction*). The scripture quoted (Hab 2:4) is not itself the text of the letter (Luz, "Aufbau"; against Nygren, Cranfield), but, as usual with Paul, is attached to the main claim to document it and to provide a scriptural basis for it.

The two key terms clearly have programmatic significance in what follows:

> *Faith*—after dominating the key section, 3:21–5:21 (3:22, 25, 27–28, 30–31; 4:3, 5, 9, 11–14, 16–20; 5:1–2), it disappears from view in chaps. 6–8 to reappear at crucial points in chaps. 9–11 (9:30, 32, 33; 10:4, 6, 8–9, 11, 14, 17; 11:20) and again in chaps. 12–15 (12:3, 6; 14:1, 2, 22–23).
>
> *Righteous, righteousness, to hold righteous*—equally the dominant theme in the same sections (3:20–22, 24–26, 28, 30;   4:2–3, 5–6, 9, 11, 13, 22;   5:1, 7, 9, 17, 19, 21; 9:30–31; 10:3–6), but more than "faith" providing a link into the intervening discussions (2:13; 3:4–5, 10; 6:7, 13, 16, 19, 20; 7:12; 8:10, 30, 33).

Ellis, "Exegetical Patterns," 217–18, sees a midrashic structure in 1:17–18, with 1:17 as the proem text followed by a sequence of expositions and supporting texts.

Achtemeier takes 1:14–2:16 as a complete unit, arguing that vv 16, 17, and 18 ff. are grammatically subordinate to v 15. But that is to overload the significance of γάρ, which may denote lighter connections of thought or introduce an explanation without indicating where the weight of emphasis lies (cf. Harrisville—"throughout the epistle, and with only one exception . . . 'for' does not conclude but begins an argument, with or without any link to what precedes"; see also on 1:18). There is no reason here to depart from the usual recognition that 1:16–17 are the climax of the introduction and theme for what follows.

Comment

16 οὐ γὰρ ἐπαισχύνομαι τὸ εὐαγγέλιον, "for I am not ashamed of the gospel." For "shame" as the consequence of being shown to have acted on a false assumption or misplaced confidence, see particularly the Psalms (35:26; 40:14–15; 69:19; 71:13; 119:6; etc.); see also καταισχύνω in 5:5 and 9:33. This usage also fits Jewett's "Ambassadorial Letter" thesis (15), since it may include the thought of the representative (of "the gospel of God") not being put to shame in the face of a superior power.

As Barrett has shown, it is likely that some connection between this assertion and the Jesus tradition preserved in Mark 8:38 // Luke 9:26 should be recognized ("Not Ashamed"). Paul herein shows awareness of the tradition of Jesus' teaching and includes it within his own understanding of "the gospel"—the post-Easter interpretation of the "Christ-event" being consciously formulated in continuity with the proclamation of Jesus (see further on 1:1 and 12:14). This also means that Paul quite deliberately makes his own what must have been a shared affirmation among other early Christian communities who expressed their solidarity precisely in terms of their confidence in and loyalty to Jesus (Barrett, "Not Ashamed," 128). As Michel had already pointed out, this likelihood of a firm connection between 1:16 and the tradition of Mark

8:38 // Luke 9:26 confirms that the οὐκ ἐπαισχύνομαι should be taken in the sense of "confess," "bear witness" against the older "psychological" interpretation ("Sprachgebrauch"; cf. particularly 2 Tim 1:8, 12). Herold, however, presses hard the overtones of legal procedure in ἐπαισχύνομαι ("it describes a forensic not a psychological process") to argue that Paul speaks with a view to opponents in Rome (*Zorn,* chap. 1, esp. 140).

δύναμις γὰρ θεοῦ ἐστιν, "for it is the power of God," is a regular concept in Paul (particularly 1:20; 9:17; 1 Cor 1:18, 24; 2:5; 6:14; 2 Cor 4:7; 6:7; 13:4). By it he clearly has in mind a force that operates with marked effect on people, transforming them—as evident particularly in conversion (1 Cor 2:4–5; 1 Thess 1:5) and resurrection (1:4; 1 Cor 6:14; 15:43; 2 Cor 13:4; Phil 3:10)—and providing a source of energy to sustain that qualitatively different life (1 Cor 1:18; 2 Cor 4:7; 6:7; 12:9; 13:4; Col 1:11, 29; 2 Thess 1:11; see also on 15:13). It was not a matter of blind trust that such a power must be operative whatever the appearances, but rather a matter of actual experience as indicated also by the plural = "miracles," a visible and marked alteration in a current condition that could not be attributed to human causation (1 Cor 12:10, 28–29; 2 Cor 12:12; Gal 3:5; see also on 15:19). That Paul could be confident that the source of this power was God presumably follows from its context (a consequence of preaching the gospel) and continuing effects (cf. 1 Cor 4:20; 2 Cor 1:8; 6:7; 12:9; 2 Thess 1:11). In contrast to the strongly magical overtones which often gathered round the word in non-Jewish circles (*TDNT* 2:288–90, 309; MM), Paul's emphasis on the power of God as embodied in and mediated through the gospel would have had a marked significance for his readers (cf. 1 Cor 1:18–25). Of the OT passages which speak of the effectiveness of God's word and which Paul might have had in mind, Ps 107:20 is the most suggestive, particularly in view of its use in the ancient form of the kerygma preserved in Acts 10:36–38. On the power of the word of preaching cf. again 1 Cor 2:4–5 and 1 Thess 1:5; also John 6:63; 15:3; 1 Cor 4:15; James 1:18; 1 Pet 1:23. See also on 1:20; 4:21; and 8:38.

εἰς σωτηρίαν, "with the effect of bringing about salvation." σωτηρία would be familiar to Paul's readers in the everyday sense of "bodily health, preservation, safety" (LSJ, MM); cf. e.g., Mark 5:23, 28, 34; 6:56; 10:52; Acts 27:34. In the religious meaning, which was of course known in Greek thought, but which dominates the LXX (34 times in the Psalms, 18 in Isaiah) and NT usage (BGD), the physical imagery is retained in its sense of deliverance from peril and restoration to wholeness; see further Lagrange. As such in Paul it is primarily eschatological, a hope for the future, deliverance from final destruction (ἀπώλεια), the end product of God's good purpose for humankind (see particularly 5:9–10; 13:11; 1 Cor 3:15; 5:5; Phil 2:12; 1 Thess 5:8–9; see further on 5:9 and 11:11). But through the power of the gospel (conversion—see above), the believer has already been launched toward salvation; hence the use of the verb in the present tense in 1 Cor 1:18, 15:2, and 2 Cor 2:15—God's preservation through to final safety; and here the preposition εἰς has the force not simply of movement toward but of movement right up to and into, so "with the effect of bringing about" (cf. 10:10; 2 Cor 7:10; Phil 1:19; 2 Thess 2:13; 2 Tim 3:15; and see also on 6:16).

παντὶ τῷ πιστεύοντι, "to all who believe." Here as in other similar references to believers Paul uses the present rather than the aorist tense (3:22; 4:5, 11, 24; 9:33; 10:4, 10–11; 15:13; 1 Cor 1:21; 14:22; 2 Cor 4:13; Gal 3:22; Phil 1:29; 1 Thess 1:7; 2:10, 13; also Eph 1:19; aorist in 2 Thess 1:10). The significance presumably is that in such passages he wishes to focus not solely on the initial act of faith but on faith as a continuing orientation and motivation for life. For πίστις see on 1:17. The emphasis on "*all* who *believe*" has the ring of a "war cry" (Michel) and is fundamental for the rest of the letter (cf. particularly 3:22; 4:11; 10:4, 11): "all" is a key word for the letter (Gaston, *Paul*, 116; see further on 11:32). Faith is both the initial and the continuing access point for the saving power of God into human life, the common denominator which God looks for in every case. See further *Form and Structure* and on 3:22.

Ἰουδαίῳ τε πρῶτον καὶ ῞Ελληνι, "to Jew first, but also to Greek." "Jew and Greek" is the Jewish equivalent to the Gentile categorization of the world given in v 14, only here with "Greek" replacing "Gentile," reflecting the all-pervasiveness of Greek culture (cf. 2 Macc 4:36; 11:2; *3 Macc* 3.8; *4 Macc* 18.20; *Sib. Or.* 5.264). The two terms form a regular combination in Paul (2:9–10; 3:9, 29; 9:24; 10:12; 1 Cor 1:22–24; 10:32; 12:13; Gal 2:14–15; 3:28; Col 3:11); and note also 3:1–4 and 11:18, 28–29. The stepping back into a Jewish perspective (following on from v 14) will be deliberate. The phrase here reflects Paul's consciousness that he was a Jew who believed in a Jewish Messiah yet whose life's work was to take the gospel beyond the national and religious boundaries of Judaism. The πρῶτον here balances the παντί of the preceding phrase: he does not for a moment forget, nor does he want his Gentile readers to forget ("a certain polemical overtone"— Zeller, *Juden*, 145) Jewish priority in God's saving purpose (cf. 3:3–4; chaps. 9–11); but equally fundamental is his conviction that Jewish priority does not shift the "terms of salvation" one whit beyond faith. The need to explain and defend this double emphasis is the driving force behind the whole epistle. For Ἰουδαῖος see further on 2:17.

The sequence "Jew first but also Gentile" should not be taken as directly indicative of Paul's missionary strategy, since he saw himself as first and foremost "apostle to the Gentiles" (11:13; 15:16); but since his natural constituency was the body of Gentiles who had already been attracted to or influenced by Judaism (proselytes and "God-worshipers"—see *Introduction* §2.2.2), it has some bearing on his evangelistic practice since the synagogue provided the most obvious platform for his message—"to the synagogue first and so to the God-fearing Gentile."

17 δικαιοσύνη γὰρ θεοῦ, "for the righteousness of God." δικαιοσύνη is a good example of the need to penetrate through Paul's Greek language in order to understand it in the light of his Jewish background and training. The concept which emerged from the Greco-Roman tradition to dominate Western thought was of righteousness/justice as an ideal or absolute ethical norm against which particular claims and duties could be measured (cf. von Rad, 370–71; Stuhlmacher, *Gerechtigkeit*, 103). But since the fundamental study of H. Cremer it has been recognized that in Hebrew thought צֶדֶק // צְדָקָה is essentially a concept of *relation*. Righteousness is not something which an individual has on his or her own, independently of anyone else; it is something which one has precisely in one's relationships as a social being. People are righteous when they meet the claims which others have on them by virtue of their relationship (see particularly Cremer, 34–38; hence the possibility of using δικαιοσύνη to translate חֶסֶד "loving-kindness," in Gen 19:19; 20:13; 21:23; 24:27; 32:10 [LXX 11]; etc.; see further Hill, *Greek Words*, 106; Ziesler, 60–61). So too when it is predicated of God—in this case the relationship being the covenant which God entered into with his people (discussion of the background should not be confined to occurrences of the actual phrase δικαιοσύνη θεοῦ—cf. Hultgren, *Gospel*, 18–21). God is "righteous" when he fulfills the obligations he took upon himself to be Israel's God, that is, to rescue Israel and punish Israel's enemies (e.g., Exod 9:27; 1 Sam 12:7; Dan 9:16; Mic 6:5)—"righteousness" as "covenant faithfulness" (3:3–5, 25; 10:3; also 9:6 and 15:8). Particularly in the Psalms and Second Isaiah the logic of covenant grace is followed through with the result that righteousness and salvation become virtually synonymous: the righteousness of God as God's act to restore his own and to sustain them within the covenant (Ps 31:1; 35:24; 51:14; 65:5; 71:2, 15; 98:2; 143:11; Isa 45:8, 21; 46:13; 51:5, 6, 8; 62:1–2; 63:1, 7; in the DSS see particularly 1QS 11.2–5, 12–15; 1QH 4.37; 11.17–18, 30–31; elsewhere see, e.g., Bar 5:2, 4, 9; *1 Enoch* 71.14; *Apoc. Mos.* 20.1; *4 Ezra* 8.36; see further, e.g., Cremer, 11–17; Eichrodt; von Rad; E. R. Achtemeier; Stuhlmacher, *Gerechtigkeit*, 115, 141, 166, 175; Kertelge, *Rechtfertigung*, 15–24; Ziesler, 38–43, 82, 93–94, 186; on the Qumran texts see particularly Kertelge, 28–33, and Sanders, *Paul*, 305–10). It is clearly this concept of God's righteousness which Paul takes over here; the "righteousness of God" being his way of explicating "the power of God for salvation" (v 16; cf. Gyllenberg, 41; Hill, 156; NEB catches only one side of it with the translation "God's way of righting wrong"). It is with this sense that the phrase provides a key to his exposition in Romans (3:5, 21–22, 25–26; 10:3), as elsewhere in his theology (2 Cor 5:21; Phil 3:9). See further on 5:21 and 6:13.

This understanding of Paul's language largely removes two issues which have troubled Christian theology for centuries. (1) Is "the righteousness of God" subjective genitive or objective genitive; is it an attitude of God or something he does? Seen as God's meeting of the claims of his covenant relationship, the answer is not a strict either-or, but both-and, with the emphasis on the latter. Williams's attempt to argue that "God's righteousness" denotes an aspect of the divine nature (261–62) strains against the clear thrust of the evidence. So too Cranfield's insistence on the either-or of "a gift bestowed by God" (objective genitive), as against "an activity of God" (subjective genitive) (so also Bultmann and Ridderbos, *Paul*, 163), allows nothing for the dynamism of relationship which can embrace both senses—God's activity in drawing into and sustaining within covenant relationship (cf., e.g., *Apoc. Mos.* 20.1, where loss of righteousness = estrangement from the glory of God). See further on 5:17, 6:16, 6:18, and 6:22. (2) δικαιοῦν, "to justify": does it mean "to *make* righteous" or "to *count* righteous?" This is the classic dispute between Catholic and Protestant exegesis (see particularly Ziesler whose whole analysis revolves round this question; and the Lutheran-Roman Catholic dialogue in Reumann). Since the basic idea is of a *relationship* in which God acts even for the defective partner, an action whereby God sustains the weaker partner

of his covenant relationship within the relationship, the answer again is really
both (cf. Barrett, 75–76). This is the basis of Käsemann's quite proper and
influential understanding of divine righteousness as a gift which has the character of power, because God is savingly active in it. Note the close parallelism
here, "power of God" // "righteousness of God" ("Righteousness," esp. 170,
172–76; cf., e.g., Althaus; Murray; Bornkamm, *Paul*, 147; Ziesler, 186–89;
Kümmel, *Theology*, 197–98; Strecker, "Rechtfertigung," esp. 508; Hübner,
Law, 130; Reumann—"righteousness/justice/justification terminology in the
Hebrew scriptures is 'action-oriented,' not just 'status' or 'being' language"
[15–16]; despite Bultmann, "ΔΙΚΑΙΟΣΥΝΗ," and Klein, "Gerechtigkeit"). It
is God's righteousness which enables and in fact achieves man's righteousness.
See also Robinson, *Wrestling*, 38–44.

What marks Paul's use of the concept off from that given to him in his
Jewish heritage, however, is precisely his conviction that the covenantal framework of God's righteousness has to be understood afresh in terms of faith—
"to all who believe, Jew first but also Gentile." It is the fact that man's righteousness is always to be understood as faith which explains why man's righteousness
is nothing other than God's righteousness (see below on πίστις). And it is
his fellow Jews' forgetfulness of this fact which, in Paul's view, has resulted
in a distorted understanding of their part within the covenant ("their own
righteousness") and so in a missing of "God's righteousness" (see on 10:3
and *Introduction* §5.3). In stressing this point Paul develops an emphasis which
was already present in principle in the Jesus tradition (particularly Luke 18:10–
14) but which had not been brought to the same sharpness of focus in the
pre-Pauline tradition (as represented in 3:24–26 and 4:24–25, q.v.). Hultgren,
Gospel, 86–98, suggests that in Paul the conviction of God's saving righteousness
to all is prior to his more specific talk of justification by faith. This, however,
is not quite to the point: for Paul justification is always by faith in the sense
that the correlative of God's creative and sustaining power is always the human
creature's dependent trust (faith), of which justification (of Jew and Gentile
equally) by faith is a specific expression, and which indeed provides the existential context in and through which Paul's understanding of God's righteousness
comes to clarity and focus.

Does "the righteousness of God" also include the thought of judgment
("the wrath of God" [1:18 ff.])? That is less likely in 1:17 itself since it is
righteousness as "gospel/good news" which dominates the thematic statement
(1:16–17); vv 18 ff. go on then to ground the exclusivity of the claim made
in vv 16b, 17 (Zeller, *Juden*, 147). Yet it should not be forgotten that the
very idea of righteousness (i.e., fulfillment of covenant obligation) would
preclude any thought of this saving outreach being arbitrary or impulsive
in character (cf. 3:26); and "righteousness" is used occasionally for God's
punitive action against offending Israel (particularly Isa 5:16; 10:22; Lam
1:18; see Piper, *Justification*, 86–89; cf. also Berger, "Neues Material"). More
important, when the concept of relationship between God and man broadens
out from that of covenant with Israel to that of Creator and creature (as in
1:18 ff.) the broader perspective includes also the sovereignty of God (9:14–
24) and the inevitability of final judgment (3:4–6; but see on 3:5). Cf. Schmid,
Reumann, 68; but note also the critical comments of Fitzmyer in Reumann,
199–200.

ἐν αὐτῷ ἀποκαλύπτεται, "in it is being revealed." Notice that this is present tense, not aorist (cf., e.g., 16:25–26; 1 Cor 2:9–10; Eph 3:3–5). ἀποκαλύπτω is predominantly Pauline within the NT. The sense of a disclosure divinely given (divine passive) is fundamental to the word, with all its connotations of heavenly authority (as in Matt 11:25, 27 // Luke 10:21–22; Matt 16:17; 1 Cor 2:10; 14:30; Gal 1:12, 16; 2:2; Eph 1:17; Phil 3:15). But it is difficult to escape the twin notes typical of Jewish apocalyptic: revelation as the disclosure of a heavenly mystery (as in 2 Cor 12:1, 7; see particularly Rowland, *Open Heaven*); and the *eschatological* character of the revelation in speaking both of the revelation already given (16:25; 1 Cor 1:7; Gal 3:23; Eph 3:3, 5; 1 Pet 1:12) and of the final acts themselves (Luke 17:30; Rom 2:5; 8:18–19; 1 Cor 3:13; 2 Thess 1:7; 2:3, 6, 8; 1 Pet 1:5, 7, 13; 4:13; 5:1; Rev 1:1). So here the implication is of an eschatologically new and decisive disclosure of God's purpose (cf. 3:21), with reference to the Christ event as introducing the new age in which God's offer of salvation, previously restricted to and by Israel, will now be open to all who believe. See also Schlier and Wilckens.

ἐκ πίστεως εἰς πίστιν, "from faith to faith." As the verb πιστεύειν ("believe") shows, πίστις for Paul has the twofold sense: both of *belief that*—acceptance of the truth/reliability of what has been said (cf. 4:3; 6:8; 10:9, 16; 1 Cor 11:18; Gal 3:6; 1 Thess 4:14; 2 Thess 2:11–12); but also of consequent *trust in*, reliance upon (4:5, 24; 9:33; 10:11; Gal 2:16; Phil 1:29), as expressed particularly in the initial act of being baptized, that is, identifying with Jesus in his death (6:3–4) and placing oneself under his lordship (10:9). The old debate polarizing "objective" faith and "subjective" faith is passé (cf. further Kuss, 131–54; Lührmann, *Glaube*, 55–59). Paul will go on to analyze the plight of man as his failure to accept this status of complete dependence on God (1:21, 25, 28), including his fellow Jews whose narrower definition of covenant righteousness in terms of ethnic identity and "works" (9:6–13) in Paul's view involved a departure from the fundamental recognition that faith on man's side is the only possible and sufficient basis to sustain a relation with God, as exemplified above all in Abraham's unconditional trust and total dependence on God and his promise (see further on 4:4–5, 18–21). Nygren's warning of the danger of understanding Paul's *sola fide* legalistically (67–72) runs ahead of Paul's exposition but is nevertheless important and valid. That πίστις can also mean "faithfulness" (quite likely in Gal 5:22 and 2 Thess 1:4; in the latter it stands alongside ὑπομονή, "patience, steadfastness") and is used by Paul of *God's* faithfulness (3:3, which is the next passage in which it appears) is certainly significant, as his use of the Habakkuk quotation shows.

ἐκ . . . εἰς . . . , "from . . . to . . . ." The idiom is clearly one denoting some sort of progression, where ἐκ refers to the starting point and εἰς the end (cf. Ps 83:8; Jer 9:2; 2 Cor 2:16; 3:18; Fridrichsen cites also Plutarch, *Mor.* 1129A and *Galba* 14). As such it could mean starting with (man's) faith and ending with (man's) faith; "faith from first to last" (Denney, NIV). That the ἐκ πίστεως can mean "by faith" is clear from Paul's use of the Habakkuk quotation and subsequently (1:17; 3:26, 30; 4:16; 5:1; 9:30, 32; 10:6; 14:23). And so the full phrase is usually understood (Paul thus expresses the Reformation's *sola fide*, "by faith *alone*"; cf. Schlatter; for this and the full range of interpretations which have been canvassed see particularly Kuss). It should however be considered more fully than do most commentators whether Paul intended the ἐκ πίστεως to refer to God's faithfulness and only the εἰς πίστιν to man's faith—from (God's) faithfulness to (man's) faith (so K. Barth; T. W. Manson; Hebert, 375; Gaston, *Paul*)—a matter of πίστις throughout. (1) In both written and spoken media, where there is a word with a double meaning, it is universally recognized to be characteristic of good style to play on that double meaning; non-Greek commentators are unduly put off by the awkwardness of having to translate with *different* words; Barrett's objection to Barth—"to ascribe different meanings to the same word in one phrase is very harsh" (similarly Black)—is thus misconceived. (2) Following a verb like "reveal" the ἐκ is more naturally to be understood as denoting the source of the revelation (cf. 1:18; 2 Thess 1:7) and the εἰς as denoting that to which the revelation is directed. (3) To take both ἐκ and εἰς as referring to man's appropriation of God's righteousness is somewhat odd. If in this instance εἰς is the more appropriate preposition for that purpose (as in 3:21–22), the ἐκ is again better taken to refer to the starting point = source. (4) Not least important is the fact that the ἐκ πίστεως of the Hab 2:4 quotation is probably intended by Paul to be understood with an ambiguity which embraces both God's faithfulness and man's faith (see below). (5) The very next reference to πίστις subsequent to the thematic statement of 1:16–17 is certainly to God's faithfulness (3:3). (6) Indeed, the extent to which the faithfulness of God is *also* a theme of Romans (as part of the theme of God's righteousness) is obscured by the fact that "faithfulness" (אֱמוּנָה, אֱמֶת) can be translated equally by ἀλήθεια ("truth") as by πίστις ("faith") (see HR; in Romans note particularly 3:3, 4, 7 and 15:8, 11). (7) Not least, of course, is the fact that the righteousness of God can be defined quite accurately as "God's covenant-faithfulness" (Käsemann, "Righteousness," 177), as we have seen above.

καθὼς γέγραπται, "as it is written." γέγραπται is a well known legal expression (BGD, γράφω 2c), but in our writings the phrase is used as a formula to introduce quotations from the OT—not least in Romans, and consistently as an appeal to Scripture to document or prove an assertion just made (2:24; 3:4, 10; 4:17; 8:36; 9:13, 33; 10:15; 11:8, 26; 15:3, 21). See further Ellis, *Paul's Use*, 22–25; Fitzmyer, "Old Testament Quotations," 7–16.

The quotation from Hab 2:4 is known to us in basically four different versions, including Heb 10:38:

MT	וְצַדִּיק בֶּאֱמוּנָתוֹ יִחְיֶה	the righteous (man) by his faith(fulness) shall live
LXX	ὁ δὲ δίκαιος ἐκ πίστεώς μου ζήσεται	the righteous out of my faith(fulness) shall live
Paul	ὁ δὲ δίκαιος ἐκ πίστεως ζήσεται	the righteous out of faith/faithfulness(?) shall live
Heb	ὁ δὲ δίκαιός μου ἐκ πίστεως ζήσεται	my righteous one out of faith/faithful-ness(?) shall live

The MT form is read also by the Habakkuk commentary in the DSS, where, although the quotation itself has been obliterated at the foot of column 7, the interpretation of it at the beginning of the next column makes the reading clear: "The interpretation of it concerns the observers of the law in the house of Judah, whom God shall deliver from the house of judgment because of their struggle and their fidelity to the Teacher of Righteousness" (1QpHab 8.1–3, Fitzmyer). Other Greek versions of Habakkuk also follow the MT (Fitzmyer, 240–41). Paul's version appears also in Gal 3:11.

The MT clearly has in view the *ṣadîq*, the righteous man. At the time of Paul this would be understood to be the man who is a faithful member of the covenant, who fulfills the obligations laid upon him by the law of the covenant as a loyal Jew; namely, faithful observance of and devotion to the law as the ideal of Jewish piety. This self-understanding of "the righteous" is particularly prominent in the Psalms (1:5–6; 5:12; 7:9–10; 14:5; etc.), in the wisdom literature (e.g., Prov 3:32–33; 4:18; 9:9; 10:3, 6–7; etc.; Wisd Sol 2:10, 12, 16, 18; 3:1, 10; etc.), in *1 Enoch* (e.g., 1.8; 5.4–6; 82.4; 95.3; 100.5), and in the *Psalms of Solomon* (2.38–39 [LXX 34–35]; 3.3–8, 14 [LXX 11]; 4.9 [LXX 8]; etc.). The same understanding of the Hebrew of Hab 2:4 is evident both in the Qumran *pesher* ("it concerns the observers of the law . . ."; cf. 1QpHab 7.11; 12.4–5; 4QpPs37 2.14, 22), in the range of Greek versions which held more closely to the MT form of the text despite the LXX, and in the rendering of the Targum. "One believes in that one obeys the law" (Michel). See further on 2:13; 4:2–3; 10:2–3; also 5:19. The LXX in some contrast embodies an assertion with which Paul would certainly have had no quarrel—that individual righteousness is a product of God's fidelity to his obligations to humankind, to Israel in particular by virtue of Israel's being his chosen people.

Paul (like Hebrews) seems to be more dependent on the LXX tradition, as in most of his other OT quotations, not least in Romans (Ellis, *Paul's Use*, 12–15; Koch argues that the LXX reading as above is the oldest and original text). But since the different MT form was obviously well established and well known, he was probably aware of it also (cf. Kertelge, *Rechtfertigung*, 93), whether from the Hebrew text or from another Greek rendering of it. In this case his dropping of the ʾpersonal adjective ("my"/"his"—but in no case changing the word order) was probably, in part at least, prompted by a desire both to avoid choosing between the two different renderings and to embrace both forms (against Gaston, *Paul*, 111, 170, who argues that Paul means *God's* faithfulness here; but why then did he depart from the LXX?). In view of longstanding misunderstandings this point needs to be stressed: that the omission of the personal adjective does not necessarily amount to an exclusion of these other renderings. In the tradition of Jewish exegesis Paul would not necessarily want to narrow the meaning to *exclude* other meanings self-evident in the text forms used elsewhere, so much as to *extend* and broaden the meaning to include the sense he was most concerned to bring out. The various rules of interpretation already current in Pharisaic circles at the time of Paul (the "seven middoth of Hillel"—see, e.g., H. L. Strack, *Introduction to the Talmud and Midrash* [1931; reprint, New York: Harper Torchbook, 1965], 93–94) were designed to draw out as much meaning as possible from the text. In this case the fuller meaning would include the possibility of taking the ἐκ πίστεως with both ὁ δίκαιος and ζήσεται (cf. T. W. Manson and Moody). Here too the continuing sharp division between translators and commentators who insist on "either-or exegesis" underlines its unreality (those who insist on taking ἐκ πίστεως only with ὁ δίκαιος include NEB, Nygren, Barrett, Käsemann, Cranfield, and Wilckens; those who prefer to take ὁ δίκαιος with ζήσεται include NIV; Althaus; Michel; Murray; Smith, 18–20; Schlier; Cavallin; Hendriksen; and Wright, *Messiah*, 126): how could Paul have expected his readers to opt one way or other without clearer guidance?

The real significance of his dropping the personal adjective only becomes clear as his argument progresses, though the Christian readership would probably recognize the point right away: viz., to give πίστις his own, or its particularly Christian force ("trust in"), in a way which ran counter to the generally understood meaning of the MT form; that is, to free πίστις from the interpretation usually put upon it by virtue of the MT's "his." When πίστις is understood as "trust," better sense can be made of *both* the chief alternative text forms: that is to say, for Paul the counterpart of God's faithfulness is not man's *faithfulness* (at any rate as understood within Judaism), but *faith,* his trust in and total reliance upon God. If man's faithfulness is a consistent expression of that faith, good and well. But Paul's charge against Israel will be that the definition of faithfulness as observance of the law amounts to a serious misunderstanding of faith—and so of righteousness (both God's and man's), and so also of the life which follows from it (see further on 3:3, 20, 27; 4:2–3; 9:31–32; 10:2–3). To expound his theme with Hab 2:4 understood thus is the task he sets himself in this letter. For ζήσεται see on 6:11, 8:13, and 10:5; as denoting eschatological salvation and equivalent to life with Christ see 1 Thess 5:9–10.

Explanation

These two verses serve as the launching pad and provide the primary thrust and direction for the rest of the letter, with the double explanation concerning the gospel ("for . . . for . . .") giving both the raison d'être for Paul's missionary endeavor and the outline of the main argument to be developed through chaps. 1–15. That this is the purpose of vv 16–17 has always been recognized; but too often the point has been focused on the quotation from Hab 2:4, as though Paul was putting it forward as his text, with what followed as the sermon on the text. However, in the light of what we know of first-century midrashic technique and forms, it is difficult to classify Romans (even Rom 1–11) as a midrash on Hab 2:4 (contrast Rom 4 as a midrash on Gen 15:6). We are probably closer to Paul's intention if we take the whole of vv 16–17 as the text for or thematic statement of what follows, with the Habakkuk citation giving the first or primary proof text, as the introductory formula ("as it is written") indicates. The role of the proof text is to provide the initial underpinning and prima facie justification for the thematic assertion to which it is attached.

Paul's buildup to this point enables him to introduce it with great force in a bold and confident affirmation. He is not ashamed or afraid to confess the gospel even in face of the distinctions made in v 14, even though the gospel as to its origin or content, or he himself, might be classified as barbarian and lacking in wisdom (cf. 1 Cor 1–2). The reason for his confidence is not because he can dispute such an inference, nor because of the gospel's sophistication or appeal to the rational mind, but because it is the power of God to salvation. It not merely contains somewhere in it the secret of or bears witness to the power of God through other channels, but *is itself* the power of God to salvation. That is to say, his confidence in the gospel rests in what is for him a clear and simple fact: the gospel is the effective means by which God brings about the wholeness and preservation of the whole person. He does not say *when* this goal will be achieved, and there is certainly no implication that it will be instantaneous; his confidence is simply that the goal *will* be achieved. This is a point worth grasping even at this early stage: Paul does not see the gospel as something which merely *begins* someone on the way to salvation, but as something which embraces the totality of the process toward and into salvation. The gospel is not merely the initial proclamation of Christ which wins converts, but is the whole Christian message and claim—in terms of the rest of the letter, not just chaps. 1–5, or 1–8, or even 1–11, but the whole letter.

This observation bears also on the next phrase—"to all who believe"—for it follows from what has just been said that Paul here is talking not just about the initial acceptance of the proclamation of the crucified and risen Christ, but about that together with the life which follows from it as the whole process which leads into final wholeness. This is the point of the present tense—"to all who believe and go on believing"; namely, to all who not only come to a decision of faith, but whose whole life is characterized as a trustful acceptance of and commitment to the gospel which is God's power to salvation.

"To Jew first and to Greek." The phrase might well jolt the addressees out of any complacency or pride encouraged by Paul's repeated reminder that his life's work was directed toward the Gentiles (vv 5, 13–14). But the emphasis is clearly deliberate, and, given its place in these key sentences, almost certainly programmatic for the whole letter. Once again the correlation between Jewish prerogative and Gentile outreach is thrust to the fore as something the Gentile readership needs reminding of, and something fundamental to Paul's understanding of the gospel.

V 17 provides a further explanation of the central assertion of v 16 ("the power of God to salvation to all who believe"), but without ignoring the final phrase of v 16 ("to Jew first and Greek"). "The righteousness of God" would not necessarily be understood at once by all those listening to his letter. The purpose of the first few chapters, particularly chaps. 3 and 4, is precisely to explain what the phrase does mean for Paul. But those familiar with the Jewish scriptures, including many of the Gentile converts who had first been proselytes or God-worshipers, would probably understand it as the power of God put forth to effect his part in his covenant relation with Israel, that is, particularly his saving actions, his power put forth to restore Israel to and sustain Israel within its covenant relationship with God.

The choice of verb is also significant—"is being revealed." Paul evidently has in mind not merely the content of the gospel; the aorist tense would have been more suitable in that case ("has been revealed"). Nor is he thinking of preaching as a transfer of such information about God, a merely rational exercise; a word like "announce" or "proclaim" would have served better in that case. Paul, however, probably chose the verb and tense because it best describes the ongoing impact of the gospel, as an unveiling of God's final purpose with all the authority of heaven. That is to say, Paul's experience of evangelizing the Gentiles gives him firm confidence that in the gospel as the power of God to salvation such early converts are being given to see the righteousness of God actually happening, taking effect in their own conversion. Gentiles can see that they are being brought into that relationship with God hitherto regarded as a distinctively Jewish prerogative as an ongoing process having the force of eschatological disclosure and the stamp of heavenly authority (cf 1:18).

The nub of what is being revealed is contained in the next four words—"from faith to faith." The phrase can and probably should be taken as a play on the ambiguity of the word faith/faithfulness, in the sense "from *God's* faithfulness (to his covenant promises) to man's response of faith." This fits well with the concept of God's righteousness and with the quotation from Habakkuk about to follow. Moreover, as we shall see, it provides a better integrating theme for the major part of the letter than the alternative ("from man's faith to man's faith"), since chaps. 1–11 can be well characterized as Paul's exploration of the interface between God's faithfulness and man's faith, with faith understood as unconditional trust rather than covenant loyalty and so possible for Gentile as well as Jew.

Paul now indicates that his understanding of the gospel just outlined is based on Scripture and that the revelation he claims to be taking place in the saving power of the gospel is in full continuity with the revelation in the (Jewish) Scriptures. What should not escape notice is the fact that Hab 2:4 can serve as a proof text for his thematic statement precisely because its central phrase ("from faith") can be understood to embrace *both* the preceding "faith" phrases. This point is so important for the exegesis of Romans that it is worth emphasizing.

It is unlikely that Paul in dictating these words was unaware of the two alternative renderings of the text—"by *his* faith(fulness)" and "by *my* (= God's) faith(fulness)." Nor is it likely that he removed or ignored the possessive pronouns ("his," "my") with a view to persuading his addressees to take the verse in a wholly new and unexpected way. Had he entertained such an intention we would have expected a clearer formulation of the Habakkuk quotation, whereas in fact his quotation is so ambiguous that commentators have never been able to agree on how it should be read. The point which has usually been missed is that Paul's citation is *deliberately* ambiguous. That is to say, Paul does not want to give Hab 2:4 a new sense and to do so by *excluding* the alternative understandings; if so he made a bad job of it. Rather he wants to read *as much meaning* into the verse as possible—just what we would expect a Jewish exegete, especially a Pharisee, to do with a text of Scripture. In other words, the "from faith" is probably intended by Paul to be read as including the sense of the LXX ("from God's faith"), and so as providing the proof text for the "from faith" (from God's faithfulness) in the preceding line (cf. 3:3). But most probably he also intended it to be read as including the sense of the phrase "to faith" as well; that is, the righteousness of God revealed to faith (cf. 3:21–22). And "faith" here will include both the initial act of receiving the gospel and the continuing process toward salvation = all who go on believing (v 16) = the righteous from (his) faith shall live (v 17).

In short, Paul probably intends the Habakkuk quotation to be understood with a richness of meaning which can embrace within it the fuller understanding of the gospel for which Paul stands, in its continuity with the revelation to Israel. He who is maintained within or has been brought into the relationship with God which brings about salvation, by the outreach of God's faithfulness to his own faith, shall experience the fullness of life which God intended for humankind as he lives in the dependence of faith on the continuing faithfulness of God. Such an elaboration may seem to modern ears unduly complex, since we today are more familiar with the convention that if a statement has one meaning it cannot simultaneously have a different meaning. But it would be quite otherwise for Paul. At any rate it is this richer meaning which seems to provide most substantiation of the thematic statement to which it is attached, and as such it is this richer meaning which Paul goes on to expound, together with the issues and questions it raises, in the rest of the letter.

II–V. The Righteousness of God—from God's Faithfulness to Man's Faith (1:18–11:36)

Introduction

The treatise begins with a universal indictment which plays variations on the "Jew first but also Gentile" theme (1:18–3:20), goes on to expound how God's righteousness operates through faith for all (3:21–5:21) and what that means for the life of the believer (6:1–8:39), and climaxes in a defense of God's faithfulness to Israel—"to the Jew first" (9:1–11:36).

In this connection it is important to note how Paul holds the whole discussion within a cosmic framework. Structurally this is indicated by the way the opening paragraph (1:18–32) is balanced by the concluding section of each of the four main sections (II–V). Thus:

1:18–32 is summed up by 3:9–20—the universal indictment;

1:18–32, the section beginning with the plight of man in terms of Adam's abandonment of the truth of God, correlates with the climax consisting of the sustained contrast between Adam's disobedience and Christ's obedience in 5:12–20;

1:18–32, the analysis of man's tragic decline, is matched by the glowing hope of a cosmic redemption in 8:18–39;

1:18–32, the section beginning with the universal indictment from which Paul's Jewish contemporaries thought themselves exempt, is answered by the conclusion of 11:25–36, holding out firm assurance of salvation on a universal scale, for Gentiles certainly, but also Jews!

We might add that the emphasis on "the truth of God" in 1:18 (the summary and heading for 1:18–3:20) is answered by a similar emphasis on "the truth of God" in 15:8 (the paragraph which concludes the body of the letter—1:18–15:13), thus making an effective *inclusio*.

A feature of the treatise section is the repeated use of diatribe style (dialogue with an imagined interlocutor)—particularly 2:1–5, 17–29; 3:27–4:2; 9:19–21; 11:17–24; see *Introduction* §4.2.2.

II–III. The Righteousness of God—to Man's Faith (1:18–5:21)

II. The Wrath of God on Man's Unrighteousness (1:18–3:20)

Introduction

1:18, with its double use of ἀδικία as a summary of human failure, serves as a heading for the whole section, to which the repetition of the word in 1:29, 2:8, and 3:5 recalls the reader. The indictment focuses first on man as such, but in effect on the Gentile "them" over against the Jewish "us" (1:18–32), then on "the Jew" himself (2:1–3:8), before summing up in 3:9–20. That is to say, the principal focus of critique is Jewish self-assurance that the typically Jewish indictment of Gentile sin (1:18–32) is not applicable to the covenant people themselves (2:1–3:20; cf. Synofzik, 87–88).

A. God's Wrath on Humankind—from a Jewish Perspective (1:18–32)

Bibliography

Barth, M. "Speaking of Sin: Some Interpretative Notes on Romans 1:18–3:20." *SJT* 8 (1955) 288–96. **Bassler, J. M.** *Divine Impartiality.* 195–97, 201–4. **Bietenhard, H.** "Natürliche Gotteserkenntnis der Heiden? Eine Erwägung zu Röm 1." *TZ* 12 (1956) 275–88. **Bornkamm, G.** "Revelation." **Bussmann, C.** *Themen der paulinischen Missionspredigt auf dem Hintergrund der spätjüdisch-hellenistischen Missionsliteratur.* Bern/Frankfurt: Lang, 1975. 108–22. **Castellino, G. R.** "Il paganesimo di Romani 1, Sapienza 13–14 e la storia della religioni." *SPCIC* 2:255–63. **Dabelstein, R.** *Beurteilung.* 73–86. **Daxer, H.** *Römer 1:18–2:10.* **Dupont, J.** *Gnosis.* 20–30. **Easton, B. S.** "New Testament Ethical Lists." *JBL* 51 (1932) 1–12. **Eckstein, H.-J.** "'Denn Gottes Zorn wird vom Himmel her offenbar werden.' Exegetische Erwägungen zu Röm 1:18." *ZNW* 78 (1987) 74–89. **Eichholz, G.** *Theologie.* 63–81. **Feuillet, A.** "La connaissance naturelle de Dieu par les hommes d'après Rom 1:18–23." *LumVie* 14 (1954) 63–80. **Filson, F. V.** *St. Paul's Conception of Recompense.* UNT 21. Leipzig: Hinrichs, 1931. **Flückiger, F.** "Zur Unterscheidung von Heiden und Juden in Röm 1:18–2:3." *TZ* 10 (1954) 154–58. **Fridrichsen, A.** "Zur Auslegung von Röm 1:19f." *ZNW* 17 (1916) 159–68. **Hanson, A. T.** *Wrath.* **Herold, G.** *Zorn.* **Hooker, M. D.** "Adam in Romans 1." *NTS* 6 (1959–60) 297–306. ———. "A Further Note on Romans 1." *NTS* 13 (1966–67) 181–83. **Hyldahl, N.** "A Reminiscence of the Old Testament at Romans 1:23." *NTS* 2 (1955–

56) 285–88. **Jeremias, J.** "Zu Röm 1:22–32." *ZNW* 45 (1954) 119–23. Reprinted in *Abba.* Göttingen: Vandenhoeck, 1966. 290–92. **Jervell, J.** *Imago Dei: Gen 1:26f. im Spätjudentum, in der Gnosis und in den paulinischen Briefen.* FRLANT 76. Göttingen: Vandenhoeck, 1960. **Kamlah, E.** *Die Form der katalogischen Paränese im Neuen Testament.* Tübingen: Mohr, 1964. **Klostermann, A.** "Die adäquate Vergeltung in Röm 1:22–31." *ZNW* 32 (1933) 1–6. **Langerbeck, H.** "Paulus und das Griechentum. Zum Problem des Verhältnisses der christlichen Botschaft zum antiken Erkenntnisideal." In *Aufsätze zur Gnosis.* Göttingen: Vandenhoeck, 1967. 83–145, esp. 96–99. **Lührmann, D.** *Offenbarungsverständnis.* 21–26. **Macgregor, G. H. C.** "The Concept of the Wrath of God in the New Testament." *NTS* 7 (1960–61) 101–9. **Pohlenz, M.** "Paulus." 523–27. **Popkes, W.** "Zum Aufbau und Charakter von Röm 1:18–32." *NTS* 28 (1982) 490–501. **Ridderbos, H.** *Paul.* 108–14. **Rosin, H.** "To gnoston tou Theou." *TZ* 17 (1961) 161–65. **Schlier, H.** "Von den Heiden. Röm 1:18–32." In *Zeit der Kirche.* 29–37. ———. "Doxa bei Paulus als heilsgeschichtlicher Begriff." *SPCIC* 1:45–56. **Schulz, S.** "Die Anklage in Röm 1:18–32." *TZ* 14 (1958) 161–73. **Schweizer, E.** "Gottesgerechtigkeit und Lasterkataloge bei Paulus." In *Rechtfertigung,* FS E. Käsemann, ed. J. Friedrich et al. Tübingen: Mohr, 1976. 461–77. **Scroggs, R.** *The New Testament and Homosexuality.* Philadelphia: Fortress, 1983. **Sullivan, K.** "Epignosis in the Epistles of St Paul." *SPCIC* 2:405–16. **Synofzik, E.** *Vergeltungsaussagen.* 78–80, 86–88. **Travis, S. H.** *Judgment.* Esp. 36–38. **Vögtle, A.** *Die Tugend- und Lasterkataloge im Neuen Testament.* Munster: Aschendorff, 1936. **Wedderburn, A. J. M.** "Adam in Paul's Letter to the Romans." *Studia Biblica 1978.* Vol. 3. *JSNTSup* (1980) 413–30. **Wibbing, S.** *Die Tugend- und Lasterkataloge im Neuen Testament und ihre Traditionsgeschichte unter besonderer Berücksichtigung der Qumran-Texte.* BZNW 25. Berlin: Töpelmann, 1959. **Willer, A.** *Der Römerbrief—eine dekalogische Komposition.* Stuttgart: Calwer, 1981.

Translation

[18] *For the wrath of God* [a] *is being revealed from heaven against all impiety and unrighteousness of men who suppress the truth* [b] *in unrighteousness,* [19] *because what can be known about God is evident to them. For God has shown it to them.* [20] *For his invisible attributes from the creation of the world are perceived rationally in the things which have been made, both his eternal power and deity, so that they are without excuse.* [21] *Because though they knew God they did not glorify him as God or give him thanks, but became futile in their thinking, and their foolish hearts were darkened.* [22] *Claiming to be wise they became fools,* [23] *and changed the glory of the incorruptible God for the mere likeness of corruptible man, birds, beasts, and reptiles.* [24] *Wherefore God handed them in the desires of their hearts to uncleanness to the dishonoring of their bodies among themselves:* [c] [25] *they exchanged the truth of God for falsehood and worshiped and served the creature rather than the Creator, who is blessed for ever. Amen.*

[26] *For this reason God handed them over to disgraceful passions. For their females changed natural relations into what is contrary to nature.* [27] *Likewise also the males gave up natural relations with the female and were inflamed with desire for one another, males with males committing what is shameless and receiving back* [d] *in themselves* [c] *the appropriate penalty for their error.* [28] *And as they did not think God qualified for continued recognition, God* [e] *gave them over to a disqualified mind, to do what is improper—* [29] *filled with all unrighteousness, wickedness,* [f] *greediness,* [f] *badness* [f] *—full of jealousy, murder, rivalry, deceit, spite—rumor-mongers,* [30] *slanderers, God-haters, insolent, arrogant, braggarts, contrivers of evil, disobedient*

to parents—[31] *senseless, faithless, loveless, merciless.* [32] *Although they have known the just decree of God, that those who practice such things deserve death, they not only do the same but approve of those who practice them.*g

Notes

aMarcion suppressed the "of God" since it did not fit with his view of God.

bA few Western textual traditions add "of God," presumably in view of v 25.

cThe ἑαυτοῖς of G and some others is a scribal improvement to give greater precision. For the same reason the text could be read αὐτοῖς; but αὐτοῖς as such could have a reflexive meaning (Metzger). Cf. v 27 where some MSS including B and K read αὐτοῖς for ἑαυτοῖς.

dG increases the reciprocal force by replacing the prefix ἀπο- with ἀντι-.

eὁ θεός may originally have been absent (ℵ* A 0172*) and added at a very early stage to match vv 24 and 26.

fThese words appear in different order with πορνείᾳ sometimes replacing πονηρίᾳ and sometimes added to the list in various MSS, probably as an early copyist's mistake (though cf. Gal 5:19).

gFor various modifications of the text of v 32 to make what would have been judged better or more appropriate sense of Paul, see Cranfield.

Form and Structure

Significant for the initial setting up of the argument is the obviously deliberate echo of the Adam narratives (Gen 2–3) in vv 19–25: it was Adam who above all perverted his knowledge of God and sought to escape the status of creature, but who believed a lie and became a fool and thus set the pattern (Adam = man) for a mankind which worshiped the idol rather than the Creator (Hooker, Wedderburn). The use of more widely known Stoic categories, particularly in vv 19–20, 23, and 28 (Pohlenz), would increase the universal appeal of the argument.

Equally significant, however, is the fact that in v 21 and overwhelmingly from v 23 onward Paul speaks as a Jew and makes use of the standard Hellenistic Jewish polemic against idolatry; the influence of Wisd Sol 11–15 is particularly noticeable (Daxer, Bussmann). The effect is to characterize human (Adam) unrighteousness from a Jewish perspective; that is, human unrighteousness typified by the Jewish abhorrence of idolatry and the degradation of Gentile sexual ethics. Note also the use of a vice list in vv 29–30, such as were common in Hellenistic (again particularly Stoic) and Jewish circles (e.g., Daxer, 46–52; Lietzmann).

Structurally significant for the development of the exposition in 1:18–32 is the threefold repetition of (μετ)ήλλαξαν in vv 23, 25, and 26, matched by the threefold repetition of παρέδωκεν in vv 24, 26, and 28. These create a powerful sense of the vicious circle of human sin—failure to acknowledge God leading to degenerate religion and behavior, human pride reaping the fruit of human depravity (vv 24, 26–27) and general nastiness (vv 29–31). Popkes's structural analysis points to vv 19–20 as focusing the principal emphasis on human inexcusableness. Quite influential has been Klostermann's division of vv 22–32 into three sections (vv 22–24, 25–27, 28–32), determined by the idea of the appropriateness of the judgment to the sin described. Maillot notes the threefold development: vv 19–23—sin against the truth of God; vv 24–27—sin against nature; vv 28–32—sin against others.

Also indicative of Paul's ability as a writer are the neat wordplays ἀφθάρτου // φθαρτοῦ, κτίσει // κτίσαντα, ἄρσενες // ἄρσεσιν, ἐδοκίμασαν // ἀδόκιμον, φθόνου // φόνου, and ἀσυνέτους // ἀσυνθέτους in vv 23, 25, 27, 28, 29, and 31, and the formulation of the vice list in vv 29–31, starting with its four general words ending with -ία, and rounded off with the alliterative sequence of four (or five!) beginning with the negative ἀ-. Black notes that vv 28–32 read like part of a spoken diatribe: "they resemble, in some respects, the section in Attic comedy known to the ancient rhetoricians as the *pnigos,* a long passage to be spoken in a single breath."

Comment

1:18 ἀποκαλύπτεται γὰρ ὀργὴ θεοῦ ἀπ' οὐρανοῦ, "for the wrath of God is being revealed from heaven." γάρ, "for," can express simply connection or continuation of thought without specifying what precisely the connection is (BGD). That a connection of thought is certainly intended is clear from the parallel structuring of vv 17 and 18. But the ὀργὴ θεοῦ ἐπὶ ἀδικίαν as against the δικαιοσύνη θεοῦ εἰς πίστιν (v 17) strongly suggests that the connection is as much of contrast as of cause (Stuhlmacher, *Gerechtigkeit,* 80; and Kertelge, *Rechtfertigung,* 88; despite Gaugler and Herold, 329–30). However, see on 1:17 (δικαιοσύνη θεοῦ, final paragraph) and Schlatter, 52–54.

The repetition of ἀποκαλύπτεται is obviously deliberate (cf. particularly Schmidt). It conveys the same idea of heavenly revelation (here explicitly— ἀπ' οὐρανοῦ), that is, from God. And the eschatological overtone is confirmed by the fact that the ὀργὴ θεοῦ is of a piece with God's final judgment (2:5, 8; 3:5; 5:9; 1 Thess 1:10; 5:9; in Jewish thought divine wrath is not a particularly eschatological concept—but note Isa 13:9, 13; Zeph 1:15, 18; 2:2–3; 3:8; Dan 8:19; *Jub.* 24.30); God's final judgment is simply the end of a process already in train (cf. particularly *1 Enoch* 84.4; 91.7–9)! The clear implication is that the two heavenly revelations are happening concurrently, as well as divine righteousness, so also divine wrath; to take the second ἀποκαλύπτεται as future (Eckstein) destroys the parallel and draws an unnecessary distinction between God's wrath and the divine action in "he handed over" in παρέδωκεν (vv 24, 26, 28). In the OT the wrath of God has special reference to the covenant relation (SH), but here the implication, quickly confirmed (vv 19ff.), is that Paul is shifting from a narrower covenant perspective to a more cosmic or universal perspective, from God understood primarily as the God of Israel to God as Creator of all. However, if the covenant is seen as God restoring Israel to man's proper place as creature (for the Adam theology of the section, see on 1:22), then Creatorly wrath can be seen as the full scope of the other side of the coin from covenant righteousness (cf. Isa 63:6–7; Sir 5:6; 16:11); and see also 2:5.

The ὀργὴ θεοῦ was a familiar concept in the ancient world—divine indignation as heaven's response to human impiety or transgression of divinely approved laws, or as a way of explaining communal catastrophes or unlooked-for sickness or death (*TDNT* 5:383–409). Paul takes up this well-known language as a way of describing the effect of human unrighteousness in the world (vv 19–32), though clearly, in Paul's view, "wrath" is not something for which God is merely responsible, "an inevitable process of cause and effect in a moral universe" (Dodd; Macgregor, 105; similarly Hanson, *Wrath*, 85, 110), nor merely an attitude of God (far less a vengeful attitude of God), but something God *does* (see Travis, 37–38). The parallel with "the righteousness of God" would be sufficient indication of this, especially when taken in conjunction with other references to God's wrath later in Romans (3:5; 9:22; 12:19), and the repeated παρέδωκεν of vv 24, 26, and 28 puts the issue beyond dispute (cf. Ladd, *Theology*, 407; Robinson, *Wrestling*, 18–21; Maillot, 62). Not merely a psychological or sociological process is in view but a process on earth in which heaven (ἀπ᾿ οὐρανοῦ) is involved.

That a degree of irrationality or incalculability was often manifest in the operation of divine wrath was also evident to classical thought (as expressed particularly in the concept of "fate"—see, e.g., *OCD*). Jewish thought is familiar with the same feature, but within its monotheistic system found it more of a problem; cf. 2 Sam 24:1 and 15–16 with 1 Chron 21:1, 14–15; Job 19:11; Ps 88:16 (*TDNT* 5:402); and the apocalyptist's puzzled "How long?" Paul too is conscious of the same problem (3:5; 9:22). Here he expounds the concept in highly moral terms (vv 19–32), but these verses contain the beginning of an answer which he elaborates later in terms of the individual (chaps. 6–8) and of humankind as a whole, Jew and Gentile (chaps. 9–11). In brief, his resolution is that the effect of divine wrath upon man is to show that man who rebels against his relation of creaturely dependence on God (which is what faith is) becomes subject to degenerative processes. Deliverance from these comes through returning to the relation of faith. Such a return does not mean that wrath ceases to operate against man in his fleshliness, but that it becomes part of a larger process whose end is liberation and redemption from all that occasions and involves wrath; cf. Herold—"The eschatological judgment of wrath comes about in accordance with covenant and promise, because it will lead to redemption and to salvation" (*Zorn*, 301). That this fuller understanding of God's wrath emerges from the gospel (or at least Paul's expression thereof) is true, but the actual operation of wrath Paul affirms to be clearly visible in human behavior (Althaus; Michel; Bruce; Travis, 36; against Barth, *Shorter*; Leenhardt; Schenke, 888; Cranfield; cf. Filson, 39–48; Kuss; Wilckens). For the eschatological dimension of "wrath" see above under ἀποκαλύπτεται and on 2:5.

πᾶσαν ἀσέβειαν καὶ ἀδικίαν ἀνθρώπων, "all impiety and unrighteousness of men," is an all-embracing phrase. In Greek thought it would include hostility to or disregard for what was generally accepted to be good religious practice (typically failure to observe the state cultus) and unlawful conduct toward others (*TDNT* 1:154). That Paul intends a clear distinction between the words is unlikely, as also the suggestion that he had in mind the two tables of the law (as suggested by Schlatter, 49, and implausibly elaborated by Willer, 12ff.; but see *TDNT* 5:190). Such sins were all of a piece in Jewish thought and the phrase is comprehensive, not analytic (cf. Philo, *Immut.* 112; *Spec. Leg.* 1.215; *Praem.* 105). In fact ἀσέβεια is hardly used by Paul (only here and 11:26 in the undisputed Paulines; ἀσεβής only in 4:5 and 5:6), whereas ἀδικία is the more dominant concept (1:29; 2:8; 3:5; 6:13; 9:14; also 1 Cor 13:6; 2 Cor 12:13; 2 Thess 2:10, 12), and, as its repetition here shows, it clearly embraces the full range covered by the more comprehensive phrase in itself.

Not least in significance is the fact that the ἀδικία of men is clearly set in antithesis to the δικαιοσύνη of God (v 17; note also 3:5; cf. 1QS 3.20). "Unrighteousness" is thus more precisely defined as failure to meet the obligations toward God and man which arise out of relationship with God and man. That the two aspects of unrighteousness go together and follow from failure to recognize and accept what is man's proper relation to God is the thrust of what follows. It is this unrighteousness on the part of men which makes necessary the initiative of God's righteousness. Moreover, the fact that the argument can be transposed from the narrower question of Jew/Gentile relation within the saving purpose of God to that of humankind as a whole, and precisely in terms of the play on δικαιοσύνη/ἀδικία strengthens the view of Käsemann, C. Müller, and Stuhlmacher that God's righteousness is his power and faithfulness as Creator. The πᾶσαν has a polemical edge, since Paul has in view his devout Jewish contemporaries who thought that as δίκαιοι they were distanced from all ἀδικία (see on 1:17 and *Introduction* §5.3.1). That is to say, v 18 already looks to the fuller exposition of ἀδικία in chap. 2 and thus serves as the opening statement of the whole section (1:18–3:20).

τῶν τὴν ἀλήθειαν ἐν ἀδικίᾳ κατεχόντων, "who suppress the truth in unrighteousness." ἀλήθεια, "truth"—specifically of God (v 25), but here probably intended more broadly in the sense of "the real state of affairs," things as they actually are (*TDNT* 1:243). The idea of "holding down, suppressing" (κατεχόντων—BGD), "holding back, restraining" (Murray; see also on 7:6) the truth implies not only the willfulness of man (vv 19–20, 23, 25; so also 2:8), but also that truth not thus suppressed would have effect. In particular "the truth of God" in a Jewish or Jewish-influenced context would carry the connotation of God's reliability and trustworthiness. Paul thus already prepares the way to tie in the theme of universal indictment with the special issue of God's faithfulness as Israel's covenant God (see further *Introduction* §4.2.2 and on 1:17 [ἐκ . . . ἐκ . . .] and 3:3–4, 7). The indictment here is that failure to acknowledge God as Creator results inevitably in a sequence of false relations toward God, toward man, and toward creation itself. See further on 1:25.

19 διότι τὸ γνωστὸν τοῦ θεοῦ φανερόν ἐστιν ἐν αὐτοῖς, "because what can be known about God is evident to them." τὸ γνωστὸν τοῦ θεοῦ, "what can be known about God, God to the extent that he can be known, God in his knowability" (BGD, *TDNT* 1:719; only here in Paul). Clearly implicit here is the conviction that God is not knowable in himself (a very strong conviction in Judaism—e.g., Exod 33:20; Deut 4:12; Sir 43:31; *Sib. Or.* 3.17; Philo, *Som.* 1.65–66, 68–69; *Post.* 16–20; Josephus, *War* 7.346; *Ap.* 2.167), but that he has made himself known to some extent. The phrase here probably includes the sense of what is common knowledge about God (so also φανερόν, "visible, clear, plainly to be seen, open, evident"), hence the severity of the indictment at the end of v 20.

Also clear is the fact that some sort of natural theology is involved here. The claim is more or less explicit in vv 19–20. And Paul is certainly conversant with and indeed indebted to a strong strand of like-minded Hellenistic Jewish wisdom theology. The parallel between Wisd Sol 12–15 and vv 19–32 is too close to be accidental; note Wisd Sol 13:1–9 (see further on 1:20c, 21b, 23, 24, 26–27, 29–31; also SH 51–52 and those cited in Dunn, *Christology*, 306 n.9; and for a broader survey Daxer, 3–58; Herold, 188–209, sees the same scheme of thought in 1:16–18 and Wisdom; *Sib. Or.* 3.8–45 shows a strikingly similar influence; and cf. already Job 12:7–9 and Ps 19:1–4). Very relevant for the background of Paul's thought at this point, then, is the interplay in Jewish wisdom between the hiddenness and revelation of divine wisdom (see particularly Job 28; Bar 3:15–4:4), which forms the warp and woof of a natural theology. In Philo in particular the Logos can be defined precisely as "God in his knowability," with creation as it were a "shadow" cast by God by means of which the Creator may to some extent be discerned (*Leg. All.* 3.97–99; see Dunn, *Christology*, 220–28). ἐν αὐτοῖς could be translated "in them," or "among them," but also "to them" with ἐν standing for the dative (BGD, ἐν IV.4.a). The ambiguity probably reflects the common belief in a direct continuity between human rationality and the rationality evident in the cosmos.

ὁ θεὸς γὰρ αὐτοῖς ἐφανέρωσεν, "for God has shown them." Φανερόω appears little outside the NT (including other pre-Christian Jewish writings—only once in LXX and in Philo; see *TDNT* 9:3–4). Consequently its frequent occurrence in the NT (49 times) is rather striking and helps underline the early Christian sense of being a religion of revelation (cf. particularly 3:21; 16:26; 1 Cor 4:5; Col 1:26; 3:4; 1 Tim 3:16; 2 Tim 1:10; Titus 1:3; Heb 9:26; 1 Pet 1:20). The clause here emphasizes that God's knowability is not merely a characteristic or "spin-off" of creation but was willed and effected by God. Even so, and despite Käsemann's careful qualifications, we still have to speak of a "natural theology"—that is here, of a revelation of God through the cosmos, to humankind as a whole, and operative since the creation of the cosmos. "Observation of created life is sufficient to show that creation does not provide the key to its own existence" (Barrett). That is well said; but Paul speaks primarily (v 21) of an actual knowing of God (Kuss, 45; Rosin; Lührmann, 26; Harrisville; see also Lyonnet, *Quaestiones*, 1:78–88). Whether it is a saving knowledge is another question which Paul does not address here (cf. particularly Nygren and Robinson, *Wrestling*, 22–23); see further 2:6–16.

20 τὰ γὰρ ἀόρατα αὐτοῦ ἀπὸ κτίσεως κόσμου τοῖς ποιήμασιν νοούμενα καθορᾶται, ἥ τε ἀΐδιος αὐτοῦ δύναμις καὶ θειότης, "for his invisible characteristics from the creation of the world are perceived intellectually in the things which have been made, both his eternal power and deity." The language here is scarcely characteristic of earliest Christian thought (καθοράω, "perceive," and θειότης, "divinity, divine nature," occur only here in the NT; ἀΐδιος, "eternal," elsewhere only in Jude 6; and ποίημα, "what is made," only here and Eph 2:10). It also for the most part plays an insignificant role in the OT. But it is familiar in Stoic thought: the closest parallel to the ἀόρατα/καθορᾶται word-play comes in Pseudo-Aristotle, *de Mundo* 399b.14 ff. (ἀόρατος τοῖς ἔργοις ὁρᾶται); and for θειότης cf. particularly Plutarch, *Mor.* 398A; 665A (see further Lietzmann). And it is presumably through Stoic influence that the language entered the Jewish wisdom tradition (ἀΐδιος—cf. Wisd Sol 2:23; 7:26 = a description of Wisdom; θειότης—in LXX only in Wisd Sol 18:19) and influenced

Philo (for whom ἀόρατος and ἀίδιος in particular are favorite terms; see, e.g.,
TDNT 5:368–69; 1:168); hence also the only other occurrence of ἀόρατος
("unseen, invisible") in Paul comes in the Wisdom hymn of Col 1:15–16.
The same is in large part true of both the term and concept κόσμος (TDNT
3:877–78, 880–82). The concept of κτίσις, "creation," was also common to
Greek as well as Hebrew thought; though it should be noted that the Christian
exclusive use of κτίζω/κτίσις for the act and fact of divine creation reflects
the same Hebrew exclusiveness in the use of בָּרָא "to create" (see TDNT
3:1000–1035; TDOT 2:242–49), in distinction to the much less discriminating
use of Greek thought (see LSJ). The verb maintains the sense of qualitative
distinction between Creator and creature which is such a fundamental feature
of Judeo-Christian theology (see also on 9:20). δύναμις, "power," though more
common in other connections (see on 1:16), here belongs within the same
frame of reference (cf. Wisd Sol 13:4; Ep. Arist. 132; Josephus, Ap. 2.167),
so that it can be used as a way of speaking of God's self-revelation and creative
energy both in the singular (Wisd Sol 7:25; Mark 14:62; cf. Acts 8:10) and
in the plural (particularly Philo, where the Logos can be described as the
"sum" of the powers; cf. Dunn, Christology, 225).

Paul thus is clearly and deliberately following Hellenistic Judaism in using
this kind of language as an apologetic bridge to non-Jewish religious philosophy (Fridrichsen; Pohlenz; Bornkamm, "Revelation," 50–53; Bietenhard's
discussion is too narrowly focused)—a fact which must decisively influence
our understanding of the meaning he intended his readers to derive from
it. Paul is trading upon, without necessarily committing himself to, the Greek
(particularly Stoic) understanding of an invisible realm of reality, invisible
to sense perception, which can be known only through the rational power
of the mind. With Philo he presumably would not want to say that the rational
mind is able to reach or grasp God. And he ensures that his language, however
indebted to Stoic thought, should not be understood in terms of Stoicism by
giving prominence to the thought of creation ("from the act of creation . . . the
things which have been made"; "Paul speaks not of Ideas, but of things and
events which manifest God's power" [Schlatter; cf. Acts 14:17]), and by setting
it within an apocalyptic framework (the revelation of divine wrath from heaven;
cf. Michel, Wilckens). "The intention of the Apostle is not to infer God's
being from the world, but to uncover the being of the world from God's
revelation" (Bornkamm, "Revelation," 59). The value of the language, however, is that it enables him to appeal to this commonplace of Greek religious
philosophy: that rational man recognizes the existence of God (even though
invisible) and his nature as eternal power and deity. That is to say, however
precisely the phrase νοούμενα καθορᾶται should be rendered ("clearly perceived"
[RSV]; "visible to the eye of reason" [NEB]), it is scarcely possible that Paul
did not intend his readers to think in terms of some kind of rational perception
of the fuller reality in and behind the created cosmos (cf. BGD, νοέω 1a;
TDNT 5:380). That this is no longer a widely acceptable world-view should
not, of course, influence our exegesis of Paul. At the same time, the extent
to which Paul was prepared to build his argument on what was not a traditional
Jewish world-view, and indeed to commit himself to it at this crucial opening
stage of his exposition, even if as an ad hominem argument, reveals a breadth
and a boldness in his apologetic strategy.

εἰς τὸ εἶναι αὐτοὺς ἀναπολογήτους, "so that they are without excuse." ἀναπολόγητος, "inexcusable"; in biblical Greek only here and in 2:1; see Althaus. The construction can be taken as causative ("so that") rather than as final ("in order that") and probably was intended to be so taken (*TDNT* 2:430–31). The point is the same as in Wisd Sol 13:8–9; cf. also *4 Ezra* 7.22–24 and *T. Mos.* 1.13. This is Paul's object; namely, to build his indictment on a large area of common ground. That his elaboration of it in more distinctively Jewish terms (vv 21ff.) would narrow the common ground quite rapidly is a risk he takes. The object is to begin from a common sense of the disproportion between human conduct (including religious conduct) and "what is known of God." The hope presumably is that the initial common assent will make even the fringe members of the audience more open to the subsequent more Jewish analysis.

21 διότι γνόντες τὸν θεὸν οὐχ ὡς θεὸν ἐδόξασαν ἢ ηὐχαρίστησαν, "because though they knew God they did not glorify him as God or give him thanks." Paul begins here to make the transition into more familiar Jewish categories. γνόντες τὸν θεόν, "having known God" (cf. 1 Cor 1:21; Gal 4:9; John 10:15; 17:3; 1 John 4:7–8). If in Greek thought "to know God" is to perceive God as he really is (*TDNT* 1:690–91; cf. v 18), in Hebrew thought there was a strong sense of knowledge as an acknowledging, a motivational recognition which expressed itself in the appropriate worship and obedience (as in Judg 2:10; 1 Sam 3:7; Ps 79:6; Hos 8:2; cf. *TDNT* 1:704–7; Bultmann, *Theology*, 1:213 ["knowledge of God is a lie if it is not acknowledgment of him"]); note Wisd Sol 16:16. With δοξάζω, "glorify, honor," however, we move more fully into Jewish categories (cf. already Exod 15:1, 2, 6, 11, 21). To "glorify God" is to render the appropriate response due to his δόξα, "glory," the awesome radiance of deity which becomes the visible manifestation of God in theophany and vision and which can only bring home to the individual concerned his finite weakness and corruption (e.g., Exod 24:15–17; cf. 20:18–20; Isa 6:1–5; Ezek 1; see also on 6:4 and 9:4; *TDNT* 2:238–42). So elsewhere in Paul (15:6, 9; 1 Cor 6:20; 2 Cor 9:13; Gal 1:24) and the NT (e.g., Mark 2:12; Luke 23:47; Acts 4:21; 1 Pet 2:12).

The οὐχ ηὐχαρίστησαν, "were not thankful," is not to be understood as a kind of standard formality (as could the earlier epistolary use; see on 1:8). In contrast here Paul is obviously thinking more in terms of thanksgiving as characteristic of a whole life, as the appropriate response of one whose daily experience is shaped by the recognition that he stands in debt to God, that his very life and experience of living is a gift from God (cf. *4 Ezra* 8.60); cf. Kuss. In Paul's perspective this attitude of awe (the fear of the Lord) and thankful dependence is how knowledge of God should express itself. But human behavior is marked by an irrational disjunction between what man knows to be the true state of affairs and a life at odds with that knowledge. This failure to give God his due and to receive life as God's gift is Paul's way of expressing the primal sin of humankind.

ἐματαιώθησαν ἐν τοῖς διαλογισμοῖς αὐτῶν, "they became futile in their thinking." διαλογισμός, "thought, opinion, reasoning": see also on 14:1. Although μάταιος is well enough known in Greek literature in the sense "vain, empty," ματαιότης (8:20; Eph 4:17; 2 Pet 2:18) and ματαιόω (only here in NT) are almost exclusively biblical in usage. As such Paul's commentary will be heavily influenced by the ruthless negative judgment of the psalmist (39:4–5; 62:9; 78:33; 144:4; esp. 94:11) and particularly Ecclesiastes (1:2, 14; 2:1, 11, 15, 17; etc.) on the brevity of life and on the worthless character of so much that takes place in life. And note again the close parallel in Wisd Sol 13:1; also Jer 2:5 (see also Lagrange). Paul's implication is plain: where life is not experienced as a gift from God it has lost touch with reality and condemns itself to futility. See also on 8:20.

ἐσκοτίσθη ἡ ἀσύνετος αὐτῶν καρδία, "their foolish hearts were darkened." Cf. particularly Ps 75:6 LXX [76:5]: οἱ ἀσύνετοι τῇ καρδίᾳ . . . , which begins, γνωστὸς ἐν τῇ Ἰουδαίᾳ ὁ θεός (75:2 LXX [76:1]); 1 Enoch 99.8. For σκοτίζω in the figurative sense with reference to the organs of religious and moral perception, cf. 11:10 (quoting Ps 68:24) and T. 12 Patr. (T. Reub. 3.8; T. Levi 14.4; T. Gad 6.2). ἀσύνετος, "void of understanding, not able to understand" (cf. 1:31; 10:19). καρδία had a broader use than its modern equivalent ("heart"), denoting the seat of the inner life, the inner experiencing "I," but not only in reference to emotions, wishes, or desires (e.g., 1:24; 9:2), but also in reference to the will and decision making (e.g., 2 Cor 9:7) and to the faculty of thought and understanding, as here (see BGD; Jewett, Anthropological Terms, 305–33); see also on 2:15 and 8:27. Paul's point is that man's whole ability to respond and function not least as a rational being has been damaged; without the illumination and orientation which comes from the proper recognition of God his whole center is operating in the dark, lacking direction and dissipating itself in what are essentially trifles.

22 φάσκοντες εἶναι σοφοὶ ἐμωράνθησαν, "claiming to be wise they became fools." σοφία, "wisdom," was highly prized throughout the ancient world, as the wisdom tradition within Judaism itself demonstrates. In Stoicism in particular, the σοφός, "wise man," was the ideal to be aspired to (cf. TDNT 7:473). In using ἐμωράνθην Paul may have in mind Jer 10:14, particularly since it is part of the Jewish polemic against idolatry which Paul takes up in the following verses. Whether its use in Matt 5:13 // Luke 14:34 throws light on its usage here is unclear: salt μωρανθῇ, "became insipid," in the sense of being unfitted to fulfill its function as salt.

The irony here is intentional and heavy: men claim to be wise, to have achieved the appropriate balance between their theoretical (rational) knowledge and its practical application. But their lives demonstrate the contrary, that their conduct does *not* match what they know of God. The tragedy is that they do not recognize the disparity: despite this folly they still claim to be wise; their futility is the measure of their wisdom (cf. 1 Cor 1:18–25; TDNT 4:845–47; 7:521).

Here the echo of the Adam narratives becomes quite strong. Not that Paul alludes to it explicitly, although the γνωστόν of v 19 may recall Gen 2:9. It is rather that the description of human aspiration for greater knowledge and a position of high regard which actually results in a decline into disadvantage and a position of low regard, set as it is in aorist terms, is obviously modeled on the account of man's fall in Gen 3. The emphasis in the fall narratives on "knowledge" invites the use Paul makes of it, and enables him to formulate the same emphasis as Gen 3 in terms which a Greco-Roman and Hellenistic Jewish audience would recognize and respond to. Considerable use was made of the Genesis account of man's fall in Jewish theology of this period (here note Wisd Sol 2:23–24; *Jub.* 3.28–32; *Adam and Eve*; *4 Ezra* 4.30; and particularly *2 Apoc. Bar.* 54.17–19, which uses Adam in a similar piece of polemic; see further on 5:12); and the influence of the Genesis narratives is also evidenced outside the Judeo-Christian tradition proper, as the Hermetic tractate *Poimandres* in particular demonstrates (see Dodd, *Greeks,* esp. 145–69). That v 23 has in mind also the idolatry of the golden calf at Mount Sinai (Ps 106:20; see on 1:23) does not weaken the conclusion drawn here (*pace* Bassler, *Divine Impartiality,* 197), since in Jewish tradition the idolatry of the golden calf was frequently associated with the fall of Adam: idolatry was the prime indication of the depth of man's fall, and Israel's own fall into idolatry at Sinai after God had chosen them to be his people was seen as the equivalent in Israel's history to Adam's fall after creation (cf. Jervell, *Imago,* 115–16, 321–22). See further Hooker, "Adam"; Wedderburn, "Adam," 413–19; Dunn, *Christology,* 101–2.

23 ἤλλαξαν τὴν δόξαν τοῦ ἀφθάρτου θεοῦ ἐν ὁμοιώματι εἰκόνος φθαρτοῦ ἀνθρώπου καὶ πετεινῶν καὶ τετραπόδων καὶ ἑρπετῶν, "they changed the glory of the incorruptible God for the likeness of the image of corruptible man, and of birds, and of beasts and of reptiles." The argument now becomes almost wholly Jewish by drawing on the standard Jewish polemic against idolatry. The language here has been determined particularly by Ps 106 [LXX 105]:20: ἠλλάξαντο τὴν δόξαν . . . ἐν ὁμοιώματι . . . (the ἐν derived from the adaptable Hebrew preposition ⊃; BGD ἀλλάσσω), referring to the idolatry of the golden calf, though Jer 2:11 is probably also in view (. . . ἠλλάξατο τὴν δόξαν . . .) and Paul no doubt had in mind the magnificent satire of Isa 44:9–20 (of which there are several echoes in vv 22–23). Not least in influence would be the sustained polemic in the second half of Wisd Sol: note particularly 11:15; 12:24; 13:10, 13–14; 14:8; 15:18–19 (cf. also *Ep. Arist.* 138). Typical also for the background here is the sustained polemic of the Letter of Jeremiah (Ep Jer) and the repeated attacks of *Sib. Or.* 3 (note particularly again 3:8–45). Jeremias, "Röm 1:22–32," draws particular attention to *T. Naph.* 3.2–4. Schulz sees the background as rooted more in Jewish apocalyptic (cf. *1 Enoch* 91.4 ff.; 99.2 ff.; *Sib. Or.* 3.6 ff.; *T. Mos.* 1.13; *2 Apoc. Bar.* 54.17–22). See further Str-B, 3:53–60, 60–62. For δόξα θεοῦ, "glory of God," see on 1:21, 3:23, 6:4, and 9:4.

The use of ὁμοίωμα, "close likeness" (see on 5:14, 6:5, and 8:3), and εἰκών, "image" (cf. particularly Rev 13:14–15; 14:9, 11; 15:2; 16:2; see on 8:29), may have been prompted by the fact that the same terms are used as equivalents in Deut 4:16–18. The deliberate use of both, when one or other might have been thought sufficient, may be an example of the Semitic habit of repeating an idea for effect (cf. Moulton, *Grammar* 2:419–20); but here it is probably intended to increase the distance between the reality and that which the idol is supposed to depict—a copy of a copy, inadequate even as a representation ("the inferior, shadowy character" [Barrett]); Lagrange cites the possibly parallel 1 Macc 3:48; we might also compare Plato's allegory of the cave: what man sees is but the shadow of the figures on the wall (*Republic* 7.514–17). That εἰκών is prompted by the thought of man as God's image is possible but less likely, since it refers also to "birds, beasts, and reptiles" (see discussion in Wedderburn, "Adam," 416–19), though the influence of Gen 1:20–25 may nevertheless be discernible in the choice of the last four nouns (Hyldahl).

The ἄφθαρτος/φθαρτός antithesis ("incorruptible/corruptible, immortal/ mortal") is probably drawn ultimately from Stoic philosophy (cf. *TDNT* 9:96) via Hellenistic Judaism, where we see it already established by implication in Wisd Sol 2:23 (which again has several points of contact with Paul's exposition here) and in Philo, *Leg. All.* 3.36 (where it also forms part of a Jewish polemic against idolatry).

We may note that the Judeo-Christian polemic against idolatry foreshadows Feuerbach's critique of theism in general (cf. Gaugler); the critique of human *religion* is already given within the Judeo-Christian tradition (Barth; Eichholz, *Theology*, 70–76).

24 διὸ παρέδωκεν αὐτοὺς ὁ θεὸς ἐν ταῖς ἐπιθυμίαις τῶν καρδιῶν αὐτῶν, "wherefore God handed them over in the desires of their hearts." παρέδωκεν, "hand over," in the sense of hand over control of, responsibility for. For the usage here, cf. Acts 7:42; Rom 6:17. The threefold repetition of the same word (vv 24, 26, 28) is very effective; but the divine judgment has already been implied in the "divine passives" of vv 21–22. ἐπιθυμία, "desire," can be used in a good sense (so in Phil 1:23 and 1 Thess 2:17), but more often in a bad sense, as desire for something forbidden, including, not least, sexual desire, lust. It is found regularly in the Stoics (BGD) and in this sense also in the wisdom literature (Wisd Sol 4:12; Sir 5:2; 18:30–31; 23:5). Paul has in view man's animal appetites, specifically the desires of the flesh, the mortal body (6:12; 7:7–8; 13:14; Gal 5:16, 24; Col 3:5; 1 Thess 4:5; also Eph 2:3; 4:22). Paul is still operating within the framework of the fall narratives: man's desire for freedom from constraint to do what he wants as the primal sin (see on 7:7). But he probably also has in mind another classic example of human craving which brought divine wrath upon it (Num 11:31–35) which is twice referred to in the Psalms with the formula that God gave them their desire (Pss 78 [LXX 77]:29: καὶ τὴν ἐπιθυμίαν αὐτῶν ἔδωκεν αὐτοῖς [S]; 106 [105]: 14–15).

εἰς ἀκαθαρσίαν, "to uncleanness." ἀκαθαρσία, "uncleanness," has by now almost entirely lost its earlier cultic connotation and bears a clear moral sense (as in Wisd Sol 2:16; 1 Esd 1:42 [LXX 40]), especially sexual immorality (*1 Enoch* 10.11; *T. Jud.* 14–15; *T. Jos.* 4.6). For a somewhat similar train of thought cf. Philo, *Leg. All.* 3.139. In the NT it is almost exclusively a Pauline word (9 times in the Pauline corpus); here cf. particularly 6:19; Gal 5:19; Eph 4:19; Col 3:5.

ἀτιμάζεσθαι τὰ σώματα αὐτῶν ἐν αὐτοῖς, "that their bodies might be dishonored among themselves," i.e., might be treated in a way lacking in respect for them (in accordance with the purpose for which they were created); so, "degraded." In linking idolatry and sexual license Paul continues to follow the line of Jewish polemic, as expressed not least Wisd Sol 14:12–27. For the denunciation of homosexual practice see on 1:26–27.

Paul would see the act of handing over as punitive, but not as spiteful or vengeful. For him it is simply the case that man apart from God regresses to a lower level of animality. God has handed them over in the sense that he has accepted the fact of man's rebellious desire to be free of God (in terms of Gen 3, to be "as God"), and has let go of the control which restrained them from their baser instincts. The rationale is, presumably, that God does not retain control over those who do not desire it; he who wants to be on his own is granted his wish. The important corollary also follows that Paul does not indict all human, including sexual, desire as unclean. Rather it is only when such desire has control of man, when it becomes the most important aspect of human life, that it is condemned. Paul would also, presumably, see the divine handing over as at least potentially redemptive, if it resulted in man's recoiling from the degenerate outworking of his own freedom (cf. 1 Cor 5:5), as no doubt had been the case with many of the Gentile God-worshipers who made up his audience.

25 οἴτινες μετήλλαξαν τὴν ἀλήθειαν τοῦ θεοῦ ἐν τῷ ψεύδει, "who changed the truth of God by the lie." This is a stronger version of v 23. "The truth of God" is thus partly his invisible nature and partly his cosmic power as Creator (see on 1:20). But for those familiar with Jewish thought ἀλήθεια inevitably includes also the implication of God's reliability and trustworthiness (אֱמֶת; cf. TDNT 1:242; TDOT 1:313–16; see also on 3:3–4). The indictment in these terms has thematic importance within the thought of the letter (see Introduction §4.2.2 and on 1:17): misunderstanding of God's trustworthiness = faithfulness lies at the root of both Gentile and Jewish failure; but the only hope for both lies in that same "truth of God." τὸ ψεῦδος can be used collectively, meaning "lies," and as an obvious antithesis to man's proper response to God (Pss 4:2; 5:6; Jer 3:10; 13:25); in Ep Jer 47 in anti-idol polemic, as here. But NEB's "bartered away the true God for a false one" is a little too free.

ἐσεβάσθησαν καὶ ἐλάτρευσαν τῇ κτίσει παρὰ τὸν κτίσαντα, "they worshiped and served the creature rather than the creator." σεβάζομαι, "worship," occurs only here in the NT and rarely elsewhere (TDNT 7:172–73). For λατρεύω see on 1:9; here cf. particularly Acts 7:42. In this case Paul is obviously thinking of cultic worship as such, or the pagan worship of idols which Jews found so abhorrent; though if the ἐσεβάσθησαν καὶ ἐλάτρευσαν is intended to balance the ἐδόξασαν ἢ ηὐχαρίστησαν of v 21, a broader reference is by no means excluded. On the fundamental perception of God as Creator in the Jewish piety of the period see TDNT 3:1019; see also on 1:20.

For the typical Jew it was always an indication of the ludicrous folly of other religions that they preferred to worship the creature rather than the Creator, to worship indeed the creation of their own hands (see on 1:23). The reply that the images were only representations of deity is already met by the emphasis on God's invisibility (v 20), glory, and incorruptibility (v 23). The idol is a lie (ἐν τῷ ψεύδει), a falsification of reality which distorts all man's perception (vv 21–22) and consequent attitudes and conduct. Paul would certainly affirm that the typical association between pagan idolatry and sexual license was no accident: the more base the perception of God, the more base the worship and corresponding conduct appropriate to it (cf. Wisd Sol 14:12).

ὅς ἐστιν εὐλογητὸς εἰς τοὺς αἰῶνος, ἀμήν, "who is blessed for ever, Amen." A thoroughly and typically Jewish benediction (Gen 9:26; 14:20; 1 Sam 25:32; 2 Sam 18:28; 1 Kgs 1:48; 8:15; 2 Chron 2:12; Ps 41:13; Tob 3:11; 8:5;

Luke 1:68); like all devout Jews, Paul would declare God's blessedness in his daily prayers (the Eighteen Benedictions; בָּרוּךְ = εὐλογητός). The formula, "Blessed be the God and Father of our Lord" quickly became established in Christianity (2 Cor 1:3; Eph 1:3; 1 Pet 1:3). See also 9:5; *TDNT* 2:760, 764; and further on 12:14. Here Paul uses the blessing as a way of distancing himself from worship which does not recognize that all blessing and blessedness lies in God alone and from any life not lived in dependence on that blessing before all else. The "Amen" underlines Paul's commitment to this truth; for the established place of ἀμήν in Jewish and Christian prayer and doxology as signifying the worshiper's concurrence see *TDNT* 1:335–37; in Paul see 9:5; 11:36; 15:33; 1 Cor 16:24; Gal 1:5; 6:18; Phil 4:20; 1 Thess 3:13; also Eph 3:21; 1 Tim 1:17; 6:16; 2 Tim 4:18.

26 διὰ τοῦτο παρέδωκεν αὐτοὺς ὁ θεὸς εἰς πάθη ἀτιμίας, "for this reason God handed them over to disgraceful passions." For παρέδωκεν see on 1:24. εἰς πάθη ἀτιμίας is a reformulation of v 24 (ἐν ταῖς ἐπιθυμίας . . . τοῦ ἀτιμάζεσ-θαι . . .). "Moral perversion is the result of God's wrath, not the reason for it" (Käsemann). For πάθος in the sense of "passion," especially of a sexual nature, see BGD (particularly *4 Macc*; elsewhere in the NT only Col 3:5; 1 Thess 4:5 where the phrase is used as in *T. Jos.* 7.8). Not just the acts, but the passions are dishonoring (Schlier). ἀτιμία means "dishonor, disgrace, shame," worthy of no respect. The outcome of failing to give God his due honor is the dishonoring of oneself: human respect (both self-respect and respect for others) is rooted in the recognition that only God has authority as Creator to order and dispose of that which is created.

αἵ τε γὰρ θήλειαι αὐτῶν μετήλλαξαν τὴν φυσικὴν χρῆσιν εἰς τὴν παρὰ φύσιν, "for their females changed the natural function into what is contrary to nature." Both θήλειαι and ἄρσενες (v 27), "females, males," are used presumably because Paul has in mind particularly their sexual relationship, and indeed sexual compatibility (cf. Mark 10:6 // Matt 19:4; Gen 1:27; Gal 3:28). Female homosexual practice is mentioned before male, possibly because the more aggressive character of male sexuality, as indicated in v 27, makes for a better crescendo. χρῆσις can be used, as here, in the sense of "relations, function," especially with reference to sexual intercourse (BGD).

φύσις, "nature," is not a Hebrew concept; the term only comes into the LXX in the later works which originated in Greek (Wisd Sol 3 and *4 Macc*). Note again Wisd Sol 13:1, though the point is different; much closer is *T. Naph.* 3.4–5, where the line of thought is very similar. The concept is primarily Greek, and typically Stoic—to live in harmony with the natural order and its divine rationality being the Stoic ideal; τὸ κατὰ φύσιν ζῆν is equivalent to τὸ καλῶς/εὖ ζῆν, "to live well." The idea of actions as "against nature" (παρὰ φύσιν) is also present, and with particular reference to sexual relations such as pederasty (see further *TDNT* 9:252–71, particularly 262–67). But abhorrence of homosexual practice as such is particularly Jewish (see on 1:27).

27 ὁμοίως τε καὶ οἱ ἄρσενες ἀφέντες τὴν φυσικὴν χρῆσιν τῆς θηλείας, "likewise also the males gave up the natural function of the female"; see on 1:26.

ἐξεκαύθησαν ἐν τῇ ὀρέξει αὐτῶν εἰς ἀλλήλους, "they were inflamed with their desire for one another." Both ἐκκαίομαι, "be inflamed," and ὄρεξις, "longing, desire, particularly of sexual desire," occur only here in the NT (BGD); but ὄρεξις is used in Wisd Sol 14:2, 15:5, and 16:2–3, though the closer parallel is found in Sir 23:6, 16.

ἄρσενες ἐν ἄρσεσιν τὴν ἀσχημοσύνην κατεργαζόμενοι, "males with males committing what is shameless." ἀσχημοσύνη, "shameless deed," "indecent act" (NIV). Like the cognate adjective it can be used with reference to the exposure of the sexual organs (as regularly in the LXX, e.g., Exod 28:42; Nah 3:5; Ezek 16:8; and particularly Lev 18 and 20, where more than two-thirds of the LXX references occur; in the NT only 1 Cor 12:23 and Rev 16:15; see also BGD). The whole phrase (τὴν ἀσχημοσύνην κατεργαζόμενοι, "committing the shameless act") indicates clearly that not merely homosexual tendency or desire is in view, but the genital act itself. Scroggs, *Homosexuality*, 115, suggests that Paul has in mind here pederasty in particular, but Paul's indictment seems to include all kinds of homosexual practice, female as well as male, and was not directed against one kind of homosexual practice in distinction from another.

τὴν ἀντιμισθίαν ἣν ἔδει τῆς πλάνης αὐτῶν ἐν ἑαυτοῖς ἀπολαμβάνοντες, "receiving in themselves the penalty which was fitting for their error." In ἀντιμισθία, "penalty, reward," so far only in Christian writers (elsewhere in the NT only 2 Cor 6:13), as also in ἀπολαμβάνω, "receive back," there is some emphasis on the reciprocal nature of the transaction (ἀντι-, ἀπο-); cf. *m. 'Abot* 4.2. πλάνη, "wandering, roaming," in Christian literature is used only figuratively of wandering from the path of truth, as in "error, delusion, deceit, deception" (BGD); cf. particularly James 5:20; 2 Pet 2:18; Jude 11. The influence of Wisd Sol 12:24 at this point is very probable. The implication is that unnatural sexual practice is its own penalty, the inevitable outcome of wandering from God. That the divinely ordered punishment for sin is to be handed over to the power of that sin, to be left to its consequences, is the theme throughout this section (παρέδωκεν: vv 24, 26, 28), which is given further emphasis here (cf. particularly Wisd Sol 11:16; 12:23, 27; *T. Gad* 5.10).

In the Greco-Roman world homosexuality was quite common and even highly regarded, as is evident from Plato's *Symposium* and Plutarch's *Lycurgus*. It was a feature of social life, indulged in not least by the gods (e.g., Zeus' attraction to Ganymede) and emperors (e.g., Nero's seduction of free-born boys was soon to become notorious). The homosexual reputations of the women of Lesbos was well established long before Lucian made it the theme of his fifth *Dialogue of the Courtesans* (second century A.D.). But Jewish reaction to it as a perversion, a pagan abomination, is consistent throughout the OT (Lev 18:22; 20:13; 1 Kgs 14:24; 15:12; 22:46; 2 Kgs 23:7), with the sin of Sodom often recalled as a terrible warning (e.g., Gen 19:1–28; Deut 23:18; Isa 1:9–10; 3:9; Jer 23:14; Lam 4:6; Ezek 16:43–58). In the period of early Judaism, abhorrence of homosexuality is not just part of the reaction against Greek mores, since we find it also in those most influenced by Greek thought (Wisd Sol 14:26; *Ep. Arist.* 152; Philo, *Abr.* 135–37; *Spec. Leg.* 3.37–42; *Sib. Or.* 3:184–86, 764; Ps. Phoc. 3, 190–92, 213–14; Josephus, *Ap.* 2.273–75); note also the sustained polemic against sexual promiscuity and homosexuality in *T. 12 Patr.* (particularly *T. Lev.* 14.6; 17.11; *T. Naph.* 4.1) and in *Sib. Or.* (e.g., 3.185–87, 594–600, 763); see further Str-B, 3:68–74. In other words, antipathy to homosexuality remains a consistent and distinctive feature of

Jewish understanding of what man's createdness involves and requires. That homosexuality is of a piece with idolatry is taken for granted (as several of the same passages show), both understood as a demeaning of the people who indulge in them. The link between man's fall (Gen 3) and sexual perversion (as here) is also typically Jewish, since Gen 6:1–4 also played a considerable part in Jewish attempts to account for the origin of sin (*Jub.* 4.22; 5.1–10; 7.21; *1 Enoch* 6–11; 86; *T. Reub.* 5; *T. Naph.* 3.5; CD 2.18–21; etc.). Elsewhere in the NT see 1 Cor 6:9; 1 Tim 1:10; 2 Pet 2; Jude 7.

28 καθὼς οὐκ ἐδοκίμασαν τὸν θεὸν ἔχειν ἐν ἐπιγνώσει, "as they did not think fit to keep God in mind"—a fifth repetition of the same accusation (vv 18, 21, 23, 25). καθώς, "just as" (BDF, § 453.2). δοκιμάζω usually has the sense of "test, examine, prove by testing, accept as proved"; cf. 14:22; 1 Cor 16:3; 2 Cor 8:22 (BGD); see also on 5:4. The implication then is of a deliberate act of disqualification. It was not simply a case of humans being distracted by something else and losing sight of God; they gave God their consideration, and concluded that God was unnecessary to their living (that is, presumably God as Creator with rights over his creation); cf. more modern disclaimers of God as an "unnecessary hypothesis," an infantile projection no longer needed by man "come of age." ἐπίγνωσις, "knowledge, recognition," is found in our literature only with reference to religious or moral knowledge. Used in the absolute (as in 10:2, Phil 1:9, and Col 3:10), and with δοκιμάζειν, it probably has a more intensive sense; that is, knowledge as deliberately acquired to serve as the information resource for daily living (see also Sullivan, 406). They discounted God as a factor in shaping their lives.

παρέδωκεν αὐτοὺς ὁ θεὸς εἰς ἀδόκιμον νοῦν, "God handed them over to a disqualified mind"—the third use of παρέδωκεν (see on 1:24 and 26). The wordplay ἐδοκίμασαν/ἀδόκιμον is obviously deliberate. The point is not that *God* chose to test and to disqualify their minds, or caused their minds to degenerate, but that the act of making God the subject of a test was itself the act of an unqualified mind, of an intelligence "below par." The mind of the creature depends on the light of God (cf. v 21) for it to function properly. When God leaves it to itself it is not adequate, insufficiently qualified for its task of informing relationships with others and with the rest of creation. Paul uses the image of failing the test, being disqualified, elsewhere (1 Cor 9:27; 2 Cor 13:5–7). That the mind has a crucial part in shaping conduct for Paul is clear from its usage here and elsewhere in Romans (12:2; 14:5); Paul has no desire to dissociate man's rational processes from the gospel (cf. 1 Cor 14:14–15, 19); it is the mind which leaves God out of consideration, which befogs its own function (v 21) and disqualifies itself. For νοῦς see further on 7:23 and 12:2. On the theme of "the punishment fitting the crime" see further Klostermann.

ποιεῖν τὰ μὴ καθήκοντα, "to do what is not fitting." τὸ καθῆκον/τὰ καθήκοντα, "what is fitting, proper," is certainly a Stoic phrase, known as such as a technical term in philosophy, as Philo demonstrates (*Leg. All.* 1.56). The negative form, as here, is found also in 2 Macc 6:4, *3 Macc* 4.16, and Philo, *Cher.* 14, though the more regular Stoic expression is τὸ παρὰ τὸ καθῆκον (as in Philo, *Leg. All.* 2.32). Within Stoic thought the positive phrase denotes what is fitting, what is one's duty, what is in harmony with nature. See further BGD, καθήκω;

TDNT 3:438–40. As with his appeal to what is "natural" and "contrary to nature" in v 26, so here, Paul's use of these more broadly appealing concepts is obviously deliberate. He is not content simply to "rehash" Jewish polemic in traditional Jewish terms (NJB is wrong to refer back to 1:26–27 with its translation "their indecent behavior"). He is clearly attempting not merely to frame his indictment in non-Jewish terms, but also to appeal to the broader recognition within Greek thought that there are many things which cannot be regarded as proper and fitting (see also on 2:7, 10; 12:17; 13:3, 5, 10, 13; 14:18). This also implies that his argument here should not be taken as a blanket condemnation of Gentile morals and lifestyle as a whole (as though the description of vv 26–27 and 29–31 referred to all Gentiles); that would have left his indictment open to rejection as merely demonstrating Jewish prudery and bias. His argument is rather that the presence of such features in human society (though using Jewish polemic, he has never restricted his condemnation to the Gentiles), features which thoughtful Gentiles should also be willing to recognize as unnatural and improper, is best explained on Jewish premises, as evidence of man's self-displacement from his proper role as creature and worshiper of the invisible Creator.

29–31 Such catalogs of vice are well known in the ancient world, particularly, as we might expect from the preceding phrase, among the Stoics (see particularly Lietzmann). But similar lists also appear in different strands of Judaism; again, significantly, Wisd Sol 14:25–26; but see also, e.g., *4 Macc* 1.26–27; 2.15; *T. Reub.* 3.3–6; *T. Lev.* 17.11; 1QS 4.9–11; *2 Enoch* 10.4–5; *3 Apoc. Bar.* 8.5; 13.4; the list in Philo, *Sac.* 32 has more than 140 items! (see further Daxer, 46–52; Easton, 1–8; Wibbing, 14–76; Vögtle, esp. 227–32; Kamlah, chap. 2). They are common also in the earliest Christian literature (see especially Mark 7:21–22; Rom 13:13; 1 Cor 5:10–11; 6:9–10; 2 Cor 12:20; Gal 5:19–21; Col 3:5, 8; 1 Tim 1:9–10; 2 Tim 3:2–5; Titus 3:3; 1 Pet 4:3; Rev 22:15; *1 Clem.* 35.5, which is almost certainly modeled on Rom 1:29–31; *Did.* 2–5; and *Barn.* 18–20); see also on 13:13. The difference in contents (e.g., Paul's lengthy list here has only two or three items in common with Philo's in *Sac.* 32), as also indeed with the similar lists in Paul himself, indicates that Paul is not simply taking over a standard catalog from elsewhere or adapting his message completely to the moral perspective of other systems. So too the degree to which its structuring depends on verbal features (association of sounds, grouping of words with initial ἀ-; see *Form and Structure*) implies that Paul is not concerned to castigate particular sins above all others as distinctively non-Christian. Rather the implication is that he is simply appealing to a widespread recognition in conventional morality that there are features of social life which are to be condemned. The more distinctive Judeo-Christian emphasis comes not with the list itself (which is not to be characterized as anti-Gentile [Dabelstein, 85]), but in the understanding of such a state of affairs as the consequence of God's "handing over," as evidence of God's final wrath on his rebellious and disordered creation (cf. further Wilckens).

πεπληρωμένους πάσῃ ἀδικίᾳ πονηρίᾳ πλεονεξίᾳ κακίᾳ, "filled with all unrighteousness, wickedness, greediness, badness." πεπληρωμένους, "filled with"; cf. 2 Macc 7:21; *3 Macc* 4.16; 5.30; Luke 2:40; 2 Cor 7:4; see also on 15:14. The positioning of ἀδικία, "unrighteousness," at the head of the list is no doubt deliberate, linking back to the double usage at the beginning of the section (v 18) and maintaining the implication that all which is to follow characterizes man as forgetful of the Creator's claim on him as creature; cf. particularly 3:5; also the list in *1 Clem.* 35.5. πονηρία, "wickedness, maliciousness"; with κακία in 1 Cor 5:8 and in vice lists in Philo, *Ebr.* 223, and *1 Clem.* 35.5. πλεονεξία, literally, "a desire to have more," so "greediness, insatiableness, covetousness"—"ruthless self-assertion" (Dodd); a widely condemned vice and an obvious item for inclusion in the Stoic and other catalogs (BGD; *TDNT* 6:267–70); so in Mark 7:22; Col 3:5; *1 Clem.* 35.5; and *Barn.* 20.1 (also 2 Cor 9:5; Eph 4:19; 5:3; 1 Thess 2:5). κακία, "badness, wickedness," though possibly more specific, "malice, ill-will," as in other lists (Eph 4:31; Col 3:8; Titus 3:3; 1 Pet 2:1; *Did.* 5.1; *Barn.* 20.1).

μεστοὺς φθόνου φόνου ἔριδος δόλου κακοηθείας, "full of envy, murder, rivalry, deceit, spite." μεστοὺς, "full of," governs the next five words; see further on 15:14. φθόνος, "envy, jealousy"; in lists of vice also in Gal 5:21; 1 Tim 6:4; and 1 Pet 2:1 (see Spicq, 919–21). φόνος, "murder, killing," found in similar lists in Hos 4:2; Mark 7:21; Rev 9:21; and *Barn.* 20.1. The φθόνος/φόνος wordplay occurs also in Euripides, *Troades* 766ff. ἔρις, "rivalry, strife"; so also Rom 13:13; 1 Cor 3:3; 2 Cor 12:20; Gal 5:20; and *1 Clem.* 35.5 (see also Spicq, 291). δόλος, "deceit, treachery"; so also Mark 7:22; *1 Clem.* 35.5; *Did.* 5.1, and *Barn.* 20.1. κακοήθεια, "malice, spite"; only here in the NT; see Spicq, 392–93.

ψιθυριστάς, καταλάλους, θεοστυγεῖς, ὑβριστάς, ὑπερηφάνους, ἀλαζόνας, ἐφευρετὰς κακῶν, γονεῦσιν ἀπειθεῖς. As with κακοήθεια, ψιθυριστής, "whisperer, rumor-monger, tale-bearer," κατάλαλος, "slanderer," and θεοστυγής, "hating God," all occur only here in the NT and are little used elsewhere (though note again *1 Clem.* 35.5); such piling up of epithets invites the use of less familiar terms. Elsewhere θεοστυγής has the sense "hated by God, God-forsaken" ("hateful to God" [NEB]), but the active meaning is presumably intended here (BGD), unless we should take it adjectively with the following word, "despisers hated by God" (*TDNT* 8:306); see also 5:10. ὑβριστής, "violent, insolent" (in the NT only here and 1 Tim 1:13), ὑπερήφανος, "arrogant, proud," and ἀλαζών, "boaster, braggart" are all obvious candidates for inclusion in a list of socially undesirable characteristics (e.g., *T. Lev.* 17.11; Mark 7:22; *1 Clem.* 35.5) and make a natural association elsewhere, as in Wisd Sol 5:8 and 2 Tim 3:2 (see BGD in each case). ἐφευρετής, "inventor, contriver"; only here in NT; similar phrases in 2 Macc 7:31; Philo, *Flacc.* 20; and Virgil, *Aen.* 2.164. γονεῦσιν ἀπειθεῖς, "disobedient to parents"; particularly abhorrent for a Jew (Deut 21:18) and a mark of "the last days" according to 2 Tim 3:2.

ἀσυνέτους, ἀσυνθέτους, ἀστόργους, ἀνελεήμονας, "senseless, faithless, loveless, merciless," "without brains, honor, love or pity" (NJB). For ἀσύνετος see on 1:21. ἀσύνθετος, "faithless"; perhaps pointedly chosen since its literal meaning is "covenant breaking" (cf. particularly its use in LXX [Jer 3:7–11]), though in a list of vices in its present context the sense "undutiful" may be more in Paul's mind (BGD). ἄστοργος, "unloving, lacking family affection," and ἀνελεήμων, "unmerciful," occur elsewhere in the lists of 2 Tim 3:3 and Titus 1:9 (late variant reading) respectively.

32 οἵτινες τὸ δικαίωμα τοῦ θεοῦ ἐπιγνόντες, "who having known the just

decree of God." ἐπιγνόντες clearly harks back to the similar emphasis in vv
19, 21, and 28, and so constitutes a concluding summary of the preceding
denunciation (against Flückiger's implausible suggestion that with 1:32 Paul
turns to his indictment of his fellow Jews). δικαίωμα, "regulation, requirement,
decree." Paul speaks here of "the decree of God," not of "the requirement
of the law," as in 2:26 and 8:4. Of course Paul sees the law as the clear
expression of what God requires of man (so also 2:13). But the same references
show that in using this word he is not thinking of requirements of the law
as normally understood in Judaism (2:26; and see further on 8:4); obedience
to what the law requires is possible to those who do not know the law as
such, but it is an obedience of a different order (cf. 2:28–29; 7:6). Here he
is thinking rather of a knowledge which is obviously part of man's knowledge
of God (1:21), a consequence of his creatureliness, although he may possibly
have in mind specifically the so-called Adamic and Noahic commandments
(cf. particularly *Jub.* 7.20; see further Str-B, 3:36–38 and on 2:14). Evidently,
however, Paul felt no need to be more specific: the appeal to things unfit (v
28) shows he is sufficiently in tune with a strong strand of moral sensibility
then current. This sense of a moral "ought" even in fallen man is for Paul's
purposes here sufficient evidence of man's continuing, albeit unwilling, recognition of his status as creature, as standing under a transcendent requirement,
and therefore sufficient common ground for an apologetic which looks to
move beyond Jewish condemnation of Gentile idolatry.

ὅτι οἱ τὰ τοιαῦτα πράσσοντες ἄξιοι θανάτου εἰσίν, "that those who practice such
things are worthy of death." This is the first appearance of a word ("death")
which will play a leading role (see chaps. 6–8 *Form and Structure*), but it
does not yet have the full force of that later usage. That he is thinking here
of the death penalty for particular sins is hardly likely (Dupont, *Gnosis*, 27,
cites Philo, *Mos.* 2.171, but there the thought is directed solely against idolatry).
Nor that he has simply indulged in a too sweeping denunciation which disre-
gards the difference between private vice and public crime. More likely is it
that he deliberately reverts to the Gen 2–3 narratives, which provided the
basic paradigm for the earlier part of the analysis (vv 19–25; see above on
1:22), so that in this way too v 32 provides a concluding summary of the
preceding verses. All these examples of things unfit (vv 29–31) are of a piece
with Adam's/man's rebellion, and evidence of his continuing distance from
God and of his standing under the primeval sentence of death (Gen 2:16).
In reverting to a more Jewish analysis Paul might be in danger of losing
some of his audience, though he probably had done enough to gain the
assent of those less familiar with the Jewish scriptures; but to express his
judgment in more specifically Jewish terms is important in providing a transition to the next stage of the indictment (cf. Kamlah, 18–19).

οὐ μόνον αὐτὰ ποιοῦσιν ἀλλὰ καὶ συνευδοκοῦσιν τοῖς πράσσουσιν, "not only do
them but give approval to those who practice them." There is a striking
parallel in *T. Ash.* 6.2, but regarded as an addition by de Jonge; Käsemann
also cites Seneca, *Ep.* 39.6. Having shown his awareness of the fair degree
of moral sensibility particularly among his Stoic contemporaries, Paul thinks
here more of another prominent side of Greco-Roman society where the
moral sensibility is not in evidence, but only delight in political intrigue,

manipulation, and power or pleasure in human vice as popularly portrayed in comedy and mime (Bultmann, "Glossen," 281 n.6). That his denunciation is overdrawn and too all-embracing should not be made grounds for criticism. The analysis here is not to be judged in relation to a modern carefully documented survey of social trends. This is written with the flourish of ancient rhetoric, in the style of the preacher of all ages, and would be recognized for what it is—a dramatic expression of a widespread malaise, of a human condition whose character as a whole is demonstrated by its failure to control or to find an answer to its most depressing features and worst excesses. See also on 2:1; and for a possible distinction between πράσσειν and ποιεῖν see on 2:3.

Explanation

1:18 The first main section of Paul's argument opens in a surprising way. Having announced his subject as the gospel revealing the righteousness of God, he immediately goes on: "for the wrath of God is being revealed from heaven." The linking "for" sounds as though it is introducing an explanation of the thematic statement. And this indeed was probably Paul's intention: either to depict the wrath of God as *part* of God's righteousness—in which case "God's righteousness" is at once being expanded as a two-edged concept, as unfolding in a two-sided revelatory process (salvation to faith, wrath to ungodliness and wickedness); or to demonstrate that wrath is the presupposition of or preliminary to righteousness—the need for and nature of God's righteousness can be understood only when we have first understood the outworking of divine wrath ("righteousness to life through faith," because the alternative is wrath to death through disobedience). But the causal force of the conjunction need not be pressed, and it may function here simply as a linking word ("indeed"), so that some listeners could well hear it simply as introducing the first stage of the larger argument.

The "wrath of God" which is thus abruptly introduced would not be a concept unfamiliar to Paul's readers. Both Jew and Greek would be familiar with the idea of divine indignation, of judicial anger against evil. Paul assumes this kind of preunderstanding before he goes on to develop his own exposition. This wrath, Paul affirms, is already being revealed from heaven; just as the righteousness of God is being revealed in the Jewish and Gentile response to the gospel, so the divine anger can be readily recognized in what is already actually taking place. The listener is thus prepared for a description or analysis of the current state of affairs—wrath not as God's final judgment, but as God's response to and indeed part in the unfolding of events and relationships at both personal and corporate level (vv 21–31).

The evil against which the divine wrath is initially directed is described in the most general and all-embracing terms: against *all* disregard or contempt for God and for the rights of our fellow human beings. It is not impossible that Paul thinks of the heavenly indignation being directed against deeds and not against persons as such, but lest any might infer that his or her own responsibility is thereby diminished, Paul defines the impiety and injustice as the work of those "who suppress or keep back the truth in unrighteousness." Here again the description is as broad and as inescapable as possible—"the truth" here being understood not in terms of some absolute ideal ("the good"), but as the truth of God (v 25), the truth of God in relation to man, of man in relation to God, and of man in relation to man, the reality which should determine these relations but which has been so effectively suppressed in and by the relationships which people have actually promoted. Here already is the implication that the truth of God and truth of man are interdependent, and that one person's relationship with another cannot be considered in isolation from that person's relationship with God.

19–20 The general charge of human wickedness is now made more precise by defining or justifying it in terms of the knowledge of God. Here too the charge is framed in broad terms and Paul is evidently concerned that it should be as meaningful and as widely admitted as possible. For the phrase used, "what can be known of God," takes up the well known premise of the time that God is knowable, and his brief elaboration of it (vv 19–20) draws principally on influential Stoic ideas: that there is an innate rapport between the divine and the human because the divine logos immanent throughout the world is immanent also in man as the power of reason; and that consequently the invisible realities and eternal power of divinity behind the visible cosmos are clearly seen by the eye of understanding (that same rational power) in and through the creation. At the same time, however, it is Paul's more Jewish perception of this divine human relation which remains primary: what is known of God is an act of revelation personally willed by God (v 19b) in relation to a created order (v 20); and man is recognized as a responsible agent in face of this revelation, so that his failure to respond appropriately is not simply a lack of perception, a defect in spiritual capacity, but a moral failure, a culpable act, "without excuse" (v 20b).

21 With v 21 the accusation becomes more specific and more Jewish in tone. Humankind is inexcusable because the human response called for by God's self-revelation in and to his creation is acknowledgment of his magnificent splendor and power as Creator, and the humble gratitude due from the creature to the Creator. Yet, despite having this knowledge of God, despite knowing God insofar as he had made himself known to them, humankind refused that response. In consequence their reasoning became futile, their foolish heart darkened. That is to say, by closing the eye of understanding which has the capacity to receive and recognize God's self-revelation (vv 19–20), they shut off the light of the mind and left it fumbling with inane trifles and relatively worthless side issues. Their whole intellectual and emotional life ("heart") by thus demonstrating this foolishness became clouded and less capable of receiving or responding to that light. In other words, by withholding the appropriate recognition of God they became less (not more) able to function as rational beings; failure to recognize their own creatureliness brought with it a decreasing ability to function as a human being.

22 The accusation is given still greater sharpness by the next cutting phrase (v 22). This failure to respond aright to God was not simply an oversight or an act of thoughtless petulance. They actually claimed they were being wise in thus turning their back on God, that it was an act of sophistication and sign of high intelligence to declare their independence from God, as though the refusal to acknowledge God as God in their daily living made them something more than creature. But what they took to be an attitude of great wisdom simply demonstrated their folly. The consequence was that they became less, not more capable of directing their own life. Seeking to rise above their creatureliness they actually regressed rather than progressed.

23 The *reductio ad absurdum* is reached with v 23: they exchanged the glory which they refused to recognize or acknowledge in the incorruptible God, in preference for not merely created beings in all their corruptibility, but for the image of such beings, or rather, and even more ridiculous, the likeness of the image of such beings. They preferred the imperfect copy of what God had made to God himself. They preferred the flickering shadows of their darkened minds to the strong light of the knowledge of God. Their desire for the role of creator came to fulfillment in the making of images of wood and stone! Nor could it be otherwise, because in thus turning their back on God they made it impossible for themselves to see things as they are and for what they are. Their sense of values became distorted, because they had abandoned the one firm reference point by relating to which all other shifting relativities of meaning and worth become stable and clear.

By this time it would be clear to Paul's readers and listeners that he was leading them along the familiar path of Jewish polemic against idolatry. It is probable indeed that Paul was consciously modeling his exposition on the Wisdom of Solomon: the echoes of Wisdom's thought and language are quite marked in this section of the argument, particularly Wisd Sol 13–15, so much so that vv 19–21 almost constitute a summary of Wisd Sol 13:1–9 and vv 23–25 of the powerful anti-idol polemic in Wisd Sol 13:10–15:19; and both make effective use of widely familiar concepts, like the contrast between incorruptible (God) and corruptible (man), so that the polemic gains maximum leverage from contemporary thought. Paul can assume the line of argument without needing to elaborate it in any detail, confident that his Roman audience would accept it readily enough, since almost certainly it was the Jewish attitude to idolatry which had attracted many of them to the synagogue in the first place as God-worshipers and proselytes, from which they had gone on to faith in Jesus the Christ.

It is sufficiently clear that Paul also had in mind the figure of Adam and the narrative of the fall (Gen 3), as of course is true also of the Wisdom of Solomon (2:23–24). There is no specific allusion to Genesis, but it was hardly possible for a Jew to think of man's place in creation, his knowledge of God, and his loss of that knowledge in a (single) act of willful rebellion, without reference to Gen 2–3. Paul's indictment of humankind is also his description of Adam (= man): Adam/man who did not honor God as God or acknowledge his creaturely dependence on him, Adam/man who thought he himself could be as God, wise in his own right without need of God's wisdom, and who by that very act darkened his own counsel and clothed himself in folly. Thus it is that the Genesis narrative provides Paul with a penetrating analysis of contemporary man.

Still more interesting in v 23 is Paul's clearly deliberate use of Ps 106:20 (the psalmist's brief description of Israel's earliest apostasy in the idolatry of the golden calf at Sinai [Exod 32]). This association between the fall of Adam and the fall of Israel was probably already established in Jewish thought, the disobedience of Adam and the idolatry at Sinai itself being seen as the two archetypal sins threatening humankind and Israel. But it would probably not escape notice that the illustration Paul uses to document the typical Jewish polemic against idolatry is Israel itself! It is Israel who stands as a perpetual warning of how quickly man can turn from God and lose himself in things. The most devastating example of humankind's folly in turning its back on God is given by Paul's own people. Those among his largely Gentile audience who recognized the allusion would probably appreciate this unexpected twist in the Pauline emphasis—"Jew first and also Greek."

24 Up till this point Paul has been content to highlight the basic consequence of man's refusal to acknowledge God, where the wrath of God can be understood in terms of the inevitable consequences of man's chosen course of action. When the creature cuts itself off from the Creator the inevitable result is that the creature can no longer function aright. But now the spiral of man's sin and sinning is given a sharper twist: God determines the consequence of man's sin. "God handed them over"; the word denotes a measured and deliberate act, but also the resigning of direct control over what is thus passed on. It is this last aspect which is the clue to what follows. They wanted to pursue the desire of their own hearts, and so God gave them over to what they desired; he did not, it should be noted, give them their desires, rather he gave them to what they desired and the consequences of what they desired (more explicit in vv 26–27). God handed them over to the freedom for which they yearned; not their freedom to them, but them to their freedom. The control of God once removed left them like a faulty rocket plunging out of control. For what this vaunted liberty consisted in was nothing other than freedom to indulge in immorality which insulted themselves and their bodies. The desire to be independent of God in achieving its end showed itself to be nothing higher than the desire for a degrading impurity.

25 And, lest the reason be forgotten, Paul points again to the root cause of humankind's corrupted and dishonoring state. They exchanged what they knew to be the truth of God for a lie; they preferred to direct their devotion to the creature instead of the Creator. Here the echo of Gen 3 is even stronger. Adam/man believed the serpent's calumny and deception ("You will not die . . . ; you will be like God" [Gen 3:4–5]). And the result? Not that he became independent and godlike, but rather that he became caught in a baser dependence, a dependence on things; he became less than human, the creature of creatures rather than of the Creator. As Paul himself implies so clearly, man the creature is bound by his very nature to worship and serve something beyond himself. So that if he rejects the only one worthy of his worship and service, it is inevitable that he will direct that basic drive toward an inferior object and thus reduce his own stature in consequence. Who would think to choose as one's master the created thing rather than the glorious Creator? But that is just what man has done. The thought so appalls Paul that in typically Jewish fashion he utters a benediction to distance God from such perverse folly.

26–27 The effect of the repeated "handed over" is not to imply any increasing depth of depravity, implying a downward spiral of degradation, since what is described in vv 26–27 is no different from and no worse than the state depicted more briefly in v 24. But the repetition of the same phrase, "For this cause God handed them over," increases the solemnity and seriousness of the charge being made, the awfulness of the state to which man has come by virtue of turning his back on God, literally, the God-forsaken character of his plight. The description which follows is a characteristic expression of Jewish antipathy toward the practice of homosexuality so prevalent in the Greco-Roman world.

Paul's attitude to homosexual practice is unambiguous. The third appearance of the word "changed" (cf. vv 23 and 25) seems to imply that the action described ("changing the natural use to that which is contrary to nature") is of a piece with and direct result of the basic corruption of the glory and truth of God in idolatry, a similar turning from the role of creature to what is simply a perversion of the creature's share in creating. But more striking still is his use of a sequence of words whose import is unmistakable. Homosexuality is seen as a passion which is "worthy of no respect." Homosexual practice is characterized with the emphasis of repetition as "unnatural," where Paul uses very Greek and particularly Stoic language to broaden the appeal of the more characteristically Jewish rejection of homosexuality, and where he in effect appeals to his own readers' common sense to recognize that homosexual practice is a violation of the natural order (as determined by God). "Inflamed with desire": taken individually the two words do not necessarily have a negative connotation, but together the implication is of something immoderate and ultimately self-destructive. "Committing the shameless deed": Paul could not help but be thinking here of Lev 18 and 20, which include the homosexual act within the category of illicit sexual relationships, as one of the "abominations" of the surrounding peoples which Israel should avoid on pain of being cut off from the covenant (Lev 18:22; 20:13). The final clause with heavy and repeated strokes completes the picture of a perversion which is turned in upon itself in a tightening spiral of self-destruction—literally, "receiving in return in themselves the penalty which matches the deed and which is proper to their error"—sex treated as an end in itself becomes a dead end in itself, and sexual perversion is its own inevitable penalty.

In all this Paul had evidently no need to mount a strong argument to establish his point. No doubt the reason was that those present to hear his letter read would already be largely sympathetic to Jewish standards of sexual morality; indeed it was no doubt precisely this tighter ethical discipline which had previously helped attract many of them to the synagogue in the first place. But the effect of Paul's argument at this point in the context of his whole letter should not be ignored. For it is designed not merely to placard pagan perversion, but to draw his listeners in their reaction against that perversion within the circle of the moral standards which had always marked Israel off from the surrounding nations. That Paul simply takes it for granted that the Jewish abhorrence of Gentile sexual license is still the appropriate ethical response of the Gentile believer in Christ means that he recognizes at least one distinctive element of Israel's covenant righteousness which remains unchanged within the wider freedom of the new covenant.

28 For one last time, lest there should remain any doubt, Paul emphasizes the direct link between humankind's rejection of God and its disordered state.

It all stems from the basic refusal to recognize God. The first clause brings out the character of this refusal as a deliberate act of human pride and self-sufficiency: they considered whether God should be retained as a factor of importance within their fuller reflective knowledge and decided against it; they tested the worth of acknowledging God and found him wanting. And once again, as in v 22, the consequence is phrased in a biting epigram: God handed them over to a disqualified mind. The test they thought they were applying to the knowledge of God was actually a test of their own understanding. The judgment they cast against God condemned themselves and condemned themselves to themselves. In claiming the ability to evaluate God they simply proved the unfitness of their own rational powers. And so God handed them over to the maturity they claimed—the maturity which only the immature would be bold enough to claim in the first place.

The use of the same phrase, "God handed them over," for yet a third time is somber and sobering in its effect. Just as the thrice repeated "they changed" underscores humankind's responsibility for the state of affairs they find themselves in, man's own choice to be free of God is at the root of all evil. So the thrice repeated "God handed them over" underscores the point that in striking free of God's immediate control, man has not escaped God's overall ordering of his creation. He has certainly not escaped into godlike independence, but neither has he left himself prey to an impersonal and arbitrary fate. The simple fact is that man cannot escape his own nature and the nature of the world as God made it. It is God who has handed man over to his desires and the endless pursuit of their satisfaction; man's freedom to go his own way still leaves him within the limits set by God. The believer then should not be depressed at the disorder of society and the evidence of man's degradation; it actually constitutes evidence of God's overall control. Man is still the creature whom God made, and even when he refuses to recognize God his essentially creaturely instincts and their outworkings nevertheless bear witness to the Creator his conscious mind denies. In short, human fallenness is an ellipse caught by the twin foci of man's freely chosen willfulness and God's ordering of his creation. And thus it becomes clearer that God's wrath is indeed the converse of his righteousness, since both express and bring to effect the world as God intends it to be: righteousness through faithful dependence on the Creator leads to salvation; wrath through self-deceitful pride and self-indulgent desire leads to self-destruction.

29–31 The expression and outworking of the "disqualified mind" is a catalog of vice which would be familiar to the addressees as a type. No doubt deliberately, Paul again alludes to established Stoic terminology ("what is improper") to describe the sort of antisocial attitude and behavior which thoughtful people generally would condemn. No real attempt is made to put the list in any particular order; it floods out in something of a jumble. Some of the words are clearly prompted by association of ideas ("rumor-mongers, gossips, slanderers," "insolent, arrogant, boastful"), others by association of sounds ("envy, murder," "foolish, faithless"). So obviously Paul has no intention of focusing on any particular sin or on any particular kind of sin; his object is simply to give an impression of the whole range of attitude and conduct which all fair-minded people would count as unacceptable. These too are all the direct consequence of man's basic failure to acknowledge God. It is not simply sexual irregularity which marks man's breakaway from God. The climax of Paul's analysis of man's fall and its consequences, if climax it be, is a picture of the general disorder of human society. The daily envy, deceit, whispering behind backs, heartlessness, ruthlessness, and so on, manifest human corruption quite as much, if not more than homosexual acts. Such homely, everyday vices which poison human relationships are as much a sign of man's loss of God as any sexual perversion.

32 Paul refuses to accept that people generally are not aware of the negative character and ultimately destructive effect of such conduct. The Stoic recognition that such things are "not fitting, improper" shows this. But as Paul draws the first stage of his argument to a close it is the Adam background which shines through most clearly once again. Adam/man knew God's warning ("In the day you eat of it you shall die" [Gen 2:16]), and yet went ahead and ate. In this way Paul interprets the less specifically theistic "good sense" of Stoicism in terms of Jewish monotheism. The Stoic recognition of what is proper, in accord with good order, constitutes evidence for Paul that man generally (not just the Jew) knows what is right, knows it in fact (or in effect) to be the requirement of God, and knows that to flout it is to court death, a death justly deserved.

It is this character of so much of man's social relations, as deliberate rejection of what is known to be best, as willful rebellion against God's ordering of things, which Paul reemphasizes with one final flourish. "They not only do such things but give their approval to those who do so too." Their rejection of God is not merely a spur of the moment, heat of the instant flouting of his authority, but a considered and measured act of defiance. This is an important insight into one aspect of human sinfulness—its character of rebellion against what is known to be right (or best), its act of defiance in the face of known and perilous consequences of the act, its seemingly heroic "I/we will do what I/we will do and damn the outcome!" The miserable list of antisocial behavior (vv 29–31) illustrates just what human wisdom in its vaunted independence from God ends up justifying to itself (it would not be difficult to extend the list with twentieth-century examples). It is such self-delusion which lies at the heart of so much human conduct. And precisely because it is self-delusion, a self-destructive and society-destructive delusion, Paul attacks it so fiercely as the opening argument of his broader indictment.

B. God's Wrath—on Jew First As Well As Gentile (2:1–3:8)

Introduction

The exposition of 2:1–29 can be characterized as a kind of spiral argument, structurally parallel in fact to the spiral of sin and sinning described in 1:18–32. Here the spiral consists of the increasing specificity of the Jewish identity of the viewpoint rebutted. In vv 1–11 the indictment is posed in general terms which would command widespread assent (from both Jew and Gentile); vv 12–16 introduce the key criterion of the law; and in vv 17–29 the indictment becomes specific, though in fact it is simply the specific application to Jewish presumption of the more generally worded indictment of vv 1–11 (equally characterized by personal address to an imagined interlocutor). 3:1–8 provide a link to the concluding overall indictment and give a first indication of issues which will loom large in the later discussion. The connecting thread is judgment, which binds 2:1–3:8 into a unity (2:1–3, 5, 12, 16, 27; 3:4, 6–8), with ἀδικία (1:18, 29; 2:8; 3:5) and ἀλήθεια (1:18, 25; 2:2, 8, 20; 3:4, 7) providing the link with the preceding section.

Failure to recognize the specific diatribal objective of deflating Jewish presumption (that Israel's being the people of the law indicates God's predisposition in Israel's favor) is the root of the confusion among commentators over the purpose and theology of chap. 2, including vv 12–13 (most recently Sanders, *Law*, 123–35, and Räisänen, *Law*, 101–9; O'Neill's decision to excise the whole of 1:18–2:29 is still less warranted). Paul's point is that the law must be allowed its function as a *universal* standard set by God, and not be reduced to the level of an identity marker which distinguishes Jew from Gentile or be characterized too superficially by a rite like circumcision which separates the Jewish "us" from the Gentile "them."

1. The Impartiality of God   (2:1–11)

Bibliography

Bassler, J. M. *Impartiality.* ———. "Divine Impartiality in Paul's Letter to the Romans." *NovT* 26 (1984) 43–58. Dabelstein, R. *Beurteilung.* 64–73, 86–97. Daxer, H. *Römer 1:18–2:10.* 59–87. Filson, F. V. *St Paul's Conception of Recompense.* Leipzig: Hinrichs, 1931. Grobel, K. "A Chiastic Retribution-Formula in Romans." In *Zeit und Geschichte,* FS R. Bultmann, ed. E. Dinkler. Tübingen: Mohr, 1964. 255–61. Hanson, A. T. *Wrath.* 85–88. Heiligenthal, R. *Werke,* 165–97. Mattern, L. *Verständnis.* 123–40. Pregeant, R. "Grace and Recompense: Reflections on a Pauline Paradox." *JAAR* 47 (1979) 73–96. Roetzel, C. J. *Judgment in the Community.* Leiden: Brill, 1972, esp. 79–83. Schlier, H. "Röm 2:1–29." Siotis, M. A. "La 'ΧΡΗΣΤΟΤΗΣ' de Dieu selon l'Apôtre Paul." In *Paul de Tarse: apôtre du notre temps,* ed. L. de Lorenzi. Rome: Abbaye de S. Paul, 1979. 201–32. Stendahl, K. "Rechtfertigung und Endgericht." *LR* 11 (1961) 3–10. Stowers, S. K. *Diatribe.* 93–96, 100–112. Synofzik, E. *Vergeltungsaussagen.* 78–90. Travis, S. H. *Judgment.* 58–64. Watson, N. M. "Justified by Faith, Judged by Works—An Antinomy." *NTS* 29 (1983) 209–21.

Translation

¹*For this reason you are without excuse, you sir, each one of you who passes judgment. For in that you pass judgment on the other you condemn yourself; for you practice the very things on which you pass judgment.*ᵃ ²*And*ᵇ *we know that the condemnation of God is in accordance with truth against those who practice*

such things. ³*Do you suppose then, you sir, you who pass judgment on those who practice such things and do the same, that you will escape the condemnation of God?* ⁴*Or do you think lightly of the wealth of his goodness and of his forbearance and patience, disregarding the fact that the kindness of God is to lead you to repentance?* ⁵*As a result of your hardness and impenitent heart you are storing up for yourself wrath in the day of wrath when will be revealed the righteous judgment of God,* ⁶*"who will render to each in accordance with his works."* ⁷*To those who seek for glory and honor and immortality by perseverance in doing good, eternal life.* ⁸*But to those who out of selfish ambition also disobey the truth, being persuaded to unrighteousness, wrath and anger.* ⁹*Affliction and distress on every living person who brings about what is evil, Jew first and Gentile as well.* ¹⁰*But glory and honor and peace to everyone who brings about what is good, Jew first and Gentile as well.* ¹¹*For there is no partiality with God.*

Notes

a Bultmann's suggestion that v 1 is an early marginal gloss which was originally intended to draw an appropriate conclusion from v 3 ("Glossen," 281; followed by Käsemann) is unnecessary. Paul's style is hardly so polished that some awkwardness in syntax can be regarded as un-Pauline (Schmithals, *Römerbrief,* 204, offers the unnecessarily complicated suggestion that v 1 may be "a Pauline explanation of the unsatisfactory new start in 2:3, written in the margin of the letter and wrongly inserted in a copy"). V 1 answers to 1:20 in the lively style of personal address (diatribe) which Paul here adopts.

b Some MSS (including ℵ C) read γάρ instead of δέ, the result of a scribe's failing to realize that v 2 is not intended as a reason for the insertion of v 1, but is intended as a further consideration.

Form and Structure

In vigorous diatribe style Paul turns on a fellow student of human degeneracy who evidently counts the preceding indictment as his own. Who this interlocutor may be is not specified at first, and Paul takes care to frame his proposition about God's impartiality (vv 1–11) in terms general enough ("the good," "the evil") to command wide assent. At the same time it is evident from the Jewish perspective of 1:19–32 that the interlocutor is envisaged as a Jew (e.g., Lagrange; Feuillet, "Plan," 347; Bornkamm, "Revelation," 59; Murray; Eichholz, *Theologie,* 81–85; Cranfield; Maillot; against Leenhardt; Boers, "Problem," 6; Stowers, *Diatribe,* 112; Gaston, *Paul,* 120), and the centrality in the argument (v 6) of the established Jewish principle of the evenhandedness of divine retribution (Ps 62:12; Prov 24:12) is calculated to win specifically Jewish assent (cf. Bassler). More subtly, the echo of Wisd Sol 15:1 ff. in v 4 seems designed to undermine any Jewish assumption that God's people are free of the grosser gentile sins and that any Jewish sin is insufficient to disturb Israel's favored status as the people chosen by God.

Indicative of Paul's rhetorical skill is the diatribe style (Stowers, *Diatribe,* 93–96), with its repeated personal address to a single individual in vv 1–5, and the ABBA structure of vv 7–10 (Jeremias, "Chiasmus," 282; Grobel's suggestion of a larger chiasm, vv 6–11, becomes less persuasive with its greater complexity). Bassler, "Romans," justifiably emphasizes the pivotal role of v 11 in the whole argument, but her own claim that 2:11 closes the unit 1:16–

2:11 (*Divine Impartiality*, 121–37) makes too much of a break in the developing indictment of chap. 2 itself. She does also demonstrate that v 11 serves as the thematic introduction to vv 12–29 (*Impartiality*, 137, 152), but the lack of clear identification of the one indicted in vv 1–11 suggests that it would be better to see 2:1–11 as an overlapping section binding the two more specific indictments of 1:18–32 and 2:12–3:8 together.

Comment

2:1 διὸ ἀναπολόγητος εἶ, ὦ ἄνθρωπε πᾶς ὁ κρίνων, "therefore you are without excuse, you sir, whoever you are who acts as judge." διό usually denotes an inference or conclusion drawn from what went before: "therefore, for this reason," as elsewhere in Romans (1:24; 4:22; 13:5; though 15:7 and 22 show that the connection with the preceding context can be looser); see also Bassler, *Divine Impartiality*, 131–34. The connection here depends on recognition of the diatribe style adopted by Paul. The unexpected conclusion takes the form of a challenge to anyone who thought himself exempt from the preceding indictment, with something of the force of Nathan's conclusion to David: "You are the man" (2 Sam 12:7: SH; Wilckens, 1:116, 124). The repetition of ἀναπολόγητος, "without excuse," which is not a word commonly used by Paul (only here and in 1:20 in the NT), confirms that Paul is drawing out an inference from the preceding indictment where human inexcusability was stressed (1:20).

With εἶ, ὦ ἄνθρωπε, "you sir," Paul deliberately adopts the haranguing style of the popular preacher (so also 2:3; cf. 9:20; for examples of the reproachful vocative in rhetorical address see BGD, ἄνθρωπος 1αγ, and Stowers, *Diatribe*, 85–93; used also by James 2:20). Perhaps he is here following a line of argument which had already taken shape in preaching and debating in the synagogue and marketplace (Barrett). The imaginary interlocutor is envisaged not as objecting to what Paul had said but as agreeing with it very strongly.

ὁ κρίνων, "you who judge." κρίνω appears throughout the chapter (8 times), always in the typical judicial sense, "judge, pass judgment on" (see also on 2:12). Possibly in view here is the sophisticated Greek like Juvenal, *Sat.* 15.1 ff., who could mock the animal idols of the Egyptians as heartily as the Jews (1:23); or the Stoic who would agree that such vices as those listed in 1:29–31 were "unfitting" (cf. Bruce; Stowers draws attention to the philosophical treatment of the theme of inconsistency—in particular, Epictetus, *Diss.* 2.21.11–12 and 3.2.14–16 providing a good parallel—*Diatribe*, 103–4). But the degree to which 1:18–32 echoes Hellenistic Jewish polemic against idolatry and its outworkings confirms that it is probably a Jewish interlocutor whom Paul has primarily in mind (so most commentators today); though at this stage the discussion relates more to a difference determined by response to what is known of God, which to some extent cuts across the more clear-cut ethnically determined Jew/Gentile distinction (cf. Dabelstein, 64–73, 87). As an example of the attitude attacked here Schlier appropriately cites *4 Ezra* 3.32–36; see also on 14:3. The contrast between human and divine judgment becomes a key theme in the remainder of the indictment (2:1–3, 12, 16, 27;

3:4, 6–8). The idea of "measure for measure" was probably already an old one at this time (cf. Mark 4:24 pars. with *m. Sota* 1.7), but the particular expression of it in terms of the one who judges being condemned by his own judgment is too similar to Matt 7:1–2 to be accidental; that is to say, Paul's formulation probably shows the influence of (or interaction with) the Jesus tradition at this point (see further on 12:14).

ἐν ᾧ κρίνεις τὸν ἕτερον, "in that you judge the other," not ἐν τῷ κρίνειν, "in and by the act of judgment."

σεαυτὸν κατακρίνεις, "you condemn yourself." κατά—"against"; κρίνω—"judge"; so κατακρίνω—"condemn." The word is infrequent in Paul (in Romans see 8:3, 34 and 14:23; otherwise only in 1 Cor 11:32).

τὰ . . . αὐτὰ πράσσεις, "you practice the same things." The close echo of 1:32 implies that the τὰ αὐτά Paul particularly has in mind are the sort of things listed in 1:29–31. A line of argument which accused Jews of idolatry and homosexual practice would be unlikely to commend much support, either from the judgmental Jew or from the God-worshiping Gentile who had previously been attracted to Judaism, particularly because of the sublimity of its idea of God and of its high moral standards. But the list of 1:29–31 largely consists of vices into which an individual can slide without being fully aware of it. In particular, the last five items are applicable to the sort of attitude among the Pharisees already criticized within the Jesus tradition (Mark 7:9–13; cf. also Mark 7:21–22 with Rom 1:29–31). The prominence given in that list to sins of pride and presumption (ὑβριστάς, ὑπερηφάνους, ἀλαζόνας) may well already have had the Jewish interlocutor in mind, since it is precisely Jewish presumption regarding their favored status as the people of God which underlay so much Jewish disparagement of Gentile religion; that Paul here makes use of a more widely attested diatribal style (Stowers, *Diatribe*, 108–110) does not detract from this suggestion. Paul himself had certainly been a victim of whispered slander within the Jewish communities of the diaspora (cf. 3:8).

2 οἴδαμεν δὲ ὅτι τὸ κρίμα τοῦ θεοῦ ἐστιν κατὰ ἀλήθειαν ἐπὶ τοὺς τὰ τοιαῦτα πράσσοντας, "and we know that the judgment of God is in accordance with truth on those who practice such things." οἴδαμεν ὅτι, "we know that," is a frequently used formula to introduce a fact which is generally accepted, not least in Romans (3:19; 7:14; 8:22, 28). κρίμα, "judgment," or more specifically, "judicial verdict" in an unfavorable sense, "condemnation" (*TDNT* 3:942; see also on 3:8 and 11:33). The appeal to the idea of divine judgment ("the judgment of God") would indeed meet with general acceptance: it was familiar in Greek thought, but particularly prominent in the Jewish tradition (e.g., Isa 13:6–16; 34:8; Dan 7:9–11; Joel 2:1–2; Zeph 1:14–2:3; 3:8; Mal 4:1; *Jub.* 5.10–16; *1 Enoch* 90.20–27; see further *TDNT* 3:933–35); and the mixed congregations at Rome would certainly assent readily to Paul's assertion.

κατὰ ἀλήθειαν, "according to truth." Note the reappearance of one of the letter's key linking motifs—God's ἀλήθεια (see *Introduction* §4.2.2 and on 1:18). The phrase could have a depth of meaning: "rightly" (BGD), or "in terms of the real state of affairs"; but also, and more likely in view of its thematic importance, "in terms of God's reliability" (cf. 1QS 4.19–20; CD 20.30; *4*

Ezra 7.34; *2 Apoc. Bar.* 85.9; *m.* ʿ*Abot* 3.16 as given in Str-B, 3:76; other references in Schlier). In expressing himself thus Paul may well be "playing his imagined opponent along," since a pious Jew would readily think of God's judgment "according to truth" as judgment in which God displayed his choice of and commitment to Israel. It is precisely this presupposition of divine bias towards Israel which in Paul's eyes becomes the excuse and cloak for practices among Jews which they would condemn in Gentile society (2:17–24).

3 λογίζῃ δὲ τοῦτο, ὦ ἄνθρωπε ὁ κρίνων τοὺς τὰ τοιαῦτα πράσσοντας καὶ ποιῶν αὐτά, ὅτι σὺ ἐκφεύξῃ τὸ κρίμα τοῦ θεοῦ;, "Do you suppose then, you, sir, who pass judgment on those who practice such things and do the same, that you will escape the judgment of God?" λογίζῃ, "do you think, entertain the opinion, suppose?"—the first appearance of an important word, particularly in chap. 4 (2:26; 3:28; 11 times in chap. 4; 6:11; 8:18, 36; 9:8; 14:14; see on 3:28); but also used in diatribe (Stowers, *Diatribe,* 229, n.67). There may be some distinction between πράσσειν ("practice") and ποιεῖν ("do") in this section (1:32–2:3) which comes to a small climax here, πράσσειν having a more general sense and ποιεῖν denoting a more deliberate act (*TDNT* 6:636); cf. 7:19 and 9:11. The σύ is emphatic. For κρίμα see on 2:2.

There is a striking parallel between this verse and *Pss. Sol.* 15.8.

Pss. Sol.	καὶ οὐκ ἐκφεύξονται οἱ ποιοῦντες ἀνομίαν τὸ κρίμα κυρίου
Rom	καὶ ποιῶν αὐτά, ὅτι σὺ ἐκφεύξῃ τὸ κρίμα τοῦ θεοῦ;
Pss. Sol.	And those who do lawlessness shall not escape the judgment of the Lord.
Rom	(Do you suppose you) who do the same things that you shall escape the judgment of God?

The attitude that Paul hits out against is just that expressed in *Psalms of Solomon* and in almost the precise words used by Paul. The implication, which comes to clear expression in *Psalms of Solomon,* is that the law was a critical factor in Jewish "judging" of the Gentiles; but Paul implies also that Jewish pride in the law (2:17–20) obscured the degree to which Jews themselves failed to "do" the law (2:21–29). Not surprisingly, the law soon enters the discussion and becomes the dominant factor (2:12 ff.), confirming that it lies in the back of Paul's mind here. But at this point he keeps the indictment open and of more general application. Cf. the critique in Matt 3:8–9 and Justin, *Dial.* 140.

4 ἢ τοῦ πλούτου τῆς χρηστότητος αὐτοῦ καὶ τῆς ἀνοχῆς καὶ τῆς μακροθυμίας καταφρονεῖς, ἀγνοῶν ὅτι τὸ χρηστὸν τοῦ θεοῦ εἰς μετάνοιάν σε ἄγει, "or do you think lightly of the wealth of his goodness and of his forbearance and patience, disregarding the fact that the kindness of God leads you to repentance?" That Paul has in mind a *Jewish* interlocutor is confirmed by several factors. (1) He uses here a sequence of terms which he uses little elsewhere (ἀνοχή, "forbearance" = delay of wrath, only here and 3:26 in the NT), but several of which reappear in chaps. 9–11: πλοῦτος ("wealth")—9:23; (10:12); 11:12, 33 (see further on 11:12); χρηστότης ("goodness")—three times in 11:22; μακροθυμία ("patience")—9:22. The implication is that Paul's thought is moving within the same circle of reflection in both cases.

(2) τὸ χρηστόν ("kindness") and χρηστότης ("goodness") in Greek thought
are only attributed to the gods in exceptional cases, whereas in the Jewish
scriptures, particularly in the Psalms, the praise of God for his goodness
and mercy is typical (Pss 25:7; 69:16; 86:5; 100:5; 106:1; 109:21; 136:1;
145:8–9). "When in ἔλεος (mercy) God acts with faithfulness to his covenant
promises and to his own nature as the covenant God he shows himself to be
χρηστός thereby" (TDNT 9:485–86). For χρηστότης see Siotis, 217–20. On
God's μακροθυμία in Jewish thought see Str-B, 3:77–78; Zeller notes the emphasis particularly of Sir 5:4–7 and Philo, Leg. All. 3.106, on God's giving time
for repentance; see further on 9:15 and 9:22.

(3) μετάνοια, "repentance," is a concept not prominent but well enough
known in Greek, not least in Stoic thought, though in the less weighty sense
of "change of mind," or, more commonly, "remorse" (TDNT 4:978–79; BGD).
In the earliest Christian tradition, however, it is the more pregnant sense of
"conversion" which dominates, with the verb μετανοέω, "repent, convert,"
being used as the equivalent of the Hebrew שׁוּב, "turn back, return." Paul's
use here is notable for two reasons. (a) Repentance held a very important
place within Jewish teaching on salvation. It was a fundamental tenet for
the pious Jew of Paul's time that God had provided a way of dealing with
sin for his covenant people through repentance and atonement (e.g., Lev
4–5 with the repeated refrain, "and he shall be forgiven"—4:20, 26, 31, 35,
etc.; Ps 116; Isa 1:27; Jer 3:12–14, 22; Sir 17:24–26; Jub. 5.17–18; Pss. Sol.
9; T. Gad 5.3–8; see further TDNT 4:991–92, 995–99, and Sanders, Paul,
index, particularly 157). Paul thus seems here to turn one of the Jewish
interlocutor's own key beliefs against him. Somewhat similar is the warning
of Sir 5:4–7 (Zeller). (b) Although common enough as an important element
in the preaching and teaching of John the Baptist (Matt 3:2, 8, 11; Mark
1:4) and of Jesus (Matt 11:20-21; 12:41; Mark 1:15; etc.), as of the first
disciples (Mark 6:12; Acts 2:38; 3:19; etc.), the concept of "repentance" appears
in only two other passages in the undisputed Paulines (2 Cor 7:9–10; 12:21;
cf. 2 Tim 2:25; and nowhere in the Gospel or Epistles of John!). Its strongly
Jewish and covenant character might provide the reason here too: "repentance" as a concept was too much bound up with the accepted understanding
of God's covenant goodness, so that Paul prefers the more widely embracing
concept of "faith" as one through which he can develop his (Christian) reinterpretation of the covenant more readily (see on 1:17). Hence it is the more
"Jewish" language of goodness and repentance (χρηστότης, μετάνοια) which
Paul uses here rather than the more distinctively "Christian" language of
grace (see on 1:5) and faith (χάρις, πίστις); see also on 4:7–8.

(4) Equally striking is the way once again Paul seems to have in mind the
language and standpoint of the Wisdom of Solomon as an expression of
Jewish, and not least of diaspora Jewish piety. Typical of Wisdom of Solomon
is the confident assumption that God's mercy is upon his elect (3:9; 4:15),
with a clear distinction drawn between God's mercy to his own (even when
disciplining them) and his wrathful judgment on the ungodly (3:10; 11:9-
10; 12:22; 16:9–10), and with repentance seen as something which the Gentiles
need to be granted more than Israel (11:23—εἰς μετάνοιαν; 12:8–11, 19–22).
The particular passage which Paul may well have in mind is Wisd Sol 15:1 ff.:

But you, our God, are kind and true [χρηστὸς καὶ ἀληθής],
patient [μακρόθυμος] and in mercy governing all things.
² For even if we sin, we are yours, knowing your power;
but we will not sin, knowing that we are reckoned [λελογίσμεθα] yours.
³ For to know you is complete righteousness [δικαιοσύνη],
and to know your power [cf. Rom 1:19–20] is the root of immortality.
⁴ For neither has the evil intent of human art misled (ἐπλάνησεν) us,
nor the fruitless toil of painters . . . [with the polemic against idolatry being
taken up again by way of disavowal].

We will not go far wrong if we assume that it was the attitude expressed
particularly in Wisd Sol 15:1–6 which Paul "heard" being expressed by his
Jewish interlocutor and as requiring the strong response of v 4 (see also
especially Nygren).

For use of ἤ in diatribe see Stowers, *Diatribe*, 229 n.69. In the first clause
the force of καταφρονέω should not be exaggerated: "despise, show contempt
for" (NIV), though appropriate in Paul's only other use (1 Cor 11:22; cf. 1
Tim 4:12), is too strong here. The interlocutor's mistake is that he "has the
wrong idea, thinks too lightly about" God's goodness (BGD; cf. 1 Tim 6:2).
Cf. *2 Apoc. Bar.* 21.20 which refers to those who think God's long-suffering
means weakness.

In the second clause the σέ of individual address, which Paul uses only
rarely, gives deliberate emphasis, as in 2:27 and 11:22, and as the σύ in 2:3.
The interlocutor of typical Jewish piety knows well about the importance of
repentance within the divine-human relationship, but is unaware, does not
understand, that he stands in the same need of repentance as the Gentiles
(cf. particularly 10:3). εἰς μετάνοιαν ἄγει: the thought is more of giving opportunity for repentance (as in Wisd Sol 11:23; 12:10; cf. *Ap. Const.* 7.35.1) than
of giving repentance itself (as in Wisd Sol 12:19). Cf. the somewhat similar
warning of Sir 5:4–7.

5 κατὰ δὲ τὴν σκληρότητά σου καὶ ἀμετανόητον καρδίαν θησαυρίζεις σεαυτῷ
ὀργὴν ἐν ἡμέρᾳ ὀργῆς καὶ ἀποκαλύψεως δικαιοκρισίας τοῦ θεοῦ, "in accordance
with your hardness and impenitent heart you are storing up for yourself
wrath in the day of wrath and of the revelation of the righteous judgment
of God." The verse contains a surprising number of *hapax legomena* (σκληρότης,
ἀμετανόητος, and δικαιοκρισία) all occurring only here in the NT, which strongly
suggests that Paul is striving to find words which will maximize the impact
of what he is saying and not be shrugged off as merely formulaic or commonplace.

σκληρότης, "hardness, stubbornness," is used only four times in the LXX
(most relevantly in Deut 9:27). But Paul is clearly evoking the fuller concept
σκληροκαρδία, "hardness of heart, obstinacy," and giving it greater force by
inserting (perhaps formulating for himself) the hardly known word
ἀμετανόητος, "impenitent" (cf. *T. Gad* 7.5). The danger of the "hardened
heart" is one which keeps recurring in Jewish thought (Jer 4:4; Ezek 3:7;
Sir 16:10; *1 Enoch* 16.3; *T. Sim.* 6.2; Philo, *Spec. Leg.* 1.305; Qumran references
in Michel, 114 n.10), passages which all hark back in one degree or other to
the initial warning of Deut 10:16. Paul clearly aligns himself with this series

of warnings, with 2:29 echoing in climactic manner the call of Deuteronomy and Jeremiah for the *heart* to be circumcised. The inference Paul obviously intends the careful listener to draw is that there is a dimension of the whole legal relationship with God which his Jewish interlocutor fails to appreciate (as Deut 10:16 warned) and that the judgmental pose towards Gentile vices, with its readiness to discount the equivalent failings of the pious of Israel, simply shows that the danger of the hardened heart has been succumbed to.

For κατά meaning "as a result of" see BGD, κατά 5αδ. θησαυρίζεις σεαυτῷ ὀργήν, "you are storing up wrath for yourself," is a transformation of the idea of laying up treasure in heaven, which seems to have been particularly Jewish in character. We may not assume that a concept of a heavenly "treasury of merits" was already developed within Judaism (Sanders, *Paul*, 183–98). But certainly the idea was already current that faithfulness to covenant obligations provided a sort of heavenly bank account for the individual himself. Tob 4:9–10 provides a rather striking parallel which Paul might even be echoing: ἀγαθὸν θησαυρίζεις σεαυτῷ εἰς ἡμέραν ἀνάγκης, "you are storing up good for yourself for the day of distress" (ἀνάγκη having its eschatological force as in Zeph 1:15 and Luke 21:23). And *Pss. Sol.* 9.3–5 climaxes talk of the righteous deeds and works of the pious (αἱ δικαιοσύναι τῶν ὁσίων . . . τὰ ἔργα ἡμῶν) with the line ὁ ποιῶν δικαιοσύνην θησαυρίζει ζωὴν αὑτῷ παρὰ κυρίῳ, "he who does righteousness stores up life for himself with the Lord." The more explicit talk of a "treasury of works," which we find in 4 *Ezra* 6.5; 7.77; 8.33, 36 and 2 *Apoc. Bar.* 14.12 (cf. 24.1), may already have been current at the time of Paul, but it cannot be taken for granted (see also on 4:4–5 and 11:28). At all events, it is this line of thought which Paul here turns on its head: the pious interlocutor assumes that by his faithfulness to the covenant he is laying up treasure in heaven; but by his failure to recognize the need for a more radical repentance he is actually storing up not "good," not "life," but wrath.

ἐν ἡμέρᾳ ὀργῆς καὶ ἀποκαλύψεως δικαιοκρισίας τοῦ θεοῦ, "in the day of wrath and of the revelation of the righteous judgment of God." For ὀργή see on 1:18. The last day as a "day of wrath" is a particular emphasis of Zephaniah (Zeph 1:15, 18; 2:2–3; cf. 3:8; other references in SH and Str-B, 4:1093–1118; in Paul cf. 2:16; 1 Cor 1:8; 5:5; Phil 1:6, 10; 2:16; 1 Thess 5:2, 4). For "wrath" as Paul's description of God's final judgment on human rebellion see 2:8; 3:5; 5:9; 9:22; 1 Thess 1:10; 5:9. ἀποκάλυψις, "revelation," is used here with full eschatological flavor (see on 1:17); only in the end will it become fully clear that the human condition (of 1:18–2:5) is the outworking of God's wrath (cf. Knox). δικαιοκρισία, "righteous judgment," has the same reference to the day of God's final judgment as unfavorable as in *T. Levi* 3.2 and 15.2 (see also on 2:2). The phrase confirms that wrath can be seen also as an expression of God's righteousness as Creator (see Käsemann and above on 1:17 and 1:18). Wilckens points out that there is probably a polemical note here too, since for the pious Jew God's "righteous judgment" is usually understood as taking place for the benefit of his chosen ones (cf. particularly 1QM 18.7–8; *Sib. Or.* 3.702–9). Once again, then, Paul turns a concept of covenant confidence against that confidence itself.

6 ὃς ἀποδώσει ἑκάστῳ κατὰ τὰ ἔργα αὐτοῦ, "who will render to each according to his works." This is intended as a direct quotation of an established principle of Jewish faith, with the formulation of Ps 62:12 (LXX 61:13) and Prov 24:12 at the forefront of Paul's mind:

Psalms	σὺ ἀποδώσεις	
Proverbs	ὃς ἀποδίδωσιν	ἑκάστῳ κατὰ τὰ ἔργα αὐτοῦ.
Romans	ὃς ἀποδώσει	

but see also Job 34:11; Jer 17:10; Hos 12:2; Sir 16:12–14; *1 Enoch* 100.7; *Jos. Asen.* 28.3; Ps-Philo, *Lib. Ant.* 3.10. It is important to note that the principle is embraced no less by the first Christians (cf. Matt 16:27; 2 Cor 5:10; Col 3:25; 2 Tim 4:14; 1 Pet 1:17; Rev 2:23; etc.; see further Heiligenthal, 172–75). As such it provides an interesting example of how the same principle could be read differently within a different framework or pattern of religious thought. Paul's typical Jewish interlocutor would probably assume that in his own case the works in question were his faithful practice of his covenant obligations, including his acts of charity and his observance of the ritual law (cf. again Tob 4:9–11; *Pss. Sol.* 9.3–5)—precisely the presupposition which Paul wants to challenge in this chapter, whereas Paul would understand the principle in terms of what he would see and intend as the more universal and more fundamental "work" of trusting in God through Jesus Christ ("the obedience of faith"—1:5). In contrast, simply to deny that Paul demonstrates here "a rabbinic works theology" (as in Synozik, 81) is to miss the point and to force Paul's dialectic between grace and judgment into an antithesis which throws his theology into confusion (as the typical confusion regarding the function of chap. 2 within Paul's theology clearly shows).

7 τοῖς μὲν καθ᾽ ὑπομονὴν ἔργου ἀγαθοῦ δόξαν καὶ τιμὴν καὶ ἀφθαρσίαν ζητοῦσιν, ζωὴν αἰώνιον, "to those who, by perseverance in doing what is good, seek for glory and honor and immortality, eternal life." Paul here seems deliberately to choose language of broad appeal, particularly in describing the goal sought after. δόξα καὶ τιμή, "glory and honor," is familiar enough to Jewish ears as a description of what God desires for man (Job 40:10; Ps 8:5), or what man should ascribe to God (Pss 29:1; 96:7), but in Greek ears this conjunction would speak of the honor and high repute which properly accrues to the name of a good man (see LSJ in each case; BGD, τιμή 2b). ἀφθαρσία, "incorruption, immortality," is more Greek, in LXX occurring only in the Hellenistic Jewish writings Wisdom of Solomon and *4 Maccabees*: Wisd Sol 2:23 describes it as the end God had in view in creating man; and *4 Macc* 17.12 provides quite a close parallel in language to what Paul says here (cf. also 1 Cor 15:42, 50, 53–54; and also on 1:23). ζωὴ αἰώνιος, "eternal life," "life without end," is more Jewish, though it appears only in later Jewish writings (Dan 12:2; 2 Macc 7:9; *4 Macc* 15.3; 1QS 4.7), but would be readily comprehensible to Greeks (elsewhere in the Paulines—5:21; 6:22–23; Gal 6:8; 1 Tim 1:16; 6:12; Titus 1:2; 3:7; and in the rest of the NT—Mark 10:17 and 30 pars.; Luke 10:25; John 3:15–16, 36; etc.; Acts 13:46, 48; 1 John 1:2; 2:25, etc.; Jude 21).

The rest of the verse is also expressed in broad terms. The καθ᾽ ὑπομονὴν ἔργου ἀγαθοῦ can hardly be understood in anything other than its obvious sense: patient persistence in doing what is recognized to be good (Barrett's rendering is impossibly tortuous; equally questionable is Barth's narrowing the "good work" to that of repentance—[*Shorter*]). For ὑπομονή see further on 5:3–4, and for ἔργον see further on 13:12. The verb used (ζητεῖν, "seek") reinforces the ὑπομονή: what is in mind is a sustained and deliberate application (present participle), rather than a casual or spasmodic pursuit of the goal; see also on 10:3.

As in v 6, therefore, Paul expresses a broad principle which would gain wide acceptance among people with any degree of moral sensibility (see also on 1:28 and 12:17). Among Paul's typically devout Hellenistic Jewish contemporaries, however, it would probably be understood in more restrictive terms—as "the patience of the godly" (Sir 16:13; 17:24), as the persistence of covenant faithfulness (Sir 11:20); "giving heed to Wisdom's laws is assurance of immortality" (Wisd Sol 6:18–19). But Paul's object here is evidently to provide an expression of what we might call "natural justice"—the eschatological outworking of the earlier "natural theology" of chap. 1—the statement of a principle which anyone with a moral conception of God (or the good) would accept: the person who persists in doing good will receive honor. The implication once again is that Paul intends the formulation as a critique of the narrower Jewish view which discounts the good done outside the covenant just as it discounts the unrighteousness committed by those within the covenant.

We might add that Paul is here giving no hostages to fortune in promulgating a doctrine of judgment according to "good works." For as the indictment of 1:18 ff. implies, and as he will later make clearer in other terms (chaps. 6–8), such "patient persistence in good work" is possible only for those who recognize their creaturely dependence on God, and who live their lives out of a spirit of gratitude and worship; (in contesting *sola gratia* as "a deep misunderstanding of Paul," Watson, *Paul*, 120, ignores this fundamental feature in Paul's theology; see also 4:16–21 and 14:23). And that open and complete trust in God he finds only possible through Jesus Christ. But here it is the broadly stated principle which is in view—a principle all would accept, even if they fail to recognize that the ideal cannot be achieved apart from such faith. The underlying claim is that the narrower Jewish interpretation of the principle in fact fails to appreciate the breadth of its applicability, whereas his own is open to Jew and Gentile alike on the same terms (see also on 2:13 and 15). The problem which this verse has caused for the doctrine of "justification by faith" (which has exercised many commentators since the Reformation) only emerges when the passage is treated as an exercise in dogmatics; whereas when its more specific focus is thus recognized, the problem becomes much more manageable and indeed largely disappears (cf. Watson, *Paul*, 118–19).

8 τοῖς δὲ ἐξ ἐριθείας καὶ ἀπειθοῦσι τῇ ἀληθείᾳ, "but to those who, out of selfish ambition, also disobey the truth." The debate regarding the meaning of ἐριθεία, occasioned by its almost complete absence from pre-NT documentation (only in Aristotle, *Polit.*, 1302b:4 and 1303a:14, where it describes the self-seeking pursuit of public office by intrigue), has now reached a large measure of consensus, with the sense of "selfish" ambition being preferred

against that of "factious" ambition (dependent on a derivation from ἔρις, "strife, contention"—as still in RSV, Murray); see BGD, Cranfield. Cf. particularly Phil 2:3–4; elsewhere in Phil 1:17 and in the vice-catalogs of 2 Cor 12:20 and Gal 5:20. That the most Jewish writing of the NT also recognizes ἐριθεία, "selfishness, selfish ambition," as a danger is significant (James 3:14, 16); Rom 2:8 is not to be dismissed as the jaundiced view of a failed or renegade Pharisee.

ἀπειθοῦσι τῇ ἀληθείᾳ, "to those who disobey the truth." Once again the indictment is posed in general terms, echoing 1:18. But that Paul also has in mind his Jewish contemporaries in particular is confirmed from his description of them later (10:21; 11:31; 15:31; cf. Acts 14:2; 19:9; Heb 3:18; 4:6; 1 Pet 2:8). In the light of these later references "the truth" could be said to be specifically the gospel. But here Paul has not yet defined "the truth" so precisely. It is still the more broadly understood "truth of God," of God as Creator, of the creature's need to acknowledge dependence on him. Insofar as Israel has changed that truth into a presumption of God's reliability (= truth; see on 1:18) in treating Israel on different terms (and thus making more demands of the believing Gentile than God makes), they have "disobeyed the truth."

πειθομένοις δὲ τῇ ἀδικίᾳ, "persuaded to unrighteousness." Paul obviously chooses the verb to provide an antithesis with ἀπειθοῦσι. Even so the straightforward translation "obey" probably cloaks the force of πειθομένοις (the play on words in the Greek of course remains even if we fail to reflect it in English translation). The meaning of πείθω in the middle and passive moves out from the sense "be persuaded, be convinced, be won over" (LSJ, BGD). So here what Paul seems to have in mind is that situation in life where one principle is (reluctantly) allowed to give way in face of what is regarded as a higher principle, where for the sake of a purer end a baser means is (unwillingly) justified. Paul's formulation, in other words, is more sensitive to the moral ambiguities and possible compromises which inevitably confront even people of the most undiluted good will (whereas in 6:12, 16–17 and 10:16 he uses the less excusable ὑπακούω, "obey"). Nevertheless, his charge against his Jewish interlocutor (now broadened out into more generalized description) is that the typical Jewish understanding of Israel's special relation with God has become a justification for practices within the covenant people and for attitudes toward those without, which in fact constitute a breach of the more fundamental relation of man to God as creature to his Creator (ἀδικία—see on 1:18).

ὀργὴ καὶ θυμός, "wrath and anger." The two words are regularly associated in the LXX, usually in the form ὀργὴ θυμοῦ, but also as here with reference to divine anger (Deut 29:27; Ps 78 [LXX 77]:49; Sir 45:18; Jer 7:20; 21:5), though not usually with reference to final judgment (but cf. Isa 13:9; 30:30). See also Hanson, Wrath, 206–9, and for ὀργή see further on 1:18 and 2:5. Since the thought is clearly of God's wrath (as the OT association of the two words confirms), the θυμός underscores the personal and "deeply felt" indignation of God at injustice. There is little of the "impassibility of God" here.

9–10 Since the verses stand in close parallel it is easier to consider the corresponding elements in each in order.

θλῖψις καὶ στενοχωρία, "affliction and distress." As with the preceding phrase, these two words are also linked in the OT (in 5 out of the 6 uses of στενοχωρία)— Deut 28:53, 55, 57; Isa 8:22; 30:6. Judgment is depicted by evoking those experiences of life where outward circumstances put the individual under pressure and stress and cause personal distress; the stronger word is στενοχωρία = hemmed in with no way out (cf. particularly 8:35; 2 Cor 6:4; 12:10—the other occurrences of στενοχωρία in the NT, the first two also in association with θλῖψις; also 2 Cor 4:8). See also *TDNT* 7:607; and on 5:3.

δόξα . . . καὶ τιμὴ καὶ εἰρήνη, "glory and honor and peace." The thought is partly a repeat of v 7, with εἰρήνη, "peace," replacing ἀφθαρσία, "immortality." For δόξα καὶ τιμή see on 2:7; and for εἰρήνη see on 1:7. Again concepts more often applied to conditions of this life (see again on 2:7) are raised to an eschatological degree to describe the final state of the good individual.

ἐπὶ πᾶσαν ψυχὴν ἀνθρώπου, "on every single person," reflects the Semitic understanding of man as (not simply having) a soul (נֶפֶשׁ), as a living being (given life by God—Gen 2:7; 1 Cor 15:45; cf. also Acts 2:41, 43; 3:23; 7:14; 27:37; 1 Pet 3:20; *1 Clem.* 64; see BGD with bibliography, and on 13:1; against Lagrange). The parallel element in v 10 is simply παντί. In both cases the πᾶσαν and the παντί add emphasis, stressing the final phrase ("Jew first and also Greek").

τοῦ κατεργαζομένου τὸ κακόν / τῷ ἐργαζομένῳ τὸ ἀγαθόν, "who brings about what is evil / who brings about what is good." The two forms of ἐργάζεσθαι are simply stylistic variations, since both have the meaning "accomplish, do, bring about," the verbal equivalent to ἔργον (vv 6, 7). τὸ κακόν / τὸ ἀγαθόν, "the bad thing / the good thing." The use of the adjectives as substantives would be very familiar to Greek ears, including the antithesis between "the bad" and "the good," particularly to Stoics (*TDNT* 3:473; see also LSJ). But the contrast would be quite familiar to Jewish ears too (see particularly Deut 30:15; 1 Kgs 3:9; Job 2:10; Pss 34:14 [LXX 33:15]; 37[LXX 36]:27; Lam 3:38; Ep Jer 34; Sir 12:5; 13:25; 17:7; 18:8; 33:14; 37:18). In Romans Paul makes repeated use of the antithesis—3:8; 7:19, 21; 12:21; 13:3; 16:19; see also 1 Pet 3:11 (citing Ps 33:15 LXX [34:14]); 3 John 11.

Ἰουδαίου τε πρῶτον καὶ ῞Ελληνος // Ἰουδαίῳ τε πρῶτον καὶ ῞Ελληνι, "Jew first and also Greek"; see on 1:16. The underlying thrust of 2:1–11 now becomes explicit: the target is Jewish presumption of priority of privilege, which however soundly rooted in God's election of Israel—a fact which Paul does not dispute (1:16) and to which he will return (3:1–4; chaps. 9–11)— has led Paul's kinsfolk to the effective conclusion that God's judgment of Israel will be on different terms from his judgment of the nations as a whole (where v 7 can be safely applied to the devout Jew and v 8 to the uncovenanted Gentile). In reformulating vv 7–8 Paul insists that *both* verses apply equally to *both* Jew and Gentile. Paul's whole point here is that the terms of judgment are precisely the *same* for *everyone*.

11 οὐ γάρ ἐστιν προσωπολημψία παρὰ τῷ θεῷ, "for there is no partiality with God." προσωπολημψία may well be a Christian formulation since it first appears in the NT (Eph 6:9; Col 3:25; James 2:1; note also the cognates in James 2:9; 1 Pet 1:17; Acts 10:34 and the fuller idiom in Gal 2:6); though see *T. Job* 43:13 and cf. 4:8. At all events, the Greek is obviously modeled

on the Hebrew פָּנִים נָשָׂא = λαμβάνειν πρόσωπον. In the Middle East the respectful greeting of a superior would require the bowing of the head, if not complete prostration, and the "raising of the face" would be the sign of acceptance and welcome. From this derives the unfavorable meaning, whereby the acceptance and esteem expressed in "receiving the face" is unwarranted, an act of uncalled-for favor (i.e., favoritism). Judges in particular are warned against this (Lev 19:15; Deut 1:17; 16:19). And in Jewish thought God is presented consistently as the model of impartiality (Deut 10:17; 2 Chron 19:7; Sir 35:12–13; *Jub.* 5.16; 21.4; 30.16; 33.18; *Pss. Sol.* 2.18; *2 Apoc. Bar.* 13.8; 44.4; *1 Enoch* 63.8; Ps-Philo, *Lib. Ant.* 20.4; see further *TDNT* 6:779–80; *EWNT* 3:434; Bassler, *Divine Impartiality*). But whereas Deut 10:17 could be interpreted simply in terms of covenant obligations (Deut 10:18–19; likewise *Jub.* 5.17–18; 33.16–20), and *Pss. Sol.* 2.18 seems to be an expression of covenant confidence that God will not fail to recompense the nations for their despoiling of Jerusalem (cf. *Pss. Sol.* 4.9, 26–28; 8.25–32; 17.12; cf. also Str-B, 3:81–83), Paul extracts the theologoumenon from such a narrower context and turns it against such presumptive confidence, in much the same way as Acts 10:34, and with something of the force of a new realization or revelation which belongs to that passage. The critique of course is not new within Israel's prophetic tradition—implied in Deut 10:16, Jer 4:4 and explicit in Amos 9:7, but evidently too easily forgotten in the Maccabean and post-Maccabean period (cf. Matt 3:9 // Luke 3:8). The movement of thought from 2:5–11 is in effect Paul's elaboration of Deut 10:16–17.

Explanation

2:1–2 Paul now switches from third person plural to second person singular, swinging round, as it were, in good diatribe style, to confront an imaginary onlooker. Who is this hidden interlocutor who provides a foil for Paul's argument but seems to say nothing? The answer is not immediately obvious. Paul addresses him simply as "you who pass judgment on those who practice such things" (v 3). Presumably then his readers would imagine someone listening to the polemic of 1:18–32 and heartily joining in its condemnation of idolatry, homosexual practice, and the rest. Such a one would feel safe in passing judgment on "the other," either because he thought himself free of such vices, or because he thought the attack was directed against others and not himself. This silent onlooker is envisaged then as striking a judgmental pose either thoughtlessly or as one who presumes himself exempt from such criticism. Paul's rhetorical tactic is designed to expose the self-deceitfulness of such a pose.

Paul's denunciation is abrupt: "you do the same things." Paul could mean that the very attitude of passing judgment on others was in effect an attempt to usurp the role of the Creator and so improper to the creature. That is to say, "the same things" here would be the adoption of an attitude as much expressive of man's rebellion from God as any of the evils and improprieties itemized earlier. The reappearance of the word "truth" in v 2 somewhat strengthens this possibility, since the reminder that "the judgment *of God* is according to truth" could well be taken to imply in contrast that the judgment of the critical onlooker was *not* according to truth, was a misapprehension of God's truth (that only the Creator can deliver such a judgment), was in fact a form of suppressing the truth (1:18).

On the whole, however, Paul's formulation suggests rather that he had in mind someone who actually does at least some of "the same things" (vv 1, 3) or "such things" (vv 2, 3) as those listed in 1:29–31, but who needs to be reminded of it. That is to say, he seems to be aiming at an attitude that can condemn such things in others but somehow ignore or excuse them in oneself. The phrasing is so general as to include the sophisticated Stoic proud of his living in accord with reason: v 2 echoes 1:32 in drawing the Stoic recognition of "what is improper" under an explicitly theistic banner ("the judgment of God"); and Paul may still have in mind the defiant attitude of 1:32 which can condemn in general what it justifies for itself (the plea of "special circumstances" and worthy ends can be used to excuse all sorts of unsavory actions).

It is much more likely, however, that Paul's attack is aimed most directly at what he sees to be a typically Jewish attitude. Paul probably has in mind someone who would identify with his typically Jewish polemic against idolatry, who would applaud the typically Jewish condemnation of homosexual practice (1:23–27), and who consequently might miss the wider relevance of the final and broader list of anti-social vices. This indeed may help explain the order of the polemic in 1:18–32: having played to the gallery of Jewish assurance of moral superiority over the Gentile, he then broadened out his description of human corruption in order to provide a base for his attack on that very assurance. Hence also the appeal of 2:2: the "we" who know God's judgment are most obviously those familiar with the Jewish scriptures—that is, an imagined Jewish interlocutor, or indeed any among those listening to his letter who knew and approved the typically Jewish polemic of chap. 1, and who might not unnaturally assume that whoever Paul had been attacking, it was not them!

3–4 The impression that Paul has in mind a Jewish overconfidence in God's favor for and obligation to Israel is strengthened by vv 3–4 with their rather striking parallels in literature which was known to Paul and which expresses something of this assurance of a favored status based on and protected by God's election. In *Pss. Sol.* 15 the confident assurance of "the righteous" and "the devout" is also expressed not least in the contrasting affirmation, "they that do lawlessness shall not escape the judgment of God" (*Pss. Sol.* 15.8). To such an attitude Paul says in effect, "Do you think that because you are marked off from 'the lawless' and protected by the covenant that you can still do such things and yet escape God's judgment?" (v 3). In the Wisd Sol 15 a somewhat similar assurance of God's "kindness" and "patience" seems to make light of sin, not least because idolatry has been so completely avoided (vv 1–6). To such an attitude—and we have already seen how probable it is that Paul had Wisd Sol 11–15 in mind when he wrote chap. 1—Paul says in effect, "Such overconfidence is in fact a despising of the goodness and forbearance and patience of God of which you are so confident." Whereas Wisdom of Solomon can assume that God's mercy is on his elect (15:1–2) and that it is the nations who need to be given opportunity to repent (11:23), Paul says to such a Jew, "Do you not realize that the kindness of God seeks to lead you also to repentance" (v 4). All men need to repent—Jew first, as well as Gentile!

5–6 The echo in v 5 goes further back. Talk of "hardness (of heart)" cannot but be intended to recall Deut 10:16 and Jer 4:4 ("circumcise your hardened hearts"), especially when the contrast with the circumcised heart is already in view (2:29). Paul fills out this idea of the hardened heart warned against by Torah and prophet by relating it to the lack of repentance for which Jewish apologetic chided the Gentiles. He thus associates his own argument here with the prophetic warning from the earlier period of Israel's history: an attitude such as that in the Wisdom of Solomon, such as that of the interlocutor, manifests the very attitude against which Moses and Jeremiah warned, a faith which has not penetrated deeply enough, a false confidence resting too much on loyalty to the covenant understood too superficially. The very act of passing judgment on others presumes a favorable judgment of God on oneself, and so manifests an equal if not greater hardness of heart, an equal if not greater need to repent.

In all this it is very difficult to avoid the conclusion that Paul's aim is directed at what he sees to be the overconfidence in their election on the part of many of his fellow Jews. We of the twentieth century listening to this can point to other statements from the Judaism of the same period which express a greater humility and rejoice that opportunity for repentance and means of atonement are provided within the covenant. But we cannot assume that these writings are typical of the actual Judaism of Paul's time, any more than we can assume that Deuteronomy and Jeremiah are representative of the Israelite religion of their time. The passages from Jewish writings already adduced, when set alongside the attitude Paul attacks, provide sufficient evidence that Paul's interlocutor was no straw man. The dominant or at least a prominent mood within Judaism prior to A.D. 70 may well have been more buoyant and self-confident than that which the sayings and writings actually preserved from the period represent. Indeed we know from Phil 3:4–6 that such self-confidence had been typical of Paul himself in his days as a Pharisee before Christ, apparently oblivious of his own need of a fundamental repentance. In fact we would probably not be far from the mark if we were to conclude that Paul's interlocutor is Paul himself—Paul the unconverted Pharisee, expressing attitudes Paul remembered so well as having been his own!

To such a one Paul gives forthright warning of impending wrath. This wrath is not to be sharply distinguished from the wrath of 1:18: it is rather the outworking of the same divine retribution. The only difference is that the process of divine retribution is already in clear evidence among the Gentiles (1:18–32, particularly 18–27), whereas the too-confident Jew is simply storing it up for the future, for the day of final judgment. In that day such a one will be surprised to find that he has stored up not treasures of good (Tob 4:9–10), but treasures of divine wrath! The Scriptures (Prov 24:12; Ps 62:12) allow of no special cases: God will render what is due a man for his works—Jew as well as Greek. Such a word does not allow anyone to rest in the assurance of election. "According to his works" denotes the conduct that follows from Jewish presumption of God's mercy as well as that which follows from Gentile idolatry.

7 That Paul is tilting against what he sees to be typical Jewish overconfidence is given further confirmation in the way he enlarges on this scriptural quotation. He sets in antithesis two kinds of works and their matching rewards. On the one hand, there are those who seek for glory, honor, and immortality by enduring patience in doing good. The language is carefully chosen by Paul and the addressees would have had to listen attentively to catch the full sense. Their goal he describes in very broad terms which would be widely accepted in the Hellenistic world—the highest respect from subsequent generations and a full participation in the life of heaven. The verb with its present continuous tense ("go on seeking") implies that they have not yet attained their goal, that it is not yet assured. The qualifying phrase ("by patient persistence in doing good") makes the same point all the more forcefully: their goal will not easily or soon be achieved; it requires a lifelong perseverance. To them God will render the eternal life appropriate to that lifelong seeking and persevering in good.

8 On the other hand, there are those who out of selfishness, selfish ambition, are also disobedient to the truth and let themselves be persuaded to injustice. The contrast is striking and is carefully drawn. The horizon is now not future generations and heaven, but is narrowed to self; the governing and motivating aim is directed to their own advantage. This is not to be understood as an irreligious attitude in contrast to the religious attitude of v 7. We are not back in chap. 1 with the particularly Gentile sins condemned by the Jews in view. The thought is still on the self-confident Jew, as the immediate context, both before and after, makes clear. That is to say, Paul here is not thinking of a life of flagrant falsehood and gross injustice, but of the self-seeking of the self-consciously righteous—those whose concern is so much for their own moral standing and purity, focused so much upon their own salvation, that they can actually stifle truth and love in the process. They are disobedient to the same truth of which Paul speaks in 1:18—the truth here of man's creaturely dependence on the Creator for himself, for his self-esteem, for his future good and salvation. They can be persuaded to justify injustice in the name of their religion, in advancement of their own piety, even some of "the same things" as those listed in 1:29–31. To them the just reward is the retribution and anger which they self-confidently predicted would be the lot of others.

9–11 Vv 9–10 repeat the same contrast, with two significant differences. The contrasting character of the two lives, having been carefully outlined in vv 7–8, can now be stated in blunt and simplified terms: everyone who does what is bad, everyone who does what is good. This is what the contrast amounts to when reduced to its bare bones: one does evil, whatever else he thinks he is doing; the other does good, however incomplete he feels his life-search to be. Again the definition of the contrast in broad Hellenistic, or perhaps more accurately, universal terms ("the bad," "the good") signals an attempt to rise above the narrower categories of Jewish particularity, even though the evil-worker is described with a Semitic phrase, and in the reward of the good-worker the rich Semitic concept of "peace" replaces the more Hellenistic concept of "immortality."

The contrasting characters can be thus simplified because the contrast is also elaborated: "Jew first and also Greek." Here becomes explicit what has been implicit since 1:18, as 1:23 in particular made clear, that Paul's description of God's wrath has in view mankind as a whole (Adam)—everyone, Jew as well as Greek. Here too what has been more clearly implied in chap. 2 becomes also explicit, not only that the Jew also stands under God's judgment, but that he stands in the first rank of those who are to be judged. Jewish priority (in the history of salvation) is also a priority in judgment—first to receive God's wrath as well as first to receive his blessing. So far as judgment is concerned, Jewish priority does not mean a priority of privilege. So far as judgment is concerned the Jew is not in a privileged position. As Paul points out with the devastating simplicity of a generalization whose breadth of application has come home with something of a shock, "God has no favorites" (v 11); he shows none of the partiality between Jew and Gentile that Jewish self-confidence in divine election had come to assume.

Here then it becomes clear that in vv 7–10 two kinds of religiosity are in view. The one is a religiosity which is not specifically or exclusively Jewish (vv 7, 10). Whether it is an ideal or a practical possibility is not at issue here; it is simply the description of a good religious life which all would recognize as such. By expressing it in broader terms, which Jew as well as Gentile would have to acknowledge, he provides one check against Jewish self-assurance that in religious terms Jewish religiosity is well in advance of all others. The other is also a kind of religiosity, a religious mentality which makes its own religious improvement the primary goal and which subordinates even truth and justice to that end. We today, as well as those listening to Paul's letter on its first reading, would have little difficulty in imagining examples of such religiosity—a religiosity, for example, which out of an overmastering desire for consistency will fail to acknowledge some truth because its particular expressions are not always consistent, at least with that degree of consistency their self-approved system requires; or a religiosity which will be persuaded to countenance unjust actions because even natural justice has been squeezed out by the narrow horizon dominated by their own fears and ambitions. It was just such a religiosity, some might well recall, which was exemplified by Jesus' opponents in the Sabbath day controversies and corban issue (Mark 2:23–3:5; 7:10–13), just such a rigid mind-set and unbending consistency which Paul had indicted earlier in the same sentence (v 5).

2. Possession of the Law No Safeguard (2:12–16)

Bibliography

Bassler, J. M. *Divine Impartiality.* 139–49. **Bornkamm, G.** "Gesetz und Natur: Röm 2:14–16." *Studien zu Antike und Urchristentum.* Munich: Kaiser, 1963[2]. 93–118. **Cambier, J.-M.** "Le jugement de tous les hommes par Dieu seul, selon la vérité, dans Rom

2:1–3:20." *ZNW* 67 (1976) 187–213. **Deidun, T. J.** *Morality.* 162–68. **Donfried, K. P.**
"Justification." **Dülmen, A. van.** *Theologie.* 74–78. **Eckstein, H.-J.** *Syneidesis.* 137–79.
Eichholz, G. *Theologie.* 89–96. **Fluckiger, F.** "Die Werke des Gesetzes bei den Heiden."
TZ 8 (1952) 17–42. **Haacker, K.** "Probleme." 6–9. **Jewett, R.** *Anthropological Terms.*
402–421, 441–45. **Kertelge, K.** *Rechtfertigung.* 112–60. **Kranz, W.** "Das Gesetz des
Herzens." *Rheinisches Museum für Philologie.* N.F. 94 (1951) 222–41. **Kuhr, F.** "Römer
2:14 f. und die Verheissung bei Jeremia 31:31 ff." *ZNW* 55 (1964) 243–61. **Kuss, O.**
"Die Heiden und die Werke des Gesetzes (nach Röm 2:14–16)." *MTZ* 5/2 (1954)
77–98. Repr. in *Auslegung* 1:213–45. **Lyonnet, S.** "Lex naturalis et iustificatio Gen-
tilium." *VD* 41 (1963) 238–42. **Mattern, L.** *Verständnis.* 123–40. **Mundle, W.** "Zur
Auslegung von Röm 2:13 ff." *ThBl* 13 (1934) 249–56. **Pierce, C. A.** *Conscience in the
New Testament.* SBT 15. London: SCM, 1955. **Pohlenz, M.** "Paulus." 528–35. **Räisänen,
H.** *Law.* 101–9. **Reicke, B.** "Syneidesis in Röm 2:15." *TZ* 12 (1956) 157–61. ———.
"Natürliche Theologie nach Paulus." *SEÅ* 22/23 (1957/58) 154–67. **Riedl, J.** "Die
Auslegung von Röm 2:14–16 in Vergangenheit und Gegenwart." *SPCIC* I. 271–81.
———. *Das Heil der Heiden nach Röm 2:14–16, 26, 27.* Mödling bei Wien: St. Gabriel,
1965. **Saake, H.** "Echtheitskritische Überlegungen zur Interpolationshypothese von
Römer 2:16." *NTS* 19 (1972–73) 486–89. **Sahlin, H.** "Textemendationen." 93–95.
Schlier, H. "Röm 2:1–29." **Snodgrass, K. R.** "Justification by Grace—to the Doers:
An Analysis of the Place of Romans 2 in the Theology of Paul." *NTS* 32 (1986) 72–
93. **Stuhlmacher, P.** *Gerechtigkeit.* 228–36. **Synofzik, E.** *Vergeltungsaussagen.* 81–82.
Theissen, G. *Psychological Aspects of Pauline Theology.* Edinburgh: T. & T. Clark, 1987.
66–74. **Walker, R.** "Die Heiden und das Gericht: Zur Auslegung von Röm 2:12–
16." *EvT* 20 (1960) 302–314.

Translation

[12] *For as many as have sinned without the law shall also perish without the
law; and as many as have sinned within the law shall be condemned through
the law.* [13] *For it is not the hearers of the law who are righteous before God,*[a] *but
the doers of the law will be counted righteous.* [14] *For when Gentiles who have not
the law do by nature what the law requires, they*[b] *not having the law are the law
for themselves:* [15] *they demonstrate the business of the law written in their hearts,
their conscience also bearing witness, while their thoughts*[b] *bring accusation or
even make defense among themselves,* [16] *in the day when God is to judge*[c] *the secrets
of mankind in accordance with my gospel through Christ Jesus.*

Notes

[a]The absence or presence of the definite article with θεός (equally attested in important
manuscripts) confirms that the use of the definite article in such cases was usually a matter of
stylistic preference.

[b]Further attempts within the G textual tradition at stylistic improvement at these points.

[c]The apparent sudden switch from present to future judgment encouraged several attempts
at improvement in the history of transmission, including J. Weiss's suggestion that vv 14–15
are a gloss, Bultmann's suggestion that v 16 is an interpolation ("Glossen," 282–83), Sahlin's
more modest suggestion that only ἡμέρᾳ need be regarded as an insertion, Schmithal's suggestion
that v 13 as well as v 16 are interpolations (*Römerbrief*, 204–5), and Moffatt's placing v 16 after
v 13 (see further Schlier). But the principle of *difficilior lectio* rules against all emendations to
the best attested text.

Form and Structure

The thrust of Paul's argument becomes still more clear in vv 12–16 where
the law enters the discussion for the first time, to dominate the rest of the

chapter (νόμος—19 times in 16 verses; 9 times in vv 12–16; ἀνόμως twice), and to serve as the major counterpoint in the argument thereafter (see further *Introduction* §5.2). The terms in which it is introduced are significant. For Paul is seeking to deny any false distinction between Jew and Gentile (vv 9–10), and the law is introduced as providing just such a distinction—Gentiles being characterized as those "without the law," "not having the law" (vv 12, 14), and Jews as those "within the law," "hearers of the law" (vv 12, 13). The point is that there is no advantage in merely having the law, that is, in belonging to the people who hear the law sabbath by sabbath (cf. Acts 15:21). The possibility of a "doing" of the law acceptable to God is not dependent on such an understanding of covenant status but on an obedience from the heart unrestricted by ethnic boundaries (vv 13–15). As Snodgrass rightly argues, Paul does clearly believe here in "judgment according to works," and is expounding an essentially Jewish view of judgment (in which mercy and judgment were held together without any thought of incongruity), but radicalized to warn against Jewish overconfidence in election.

The sequence of thought from v 13 to v 16 is awkward (e.g., NIV has vv 14–15 as a parenthesis, and NJB shows v 15 as unfinished—anacoluthon; see also *Notes* on v 16); but the transition from v 15 to v 16 in particular is just the kind of awkwardness which would arise in dictation—a viable connection of thought (using law court imagery), and not so awkward as to require the sort of substantial revision which would be difficult in the middle of a completed scroll.

Comment

2:12 ὅσοι γὰρ ἀνόμως ἥμαρτον, ἀνόμως καὶ ἀπολοῦνται· καὶ ὅσοι ἐν νόμῳ ἥμαρτον, διὰ νόμου κριθήσονται, "for as many as sinned without the law, shall also perish without the law; and as many as sinned within the law, shall be condemned through the law." In this way the concept of the law is first introduced to the discussion, to become a dominant element in the rest of the chapter (see *Form and Structure*).

ἀνόμως/ἐν νόμῳ, ἀνόμως/διὰ νόμου, "without the law/within the law," "without the law/through the law." It is not by chance that Paul introduces this crucial factor (the law) in this way (this is the only time he, or any other NT writer, uses ἀνόμως). As the sequence of thought from the preceding context suggests, and the parallels with v 14 ("without the law" = "not having the law"), with 3:19, 21 ("within the law," "apart from the law"), and with 1 Cor 9:21 confirm, Paul is clearly drawing on one of the standard Jewish definitions of the distinction between Jew and Gentile: the Jews as the people of the law (cf. 4:14, 16), the Gentiles as those without the law, "outside the pale of the law of Moses" (NEB); similarly Murray. In fact the point here turns on this Jewish perception of the distinction between Jew and Gentile, that is, on the degree to which the Judaism of Paul's day defined itself in terms of the law, on the fact that the law constituted one of the chief, indeed, for most devout Jews, the chief identity factor and boundary marker which evidenced Israel's distinctiveness among the (other) nations as the people of (the one) God—so ἀνόμως in the sense of "*lacking* the law" and "*outside* the law," and ἐν νόμῳ in the sense of "*with* the law" and "*within* the law" (within the terms and boundary formulated by the law). See further *Introduction* §5.3.1 and on 6:14.

It is important to grasp Paul's point here carefully. On the one hand he starts by taking up the distinction between Jew and Gentile as between those who have the law and those who don't. But his main emphasis is that there is *no* distinction so far as the final outcome of a sinning life is concerned. His real point then is that judgment will *not* depend on whether the individual starts from within the people of the law or from outside. Both will be judged; sin in both cases will be condemned. The equivalence of the sin (ἥμαρτον) and of its consequences (κριθήσονται/ἀπολοῦνται—"condemned" as no less serious than "perish") in fact undermines the initial distinction between ἀνόμως and ἐν νόμῳ. Since judgment will actually take account of the law (v 13) it confirms that the ἀνόμως refers to the perception of Jewish nationalism and not to a "lawless" judgment of God.

ἁμαρτάνειν was widely familiar in Greek as well as Jewish thought in the sense of "to transgress, sin" against divinity, custom, or law (BGD; bibliography under ἁμαρτία; in the undisputed Paulines somewhat surprisingly only in 2:12; 3:23; 5:12, 14, 16; 6:15; and 6 times in 1 Cor; but see also 3:9 where ἁμαρτία appears for the first time). Here the aorist (ἥμαρτον) is used, since at the final judgment the whole of life can be summed up as a single past event (though cf. 3:23 and 5:12); and if the character of any lives is most adequately summed up by the word "they sinned," then the consequence is wholly negative, whether the sinner was a Gentile or a member of the covenant people. Though this is the first time that the concept of "sinning" is introduced in the letter, its use here confirms that Paul would be ready to sum up the previous description of human vice under the catchword "sin." Snodgrass (76) reacts too strongly against the usual view that 1:18–3:8 constitute Paul's indictment of Jew as well as Gentile, though it is true that the vindication of God (in judgment) is an important theme of these chapters usually given too little weight (hence 3:4–6).

ἀπολοῦνται, "will perish": death used as an analogy (cf. 2:8–9) to denote the final outcome of a life determined by sin (cf. 1 Cor 1:18; 15:18; 2 Cor 2:15; 4:3; 2 Thess 2:10; John 3:16; 10:28; 17:12). It is not merely coincidental that in the LXX the psalmist regularly uses this word to describe the (hoped for) fate of Israel's enemies, the wicked (9:3, 5–6 [LXX 9:4, 6–7]; 10:16 [LXX 9:37]; 37 [LXX 36]:20; 68 [LXX 67]:2; 73 [LXX 72]:27; 80 [LXX 79]:16; etc.), but also that it appears regularly in Deuteronomy as a warning to Israel of what will happen if they prove unfaithful to the Lord (Deut 4:26; 8:19–20; 11:17; 28:20, 22, 24, 45, 52; 30:18). See also on 14:15.

κριθήσονται, "will be condemned" (that is, by God)—here clearly "judge" in the sense of "give a negative verdict, condemn," as in 3:6–7 and 2 Thess 2:12 (cf. John 3:17–18; 12:47–48; Acts 7:7; Heb 13:4; James 5:9; 1 Pet 4:6; Rev 18:8; 19:2). Did Paul have in mind Deut 32:36 (= Ps 135 [LXX 134]:14, cited in Heb 10:30), where κρίνειν is used in the sense of God's judgment of vindication of his people? But even without such a reference in mind, Paul certainly seems to be taking up key elements of Jewish national self-confidence in order to undermine it (see also on 2:4 in reference to Wisd Sol 15:1–4).

διὰ νόμου, "through, that is, in accordance with the law." The presence or absence of the definite article is merely stylistic (so now most commentators; see on 2:14). To belong to the people of the law only makes the difference that that law serves as the instrument of condemnation (not of vindication). For the law as the measure of judgment in Jewish thought see particularly *Jub.* 5.13; *2 Apoc. Bar.* 48.47; Ps-Philo, *Lib. Ant.* 11.1–2—for Gentiles as well; further Str-B, 3:84.

13 οὐ γὰρ οἱ ἀκροαταὶ νόμου δίκαιοι παρὰ τῷ θεῷ, ἀλλ᾽ οἱ ποιηταὶ νόμου δικαιωθήσονται, "for not the hearers of the law are righteous before God, but the doers of the law shall be counted righteous." Here again Paul's wording is significant. Emphasis on doing the law was of course characteristic of Judaism (cf., e.g., Deut 4:1, 5–6, 13–14; 30:11–14; 1 Macc 2:67; 13:48; for Qumran see on 1:17), and exhortations to the same effect can be readily documented from Jewish sources (e.g., Philo, *Cong.* 70; *Praem.* 79; Josephus, *Ant.* 20.44; *m. 'Abot* 1.17; 5.14; see further Str-B, 3:84–88, and on 10:5). What would probably ring somewhat oddly in the ears of a devout Jew, however, would be the contrast between *hearing* and doing. In Jewish thought the idea of hearing (עָמַע) had a more positive content (attentive hearing, heedful hearing; see on 1:5; and again Deut 30:12–13; other examples in Cranfield). Jews could thus be properly described as hearers of the law (Josephus, *Ant.* 5.107, 132; cf. *Sib. Or.* 3.70; Acts 15:21); indeed the two descriptions "hearers of the law" and "righteous" were closely complementary and overlapped in large measure. Here then, once again, Paul drives a wedge between the interconnected elements of Jewish self-understanding. The implication is that he has in mind a different kind of "doing the law," different from the heedful hearing characteristic of Judaism. Similarly, the most characteristic Jewish Christian documents within the NT (Matthew and James) make the same distinction (Matt 7:24–27; James 1:22–25), since a radical reinterpretation of the law and of what fulfillment of the law really means is a fundamental part of all the strands of earliest Christianity's distinctiveness over against the prevailing Jewish piety of the day.

For the self-understanding of the devout Jew as δίκαιος, "righteous," see on 1:17. The important verb δικαιοῦν (15 times in Romans; see on 1:16–17 *Form and Structure*) appears here for the first time in the letter. The future tense underlines its eschatological dimension (δικαιωθήσονται, "shall be justified, acquitted," that is, by God); cf. 3:20, 30; Ziesler, *Righteousness*, 189–90, takes the future as logical, but as thus including the last judgment. Paul's teaching here is not at odds with his emphasis elsewhere, either on justification as something believers already enjoy, or on justification by faith (e.g., 5:1); here too Sanders's argument that in 2:13 there is a shift in the meaning of the word "justified" (no longer = "become Christian" = transfer terminology) (so *ANRW* II.25.1 438) poses a too sharp dichotomy (for both Judaism and Christianity) between "getting in" and "staying in." The "righteousness of God" is nowhere conceived as a single, once-for-all action of God, but as his accepting, sustaining, and finally vindicating grace (cf. Reumann, 83; SH miss this point; the still future dimension of God's "enrighteousing" needs more emphasis than Kertelge, *Rechtfertigung*, 159, finally allows; cf. particularly Gal 5:5; and see further on 1:17; 5:16–18; 6:16; 8:30 and 33). And Paul has already indicated that there is a *doing* (of the law, indeed an obedient hearing) which is necessary and which shall be commended by God (see on 1:5 and 2:7); cf. Donfried, "Justification," though he oversystematizes the distinctions between justification, sanctification, and salvation, and the discussion in Wilckens, 1:142–46. But Paul's concern here is not to provide a carefully worded statement of the Christian gospel; that will come later. Rather his concern is to put in question the prevailing Jewish understanding of who "the righteous" are and of the grounds on which they can hope for final justification. For Judaism knew a similar tension between present righteousness and final acquittal (that is why in putting the typical Jewish understanding in question his statement seems to cut across some of his own teaching elsewhere). The difference is that the dominant strands in the Judaism of Paul's time started from the presupposition of a favored status before God by virtue of membership of the covenant people, which could be characterized by the very link between "hearing the law" and "the righteous" which Paul here puts in question. Like his fellow Jews and the whole prophetic tradition, Paul is ready to insist that a doing of the law is necessary for final acquittal before God; but that doing is neither synonymous with nor dependent upon maintaining a loyal membership of the covenant people.

14 ὅταν γὰρ ἔθνη τὰ μὴ νόμον ἔχοντα, "for when Gentiles [not 'the Gentiles'] who do not have the law." Even more clearly than in v 12 the Jewish perspective of the law (possession of the law), as that which marks the difference between Jew and Gentile, is evoked (see further on 2:12 and *Introduction* §5.3.1).

φύσει τὰ τοῦ νόμου ποιῶσιν, "do by nature the things of the law, what the law requires"; "through their own innate sense behave as the law commands" (NJB). Syntax and balance of the sentence require that φύσει be taken with what follows (against Cranfield and Achtemeier); had Paul wanted to speak of "those who do not have the law by nature" he would have put the φύσει *within* the phrase (that is, preceding ἔχοντα, as the parallels cited by Cranfield indicate [2:27; Gal 2:15; Eph 2:3]; cf. already Leenhardt against Bengel). Paul therefore hardly has in view Gentile Christians here: they "do what the law requires" *not* "by nature" but insofar as they "walk in accordance with the Spirit" (8:4; see, e.g., Althaus; Bornkamm, "Gesetz," 108–9; Eichholz, *Theologie,* 94–96; Hendriksen; Bassler, *Divine Impartiality,* 141–45; Zeller; and particularly Kuhr; against Barth, *Shorter;* Fluckiger; and Minear, *Obedience,* 51; others in Snodgrass, 88 n.10). Rather Paul is still intent to make a broader statement of more open-ended principle which will undermine the presuppositions of Jewish particularity. The appeal is to the same more widespread sense of the rightness or wrongness of certain conduct to which appeal has already been made in 1:26–27 (φυσικός, παρὰ φύσιν) and in 1:28 ("what is not fitting")—the appeal, in other words, to the reality of "the godly pagan." He does not, it should be noted, envisage some Gentiles as *always* "doing what the law requires," but simply the fact that there are Gentiles who for some of the time at least live as the law lays down (cf. Bassler, *Divine Impartiality,* 146, and those cited by her). Nor does Paul, of course, attribute this "doing the law" to man's unaided effort (φύσει in that sense). "Doing the things of *the law,*" even when the law itself is unknown, is possible only where "what is known/knowable of God" (1:19, 21) is the basis of conduct, rather than the rebellion that characterizes humankind as a whole (1:18–32), and only because in Paul's mind there is an immediate connection between knowing God and doing what God wants (1:21a). If Paul makes use of Stoic ideas (see Lietzmann, Bornkamm, "Gesetz," 101–7; see also on 1:26–27; but see also Eckstein, 150–51, and those cited by him), he does so without surrendering his thought to them, just as, in a somewhat similar way, Philo makes use of the Stoic concept of "right reason" as the rule of life (*Opif.* 143; *Leg. All.* 1:46, 93; etc.), while assuming the identification between the divine reason (λόγος) and the law (explicitly, *Migr.* 130); though, of course, in contrast to Paul's, Philo's treatment constitutes an apologetic on behalf of the Jewish view of the law.

Paul's openness here to the reality, not just hypothetical possibility (cf. particularly Lietzmann; Knox; Räisänen, *Law,* 103–4; review of history of interpretation in Riedl, *Heil;* others in Snodgrass, 88 n.9) of Gentile goodness (cf. 2:26–27) can be paralleled within Judaism by *4 Ezra* 3:36 and by the more broadly positive Jewish attitude toward Gentiles, as illustrated (probably) by Acts 10:22, by the readiness of the Temple to receive gifts and sacrifices from foreigners, and by the relative openness of Judaism to resident alien and "God-worshiper" as well as to proselyte; though within the Pharisaic Judaism with which Paul was most familiar, such Gentiles were probably only tolerated and were counted acceptable to God only when they actually became members of the covenant people as proselytes (see further Dunn, "Antioch Incident," especially 17–24; cf. SH; Str-B, 3:88; and particularly Dabelstein, 88–91). On the possibility of a general knowledge of the commandments given to Adam and Moses see on 1:32 and 7:7.

οὗτοι νόμον μὴ ἔχοντες ἑαυτοῖς εἰσιν νόμος, "these not having the law (see on 2:12) are the law for themselves"; not "a law unto themselves," or "their own law" (NEB), which superficially makes a more attractive rendering, and which would be a more appropriate rendering within a more Greek and less Jewish context (parallels, e.g., in Wettstein; but see Lightfoot). It is not some other universal or "unwritten law" (full documentation in Kranz) which Paul has in view. The measure of what is pleasing to God is the law, as much for Paul as for his fellow Jews (cf. Philo, *Abr.* 275–76; *2 Apoc. Bar.* 57.2; *Ap. Const.* 8.98; see particularly the discussion in Michel); though the possibility of a broader view is provided by the Jewish Wisdom tradition's identification of universal divine wisdom with the law (Sir 24:23; Bar 4:1). Indeed the whole point of what Paul is saying here would be lost if νόμος was understood other than as a reference to *the* law, the law given to Israel (see particularly Walker, 306–8; against the older view of Lightfoot, SH, still in Black, and especially Riedl, *Heil,* 196–203; see also on 4:13). For Paul's object is precisely to undercut the assumption that Israel and the law are coterminous, that the law is known only within Israel and possible of fulfillment only by Jews and proselytes. "The intention of Paul is not to reflect systematically on the possibility of moral norms among the Gentiles, but to emphasize the one point, that the exclusively understood pledge of election, the law, is also present among the Gentiles, so that the 'boasting' of the Jews is 'excluded' (3:27)" (Eckstein, *Syneidesis,* 152). In what sense Gentiles "are the law" is explained in the next verse.

15 οἴτινες ἐνδείκνυνται τὸ ἔργον τοῦ νόμου γραπτὸν ἐν ταῖς καρδίαις αὐτῶν, "who demonstrate the business of the law written in their hearts." ἐνδείκνυσθαι, "demonstrate, give proof of," as in 9:22 and 2 Cor 8:24. With the rest of the clause (τὸ ἔργον τοῦ νόμου κτλ.), Paul seems deliberately to have chosen what for him is an unusual phrase which falls between two more familiar ideas, which can be identified completely with neither, but which is probably intended to evoke both. One is (τὰ) ἔργα (τοῦ) νόμου, "works (plural) of the law." This always has a negative force in Paul (3:20, 28; Gal 2:16; 3:2, 5, 10; cf. Rom 4:2, 6; 9:11, 32; 11:6); so the singular here ("the work of the law") is clearly not intended to be a synonym, since here the phrase denotes something commendable. What makes it commendable, and, in Paul's mind, marks it off from the plural phrase, is that this work of the law happens "in the heart." Here, as elsewhere, the "heart" denotes the inward person ("the real you"—as in 8:27; 1 Cor 4:5; 14:25; 2 Cor 3:2–3; 5:12), with overtones of wholehearted, sincere, complete commitment stemming from the integrating center of man as a rational, emotional, volitional being (as in 2:29; 6:17; 10:1, 9–10; 1 Cor 7:37; 2 Cor 9:7; see also on 1:21 and 8:27). The evocation of the plural phrase is thus one of implied contrast, of an inward "work of the law" in contrast to "works of the law," which for Paul are something outward, lacking in depth (see on 2:28 and 3:20); the distinction is missed, e.g., by Nygren, but cf. Schlatter.

The other phrase probably evoked is the new covenant promise of God's law written on the heart (Jer 31 [LXX 38]:33: ἐπὶ καρδίας αὐτῶν γράψω αὐτούς, "I will write them [my laws] on their hearts"; cf. also Isa 51:7: ὁ νόμος μου ἐν τῇ καρδίᾳ ὑμῶν, "[my people] in whose heart is my law"). Elsewhere Paul clearly sees this promise to have been fulfilled in the gift of the Spirit to Christians (2 Cor 3:3, 6; cf. Rom 2:29; Phil 3:3). But here Paul is not thinking explicitly or exclusively of Christians (Christian Gentiles—see on 2:14; against Mundle, Mattern, Cranfield, and others cited by Michel and Käsemann), but is intent on providing a more open-ended formula which has at least the potential of a wider application. It evokes the more explicitly Christian claim because what Paul has in mind is the kind of true inward dependence on God, of a commitment stemming from the heart which he had found only through faith in Christ. He allows the possibility of such religiosity among Gentiles which actually produces what the law is really (or should be really) concerned with. Hence the translation "business" for ἔργον to signal the distinctiveness of Paul's formulation here and to express the breadth of meaning which ἔργον has (BGD) and the undefined breadth of Paul's thought at this point (cf. Barrett, NEB, NJB—"the effect of the law"; Heiligenthal, 195—"sign of a man's 'inner' reality"; but not "the requirements of the law" [NIV]). The fact that "the law" is still the measure of what God requires is a further reminder that Paul's object in separating the law from its identification with Israel is not to discount the law but rather to free the whole understanding of God's concern for man from the narrowness of the prevailing Jewish perspective and presupposition. "Law" (vv 13–15) and "gospel" (v 16) are not at odds in this.

συμμαρτυρούσης αὐτῶν τῆς συνειδήσεως, "their conscience also bearing witness." The language here owes very little to Jewish thought, but would be quite familiar to Greek ears. Here too Paul is evidently making a deliberate effort to express himself in a way which transcends the limitations of the traditional Jewish perspective. συμμαρτυρέω, "bear witness with, attest or confirm something as one witness along with another or several others"; so in various Greek sources (*TDNT* 4:508–9), but unknown in LXX, and in the NT only here and 8:16 and 9:1. As in these other references, the συν- prefix (much loved by Paul; see on 6:4) reinforces its force of "(together) with" (Wilckens; against Cranfield). The implication is that "conscience" is not to be identified as "the work of the law" (far less that Paul understands it as an inner law), but constitutes a further confirmatory witness (see further Eckstein, 161–63).

By first century B.C.E. the sense of συνείδησις as "(moral) conscience" was well established in the popular usage of Greek thought (*TDNT* 7:902–4; Spicq, 854–57), where it normally denoted a painful or disturbing awareness of the wrongness of what one had done: "the normal case is the bad conscience; the good conscience is an exception" (*TDNT* 7:904; see also Pierce and Eckstein, *Syneidesis*; regularly cited are Seneca, *De Ira* 3.36.1 and *Ep.* 28.10). In the OT and rabbinic Judaism the experience of conscience is attested, but not the conception as such (see particularly Str-B, 3:91–96). But certainly in Hellenistic Judaism the concept of the bad conscience is clear—Wisd Sol 17:11; Philo, *Det.* 146, *Spec. Leg.* 2:49, *Virt.* 124 (all in terms of "consciousness of wrongdoing"); *T. Reub.* 4.3; Josephus, *Ant.* 16.103 (the thought is close to Paul's here in *T. Jud.* 20.2 and Josephus, *Ap.* 2.218). So elsewhere in Paul (particularly 1 Cor 8:7, 10, 12; cf. 1 Tim 4:2; Titus 1:15; Heb 10:2, 22), though also in the more positive sense of good conscience, that is, lacking that painful sense that one's attitude or action is wrong (9:1; 2 Cor 1:12; cf. 1 Tim 1:5, 19; 3:9; 2 Tim 1:3; Acts 23:1; 24:16; Heb 13:18; 1 Pet 3:16, 21), so that the prospect of whether that disturbing awareness will result from an action or not becomes itself a test of or guide for the appropriateness of that action (13:5; 1 Cor 10:25–29; see also on 13:5). Since the reference here is evidently commendatory, Paul is presumably envisaging Gentiles who at the final judgment will have lived responsibly by avoiding such actions as would have aroused their conscience. The rationale is still that of 1:18–32, of a "natural" sense of responsibility, consequent upon what is known of God and of the kind of life appropriate to that knowledge, present in wider society. But the reference here is more positive, since Paul appeals not simply to the fact or activity of conscience, but to its testimony confirming the evidence of "the law's effect on the heart." Dahl suggests that Paul here is countering a Jewish claim that the law and its commands would provide Israel with special advocates to witness for (or against) them in the final judgment; so Gentiles will have the advocacy of conscience and thoughts (taken up by Bassler, *Divine Impartiality*, 148). If so, once again, the point would be that possession of the law provides no special privilege advantaging Jew over Gentile.

καὶ μεταξὺ ἀλλήλων τῶν λογισμῶν κατηγορούντων ἢ καὶ ἀπολογουμένων, "and their thoughts bringing accusation or even making defense among themselves." λογισμός, "thought, reasoning" is found only here and in 2 Cor 10:5; note its use in Wisd Sol 11:15 and 12:10 and a sort of parallel in Sir 27:5, 7. κατηγορέω, "accuse, bring charges against," a legal technical term as elsewhere in the NT, occurs only here in Paul. ἀπολογεῖσθαι, "make a defense, defend oneself," is found elsewhere in Paul only in 2 Cor 12:19. The implication of the ἢ καί, "or even," is that Paul expects the former to be more the rule and the latter more the exception. While not turning a blind eye to the reality of Gentile goodness, the overwhelming weight of the indictment of 1:18–32 remains unaffected. This is probably not intended as an explanation of the preceding clause, of how conscience works (as many commentators simply assume), but forms a second genitive absolute construction which provides a third indication or way of speaking about the moral consciousness evident among those outside the law (possibly a natural reflex on Paul's part in view of Deut 17:6 and 19:15). The two clauses are of course complementary, and indeed describe the same range of phenomena, but it would be unjustified to conclude from this verse that for Paul conscience consists of conflicting thoughts. In Paul conscience is not to be identified simply with either heart or mind (see particularly Jewett, *Anthropological Terms*, 442–44, and Eckstein, *Syneidesis*, 164–68; otherwise, e.g., Reicke, "Syneidesis," and Schlier). Paul in fact is probably appealing to a sense of moral confusion or self-contradiction similar to that he himself expounds in 7:14–25, as attested elsewhere in the Greco-Roman literature of the day (see particularly Ovid, *Met.* 7.19–21; Epictetus, *Diss.* 2.26.3–4; see further on 7:15), and in the Jewish concept of the struggle between the evil and good impulses (יֵצֶר; see Davies, *Paul*, 20–23). Paul "speaks of the great disturbance which affects those who encounter in themselves what is written by another hand and who find themselves engaging in self-criticism and self-defense before an alien forum. Precisely in his innermost being a person is not his own master" (Käsemann).

16 ἐν ἡμέρᾳ ὅτε κρίνει ὁ θεός, "in the day when God is to judge." For the concept of a day of judgment, see on 2:5, and on God as judge, see on 2:2. That final judgment is in view is not to be doubted, despite the present tense (though Haacker suggests that ἡμέρα should be taken in a "non-temporal" sense). The verb could be taken as a future (κρινεῖ rather than κρίνει), but the present can be used with future reference (BDF, §323). However, it is characteristic of Paul's thought that there is a continuity between present and future, with regard both to justification (see on 2:13) and to divine wrath (see on 1:18; 2:5, 8)—eschatological judgment as the completed outworking of and final verdict on already evident traits (cf. particularly Saake). The thought is still of God as universal Creator and judge of all, without respect to any election of Israel.

τὰ κρυπτὰ τῶν ἀνθρώπων, "the secrets of men" (that is, all humankind individually). A contrast with what is open, visible is clearly in view, as usual with κρυπτός (see, e.g., Mark 4:22; John 7:4; 1 Cor 14:25; and particularly Rom 2:28–29). The thought that God knows the secrets of men's hearts would be familiar to an audience well versed in the scriptures of Judaism (Cranfield cites 1 Sam 16:7; 1 Chron 28:9; Ps 139:1–2, 23; Jer 17:10; see also, e.g., *Pss. Sol.* 14.8 and 17.25). Once again then Paul takes up a familiar scriptural theme as part of his mounting warning against his own people's presumption: what the final judgment uncovers will not necessarily work in favor of the covenant people or against the Gentiles (vv 28–29). The emphasis on inwardness is clear, but it should not be taken as a straight inward/outward contrast (they *"demonstrate"* what is *"in their hearts"*—v 15), rather it is a reminder that inner motives and governing principles are a truer guide in assessing the (outward) relationships between individuals (and races). See further on 2:28–29.

κατὰ τὸ εὐαγγέλιόν μου, "in accordance with my gospel." Prepositional phrases with εὐαγγέλιον are characteristic in the Pauline corpus, but with κατά only in 11:28 and 1 Tim 1:11, though the full phrase used here appears also in 16:25 and 2 Tim 2:8. For εὐαγγέλιον see on 1:1, 16. κατά with κρίνει must mean that Paul sees the gospel as the criterion either for the assertion or for the judgment itself (or both); the effective difference is not substantial. The μοῦ should perhaps not be stressed (cf. on 1:8; also 16:25), unless it is that Paul was conscious that here he was expounding the gospel in terms of Jew-Gentile relations in a way which was indeed distinctive (cf. 1 Cor 15:1; 2 Cor 11:7; Gal 1:11); see also Schlatter.

The introduction of the gospel as criterion is not at odds with the preceding argument, as though in speaking of divine judgment Paul suddenly narrowed the much broader criteria with which he had been operating to the narrower one of faith in Christ. On the contrary, his point is precisely that his gospel operates with those broader factors, with faith in Christ seen as of a piece with a less well defined responsiveness to the Creator (the κατὰ εὐαγγέλιον parallels the κατὰ ἀλήθειαν of 2:2); cf. Synofzik, 82. Faith in Christ is of course the goal of his own mission and preaching (cf. 10:14–17), but as a fuller and normative rather than exclusive expression of such responsiveness (and embracing the content of chaps. 12–15 as well as of chaps. 1–11); see again on 2:7, 13, 15. It is precisely the exclusiveness of the more typically Jewish assessment of how Gentiles will fare in the final judgment which Paul seeks to undercut; so it is probably significant that "the gospel" here replaces "the law" as the measure of judgment (for the idea of the law as measure of judgment see on 2:12).

διὰ Χριστοῦ Ἰησοῦ, "through Christ Jesus," is not to be taken independently as a literary conclusion (Käsemann) or with τὸ εὐαγγέλιον (Schlier), but probably with κρίνει (as most prefer). The idea of the exalted Christ acting as judge in the final reckoning is familiar in earliest Christian thought (see particularly Matt 25:31–33; John 5:22, 27; Acts 10:42; 17:31; 1 Cor 4:5; 2 Cor 5:10; 2 Thess 1:7–10; 2 Tim 4:1; Rev 22:12). That he is given this role by God, or that God acts through him in the final judgment, is also a strong feature of the same texts. During this period there was a good deal of speculation in Jewish circles about figures involved in the final judgment. Most speculation focused on Enoch (*Jub.* 4:22–23; *1 Enoch* 12–16), though *T. Abr.* 11 (Recension B) makes a point of insisting that Enoch's role was confined to that of court scribe. But the role of judge is attributed both to the mysterious Melchizedek figure in 11QMelch and to Abel in *T. Abr.* 11 (B). The closest parallel is that of the Son of Man in the *Similitudes of Enoch*: "he shall judge the secret things" (*1 Enoch* 49.4; 61.9) and does so "in the name of the Lord of Spirits" (45.26; 55.4; 61.8–9; 62.2–5); cf. the role given to the Messiah in *4 Ezra* 12.31–33 and *2 Apoc. Bar.* 40.1–2. The Christian assertion of the uniquely representative and mediatorial role of the exalted Christ forms part of this broader speculation, but is more thoroughgoing and consistent in its claim (see further on 1:7, 8 and 5:1).

Explanation

With v 12 the thrust of the argument becomes still clearer as Paul for the first time refers to the law. Those listening would be in no doubt that he was referring primarily to the Jewish law, the Torah—not least because he begins with a contrast between in effect those outside the law and those inside the law, that is, between Gentile and Jew. In vv 7–11 he has just made the point that Jews as well as Gentiles will be counted among "those who do evil," just as Gentiles as well as Jews will be counted among "those who do good." Now he begins to develop the argument that even the law does not mark a clear distinction between Jew and Gentile, that Jew is not better than Gentile for having the law, that so far as the real business of the law is concerned there are Gentiles who stand a better chance of acquittal at the final judgment than many Jews. The implication quickly becomes clear that the religiosity attacked in vv 1–11 is the religiosity of the Jew who thinks he is secure before God by virtue of his having the law.

2:12 The point is first made negatively. As many as sinned without the law will also perish without the law; they will be lost not because they did not have the law but because they sinned. And as many (the same equal-handed measure applies) as sinned within the law, they will be judged through the law; they will be judged not by whether they were within the law (Jew) or without the law (Gentile), but because they sinned. In other words, neither interlocutor nor readers should confuse the role of the law as identity factor (the people of the law) with its role as standard of judgment; the law may be a badge marking off Jew from Gentile, but possession of the law does not of itself secure the Jew from condemnation.

13 The explanation of this assertion (v 12) uses a theologoumenon which is not peculiar to Paul or entirely distinctive: not the hearing of the law constitutes individuals as righteous before God, but those who do the law shall be acquitted at the final judgment. Warnings against the dangers of not doing (= keeping) the law are characteristic of Jewish writing from the Torah onwards, and similar rebukes would probably be familiar to a Jewish congregation of Paul's time, though not usually in terms of a contrast between "hearing" and "doing." But Paul's formulation gives it a different slant. It is no longer an exhortation from one member of the covenant people to others, but a claim that breaks through the boundaries of the covenant, whose reference stretches beyond the covenant people. The double contrast of the antithesis is significant—not only between those who are merely hearers and those who do what the law wants, but between the idea that there are those who can be called "righteous" (here and now) and the idea of an acquittal yet in the future. What is attacked, therefore, is the self-confidence of the synagogue attender who faithfully hears the law being read Sabbath by Sabbath and who in consequence counts himself as one of the righteous, one of the chosen people (an equation encouraged not least once again by the Wisdom of Solomon and *Psalms of Solomon*), that is, one who is already assured of a favorable final verdict because as a member of the covenant people he has remained within the covenant, loyal to the covenant. Likewise the positive affirmation of the second clause stretches beyond the covenant people: the doers of the law are not simply those who both have *and* obey the law; there is a "doing of the law" which happens outside the covenant people. The "workers of the good" (v 10) = "the doers of the law" (v 13) will include Gentiles as well as Jews.

14–15 The point is justified once again by alluding to the same broader religiosity already evoked in 1:19–20, 28 and 2:7, 10—in particular the Stoic belief that there is a natural bond of sympathy between man and the cosmos, that man by nature knows the proper order of things and so knows what is fitting in matters of conduct. There are Gentiles (not all Gentiles) whose lives do in fact manifest the concerns of the law even though they have no knowledge of the law. "They do the things of the law by nature." In so saying, Paul is not asserting the existence of a natural law as such; the law in question is still the Jewish law. He is simply noting that there are Gentiles who, despite their ignorance of the law, give evidence of a moral sensitivity which one would sooner expect to find in the people of the law. His readers would probably think back to the Stoic idea of what is proper (1:28), or the broader (Hellenistic) ideal of "the good" (2:10). Such moral awareness will serve in place of the law in the day of judgment, the measure by which those who sinned outside the law will be judged (v 12); the implication being that those who responded to such "natural" promptings would fare better in the day of judgment than the Jew who sinned within the law.

"Those who do the things of the law" is a deliberately vague phrase. What Paul means by it is spelled out more clearly in v 15, whose three clauses provide the evidence and proof for the more controversial assertion of v 14. "They demonstrate the work of the law written in the hearts": not the *law* written in their hearts (which is a specifically Christian claim that Christians experience the new covenant fulfillment of old covenant hope—2 Cor 3:3, 6); and not the *works* of the law (which would evoke the specifically Jewish claim attacked by Paul—Gal 2:16; Rom 3:20). By "work of the law" Paul must mean the business of the law, what it is the law's business to produce (= work). And he must be referring again to that same moral sensibility evident in so many Gentiles: the moral sensibility that he would have expected the law to produce in Jews he actually sees in greater measure in many Gentiles. Whereas by implication, in his view, Jewish concern for (outward) *works* of the law does not demonstrate the same (inward) work of the law.

The second witness he calls to give evidence of Gentile awareness of moral responsibility is "conscience." The idea of conscience as an inward monitor which assesses and condemns deeds already committed was widespread in Hellenism, but the idea as such is hardly to be found in Judaism prior to

Wisd Sol 17:11. It thus illustrates Paul's point well of a moral consciousness outside the Jewish people and independent of the law as such. The third proof he calls is the evidence of inward moral conflict among the Gentiles. He who knows what he should do and yet fails to do it, provides the testimony of conflicting thoughts, some condemning the failure, others offering excuses for it. Here, Paul's readers would note, is a doing of (the things of) the law which is essentially an inward matter, at the level of heart and conscience and thought, and which Paul sets in approving antithesis over against Jewish pride and confidence in possessing the law.

16 It is this doing of the law which will become evident to all in the day of judgment. The unveiling of these inner secrets of heart and conscience and thought will demonstrate the extent to which such Gentiles can be called "doers of the law" and will result in many Gentiles faring better than many Jews in that day. Significantly, Paul adds "in accordance with my gospel." Paul's addressees would probably understand the phrase thus: it will be by measuring them against the gospel which will show the extent to which these Gentiles "do the things of the law"; it will be comparison with the law written in the heart (cf. 2 Cor 3:3) which will reveal whether their moral sensibility is indeed what the law is about. The significance of the addition is not least that the gospel is thus accorded a role in the final judgment not dissimilar to that more usually attributable to the law (cf. v 12). Here again then the implication comes through with some strength that gospel and law are not antithetical opposites for Paul; Paul's gospel can be a measure of inner secrets because it shows what obedience to the law means and it opens the heart to the writing of the law in the heart. The same point is implicit in the final phrase which attributes to Christ Jesus the role of mediator or representative of God's judgment in that final day. It is the fact of Christ (1:3–4) and the gospel he gave to Paul (1:1, 5) which freed Paul to recognize the positive features of Gentile religiosity (as well as confirming the negative features already evident to him from earlier Jewish apologetic—1:18–2:11), and which undermined the Jewish presumption that being a member of the people of the law would be sufficient to secure acquittal on that day (2:12–16).

Modern commentators need to take care at this point that they do not attempt to squeeze these verses (12–16) into a later dogmatic mold. Too many indeed have made the mistake of attempting at once to explain, or explain away, Paul's language here in the light of what they take to be his doctrine of justification by faith. So, for example, v 13 cannot mean that people will be justified by virtue of being "doers of the law," since that would mean justification by works. And v 14 cannot be speaking of Gentiles in general since that would imply a doctrine not just of natural law but of justification by living in accordance with the natural law—and what need then would there be for the gospel? To be sure, there is some ground for such an interpretation—in particular the allusion to Jer 31:33 in v 15 could well be taken as a description of Gentile Christians (as in 2 Cor 3:3), even though it is "the work of the Law" rather than the law itself which is here said to be "written in their hearts." But it is hardly possible to imagine Paul describing Gentile Christians as those "who do the things of the law by nature" (v 14); and Paul would probably be well aware that the activity of conscience and the presence of inward moral conflict was well attested within Hellenism at large and not confined merely to Gentile Christians.

If we are to understand Paul's argument here within his wider thought we must first see its function within its immediate context. After all, Paul could not assume that all those listening to his letter would be already familiar with his teaching on justification by faith; it is precisely with a view to introducing and expounding his teaching that he wrote them in the first place. So at this stage of the exposition he could only assume that they would understand his language in its most straightforward and obvious sense within the immediate context of his argument in chap. 2. The aim of this argument is clearly to puncture a Jewish assurance falsely based on the fact of having the law, of being the chosen people of God. His argument is that this assurance must be false simply because there are Gentiles who show more evidence in themselves of what the law points to than many Jews (vv 12–16), just as there are Jews, members of the people of the law, who break the law (vv 17–24), Jews who keep the law at one level (circumcision) but who are not properly to be described as real Jews, as "doers of the law" (vv 25–29).

There is no doubt then that "doing (the things of) the law" is important for Paul; but already it is becoming evident that this is not a "doing of the law" in just the sense that the typical Jew would think of it. What "doing the law" could be for Paul is hinted at in v 15: something inward, rooted in and stemming from the heart. He will develop the idea steadily by allusion in 2:29; 3:31; 6:19–22; 7:6 until its most explicit expression in 8:4 and fuller exemplification in 12:1–15:6. In the meantime he can express the point with some vagueness, simply because he need not be specific yet. It is enough for his present argument to adduce the example of Gentiles who show a moral sensibility such as the law looks for and greater than that shown by many Jews. He does not actually say that this "work of the law" will guarantee their acquittal on the day of judgment; if anything his language is designed rather to explain how it is that Gentiles who sin without the law can yet be held responsible (vv 12, 15bc). Their own talk of conscience and of inward moral conflict demonstrates their sense of moral responsibility. To that extent at least they know the just decree of God regulating such matters (1:32). But neither does he deny the possibility that there are among the unevangelized Gentiles "doers of the law" who shall be acquitted (v 13); he does not ask the question and his treatment leaves the answer open. He himself, however, had found the possibility of acquittal only through and in terms of the gospel given him by Christ Jesus (v 16); and no doubt he would direct the patient good-working seeker for glory and honor and immortality (v 7) to the gospel; just as he would seek to lead any Gentile who by nature "showed the work of the law written in his heart" (v 15) into the fuller experience of the Spirit which provides the effective motivating power from the heart (2:29; 7:6; 8:4; 2 Cor 3:3, 6).

3. Favored Status No Security   (2:17–24)

Bibliography

Bornkamm, G. "Anakoluthe." 76–78. **Fridrichsen, A.** "Der wahre Jude und sein Lob: Röm 2:28 f." *Symbolae Arctoae* 1 (1927) 39–49. **Goppelt, L.** "Der Missionar des Gesetzes: Zu Röm 2:21 f." *Christologie und Ethik*. Göttingen: Vandenhoeck und Ruprecht, 1968. 137–46. **Murphy-O'Connor, J.** "Truth: Paul and Qumran." In *Paul and Qumran*, ed. J. Murphy-O'Connor. London: Chapman, 1968. 186–92. **Räisänen, H.** *Law*. 98–101. **Schnabel, E. J.** *Law*. 232–34. **Stowers, S. K.** *Diatribe*. 96–98, 112–13.

Translation

[17]*But if you are called a "Jew" and rely on the law and boast in God,* [18]*and know his will and approve the things that matter, being instructed from the law,* [19]*and are confident that you are a guide of the blind, a light for those in darkness,* [20]*an instructor of the foolish, a teacher of the young, having the embodiment of knowledge and of truth in the law . . .*[a] [21]*You then who teach another, do you not teach yourself? You who preach "Do not steal," do you steal?* [22]*You who say, "Do not commit adultery," do you commit adultery? You who abhor idols, do you commit sacrilege?* [23]*You who boast in the law—through transgression of the law you dishonor God.* [24]*For "the name of God is blasphemed among the Gentiles through you," as it is written.*

Notes

[a]For discussion of anacoluthon, see following *Form and Structure*.

Form and Structure

With vv 17–24 the identity of the interlocutor becomes explicit: a (typical) Jew whose views Paul knew "from inside." The diatribe style of the opening verses (2:1ff.), which had been allowed to lapse from 2:6, is now resumed, as an appropriate medium for conducting this "in-house" critique of Jewish presumption. The detail indicates that the indictment is not intended as an accusation of wholesale Jewish profligacy, but as a pricking of the balloon of Jewish pride and presumption that being the people of God's law puts them in a uniquely privileged position in relation to the rest of humankind. If a Jew is guilty of the sins he condemns in others, he is equally condemned. A Gentile who does not have the law but keeps it can hardly be in a less advantageous position than a Jew who has the law but fails to keep it. Not to be ignored is the fact that it is the law as ethical standard which is commended here (vv 21–23), over against the law in its function as a boundary marking off Jews as an entity from the rest of humankind (vv 25–29).

Structurally the passage falls into two halves, vv 17–20 and 21–23, with v 24 providing a conclusive confirmatory scriptural proof. Vv 17–20 are built on a sequence of pairs, the first set consisting of verbal phrases, and the second set contained within a single clause, with both sets rounded off with participial clauses.

εἰ δὲ σὺ Ἰουδαῖος ἐπονομάζῃ
καὶ ἐπαναπαύῃ νόμῳ   καὶ καυχᾶσαι ἐν θεῷ
καὶ γινώσκεις τὸ θέλημα   καὶ δοκιμάζεις τὰ διαφέροντα
κατηχούμενος ἐκ τοῦ νόμου,

πέποιθάς τε σεαυτὸν
ὁδηγὸν εἶναι τυφλῶν   φῶς τῶν ἐν σκότει
παιδευτὴν ἀφρόνων   διδάσκαλον νηπίων
ἔχοντα τὴν μόρφωσιν
τῆς γνώσεως   καὶ τῆς ἀληθείας
ἐν τῷ νόμῳ . . .

Both parts climax in an assertion about the law, and the effect of the anacoluthon is to leave the thought unfinished: these are not all the claims which the devout Jew could make of the law, but they are a good representation, and the final clause is a fitting climax to express the high regard in which Jews hold the law.

The second half is built up of a sequence of four rhetorical questions in participial construction, with a neat stylistic variation between διδάσκων, κηρύσσων, and λέγων (vv 21–22), and the final statement couched in the indicative forming a natural climax, again with explicit reference to the law (v 23); cf. Byrne, *Reading*, 66–67. For parallels to the anacoluthon of vv 17–20 and the posing of rhetorical questions in vv 21–22, see Stowers, *Diatribe*, 96–97: almost "a classic example of indictment of the pretentious philosopher" (112).

Comment

2:17 εἰ δὲ σὺ Ἰουδαῖος ἐπονομάζῃ, "but if you are called a 'Jew.'" ἐπονομάζομαι occurs only here in the NT. Already for some centuries Ἰουδαῖος had been the name used by foreigners for a person belonging to Judea. But increasingly from the time of the Maccabean period it was also accepted and used by the Jews themselves as a self-designation in place of the older designations, "Israelite" or "Hebrew" (*TDNT* 3:369–75; but see further on 9:4). As such the function of the name was to distinguish Jew from Gentile, or simply from non-Jew—so almost always in Paul (1:16; 2:9–10; 3:9, 29; 9:24; 10:12; 1 Cor 1:22–24; 9:20–21; 10:32; 12:13; Gal 2:14–15; 3:28; Col 3:11); as also in rabbinic teaching (Str-B, 3:96–97). Its emergence as an accepted self-designation was probably tied into the emergence also of Ἰουδαϊσμός in the same period (first in 2 Macc 2:21; 8:1; 14:38) as a designation for the national religion of the Jews in its self-conscious distinctiveness and fierce loyalty to the law and the traditional customs (see also Amir). Ἰουδαῖος therefore would be a name accepted with pride by Paul's contemporaries (cf. *4 Ezra* 6:55–59). In addressing a single Jew Paul has in mind no particular Jew, of course, but the typical Jew (*TDNT* 3:380–81), that is, the Jew per se, conscious of his Jewishness, of his distinctiveness from the nations (see also on 3:1). Subsequently, in Acts and John οἱ Ἰουδαῖοι became established as a designation for the opponents of Christianity. But here the distinction is still simply that between Jew and Gentile, and what is at stake is the status of the new movement in relation to that distinction. For Paul himself it is still a debate between Jews (though noticeably for his own self-designation he uses the older name "Israelite"—11:1; 2 Cor 11:22), and the issue is the real meaning of "Jew" or what being a "Jew" involves (2:28–29; against Watson, *Paul*, 113–15, who argues that Paul is attacking primarily the leaders of the Jewish community).

καὶ ἐπαναπαύῃ νόμῳ, "and rest on the law." ἐπαναπαύω has the basic sense of "rest upon," but with overtones of leaning upon, relying upon, finding one's foundation and support in, resting one's hopes upon, or even resting content with. The phrase thus catches well the Jewish attitude to the law which Paul is here confronting—a confidence born of the gift of the law to Israel, a confidence that possession of the law is a sure mark of God's favor (cf. Mic 3:11); Hübner's critique at this point is off target (*Law*, 113): Jewish "possession of the law" was hardly "illusory" nor regarded as a "merit." Paul does not imply that the typical Jew is content simply to have the law; what the law supports is a whole way of life, as Paul knew well (Gal 1:14; Phil 3:6). But it was a way of life where distinctiveness of the Jew from the non-Jew was always to the fore (as the next clauses confirm). What Paul is attacking, therefore, is precisely the Jewish reliance on this distinctiveness. The attitude in view is well expressed in 2 *Apoc. Bar.* 48:22–24 (tr. Charlesworth):

In you we have put our trust, because, behold, your Law is with us,
and we know that we do not fall as long as we keep your statutes.
We shall always be blessed; at least, we did not mingle with the nations.
For we are all a people of the Name;
we, who received one Law from the One.
And that Law which is among us will help us,
and that excellent wisdom which is in us will support us.

See further *Introduction* §5.3.1–2.

καὶ καυχᾶσαι ἐν θεῷ, "and boast in God." καυχάομαι was not a widely used word, but was well enough known in Greek usage (including the LXX). As in the modern equivalent, the sense of "boast" could have a negative force (boast without due cause, boast in an unworthy object); but it could also signify a justifiable boast (cf., e.g., Ps 49:6 [LXX 48:7] with 149:5 and Sir 11:4 with 30:2). In the NT it is an almost exclusively Pauline word (35 out of 37 occurrences are in the Pauline corpus). For this particular boast of the typical Jew see Deut 10:21; Pss 5:11 [LXX 12]; 89:17 [LXX 88:18]; Jer 9:23–24; Sir 50:20; *Pss. Sol.* 17:1. Paul of course makes no (implied) criticism of boasting in God. On the contrary, he makes such boasts himself (5:11; 1 Cor 1:31 and 2 Cor 10:17 both citing Jer 9:23). From the context, however, the implication is that such Jewish boasting tends to be nationalistically exclusive: Jewish boasting in God as theirs alone (cf 3:27–29). Hence it gathers (by implication) the more negative force which Paul uses in criticizing a boasting based on outward evaluation and physical relationship (2 Cor 5:12; 11:18; Gal 6:13; Phil 3:3). Bultmann's understanding of this boasting as "self-confidence" (*TDNT* 3:648–49; also *NT Theology* 1:243) overindividualizes the concept and fails to appreciate the nationalistic character of the "boasting" envisaged here.

18 καὶ γινώσκεις τὸ θέλημα, "and you know the will (of God), or his will." The absolute use of "the will" = God's will reflects Jewish usage (Michel). Knowing what God wanted of his people was naturally a matter of concern in Jewish piety, though not so frequently expressed in just these terms (cf. Pss 40:8; 143:10; *T. Iss.* 4:3). The attitude Paul has in mind is most clearly expressed in 2 Macc 1:3–4. Again Paul makes no criticism of the desire to do God's will; on the contrary, that is fundamental for him too (cf. 1:10 and 15:32). What he sets his sights on is rather the too easy assumption of a privileged knowledge by virtue of being instructed in the law (v 18c; cf. Bar 4:4—"Happy are we, Israel, because we know what is pleasing to God"; Wisd Sol 15:2–3; *4 Ezra* 8:12, whereas for Paul such knowledge is possible only at a deeper level, through a transformed mind (12:2).

καὶ δοκιμάζεις τὰ διαφέροντα, "and you approve the things which matter"; "you know right from wrong" (NEB). The same phrase is used in Phil 1:10, and in both instances Paul probably has in mind the act of applying a test which will show what in any particular case are the essential matters and what the nonessentials. τὰ διαφέροντα is probably used in conscious contrast to τὰ ἀδιάφορα, which was already established as a technical term in Cynic-Stoic ethics in the sense of "things indifferent, neither good nor bad" (LSJ; Lietzmann; *TDNT* 9:63). For δοκιμάζειν see on 1:28. To translate "*can* approve" would weaken the point somewhat. The assumption criticized is not simply that of having a test ready to hand (= the Torah), but rather the assumption that the law has already decided such questions (cf. v 20c). Paul has in mind the Jew who consults the Torah not to apply the test, but to find the answer. The law makes plain what is essential. The criticism Paul is building up to is that discrimination as to what God counts important in any particular case is not such a superficial business (cf. 12:2; Phil 1:10), and that this too Jewish attitude has resulted in giving false priority to the whole matter of Jewish distinctiveness, not least to the rite of circumcision (2:25–29).

κατηχούμενος ἐκ τοῦ νόμου, "being instructed from the law." The phrase probably goes with both preceding phrases (Cranfield). κατηχέω had not long become current (BGD), but its sense is already clearly established as "instruct, teach." Paul uses it in this sense, particularly for religious instruction, in 1 Cor 14:19 and Gal 6:6 (cf. Acts 18:25), from which comes the English transliteration "catechesis" (Käsemann is confident that the verb denoted "the fixed catechetical traditions of Judaism"). The phrase characterizes well the Jewish sense of dependence for their knowledge of God's will and conduct of life both on their instruction in the law as children and in the weekly reading from the law in the synagogue (cf. Josephus, *Ap.* 2:183). The ἐκ τοῦ νόμου probably has something of the same force which we find in 4:14, 16; it is precisely the completeness of the identification between law and people which Paul has reacted against.

19–20 These verses consist of a sequence of phrases which continue the characterization of what Paul clearly regards as typical Jewish attitudes. There are clear echoes of the first two in particular in Jewish sources, and the overall attitude is so much of a piece that we can be confident that Paul is not exaggerating or painting an unfair picture. To do so would have been tactically unwise anyway, since his device of putting his case to the Jewish interlocutor would only succeed if his representation was fair. Paul's target at this point, however, is more likely to be the diaspora than the Palestinian Jew, since the former naturally had an apologetic and even missionary concern which was mostly lacking in the latter (Str-B, 3:98–105). The point which is repeated four times is the distinction made between the more privileged and the less. And once again the sense of privilege is expressed in terms of the law, not in terms of election or of God's covenant of faithfulness (it is in these latter terms that the problem of Israel's distinctive position confronts Paul—3:1–4 and chaps. 9–11). For most Jews, of course, such a distinction (between covenant and law) would be unreal: the law to all intents and purposes of Israel's existence is the covenant. But for Paul the law had become so identified with the people of God as a national entity with distinctively national characteristics that it was now preventing the covenant and covenant promise from opening out in full extent to the Gentiles. Those same phrases used here had become an expression of privileged status over against the Gentiles rather than of responsibility toward the Gentiles.

πέποιθάς τε σεαυτόν, "you are confident that you yourself." Paul chooses this word rather than "know" to indicate that this is a conviction which in its present form (as an expression of privileged status) is something to which they have persuaded themselves rather than something God-given (cf. 2 Cor 10:7).

ὁδηγὸν εἶναι τυφλῶν, "are a guide of the blind." Cf. Isa 42:7: the servant's task is "to open the eyes of the blind"; 1 Enoch 105:1: "you are their (the children of the earth) guides"; Sib. Or. 3:195: "that nation shall be to all mortals the guide of life"; Josephus, Ap. 2:291–95; Philo, Abr. 98. Matt 15:14 and 23:16, 24 hit at the same confident Jewish attitudes, but more bitingly.

φῶς τῶν ἐν σκότει, "a light to those in darkness." Cf. Isa 42:6–7: φῶς ἐθνῶν . . . ἐν σκότει; 49:6. The light which Israel had been given is characteristically and quite naturally thought of as the law: Ps 119:105—"a light to my path"; Wisd Sol 18:4—"your sons . . . through whom the imperishable light of the law is given to the world"; Sir 24:27—the law "makes instruction shine forth like light"; 45:17—"to enlighten Israel with his law"; T. Lev. 14.4—"the light of the Law"; 1QSb 4.27; Ps-Philo, Lib. Ant. 23.10; see further Wilckens 1:148–49 and n. 382; and on 13:12. None of these phrases necessarily implies an actively outgoing missionary concern (despite e.g., Bassler, Divine Impartiality, 150), more a sense of superior privilege (see Introduction §5.3.2) and readiness to accept those who acknowledge their blindness and come for light and teaching.

παιδευτὴν ἀφρόνων, διδάσκαλον νηπίων, "an instructor of the foolish, a teacher of the young/immature." These phrases are less easy to parallel from contemporary Jewish literature (though cf. Hos 5:2; Sir 37:19; Pss. Sol. 8:29; 4 Macc 5:34). But the conviction of having received insight into the divine mysteries and responsibility for giving instruction in them is clearly evident in the Qumran scrolls (1QS 3.13; 8.11–12; 9.12–21; 1QH 2.13; 4.27–29; 1QpHab 7.4–5; see also on 11.25), and in the wisdom tradition there is something of a similar distinction between the self-consciously wise and the νήπιοι (Prov 1:22; 16:22; Wisd Sol 10:21; 12:24; 15:14; 1QH 2:9; cf. Matt 11:25 //

Luke 10:21 where Jesus is remembered as countering a similar attitude). The two phrases are almost synonymous, the structural pairing (see *Form and Structure*) here producing a degree of redundancy. But παιδευτής may also have the overtone of "corrector," as in its only other NT use (Heb 12:9).

ἔχοντα τὴν μόρφωσιν τῆς γνώσεως καὶ τῆς ἀληθείας ἐν τῷ νόμῳ, "having the embodiment of knowledge and of truth in the law." There is now general agreement that μόρφωσις must mean "embodiment, complete expression"— the usage of *koine* rather than of classical Greek (Käsemann). "Knowledge" and "truth" refer to no specific content or claim; it is knowledge and truth as such which are in mind (ἡ γνῶσις, ἡ ἀλήθεια). Together the words encompass the highest claims and aspirations of religion and philosophy in the ancient world. The Jewish claim is that what everyone of *gravitas* aspires after has been given to Israel in the law. That Paul echoes some actual formulation of the diaspora synagogues is certainly possible (Lietzmann; Michel; here cf. Sir 17:11; 45:5; Bar 3:36; 2 Apoc. Bar. 44.14). But the closest parallels known to us are the claims of ben Sira and Baruch that the divine Wisdom sought by all is now embodied in the law (Sir 24:23; Bar 4:1). Bar 4:1–4 in fact provides a good representation of the attitude being characterized here; see also Murphy-O'Connor, *Paul and Qumran*, 186–92; Schabel, 234, notes that this was the only explicit correlation of law and wisdom in the Pauline corpus. Certainly the way in which Paul focuses this statement of Jewish confidence on the law, including the two points of climax (vv 17, 18, 20— see *Form and Structure*) makes it clear enough that this is where *his* criticism of that confidence also focuses—not least on the assumption that all they need or can aspire to in terms of knowledge and truth has already been given to them in the form of the law. For Paul who had come to recognize that truth (1:18, 25; 2:8) and knowledge (15:14 q.v.) could be encountered outside the boundaries marked by the law, this too close identification of them with the law was bound to be resisted.

21–23 Each of the clauses in vv 21–23 could be punctuated either as statements or as questions (so most; otherwise Zeller). The rhetorical style suggests that the four sentences of vv 21–22 are intended as questions, whereas the scriptural proof (v 24) attached to the fifth clause (v 23) indicates that it should be taken as a statement, indeed as the explicit conclusion to what had been implied in the preceding verses (so, e.g., SH, Lagrange, Lietzmann, Cranfield, NEB, NJB; against RSV, NIV). The challenges posed here have puzzled many commentators, since the moral caliber of Judaism was one of the features which made it most attractive to God-worshipers and proselytes. But it is unnecessary to conclude that Paul is exaggerating or generalizing from a few isolated cases or disqualifying the whole for the crimes of a few (Trocmé, "The Jews," 153) or condemning the Jewish nation *in toto* (Räisänen, *Law*, 100; still less that Paul has Jewish rejection of Jesus in mind here, as Barth, *Shorter*, suggests). It is the rhetorical flourish which constitutes the exaggeration and it would be unlikely to mislead Paul's listeners. Fridrichsen justly calls attention to the similar challenges in Epictetus to those who call themselves Stoics (*Diss.* 2.19.19–28; 3.7.17; 3.24.40—"Jude," 45). And there are sufficient challenges of a not dissimilar kind both in the prophets (e.g., Isa 3:14–15; Jer 7:8–11; Ezek 22:6–12; Mal 3:5), and in subsequent rabbinic literature (see Str-B, 3:105–111), not to mention Luke 11:39–52 // Matt 23, to show that Paul's diatribe is not by any means out of the ordinary (contrast Räisänen, *Law*, 101—"a piece of propagandist denigration"). Indeed the similarity of the sequence of charges leveled in Jewish literature of the time (*Pss. Sol.* 8.8–14; Philo, *Conf.* 163; *T. Lev.* 14.4–8; CD 6.16–17; and already Ps 50:16–21; elsewhere in Greek vice-catalogs, see *TDNT* 3:256) suggests that Paul was in fact drawing on a well-known tradition of rebuke and exhortation. So Barrett's attempt (cf. Goppelt, "Missionar") to interpret the passage along the lines of Matt 5:21–48 is unnecessary, and in fact misses the point. For Paul's target is not any or all Jews as individuals, but Jewish assurance of standing in a position of ethical privilege by virtue of the law (cf. particularly Wilckens). For Paul the very fact that there are Jews who do what their law clearly forbids should be enough to undermine the confidence that the Jew per se stands in a position of superiority or advantage over the non-Jew by virtue of being a member of the people of the law. See also on 3:3.

ὁ οὖν διδάσκων ἕτερον σεαυτὸν οὐ διδάσκεις; ὁ κηρύσσων μὴ κλέπτειν κλέπτεις; ὁ λέγων μὴ μοιχεύειν μοιχεύεις; ὁ βδελυσσόμενος τὰ εἴδωλα ἱεροσυλεῖς; "You therefore who teach another, do you not teach yourself? You who preach 'Do not steal,' do you steal? You who say, 'Do not commit adultery,' do you commit adultery? You who abhor idols, do you commit sacrilege?" The fact that in vv 21–22 Paul focuses on three charges arising directly from the decalogue (Exod 20:15, 14, 4–5; Deut 5:19, 18, 8–9), and not at all on cultic requirements, such as circumcision and the food laws, which are laid down with equal clarity in the Torah, may be significant. It may, of course, be the result simply of following an established sequence of Jewish exhortation (see above). But it may also indicate that in Paul's mind there was an important distinction between these commands of the decalogue and the ritual of the Jewish cult. Paul would hardly criticize Jews for *not* being circumcised (2:25–29), whereas he asks his questions here with as much heartfelt moral intensity as any of his fellow Jews. See further on 13:9.

It is inaccurate to say that "in the LXX βδελύσσεσθαι is frequently used to denote abhorrence of idolatry" (Cranfield, 169 n.4). But βδέλυγμα, "abomination," *is* frequently used as a reference to idolatry (e.g., Isa 2:8, 20; Dan 11:31; 1 Macc 1:54; Wisd Sol 14:11). So Rev 21:8: ἐβδελυγμένοις, "those abhorred as idolaters." For Jewish polemic against idolatry see further on 1:23. There was quite a strong sense of self-congratulation among the rabbis that idolatry had been entirely rooted out of Israel (Str-B, 3:111–12; already Jud 8:18).

ἱεροσυλεῖν usually means "to rob a temple" (as in its only LXX reference, 2 Macc 9:2; also Josephus, *Ant.* 17.163), but it can also have the less precise sense of "to commit sacrilege" (LSJ—so, probably, Acts 19:37), "desecrate holy things" (NJB). That the accusation was of robbing the Jerusalem temple is possible in view of *T. Lev.* 14.5 and *Pss. Sol.* 8.12, presumably the equivalent to Ep Jer 10, 33 or Acts 5:2–5 being in view; since 2:24 here is paralleled by Mal 1:12, Paul could conceivably have had Mal 1:14 in mind; and we can document at least one case of a Jew in Rome misappropriating funds and gifts intended for the temple—a scandal that resulted in the expulsion of the Jewish community from Rome in A.D. 19 (Josephus, *Ant.* 18.81–84). But in context the thought more probably has pagan temples and idols in view—the danger being that of actual plunder (as in Josephus, *Ant.* 4.207), or of use of items taken from idol shrines (since they lacked an owner anyway!), despite the clear warning of Deut 7:25–26 (see Str-B, 3:114; *TDNT* 3:255).

23 ἐν νόμῳ καυχᾶσαι, "you boast in the law," understood as in Sir 39:8, "he glories in the law of the Lord's covenant" (see further Str-B, 3:115–18). Here once again the focus is on the law, and again at the climactic point of the sequence of accusations. And once again the theme is of Jewish boasting (as in v 17), here too not as a boasting in self-righteousness, but, significantly, in the law. They can boast in it, because their having it is a mark of God's favor. Where the boasting becomes more open to criticism is that it becomes a cause of boasting over those who do not have the law.

διὰ τῆς παραβάσεως τοῦ νόμου τὸν θεὸν ἀτιμάζεις, "through transgressing the law you dishonor God." The clause sums up the preceding charges, now as a blunt statement, implying that the point of the previous questions cannot be denied. Delight in the law of the covenant has not been proof against breach of the law, and the very distinctiveness in which the Jewish interlocutor glories has been contradicted by Jewish actions. It should be noted that Paul affirms on his own part that transgression of the law dishonors God, and no doubt also its corollary, that keeping the law honors God. In view of the strong tradition of Protestant exegesis which climaxed in Bultmann, it needs to be said repeatedly that Paul regards the doing of the law as something desirable and necessary (2:13). His criticism of the Jewish interlocutor is that his national pride in the law has resulted in his *failing* to do what the law requires, the real business of the law (2:14–15). The accusation so often laid at Paul's door (antinomianism—3:8), he levels in turn against his typical Jewish interlocutor! For παράβασις see on 4:15 and 5:14.

24 τὸ γὰρ ὄνομα τοῦ θεοῦ δι' ὑμᾶς βλασφημεῖται ἐν τοῖς ἔθνεσιν, καθὼς γέγραπται, "for the name of God through you is blasphemed among the Gentiles, as it is written." As with the previous scriptural quotation (καθὼς γέγραπται—see on 1:17), Paul turns to Scripture for clinching confirmation of his argument. The formula of appeal ("as it is written") is, unusually, left to the end. The quotation is from Isa 52:5:

Paul—τὸ ὄνομα τοῦ θεοῦ δι' ὑμᾶς βλασφημεῖται ἐν τοῖς ἔθνεσιν·
Isa—δι' ὑμᾶς διὰ παντὸς τὸ ὄνομά μου βλασφημεῖται ἐν τοῖς ἔθνεσιν.

The LXX addition of δι' ὑμᾶς and ἐν τοῖς ἔθνεσιν to the Hebrew (if that is the proper way to describe the passage's textual history; Schlatter conjectures that the LXX text was altered on the basis of Romans), enables Paul to make his point with greater force. For βλασφημεῖν see on 3:8. There is a clearer and sharper note of condemnation in Ezek 36:17–23 (. . . τὸ ὄνομά μου τὸ ἅγιον, ὃ ἐβεβήλωσαν οἶκος Ἰσραὴλ ἐν τοῖς ἔθνεσιν . . .), which Paul probably also had in mind (see also on 15:16: ἡγιασμένη), and which in effect enables him to give Isa 52:5 a more accusing note: it is Israel's subjugation at the hands of pagan nations (as a consequence of Israel's sin) which caused Israel's God to be despised by these nations. This suggests that Paul was thinking not simply of the contrast between profession and conduct (cf. CD 12:7–8; *T. Naph.* 8:6), but had more of the original force of these passages in view.

For if we extend Paul's thought as far ahead as 3:27–30, the line of Paul's
eschatological interpretation of these passages may be conjectured thus: it is
not just particular acts of transgression, but the whole attitude to the law
expressed in the previous verses, which amounts to a perversion of God's
purpose for Israel and the nations, and which results in the nations continuing
to regard God simply as the national God of a small nation and thus to
dishonor him who is the only God, God of all (3:29); cf. Lindars, *Apologetic*, 22.

Explanation

The argument proceeds by tightening still further the circle of reference:
no longer simply in terms of the law (vv 12–16), but now, in a resumption
of the diatribe style, the Jewish dialogue partner is addressed specifically by
name. At first the point seems to be simply that as there are Gentiles who
"do the things of the law," so there are Jews who flagrantly break the law.
But the accusation is a little more complex than that. The Jew who is addressed
as such ("you call yourself a Jew") is not any particular Jew, or any group
of Jews; he is the Jew in general, the Jew per se, the Jew conscious of his
people's special privilege in being given the law, conscious that his people
had been specially chosen by God, the Jew who claims the special prerogatives
of his people. And the Jew who is accused of flagrant transgression of the
law is not any particular Jew, let alone Jews in general; Paul would be well
enough aware that accusations of wholesale theft, adultery and idolatry would
weaken rather than strengthen his argument. He is simply any Jew who has
been guilty of such offenses against the law. What is set in contrast, therefore,
are the national pride of the typical Jew in the law, over against instances
of transgression of the law by Jews. The argument is that the transgression of any individual Jew is enough to call in question the Jewish assumption that as a Jew he stands in a position of privilege and superiority before
God as compared with the Gentile. The point is that once the typical
Jew's *a priori* status as Jew before God by virtue of his people's election
is seen to be called in question, then the broader indictment of man in general (1:18–32) can be seen to apply more clearly to Jew as well as Gentile
(2:9–11).

2:17–20   Paul begins by giving voice to this national pride of the "Jew."
The interlocutor is proud of the name "Jew," self-confident in the privileges
of being a Jew, conscious of his responsibilities to those less highly favored
than himself. His confidence is based on the fact that he has been given the
law; he rests his hope on the law; his sense of security as a Jew is focused
on the law. He boasts in God—not necessarily a bad thing in Paul's eyes (cf.
5:11), but here the implication is plain that it is a boasting in God as the
God of Israel, the God who has specially chosen the Jewish nation. As Paul
proceeds it becomes still clearer that the interlocutor's Jewishness is wholly
bound up with the law, with his possession of the law and the privileged
position this gives him. As the syntax shows, the recital of vv 18–20 springs
from and revolves round this pride in being the people of the law. It is
instruction from the law which provides the "Jew" with the key to those
important recurring questions of daily life and otherwise so demanding ques-

tions: What does God want of us? What are the things which really matter? The "Jew" is confident that God's law contains the answer. It is because the "Jew" is thus convinced that the law is the very embodiment of knowledge and truth that he can be so confident that he is fulfilling Israel's task to be a guide of the blind, a light to those in darkness (Isa 42:6–7), confident that as a Jew having the law he can be educator and teacher of those who not having the law are ignorant and immature.

This is the voice of Jewish fundamentalism—the voice of one who sees the law as a sure and certain sign of God's continuing favor to Israel, who believes the Torah is God's word *tout simple*. It is not merely a charter or constitution; it does not merely give guidelines and norms to be worked out in daily living; it is a complete and comprehensive manual for the whole of life. Having been instructed in it he has no doubts as to God's will; the right answer in matters of disputed priorities is clear. The very fact of having the law puts him in a position of advantage and superiority over the Gentile, as leader to blind, as light to those in darkness, as one who corrects the foolish, as teacher to young children. Paul does not contest the fact that such claims can be made and can be valid. But implicit in his diatribe is the question of whether all this can be said of the Jew per se, by virtue of his being a member of the people chosen by God, by virtue of his having the law. The implication indeed is that the Jew as such is *not* fulfilling the role of Israel, that he is mistaking his priorities, that he has misunderstood God's will, boasts in God misguidedly, and has a false confidence in the law. Implicit also for many of those listening to Paul's letter being read would be the assertion that discernment of God's will and God's priorities in any instance is not to be read off the Torah but comes through a much more existential openness to God and his Spirit (cf. 12:2; Phil 1:9–10), that Christ is the true embodiment of God's wisdom, not the law (1 Cor 1:24, 30), and that it is only through the gospel that Israel's role as leader of the blind and light to those in darkness can be fulfilled (cf. 1 Cor 4:5; 2 Cor 4:6)—the very role the Jew per se is rejecting by his rejection of the gospel and Christ. This will begin to become clearer shortly in vv 25–29—even that the interlocutor's right to the name "Jew" stands in question (vv 28–29).

21–23 But first Paul tries to puncture this national pride by forthright denunciation. You who are so sure that having the law puts you in a position to teach someone else (the Gentile), do you teach yourself? Have you made the effort to understand it yourself? (The implication is again clear that this Jew who speaks for the Jewish nation as a whole has indeed failed to understand the law of which he boasts so confidently, or more precisely, that he has understood the law, but only at one level, and has missed its real import). The fact is, Paul reminds his dialogue partner, that there are Jews who have acted in flagrant contradiction of the law. Resting on the law, being instructed out of the law, having the law as an embodiment of knowledge and truth is not enough. They have the command in the law not to steal, yet there are Jews who steal. They read in the law that one should not commit adultery, yet there are Jews who commit adultery. The Jew abhors idols, and yet Jews commit sacrilege. In short, the national boasting in the law has to be set alongside the fact that Jews dishonor God by breaking the same law. The implication is again clear: the national pride in the law is misplaced; the

Jew as Jew is no better than the Gentile as Gentile, and his sin will be judged as severely as that of the Gentile (v 12).

24 The point is nailed firmly by the quotation from Isa 52:5 and probable allusion to Ezek 36:20–23. Almost certainly in each case Paul had the context in mind and used one to interpret the other. It was the very fact of exile, as well as the conduct which made exile inevitable, which caused the Gentiles to despise the name of Yahweh. The people of Israel had boasted in being God's chosen nation and had rested in the covenant given them by God. But their land had been wasted, Jerusalem destroyed, and the people taken into exile. In consequence the Gentiles despised the God of such a defeated nation and sneered at a God who could not save his own people. Paul sees a clear parallel between the situation described by Isaiah and Ezekiel and the situation of his own day. Once again the "Jew" is resting with false confidence on the fact of God's election of Israel, presuming upon the prerogative of having the law. And as the exile showed the consequences of such pride then, so the transgressions of particular Jews now make the same pride an occasion for Gentile jibes at the God who has chosen such a race. The implication is that just as the exile should have caused Israel then to recognize that they had been resting on a misunderstanding of what the covenant meant, so the Jew now should be reassessing the significance of his covenant status and not simply relying on the fact of his being a Jew and having the law.

4. Circumcision No Guarantee   (2:25–29)

Bibliography

Borgen, P. "Debates on Circumcision in Philo and Paul." *Paul Preaches Circumcision and Pleases Men.* Trondheim: Tapir, 1983. 15–32. **Collins, J. J.** "A Symbol of Otherness." **Fridrichsen, A.** "Der wahre Jude und sein Lob: Röm 2:28 f." *Symbolae Arctoae* 1 (1927) 39–49. **Käsemann, E.** "The Spirit and the Letter." *Perspectives.* 138–66. **McEleney, N. J.** "Conversion, Circumcision and the Law." *NTS* 20 (1973–74) 319–41. **Marcus, J.** "Περιτομή and Ἀκροβυστία in the New Testament." Forthcoming in *NTS.* **Nolland, J.** "Uncircumcised Proselytes?" *JSJ* 12 (1981) 173–94. **Sahlin, H.** "Textemendationen." 95–96. **Schneider, B.** "The Meaning of St Paul's Antithesis 'The Letter and the Spirit.'" *CBQ* 15 (1953) 163–207. **Schneider, N.** *Die rhetorische Eigenart der paulinischen Antithese.* Tübingen: Mohr, 1970. 79–83. **Schweizer, E.** "'Der Jude im Verborgenen . . . , dessen Lob nicht von Menschen, sondern von Gott kommt.' Zu Röm 2:28 f. und Matt 6:1–18." In *Neues Testament und Kirche,* FS R. Schnackenburg, ed. J. Gnilka. Freiburg: Herder, 1974. 115–25. **Snodgrass, K. R.** "Justification by Grace—to the Doers: An Analysis of the Place of Romans 2 in the Theology of Paul." *NTS* 32 (1986) 72–93.

Translation

25 For circumcision is of benefit if you practice the law. But if you are a transgressor of the law your circumcision has become uncircumcision. 26 If then the uncircumcised keeps the requirements of the law, will not his uncircumcision be reckoned as circumci-

sion? *27 And the naturally uncircumcised who fulfills the law will pass judgment on you who through letter and circumcision are a transgressor of the law. 28 For the true Jew is not the one visibly marked as such, nor circumcision that which is performed visibly in the flesh, 29 but one who is so in a hidden way, and circumcision is of the heart, in Spirit not in letter. His praise comes not from men but from God.*

Form and Structure

The argument settles back to more measured accusations as the indictment reaches its climax. The return to the opening theme of passing judgment makes for a rounded whole, the thought having started with the Jewish interlocutor's judgment of Gentiles (vv 1–3), and passed through the assertion of God's righteous judgment (vv 5, 12–16) to the climactic reverse where the law-keeping Gentile passes judgment on the too literal Jew (v 27). The degree to which the thought of vv 25–29 parallels that of vv 12–16 confirms that Paul's purpose was not so much to break fresh ground at each stage as to bring home the same charge with increasing pointedness to his Jewish contemporaries. The climactic focus on circumcision is a measure both of the degree to which it marked out distinctive Jewish identity and of the danger to which the typical Jew was exposed by over-reliance on it. To set such a value on ethnic identity and outward ritual is of a piece with the presumptuous wisdom of 1:22 and so draws the interlocutor under the same indictment of impiety and unrighteousness (1:18). Vv 28–29 are written in a very compressed, epigrammatic style (though the meaning is clear), and function as a final summary statement of the whole preceding argument. They are built on a series of antitheses (see *Comment*) made more effective by their being interwoven.

Comment

2:25 The argument has narrowed from a vaguely defined "doing good," through the more specific "doing the law," and now to the single issue of circumcision, in a progression the devout Jewish interlocutor would have appreciated. For such a one, all that had so far been discussed—what God approves, the point of the law, the privilege of the Jew—could quite properly and fittingly be focused on the one question of circumcision.

The irreducibly fundamental importance of circumcision for the Jew of Paul's time can be easily documented. Nothing could be clearer than Gen 17:9–14: "This is my covenant which you shall keep, between me and you and your descendants after you: Every male among you shall be circumcised . . . and it shall be a sign of the covenant between me and you. . . . So shall my covenant be in your flesh an everlasting covenant. Any uncircumcised male who is not circumcised in the flesh of his foreskin shall be cut off from his people; he has broken my covenant." The central importance of circumcision as a test of covenant loyalty and mark of Jewish national distinctiveness in the Maccabean period is clear in 1 Macc 1:48, 60–61; 2:46; and 2 Macc 6:10. Hence the mass circumcisions of the Idumeans and Itureans by the Hasmoneans when they conquered and incorporated their territory: they

could not be counted as belonging to the people of the covenant without
circumcision (Josephus, *Ant.* 13.257–58, 318; Timagenes in *GLAJJ* §81). The
Book of Jubilees, probably written in this period, follows Gen 17 fairly closely
and then continues: "This law is for all generations for ever . . . it is an
eternal ordinance, ordained and written on the heavenly tablets. And everyone
who is born, the flesh of whose foreskin is not circumcised on the eighth
day, belongs not to the children of the covenant which the Lord made with
Abraham, but to the children of destruction . . ." (*Jub.* 15.25–34).

Correspondingly, it is evident from various Greco-Roman writers of our
period that circumcision was generally regarded as a particularly Jewish rite.
Even though it was known that other peoples practiced circumcision (Samari-
tans, Arabs, Egyptians—cf. Jer 9:25–26; Philo, *Spec. Leg.* 1.2), circumcision
was nevertheless recognized to be a rite which marked out the Jews (see
particularly Petronius, *Satyricon* 102.14; *Fragmenta* 37; Tacitus, *Hist.* 5.5.2;
Juvenal, *Sat.* 14.99—texts in *GLAJJ* §§194, 195, 281, 301). This can only be
a reflection of the high evaluation placed on circumcision by Jews themselves
in defining their national and religious distinctiveness. The fact that Paul
can simply assume the distinction "circumcision/uncircumcision" as fully
equivalent to "Jew/Gentile" makes the same point (2:26; 3:30; Gal 2:7; Col
3:11). Within the dispersion God-worshipers were welcome in the synagogue;
but only by accepting circumcision could they become proselytes, members
of the covenant people. (In view of Sanders's distinction between "getting
in" and "staying in" [*Law,* chap. 1], Borgen's observation should be noted
that for Philo and Hillel "bodily circumcision was not the requirement for
entering the Jewish community, but was one of the commandments which
they had to obey upon receiving status as a Jew" ["Observations," 18]). To
be sure, questions about the necessity of circumcision in untypical cases were
raised (Philo, *Migr.* 92; Josephus, *Ant.* 20.38–42), but in each case the answer
given is that the rite of circumcision was too fundamental to be dispensed
with (*Migr.* 93–94; *Ant.* 20.43–48); see Nolland, "Uncircumcised," and SVMG,
3:169, against McEleney, "Conversion," 328–33; see also the discussion in
Collins, "Symbol," and more generally L. H. Feldman, "The Orthodoxy of
the Jews in Hellenistic Egypt" (*Jewish Social Studies* 22 [1960] 215–37). For
Qumran, note particularly 1QH 6.20–21, and for the continuing high evaluation of circumcision in rabbinic Judaism subsequent to our period, see
Str-B, 4:31–40.

In short, whatever else the covenant required of its members, Paul's Jewish
interlocutor could be in no doubt that circumcision was obligatory and fundamental, the single clearest distinguishing feature of the covenant people,
the most obvious boundary line which divided Jew from Gentile, those within
the covenant from those without (see further on 4:9 and 4:11). Marcus argues
that both περιτομή and ἀκροβυστία are identification words, betraying their
origin as nicknames used to characterize Jew and Gentile by their opponents,
and reflecting the Jewish dimension of what was at stake, just as "strong"
and "weak" (14:1–15:6) are nicknames which reflect a more Gentile perspective.

περιτομή μὲν γὰρ ὠφελεῖ ἐὰν νόμον πράσσῃς, "for circumcision is of benefit
if you practice the law." For ὠφελεῖν cf. 1 Cor 13:3, 14:6 and Gal 5:2. For

πράσσειν νόμον, "to do, practice the law," cf. 2:13 and see on 2:3. The Jewish interlocutor would almost certainly accept the first part of Paul's assertion, the difference being that he would see circumcision as a fundamental part of that practice of the law. On the other hand, the fact that Paul affirms on his own account that circumcision is of value is also important; he does not wish the command of God to be disregarded (cf. Hübner, *Law,* 55; see also 4:11–12). Here the difference is that in Paul's view the interpretation of that command made necessary by the circumstances of the new age calls for a practice of the law (including circumcision) that need not include the outward rite (vv 27–29). Käsemann's suggestion that Paul's language here echoes a polemic against enthusiasm detracts from the point; but Schlatter is probably correct in deducing that circumcision was not an issue among the Christians in Rome (otherwise Paul would not have expressed himself in these terms).

ἐὰν δὲ παραβάτης νόμου ᾖς, ἡ περιτομή σου ἀκροβυστία γέγονεν, "but if you are a transgressor of the law, your circumcision has become uncircumcision." This second half of Paul's assertion would be more controversial. The idea of Jews failing to live in accordance with the law was not at all new or strange: the prophetic rebuke of ritual form lacking ethical substance, the ideal of "the righteous" self-attested in writings like the Wisdom of Solomon, the *Psalms of Solomon* and the Dead Sea Scrolls, and the (subsequent) rabbinic distancing of themselves from "the people of the land," were all attempts to cope with what was perceived to be an inadequate level of law-keeping among the chosen people (see also on 2:21–23). But that such failure could cost a circumcised Jew his place in the covenant and in the blessings of the new age was a prospect that devout Jews did not care to contemplate. The sustained hope that the lost sheep of the house of Israel would be brought in even at the last and the confidence expressed subsequently by various rabbinic authorities that circumcision would save from hell (examples in Cranfield, 172 n.1), suggest rather that the sort of qualification used by Paul himself in 1 Cor 3:15 would have prevailed. And even where the distinctions seem to be drawn more sharply, as at Qumran, the accepted answer was to withdraw more deeply within the boundaries marked out by the law (cf. Sanders, *Paul,* 242–57). Paul's assertion that circumcision could actually count for nothing would therefore be shocking to many Jews. And if he was alluding to or could be understood as alluding to the practice of epispasm, by which hellenizing Jews had somehow removed or disguised the mark of circumcision (cf. 1 Macc 1:15; see SVM, 1:149 n.28), his assertion would be additionally offensive. But Paul evidently was of the opinion that such a sharp challenge was necessary to undermine so central a pillar of Jewish self-understanding and identity.

26 ἐὰν οὖν ἡ ἀκροβυστία τὰ δικαιώματα τοῦ νόμου φυλάσσῃ, "if then the uncircumcised keeps the just requirements of the law." By a natural progression of meaning ἀκροβυστία, "foreskin," means "uncircumcision," and so the uncircumcised person (see also on 4:9). The importance of the issue for Paul at this point is indicated by the fact that more than half the occurrences of ἀκροβυστία in the NT occur in chaps. 2–4. δικαίωμα is used in the sense of "(just) requirement or decree," as in 8:4 (see on 1:32). φυλάσσω in the sense of "keep" a law was familiar in contemporary Greek (LSJ; cf. Acts 7:53; 21:24; Gal 6:13). The full phrase, "keep the (God's) ordinances" occurs regularly in Deuteronomy (4:40; 6:2; 7:11; etc.) and Ezekiel (11:20; 18:9; 20:18; etc.). V 26a is a restatement of 2:14, with the boundary-marking character of circumcision and the degree to which the requirement of circumcision could serve as a summary expression of the law clearly indicated in the equivalence of "Gentiles who do not have the law" and "the uncircumcised."

οὐχ ἡ ἀκροβυστία αὐτοῦ εἰς περιτομὴν λογισθήσεται;, "shall not his uncircumcision be reckoned as circumcision?" In view of the important role filled by λογίζεσθαι from 3:28 through chap. 4, the word will be pregnant with significance as the focus steadily narrows to the *Christian* Gentile as such. The future is probably temporal (i.e., at the final judgment), but may be logical. The argument is *ad hominem*. Paul would not want to argue for himself that people should be assessed in terms of having circumcision; his own view is expressed in 1 Cor 7:19; Gal 5:6; and 6:15. The point here is that the Jew who truly approves the business of the law (v 15) should recognize the acceptability to God of those who meet the demands of the law (apart from circumcision and other "works of the law"). Such a non-Jew who lacked only the physical mark of the covenant (which was true of many God-worshipers; cf. Dunn, "Antioch Incident," 21–23, 26–27; and see *Introduction* §2.2.2) was surely in reality the equivalent in God's eyes to the full member of the covenant people (cf. 2:13). Paul's object, of course, in pressing for such agreement is precisely to undermine the assumption that the distinction between those within and those without the covenant, those acceptable and those unacceptable to God, cannot be determined except by reference to the rite of circumcision. The rabbis would not have accepted the line of argument (Str-B, 3:119–21; Michel), but Paul could expect his Roman audience to be more sympathetic to the point.

27 καὶ κρινεῖ ἡ ἐκ φύσεως ἀκροβυστία τὸν νόμον τελοῦσα σε, "and the naturally uncircumcised who fulfills the law will judge you"—a further variation on 2:14, making the same claim. For φύσις see on 2:14; but the thought is slightly different from 2:14, where the φύσει refers to the "doing the law" (see on 2:14)—is Paul beginning to think of Gentile Christians as such (see on 2:28–29)? That Jews can be regarded by implication as "naturally circumcised" is a further indication of the close identification between circumcision and the Jewish race (cf. Gal 2:15). τελέω in the sense of "fulfill, accomplish, perform" is well known in the poets from Homer onwards (LSJ, BGD; "give full effect to"—Barrett). What is intended here, of course, is not fulfillment of the law quantitatively in all the ritual requirements (they are uncircumcised!), but presumably more in a qualitative sense (cf. James 2:8)—fulfillment by performance at a deeper level. Something along these lines is clearly implied by v 27b.

κρινεῖ . . . σε, "shall pass judgment on you." Paul does not hereby encourage his Gentile Christian readers to adopt the same judgmental attitude against the Jews which he had condemned in the Jewish interlocutor at the beginning (2:1, 3), as his own subsequent warning makes clear (cf. 11:17–24). Paul still writes in the spirit of the diatribe. Some influence from Matt 12:41–42 // Luke 11:31–32 is possible (Schlatter, Lagrange, Dodd, Nygren; cf. Matt 19:28 // Luke 22:30; 1 Cor 6:2).

τὸν διὰ γράμματος καὶ περιτομῆς παραβάτην νόμου, "who through letter and circumcision are a transgressor of the law." The association of γράμμα with περιτομή, and their both being accounted the means of breaking the law, is striking and poses as a sharp alternative what the devout Jew would normally assume must go together—literal obedience as part of complete obedience. γράμμα, having the basic sense of written letter (LSJ, BGD), encouraged the distinction between outward form ("the Mosaic Torah in its written documentation"—Käsemann, "Spirit," 143) and deeper meaning, between superficial and real (see further on 2:28–29). By associating περιτομή with γράμμα in this way (whether he refers γράμμα to the law as written code or intends the phrase to be taken as a hendiadys, "literal circumcision," the force is the same), Paul makes the substantive charge that circumcision as valued typically within Judaism focused too much on the outward rite. But unlike the traditional Deuteronomic exhortation (Deut 10:16; Jer 4:4), Paul regarded this emphasis not simply as an inadequate meeting of the law's demands, but as an actual breach of the law (Paul probably intends the διά to be taken instrumentally—Schlatter; TDNT 1:765). To continue to identify the point of the law with Israel as a national entity (clearly distinguished from the other nations by circumcision) was actually to prevent God's purpose in the law attaining fulfillment. This has been Paul's critique consistently throughout the chapter.

28–29 οὐ γὰρ ὁ ἐν τῷ φανερῷ Ἰουδαῖός ἐστιν, οὐδὲ ἡ ἐν τῷ φανερῷ ἐν σαρκὶ περιτομή· ἀλλ' ὁ ἐν τῷ κρυπτῷ Ἰουδαῖος, καὶ περιτομὴ καρδίας ἐν πνεύματι οὐ γράμματι, οὗ ὁ ἔπαινος οὐκ ἐξ ἀνθρώπων ἀλλ' ἐκ τοῦ θεοῦ, "for the 'Jew' is not a matter of being visibly so marked, nor is circumcision a matter of visible marking in the flesh; but the 'Jew' is something inward, and circumcision is of the heart, in Spirit not in letter, whose praise comes not from men but from God." The verses are clearly the climax and conclusion of Paul's argument against the typical Jew characterized in the preceding verses. Consequently these verses are particularly important for our understanding of Paul's complaint against his fellow Jews. Of course he uses contrasts and themes known elsewhere. The ἐν τῷ φανερῷ/ἐν τῷ κρυπτῷ antithesis, "in the open/in secret," plays upon the importance of God's knowing the hidden truth of a person (see on 2:16 and cf. Matt 6:4, 6 [Schweizer]; 1 Pet 3:4); the φανερός // κρυπτός distinction is familiar elsewhere in earliest Christian tradition in other forms (Mark 4:22; Luke 8:17; John 7:4; 1 Cor 14:25); and the unsatisfactoriness of a praise which is based on appearances is a theme used several times by Epictetus (e.g., Diss. 2.16.5–11; 3.12.16—see Fridrichsen, "Jude"). The thought is not to be reduced to a merely inward/outward antithesis, but focuses attention on the hiddenness of the real person, especially when that reality is obscured by what comes more immediately to the onlooker's perception. Likewise the question about who is a Jew or what is a true Jew is raised in John 1:47 and Rev 2:9, 3:9, and touched on in Epictetus 2.9.20–21 (cf. again Jer 9:25–26); and in the final clause Paul may be making use of a familiar wordplay based on Gen 29:35 and 49:8 (Judah/hodah = praise; יהודה/הודה), even though he could not expect it to be grasped by all or many of his Greek-speaking hearers. For ἔπαινος see further on 13:3.

But this does not mean that Paul's contrast is purely formal or stereotyped. For in the rest of the clauses we are confronted with distinctively Pauline themes and assertions. The description of circumcision as ἐν σαρκί, "in the flesh," catches the breadth and ambivalence of the word as characteristically used by Paul. On the one hand it describes circumcision in a purely factual way—a physical rite, a cutting of the flesh. But in context it carries the sense also of racial kinship and national identity (as in 4:1; 9:3, 5; 11:14). And in conjunction with ἐν τῷ φανερῷ and in contrast to καρδίας, "of the heart," it has a clearly pejorative overtone, as so often elsewhere in Paul (see further on 1:3 and 7:5)—an overtone completely lacking, of course, in rabbinic talk of circumcision "in the flesh" (examples in Cranfield, 175 n.2). Likewise, though the desirability of a circumcised heart was familiar in Jewish thought (Deut 10:16; Jer 4:4; 9:25-26; Ezek 44:9; 1QpHab 11.13; 1QS 5.5; 1QH 2.18; 18.20; Philo, *Spec. Leg.* 1.305), and the hope of its future realization cherished (Deut 30:6; *Jub.* 1.23), it is Paul's distinctively Christian claim that this hope has been already realized. The point is not simply that the eschatological hope of the gift of the Spirit has been realized, but that it has been realized in a way which, while fulfilling the Torah as promise, also stands in contrast to the Torah as letter (γράμμα—7:6; 2 Cor 3:6; Phil 3:3; Col 2:11; cf. *Odes Sol.* 11.1-3), whereas the more typically Jewish hope for the fulfillment of Jer 31:31-34 would hardly conceive of such a contrast (as Ezek 36:26-27 illustrates). For καρδία, "heart," as the experiencing, motivating center of man see on 1:21; as the focus of God's work of renewal see also 2:15; 5:5; 6:17; 10:9-10. On πνεῦμα, "Spirit," as the divine agent of renewal and enabler of a life acceptable to God see on 5:5, 7:6 and 8:4; the older view that the contrast is between the *literal* sense of the law/OT and the *spiritual* sense, has generally been abandoned (see B. Schneider's review of the older debate).

Particularly significant is the association between the different contrasts.

(1) ἐν τῷ φανερῷ   ἐν τῷ κρυπτῷ
(2) ἐν τῷ φανερῷ, ἐν σαρκί   καρδίας
(3) (ἐν) γράμματι   ἐν πνεύματι

Since (3) is an alternative formulation equivalent to (2) (both referring to circumcision), and since ἐν τῷ φανερῷ appears in both (1) and (2), with ἐν σαρκί as an elaboration, it is clear that Paul intends here a sequence of synonyms or closely complementary concepts.

ἐν τῷ φανερῷ = ἐν σαρκί = ἐν γράμματι (ἐξ ἀνθρώπων)
ἐν τῷ κρυπτῷ = καρδίας = ἐν πνεύματι (ἐκ τοῦ θεοῦ)

As the summation of his indictment of the Jewish interlocutor, this is what constitutes Paul's critique of his own native religion: it puts too much stress on the outward and visible, on physical kinship and ritual and in consequence treats the law superficially. What makes the true Jew, the Jew whom *God* praises, is precisely that which can never be measured in physical, visible, and ritual terms—it is something hidden, of the heart, by the Spirit.

These contrasts should not be read merely as a plea for inwardness in religion (it is now usually agreed by comparison with 7:6 and 2 Cor 3:6 that in Paul's intention πνεῦμα = Holy Spirit, not the human spirit = the true I); nor as an attack on ritual(ism) (Robinson, *Wrestling*: the contrast is the same as that between baptism "in water" and baptism "in/by Spirit" in Mark 1:8

pars.), nor as a championing of morality against legality. Paul directs his challenge against the specific fact that the Judaism of his day had become too much identified with one ethnic group: it was *merely* a national religion, it had been *mis*understood by being too much understood in terms of the physical characteristics and visible rituals which marked it out as Jewish. Nor is his denunciation of this Judaism wholesale and sweeping. It is on this one major point that his criticism turns, though for Paul it was a point of decisive significance. In holding up the concepts of "Jew," "circumcision," and "law" to closer inspection, he does not deny them to his own people. Rather his is an assertion of what Judaism, what the covenant, what the law and circumcision are all about, a reality which he implicitly claims to have been realized in the eschatological working of the Spirit in the hearts of Gentiles as well as of Jews, a working which had transcended the old division between Jew and Gentile and rendered the old boundary markers between Jew and Gentile redundant. Thus in narrowing his charge against the Jewish interlocutor to the very specific charge focusing on circumcision, at the same time he has narrowed the more vaguely defined category of the righteous Gentile to the Christian Gentile (disputed by Snodgrass, 81) rejoicing in the gift of the eschatological Spirit—the eschatological Jew is Gentile as well as Jew! (cf. particularly Käsemann, "Spirit," 144–46). This "both/and" needs to be borne in mind in assessing Watson's otherwise perceptive point that Paul's argument amounts to a "sectarian claim to sole legitimate possession of the religious traditions of the community as a whole" (*Paul*, 122).

Explanation

2:25 The argument takes a final tightening turn by abruptly introducing the subject of circumcision: "For circumcision is of value if you keep the law . . . ." To understand how it is that this large discussion can be narrowed down to such a specific focus we must recall how fundamental circumcision was for the Jews of Paul's day. According to Gen 17:9–14 circumcision was the single most important act which established the covenant between Yahweh and Abraham's descendants: it was the act of circumcision which secured the covenant as an everlasting covenant; failure to circumcise constituted a fatal breach of the covenant. This sense of circumcision's importance had been strengthened in the Hellenistic period by way of reaction to Hellenism's distaste for the rite, and ever since the Maccabees, circumcision had been seen as an absolutely essential expression of Israel's national identity and religion. Even the Herods, Idumean and thoroughly Hellenist though they were in culture and lifestyle, recognized that circumcision had the force of a national taboo which could not be broken. Significant also are the number of Greco-Roman authors who simply identify circumcision with being a Jew— indicative of the image projected by Jews in Roman society at the time Paul was writing; such an image prevented many "God-worshipers" attracted by Judaism from taking the final step and becoming proselytes. Those listening to Paul's letter would thus recognize the connection of thought without difficulty: circumcision was fundamental to the typical Jew's self-understanding, the mark of his religious distinctiveness, the badge of national privilege, the

seal of God's covenant favor to Israel his chosen people. The confidence
that circumcision secured the Israelite's salvation, which we find coming to
expression within the sayings of later rabbinic Judaism, is the confidence of
Paul's interlocutor, the same presumption of God's favor which long before
had resulted in the exile (v 24).

This is the false confidence Paul now attacks head-on: circumcision in
and of itself makes no difference; circumcision will not be sufficient to secure
the salvation of anyone who is a transgressor of the law. Paul would be well
aware that such a blunt antithesis between circumcision and keeping the
law would surprise, even shock, a devout Jew. For the interlocutor, circumcision
was not something other than law-keeping; on the contrary, it was the most
fundamental act of the covenant and its law; *failure to circumcise* excluded
from the covenant (Gen 17:14). Once a man had been circumcised the terms
of the divine-human relationship were different: keeping the law was the
way of life within the covenant; it did not affect the basic covenant status as
such (as did circumcision). But Paul will have none of this: the law-breaking
Jew is in just the same position as the sinful Gentile (whom he so often
despised and condemned—1:19–2:3). His circumcision has become uncircumcision—a shocking charge for the pious Jew, for Paul could be understood
as alluding to those hellenizing Jews of the Maccabean period who tried to
turn their circumcision into uncircumcision by having the mark of circumcision
removed or disguised, a course of action both heretical and treasonable in
the eyes of the devout. To such covenant-confident piety Paul says bluntly:
your law-breaking has the same effect on *your* covenant status; transgression
of the law in effect puts even the circumcised Jew *outside* the covenant.

On the other hand, we should not ignore the fact that Paul also says,
"Circumcision *is of value* if you keep the law." Paul does not turn his back
on the idea of a covenant, a special relationship between God and (some
of) his creatures; certainly he does not turn away from the covenant made
by God with Abraham and his descendants and sealed by circumcision, not
even from a close tie-up between God's covenant people and the law. "What
is this value in circumcision and in being a Jew?" is a question which his
argument is forcing steadily closer to the surface, and he will shortly offer a
brief answer to it (3:1–2). For the moment we may simply note the further
hint of continuity between the law and Paul's gospel, that keeping the law
in at least some sense is important for Paul, though clearly not in a sense
which equates law-keeping with being a circumcised Jew.

26 The same point is reinforced in v 26. It is this keeping of the law
which really counts: the Gentile who thus keeps the requirements of the
law shall be reckoned as in effect one of the circumcised, a member of the
covenant people, even without circumcision. Such a flagrant departure from
Gen 17:9–14 and Exod 12:43–49 would appall most devout Jews, but the
Gentile believers at Rome would no doubt recognize that the argument was
driving strongly in their favor and would be expecting some exposition of
what "keeping the requirements of the law" meant in their case at a later
stage in the letter. Those who had attended the synagogue as God-worshipers
in particular would rejoice at the clear implication of Paul's teaching: that
in order to become a full member of the covenant, a full participator in the

blessings God had promised to the people of Israel, it was *not* necessary to be circumcised.

27 With v 27 the charge is honed to its final sharpness. Once more, as throughout the chapter, we find set in antithesis the Gentile who keeps the law and the Jew who does not. On the one hand is he who never has been circumcised and yet "fulfills the law"; in this last phrase there is presumably an implication of an accomplishing of the law which is more than simply a matter of carrying out its ritual and outward requirements (cf. 13:8 with James 2:8). In contrast, and in confirmation of the last suggestion, stands the same interlocutor "who through the letter and circumcision is a transgressor of the law." In contrast to "fulfilling the law" "the letter" must mean something like the literal meaning, an understanding of the law which stays at the level of the ritual act and outward deed. The charge is sharp indeed! By resting on the law, in the false confidence that what the law requires is a strict observance of the practice of circumcision and the maintenance of the cult with its attendant laws, the devout Jew is actually transgressing the law. He has missed the point of the law and of circumcision. What he counts as "doing the law" Paul counts as transgressing the law! In consequence it will not be a case of the faithful Jew passing judgment on the lawless Gentile, as the interlocutor began by thinking (2:1–3), but rather a case of the law-fulfilling Gentile (by his faith and life) passing judgment on the law-transgressing Jew— this is what God's judgment of human secrets will reveal in the day of judgment (2:16). In a fitting climax to the argument the tables are neatly turned on the interlocutor, and the counsel for the prosecution (2:1–3) finds himself in the dock!

28–29 The reason for this surprising turn-around, and the theological thesis underlying the whole line of argument with the interlocutor in chap. 2, is summed up in the last two verses with terse and devastating simplicity. Throughout the chapter it has been becoming increasingly clear that Paul has in view different levels of law-keeping and that in this last paragraph he is using circumcision in two senses. But what is this circumcision which can be credited to Gentiles without actual circumcision? And how is it that physical circumcision can be a means of transgressing the law? Paul's answer is that the circumcision God looks for is *not* an outward visible cutting of the flesh, that the law is not to be thought of as *fulfilled* at that level. The circumcision God looks for is the circumcision of the heart, what the prophets had called for (Deut 10:16; Jer 4:4) and promised (Deut 30:6; Ezek 36:26–27; *Jub.* 1.23), something which various Gentiles had given greater evidence of (2:15), something which could be fully accomplished only by the Spirit of God. With this last phrase Paul begins to construct his answer to the question "How is the law to be properly carried out, fulfilled?"—a first hint which will be taken up again later, particularly in 7:6, 8:4 and illustratively in 12:1–15:6. It is already clear, however, that unlike the prophets in their criticism of the cult, Paul looks for a circumcision of the heart that completely *replaces* the physical rite and does not merely complement it, for a law-keeping which can be completely independent of so much of the law, the ritual law, which Jews regarded as fundamental, with all the authority of Moses behind them.

But not only is it the law and circumcision that Paul seeks to remove from the domain of Jewish national pride and self-assurance; even the title "Jew" itself comes into radical question. In a final confirmation of what had become increasingly evident throughout, that Paul is attacking a concept of law-keeping which was tightly tied to membership of the Jewish nation (what we can properly call "national righteousness"), comes this explicit association of "Jew," "circumcision," and "letter/written code." Paul will not allow this false understanding of God's covenant righteousness to retain even the title "Jew." Not only is the requirement of circumcision to be redefined (properly defined) in a way which renders the outward rite unnecessary, but the very name "Jew" is to be redefined (properly defined) also, as one whose Jewishness (= praiseworthiness) is dependent not on what spectators can see and approve, but on what God alone can see and approve (the hidden secrets of the heart— 2:16). With this final thrust Paul's readers would recognize once again that he was not turning his back on, far less rejecting, all these fundamental elements of Jewish self-understanding. On the contrary, he was affirming them and claiming them anew so that Jew first but also Gentile could appropriate them as something eschatologically fresh from God, but at the deeper level previously called for and hitherto promised (of the heart and by the Spirit), and now at last a present possibility and reality for those listening to his words in the congregations of Rome.

5. What Then of God's Faithfulness?   (3:1–8)

Bibliography

Barr, J. *The Semantics of Biblical Language.* Oxford: Oxford UP, 1961. 187–94. **Bornkamm, G.** "Theologie als Teufelskunst." *Geschichte und Glaube* II. Munich: Kaiser, 1971. 140–48. **Campbell, W. S.** "Romans 3." **Canales, I. J.** "Paul's Accusers in Romans 3:8 and 6:1." *EvQ* 57 (1985) 237–45. **Cosgrove, C. H.** "What If Some Have Not Believed? The Occasion and Thrust of Romans 3:1–8." *ZNW* 78 (1987) 90–105. **Doeve, J. W.** "Some Notes with Reference to ΤΑ ΛΟΓΙΑ ΤΟΥ ΘΕΟΥ in Romans 3:2." In *Studia Paulina*, FS J. de Zwaan, ed. J. N. Sevenster and W. C. van Unnik. Haarlem: Bohn, 1953. 111–23. **Hall, D. R.** "Romans 3:1–8 Reconsidered." *NTS* 29 (1983) 183–97. **Jeremias, J.** "Gedankenführung." *Abba.* 269–71. ———. "Chiasmus in den Paulusbriefen." *Abba.* 287–89. **Kertelge, K.** *Rechtfertigung.* 63–70. **Lüdemann, G.** *Paulus, der Heidenapostel.* II. *Antipaulinismus im frühen Christentum.* Göttingen: Vandenhoeck & Ruprecht, 1983. 158–61. **Ljungman, H.** *Pistis,* 13–36. **Manson, T. W.** "Appendix on ΛΟΓΙΑ." *Studies.* 87–104. **Müller, C.** *Gerechtigkeit.* 65–67. **Piper, J.** "The Righteousness of God in Romans 3:1–8." *TZ* 36 (1980) 3–16. ———. *Justification.* 103–13. **Räisänen, H.** "Zum Verständnis von Röm 3:1–8." *SNTU* 10 (1985) 93–108. In *Torah,* 185–205. **Stowers, S. K.** "Paul's Dialogue with a Fellow Jew in Romans 3:1–9." *CBQ* 46 (1984) 707–22. **Stuhlmacher, P.** *Gerechtigkeit.* 84–86. **Synofzik, E.** *Vergeltungsaussagen.* 34–35, 83–85. **Theobald, M.** *Gnade.* 133–39. **Watson, F.** *Paul.* 124–29. **Williams, S. K.** "Righteousness." 265–70.

Translation

¹ *What then is the advantage of the Jew, or what is the value of circumcision?* ² *Much in every way! In the first place,*ª *they were entrusted with the oracles of*

God. ³ *So, where does that leave us? If some have been unfaithful, has their unfaithful-ness done away with the faithfulness of God?* ⁴ *Not at all! Let God be true and "every man a liar." As it is written,* ᵇ

> *"that you might be justified in your words*
> *and shall overcome* ᶜ *when you are on trial."*

⁵ *But if our unrighteousness demonstrates the righteousness of God, what shall we say? Is God unjust in inflicting wrath? (I speak from a human standpoint.)* ⁶ *Not at all! Otherwise, how will God judge the world?* ⁷ *But* ᵈ *if the truth of God has by my lie overflowed to his glory, why am I still judged as a sinner?* ⁸ *Why do we not say, as some slanderously report us to say, "Let us do evil that good might come of it"? Their condemnation is well deserved.*

Notes

ᵃThe fact that the πρῶτον is not followed by an ἔπειτα, "first, then, . . . ," resulted in some attempts at stylistic improvement, notably Origen's reading of πρῶτοι, "they were the first to be entrusted . . . ."

ᵇNestle²⁶ reads καθώς despite the superior attestation of καθάπερ, which Paul may well have used as a variant on the more familiar καθὼς γέγραπται elsewhere in Romans (9:13; 10:15; 11:8), though in each case Nestle²⁶ reads καθώς with the support of P⁴⁶ which is lacking here.

ᶜSince νικήσῃς is the more natural reading (both grammatically and as the LXX reading) and since νικήσεις could have been a slip on the part of a very early (even the earliest) amanuensis, it could be argued that νικήσῃς is original. But as things stand in the manuscript tradition the future indicative must be regarded as earlier—it is certainly grammatically possible (BDF §369.3)—with the subjunctive a subsequent correction to improve the construction and to assimilate the text to LXX.

ᵈεἰ δέ (ℵ A etc.) should certainly be read against εἰ γάρ (B G D etc.). V 7 is not an explanation of v 6 but a repetition of v 5, since v 6 has not provided a sufficient answer.

Form and Structure

That the target of Paul's indictment in chap. 2 is not gross law-breaking (such as Gentiles were accused of in 1:19–32) but the (equally "unrighteous") Jewish assumption of advantage vis-à-vis the non-Jew, by being the people of God as marked out by circumcision, is confirmed by v 1. Paul is well aware that his argument puts in question the traditional understanding of God's election of Israel. But he reasserts God's faithfulness as strongly as any covenant-conscious Jew (v 3; against Räisänen). The point is that it is God's faithfulness as righteous Creator and Judge, and not just as God of Israel, and certainly not as determined by criteria of ethnic identity. But this point depends on a more detailed argument over the following chapters and cannot be developed yet.

The section is transitional. Paul at first perseveres with the diatribe style (Stowers, "Romans 3:1–9"; despite Hall); but the debate becomes increasingly with himself. The questions are no longer merely rhetorical devices to help forward his own exposition, but hard questions with existential bite for his own faith (note the first-person usage, particularly in vv 5–7). Although he is not ready to tackle these questions, the momentum of the diatribe and his own integrity force him to bring them into the open at once. But since he cannot provide a proper response to them at this stage the dialogue loses momentum and direction. The unsatisfactory character of Paul's response (because at this point he can only deal in slogans and assert axioms) has often obscured from commentators the way in which Paul uses the opportunity not only to point forward to subsequent discussion (particularly chaps. 6 and 9–11), but also to tie his discussion back into the first part of his indictment: note particularly

         3.3—1.17;   3.5—1.17–18;   3.7—1.25.

3:1–8 therefore is something of a bridge between earlier and later parts of the letter, or like a railway junction through which many of the key ideas and themes of the epistle pass (cf. Campbell, "Romans 3").

Jeremias, "Chiasmus," notes the chiastic structure of vv 4–8, where the first objection (v 5) takes up the second scriptural quotation (v 4b), and the second objection (vv 7–8a) takes up the first scriptural reference (v 4a). "The antinomy 'sin of men and faithfulness of God' is the constant of the passage" (Theobald, 138).

Comment

3:1 τί οὖν . . . ἢ τίς . . ., "what then . . . or what . . . ?" For the double question as a feature of Paul's style, cf. 10:6–7 and 11:34–35.

τὸ περισσὸν τοῦ Ἰουδαίου, "the advantage of the Jew." From περισσός in the sense of "exceeding the usual amount" is derived the substantive, τὸ περισσόν (= "the advantage, benefit" [BGD; cf. Prov 14:23; Matt 5:47]). Paul's speaking of "the Jew" here confirms the observation on 2:17 that by Ἰουδαῖος Paul means the typical Jew, "the Jew" as a national type. Such characterization of a people is a feature of all ages and as such can be appropriate and valid without being disparaging or necessarily of universal application.

ἡ ὠφέλεια τῆς περιτομῆς, "the value of circumcision." ὠφέλεια means "utility, gain, profit, advantage." Both questions presuppose the standpoint of one who has hitherto assumed that being a Jew is an advantage, that being circumcised is of value—the presumption of "the Jew." The close conjunction of the questions also confirms that circumcision was closely bound up with the identity of "the Jew" (see on 2:25).

2 πολὺ κατὰ πάντα τρόπον, "much in every way." For the idiom see BGD, τρόπος. Dodd's comment "The logical answer on the basis of Paul's argument is, "None whatever!' " shows that he has missed the real point of the preceding indictment.

πρῶτον μὲν ὅτι ἐπιστεύθησαν τὰ λόγια τοῦ θεοῦ, "In the first place, they were entrusted with the oracles of God" ("the very words of God"—NIV). πρῶτον usually denotes the first of a series (as in 1 Cor 12:28), but Paul begins thus without completing the sequence elsewhere (see on 1:8), although he certainly had other advantages in mind (9:4–5). πιστεύειν in the sense of "entrust with" is fairly common, and not specifically Christian (see BGD, πιστεύω 3). By τὰ λόγια (only here in Paul) Paul means the utterances of God, given through

Moses and the prophets (he makes no closer specification) and now constituting the holy scriptures (1:2). This usage is already established in the LXX (Deut 33:9; Isa 5:24; Pss 12:6 [LXX 11:7]; 18:30 [LXX 17:31]; 107 [LXX 106]:11; 119 [LXX 118]:11, 25 (S), 38, etc.; cf. Philo, *Praem.* 1; *Vit. Cont.* 25; Josephus, *War* 6.311; Heb 5:12). But elsewhere in Greek usage λόγιον means an "oracle" or "oracular saying" (LSJ, BGD), and this sense of the numinous quality of an inspired utterance is also present in Num 24:4, 16 and reflected in Acts 7:38 ("living oracles") and 1 Pet 4:11 (charismatic utterance). See further Manson, *Studies*, 87–96. For the view that Paul refers specifically to the promises of God see Williams, "Righteousness," 267, and *Notes* (the debate goes back to the Fathers—see Lagrange). But Paul does not yet so restrict his thought (cf. 9:4–5).

A play on the concept of πίστις is clearly intended in vv 2–3 (ἐπιστεύθησαν, ἠπίστησαν, ἀπιστία, πίστιν), but its scope is not clear. If ἐπιστεύθησαν is intended to evoke Jewish responsibility within the covenant, with reference to the δικαιώματα of 2:26 (as Stuhlmacher, *Gerechtigkeit*, 85 suggests), the point is that the δικαιώματα are not conceived in the terms used by Deut 4:7–8 or Ps 147:19–20, but as "oracles" given to the Jews to hold in trust for others. This is the implication of πιστεύω when Paul uses it in this way of his own commissioning and gospel (1 Cor 9:17; Gal 2:7; 1 Thess 2:4; also 1 Tim 1:11; Titus 1:3), and may be implied in the choice of λόγια to indicate divine oracles whose interpretation had only become clear through the gospel of Christ.

3 τί γάρ; "So, where does that leave us?" ("what, then, is the situation?"— BGD); cf. Phil 1:18. For different possible punctuations see Cranfield.

εἰ ἠπίστησάν τινες, "if some have been unfaithful." As in 11:17 τινές, "some," denotes the bulk of Paul's Jewish contemporaries (= "the Jew" in the preceding diatribe—a further indication that 2:1–29 is not a blanket condemnation of all Jews by any means; see on 2:21–23). But Paul assumes this current lack of faith is temporary (chap. 11) and so may be speaking from a much larger perspective (cf. Althaus, Schlier). ἠπίστησαν and ἀπιστία could be taken as denoting unbelief (= failure to believe), as in 4:20 and 11:20, 23 (SH, Schlatter, Gaugler, Cranfield, Räisänen, "Röm 3:1–8," Cosgrove), or in the sense "unfaithful, faithless" (RSV, NEB, Lightfoot and most commentators). In the context where ἐπιστεύθησαν means "entrusted" and πίστις denotes the faithfulness of God (see below), the latter is the more obvious sense. The thought focuses wholly on the covenant relationship between God and Israel, and so on "the Jew's" obligation under that covenant, faithfulness within that covenant (against Räisänen, the argument is still at the stage of the indictment outlined in 2:17–29, and not yet at chaps. 9–11). The typical Jew saw that faithfulness simply in terms of keeping the commandments (Sir 32:24; 2 Apoc. Bar. 48.22) and could take pride in the fact that Israel's belief in God's covenant(s) marked them out from other nations (4 Ezra 3.32)—as had Paul himself (Gal 1:14; Phil 3:5–6); see further *Introduction* §5. Paul, however, now saw that covenant obligation at a deeper level (2:28–29), as always having had the nations in mind for the eschatological future (cf. 4:11–18), but in such a way as to nullify the presumption that (physical) membership of the Jewish nation was still fundamental to covenant membership (2:17–29). Jewish unfaithfulness

for Paul means the failure of "some" Jews to recognize the meaning of what
had been entrusted to them for the epoch now dawned (see also on 4:20).
Thus ἀπιστία does not exclude the sense of unbelief (cf. 10:16). The range
of meaning possible here confirms the danger of treating the meanings of
πίστις as though they were sharply distinct (or even polarized points), rather
than a continuous spectrum where the meaning "faith" merges into the meaning "faithful" (see further on 1:17).

μὴ ἡ ἀπιστία αὐτῶν τὴν πίστιν τοῦ θεοῦ καταργήσει, "has their unfaithfulness
done away with the faithfulness of God?" πίστις in the sense of "faithfulness"
was quite common in Greek thought (BGD, πίστις 1), and appears elsewhere
in the NT (Matt 23:23; Gal 5:22; 2 Thess 1:4; Titus 2:10), though swamped
by the dominant usage as "faith." In the LXX it is comparatively infrequent,
but is used several times to denote God's faithfulness (Ps 33 [LXX 32]:4;
Hos 2:22 [LXX 20]; Hab 2:4; Lam 3:23; also *Pss. Sol.* 8.35), always as a
translation for אֱמוּנָה, so denoting his firmness and reliability, his constant
faithfulness (BDB, *TDOT* 1:309–20). The fact that in reverting to the theme
of πίστις (for the first time since 1:17) Paul speaks of God's faithfulness has
not been given enough weight in the exegesis of 1:17 and of the epistle as
a whole, which can be characterized precisely as an attempt on Paul's part
to work out the tension between πίστις = God's faithfulness (to Israel) and
πίστις as faith (in Christ Jesus). Cf. the formula πιστὸς ὁ θεός: "God is faithful"
(1 Cor 1:9; 10:13; 2 Cor 1:18; cf. 1 Thess 5:24; 2 Thess 3:3). Despite Käsemann,
the thought of the new covenant is not present here, but rather the continuity
of God's purpose in his original covenant commitment to Israel. Williams's
argument that Paul has in view God's promises (through Abraham to the
nations—"Righteousness," 268–69) likewise distinguishes too sharply between
the election of Israel and the promise made with a view to the nations (but
contrast 4:16); but the question of 3:3 is posed precisely in response to 2:17–
29.

καταργεῖν can have the stronger sense of "abolish, do away with" (as in 1
Cor 6:13; 15:24). But here the sense of "nullify, render ineffective" is presumably more what Paul had in mind (cf. 3:31; 4:14). See further on 3:31 and
6:6.

4 μὴ γένοιτο, literally, "may it not be," is a strong negation, which Paul
uses quite frequently after rhetorical questions, chiefly in Romans (3:6, 31;
6:2, 15; 7:7, 13; 9:14; 11:1, 11; also 1 Cor 6:15; Gal 2:17; 3:21; the usage is
quite common in Epictetus—20 times in *Diss.* [Lagrange]; but it also occurs
occasionally in the LXX—Gen 44:7, 17; Deut 24:16; 1 Kgs 21:3 [LXX 3
Kgs 20:3]; 1 Macc 9:10; 13:5). Hence the translation can be flexible in order
to bring out the strength of Paul's repugnance at the idea suggested: "By
no means!" "God forbid!" etc. (BGD, γίνομαι 3a); "Impossible" (Maillot). Here
the force of Paul's rejoinder underlines the extent to which he sees
(a) God's covenant with Israel as still in force, (b) the current typical Jewish
understanding of the covenant as a misunderstanding, and (c) his gospel as
continuous with and the fulfillment of God's covenant purpose with Israel.
Unless this triple theme is clearly perceived as a determining factor of primary
importance in the construction of this letter, Paul's language here and elsewhere will seem like empty rhetoric.

γινέσθω δὲ ὁ θεὸς ἀληθής, "let God be true." There is a Hebraic connection of thought between the ἀλήθεια of God here and the πίστις of God in v 3, which would probably be lost on Paul's readers unless they were very familiar with the LXX. אֱמוּנָה, usually translated by πίστις elsewhere in the LXX (see on 3:3), is almost always translated ἀλήθεια in the Psalms, regularly to denote God's covenant faithfulness to Israel (see particularly Ps 89:1, 2, 5, 8, 14, 24, 33, 49 [LXX 88:2, 3, 6, 9, 25, 34, 50]; 98 [LXX 97]:3), with Ps 33 [LXX 32]:4 the interesting exception. In both cases Paul will have had in mind the constancy and reliability of God, but the Greek word allows him to extend the meaning to "real, true" (see further on 1:18; also Ljungman, 17–21; and note Barr's cautionary remarks, *Semantics,* 187–94), implying once again that "the Jew" has misconceived the true character and real purpose of the covenant made with Israel. The ἀληθής here helps link this section of Paul's indictment back into the earlier indictment where he used ἀλήθεια regularly (1:18, 25; 2:2, 8, 20). γίνομαι is often used, as possibly here, simply with the force of the verb "to be" (BGD, γίνομαι II), though Paul probably uses it here with eschatological force: "let God become" = "be seen to be true" (Schlatter, Käsemann).

πᾶς δὲ ἄνθρωπος ψεύστης, καθάπερ γέγραπται, "and every man a liar, as it is written," is probably intended as a quotation from Ps 116:11[LXX 115:2].

Ps 115:2: πᾶς   ἄνθρωπος ψεύστης
Rom 3:4:   πᾶς δὲ ἄνθρωπος ψεύστης

In such a brief allusion it is quite possible that Paul simply fell into scriptural language without intending a particular reference. But in this case the language is fairly distinct (ψεύστης occurs only in Prov 19:22 and Sir 15:8; 25:2 elsewhere in the LXX). On the other hand, the καθάπερ γέγραπται, "as it is written" (see *Notes* and on 1:17) clearly refers to the following quotation, and if the words are indeed intended as a direct quotation it is atomistic in character since the context of Ps 116 [LXX 115] seems to add nothing to its use here.

ὅπως ἂν δικαιωθῇς ἐν τοῖς λόγοις σου
καὶ νικήσεις ἐν τῷ κρίνεσθαί σε
"that you might be justified in your words
and shall overcome when you are on trial."

The quotation from Ps 50:6 LXX [= Ps 51:4] is exact except that LXX reads νικήσῃς in the second line. The psalmist uses the picture of the heavenly law court and of the manifest justice of God's judgment as a vivid way of expressing his own lawlessness and sin. The repeated confession of ἀνομία and ἁμαρτία (LXX Ps 50:4, 5, 7, 11) is unusual (elsewhere in the Psalms only in LXX 31:5; 37:19; 58:4; 78:8–9; 84:3; 102:10; 108:14; 140:4). That David confesses to "lawlessness" is presumably a factor in Paul's citing of the psalm, since in the eyes of the Jewish interlocutor lawlessness = faithlessness. Ljungman draws out the importance of the lawsuit imagery in Second Isaiah, particularly Isa 43:9—"Israel's litigation with God . . . means that Israel deserts its mission, according to Isa 43:9 ff." (*Pistis,* 23). LXX's second line is surprising (but cf. particularly *Pss. Sol.* 2.15; 3.5; 4.8; 8.7, 26; 9.2) since it depicts God as defendant in a lawsuit (to take κρίνεσθαι as a middle [cf. 1 Cor 6:1] would not completely resolve the problem; "when you give judgment" [NJB; cf. NIV] is inadmissible). Paul does not question or try to escape this sense, since he sees all too well that his indictment of his own people necessarily carries with it an indictment of the God who remains faithful to such a people. He is confident, however, that the reality of God's covenant purpose and God's faithfulness to Israel (not his punitive judgment, as Piper, *Justification*, 110–12, argues) will be vindicated in the final judgment. Only from the perspective of the eschaton can God's truth and faithfulness be properly understood (cf. Rom 11). The vision of the whole of human history as a trial between the truth of God and the claims of man is impressive (cf. again Käsemann). God will be God, whatever man says. "In this verse lies the deepest *motif* of Paul's teaching on justification" (Michel).

Similar assertions of the justice of God's judgment are a constant refrain in *Pss. Sol.* (2.16–19; 3.3; 4.9, 28; 5.1; 8.7–8, 27, 29–32, 40; 9.3–4; 10.6; 17.12), but there as an expression of trust in the covenant God. It is precisely because Paul has questioned the usual assumption of his "righteous" countrymen, that Israel can rest confidently in God's judgment because of his covenant obligation (righteousness) to Israel, that this line of questioning has been forced upon Paul. To question the terms of God's commitment to Israel (so he replies in effect) is *not* to question that commitment or the ground for trusting in the righteousness of God's judgment. Cf. also Wilckens 1:164–65, 168.

5 εἰ δὲ ἡ ἀδικία ἡμῶν θεοῦ δικαιοσύνην συνίστησιν, "but if our unrighteousness brings out the righteousness of God." συνίστημι has the sense of "put together" and so "demonstrate, show" (as in 5:8; 2 Cor 7:11; Gal 2:18). The ἀδικία/δικαιοσύνη wordplay is obviously deliberate (as also in 1:17–18). ἀδικία is resumptive both of ἀπιστία (v 3) and of the summary ἀδικία in the introduction to the whole section (1:18; also 1:29; 2:8). It thus embraces the thought of Jewish unfaithfulness and treats it as part of the universal ἀδικία (cf. Müller, *Gerechtigkeit*, 66–67, 112; Kertelge, *Rechtfertigung*, 68). Likewise the δικαιοσύνη θεοῦ must be resumptive of ἡ πιστίς τοῦ θεοῦ (v 3), confirming its strong covenant significance for Paul, as denoting God's action in favor of his people, or of humankind in general, despite their failure to respond appropriately (see on 1:17; and see Piper, *Justification*, 105–10, and Achtemeier). Hence the problem posed here. Paul thus uses covenant language to reaffirm the basic covenant concepts of the Jewish scriptures which had hitherto prevailed. In speaking of "our unrighteousness" he speaks as everyman, or more precisely as a Jew who now sees the universal implications of what had hitherto been an exclusively Jewish insight. Bornkamm, "Theologie," 145–46, and Williams, "Righteousness," 268 n.82, underplay in different directions the degree of continuity in Paul's thought between God's righteousness as covenant faithfulness and this more universal perspective (cf. Reumann, 73–74; Zeller).

τί ἐροῦμεν, "what shall we say?" is a regular feature of Paul's style in this letter (4:1; 6:1; 7:7; 8:31; 9:14, 30). See on 6:1.

μὴ ἄδικος ὁ θεὸς ὁ ἐπιφέρων τὴν ὀργήν; "is God unjust in inflicting wrath?" By introducing the question with μὴ Paul indicates a question expecting a negative answer. For ἐπιφέρειν in the sense of "inflict, bring to bear," cf. *Ep. Arist.* 253; Josephus, *Ant.* 2.296. The ὀργή is primarily eschatological (v 6), but includes the "wrath" already being displayed—ἐπιφέρων, present tense (see on 1:18 and 2:5). The very fact that the thought of God's wrath could prompt the suggestion of God as *unjust* is a further indication of the extent to which the concept of God's righteousness is dominated by the sense of his gratuitous favor toward man (see also on 9:14). "Wrath" is not just one aspect of "righteousness"; otherwise the question would not arise (cf. Bornkamm, "Wrath," 63–64; Kertelge, *Rechtfertigung*, 70).

κατὰ ἄνθρωπον λέγω, "I speak in a human way, from a human standpoint" (cf. 6:19; 1 Cor 9:8; Gal 3:15 [BGD, ἄνθρωπος 1c; cf. Str-B, 3:136–39]), is a parenthetic apology for the blasphemous thought of God as unjust (cf. Harrisville). Paul is forced into this train of thought not because of the logic of his own position, but because it sets up such a tension with what he himself had previously always assumed to be the proper understanding of the relation between God's righteousness and Israel's covenant privileges and obligations. It is precisely because Paul speaks from the standpoint of everyman and no longer from the standpoint of the typical Jew that the previously clear-cut lines of divine-human relationship appear (in Jewish eyes at least) to have become wholly confused.

6 μὴ γένοιτο, "God forbid": see on 3:4.

ἐπεὶ πῶς κρινεῖ ὁ θεὸς τὸν κόσμον; "otherwise how will God judge the world?" ἐπεί in this sense has classical precedent (BGD; also 11:6, 22; 1 Cor 14:16; 15:29; Heb 10:2). κρινεῖ could be punctuated as a present (κρίνει—see Lightfoot, referring to Gen 18:25), in which case the present tenses of vv 5–6 could be taken as describing divine functions rather than as temporal (God is one who . . .). But it is more likely that it should be taken as a direct reference to the final judgment as such. κόσμος can be used for the totality of the universe (as in 1:20), but also for humankind, as also in 3:19 and 11:12, 15. Worthy of note is the fact that κόσμος in Romans lacks the pejorative note prominent in 1 Cor 1:20–21, 27–28; 3:19, etc. and present elsewhere in Paul's writings (especially 2 Cor 7:10; Gal 6:14; Col 2:20) and particularly in the Fourth Gospel (1:10; 7:7; 8:23; etc.). See further BGD; on Pauline usage *TDNT* 3:892–93. It is the axiomatic character of this belief (God as final judge—see on 2:2) which rules out of order the more loosely formulated thought of v 5. Paul presumably felt able to respond to the awkward train of thought at this point only by noting that its corollary is a *reductio ad absurdum*. Paul did not shirk the fact that faith in God has to operate from certain fixed axioms; his problems arose from his questioning of the hitherto accepted meaning of what had always been one of the other axioms of Jewish faith (God's choice of Israel to be his people). That God's judgment was "righteous" was also fundamental (e.g., Gen 18:25; Deut 32:4; Job 34:10–12); but Paul's broadening out of the concept of God's righteousness (χωρὶς νόμου—3:21) had upset one of the touchstones by which his own people had previously escaped such conundrums (v 5).

7 εἰ δὲ ἡ ἀλήθεια τοῦ θεοῦ, "but if the truth of God." With ἀλήθεια one of the key linking words of this whole opening section (1:18–3:20) is repeated for the last time (1:18, 25; 2:2, 8, 20; 3:7). Note again that the Hebrew concept of God's reliability (אֱמֶת, אֱמוּנָה) underlies the Greek here (see on 1:18 and 3:4; BGD, ἀλήθεια 1), tying the thought back into the preceding context. In the sequence of parallel questions in vv 3, 5, and 7 the parallel concepts are ἡ πίστις τοῦ θεοῦ, ἡ δικαιοσύνη τοῦ θεοῦ and ἡ ἀλήθεια τοῦ θεοῦ (Stuhlmacher, *Gerechtigkeit*, 86; Schlier; "virtual equivalents"—Williams, "Righteousness," 268).

ἐν τῷ ἐμῷ ψεύσματι, "by my lie." As the opposite of ἀλήθεια, ψεῦσμα for Paul would have the connotation of "untruthfulness, undependability" (BGD). As with the parallel question in v 5 Paul endeavors to link up with the earlier part of the indictment: 3:5—1:17–18; 3:7—1:25 (τὴν ἀλήθειαν τοῦ θεοῦ ἐν τῷ ψεύδει). The allusion sharpens the problem: in 1:25 the contrast between divine truth and human lie was the occasion for outright condemnation; but here the same response to God (lying) provokes not wrath but the demonstration of God's reliability as faithfulness to the liar! ἐμῷ ψεύσματι, "my lie"— even though he speaks from the far side of 3:20 Paul is not able to distance himself from the plight of unrighteous Gentile and unfaithful Jew (cf. Schlatter); the "my" is not merely rhetorical, as Murray suggests.

ἐπερίσσευσεν εἰς τὴν δόξαν αὐτοῦ, "has overflowed to his glory." περισσεύειν has the sense of existing in excess, "to be more than enough, have in abundance." The meaning is clear though difficult to translate felicitously: God in his faithfulness as Creator and covenant God discounts the falsehood and infidelity of man by continuing to uphold him as creature and covenant partner. It is this overflowing of generosity which brings God honor and renown (see further on 5:15; on God's δόξα see on 1:21 and 3:23). It is a striking feature of Paul's theology that what brings God glory (brightens his image, we might say) is the exercise of his mercy and grace (cf. particularly 9:23; 2 Cor 4:15); he does not speak in the same way of God's wrath. It is of the essence of his faith that God is first and foremost a God of grace (see also on 9:15).

τί ἔτι κἀγὼ ὡς ἁμαρτωλὸς κρίνομαι; "why am I still judged as a sinner?" ἁμαρτωλός is a particularly Jewish word, denoting those who are lawbreakers, either as knowing but disobeying the law, or as ignorant of the law in the first place (= Gentiles; e.g., Ps 119 [118 LXX]:53, 155; 1 Macc 2:44, 48; *Pss. Sol.* 2.1–2; Matt 5:47//Luke 6:33; Mark 2:15–17 pars.; Gal 2:15; see further on 4:5 and *Introduction* §5.3.1). The problem is that such an understanding of God's faithfulness calls into question the concept of judgment and of the law in terms of which the verdict is reached. When God is so gracious, what is the part and function of the law? As so often in Romans the real problematic feature of Paul's gospel is not so much man as the law.

8 καὶ μὴ καθὼς βλασφημούμεθα καὶ καθώς φασίν τινες ἡμᾶς λέγειν ὅτι ποιήσωμεν τὰ κακὰ ἵνα ἔλθῃ τὰ ἀγαθά; "and not as we are slanderously reported and as some allege that we say, 'Let us do evil in order that good might come'?" βλασφημεῖν in the sense of "defame, libel" is well enough known in the Greek of the time (BGD; cf. Acts 13:45; 18:6; 1 Cor 10:30; Titus 3:2), but already in the LXX it had gained the technical sense "blaspheme," referring to a word (or action) directed against God. Since the assumption is regularly that "blasphemy" is what Gentiles do by failing to recognize the special favor in which God holds Israel (see particularly 2 Kgs 19:4, 6, 22; Ezek 35:12; 2

Macc 15:24; cf. Josephus, *Ap.* 1.59; cf. *TDNT* 1:621–22), there may be the overtone here that many of Paul's Jewish and/or Jewish Christian opponents thought him treacherously blasphemous (see also 14:16). Paul, of course, has already leveled the equivalent charge in the opposite direction (2:24 = Isa 52:5).

φασίν τινες . . ., "some say . . .," is the first hint in Romans of explicit opposition to Paul, though the preceding diatribe almost certainly drew on earlier controversies and arguments. The vagueness of the allusion tells against the view that Paul was directing his comment against particular individuals among the Roman congregations. The evidence of his other letters is that Paul was much more direct in his address to those who criticized his teaching. And though the challenge posed is an important one for him (6:1), and had certainly been raised against his teaching elsewhere (but not necessarily just from the Jewish side—e.g., Schlatter, Althaus, and Zeller; against Schlier and Wilckens), both here and in 6:1 it appears as a corollary to his own exposition and not as a question asked by his readers. The fact that he can pose the issue quite so bluntly (does his teaching amount to saying, "Let us do evil that good may result"?) clearly shows the risk Paul was taking in freeing the righteousness of God from its close correlation with the law as delivered to the covenant people: to break the link between covenant righteousness and covenant law seemed to many a slight on God's own morality. Hence the need on Paul's part to clarify the ethical outworking of his redefinition of covenant righteousness, in general terms in chaps. 6–8, and in more detail in 12:1–15:6 (see further 12:1–15:13 *Introduction*).

ὧν τὸ κρίμα ἔνδικόν ἐστιν, "whose condemnation is just," "they deserve what's coming to them." The ὧν is more naturally taken as a reference to the τινές rather than to what they say. For κρίμα, "judgment, condemnation," see on 2:2 and 11:33; elsewhere in Paul (2:2, 3; 5:16; 11:33; 13:2; 1 Cor 6:7; 11:29, 34; Gal 5:10). ἔνδικος, "based on what is right," hence "just, deserved" is found elsewhere in the NT only in Heb 2:2. Paul curtails the line of questioning abruptly, trusting in his own conviction as to the rightness of his message and in the same assurance that God's judgment is just (cf. 9:20). Canales suggests that 3:8–31 forms an answer to the question (v 8), without giving thought to the character of 3:9 as introducing a conclusion to the preceding indictment, particularly 2:1–3:8 (see on 3:9).

Explanation

3:1 To anyone following the line and force of Paul's argument with his interlocutor the inevitable response can no longer be put off: "What then is the advantage of being a Jew? What value has circumcision?" If being a member of the Jewish nation, if the authenticating badge of covenant membership in the people of Israel counts for so little, has the Jew any advantage whatsoever in God's dealings with humankind? The very fact that the question can be put and put in such terms is clear confirmation of Paul's target in chap. 2: the "Jew" in his self-assurance as a Jew, i.e., Jewish overconfidence in the privilege of being God's chosen people. It is the *assumption* that being a Jew *is* an advantage, that circumcision *is* of value even when one goes on to break the law (2:25), that Paul has attacked—and attacked so effectively that the slightly agonized cry of Jewish self-identity responds in bewildered protest.

2 Paul's reply is at first sight surprising: "Much, in every way." However, it would be a complete surprise only for those who had understood Paul's argument so far in too sharply antithetical terms, as though in rejecting covenant presumption he had rejected the whole idea of the covenant as well, and as though in questioning the value of possessing the law and performing the outward rite he had denied any role to the law or any significance to circumcision. But as we have noted frequently in chaps. 1 and 2, Paul by no means turns his back on his heritage as a Jew. On the contrary, fundamental to his understanding of the gospel is the conviction that it stands in complete continuity with what the prophets preached beforehand in the scriptures (1:2). God intended that the law should be done, that it should be fulfilled (2:13, 27). Circumcision *has* an important meaning (2:26, 29). Hence Paul's immediate response.

He begins to expand this initial answer in a way which suggests he wants to say a good deal more ("In the first place"). That may simply be a stylistic device to signal to his addressees that he has much more to say on the subject, but that it is inappropriate to the development of his argument to present that fuller treatment here. Or he may indeed have been caught up in the spirit of the diatribe and found himself forced by the logic of his argument to raise the issue of Israel's special status with God before he was ready to tackle it in detail. Either way he does not really come to grips with the issue at this point and cuts off the interlocutor's line of questioning with some rather abrupt generalizations. His awkwardness in handling the issue in these verses is partly explained by the fact that the issue is of such fundamental importance to him, himself being a Jew, that he cannot suppress it any longer, even though he is not yet in a position to deal with it adequately. (It is worth following Paul's train of thought in some detail, however, despite its incomplete and unsatisfactory development, since in wrestling with the issue raised he exposes some of the basic presuppositions and foundational elements in his thought and gospel.)

The answer Paul actually does give, though only partial and the beginning of a much larger exposition (to be resumed in chaps. 9–11), does pick out by implication one of the chief points underlying this whole opening section of the letter: the continuity between the revelation given to Israel and the gospel of God's Son. The advantage experienced by the Jewish people was that "they had been entrusted with the oracles of God." The last phrase is unique in Paul and was no doubt deliberately chosen (in preference to "word(s)" or "promises"). It would certainly be taken to refer to the words of God spoken and written in the Jewish scriptures. But for a gentile readership the word "oracle" would evoke the thought of inspired utterances preserved from the past, often mysterious and puzzling in character, awaiting some key to unlock their meaning. Paul may well imply then that the Jews had been entrusted with the stewardship of safeguarding and preserving these oracles of God until the coming of the key, that is, the gospel of Christ Jesus, which unlocked the mystery of what had always been God's purpose but which had remained hidden hitherto until this time of the End (cf. 11:25–27; 16:25–26). Alternatively, Paul could be taken to imply that the Jews should have understood what God was saying to them all the time ("the oracles of God" being clearer than "what may be known of God"—1:19), and that their stewardship was a commissioning (cf. Gal 2:7) to make these revelations known to the wider world.

3 Either way they had failed, or at least "some" had—Paul's delicate way of reminding his readers that not all Jews had rejected the gospel. They had failed God's trust: either because having preserved the oracles of God for so many generations they had now failed to recognize the real meaning of them as given by the gospel; or because they had never recognized the real meaning in the first place, and in discharging their responsibility to the Gentiles as they saw it (2:19–20), they were presenting and living by a misconception of their covenant and the law (2:21–29).

The question which this Jewish unfaithfulness raises for Paul is striking: Does their faithlessness render ineffective the faithfulness of God? Why this question? The answer must be that behind Paul's thinking is the recognition that the covenant with Israel had been given by God, i.e., that the relationship between God and his chosen people had been established and maintained by God, by God's faithfulness. Paul in fact himself holds to the same basic conviction which lies behind the Jewish presumption attacked by him in chap. 2! It is his own attack on that presumption which inevitably puts a question mark also against the common underlying conviction. The question which cannot be avoided is whether the Jewish failure denounced in chap. 2, the failure to recognize God's purpose and the significance of "the oracles of God," means that God's loyalty to Israel has been in vain, or should result in God washing his hands of Israel, abolishing his covenant with the Jews. Was the choice of Israel and the entrusting of the oracles of God to the Jews a mistake from the beginning? Should God abandon Israel and start afresh? Paul's answer in effect is a firm negative: God's faithfulness is not determined by Jewish unfaithfulness. As God remained faithful to his covenant with Israel in the past, despite Israel's unfaithfulness, so he will remain faithful to Israel in the present and future, despite Israel's continuing unfaithfulness in rejecting the gospel.

The significance of this verse is not least that here for the first time in the letter we find the other key element ("from faith to faith") in the thematic statement of 1:17 being taken up—"righteousness from God's faithfulness." The implications of this are profound. God's faithfulness is thought of as in the first place directed toward *Israel*. This confirms the earlier suggestion that behind 1:17 in Paul's mind stood the Old Testament understanding of God's righteousness as God's saving action on behalf of Israel, more particularly on behalf of undeserving Israel. Paul cannot allow that Israel's unfaithfulness has nullified God's choice of Israel, his righteousness towards Israel, for the simple reason that such an admission would undermine his own gospel; such is the continuity between God's purpose for Israel and the gospel of his Son. On the contrary, God's *continuing* faithfulness towards Israel is for Paul a primary confirmation of Paul's belief that God's righteousness is from faith to faith, is neither dependent on nor destroyed by Israel's misunderstanding of the law and its role, and is neither dependent on nor destroyed by man's works of unfaithfulness.

4 But here he can only hint at such profounder implications. He is not yet ready to develop that line of argument, and will not be ready to do so until he can expound the "from God's faithfulness" (chaps. 9–11) in the light of "to man's faith" (3:21–5:21). In the meantime he contents himself with a brusque rejection of the very idea of God's being unfaithful by two terse citations from the Psalms. "Let God be true and 'every man a liar' (Ps 116:11)." The response is prompted by the fact that in the Hebraic categories which would often influence or shape Paul's train of thought the idea of God's faithfulness readily merged into that of God as true. God's faithfulness is not determined by man's response, whether of faith or of unfaith. God's truth is not called in question by man's misconstrual and perversion of it. The allusion back to the earlier stages of the argument will be deliberate, and would probably not have been lost on the attentive listener, since God's "truth" has been such a consistent motif throughout the argument, not only in the indictment of man in general (1:18, 25), but also in the indictment of Jewish religiosity in its falsely based pride (2:2, 8, 20). Here the connection of thought between vv 3 and 4 confirms that the Jews in general are included in the "every man a liar" (the "liar" includes the "unfaithful" Jew). The quotation therefore has the effect of including the Jewish interlocutor within the psalm's general indictment of humankind in general: the "Jew" in his unfaithfulness has suppressed the truth (1:18), has perverted the truth into a lie (1:25), and has disobeyed the truth (2:8), as much as anyone else. Nevertheless God will be true to his original purpose both in creating man (1:18, 25) and in choosing Israel (2:8, 20), Israel's "falseness" notwithstanding.

The second quotation (Ps 51:4) seems to contain the complex thought of God's final judgment (as in 2:16), in which both his condemnation of man's unrighteousness and lie will be seen to be just and according to truth (2:2), and his continuing faithfulness to Israel will be vindicated despite Israel's unfaithfulness:

> That you might be vindicated in your words,
> and shall overcome when you go to court/are on trial.

The previous context (chap. 2) and the context of Ps 51 itself suggest the thought of God's judgment of wrath. The psalmist confesses his "lawlessness and sin" repeatedly; it is because his sin is against God ("against you only have I sinned"—51:4) that God is justified in condemning it. The implication then is that here is a Jew (David himself!) who recognized his transgression of the law and his sin against God, and who made no attempt to argue a special relationship or prerogative as a way of averting God's wrath, but accepted God's condemnation as wholly justified—Jewish objector, take note! It may be this way of reading the verse which prompted the reference to wrath and God's final judgment in vv 5–6.

On the other hand, the verse from Ps 51:4 on its own speaks of God as having to be justified, of God as having to contest a case lodged against him. And the most obvious objection against God is not that he will exercise final judgment—that can be taken for granted as axiomatic (2:2; 3:6)—but rather that he has been unjustifiably faithful to Israel (v 3). Indeed the principal thread of argument running through vv 3–8 as a whole is the suggestion that there is something unreasonable or objectionable about God's remaining loyal to a disloyal covenant partner. What Paul is sure of is that in that day God will overcome any objections or counter-suits against him, not, of course, by sheer force or by arbitrary power of majesty, but by the demonstration of the justice of his case, and by the truth of his words being recognized (in that sense "becoming true"—v 4). In that day his righteousness (= saving action toward Israel) will be demonstrated (v 5).

5 This brusque treatment of the problem prompts an almost inevitable further rejoinder: "But if our unrighteousness demonstrates the righteousness of God, what shall we say?" Is there not something wrong here: if our unfaithfulness makes no difference to God's faithfulness, what point or need is there for us to be faithful and why should we be blamed for being unfaithful? Here the voice of the interlocutor is finally merged into Paul's own debate with himself; in using the first person plural ("our") Paul identifies himself with the unfaithful Jews, and their common (= national) unfaithfulness is identified with the unrighteousness condemned in both of the earlier stages of the argument (1:18, 29; 2:8). Here too the character of God's righteousness as undeserved goodness to the unrighteous, as faithfulness even to the unfaithful, is underlined. And thus by way of contrast the heart of Israel's presumption begins to be exposed, as being the assumption that a special status (righteousness) of Israel is the inevitable corollary of God's righteousness, or more precisely that God's righteousness (his obligation towards Israel) is demonstrated (to be just) by Israel's righteousness (Israel's fulfillment of its covenant obligations, particularly circumcision). To such a view Paul's counterassertion (that it is Israel's *un*righteousness which shows God's righteousness) can only lead to puzzle and bewilderment: "what shall we say?"

So the question is posed again: "Is God unjust who brings wrath to bear?" Once abandon the idea that Israel is righteous through its loyalty to the covenant and the ground for maintaining God's faithfulness to Israel has been undermined; to assert God's righteousness towards Israel in these terms is tantamount to denying God's right to condemn Israel. To put it in terms of the developing argument of the whole section: Paul has spoken of God's wrath being revealed against *all* human unrighteousness (1:18), Jew first as well as Greek (2:8–9). Now he says that Jewish unrighteousness demonstrates God's righteousness (as undeserved kindness to the unrighteous). So how can Paul say that God condemns the very attitudes and actions which provide the clearest occasion for demonstrating his righteousness? If God's righteousness is understood in this way, what room does it leave for God's wrath? The trouble is that Paul's argument now seems to be going in two contradictory directions. The powerful exposition of God's wrath in chaps. 1–2 has been thrown completely off course by the gratuitous assertion that God nevertheless remains faithful to faithless Israel.

5c–6 Paul is clearly conscious of the sharpness of the problem he has set himself. Even to pose it causes him some embarrassment: "I am speaking in human terms" (v 5). The very idea that God can be criticized as "unjust"

appalls him, and he dismisses it at once: "By no means!" But at this stage in
his overall argument he can do no more than counter the question by falling
back on what for him was obviously a basic conviction—that God will in the
last day judge the world. He need not defend or explain this counterassertion;
it is axiomatic for anyone who stands in the tradition of the prophets; it is
common ground for all Jews. The world we inhabit is a morally ordered
world; man's sense of being morally responsible, whether in terms of gentile
conscience or of Jewish law, simply confirms the revelatory postulate that
there will be a final day of reckoning at which God will provide and "render
to each according to his works" (2:6).

However, Paul has now boxed himself completely into a corner, from
which he cannot escape. All he can do is hang on to these two basic assertions
of his faith: that God is eschatological judge, and his judgment will be according
to truth and seen to be so; and that God has not abandoned his purpose
for Israel, his saving outreach through Israel to the world, and his continuing
faithfulness to Israel despite Israel's unfaithfulness and unrighteousness.
These two axioms seem to run counter to each other and he can do no
more at this stage than acknowledge that fact, while continuing to hang on
firmly to both. The irony is that the problem is caused to the human mind
more by God's faithfulness than by man's unrighteousness.

7 But in loyalty to the logical correctness of the objection posed Paul
cannot simply let it go. Despite increasing discomfort he cannot suppress or
ignore even this kind of blasphemous questioning. Even such faith-disturbing
questions must be asked openly despite his inability or unreadiness to tackle
them here. So yet again he asks: "But if the truth of God brings still greater
glory to God by means of my falsehood, why am I still condemned as a
sinner?" The connection of thought with vv 3–4, the implicit link for the
Hebrew mind between God's truth and God's faithfulness, and the very question
itself, all indicate clearly enough that the thought is still on the problems
caused by God's faithfulness to unfaithful Israel. But the combination of
the conception of God's truth, human falseness, and divine glory would almost
inevitably recall the initial section of the exposé of humankind's unrighteousness
(1:18, 23, 25). It is not only God's faithfulness in the face of Jewish
unfaithfulness, but also God's truth sustained in the face of man's lie, which
pose the problem. For one who proclaims God's righteousness to unrighteous
Gentile as well as to unfaithful Jew (1:16–17), the problem of how to understand
this righteousness of God in relation to his wrath is one and the same,
and quite as sharp on both fronts.

Also striking is the way in which in these verses once again Paul focuses
the whole debate on himself: "my falseness," "me a sinner." In his indictment
of man in general as of the Jew in particular he indicts first and foremost
himself. The problem posed in these verses is not one he can easily distance
himself from or treat dispassionately. For he himself is personally involved
on both sides of the problem—himself still the sinner, himself already a recipient
of God's saving righteousness. It is just possible that in the question
"Why am I still condemned as a sinner?" we also overhear an echo of the
fierce interchange between Paul and Peter referred to by Paul in Gal 2:14–
17, where the implication is that the phrase "gentile sinners" was used by

the group from Jerusalem to refer to the Jewish Christian practice (Peter, Paul, etc.) of eating with uncircumcised and ritually unclean Gentiles (Gal 2:12). In this case Paul begins to turn the question asked away from the thought of God's final judgment, and so away from a mere repetition of v 5, back to the theme of Jewish condemnation of Gentiles (as in 1:19–2:3). The point here would then be that Jew should not condemn Gentile (including gentile Christian) as "sinner" because he is in the same boat—his faithlessness is as liable to God's wrath as humankind's falseness in general. This may be overloading Paul's meaning, and even if the thought was present to Paul it would most probably be lost on his Roman audiences.

8 Nevertheless, the fact is that in v 8 Paul's thought does clearly slide from the objection against his defense of God's faithfulness to faithless Israel, to what was probably a Jewish or Jewish Christian objection against his gospel to the Gentiles: "and not as we are maligned and as some affirm that we say, 'Let us do evil that good may come.'" The awkwardness of the phrasing is evidence enough that Paul's patience was running out with this discussion. Clearly Paul's teaching on God's righteousness from faith to faith was coming under attack as being in effect an encouragement to sin, and Paul's feelings were rather sensitive to the jibe: he describes it as a slander, a deliberate turning of white into black; the very suggestion that he could consent to elide so completely the difference between good and evil (cf. 2:9–10) he thinks is so manifestly unjust as to be self-condemned. The trouble was that he could not begin to respond to the charge—he has not yet even explained what he means by "righteousness to faith," though it must already have been becoming clear from the present argument about God's faithfulness (= God's righteousness to faith), even for those not yet familiar with his gospel. In the event it is not till the beginning of chap. 6 that he felt able to return to the issue. In the meantime, even to raise the question was taking him too far ahead of his more measured exposition, and he evidently decided to cut it off before it threw his whole argument irretrievably off-course. So that is what he does; he dismisses the complete insistent line of questioning with a curt five words: "whose condemnation is justly deserved." Anyone who could think Paul was so perverse in his reasoning is hardly worth arguing with!

At least, however, Paul's brief diversion has achieved something of value. It has underscored Israel's faithlessness and confirmed the Jew's solidarity with the Gentile in humankind's lie and unrighteousness. To accept that there is a problem here (if indeed the interlocutor is imagined as doing so) is a positive step in this first main section of his argument (1:18–3:20), for the problem starts with the recognition of Israel's unfaithfulness and develops with the recognition that this leaves the overconfident Jew as defenseless as the ungodly Gentile. This is the point to which Paul returns in v 9. But more important for the argument of the whole letter is the very clear implication that God's faithfulness to Israel is of a piece with his offer of righteousness to all men. The very fact that Paul (the bearer of the gospel to the Gentiles) can identify himself so completely with Israel's failure ("their faithlessness," v 3; "our unrighteousness," v 5; "my falseness," v 7), and in his thinking can slide so naturally from the objection which starts with God's faithfulness to unfaithful Israel to the objection against his own gospel (v 8), shows clearly that for Paul the model of the gospel is already given in God's covenant with Israel, i.e., in his keeping faith with his faithless people. His own people should have understood this so readily (the same objection could be brought against Isaiah's understanding of God's righteousness as against Paul's), and yet they have compounded their earlier unfaithfulness by rejecting the gospel which simply extends the same offer of God's undeserved goodness to all humankind. Thus the gospel indeed is to Jew first as well as Gentile (1:16), but Israel's failure to accept it ensures that God's wrath is also to Jew first as well as Gentile.

C. Conclusion: God's Judgment on All without Exception (3:9–20)

Bibliography

Blank, J. "Warum sagt Paulus: 'Aus Werken des Gesetzes wird niemand gerecht'?" EKK. *Vorarbeiten 1* (1969). Repr. in *Paulus*. 42–68. **Dahl, N. A.** "Romans 3:9: Text and Meaning." In *Paul and Paulinism*, FS C. K. Barrett, ed. M. D. Hooker and S. G. Wilson. London: SPCK, 1982. 184–204. **Dunn, J. D. G.** "New Perspective." ———. "Works of the Law." **Feuillet, A.** "La situation privilégiée des Juifs d'après Rom 3:9: Comparaison avec Rom 1:16 et 3:1–2." *NRT* 105 (1983) 33–46. **Fitzmyer, J. A.** "4Q Testimonia" 66–67. **Gaston, L.** "Works of Law as a Subjective Genitive." *Paul.* 100–106. **Hays, R. B.** "Psalm 143 and the Logic of Romans 3." *JBL* 99 (1980) 107–15. **Hübner, H.** "Was heisst bei Paulus 'Werke des Gesetzes'?" In *Glaube und Eschatologie*, FS W. G. Kümmel, ed. E. Grässer and O. Merk. Tübingen: Mohr, 1985. 123–33. **Keck, L. E.** "The Function of Romans 3:10–18—Observations and Suggestions." In *God's Christ and His People*, FS N. A. Dahl, ed. J. Jervell and W. A. Meeks. Oslo-Bergen Tromsö: Universitetsforlaget, 1977. 141–57. **Lohmeyer, E.** "Gesetzeswerke." *Probleme*. 33–74. **Minde, H. J. van der.** *Schrift*. 54–58. **Moo, D. J.** "'Law,' 'Works of the Law,' and Legalism in Paul." *WTJ* 45 (1983) 73–100. **Tyson, J. B.** "'Works of Law' in Galatians." *JBL* 92 (1973) 423–31. **Wilckens, U.** "Was heisst bei Paulus: 'Aus Werken des Gesetzes wird kein Mensch gerecht'?" (1969). *Rechtfertigung*. 77–109.

Translation

[9] *What then [a] do we plead in our defense? [b] For we have now charged both Jews and Greeks as all alike under sin,* [10] *as it is written,*
"There is none righteous, not even one."
[11] *"There is none who understands*
there is none who [c] seeks out God.
[12] *All have turned aside, they have together become worthless;*
there is none who [c] does good
there is none, [c] not so much as one."
[13] *"Their throat is an open grave,*
they use their tongues to deceive."
"The venom of asps is under their lips."

14 *"Whose mouth is full of curses and bitterness."*
15 *"Their feet are swift when it comes to shedding blood,*
16 *ruin and wretchedness are in their ways,*
17 *and the way of peace they have not known."*
18 *"There is no fear of God before their eyes."*
19 *Now we know that whatever the law says it says to those within the law, in order that every mouth might be stopped and all the world become liable to God's judgment.* 20 *For by works of the law shall no flesh be justified before him, for through the law comes the knowledge of sin.*

Notes

ªTί οὖν is usually punctuated as a separate question: "What then?" But the division here depends on the meaning of the next word (see *Note* b).

ᵇThe weight of MS tradition reads οὐ πάντως, "not at all," or "not altogether," after the verb. But Dahl, "Romans 3:9," has shown that P (which omits οὐ πάντως) probably preserves a text which was earlier well known in Syria and the West ("Antiochene"), and that the addition of οὐ πάντως (since προεχόμεθα seems to demand an answer) is much easier to explain than its omission. He concludes justifiably that the οὐ πάντως was probably a very early gloss or supplement inserted to fill out the sense as then perceived by the scribe at the time. Dahl goes on to note that οὐ πάντως is absent only in manuscripts whose ancestry can be traced to the edition of Romans which lacked chaps. 15–16, and to argue that the weak attestation of the shorter 3:9 text is due to the lack of continuing popularity of the Antiochene textual tradition in face of the longer version of Romans.

ᶜAt these points the MS tradition shows evidence of attempts to make what Paul wrote match the LXX more precisely; though see Metzger on 3:12.

Form and Structure

The opening question is the final spasm of the diatribe which dominated most of 2:1–3:9, but which had already begun to get out of hand in the preceding section. The response sums up Paul's claim: Jew as well as Greek, possession of the law notwithstanding, is equally "under sin."

The carefully constructed catena of scriptural passages which follows (with near contemporary parallel in CD 5:13–17 and *4 Ezra* 7.22–24) may be drawn from preformed material (Keck) and serves again to underpin the claim just made with scriptural proof. The point becomes clearer when it is recalled that all the Psalm citations presuppose an antithesis between the righteous (the faithful member of the covenant) and the unrighteous. The implication is that when that presupposition of favored status before God is set aside, the scriptures serve as a condemnation of *all* humankind (in suggesting that vv 10–18 are a secondary insertion, Schenke, "Aporien," 885–87, misses this crucial function of the catena within Paul's argument). The point becomes explicit in v 19: the law speaks to those "within the law," that is, to those whose confidence rests in the fact that they belong to the people defined and marked out by the law. Michel sees a strophe structure—vv 10–12 (2 x 3 lines), vv 13–14 (2 x 2) and vv 15–18 (2 x 2)—which is hardly self-evident. More impressive and effective is the sixfold repetition of οὐκ ἔστιν (vv 10, 11, 12, 18; cf. Heil).

V 20 provides the conclusion to the whole preceding argument (1:18–

3:20). But as usual with Romans (see on 5:21 *Form and Structure*), Paul so frames his conclusion as to introduce themes which will be important in the subsequent discussion: ἐξ ἔργων νόμου—3:27, 28; 4:2, 6; 9:11, 32; 11:6; δικαιωθήσεται—3:24, 26, 28, 30; 4:2, 5; 5:1, 9; 6:7; 8:30, 33; διὰ νόμου ἐπίγνωσις ἁμαρτίας—4:15; 5:13; 7:13.

Comment

3:9 τί οὖν προεχόμεθα; "what then do we put forward on our own behalf?" The text is usually read τί οὖν; προεχόμεθα; οὐ πάντως, "What then? Are we Jews any better off? No, not at all" (RSV, NEB; similarly NJB, NIV). But (1) to render προεχόμεθα as "Are we better off?" involves treating the middle (or passive) form as equivalent to the active—a usage nowhere else attested. (2) To take the first person plural as "we Jews" is to narrow the discussion back into the terms of 3:1, with either the speaker again imagined as "the Jew," but now speaking in the plural, or the speaker as Paul identifying himself with his own people. But the force of the sequence of first person forms in vv 5–8 was precisely to broaden the scope of the discussion beyond the more narrowly Jewish perspective (see on 3:5—note the distinction between "they" and "we" in 3:3, 5); and the immediately following first person plural (προῃτιασάμεθα) continues to maintain this broader perspective since the "we" is set over against "both Jews and Gentiles" and is clearly not intended to be identified with either group as such. To render προεχόμεθα "we Jews" is thus disruptive of Paul's flow of thought. (3) The usual rendering of 3:9 makes it a restatement of 3:1, but now with a contradictory (or at least contrary) answer—which again makes no sense of 3:1–8 since the sequence of questions was the result of Paul's firm assertion that "the Jew" *was* after all better off ("a direct contradiction"—Dodd). Had Paul been about to answer the same question (3:1, 9) negatively he would not have embroiled himself in the frustration of posing questions he could not yet answer. The only way to escape (or soften) the contradiction is to render the οὐ πάντως, which means "not at all" (BGD; BDF, §433.2; cf. 1 Cor 16:12), in the less natural sense "not altogether," which would be without parallel elsewhere (1 Cor 5:10 should not be cited since the rendering "not at all" is perfectly proper as, e.g., RSV and NIV recognize; the parallels suggested by Feuillet, "Situation," 36–37, fare no better). (4) Paul's use of τί οὖν elsewhere does not help, since he uses it both as an independent question (6:15; 11:7; cf. 3:3; 9:32) but also as a predicate of a fuller question—most regularly τί οὖν ἐροῦμεν at points where a new (or concluding) phase of the argument is introduced (4:1; 6:1; 7:7; 8:31; 9:14, 30).

προεχόμεθα could be rendered as a passive, "Are we worse off?" But again "we Jews" jars with the preceding context, and on any other understanding of "we" the οὐ πάντως jars with the subsequent blanket indictment. Dahl in his magisterial study ("Romans 3:9") therefore advocates rendering it as a genuine middle (literally, "to hold, have, set or put something before oneself"), with τί οὖν προεχόμεθα read as a single question. Against those who point out that the few examples of προέχεσθαι (middle) denote an alleged pretext or excuse, he draws attention to 1 *Enoch* 99.3–4: "Then prepare yourselves, you righteous, and hold your supplications before you, that they may be remembered (προέχεσθε τὰς ἐντεύξεις ὑμῶν εἰς μνημόσυνον); make them a solemn testimony before the angels, that the angels may bring the sins of the wicked ones before the Most High God that they may be remembered; and then they (the sinners) shall be terrified on the day when unrighteousness is destroyed." The alternative, put forward by BGD, of taking the "we" of v 9a as a self-reference, as in v 9b ("Am I protecting myself? Am I making excuses?") in fact makes for more discontinuity between v 9a and v 9b, since then v 9a would continue with the personal issue raised in v 8, while v 9b reverts to the universal indictment. Better to regard the closing words of v 8 as a guillotine on the preceding line of questioning.

Understood as Dahl suggests ("What then do we plead in defense?"; followed by Gaston, *Paul*, 121), the question is highly appropriate in its context. It is not a restatement of 3:1 or a supplementary question which would require the sort of discussion opened up in 3:1–8 to be taken further. Its function is rather to bring the dialogue which has dominated the preceding paragraph to a close. It is the beginning of the conclusion to the first main section of the argument. "In the light of all that we have said, what do we human beings put forward as a defense?" The question is rhetorical, and the answer so obvious that it need not be stated (the οὐ πάντως being an early addition to provide an answer to the question whose point was not clearly taken). In fact, however, an answer is given at the end of the intervening catena of OT passages; these demonstrate that no defense is possible (3:19).

Dahl's exegesis may, however, require some qualification in its understanding of the force of "we." While it is true that the rendering "we Jews" sets the argument back to 3:1, and while the first person plurals of 3:5–8 have broadened the argument out beyond the Jews as such, the fact remains that the broadening out of 3:5–8 was intended as a way of undermining the misconceived Jewish claim to distinctiveness, a reminder that Jewish ἀπιστία was of a piece with human ἀδικία and ψεῦσμα in general. The "we" of 3:9 is Paul's signal that in rounding off his indictment this is the point he wants to keep making. The main thrust of his attack is still to expose the falseness of the typical Jewish presumption of distinctiveness so far as righteousness/unrighteousness is concerned. In order to make firm his charge that *all* human beings are in the same boat ("under sin") it is the *Jewish* presumption of righteousness by virtue of maintaining covenant status which he has had to undermine (Jew and God-worshiper needed no convincing as to gentile sinfulness—1:18–32).

(1) Had the "we" of 3:9 been aimed as much at the Gentile as at the Jew, an obvious response would have been to recall 2:14–15, 26—such Gentiles can make some defense. Such a response becomes inappropriate, however, as soon as we realize that the function of 2:14–15, 26, as of 3:5–9, is to prick the bubble of Jewish confidence in a covenant prerogative which marks them off from gentile "sinners." "The Jew" is still very much in mind, *not* in his distinctiveness, but precisely in his solidarity in human failure. (2) This also makes best sense of the following catena of OT quotations (3:10–18), where Paul (no doubt deliberately) quotes a sequence of Psalm passages which formed the *Jewish* indictment of *others*. Paul cites them not because they can be read in isolation as universal indictments, but because in the light of his

preceding exposition of Jewish unfaithfulness they function as self-indictments *as well,* and *therefore* as universal indictments. (3) Here too, as Dahl notes, the parallel with *1 Enoch* 99.3–4 may have greater value, and indeed provide a key to Paul's meaning here. Far from being a ground of complaint against Israel's oppressors which the righteous can hold before themselves in pleading before God (as in *1 Enoch*), the scriptural catena functions as an indictment of both Jew as well as Gentile. The *1 Enoch* 99:3–4 parallel thus helps to clarify how the opening question of the conclusion (3:9) leads into the following verses. Paul is probably deliberately attacking the sort of attitude which comes to expression in the Enoch passage and which found scriptural expression in the Psalms cited by Paul.

προῃτιασάμεθα γὰρ Ἰουδαίους τε καὶ Ἕλληνας, "for we have already charged that, we previously accused both Jews and Greeks." LSJ lists 3:9 as the only occurrence of this verbal form, but the meaning is quite clear. Paul sums up the overall conclusion of 1:18–3:8. The proper force of his argument will be grasped if we see the summary thus: *not* "previous accusation of Gentiles" (1:18–32) and "previous accusation of Jews" (2:1–29); *but,* previous accusation of humankind as a whole in terms of the typical Jewish condemnation of Gentiles (1:18–32), i.e., previous accusation of the Jews having shown that their covenant privileges (although real) have been misunderstood and abused and that this misunderstanding and abuse demonstrates the condemnation of 1:18–32 to be in fact a condemnation of humankind as a whole, Jews as well as Gentiles (2:1–3:8). Ἰουδαίους τε καὶ Ἕλληνας, "Jews and Greeks" (see on 1:16): the plural (as distinct from 1:16 and 2:9–10 and the formulaic use of 10:12; Gal 3:28; Col 3:11) being a further indication that Paul has now departed completely from the dialogue with the typical "Jew" of 2:1–3:8 (cf. 1 Cor 1:24; 10:32; 12:13).

πάντας ὑφ᾿ ἁμαρτίαν εἶναι, "all to be under sin." The πάντας, "all," is of course emphatic, as one would expect in view of the scope of the indictment in such a summary statement (cf. particularly 1:16; 2:1; 3:20, 22, 23; 4:16; 10:4; see also on 1:16 and 3:22). With ὑφ᾿ ἁμαρτίαν we have the first occurrence of a word that will largely dominate chaps. 6 and 7. The prepositional formula *"under* sin" (as in 7:14 and Gal 3:22) and the personification subsequently (most clearly 5:12, 21; 6:6, 12–23; 7:8–11) indicate that Paul understands "sin" as a force (or power) within the world, which functions in and upon man to negative effect (cf. Sir 21:2; 27:10; 1QH 1:27; 4:29–30). The strength of the imagery of kingly rule or slave ownership (5:21; 6:12–23; 7:14) should not be discounted, since evidently this power can exercise a *force majeure* which results in death (5:21; 6:16, 21, 23; 7:9, 11). Just how Paul conceptualized "sin" as a power is not clear. He never speaks of it in conjunction with "Satan" (see on 16:20), or the "devil," or any of the "principalities and powers" (see on 8:38–39 and 8:31–39 *Form and Structure*), and while it could be said that these other conceptions occur in more formalized contexts (8:38–89; 16:20; 1 Cor 5:5; 7:5; 2 Cor 11:14; etc.), it cannot be said that (Romans apart) the concept of sin as a power is any more prominent in Paul's thought. Nevertheless the fact remains that in Romans Paul sees sin (along with death) as the most negative and most dangerous force in human experience. The question of conceptualization is therefore secondary. The one fact which matters is that man experiences (consciously or unconsciously) a power which works in him to bind him wholly to his mortality and corruptibility, to render impotent any knowledge of God or concern to do God's will, to provoke his merely animal appetites in forgetfulness that he is a creature of God—and that power Paul calls "sin." ("The mythical concept of ἁμαρτία describes a concrete anthropological fact [Sachverhalt]"—Michel; cf. SH, 145–46.) See further particularly chaps. 6–7, where Paul treats in some detail the interaction of sin and death, sin and flesh, and, not least of importance for his overall argument, sin and the law. Since it is sometimes said that Paul rarely uses ἁμαρτία of individual acts (cf. Bornkamm, Paul, 133; Cranfield), we should note the use of the plural in 4:7, (8); 7:5; 11:27 and the ambiguity of 3:20; 5:13, 20; 6:1; 7:7; 14:23 (see on 5:20; 7:7; and even 6:16), and that the majority of the references to ἁμαρτία in the Pauline corpus outside of Romans denote (the) sinful act(s); Kaye indeed argues that ἁμαρτία consistently in Romans means "sinful act, or the guilt consequent upon such acts" (Chapter 6, 30–57), without giving enough weight to the force of the language Paul uses (indicated above). The fact that the two uses merge into each other reflects the reality of experience where motive force and actual performance can not always be easily distinguished.

10–18 καθὼς γέγραπται, "as it is written": see on 1:17. The summary indictment is underpinned by a sequence of scriptural texts. Once again it needs to be stressed that the point of the catena is not simply to demonstrate that scripture condemns all humankind, but more precisely to demonstrate that scriptures which had been read from the presupposition of a clear distinction between the righteous and the unrighteous (cf. Jub. 21.21–22; and see further on 1:17, δίκαιος) in fact condemned all humankind as soon as that clear distinction was undermined.

¹⁰οὐκ ἔστιν δίκαιος οὐδὲ εἷς,

¹¹οὐκ ἔστιν ὁ συνίων,
οὐκ ἔστιν ὁ ἐκζητῶν τὸν θεόν.
¹²πάντες ἐξέκλιναν ἅμα ἠχρεώθησαν·
οὐκ ἔστιν ὁ ποιῶν χρηστότητα,
οὐκ ἔστιν ἕως ἑνός.
¹³τάφος ἀνεῳγμένος ὁ λάρυγξ αὐτῶν,
ταῖς γλώσσαις αὐτῶν ἐδολιοῦσαν,
ἰὸς ἀσπίδων ὑπὸ τὰ χείλη αὐτῶν·
¹⁴ὧν τὸ στόμα ἀρᾶς καὶ πικρίας γέμει,

¹⁵ὀξεῖς οἱ πόδες αὐτῶν ἐκχέαι αἷμα,

¹⁶σύντριμμα καὶ ταλαιπωρία ἐν ταῖς ὁδοῖς αὐτῶν.
¹⁷καὶ ὁδὸν εἰρήνης οὐκ ἔγνωσαν
¹⁸οὐκ ἔστιν φόβος θεοῦ ἀπέναντι τῶν ὀφθαλμῶν αὐτῶν.

Eccl 7:20—ἄνθρωπος οὐκ ἔστιν δίκαιος ἐν τῇ γῇ, ὃς ποιήσει ἀγαθὸν καὶ οὐχ ἁμαρτήσεται.
Ps 13:2–3— . . . εἰ ἔστιν συνίων ἢ ἐκζητῶν τὸν θεόν.
πάντες ἐξέκλιναν, ἅμα ἠχρεώθησαν,
οὐκ ἔστιν ποιῶν χρηστότητα,
οὐκ ἔστιν ἕως ἑνός.
Ps 5:10—τάφος ἀνεῳγμένος ὁ λάρυγξ αὐτῶν,
ταῖς γλώσσαις αὐτῶν ἐδολιοῦσαν.
Ps 139:4—ἰὸς ἀσπίδων ὑπὸ τὰ χείλη αὐτῶν.
Ps 9:28—οὗ ἀρᾶς τὸ στόμα αὐτοῦ γέμει καὶ πικρίας καὶ δόλου.
Isa 59:7–8—οἱ δὲ πόδες αὐτῶν ἐπὶ πονηρίαν τρέχουσιν ταχινοὶ ἐκχέαι αἷμα· . . . .
σύντριμμα καὶ ταλαιπωρία ἐν ταῖς ὁδοῖς αὐτῶν.
καὶ ὁδὸν εἰρήνης οὐκ οἴδασιν.
Ps 35:2—οὐκ ἔστιν φόβος θεοῦ ἀπέναντι τῶν ὀφθαλμῶν αὐτοῦ.

The catena consists of seven citations of varying lengths, five of them from the Psalms. As can be readily seen, the LXX is followed in every case, with the opening lines modified (but not the sense) to fit the pattern of the catena (vv 10–11), some later lines abbreviated (again without affecting the sense—vv 14–15), and only minor modifications elsewhere (vv 12b, 15, 17). That Paul is drawing on a catalog previously minted by others is possible (van der Minde, 57; Keck; cf. particularly Justin, *Dial.* 27.3), but the degree to which the verses fit his particular point (Jewish condemnation of Gentiles becomes self-accusation) makes it unlikely (despite Keck, Justin's catena could well have been inspired by Paul's); see particularly Zeller. Of course, the sequence may have been formulated by Paul himself on a previous occasion with the same object in view (the degree of structuring evident suggests a more formal rather than a spontaneous composition while dictating the letter).

10 Commentators generally assume that the opening line of the catena is an adaptation of Ps 13:1, where the same words appear as in v 3 (οὐκ ἔστιν ποιῶν χρηστότητα, οὐκ ἔστιν ἕως ἑνός). But the parallel with Eccl 7:20 is clearly closer: Paul indeed probably recalled it precisely because it used δίκαιος and provided just the denial that there is such a distinct group as "the righteous" which Paul wanted as his opening reference. The somewhat jaundiced view of Qoheleth confirms Paul's own argument that Jewish national understanding of themselves as "the righteous" (see on 1:17) is a misunderstanding of covenant privilege and responsibility. In this case this is the only explicit quotation from Eccl in the NT. Cranfield notes that a rabbi of the next generation (Eliezer ben Hyrcanus) made much of the same verse (*b. Sanh.* 101a—Cranfield, 192 n.1). Cf. particularly the repeated confessions in the Qumran Hymn scroll (especially 1QH 4.30–31; 7.17, 28–29; 13.16–17; 16.11; also 11QPsa 155.8).

11–12 Next the catena draws on Pss 14:1–3 [LXX 13:2–3] and 53:2–3 [LXX 52:3–4]. Significantly it is "the fool" who is indicted, and those described are set over against God's people, "the righteous generation" (Ps 14:4, 5, 7), those who *do* seek after God (cf. Pss 9:10; 22:26; 24:6; 27:8; etc.). Str-B note that by "the fool" rabbinic exegetes understood Esau and then Rome (3:157). But when used as an elaboration of Eccl 7:10, according to the conventions of Jewish interpretation, the Psalm passages can be understood to fill out the universal condemnation of Qoheleth ("the principal method by which the rabbis clarify the sacred text and probe its depths is by recourse to parallel passages"—Bloch, "Midrash," 32). Those who recognized the quotation (whose repetition in the Psalms would make it all the more familiar) would recognize too the shocking implication that Paul was in effect lumping Jewish presumption with gentile idolatry and sexual perversion (cf. Ps 14:1) as equally an expression of the fool's denial of God. ἠχρεώθησαν is the LXX translation of נֶאֱלָ֑חוּ, "become sour" (of milk)—hence NJB: "all alike turned sour."

13 Pss 5:9 [LXX 10] and 140:3 [LXX 139:4] are used with the same force as the preceding verses. For in both psalms the psalmist again distinguishes himself, as one who could expect to be led by God's righteousness (5:8) and to be counted among "the righteous" (5:12; 140:13), from those described in 5:5 and 140:4, "the workers of lawlessness" so often alluded to in the Psalms (the "unrighteous," "sinners"). But here again Paul implies that there is no distinction between Jew and Gentile, between Jewish "righteousness" and gentile "unrighteousness" so far as their standing before

God is concerned. Whatever the psalmist meant by saying "their throat is an open grave," the overall imagery is powerfully evocative and the sense sufficiently clear.

14 Citing Ps 10:7 [LXX 9:28] has the same effect as the earlier quotation from Ps 14, with the indictment of the wicked who scorns God (10:2–4, 6, 11) again used as a description of all, Jew and Gentile alike (Maillot).

15–17 The catena is given still greater force by drawing in the powerful psalmlike passage from Isa 59:7–8. It will be no accident that that passage is a lament for *Israel's* sins, for Israel's *lack* of righteousness (59:12–15). And the implication is the same as in Paul's earlier use of Isa 52:5 in 2:24: Jews *now* are like Israel then; they have presumed upon their covenant standing before God; their sins have been sufficient to cut them off completely from God (Isa 59:2), even though there is still hope in God's righteousness and salvation (59:17). For the richness of the concept "peace" in the phrase "the way of peace" see on 1:7; and contrast 5:1. We may note in passing that Paul's use of this passage strengthens the impression that Paul's understanding of God's righteousness has been largely influenced by Second Isaiah (see on 1:17).

18 The catena is rounded off with reference to Ps 36:1 [LXX 35:2], where once again the contrast is made between the law-breaker (36:1–4, 11–12) and those who can rely on God's righteousness (36:10), and once again the implication is that the description of the former can be applied to all. Since "the fear of God" is such an important motif in Jewish scripture and religion (e.g., Gen 22:12; Deut 6:2; Prov 1:7; *T. Lev.* 13.1; 1QH 12.3; see further *TDNT* 9:201–3, 205–7) the final verse is particularly damning and makes an effective conclusion: "there is no fear of God before their eyes."

Of all these passages only the two which do not come from the Psalms might be seen to be fairly quoted, since it is only these two which can on any straightforward reading be applied to the Jews as a whole. But, as already noted (see on 3:11–12), it would be quite proper in terms of the hermeneutical principles then current to use similarly worded passages to expand on the initial description from Ecclesiastes. And while modern commentators should beware of *assuming* that such composite proof-texting would have carried with it any allusion to the contexts from which the texts or part-texts were taken, it can hardly be accidental that in this case all the Psalm quotations work with an antithesis between those self-consciously favored by God and the rest variously described as the fool, the unrighteous, the lawless, the wicked, the sinner. Whether his first readers would have recognized the allusions or not, it is hard to doubt that Paul intended the Psalm citations as a turning of the tables on Jewish overconfidence in their nation's favored status before God. The very descriptions which the psalmist used for those outside of God's favor and righteousness can be seen in the light of the Ecclesiastes and Isaiah passages as a self-description and self-condemnation.

19 οἴδαμεν δὲ ὅτι, "and we know that": see on 2:2. Paul uses the same appeal to common knowledge in Gal 2:16, one of the points at which the arguments of Galatians and Romans come very close. The exposition of Romans to this point (especially from 2:1) can be regarded as Paul's attempt to defend and make clear his understanding of the crucial principle (Gal 2:16) on which his earlier rebuke of Peter turned.

ὄσα ὁ νόμος λέγει τοῖς ἐν τῷ νόμῳ λαλεῖ, "whatever the law says it says to those within the law"; not "under the law" [NIV]—the distinction in Paul's choice of prepositions should be observed. οἱ ἐν τῷ νόμῳ, "those within the law"; cf. οἱ τὸν νόμον ἔχοντες, "those having the law" (2:14), οἱ ὑπὸ νόμον, "those under the law" (1 Cor 9:20; Gal 4:5) and οἱ ἐκ νόμου, "those from the law" (4:14, 16). Here, even more clearly than in 2:12, the character and function of the law as marking the boundary between Jew and Gentile comes to expression. The Jews are defined as "those within the law," within the area circumscribed by the law, whose religion, nationality, and lifestyle bears the distinctive marks of the Torah (see on 2:12 and *Introduction* §5; by arguing that "in the law" includes Gentiles, Murray and Hendriksen weaken Paul's point). The ὄσα is emphatic: "*all* that the law says." Since the law has this character of separating those within from those without, it could hardly be denied that it is addressed to those within. But that means everything in the law, including what should be read as an indictment of those within the law as well as of those without (3:10–18). It should be noted that Paul does not distinguish "the law" from the rest of the Jewish scriptures (none of the quotations in 3:10–18 came from the Pentateuch). This ambivalence reflects Jewish usage (cf. 1 Cor 14:21; John 10:34; 15:25; Str-B, 3:159, 463). The way in which νόμος once again suddenly dominates the discussion is striking (6 times in three verses, just as in 2:12–15 [9 times]), but here Paul is at the climax of the first stage of his exposition and the crucial transition to the vital next stage.

ἵνα πᾶν στόμα φραγῇ, "that every mouth may be stopped." The metaphor is of someone being prevented from speaking (cf. particularly 1 Macc 9:55)—here not simply by the weight of evidence brought in accusation, but also by its authority as the law of God, the scriptures, the sacred oracles entrusted to Israel (3:2).

καὶ ὑπόδικος γένηται πᾶς ὁ κόσμος τῷ θεῷ, "and all the world become liable to God's judgment." ὑπόδικος (only here in the NT) means "answerable, accountable," so either "judicially actionable" or "liable to punishment" as having been already found guilty (see LSJ). So here, "it describes the state of an accused person who cannot reply at the trial initiated against him because he has exhausted all possibilities of refuting the charge against him and averting the condemnation and its consequences which ineluctably follow" (*TDNT* 8:558). ὁ κόσμος again means humankind as a whole (see 3:6), though Paul's concept of final judgment includes judgment of all created beings (1 Cor 6:3; cf. Phil 2:10–11).

That *every* mouth (πᾶν στόμα) and *all* the world (πᾶς ὁ κόσμος) are thus left defenseless (3:9) before the indictment of the *Jewish* scriptures, confirms that Paul pens his *universal* indictment with a view to denying *Jewish* claims to a special defense at the final judgment. He does not question here the Jewish assumption of gentile wickedness (he only did so in 2:1–29 in order to prick the bubble of Jewish presumption of covenant righteousness); his object is rather to show that their own scriptures place his own people just as firmly "in the dock" along with everyone else.

20 Almost certainly intended here is an allusion to Ps 143 [LXX 142]:2 or at least the thought is modeled on that verse:

142:2—ὅτι οὐ δικαιωθήσεται πᾶς ζῶν ἐνώπιόν σου
3:20— διότι ἐξ ἔργων νόμου οὐ δικαιωθήσεται πᾶσα σάρξ ἐνώπιον αὐτοῦ
142:2—"because no living person will be justified before you."
3:20— "because by works of the law no flesh will be justified before him."

Paul uses the text in the same form as in Gal 2:16, but there without the ἐνώπιον σου/αὐτοῦ. Its inclusion here puts the allusion to the psalm beyond reasonable doubt. It is possible that the other variations from the psalm come from a different text tradition, particularly so far as the πᾶσα σάρξ is concerned (see below), but since the variations fit so well into the line of Paul's argument it is more likely that Paul has introduced them himself. The fact that he introduces the text simply with διότι, "for, because," rather than with γέγραπται (as is his normal practice—see on 1:17), probably indicates Paul's awareness that he was quoting the text in a tendentious (but he would say, legitimate) form. Such an interpretative rendering of a text would be quite acceptable to Jewish ears, so long as the interpretation could be justified.

οὐ δικαιωθήσεται . . . ἐνώπιον αὐτοῦ, "shall not be justified/acquitted before him." The metaphor in the psalm is of a servant being called to account before his master, but in the context here the imagery of final judgment is to the fore (though of course since the final judgment is on the whole life it can be invoked for different parts and stages of that life). Against the view that Paul sees "justification" simply as an act which marks the beginning of a believer's life, as believer, here is a further example of the verb used for a final verdict, not excluding the idea of the final verdict at the end of a life (see on 2:13). The thought that no one could stand before God on his own terms, in his own strength, or could hope for acquittal on the merit of his own deeds, was thoroughly Jewish (cf. particularly Job 9:2; *1 Enoch* 81.5; 1QH 9.14–16; *4 Ezra* 7.46; as well as Ps 14 and Isa 59 quoted in 3:11–12, 15–17; see also Str-B, 3:156; Zeller, 81–82); "even in his radicalizing of the knowledge of sin Paul remains bound up with Judaism" (Michel, 145 n.10). The variations introduced by Paul to Ps 143:2 therefore are all the more important as a clue to the particular point he is trying to make.

ἐξ ἔργων νόμου, "by works of the law, by nomistic service." The way in which this most striking variation from the LXX text of the psalm brings out Paul's point is indicated by several factors. (1) Its use here and in Galatians shows that it is a key phrase in Paul's polemic against what he regards as the typical Jewish misunderstanding of how God's righteousness manifests itself, since it occurs only in the immediate context of that polemic, with the full phrase either explicit (3:20, 28; Gal 2:16; 3:2, 5, 10; cf. Eph 2:9) or implicit (3:27; 4:2, 6; 9:12, 32; 11:6). The contrast with 2:13 confirms that ἔργα νόμου is thus more narrowly and polemically focused than οἱ ποιηταὶ νόμου. For the different sense of the singular (τὸ ἔργον τοῦ νόμου), though with a complementary polemical thrust, see on 2:15. (2) Paul's purpose throughout the preceding paragraphs was to show that the Jewish particular should be merged with the human universal as "all alike under sin." The ἐξ ἔργων νόμου are another example of the Jewish particular. Throughout the preceding paragraphs the Jewish particular consisted of the assumption that God's covenant with Israel

gave them a special ground of justification, a special defense in the final
judgment. The ἔργα νόμου are Paul's concluding summary reference to that
special defense. Since "works of the law" are no defense, the verdict of Ps
143:2 is truly universal. (3) As Lohmeyer has argued, the phrase ἔργα νόμου
means "service of the law" ("nomistic service"—Tyson, "Works," 424–25),
service not so much in the sense of particular actions already accomplished,
but in the sense of the obligations set by the law, the religious system determined by the law ("Gesetzeswerke"; cf. Schlatter). Lohmeyer's insight is borne
out by the way in which the equivalent phrase is used in the Qumran writings—
מעשי תורה, "deeds of the law" (cf. Moo, 91). For it was precisely by reference
to his "deeds," his "deeds within, or by means of, or with reference to the
law," his "observance of the law" as understood within the community, that
an individual's membership in the covenant was tested (1QS 5.21, 23; 6:18;
cf. similar phrases, particularly מעשי (ה)צדקה, "deeds/works of righteousness"—1QH 1.26; 4.31; and מעשיהם באמתכה, "their deeds in your truth"—
1QH 6.9). Likewise מעשי תורה were what marked out the community of
the end days in its distinctiveness from the outsiders and enemies (4QFlor
1.1–7). The precisely equivalent phrase מעשי התורה apparently occurs in
an as yet unpublished 4Q scroll in the hands of J. Strugnell. Cf. also 2 Apoc.
Bar. 57.2: "the works of the commandments." The phrase therefore as used
also here refers to a religious mode of existence, but a mode of existence
marked out in its distinctiveness as determined by the law, the religious practices which set those "within the law" (v 19) apart as the people of the law.
(4) This is what we would have expected anyway in the context here and in
Galatians. The concluding summary of the first main stage of the argument
must refer back to what Paul had been attacking for the last chapter and a
half, particularly Jewish pride in the law, and especially in circumcision as
the most fundamental distinctive marker of the people of the law (see on
2:25). Just as in Galatians the phrase is introduced (Gal 2:16) immediately
following and in clear reference to the preceding controversies regarding
circumcision and food laws (2:1–15)—two obligations laid upon the devout
Jew which most clearly functioned as boundary markers, distinguishing him
clearly from the Gentiles. See also *Introduction* §5, on 9:32 and 11:6, and,
further, Dunn, "New Perspective" and "Works of the Law." Gager, *Origins*,
200, 222, follows M. Barth, *Ephesians* (AB [New York: Doubleday, 1974] 244–
48), in arguing that Paul's polemic against "works of the law" is not directed
against the Jews and that the phrase itself never occurs in Jewish texts and
refers only to the adoption of Jewish practices by Gentiles. But this ignores
the DSS evidence cited above and the clear implication that ἔργα in 3:27;
4:2, 6; 9:12, 32; and 11:6 is shorthand for the ἔργα νόμου of 3:20 and 28.
Gaston, "Works," surprisingly ignores the same data and argues the idiosyncratic view that the work(s) of the law are the law's "work" of wrath (4:15);
though why then Paul should bother to deny that justification comes through
wrath (3:20) becomes rather baffling. Contrast also Cosgrove's dubious distinction between justification *by means of* and *on the basis of* works ("Justification").

Paul's polemic here therefore is quite specific and particular. He has the
devout Jew in view, but not as a type of the universal *homo religiosus* who
thinks that his piety somehow puts God in his debt (Käsemann); the devout

Jew was usually conscious of his need of repentance and for the atonement provided within the law (see on 2:4, and further Sanders, *Paul*, index, "atonement," "repentance," "sin"). His target was rather the devout Jew in his presupposition that as a member of the covenant people he could expect God's righteousness to be put forth in his favor because he was "within the law." Nor is Paul attacking a general human presumption that by good works one can earn God's favor, that starting from scratch, as it were, one can achieve God's recognition by hard work (still misunderstood by Moo, 96–97; contrast *Ep. Arist.* 231: "it is a gift of God to be a doer of good works"). His target was rather the devout Jew who reckoned himself already a member of the covenant people and as such already accepted by God, who saw his responsibility as maintaining his covenant identity and status and who thought that his obligation under the law found characteristic expression in a distinctive religious lifestyle in which the distinctively Jewish rites inevitably came into prominence precisely because they were the rites which marked the Jews off from the other nations as distinctively God's people; see further on 3:27 (also 13:12), and cf. Wilckens, 1:176–77, and Watson, *Paul*, 119, 130.

πᾶσα σάρξ, "all flesh," could be taken simply as a variant translation of the Hebrew כָּל־חָי, "all living," since it is in fact synonymous with כָּל־בָּשָׂר, "all flesh"; cf. again *1 Enoch* 81.5. But there are no other examples of this variation in the LXX, so we should probably regard it as deliberate on Paul's part. For πᾶσα σάρξ as a way of describing human finitude, weakness and corruptibility in contrast to God, see particularly its prominence in the story of the flood (e.g., Gen 6:12, 17; 7:21; 9:11). For Paul see on 1:3. But here too Paul probably introduces σάρξ with the Jewish particular in mind: "all flesh" includes not least the fleshly distinctiveness of which the loyal Jew makes boast, particularly his circumcision "in the flesh" (2:27; note the prominence of the word "flesh" in Gen 17, the scriptural charter for circumcision—17:11, 13, 14, 24, 25). It is this nationalistic, or ethnic narrowing of the terms of God's righteousness which Paul continues to combat in 4:1 and 9:8, as in Gal 3:3; 4:23, 29; and particularly 6:13.

διὰ γὰρ νόμου ἐπίγνωσις ἁμαρτίας, "for through the law comes knowledge of sin." The prefix in ἐπίγνωσις probably indicates some intensifying in the concept—effective knowledge, a knowing which informs character of life and influences conduct (see on 1:28). So here Paul probably means awareness, consciousness of sin. But the meaning of ἁμαρτία is also somewhat uncertain (see on 3:9): the phrase could mean consciousness of sin as a power dominating life ("under sin"—3:9), or conviction regarding the sinful act, conviction of guilt (cf. 4:15; 5:13; 7:13). Here too we should not necessarily assume that Paul had clarified all such ambiguities in his thinking. On the other hand, it is less likely that he intended ἐπίγνωσις in a still more pregnant sense (law as provoking experience of sin, the commission of the sinful act), since that would be a huge leap in his argument (not otherwise properly reached till chap.7), which would be likely to confuse the listener and detract from the point being made (so rightly Cranfield, Zeller; against Althaus, Gaugler, Schlier). The point clearly being made here does not extend so far: it simply revolves round the contrast with the more typical Jewish attitude which saw the law as the means and measure of life within the covenant (as in Sir 45:5; *Pss. Sol.* 14.2) and as a bulwark and hedge against the sinfulness of the Gentiles (as in *Ep. Arist.* 139, 142). In contrast Paul's point is that the law was *not* intended to provoke a sense of distinctiveness and security, but to make those to whom it was addressed conscious of the fact that even as members of the people of God their continuing need of grace was no different from that of the gentile sinner. See also on 4:15 and 5:13.

Explanation

3:9 The line of questioning in 3:1–8, while enabling important ties backward and forward, had nevertheless run too far ahead. Having decided he could follow it no further at this stage and abruptly having terminated it, Paul turns at once to the task of summing up his overall indictment of Jew and Gentile (1:18–3:8). Unfortunately we cannot be entirely sure just what it was that Paul wrote here, and since he used a verb which seems not to have been very familiar, his Roman audience may have been uncertain as to his precise meaning too (though, of course, the way the text was read out would help inform the sense). But at least it is clear that, despite the cut-off at the end of v 8, the thought runs over from the immediately preceding context, as the temporary continuation of the diatribe format and of the "we" style shows. This indicates that in beginning his conclusion Paul does not move back to an earlier perspective and sum up, evenhandedly as it were, the indictment against Gentiles (1:18–32) and against Jews (2:1–29). Rather, in continuation from 3:1–8, Paul starts his summing up by denying that within the generality of human ("our") unrighteousness any defense can be made, any special plea put forward. The Jews' condemnation of gentile depravity (2:1, 3) has indeed become a self-condemnation, a condemnation of national presumption which takes for granted a clear distancing between Jewish faithfulness and gentile unrighteousness. The denial of any excuse to Jew (2:1) as well as to man in general (1:20) has been made good. The special defense of covenant, law, and circumcision, behind which "the Jew" thought he could shelter, has been shown to be a misunderstanding and a false confidence. What defense remains for any man? None at all.

"For we have already charged both Jews and Greeks as all alike under the power of sin." The force of 1:18–2:29 here becomes fully clear. Denied his special plea of being marked out for God, of having the law and being the covenant people of God, "the Jew" is like everyone else, and falls under the general condemnation of humankind (Adam) in chap. 1. Where previously Paul has spoken of Jew and Greek (singular), here he uses the plural—that is, Jews and Greeks as a whole. Not that he is thinking of everyone as specific individuals, but of Jews and Gentiles in general, as an ethnic and social solidarity to which the particular "I" belongs. And for the first time the significant word "sin" occurs (though the verb had been used in 2:12). The use of the singular and the prepositional phrase ("under sin") would strike a solemn note for the readership. "Sin" is clearly presented as an external power which can and does dominate all humankind, giving rise (so it is implied) to the unrighteousness, all the pride, selfish ambition and disregard for the truth documented in chaps. 1 and 2. To highlight the plight of humankind the singular (sin) is deliberately set over against the plural (Jews and Greeks):

for all the differences of race, culture and religion which distinguish and divide human beings, they are all alike under the same domination—the power of a force which binds them to their creatureliness in forgetfulness of their creatureliness.

10–18 The final nail in the coffin for any special pleading or defense is provided by a powerful string of quotations from the Jewish scriptures— entirely appropriate, since the only defense in view is the Jewish claim to special status and consideration before God. The point is given by v 19: the law speaks to those to whom it was given; and what does it say? That every one is unrighteous. The opening quotation, probably from Eccl 7:20, provides a damning and, more important, universal indictment: "There is no righteous person on the earth." The message is clear beyond peradventure: no one within the law can claim to be righteous either because he is within the law or because (he thinks) he keeps the law. Paul's adaptation of the quotation reemphasizes the point: "There is none righteous, *not even one.*" The later, larger quotation from Isa 59:7–8 (vv 15–17) makes the same point: this is Israel being challenged from within its own scriptures for its own lawlessness and lack of righteousness (though Paul no doubt already had it in mind that the same chapter would provide the same Israel with one of the clearest statements of its eschatological hope—Isa 59:20–21 = Rom 11:26–27).

The other five quotations (vv 11–14, 18), all from the Psalms, are the more interesting, since all would normally be read within the synagogue as bolstering the assumption that the (Jewish) righteous could plead against the (gentile) wicked, very much in the spirit of *1 Enoch* 99.3–4 (cited in 3:9, *Comment*). But that assumption has now been decisively undermined (all are "under sin"—v 10). And by linking these passages in with Eccl 7:20 and Isa 59:7–8, Paul effectively makes the same point in a way which those in the Roman congregations familiar with Jewish exegesis would appreciate. *No* defense remains. As soon as these scriptures are read without the blinkers of Jewish presumption of privilege, they become a devastating indictment of all peoples, Jews as well as Gentiles. Whatever distinction between Jew and Gentile remains, whatever is the continuing advantage of the Jew (3:1–2), it does not apply here. When such scriptures assert that no one is righteous, no one understands, no one seeks for God, no one does good, no one fears God, they mean *no one.*

19 The point is hammered home by v 19, if it was not already sufficiently obvious: all that the law says it says to those within the law; so when the law speaks a word of condemnation from which "not even one" can escape, it says it above all to the people of the law. As in 2:2 the "we know" both appeals to what all those familiar with the Jewish scriptures would take for granted and identifies Paul with them. If some Jews had accused Paul of identifying himself with "gentile sinners" (Gal 2:15), Paul's response is to identify himself with his own people, but in the solidarity of all humankind "under the power of sin" (cf. Gal 3:22).

The purpose of the catena of scriptural indictment, overwhelming in its sustained denunciation of human unrighteousness, is to silence all protest and any attempted self-defense, to make it clear that all the world without exception is answerable to God and liable to judgment. When both halves of the verse are read together the implication is obvious that it is the Jews, those within the law, who need to be convinced on this point. The people of Israel cannot distinguish themselves from the rest of the world or claim a national righteousness which makes them any less liable to judgment. And if the Jew can make no plea for special consideration, then no one can.

20 This verse delivers the *coup de grâce,* the final and fundamental reason which actually serves as the basic theological underpinning of the whole argument. All this must be so (the *whole* world answerable to God for its unrighteousness) because "by works of the law shall no flesh be justified before him." Its importance for Paul is confirmed by his use of the very same assertion in Gal 2:16, where it clearly fills the same role of expressing a fundamental axiom of Christian thought (agreed by Christians from both Palestine and beyond).

The assertion is obviously drawn from Ps 143:2, where the psalmist appeals to God:

> Lord, hear my prayer,
> Give ear to my supplication in your truth,
> Listen to me in your righteousness,
> And do not enter into judgment with your servant,
> For before you no one living shall be justified.

In itself the psalm provides a substantial and clinching reference to round off the preceding catena: the psalmist confesses his own liability to judgment because he, like all the rest of humankind, can make no assumption that he will be acquitted or vindicated by God. But Paul makes the point doubly applicable by using a modified text.

First, he adds, as again also in Gal 2:16, "by works of the law." This is the first appearance of a key phrase whose importance for understanding Paul's thought in this letter can hardly be overemphasized, but which has in fact frequently been misunderstood by successive generations of commentators. How did Paul intend his Roman readership to understand it? That must be the first question. And given that this verse is clearly the climax to the first main section, given also the emphasis put on the law in 2:12–29 and Paul's polemic against Jewish over-confidence based on having the law, the answer is not difficult. "Works of the law" must refer to the attitude attacked in chap. 2; it must denote the "works" referred to there, particularly circumcision. That is to say, the first Roman listeners would most probably and rightly understand "works of the law" as referring to those actions which were performed at the behest of the law, in service of the Torah; that is, those actions which marked out those involved as the people of the law, those acts prescribed by the law by which a member of the covenant people identified himself as a Jew and maintained his status within the covenant.

This is confirmed by the twofold distinction implicit by reference to chap. 2: "works of the law" are *not* the same as *doing* the law (2:13–14), or *fulfilling* the law (2:27); "works of the law" are *not* the same as "the work of the law written in the heart" (2:15), "the circumcision of heart by the Spirit" (2:29). "Works of the law" are rather something more superficial, at the level of "the letter" (2:27, 29), an outward mark indicative of ethnic solidarity (2:28), something more limited than "the patient perseverance in good work" (2:7). In the context of the argument in 2:1–3:8 then, "works of the law" can be defined somewhat crudely as doing what is necessary to be (become, or remain) within the covenant. This, we may recall, was the point at issue also in the Antioch incident (Gal 2:11–18), where the Palestinian believers were clearly anxious to maintain their own obedience to the law (food and purity laws) and so to retain their covenant standing within Judaism. In consequence they were in effect requiring the gentile believers to "judaize," that is, to enter within the boundaries marked out by these laws, in order to make possible a full table-fellowship within the circumference marked out by these laws. Here too the works of the law by which no flesh shall be justified (Gal 2:16) clearly refer to the actions and conduct required by the law if one is to be fully recognized and retain one's status as a member of the people of God.

There is, we might say, therefore, a hidden middle term in 3:20 between "works of the law" and "shall be justified"—a middle term which Reformation exegesis largely missed, as indeed also most exegesis deriving from the controversies of the Reformation period in general. The connection of thought in 3:20 does not run directly from "works of the law" to "shall be justified" and is not aimed directly at works of the law *as a means to achieving* righteousness and acquittal. The connection of thought is more indirect, of works of the law *as a way of identifying the individual with* the people whom God has chosen and will vindicate and of *maintaining his status within* that people. In a word, the hidden middle term is the function of the law as an identity factor, the social function of the law as marking out the people of the law in their distinctiveness (circumcision, food laws, etc.). It is "hidden" at 3:20 simply because it could be taken for granted in the Roman world of this period when talking about the Jews with their religious and national peculiarities; "hidden" too simply because it was clear enough already in 2:1–3:8 and need not complicate the final summary statement beyond the sufficiently clear phrase "works of the law."

As a second modification of Ps 143:2, Paul reads "no flesh" instead of "no one living," the point being no doubt that "flesh" denotes man in his weakness and corruptibility, man in his dependency on this world. It is precisely man in his independence from God, choosing to live on his own terms, for himself, man the creature of his appetites, subservient to his mortality, man taking his sense of value from this world, its society and its standards, man, in a word, as "flesh," who can have no hope of acquittal on the day of judgment. By associating the two phrases ("works of law," "all flesh") Paul implies that the Jewish assumption of a special covenant prerogative which assures a verdict of acquittal at the day of judgment is a living on the level of the flesh. Those who think that to perform "the works of the law" is the same as "doing the law," who think that hearing the law, being a Jew, or bearing the physical mark of circumcision, is what the law is about (the work of the law), are thinking and living as (men of) flesh and consequently can cherish no such confident hope of vindication in that final day; their fleshly understanding of the law is in fact the very transgression of the law (2:27) for which they shall be judged. By implication also there is a play on the word "flesh": it is precisely the equation of covenant membership with physical rite and national kinship, the definition of the people of God in terms of the flesh, which reveals and characterizes the thought of the man of flesh. "All flesh" includes not least "the Jew," precisely because he puts such emphasis on the flesh.

In contrast to this too superficial understanding of the law, Paul offers an alternative understanding of the role of the law: "for through the law comes knowledge of sin." We should not be too hasty in exalting this to a general principle, even though Paul does use it with axiomatic force in his conclusion to the first major section of the letter. In hermeneutical terms the scope of v 20b is determined by what it is set in antithesis to: its primary reference is to the immediate context; its primary function is as a criticism of Paul's fellow Jews for their failure to recognize the role of the law as demonstrated in 3:10–18. If they had properly understood the law they would have realized it was not intended to provide a ground of confidence or boasting (2:17, 23), but rather to eliminate such confidence or boasting (cf. 1 Cor 1:29, 31); it was addressed to the covenant people to make them conscious of sin, aware of being under the power of sin even as members of the covenant people (3:9, 19).

Recognizing thus the primary thrust of v 20b also helps us to recognize why it is that Paul puts only this alternative to the misunderstanding of the law in v 20a. Not because this is the only function he is still willing to accord to the law. On the contrary, there is the other very positive role for the law already alluded to in a phrase like "the obedience of faith" (1:5) and at several points in chap. 2 (2:13–15, 25–29). Rather he posits this function of the law because it highlights most sharply the Jewish failure to understand the role of the law: they have seen it as a confirmation of their special status before God and special favor from God, whereas they should have felt its "work" more deeply (as in some degree some Gentiles did—2:14–15, 26–27), in making them more aware of their *continuing* need of God's grace.

III. God's Saving Righteousness to Faith (3:21–5:21)

Introduction

No one disputes that with the *νυνὶ δέ* of v 21 Paul intends a decisive shift in the argument to a new stage: the eschatological state of affairs brought about by Christ. But Paul is also careful to pick up the terms of the preceding conclusion (Hays, "Psalm 143"), particularly the double negative-positive reference to the law:

> v 20—righteousness not by works of the law . . . through the law knowledge of sin;
> v 21—righteousness apart from the law . . . but attested by the law.

Thus he underscores the point that his argument is not against the law as such, but against an assumption that God's righteousness is his commitment to the people of the law so that a righteousness *χωρὶς νόμου*, "without the law," outside the bounds of the covenant people, would be scarcely conceivable. Paul's objective is to argue the contrary: Jesus' sacrificial death provides a different criterion for the understanding of God's righteousness; the one God must by definition be concerned for Gentile as well as Jew (3:21–31). The case is then made in terms of the determinative precedent of Abraham (chap. 4). And this crucial central section of the argument is summed up in individual and universal salvation-history terms in chap. 5.

A. To Faith in Christ Jesus (3:21–31)

1. The Decisive Demonstration of God's Righteousness in the Death of Jesus (3:21–26)

Bibliography

Bader, G. "Jesu Tod als Opfer." *ZTK* 80 (1983) 411–31. **Barth, M.** *Was Christ's Death a Sacrifice?* SJTOP 9. Edinburgh: Oliver & Boyd, 1961. ———. "The Faith of the Messiah." *HeyJ* 10 (1969) 363–70. **Daly, R. J.** *Christian Sacrifice.* Washington: Catholic University of America, 1978. **Dodd, C. H.** "Atonement." *Bible.* 82–95. **Dunn,**

J. D. G. "Death of Jesus." **Eichholz, G.** *Theologie.* 189–97. **Fitzer, G.** "Der Ort der Versöhnung: Zu Frage des 'Sühnopfers Jesu'." *TZ* 22 (1966) 161–83. **Fryer, N. S. L.** "The Meaning and Translation of *Hilastērion* in Romans 3:25." *EvQ* 59 (1987) 99–116. **Friedrich, G.** *Verkündigung.* 57–67. **Gese, H.** "The Atonement." *Essays on Biblical Theology.* Minneapolis: Augsburg, 1981. 93–116. **Hays, R. B.** *The Faith of Jesus Christ.* SBLDS 56. Chico: Scholars Press, 1983. 170–74. **Hill, D.** *Greek Words.* 23–81. **Hofius, O.** "Sühne und Versöhnung: Zum paulinischen Verständnis des Kreuzestodes Jesu." In *Versuche, das Leiden und Sterben Jesu zu verstehen,* ed. W. Maas. Munich: Schnell & Steiner, 1983. 25–46. **Hooker, M. D.** "Interchange in Christ." *JTS* 22 (1971) 349–61. ———. "Interchange and Atonement." *BJRL* 60 (1978) 462–81. ———. "Interchange and Suffering." In *Suffering and Martyrdom in the New Testament,* ed. W. Horbury and B. McNeill. Cambridge: CUP, 1981. 70–83. **Howard, G.** "On the 'Faith of Christ'." *HTR* 60 (1967) 459–65. ———. "Romans 3:21–31 and the Inclusion of the Gentiles." *HTR* 63 (1970) 223–33. **Hübner, H.** "Paulusforschung." 2709–21. ———. "Sühne und Versöhnung." *KD* 29 (1983) 284–305. **Hultgren, A. J.** "The *Pistis Christou* Formulation in Paul." *NovT* 22 (1980) 248–63. ———. *Gospel.* 47–81. **Janowski, B.** *Sühne als Heilsgeschehen.* WMANT 55. Neukirchen: Neukirchener, 1982. **Johnson, L. T.** "Romans 3:21–26 and the Faith of Jesus." *CBQ* 44 (1982) 77–90. **Käsemann, E.** "Zum Verständnis von Röm 3:24–26." *Exegetische Versuche und Besinnungen I.* Göttingen: Vandenhoeck & Ruprecht, 1960. 96–100. **Kertelge, K.** *Rechtfertigung.* 48–62, 71–84. ———. "Das Verständnis des Todes Jesu bei Paulus." In *Der Tod Jesu: Deutungen im Neuen Testament,* ed. K. Kertelge. Freiburg: Herder, 1976. 114–36. **Kümmel, W. G.** "Πάρεσις und ἔνδειξις." *Heilsgeschehen und Geschichte.* Marburg: Elwert, 1965. 260–70. **Lohse, E.** *Märtyrer und Gottesknecht.* Göttingen: Vandenhoeck & Ruprecht, 1963². 149–54. **Lührmann, D.** "Rechtfertigung und Versöhnung: Zur Geschichte der paulinischen Tradition." *ZTK* 67 (1970) 437–52. **Ljungman, H.** *Pistis.* 37–47. **Lyonnet, S.** *Sin, Redemption and Sacrifice.* AnBib 48. Rome: Pontifical Biblical Institute, 1970. 155–66. **Manson, T. W.** "ἹΛΑΣΤΗΡΙΟΝ." *JTS* 46 (1945) 1–10. **Marshall, I. H.** "The Development of the Concept of Redemption in the New Testament." In *Reconciliation and Hope,* FS L. L. Morris, ed. R. J. Banks. Exeter: Paternoster, 1974. 153–69. **Meyer, B. F.** "The Pre-Pauline Formula in Rom 3:25–26a." *NTS* 29 (1983) 198–208. **Morris, L. L.** "The Meaning of ἱλαστήριον in Romans 3:25." *NTS* 2 (1955–56) 33–43. ———. *The Apostolic Preaching of the Cross.* London: Tyndale, 1955. **Müller, C.** *Gerechtigkeit.* 108–13. **Piper, J.** "The Demonstration of the Righteousness of God in Rom 3:25, 26." *JSNT* 7 (1980) 2–32. ———. *Justification.* 115–30. **Pluta, A.** *Gottes Bundestreue: Ein Schlüsselbegriff in Röm 3:25a.* SBS 34. Stuttgart: Katholisches Bibelwerk, 1969. **Reumann, J.** "The Gospel of the Righteousness of God: Pauline Interpretation in Rom 3:21–31." *Int* 20 (1966) 432–52. **Schrage, W.** "Römer 3:21–26 und die Bedeutung des Todes Jesu Christi bei Paulus." In *Das Kreuz Jesu,* ed. P. Rieger. Göttingen: Vandenhoeck & Ruprecht, 1969. 65–88. **Scroggs, R.** *Last Adam.* **Stuhlmacher, P.** *Gerechtigkeit.* 86–91. ———. "Zur neueren Exegese von Röm 3:24–26." *Versöhnung, Gesetz und Gerechtigkeit.* Göttingen: Vandenhoeck & Ruprecht, 1981. 117–35. ———. "Sühne oder Versöhnung." **Talbert, C. H.** "A Non-Pauline Fragment at Romans 3:24–26." *JBL* 85 (1966) 287–96. **Taylor, V.** *The Atonement in New Testament Teaching.* London: Epworth, 1958³. **Thyen, H.** *Studien.* 163–72. **Wegenast, K.** *Tradition.* 76–80. **Wengst, K.** *Formeln.* 87–90. **Wennemer, K.** "ἈΠΟΛΥΤΡΩΣΙΣ Römer 3:24–25a." *SPCIC* 1:283–88. **Whiteley, D. E. H.** *Theology.* 130–51. **Williams, S. K.** *Jesus' Death as Saving Event: The Background and Origin of a Concept.* HDR 2. Missoula: Scholars Press, 1975. ———. "Righteousness." 270–78. ———. "Again *Pistis Christou.*" *CBQ* 49 (1987) 431–47. **Young, N. H.** "'Hilaskesthai' and Related Words in the New Testament." *EvQ* 55 (1983) 169–76. **Zeller, D.** "Sühne und Langmut: Zur Traditionsgeschichte von Röm 3:24–26." *TP* 43 (1968) 51–75. ———. *Juden.* 157–61, 182–88. **Ziesler, J.** *Righteousness.* 190–94. ———. "Romans 3:21–26." *ExpT* 93 (1981–82) 356–59.

Translation

²¹*But now apart from the law the righteousness of God has been revealed, as attested by the law and the prophets, ²²that is, the righteousness of God through faith in Christ Jesus to all who believe.*ᵃ *For there is no distinction, ²³for all have sinned and lack the glory of God. ²⁴They are justified as a gift by his grace through the redemption which is in Christ Jesus, ²⁵whom God set forth as an expiation, through faith,*ᵇ *in his blood, to demonstrate his righteousness in passing over the sins committed in former times ²⁶in the forbearance of God, to demonstrate his righteousness in the present time, that he might be just and the one who justifies him who believes in Jesus.*ᶜ

Notes

ᵃSome witnesses replaced the εἰς πάντας with ἐπὶ πάντας which resulted in later versions conflating the two readings (Nygren takes the conflated reading as original).

ᵇThere is disagreement as to whether the definite article was part of the original text—διὰ (τῆς) πίστεως. The phrase is omitted by A, presumably by accident, but possibly in recognition of its awkwardness.

ᶜSome witnesses naturally added Χριστοῦ; other variations are probably scribal blunders (see Metzger on 3:26).

Form and Structure

The centrality of this passage in the development of Paul's argument is clearly indicated by the re-emergence of the two key terms in the thematic statement of 1.17: δικαιοσύνη—3:21, 22, 25, 26; πίστις—3:22, 25, 26, 27, 28, 30, 31.

The most striking feature is the syntactical construction of vv 24–26, particularly the awkward participial opening of v 24 (δικαιούμενοι) and the sequence of prepositional phrases which carry the thought forward from v 25 without making clear what their mutual relationship is (sequential, or each directly dependent on v 25a):

²⁵ὃν προέθετο ὁ θεὸς ἱλαστήριον διὰ τῆς πίστεως ἐν τῷ αὐτοῦ αἵματι
εἰς ἔνδειξιν τῆς δικαιοσύνης αὐτοῦ διὰ τὴν πάρεσιν τῶν προγεγονότων
ἁμαρτημάτων ²⁶ἐν τῇ ἀνοχῇ τοῦ θεοῦ,
πρὸς τὴν ἔνδειξιν τῆς δικαιοσύνης αὐτοῦ ἐν τῷ νῦν καιρῷ
εἰς τὸ εἶναι αὐτὸν δίκαιον . . .

(See discussion particularly in Meyer, "Formula," 201–4.)

There is a widespread measure of agreement (though see Kuss, Cranfield, and Schlier) that vv 25–26a (. . . ἐν τῇ ἀνοχῇ τοῦ θεοῦ) is a pre-Pauline formula. The surprising cluster of Pauline *hapax legomena* (*hap. leg.*) within such a short compass certainly encourages such a conclusion: προτίθημι (only in 1:13, but probably not in the same sense), ἱλαστήριον (*hap. leg.*), ἔνδειξις (only in 2 Cor 8:24 in the same sense), πάρεσις (*hap. leg.*), προγίνομαι (*hap. leg.*), ἁμάρτημα (only in 1 Cor 6:18), and ἀνοχή (only in 2:4). Paul would then have inserted the διὰ τῆς πίστεως (thus explaining its awkwardness) and have formed the second ἔνδειξις phrase to balance (past and present) and broaden (Israel and all ἐκ πίστεως) the first ἔνδειξις phrase. Against the alternative suggestions of post-Pauline glosses (Fitzer, 163–66—εἰς ἔνδειξιν . . . ἀνοχῇ τοῦ θεοῦ; Talbert—vv 25–26) see Williams, *Saving Event*, 6–11. Hultgren, *Gospel*, 60–62, sees a chiastic structure embracing vv 23–26a, of which vv 25–26a form the second part, but becomes unnecessarily speculative in suggesting that Paul had previously formulated vv 23–26a as part of a homily delivered at Ephesus on the Day of Atonement (62–64).

More disputed is whether v 24 is also pre-Pauline (the affirmative case is made particularly by Käsemann, "Verständnis"; followed, e.g., by Wegenast; Reumann, "Gospel"; and Eichholz, *Theologie*, 190–91). The case here can hardly depend on the unusualness of the vocabulary, since every element can be paralleled without much difficulty from elsewhere in Paul. It boils down basically to the syntactical awkwardness of the δικαιούμενοι. But even that is not without parallel in Paul; Wengst draws attention to 2 Cor 5:12; 7:5; and 10:14–15 (*Formeln*, 87; see further Williams, *Saving Event*, 11–16). An intermediate solution is also possible: that the awkwardness is the result of Paul's adapting the beginning of a preformed formula to make it fit to his flow of thought; or, alternatively, of his adapting his own terminology to make the incorporation of the preformed formula possible.

The resulting claim is simple: Christ's death, a sacrifice for sin provided by God in accordance with the law, is God's means of extending his righteousness to all who believe (including those outside the law). The fact that Paul can put this forward as a bare assertion, without substantive supporting argument, confirms that the pre-Pauline formula expressed a fundamental element of the confession of the first Christian churches. As such the recipients of the letter would accept it without argument, as part of their shared faith (hence the unlikelihood of Paul's "correcting" the earlier formula; see further the penultimate paragraph on 3:26). Paul's concern here is more for what this means for Jew and Gentile (3:27–31); cf. particularly Howard, "Romans 3:21–31," 228.

Comment

3:21   νυνὶ δέ, "but now," is a characteristic feature of Paul's style, sometimes denoting a logical contrast (7:17; 1 Cor 12:18; 13:13), but usually with a clear temporal force (as in 15:23, 25; 2 Cor 8:22; Philem 9, 11). Here it clearly marks a significant transition point, a contrast with what has just been described (1:18–3:20)—not just the before and after contrast of individual conversion (as in 6:22; 7:6; Col 1:22; 3:8), but more the transition from one epoch to another, where a decisive new element has transformed the circumstances which previously pertained (as in 5:9–11; 8:1; 11:30–31; 13:11; elsewhere especially 1 Cor 15:20; Eph 2:13), i.e., the eschatological "now" (cf. also particularly 2 Cor 6:2).

χωρὶς νόμου, "without, apart from the law." χωρὶς is "the most typical Hellenistic word for 'without'" (BGD). Given the close parallel of thought between vv 21–22 and 27–28, the phrase is obviously synonymous with χωρὶς ἔργων νόμου (v 28); also χωρὶς ἔργων (4:6). It is thus intended to be understood in contrast (νυνὶ δέ) to the ἐν τῷ νόμῳ and ἐξ ἔργων νόμου of vv 19–20, implying that Paul thinks of the law in the same way in each of the phrases—the law as a boundary marker ("those within the law"), where "works of the law" is the distinctive pattern of religion and lifestyle demanded of those marked out by the law. "Without the law" then means outside the national and religious parameters set by the law, without reference to the normal Jewish hallmarks (cf. NEB: "quite independently of the law").

δικαιοσύνη θεοῦ, "the righteousness of God." Given the heavily covenantal overtones of the phrase (God's saving action on behalf of his people—see on 1:17 and 3:5), the shocking thing here would be Paul's juxtaposition of the two phrases ("apart from the law," "the righteousness of God"), since in Jewish tradition righteousness and the law were two closely correlative terms (see Introduction §5). Cf. the similar expressions of trust in God's righteousness in Isa 51:5–6, 8 and Dan 9:16, where the confidence is precisely in God's commitment to Israel.

πεφανέρωται, "has been revealed." Paul reiterates the thematic assertion of 1:17, with φανερόω used in place of ἀποκαλύπτω (but obviously as synonyms—TDNT 9:4; EWNT 3:988), and the perfect tense emphasizing that a decisive act has already taken place which has proved to be the eschatological turning point in the history of salvation; cf. particularly 16:26, which recalls the fulcrum effect of 3:21 in the exposition, and Col 1:26. As the χωρὶς νόμου and these parallels confirm, the salvation-history transition Paul has in view is precisely the transition from a salvation-history conceived in too narrowly Jewish terms to a salvation-history which embraces Gentiles as well as Jews on the same terms. The thought is not of the incarnation (Lagrange) but of the salvation-effective events of Christ's death (and resurrection), as the subsequent exposition makes clear (3:25; 4:24–25; etc.), and of these events made known in the gospel (1:16–17).

μαρτυρουμένη ὑπὸ τοῦ νόμου καὶ τῶν προφητῶν, "attested by the law and the prophets." The imagery of the law court (vv 19–20) still influences Paul's language—"the law and the prophets" summoned as witnesses. Somewhat surprisingly Paul rarely speaks of the OT prophets (only 1:2 and 3:21 in his own words) and nowhere else does he use the phrase "the law and the prophets" (though it was certainly familiar elsewhere as a way of speaking of the Jewish sacred writings as a whole—Matt 11:13 // Luke 16:16; Matt 5:17; 7:12; 22:40; Luke 24:44; John 1:45; Acts 13:15; 24:14; 28:23; and not a Christian creation—Sirach, prologue; 2 Macc 15:9; 4 Macc 18.10; Str-B, 3:164–65). Coming at such a crucial point in the argument, the emphasis is certainly deliberate, and almost certainly is intended to safeguard the χωρὶς νόμου from misunderstanding: the continuity of divine purpose runs right through the scriptures, both law and prophets; see also on 1:2. To be able to appeal to the (Jewish) scriptures was of course fundamental for the earliest Christians (with the terminology here cf. particularly John 5:19 and Acts 10:43). But it was even more important for Paul, with his too easily misunderstood attempt to put space between the gospel and the law. The testimony he will subsequently elaborate, particularly in chaps. 4 and 9–11, is of a continuity in the *character* of God's saving purpose through Israel, which is not to be confused with a national or ethnic continuity as such.

22 δικαιοσύνη δὲ θεοῦ, "that is, the righteousness of God." The repetition with δέ indicates a fuller definition of the key phrase (as particularly in 9:30 and 1 Cor 2:6). The absence of a verb in this fuller definition confirms the dynamic force of the concept itself—God's action on behalf of those to whom he has committed himself (cf. Stuhlmacher, *Gerechtigkeit,* 87; Kertelge, *Rechtfertigung,* 75; Williams, "Righteousness," 272, has to supply the verb "to be" in order to defend his interpretation of God's righteousness as "an aspect of his nature"; but see again on 1:17 and 3:5). Those who continue to treat the phrase as objective genitive, a status conferred by God himself, include Cranfield and Schlier.

διὰ πίστεως Ἰησοῦ Χριστοῦ, "through faith in Jesus Christ." The phrase is potentially ambiguous, since πίστις can mean both "faith" and "faithfulness" (see on 1:17), and since the genitive construction can be taken in different ways ("faith given by Jesus Christ," "Jesus Christ's faith = faithfulness"); as the debate between Hultgren, *"Pistis Christou,"* and Williams, "Again," shows, the matter cannot be resolved on syntactical grounds alone (but cf. Gaston's argument regarding ἔργα νόμου—see on 3:20). The latter alternative, "the faith(fulness) of Jesus Christ" (cf. 4:16) continues to find advocates and has recently gained a wave of renewed support (Barth [but not *Shorter*]; Schmidt; Longenecker, *Paul,* 149–50; Howard, "Faith of Christ"; M. Barth, "Faith," 368; Williams, "Righteousness," 272–78; Johnson, "Rom 3:21–26"; Hays, *Faith,* 170–74; Byrne, *Reckoning,* 79–80; Gaston, *Paul,* 117, 172; Ljungman 38–40, 47, argues for both senses), in which case the thought would be almost synonymous with v 24 (δικαιούμενοι . . . διὰ τῆς ἀπολυτρώσεως τῆς ἐν Χριστῷ Ἰησοῦ), the "faithfulness of Christ" being Christ's faithful obedience to the death of the cross. But Christ's faithfulness is not something which Paul draws attention to elsewhere in the extended exposition of Romans, even where it would have been highly appropriate—particularly chap. 4, where Abraham's πίστις is the model for the believer, *not* for Christ, and 5:15–19, where the antithesis ἀπιστία/πίστις would have been very natural, had Christ's faith been a factor in his thought (against Johnson, "Rom 3:21–26," 87–89). That some repetition is involved on either rendering is clear. But repetition is a means of emphasis, and the emphasis in the section as a whole (vv 21–31, or indeed 3:21–4:25) is clearly on faith, the faith of those who believe. The central issue is how God's righteousness operates, the means by which or "terms" on which he acts on man's behalf (Hays, 172, misses this). What Paul has been objecting to with increasing clarity and emphasis is his own people's assumption that the righteousness of God is coterminous with Israel, the people of the law, those marked out as members of the covenant (= recipients of his righteousness). Paul's response is that God's righteousness is *not* thus determined; it works through faith without regard to the law understood in these terms. Faith is the human condition or attitude which is set in contrast to "works of the law" (vv 20–22, 27–28; cf. Schlatter). This sense was clearly central to the thematic statement of 1:17, and it is clearly this statement which Paul picks up here. In the same way and at the equivalent fulcrum point in Galatians (2:16), Paul had sharpened the contrast between "works of the law" and "faith" into outright antithesis. Since the line of thought and the terminology at the two points is so similar, it is hard to set aside the explicit evidence of Gal 2:16 where διὰ πίστεως Ἰησοῦ Χριστοῦ is rendered equivalently by εἰς Χριστὸν Ἰησοῦν ἐπιστεύσαμεν (πίστις [Χριστοῦ] is clearly the same antithesis to ἔργα νόμου in Gal 2:16 as in 3:2, 5); Williams's counterargument that Paul was not accustomed to thinking of Christ as the "object" of faith ("Again," 434–35, 442–43) makes too little sense of 10:14, Gal 2:16 and Phil 1:29. This does not mean that Paul regarded man's faith as the manifestation of God's righteousness (against Hays, *Faith*, 172). What Paul says is that God's righteousness comes to expression *through* faith in Christ (rather than through those acts which set Jews apart in their national distinctiveness). Wilckens criticizes Bultmann's subordination of Christology to justification in his interpretation of Paul by noting that the faith by which Paul says a person is justified is characteristically πίστις Χριστοῦ, that is, in the crucified (3:25; "Christologie").

εἰς πάντας τοὺς πιστεύοντας, "to all who believe." The πάντας is obviously the point of the repetition (the phrase is neither a mere repetition nor a new thought)—emphatic, both to balance the repeated "all/every" of vv 19–20 and 23, and at the same time to emphasize the universal outreach of God's saving purpose and action (as in 1:5, 16; 2:10; 4:11, 16; 10:4, 11–13). See further on 1:16. For οἱ πιστεύοντες/πιστεύσαντες, "the believers," as one of the earliest self-descriptions of the new movement see also Acts 2:44; 4:32; 5:14; and 22:19. That it was a self-description is evident (πίστις as such not being an exclusively Christian trait). Nevertheless it is significant that it was faith (in Christ) which they regarded as their distinguishing feature, not any equivalent to the rituals of the law ("the believers," not, e.g., "the baptized").

οὐ γάρ ἐστιν διαστολή, "for there is no difference, distinction," explains both the preceding and the immediately following "all," meaning, in particular, both Jew and Gentile (see further on 10:12). The familiarity of the assertion to present-day readers should not be allowed to dull the shocking character of what Paul says: the established character of the phrase "Jew and Gentile/Greek" (see on 1:16) expressed the axiomatic nature of the Jewish self-understanding of the people of Israel as different. The object of 1:18–3:20, however, had been precisely to destroy the Jewish presumption of special prerogative and defense even before the faithful covenant God (the point reiterated in v 23). If that special claim on God is not allowed, the way is open for Paul to expound faith as the only means for anyone, everyone, to receive God's righteousness.

23 πάντες γὰρ ἥμαρτον, "for all have sinned." "All" continues the emphasis of 3:4, 9, 12, 19, 20. The aorist is used either because the perspective is that of the final judgment (as in 2:12, q.v.) or because the perspective is that of the decisive and universal character of man's fall (see further on 5:12).

ὑστεροῦνται τῆς δόξης τοῦ θεοῦ, "lack the glory of God." ὑστερέω is an antonym of περισσεύω (see on 3:7), meaning "to lack, be deficient, fall short of" (cf. 1 Cor 1:7; 8:8; 12:24; 2 Cor 11:5, 9; 12:11; Phil 4:12). Linked with "the glory of God" (see on 1:21), it almost certainly alludes to Adam's fall (the aorist [ἥμαρτον] and present combined having the same epochal implication as the perfect in 3:21). The thought of Adam's fall as his being deprived of the glory of God was probably already a feature of Jewish reflection on the Genesis narratives (cf. particularly *Apoc. Mos.* 21.6—Adam accuses Eve, "you have deprived me of the glory of God"; see further Scroggs, *Adam*, 26, 48–49); although "image" and "glory" are closely related at this point, Jewish theology did not share the later Christian fascination with the question of whether Adam had lost the divine image (see Dunn, *Christology*, 105; and further on 8:29). Correspondingly, the hope of the end time could be expressed in terms of the restoration or enhancement of the original glory (*Apoc. Mos.* 39.2; *1 Enoch* 50.1; *4 Ezra* 7.122–25; *2 Apoc. Bar.* 51.1, 3; 54.15, 21; cf. 1QS 4.23; CD 3:20; 1QH 17.15; see also Scroggs, *Adam*, 26–27, 54–56; Dunn, *Christology*, 106). Christian reflection is of a piece with the broader Jewish theology at this point; cf. particularly the way in which Heb 2:6–10 gives a Christological and eschatological interpretation to Ps 8:4–6 which talks of the glory which God had in view in making man (see further Dunn, *Christology*, 102–3, 109–110). Paul's own use of the δόξα motif elsewhere in Romans shows how much he was influenced by the same line of reflection (cf. particularly 1:23 with 8:18–21). So Paul probably refers here *both* to the glory lost in man's fall *and* to the glory that fallen man is failing to reach in consequence. The reference confirms the double thrust of Paul's polemic: he reduces the difference between Jew and Gentile to the same level of their common creature-liness, so that this recognition of their creaturely dependence on the Creator's power can be put to all as the paradigm of faith (cf. 4:17).

24 δικαιούμενοι, "being justified." The syntactical link with the preceding context is obscure (see Cranfield). But the sense is clear enough: Paul is describing, possibly by adapting preformed material (see *Form and Structure*), how "the righteousness of God" comes to effect "through faith in Jesus Christ." The abruptness of the construction also helps underline the fact that it is precisely those who have sinned and fall short of God's glory who are justified; cf. 5:20 (Wilckens). The passive indicative participle of δικαιόω is without parallel in Paul, but he does speak of God as ὁ δικαιῶν, "the one who justifies," on several occasions (3:26; 4:5; 8:33; Gal 3:11), and the same tense is used in the passive to describe how justification happens as a general rule (3:28; Gal 2:16). The present tense also serves to span the temporal gap between the two decisive epochal moments in salvation history which he has in view: Christ's atoning death (v 25) and the final judgment (v 20). Cf. the switch from present to future in 3:28, 30; and see further on 1:17.

δωρεάν, "as a gift, without payment." Cf. Gen 29:15; Exod 21:11; Josephus, *Life* 38, 425; *War* 1.274; Matt 10:8; 2 Cor 11:7; 2 Thess 3:8; Rev 21:6; 22:17.

τῇ αὐτοῦ χάριτι, "by his grace." For χάρις, a dynamic word like δικαιοσύνη, as denoting God's outreach in gracious power, see on 1:5. Where δικαιοσύνη, however, is qualified by the relationship to which it refers, χάρις denotes the unconditional character of God's action—an emphasis doubled by conjoining it here with δωρεάν; cf. particularly 5:15: ἡ δωρεὰ ἐν χάριτι. It is important to recall that Judaism also saw its covenant relationship with God as given by grace (cf. Philo, *Sac.* 57; *2 Apoc. Bar.* 48.18–20; 75.5–7; and see further

Introduction §§5.1 and 5.3)—an emphasis which Paul would not dispute (11:5); see also *EWNT* 3:1098–99. But in Paul's perspective this recognition of God's covenant choice had been too much obscured by current Jewish emphasis on law and works of law. Paul is here, therefore, developing a different understanding of God's covenant choice and righteousness, by setting grace in antithesis to the law and works (implicit here; explicit in 6:14–15 and 11:6) and asserting the human correlative to be *faith* (cf. particularly 4:16).

διὰ τῆς ἀπολυτρώσεως, "through the redemption," "act of liberation" (NEB). ἀπολύτρωσις is a little used word, but certainly known not least in Jewish writers in the sense of ransoming a captive or prisoner of war from slavery (*Ep. Arist.* 12, 33; Philo, *Prob.* 114; Josephus, *Ant.* 12.27; see further BGD); Deissmann's famous example of its use in reference to sacral manumission (*Light*, 327) should not be allowed to dominate the interpretation, since it is only a particular application of a broader concept; on the other hand, we should not forget that many of Paul's audience in Rome were themselves slaves or ex-slaves (Leenhardt; see *Introduction* §2.4.2). The uncompounded word (λύτρωσις) is more widely used, in the LXX at any rate (about 10 times), in the same sense of "ransoming"; it is quite possible that Christian tradition or Paul himself deliberately chose the weightier compound form to strengthen the sense of ransoming from (sin) or back (to God; cf. Moulton, *Grammar* 2:298, 299). But it is almost impossible to doubt that behind the text lies the strong OT motif, expressed in regular use of the verb λυτροῦν, particularly of God as redeemer of his people Israel and especially of Israel's being ransomed (from slavery) in Egypt—prominent in Deut (7:8; 9:26; 13:5 [LXX6]; 15:15; 21:8; 24:18), the Psalms (25 [24]:22; 26 [25]:11; 31:5 [30:6]; 32 [31]:7; etc.) and Second Isaiah (41:14; 43:1, 14; 44:22–24; 51:11; 52:3; 62:12; 63:9). That Paul is drawing on typical emphases of Israel's covenant faith is indicated also particularly by Pss 111 [110]:9 and 130 [129]:7–8. The distinctively Christian note is not given in the ἀπολύτρωσις, but in the ἐν Χριστῷ Ἰησοῦ. For the debate on whether the concept of "redemption" includes the idea of paying a price (the stronger the LXX background is thought to be, the less is it likely that the two go necessarily together) see particularly Marshall, who makes a helpful clarification of the distinction between "price" and "cost" ("Redemption," 153 n.4). See further especially Kertelge, *Rechtfertigung*, 53–55; also *EWNT* 1:332–34. The word includes the process of redemption, not just the event of crucifixion (see Wennemer); in the Pauline literature ἀπολύτρωσις (like δικαιόω) contains the "already/not yet" tension within itself (8:23; 1 Cor 1:30; Eph 1:7, 14; 4:30; Col 1:14); note the striking parallels in 1QM 1:12; 14:5; 15:1.

ἐν Χριστῷ Ἰησοῦ, "in Christ Jesus," is the first occurrence in Romans of a phrase much loved by Paul and distinctive of his theology (6:11, 23; 8:1, 2; 9:1; 12:5; 15:17; 16:3, 7, 9, 10; etc.—more than 80 times in the Pauline corpus); outside the Pauline corpus as such in this distinctive Pauline usage elsewhere only in 1 Pet 3:16 and 5:10, 14; the use of the phrase in Clement and Ignatius (e.g., *1 Clem.* 32.4; 38.1; Ign. *Eph.* 1.1; *Trall.* 9.2) is almost certainly a reflection of Pauline influence. That in this phrase here at least Paul looks back to the decisive act of Christ's death and resurrection by which the new epoch had been introduced is certainly indicated by the context (vv

21, 25)—"through Christ Jesus," "determined by the fact that Jesus Christ died and rose" (Neugebauer, quoted by Kramer, 143). But since this new epoch is also characterized by the continuing Lordship of Christ (not just initiated by him), it is difficult to exclude the thought of a redemption which is "in Christ" for those who are "in Christ Jesus" (cf. ἐν νόμῳ—3:19). Since deliverance from sin comes about through death (6:7), it is only by participation in Christ in his death and new life that redemption from sin can begin to be experienced now (6:1–11); to the usage here cf. particularly 8:2; 1 Cor 1:4; 2 Cor 4:10–12; 13:4; and Gal 2:19–20. This fuller connotation should remind us that Paul's concept of the risen Christ as "person" is by no means simple or easy to accommodate to modern understanding of persons; for Paul to be or share "in Christ Jesus" is to experience a (personal) power which embraces the individual, which has the character of Christ's dying and rising and which effects an equivalent dying and rising in the one "in Christ" (see further Dunn, *Jesus,* 324 and 326–38; and below on 6:11 and 15:17).

25 ὃν προέθετο ὁ θεὸς ἱλαστήριον διὰ πίστεως ἐν τῷ αὐτοῦ αἵματι, "whom God set forth as an expiation, through faith, in his blood." προτίθημι can have the sense of "purpose, intend" (as in 1:13); Zeller, "Sühne," 58, and Cranfield argue strongly for this sense here (cf. Lagrange, NEB, Hendriksen). But "set forth, present" is more likely (BGD, RSV, NIV; so, e.g., SH, Murray, Käsemann, Schlier, Hultgren, *Gospel,* 56–57; Williams, *Saving Event,* 34–38, gives this meaning too little consideration). The word was probably chosen to evoke or emerged as summary of a complex of ideas: the undeniable because public fact of Christ's shameful death which earliest Christian apologetic turned to good account (Acts 5:30; 10:39; Gal 3:1); the contrast between the manipulation of the sacrificial blood in the inner sanctum of the Temple on the Day of Atonement and the open character of Christ's death as the eschatologically decisive sin offering (T. W. Manson, "ΙΛΑΣΤΗΡΙΟΝ," 5; Bruce; see below); and probably also the idea of the public use of sacrificial blood to symbolize the introduction of the new covenant (cf. Exod 24:3–8). Stuhlmacher notes its cultic use in reference to the bread of the presence in Exod 29:23; 40:23; Lev 24:8; 2 Macc 1:8, 15 ("Exegese," 130). The affirmation that God provided the sacrifice is an important supplementary corrective to the (probably) older antithesis, "You (Jews) killed him, but God raised him up" (Acts 2:23–24; 3:15; 4:10; 5:30–31; 10:39–40), since it not only underscores the divine initiative, but allows the thought that it was God himself who acted to establish the new covenant/epoch in the death as well as resurrection of Christ. The possibility of some play on the Akedah theme (the offering of Isaac, Gen 22) cannot be excluded (see further on 8:32). The metaphor is different of course from the idea of "God *in* Christ reconciling the world to himself" (2 Cor 5:19), but Paul could hold the two together without difficulty (2 Cor 5:21); that he can use such apparently conflicting imagery should warn us against pressing the metaphorical language for a too literal or allegorical sense.

ἱλαστήριον is almost exclusively an LXX word, used 21 times in Exodus, Leviticus, and Numbers for the lid of the ark ("the mercy seat"), the "place of expiation" (see particularly Exod 25 and Lev 16); similarly Amos 9:1 (not in all MSS), 5 times in Ezek 43 (the temple vision), and in four passages in Philo (usually citing LXX); so also Heb 9:5 (so here, e.g., Nygren; Bruce; Hultgren, *Gospel*, 55–60, with further bibliography, 53; Fryer). But the sense "means of expiation" is also clear enough in *4 Macc* 17.22, Josephus, *Ant.* 16.182, Gen 6:16 (Sym.) and elsewhere (see BGD, *TDNT* 3:319–20), and is the more obvious meaning here (Denney; Morris, "ἱλαστήριον"; Thyen, 167; Kertelge, *Rechtfertigung*, 55–57; Eichholz, 192–94; Zeller; others in Hultgren, *Gospel*, 54–55); although, once again, it would be unwise to press for a clear-cut either/or (cf. Str-B, 3:175–78; Black; Stuhlmacher, "Exegese"; Goppelt, *Theology*, 2:95; Wilckens)—"medium of atonement" would preserve the ambiguity.

At all events, in view of this background, it can hardly be doubted that Paul (and the pre-Pauline tradition) was thinking of Jesus' death as a sacrifice (so explicitly NEB, NIV, and NJB), a judgment that is confirmed by the reference to Jesus' blood. Since Jesus' death was not particularly bloody in the earliest traditions, the notice of the blood here is to be explained precisely by the association of ideas within Jewish traditions, "blood of sacrifice"— the manipulation of the blood being a crucial part of the ritual, particularly of the Day of Atonement sin offering (Lev 16), as would have been well known in diaspora communities (cf. also Mark 14:24 par.; Heb 9:11–14; 1 Pet 1:19; so, e.g., Taylor, *Atonement*, 63–64; Davies, *Paul*, 236; Lohse, *Märtyrer*, 138–39; Ladd, *Theology*, 425–26; Daly, 239–40; Stuhlmacher, "Sühne," especially 297–304; Maillot; against Fitzer, Schrage, 81–82, Kümmel, *Theology*, 198–99, Friedrich). It is possible that Paul was aware of the same language being used to describe the significance of the Maccabean martyrs' death (as presented in *4 Macc* 17.22; cf. Lohse, "Märtyrer," 152 n.4; Hill, *Greek Words*, 41–45; Williams, *Saving Event*, 248); see also 5:9. But this possibility should not be understood as an alternative to the view that Paul thought of Jesus' death as a sacrifice and in specifically Day of Atonement terms. The *4 Maccabees* tradition is simply another example, roughly contemporaneous with Paul, of sacrificial imagery being used to give meaning to what would otherwise have been horrific and faith-disturbing deaths. In contrast to Rom 3:25–26, *4 Macc* 17.22 sees the martyrs' death as a ground of hope for the continuance of God's special care for Israel; and in contrast to *4 Macc* 17, Rom 3:25 stresses the initiative of God in providing the sacrifice (cf. Kertelge, *Rechtfertigung*, 57–58). The older dispute as to whether ἱλαστήριον should be rendered "propitiation" or "expiation" (in which Dodd ["Atonement"] and Morris [*Apostolic Preaching*, chaps. 4 and 5] were the chief protagonists), has also suffered from an unnecessary polarizing of alternatives (cf. Young, 175; Hofius, "Sühne," 26–31, in effect restates Dodd's position, with the same imbalance; while Ridderbos, *Paul*, 189–90, is surprisingly and unjustifiably dogmatic on the issue on the side of Morris). Assuredly, the logic of Paul's exposition is that the wrath of God (expounded in 1:18–3:20) is somehow averted by Jesus' death (cf. 2 Macc 7:38), but the passage also portrays God as offerer of the sacrifice rather than its object (cf. Schlatter, Barrett, Gaugler, Robinson, *Wrestling*, 44–47).

Although the theology of sacrifice within Judaism is obscure (see, e.g., M. Barth, *Sacrifice*, 13, with bibliography), it is possible to say something more positive about Paul's own theology of sacrifice, from (1) his own use of sacrificial language in speaking of Christ's death, and (2) the not dissimilar use of sacrificial imagery in martyr theology, bearing in mind (3) that Paul seems to have shared his views with his readers (hence the possibility of such brief and undeveloped references as 3:25; 4:25; and 8:3). (a) The sin offering dealt with sin. In some sense or other the killing of the sacrifice dealt with the sin or removed the sin of the sacrificer: 8:3—"condemned sin"; 2 Cor 5:21—sin removed; cf. 2 Macc 7:38—wrath ended by means of martyr death; *4 Macc* 17.21–22—the country purified. (b) The sin offering represented the offerer in his sin, the sinner *qua* sinner. This is the most obvious significance of that part of the ritual where the offerer laid his hands on the animal's head (Lev 4:4, 15, 24, 29, 33); thereby the sinner identified himself with the animal, or at least indicated that the animal in some sense represented him (Leenhardt; H. H. Rowley, *Worship in Ancient Israel* [London: SPCK, 1967] 133; Gese, "Atonement," 105–6; Daly, 100–106; Janowski, 199–221; Hofius, "Sühne," 35–36). This is what we would expect from other references to the laying on of hand(s), where identification seems again to be the chief rationale (particularly Num 8:10; 27:18, 23; Deut 34:9). In the Day of Atonement ritual, which Paul certainly has in mind here, the action explicitly lays the sins of the people on the head of the goat (Lev 16:21), which then literally removes the sins from the camp; but this seems simply to be an alternative way of describing what the more normal sin offering achieves, since the same formula can be used for both sin offering and scapegoat (11Q Temple 26.9–27.2—"so that they will be forgiven"; *m. Seb.* 1.7—"makes atonement for"). This dovetails completely with Paul's use of Adam Christology in 8:3 (Christ identified with sinful flesh—see on 8:3), 2 Cor 5:14 (Christ died, therefore all died, because Christ was identified with man) and 5:21 (Christ became sin); cf. Whiteley's formulation—"salvation through participation" (*Theology*, 130). (c) Only with such an understanding can we make sufficient sense of the sacrificial "interchange" (so particularly Hooker, "Interchange in Christ," 358; "Interchange and Suffering," 77) which seems to be a fundamental feature of Paul's understanding of Jesus' death: the sinner lives, the sinless dies. The implication is that as the sinner's sin was transferred to the spotless sacrifice, so the spotless life of the sacrifice was transferred (or reckoned) to the sinner (so in varying forms 2 Cor 5:21; Rom 8:3; Gal 3:13; and 4:4). See further on 8:3 and Dunn, "Death"; Wilckens, 1:236–40.

διὰ πίστεως, "through faith." This should probably be taken as a parenthesis, and not with ἐν τῷ αἵματι, which would be without parallel in the NT; besides which Paul does not use πίστις with ἐν (see further Käsemann). Hebert's ("Faithfulness," 376) and Pluta's suggestion that πίστις here refers to God's covenant faithfulness is attractive, in view of the emphasis of 3:3–4, 7 and the strong likelihood that Paul had the same thought in mind in 1:17 (see on 1:17); cf. 1 John 1:9. The possibility is not to be entirely excluded, but it is much more likely that Paul took the opportunity to stress once again that God reaches out to faith. Whereas the concomitant of the system of atonement for the devout Jew was faithful attention to the rules of the covenant ("works of the law"), Paul insists on a faith which is not tied into a continued practice of the cult (faithfulness) but which can only be an acceptance of the decisive sacrifice already provided by God. Those who take πίστις Ἰησοῦ Χριστοῦ in v 22 as "the faith/faithfulness of Jesus Christ" naturally incline to the same sense for πίστις here (e.g., Barth, Williams, *Saving Event*, 47–50); but see on 3:22.

εἰς ἔνδειξιν τῆς δικαιοσύνης αὐτοῦ, "to demonstrate his righteousness." ἔνδειξις, "indication, proof, demonstration" (LSJ; Kümmel, "Πάρεσις," 263); cf. particularly 2 Cor 8:24. The exegesis of δικαιοσύνη should again not be forced into the either/or of righteous status given by God, or God's own righteousness (as again Cranfield). The sense is still that of God's action on behalf of those to whom he has pledged himself (see on 1:17 and 3:5). He demonstrates his righteousness by providing a sacrifice which fulfills the terms laid down in his covenant with Israel (sin offering—cf. 8:3); see also Nygren; Kertelge, *Rechtfertigung*, 59–60; Ziesler, *Righteousness*, 194; Wilckens. That the shameful death of crucifixion could be thus presented as an expression of God's saving grace is a classic example of the gospel's transformation of normal human values.

διὰ τὴν πάρεσιν τῶν προγεγονότων ἁμαρτημάτων, "on account of the passing over of the sins committed in former times." πάρεσις, only here in the Greek Bible, means "passing over," but not in the sense of "overlooking, disregarding." Rather it has the more strictly legal sense of "letting go unpunished, remission of penalty" (BGD). For the ambiguity of διά cf. 4:25 and 8:10, 20. That gentile sins as such are in view (Gager, *Origins*, 216, following Howard) is less likely, particularly if the formula was first framed within Jewish Christianity. What is not clear is the relation between the ἔνδειξις and the πάρεσις, particularly whether Paul envisaged the πάρεσις as taking place in the past or present and whether any remission in the past was simply provisional or a postponement of the reckoning (see Meyer, "Formula," 200–201). Paul presumably at least meant that while the sacrificial system was a legitimate way of dealing with sin in the past, it did not constitute an adequate or final answer to the problem of sin and sinning. Only the sacrifice of Christ could do that (presumably because with his resurrection came the possibility for the power of sin to be countered through union with him). But still unclear is what Paul's language implies about the validity of the sacrificial system in the past. Did he regard it as only provisional, merely a "holding operation" with sentence suspended, as it were, till the coming of Christ, with Christ's death the one and only properly effective sacrifice (cf. Heb 9:25–26; 10:12, 14; cf. Williams, *Saving Event*, 29–34; Hübner, "Sühne," 301)? Or did he regard it as effective (and therefore Christ's death as sacrifice, effective by being a sacrifice—Maillot), but now (presumably) no longer necessary in view of the effectiveness of Christ's death?

In all this the question remains unresolved as to how the sacrificial cult, still in operation at this time in Jerusalem, of course, was regarded across the spectrum of earliest Christianity. That the Hellenists broke with a still Temple-centered faith is the testimony of Acts (chaps. 1–7); and that breach presumably helped determine the character of the Christianity which followed from it (including Paul's own missionary work and theology). But whether the Jewish Christians in Jerusalem itself held aloof from the regular offering of sacrifices (for which the Temple primarily existed) remains unclear; it is difficult to envisage a continuing loyalty to Temple and law within Jerusalem itself (such as Acts 21:20–26 attests) which did not include some involvement in the sacrificial cult; but the practice of the last supper as a commemoration of Jesus' death as sacrifice, indeed as sacrifice of the new covenant, probably belongs already to that very early period (cf. 1 Cor 15:3), and attitudes to the continuing Temple sacrifices cannot have been unaffected. Unfortunately Paul's language here, both as a pre-Pauline formula and in Paul's use of it, is too ambiguous to provide further clarification. On this too we are left with more questions than answers.

The puzzle of why Paul uses πάρεσις and not ἄφεσις, "forgiveness" (only in Col 1:14 and Eph 1:7 in the Pauline corpus, with ἀφίημι used in the sense of "forgive" only in the quotation of Rom 4:7; Kümmel, "Πάρεσις," 262–63, presses too hard in arguing for the sense of "forgiveness" for πάρεσις), has not yet been adequately solved either. It may simply reflect the fact that no single technical term had clearly established itself in Greek to express the various Hebrew metaphors which functioned in this area; but Paul seems to avoid overlapping alternatives like ἱλάσκομαι/ἱλασμός, καλύπτω, and ἐξαλείφω (Col 2:14) as well. The issue is presumably related to the fact that Paul seems deliberately to avoid using the correlated term "repentance" (μετάνοια—only 2:4 and 2 Cor 7:9–10; μετανοέω—only 2 Cor 12:21). Taken together these facts may simply indicate that Paul wanted to establish his own technical terminology ("grace" and "faith") in a way which made them usable and understandable without reference to Judaism's continuing sacrificial cult (see also on 2:4; and further on 4:7–8; 12:1; and 15:16).

26 ἐν τῇ ἀνοχῇ τοῦ θεοῦ, "in the forbearance of God." The phrase simply strengthens the clear implication of the preceding phrases that whatever the rationale of God's not pressing for punishment of the sins committed by his covenant people in the preceding epoch (whether the sacrificial system "worked" or merely foreshadowed Christ's sacrificial death), it was an act of divine forbearance or "restraint" (Williams, *Saving Event*, 28). The thought was hardly strange to Jewish ears (cf. particularly the often repeated theme of Exod 34:6–7—see on 9:15, and further 11:31, 32; Wilckens; and further Zeller, "Sühne," 64–70); yet it would be easy to fall into the habit of taking that forbearance for granted simply because the sacrificial system was so well established (see again on 2:4). Käsemann's conclusion that the motivation here contradicts Paul's earlier description of the wrath of God (1:18–3:20) is built on the fallacious assumption that Paul made a blanket condemnation of his ancestral faith as such.

πρὸς τὴν ἔνδειξιν τῆς δικαιοσύνης αὐτοῦ ἐν τῷ νῦν καιρῷ, "to demonstrate his righteousness in the present time." The repetition of more or less the same phrase (as v 25b) is obviously deliberate, and a balance is clearly intended with the preceding lines, with ἐν τῷ νῦν καιρῷ balancing διὰ τὴν πάρεσιν τῶν προγεγονότων ἁμαρτημάτων. . . . The death of Christ is envisaged as forming a pivotal point in history with God's righteousness demonstrated there having effect for both the past and the future. καιρός here denotes not just a moment in time or the passage of time, but time pregnant with significance—the appointed time, the time of opportunity, whose decisions and actions will determine the future. In Paul, see particularly 13:11; 1 Cor 7:29; 2 Cor

6:2; Gal 6:10 (cf. *EWNT* 2:572–74). ὁ νῦν καιρός has a particularly strong eschatological overtone (as also in 8:18; 11:5; 2 Cor 6:2; less so in 2 Cor 8:14), as denoting the time between the death and resurrection of Christ and the consummation—the time when the eschatological promises are being realized but not yet completely.

εἰς τὸ εἶναι αὐτὸν δίκαιον, "that he might be just," is the third compressed purpose clause whose precise relation to the preceding (sequential, or each dependent directly on v 25a) is unclear, though the sense is not dissimilar to 2 Thess 1:5–6 or indeed Rom 3:4. God is "just" not because he acts in accordance with some abstract ideal of justice, but because he has acted in fulfillment of the obligation he took upon himself as covenant God of Israel (see on 1:17). Since the reference here is directly (or indirectly) to the death of Jesus as ἱλαστήριον, the implication is that Jesus' sacrificial death was God's effective way of dealing with his people's sin (had he simply disregarded it, he would not have acted in accord with the covenant and would not have been just). Still unclear, however, is whether Jesus' death was effective because it was a sacrifice, or whether Israel's sacrificial system gained its efficacy and point retrospectively from Jesus' death (see on 3:25—διὰ τὴν πάρεσιν . . .). Nor is it indicated in this text that Jesus' fulfillment of the OT cultic law constituted also its annulment (as in Luz, *Gesetz*, 106), even though the point may be strongly argued from other passages.

καὶ δικαιοῦντα τὸν ἐκ πίστεως Ἰησοῦ, "and the one who justifies him who believes in Jesus." The δικαιοῦντα is not simply a more active expression of what is already implicit in the δίκαιον. The difference is provided by the predicate: "him who believes in Jesus." Strictly speaking, that possibility was not covered by the earlier covenant (cf. Eichholz, *Theologie*, 197). Paul's point, however, is precisely that in Christ's death the terms of the old covenant were both fulfilled and enlarged (to its originally intended scope, he would add—chap. 4). So the unifying and continuity factors are Jesus' death as sacrifice and faith in this Jesus: not just Jesus' death, but his death as a sacrifice in accordance with covenant provision; and not just faith, but faith in Jesus as the one in whom the conditions previously pertaining have been fully met. As more explicitly in Gal 3, Jesus' death and continuing risen reality are what both fulfill the covenant promise and open it to the Gentiles without losing its character as the covenant promise. Thus the "just *and* justifier" is not so much Paul's way of saying God both punishes sin and accepts the sinner despite his sin ("just and *yet* justifier," "just and *therefore* justifier"—though see Denney, Fitzmyer), but rather of insisting that God has acted in accordance with his covenant obligations (passing over former sins) while in one and the same act he has extended his acceptance more widely (in the now time to faith in Jesus). The argument of Käsemann ("Verständnis," 100), Müller (*Gerechtigkeit*, 110–13), and Stuhlmacher (*Gerechtigkeit*, 90), that v 26 replaces or corrects(!) the pre-Pauline concept of God's righteousness as covenant faithfulness (v 25) with the concept of righteousness as the faithfulness of the Creator to his creation (followed by Schrage, 86–87; cf. Lührmann, "Recht- fertigung"), sets too little store by the central fact that the righteousness is still thought of as demonstrated in Christ's death as sacrifice (as provided under the covenant). Zeller, *Juden*, 185–86, likewise misses the element of continuity central to Paul's argument here. But see Piper, "Demonstration," though he underplays too much the relational character of God's righteousness.

For the present tense, δικαιοῦντα, see on 3:24; for πίστις Ἰησοῦ, "faith in Jesus," see on 3:22 (against Williams, *Saving Event*, 54, and others cited at 3:22). The use of the personal name "Jesus" by itself is not usual in Paul, but neither is it exceptional; it occurs mostly in passages referring to Christ's death and resurrection (8:11; 2 Cor 4:10–11, 14; Gal 6:17; 1 Thess 1:10; 4:14; note also 1 Cor 12:3; Phil 2:10). ὁ ἐκ πίστεως is the one whose life has been determined by an act of faith (commitment) to Jesus (as Lord) and continues to be characterized by the attitude of trust in Jesus; for the phrase cf. particularly 4:16 and Gal 3:7, 9; and contrast οἱ ἐκ περιτομῆς (4:12) and οἱ ἐκ νόμου (4:14, 16).

Explanation

In exegetical analysis we mark off here the beginning of a new section of the overall argument, and it is clear enough that Paul at this point switches from indictment of all, Jew and Greek, to outline in fuller terms what his gospel actually says to this otherwise depressing analysis. But the transition does not involve a complete discontinuity in the thought, and it will be necessary to bear in mind the preceding context if we are fully to understand Paul's exposition of his gospel. The point, which bears some reiteration, is that *his gospel is good news precisely to the situation elaborated in 1:18–3:20*, the good news of God's action on behalf of man, to and in the believer, to establish him in the relation with God broken by man's (Adam's) unrighteousness and distorted by Israel's misunderstanding of the law.

3:21 The opening word, "Now," and the perfect tense of the verb ("has been manifested") indicate that Paul has shifted his gaze to a new state of affairs which puts a completely different complexion on the depressing conclusion of vv 19–20. The "now" does not have eschatological overtones in and of itself, but those who knew Paul's thinking would be aware that for him the "now" was the "now" of eschatological salvation, the time when God is putting into action his final purpose for Israel and humankind (cf. 2 Cor 6:2). The perfect tense of the verb has a different significance from the present tense in 1:17 ("is being revealed"), indicating that the new state of affairs was introduced by a decisive act in the past whose effect still remains in force. God made his righteousness visible in this act, and he brought his outreach for man's salvation to clear expression at that time, in such a way that it remains clearly manifest and determinative for the "now." What that action was which has made such a difference would be obvious enough to the already informed and committed members of the house churches in Rome: the act of Jesus Christ, as Paul goes on to explain anyway. More precisely the decisive act which has made all the difference is the righteousness of God revealed in terms of Jesus Christ, God's saving outreach achieved through Jesus Christ and to faith in Christ Jesus.

Such an assertion in such terms would not be too surprising or difficult for Jews to accept—God's eschatological act of salvation related to the coming of a messiah (cf., e.g., Isa 11:5; 42:6; 61:3). But Paul takes pains to mark off the distinctiveness of his own understanding of the righteousness of God by giving prominence to the phrase "without or apart from the law": "but now the righteousness of God has been manifested quite apart from the law." Once again we must beware of taking the phrase as the statement of an absolute, for Paul can hardly intend, for example, that his readers should understand it in complete antithesis to 2:13 ("the doers of the law shall be justified"). Rather he must have intended us to understand the "apart from the law" in relation to and in antithesis to the misunderstanding of the law just dismissed. That is to say, "apart from the law" means apart from the law understood as a badge of Jewishness, understood as the chief identifying characteristic of covenant membership by those "within the law." It is precisely this link between law and God's righteousness which Paul the Jew called to be an apostle to the Gentiles seeks to sever; it is precisely this presumption, that works of the law ensure the Jew's final vindication by God because they maintain his status and identity as a member of God's people, that Paul seeks to destroy by his abrupt "apart from the law." The new situation now made clear since the act of Jesus Christ and by the act of Jesus Christ is that God's saving outreach is not determined by an individual's being a Jew; it is not dependent upon his being within the religious space bounded by the law.

At the same time Paul immediately adds that this righteousness is "borne witness to by the law and the prophets." Even in the very process of breaking the link between God's righteousness and the law, at least as understood by most of his fellow Jews at the time of writing, Paul hastens to stress the *continuity* between his gospel of the righteousness of God and the same law. To heighten the antithesis implicit in this twin assertion of discontinuity and continuity Paul phrases the point differently from the same point made at the very beginning of his letter: "the gospel of God promised beforehand through his prophets" (1:2). Here he adds explicitly that this testimony is given by the *law* and the prophets, implying once again that the gospel is the continuation or completion or fulfillment of the law properly understood within the scriptures as a whole. Moreover, he no doubt deliberately puts the verb in the present rather than past tense: this was not a testimony given once for all in the past, but is still being given; the law gives not only knowledge of sin (3:19–20) but also continuing testimony to the gospel (as chap. 4 will demonstrate). Any interpretation of "apart from the law" which does not give adequate weight to "the law also bearing witness" will inevitably result in a misconception of "the righteousness of God."

22 With v 22 "the righteousness of God" (repeated for emphasis) is further defined in terms which for the first time take up the other half of the thematic statement in 1:17 ("to faith"): "the righteousness of God through faith . . . to faith." The attentive reader who had seen how the first stage of the argument (1:18–3:20) had raised the question of God's faithfulness ("from faith"—1:17; 3:3–4) would also recognize that Paul was now beginning to expound and explain the role of *man's* faith, man's proper response to the faithfulness of God.

This faith is more precisely defined as "faith in Jesus Christ." The phrase could be taken to mean "the faith exercised by Jesus Christ" (cf. 3:26), but though we should not finally exclude the possibility of a deliberate secondary ambiguity in the phrase (cf. 3:24), it is much more likely that the primary meaning intended by Paul is "faith directed toward Christ as the object" (as 3:25 probably confirms). The word "faith" has already been used several times in chap. 1 (1:5, 8, 12, 17), and Paul evidently assumed that its significance was clear enough to his readers at this point (though he does expound it more fully in chap. 4). We may presume they would think in terms of trust in, commitment and obedience to, this Jesus (cf. again Gal 2:16). Expressed as an antithesis to "works of the law" (3:20), it is clearly intended to denote *the basis of a relationship which is not dependent on specific ritual acts, but is direct and immediate, a relying on the risen Christ rather than a resting on the law.* The fact that Paul can describe those who participate in this relationship with Christ simply as "those who believe, the believers," confirms that it was faith more than anything else which distinguished such groups of earliest Christians—faith rather than, here especially, any particular relationship with the law. As with 1:16 the present tense of the verb ("to all who believe") may well imply that Paul was thinking of this attitude of reliance on Christ not simply as the beginning of the relationship with God (experience of God's righteousness) but also as the continuing (indeed lifelong) basis of that relationship (a point he had had to make with some force in Gal 3:2–3).

23 The emphasis on *all* ("all who believe") leads to the brief parenthesis of vv 22c–23: "for there is no distinction; for all have sinned and lack the glory of God." If it were not clear enough already, this parenthesis would confirm that in Paul's mind we have by no means left the argument with Jewish self-understanding behind. The basis of God's saving outreach to man, on man's side that is, has to be the same for all ("all who believe"), not one for the Jew (God's covenant choice) and another for the Gentile. Why so? Because there is no distinction between Jew and Gentile, such as Jewish attitude to the law implies; they are all in the same boat, Jew as well as Gentile: *all* have sinned (cf. 2:12) and are missing out on the glory intended for them— the tenses denoting a continuing consequence of past sins.

Almost certainly Paul is thinking once again of Adam in Gen 1–3, or of humankind in Adamic terms—Adam who sinned and who in consequence both forfeited the glory he originally had (the immediate presence of God and a share in the Creator's dominion over the rest of creation) and also failed to reach the eschatological glory intended for him (an ever fuller share in the immortal life of God—Gen 3:22–24). Both ideas (forfeiting what one had, and failing to reach or falling short of an intended goal) are probably contained within the one verb (here translated "lack"), and were probably already current in Jewish theology of that period. So Paul could have some confidence that his readership would recognize the allusion. In effect v 23 gives a concise summary of Paul's analysis of humankind's plight "under sin": man's attempt to escape his creatureliness has resulted in his forfeiting that which most distinguished him from the other creatures and has resulted in his falling short of his intended role as a companion of God. It is the catastrophe and continuing hopelessness of man's self-achievements which have made it indispensable that God himself should take the initiative and that his offer of restoration should come to effect only to faith and through faith.

24 V 24 resumes the exposition of "the righteousness of God" (v 22). The awkwardness of the syntax is not so untypically Pauline as to occasion much surprise, though it could signal the beginning of a quotation of an earlier Christian formulation. Either way it is clear enough that it is the "all" who are here being described—the "all" who believe, who have also sinned and lack God's glory. The "who are (being) justified" would hardly be understood by Paul's readership in a sense different from its earlier usage in 2:13; 3:4; and 3:20; that is, as a reference to God's final verdict in the day of judgment. The present tense, however, does mark some difference from these earlier references. It could conceivably be taken to denote God's vindication as an ongoing process, in which God brings man into and sustains man in a positive relationship with himself and which will be manifested in its completion at that day (cf. Phil 1:6). And if v 24 is an earlier formulation, the considerations against that possibility are weakened. But as it now stands within the context of the letter, the present tense is better understood as denoting a general rule: this is how God justifies (as in 3:26). In addition Paul may well intend the implication that the final verdict is already being delivered (cf. 5:1, 9), or perhaps more precisely, that the ground of the final acquittal is already established—"by grace . . . through faith."

That a final verdict is in view, rather than an ongoing process, is also made more likely by the addition of the double qualifier: "as a gift, by his grace" (though Paul may well have added both to an earlier formulation). Clearly as the text stands, the juxtaposition of the two phrases with the verb ("being justified") is intended to indicate a different ground of acquittal from that mentioned either in 2:13 or in 3:20, and the double emphasis of the two phrases powerfully reinforces this sense of difference attaching to the gospel in the "now." *The gospel is that God sets to rights man's relationship with himself by an act of sheer generosity which depends on no payment man can make,* which is without reference to whether any individual in particular is inside the law/covenant or outside, and which applies to all human beings without exception. It is this humbling recognition—that he has no grounds for appeal either in covenant status or in particular "works of the law," that he has to depend *entirely* from start to finish on God's gracious power, that he can receive acquittal only as a gift—which lies at the heart of faith for Paul. His readers might well understand that the exercise of such faith can properly be defined as "obedience" (1:5), or indeed as "a doing of the law" (2:13), but that is not the point he wants to make here. For at this stage *everything*, the whole argument, the gospel itself, depends on the most fundamental insight of all: that man's dependency on God for *all* good (cf. 2:7, 10) is total, and that the indispensable starting point for any good that man does is his acceptance of God's embrace and his continual reliance on God's enabling to accomplish that good.

God's free gift of justification/acquittal is further defined as taking place by means of or on the basis of "the redemption which is in Christ Jesus." The word "redemption" would probably conjure up for those listening to Paul's letter the image of prisoners of war being ransomed (or of slaves being

set free). Those familiar with the LXX would almost certainly think of Israel's
redemption from Egyptian slavery and Babylonian exile spoken of by Deuteronomy and Isaiah. "Which is in Christ Jesus" may well be deliberately phrased
to suggest a complex thought (somewhat in the same way as the present
tense of v 22). On the one hand it certainly denotes a historical action of
Christ, the act of ransoming, the provision of a ransom payment, though as
a metaphor (rather than an allegory) the question of whether the payment
was made to anyone in particular need not have arisen (the most obvious
answer would have been the personified power "sin"—3:9). This would probably be the intended meaning at the pre-Pauline level (if Paul is quoting here),
though Paul would certainly link it with v 21: it was this action of Christ
which began the "now" by manifesting (as never before) the righteousness
of God apart from the law. But on the other hand, in Paul's mind there
may well have been also the implication that this redemption is an offer still
available "in Christ Jesus." If so, the two aspects would be held together in
Paul's mind by his "Christ-mysticism," his conviction that the believer is united
with Christ not only in the here and now, but also with Christ in his dying
and rising again.

Taking v 24 as a whole, it thus becomes clear that God's act of acquittal
is not an act of arbitrary caprice. There was a cost to pay, a ransom to be
secured. The acquittal depends on this ransom having been given: God's
sentence is based on it, comes to effect through it, and can be pronounced
already in the "now" in favor of all who believe by virtue of it. But at the
same time the point most emphasized by Paul remains unobscured: that the
payment was *not* made by man, and, by implication, no payment is yet outstanding to be required from man. The price was paid by God's free generosity;
the ransom was provided by God alone. It is this point which Paul (and the
earlier quotation?) takes further in v 25.

25 If the primary reference of "the act of ransom" was not already clear,
Paul puts it beyond doubt by following through the definition of it as "a
means of expiation." Anyone familiar with the LXX could hardly be unaware
that the word was always used in the LXX to refer to the golden cover of
the ark of the covenant (Exod 25:17–22). And the addition of "in his blood"
must surely indicate that Paul (and the earlier formula) had in mind the
one occasion in the Jewish year when blood was sprinkled on the cover of
the ark—namely, the blood of the two sin offerings on the Day of Atonement
(Lev 16:12–19). The clear implication then is that Paul was thinking of Christ's
death, and thinking of it as a sin offering, probably specifically in terms of
the sin offerings of the Day of Atonement ritual. An allusion to martyr theology
is possible, but it is more likely that *4 Macc* 17.21–22 (the atoning significance
of the Maccabean martyrs' deaths) and Rom 3:25 are parallel extensions of
the same cultic language and show how sacrifical imagery used to describe
the death of a human being (rather than an animal) would have been readily
understood in the diaspora Judaism of Paul's time.

Not least in importance is the assertion that it is God who presented (publicly)
Christ as the "means of expiation," a thought not present in Jewish martyr
theology, but a natural inference to be drawn from the fact that it was God
himself who through Moses had made provision for dealing with sin in the

sacrificial cult. Here again we should not ignore Paul's emphasis on the continuity between the religion given to Israel and the manifestation of God's righteousness in Christ, although there may also be a contrast between the public character of Christ's death and the hiddenness of the blood sprinkling in the inner sanctum of the tent and Temple on the Day of Atonement. At all events it is the God who provided the sacrificial cult for Israel who also put forward Christ as *the* decisive sin offering for *all* who believe.

"Through faith" may well be another addition by Paul, since it seems to disrupt what would be a more coherent phrase, "means of expiation in his blood." In this case Paul may have inserted the words in order to provide a balance to the (Jewish) emphasis on God's provision of the sacrificial cult. Jewish overconfidence, he may imply, takes the cult too much for granted. Certainly it was provided by God; however, the proper response is not presumption but humble trust, something which in reference to Christ's sacrifice everyone can exercise, Gentile as well as Jew.

Unfortunately, the rationale of sacrifice in Judaism and in the earlier religion of Israel is not at all clear, and indeed continues to be much disputed in modern scholarship. However, we do have some substantial grounds for claiming that we can in fact reconstruct Paul's own understanding of how sacrifice "works" at the point which concerns us, viz., in his use of the sin offering to speak of Christ's death. In brief, Paul's view seems to be that Christ's death was effective in dealing with human sins because he represented the sinners and by his death destroyed their sins (cf. 8:3; 2 Cor 5:21), that is, brought to an end man as sinner, man under the power of sin (cf. 2 Cor 5:14). Consequently, for those in Christ Jesus no further action need be taken by God against their sin (the wrath of God), for being "in Christ" they share in his death and thus can also have firm hope of sharing fully in his resurrection (cf. 6:3–11). While all this may well have been in Paul's mind, it is of course much less certain that his readers would have been aware of such a fully thought-out theology of sacrifice. On the other hand, the brief allusion both here and in 8:3 may well imply that there was a quite coherent rationale of sacrifice current in Judaism whose very familiarity to synagogue congregations would have rendered fuller exposition superfluous.

Paul does, however, go on to clarify the theology to some degree by saying something about how Christ's sacrificial death relates both to past and present—the reference to the past most likely being part of the original quotation, the reference to the present being Paul's addition. The purpose of Christ's expiatory sacrifice, in the first place, was to demonstrate or provide proof of God's saving action on account of the fact that in his forbearance he had let former sins go unpunished. This must mean God's purpose was to demonstrate that his saving action on Israel's behalf was in accord with the covenant obligations he had taken upon himself and laid upon Israel. His failure to punish Israel's sins, that is, by completely rejecting Israel as his people, did not mean that he was unfairly generous (one of the questions raised by the aborted discussion in 3:1–8). Former sins were passed over, either because Jesus' death demonstrates the sacrificial system to be effective (at least so far as inadvertent sins were concerned), or because Jesus' death as the death of sinful man is effective for the persons of faith who came before him as well as for those who come after. The suggestion that such a view is at odds with the exposition of God's wrath in 1:18–3:20 neglects the fact that chap. 2 more or less throughout envisages that there could be those who will be acquitted at the final judgment (workers of the good, doers of the law, etc.)— those whose sins, Paul would presumably say, were left unpunished in the past by virtue of Christ's death.

26 In the second place, the purpose of Christ's expiatory death was to demonstrate God's righteousness in the "now" time, that he might be just and the justifier of the one who believes in Jesus. Jesus' death has the same effect for present sins—that is, if we have understood Paul's theology of sacrifice correctly, the identification between Christ and the believer means that Christ's death deals with the believer's sins and destroys the power of sin for the one "in Christ." In the same way it also demonstrates both God's justice and his effectively saving purpose, for in accordance with the sacrificial ritual and in effective reality, it actually deals with the power of sin, destroying the malignant cancer in death and restoring to communion with God the one who identifies himself with the dead and risen Christ in trustful commitment.

Both elements in God's purpose defined here give a very important insight into what Paul means by "God's righteousness" (the repetition of "to demonstrate his righteousness" will not have been accidental)—namely, that "God's righteousness" means not just his saving acts, but his saving action in terms of the covenant he entered into with Israel. God's righteousness is indeed God's fulfilling of his covenant obligation to be Israel's God, to save and sustain Israel, as the devout Jew would well understand. The sacrificial system demonstrates this: that God provided a way for dealing with failure, for Israel's breach of the covenant. And now Christ's death demonstrates God's righteousness in the same way, for both past and present; that is to say, Christ's death demonstrates God's righteousness *precisely by being a sacrifice*, by doing with effective finality what the sacrificial system had done only in part (that is only for some sins, or only for Israel's sins). Once again, then, the very important emphasis comes through that God's saving action for and to faith is *not* a departure from the covenant with Israel, but is continuous with it and in accordance with it; God's righteousness is not an arbitrary choosing of Israel and then dropping of Israel, but his choice of Israel is always with the *all* in view, the extension of his saving purpose to all in accordance with his covenant obligation to Israel.

The force of Paul's own particular emphases may become clearer if indeed Paul is drawing on an older formulation in vv (24) 25–26a. For if we exclude the material most likely added by Paul—the references (to free grace in v 24) to faith in v 25 and the bulk of v 26—we find a formulation which focuses primarily on the meaning of Jesus' death for Israel's self-understanding. This suggests that it originated (in Greek, in the diaspora) as a Jewish Christian statement which understood God's obligation to save Israel as being met by his provision of the Messiah Jesus as a ransom and expiatory sacrifice in accordance with the terms God himself laid down in the Torah. For this Jewish-Christian credo Jesus' death and resurrection provides a ransom analogous to and even more epochal than the deliverance from Egypt and the return from Babylon. For this Jewish-Christian credo the sacrificial system makes sense of Jesus' death, and Jesus' death makes sense of the sacrificial system in the past. Paul in adopting this formulation affirms its emphasis on continuity with God's faithfulness to Israel and Israel's sacrificial system and affirms on his own account its emphasis on God's acting in accordance with his covenanted obligation to Israel. But he also emphasizes that God's provision of Christ as a ransom is nevertheless an act of his wholly free generosity (not restricted to the covenant with Israel as such), and he adds that his expiation of sin is dependent solely on faith on man's side (not on any continuation of the sacrificial cult) and that this demonstrated righteousness is effective not only for Israel's sins in history but for the present sins too of the one who has faith, whoever that one may be (the whole sentence on Paul's construction being an elaboration of "all who believe").

This section (vv 21–26) is clearly of crucial significance in the development of Paul's argument and exposition of his gospel, as is confirmed by the repeated emphasis on the key words of his earlier thematic statement (1:17): in the six verses, "righteousness" and its cognates occur no less than seven times, while "faith" (noun and verb) appears four times. So it is well worth pausing to summarize the central points made. (1) The answer to the plight of all humankind "under sin" has been given by God in his provision of Christ as a ransom and expiatory sacrifice. (2) This saving act of God is in complete continuity with and fulfillment of his covenanted promises to Israel. (3) Participation in or benefit from this righteousness of God comes through faith— trust that Christ's ransom and expiatory sacrifice has been effective, and trust in Jesus himself; and since all alike have the same need of God's righteousness, so it comes to all alike in the same way—through faith. We should note that of these three propositions it is only the third which Paul regards as contentious. The first two are simply asserted and not argued; he makes no attempt to prove that Jesus' death must be understood as a ransom and sacrifice. The first two are evidently not controversial; he can safely assume that his readership will accept, even take for granted, this characterization of Jesus' death in explicitly Jewish sacrificial terms (a fact which strengthens the case for seeing a pre-Pauline formula here). The focus of his argument therefore is on the third proposition, "to all who believe"; the contention which has to be argued is that this understanding of the righteousness of God is in full continuity with and fulfillment of "the law and the prophets."

2. The Consequences for the Self-Understanding of the Jewish People (3:27–31)

Bibliography

Barrett, C. K. "Boasting (καυχᾶσθαι, κτλ.) in the Pauline Epistles." In *L'Apôtre Paul: Personalité, style et conception du ministère,* ed. A. Vanhoye. BETL 73. Leuven: University Press, 1986. 363–68. **Dahl, N. A.** "The One God of Jews and Gentiles." *Studies.* 178–91. **Dülmen, A. van.** *Theologie.* 86–88. **Friedrich, G.** "Das Gesetz des Glaubens: Röm

3:27." *TZ* 10 (1954) 401–417. **Gager, J. G.** *Origins.* 214–17, 248–49. **Giblin, C. H.**
"Three Monotheistic Texts in Paul." *CBQ* 37 (1975) 543–45. **Grässer, E.** " 'Ein einziger
ist Gott' (Röm 3:30)." *Der Alte Bund im Neuen.* Tübingen: Mohr, 1985. 231–58. **Howard,
G.** "Rom 3:21–31 and the Inclusion of the Gentiles." *HTR* 63 (1970) 223–33. **Hübner,
H.** *Law.* 113–18, 137–44. **Lambrecht, J.** "Why Is Boasting Excluded? A Note on Rom
3:27 and 4:2." *ETL* 61 (1985) 365–69. **Räisänen, H.** "Das 'Gesetz' des Glaubens und
des Geistes." *NTS* 26 (1979–80) 101–117. Repr. in *Torah,* 95–118. ———. *Law.* 50–
52, 69–72, 170–71. **Rhyne, C. T.** *Faith.* 25–74. **Sanders, E. P.** *Law.* 29–36. **Schnabel,
E. J.** *Law.* 285–88. **Snodgrass, K.** "Spheres of Influence." 100–103. **Stowers, S. K.**
Diatribe. 155–67. **Thompson, R. W.** "Paul's Double Critique of Jewish Boasting: A
Study of Rom 3:27 in Its Context." *Bib* 67 (1986) 520–31. **Watson, F.** *Paul.* 131–35.

Translation

[27] *Where then is* [a] *boasting? It has been excluded. By what kind of law? Of
works? No, on the contrary, by the law of faith.* [28] *For* [b] *we reckon that a man is
justified by faith,* [c] *apart from works of the law.* [29] *Or is he God of Jews only?* [d] *Is
he not also God of Gentiles? Yes, of Gentiles too,* [30] *since, after all,* [e] *"God is one,"
who will justify circumcision from faith and uncircumcision through faith.* [31] *Do
we then make the law invalid through faith? Not at all. On the contrary, we
establish the law.*

Notes

[a] Some MSS, principally of the Western tradition, add σοῦ ("your boasting") to make the
resumption of the dialogue style more explicit.

[b] A strong tradition reads οὖν instead of γάρ. But the context clearly favors γάρ. The οὖν was
probably introduced by scribes who took λογιζόμεθα as a conclusion: "we infer, conclude."

[c] Another improving modification by the same group as in *Note* a, who replaced the unusual
πίστει with διὰ πίστεως to accord better with vv 30–31.

[d] Further attempted improvements, altering the adverbial μόνον into an adjective agreeing
with either θεός (the only God) or Ἰουδαίων (Jews by themselves)—the latter including B and
Clement.

[e] Another slight improvement from the same stable as *Notes* a and c—reading ἐπείπερ ("since
indeed") for the much better attested εἴπερ.

Form and Structure

The resumption of diatribe style (Stowers, *Diatribe,* 155–67), though now
in less confrontational "we" terms, again indicates the objective of puncturing
Jewish presumption. The conclusion of 3:20, that God's justifying does not
operate by reference to those requirements of the law which mark out Jewish
identity, is now supplemented by the central assertion of vv 21–26 that God
justifies through faith (v 28). In terms of the main issue of the letter (Jew
and/or Gentile?), what this means is that the sort of boasting (καυχᾶσθαι)
envisaged in 2:17 and 2:23 is excluded—not by the law understood in terms
of works in which the Jew can take such pride (as documenting his membership
of the people chosen by God), but by the law understood in terms of faith
(v 27). Only so can Israel's basic confession of God as one be meaningfully
maintained (v 29). For law understood as marking off Jew from Gentile makes

God, the law-giver, God only of the people of the law. But law understood in terms of faith means that the law-giver can be God of both circumcised and uncircumcised, since his righteousness is not limited to the circumcised but extends to all who believe (v 30). In this way the law as given by the one God is truly understood, affirmed, and established (v 31).

Following the log-jam of prepositional phrases and somewhat tortuous syntax of the preceding paragraph (vv 21–26), the change of style is abrupt. The staccato interchange of brief question and answer would give relief after the intensity of concentration required to catch the full force of what had obviously been a major statement of the letter's central theme. The change is certainly deliberate and shows Paul's awareness of the need to vary his style in order to retain the attention of those listening to his letter read out.

Comment

3:27 ποῦ οὖν ἡ καύχησις; "where then is boasting?" The allusion to 2:17, 23 is indisputable. What is in view is not the self-confidence of the religious person, as Käsemann in particular argues, universalizing the godly Jew as the classic type of that piety which boasts in its own achievements ("sinful self-reliance"—Bultmann, *Theology*, 1:242; "the religious man"—Bornkamm, *Paul*, 95; "self-glorying"—Hübner, *Law*, 116; Leenhardt, and Ladd, *Theology*, 447, provide other good examples of such classic "Protestant" exegesis). Rather Paul attacks the self-confidence of the Jew as Jew, the boasting in God as Israel's God, the pride in the law as indicating God's commitment to his people and as marking them off from the other nations; so rightly Howard, "Romans 3:21–31," 232; Sanders, *Law*, 33–34; Räisänen, *Law*, 170–71; Watson, *Paul*, 133–35; Moxnes, "Honour," 71. It is important to recognize that it is such boasting (in the law), not the Torah itself, which is under attack (Gager, *Origins*, 215). See further *Introduction*, §5.3 and on 2:17, 23; also on 15:17, where Paul uses καύχησις in positive sense.

ἐξεκλείσθη, 'it has been excluded, made impossible" (BGD). ἐκκλείω is found elsewhere in the NT only in Gal 4:17. The passive implies that it has been excluded by God or at least by divine intention. The aorist refers to what has just been described in v 25: the death of Christ as expiation has altered the terms of God's dealing with sin by breaking the previously exclusive link with Israel, the Day of Atonement ritual being a peculiar and distinctive provision of the Jewish law. In the eschatological present Christ's expiatory death avails for all and demonstrates God's righteousness to all who believe. The exclusive relationship to God in which Paul's kinsfolk boasted therefore no longer pertains, and so no room for boasting is left.

διὰ ποίου νόμου; "by what kind of law?" The argument is regularly made that νόμος here and in the following phrases should not be taken as the Torah, but in the more general sense of "law" (any kind of law, with the subsequent phrase νόμος πίστεως understood as "a law or principle of faith"; cf. 7:21, 23; 8:2; Gal 6:2 (see, e.g., BGD, νόμος 1, 2, 5; *TDNT* 4:1071; RSV, NEB, NIV, NJB; Bultmann, *Theology* 1:259; Barrett; Murray; Sanders, *Law*, 33; Räisänen, *Law*, 50–52; Watson, *Paul*, 131; "a new 'law' or dispensation"—

Lambrecht, 368). But νόμος τῶν ἔργων can hardly be understood otherwise than as a reference to the Torah (van Dülmen, 87; Schnabel, 286); it is simply the reverse form of τὰ ἔργα νόμου—both denoting the law understood in terms of its characteristic obligations (see below). And equally clearly v 31 is an expansion of νόμος πίστεως; and in v 31 νόμος as Torah is not to be denied (cf. Friedrich, "Gesetz"; Hahn, "Gesetzesverständnis," 38; Cranfield; Wilckens; Rhyne, 69–70; Snodgrass, 100–103; other bibliography in Räisänen, *Law*, 51 n.37). Consequently the question posed here is equivalent to "What kind of understanding of the law is this?" The question catches the taken-for-granted character of Jewish pride in the law (2:23). See also on 7:21, 23, and 8:2.

τῶν ἔργων; "of works?" The key to exegesis here is the axiomatic three-way association in Jewish thought between the national pride of the covenant people, the law as the particular focus and reason for that pride, and works of the law as the expression of Jewish devotion to their God and his law particularly through these obligations which marked them out in their distinctiveness as his people, the people of the law (cf. Wright, *Messiah*, 97: "Paul's critique of 'works' . . . functions *within* his critique of 'national righteousness'"; also 118). The question arises because the typical Jew of Paul's time could not think of the law other than in its distinctiveness as the Jewish law; "the law of works" is the law shown to be the *Jewish* law by what it required (*not* "the law of God insofar as it has been degraded and depraved [!] into a means of having to assert oneself before God," as Hübner, *Law*, 138, continues to assert). Once again it is not a question of "*good* works" (boasting excluded because of an insufficiency of good works; a continued misunderstanding which leads Thompson off on a false trail), but of works as denoting covenant obligation and distinctiveness ("covenantal nomism"); the law thus kept (cf. Phil 3:6) did *not* exclude boasting (2:17, 23). See further *Introduction* §5.3 and on 3:20.

οὐχί, ἀλλὰ διὰ νόμου πίστεως, "No! On the contrary, by the law of faith." Granted that νόμος here too refers to the Torah (see above), Paul's meaning should not be short-changed. He does not mean simply the law as bearing witness to faith or even summoning people to faith (Friedrich, "Gesetz"; Cranfield; Stuhlmacher, "Law," 97). Nor does he have in view the law reduced to some core and shorn of its peculiarly Jewish ritual requirements (cf. Räisänen, *Law*, 27–28, 64), nor even the law in Matthew's sense, reinterpreted by reference to Christ's ministry (Matt 5:17–20; cf. Gal 6:2)—though in the event his approach gives scope to both these alternatives because of the liberty it offers in regard to the law. In both phrases, "law of works" and "law of faith," Paul has the law as such, the whole law, in view; otherwise his response here would be deficient from the start, and his concluding assertion (v 31) critically undermined. "The law of faith" then must mean the law understood in terms of faith (not "of God's faithfulness" [Gaston, *Paul*, 172], which destroys the "works"/"faith" antithesis). It is two ways of looking at the law as a whole which he here sets in opposition: when the law is understood in terms of works it is seen as distinctively Jewish and particular features come into prominence (particularly circumcision); but when the law is understood in terms of faith its distinctive Jewish character ceases to hold center stage, and the distinctively Jewish works become subsidiary and secondary matters which cannot be required of all and which can be disregarded by Gentiles in particular without damaging (indeed thereby enhancing—v 31) its faith character. νόμος πίστεως is therefore best taken in a full sense as the law addressed to faith and fulfilled through faith. Räisänen's objection that this gives νόμος "a very active role" (Law, 51; also "Gesetz," 109–111) is not to the point: the διά has the same force as in the nearly synonymous phrase διὰ πίστεως in 3:22, 25, 31. And Sanders, Law, 33, misses the point that "the law of faith" is the opposite of "the law of works," that is, not the opposite of the law as such, but of the law precisely as the law of the Jews (alone). On the other hand, Watson's shrewd observation that Paul replaces "works of the law" by "faith" as the principle of sectarian self-definition (Paul, 134–35) at least runs counter to Paul's intention. The paraphrases of NEB and NJB move too far away from the text.

28 λογιζόμεθα γὰρ δικαιοῦσθαι πίστει ἄνθρωπον χωρὶς ἔργων νόμου, "for we reckon that a person is justified by faith without works of the law." Here again, as in 3:20, the train of thought comes so close to that of Paul's argument in Galatians that the phrasing of the earlier letter is closely reproduced: Gal 2:16—εἰδότες ὅτι οὐ δικαιοῦται ἄνθρωπος ἐξ ἔργων νόμου ἐὰν μὴ διὰ πίστεως . . . . Since it was also Gal 2:16 which was paralleled in 3:20, and since Paul was hardly writing Romans with a copy of Galatians to hand, the obvious conclusion is that the theological assertions formulated in Gal 2:16 were a fundamental part of Paul's understanding of the gospel, and fundamental in these terms. The line of argument here therefore cannot be thought of as freshly minted for the purposes of this letter. It is rather to be seen as a mature formulation of an argument sharpened and polished over the years in not a few discussions and controversies. (On Gal 2:16 see Dunn, "New Perspective"). Barth again takes πίστει as a reference to God's faithfulness.

The λογιζόμεθα, "we reckon," makes the same appeal as the εἰδότες of Gal 2:16, to what is the common opinion among all the Christian communities. λογίζομαι is preferred here presumably because Paul was conscious of the key role it was about to play in the next stage of the argument, human "reckoning" being a reflection of God's (note particularly 4:6). That it is a forceful word, denoting conviction with practical consequences, and not just an abstract decision in the mind, is confirmed by its use in 6:11 and 14:14. For δικαιόω used in the present tense of God's act in justifying, see on 3:24. The πίστει reflects the sharper antithesis between faith and works to which Paul pushed the contrast in the second half of Gal 2:16; Luther's translation, "by faith alone," may be regarded as faithful to the thrust of Paul's argument so long as the scope of Paul's contrast is borne in mind. ἄνθρωπος is "man [in general], one" (cf. 1 Cor 4:1; BGD, ἄνθρωπος 3aγ); see also Howard, "Romans 3:21–31," 232–33. The χωρίς, however, is determined by the more immediate line of the present argument, clearly harking back to 3:21 and the contrast between Jew and Gentile as within and without the law (Käsemann continues to read the text through Lutheran spectacles; Kuss and Schlier bridge the gap between traditional Catholic and Lutheran exegesis but still miss the Pauline emphasis in "works of the law"; so too NEB—"quite apart from success in keeping the law"). The parallel with 3:21 confirms that "law"

and "works of law" are more or less synonymous, when, that is to say, the
law is regarded as something exclusively and distinctively Jewish. The only
difference between οὐκ ἐξ ἔργων νόμου and χωρὶς ἔργων νόμου is that the former
regards works of the law as characteristically and distinctively Jewish practices
("identity marker"), while the latter depicts works of the law as marking the
boundary between Jew and Gentile ("boundary marker"). This more precise
specification of "works of the law" means that there is no real contradiction
with 2:13 (cf. particularly Sanders, Law, 35–36, 129). On the contrary, the
antitheses in 2:12–13 can be seen to parallel the contrast here:

ὅσοι ἐν νόμῳ = οἱ ἀκροαταὶ νόμου = οἱ ἐξ ἔργων νόμου·
ὅσοι ἀνόμως = οἱ ποιηταὶ νόμου = οἱ χωρὶς (ἔργων) νόμου = οἱ ἐκ (νόμου) πίστεως.

29 ἢ Ἰουδαίων ὁ θεὸς μόνον; οὐχὶ καὶ ἐθνῶν; "Or is he God of Jews only? Is
he not also (God) of Gentiles?" The rapid-fire style suggests a line of argument
finely tuned as a result of many exposures in debate. For Ἰουδαῖος see on
1:16. The contrast is not now between Jew and Greek, as hitherto in the
formulaic "Jew first but also Greek" (1:16; 2:9–10), but between Jew and
Gentile, the more typical contrast of Jewish national self-consciousness as
the people of God in distinction from "the nations." The train of thought
again reflects the sequence of antitheses in 2:12–14.

Paul here exploits a tension in Jewish thought between God as Creator
(and so Lord of all) and God as Israel's Lord. Regularly quoted is the saying
attributed to Rabbi Simeon ben Jochai (about a century later than Paul):
"God spoke to the Israelites: I am God over all who come into the world,
but my name have I associated only with you; I do not call myself the God
of the nations of the world, but the God of Israel" (Str-B, 3:185; though
note Dahl, 'One God," 183). But the tension is clearly present in the literature
already current in our period. Compare, e.g., 1 Enoch 84.2—". . . King of
kings and God of the whole world . . . ," and Ps 44:4—"You are my king,
who ordains victories for Jacob." In Jub. 15.31–32 the tension is explicit—
". . . He chose Israel to be his people . . . for there are many nations and
many peoples, and all are his. . . ." Similarly other passages speak of God's
appointing angels to rule other nations, but keeping Israel for himself (Deut
32:8–9; Sir 17:17). And the thought of a particular election by the God of
all is clearly implicit in the assertion of ben Sira and Baruch that cosmic
Wisdom has been given specifically to Israel in the law (Sir 24:23; Bar
4:1–4). See further Sanders, Paul, index "election." To Paul's questions here,
therefore, the devout Jew would answer "yes," however he might want to
qualify it. Important at these points is Dahl's warning against speaking here
too quickly of Jewish "particularism" as a foil to Christian "universalism";
no Jew would deny the universal monotheism which Paul here propounds
("One God"; cf. e.g., Ps 145:8–9; Jonah 4:2; Wisd Sol 11:24–26). The issue
is whether Israel's special relation to God through election and as embodied
in the Torah actually undercuts that universal monotheism in fact, and whether
justification by faith (v 30) is a better effective safeguard of universal monotheism (cf. Grässer, 256–58).

29–30 ναὶ καὶ ἐθνῶν, εἴπερ εἷς ὁ θεός, "of course, of the Gentiles too, since, after all, "God is one.'" ναί, is an affirmative particle not much used by Paul; but note particularly 1 Cor 1:17–20. εἴπερ means 'if indeed, if after all, provided that, since" (BGD, εἰ vi.11); it introduces the necessary and sufficient condition for the affirmation just made (cf. 8:9, 17). εἷς ὁ θεός is certainly intended as an evocation of the basic creed of Jewish monotheism: κύριος ὁ θεὸς ἡμῶν κύριος εἷς ἐστιν (Deut 6:4); Paul takes it up again in 1 Cor 8:6 (see Dunn, *Christology*, 179–80); cf. Mark 12:29 = Deut 6:4; James 2:19—εἷς ἐστιν ὁ θεός (on the parallel with James see 4:1–25 *Form and Structure*). The appeal in fact is to God as Creator, from one arm of the twofold dogma (God as Israel's Lord) to the other (God as Lord of all). Here in effect Paul does go behind Israel's salvation-history claim to have been specially chosen by God. God's Lordship as Creator is even more fundamental, and belongs to salvation history no less than his election of Israel.

ὃς δικαιώσει περιτομὴν ἐκ πίστεως καὶ ἀκροβυστίαν διὰ τῆς πίστεως, "who will justify circumcised from faith and uncircumcised through faith." The logic of Paul's train of thought (as indicated by use of the relative, ὅς) is that God looks for one basic attitude and relationship with all humankind—viz., faith. In the light of 1:18 ff. faith must be another word for that responsive dependence on God as Creator which man has failed to give; and this indeed is how Paul goes on to define it in 4:18–21. In the light of the preceding section (3:21–26) the death of Christ must (in Paul's view) mark the turn of the ages, when the epoch of Israel's special relationship as understood by most Jews has been superseded by the final age, the age in which the "terms of association" between God and man can be more clearly seen to be the same as those required of man the creature from the beginning, trust-dependence on the Creator God. Now it can also be described as faith in Jesus, because his death both confirms that God is Redeemer as well as Creator and opens the scope of that redemption beyond Israel "according to the flesh." But here it is described simply as "faith" since it is the basic trust-reliance of creature on the only Creator which is in view. The future tense (δικαιώσει) is not simply a logical future (so, e.g., Kuss, Cranfield), but, as so often with this verb, and as appropriate when the one God, Creator and Judge, beginning and end, is in view, it looks forward also to the final judgment (see on 2:13). The characterization of humankind under the two catchwords "circumcision" and "uncircumcision" harks back to 2:25–27 by evoking the Jewish perspective and distinction, but only in order to show that it is no longer valid, no longer in accord with the perspective and purpose of the one God. The distinction between ἐκ and διά ("from faith," "through faith") is probably merely stylistic (Denney, Lagrange, Lietzmann, Cranfield, Schlier): Paul would not want to imply a continuing distinction, since it is precisely the common ground and medium of faith which has rendered insignificant the distinction circumcision/uncircumcision so far as relationship with the God who is one is concerned; "it is the faith which counts, not the preposition" (Maillot). On the other hand Paul may use ἐκ πίστεως in reference to the circumcised precisely in order to recall the quotation from Hab 2:4 in 1:17 and its probable ambiguity: the Creator God's saving action through faith is an expression of his covenant faithfulness in the case of the Jew. Gager, *Origins*, 217, follows Gaston's thesis that the first πίστις denotes Israel's faithfulness ("for Jews . . . faith means doing the Torah rather than merely having it"). But it is just such an under-standing of πίστις, as Abraham's faithfulness, which Paul goes on to dispute in chap. 4 (see on 4:2; πίστις = "trust," 4:17–21). In his own translation (*Paul*, 173) Gaston refers πίστις both times to God's faithfulness. But this position also cannot be sustained, as is evident in his translation of chap. 4, where the clear thread of the argument is lost by rendering πίστις sometimes as (Abraham's) trust (vv 5, 9, 11, 12, 19, 20), sometimes as (God's) faithfulness (vv 13, 14, 16), and once as (Abraham's) faithfulness (v 16).

31 ὄνομον οὖν καταργοῦμεν διὰ τῆς πίστεως, 'do we then nullify the law through faith?" V 31 is best taken as the conclusion to the brief section of dialogue (vv 27–31), rather than as the introduction to chap. 4 (as has been argued in the past, though less frequently now—e.g., Barth, Lagrange, Knox, Achtemeier). But as elsewhere in the letter, Paul winds up one phase of his argument in a way which provides a lead into the next section (see on 5:12–21 *Form and Structure;* and cf. particularly Rhyne, 59–61)—good evidence that the epistle's line of argument was carefully planned in Paul's mind before he started dictating. The question asked here is also of a piece with the questions posed at the beginning of chap. 3 and could have been posed there (except that the emphasis on faith has strengthened in the interim), indicating the transitional character of both the beginning and the end of the chapter.

καταργέω can have the sense "abolish, do away with" as well as "nullify, render ineffective" (see on 6:6). Its precise sense here is in large part deter-mined by the fact that it stands in antithesis to ἱστάνω, "establish, confirm, make valid" (a form of ἵστημι—BGD). This certainly reflects and may indeed be a rendering of the contrast we know to have been used by the rabbis between בטל ("neglect, render futile, break") and קום ("uphold, fulfill, con-firm"), as in *m.* '*Abot* 4.9; (cf. also *4 Macc* 5.25 and 33). That it could be rendered more strongly as "destroy/fulfill" is suggested by Matt 5:17 (Str-B, 1:241; Michel; cf. Daube, *Rabbinic Judaism*, 60–61). Paul's rejoinder here was probably taking up actual objections which had been put to him by fellow Jews and Jewish Christians.

"The Jew" (3:1) would regard Paul's exposition as destructive of the law precisely because the law for him was so much bound up with his identity as a Jew, as marking out the distinctiveness of his people. The attitude is evident in *4 Macc* 5:25: "since we believe that the law was *established* by God, we know that in the nature of things the Creator of the *world* in giving *us* the law has shown sympathy toward us" (my emphasis). Paul's argument, by undermining that special link between Israel and the law, seems to render it invalid and futile. If this character of the law as a crucial identity factor in Judaism's self-understanding is not clearly grasped (see further *Introduction* §5.3), the point of v 31 is lost—as Käsemann's treatment demonstrates, as well as the other views noted by him (Wilckens again comes closest). Dodd again believes he is more faithful to the logic of Paul's thought than Paul himself: "He hesitates to draw the conclusion. It would have made things clearer if he had boldly done so!"

μὴ γένοιτο, "Not at all, God forbid" (see on 3:4).

ἀλλὰ νόμον ἱστάνομεν, "but we establish the law," "we are placing the law on its true footing" (NJB), that is, through faith. On ἱστάνω see above. Paul's object is not to make the law as though it had never been, but by universalizing it to confirm it in its proper function. When seen as directed to faith rather than to works, to bring all humankind under the Creator's rule rather than to divide off Israel from the nations, the law's role in the eschatological age (the "now" time) is established (cf. Schlier); see further on 10:3. Paul's point in fact is the same as in 2:12–16: only when the *universal* function of the law is recognized can it fulfill its proper role, as the word of the Creator to his creatures by which he calls them to their proper creaturely response and by which he will in the end judge them all—Jew and Gentile. The law "understood thus (κατὰ τὸ εὐαγγέλιον—2:16) is "the law of faith" (see on 3:27). Since νόμος can be thus understood consistently through the paragraph, it is unnecessary to seek here a different sense, νόμος, *not* Sinai-Torah, but the Old Testament (as most recently in Luz, *Gesetz,* 105, and Hofius, "Gesetz," 278).

In view of continuing blanket assertions that Paul "broke" with the law, or abandoned the law, or regarded it as superseded and abolished (as in Sanders, *Law,* 3; Räisänen, *Law,* 50, 69, 71), it cannot be stressed too much that Paul had no intention of destroying the law. He sought only to undermine the law in its function as marking out Jewish privilege and prerogative (so characterized by "works of the law, nomistic service")—what was in fact its most fundamental and distinctive function in Jewish eyes. Once that point is grasped the continuing positive value he attributes to the law can be appreciated, and 3:31 (as well particularly as 6:16; 8:4; and 13:8–10) ceases to be a contradiction (cf. particularly Hahn, "Gesetzesverständnis," 40–41; Cranfield). We should do Paul the courtesy of taking his various assertions about the law seriously and of assuming that they made sufficiently coherent sense within his own theology. The conclusion that Paul's various statements on the law cannot be saved from outright contradiction should be a last resort and is more likely to indicate that the exegete has failed to enter sufficiently into the concerns and contexts of Paul's writing on the subject. See again *Introduction* §5.3 and on 8:2.

Explanation

3:27 Once the centrality of "faith" in the preceding section is grasped, the movement of thought to v 27 becomes clear, for in the resumed diatribe of vv 27–31 it is precisely this point which is hammered home: faith as the proper understanding of the law, faith as the indispensable basis of "doing the law." V 27, "Where then is boasting?," clearly harks back to the characterization of Jewish pride in their election and in their law in 2:17, 23. The very fact that Paul follows on v 26 with just this question is clear confirmation that all the while Paul has in view Jewish overconfidence in their privileged status. It is precisely the assertion that God's saving act is for all who believe, without distinction (v 22), which puts a question mark against what would otherwise be just cause for confidence and gratitude (not least in the death of Christ illuminated by the law).

"It is excluded, eliminated." Why? The answer is obvious enough, if Paul's argument has been followed: confidence cannot be based simply on the fact that one belongs to the chosen people; true confidence in God consists of each individual's own humble reliance upon God's saving act through Christ and trust in this Jesus, and such faith is no basis for the overconfidence of Jewish boasting. But to make the point firmer Paul continues the dialogue. "By what (kind of) law?" The order of the questions shows clearly that boasting and (the) law go together in Paul's thinking at this point, and again confirm, if confirmation was necessary, that it is the Torah which Paul has in mind, and Jewish national self-confidence based on their being the people of the law.

Hence the next question: "Of works?" The question is put only to be dismissed. But again the fact that it is put indicates clearly that this was the primary alternative to Paul's view, the one he is most anxious to deny. "The law of works" cannot mean other than the law understood in terms of "works of the law" (v 20), the law seen as at basis consisting of particular acts by which the devoted Jew affirms his continued membership in the people of the law. That (kind of) law might have provided a ground of boasting, although the argument of 2:1–3:20 should have punctured that illusion. No, what really destroys Jewish overconfidence is the realization that the law is properly to be understood in terms of faith, faith which all can exercise, including those "outside the law." It is the recognition that the purpose of the law is to produce faith and not works which eliminates such boasting.

Here we might pause long enough to notice that Paul's antithesis is not between faith and the law, but between faith and *works* of the law, and that faith can be described in terms of the law: "the law of faith!" (cf. 1:5). This one phrase confirms beyond dispute that Paul sees his gospel as standing in complete continuity with the revelation of God given to Israel, and in complete continuity with the law. It is his basic contention that most of Israel has misunderstood the law, by taking it as a badge of national and covenant identity. And it is this false understanding of the law (the law of works) which he seeks to eliminate. The law properly understood is fulfilled or "done" by faith. Any antinomian interpretation of Paul's thought is thus to be rejected and his teaching on faith is to be seen as the basis of his parenesis. Similarly any attempt to give "law of faith" a reference to other than the (Jewish) law is self-condemned as a misunderstanding of the basic thrust of Paul's argument.

28 The explanation and justification of the epigrammatic assertion of v 27 is given in v 28: "For we reckon that a person is justified by faith, apart from works of the law." The parallel with Gal 2:16 is again very close, and it is quite clear that here as there Paul is able to appeal to what was a basic and agreed statement of the gospel common to all the earliest Christians, loyal Jews as well as Gentiles. It was an agreed statement which Paul had probably secured on his second visit to Jerusalem (Gal 2:1–10), and it provided the basis for his response to the Antioch incident, as outlined in Gal 2:15–18. There the question at issue seems to have been, Given that a person is justified primarily by faith and not (just) by works of the law (Gal 2:16a), how should the believer live? How should the Jewish believer in particular conduct himself in relation to the food and purity laws? Here the question is different, although the agreed premise is the same: Given that a person is justified by faith apart from works of the law, what is the significance of God's choice of Israel, and of his giving Israel the law in the first place?

Paul's answer in Galatians had pushed to a sharper antithesis between the law and faith than he does here. And one of his reasons for writing the letter to Rome may well have been to provide a more carefully stated exposition of the continuity as well as of the discontinuity in God's purpose for Israel and between the law and the gospel. The most striking difference between v 28 and Gal 2:16 is the reappearance of the word "apart from." The echo of 3:21 will have been intended, and confirms that being within the law, "works of the law," and boasting in the law are all closely integrated phrases for Paul; that they all denote more or less synonymously Jewish assumption of God's favor and overconfidence in election; that in Paul's thinking they are to be distinguished from "doing the law," "fulfilling the law" and being testified to by the law (2:13, 27; 3:21).

29–30 "Or is he the God only of Jews? Is he not also the God of Gentiles?" Again the connection of thought is clear: "works of the law" signify that attitude which affirms that in effect God is only God of the Jews. His favor has been so clearly directed to the people of Israel that Gentiles as such can hardly count before him. To this basic presupposition of Jewish nationhood Paul has a neat rejoinder (v 30): But if God is one (and what Jew would deny that?—Deut 6:4), then he must be the God for all humankind, Jew first no doubt, but also Gentile. The relevance of God's oneness is the fact that he alone is related to all creation as Creator, and that as Creator he demands a common response from all his creatures, Gentile as well as Jew, Jew as well as Gentile—the response of creaturely dependence (= faith). To continue to set store on the law and works as that which marks off Jew from Gentile is to distort and obscure the oneness of that response, and so the oneness of the God who requires it. Jewish pride in election by the one God is therefore actually at odds with their own monotheism. Only if God justifies all humankind by faith can he be seen as the God of Gentile as well as Jew and be confessed as the one God. Paul sounds somewhat pleased with himself here, as though the fact that he could derive his gospel from first principles and could use Israel's own basic credo to undermine Jewish claims to exclusive rights before God pleased him greatly.

31 With v 31 the argument of this section is summed up. That the concluding word is on the relation of the law to faith confirms once again that it was precisely this relation which Paul has been seeking to elucidate (not, for example, a particular doctrine of atonement). "Do we then make the law invalid through faith?" The fact that this question can be asked, and that it was evidently a real question, also confirms once more that Paul's target is Jewish national righteousness. Many Jews would think that Paul's line of argument *did* nullify the law, precisely because they identified the law so completely with their nationhood and self-understanding as Jews. Paul's response is clearly that the law is nullified only when it is taken as the law (= identity and boundary marker) of the Jews, only when it is taken (wrongly) as "the law of works." When it is taken as "the law of faith," when it is seen as speaking to Gentiles as well, it is established and its validity confirmed. The fact that God is one does not nullify his giving of the law to the Jews; rather it shows that his giving of the law had the Gentiles in view as well, and that the law is only properly understood when it is seen as something

Gentile as well as Jew can "do" without thereby becoming a Jew, as something which can only be fulfilled by faith. The real object of Paul's argument here is to break the too exclusive Jewish claim to the law, to the revelation of God in the (Jewish) scriptures and its fulfillment in Christ.

B. Abraham as a Test Case (4:1-25)

Bibliography

Beker, J. C. Paul. 95–104. Berger, K. "Abraham in den paulinischen Hauptbriefen." MTZ 17 (1966) 47–89, esp. 63–77. Boers, H. Theology out of the Ghetto: A New Testament Exegetical Study concerning Exclusiveness. Leiden: Brill, 1970. 82–104. Bruce, F. F. "Abraham Our Father (Romans 4:1)." In The Time Is Fulfilled. Exeter: Paternoster, 1978. 57–74. Davies, W. D. Land. 168–79. Dülmen, A. van. Theologie. 88–94. Dunn, J. D. G. "Some Ecumenical Reflections on Romans 4." In Aksum Thyateira, FS Archbishop Methodius, ed. G. D. Dragas. London: Thyateira House, 1985. 423–26. Flusser, D., and Safrai, S. "Who Sanctified the Beloved in the Womb?" Immanuel 11 (1980) 46–55. Gager, J. G. Origins. 217–20. Gale, H. M. Analogy. 173–75. Gaston, L. "Abraham and the Righteousness of God." HBT 2 (1980) 39–68 = Paul. 45–63. Goppelt, L. Typos: The Typological Interpretation of the Old Testament in the New. 1939; ET Grand Rapids: Eerdmans, 1982. ———. "Apocalypticism and Typology in Paul" (1964). In Typos. 209–37. ———. "Paulus und die Heilsgeschichte: Schlussfolgerungen aus Röm 4 und 1 Kor 10:1–13" (1966). In Christologie und Ethik. Aufsätze zum Neuen Testament. Göttingen: Vandenhoeck & Ruprecht, 1968. 220–33. Hahn, F. "Genesis 15:6 im Neuen Testament." In Probleme biblischer Theologie, FS G. von Rad, ed. H. W. Wolff. Munich: Kaiser, 1971. 90–107. Hanson, A. T. "Abraham the Justified Sinner." In Studies. 52–66. Hays, R. B. "'Have We Found Abraham to Be Our Forefather according to the Flesh?' A Reconsideration of Rom 4:1." NovT 27 (1985) 76–98. Hester, J. D. Paul's Concept of Inheritance. SJTOP 14. Edinburgh: Oliver & Boyd, 1968. Hofius, O. "Eine altjüdische Parallele zu Röm 4:17b." NTS 18 (1971–72) 93–94. Hübner, H. Law. 51–57, 79–80, 118–23. Jeremias, J. "Gedankenführung." 271–72. ———. "Die Gedankenführung in Röm 4. Zum paulinischen Glaubensverständnis." Foi et Salut selon S. Paul. AnBib 42. Rome: Biblical Institute, 1970. 51–58. Käsemann, E. "The Faith of Abraham in Romans 4." In Perspectives. 79–101. Kertelge, K. Rechtfertigung. 185–95. Klein, G. "Römer 4 und die Idee der Heilsgeschichte." In Rekonstruktion und Interpretation. Munich: Kaiser, 1969. 145–69. ———. "Exegetische Probleme in Röm 3:21–4:25." In Rekonstruktion. 170–79. Kolenkow, A. "The Ascription of Romans 4:5." HTR 60 (1967) 228–30. Lafon, G. "La pensée du social et la théologie: Loi et grâce en Romains 4:13–16." RSR 75 (1987) 9–38. Longenecker, R. N. "The 'Faith of Abraham' Theme in Paul, James and Hebrews: A Study in the Circumstantial Nature of New Testament Teaching." JETS 20 (1977) 203–12. Lührmann, D. Glaube. 46–48. Luz, U. Geschichtsverständnis. 113–16, 168–86. McNeil, B. "Raised for Our Justification." ITQ 42 (1975) 97–105. Minde, H. J. van der. Schrift. 68–106. Moxnes, H. Theology in Conflict: Studies in Paul's Understanding of God in Romans. Leiden: Brill, 1980. Patsch, H. "Zum alttestamentlichen Hintergrund von Römer 4:25." ZNW 60 (1969) 273–79. Rad, G. von. "Faith Reckoned as Righteousness" (1951). In The Problem of the Hexateuch and Other Essays. Edinburgh: Oliver & Boyd, 1966. 125–30. Reicke, B. "Paul's Understanding of Righteousness." In Soli Deo Gloria, FS W. C. Robinson, ed. J. M. Richards. Richmond: John Knox, 1968. 37–49. **Sanders, E. P.** *Law.* 32–36. **Stowers, S. K.** *Diatribe.* 168–74. **Swetnam, J.** "The Curious Crux at Romans 4:12." *Bib* 61 (1980) 110–15. **Vielhauer, P.** "Paulus und das Alte Testament" (1969). In *Oikodome. Aufsätze 2.* Munich: Kaiser, 1979. 196–228. **Watson, F.** *Paul.* 135–42. **Wengst, K.** *Formeln.* 101–4. **Wilckens, U.** "Die Rechtfertigung Abrahams nach Röm 4" (1961). In *Rechtfertigung.* 33–49. ———. "Zu Römer 3:21–4:25. Antwort an G. Klein." In *Rechtfertigung.* 50–76. **Zeller, D.** *Juden.* 88–108. **Ziesler, J. A.** *Righteousness.* 180–85, 195–96.

Translation

[1] *What then shall we say that Abraham our forefather* [a] *according to the flesh has found?* [b] [2] *For if Abraham was justified from works, he has something to boast about—but not before God.* [3] *For what says the scripture? "Abraham believed God and it was reckoned to him for righteousness."* [4] *Now to him who works the reward is not reckoned as a favor but as a debt.* [5] *Whereas to him who does not work but believes on him who justifies the ungodly, his faith is "reckoned for righteousness."* [6] *As also* [c] *David speaks of the blessedness of the person to whom God reckons righteousness without works:*

[7] *"Blessed are those whose lawless deeds have been forgiven,*
   and whose sins have been covered;
[8] *Blessed is the one whose* [d] *sin the Lord will by no means reckon."*

[9] *This blessedness then, does it come on the circumcised* [e] *or also on the uncircumcised? For we say, faith "was reckoned" to Abraham "for righteousness."* [10] *How then was it "reckoned"? When he was in circumcision or in uncircumcision? Not in circumcision, but in uncircumcision.* [11] *And he received the sign of circumcision, a seal of the righteousness of the faith which he had in his uncircumcision, in order that he might be father of all who believe through uncircumcision, that righteousness might be reckoned to them as well,* [f] [12] *and father of circumcision to those who are not only men of circumcision but also who* [g] *follow in the footsteps of the faith of our father Abraham which he had in his uncircumcision.*

[13] *For the promise to Abraham and his seed, that he should be heir of the world, did not come through the law but through the righteousness of faith.* [14] *For if the people of the law are heirs, faith is rendered invalid and the promise is nullified;* [15] *for the law brings about wrath, and* [h] *where there is no law there is also no transgression.* [16] *For this reason it is of faith, in order that it might be in accordance with grace, that the promise might be certain to all the seed, not to him who is of the law only, but also to him who is of the faith of Abraham. He is the father of us all,* [17] *as it is written, "I have made you father of many nations," before God in whom "he believed," who gives life to the dead and calls things which have no existence into existence.* [18] *Against hope, in hope "he believed," in order that he might become "father of many nations" in accordance with what had been said, "So shall your seed be."* [i] [19] *Without weakening in faith he* [j] *considered his own body already* [k] *dead, being about one hundred years old, and the deadness of Sarah's womb.* [20] *He did not doubt the promise of God in disbelief, but was strengthened in faith, giving glory to God,* [21] *being fully convinced that what he had promised he was able also to do.*

[22] *Therefore* [l] *"it was reckoned to him for righteousness."*

23 *Nor was it written down for his sake alone that "it was reckoned to him,"*
24 *but also for us, to whom it is to be reckoned, who believe in*
  him who raised Jesus our Lord from the dead,
25 *who was handed over for our transgressions*
  and raised for our vindication.

Notes

a Several versions read πάτερα, reflecting scribal awareness of the unusualness of προπάτωρ.

b The absence of εὑρηκέναι from B and its different positioning in other witnesses attests the sense of various copyists that the verb was being used somewhat awkwardly here. See the discussion, for example, in Cranfield and Wilckens against the older view that εὑρηκέναι did not belong to the text (so, e.g., SH, O'Neill; also RSV, NEB, NJB).

c As often there is manuscript variation between καθάπερ and καθώς (see *Notes* on 3:4).

d A quite popular correction substituted ᾧ for οὗ, making the easier reading "to whom the Lord will not reckon sin."

e A Western tradition inserted μόνον in light of its use later (vv 12, 16).

f The omission of καί is strongly attested. A decision between the two readings is difficult to achieve, since there is a tension in Paul's thought between the assertion of the continuing priority of Israel in God's purpose and his own conviction that the promise always had the Gentiles in view ("to the Jew first, but also the Gentile"). See also Metzger.

g The second τοῖς is surprising but there is no textual tradition which omits it. A slip by the amanuensis or the earliest copyists is likely (see, e.g., SH).

h The reading γάρ appears to be secondary on the MSS attestation, and was probably substituted for the δέ to make the flow of reasoning read more sequentially.

i F G a supplement the quotation of Gen 15:5 with words drawn from Gen 22:17—"as the stars of heaven and the sand of the sea."

j Quite a strong, but clearly secondary, tradition of Western origin reads a negative in front of κατενόησεν: Abraham was so strong in faith that he did not consider. . . . The more strongly attested reading also gives the stronger sense: Abraham's faith took account of the actual circumstances.

k Though the weight of manuscript evidence favors the retention of ἤδη, the sense would not suffer by its omission. As strengthening the point, however, it is perhaps more likely that ἤδη has been added than that its (accidental) omission should have gained such influence.

l The textual tradition is equally balanced between the reading διό with and without καί. The καί simply strengthens the force of διό as introducing a conclusion, and for that reason may have been added.

Form and Structure

The continuity of thought (Rhyne, *Faith*, 59–61, 75) and form (Stowers, *Diatribe*, 164–68) from the preceding section is clearly indicated by the way the issue is posed (v 2: . . . ἐξ ἔργων ἐδικαιώθη . . . καύχημα . . . ; cf. 3:27). But the issue is not a theoretical one of how faith confirms the law (3:31). It is rather an exposition of the basic theme of the argument so far (as summarized in 3:28)—that God justifies through faith (so Gentile as well as Jew) and does not limit his saving righteousness to the circumcised (cf. Berger). In this regard Abraham provides a crucial test case, since he was characteristically understood within Judaism as the archetype of the devout Jew who demonstrated his faithfulness to the covenant by keeping the law and who thus was reckoned righteous. Paul's decision to focus on Gen 15:6 was also determined by the way the verse was currently understood within Judaism—

as describing a righteousness coterminous with faithfulness to the covenant God. Fundamental is the salvation-history dimension: "Abraham in Rom 4 is not simply an illustration of 'the justified sinner' but stands as the first of the people of God" (Campbell, "Freedom" 39). In the lengthy debate between Wilckens and Klein on this topic, the former must be judged to have the stronger case, since Klein both overstates the discontinuity between the before-and-after of 3:21 (see not least on 3:31) and gives too little weight to the continuity of *covenant* promise so fundamental to the argument of 4:13–17 (cf. Luz, *Geschichtsverständnis*, 182). Even if he does not speak to the point, Paul would not deny a continuity of God's righteousness (faithfulness) through the period from Abraham to Christ (he draws the motif from the OT!). It is the failure to realize that God's righteousness is *now* being revealed to *all* who *believe* (3:21–22) to which Paul takes such exception.

The exposition of Gen 15:6 of which chap. 4 consists is one of the finest examples of Jewish midrash available to us from this era. Van der Minde has developed a suggestion of Michel and attempted to trace a pre-Pauline midrash (comprising vv 3, 11, 12, 13, 16, 17a, and 18c) which originated among non-Jewish Christians (*Schrift*, 78–83). More likely is Moxnes's thesis that Rom 4 is a composition of Paul himself in which he has followed a traditional homiletic pattern and included traditional Jewish material (particularly vv 13–22) with clear parallels in Philo and in Heb 11 in particular (*Theology*, 195–205; see particularly on 4:17 and 22). Moreover, the fact that James 2:18–24 poses a point-by-point counterargument to that of 3:27–4:25, calling on the more typically Jewish understanding of Gen 15:6 (but with "works" now understood as good works), suggests that Paul was drawing on a line of argument in 3:21–4:25 which he had used elsewhere.

	Romans	James
Issue posed in terms of faith and works	3:27–28	2:18
Significance of claiming "God is one"	3:29–30	2:19
Appeal to Abraham as test case	4:1–2	2:20–22
Citation of proof text—Gen 15:6	4:3	2:20–22
Interpretation of Gen 15:6	4:4–21	2:23
Conclusion	4:22	2:24

The exposition proper (vv 3–22) is bracketed by explicit citation of the text itself (vv 3, 22), with several other references or echoes incorporated within the body of the midrash (vv 5, 6, 9 and 11, 17 and 18), and consists of Paul's explanation of the two key verbs, ἐλογίσθη and ἐπίστευσεν. Typical of the midrashic form is the use of Ps 32:1 to elucidate the text from the Torah (vv 3, 7–8; $g^{e}z\bar{e}r\bar{a}h$ $\check{s}\bar{a}w\bar{a}h$—Jeremias) and the interweaving of Gen 17:5 into the exposition (v 17), to provide the fatherhood of Abraham as the counterpoint to the principal theme (vv 1, 11–12, 16–18); cf. particularly Hays, "Rom 4:1."

The midrash falls into fairly clear stages, but each stage is interrelated, with thematic words (faith, promise) appearing outside the stage in which they are most prominent, with no clear division at v 17 in particular.

vv 1-2   Introduction (in continued diatribe style)
3   The text to be explained—ἐπίστευσεν δὲ Ἀβραὰμ τῷ θεῷ καὶ
                ἐλογίσθη αὐτῷ εἰς δικαιοσύνην
4-8   The meaning of ἐλογίσθη
        4-5   from the logic of divine-human relations
        6-8   from its use in Ps 32:1
9-21   The meaning of ἐπίστευσεν
        9-12   from the order of events in Abraham's case
        13-17   from the link between faith and promise in Abraham's case
        17-21   from the character of Abraham's faith
22   Conclusion—the text explained
23-25   Corollary—its wider application as thus understood.

The concluding verses (24–25) use traditional formulations, focusing once again on the saving function of Christ's death (cf. 3:25–26) and resurrection (cf. 1:3–4), and prepare the reader for the two-sidedness of the salvation process set out in the following chapters (see on 5:12–21 *Form and Structure*).

Comment

1 τί οὖν ἐροῦμεν, "what then shall we say?" See on 3:5. The object is not to demonstrate the truth of 3:31 as such (cf., e.g., SH, Lietzmann, Schmidt, Jeremias, "Röm 4"), for which a conjunction like "for" would have been more appropriate, but to build on and further defend the conclusions drawn in 3:27–31 as a whole (cf. particularly Cranfield, 223–24; Moxnes, 228–29; Rhyne, *Faith*; chap. 4: "a kind of scripture proof attached to 3:21–31"—Kuss, 178).

εὑρηκέναι, "has found." Paul may well have intended to evoke the phrase which occurs quite frequently in the LXX: εὑρίσκειν χάριν (or ἔλεος), "to find grace (or mercy)." It is prominent particularly in Genesis (13 times), but also in Exod 33 (4 times), 1 Samuel (6 times), and Sirach (7 times). Elsewhere cf., e.g., Deut 24:1, Dan 3:38 (LXX), Bar 1:12, and 1 Macc 11:24. Note particularly Gen 18:3—Abraham himself speaks of "finding favor in God's sight." That the phrase was still in familiar usage in the first century in Jewish circles is indicated by Luke 1:30, Acts 7:46, Heb 4:16, and 4 Ezra 12.7. BGD's suggested translation "obtain" is inadequate. The dominant thought in this usage is of being granted a favored standing before someone who has the power to withhold or bestow the favor as he chooses; even though the idea was also included in the context of gaining that favor by giving presents to the one who has the power to bestow it (as in Gen 33:10; 1 Macc 10:60). Paul's purpose in evoking the phrase would probably be to prepare the ground for the following exposition in which χάρις features (vv 4, 16), by implying from the outset that Abraham's standing before God was an act of divine favor. It is not necessary, however, to assume that Paul intended χάρις to answer the opening τί. We could translate simply, "What did Abraham find to be the case . . . ?" The perfect tense also is a subtle indication that what Abraham found to be the case when he first found favor with God determined his standing with God thereafter. Black offers "a Hebrew sense" for the verb and the rendering, "What then shall we say befell Abraham . . . ?" (cf. Josh

2:23; *Pss. Sol.* 17.8 [not 18]). An alternative or additional and just as likely explanation for the use of εὑρίσκειν here is that Paul consciously or unconsciously had in mind its use with reference to Abraham in the formula used in Sir 44:20 and 1 Macc 2:52 (see on 4:2).

Ἀβραὰμ τὸν προπάτορα ἡμῶν κατὰ σάρκα, "Abraham our forefather according to the flesh." Abraham is naturally appealed to as father of the race, in view of his place within God's salvation-history (Gen 12–24). Among the founders of the people, he had first claim on the title "father" (see *TDNT* 5:976). Josephus also speaks of him as προπάτωρ (*War* 5.380); note also *Ap. Const.* 7.33.4. Hence Israel can regard itself simply as "the seed of Abraham" (as in Ps 105:6; Isa 41:8). He was highly regarded within Judaism for the closeness of his relationship with God: "the friend of God" (2 Chron 20:7; Isa 41:8; *Jub.* 19.9; Philo, *Abr.* 273; *Jos. As.* 23.10; James 2:23). See further on 4:2.

When Paul speaks of *"our* forefather" (cf. 9:10—"Isaac our father"), it is not entirely clear whether he was thinking in exclusively Jewish terms (having resumed his dialogue with the Jewish interlocutor of the earlier diatribe—2:1ff.), or intended to include Gentiles as well (as the immediately preceding argument and the subsequent exposition of Gen 15:6 would suggest—vv 13–18); cf. 1 Cor 10:1, and contrast Davies's observation that in Judaism "even proselytes were not allowed to call Abraham 'our father'" (*Land,* 177). Such transitions in his thought are fairly typical (e.g., Gal 3:10–14; 4:1–5) and indicate the extent to which he both still thought of himself as a Jew and still regarded the debate in which he was involved as intra-Jewish (Lietzmann indeed adds "I speak as a Jew" to the translation); Schlatter catches the nuance nicely.

κατὰ σάρκα, "according to the flesh," should certainly be taken with the preceding noun in accordance with the weight of manuscript tradition (as is now generally agreed); Paul writes thus to provide a foil for his later exposition of Abraham's fatherhood (vv 13ff.). The phrase should not be regarded as a "neutral" use of σάρξ; as usual in Paul the phrase has a somewhat negative, even slightly pejorative overtone (see further on 1:3 and 9:3). The overtone is the same as that attaching to ἐν σαρκί in 2:28. The implication is that boasting, works of the law (v 2), and Jewish insistence on circumcision of the flesh all belong together and fall under the negative sign of κατὰ σάρκα.

Hays, "Rom 4:1," follows Zahn in arguing that v 1 should be punctuated to read, "What then shall we say? Have we found Abraham (to be) our forefather according to the flesh?" But while his rendering strengthens the link to vv 11ff. (Abraham's fatherhood), it weakens the more immediate link. Nor is it required by the form (cf. 8:31; 9:30; and 3:9 q.v.); and the beginning of a sentence with an accusative and infinitive construction where the accusative was unstated would be rather odd. Despite Zahn and Hays, it still seems to read more naturally to take Abraham as the subject of εὑρηκέναι; it at once focuses attention on the one who would be generally accepted as a decisive test case; it echoes familiar language used of Abraham and introduces the grace/works antithesis which follows immediately; and the line of argument from 3:27 seems to have been one which Paul had used more than once (see *Form and Structure*—parallel with James 2).

2 εἰ γὰρ Ἀβραὰμ ἐξ ἔργων ἐδικαιώθη, ἔχει καύχημα, ἀλλ᾽ οὐ πρὸς θεόν, "for

if Abraham was justified from works he has something to boast about, but
not towards God." The opening clause picks up what was explicitly denied
in the summary conclusion to the first section of the argument (3:20). For
ἐδικαιώθη see on 2:13; this is the link word between the preceding discussion
(3:21–31) and the key text (Gen 15:6—v 3). The ἐξ ἔργων should not be
taken as a more generalized statement than ἐξ ἔργων νόμου, as the parallel
with 3:20 and the similar usage in 3:27–28 clearly indicate. Paul is not speaking
about "good works" done by Abraham, but about faithful obedience to what
God requires (see on 3:20 and further below). For the use of καύχημα cf.
particularly 1 Cor 9:16 and Gal 6:4; and see on 2:17. πρὸς θεόν, "in reference
to God, looking towards God" (cf. Luke 18:1; Gal 2:14; Heb 1:7; and particularly Rom 15:17 and 2 Cor 3:4).

Paul here attacks head-on the normal or at least widely accepted way of
thinking about Abraham among his fellow Jews (cf. particularly Luz, Geschichtsverständnis, 177–80; Hahn, "Gen 15:6," 94–97; Longenecker, "Faith,"
204–5; Watson, Paul, 136–38). For precisely as the father of the nation, the
friend of God (see on 4:1), Abraham was at this time regularly presented as
a type of or model for the devout Jew. Already it was being said that he
had observed the law in its as yet unwritten state (Gen 26:5; Jub. 16.28;
24.11; 2 Apoc. Bar. 57.1–2; m. Qidd. 4.14; Abraham "was accounted a friend
of God because he kept the commandments of God"—CD 3.2); note also Pr
Man 8—"you did not appoint grace for the righteous ones, such as Abraham
and Isaac and Jacob, those who did not sin against you." More frequently
recalled was the folk memory of how Abraham had been tested and yet
found faithful, with particular reference to the sacrifice of Isaac (Jud. 8:26;
Jub. 17.15–18; 18.16; 19.8; m. ʾAbot 5.3; see also Philo, Abr. 192; Josephus,
Ant. 1.223–25; Ps-Philo, Lib. Ant. 40.2, 5; 4 Macc 14.20). Here particularly
noteworthy is Sir 44:19–21:

> Abraham was the great father of a multitude of nations,
>   and no one has been found like him in glory;
> he kept the law of the Most High,
>   and was taken into covenant with him;
> he established the covenant in his flesh,
>   and when he was tested he was found faithful.
> Therefore the Lord assured him by an oath
>   that the nations would be blessed through his posterity;
> that he would multiply him like the dust of the earth,
>   and exalt his posterity like the stars,
> and cause them to inherit from sea to sea
>   and from the River to the ends of the earth.

Paul could well have had this passage in mind, since it associates so many
of the same themes (father Abraham, his preeminence, law-keeping, covenant,
flesh, blessing promised to the nations, posterity, even the use of εὑρίσκειν).
What catches immediate attention is the marked divergence between ben
Sira's handling of these themes and Paul's: for ben Sira the covenant promise
of blessing to the nations is a consequence of Abraham's faithfulness and

presupposes Israel's supremacy; Paul reads the same scriptural tradition differently at both points (see 4:9–21). Even if Paul did not have this passage as such in mind, he certainly had in view the train of thought expressed by ben Sira.

More striking still is the fact that another expression of the same motif uses just the same phrases as we find in Sir 44:20, ἐν πειρασμῷ εὑρέθη πιστός, and immediately adds καὶ ἐλογίσθη αὐτῷ εἰς δικαιοσύνην, "when he was tested he was found faithful, and it was reckoned to him for righteousness" (1 Macc 2:52)—the same appeal to Gen 15:6 which Paul himself makes in v 3. Clearly then Paul has in view a well established theme of Jewish theology at that time, which tied the covenant promise made to Abraham to Abraham's faithfulness under testing, and which regarded Abraham's offering of Isaac as the key to understanding Gen 15:6. Equally clearly James 2:22–23 shows a similar dependence on the same theme, using the same exegesis; but whereas Paul severely questions the association of πίστις and works as the way to interpret Gen 15:6, James affirms the association and remains much more within the tradition which Paul here questions (see further *Form and Structure*); cf. also Heb 11:17–18. Much disputed is the question of whether Jewish reflection about Abraham's offering of Isaac had been elaborated still further by this time (see further on 8:32), but the dispute makes little difference to the exegesis here. More questionable is the use of later rabbinic interpretations of Gen 15:6 (even when attributed to earlier rabbis) to illustrate the views of the Pharisees at the time of Paul, such as are cited by Str-B, 3:199–201, Leenhardt and Cranfield. Boers, 86–87, and Hübner, *Law*, 119, miss the point precisely because they fail to ask why Abraham was so highly regarded in the Judaism of Paul's time.

Paul evokes and sums up this strong theme of Jewish exposition with the catchwords which characterized the preceding stages of his argument—"works" and "boasting." In Jewish perspective Abraham's faithfulness under testing provided the same ground for confidence before God as that enjoyed by the second-temple Jew who showed the equivalent loyalty under the Maccabees and in face of current pressure from the Roman overlords, a faithfulness focused particularly in the obligations which marked them off most clearly as the seed of Abraham, the children of Israel, the people of the law (circumcision, food laws, Sabbath, in particular; see *Introduction* §5.3.3). Paul's formulation seems at first to allow the possibility that this traditional association of faithfulness in nomistic service (works of the law—see on 3:20) was what established the covenant member's righteousness and confirmed his prerogative before God wherein he could boast (2:17, 23). But he poses it as a theoretical possibility only to deny its central affirmation completely: in relation to God boasting such as characterizes his fellow Jews has no place, because righteousness is not "from works." Gaston, too much influenced by his understandable reaction against an overstressing of the discontinuities between Jew and Christian on the significance of God's righteousness and Abraham's faith, ignores the extent to which Paul clearly is contesting a strong line of Jewish interpretation.

3 τί γὰρ ἡ γραφὴ λέγει, "for what says the scripture?" "The scripture" documents the claim "not before God." ἡ γραφή here is probably a designation for the scriptures as a single collectivity (as in Philo, *Mos.* 2.84; *Ep. Arist.* 155, 168); so also in 9:17; 10:11; and Gal 4:30 (see BGD, γραφή 2bβ). For the plural see on 1:2. The singular need not imply an already established concept of a closed canon of scripture, but it does imply the presupposition that a single mind and purpose (God's) inspired and informed the several writings so designated (see B. B. Warfield, *The Inspiration and Authority of the Bible* [London: Marshall, 1951], 235, 316–17; *TDNT* 1:753–55). Hanson's suggestion that Paul would think of the divine speaker in Gen 15:6 as the preexistent Christ, so that Abraham's faith was directed to Christ ("Abraham," 53, 66), is farfetched. Had Paul wanted to establish such a complete continuity between Abraham's faith and the faith he himself now proclaimed he would have brought it out much more clearly. In contrast, however, the continuity he emphasizes is faith in God (v 24).

ἐπίστευσεν δὲ ᾿Αβραὰμ τῷ θεῷ καὶ ἐλογίσθη αὐτῷ εἰς δικαιοσύνην, "Abraham believed God and it was reckoned to him for righteousness." Paul quotes the LXX almost exactly, which in turn is a quite satisfactory rendering of the Hebrew. The one difference is that in Gen 15:6 Abraham still had his old name Abram. It was not changed till the covenant was agreed in Gen 17:5. The point may be significant since the promise made to Abraham (that he would be "father of a multitude" = "Abraham") was given many times (Gen 12:2–3; 15:5; 17:4–5; 18:18; 22:17–18), and there were two versions of the giving of the covenant as well (15:18; 17:2–21). It would be natural for these various accounts to be merged together in Jewish thought about the giving of the promise and the covenant. Hence the quite natural running together of Gen 15:6 with Gen 22. Paul's use of "Abraham" (rather than Abram) here (as also in Gal 3:6) and his quotation of the promise in a mixed form in Gal 3:8 (Gen 12:3; 18:18) reflects the same tendency.

Gen 15:6 is the only passage in the Abraham complex which speaks of Abraham's faith as such and of righteousness as something attributed by God, so it is natural that Paul should focus on it (see on 4:2; on its original force probably as a declaration of God independent of the cult, see von Rad). The fact, however, that 1 Macc 2:52 and James 2:23 also appeal to it shows that Paul's focusing the discussion on it is not idiosyncratic. Jewish exposition of the verse by reference to Abraham's faithfulness to God's command in Gen 22 would be assisted by Ps 106 [LXX 105]:31 where Phinehas's zeal (for the law) is commended and the same phrase is used: καὶ ἐλογίσθη αὐτῷ εἰς δικαιοσύνην. For Phinehas was held forth as the ideal of zealous devotion to Israel's covenant with Yahweh, as one who had preserved Israel's exclusiveness and separateness from other nations (Num 25:6–13); see Hengel, *Zeloten,* 154–81. To the same effect cf. also *Jub.* 30.17–19; and see further on 10.2. Philo's use of the text to emphasize the example of Abraham's faith in God's faithfulness is to that extent not dissimilar to Paul's (*Leg. All.* 3.228; *Immut.* 4; *Migr.* 44; *Heres* 90–95; etc.), but as usual, Philo's exegesis is determined by his own apologetic religious and philosophic concerns and shows no other points of contact with Paul (see Moxnes, 130–64, particularly 155–63; and further on 4:17 and 21).

The subsequent exposition (vv 4–21) focuses on the meaning of the two verbs used in Gen 15:6: ἐπίστευσεν (vv 9–21) and ἐλογίσθη (vv 4–8); see *Form and Structure.* The meaning of εἰς δικαιοσύνην evidently needed no discussion, since all parties presumably agreed that to be "righteous" is to be not so much acceptable to God as accepted by God—righteousness as the status which God accorded to his covenant people and in which he sustained them. What was at issue was what membership in the covenant people involved, what counted for righteousness—the typical Jewish answer being given by the interpretation of Gen 15:6 by means of Gen 22 (see further on 4:6 and 9). In the following verses note the different ways in which Paul can express the relationship between righteousness and faith: πίστις εἰς δικαιοσύνην (vv 5, 9), δικαιοσύνη τῆς πίστεως (vv 11, 13). In expounding ἐπίστευσεν here Käsemann becomes almost lyrical in his Lutheranism; but it is better to await Paul's own exposition.

4–5 τῷ δὲ ἐργαζομένῳ ὁ μισθὸς οὐ λογίζεται κατὰ χάριν ἀλλὰ κατὰ ὀφείλημα· τῷ δὲ μὴ ἐργαζομένῳ, πιστεύοντι δὲ ἐπὶ τὸν δικαιοῦντα τὸν ἀσεβῆ, λογίζεται ἡ πίστις αὐτοῦ εἰς δικαιοσύνην, "now to him who works the reward is not reckoned as a favor but as a debt; but to him who does not work but believes on him who justifies the ungodly, his faith is 'reckoned for righteousness.'" For ἐργάζομαι used positively in Paul see particularly 2:10; 1 Cor 16:10; Gal 6:10; and Col 3:23. For μισθός, "reward," as a Christian concept see, e.g., Matt 5:12; 6:1; Mark 9:41; Luke 10:7; 1 Cor 3:8, 14; Rev 11:18. λογίζεται, "is reckoned," appears 11 times in this chapter; Paul seeks to clarify the weight to be given to the ἐλογίσθη of Gen 15:6. Cranfield argues that Paul's concern from the start is with the ἐπίστευσεν, but he ignores the fact that λογίζεσθαι appears again in vv 6 and 8, the clear implication being that Paul cites Ps 32:1–2 in order to justify his interpretation of ἐλογίσθη (NEB rightly puts the λογίζεσθαι references in vv 5–6 in quotation marks). The fact that it was a t.t. in commercial dealings ("reckon or put to someone's account"; see BGD, TDNT 4:284) obviously suggested an analogy from the business world, as also the talk of "works." In terms of the contractual relationships of commerce λογίζεσθαι must mean a reckoning of payment for work done. No business could survive which simply gave away its stock or paid its employees for not working.

κατὰ χάριν, "as a favor, out of goodwill" (BGD, χάρις 2a). Paul uses the language mindful of the centrality of χάρις in his own understanding of the gospel (see on 1:5), and perhaps also conscious of OT usage in the phrase "to find grace" (see on 4:1). But here it is part of the business world analogy, and would be sufficiently familiar as such (see LSJ). ὀφείλημα, "debt," is used only here in Paul, but again the language would be familiar; the contrast χάρις/ὀφείλημα occurs also in Thucydides 2.40.4. That Paul substitutes πιστεύειν ἐπί for πιστεύειν with the dative (v 3) presumably signifies that here at least he sees no great difference between believing someone (God's promise) and believing in him (see further vv 17–21 and on 4:24). For the indicative of πιστεύειν see on 1:16.

Paul's point seems to be (1) that Gen 15:6 does not use ἐργάζεσθαι but πιστεύειν, with the implication (2) that in divine-human relations the parallel of a contractual relationship between those who relatively speaking are equals is inappropriate. His Jewish interlocutor would not be convinced at this initial attempt to separate Gen 15:6 from Abraham's faithfulness, but at least so

far as the λογίζεσθαι in Gen 15:6 is concerned the point has weight: in Gen
15:6 it is *faith* which is so "reckoned." That Paul was not indulging in special
pleading by rewording Gen 15:6 with πίστις as the subject (v 5) is confirmed
from Philo's similar rewording of the same passage in *Heres* 94: λογισθῆναι
τὴν πίστιν εἰς δικαιοσύνην αὐτῷ. The difference is that where πίστις would be
taken in the sense "faithfulness" by most Jews, and quite properly so in terms
of common usage (Spicq, 701–2), the balance of the sentence and the contrast
drawn restricts the sense here to "faith" as belief, trust.

The language used here (working, reckoning, reward) should not be taken
as a description of the Judaism of Paul's day. In particular, Paul is not castigat-
ing contemporary Judaism for a theology of (self-achieved) merit and reward
(contrast, e.g., Hübner, *Law*, 121–22: "he shows how good he is . . . this
egocentric use of the Law . . . man's effort to achieve his salvation by keeping
the Law"). The wording is used simply as part of the analogy drawn from
the world of contract and employment. He does *not* say, "If you think of
Abraham's faith as a work, you must think of his righteousness as a reward."
The contrast is solely between working and believing, between what the worker
is due and what is given as a complete favor. The first-century Jew did of
course have a concept of divine recompense and reward for covenant loyalty
(as in Ps 18:20–24), though we should beware of assuming that the later
doctrine of merits, first clearly evident in *4 Ezra* 8.33, was already characteristic
of Pharisaic Judaism (for rabbinic Judaism itself, see particularly Sanders,
Paul, 117–47; see also on 2:5). But it is not the concept of reward as such
which Paul disputes. He himself has already described God's judgment as a
rendering to everyone according to his works (2:6; note particularly 2:10),
and he had not hesitated to use the word "reward" in a similar context in
his own teaching in an earlier letter (1 Cor 3:8, 14). His point is simply that
in the case of Gen 15:6 the whole language of "payment due" is inappropriate.
Or rather, that is what he is going to demonstrate. Here he simply poses
the alternatives, work → reckon → debt, faith → reckon → favor, as a way
of setting up the exposition which is about to follow and as a way of shaking
his Jewish interlocutor out of a too ready equation of Abraham's believing
with his covenant loyalty. Where (Abraham's) faith is in view, the righteousness
is surely reckoned in terms of grace, not of payment due. There is a danger
therefore that expositions of Paul's theology of justification will focus too
heavily on these verses without sufficient regard for the movement of his
thought in them (cf., e.g., Kertelge, *Rechtfertigung*, 185–95). Contrast Gale,
Analogy, 174: "for the reader, as for Paul, the picture offered in v 4 possesses
relatively little significance in and of itself."

τὸν δικαιοῦντα τὸν ἀσεβῆ, "the one who justifies the ungodly." This would
be distinctly more provocative. To justify the ungodly or acquit the wicked
was abhorrent to a basic and frequently repeated canon of Jewish justice
(Exod 23:7; Prov 17:15; 24:24; Isa 5:23; Sir 42:2; CD 1.19). As such it also
offended against the whole basis of the covenant, since Israel's judicial system
was posited on God's own dealings with humankind (as Exod 23:7 indicates).
Another indication of the extent to which Paul's language would jar with
normal Jewish presuppositions is the extent to which ἀσεβής, "ungodly," was
synonymous with ἁμαρτωλός, "sinner," that is, one whose conduct put him

outside the covenant (Pss 1:1, 5; 37 [LXX 36]:34–35; 58:10 [LXX 57:11]; Prov 11:9 (variant); 11:31; 12:12–13; 15:8 (variant); 24:19–20; Ezek 33:8–11; Sir 7:16–17; 9:11–12; 41:5–8; see also on 3:7, *Introduction* §5.3.1, and Dunn, "Antioch Incident," 27–28; in Romans note particularly the parallelism of 5:6 and 8). Paul puts together two concepts which in Jewish thought were mutually exclusive: God justifies (that is, through the covenant) the ungodly (the one who is outside the covenant, that is, outside the sphere of God's saving righteousness). In reference to Abraham himself the thought was not entirely strange to Jewish ears. For since the covenant began with Abraham, Abraham was already seen as the type of the proselyte, the Gentile who turns away from his idolatry to the one true God (*Jub.* 12.1–21; Josephus, *Ant.* 1.155; *Apoc. Abr.* 1–8; Str-B, 3:195; this line of reflection seems more pertinent than the possibility that Abraham was remembered here as one who interceded for the ungodly [= Sodom], as suggested by Kolenkow). But in Judaism he is lauded precisely as one who turned from his ungodliness and who through his obedience to the commands of God (including, not least, circumcision) entered the sphere of God's righteousness. Paul starts at the same point but reaches a radically different conclusion: his argument is that the believing and being justified were already effective prior to and apart from such works, and it is *that* fact rather than the subsequent works done by Abraham which shows that the business analogy does not determine the meaning of ἐλογίσθη in this crucial passage; "in painting Abraham in these colors Paul is taking the provocative step of making the 'Gentile' stance before God somehow the norm" (Byrne, *Reckoning,* 97).

Paul states his point as a general principle ("God who justifies the ungodly"), but it is a principle drawn from the particular case of Abraham, which has its force as a counter to the more normal interpretation of Abraham as a model of covenant righteousness. To build it up into a free-standing principle of much wider application, without reference to what it was set in opposition to, runs the risk of pushing the theological point out of balance. As an example of powerful exegesis/exposition, see Denney.

6 καθάπερ καὶ Δαυὶδ λέγει τὸν μακαρισμὸν τοῦ ἀνθρώπου, "as David also speaks of the blessedness of the person." καθάπερ, "as also," is almost exclusively Pauline (16 times?) within the NT (apart from Heb 4:2), with καθώς regularly appearing as a variant (see *Notes*). Δαυίδ, "David," is naturally regarded as the author of the psalm, an attribution established in the textual tradition itself (so also 11:9, citing Ps 69). With the dimensions of the Psalter already well (though not finally) established, David could be regarded as author of its individual components, even when tradition did not make the association (as in Acts 4:25 and Heb 4:7). In some instances the attribution was of theological importance (Mark 12:35–37; Acts 2:25–31; 13:35–37). Here, however, David is cited merely as author, not as a second example alongside Abraham. μακαρισμός, "blessedness," is found only here (vv 6, 9) and Gal 4:15 in the NT (see on μακάριος in 4:7–8).

ᾧ ὁ θεὸς λογίζεται δικαιοσύνην, "to whom God reckons righteousness." The formulation clearly indicates that Paul is still exegeting the last four words of Gen 15:6. The rewording clarifies what was implicit in the passive (ἐλογίσθη), viz., that God is the one who makes the reckoning. That Paul puts δικαιοσύνην as the direct object (in place of εἰς δικαιοσύνην in Gen 15:6) confirms that he does not think of God accepting faith merely as a substitute for righteousness, but that righteousness is actually accorded. In terms of the generally accepted understanding of the term in Jewish circles (see above on 1:17), the idea is of God treating someone as fully acceptable, as a full participant in the benefits of his covenant. Paul's point in effect is that to make that acceptability dependent on "works" is to treat it as less than full acceptability and to deny what the scripture affirmed: viz., that God fully accepted Abraham there and then on the basis of his faith.

χωρὶς ἔργων, "apart from works" (see on 3:20 and 4:2). Paul again makes explicit what was implied in vv 3–5, that he is setting in antithesis what his Jewish contemporaries usually took as interdependent (faith and works). His point is that Gen 15:6 has in view a righteousness which was not dependent on the sort of nomistic service in which the devout Jew could boast (3:27–28; 4:2); however closely the requirement of circumcision followed upon the being reckoned righteousness, the righteousness was already reckoned before circumcision was mentioned. The explicit argument of 4:9–12 is thus already foreshadowed in the exegesis of Gen 15:6 which this reformulation of it implies.

7–8 The quotation accords exactly with the LXX Ps 31:1–2 = MT 32:1–2.

μακάριοι ὧν ἀφέθησαν αἱ ἀνομίαι, "blessed are those whose acts of lawlessness have been forgiven." μακάριος, "blessed, fortunate, happy," usually has the sense of "privileged recipient of divine favor" (BGD). The form of the beatitude is not exclusive to Jewish and Christian piety. In Greek literature it usually took the form μακάριος ὅστις. The fact that in the LXX it is found predominantly in the Psalms and Wisdom literature also betokens a wider provenance (cf., e.g., Ps 1:1; Sir 14:1–2; 28:19). See further TDNT 4:362–67. It is less clear here than in the other beatitudes of the NT that "eschatological salvation" is in view (pace Käsemann). Elsewhere in Paul see 14:22 and cf. 1 Cor 7:40.

It would be significant for Paul that ἀνομία was another word associated with the ἁμαρτωλός as indicating actions which characterized those outside the covenant (Ps 28 [LXX 27]:3 [variant]; 55:3 [54:4]; 92:7 [91:8]; 101 [100]:8; 125 [124]:3; cf. 1 Macc 1:34; 2:44; cf. Paul's own use elsewhere—6:19; 2 Cor 6:14; 2 Thess 2:3, 7; see further Introduction §5.3.1). David can thus be said to envisage a forgiveness which goes beyond the bounds of the covenant, and which therefore is not dependent on the works of the covenant law.

ἀφέθησαν, "have been forgiven." Since Paul equates the blessing of forgiveness (v 7) with the blessedness of being reckoned righteous (v 6), Jeremias has grounds for concluding that "justification is forgiveness, nothing but forgiveness" (Central Message, 66; similarly Nygren), though it should be noted that such an equation can only stand if forgiveness is understood in very positive terms. The fact, however, that Paul elsewhere, and when expressing his own theology, seems to avoid so completely the thought of God's forgiveness (ἄφεσις only in Col 1:14 and Eph 1:7), as also the conjoint idea of repentance (see further on 3:25), has caused considerable perplexity, precisely because of the prominence of these themes within other strands of Judaism. "How a Jew of Paul's antecedents could ignore, and by implication deny, the great prophetic doctrine of repentance . . . that God, out of love freely forgives the sincerely penitent sinner and restores him to his favor—that seems from the Jewish point of view inexplicable" (Moore, *Judaism*, 3:151). In rabbinic Judaism the very same passage (Ps 32:1–2) was frequently cited in connection with the Day of Atonement (Str-B, 3:202–3). It may be, of course, that another attitude was more typical at the time of Paul: the belief that the righteous needed no repentance, that repentance was provided only for the sinner (ἁμαρτωλός—see on 4:5), and that Abraham was one who needed no repentance because he did no sin (Pr Man 8; cf. *Jub.* 23.10). But if Moore's observation applies also to the Judaism of Paul's time, the best answer may simply be that in Paul's perspective the talk of repentance and forgiveness was too much tied up with the assumption that it was the language of the covenant, the privilege of the covenant member who, despite his various sins, nevertheless maintained his standing within the covenant by his loyalty to its distinctive claims (works). Hence the phrase is regularly attached to the regulations governing the sin and guilt offerings in Lev 4 and 5: "and it/the sin will be forgiven"; "according to the covenant which God made with the forefathers, to forgive their sins, so shall he forgive their sins also" (CD 4.9–10 Vermes); see further on 2:4. Paul tries to counter the presuppositional framework of such language by avoiding it and by developing his own focal terms (grace and faith); see on 3:25.

καὶ ὧν ἐπεκαλύφθησαν αἱ ἁμαρτίαι, "and whose sins have been covered." ἐπικαλύπτειν, is only found here in the NT (see further Cranfield). For ἁμαρτία see on 3:9.

μακάριος ἀνὴρ οὗ οὐ μὴ λογίσηται κύριος ἁμαρτίαν, "blessed is the man whose sin the Lord by no means reckons." Paul clearly regards all these phrases as synonyms: reckon righteous = forgive acts of lawlessness = cover sins = not reckon sins. In what was very proper hermeneutical method Paul has cited Ps 32:1–2 because it used the same key word (λογίζεσθαι) in a similar context (the so-called second rule of Hillel—גְּזֵירָה שָׁוָה, "equal category"; Jeremias, "Gedankenführung," 271–72). If his point is that Ps 32:1–2 confirms the inappropriateness of the analogy from the business world (v 4), then it can be regarded as successful, since his fellow Jews would readily recognize the graciousness of the system of sacrifice and atonement by which God made provision for the sins of his people. But "without works" (v 6) would remain in dispute. On οὐ μή see BGD, μή D. As usual, the κύριος within an OT quotation denotes God rather than Christ (*TDNT* 3:1086–87). Hanson's suggestion that Paul "must have regarded the psalm as uttered originally by Abraham" ("Abraham," 57) is quite unnecessary to the exegesis and foreign to Paul's hermeneutic and thought.

9 ὁ μακαρισμὸς οὖν οὗτος ἐπὶ τὴν περιτομὴν ἢ καὶ ἐπὶ τὴν ἀκροβυστίαν; λέγομεν γάρ, Ἐλογίσθη τῷ Ἀβραὰμ ἡ πίστις εἰς δικαιοσύνην, "this blessedness then, does it come to the circumcised or also to the uncircumcised? For we say, 'Faith was reckoned to Abraham for righteousness.'" Since μακαρισμός refers back to the blessedness (v 6) which was documented by the quotation from Ps 32, and since v 9b is an explicit repetition of Gen 15:6, Paul is here showing how he wants the two OT passages to be related to each other: not simply that the blessedness of forgiveness is synonymous with the being reckoned righteous (that was already explicit in v 6), but that Ps 32:1–2 is only drawn in to help the exposition of Gen 15:6 (that is, to illuminate the force of ἐλογίσθη), not for its independent value (*David* received this blessing when already circumcised!). This is the third explicit quotation of Gen 15:6 (vv 3, 5, 6), with the noun (πίστις) again substituted for the verb (ἐπίστευσεν), as in v 5 (see on 4:5). But the further allusion to Gen 15:6 in v 6 has already made clear that the faith *is* the righteousness, not merely a substitute for it (see on 4:6). As the devout Jew would see his covenant righteousness in terms of his faithfulness to the covenant (works of the law), so Paul sees the righteousness reckoned by God in terms of faith, the total dependence on and trust in God which Abraham exemplified (4:17–21).

For περιτομή and ἀκροβυστία as signifying people, the circumcised and the uncircumcised, respectively, see on 2:26. They are equivalent to Jew and Gentile, someone inside the law and someone outside the law (see on 2:12). It is significant that Paul does not pose the question with reference to Abraham as such yet; it is the circumcised and uncircumcised in general he has in view. The metonymy (part for the whole) is an excellent illustration of the social function of the ritual, as establishing and confirming the identity of a social group and marking out the boundary which separates it from other social groups (see further *Introduction* §§5.3.1, 5.3.3, and on 2:12 and 17). In particular it is a striking indication of the fact that the difference between Jew and Gentile could be summed up and focused in the one ritual act of circumcision, and underlines the importance of circumcision for Jewish self-understanding as epitomizing their distinctiveness as the people of God and the particular work of the law which brought that distinctiveness to clearest expression; cf. v 12: οἱ ἐκ περιτομῆς, those whose whole being and life, individually and collectively, is determined and characterized by the fact of their having been circumcised (see further on 2:25).

The καί should be noted. Paul does not pose the question as an either-or, either circumcised *or* uncircumcised. He accepts that the blessedness (of righteousness, forgiveness) comes to the circumcised. His question is whether it comes to the uncircumcised *as well.* Is it confined to the Jew as Jew, so that the Gentile can enter into it only by entering into the covenant people distinguished as such by their circumcision?

10 πῶς οὖν ἐλογίσθη; "how was it reckoned?" The sequence of questions in vv 9–10 brings the issue back to Abraham and focuses it on the circumstances of his particular case. The general question, "on the circumcised or also on the uncircumcised?" (v 9), is narrowed to the particular question, "on Abraham when he had already been circumcised, or while he was still uncircumcised?" The paradigmatic importance of Abraham's own relationship with God is underlined and would not be disputed by Paul's Jewish and God-worshiping readers (see on 4:2).

οὐκ ἐν περιτομῇ ἀλλ' ἐν ἀκροβυστίᾳ, "not in circumcision but in uncircumcision." Gen 15:6 precedes Gen 17 by several years (29 on Jewish reckoning—Str-B, 3:203)! The argument is more subtle than the equivalent argument in Gal 3 which similarly depended on the time gap between the promise to Abraham and the giving of the law (Gal 3:15–18). Since the issue in both cases was the law as focused in particular works, circumcision in particular,

the real question in this debate between Jews was whether or to what extent
the promise depended on circumcision. Since Paul is not arguing for an
either-or (4:9) all that his argument requires at this point is to demonstrate
that God had fully accepted Abraham while he was still uncircumcised.

11 καὶ σημεῖον ἔλαβεν περιτομῆς, "and he received the sign of circumcision."
The first clause of v 11 should not be taken as a parenthesis (against Barrett):
since vv 11b–12 speak of the double relationship in which Abraham stands,
to the circumcised who also believe and the uncircumcised who believe, it is
necessary in v 11a to explain the significance of (Abraham's) circumcision in
relation to (Abraham's) faith—he is father of the circumcised as one whose
own circumcision was the seal of his faith.

σημεῖον, "sign, distinguishing mark," by which something is known (BGD).
The phrase certainly means "a sign which is circumcision," "the symbolic
rite of circumcision" (NEB). Equally clearly Paul has in mind Gen 17:11 where
circumcision is described as the "sign of the covenant" (ἐν σημείῳ διαθήκης),
that is, the mark which distinguishes those who bear it as members of the
covenant (so also *Jub.* 15:26–28: circumcision the sign that the circumcised
"belongs to the children of the covenant," "that he is the Lord's," "the sign
of this covenant"). No Jew could miss the allusion (see further on 2:25).
Paul does not use the word "covenant" here. The passage is a clear indication,
however, that the covenant context of circumcision was integral to the complex
of ideas with which Paul was working (see also 1:17 on δικαιοσύνη). But it
indicates that he was also *re*-working them: circumcision not so much a direct
sign of the covenant, but a sign of the righteousness Abraham received through
faith—with the clear implication that this covenant righteousness did not
depend on circumcision but on faith (cf. Althaus; Berger, "Abraham," 67–
68; Hahn, "Gen 15:6," 103; Zeller). Note again the positive role Paul ascribes
to circumcision (see 2:25).

σφραγῖδα τῆς δικαιοσύνης τῆς πίστεως, "a seal of the righteousness of his
faith." The common element in the various uses of σφραγίς is the idea of
something which clearly attests or validates the authority of a claim or status
(see, e.g., MM, σφραγίζω, σφραγίς); but a distinction between "sign" (directed
to the outside world) and "seal" (directed to the believer; as in Leenhardt)
is unfounded—the seal also attests to others; elsewhere in the Paulines only
in 1 Cor 9:2 and 2 Tim 2:19; cf. particularly Rev 9:4 and the use of the
verb in Matt 27:66 (see also on 15:28). It is probable that Paul's description
of circumcision as a seal reflects an already established usage within contemporary Judaism; although the rabbinic parallels are later (Str-B, 4:32–33; Lagrange; *TDNT* 7:947, 949 n.85), there is also the testimony of *T. Job* 5.2 (a
sealing in the context of Job's change of name and rejection of idolatry, so
possibly modeled on the similar sequence of events associated with Abraham—
Jub. 12, 15) and *Barn.* 9.6. Moreover Paul seems able to assume the association
of ideas: circumcision of the heart (Deut 30:6) = the law written on the
heart (Jer 31:33) or the new heart and new spirit (Ezek 36:26; note particularly
Jub. 1.23), being seen as fulfilled in the gift of the Spirit (2 Cor 3:3, 6) =
the seal of the Spirit (2 Cor 1:22).

It is unlikely that either "seal" here or the use of the verb in 2 Cor 1:22,
Eph 1:13 and 4:30 should be taken as a reference to baptism as such (so,

e.g., Käsemann). As the preceding complex of ideas indicates, Paul saw the gift of the Spirit as the eschatological equivalent to or fulfillment of circumcision (so also the implication of 2:29 and the clear assertion of Phil 3:3). And the "circumcision without hands" (Col 2:11) should accordingly probably be seen as a reference to the Spirit too (cf. 2 Cor 5:1–5). The description of baptism as a seal first appears only in the second century (Herm. *Sim.* 8.6.3; 9.16.3ff.; *2 Clem.* 7.6; 8.6), but the earlier equation (seal = Spirit) is still reflected in *Gos. Thom.* 53 and *Odes Sol.* 11.1–3 (see also Dunn, *Baptism*, 133–34, 156–57).

τῆς δικαιοσύνης τῆς πίστεως, "of the righteousness of faith," is a further variation of the relation between faith and righteousness (cf. vv 3, 5, 6, 9), but obviously with the same meaning—the relationship has faith as its basis and expression on Abraham's side (similarly v 13). "Faith" now clearly emerges as the key word whose significance is being drawn out, as its prominence in the following εἰς τό clause makes clear (vv 11b, 12).

εἰς τὸ εἶναι αὐτὸν πατέρα πάντων τῶν πιστευόντων δι᾽ ἀκροβυστίας, "in order that he might be father of all who believe through uncircumcision." The first εἰς τό governs both v 11 and v 12, with the second εἰς τό clause (v 11c, see below) inserted to give emphasis to v 11b. V 12 should be regarded not simply as a kind of afterthought added to "soften" the "roughness" and "exaggeration" of v 11b (Käsemann); it is more likely that Paul's intention was to make a balanced statement from the first.

Paul expresses his point very deliberately. Judaism could readily embrace the thought of Abraham as the father of Gentiles, by virtue of their becoming proselytes (Str-B, 3:211). But Paul argues that Gen 15:6 shows Abraham to be father of the uncircumcised *in their uncircumcision*, so long as they share his *faith*. It is thus precisely his own distinction between faith and works of the law which he finds validated by Gen 15:6. The emphasis on *all*, which was a feature of the earlier stages of his letter (see particularly 1:5, 16; 2:10; 3:22), reemerges to be further emphasized in v 16 (see further Zeller, *Juden*, 101–5). δι᾽ ἀκροβυστίας; note the flexibility of διά (cf. 2:27; 3:30; 8:25; 14:20).

εἰς τὸ λογισθῆναι καὶ αὐτοῖς τὴν δικαιοσύνην, "that righteousness might be reckoned to them as well." The εἰς τό is final, and not merely consecutive (Lagrange, Michel, Barrett; against Cranfield, Käsemann, Wilckens): Paul regards it as part of God's purpose that he first accepted Abraham as beneficiary of his promise prior to requiring circumcision of Abraham, in order that it might be clear that God accepted the uncircumcised as uncircumcised. It is just this point which he wants to make (hence the addition of this clause to give the point emphasis); that God always intended to reckon righteousness to Gentiles without reference to whether they became proselytes and accepted the obligations (works) of the law.

12 καὶ πατέρα περιτομῆς τοῖς οὐκ ἐκ περιτομῆς μόνον ἀλλὰ καὶ τοῖς στοιχοῦσιν τοῖς ἴχνεσιν τῆς ἐν ἀκροβυστίᾳ πίστεως τοῦ πατρὸς ἡμῶν Ἀβραάμ, "and father of circumcision to those who are not only men of circumcision but who also follow in the footsteps of the faith of our father Abraham which he had in uncircumcision." As a grammatical construction the text speaks of two groups: "those who" and "those who" (τοῖς . . . τοῖς . . .—the problem is the second τοῖς, not the καί, as Wilckens implies; see *Notes*), Jews and Jewish Christians.

But the syntax is awkward on either construction: for two groups one would expect the order οὐ τοῖς. And the flow of the argument and the use of οὐ μόνον . . . ἀλλὰ καὶ . . . (Cranfield) show that Paul has in view simply the one group—the circumcised who believe (Swetnam offers the implausible solution that πατέρα περιτομῆς = "father of *spiritual* circumcision," unlikely in a repeated περιτομή/ἀκροβυστία antithesis [vv 11–12]). That is to say, Paul follows through the logic of his argument: Abraham's faith was the determinative factor in the giving and receiving of the promise, so that it is faith like Abraham's which determines Abraham's fatherhood and the sonship of Abraham.

The use of οὐ μόνον, ἀλλὰ καί, rather than οὐ(κ), ἀλλά is significant. Paul does not deny or wholly set aside Abraham's fatherhood of the Jewish people as such (cf. 4:1). Nor does he say "not circumcision," but "not only circumcision"; he accepts circumcision's continuing role as a mark of the Jewish people. Moreover, the order of the clauses (vv 11b–12), noncircumcised followed by circumcised, should not be counted as a rejection of Jewish salvation-history (against Klein, "Röm 4," 156; cf. Boers); the order simply follows the order of events in Abraham's case, and does not constitute a denial of Paul's emphasis elsewhere ("Jew first but also Greek"—see on 1:16). Käsemann's typically vigorous and valuable comments on the salvation-history perspective here should not be allowed to obscure the fact that Paul regards Abraham at this point as the antitype of the eschatological reality of faith, and, more important, that Paul sees the promise to Abraham as always having had the Gentiles in view from the first (vv 13–17).

It is possible, however, that Paul's wording here (not circumcision only, but also . . .) is also intended to defuse the counterargument that, whatever the significance of Gen 15:6 preceding Gen 17, the fact remains that Abraham went on to receive circumcision—so why not the same for Gentile believers now? Paul's reply in effect is that Abraham was circumcised in order to establish his fatherhood over the circumcised as well (or in particular), so long as that truth leaves the primary role of faith in both cases undisputed. This relative devaluation of circumcision in relation to faith can be paralleled from the prophets (see on 2:28–29). But Paul goes beyond this in pressing the logic of Abraham's antitype: if faith is more important than outward ritual, then righteousness depends primarily on faith rather than the outward ritual, and is accorded also to those who have the faith without the outward ritual. The true Jew is ἐν κρυπτῷ and circumcision is of the heart ἐν πνεύματι (2:29). Paul "wants and must hold fast the validity and binding character of the OT salvation-history, but at the same time he must get beyond that and still more overcome a Jewish narrowing, a religious nationalistic misunderstanding of this salvation-history" (Kuss, 186).

περιτομῆς . . . ἐκ περιτομῆς, "of circumcision . . . from circumcision." That Abraham's fatherhood and Jewish existence can be focused so simply on circumcision underlines again the importance of circumcision in defining Jewish identity (see on 2:25 and 4:9).

στοιχοῦσιν τοῖς ἴχνεσιν, "who follow in the footsteps"; cf. 2 Cor 12:8 and 1 Pet 2:21. The metaphor is more widely known (*m. Nid.* 4.2; Dit., *Syll.*³, 708.6), and may already have been used of Abraham in Jewish circles (cf. *Gen. Rab.* 40.12; cited in van der Minde, 100 n.112). στοιχέω originally meant "draw up in line," so "be in line with, hold to, follow" (BGD); ἴχνος, "footprint," "the trace left by someone's conduct or journey through life" (*TDNT* 3:402). Here again the implication is clear that faith is something active, which includes an element of obedience (see on 1:5—"the obedience of faith"). But at the same time the ground is cut from under those who see conduct (ethical and/or cultic) as something ("works of law") beyond the faith of uncircumcised Abraham (cf. Zeller).

13 οὐ γὰρ διὰ νόμου ἡ ἐπαγγελία τῷ Ἀβραάμ, "for the promise to Abraham was not through the law." ἐπαγγελία now comes into play as the dominant word over the next few verses (vv 13, 14, 16; also v 20; see *Form and Structure*). Paul's use of the word usually has the promise(s) to the patriarchs explicitly in view (so also 9:4, 8–9; 15:8; Gal 3:14–29; 4:23, 28; also Eph 2:12; 3:6; so too Acts 7:17; 13:32; 26:6; Heb 4:1; 6:12–17; etc.). It has no equivalent in Hebrew (hence its almost complete absence from the LXX of the OT), but in fact the sense "promise" for ἐπαγγελία only emerged into prominence in wider Greek usage in the second century B.C.E. anyway (particularly with Polybius; cf. LSJ, BGD). But even if the formal category (promise) appears only late on the scene, the fact that God had made such a commitment was a basic element in Israel's faith (see, e.g., Exod 32:13; 1 Chron 16:14–18; Neh 9:7–8; Ps 105:6–11; Sir 44:21; Wisd Sol 12:21; Pr Man 6; *T. Jos.* 20.1; as reflected also in Luke 1:72–73; see also on 9:4). What is striking is the way in which when the concept "promise" emerges it is subordinated to or its effects seen as mediated through the law; thus 2 Macc 2:17–18 speaks of God restoring the inheritance (κληρονομία) "as he promised through the law" (καθὼς ἐπηγγείλατο διὰ τοῦ νόμου), and *Pss. Sol.* 12.6 prays: "Let the Lord's pious ones inherit the promises of the Lord" (cf. *Sib. Or.* 3.768–69; *2 Apoc. Bar.* 14.12–13, quoted with wrong reference by Wilckens; 51:3). Whether Paul knows these specific passages we cannot tell, but he must certainly have been aware of such sentiments among his fellow Jews, since they are precisely what he denies: "not through the law"—the οὐ emphatic (the absence of the definite article before νόμου is no more significant here than elsewhere in Romans—so rightly Schlier; see particularly on 2:14). The traditional Jewish tie-in between promise and law created its own problems within the traditional Jewish framework as soon as Israel's failure to keep its part in the covenant was taken seriously—already in Deut 9:25–29, but especially after the disaster of A.D. 70 (*4 Ezra* 7.119–20). With Paul that problem does not arise because he denies its premise; the priority of the promise becomes a hermeneutical key for Paul (Maillot).

ἢ τῷ σπέρματι αὐτοῦ, "or to his seed." That the promise is also (ἢ here equivalent to καί—BDF, §446) to Abraham's seed (descendants) is regularly repeated in the Genesis narratives (Gen 12:7; 13:15–16; 15:5, 18; 17:7–8, 19; 22:17–18). Paul does not pursue the Christological interpretation of σπέρμα used in Gal 3:16, 19 (otherwise as a collective noun—4:16, 18; 9:7–8, 29; 11:1; 2 Cor 11:22; Gal 3:29), if only because he wants to focus attention on the "terms" by which the promise was given. He has already made it clear that he understands Abraham's "seed" to include "all who believe," and he reemphasizes the point in the positive clause answering to the οὐ διὰ νόμου—not through the law, but through the righteousness of faith (διὰ δικαιοσύνης πίστεως—see on 4:11). He does not dispute with his kinsfolk that the promise works out "through righteousness." His point is that Gen 15:6 shows the righteousness to be "of faith" (rather than "of works"), that is, that relationship with God which is lived out of and characterized by faith.

τὸ κληρονόμον αὐτὸν εἶναι κόσμου, "that he should be heir of the world." The idea of "inheritance" was a fundamental part of Jewish understanding of their covenant relationship with God, above all, indeed almost exclusively, in connection with the land (see Gen references above)—the land of Canaan theirs by right of inheritance as promised to Abraham (see further on 8:17; TDNT 3:769–75; Hester, *Inheritance*, 22–36; Davies, *Land*, pt. 1; in the NT see particularly Mark 12:7; Acts 7:5; and Heb 11:8–9). Already before Paul the concept had been broadened out from Canaan to embrace the whole earth (Sir 44:21; *Jub.* 17.3; 22.14; 32.19; *1 Enoch* 5.7; Philo, *Som.* 1.175; *Mos.* 1.155; cf. *4 Ezra* 6.59; *Ap. Const.* 8.12.23; rabbinic references in Str-B, 3:209; the world to come—*2 Apoc. Bar.* 14.13; 51.3). Our passage therefore is a good example of the extent to which Paul's own thinking reflects ideas which were widespread in other strands of Jewish theology at that time (cf. also Matt 5:5; Heb 1:2). Paul takes up the enlarged form of the promise, of course, not because it implies Israel's worldwide dominance, but presumably because it sets the narrower strand of salvation-history centering on Israel within the larger scheme of the creation: the blessing promised to Abraham and his seed (including "the nations") is the restoration of God's created order, of man to his Adamic status as steward of the rest of God's creation; over against a more nationalistic understanding of the promise, Paul's "interpretation of the promise is a-territorial," fulfilled "in Christ" (Davies, *Land*, 179). Elsewhere Paul places the concept within an eschatological framework, with the Spirit as the first installment and guarantee (see further on 8:17). As with other related covenantal terms—"promise" (Gal 3:14) and "seal" (see on 4:11)—Paul sees the eschatological fulfillment in terms of the Spirit given to faith.

ἀλλὰ διὰ δικαιοσύνης πίστεως, "but through the righteousness of faith"; see on 4:11.

14 εἰ γὰρ οἱ ἐκ νόμου κληρονόμοι, "for if those of the law are heirs." It is important to catch the connotation of the phrase οἱ ἐκ νόμου as clearly as possible, since it is evidently an important way of expressing the viewpoint which Paul here rejects. (1) The question Paul has in view is, "Who are the heirs of the promise to Abraham?" The answer he is in the process of rejecting is, "The circumcised as such" (vv 9–12): the heirs of Abraham = the seed of Abraham = the people of Israel (vv 13–17; see further on 4:13). That is to say, in the phrase οἱ ἐκ νόμου he has in view the typical Jewish attitude and self-understanding which he attacked in chap. 2 and again from 3:27: those who quite naturally saw their participation in the inheritance promised to Abraham as identical with their membership of the covenant people, the people of the law (Michel takes the phrase as equivalent to בְּנֵי הַתּוֹרָה, "sons of the Torah"). This specific social (or national) and salvation-history dimension to the phrase should be respected (*pace* SH, Murray). (2) They are ἐκ νόμου because their continuing existence as Jews arises out of the law; the law determines what is characteristic and distinctive in all they are and do as

God's people (see further *Introduction* §5.3 and on 6:14). The phrase is thus also an abbreviated form of the fuller phrase οἱ ἐξ ἔργων νόμου, since the "works" are what the law was seen to require of "the Jew," with the work of circumcision in particular focusing the distinctiveness of the people of the law (see on 3:20). Both phrases are misunderstood therefore if they are taken to denote individuals who hope to attain entry into the heirs of the promise, or to turn a basic unacceptability to God into an acceptability to God by virtue of their "works" (contrast, e.g., Schmidt; Cranfield; Hübner; *Law*, 121–22; despite his objection to this view [*Law*, 34], Sanders in fact gives it support by pressing his distinction between "getting in" and "staying in": "works of the law" have to do with "entry"—*Law*, 105, 147; NEB's "those who hold by the law" runs the same danger). See further on 4:16.

κεκένωται ἡ πίστις, "faith is rendered invalid." κενόω, "make empty," can have the stronger sense of "destroy, render void, of no effect" (BGD). In the NT it is an exclusively Pauline term (1 Cor 1:17; 9:15; 2 Cor 9:3; Phil 2:7). πίστις has the definite article here ("the faith") as harking back specifically to Abraham's faith. The reference to Gen 15:6 is clear. If the law becomes a determinative factor, then Abraham's acceptance of the promise has become and remains (perfect tense) invalid and meaningless.

καὶ κατήργηται ἡ ἐπαγγελία, "and the promise is nullified." For καταργέω see on 6:6. Paul's point is not dependent on a pedantic definition of "promise"—that a promise must be unconditional otherwise it is not a promise (cf. Barrett). Such an argument would immediately be vulnerable to the rejoinder that the promise was given on several occasions, and usually attached to some command (Gen 12:1–3; 17:1–14; 22:15–18; note even 15:7–11). And in v 16 Paul himself makes the κατὰ χάριν a consequence of the διὰ πίστεως not of ἐκ ἐπαγγελίας. Nor does Paul's point depend on the hidden premise that the law cannot be kept (as Althaus, Zeller), which again misses the ethnic force of the οἱ ἐκ νόμου (see also above). His point again depends solely on the fact that, according to Gen 15:6, Abraham's faith was a complete and satisfactory response to the promise (otherwise Abraham would not have been "reckoned righteous"). Hence to ask more than the faith of Gen 15:6 is to nullify the promise of Gen 15:5.

15   ὁ γὰρ νόμος ὀργὴν κατεργάζεται, "for the law brings about wrath." Having denied that the law has a role in determining who are to be regarded as the heirs of the promise, Paul meets an obvious objection: What then is the role of the law? His thought probably follows the same progression as in Gal 3:18–19. His answer is to link the Torah with God's wrath rather than to God's promise—the tense implying that Paul had in mind the outworking of God's ὀργή in 1:18–32 rather than his final judgment as in 2:5, 8 (see on 1:18 and 2:5). It is clearly an antithetical or polemical assertion: against those who saw the law as a source of life (as in 2 *Apoc. Bar.* 38; see also on 7:10), Paul asserts that the function of the law in bringing God's wrath to effect and in convicting of sin (v 15b) is sufficient explanation of its role in relation to the promise.

Exegesis must respect the narrowness of the front on which Paul argues here. (1) It is possible that he had in mind some general legal maxim (*nulla poena sine lege*; cf. also Str-B, 3:210–11). But it is the Torah as such that he refers to. The degree to which he universalizes the role of the Torah in describing it as the executor of the wrath of 1:18–32 would cause no surprise to a readership which was familiar with the identification between cosmic Wisdom and the Torah (see on 10:6–8)—the law as the concrete embodiment of God's moral ordering of creation as a whole (cf. also 2:12–16). (2) Since the role ascribed to the law here is specifically antithetical to its more traditional role (as defining and marking out the covenant people of promise, and its obligations [works] as the means of maintaining covenant status), the assertion of v 15a should not be regarded as a complete description of the function of the law. Outside the framework of this particular discussion Paul has no hesitation in affirming further and positive roles for the law (as in 8:4 and 13:8–10). Within the framework of the discussion in chap. 4 Paul's point is that the function of the law was not to determine the scope of the promise but to bring those under the law to consciousness of their transgression and therefore to the same unconditional dependence and reliance on God which man in general had abandoned (1:19–25) and which Abraham displayed so clearly. Rightly understood, the law does not mark off Jew from Gentile but rather puts Jew alongside Gentile in need of the grace of God.

οὗ δὲ οὐκ ἔστιν νόμος οὐδὲ παράβασις, "where there is no law there is also no transgression"; "where there is no law there can be no breach of law" (NEB). The clause can function as either a coordinate ("and") or a sequential reason ("for"); see *Notes*. Either way the clause serves as an explanation of how the process of wrath works out. It is not simply the disobedient or selfish *act* which corrupts, but even more the act as *disobedient*, as the deliberate choice to live for oneself out of one's own resources in willful forgetfulness (or denial) of one's creatureliness (1:18–32). With the law making God's will so much more fully explicit than it had been to Adam in the beginning, the appropriate response of the people of the law should not be pride in possession of the law but the greater consciousness of transgression and so of their dependence on grace—a dependence no different from that of "Gentile" Abraham. See further on 3:20 and 5:13. This definition of a role for the law would not necessarily be offensive to Jewish ears (as Schlier suggests; cf., e.g., Lev 26); the offense comes in 5:20 and 7:5, as Paul's own response to his argument at these points makes clear (6:1ff.; 7:7 ff.).

16 διὰ τοῦτο ἐκ πίστεως, ἵνα κατὰ χάριν, "therefore it is from faith, in order that it might be in terms of grace." The διὰ τοῦτο may refer backward ("wherefore"—because the law could not serve as a medium of the promise, as demonstrated by the restrictiveness of the Jewish understanding of it and by their failure to respond adequately to its wrath-working function), or forward ("for this reason"—"that it might be in terms of grace"), or indeed both (see further Cranfield). The unstated subject is most likely the subject of the paragraph (ἡ ἐπαγγελία) which Paul leaves out here in order to avoid unnecessary repetition.

As already made clear in vv 4–5, the interlocking correlatives are ἐκ πίστεως and κατὰ χάριν: God's gracious outreach to man is of such a character that it can only be received in unconditional openness. Whatever restricts or obscures that openness, and the character of faith as sheer receptivity and dependence on God, denies and restricts that grace. The ἐκ πίστεως is formed to provide a parallel with ἐκ νόμου (see below), but διὰ πίστεως would have done as well (cf. 3:30; 4:13). To the negative trio of v 15 (law, transgression, wrath) corresponds the positive trio of v 16 (promise, faith, grace—Michel).

εἰς τὸ εἶναι βεβαίαν τὴν ἐπαγγελίαν παντὶ τῷ σπέρματι, "in order that the promise might be certain to all the seed." The construction is again final and not merely consecutive (against Käsemann). As in Gal 3, Paul's argument is controlled by the conviction that God's promise to Abraham always had the nations as a whole in view (and not just Israel). It is because most of his Jewish contemporaries took the promise in a nationally restrictive way and because the law served to focus and embody that restrictiveness that he insists so vehemently that the only two correlatives allowed by Gen 15:6 are grace and faith. God reckoned Abraham righteous solely on the grounds of his faith in order that the promise to which Abraham thus responded might be dependent on no other grounds. βέβαιος would probably be familiar in a technical sense to denote legally guaranteed security (MM). In the figurative sense of "reliable, dependable, certain" it was quite often used to describe faith (BGD); here it is intended as the antithesis to the κατήργηται of v 14 (Schmidt, Wilckens). As the phrasing makes clear, the stress comes on the final words of the clause—"all the seed" (against Cranfield).

οὐ τῷ ἐκ τοῦ νόμου μόνον ἀλλὰ καὶ τῷ ἐκ πίστεως Ἀβραάμ, "not to the one who is of the law only but also to the one who is of the faith of Abraham." For the οὐ μόνον . . . ἀλλὰ καί cf. 4:12. But this time Paul envisages the promise extending to the one who is ἐκ τοῦ νόμου without the qualification that he also shares Abraham's faith (v 12). Paul accepts that the promise to the seed of Abraham must have the Jewish people in view (cf. Rom 11), whoever else is included within its sweep, and whatever qualifications he might insert in a more careful statement of his position (v 12). Even if he has the Jewish *Christian* as such in view ("us all"—v 16d; cf. particularly Käsemann), it is the fact of the Jewish Christian's being a Jew on which he lights here. The fact that he can so write confirms the national reference in Paul's use of the phrase οἱ/ὁ ἐκ τοῦ νόμου (see on 4:14). It is because it has this reference to a member of the Jewish people that Paul can say "not *only*." Had he used it to refer to those who sought to lay claim on God by the merit of self-achievement he would have had to say "not" in outright denial. Despite the ethnic restrictiveness of the typical Jewish understanding of the law, it was wholly possible for him to speak of the promise as being given to the Jew(s), in a way which he could not have said it was given to the one who boasted of his self-achievement. By missing these nuances Cranfield (cf. van Dülmen, 94) is led into an increasingly strained line of exegesis (so too Zeller). For ὁ ἐκ πίστεως see on 3:26; against Gaston's rendering of πίστις here as "the faithfulness of Abraham," see on 3:30.

ὅς ἐστιν πατὴρ πάντων ἡμῶν, "who is father of us all." This is the third time Paul insists on Abraham's common ancestry of his readers, or of believers in general (vv 1, 11–12, 16–18). As in v 11 and earlier in v 16, the "all" is emphatic, as also earlier in the letter (see on 1:16 and 3:22). It is aimed polemically, as in vv 11–12, against those who assume that Abraham is father only of the Jews (see further on 4:1 and 11). The reiteration of the theme ties in the immediately preceding point to the earlier stage of the argument (vv 9–12), and with the following scriptural quotation rounds off the present stage of the argument (vv 13–17a).

17 καθὼς γέγραπται, "as it is written"; see on 1:17.

πατέρα πολλῶν ἐθνῶν τέθεικά σε, "I have made you father of many nations." That ἔθνη means not only "nations" but "Gentiles" (in contrast to Jews!—as in 3:29; see on 1:5) is of course part of Paul's argument, but at the implicit rather than explicit level. The quotation is verbatim from the LXX of Gen 17:5. Paul does not hesitate to draw his scriptural authority from a passage *later* than Gen 15, indeed from the very passage (Gen 17) on which the traditional Jewish argument about the necessity for circumcision as the sign of the covenant (Gen 17:11) was based (whereas in Gal 3:8 he had used Gen 12:3 and 18:18). Paul thus shows his awareness of the (likely) rationale of the argument he here opposes—that the various formulations of the promise to Abraham are interconnected (see on 4:14), with the corollary that Gen 15:6 cannot be separated from Gen 17 (as Paul had just argued—4:10). On this viewpoint the "many nations" would presumably include proselytes, or along the lines of v 13 ("heir of the world") would look to the hegemony of Abraham's seed over the other nations (as particularly in Sir 44:19–21; see further on 4:13), including presumably enforced circumcision as in the case of the conversion of the Idumeans and Itureans in the preceding two centuries (see on 2:25). By thus drawing in Gen 17, Paul of course has no intention of conceding his opponents' case. On the contrary, he probably intended the perfect tense of the verb (τέθεικα) to have its full force, signifying a status and fulfillment already established and operative before the issue of circumcision arose, with the "many nations" referring to the rapidly growing Gentile mission. See further on 4:18.

κατέναντι οὗ ἐπίστευσεν θεοῦ, "before God in whom he believed" = κατέναντι τοῦ θεοῦ ᾧ ἐπίστευσεν. For the attraction of the relative see BDF, §294, particularly (2). For parallels to the use of κατέναντι, "in the sight of, before," see BGD, 2b. Paul's formulation here may possibly be derived from the Hebrew לְפָנַי, "in front of, in the presence of," which occurs in Gen 17:1 (Wilckens; cf. also Str-B, 3:212). But of course Paul has in mind the specific exercise of faith (aorist) described in Gen 15:6.

τοῦ ζῳοποιοῦντος τοὺς νεκρούς, "who gives life to the dead." The language clearly speaks of God's power to resurrect the dead. Similar language is used in the second of the Eighteen Benedictions: "you make the dead alive" (cf. Ps 71 [LXX 70]:20; Tob 13:2; Wisd Sol 16:13; *Jos. As.* 20.7; *T. Gad* 4.6); Paul's use of ζῳοποιεῖν in 8:11 has the resurrection of believers in view (so also 1 Cor 15:22, 36, 45; and outside Paul, John 5:21; 1 Pet 3:18); and his thought here almost certainly already looks to the resurrection of Jesus with which his midrash reaches its conclusion (vv 24–25). In view of Heb 11:19, an allusion to Gen 22:1–14 cannot be ruled out (Barrett). But Paul also has more immediately in view the deadness of Abraham's body and of Sarah's womb (v 19), and so presumably also the broader usage of ζῳοποιεῖν where it can denote God's creative, sustaining (keeping alive) or renewing power (cf. Neh 9:6; Job 36:6; Eccl 7:12; *Jos. As.* 8.9; John 6:63; 2 Cor 3:6; Gal 3:21). Either way it is the creative power of God to which reference is made:

the impartation of life understood as a miracle attributed directly to God—God characterized precisely as the one whose power brings this miracle about. And if it is God's resurrecting power which is to the forefront of Paul's thought, that is because it is the same power bringing about the final act of creation which is of a piece with the first. In view of the spread of parallels cited above it may be fair to conclude that Paul here echoes familiar theological or liturgical language.

καλοῦντος τὰ μὴ ὄντα ὡς ὄντα, "who calls things that have no existence into existence." καλέω here has the strong sense of an effectual summons (see further on 1:1 and BGD, 2), and the use of ὡς to express a consequence ("call things that are not so that they are") is well attested elsewhere (LSJ B.3; in the parallel of Philo, *Jos.* 126, though verbally close, the ὡς has more the sense "as though," which NIV uses here giving too weak a sense—"as though they were"; the closer parallel in fact is Philo's more regular formula τὰ μὴ ὄντα . . . εἰς τὸ εἶναι—see below). Both elements of the formulation are firmly rooted in Jewish thought: the idea of God's act of creation as an effective "calling" (Isa 41:4; 48:13; Wisd Sol 11:25; Philo, *Spec. Leg.* 4.187; 2 *Apoc. Bar.* 21.4; *Jos. As.* 8.9) and the belief that God created "out of nothing," *creatio ex nihilo* (2 Macc 7:28; *Jos. As.* 12.2; 2 *Apoc. Bar.* 21.4; 48.8; 2 *Enoch* 24.2; *Ap. Const.* 8.12.7)—a particular feature of Philo's theology, for whom God is τὸ ὄν who brings non-being into being (*Opif.* 81; *Leg. All.* 3.10; *Migr.* 183; *Heres* 36; *Mut.* 46; *Som.* 1.76; *Mos.* 2.100, 267; note especially *Spec. Leg.* 4.187—τὰ μὴ ὄντα ἐκάλεσεν εἰς τὸ εἶναι). As with the preceding phrase, Paul is obviously drawing on language which was well established in Jewish theological reflection, particularly in Hellenistic Jewish circles. Noteworthy is the parallel to the complete formulation in *Jos. As.* 8.9 (. . . θεός ὁ ζωοποιήσας τὰ πάντα καὶ καλέσας . . . ἀπὸ τοῦ θανάτου εἰς τὴν ζωήν). See further Moxnes, 241–47.

Paul thus turns his back on any dualistic tendency which would set creation and salvation in antithesis: God's redemptive purpose through Abraham expresses the same power which created being out of non-being. Although Paul uses language elsewhere which later Gnostic systems could take up, he provides here a statement of principle which sets him clearly apart from these later systems (it was not simply for Paul's use of the OT here that Marcion omitted chap. 4). That he can link God's reckoning Abraham righteous with his giving life to that which does not exist confirms the close link between God's righteousness and his power as Creator (Stuhlmacher, *Gerechtigkeit,* 227; more cautiously Moxnes, 105) and shows how radically Paul understood man's creatureliness before God (see further Käsemann; and on 4:20). It may not be accidental that in contrast, *T. Gad* 4.6–7 depicts the love which "wants to bring the dead back to life" as working "by the law of God . . . for the salvation of mankind." It is characteristic of Paul that he sees God's saving as well as his creating power working immediately and directly on man (Gal 3:19–22).

18 ὃς παρ' ἐλπίδα ἐπ' ἐλπίδι ἐπίστευσεν, "who against hope, in hope believed." Hays, "Rom 4:1," 90 n.44, notes that this ὃς clause, followed by a proof text, parallels the similar construction of vv 16d–17. The second use of ἐπίστευσεν in two verses, echoing the ἐπίστευσεν of Gen 15:6, focuses attention on the nature of Abraham's faith itself, as the exposition moves into its final stage. Both prepositional forms with ἐλπίς would be familiar to Greek speakers (BGD, ἐλπίς 1 and 2a; for παρ' ἐλπίδα in Philo see Moxnes, 152 n.111). The verbal play on the idea of hope would be pleasing to the ear, and though the content of the contrast is not explicit, the contrast itself makes the point sufficiently clear. "Against, contrary to" (see BGD, παρά III.6) what man can hope for as humanly possible, Abraham's faith was characterized by (or based on) a hope which was determined solely by the promise of God. It may be that a further dimension to the contrast is that between ἐλπίς in its classic Greek sense and ἐλπίς as experienced within the Jewish tradition. For in classical thought the uncertainty of the future is fundamental to the concept of ἐλπίς, which regularly means simply "expectation," with ἐλπίζω often used in the sense of fearing evil (see LSJ; TDNT 2:519–20). In the OT, however, hope is something different from fear, hope as expectation of good. It is thus closely allied to trust, trustful hope, hope as confidence in God (see documentation in TDNT 2:521–23); Lagrange appositely cites Sir 49:10. We can therefore say that Paul here plays the Hebrew concept of hope off against the Greek: against a hope characterized by uncertainty and fear of the unknown future, Abraham's faith was a firm confidence in God as the one who determines the future according to what he has promised. The word plays an important role in the letter (5:2, 4–5; 8:20, 24; 12:12; 15:4, 13); see further on 5:4.

εἰς τὸ γενέσθαι αὐτόν, "in order that he might become." The εἰς τό with the infinitive hardly goes with the ἐπίστευσεν to describe the content of Abraham's hope (against TDNT 6:206; Kuss), and the construction is again (as in v 16) better taken as final rather than consecutive (SH; against Käsemann, Cranfield, Schlier). The perspective is that of God's purpose: God acted as he did (Gen 15:6) precisely with a view to determining the way in which Abraham's fatherhood of "many nations" would come about—that is, by faith.

πατέρα πολλῶν ἐθνῶν κατὰ τὸ εἰρημένον, "father of many nations (Gen 17:5), in accordance with what had been said"; then follows a verbatim quotation from the LXX of Gen 15:5: οὕτως ἔσται τὸ σπέρμα σου, "so shall your seed be." By relating Gen 17:5 back to Gen 15:5 Paul again shows his awareness of how his opposition would argue, by interpreting Gen 15:5–6 in the light of the subsequent formulations of the promise where conditions are attached (Gen 17) or faithfulness presupposed (Gen 22). Paul here therefore insists that the meaning of the later formulation (Gen 17:5) has to be determined in accordance with (κατά) the earlier (Gen 15:5), where its acceptance by Abraham is related and his consequent status before God clearly expressed (Gen 15:6). Cf. Philo's argument in Mut. 177–78 that Gen 17:17 has to be understood in the light of Gen 15:6. See also on 4:17. κατὰ τὸ εἰρημένον: so also Luke 2:24; cf. Acts 2:16 and 13:40 (see further BGD, εἶπον 4). For σπέρμα see on 4:13.

19 καὶ μὴ ἀσθενήσας τῇ πίστει κατενόησεν τὸ ἑαυτοῦ σῶμα ἤδη νενεκρωμένον, ἑκατονταετής που ὑπάρχων, καὶ τὴν νέκρωσιν τῆς μήτρας Σάρρας, "and not weakening in faith he considered his own body already dead, being about one hundred years old, and the deadness of Sarah's womb." The sense revolves round the juxtaposition of μὴ ἀσθενήσας, "not weakening (in faith)," and κατενόησεν, "he considered, contemplated (his own body already dead)," "he faced the fact that" (NIV). For ἀσθενέω used figuratively of religious or moral weakness (in the NT only in Paul), cf. 14:1–2; 14:21 *v.1.;* 1 Cor 8:11–12; 2 Cor 11:29. For the reading of κατενόησεν without the negative, see *Notes;* and for the sense see BGD, κατανόεω 2 (only here in Paul). The point of this section of the argument begins to become clear: faith is strong precisely because it looks solely to God and does not depend on human possibilities (Nygren). It is not that faith ignores or denies the historical realities (as the reading with οὐ would imply); rather, says Paul, Abraham took them fully into account (thinking presumably of Gen 17:17); that is why his faith can be called strong (cf. Schlier). By implication faith is weak when it allows itself to be determined by or depend upon what lies within human power. By implication too the insistence on making faith depend in any degree on what man can do (works of the law) is not the faith of Abraham. The uses of νεκρόω and νέκρωσις here are paralleled by Deissmann, *Light,* 97 n.1 (σῶμα τὸ νενεκρωμένον, "body now dead"; cf. also Heb 11:12) and 98 n.3 (cf. 2 Cor 4:10). Paul clearly intends to recall the description of God as ὁ ζῳοποιῶν τοὺς νεκρούς (v 17). Abraham's age ("approximately a hundred years old") is derived from Gen 17:1, 17 and 21:5. His later ability to father children (Gen 25:1–2) is not in view; had Paul been asked he would either have answered that Abraham's being made alive from the dead continued to have effect after Sarah's death, or more likely that his argument concerned only the seed of promise.

20 εἰς δὲ τὴν ἐπαγγελίαν τοῦ θεοῦ οὐ διεκρίθη τῇ ἀπιστίᾳ ἀλλ᾽ ἐνεδυναμώθη τῇ πίστει, δοὺς δόξαν τῷ θεῷ, "he did not doubt the promise of God in unbelief, but was strengthened in faith, giving glory to God." Once again Paul seeks to bring out the character of Abraham's faith by posing a contrast (the development from v 19 is that of Paul's exposition, not of Abraham's faith—Michel). Here it is a double contrast. First the negative. (1) Abraham's faith did not waver or doubt with reference to the promise of God—διακρίνεσθαι in the sense "be at odds with oneself, hesitate, doubt," appears first in the NT (BGD, 2b, SH); elsewhere in Paul in this sense only in 14:23 (see on 14:23); J. R. Mantey, "The Causal Use of ΕΙΣ in the New Testament," *JBL* 70 (1951) 45–48, notes the possibility of reading the εἰς with causal force, "because of." Faith means accepting and trusting God's promise. (2) Faith is the opposite of ἀπιστία, which here clearly cannot mean "unfaithfulness" in the observance of the law, but must mean failure to accept God's promise as to its scope (the many nations) and its terms (faith). In that sense ἀπιστία can be described as the refusal of faith, the renunciation of God's promise (Michel); see further on 3:3.

Second, the positive side of the double contrast. (1) ἐνεδυναμώθη τῇ πίστει, "he was strengthened in faith." The contrast with (1) above is immediate. The passive may well be a divine passive, "was strengthened by God" (Cranfield, Wilckens); otherwise "became or grew strong" (BGD, RSV, NEB, Schlier; cf. Eph 6:10 and 2 Tim 2:1). τῇ πίστει could mean either "with respect to (his) faith" (cf. BDF §197), or possibly "by means of faith" (cf. Heb 11:11). The ambiguity should not be allowed to become a theological one, since it is faith as complete trust in God which Paul has in mind, and whether it is the faith which was strengthened or which was the means of strengthening, the point is the same: Abraham's reliance on God became stronger (NJB's "drew strength from faith," however, moves too far from the sense intended by Paul). Paul takes for granted that faith is not a fixed packet but can grow strong and grow weak (see on 4:19). (2) δοὺς δόξαν τῷ θεῷ, "giving glory to God." Note the contrast with 1:21—γνόντες τὸν θεὸν οὐχ ὡς θεὸν ἐδόξασαν; Abraham did what man failed to do in the primal sin (see on 1:21). The phrase is familiar in biblical Greek (see Cranfield's examples), but here it functions as a further description of πίστις and as the opposite of ἀπιστία (see (2) above): faith as the proper response of the creature to his Creator; unfaith as the denial of creaturely dependence on God. As in v 17 the implied broadening of the perspective to the full sweep of human history will be deliberate. In characterizing Abraham's faith here as "strenuous human response" and therefore as incompatible with the view that for Paul salvation is by grace alone, Watson (*Paul*, 140) ignores the clear thrust of Paul's argument—faith as unqualified trust in God (cf. Hultgren, *Gospel*, 39–40).

21 καὶ πληροφορηθεὶς ὅτι ὃ ἐπήγγελται, "and being fully convinced that what he had promised." πληροφορεῖσθαι, "be fully convinced, wholly certain," is a late compound, used in the LXX only at Eccl 8:11 (see *TDNT* 6:309– 10). Note the same sense in 14:5, and the use of the noun in Col 2:2, 1 Thess 1:5; Heb 6:11; and 10:22 (πληροφορία πίστεως). On ἐπήγγελται, "has been promised," or "he has promised," see Lightfoot.

δυνατός ἐστιν καὶ ποιῆσαι, "he is able also to do." The point is drawn from Gen 18:14 (μὴ ἀδυνατεῖ παρὰ τῷ θεῷ ῥῆμα; the Lord's response to Sarah's laughter) and ignores Abraham's own similar response in Gen 17:17 (though see above on 4:19). Here too, however, as in v 17, Paul is not formulating a fresh line of theological reflection, but drawing on an already well established theme of Jewish theology with, once again, Philo's confidence in God's power to do all things providing the nearest parallels (*Som.* 2.136; *Jos.* 244; *Spec. Leg.* 1.282), not least with reference to the same episode in Genesis (*Abr.* 112; note also 175; *Qu. Gen.* 3.2, 56); see further Moxnes, 146–55, and add *Ap. Const.* 7.35.7. Within the NT cf. particularly Heb 11:19. Paul appeals to God's all-powerfulness elsewhere in Romans (9:22; 11:23 q.v.), as did Jesus himself according to Mark 10:27 pars., 14:36. See further on 1:16 and 1:20. The formulation here "underlines the fact that Abraham's faith was faith in the God who had promised, not merely in what had been promised" (Cranfield; similarly Leenhardt). See also Heil, *Hope*, 33.

22 διὸ (καὶ) ἐλογίσθη αὐτῷ εἰς δικαιοσύνην, "therefore it was reckoned to him for righteousness." διὸ καί denotes that the inference is self evident (cf. Luke 1:35; Acts 10:29; 24:26; Rom 15:22; 2 Cor 1:20; 5:9); but διό alone still has the force of a conclusion drawn from what has preceded (BGD). This then is the conclusion to the preceding exposition as a whole; the second exact quotation from Gen 15:6 forming a frame with v 3 in which the intervening exposition is set. The exposition has demonstrated that what was reckoned to Abraham was Abraham's believing, the "faith," whose circumstances (vv 9–12), object (vv 13–17) and nature (vv 17–21) had been clarified in vv 9– 21. See further on 4:3 and *Form and Structure*. Dodd's strictures on the remoteness of Paul's discussion here for modern use of his theology completely underestimates the importance of vv 5b, 17b, and 22b in particular as fundamental theological assertions about God (Moxnes, 105).

23–24 οὐκ ἐγράφη δὲ δι᾽ αὐτὸν μόνον ὅτι ἐλογίσθη αὐτῷ, ἀλλὰ καὶ δι᾽ ἡμᾶς, "it
was not written for his sake alone that 'it was reckoned to him,' but also for
ours"—the third use of the "not only . . . but also" construction in chap. 4
(vv 12, 16; also 5:3, 11). Paul's appeal to Abraham as a pattern and type for
his heirs would be quite acceptable to Jewish(-Christian) ears (see on 4:2).
He is able to focus the type in one verse (Gen 15:6), not least because that
was a focal point of the wider Jewish reflection on Abraham as well (see on
4:2 and 4:3). But he is able to invest the verse with such significance because
its distinctive association of πίστις and δικαιοσύνη in the case of Abraham gave
it an archetypal significance for clarifying the meaning and relation of these
concepts and of the reality they expressed in Paul's own day; and because
the promise which drew forth Abraham's faith and resulted in his righteousness
concerned the scope of his fatherhood ("many nations"—hence the counterpoint theme of Abraham as father; see *Form and Structure*). Thus although
he reads the scriptural passage in the light of his faith in Christ (Goppelt,
Typos, 136), his choice of text is not arbitrary, nor does he force upon it a
meaning strange to it or difficult for it to bear. For the same reason Goppelt's
assertion that "Paul views Abraham in a basically different way than Judaism
does" (*Typos*, 224) must be severely qualified. Of course Paul's interpretation
called in question one of Judaism's hermeneutical presuppositions, but otherwise it was entirely proper in terms of current hermeneutical rubrics and
must have had compelling force for many Jews and God-worshipers involved
in a self-critical reappraisal of their own inherited beliefs.

The theory of scripture involved here (ἐγράφη) has two important features.
(1) It was written "for our sake" (the "our" including Gentiles as well as
Jews as Abraham's seed—vv 11–12, 16–17). This is not a belief in the timeless-
ness of a scriptural statement so that it can be related to any time and every
circumstance: the links between the text and Paul's context are specific (as
we have just seen); and the broader principle involved is that of eschatological
equivalence—what happened in the formative period of Israel and the covenant foreshadowing and prefiguring the full(er) reality of the end time (cf.
15:4; 1 Cor 9:10, and particularly 10:11). (2) It was written for *Abraham's*
sake. This could mean simply that the writing of Gen 15:6 preserved the
memory of Abraham and so benefited him that way (cf. Sir 44:10–15). But
if Paul's chief thought is of the historical actuality which Gen 15:6 records
(that Abraham was benefited by being reckoned righteous), and if the ἐγράφη
is not determined wholly by the "for us," then it may imply that Paul saw
scripture as somehow embodying the historical event—scripture being more
than merely a record of or witness to something other than itself. That may
be reading too much into the text, but certainly the οὐ μόνον should be given
due weight. This two-sided character of Paul's hermeneutic should be noted
and distinguishes what can properly be called typological interpretation from
that of promise-fulfillment or allegory (see further Goppelt, all three terms
in bibliog.; Käsemann; also Wilckens 1:284–85).

24 οἷς μέλλει λογίζεσθαι, "to whom it is to be reckoned." Commentators
are divided as to whether the phrase should be taken as having (1) present
or (2) future reference. (1) μέλλω can denote an action which necessarily
follows from divine purpose or decree, "must, is certainly to be" (BGD, 1.c.δ);

and the presumption is that the λογίζεσθαι takes place in "our" case as in Abraham's—there and then on believing; cf. 5:1 (so Cranfield, and Wilckens with further bibliog.). (2) The future eschatological reference (to final judgment) fits better with Paul's use of μέλλω in 8:13, 18, and accords with the future reference of δικαιόω already noted several times (2:13; 3:20, 30); so Schlatter, Barrett, Michel, Käsemann, Schlier. At the very least Paul's language probably reflects the fact that he saw God's reckoning righteous as not merely an initial acceptance but as an acceptance which looked to the final judgment and the need for a continued sustaining in the time between (see on 1:17 and 2:13); cf. the description of "believers" (present tense) below.

τοῖς πιστεύουσιν ἐπί, "who believe in." The subject of ἐλογίσθη in vv 22 and 23 was not stated, though it was quite clear (Abraham's believing). But by leaving it unstated Paul makes the τοῖς πιστεύουσιν all the more effective: the listener/reader is forced to reflect that since it was Abraham's believing which was so reckoned, then obviously the paradigm he provides is for believers; by thus requiring the reader to draw the obvious deduction from the unstated logic Paul makes it part of the reader's own thought. For the use of πιστεύω in the present tense see on 1:16. πιστεύειν ἐπί can be taken as a stronger form of πιστεύειν with the dative (see on 4:5), denoting a trusting acceptance which has the force of personal commitment to the object of the ἐπί (cf. particularly Acts 9:42; 11:17; 16:31; 22:19). Paul's seeming preference for it in Romans (4:5, 24; 9:33; 10:11), instead of the elsewhere more common πιστεύειν εἰς, perhaps suggests that the influence of Isa 28:16 which determines the form in 9:33 and 10:11 has already affected Paul's formulation in chap. 4; a construction after the analogy of ἐλπίζειν ἐπί (TDNT 6:211 n.273) is less likely.

τὸν ἐγείραντα Ἰησοῦν τὸν κύριον ἡμῶν ἐκ νεκρῶν, "who raised Jesus our Lord from the dead." Paul falls naturally into the rhythm of a familiar formulation. "God raised him from the dead" was evidently one of the earliest credal-type affirmations of the first Christians (cf. Acts 3:15; 4:10; 13:30; Rom 7:4; 8:11; 10:9; 1 Cor 15:12, 20; Gal 1:1; Eph 1:20; Col 2:12; 1 Thess 1:10; 1 Pet 1:21; see particularly Kramer, Christ, 20–26). For the use of "Jesus" (rather than Jesus Christ) in the formula, cf. 8:11, 10:9, and 1 Thess 1:10. The less usual κύριος is paralleled in 1 Cor 6:14 and 2 Cor 4:14, and may be explained at least partly by the fact that Paul tends to use fuller Christological titles in closing passages (Kramer, 25). The distinctive features of the formulation here result from Paul's concern to adapt his language to the immediate context: faith as directed to God (rather than the normal Christian talk of faith in Christ—see TDNT 6:210–12), thus bringing out more explicitly the parallel with Abraham's faith; and the use of ἐκ νεκρῶν, in accordance with the regular formulation (though not in 1 Cor 6:14; 2 Cor 4:14), but here clearly to bring out the parallel with vv 17 and 19 and so the degree of similarity with Abraham's faith. So far as providing an occasion for faith is concerned, God's ζωοποίησαι of Jesus (ζωοποιεῖν can be used as a synonym for ἐγείρειν—cf. particularly John 5:21; Rom 8:11; 1 Pet 3:18) is the eschatological counterpart of his ζωοποίησαι in Sarah's womb, both paradigmatic expressions of God's creative power. In salvation-history terms both are literally epoch-creating events. In arguing that the "us" are involved vicariously in God's reckoning of righteousness ("vicariously, because we are Abraham's seed"), Hays ignores the more obvious typological paralleling ("Rom 4:1," 94).

The significance of Paul's formulation here for theo-christology should not go unnoticed. (1) Christian faith can be described as faith in God equally as faith in Christ, but faith in God by virtue of what he has done in reference to Christ (cf. particularly 1 Thess 1:8–10); the two are not different stages, far less alternatives, but different aspects of the one faith. (2) That the earliest formulation is "God raised Jesus" rather than "Jesus rose" (though cf. 1 Thess 4:14) retains the event of Christ's resurrection within the sweep of God's unfolding purpose, and keeps it or Jesus from becoming an alternative object of faith or independent subject of theological speculation. (3) κύριος here is not simply a status which results from Jesus' resurrection (see further on 1:4 and 10:9), but describes the one raised. Here too it is clear that we are dealing with a unified conception which makes no room for a sharp distinction between the earthly Jesus and exalted Lord or which allows one to be played off against the other; it is precisely the crucified and buried Jesus who is the Lord. (4) God raised the Lord: for all the divine status implied in κύριος (see further on 1:7, 8, and 10:9), the status is clearly conceived as different from and subject to that of God; it is as *Lord* that *God* raised him up (cf. 1 Cor 15:20–28); see also on 11:36 and 14:3.

25 ὃς παρεδόθη διὰ τὰ παραπτώματα ἡμῶν, "who was handed over because of our transgressions." This is a variation of quite a well established formulation in earliest Christianity; cf. particularly 8:32; Gal 2:20; Eph 5:2, 25. The distinctive features are the passive, which is certainly to be counted as a divine passive (God handed him over; cf. 8:32 and contrast the other three references), and the διά clause in contrast to the usual ὑπέρ clause. These are to be explained by the fact that this formulation is a meeting point between two strands of Christian tradition: (1) the passion narratives and (2) Christian reflection on Jesus' death using Isa 53. (1) παραδίδωμι had the important function of being able to embrace the double thought of Jesus' betrayal by man (Judas) and his being handed over by God: so, on the one hand, e.g., Mark 9:31; 10:33; 14:1–2; and Matt 10:4; and, on the other, Acts 3:13; Rom 4:25; and 8:32; with 1 Cor 11:23 well reflecting the ambiguity. It thus provided, particularly of course in its passive form, a ready means of reconciling the tension between the horrific act of Judas (cf. Mark 14:21) and the overarching purpose of God (cf. Acts 2:23). See further the discussion by N. Perrin, "The Use of (*Para*)*didonai* in Connection with the Passion of Jesus in the New Testament," in *A Modern Pilgrimage in New Testament Christology* (Philadelphia: Fortress, 1974), 94–103; A. E. Harvey, *Jesus and the Constraints of History* (London: Duckworth, 1982), 23–26. (2) The influence of Isa 53 LXX is hard to dispute; cf. particularly Isa 53:12: καὶ διὰ τὰς ἁμαρτίας αὐτῶν παρεδόθη. Since the threefold use of παραδίδωμι in Isa 53 (vv 6, 12) involves somewhat surprising renderings of the underlying Hebrew, we should probably recognize that the formulation here reflects Hellenistic Jewish (Christian) use of the LXX (Wengst, *Formeln*, 103). However, that need not mean that the use of Isa 53 was introduced only at the Greek-speaking stage. On the contrary, the divergence of v 25 from Isa 53:12 probably resulted from an awareness of the Aramaic rendering (or indeed direct use) of Isa 53:5, since παρεδόθη

διὰ τὰ παραπτώματα ἡμῶν corresponds to *Targ. Isa.* 53.5b—אַתְמְסַר בַּעֲוָיָתַנָא
(J. Jeremias, *The Servant of God,* 2d ed. [London: SCM, 1965], 89 n.397)—
though there said in reference to the temple (Bruce); see further Patsch,
274–78. Taken together therefore the distinctive features of v 25a probably
indicate that we have here a Greek rendering of one of the earliest theological
reflections about Jesus' death. Certainly its reference to Jesus' passion is firm
beyond dispute; Kramer's attempt to broaden it to include thought of the
coming of the Son of God into the life of the world (*Christ,* 117) lacks exegetical
foundation. For παράπτωμα see further on 5:15.

καὶ ἠγέρθη διὰ τὴν δικαίωσιν ἡμῶν, "and was raised because of our vindication."
The marks of an established formula are less clear here. When ἐγείρω is
used in the passive of Jesus, the form is regularly ἠγέρθη ἐκ νεκρῶν (6:4, 9;
7:4; 1 Cor 15:12; see *Notes* on Rom 8:34); the nearest parallel is 2 Cor 5:15
(ὑπὲρ αὐτῶν . . . ἐγερθέντι). On the other hand the δικαίωσις, "justification,
vindication, acquittal," is not a particularly Pauline expression (its one other
occurrence in the NT, Rom 5:18, is best explained as an attempt to avoid
undue repetition—see on 5:18); its sense here is untypical of its wider usage
(LSJ); and its link with the resurrection somewhat surprising (but cf. the
unusual formulations of 6:7; 1 Tim 3:16; and John 16:10). Cranfield suggests
some influence from the Hebrew text of Isa 53:11 (LXX uses δικαιῶσαι but
again differs from the MT). The διά is clearly used to provide a rhetorical
parallel with the preceding clause; as most recognize, the parallel is not disrupted by reading the first διά in a more causal sense and the second in a
more final sense ("because of" has the same ambiguity; *pace* Schlatter, Zeller;
but NEB abandons the parallelism too completely). And the two clauses may
well be modeled in relation to each other somewhat in accordance with the
parallelism of Hebrew poetic style (Dodd). It remains unclear, however,
whether Paul has incorporated (adapted) an already existing formula or has
constructed the second line to match the more established first line (Wilckens).
Either way it would be a mistake to read theological significance into distinctions
(between the effect of Jesus' death and the effect of his resurrection) which
are purely rhetorical (see particularly Kuss and McNeil, 104–5; contrast Murray; cf. 10:10). It does at least, however, underscore the soteriological significance of Jesus' resurrection and prevent its being regarded solely in terms
of Jesus' vindication (cf. 7:4, 8:34, and 1 Cor 15:17 with the different emphasis
of Rom 1:4 and 1 Tim 3:16).

Explanation

Paul's claim that his gospel was promised beforehand in the prophets and
continues to be attested by the law and the prophets (1:2; 3:21) has so far
been documented in primarily christological terms—that Jesus was the promised Son of David and that his death was in accord with the law of the sin-
offering on the Day of Atonement (1:3–4; 3:24–26), both claims using earlier
Christian formulations. However, the more provocative claim that God's righteousness reaches out to faith in Jesus Christ to all who believe without regard
to works of the law (3:21–22, 27–31), has not yet been demonstrated from
the scriptures. But this is precisely where Paul's gospel becomes most objection-

able to his fellow Jews, both followers of the older ways and fellow believers in Messiah Jesus. So if Paul is to have any hope of winning the argument already begun with his Jewish interlocutor (2:1–3:8), he must make good his claim at this point. Unless he can demonstrate from scripture that a person is justified by faith and not by works of law (3:28) he will be unable to maintain the continuity between the gospel and his central faith. To that essential task he now turns.

4:1–3: INTRODUCTION

1 He turns at once to Abraham. The reasons are obvious: Abraham was the first and most highly regarded of the fathers of the nation ("the friend of God"); to him the founding promises had been given, the covenant of the land and of circumcision (Gen 17). If the operation of God's righteousness in the case of Abraham could be clearly ascertained it would provide a crucial precedent and indeed pattern for those who claimed to be his seed and heirs. Moreover, and more to the point, Paul was not alone in so regarding Abraham. For within the Judaism of Paul's day Abraham had long been lauded as, in effect, the prototype of the devout Jew—that is, as one who demonstrated his faithfulness to the Lord under testing, as one who "in testing was found faithful" (Sir 44:20; 1 Macc 2:52). The repetition of the same phrase within the more extensive motif (of Abraham's faithfulness), and the fact that Paul uses the same verb ("was found") here (somewhat awkwardly), suggests that we are dealing with a fairly well established way of speaking about Abraham to which Paul here alludes. In other words, it looks as though Paul is about to meet head on a widely current view of Abraham's faith as his *covenant faithfulness*—his loyalty to God and obedience to God's command even under extreme provocation.

Paul's readers might also be aware of the tradition of exposition attested in 1 Macc 2:52 and James 2:22–23 which explicitly linked Gen 15:6 into this theme; Abraham's believing in God and his being counted righteous has to be understood in terms of his faithfulness in the offering of Isaac. They especially would not be surprised therefore when Paul too immediately focuses on Gen 15:6 (v 3), for unless Paul can sustain an alternative understanding of that key passage his claim to root the gospel of righteousness to faith in the law itself will have failed a crucial test. In short, it becomes increasingly apparent that what we have here in the following verses is much more than a mere illustration or example of a man of faith. There was evidently an already well established and influential view of Abraham as pattern for the faithful Jew, which ran almost directly counter to Paul's gospel. Paul would have been very conscious therefore that the very viability of his gospel was at stake in the following exposition.

The Roman congregation could also hardly fail to notice the way Paul speaks of Abraham—"our forefather, according to the flesh." He probably indicates thereby that he is resuming his dialogue (diatribe) with the Jewish interlocutor of 2:1–3:8—Gentile Christians could call Abraham "father" (as Paul had argued so forcefully in Gal 3 and would again in the following verses here), but "father" in terms of faith, not in terms of physical descent.

But the slightly pejorative note in the phrase "according to the flesh" further implies that to understand that inheritance from Abraham in merely fleshly, ethnic terms is inadequate. Paul at once hints at the line of argument he is shortly to develop—that Abraham's paternity extends beyond the realm of the physical and visible (cf. 2:28–29), embracing Gentile as well as Jew. This somewhat beguiling opening, apparently so reassuring to Jewish sensibilities (Abraham is our father, and we are his promised seed), is actually the opening thrust in Paul's attempt to challenge these axioms of Jewish self-understanding as a people by his assertion that God's covenant righteousness extends to believing Gentile as well as to Jew without regard to national identity as determined by the law.

2 How was it in the case of Abraham? One possible answer to the question of v 1 is the alternative already dismissed by Paul—that Abraham was justified from works. If that were true, Paul concludes, then Abraham has something to boast about. The recurrence of the key themes, "works" and "boasting," indicates clearly that Paul once again is thinking of the typical national confidence of his own people as to their election by God and privileged position under the law (2:17, 23; 3:27–30). In other words, this is the answer Paul would expect his fellow Jewish interlocutor to give. Even if the categorization of this attitude in terms of "works of law" has been given its polemical edge by Paul, it was language already familiar in Jewish Christian circles (Gal 2:16— "we know . . . "). And the close parallel between James 2:23 and 1 Macc 2:52 implies that most Jews of Paul's day would readily enough recognize and identify with the position Paul attacks here: Abraham was justified by works (cf. James 2:21), that is, by demonstrating his covenant faithfulness and obedience to God's command in the offering of Isaac; he *can* boast in his God-given privilege and steadfastness under trial.

But, adds Paul, even so, he cannot boast in reference to God. Herein lies the crucial flaw in the typical Jewish answer for Paul. Their pride in having a privileged position among the nations became a pride before God and so fell under the same judgment outlined in 1:21–22. This was the tragedy of Jewish boasting: their boast in having a special status before God (attested by their works of the law) was preventing them from recognizing that the only way anyone can stand before God is by humble faith.

3 How is such an issue, such a dispute between Jews to be resolved? How else but by appeal to scripture, to the law itself? Paul at once appeals to Gen 15:6, following the LXX almost exactly: "Abraham believed God and it was reckoned to him for righteousness." To use the text of scripture presumably most familiar to diaspora Judaism would obviously be important if his exposition was to be persuasive to diaspora Jews. Almost certainly he turns to this verse because he was aware of the already typical understanding of it as attesting Abraham's covenant faithfulness (1 Macc 2:52). No doubt that had been his own understanding of Gen 15:6 prior to "the revelation of Jesus Christ." But now, in the light of the revelation of Christ, he reads it differently, and of this different reading he seeks to persuade the Roman congregations, Jews as well as Gentiles.

We should not imagine that Paul here saw himself as alienated from the traditional Jewish self-understanding and making, as it were, a raid into the traditionalists' territory to steal one of their chief texts away from them. Paul would rather say that he had come to a clearer perception of what the mainstream of God's covenant purpose was, and with that clearer perception had come the realization that the usual interpretation of Abraham and of Gen 15:6 in particular was a misinterpretation. Paul appeals to this text now because he is confident that he himself stands within that main stream of God's covenant purpose, and that he can demonstrate what he sees now to be the proper interpretation of Gen 15:6.

In the text thus announced there are two key words on which the understanding of Abraham's righteousness turns—the two verbs "believed" and "reckoned." Paul proceeds, in classic Jewish midrashic style, to expound each in turn, starting with "reckoned."

4:4–8: THE MEANING OF "RECKONED"

4–5 Paul begins by taking up the link between work and the idea of "reckoning." When "working" and "reckoning" are put together then self-evidently we are talking in the accounting terms of everyday transaction, where the payment for the work done is the amount due for the work and not a favor. But in Gen 15:6 the link is between *belief* and "reckoning." And if someone does not work and only "believes" in the God who justifies the impious, then it must be his *belief* which is "reckoned for righteousness."

Clearly Paul is playing on the idea of "work," as between "works of the law" in the sense of covenant obligations and "work" in the everyday sense of contractual employment. To take the force of Paul's contrast, however, it is not necessary to assume that his Jewish interlocutor would accept a straight equation between works of law and the payment-earning work of day-to-day life. Nor is it necessary to assume that Paul was accusing his fellow Jews of making that equation. He simply points out that to interpret Gen 15:6 in terms of Abraham's acts (works) of covenant loyalty, leaves no room in the common-sense logic of the work-a-day world for grace.

Paul's line of exposition is already foreshadowed in the most provocative phrase of all: "him (God) who justifies the ungodly." This description of God would certainly come as a shock to Paul's Jewish readers, and devout God-worshipers as well, for it runs so directly counter to a basic principle of Jewish justice, one which was rooted in the Lord's own self-declaration (Exod 23:7). Why does Paul risk losing Jewish and God-worshipers' sympathy with what appears at first an unnecessary slighting of divine righteousness? The answer presumably lies once again in the degree to which Paul is angling his exposition to the typical Judaism of his own day. Paul will almost certainly have been aware that for the devout Jew "godliness" was more or less synonymous with covenant loyalty, faithfulness to the obligations laid upon Israel by the covenant God of Israel; and "ungodliness" accordingly denoted disregard for the law and its prescriptions (e.g., Ps 1:1–2, 5; Prov 15:8; Sir 41:8). What he is implying then, very clearly and with epigrammatic sharpness, is that God's righteousness is not determined by reference to covenant loyalty. Like his master before him, Paul asserts in one shockingly crisp phrase that God accepts sinners who put their trust in him without requiring them to express that trust through the hallowed rituals of cult and law. In the first instance, of course, that means Abraham: Abraham was declared righteous before fulfilling any covenant obligation when he was still, in the terms used by the devout Jew, "ungodly"; that is the thesis which Paul is going to demonstrate in the following verses. But beyond Abraham in particular Paul has in view the whole of the contemporary Judaism he himself had once practiced. This is why Abraham is such a crucial test case. If he was declared righteous by God apart from any covenant ritual or obligation then he demonstrates that God's righteousness extends to all who have faith without reference to any such works of the law.

6–8   In a manner typical of Jewish exegesis, Paul turns to another scripture which might throw light on the word "reckon," the closest parallel being the opening words of Ps 32. There the psalmist (David) describes the blessing of the one whose sin the Lord will not "reckon" (Ps 32:2). In the parallelism of word and thought in these opening lines of the psalm, the non-reckoning of sin is the same as the forgiveness of acts of lawlessness and the covering of sins.

Paul's argument appears deceptively simple. The language of calculating payment due is *in*appropriate to describe God's dealings with human beings where the initiative lies with God. In the nearest parallel to Gen 15:6, the idea of God "reckoning" is used with reference to forgiveness, an act of divine grace, something freely given, without calculation of the number of sins or the gravity of the deeds done in *disregard* of the law. This blessedness of forgiveness, of sins not reckoned, Paul affirms with full confidence, is also the blessing of righteousness reckoned by God without regard to works. David's words provide a fully equivalent description of Abraham's standing before God in Gen 15:6.

Would Paul's Jewish interlocutor find this argument as just stated wholly convincing? Probably not. It is not that he would have had difficulty with the near equation of "righteousness" and "forgiveness": the idea of God's righteousness as his action to rescue and sustain his undeserving people was too well established in psalmist and prophet for that. It is rather Paul's slipping in once again the words "apart from works" which would cause the problem. For the typical Jew would *not* see forgiveness as happening "apart from works." On the contrary, the whole point of sacrifice for sin and the Day of Atonement was to provide the means of forgiveness—the cultic works of the law which expressed the sinner's repentance and provided expiation.

What is Paul's point then? That the psalmist was not speaking in a cultic context? That the psalm speaks of a forgiveness which is independent of sacrifice and atonement? This might be an inference drawn in a diaspora Jewish context since the reality of the sacrificial and atoning ritual in far-off Jerusalem must have been very distant for many. But for the devout who contributed their temple tax regularly, and certainly for mainstream Palestinian Judaism, the link between repentance, atonement (sacrificial expiation) and forgiveness would be largely axiomatic, and Ps 32 would hardly constitute evidence to the contrary. Nor does any distinction between inadvertent sins and sins "with a high hand" (Deut 17:12) seem to be relevant here. Nor would a Jewish reader be likely to see here implied a universalism which disputed Israel's claim to a distinctive righteousness. Paul's point could be, of course, that God's readiness to *dis*count sin, to forgive acts of lawlessness, and to cover sins, is manifestly an act of sheer grace, however that forgiveness comes to effect. And the point could be pushed quite far: God's forgiveness is out of all proportion to the number of sins committed or rituals observed; he does not keep a score of wrongs done or atonement made (cf. 1 Cor 13:5). But most devout Jews would not demur at any of that, yet still find Paul's "apart from works" an unjustified dichotomy between God's righteousness and Israel's covenant obligations.

On the other hand, we should not expect too much from Paul's use of Ps 32, since the next verse begins by asking to whom this blessing comes. In other words, Paul does not actually treat Ps 32:1–2 as self-evidently proof of his case. And in the event he develops the point solely with reference to Abraham; had he wanted to shift the argument to David himself his argument would have been in trouble (David was certainly already circumcised when he received the blessing of forgiveness). In point of fact then Paul's reference to Ps 32 does not advance the argument very far. He is content simply to draw attention to the other most relevant use of "reckon" in scripture, with the implication that when God "reckons" something to someone it is a reckoning of grace which cannot be measured in accounting terms. He *claims* that this act of divine forgiveness is the same as God's reckoning a person righteous apart from works (v 1). But that claim has not yet been established.

4:9–21: THE MEANING OF "BELIEVED"

All that Paul has done so far is to show that the issue of the meaning of Gen 15:6 cannot be resolved by reference to the verb "reckon": God's reckoning in favor of man is always a matter of his generous favor; man is never able to put God in his debt. The argument must shift therefore to the other key verb: "Abraham *believed* God." The reference to Ps 32:1–2 simply provides the occasion to frame the key question differently: to whom and how does this blessing (of forgiveness granted, of righteousness reckoned) come? The Ps 32 reference makes no further contribution to the midrash and its language of "acts of lawlessness forgiven" and "sins (plural) covered" is not picked up again. Instead Paul swings the argument back to Abraham and focuses on the central issue of Abraham's *faith*.

4:9–12: ABRAHAM'S FAITH WAS QUITE SEPARATE FROM ANY WORK

Paul's first step in expounding "Abraham believed God" is to demonstrate that in Abraham's case the faith to which righteousness was reckoned was exercised quite apart from any work of Abraham. That is to say, Gen 15:6 speaks of faith, not of faithfulness—of faith, not of covenant loyalty.

9 By means of a carefully formulated question v 9 swings the argument back to the key text (Gen 15:6): how does the blessing spoken of by David come to others? Ps 32:1–2 having been drawn in to clarify the meaning of "reckoned" is now in its turn clarified by harking back to Gen 15:6: what does Abraham's experience tell us about David's blessing? Granted that the blessing of acts of lawlessness forgiven and of sins covered is the same as the blessing of being reckoned righteous, how did this blessing come to Abraham?

Paul poses the alternatives in his own terms—on the circumcised or on the uncircumcised? The narrowing of the issue (by works or apart from works) to the specific question of circumcision or uncircumcision would be hard to criticize. For the devout Jew, proud of his national and religious distinctiveness, circumcision was *the* work of covenant loyalty (cf. 2:25–29). It was precisely for this reason that its discontinuation in the gentile mission was a cause of such controversy within first-generation Christianity. And it was the command to Abraham above all which showed circumcision to be a divinely sanctioned mark of the covenant people for all time (Gen 17:9–14). The shrewdness of Paul's switch back from David to Abraham is that while no one could argue convincingly that David's forgiveness was independent of David's circumcision (and the functioning of the cult), with Abraham it is a different matter. The blessing described by David could also be experienced by someone, Abraham no less, apart from circumcision. The point is that Paul's case does not depend on showing that righteousness is always and only accounted apart from circumcision, apart from works, in every case. That is to say, he need not demonstrate that David received his forgiveness independently of his circumcision and participation in the cult. All that is required for him is to show that the blessing of which both Genesis and the psalmist spoke came outside the covenant and its works in one clear instance, the paradigmatic case of Abraham himself.

10 Paul's argument is straightforward: the event of which Gen 15:6 speaks precedes the event described in Gen 17:23–27. Paul insists on separating into distinct phases what his fellow Jews, and no doubt he himself previously, had always taken as a whole. After all, Abraham's faithfulness did not begin at Gen 17. If it began anywhere, it began at Gen 12; it began with the first enunciation of the central covenant promise (Gen 12:1–5). The still later episode, the offering of Isaac, could be cited as an example of Abraham's faithfulness, indeed as an exposition of Gen 15:6 (1 Macc 2:52; James 2:23), precisely because it was simply the best example of the faithfulness which had characterized Abraham's obedience to God throughout. Nevertheless by narrowing the issue to circumcision as such, Paul takes up a strong position, and one difficult to contest. For the evidence of scripture is that Abraham was reckoned righteous, accepted in covenant relationship by God, prior to his being circumcised and without reference to circumcision. That one fact is sufficient to establish the point that God's righteousness was not dependent upon works of the law, on any cultic observance, in the case of Abraham. And if Abraham is the paradigm for God's dealings with humankind, including his covenant dealings with the seed of Abraham, that also means that God's acceptance in general is or at least can be "apart from works."

11a This is the argument Paul proceeds to draw out. Abraham's circumcision came after the righteousness which is characterized both by his faith and by the fact that it was reckoned to him when he was still uncircumcised. As such, circumcision is to be reckoned as a sign and seal of the divine acceptance effected some time before, as a ratification of the divine initiative nearly thirty years earlier, as a distinguishing mark of God's ownership already long in operation. That is to say, Abraham's circumcision was dependent on his *previously* having been accepted by God and on his already having been reckoned righteous—not the other way round.

It is important to note here that Paul deliberately uses language with strong covenantal overtones. He calls circumcision a "sign," a term certainly given him from Gen 17:11. His Jewish interlocutor and probably most of his Jewish and God-worshiping readers would inevitably think of circumcision as the "sign of the covenant" (Gen 17:11; *Jub.* 15.26–28). Likewise the word "seal" almost inevitably evokes the correlative idea of a formal agreement, that is, of a covenant (cf., e.g., Neh 9:38–39), and it may already have been used in Jewish thought for circumcision as the visible mark of the Lord's covenant with Israel. In other words, Paul does not disparage circumcision here; he does not hesitate to acknowledge that Abraham's circumcision was part of God's covenant with Abraham and that it stood in a positive relationship to God's righteousness to Abraham. He is and remains a Jew and has no intention of denying God's covenant with Israel. His concern rather is to understand properly the terms of that covenant. And his point is that the positive relation between God's righteousness to Abraham and Abraham's circumcision is not what the Judaism of his day took it for granted to be. Abraham's righteousness from God was *not* dependent on his circumcision. Abraham's circumcision was a ratification that Abraham had been accepted by God; it did not restrict that acceptance only to the circumcised. Paul can readily acknowledge that positive link between circumcision and covenant, since circumcision manifestly at this point only has a secondary role and is not integral to Abraham's already established righteousness, and since he also believes that in the eschatological fulfillment of the covenant the palpable impact of the Spirit is just as clear a mark of divine ownership as ever circumcision was (2:28–29; 2 Cor 1:22; Phil 3:3).

11b–12 The point has thus been established that Abraham's righteousness was dependent solely on a believing which clearly preceded circumcision and which therefore is clearly distinct from works of the law. This means that Abraham's faith was the crucial element in the covenant with Abraham as a whole, with circumcision functioning as a *post hoc* ratification. But this also means that the terms of the covenant *promise* are determined by faith, not by circumcision, and that the heritage of the covenant is likewise dependent on the same faith and not restricted solely to the circumcised. Here too Paul does not hesitate to take up the covenant language first explicitly used in Gen 17:4 ff. ("you shall be the father of a multitude of nations") and interpret it by reference to its less developed earlier form (Gen 15:5: "So shall your descendants be. And he believed the Lord; and he reckoned it to him as righteousness."). As Abraham's participation in God's righteousness was dependent on his faith, so his fatherhood of many nations was a promise to faith, and so its fulfillment is defined in terms of faith. Precisely in contrast to the Jewish theologoumenon of Abraham as the father of all proselytes, that is of Gentiles so long as they are circumcised, Paul asserts that Abraham's fatherhood is not restricted to the circumcised. On the contrary, because faith is the crucial factor, all those who believe as he did are his children, whether circumcised or uncircumcised. He is father of the circumcised, but they enter into their full sonship only when they exercise faith as Abraham did, in a way which shows it to be independent of circumcision. And uncircumcised Gentiles who believe can properly call Abraham "our father" too. This is the way God intended it to be—otherwise he would not have reckoned Abraham righteous apart from circumcision.

4:13–17A: THE COVENANT PROMISE DEPENDENT ON FAITH, NOT LAW

13 Paul now reformulates his exposition of Abraham's faith and moves it on to a second stage by focusing on the word "promise." The context of Gen 15:6 drawn in by implication in vv 11–12, is now brought clearly to the fore: what Abraham believed was God's promise of innumerable descendants (Gen 15:5). Accordingly Gen 15:6 speaks of a righteousness reckoned to Abraham by virtue of his believing, i.e., accepting God's promise. It was not through the law that the promise was given to Abraham but through the righteousness of faith.

The degree to which Paul's argument is determined by the current self-understanding of his own people is clearly indicated by his careful wording which picks up four key elements in that self-understanding: the covenant promise to Abraham and his seed, the inheritance (of the land) as its central element, the conviction that the beneficiaries of this promise are coterminous with the people of the law, and the importance of covenant righteousness. Paul picks up these emphases in order to redefine them.

That Abraham should be "heir of the world" might seem an odd rendering of the promises of Gen 12:2–3 and 15:5, even in their subsequent form (17:4; 18:18; 22:17–18). But in fact this was how the promise to Abraham was regularly understood. Indeed it had become almost a commonplace of Jewish teaching that the covenant promised that Abraham's seed would "inherit the earth." It is not by accident that Paul takes up this more grandiose form of the promise—the promise to Abraham or his seed (we might say "through his seed") that he should inherit the world. For the promise thus interpreted was fundamental to Israel's self-consciousness as God's covenant people: it was the reason why God had chosen them in the first place from among all the other nations of the earth, the justification for holding themselves distinct from the other nations, and the comforting hope that made their current national humiliation endurable.

It is this promise to Abraham in its apparently most nationalistic formulation which Paul abruptly severs from any connection with the law ("Not through the law . . . "). He thus strikes away one of the basic underpinnings of Jewish self-understanding. It was self-evident to most of Paul's Jewish contemporaries that the law provided the God-given structure for the outworking of his promises; because the law was what God required of his covenant partners, his covenant promises could properly be said to operate "through the law" (as in 2 Macc 2:17). It is precisely this which Paul denies. His reasoning is plain and follows directly from the preceding verses: the promise was not only made to Abraham but wholly accepted by him many years before the law as focused in the requirement of circumcision came into play. He had previously made the same point more emphatically in Gal 3:17 (the giving of the law at Sinai came several centuries later); but given that the key issue was circumcision, that was a dangerous overstatement of his case; the present argument is more modest, and the more effective in consequence.

What Paul puts forward as the positive alternative also contributes to his redefinition of the covenant: the promise operates through the righteousness of faith. Correlative with the concepts of covenant inheritance and the law was the concept of righteousness—the righteousness which sustained the covenant relation with the people of the law. Paul by no means disputes that righteousness is fundamental for the maintenance of the covenant relationship. But once again he insists on the unthinkable for most Jews—that this righteousness is not to be determined by reference to the law; it is the righteousness of faith.

This restatement of Paul's case, which follows immediately from his exposition of Gen 15:6, reveals both the strong continuity he saw between his faith and the fundamental promise of his people's scriptures, and his disagreement with its traditional interpretation within Jewish circles. Paul had no doubt that the gospel he proclaimed was a continuation and fulfillment of God's promise to Abraham. But he was equally clear that the heirs of Abraham's promise were no longer to be identified in terms of the law, no longer to be understood as coterminous with the law. For Gen 15:6 showed with sufficient clarity that the promise was given and accepted through faith, quite apart from the law in whole or part.

14 Paul rephrases the point with added emphasis: if it is the people of the covenant who are heirs, then Abraham's faith has been made an empty cipher and the promise given to Abraham rendered ineffective. The phrase rendered here "the people of the law" (literally "those from the law") is usually taken in the somewhat unnatural sense of "those who keep the law." The more natural reference is to those whose character as an identifiable group arises "out of" the law and is given by their relation to the law. In other words, it is a phrase which neatly catches the sense of national identity which the Torah and its works gave to the Jewish people of Paul's day. It is this assumption of total integration between covenant and promise, Jewish nation and the law, which Paul has been forced to question by his own experience of God's grace—this closely woven pattern of Jewish faith which he now unpicks with the sharp point of Gen 15:6.

His claim is again simple and does not depend on special pleading or hermeneutical artifice. The traditional Jewish understanding of the covenant promise cannot be correct, because it perverts the clear sense of Gen 15:6. It makes Abraham's faith empty and ineffective, whereas according to Gen 15:6 God reckoned it to him for righteousness. And it renders the promise to Abraham null and invalid because it denies that it was given to Abraham and accepted by Abraham there and then as a binding commitment which God had taken upon himself. Again the argument is not simply a re-run of Gal 3:18 (a promise is a promise and cannot have conditions added to it subsequently), nor is it a statement of some general principle (faith and promise do not cohere with law). It is strictly limited to the case in point—the proper understanding of the faith (of Abraham) and the promise (to Abraham) in relation to the people of the law.

15 "For the law produces wrath; where there is no law neither is there transgression." This definition of what the law does comes in rather abruptly. But Paul's thought is presumably still on the separation of the law from righteousness. Where most of his Jewish contemporaries would prefer to say "the law brings about righteousness," Paul has argued resolutely that righteousness comes about through faith. What then is the role of the law? It produces wrath. The law has more to do with the situation described in 1:18–3:20 than with its solution (3:21 ff.); it is more a tool of God's wrath than of his righteousness. Paul's point is that the law is the correlative of transgression. Where his typical compatriot would see the law first and foremost as determining life within the covenant, including the provision of atonement, Paul asserts the prior point that were it not for the law there would be no transgression (and so no need of atonement). The primary function of the law is to condemn, not to serve as a medium of the promise. That role is filled by faith.

16 That is why God gave the promise to Abraham in the way he did. The way in which God gave the promise to Abraham determines how the promise itself is to be understood and who its heirs are. The promise to Abraham, without reference to any act of covenant loyalty, when he was not yet a father, was an act of complete generosity, so that the promise and its beneficiaries might be expressions of the same grace. Consequently the issue of who belongs to Abraham's descendants, heirs of the promise, is not dependent on whether they perform acts which demonstrate covenant loyalty and is not dependent on their being members of the people of the law. To restrict the promise to the Jews would be to deny the terms of its original acceptance and to diminish the promise itself. God's intention, as attested by Gen 15:6, was that the promise of grace through faith might embrace all who are willing to accept that same grace, whether Jews or not, just as Abraham did.

16c–17a Only so can the promise that Abraham would be "the father of many nations" be actually fulfilled. Once again Paul does not hesitate to refer to the promise as given in Gen 17:5. For its terms can only be fulfilled if Gentiles are reckoned as Abraham's seed in far greater numbers than ever became proselytes. The loyal Jew was more inclined to interpret that promise by reference to its context in Gen 17, where it can plausibly be argued that Abraham's circumcision was an act of law-keeping and so his fatherhood of many nations can be interpreted in terms of Jewish national or religious hegemony (cf. Sir 44:19–21). But in Paul's view the terms of the promise, even in Gen 17, can only be fulfilled if the definition of Abraham's promised descendants is not determined by national or cultic criteria but by the faith through which Abraham received the promise in the first place. What is at issue here is not whether Gentiles can be included among Abraham's descendants along with the Jews who are there as of right, but how anyone, Jew as well as Gentile, may come to be counted a descendant of Abraham. Paul's answer rings with increasing strength as his argument proceeds—by faith, apart from (works of) the law.

4:17B–21: ABRAHAM'S FAITH WAS NOTHING OTHER THAN UNQUESTIONING
TRUST IN GOD'S POWER

As the argument progresses, the reader suddenly becomes aware that it
has moved on to a new point, the third stage of the exposition of the assertion
in Gen 15:6 that "Abraham believed God." Paul is clearly not concerned to
divide up the exposition into three neatly discrete exegetical observations.
The exposition is a whole and each observation is mutually interdependent
on the others. Thus vv 11–12 presupposed and ushered in the argument of
vv 13–17a, just as v 17b now states a principle which is fundamental to the
argument of vv 18–21. And the definition of Abraham's faith which is now
to be developed has already been presupposed in the sharpness of the distinction between law and faith which motivated vv 13–16.

17b The transition to the new stage of the argument is made by attaching
rather awkwardly a description of the God in whom Abraham believed: "before
whom he believed, that is the God who makes the dead alive and calls what
has no existence into existence." The transition is so awkward presumably
because Paul wanted to base his final observation about Gen 15:6 on this
description of God, even at the cost of syntactical inelegance. The rationale
is plain: fundamental to the character of any theistic religion is the character
of the God believed in. Here Paul goes out of his way to give a basic definition
of the God whom he worshiped, the same God in whom Abraham believed.
His point is that if we understand aright the God in whom Abraham believed,
we will understand also what it means when it says "Abraham believed God."
The character of Abraham's faith is determined by the character of the God
in whom he believed.

The description he gives is thoroughly Jewish, and its individual elements
would have been thoroughly familiar to anyone in touch with contemporary
Jewish thought and worship. In particular, God "who gives life to the dead"
is the chief theme of the second of the Eighteen Benedictions, probably already
familiar in this form in the daily prayers of the devout Jew. And God "who
calls the nonexistent into being" was a characteristic credo especially of Hellenistic Judaism, as we see from its frequent use by Philo. It is clearly important
for Paul (as for our understanding of Paul) that he can thus ground his
exposition of Gen 15:6 on such a fundamental tenet of Jewish theology. It
is not a new understanding of God which made Paul abandon the traditional
understanding of the Jewish faith and its covenant. He would not accept
that his exposition of Abraham's faith was an innovation justified by new
revelation, a departure from the original terms of the covenant. On the contrary, his understanding of Abraham's faith is wholly consistent with Israel's
own understanding of God and indeed derives from it. It is because Paul
now sees more clearly the character of Israel's God that he can now also
appreciate more clearly the character of Israel's covenant with God. For the
meaning of the promise to Abraham and his seed is determined by the character
both of Abraham's God and of Abraham's faith—these two interlock and
reinforce each other.

Equally important is the fact that this is a description of God the creator.
It is precisely as creator that he is the life-giver and life-sustainer (Neh 9:6;
Jos. As. 8.9). Of course the thought here is of God who gives life to the

dead, but in this way of speaking about God the eschatological manifestation of his life-giving power is simply the supreme example of his creative power—the same creative power which first gave life will have the final say over that which seems most to threaten the life he gave us in the beginning. It is the assurance that God's life-giving power can make even the dead alive which gives confidence in situations of challenge or despair during this life (Ps 71:20; 2 Cor 1:9). Even more clearly is the second phrase a celebration of God's creative power—God whose effective summons brings into existence what previously had no existence. And even if Paul's readers thought of creation as a product from formless matter (as in Wisd Sol 11:17) rather than as *creatio ex nihilo* (as in 2 Macc 7:28), the formula would have been sufficiently familiar and acceptable in its epigrammatic conciseness as an expression of the total sovereignty of God's power as creator.

Paul calls on this theological axiom not simply because it is a formula few if any of his readers would dispute, but because it clearly implies also the relationship which must pertain between this creator and his creation. As creator he creates without any precondition: he makes alive where there was only death, and he calls into existence where there was nothing at all. Consequently that which has been created, made alive in this way, must be totally dependent on the creator, the life-giver, for its very existence and life. Expressed in such terms the statement provides the governing principle by which all God's relationship with humankind must be understood, including salvation and redemption. Unless God is inconsistent, the same principle will govern God's dealings as savior: he redeems as he creates, and he reckons righteous in the same way in which he makes alive. That is to say, his saving work depends on nothing in that which is saved; redemption, righteous-reckoning, is not contingent on any precondition on the part of the recipient; the dead cannot make terms, that which does not exist cannot place God under any obligation—which is also to say that the individual or nation is dependent on the unconditional grace of God as much for covenant life as for created life. It was this total dependence on God for very existence itself which man forgot, his rejection of that dependence which lies at the root of his malaise (1:18–28). The tragedy of contemporary Judaism for Paul is that his compatriots were actually making the same mistake—thinking that in the covenant with Abraham God had taken upon himself obligations on which all loyal Jews, but only loyal Jews, could count. In Paul's view, no matter what Gen 17 may seem to say, that cannot be the case, precisely because it conflicts so sharply with what all Jews recognize to be the basic character of God both in creating and in renewing life.

18 The strength of Paul's case is that the key text relating to Abraham is such a good illustration of the relation between the creature and his creator, between the recipient of God's covenant promise and its giver. For Abraham knew that the fulfillment of the promise depended on no life or power that was his. There was no ground of hope in himself or in his human condition. All he had to cling to was the promise, "So shall your seed be" (Gen 15:5). Here Paul insists in effect that Gen 15:6 must be interpreted in relation to its immediate context. The promise God gave at that point was wholly without condition. It is that promise which Abraham believed. It was that belief which God acknowledged in declaring Abraham righteous. Indeed he makes a point of referring his readers back from the promise in its Gen 17 form to the prior version of Gen 15:5. The implication is that the requirements attached to the later version (Gen 17), as indeed the testing of Gen 22, need not and should not be drawn in to interpret Gen 15:5–6 when that passage is sufficiently clear and coherent in itself. Rather it is Gen 15:5–6, a giving and receiving complete in itself, which should determine the significance given to the later version of the promise and to these subsequent events. Paul thus makes it clear beyond dispute that the keystone of his whole argument is not Gen 15:6 on its own, but the fact that Gen 15:6 is the response to the promise of 15:5; without that connection the argument would collapse.

19 The importance of Gen 15:5–6 in controlling the interpretation of what followed becomes even clearer when we realize that the documentation of Abraham's faith is actually drawn from Gen 17. In the light of Gen 15:5–6 the significance of Gen 17 lies not so much in vv 9–14 (the requirement of circumcision) as in the specific promise that Sarah would have a son (vv 15 ff.). Paul deliberately picks up Abraham's recognition of the hopelessness of his human condition (Gen 17:17) and sets his complete powerlessness in sharpest contrast to the divine omnipotence. Such strength as Abraham had lay not in his body or Sarah's. It lay only in his faith. Abraham himself was fully aware of this. He took full account of the deadness of his own body and of the deadness of Sarah's womb (the double evocation of the description of God's creative power in v 17 is deliberate). He knew that only the life-giver could fulfill his own promise and only by the exercise of his own power. The strength of his faith was precisely his recognition that there was nothing in him which could make the fulfillment of the promise possible, his recognition, that is to say, that he had to rely wholly and solely on God who alone can give life to that which is dead, who alone can make something out of nothing.

20 Abraham did not doubt the promise of God in unbelief but became strong, or was strengthened (by God), in his faith. All he had to hang on to was the bare word of God; but that was enough, for it was the promise of the creator. The repeated emphasis on Abraham's faith here is deliberate. For it is here that Paul brings out most clearly the character of Abraham's faith. Gen 15:5–6 shows that Abraham's faith was nothing other and nothing more than trust in God's promise; it was not faithfulness; it was not covenant loyalty. The strength of Abraham's faith was precisely that it was unsupported by anything else; it was not something which Abraham could do. It was trust, simple trust, nothing but trust.

By thus living in unconditional and helpless trust Abraham gave glory to God; for as Paul had indicated earlier, it is by acknowledging his total dependence on God that the creature gives glory to the creator (1:21). The echo of chap. 1 is deliberate. Thereby Paul confirms his transformation of Abraham from being the pattern of the devout Jew to being the pattern of man as he was created to be—a universalizing of Abraham which further undermines Israel's otherwise exclusive claim to him. Abraham is now clearly to be seen as the model of the proper creature, the man of faith who holds his whole life in total dependence on the life-giver, the model for all who thus believe, Gentile as well as Jew.

21 The exposition is rounded off with a repetition of the crucial factors: Abraham's faith and God's ability to perform his promise. The repetition of the word "faith" and its cognates gives way to a rich alternative—"full assurance." Abraham's faith is thus presented in a strongly positive light. It was not simply a form of fatalistic passivity ("let's see what happens"), nor a fearful reliance on the goodness of some blind providence. It was confidence in God, a positive acknowledgment of God's power as creator, a calm certainty that God had made known to Abraham his purpose and could be relied on to perform it without further question or condition. Here from another aspect is the same reason why Abraham's faith should not be thought of in terms of covenant loyalty or as incomplete apart from works, for faith is confidence in God's loyalty as alone necessary, as alone able, as alone sufficient to bring God's promise to full effect.

4:22–25: CONCLUSION AND APPLICATION

22 "Therefore it was reckoned to him for righteousness." Paul's exposition of Gen 15:6 is complete and he concludes his midrash by reverting to its starting point: and so we see what Gen 15:6 means—Q.E.D., the conclusion is self-evident. It was just this faith which God looked for and accepted in reckoning Abraham righteous—a faith exercised prior to and independently of any work, circumcision in particular; a faith which responded simply to a promise which always had a wider scope than the people of the law; a faith which was nothing more than naked trust in the power of the creator. Consequently, since it was just this faith which God accepted, his reckoning of Abraham as righteous must indeed be, as Paul had asserted at the beginning of the midrash, an act of sheer grace. For the one who is thus reckoned righteous has done and can do nothing except trust, the very opposite of any status or act which might be thought to lay an obligation on God. It is this complete match between divine ability and human inability, as indeed the complete mismatch between a wholly generous promise and a confidence based on race and law, which emerges so clearly for Paul from his text.

23–24 Paul immediately applies his conclusion. Gen 15:6 was written not simply to describe how Abraham came to be reckoned righteous, but to provide a pattern for his descendants. The Jewish interlocutor addressed at the beginning of chap. 4 has presumably been silenced by the exposition of vv 3–22, but he would not dispute the propriety of Paul's application of his conclusion. As we noted at the beginning of chap. 4, Abraham's example of covenant loyalty was a well-established motif in Jewish parenesis. The crucial difference in this case, of course, is that Paul has now succeeded in showing Abraham's faith to be distinct from the law-keeping for which he was lauded in Jewish circles (as in Sir 44:10–15, 19–21). It is the paradigm of Abraham's faith as just expounded which Paul now seeks to impress upon his readers— Abraham's faith as the archetype of Christian belief in (relation to) Jesus.

The parallel can be drawn and the application made since the same two key elements are present in both: belief in God, and in God precisely as the one who gives life to the dead, or, alternatively expressed, in God as the one who raises from the dead. Paul by his terminology deliberately evokes the parallel between God's creation of life out of the deadness of Abraham's body and Sarah's womb (v 19) and God's raising of Jesus from the dead. What Paul's gospel calls for is faith in the same creator God, belief in the same exercise of life-giving power—the same faith, the same belief. The logic is clear: since the exercise of divine power is of the same order in both cases, so too the faith it evokes should have the same character in both cases; the unconditional act of God's life-giving power is met only by a faith which relies on nothing other than that life-giving power.

It is worth observing that the point made here does not depend on any particular theory of typology—the *Urzeit* faith of Abraham as the type of *Endzeit* faith of Christians. Such a theory (End will correspond to beginning) cannot explain why one episode from Israel's beginnings should provide the type and not another. On such a typological rationale there is no good reason why believing Abraham should provide the type and not law-giving Moses, or why Abraham's believing in Gen 15 should serve as the type and not his being circumcised in Gen 17. The general principle for Paul here at least is rather that what is written in scripture, particularly about matters of faith and unbelief, was always intended by the one who inspired the scripture to have application to believers, not least to those who came to faith in the new age introduced by Christ. And its particular application here depends on the particular correspondence between the two cases in point—a unique exercise of God's life-giving power, making possible the fulfillment of the promise that Abraham would father "many nations," as the single reference and anchor point for faith. As God's act of creative power presupposed no presence or manifestation of life in both cases, so the faith exercised in the latter case as much as the former must be a faith which looks for no precondition or support outside that act of God.

In applying the paradigm of Abraham's being reckoned righteous to his fellow Christians Paul writes ". . . to us to whom it is to be reckoned." The note of futurity (what is certain to be the case) is presumably deliberate (otherwise Paul would have used "reckoned" in the present or aorist tense). By it he may have in mind the imminent widening embrace of the gospel to the Gentiles ("the full number of the Gentiles"—11:25), or indeed the future judgment for which believers can wait confident of acquittal (cf. 2:16; 3:6; 8:33–34). Paul evidently was not concerned to clarify the point, presumably because for Paul, as for his fellow Jews, God's extending righteousness to his human creation is not a once-for-all event, whether in the past or in the future. It is God's acceptance of persons, whether as an initial acceptance, or as a repeated sustaining (God's saving acts), or as his final acquittal. What makes a person thus acceptable to God is nothing he or she is or does, but simply the kind of faith which Abraham exercised, as described in Gen 15:6.

25 The whole midrash and application is then fittingly rounded off with what looks like the sort of formula which may often have been used in the worship and teaching of the early Christian congregations. We should however by no means exclude the possibility that Paul created such a creedal description on his own account (even where a written liturgy is well established individuals will often use similarly formulated ascriptions in the liberty of their own inspiration). This possibility gains strength from the fact that Paul has shaped the two clauses to match the context, and indeed to provide a bridge between the two sections of his argument: the unusual link between justification and Jesus' resurrection is obviously determined by the earlier description of Abraham's justifying faith in God who makes alive the dead (v 17), just as the link between death and "transgressions" (where we might have expected "sins") evidently foreshadows the train of thought in 5:15–20.

The talk of Jesus being "handed over" is thoroughly rooted in the earliest Christians' memory and interpretation of Jesus' passion, as Paul himself is well aware (8:32; 1 Cor 11:23); so it must have become quickly established and widely used throughout the churches. Here in particular it is clear that the language has been modeled on the description of the servant in Isa 53 in both its Aramaic and LXX rendering. How far we can generalize from this occurrence to the whole "handed over" motif is much less clear, and tradition-historical analysis of Luke 22:37; Mark 10:45; and 14:24 does not permit a confident conclusion that the explicit use of Isa 53 goes back to Jesus. But Rom 4:25 is evidence enough that Isa 53 provided the first generation Christians with an important scriptural means of understanding the death of Jesus, and the fact that the reference is a formulaic allusion rather than a carefully argued scriptural proof (such as Paul has just provided for Gen 15:6) strongly suggests that the use of Isa 53 was widespread in earliest Christian apologetic and exercised a major influence on earliest Christian thought.

The two parts of the formula are obviously two sides of the same theological assertion. Paul of course does not intend his readers to distinguish between Jesus' death and his resurrection as effecting quite separate results. The distinction here is purely rhetorical. At the same time it was most natural to link human transgressions with Jesus' betrayal and death, especially since sacrificial categories were so much part and parcel of the Jewish understanding of God's way of dealing with sin. Having succeeded in separating Abraham's faith so clearly from cultic works, Paul is in no way embarrassed by the interpretation of Jesus' death within the framework of the major cultic work of sacrifice, as was evident already in chap. 3 (even if the imagery here is mediated through the allusion to Isa 53). And the link between justification and Jesus' resurrection was not merely prompted by the preceding exposition, but also further underscores its point—that the justifying grace of God is all of a piece with his creative, life-giving power. Abraham's trust would have been wholly vain if in the event God had not given him and Sarah seed after all. Just so, Christian faith would be vain unless God actually raised Jesus. Had Jesus' death not been followed by his resurrection, any understanding of his death as sacrifice would only have become part of Israel's martyr theology, without power of itself to provide the eschatological breakthrough which his resurrection demonstrated. Jesus' resurrection is proof positive that the same life-giving power which wrought for Abraham and Sarah is still at work in this new stage of God's dealing with humankind and at work in eschatological strength. Faith knows it is accepted precisely because its acceptance is the same effective power which raised Jesus and which will also give life to these mortal bodies (8:11) in the final reckoning.

C. First Conclusions: The New Perspective of Faith in Relation to the Individual and to Humanity at Large (5:1–21)

Introduction

Paul now draws out the consequences of this new perspective of faith, first for the individual believer in the present and the future—suffering but with sure hope of salvation (vv 1–11); and then on a salvation-history scale which sums up the whole sweep of human history from creation to consummation in the two men Adam and Christ—the one marking out the era of sin and death, the other of grace and life (vv 12–21); cf. Dupont, "Probleme," 381–82, who suggests that 5:12–21 functions in relation to 5:1–11 as chap. 4 to 3:21 ff.

The chapter is now regularly taken as the beginning of a new section (e.g., Dahl, "Notes"; Knox; Althaus; Michel; Fitzmyer; White, *Body*, 58–59; Cranfield; Schlier). Scroggs regards chaps. 5–8 as a unified homily originally separate from chaps. 1–4, 9–11 (cf. Zeller, *Juden*, which contains no discussion of chaps. 5–8). The categorization suggested by Nygren (elaborating the old analysis that chaps. 1–4/5 concern justification, chaps. 5/6–8, sanctification) has been influential—chap. 5: Free from the Wrath of God; chap. 6: Free from Sin; chap. 7: Free from the Law; chap. 8: Free from Death. Popular in French scholarship has been the suggestion that 5:12 to chap. 7 or 8 forms a single unit (Feuillet, "Plan"; Leenhardt; NJB; also Black; Paulsen, *Röm 8*, 13–21; Robinson, *Wrestling*, 59; otherwise Leon-Dufour); on the whole issue see Beker, *Paul*, 64–69 (with further bibliography in Fitzmyer).

However, chap. 5 as a whole must be regarded as a conclusion to the argument so far. 5:1–11 certainly functions in this way (Wolter, 207–16; Wilckens, 1:181–82, 286–87; Achtemeier treats 4:23–5:11 as a single paragraph). The backward links are too many and deliberate: δικαιοσύνη/δικαιόω ἐκ πίστεως as the chief theme of the letter as announced in 1:17 and developed through 3:21–4:25, is now summed up in vv 1 and 9. Likewise the sudden reappearance of "salvation" language in vv 9–10, recalls the only earlier but important reference in 1:16. There are echoes of the central argument (3:21–26) in vv 2 (grace, hope of glory), v 9 ("in his blood") and vv 9, 11 ("now"); central themes of the indictment of 1:18–2:29 are picked up in reverse—1:18 // 5:9 (ὀργή), 1:18 // 5:6 (ἀσέβεια/ἀσεβής), 1:21, 23 // 5:2 (δόξα), 1:28 // 5:4 (ἀδόκιμος/δοκιμή), 2:17 // 5:11 (καυχᾶσθαι ἐν θεῷ); and the climactic sequence of 5:6–10 (weak, ungodly, sinners, enemies) answers the reverse sequence of 1:19–32. This recollection of the indictment of humanity in Adamic terms (1:19–25) and its reversal "through Christ" prepares the way for the explicit Adam/Christ contrast of the following paragraph (5:12–21).

With 5:12 the perspective pulls back to cosmic focus (marked also by the shift from first person plural to third person singular). The continuity with vv 1–11 is indicated particularly by the re-emergence of the reversal theme in explicit terms of the two men whose single acts of disobedience and obedience encapsulate and determine the character of the two epochs, which together span human history. A very effective conclusion is thus achieved by showing how the sweeping indictment of Adamic humanity in 1:19 ff., repeated summarily in 3:23, is more than answered by the abundance of grace through Christ. Indeed, the whole course of the argument so far is contained within 5:12–21, with the rule of sin corresponding to 1:18–3:20 and the rule of grace corresponding to 3:21–5:11 (cf. Grayston, "Romans 1:16a," 572). The prominence of the δικαιοσύνη language in vv 16–21 also serves as a recall to the theme announced in 1:17 and provides a fitting summary of the exposition of 3:21–4:25 already recalled in 5:1 and 9.

At the same time, the ground is prepared in vv 1–11 for the "already/ not yet" tension which becomes such a mark of chaps. 6–8, and, as usual, the concluding verses (vv 20–21) provide a springboard for the next section (Dahl, "Notes," 41; *Studies*, 91) by linking law in a provocative way with the two quasi-powers which dominate the old epoch (sin and death); see further on 5:12–21 *Form and Structure*. The degree to which the two paragraphs are integrated into each other and into their context contradicts the wholly implausible thesis that they were later insertions (with reference to vv 1–11—Schmithals, *Römerbrief*, 197–202, but see particularly Wolter, 205–7; with reference to vv 12–21—O'Neill) and counts against Luz's description of vv 12–21 as "an erratic block" (*Geschichtsverständnis*, 193).

The centrality of 3:21–5:21 is further indicated by the way in which each of the following sections can be said to function as an outworking of the gospel as thus expounded. So 6:1–8:39 can be described as the outworking of the gospel in relation to the individual believer, 9:1–11:36 as the outworking of the gospel in relation to the election of grace, and even 12:1–15:13 as the outworking of the gospel for the redefined people of God in practical terms (cf. particularly Feuillet, "Plan").

In particular, it is helpful to see chaps. 6–8 and 9–11 as working out the conclusions of chap. 5 regarding the individual (5:1–11) and regarding humanity as a whole (5:12–21), in relation to the harsh realities of the present stage of God's purpose as those conclusions bear upon both the individual (chaps. 6–8; hence the parallels between 5:1–11 and chap. 8—Dahl, "Notes," 37–42, *Studies*, 88–89) and Israel (chaps. 9–11); in this sense chap. 5 can be called a "bridging" chapter (Kaye, *Chapter 6*, 7–13). The structural parallels can thus be set out as follows:

> 5:1-11 equivalent to chaps. 6-8
> 5:12-21 equivalent to chaps. 9-11.

The movement from the particular to the universal, which is a feature of 5:1–11 and 5:12–21, is also mirrored within the following chapters. In chaps. 6–8 the focus is primarily on the individual believer, but from 8:14 onwards there is a steadily mounting climax in which the tensions of the present stage of God's saving purpose are set more and more fully within the context of the Creator's purpose for the cosmos as a whole and resolved with the assurance that nothing can defeat what God has determined and already set in motion through Christ. Similarly in chaps. 9–11 Paul can only solve the salvation-history dilemma of Israel's disobedience by lifting his eyes to the mystery of God's purpose from beginning to end, his purpose as Creator and Redeemer for all humankind (11:25–36). The particular problems confronting individual (believer) or nation (Israel) can only be resolved within the context of God's overall purpose for creation and creature. Hence the further structural parallels:

5:12-21   equivalent to   8:14-39 and 11:25-36.

It is primarily because chaps. 6–8 have the function of working out the conclusions drawn in chap. 5 that we find so many thematic and verbal links between them, particularly in the twin themes of sin and grace, and death and life. But this is simply to recognize once again that Paul makes it his regular practice in Romans to set out his conclusions in such a way as to lead into the next stage of the discussion (see further on 5:12–21 *Form and Structure*).

1. The New Perspective on the Believer's Present and Future   (5:1–11)

Bibliography

Bornkamm, G. "Anakoluthe." 78–80. **Dahl, N. A.** "Two Notes on Romans 5." *ST* 5 (1952) 37–42. ———. *Studies.* 88–90. **Deidun, T. J.** *Morality.* 126–30. **Dibelius, M.** "Vier Worte." 3–6. **Donfried, K. P.** "Justification." 100–102. **Eichholz, G.** *Theologie.* 163–69. **Fatum, L.** "Die menschliche Schwäche im Römerbrief." *ST* 29 (1975) 31–52. **Fitzmyer, J.** "Reconciliation in Pauline Theology." *To Advance the Gospel.* New York: Crossroad, 1981. 162–85. **Goppelt, L.** "Versöhnung durch Christus." *Christologie.* 147–64. **Hofius, O.** "Sühne und Versöhnung: Zum paulinischen Verständnis des Kreuzestodes Jesu." *Versuche, das Leiden und Sterben Jesu zu verstehen,* ed. W. Maas. Munich: Schnell & Steiner, 1983. 25–46. **Jacobs, L.** "'Greater Love Hath No Man . . .': The Jewish Point of View of Self-Sacrifice." *Judaism* 6 (1957) 41–47. **Käsemann, E.** "Some Thoughts on the Theme 'The Doctrine of Reconciliation in the New Testament.'" In *The Future of our Religious Past,* FS R. Bultmann, ed. J. M. Robinson. London: SCM, 1971. 49–64. **Keck, L. E.** "The Post-Pauline Interpretation on Jesus' Death in Romans 5:6–7." In *Theologia Crucis—Signum Crucis,* FS D. E. Dinkler, ed. C. Andresen and G. Klein. Tübingen: Mohr, 1979. 237–48. **Kleinknecht, K. T.** *Gerechtfertigte.* 325–32, 347–49. **Kümmel, W. G.** "Interpretation of Romans 5:1–11." *Exegetical Method: A Student's Handbook.* Ed. O. Kaiser and W. G. Kümmel. New York: Seabury, 1963. 49–58. **Lafont, F. G.** "Sur l'interprétation de Romains 5:15–21." *RSR* 45 (1957) 481–513. **Landau, Y.** "Martyrdom in Paul's Religious Ethics: An Exegetical Commentary on Romans 5:7." *Immanuel* 15 (1982–83) 24–38. **Luz, U.** "Aufbau." 177–80. **Martin, R. P.** *Reconciliation: A Study of Paul's Theology.* Atlanta: John Knox, 1981. 135–54. **Mattern, L.** *Verständnis.* 86–91. **Morris, L.** *The Apostolic Preaching of the Cross.* London: Tyndale, 1955. 186–223. **Myers, C. D.** *The Place of Romans 5:1–11 within the Argument of the Epistle.* Diss. Princeton, 1985. **Nauck, W.** "Freude im Leiden." *ZNW* 46 (1955) 68–80. **Nebe, G.** *"Hoffnung" bei Paulus: Elpis und ihre Synonyme im Zusammenhang der Eschatologie.* SUNT 16. Göttingen: Vandenhoeck & Ruprecht, 1983. 123–36. **Ridderbos, H.** *Paul.* 49–53. **Synofzik, E.** *Vergeltungsaussagen.* 97–99. **Thüsing, W.** *Per Christum.*

183–200, 205–7. **Watson, F.** *Paul.* 143–47. **Wisse, F.** "The Righteous Man and the Good Man in Romans 5:7." *NTS* 19 (1972–73) 91–93. **Wolter, M.** *Rechtfertigung und zukünftiges Heil: Untersuchungen zu Röm 5:1–11.* BZNW 43. Berlin: de Gruyter, 1978.

Translation

¹ *Therefore, having been justified from faith we have*ᵃ *peace in relation to God through our Lord Jesus Christ,* ²*through whom also we have access (by faith)*ᵇ *into this grace in which we stand and boast in hope of the glory of God.* ³*Not only so, but we also boast in afflictions, knowing that affliction produces patience,* ⁴*and patience character, and character hope.* ⁵*And hope does not put to shame, because the love of God has been poured out in our hearts through the Holy Spirit given to us.*

⁶*For while we were still*ᶜ *weak, yet*ᶜ *Christ at that time died for the ungodly.* ⁷*For only rarely will someone die for a righteous man; for perhaps someone will dare to die for the good man.*ᵈ ⁸*But God demonstrates his love to us*ᵉ *in that while we were sinners Christ died for us.* ⁹*How much more then, having now been justified by his blood, we shall be saved through him from wrath.* ¹⁰*For if when we were enemies we were reconciled to God through the death of his Son, how much more, having been reconciled, we shall be saved by his life.* ¹¹*Not only so, but we also boast*ᶠ *in God through our Lord Jesus Christ,*ᵍ *through whom we have now received this reconciliation.*

Notes

ᵃAlthough ἔχωμεν, "let us have," is supported by the greater weight of MS evidence, most now accept (though see NEB; Kuss; Martin, 135, 148; Maillot) that on grounds of intrinsic probability ἔχομεν must have been intended. If an exhortation was intended ποιήσωμεν (as in Isa 27:5) would have been the more obvious choice. As it is, the subjunctive fits at best awkwardly with the accompanying indicatives. And an amanuensis's mishearing the o for ω (being of similar sound) is inherently likely (cf. 14:8, 19; 1 Cor 15:49). See further Wolter, 89–95.

ᵇEvidence of MSS and versions is equally divided over the inclusion or exclusion of τῇ πίστει and on internal grounds the phrase is as likely to have been inserted (to maintain Paul's emphasis) as omitted (as redundant after v 1). Either way the sense is unaltered.

ᶜThe awkwardness of the double ἔτι evidently led to various attempts to improve the text, but the ἔτι γάρ . . . ἔτι seems to be the earliest, as most now agree (see, e.g., Metzger, Wilckens; otherwise SH and Black).

ᵈThat Irenaeus (lat) passes over v 7 does not mean that it was lacking in his text.

ᵉFor the likely reasons behind the different ordering of the last four words of the clause and the omission of ὁ θεός in B Ephr arm, see Cranfield, 265 n.2.

ᶠSome scribes failing to recognize this characteristic of Paul's style (see *Comment*) changed the participle into an indicative.

ᵍ B and a few others omit Χριστοῦ, but the weight of evidence points to its being part of the original text, though on grounds of intrinsic probability it was as likely to be added as omitted.

Form and Structure

For the function of this paragraph within the argument of 1:18–11:39, see 5:1–21 *Introduction.* The passage is well structured, vv 9–11 obviously answering to vv 1–3 through the repetition of δικαιωθέντες (vv 1, 9), καυχ-ᾶσθαι (vv 2, 3, 11), the strong διά formula (vv 1–2, 9–11) and the οὐ μόνον δέ, ἀλλὰ καί (vv 3, 11). In addition we may note the chain reasoning of vv 3–5 (a rhetorical "gradatio"—Heil), the climax of vv 6–10 (weak, ungodly, sinners, enemies), with the striking fourfold repetition of ἀποθανεῖν at the end of each clause in vv 6–8 (Bornkamm, "Anakoluthe," 79), and other features of vv 9–11 (repeated πολλῷ μᾶλλον and the interchange of concepts). See also Myers, *Romans 5:1–11*, 28–34, 52–53, 182–85. Kirk speaks of vv 6–11 as "the hymn of the crucified Jesus." If a dominant concept is to be found it is less likely to be "peace" (Cranfield, Hendriksen) or "reconciliation" (Martin), and more likely to be "hope" since it provides not only the link word in vv 2–5 but also characterizes the eschatological tension which is such a feature of the passage as a whole (cf. Eichholz, *Theologie,* 174; Wolter, 217–22; Watson, *Paul,* 144); Heil, *Hope,* sees hope as the leitmotif of the whole letter.

Comment

5:1 δικαιωθέντες οὖν ἐκ πίστεως, "therefore, having been justified from faith." Somewhat surprisingly, this is the first time Paul uses δικαιόω in the aorist in Romans—apart from 3:4 (God) and 4:2 (Abraham). In more general references and references to his fellow believers the present indicative (3:24, 26, 28; 4:5) and future (2:13; 3:20, 30) have predominated. The tense here certainly indicates an act of God in the past, but that should not be allowed to dominate the doctrine of justification drawn from Paul to the extent that it has, or to overwhelm the force of the other tenses. Read together with these texts and in the light of the arguments so far, δικαιωθέντες is best taken to denote God's acceptance into that relationship and status (which Abraham enjoyed as "the friend of God," "this grace in which we stand"—v 2), and which God will acknowledge and vindicate in the final judgment (denoted in the forward-looking "hope of glory"—v 2). See further on 2:13.

The ἐκ πίστεως is certainly to be construed along the same lines as the same phrase in 3:26, 30 and 4:16 (also 9:30, 32 and 10:6). With the δικαιωθέντες it is not to be separated from the *continued* act of believing (note again the characteristic use of πιστεύειν in the present tense—see on 1:16), or from the idea of life as lived ἐκ πίστεως (see on 3:26). But here it denotes the particular act in which that faith was first exercised, the initial act of commitment. Paul is able to assume that all (or most) of his readers will have gone through such a conversion, and that this is a fundamental part of their common bond; and although baptism will have been part of this process (6:4), there is nothing to suggest that at this point Paul intended to refer his readers to their baptism as such (against Schlier). At the same time, although the primary reference is to faith such as Abraham exercised (cf. 4:16), the phrase could have the richer connotations of the key text in 1:17—God's faithfulness as well as man's faith—this being precisely the point of 4:18–21: Abraham's faith is faith in God's faithfulness to his promise.

εἰρήνην ἔχομεν πρὸς τὸν θεόν, "we have peace in relation to God." The more "negative" idea of εἰρήνη as absence of war, typical of Greek thought (LSJ; in OT see e.g., Deut 20:12; Judg 4:17; 1 Sam 7:14; 1 Kings 2:5; Isa 36:16), is certainly present here (cf. v 10). But otherwise we should assume that the more positive Hebraic concept of peace is dominant (see on 1:7). In particular, although the "spiritual" dimension of peace is to the fore here ("peace toward God"), the concept should not be spiritualized or divorced from the wider Jewish concept (see again on 1:7). For the same reason it should not be reduced to a subjective feeling—von Rad indeed claims that in the OT "there is no specific text in which שָׁלוֹם denotes the specifically spiritual attitude of inward peace" (*TDNT* 2:406); so here we can say that Paul has in view an actual relationship ("reconciliation"—vv 10–11) whose outworking in life should be visible (cf. particularly 14:19; 1 Cor 14:33). Again it is worth noting that he can state it as a simple fact ("we have peace with God"; see *Notes*), confident that the assertion would ring true to the experience of his readers (cf. Gal 5:22). See also Luther's comments on the significance of the talk of peace following that of justification (cited also by Harrisville).

In view of the immediately preceding context it is important to remember the extent to which, in Jewish thought, God-given peace was bound up with the covenant (e.g., Num 6:22–27; Ps 55:18–19; Isa 48:17–22; Jer 14:19–21; Sir 47:13; 2 Macc 1:2–4) (see also Wright, *Messiah*, 136). For the "zealots for the law" it would be particularly important that the "covenant of peace" was associated especially with the priesthood and with Phinehas (Num 25:12; Mal 2:4–5; Sir 45:24; see also on 4:3). Equally significant is the degree to which within this framework of thought "peace" and "righteousness" were overlapping or complementary concepts (Pss 35:27; 72:3; 85:10; Isa 9:7; 32:17; 48:18; 60:17)—צְדָקָה as the norm for the fulfilled state of שָׁלוֹם;" (*TDNT* 2:177). Since in prophetic hope the full flowering of God's covenanted peace belonged to the future new age (Isa 9:6–7; 54:10; Ezek 34:25–31; 37:26; Mic 5:4; Hag 2:9; Zech 8:12; *1 Enoch* 5.7, 9; 10.17; 11.2), Paul's assertion amounts to a claim that Israel's eschatological hope is now already in process of fulfillment. The claim sets up the tension between "already" and "not yet" which characterizes this passage (cf. also 2:10 and 14:17). Wolter, 95–104, justly criticizes Brandenburger's talk of "peace with God" emerging from a conception of cosmic reconciliation, and suggests that behind the statements of 5:1, 10–11 stands an early Jewish interpretation of Isa 57:19 (104).

διὰ τοῦ κυρίου ἡμῶν Ἰησοῦ Χριστοῦ, "through our Lord Jesus Christ." The phrase διὰ Ἰησοῦ Χριστοῦ plays an important role in chap. 5 (vv 1, 11, 21), each verse picking out different aspects of the unique mediatorial role ascribed to the exalted Christ, both the "upward" movement of praise (5:11; see also on 1:8) and the "downward" movement of grace (5:21; see also on 2:16). The same double, two-way-interchange in this mediatorial role is indicated here (the mediator of peace) and in the immediately following phrase (the mediator of access—v 2). That this is a personal role for Jesus in his resurrected existence is taken for granted—hence διά with the genitive and not διά with the accusative ("on account of, for the sake of" some past action of Jesus). For κύριος in reference to Jesus see on 1:4 and 10:9. "*Our* Lord"—the same easy confidence that he is talking a common language to readers who share a common commitment and experience pervades the whole verse.

2 δι' οὗ καὶ τὴν προσαγωγὴν ἐσχήκαμεν, "through whom also we have access." For the δι' οὗ see on 5:1. It should not simply be assumed that the dominant imagery behind προσαγωγή is cultic ("unhindered access to the sanctuary as the place of God's presence"—Käsemann): προσαγωγή is never used and προσάγειν has no specially cultic reference in the LXX; the only other occurrences in the NT are not decisive either (Eph 2:18; 3:12); nor does Heb 10:19 necessarily provide a significant parallel since εἴσοδος there is simply the particular application of a more general concept ("entrance")—see LSJ and BGD, εἴσοδος. On the other hand, it is true that the imagery of approach to God's presence in the sanctuary would be natural to one born and bred a Jew, and the striking parallel of 1QS 11:13–15 would almost certainly have cultic overtones (see further Wolter, 107–20). Nevertheless, in the societies of the time (not least in Rome itself) the court imagery of access through the royal chamberlain into the king's presence would just as readily be evoked (Xenophon, *Cyr.* 7.5.45; so LSJ and SH), as the association of χάρις also indicates (see below); besides which, Heb 4:16 and the Emperor cult remind us that cult and court could be readily merged in such imagery. The possibility cannot be ruled out that Paul also had in mind the more nautical imagery of a "landing stage" on a favorable shore which enables the sea-weary mariner to make safe landing once more on *terra firma* (cf. LSJ II.3; MM); but that fits less well into the strong emphasis on personal relationships (as between God and believers) which characterizes 5:1–11 and leaves the mediatorial role of Jesus (pilot?) unclear.

ἐσχήκαμεν—following on from the ἔχομεν (present tense) of v 1, the perfect tense here (cf. 2 Cor 1:9; 2:13; 7:5) could be a stylistic variation, but probably is intended to denote both the initial entrance into God's presence ("having been justified") and its continuing availability and outworking ("we have peace with God"). As an alternative way of expressing the same claim as v 1 it underlines the relational character of all Paul's soteriology, including his concept of justification (see on 1:17).

τῇ πίστει, "by faith." If part of the original text (see *Notes*) this is the last time Paul uses this key noun ("faith") until the resumption of the talk of righteousness "from faith" in 9:30. Clearly he has by now established to his own satisfaction its sense as committed trust in God (particularly 4:17–21), as also his basic thesis (1:17), and can now begin to draw out the conclusion which follows from it in the confident hope that his listeners' own experience has provided sufficient confirmation and that he has carried them with him.

εἰς τὴν χάριν ταύτην ἐν ᾗ ἑστήκαμεν, "into this grace in which we stand." The use of χάρις here is somewhat unusual—"grace" as a sphere or state (a secure area) into which one enters. But it is a quite natural extension of its more normal Pauline sense, denoting the gracious power of God outreached to humanity and working in and through human beings (see on 1:5)—so here, the sphere or dimension marked out by God's grace, the status characterized by God's grace (cf. 1QH 4.21–22; 7.30–31; and the talk in 1QS of entry into "the covenant of grace"—1.8). Since a reference to royal "favor" is also a quite natural part of its broader Greek usage (cf. BGD, χάρις 2a; *TDNT* 9:375), its use here strengthens the court imagery of προσαγωγή (see above): to enter the king's presence being possible only if the king extends his royal favor to the suppliant. The preceding emphasis, by grace and not by works of the law (3:24; 4:4, 16), is of course assumed and implicit here: "*this* grace" as the overwhelmingly dominant characteristic of a positive relationship between God and man. The ἐν ᾗ together with the further use of a perfect tense ("in which we have taken our stand") underscores Paul's conviction that conversion, entry into the covenant promise, results in a relationship with God which is settled and established; though it should not be forgotten that the perfect can also carry the sense of a settled and sustained commitment on the part of the one who so stands ("stand firm"—BGD, ἵστημι II.2.c); see also Wilckens.

καυχώμεθα ἐπ᾽ ἐλπίδι τῆς δόξης τοῦ θεοῦ, "we boast in hope of the glory of God." If ἔχωμεν is read in v 1, καυχώμεθα (here and in v 3) could be taken as a subjunctive, "let us boast" (Kuss). The clause deliberately recalls and brings together language and phrases that had played a significant role at earlier stages in the argument: "boasting" (2:17, 23; 3:27; 4:2), "in hope" (4:18), "the glory of God" (1:23; 3:23). The "reversal" in the case of the first and last is also significant: "boasting" is now something Paul treats as positive and commendable; and "the glory of God" is something to be looked forward to (not something lost or departed from). Paul's point is not simply that there is a boasting which is proper, but that such boasting is only possible for the person who stands in God's grace, so that his boasting is of the God on whom he totally depends without being able to claim any special privilege (contrast 2:17, 23). As such it is a boasting which is conscious of the not-yet, but is confident of its outcome. As such it is a boasting of the creature confident in the fulfillment of the Creator's purpose for his creation. For καυχάομαι see on 2:17 and *Form and Structure;* the variation in prepositions (ἐπί—v 2; ἐν—v 3) seems to be merely stylistic (Kümmel, "Interpretation," 53). Michel speaks of "the shout of joy" (*Jubelruf*) and compares the use of ἀγαλλίασις and ἀγαλλιᾶσθαι in Luke 1:47; 10:21; and Acts 2:46. Schlier notes that the two terms often come together in the LXX (citing, e.g., Pss 5:11 [LXX 12] and 32 [LXX 31]:11); but his further suggestion that καυχᾶσθαι is synonymous with φυσιοῦσθαι ("become puffed up, conceited") fails to note that it is the national pride of his countrymen which Paul strikes at here (cf. Wright, *Messiah,* 137), rather than the more individualistic conceit more typical of the Greeks. ἐλπίς has its Hebraic sense of a confident or sure hope, rather than a tentative, uncertain expectation (see on 4:18); on what that certainty is based Paul will make clear in vv 3–5. With the reemergence of the theme "the glory of God" Paul already before 5:12 ff. reverts to the Adam motif (see on 1:21 and 3:23)—the divine purpose in salvation being understood in terms of a restoration (and completion) of fallen humanity to the glory which all now fall short of (see further on 8:17; cf. 2 Cor 3:18; 1 Thess 2:12, and Paul's similar use of the complementary but not synonymous concept of the "image" of God; see Dunn, *Christology,* 105–6). Schlier quite properly notes that δικαιοσύνη and δόξα are to some extent equivalent concepts, but underplays the degree to which "the glory of God" belongs to the future, the not-yet dimension of salvation (cf. Nebe, 126–27).

3 οὐ μόνον δέ, ἀλλὰ καί, "not only so, but also"—a typical Pauline construction (cf. 5:11; 8:23; 9:10; 2 Cor 8:19) but also in Greek and Jewish literature (BDF §479; BGD, μόνος 2c; Michel, 178 n.6).

καυχώμεθα ἐν ταῖς θλίψεσιν, "we boast in afflictions." θλῖψις can mean simply distress brought about by outward circumstances (so in Paul probably 2 Cor 1:4, 8; 2:4; 6:4; 7:4; 8:2, 13; Phil 1:17; 4:14; 1 Thess 1:6; 3:3, 7; 2 Thess

1:4). But it can also be used of the tribulations of the last days (as in Dan 12:1; Mark 13:19, 24 par.), and since the eschatological tension of the already/ not yet is such a prominent feature of this passage (vv 1–11), that overtone may be present here, as probably also in 8:35; 12:12; 1 Cor 7:28; 2 Cor 4:17; and Col 1:24 (cf. Schlier; and see also on 2:9). It is also an important aspect of his christologically determined soteriology that the sufferings believers endure in the period of overlap between the old age (of Adam) and the new age (of Christ) are bearable because they are a sharing in Christ's sufferings and death (see further Dunn, *Jesus*, 326–38). ἐν should probably not be taken as locative (we boast from the midst of our sufferings—cf. Michel), since καυχάομαι ἐν is Paul's regular formula to denote the object of the boasting (2:17, 23; 5:11; 1 Cor 1:31; 3:21; etc.).

Despite an outward attractiveness, it is unlikely that Paul intended his talk of boasting here to be taken as a further polemic against Jewish boasting in the security afforded by the law (2:17, 23), as though tribulation would always be perceived within Judaism as a contradiction of God's covenanted favor and so as something which could hardly be regarded in a positive light (Str-B, 3:221, cites Bousset, and Daube, *Rabbinic Judaism*, 117, cites Carrington as maintaining that *boasting* in sufferings was something distinctively Christian). But in fact Judaism had had a long experience in meeting the challenge of adversity, and positive responses to it are not hard to document. For example, like Heb 12:5–6, Philo also quotes Prov 3:11–12 to prove the positive value of discipline and hardship (*Cong.* 31); similarly Sir 2:4–5 and Wisd Sol 3:4–7. The high regard for the Maccabean martyrs encouraged a similarly positive evaluation of national calamity (particularly 2 Macc 6:12–16). And in the wake of the Roman conquest of Palestine the *Psalms of Solomon* reflect frequently and positively on God's chastening (παιδεία—3.3–4; 13.7–10; 16.4–5, 11–15; 18.4–5). Presumably, similar sentiments among Stoic philosophers, such as we find in Seneca's *De Providentia* (particularly chap. 4), would not be unknown among the Christians in Rome. For the particular note of rejoicing we can compare *Pss. Sol.* 10.1–2—"Happy is the man whom the Lord remembers with reproof . . . for the Lord is gracious to those who endure chastening"; 1QH 9.24–25—"Thy rebuke shall become my joy and gladness, and my scourges shall turn to (eternal) healing" (Vermes); 2 *Apoc. Bar.* 52.6—"Enjoy yourselves in the suffering which you suffer now." See further Str-B, 3:222; Daube, *Rabbinic Judaism*, 117–18; Nauck, "Freude"; and below. In taking over this theme, Paul is saying in effect that the suffering of believers is proof of their covenant membership ("evidence of membership within God's true Israel"—Wright, *Messiah*, 137), though the repetition of καυχάομαι may also be determined by the logic of the eschatological tension itself and by Paul's desire to make a transition to the chain sequence which follows.

εἰδότες ὅτι, "knowing that." The appeal is either to their common experience (the common experience of Christians which Paul could assume; "Christian experience speaks here"—Käsemann) or to their knowledge of the established homiletical pattern which Paul is about to take up (so common that Paul could assume their knowledge of it), or both (Nebe, 129). The form itself is not distinctively Christian (cf. particularly Wisd Sol 6:17–19; Maximus of

Tyre 16:3b; see further Michel, 179 n.2), and the parallels in James 1:2–4
and 1 Pet 1:6–7 strongly suggest that Paul is drawing here on a fairly well
established pattern of Christian homily (cf. particularly M. Dibelius, *Jakobus*,
KEK [1964] 103–5; cf. also 125–29). The chain sequence certainly implies a
process of maturing, but not distinguishable stages in faith (as Michel rightly
notes) since its end point is no different from the hope into which they
entered on first believing (v 2).

ἡ θλῖψις ὑπομονὴν κατεργάζεται, "affliction produces patience." For θλῖψις
see above. ὑπομονή is a strong word, as the sequence of meanings listed by
BGD, indicates—"patience, endurance, fortitude, steadfastness, perseverance." As such it was highly prized both within Greek thought, particularly
by the Stoics (*TDNT* 4:582–83) and in contemporary Judaism (*Pss. Sol.* 2.36;
T. Jos. 2.7; 10.1–2; frequently in *4 Maccabees* to describe the steadfastness of
the martyrs—1.11; 7.9; 9.8, 30; etc.; Philo, *Cher.* 78—elsewhere treating Re-
bekah as an allegory of ὑπομονή and showing the influence of Stoic thought—
TDNT 4:583 n.8 and 585 n.15; the incidence of ὑπομονή in the later Greek
translations of Job increases markedly [HR], a trend reflected also in James
5:11). Paul gives special prominence to ὑπομονή among the Christian virtues
(2:7; 5:3–4; 8:25; 15:4–5; 2 Cor 1:6; 6:4; 12:12; Col 1:11; 1 Thess 1:3; 2
Thess 1:4; 3:5). But it is also established firmly in other NT traditions (e.g.,
Luke 8:15; Heb 12:1; James 1:3–4; 1 Pet 2:20; Rev 2:2–3). Paul clearly
seeks to foster a positive attitude to "affliction," but he wisely recognizes
that the starting point must be the readiness to endure the suffering rather
than to escape it, and to endure it all the way through.

4 ἡ δὲ ὑπομονὴ δοκιμήν, "and patience [produces] character." δοκιμή is an
exclusively Pauline word within biblical Greek—here in the sense of "the
quality of being approved," hence "character," "tested character" (NJB; as
also in 2 Cor 2:9; 9:13; and Phil 2:22; in 2 Cor 8:2, "test, ordeal"; in 2 Cor
13:3, "proof"—BGD). In view of its lack of attestation elsewhere prior to
Paul, it may be that Paul was the first to coin the word. The metaphor on
which he draws, however, would have been familiar enough—the idea of
testing, particularly that of proving gold by testing it with fire (see BGD,
particularly δοκιμάζω 2a; δοκίμιον 2; *TDNT* 2:256). Here again Paul is clearly
drawing on a well established theme of Jewish wisdom (cf. Job 23:10; Prov
8:10; 17:3; Sir 2:5; Wisd Sol 3:6), and indeed the thought of Abraham's
testing which lay in the background of chap. 4 may still have been in Paul's
mind (see on 4:2; other references in Wolter, 139–42). For the combination
of testing and patience, cf. particularly *Jub.* 19.8; *T. Jos.* 2.7; and *4 Macc*
9.7–8; 17.12; and in Christian tradition independent of Paul note again
James 1:3 and cf. 1 Pet 1:7. For δοκιμάζειν see on 1:28. To regard affliction
as divinely appointed testing designed to prove and mature is the key Paul
and this broader tradition offer toward a positive attitude to suffering. Paul
probably intends his readers to pick up a contrast between the process to
salvation marked by δοκιμή and the process of wrath marked by the ἀδόκιμος
mind (1:28).

ἡ δὲ δοκιμὴ ἐλπίδα, "and character [produces] hope." It is at this point that
the Jewish and Christian response to suffering moves beyond that found in
Greek and particularly Stoic thought. Since ἐλπίς in Greek thought lacks the

positive note present in the Jewish use of the term (see on 4:18), the more natural climax for such a chain homily would be in ὑπομονή or δοκιμή (cf. TDNT 4:584). But the Jewish-Christian faith, with confidence in God, looks beyond this visible world and present age. The degree to which ὑπομονή and ἐλπίς actually overlap in Jewish thought is indicated by the fact that תִּקְוָה ("hope") is translated into Greek by both words (cf. Job 14:19; Pss 9:18 [LXX 19]; 62:5 [LXX 61:6]; and 71 [LXX 70]:5 with Job 4:6; 5:16; 6:8; etc., Prov 10:28; 11:7, 23, etc.) and by the difficulty of knowing how to render ὑπομονή in Sir 2:14; 16:13; 17:24; and 41:2. Elsewhere in Paul note the association of these ideas in 12:12; 15:5, 13; and particularly ὑπομονή τῆς ἐλπίδος in 1 Thess 1:3.

5 ἡ δὲ ἐλπὶς οὐ καταισχύνει, "and hope does not make ashamed." καταισχύνω can have the sense of "be ashamed" as well as "put to shame" (BGD). Here Paul probably has the latter more in mind; cf. particularly 1 Cor 1:27 (TDNT 1:189–90); also ἐπαισχύνομαι in 1:16; for the association of the idea of a boasting not disappointed, cf. 2 Cor 7:14. The language clearly echoes the frequent use of the same verb particularly in the Psalms (cf. 22:5 [LXX 21:6]; 25 [LXX 24]:2–3, 20; 31:1, 17 [LXX 30:2, 18]; 71 [LXX 70]:1; 119 [LXX 118]:31, 116); but note also Isa 50:7; 54:4; Joel 2:26–27; Sir 2:10; 15:4; 24:22; and the LXX of Isa 28:16 quoted by Paul in Rom 9:33 and 10:11, and found also in 1 Pet 2:6 (see also Kleinknecht, 329–30). The verb underscores the character of hope in Judeo-Christian tradition (see on 4:18 and 5:4); as usual, Paul has in mind the experience of hope, rather than the thing hoped for (Nebe, 131–35). And though the thought is of the final vindication of the hope for a complete salvation and favorable verdict in the final judgment, the verb should probably be read as a present rather than as a future (καταισχυνεῖ). Indeed the present effect of the hope may mark some distinction from the predominantly future-oriented, passive use of the verb in the Jewish tradition, since it is rooted in an eschatological fulfillment already experienced (see further below).

ὅτι ἡ ἀγάπη τοῦ θεοῦ ἐκκέχυται ἐν ταῖς καρδίαις ἡμῶν, "because the love of God has been poured out in our hearts." The ὅτι indicates that what follows is the ground of hope's confidence just expressed. For ἀγάπη see on 12:9. There is general agreement that ἀγάπη τοῦ θεοῦ means God's love to us, not our love of God (see particularly Nygren's critique of Augustine; otherwise Wright, Messiah, 137–39)—so the following three verses linked to v 5 by γάρ would indicate anyway (Käsemann). What is striking about this first reference to God's love in Romans is that Paul should speak of it in such vivid experiential terms—God's love not simply as something believed in on the basis of the gospel or the testimony of the cross (cf. even v 8), not simply the certainty of God's love (Kuss), but God's love itself (Althaus) experienced in rich measure (cf. 8:35, 39; 2 Cor 5:14; Eph 2:4; 3:18–19; 2 Thess 3:5); cf. also 1 John 2:5; 3:17; etc. The phrase itself ("the love of God") appears in the Pauline epistles only in 5:5; 8:39; and 2 Cor 13:13. For the close association between the Spirit and love in Paul, cf. particularly 15:30, Gal 5:22; Phil 2:1; Col 1:8; and 2 Tim 1:7. For the traditional dispute on the significance of the verse, see Wilckens, 1:300–305.

The ἐκκέχυται functions as the perfect tense of ἐκχέω, and although it can be used of anything bestowed from above (e.g., grace—Ps 45:2 [LXX 44:3]; mercy—Sir 18:11; see further Schlier), the association with the Spirit in the present context, which in the NT is paralleled only by Acts 2:17, 18 (citing Joel 2:28–29 [LXX 3:1–2]), 33; 10:45 (harking back to the events of chap. 2); and Tit 3:6 (an established tradition), strongly suggests that the verb had already become fixed within Christian terminology as a reference to the founding event of Pentecost (Dunn, *Jesus*, 142. The use of καταισχύνω in Joel 2:26–27 may indeed indicate that Paul's sequence of thought here was prompted by Joel 2:26–29); "with ἐκκέχυται the talk is of love, the thought is of the Holy Spirit" (Dibelius, "Vier Worte," 6). The perfect tense as usual indicates a continuing effect of a past event. Here again the experiential nature of what Paul has in mind (with some element of ecstasy not excluded— cf. Acts 2:1–4) comes strongly into view, under the vivid metaphor of a cloud-burst on a parched countryside. The ἐν ταῖς καρδίαις ἡμῶν underscores the same point since it is precisely the fact that God has effected his work at the level of their motive and emotive center (see on 1:21 and 2:15; "our inmost heart"—NEB), through the Spirit and in fulfillment of the promise of Jer 31:31–34 (cf. 2 Cor 3:3), which in Paul's view most clearly distinguished the first Christians from their typical Jewish counterparts (see on 2:29).

διὰ πνεύματος ἁγίου τοῦ δοθέντος ἡμῖν, "through the Holy Spirit given to us." The διά can designate not simply the means through which but the perceptible form in which the Spirit comes to expression (Wolter, 161–66; cf. 1 Cor 12:7, χαρίσματα, "charisms," as the manifestation of the Spirit), without reducing the Spirit to or identifying the Spirit wholly with an experi-ence of God's love. Here it is important to recall that in prophetic expectation the outpouring of the Spirit was looked for as the mark of the new age (see particularly Isa 32:15; 34:16; 44:3; Ezek 11:19; 36:26–27; 37:4–14; Joel 2:28–32). Together with the echo of Jer 31:31–34 and Joel 2:28–29 in the preceding phrase, Paul effectively brings to clear expression what had been more implicit throughout his argument from 3:21 onwards: that with Christ's death and resurrection the new age of Jewish expectation had already dawned. Within contemporary Judaism the only real parallel is the sect at Qumran (see particu-larly 1QH 7.6–7; 12.11–12; 14.13; 16.11–12; 17.26); but Qumran's outworking of that experience in increased devotion to the covenant, as marked by an intensification of the works of the law, was radically different from Paul's. For Paul in particular the eschatological character of the gift of the Spirit is clearly marked—the Spirit as the ἀρραβών, "first installment" of the eschatologi-cal harvest of redemption and "guarantee" of its completion (2 Cor 1:22; 5:5; so also Eph 1:14; see Dunn, *Jesus*, 310–12); and see further on 8:23.

It is not surprising that such a bold claim was rooted in very vivid experi-ences—here the experience of being filled with God's love. His willingness to use "Spirit vocabulary" (ἐκκέχυται) when talking of God's love suggests that Paul was not greatly concerned to make a clear distinction between the gift of the Spirit and the outpouring of love; experientially it would be hard to make such a distinction (cf. Barrett, and above on διά). Elsewhere the Spirit is associated with the experience of joy (1 Thess 1:6), of miracles (Gal 3:5), of charismatic utterances (1 Cor 1:4–7) and of moral transformation (1 Cor 6:9–11)—cf. Acts 8:17–19; 10:44–47; and 19:6 (see also on 8:14).

Nor is it surprising that within Paul's thought it is the gift of the Spirit which both determines belonging to Christ and functions as the mark of belonging to Christ (see on 8:9); the fact that Paul always conceives of the giver of the Spirit as God (rather than Christ; contrast Acts 2:33) is part of the complexity of his conception of the relationship between the exalted Christ and the Spirit (Dunn, *Christology*, 143). The Spirit as "given" or "gift" is already established Christian terminology (διδόναι, "give"—Luke 11:13; Acts 5:32; 8:18; 11:17; 15:8; 1 Thess 4:8—Ezek 37:14; with ἡ δωρεὰ τοῦ θεοῦ, "the gift of God," almost a technical term for the Spirit—John 4:10; Acts 2:38; 8:20; 10:45; 11:17; Eph 4:7; Heb 6:4). The tendency of commentators to treat the aorist (δοθέντος) as a reference to baptism (e.g., Wilckens, Zeller) reflects the long-standing ecclesiastical tradition in which the baptized is not expected to experience anything, so that any recall to someone's beginnings as a Christian has to be to the baptism itself. In contrast, the experience of the Spirit in the Pauline communities as a rule was evidently vivid enough that it could be referred to directly (as in 1 Cor 12:13; 2 Cor 1:22; Gal 3:2–5; see further Dunn, *Baptism*, pt. 3).

6 ἔτι γὰρ Χριστὸς ὄντων ἡμῶν ἀσθενῶν ἔτι κατὰ καιρὸν ὑπὲρ ἀσεβῶν ἀπέθανεν, "for while we were still weak, yet Christ at that time died for the ungodly." The sentence is awkwardly constructed, partly because Paul chooses to put the subject and verb at the two places of emphasis (beginning and end of the sentence), and partly because he wants to underscore the surprising quality of God's love both as to its object and as to its timing. The γάρ serves to link the new sequence of thought back to the preceding sequence: vv 6–8 provide further justification for the hope of vv 3–5. For the first time in Romans Paul uses Χριστός by itself. The fact that it occurs here and in v 8 in the sentence "Christ died" may well reflect the summary assertion of earliest Christian apologetic that Jesus' crucifixion was no disproof of his messiahship: it was precisely as the crucified that he was the Messiah (cf. particularly 1 Cor 1:23; Gal 2:20–3:1).

The ἀσθενής does not have any particular theological overtones here (despite BGD, "morally weak"); Paul uses it and related words simply in a general sense to characterize the human condition as such in contrast to the power of God (as in 8:26; 1 Cor 15:43; cf. Wisd Sol 9:5 and further Wolter, 170); contrast the more delimited use of 14:1–2 (the occurrence of this word in both passages is inadequate basis for Minear's suggestion, *Obedience*, 58, that the verse is directed particularly to "the strong"). The argument that "'weak' is far too mild a word to represent the state of those for whom Christ died" (O'Neill) misses the point that Paul begins a crescendo here (weak, ungodly, sinners, enemies—vv 6, 8, 10); the obvious place to begin is with the weakness of the creature over against the omnipotence of the Creator (cf 1:20; 4:21). The genitive absolute ("we being weak") thus describes not merely the previous state of the believer, as though with conversion he becomes "strong," but the continuing state of human existence in the between times of the eschatological tension and its accompanying sufferings (v 3; cf. 8:26; 2 Cor 11:29–30; 12:5, 9–10; Schlatter).

κατὰ καιρόν can mean either "at the right time," the "propitious moment," "the eschatological moment" (e.g., *TDNT* 3:460, Barrett, Michel), or more likely "at that time," that is, "when we were weak" (Fitzmyer, Käsemann, Schlier, Wilckens, n. 973). But since it is the "afflictions" of the last days (see on 5:3) which particularly demonstrate human weakness, καιρός can retain its overtone of the eschatological time as that to which God's purpose has been moving and in which he has acted decisively (see on 3:26 and 9:9); Martin, 146, appositely cites *Pss. Sol.* 17.21.

ἀποθανεῖν ὑπέρ, (Christ) "died for the sake/benefit of," is well established in the evangelistic and creedal language inherited by Paul (14:15; 1 Cor 15:3; 2 Cor 5:15; 1 Thess 5:10; cf. 1 Pet 3:18; see further Barrett and *TDNT* 8:509). But it was already familiar in Jewish circles as martyr terminology, in reference to the Maccabean martyrs (2 Macc 7:9; 8:21; 4 Macc 1:8, 10; Josephus, *Ant.* 13.5–6; cf. John 18:14). Paul was probably aware of this other usage, since his own formula is such a shocking contrast to it: Christ died for the *ungodly*. His contemporaries were familiar with this thought of dying for the law(s) or for the nation, but the ἀσεβεῖς were precisely those whose conduct put them outside the scope of such covenant faithfulness and concern (cf. v 8—ἁμαρτωλοί; see on 4:5; cf. Wilckens, 296). Paul's point is precisely that Christ died for those whose ἀσέβεια ("ungodliness") he had indicted in 1:18 ff., for humankind as a whole, Jew first as well as Gentile (see on 1:18). It is probably significant that Paul does not say ὑπὲρ ἡμῶν (as in v 8), but in effect replaces the ἀσθενῶν with ἀσεβῶν: it is not as creatures that we need Christ to die for us, but as those who have rebelled against their creaturely state; not creation per se needs redemption but fallen creation (cf. 8:19–23).

7 μόλις γὰρ ὑπὲρ δικαίου τις ἀποθανεῖται, "for only rarely will someone die for a righteous man." μόλις could be given a stronger sense—"hardly, scarcely" (see BGD), but in view of the strong martyr tradition within Judaism (see on 5:6) it is unlikely that Paul intended to play down the idea of one dying for another in itself. At the same time the choice of δίκαιος must be deliberate, since "the righteous" was one of the established self-characterizations of devout Jews (cf., e.g., Hab 2:4, and see further on 1:17; significant for the contrast Paul has in mind here, vv 6–7, is Wisd Sol 10:20—"the righteous plundered the ungodly," δίκαιοι ἐσκύλευσαν ἀσεβεῖς). Is then the singular significant? The Maccabean martyrs died for the covenant, for the sake of the nation as God's peculiar people, not for a pious individual. According to Jacobs, sacrifice of one's life for the sake of another has not been something particularly commended within Judaism. More probably there is some contrast with ἀγαθός intended, and with δίκαιος Paul recalls what to him now was the unattractiveness of his previous zeal for the law—the "pious moralist" (Landau, 34). Cf. particularly Lightfoot, "the distinction between δίκαιος and ἀγαθός is very much the same as the Aristotelian distinction between the ἀκριβοδίκαιος and the ἐπικεινής (*Eth. Nic.* 5.14), between the man, that is to say, who is scrupulously just and the man who is prepared to make allowances" (with documentation). On the other hand, the more positive the force of δίκαιος, the stronger Paul's point: if one who is faithful to the law inspires such little readiness to die on his behalf, how much greater the love which dies for the mass of the ungodly. Either way, the issue turns on the significance of δίκαιος more than on that of ἀγαθός (against Wisse).

ὑπὲρ γὰρ τοῦ ἀγαθοῦ τάχα τις καὶ τολμᾷ ἀποθανεῖν, "for perhaps someone will dare to die for the good man." The clause is poorly coordinated with v 7a, but since Paul's style quite often incorporates infelicitous features we should not be surprised here or see the awkwardness as sufficient reason to treat it as a gloss (against Jülicher; Sahlin, "Textemendationen," 96–97; Fuchs, *Freiheit*, 15–16, and Schmithals, *Römerbrief*, 198–99, regard both vv 6 and 7 as a gloss). Since its construction reduplicates rather than complements that of v 7a, it is possible that Paul in dictating intended it to replace v 7a (Lietzmann, Barrett), but just as likely that he paused after v 7a, disrupted his train of thought, and picked it up again without sufficient care. Such a pause might well have been occasioned by the realization that in v 7a he was in danger of overstating his point. The possibility of someone being willing to die for another was certainly entertained elsewhere at the time (cf. *T. Ash.* 2.3; Epictetus 2.7.3; Philostratus, *Vita Apol.* 7.12; and note particularly the passage from *Vita Philonidis*, "[For] the most beloved of his relatives or friends he would readily risk his neck"—Deissmann, *Light*, 118; further *TDNT* 9:153–54 and Wolter, 171 n.619; in the NT, John 15:13). In view of the context, ἀγαθοῦ must be construed as a masculine rather than neuter. And though Paul nowhere else so uses ἀγαθός (see Wilckens), he may well be doing what he did in 2:10—that is, appealing to a category well recognized and applauded (at least in principle), the (truly) good person (cf. Lightfoot above). It is not necessary to press for a more restricted sense—"the particularly worthy person" (Käsemann), "a really good person" (NJB), "the benefactor" (Cranfield). Although the language here moves beyond that of martyrdom "into the sphere of the heroic" the analogy is one of contrast rather than of comparison (*pace* Käsemann). Paul's point is that what God has done is "without analogy" (Eichholz, *Theologie*, 168; Kleinknecht, 349).

8 συνίστησιν δὲ τὴν ἑαυτοῦ ἀγάπην εἰς ἡμᾶς ὁ θεός, "but God demonstrates his love for us." For συνίστημι see on 3:5. The present tense complements the perfect of v 5 and probably reflects the perspective of the preacher who referred back to the death of Christ as a timeless proof of God's love (cf. 1 Cor 1:23). The ἑαυτοῦ need not be emphatic and can be rendered simply "his" (cf. BGD, ἑαυτοῦ 4). The εἰς ἡμᾶς should probably be taken with ἀγάπην, as the word order suggests (cf. e.g., 2 Cor 2:8; Col 1:4; 1 Thess 3:12), rather than with the verb ("God demonstrates to us his love"). The subject (ὁ θεός) is left to the end for emphasis: "but *God* demonstrates his love. . . ."

ὅτι ἔτι ἁμαρτωλῶν ὄντων ἡμῶν Χριστὸς ὑπὲρ ἡμῶν ἀπέθανεν, "in that while we were sinners Christ died for us." The ὅτι is explanatory—"by the fact that" (BDF §394). The fact that the phrasing is almost identical to that of v 6 (ἔτι, genitive absolute, "Christ died for") is not accidental. The effect of v 7 is to remind the Roman audience of how unusual self-sacrifice is even when the beneficiary is an attractive person. The point is simply underscored by reemphasizing that God's love is not determined by such considerations. ἁμαρτωλοί here stands in place of ἀσεβεῖς, confirming their near synonymy (see on 4:5) and bringing home the point even more forcefully that God's love is not directed solely to those within the covenant (the righteous—see on 5:7) or dependent on the degree to which the works of the law are observed (see on 3:7). As in v 6 the genitive absolute does not refer solely to a time which is past—"we being sinners" is a continuing state bound up but not synonymous with "we being weak" (v 6); see further on 7:14–25.

For the formulaic character of the phrase "Christ died for us," see on 5:6. It is important to note that Paul thinks of *Christ's* death as a demonstration of *God's* love (elsewhere particularly 3:25 and 2 Cor 5:19). That Christ's death thus benefits us as "sinners" confirms (1) the character of Christ's death as sacrifice (sin-offering), (2) provided by God to deal effectively with the sinner *qua* sinner (see further on 3:25); (3) that is, not merely with his inadvertent sins but also to cover the "lawlessness" which put us outside the law and thus, in the typical Jewish perspective, outside the scope of the atonement provided for those within the covenant (see again ἁμαρτωλός on 3:7 and 4:5). Since the point of the parallel with v 7 is the willingness of the martyr to give up his life for someone else, there is perhaps implicit here the memory of Jesus' readiness to go to the cross preserved in such traditions as Mark 10:45 and 14:24.

9 πολλῷ μᾶλλον, "how much more": the phrase is usually regarded as an example of the rabbinic קַל וְחֹמֶר (= "light and heavy") that is, an argument *a minori ad maius* (e.g., *m. 'Abot* 1.5; *m. 'Arak.* 8:4; see further Str-B, 3:223–26; Müller in 5:12–21 *Bibliography*). Paul uses it four times in chap. 5 (vv 9, 10, 15, 17); elsewhere Matt 6:30; 1 Cor 12:22; 2 Cor 3:9, 11; Phil 1:23; 2:12; cf. Matt 7:11 // Luke 11:13; Matt 10:25; Luke 12:28; Rom 11:12, 24; Philem 16; Heb 9:14.

δικαιωθέντες νῦν ἐν τῷ αἵματι αὐτοῦ, "having now been justified by his blood." The verb picks up the thought of v 1, but whereas in v 1 the immediate corollary was the present outworking of the en-righteoused state of the believer, here the immediate corollary looks to the still future completion of what has already been accomplished; see on 5:1 and below. The νῦν echoes the νυνί of 3:21—the "eschatological now"; so also 5:11; 11:30–31; 16:26; and probably also 6:19, 21; 8:1, 22; 13:11 (see on 3:21). The addition of the νῦν to the aorist, followed by the future, heightens the eschatological tension of the whole train of thought. The ἐν τῷ αἵματι αὐτοῦ is also probably intended to recall the central statement of 3:24–26 (the ἐν being either instrumental, "by means of," or reflecting a Hebrew idiom, "at the cost of"—Barrett); cf. Murray. Even without that allusion the sacrificial connotation of the phrase is hard to dispute ("Christ's sacrificial death"—NEB), whether directly in reference to the sin-offering (cf. particularly Heb 9:22), or through that language as used in the martyr theology just evoked in v 7 (cf. particularly *4 Macc* 6.29; 17.22), or in reference to sacrifice as establishing the new covenant (cf. particularly 1 Cor 11:25). The language presupposes the rationale of the covenant relationship between God and his people—that sacrifice was a fundamental part of the mechanism of the covenant (see further on 3:25). The aorist + νῦν, however, assumes the Christian perspective that Christ's sacrificial death had a once-for-all effect in establishing the new covenant relationship (including Gentiles), absorbing as it were the role of all these other sacrifices for the future (and past) and rendering further sacrifice unnecessary.

σωθησόμεθα δι' αὐτοῦ ἀπὸ τῆς ὀργῆς, "we shall be saved through him from wrath." Paul draws here on an established kerygmatic theme; cf. 1 Thess

1:9–10 (Synofzik, 98). The imagery invoked is that of rescue from a situation fraught with danger. The peril here is the same "wrath" described by Paul in 1:18–32, particularly in its final expression ("the day of wrath"—2:5), but with the implication that the latter is the outworking of the former (see further on 1:18 and 2:5). For the role of a mediator in turning away wrath, see on 5:10. As usual in Paul the concept of "salvation" is future-oriented: Paul almost always uses the verb in the future tense (5:9–10; 9:27; 10:9, 13; 11:14, 26; 1 Cor 3:15; 7:16; 9:22; cf. Rom 8:24, ἐλπίδι; for the noun see on 1:16). That righteousness leads to salvation, or that the righteous can look for salvation, is characteristically Jewish (e.g., Sir 34:13; Wisd Sol 5:2; *1 Enoch* 1.1 and 5.6 [Gr.]; *T. Naph* 8.3; 1QpHab 8:1–3). The distinctiveness of Paul's linking of the two concepts focuses in the two prepositional phrases—"in his blood" and "through him": Christ's mediation is decisive at both ends of the process. It is God's action through Christ which has transformed the categories and made them of universal application—"we" Gentiles as well as Jews, and not just "the righteous" of Israel. Here too it would be improper to push the distinction between δικαιόω (aorist) and σῴζω (future) as though two distinct operations were envisaged (so, e.g., SH and Donfried, "Justification," 100–101; vigorously contested by Reumann and Fitzmyer in Reumann, *Righteousness*, 82, 213): since the former can also be used of the future judgment (see on 2:13) it thus describes the same purposed outcome of God's gracious action using a different image; so too the use of σῴζω in the present (1 Cor 1:18; 15:2; 2 Cor 2:15) equally is a reminder that what is in view is the establishment and development of a relationship which ends in final vindication. And since the process of salvation is yet incomplete, it also means that the believer is not yet delivered from the outworking of wrath in the present (cf. 1:18–32) or from the necessity of being judged in the last day (cf. 14:10; 1 Cor 3:14–15; 2 Cor 5:10). The "much more" then signifies a process completed, not some shift in the center of Paul's theology from justification to life "in Christ" (*pace* Dodd; Schweitzer, *Mysticism*, 223–25; cf. Sanders, *Paul*, 502–8); cf. the same issue of whether a clear distinction between justification and reconciliation is in view (see on 5:10).

10 εἰ . . . πολλῷ μᾶλλον, "if . . . how much more": this is the more usual construction; see on 5:9 and BGD, μᾶλλον 2b.

ἐχθροὶ ὄντες, "being enemies." ἐχθρός can be either passive ("hated, hateful to God"—as possibly in 11:28, where it stands in parallel to ἀγαπητός) or active ("hating, hostile to God"—cf. 8:7 and Col 1:21); cf. also 1:29–31 θεοστυγεῖς. Most take it to be active here, Paul recalling man's deliberate rebellion indicted in 1:18–3:20 (e.g., BGD, *TDNT* 2:814, Kuss, Schmidt, Schlier, Wilckens); but it is also part of Paul's theology that "wrath" signifies an active hostility on God's part to that rebellion (against Hanson, *Wrath*, 89; Hofius, "Sühne," 29; see on 1:18), so that the passive may also be in view (*TDNT* 1:257; Lietzmann; Murray; Wolter, 86; Martin, 144; Zeller). Here once again we should probably avoid an "either-or" exegesis and let the translation "enemies" carry the implication of a mutual hostility (cf. Cranfield). Either way the word is evidently chosen to climax the description of the human condition apart from Christ (God's own people included—2:1–3:20). That such enmity was involved, on either side or both, highlights still more sharply the generosity of the divine initiative.

κατηλλάγημεν τῷ θεῷ, "we were reconciled to God." The metaphor of reconciliation, used infrequently in Paul, and in the NT only in the Pauline corpus (5:11; 11:15; 2 Cor 5:18–20; Col 1:20, 22; Eph 2:16), is drawn from the familiar experience of hostility between states, parties, or individuals being overcome or ended (LSJ, καταλλάσσω II; Wolter, 39) and accords with the imagery evoked in vv 1–2 (peace and acceptance into favor). It is hardly attested in cultic contexts within the wider Hellenistic usage. This may reflect the less personal conception of the relationship between the gods and men which we find in Greco-Roman religion as distinct from Judaism (*TDNT* 1:254; Goppelt, "Versöhnung," 150–52; Cranfield); but Sophocles, *Ajax* 744, and OGI 218.105 (both in LSJ) indicate that a religious reference was not unnatural. Josephus, however, shows how much more natural it was for Judaism to think in such personal terms (cf. *Ant.* 3.315; 6.143; 7.153, 295; so also Philo, *Praem.* 166). Elsewhere in Judaism the word group is little used, only achieving a degree of prominence in 2 Maccabees (1:5; 5:20; 7:33; 8:29). This latter use, however, may be important, since it clearly functions within the context of the same martyr theology which we have already found reflected in some degree in vv 7 and 9. It is quite possible therefore that Paul is moving here in the same circle of thought as the martyr theology of 2 Maccabees and may even have been prompted by it: reconciliation from divine wrath through someone's death (2 Macc 5:20; 7:33–38; 8:3–5); indeed, the association of concepts in the opening prayer of 2 Maccabees (covenant with Abraham, heart, spirit, peace, reconciliation) is surprisingly close to that of Rom 5:1–11 in its context, with the differences coming precisely at the points where Paul makes his own distinctive emphasis (2 Macc 1:2–5; we may recall also that the greeting of 2 Macc 1:1 provides probably the closest parallel in pre-Christian Judaism to Paul's standard greeting; see on 1:7).

The temptation to press for a clear distinction between "justification" and "reconciliation" should be avoided. "Reconciliation" may have a more personal connotation (Cranfield), but the imagery ranges from reconciliation between husband and wife to the more formal relations between a king and his subjects or between warring forces (see references in Wolter, 41), and at the latter end of its range of meaning it has a similar relational significance to the concept of righteousness (see on 1:17); see also Schmidt and Kuss. Here in particular the close parallel between v 9 and v 10b shows that Paul regards the one as equivalent to the other, the καταλλαγέντες of v 10b answering to the δικαιωθέντες of v 9 (Barrett); cf. also 1:16–17 with 2 Cor 5:19 (Althaus; Goppelt, "Versöhnung," 153–54). So, too, a sharp distinction between the language of sacrifice and that of reconciliation should be avoided: in martyr theology the two had already merged. Here also (ἐν τῷ αἵματι—see on 5:9) and in 2 Cor 5:18–20 the thought runs directly on to v 21 (see further Wolter, 36–45). The range of imagery is different and opens the door to different exploitation, but that Paul preferred "reconciliation" terminology to that of justification or sacrifice in his gospel reads too much into the evidence; the whole point of chap. 4, after all, was to "universalize" the language of justification, and the significance of sacrifice terminology in the key passage 3:25 should not be so discounted (*pace* Käsemann, "Reconciliation," 56–59; Martin, 152–54). Similarly the suggestion that reconciliation provides a "picture of a

seeking, caring and forgiving God who meets the sinner before he repents"
which "has no parallel in Judaism" (Martin, 151) needs to recall the message
of Hosea to which Paul later appeals (9:25–26; as also Isa 65:1–2/Rom 10:20–
21) and the fact that in Jewish theology it was God himself who had provided
the sacrificial system. The same recognition of a harmony between the concepts
of reconciliation and sacrifice, and that either can be used to speak of the
turning away or ending of divine wrath (3:25 as the answer to 1:18–3:20;
5:9–10), should also discourage a revival of the view that it is only man who
needs to be reconciled and not God; because God is the reconciler he does
not cease to be judge (cf., e.g., SH; Denney; Knox; Morris, 198–201; Ladd,
Theology, 453; Michel; Cranfield; against Hofius, "Sühne," 29–30). At the
same time it is certainly worthy of emphasis that, as with 3:25, Paul sees the
initiative wholly as God's: it is *he* alone who has effected the reconciliation
"through the death of his Son."

διὰ τοῦ θανάτου τοῦ υἱοῦ αὐτοῦ, "through the death of his Son." The idea of
reconciliation through a mediator was familiar—particularly in the case of
Moses turning away God's wrath from Israel (Ps 106:23; Josephus, *Ant.* 3.315),
but also Aaron (Wisd Sol 18:20–25) and Phinehas (Sir 45:23—hence the
priesthood and so the offering of sacrifice was given to him and to his descendants, v 24); see further Wolter, 38 n.18 and 42. That a similar role was
played by the Maccabean martyrs was of the essence of the Jewish martyr
theology—that is, by their death. The distinctive Christian emphasis here is
in the three words "of his Son," with its clear implication that this was not
simply God's initiative, but God's own action through his Son (cf. 2 Cor
5:19). The idea of divine sonship as denoting closeness to God was familiar
in the ancient world, and in Christianity this emphasis had already been
focused in Jesus as something unique: "his Son" without need to explain
the relationship any more fully (see on 1:3). Since a large proportion of
Paul's references speak of Jesus as God's Son given to death (5:10; 8:3, 32;
Gal 2:20; 4:4), a distinctive Pauline contribution to the earlier Son-Christology
(*TDNT* 8:384; Dunn, *Christology*, 38), it looks as though the formulation was
important for Paul precisely because it held together the potentially conflicting
thoughts of *God* providing a representative to turn away his own wrath. The
death of Jesus as God's *Son* was probably one of the crucial hinge points in
the development of Paul's theology.

σωθησόμεθα ἐν τῇ ζωῇ αὐτοῦ, "we shall be saved by his life." For the verb,
see on 5:9. The variation in prepositions as between vv 9 and 10 (ἐν . . . διά,
διά . . . ἐν) is probably simply a matter of style (cf. 3:30). The ζωή clearly
refers to Christ's risen life. As in 4:25 Paul's intention is not so much to
attribute separate functions to Christ's death and resurrection as to draw
out the obvious "much moreness" of life as compared with death. The death
of Jesus solved the problem of God's wrath and of the enmity between God
and man—by *death*; but God's full purpose for man is life—life from and
beyond death. The πολλῷ μᾶλλον is the "how much more" of a life no longer
confined or threatened by death. Implicit too is that the salvation will be
achieved not simply by the power of Christ's risen life but through the believer's
identification with it: the process of salvation as a sharing both in Christ's
death and in his resurrection (see again Dunn, *Jesus*, 326–38; and further
chaps. 6–8, particularly 6:3–11; 7:4; 8:17). In this motif the eschatological

tension finds some of its most powerful expression (6:4; 8:10; 2 Cor 4:10–12; Col 3:3–4). That resurrection (and so the full experience of life) is still future for the believer is clearly indicated in 6:5, 8; 8:11; 1 Cor 15:20–22; 2 Cor 4:14; and Phil 3:10–11. The hope of resurrection was familiar to contemporary Judaism, but not of resurrection as mediated through a particular salvific figure (Wilckens).

11 οὐ μόνον δέ, ἀλλὰ καί, "not only so, but also": see on 5:3. It is not necessary to decide which verb or whether any verb should be read in to complete the sense. Paul uses an open formula to indicate that for all that he has already said, he has something more to say. In fact, his chief intention seems to be to gather up the whole of the preceding paragraph by drawing into a single sentence two of the key terms from the beginning and end of the paragraph—καυχώμενοι (vv 2–3) and καταλλαγή (v 10).

καυχώμενοι ἐν τῷ θεῷ, "we boast in God." The participle here has the force of the indicative (BDF §468.1; cf. 3:24), the present tense indicating that this boasting is a continuous feature for the believer, even in the period between reconciliation and salvation, characterized by suffering (see on 5:2–3). The echo of 2:17 is almost certainly deliberate. The boasting Paul envisages here escapes the critique of 2:17 presumably because for Paul Christians boast through Christ (cf. Phil 3:3), that is, as those who have been reconciled by God's action through Christ and whose hope of salvation rests solely in God's further action through Christ. The liturgical or doxological style, to which, e.g., Michel and Käsemann draw attention, may simply be the consequence of Paul's taking over the language of Jewish worship (see on 2:17). At all events, the phrase both stresses the continuity with the traditional faith of Judaism and highlights the discontinuity, since the "we" who boast are Gentiles as well as Jews.

διὰ τοῦ κυρίου ἡμῶν Ἰησοῦ Χριστοῦ, "through our Lord Jesus Christ." For Christ as the mediator of thanksgiving to God, see on 1:8. His mediation includes both his death and his risen life (see further Kuss, 213–18). Here the use of the full title ("our Lord Jesus Christ") increases the sonority of the phrase and increases the likelihood that Paul echoes the language of Christian worship at one of its key points of distinctiveness from the rest of Jewish worship. Cf. the confidence expressed in similarly elevated style in the equivalent concluding and climactic phrase of the next stage of the argument (8:31–39).

δι' οὗ νῦν τὴν καταλλαγὴν ἐλάβομεν, "through whom we have received the reconciliation." The striking emphasis on Jesus' mediatorial role is maintained to the end (vv 1, 2, 9, 10, 11). The νῦν maintains the note of eschatological hope already being fulfilled (see 3:21 and 5:9). For καταλλαγή, see on 5:10. The final aorist brings the whole talk of hope and boasting back to the firm point that the decisive action has already taken place (on the cross and in their lives) without diminishing the repeated emphasis of vv 10 and 11 that salvation is yet to be completed.

Explanation

Paul has demonstrated from the crucial scriptural testimony concerning Abraham how scripture's talk of God's righteousness as reckoned to man should be understood. He now proceeds to draw out this basic insight and its implications not only for the individual believer but also for humankind as a whole.

5:1 "Therefore, having been justified out of *faith*." This is clearly Paul's recapitulation of the exegetical conclusion, reached in 4:22, and its extension to all who believe, in 4:23–24. The wording of Gen 15:6 had dictated the prominence of the noun "righteousness" in the midrash of chap. 4. Here he reverts to the equivalent verb "justify." His readers would, of course, have been in no doubt that the verb "justify" was fully synonymous with the verbal phrase of chap. 4, "reckon righteous" (as 3:20–26 had already clearly demonstrated anyway). What Paul asserts of himself and his readers ("having been justified") is what Gen 15:6 asserted of Abraham. The point, which he reiterates from chap. 4, is that God justifies *by faith*—God holds a person in good standing, reckons him an acceptable partner in covenant relationship, simply on the grounds of that person's trust, his humble acceptance of God's unconditional promise to act for him.

Since the covenant with Abraham is still so much in the background, the Roman congregations would be unlikely to make the mistake of reading the aorist tense ("having been justified") as though it excluded other tenses. That is to say, they would be unlikely to regard their justification, their acceptance by God, simply as an act finished and past. Paul's use is a good deal more flexible. And though his emphasis here is on what initially makes a person acceptable to God, the implication of the scriptural background and covenant connotations is that God's acceptance is no single once-for-all (far less merely passive) act; rather, it is God's reaching out to embrace and sustain up to and including the final verdict of acquittal. We might even paraphrase, therefore, "Since we too have now been drawn into God's promise and its fulfillment through our acceptance of that promise. . . ."

Paul then goes on to describe the consequences of that initial acceptance by God, the consequence of being within the sphere of God's covenant promise. Or to put it another way, he goes on to describe what the ongoing experience of God's acceptance means, how God's accepting and sustaining righteousness works out in day-to-day reality. The first is the experience of peace with God (or, less likely, the possibility of peace with God). The association between righteousness and peace is a natural one, not least for a Jew familiar with the Psalms and Isaiah, particularly Pss 72:1–7 and 85:8–13. And indeed, the sequence of Paul's thought (justification resulting in peace) may have been suggested by Isa 32:17 ("the effect of righteousness will be peace"). The Jewish or God-worshiping reader would also be familiar with the richer Jewish concept of peace—not merely cessation of war, but also material prosperity, all that makes for total well-being and harmony. More to the point, for a Jew this peace was something closely dependent on Israel's relation with its Lord—to give his people peace was an integral part of God's covenant undertaking ("my covenant of peace shall not be removed"—Isa 54:10). And the full flowering of that peace was a strong feature of the prophetic hope of the new age to come (note particularly Ezek 34:25–31 and 37:26—"I will make with them a covenant of peace").

To anyone familiar with this rich background in Jewish thought Paul's assertion here would strike a distinctive note. For one thing, he speaks of having "peace with God," whereas in Jewish thought prior to (and indeed after) Paul, "peace" denoted primarily harmonious relationships between people. Paul does not exclude that dimension; he does not spiritualize the concept or reduce it to a merely internal source of calm. Rather he "apocalypticizes" it, by focusing it on the spiritual dimension which underlies the relationships of everyday life—presumably on the grounds that without concord between God and man, Creator and creature, sustained by God, complete well–being and harmony are impossible between man and man. For another, he claims in effect that the eschatological hope of peace has already been realized through Christ ("we have peace . . ."); the covenant of peace promised in Ezekiel is now already in operation—if not in complete outworking through society, at least so far as the indispensable spiritual foundation is concerned. And not least in importance, Paul also by implication denationalizes the concept of peace. The peace which the covenant was designed to produce was often seen within the covenant people as a peace imposed by Israel on other nations (as in Isa 66:12–16 and Zech 9:10). In contrast, by use of the first person plural throughout this section, which embraces both Gentile and Jew among his readers, Paul indicates that so far as relationship with God through Christ is concerned, that kind of Israel-centered, militaristic understanding of covenant peace is no longer appropriate—the peace given by God embraces members of all races and nations without distinction.

The phrase "through our Lord Jesus Christ," which elsewhere seems sometimes to function as little more than a label to mark out the accompanying statement as Christian, here and in the immediately following clause has a much more pregnant sense. Paul is stressing the point that Christ, Jesus alive from the dead, continues to be actively involved in the relationship between God and believers. Jesus, exalted now to a position of mastery over human beings and things ("our Lord"), somehow mediates this peace with God to humankind. Integral as always to Paul's faith, his experience of faith as well as his theological expression of that faith, is the sense of personal relationship with God activated and maintained by Jesus. God reached out to Paul on the Damascus road and has continued to do so ever since, not *for the sake of* a Jesus whose personal existence ended on the cross, but *through* this same Jesus.

2   Another aspect of the believer's position in relation to God as mediated by the Lord, Jesus Christ, is given in the phrase "access into this grace." The language would probably suggest to Paul's readers the imagery of the royal chamberlain leading the suppliant into the presence of the king, both the solemnity and the fearful privilege which that involved—"grace" being the monarch's favorable disposition to the petitioner ensuring his success. The double use of the perfect tense ("we have," "we stand") is deliberate, signifying an access granted in the past and still valid—either in the sense that believers stand permanently in the royal presence or that they have the permanent privilege of immediate access when requested. Either way the perspective is still apocalyptic in character: Paul's thought is of the infinite resource of God's favor (including the royal power to translate that favor into practical effect) which lies behind the curtain of this visible world; it is that which Christ has secured for those who seek to approach God through him, trusting themselves to him.

"And we boast in our hope of the glory of God." Not by accident Paul picks up again language ("boast") which he has used only pejoratively so far (2:17, 23; 3:27; 4:2). Since boasting epitomized Jewish pride in Israel's privileged status among the nations, so Paul deliberately inserts the equivalent note into this conclusion of his argument so far. There is a boasting that is possible and proper to man—to persons as creatures—namely, to boast in his creator (cf. 1 Cor 1:29, 31). To boast in anything else, in the law, or even in divine election, is a wrong kind of boasting which thwarts rather than displays the grace of God. It is worth observing that Paul does not condemn "boasting" per se; on the contrary, it should be a natural and proper response to the wonderful favor of this divine patron; it can be a positive expression of grace experienced. No doubt it was such a surging pride in God which invigorated earliest Christian worship and emboldened its witness.

Paul's language at this point might not at first hearing have sounded so very different from the language he disparaged earlier. In fact, however, he has already safeguarded himself from such a *tu quoque* criticism. It is no longer a boasting in national privilege with its badge of law and circumcision; it is a boasting in "the hope of glory." And that is quite another matter. The glory hoped for is the glory spoken of earlier (3:23), the share in God's life and in his dominion over the rest of creation. That is to say, it is the hope of the human creature to fulfill the creator's purpose for humankind. And the hope is a confident hope because its fulfillment rests wholly with God; it relies solely on God's powerful favor, accepted in humble trust, a hope like Abraham's (4:18). In such boasting God delights—that man should be proud of his creator, of his purpose for humanity and of his power to effect that purpose.

3–4 As if to make the point with greater emphasis Paul adds a rhetorical flourish. "Not only so, but we also boast in tribulation." Here again we should give the verb its full force: Paul means to jolt his readers by the very positive attitude he takes to suffering—"we exult even in these situations of pressure and experiences of distress." The continuity of thought between vv 1–2 and v 3 presumably indicates that for Paul this too is the boasting of the person in his creatureliness, in the conscious awareness of his dependence on God which such suffering brings. For Paul such suffering is not an antithesis to the believers' experience of acceptance by God, rather its complement; such suffering does not contradict or prevent their standing in the grace of God, but rather is the condition in which that grace is experienced in its greatest strength. There would be some, at least, among the Roman readership who were aware of how deeply this personal testimony ran for Paul, who knew of the experience to which Paul bears witness in 2 Cor 12:7–10. But he does not refer to it explicitly at this point.

The reason for the boasting given here is expressed in characteristic Pauline language, though at first sight its sentiment seems to be fairly conventional, as Stoic and Jewish parallels suggest. For Paul, however, the main thrust of the process of "character formation" is eschatological: ". . . an approved character produces hope." By implication, the tribulations envisaged are not merely "the slings and arrows of outrageous fortune" but the end-time tribulations which mark the dissolution of the present age (as in Dan 12:1); and the patient endurance is the patient endurance to the end for which Jesus called (Mark 13:13), the testing in the final purgation and purification (as in Mal 3:2–3) which has already begun. The whole process produces hope because it indicates that the process of salvation is under way: when suffering is experienced not as a contradiction to faith or occasion to renounce God, but as a strengthening of patience and maturing of character, it stimulates hope in the grace that is having such effect. The whole process produces hope because for Paul it is itself the process of salvation, the process whereby God recreates humanity in his own image—what he refers to elsewhere as the wasting away of the visible man which is the necessary complement to the renewal of the hidden man (2 Cor 4:16). Once again this fuller line is not developed here (though he draws it in later in chaps. 6–8), but Paul has at least given a hint of what he probably had in mind in the way he seems to have formulated this process as the reverse of human decline into depravity, denounced in 1:21–32. The person who has abandoned the glory of God, turned to the indulgence of his baser instincts, and been given over to a disapproved mind, has nothing to look forward to but death. But believers, looking for the glory of God, find that suffering gives them a more realistic appreciation of what the world offers, tests and purifies them rather than debasing them, and so strengthens their conviction that God has a more glorious wholeness in store for them.

5 Such a hope does not put the one who holds it to shame. Paul's thought still seems to be on the contrast with the process and condition described in chap. 1. That kind of sensual indulgence should cause shame—and did for those converted from it (6:21). (Here indeed is the discomforting challenge of Paul's gospel—an indulgence to be ashamed of, a suffering to be boasted about!) But the hope that springs from salvation's reversal of the sinful process causes no shame—no shame either at the indignity and pain of the suffering, or at the possibility of its being disappointed, as though it was an unrealistic hope. Why so? By implication, because it is trust in God (as the echo of Pss 22:5 and 25:20 suggests); that is to say, it is the same trust and hope which Abraham exercised and which God honored against apparently impossible odds (4:18–21).

However, the reason Paul actually spells out is the fact that the love of God and Spirit of God have already been richly experienced in their lives. Paul uses vivid "Pentecostal" language ("poured out in our hearts"), and obviously recalls his readers to deep emotional experiences which must have been common to many of those who became Christians at that time. Described here is a sustained experience of a love that was other than merely human love—an awareness of being loved and presumably also of being filled with heartfelt love for others whom in the normal course of events one might have disregarded or even despised. Whether he thinks of the gift of the Spirit as a distinct event or experience is less clear. He certainly distinguishes the two elements conceptually—the Spirit of God given once for all (aorist), the love of God still experienced in full flood (perfect). But he may be thinking of the Spirit as the initial impact of divine power which set the whole process of salvation in movement, the hidden dynamo of divine vitality which maintains the glow of love, the hidden channel through which the flood of divine love sustains its flow. At all events, the point is clear: hope of completed salvation, of restoration to share in the divine glory, is not a vain or idle hope, because the process has already begun. The believer's hope for the future is based not only in a faithful and powerful God, but in what they have already experienced and received from that God—the end-time Spirit of God active in them already in end-time power. As hope of future resurrection is based in the resurrection of Christ already accomplished (1 Cor 15:17–22), so hope of future glory is based on the experience of grace already enjoyed (v 2), so hope of completed salvation arises out of the experience of the eschatological power of God already achieving the purposes of divine love (v 5).

6–8 Vv 6–8 introduce another ground for the confidence expressed so boldly in vv 1–5. The connection of thought is fairly loose, and the language of vv 6–7 awkward, but the point is clear enough. The confidence of vv 1–5 has another firm foundation—the death of Christ. The emphasis is striking: the thematic repetition of the word "die" at the end of each of the four sentences would scarcely be missed by those hearing the letter read out. The point is that the death of Christ is an expression of the same love of God: "God demonstrates his own love to us in that . . . Christ died for us." The love of God poured out in their hearts was the subjective counterpart of the love already expressed in the Christ's crucifixion. Reflection on the significance of Jesus' death should confirm the testimony of their own hearts, since it is the same love at work in both cases.

The thought seems to be that of martyr theology—the willing self-sacrifice of one on behalf of many. But as in the case of the Maccabean martyrs, the rationale is that of the sacrificial offering—the belief that the death of one would atone for the sins of others and remove the cause of divine wrath (as in 2 Macc 7:37–38). So here Paul recalls the brief but crucial exposition of 3:21–26, and re-expresses the obviously universal conviction among the first Christians that Jesus' death has to be seen as something willed by God to effect his purpose of love, by dealing with the factors which prevent that love coming to effect in humans. At this point it is only these disqualifying factors on the side of men and women which are listed, and not the factors which qualified Christ for this role: partly because throughout this section (vv 1–11) the focus is primarily on God and his initiative, and on Christ primarily as medium and agent of that initiative and its outcome ("through him"); but perhaps partly also because in the analogue of Jewish martyr theology it was loyalty to the law which brought about the martyrdom (2 Macc 7:30, 37), and Paul did not want to complicate his point by evoking that parallel too closely. It was enough to focus on the human factors which militate against God's love in order to bring out the completely gratuitous quality of that love.

In listing the disqualifying factors Paul reminds his readers of their human condition—not a condition they had to escape from in order to gain access to the grace of God, but the condition in which the grace first came to them, and still comes to them. They were "weak," lacking in strength. No distinction between physical and moral weakness is in view; the weakness of individuals apart from God is both the limitation and steady decay of their mortal body, and their inability before the power of sin to do God's will. They were "ungodly," their condition having already been described in 1:18ff., constantly tending to live independently of God or to live before God other than as creatures before their creator. The paradox of God's loving the ungodly recalls the sharper statement of 4:5. They were "sinners," those who did not know the law or who knowing it disregarded it. The surprising contrast of v 7 between the just man and the good man is probably best explained by reference to a similar distinction implied in the argument of chap. 2, particularly vv 7–10, where Paul seems to envisage a doing good which cuts across the clearly defined categories of the Jewish law. Perhaps then he intends to contrast the admirable but unattractive zealot for the law with the person whose goodness is less structured but acknowledged on all sides. The pedant or zealot does not inspire self-sacrificing devotion from third parties, though a truly good man might. But God did not look for any such preconditions, neither goodness in general nor more careful observance of the law in particular. It was for sinners that Christ died.

The use of the first person plural should not be passed over—"we being weak," "we being sinners." Thereby Paul affirms that he, like everyone else, is caught up in the weakness and sinfulness of humanity. That is no surprise. More surprising perhaps is his disavowal of categories which both Jew and Greek would recognize as appropriate to the truly religious man—"just" and "good." He would probably have accepted the former prior to his conversion to faith in Christ, but now he recognizes that before God no man can make such claims (1:18–3:20). God shows his love by doing for man, at the time of his need and in the sacrifice of Christ, what man could not do for himself. The twin aspects of faith are the recognition of one's helplessness, distance from God, and tendency to ignore God, and a total reliance on the divine initiative of that love.

9 Vv 6–8 constituted an elaboration of one of the twin pillars of the hope of faith—the clear evidence of the love of God in the death of Jesus (the other pillar being the believer's own experience of that love—v 5). Paul now uses the theme of vv 6–8 as a springboard for a sequence of rhetorically balanced affirmations which pulse and glow with the confidence of faith in what forms a fitting climax to his exposition of Christian hope.

The first of these (v 9) confirms what a careful reader would have seen as already implicit in vv 6–8. On the one hand, there is the sacrificial character of Jesus' death ("by his blood") and its necessary role as the ground of God's acceptance—the six words form a concise summary of the exposition of 3:21–26. The logic for Paul is that God could not be described as "righteous" if he simply disregarded unrighteousness (failure to live in creaturely or covenant conformity to the will of God); human weakness, ungodliness and submission to the power of sin must be dealt with—and the sacrificial death of Jesus is God's answer. An understanding of the rationale of sacrifice Paul could largely assume on the part of his readers (particularly 3:25–26); how God's answer works out in the ongoing life of faith is a subject to which Paul will return later (chaps. 6–8). On the other hand, the second clause of v 9 confirms that for Paul the process of "being saved" is the reversal of the process of

divine wrath described in chap. 1. What the output of divine love in Jesus'
death and resurrection achieves is the rescue of man from the vicious circle
of independence from God resulting in deeper dependence on human passions, and so also rescue from final condemnation in the day of judgment.
It achieves this result because by implication the wrath of God exhausted
itself in the death of Jesus, and so is already exhausted for believers insofar
as they identified themselves with Christ in his death—an implication probably
already present in the theology of sacrifice, which will also become clearer
in the next chapter.

10 The same balanced *a minori ad maius* formula draws in yet another
metaphor, one that would be less familiar to Paul's Hellenistic readers as
descriptive of a relationship between God and humankind, but which is so
used a number of times in 2 Macc—"reconciliation." At the same time the
catalog of indictment begun in vv 6–8 reaches its climax—"we being enemies."
The picture is clearly of a sharp hostility between God and humanity: the
human condition independent of God is not simply a state of human weakness,
disregard for God, and responsiveness to sin; it is also a state of actual rebellion
against the creaturely role of complete dependence on the creator. Man needs
to be weaned away from that delusion about "standing on his own feet,"
which is really nothing more mature than a childish tantrum. Despite the
unfamiliarity of the metaphor as applied to divine-human relationships, Paul's
readers would clearly understand "we were reconciled to God" to mean a
restoration to man's proper relationship with God. This is another way of
describing what happened through Christ's death. Here, we might note, is
another indication of the theology of sacrifice, at least according to Paul:
the death of the sacrifice reconciles God to the sinner, presumably by removing
(through its destruction) the cause of hostility (the powerful hold of sin) by
means of the sinner's identification with the sacrifice in its death. By implication
too, faith is the acceptance both of the need to be reconciled to God and of
the reconciliation itself (cf. 2 Cor 5:18–20). If believers are even now experiencing reconciliation with God as an already restored relationship, they can be
quite sure that the process of bringing the relationship to complete wholeness
will proceed to its final conclusion.

In both verses Paul obviously seeks to strike a balance between the once-
for-allness of what has already happened ("we have been justified/reconciled")
and the not yet of a salvation in process but as yet incomplete (including
"the redemption of the body"—8:23). To insist that each term (justification/
reconciliation, salvation) must be a technical term for one or other aspect
and that all three must be sharply distinguished from each other, would be
pedantic, theologically unjustified, and pastorally dangerous. So too any attempt to attach either aspect exclusively to Jesus' death or to Jesus' risen
life as soteriologically distinct entities would be equally unfounded (cf. 4:25).
The point which Paul is trying to make, on the one hand, is that the ground
of hope is not simply a past event (Jesus' death) understood as a martyrlike
sacrifice, nor simply an experience of divine power understood as Jesus' risen
life, but the cohesion of these two as completely continuous with each other
and equally manifestations of God's love. And, on the other hand, the point
also comes clearly to expression that God's purpose to draw humankind back

into proper relationship with him is something accomplished not in a once-for-all instant, either in the death of Jesus or in the event of conversion, but in an ongoing process in which the power of Christ's risen life (or alternatively expressed, the Spirit of God—v 5) plays a controlling role.

11 Paul rounds off his expression of exultant hope by catching up the sequence of thought begun some sentences earlier (vv 2–3). Christian faith boasts not only in the hope of glory, and not only in eschatological afflictions, but also in God. The sensitive reader would also catch the implication that the sentence also completes the sequence of argument begun in chap. 2 with the indictment of Jewish pride. The most striking feature of the phrase ("we boast in God") is that it is precisely the same boasting of which Paul spoke critically in 2:17. What was presented as improper there is now presented as wholly proper and appropriate. The crucial difference is that Paul now describes it as boasting "through our Lord Jesus Christ"—not a boasting in God which is coordinate with a boasting in the law (2:23). Paul encourages the Christian congregations to show their pride in their relationship with God, but the relationship has now been substantially redefined—as a relationship characterized by recognition of the need for reconciliation and determined by Christ's reconciling death and life (the repeated emphasis on Jesus' mediation in vv 9–11 is striking), not a relationship characterized and determined by factors denoting national identity (works of law). Understood thus, v 11 forms a fitting conclusion to the argument Paul has been developing patiently since chap. 2.

2. The New Perspective on God's Righteous Purpose for Humankind   (5:12–21)

Bibliography

Barth, K. *Christ and Adam: Man and Humanity in Romans 5.* SJTOP 5. Edinburgh: Oliver & Boyd, 1956. **Black, C. C.** "Pauline Perspectives on Death in Romans 5–8." *JBL* 103 (1984) 413–33. **Black, M.** "The Pauline Doctrine of the Second Adam." *SJT* 7 (1954) 170–79. **Boring, M. E.** "The Language of Universal Salvation in Paul." *JBL* 105 (1986) 269–92. **Bornkamm, G.** "Anakoluthe." 80–90. **Brandenburger, E.** *Adam und Christus. Exegetisch-religionsgeschichtliche Untersuchungen zu Röm 5:12–21 (1 Kor 15).* WMANT 7. Neukirchen: Neukirchener, 1962. **Bultmann, R.** "Adam and Christ according to Rom 5" (1959). In *Current Issues in New Testament Interpretation,* ed. W. Klassen and G. F. Snyder. London: SCM, 1962. 143–65. **Cambier, J.** "Péchés des Hommes et Péché d'Adam en Rom 5:12." *NTS* 11 (1964–65) 217–55. **Caragounis, C. C.** "Romans 5:15–16 in the Context of 5:12–21: Contrast or Comparison?" *NTS* 31 (1985) 142–48. **Cranfield, C. E. B.** "On Some Problems in the Interpretation of Rom 5:12." *SJT* 22 (1969) 324–41. **Dahl, N. A.** "Two Notes on Romans 5." *ST* 5 (1952) 42–48. ———. *Studies.* 90–91. **Danker, F. W.** "Rom 5:12: Sin under Law." *NTS* 14 (1967–68) 424–39. **Davies, W. D.** *Paul.* 31–57. **Dibelius, M.** "Vier Worte." 6–8. **Dunn, J. D. G.** *Christology.* 98–128. **Eichholz, G.** *Theologie.* 172–88. **Englezakis, B.** "Rom 5:12–15 and the Pauline Teaching on the Lord's Death: Some Observations."

Bib 58 (1977) 231–36. **Feuillet, A.** "Le règne de la mort et le règne de la vie (Rom 5:12–21)." *RB* 77 (1970) 481–521. **Haacker, K.** "Probleme." 16–19. **Hooker, M. D.** *Pauline Pieces.* London: Epworth, 1979. 36–52. **Johnson, S. L.** "Romans 5:12—An Exercise in Exegesis and Theology." In *New Dimensions in New Testament Study,* ed. R. N. Longenecker and M. C. Tenney. Grand Rapids: Zondervan, 1974. 298–316. **Jüngel, E.** "Das Gesetz zwischen Adam und Christus." *ZTK* 60 (1963) 42–69. **Kirby, J. T.** "The Syntax of Romans 5:12: A Rhetorical Approach." *NTS* 33 (1987) 283–86. **Lombard, H. A.** "The Adam-Christ 'Typology' in Romans 5:12–21." *Neotestamentica* 15 (1981) 69–100. **Luz, U.** *Geschichtsverständnis.* 193–222. **Lyonnet, S.** "Le sens de ἐφ' ᾧ en Rom 5:12 et l'exégèse des Pères grecs." *Bib* 36 (1955) 436–56. ———. "Le péché originel en Rom 5:12: L'exégèse des Pères grecs et les décrets du Concile de Trente." *Bib* 41 (1960) 325–55. **Müller, H.** "Der rabbinische Qal-Wachomer-Schluss in paulinischer Typologie." *ZNW* 58 (1967) 73–92. **Ridderbos, H.** *Paul.* 95–100. **Rogerson, J. W.** "The Hebrew Conception of Corporate Personality: A Re-examination." *JTS* 21 (1970) 1–16. **Sahlin, H.** "Adam-Christologie im Neuen Testament." *ST* 41 (1987) 11–32. **Schade, H.-H.** *Apokalyptische Christologie bei Paulus.* Göttingen: Vandenhoeck, 1981. 69–87. **Schenke, H.-M.** "Die neutestamentliche Christologie und der gnostische Erlöser." In *Gnosis und Neues Testament,* ed. H. W. Tröger. Gütersloh: Gütersloher, 1973. 205–29. **Scroggs, R.** *Last Adam.* **Stanley, D. M.** *Resurrection.* 176–80. **Theobald, M.** *Gnade.* 63–127. **Thüsing, W.** *Per Christum.* 210–19. **Vögtle, A.** "'Der Menschensohn' und die paulinische Christologie." *SPCIC* 1:199–218. **Wedderburn, A. J. M.** "The Theological Structure of Romans 5:12." *NTS* 19 (1972–73) 339–54. ———. "Philo's 'Heavenly Man.'" *NovT* 15 (1973) 301–26. **Wright, N. T.** "Adam in Pauline Christology." *SBL Seminar Papers.* Chico: Scholars, 1983. 359–89. **Ziesler, J.** *Righteousness.* 197–200.

Translation

[12] *Therefore as through one man sin entered into the world and through sin, death—and so death*[a] *came to all men, in that all sinned.* [13] *For until the law, sin was in the world, but sin is not accounted in the absence of the law.* [14] *Nevertheless death reigned from Adam until Moses, even over those who did not*[b] *sin in the very manner of Adam's transgression—he who is the type of the one to come.* [15] *But not as the trespass, so also the effect of grace; for if by the trespass of the one, the many died, how much more the grace of God and the gift in grace, which is of the one man Jesus Christ, has overflowed to the many.* [16] *And not as the one who sinned,*[c] *the gift; for the judgment is from one to condemnation, but the effect of grace is from many trespasses to justification.* [17] *For if by the trespass of the one death reigned through the one, how much more those who receive the abundance of grace and of the gift*[d] *of righteousness shall reign in life through the one, Jesus Christ.*[e] [18] *So then, as through the trespass of one*[e] *to all men to condemnation, so also through the righteous act of one to all men to righteousness of life.* [19] *For as through the disobedience of the one man, the many were made sinners, so also through the obedience of the one,*[e] *the many will be made righteous.* [20] *The law came in to increase the trespass; but where sin increased, grace overflowed in abundance,* [21] *in order that as sin reigned in death, so also grace might reign through righteousness to eternal life through Jesus Christ our Lord.*

Notes

[a] ὁ θάνατος is almost certainly original, but some Western MSS omit it.

[b] Some minuscules omit the μή, it presumably being assumed that Paul intended to liken men's sins to that of Adam (see Lightfoot).

cA mainly Western tradition reads ἁμαρτήματος, putting the emphasis on Adam's act rather than on Adam.

dThe sequence of genitives evidently led to various attempts to improve the style (see Metzger).

eSome attempted improvements to achieve conformity are evident in a few important minuscules—either by the omission of Ἰησοῦ Χριστοῦ or by the insertion of ἀνθρώπου.

Form and Structure

This paragraph is evidently intended as a conclusion to the whole opening section (1:18–5:21). The continuity with the first part of this conclusion (vv 1–11) is marked by the repeated use of the πολλῷ μᾶλλον construction in vv 9, 10, 15, and 17; by the way in which the opening emphasis on justification and grace in vv 1–2 is elaborated in vv 15–21; by the parallel between vv 11 and 21 in the use of "through our Lord Jesus Christ" as a concluding formula; and particularly by the emergence of the reversal theme implicit in vv 1–11 into the explicit contrast between Adam and Christ (see further 5:1–21 *Introduction*). More striking, however, is the transposition from the personal and individual language of vv 1–11 (marked by repeated use of first person plural) to the different key (third person) in which the whole sweep of human history is embraced by the two epochs instituted by Adam and Christ.

The paragraph is structured throughout on a ὥσπερ/ὡς . . . οὕτως καί comparison (vv 12, 18, 19, 21) with the first of these interrupted by the double clarification of vv 12c–14 and 15–17 (see the analyses in Bornkamm, "Anakoluthe," 81–82, and Cambier, "Rom 5:12," 227; the balance of similarity and difference being drawn out hardly requires us to follow Caragounis in construing vv 15a and 16a as questions). The epigrammatic compactness of the whole, but of vv 16–18 in particular, is marked. Important thematic features are the reappearance of the εἰ . . . πολλῷ μᾶλλον (vv 15, 17), the οὐχ ὡς . . . οὕτως καί of vv 15–16, and the contrasts "the one"/"the many" (vv 15, 19), παράπτωμα/χάρισμα (v 15), κρίμα/χάρισμα, κατάκριμα/δικαίωμα (v 16), παράπτωμα/δικαίωμα (v 18), παρακοή/ὑπακοή (v 19), ἁμαρτία/χάρις (vv 20–21). Indicative of Paul's emphasis and intention also is the repeated use of key concepts—εἰς (12 times), χάρις/χάρισμα (7), ἄνθρωπος (6), ἁμαρτία (6), παράπτωμα (6), δικαι- words (6), βασιλεύειν (5), πολλοί (5), πάντες (4), and cognates of περισσεύω (3). Indicative of rhetorical considerations in framing the sequence of comparisons is the predominance of words ending in -μα (παράπτωμα, χάρισμα, δώρημα, κρίμα, κατάκριμα, and δικαίωμα). As so often in Romans, the final sentence of the conclusion (vv 20–21) serves also as a transition to the next phase of the discussion, setting law alongside the two quasi-powers who dominate the old eon (sin, death), the three terms which will largely dominate chaps. 6–8 (see chaps. 6–8 *Form and Structure*); cf. particularly 3:20, 31; 4:25; 7:13; 8:17; 9:13; and 11:7.

In its basic theme, that "the excess of sin brings the fullness of grace to light," Rom 5:12–21 could be said to provide "a programmatic text" for the letter as a whole (Theobald, 120–27).

Comment

12 διὰ τοῦτο ὥσπερ δι᾽ ἑνὸς ἀνθρώπου, "therefore as through one man." The διὰ τοῦτο does not signify a conclusion drawn simply from an immediately preceding argument; v 11 had already effectively rounded off the preceding train of thought. Its function is rather to indicate that vv 12–21 serve as a conclusion to the complete argument from 1:18–5:11 (see further 5:1–21 *Introduction*). The ὥσπερ, "just as," clearly is intended to introduce the first half of a contrast which is not in fact completed until v 18 (see also *Form and Structure*). The "one man" obviously is Adam, although he is not named till v 14. Paul may have it in mind that Adam = אָדָם = "man" = ἄνθρωπος, but his argument does not depend on it. And though he will use Adam to characterize the state of humankind (vv 15–19), he does not use ἄνθρωπος here to characterize humankind as a whole; the concept of "corporate personality" (H. W. Robinson, *Man*, 121; Bruce, 126) is more of a hindrance than a help here (so rightly Käsemann; see further Rogerson); still less can it be maintained that Paul has in mind some universal mythical Man—as the distinction between "one man" and "all men" makes clear (see further on 5:14c). The further step back, already behind Moses (and the law) to Abraham (chap. 4), and now behind Abraham to Adam, is deliberate. Not only does it bring the argument back to its starting point (the indictment of human sin in terms of Adam's fall—see on 1:22) and so completes the circle of his argument (1:18–5:21—see again 5:1–21 *Introduction*), but it also highlights the universal sweep of God's saving purpose through Christ: God is Savior (vv 9–10) as Creator (cf. 4:17) and not merely as the God of Israel.

ἡ ἁμαρτία εἰς τὸν κόσμον εἰσῆλθεν καὶ διὰ τῆς ἁμαρτίας ὁ θάνατος, "sin entered into the world and through sin, death." Paul here shows himself familiar with and indeed to be a participant in what was evidently a very vigorous strand of contemporary Jewish thinking about Adam and the origin of evil and death in the world. Note particularly Sir 14:17, 25:24 ("From a woman sin had its beginning and because of her we die"); Wisd Sol 2:23–24 ("God created man for incorruption . . . but through the devil's envy death entered the world, and those who belong to his party experience it"); *Adam and Eve* 44 and *Apoc. Mos.* 14, 32; *4 Ezra* 3.7, 21–22; 4.30; 7.116–18; *2 Apoc. Bar.* 17.2–3; 23.4; 48.42–43; 54.15, 19; 56.5–6; for rabbinic references see Str-B, 3:227–29. Gen 6:1–4 was also drawn into this speculation (see on 1:27); the texts are set out by Kuss, 261–72. Unlike most of his contemporaries Paul does not speculate about the way in which sin entered the world—through Satan (as in Wisd Sol 2:24), through Eve (as in Sir 25:24; *Adam and Eve* 44; *Apoc. Mos.* 14, 32; cf. 2 Cor 11:3; 1 Tim 2:14; *2 Enoch* 30.18), through the "evil heart" (as in *4 Ezra* 4.30). Nor like the later Gnostics does he try to trace the cause further back to some primordial cosmic dualism (cf. Bornkamm, "Anakoluthe," 83–84, 90; Gaugler, who also quotes Bultmann, "Rom 5," 152— "sin came into the world through sinning"). And though he clearly personifies "sin" and "death" (see on 3:9 and 1:32 respectively) his language is not so different from that of Sir 25:24 and Wisd Sol 2:24, and his concern is not so much to designate them as cosmic powers as to characterize them as forces of existential reality: what sin entered was the world of human beings, of human experience ("all men"—v 12c; cf. 7:7–12) rather than creation (Wilckens, 315 n.1037). This is the language of universal experience, not of cosmic speculation (cf. Dodd—Paul "is not really concerned about origins, but about the facts as they are"). Where Paul does come closer to the broader Jewish thought is in the tension between sin as part of human nature and the responsibility for sinning (see below); and in the clear implication that death was a consequence of sin and so not part of God's purpose for his creation (cf. Wisd Sol 1:13; 2:23–24; see also Black, "Death," 414–15, 421). As in the broader sweep of Jewish thought also, there is no suggestion of a distinction between "spiritual" and "physical" death: human weakness (5:6), the corruptibility of the flesh (see on 1:3 and 7:5), and death are all of a piece in that they characterize the whole sweep of creaturely alienation from the Creator (cf. Kuss; against Schmidt). "Sin" and "death," appearing here for the first time as interdependent categories, will largely dominate the discussion for the next three chapters ("sin" 42 times between 5:12 and 8:10; "death" 19 times between 5:12 and 8:6; together—5:12, 21; 6:16, 23; 7:5, 13; 8:2; see further chaps. 6–8 *Introduction*).

καὶ οὕτως εἰς πάντας ἀνθρώπους ὁ θάνατος διῆλθεν, "and so death came to all men." The καὶ οὕτως does not provide the apodosis for the ὥσπερ clause (see particularly Cranfield and Schlier; otherwise Kirby—"so too [*sc.* through one man, Adam] death came to all men"—but without offering any explanation for the sequence of thought through vv 12d and 13a). Paul seems to be going off at a tangent, but his purpose is to emphasize the universal rule of death (Robinson, *Wrestling*, 61), whether as a consequence of all men's sinful acts (v 12d) or as a consequence of human sin, even if unaccounted (vv 13–14); his theme is original *death* more than original *sin* (Feuillet, "Règne," 482–92; Theobald, 80; Maillot). However, he chooses a linking phrase which prevents the transition from jarring unnecessarily (καὶ οὕτως, where the construction expects οὕτως καί, as in v 18). The διῆλθεν (usually used of journeys) may be chosen to increase the force of εἰσῆλθεν: death passed through the whole range of humankind (SH, Michel; cf. Wisd Sol 7:24). Dibelius, "Vier Worte," 8, and Englezakis emphasize the chiastic structure of v 12:

> *sin* entered and *death*
> and so *death* came to all in that all *sinned*

ἐφ' ᾧ πάντες ἥμαρτον, "in that all sinned." The classic debate on the meaning of ἐφ' ᾧ has more or less been settled in favor of the meaning "for this reason that, because" (cf. 2 Cor 5:4; Phil 3:12; 4:10; classical parallels in BGD, ἐπί IIbγ), "in view of the fact that" (Moulton, *Grammar*, 1:107); see particularly the full discussion of Cranfield; Black, however, favors the sense "wherefore, from which it follows that" (following Lyonnet) = "thus providing proof that"; unacceptable is Schmidt's interpretation, "up to which (the end [*Ziel*] of eternal death) all sinned." What comes to expression here is not some concept of "corporate personality" or cosmic Man or theology of Adam as Everyman. However much Paul wants to stress the universality of the effects of Adam's sin (vv 13–14, 18–19), the fact remains that he begins with (v 12) and maintains throughout (vv 15–19) a distinction between "one" and "all"/ "the many." The link between the "one" and the "all" is not explained, but the distinction is clear: the "one" is not the "all," and the "all" are not simply subsumed within the "one." What comes to expression is rather what we also see in the same broad stream of Jewish reflection on the Genesis account of Adam's fall—viz., the tension between the inescapableness of human sin operating as a compelling power from within or without (cf., e.g., Philo,

Mos. 2.147—συμφυὲς τὸ ἁμαρτάνειν ἐστίν; Qumran's "spirit of perversity"—1QS 3:18–4:1; *4 Ezra's* "evil heart"), and the recognition of human responsibility in sinning (particularly *4 Ezra* 8.35; *2 Apoc. Bar.* 54.15, 19—"Though Adam sinned first and has brought death upon all who were not in his own time, yet each of them who has been born from him has prepared for himself the coming torment . . ."). So here the distinction between the "one" and the "all" is matched by the distinction between ἁμαρτία and ἥμαρτον, where the latter clearly denotes human responsibility in sinful acts (as in 2:12 and 3:23)—hence the problem (v 13) of whether individuals ἥμαρτον when there was no law (Wedderburn, "Rom 5:12," 351–52; see further Denney, 627–29; Kuss, 241–48; Fitzmyer; Käsemann, 148–49; Kümmel, *Theology*, 179; Schlier, 160–63; Hendriksen; cf. Danker; against Nygren; Bruce; Murray; Ridderbos, *Paul*, 96; Johnson, 306–7; and Ladd, *Theology*, 404). In modern terms we would want to balance questions of individual responsibility against the constraints of hereditary, educational, and other social conditioning factors (cf. Dodd; Leenhardt; Robinson, *Wrestling*, 61–63). "No one sins entirely alone and no one sins without adding to the collective burden of mankind" (Byrne, *Reckoning*, 116).

13 ἄχρι γὰρ νόμου ἁμαρτία ἦν ἐν κόσμῳ, "for until the law sin was in the world." For ἁμαρτία see on 3:9 and 5:12; κόσμος is again the world of human beings, human experience (as in 5:12). νόμος clearly refers to the Torah, and the clause to the period of history prior to the giving of the law at Sinai (between Adam and Moses—v 14). Very noticeable is the speed with which Paul's thought and argument reverts to the law (cf. Jüngel, "Gesetz," 52)—a further indication that here was the chief point of tension for Paul the Jew become Christian and for his understanding of the gospel of Christ in relation to the traditional emphases of Judaism.

ἁμαρτία δὲ οὐκ ἐλλογεῖται μὴ ὄντος νόμου, "but sin is not accounted in the absence of the law." ἐλλογέω is a commercial t.t., "charge to someone's account" (BGD; cf. its only other NT use, Philem 18). Paul draws here on the idea of the heavenly tablets or books in which the sins (and righteousness) of humankind are recorded—an idea already current in Judaism (see particularly *Jub.* 30.17–23; *1 Enoch* 104.7; *2 Apoc. Bar.* 24.1); Black translates "is not entered into the ledger against." Once again νόμος does not mean "law" in general, but the law, the Torah. The meaning of ἁμαρτία has moved from that of power to that of act (see further on 3:9 and 5:20). Lietzmann appropriately compares Philo, *Immut.* 134, "For so long as the divine reason (θεῖος λόγος) has not come into our soul . . . all its (our soul's) works are free from guilt," since for Philo the law is also θεῖος λόγος (*Migr.* 130).

Paul's reasoning here has puzzled many commentators. "Verse 13 is completely unintelligible. . . . What sort of sin was it if it did not originate as contradiction of the Law? And how can it have brought death after it if it was not 'counted'? These questions cannot be answered" (Bultmann, *Theology*, 1:252). "The statement ἁμαρτία οὐκ ἐλλογεῖται is a mere verbal expedient without any real significance. Paul tries to show that, as regards man and sin, the coming of the law makes a difference; what he actually shows is that there is none" (Räisänen, *Paul*, 146 n.91). Certainly there is some tension here with what Paul says elsewhere, but such strictures are excessive. What is clear is that Paul's primary object here is to stress the universal sway of death over the epoch introduced by Adam (cf. Bultmann, *Theology*, 1:252): v 13 functions as an explanation of v 12c; and v 14 makes it clear that v 13 is to be regarded as raising a possible objection to the claim that death's sway has been unbroken from the beginning. The objection centers not on sin, because it was through sin that death entered (v 12). It centers rather on the nexus between sin and the law: that sin is not counted except as a breach of the law; and therefore in the absence of the law no acts worthy of death could have happened. Paul could have met this objection by arguing as he did in chaps. 1 and 2 that those outside the law have a knowledge of God and of his will in terms of which they will be judged (see on 2:14), or by arguing that the law itself was already known in whole or in part already in the garden (see on 7:7). That he chooses not to do so, when he was prepared to take up such ideas elsewhere in the same letter, must be significant (cf. Zeller). What the significance is, however, remains unclear. But it must be tied up with Paul's evident concern here to emphasize the role and power of sin and death as ultimately independent of the law (vv 13–14). Probably because, on the one hand, he already has in mind the argument he will have to make in chap. 7, which will leave a positive role for the law when it is not sin's catspaw (Theobald, 86–87). And probably also because he is willing to trade on the Jewish claim to a distinctive possession of the law, since he has already been able to turn it against his Jewish interlocutor: the law was given to the Jews to make them conscious of sin (see on 3:20 and 4:15)— the very point he will make with greater force in 5:20. The awkwardness of 5:13 is to be explained in large part therefore by the fact that it is like 3:1–8: it foreshadows lines of argument and emphases which Paul is not yet ready to develop.

What emerges here, however, is two potentially important distinctions. (1) Between sin as a power in human experience from which no one in the epoch can escape, and sin as something for which the individual can be charged—between sin = human sinfulness, and sin "counted" = individual "transgression" (v 14). Once again the two-sidedness of the human condition within the epoch of Adam comes to expression—sin as a given of human character and social environment ("sin was in the world"), and sin as an accountable action of individual responsibility (see also on 5:12d). Paul seems to think of both elements as present in greater or less degree in all sinning— the verb ἁμαρτάνω covering the complete range (vv 12d and 14). We may compare the distinctions already accepted within Judaism between unwitting sins and sins "with a high hand," between sins atonable within the covenant and sins which put the sinner outside the covenant = outside the scope of forgiveness (Num 15:27–31; cf. 1 John 5:16–17). (2) Between death as an inescapable part of the human condition for which the individual cannot be held responsible, and death as a consequence of the individual's responsible transgression (1:32; 6:23). It is not entirely fair to criticize Paul here by noting that it makes no difference—all die, for whatever reason (cf. Räisänen above). For, on the one hand, Paul is again giving expression to a much more widely experienced tension between unavoidable destiny and individual responsibility (see Scroggs, *Adam*, 36, and on 5:12). And, on the other, he is quite capable of distinguishing between different levels of judgment, different qualities of judgment (cf. 2:7–10; 1 Cor 3:12–15): no one can escape death as a destiny; but Paul certainly sees its hold on individuals as something which can be broken (cf. 6:7–11).

14 ἀλλὰ ἐβασίλευσεν ὁ θάνατος ἀπὸ Ἀδὰμ μέχρι Μωϋσέως, "but death ruled from Adam to Moses." For θάνατος as a power see on 1:32 and 5:12. The imagery of kingly rule appears for the first time—death reigned, "damnation carried all before it" (Lightfoot); it is used equally of "death" (vv 14, 17) and "sin" (5:21; 6:12). The personification is more vivid, but it is still the existential reality which is in view—death as exercising a power over human life which no individual can escape. Whatever the precise relation Paul has in mind between death as consequence of human sinfulness and death as "payment" for sin (6:23; see on 5:13), it is certainly the former he has in mind here—death as man's inescapable end, an oppressive power for those who delight in life, "the last enemy" (1 Cor 15:26). The period "from Adam to Moses" could hardly be regarded as an "age of innocence" (cf. Gen 6:5!). Paul's analysis here reflects the related tension in Jewish thought between, on the one hand, pride in the law as given especially to Israel and in God as Israel's God, and, on the other, the conviction that his rule reached to the ends of the earth (see on 3:29, and again on 5:13). The exception of Enoch (Gen 5:24) hardly constitutes a weakening of Paul's argument, since Paul's generalization here is shared by the wisdom and apocalyptic traditions in Judaism (see on 5:12).

καὶ ἐπὶ τοὺς μὴ ἁμαρτήσαντας ἐπὶ τῷ ὁμοιώματι τῆς παραβάσεως Ἀδάμ, "even over those who did not sin in the very manner of Adam's transgression." ἁμαρτάνω is used here in a way which implies that there is a sinning which is not a transgression, but nevertheless a responsible act whose result is death (v 12d). παράβασις obviously = "sin accounted" (v 13) = breach of the law (4:15). Adam's sin was παράβασις since it was an act of disobedience to what he knew to be a command of God (Gen 2:16–17); hence NEB's "by disobeying a direct command" (see further on 7:7). The clear implication is that even if there was sinning in the period between Adam and Moses which did not have the character of deliberate rebellion against God, it was equally pernicious in its outworking on the perpetrators (cf. 1:18–32). Paul does not mean by this that since Moses all sinning the world over has the character of "transgression." The inference here, as in 3:20 and 4:15, is that "transgression" is something of which Israel in particular is guilty, since Israel in particular has the law (so 2:1–3:20). The precise meaning of ὁμοίωμα is much disputed—probably "precise likeness," "exactly like" (Black; see on 6:5); but the meaning here is clear enough—"who did not sin in just the way that Adam transgressed." Cf. Hos 6:7 MT—"like Adam they transgressed the covenant." There is no thought of children who die in infancy here (as still in Murray).

ὅς ἐστιν τύπος τοῦ μέλλοντος, "who is the type of the one to come." τύπος was an obvious and familiar metaphor in the ancient world. The primary sense is of the impression made by a blow; so either "what is stamped," the "mark" left, or the form or outline of what made the mark. So the chief sense in Paul is "pattern, model" (6:17; Phil 3:17; 1 Thess 1:7; 2 Thess 3:9), but here and in 1 Cor 10:6 it has the more technical sense of "type";

that is, an event or person from the epoch-shaping beginning time (of the world or of Israel) which provides a pattern for the end time (see further (BGD, *TDNT* 8:246–53; Cranfield's stretching of τύπος to include every man as a human being [295] distorts the typology unacceptably). Here Jewish eschatology predominates over the use of Exod 25:40, more amenable to a Platonic view of an upper world of realities of which objects on earth are only a shadow and imperfect copy (Heb 8:5; cf. Acts 7:44). The reality to which Adam points is not a heavenly being on whom Adam was patterned, but "the one who was to come" (see further below). "The one to come" is clearly Christ (not Moses, or "man under the law" as Robinson, *Body*, 35 n.1, followed by Scroggs, *Adam*, 81, similarly Haacker, quite inappropriately suggested): Christ is the eschatological counterpart of primeval Adam; Adam is the pattern, or "prototype" (Käsemann) of Christ in that each begins an epoch and the character of each epoch is established by their action. That the actions are very different and the outcomes markedly disproportionate (vv 15–19) does not alter that basic similarity. Conceivably Paul has in mind the fact that the mark made by a stamp is precisely the converse of the pattern on the stamp itself. The μέλλοντος has an eschatological ring, but it is the realized eschatology of what Christ has already accomplished (as in Gal 3:23; Col 2:17), rather than the eschatology of what is yet to come (as in 8:18). It may be this more consistent eschatological overtone which made ὁ μέλλων more attractive to Paul than ὁ ἐρχόμενος (cf. Matt 11:3 // Luke 7:20).

The debate which was a significant feature of the earlier decades of the twentieth century still lingers on, as to Paul's source for his Adam/Christ parallel. The older History of Religions hypothesis that Paul was in fact drawing on a pre-Christian Gnostic Redeemer myth (Bultmann) is still pushed forward, but despite attempts to deduce a form of it from the Nag Hammadi codices it has increasingly taken on the appearance of a wild goose chase. Insofar as the argument affects the exegesis of Rom 5, it has now focused principally on the parallel passage in 1 Cor 15. In brief compass, the argument is that in 1 Cor 15:46 Paul attacks a distinction between spiritual man and natural man which we also find in Philo as an exegetical distinction between Gen 1:27 (the heavenly man) and the man of clay of Gen 2:7 (*Leg. All.* 1:31), where the heavenly man can also be identified with the Logos (*Conf.* 41, 62–63, 146–47; more details in Dunn, *Christology*, 100); and that both reflect a pre-Christian myth of the *Urmensch*, the pretemporal primal man in heaven. The inference drawn is that the same primal man myth lies behind Rom 5 (see particularly Bultmann, "Romans 5," 154; Brandenburger, *Adam*, 117–31; still in Kümmel, *Theology*, 156–57; Käsemann, 144; and Wilckens, 1:308–10; on the complexity of the claim being made, see Schenke, 220–221; Barth's insistence that not Adam but Jesus Christ is "first" [still in *Shorter*, 62] actually depends on a Gnostic Christology, as Bultmann, "Romans 5," 150, notes). However, the reasoning is highly suspect.

(a) Philo's treatment of Gen 1:27 can be explained wholly as a combination of three strands of his philosophical theology: (1) the Wisdom figure of the wisdom tradition; (2) the Stoic belief in the λόγος as the rational power which sustains the universe; and (3) the Platonic view of the heavenly world as the realm of eternal realities (Dunn, *Christology*, 221–22). The *Urmensch* myth is an unnecessary hypothesis; nor can it find any real foothold in the Wisdom figure of Prov 8 and Sir 24, since Wisdom there is simply a classic expression of the vivid personifications which typify Hebrew poetic style and which in this case provide a way of speaking of God's immanence without falling back into the outdated anthropomorphisms of the early tradition (ibid., 168–76). Philo's "heavenly man" is simply the ideal equivalent or pattern of the human version on earth, and otherwise is no different from the "forms" and "ideas" which provide the patterns for all earthly existents (ibid., 124). Even in the case where the heavenly man is identified with the Logos, that is simply an example of Philo's allegorical exegesis which sees the Logos, the self-revelation of God, in multifarious forms of heaven and earth (ibid., 223–28). See also Wedderburn, "Heavenly Man."

(b) The most surprising element in the hypothesis is the use made of 1 Cor 15:44–49. Paul does indeed seem to be intent on denying some philosophically based view that the spiritual must precede the natural. But we hardly need to hypothesize more than that to provide a fully adequate explanation of Paul's reasoning. Where the argument loses touch with the text is in the deduction that by "the man from heaven" (1 Cor 15:47) Paul must have in mind the preexistent Christ taking over the role of the primal Man. For clearly the logic of Paul's argument runs quite counter to that deduction: the spiritual is subsequent to the natural, as Christ is subsequent to Adam; Christ as heavenly man is the *resurrected* Christ, Christ the pattern not for the first Adam, but for resurrected believers (vv 21–22, 48–49). If Paul presupposes Christ to have been preexistent, then his whole argument at this point collapses (the "spiritual" *does* precede the "natural"). Nor does it make too much sense to argue that Paul must have been attacking even a belief like Philo's, since his argument then becomes reduced to mere assertions which could be easily countered by mere denials. Paul's argument in 1 Cor 15 is clearly governed by eschatology: Christ as the eschatological equivalent to Adam, his resurrection inaugurating a new epoch as Adam's creation in corruptible clay inaugurated the old; the importation of the idea of Christ's preexistence as heavenly man is both unnecessary and undermines what Paul himself is clearly trying to say (see, e.g., Black, "Adam," 171–72; Scroggs, 92; Ladd, *Theology*, 422; Dunn, *Christology*, 107–8, 124, with bibliog. in notes; Schade, 83). At this point the Christology of Rom 5 and that of 1 Cor 15 come close together: Adam as pattern of life leading to death—Christ as pattern of death leading to life; Christ as pattern of a new humanity (dead and risen)—Adam as pattern (in epochal significance) for the one to come. Jewish eschatology is everything here; of a primal Man mythology there is no trace. On the other hand, there is also no real ground for seeing behind the Adam language here an earlier Son of Man Christology (so rightly, e.g., Vögtle, 208–12; see further Dunn, *Christology*, 90–91, with bibliog). Nor have I been convinced by Wright's attempt to push the earlier Jewish use of Adam and creation motifs in regard to Israel to support the thesis that there is an apocalyptic belief regarding Israel as the Last Adam, which provides "the correct background against which to understand Paul's Adam-Christology" ("Adam," 372).

(c) We might simply add that Paul's thought here is close to its Jewish *Heimat* and markedly distinct from that of the later Gnostic systems at several other points—particularly in treating sin and death as quasi-cosmic powers and in his emphasis on human responsibility in sinning (see further Wedderburn, "Rom 5:12," 342–44, 348–49); see also on 5:12.

On the other hand, we should not go to the opposite extreme and attribute the whole of Paul's Adam Christology to Paul himself. There is sufficient indication in the combined use of Ps 110:1 and Ps 8:6 that the Adam Christology involved was more widely canvassed in the first generations of Christianity (Mark 12:36 // Matt 22:44; 1 Cor 15:25–27; Eph 1:20–22; Heb 1:13–2:8; 1 Pet 3:22; see further Dunn, *Christology*, 107–23); hence the fact that here Paul can assume the typological Adam/Christ correlation without pausing to prove it (Lietzmann; Eichholz, *Theologie*, 175–76). The importance of Ps 110:1 in the development of Adam Christology is a further confirmation that it is primarily as the (crucified and) risen one that Christ is last Adam.

15 ἀλλ᾽ οὐχ ὡς τὸ παράπτωμα, οὕτως καὶ τὸ χάρισμα, "but not as the trespass, so also the effect of grace." The comparison between Adam and Christ begun in v 12 and taken up again in v 14c is once more interrupted to stress the disparity between them, but with a formula (οὐχ ὡς . . . οὕτως καί) which is again similar to the one which is held in suspense (ὥσπερ . . . οὕτως καί— vv 12, 18) and which reduces the jarring effect of the long interruption (cf. v 12c). παράπτωμα (4:25; 5:15–18, 20) now replaces παράβασις (2:23; 4:15; 5:14). Whether Paul intended them to bear a different meaning is unclear: παράπτωμα can have more the sense "false step, slip, blunder" (LSJ), whereas "transgression" is the more fitting translation for παράβασις (so Cranfield). But the distinction does not amount to much (cf., e.g., Ezek 18:22, 24, 26); both refer to Adam's disobedience; and it may be that Paul switched to παράπτωμα simply because it read more euphonistically with the other -μα compounds which predominate in the following verses (see *Form and Structure*). On the other hand, since παράβασις elsewhere in Romans has the force of deliberate breach of the law, the effect of using παράπτωμα is to reinforce the idea of a broader concept of sinning (vv 12d–14). χάρισμα as usual means a concrete enactment of grace (see on 1:11). Here the act of Christ is characterized as an embodiment of grace; with the clear implication that the epoch making χάρισμα stamps the character of the whole epoch as "charismatic" (see further on 12:6).

εἰ γὰρ . . . πολλῷ μᾶλλον, "for if . . . how much more"—see on 5:9 and 10; but here the construction denotes contrast (as in v 17).

τῷ τοῦ ἑνὸς παραπτώματι οἱ πολλοὶ ἀπέθανον, "by the trespass of the one, the many died"—referring back to and rephrasing v 12. "The one . . . the many" has a Semitic ring (Michel). "The many" has an inclusive sense in Hebrew and Aramaic—"the many who cannot be counted, the great multitude, all" (*TDNT* 6:536). So here it is clearly synonymous with the "all" of vv 12 and 18; cf. 2 Cor 5:14.

ἡ χάρις τοῦ θεοῦ καὶ ἡ δωρεὰ ἐν χάριτι τῇ τοῦ ἑνὸς ἀνθρώπου Ἰησοῦ Χριστοῦ εἰς τοὺς πολλοὺς ἐπερίσσευσεν, "the grace of God and the gift in grace, which is of the one man Jesus Christ, has overflowed to the many." For χάρις see on 1:5. The double expression here should not be taken to imply that "the grace of God" is (merely) God's gracious disposition, with only the second phrase referring to his gracious giving. Both speak of God's gracious action. The redundancy partly attests Paul's concern to express the superlative quality of the act (both in its power and generosity), and partly is intended to hold together the grace (χάρις, χάρισμα) of the Christ event, and the grace actually received by those who believe in Christ. With δωρεά the gift of the Spirit in particular may be in view (see on 5:5), or the gift of righteousness (5:17), but in the description of what comes to man from God "gift," "grace," "righteousness," and "Spirit" are all near synonyms, and so can be used in various prepositional combinations (cf. 3:24; 5:17, 21; 8:10; Gal 4:4–5; Acts 2:38; 10:45; Eph 3:7; 4:7). 1 Tim 2:5 suggests that Paul's formulation "the one man Jesus Christ" became established in a creedal form in the Pauline churches; but the attempt to see behind the phrase Jesus' own self-designation as "the son of man" goes too far (Kuss; against Jeremias, *TDNT* 1:143). περισσεύειν, "overflow," is one of Paul's favorite words: he uses it both for God's generosity (see particularly 3:7; 5:17; 15:13; 2 Cor 9:8) and for believers' response (1 Cor 14:12; 15:58; 2 Cor 8:2, 7; Phil 1:9; Col 2:7). That he saw the two as interdependent and sought to pattern his own outgoingness on God's is the implication of 2 Cor 1:5; 4:15; 9:8, 12; Phil 4:12, 18; and 1 Thess 3:12. Here the implication is clearly that God's response to Adam's trespass sought not merely to make up the ground which had been lost but also to bring to completion the destiny of which Adam had fallen short (see also on 3:23). "The act of grace does not balance the act of sin; it overbalances it" (Barrett; see further, Theobald, 96–97).

16 καὶ οὐχ ὡς δι᾽ ἑνὸς ἁμαρτήσαντος τὸ δώρημα, "and not as through one who sinned, the gift." The language is very compressed, but the thought clear enough. The οὐχ ὡς . . . (οὕτως καί) of v 15 is repeated, but this time the contrast is between the gift and what came through Adam, rather than with Adam's trespass as such (v 15). The δι᾽ ἑνὸς ἁμαρτήσαντος brings together the complementary formulations of vv 12a and 14b, with ἁμαρτάνω broad enough to support the full range of παράβασις and παράπτωμα (see on 5:14 and 15). δώρημα, a word rarely used in prose (LSJ; elsewhere in the NT only James 1:17), is obviously chosen for rhetorical effect, as another -μα word.

τὸ μὲν γὰρ κρίμα ἐξ ἑνὸς εἰς κατάκριμα, "for the judgment is from one to condemnation." κρίμα can mean "judgment" in the sense of "condemnation" (see on 2:2 and 3:8), but here it is complemented by the stronger word κατάκριμα where the idea of "condemnation" includes the carrying out of the sentence (*TDNT* 3:952); elsewhere in the NT only at 5:18 and 8:1. The thought adds nothing materially to v 15 except that together with v 15 it once again highlights the two-sidedness of humankind's plight—death as a consequence of the belonging to the epoch inaugurated by Adam, and condemnation as falling upon acts of responsible trespass. As Käsemann observes, "the intensifying of κρίμα by κατάκριμα corresponds to the διὸ παρέδωκεν of 1:24ff." (see further Käsemann). In view of the rhetorical variation present in the next clause, it is quite possible that Paul intended the ἐξ ἑνός to refer either to Adam or to Adam's act or to both.

τὸ δὲ χάρισμα ἐκ πολλῶν παραπτωμάτων εἰς δικαίωμα, "but the effect of grace is from many trespasses to justification." Perhaps conscious of the danger of lapsing into mere repetition Paul varies the use of πολλοί—altering the contrast from the one and the many to the one trespass (or trespass of the one) and the many trespasses (= the trespasses of the many). "Christ stands not with the sin of the one, but with the damnation which has come to all and the transgressions of the many" (Bornkamm, "Anakoluthe," 86). For χάρισμα see on 5:15. δικαίωμα normally means "regulation, requirement" (BGD; and see on 5:18). But here it is chosen obviously as yet another -μα word to provide rhetorical balance to κατάκριμα. As such it has to be taken as the opposite of "condemnation," so "justification, acquittal." The reintroduction of δικαι- words is significant (see *Form and Structure*). The use here confirms that Paul's theology of justification always has in view (implicitly or explicitly) acquittal at the last judgment (see further on 2:13); as κατάκριμα stands at the end of the old age, so δικαίωμα is the goal of the new (Michel). Moreover the fact that he can use δικαίωμα in this way confirms that for Paul final acquittal is in no way at odds with the requirements laid down by God upon both Jew and Gentile (1:32; cf. 3:26).

17 εἰ . . . πολλῷ μᾶλλον, "if . . . how much more"—for the fourth time in 9 verses (see on 5:15).

τῷ τοῦ ἑνὸς παραπτώματι ὁ θάνατος ἐβασίλευσεν διὰ τοῦ ἑνός, "by the trespass of the one, death reigned through the one"; another recapping clause which encapsulates what had already been said in vv 12 and 14. The repetition is not merely redundant. V 14 showed that the chief focus of Paul's characterization of the age of Adam was the universal reign of death. To that he must return and show how the "much more"-ness of God's grace transforms that too. The aorist refers either to death's accession to its kingly role (through Adam's sin) or views the whole sweep of Adam's epoch as summed up in the one instant of the death to which all must bow the knee.

οἱ τὴν περισσείαν τῆς χάριτος καὶ τῆς δωρεᾶς τῆς δικαιοσύνης λαμβάνοντες, "those who receive the abundance of grace and of the gift of righteousness." Paul's piling up of language in superfluous repetition is an instinctive or deliberate attempt to mirror the superabundant quality of grace given and received. περισσεία, "surplus, abundance," a rare word (elsewhere in the NT 2 Cor 8:2; 10:15; James 1:21), is drawn in to provide a noun form of περισσεύω (see on 5:15). Paul declines the opportunity to introduce another -μα word in περίσσευμα ("abundance, fullness"—2 Cor 8:14), presumably because in this instance περισσείαν τῆς χάριτος was a more pleasing match for τῆς δωρεᾶς τῆς δικαιοσύνης. Characteristic of his understanding of "grace" is that it is abundant, more than enough (see on 5:15).

The further variation of v 15 (ἡ δωρεὰ ἐν χάριτι) allows Paul once again to recall the principal theme of 1:17–5:21 (ἡ δωρεὰ τῆς δικαιοσύνης). The fact that he can speak so explicitly of "righteousness" as a "gift received" is important. It is not merely a rhetorically stretched usage (like δικαίωμα in v 16); but neither should the usage be given determinative significance for all the other occurrences (in view of the rhetorical character of the context). The phrase signifies that the status of one acceptable to God is a gift of God. As such it is a concrete expression of the outreaching grace of God (χάρισμα) and cannot be separated from the overflowing grace of God (ἡ περισσεία τῆς χάριτος). As such it cannot be regarded as an object, a package received and retained, as if it was one's own property; on the contrary, the relational force of righteousness remains and is reemphasized—God's acceptance as always God's—a gift given not by passing the gift from God's hands but by drawing the receiver into his arms. See further on 1:17 and 6:18, 22; but also on 6:16 and 10:10.

The use of the participle form (οἱ λαμβάνοντες) is unusual in Paul. The verb he uses quite regularly, usually in a first person plural form to remind his readers of what they have received—grace (1:5), reconciliation (5:11), the Spirit (8:15; 1 Cor 2:12; Gal 3:2, 14). The participle he uses quite regularly with πιστεύειν (1:16; 3:22; 4:5, 11, 24; etc.). He can vary these more regular patterns here presumably because believing and receiving are for him two sides of the same coin. The present tense may be used for the same reason that he regularly uses πιστεύειν in the present (see on 1:16). But here part of the reason at least is to provide a contrast (together with the future tense in the next clause) to the aorist of v 17a. Where the rule of death is abrupt and peremptory, the new era of grace has an open and future character. For the significance of οἱ λαμβάνοντες taking the place of οἱ πολλοί (= πάντες), see on 5:19.

ἐν ζωῇ βασιλεύσουσιν διὰ τοῦ ἑνὸς Ἰησοῦ Χριστοῦ, "shall reign in life through the one, Jesus Christ." The future tense underlines once again the eschatological tension characteristic of the whole passage (cf. vv 2, 5, 9–10—that ἐν ζωῇ refers to Christ's life instrumentally, as in v 10, cannot be ruled out); they are already receiving grace, but they are not yet reigning (see further Käsemann; Theobald, 107). The implication clearly is that their rule will be a consequence of their δικαίωμα = final vindication (v 16); elsewhere Paul's talk is of a still future inheritance of the kingdom (see on 4:13; in 1 Cor 4:8 the ἐβασιλεύσατε is sarcastic!); cf. Bornkamm, "Anakoluthe," 87; Bultmann, "Romans 5," 157–58; Wilckens; and see further on 5:21. The expectation that the recipients of God's favor would exercise kingly rule in the coming age was, of course, a characteristic feature of Jewish hope (e.g., Dan 7:22, 27; Wisd Sol 3:8; 5:15–16; 1QM 12:14–15). But, as usual, Paul has severely transformed it: those receiving grace are those justified by faith (not those who join themselves to Israel); they will reign through Jesus Christ; also, as a further consequence of the "denationalizing" of the older Jewish hope, the idea of a rule exercised over others (the Gentiles) is lacking (they will reign "in life"). Such transformation is typical of Paul's whole understanding of God's covenant purpose through the gospel (e.g., chap. 4).

It is also significant that Paul avoids the obvious parallel: death has ruled, life will rule. The thought of "life" as exercising rule over believers is evidently inappropriate (cf. Michel). The opposite to the coldly final rule of death is the unfettered enjoyment of life—the life of a king.

18 ἄρα οὖν ὡς . . . οὕτως καί, "so then, as . . . so also." In classical Greek ἄρα is never put at the beginning of a clause (BGD), but the fuller phrase used here (ἄρα οὖν) is evidently a feature of Paul's style of reasoning (12 times in his letters, 8 in Romans); see Lagrange and also on 8:1. The οὖν also serves to resume the main line of argument (v 12) interrupted by vv 12d–17 (cf. BDF, §451.1), with ὡς corresponding to the ὥσπερ of v 12, and

the οὕτως καί introducing the long-delayed apodosis. The compressed style
(v 18 has no verb), however, is closer to that of v 16, as Paul strives to achieve
epigrammatic conciseness.

δι' ἑνὸς παραπτώματος εἰς πάντας ἀνθρώπους εἰς κατάκριμα, "through the trespass of one to all men to condemnation"—a masterly compression of the
different aspects picked out in the preceding verses (δι' ἑνός—vv 12, 16, 17;
παράπτωμα—vv 15–17; εἰς πάντας ἀνθρώπους—v 12; εἰς κατάκριμα—v 16). The
ἑνός could be taken as a neuter ("through one trespass"—so Schmidt, Murray),
but most understandably prefer to take it as a masculine ("through one man's
trespass"), since the parallel phrases being echoed all refer to Adam (vv 15–
17), and the contrast is with "all men" rather than with "many trespasses"
(as in v 16). But we should recall that the Greek allows a degree of ambiguity
not easy to retain in translation. For παράπτωμα and κατάκριμα, see 5:15 and
5:16 respectively.

δι' ἑνὸς δικαιώματος εἰς πάντας ἀνθρώπους εἰς δικαίωσιν ζωῆς, "through the
righteous act of one to all men to righteousness of life." The ἑνός here is
more obviously "the one (man) Jesus Christ" (vv 15, 17, 19), but the ambiguity
remains, since Paul evidently has in view a single action which inaugurated
a whole epoch (see further on 5:19). The focus is on the act of Christ rather
than its outcome, as in χάρισμα, δώρημα, and δικαίωμα in vv 15–16. δικαίωμα
normally means "regulation, requirement" (as in 1:32, 2:26, and 8:4; 5:16
is rhetorically determined); but the sense of "righteous act" is attested in
Aristotle and the LXX (see BGD; Lagrange also notes that in one LXX passage
[2 Sam 19:28] δικαίωμα renders צְדָקָה), and that clearly fits best here, even
though rhetorical considerations (the sequence of -μα words) again play a
part. The choice of δικαίωμα enables Paul to maintain the sequence of δικαι-
words, but the reference is not to "the gift of righteousness" (v 17; "righteous
creating act"—Wilckens). On the other hand, to see in it a reference to Christ's
whole life (TDNT 2:221–22, Leenhardt, Gaugler, Murray, Cranfield) weakens
both the point of contrast (Adam's "trespass") and the echo of 3:24–26 (God's
righteousness displayed in Christ's death as expiatory sacrifice).

On the issue of whether the "all men" implies a "universalist" view of
salvation, see on 5:19. For δικαίωσις see on 4:25. It can embrace the idea of
a process as well as its result (BGD), so although the final outcome is primarily
in view (final vindication = salvation, vv 9–10 = the still future reign in life,
v 17), the eschatological tension is again encapsulated: believers already experience something at least of the new life (cf. particularly 6:4, 11, 13), even if
its full manifestation is not yet (cf. particularly 6:5, 22–23; 8:11, 13); see further
on 2:13; 5:16; 6:5–6; and 8:23. It is unnecessary to press the genitive (ζωῆς)
for one specific sense (genitive of source, cf. v 10; genitive of result, cf.
BDF, §166; epexegetic genitive). Once again the ambiguity of the genitive
form allows a richer sense which need not necessarily exclude any of the
particular meanings (cf. Schlier).

19 ὥσπερ γάρ . . . οὕτως καί, "for just as . . . so also"—the construction
previously stretched over vv 12–18 is repeated in summary and climactic
form.

διὰ τῆς παρακοῆς τοῦ ἑνὸς ἀνθρώπου, "through the disobedience of the one
man." A further and final contrasting pair is introduced (παρακοή / ὑπακοή;

cf. vv 15–16). Adam's sin, transgression, trespass is further identified as an act of disobedience—naturally recalling the account of Gen 2–3 (2:16–17; 3:1–6). The word is little used by Paul and was probably as much prompted by the possibility of the rhetorical antithesis with ὑπακοή (so also in his only other usage—1 Cor 10:6) as by the record of Adam's disobedience. See also on 11:30–31.

ἁμαρτωλοὶ κατεστάθησαν οἱ πολλοί, "the many were made sinners." ἁμαρτωλοί probably has the more general sense of "sinners" (as in 5:8), but it is quite possible that Paul intended to recall the more specific sense in which it was then current within Judaism to denote those ignorant of or disobedient to the law (see on 3:7), especially since its antonym here (δίκαιοι) was a favorite self-description of pious Jews (see *Introduction* §5.3 and on 1:17). Paul then alludes in summary fashion to one of his main theses: the many, Jews as well, stand under the law's condemnation (cf. 4:15); Jews have not escaped the entail of Adam's disobedience by virtue of the law. Certainly the intensification of law-related words (disobedience, obedience; sinners, righteous) prepares the way for the reintroduction of the law in v 20.

The anxiety sometimes evident in commentators (e.g., Kirk, Taylor, Hendriksen, Zeller) lest καθίστημι here be too deterministic (Adam's sin caused the many to become sinners) is unnecessary. Although "make" is the simplest translation, the causal connection indicated thereby is non-specific and can be very loose, so that the passive can function simply as equivalent to γίνομαι (*TDNT* 3:445; Bultmann, "Romans 5," 159; see the range of meanings in LSJ and references in BGD; Michel compares Deut 25:6; Barrett notes that "the words 'sinners' and 'righteous' are words of relationship, not character"). The use here then expresses adequately the two-sidedness in human sinfulness which was clearly in Paul's view earlier (see on 5:12d). Certainly the only occasion when Paul reaches for this word, and in a passage where rhetorical considerations have pushed other words into less usual meanings and correlations (particularly δικαίωμα—v 18), should not be regarded as sufficient basis for an important theological thesis.

διὰ τῆς ὑπακοῆς τοῦ ἑνός, "through the obedience of the one." ὑπακοή is an important thematic word in Romans (see on 1:5). It is important for Paul that he can speak of Christ's death as an "act of obedience" and as a "righteous act" (v 18), both stressing that whereas Adam acted in breach of a divine ruling, Christ acted in accordance with God's will revealed in the law (cf. again 3:24–26). Several commentators see the reference here as embracing Christ's whole life (e.g., Michel, Cranfield; cf. 6:17 and 15:2–5), but almost certainly Paul's thought at this point focuses more or less exclusively on Christ's death. (1) In the context it stands as the antithesis to the one act of disobedience of Adam. (2) It is the answer to Adam's disobedience because it provided the counter to the consequences of Adam's trespass: by being a sin offering (3:25; 5:18; 8:3) he breaks the power of sin; by dying he breaks the rule of death (6:9). (3) In the Adam Christology being used here the theme of Christ's "obedience" refers to his submission to death (Phil 2:8; Heb 5:8). (4) Since the representative significance of "the one" is an integral part of Paul's Adam Christology, it is significant that he confines the idea of union with Christ to that of sharing in his sufferings and death as well as his resurrection (hence the closely following sequence of 6:3–11). The writ of the first Adam runs to death. It is by his death and resurrection that Christ breaks through the cul-de-sac of death and inaugurates a new humanity as last Adam (1 Cor 15:21–22, 45–49; see further Dunn, *Christology*, 127; in his criticism of my formulation in *Christology*, Wright, "Adam," 388, underplays the full statement of the theme [*Christology*, 108–13] and ignores the fact that the Adam imagery is only one formulation of Paul's Christology which should not be expected to provide a complete statement of Paul's soteriology).

δίκαιοι κατασταθήσονται οἱ πολλοί, "the many will be made righteous." For the force of καθίστημι see above. The future could be taken as a logical future, and so δίκαιοι refers to "the present life of believers" (Cranfield; similarly Althaus, Murray), as the parallel with ἀμαρτωλοί suggests. But here again Paul probably has in view the future ratification of the final judgment in part at least (cf., e.g., Dodd, Schlier with further bibliog.): as death is the final ratification of Adam's age, so it is only with the final acquittal that the divine response will be complete. Certainly it is inviting to regard δίκαιοι κατασταθήσονται as synonymous with δικαιωθήσονται of 2:13 (see on 2:13 and cf. Gal 5:5).

οἱ πολλοί = πάντες (see on 5:15). On the "universalism" of Paul's thinking here see particularly Käsemann: "all powerful grace is unthinkable without eschatological universalism"; also Hultgren, *Gospel*, 82–124. According to Boring, "Paul affirms *both* limited *and* universal salvation" ("Language," 292). Wilckens attempts to short-circuit the issue by arguing that here Christ is "not the representative of men before God, as Adam is . . . but the representative of God before men." But while it is true that for Paul "God's action comes to effect in Christ's action" (Wilckens; cf. 2 Cor 5:19, 21), that is not the point Paul is making here. Throughout this section, up to and including v 19, Paul is working with an Adam Christology, where Christ is thought of as the man Adam was intended to be and would have become had he not fallen. Here particularly (v 19) the point hangs on the representative significance of Christ as the one whose action (like Adam's) determines the character and condition of those who belong to the age he inaugurated by that action. The theme throughout the section is the solidarity of "the all/many" with the one epochal figure whether in trespass to condemnation or in grace to righteousness. What has usually been missed in the discussion is the significance of the δίκαιοι. Since it was such a favorite self-description of devout Jews (see on 1:17), the force of Paul's final phrase is to emphasize that not just Israel, or the righteous of Israel, will be finally acquitted, but "the many." The "universalism" therefore is in part at least a way of denying the limited nationalism of the normal Jewish hope—"all" = Gentiles as well as Jews (cf. Hendriksen; see also on 11:32). Alternatively, if death is truly the end of those belonging to Adam's epoch (vv 12, 14, 17, 21), the "all" may simply denote all those who through sharing Abraham's faith in the life-giving God (4:17, 23–25) can hope to share also in the life that lives beyond death (cf. 1 Cor 15:22) = "those who receive the abundance of grace" (v 17; cf. Kuss, 237). See also on 11:32.

20 νόμος δὲ παρεισῆλθεν ἵνα πλεονάσῃ τὸ παράπτωμα, "the law came in to increase the trespass." As consistently in Paul, νόμος means, of course, the Jewish law, the Torah (see on 2:12 and 14). Paul once again, as in v 13, narrows the universal sweep of his exposition by introducing the factor of Jewish particularity. His contrast between the two epochs had been neatly rounded, but he could hardly ignore the fact that for his own religious tradition the law itself had epochal significance, as marking out the people through whom God would effect his righteous and eschatological purpose (see further on 6:14). Paul challenges this positive salvation-history role for the law (cf. Michel, Schmidt); the law rather brings the force of the Adam story to existential reality (Jüngel, "Gesetz," 67–68). It is difficult to avoid the conclusion that Paul chose παρεισῆλθεν deliberately (since he could have repeated the εἰσῆλθεν of v 12). So the more negative overtone suggested by the double prefix (BGD, "slip in," "interpose") was probably intentional (cf. its only other occurrence in the NT—Gal 2:4; Wilckens; otherwise Cranfield). Taken together with the voice (active, rather than divine passive—contrast Gal 3:19), the effect is to set the law alongside sin and death who likewise "entered" human experience (v 12). This in itself may be sufficient explanation of the negative overtone, but Paul may also intend to imply that the law's purpose (to increase the trespass) is a lesser role than that of grace, or indeed that the law's entry was later and more temporary than grace's (Lightfoot, SH; cf. 5:13 and Gal 3:15–29) since its role in increasing sin ends with death and condemnation and does not (in that role at least) last into the new age of life beyond death (cf. 7:1–6); see also on 5:13 and 7:7–13.

Even if "law" is treated as a quasi-power here, analogous to "sin" and "death" (v 12), the ἵνα indicates that it serves *God's* purpose (Michel). The πλεονάζω is chosen probably as a slightly lesser equivalent to Paul's favorite περισσεύειν (though in fact they are near synonyms—cf. 6:1; 2 Cor 4:15; 1 Thess 3:12), possibly in some dependence on Sir 23:3 (cf. *Pss. Sol.* 5.16). The cutting edge of the verb is that it attributes the multiplying of the one trespass into many trespasses (v 16) to the law. This constitutes an intensifying of the role attributed to the law in 3:20 and 4:15. Here again the polemic against traditional Jewish evaluation of the law is of the essence of the point being made (*pace* Luz, *Geschichtsverständnis*, 206): God's purpose for the law was not to distinguish Jewish righteous from gentile sinners (cf. v 19; *Introduction* §5), but to make Israel more conscious of its solidarity in sin with the rest of Adam's offspring. This is not to say that Paul would thus confine the law's trespass-increasing effect to Israel: Paul was at one with his fellow Jews in his belief that the law increased the Gentiles' sins, whether by revealing the extent to which they were ἁμαρτωλοί (see on 5:19) or because the just requirements contained in the law were more widely known (1:32); but where he needed to press home the argument was in stressing this more negative role of the law for the Jewish people itself (see also on 3:20, 4:15, and 5:13). For παράπτωμα see on 5:15; no longer, of course, the one transgression of Adam, but the act characteristic of the whole epoch which his transgression began and typifies. Leenhardt lays stress on the singular—"what constitutes sin as sin."

οὗ δὲ ἐπλεόνασεν ἡ ἁμαρτία, ὑπερεπερίσσευσεν ἡ χάρις, "but where sin increased, grace abundantly overflowed." The οὗ may be intended as more than a linking word: in the very place/epoch where sin increased, there in the man Christ, in his dying the death of the old epoch, grace overwhelmed the effects of sin (cf. Schmidt). The fact that Paul replaces παράπτωμα by ἁμαρτία here should be noted—a reminder that his concept of "sin" is more flexible than commentators often allow—not just or not always a personified power, but also the act of trespass itself (see on 3:9). The use of the superlative form ὑπερπερισσεύω (elsewhere in the NT only in 2 Cor 7:4) is clearly deliberate, since πλεονάζω and περισσεύω are such close synonyms (see above). In a manner typical of Jewish apocalyptic it signifies eschatological abundance (cf. particularly *4 Ezra* 4.50; *TDNT* 6:60; Philo, *Opif.* 23, cited by Zeller, is different precisely as referring to this present creation) and makes a fitting climax to the sequence of contrasts begun in v 15, resuming and outdoing the πολλῷ μᾶλλον . . . ἐπερίσσευσεν (v 15).

21 ἵνα ὥσπερ ἐβασίλευσεν ἡ ἁμαρτία ἐν τῷ θανάτῳ, "in order that as sin ruled in death." The ἵνα matches the ἵνα of v 20a, and introduces the final ὥσπερ . . . οὕτως καί completing the sequence properly begun in v 18. NEB preserves the force of the aorist—"established its reign." ἁμαρτία shifts back in sense to personified power (see on 3:9 and 5:20), and where Paul had previously spoken of death reigning (vv 14, 17), in this concluding formulation he brings the two powers back into conjunction in a variation of v 12 (death entered through sin). The ἐν can be ambiguous: sin has exercised its rule by means of, through, or in the sphere of death. The sense is plain without pressing for greater precision: sin's power over the epoch of Adam is characterized by and summed up in its final effect—death (see also 6:16, 21, 23; 1 Cor 15:56). Since the phrase "sin ruled in death" is bound up with the increased trespass (v 20; cf. vv 15, 17), the implication is that ἵνα here as well (as in v 20) catches up sin's rule within God's plan—not as a concession or as an unplanned plight but as part of the divine structure of the world of humankind: sin's rule in death is thus another way of speaking of God's wrath (1:18–32; 4:15); God's purpose of salvation embraces death since it is through death that the epoch of Adam ends and the power of sin is broken (6:7–10).

οὕτως καὶ ἡ χάρις βασιλεύσῃ διὰ δικαιοσύνης εἰς ζωὴν αἰώνιον, "so also grace might reign through righteousness to eternal life." Whereas in v 17 the eschatological equivalent of death's reign was the reign of the saints, here the contrast to sin's reign is the reign of grace. As it is sin (power and act) which characterizes the epoch of Adam, so it is grace which characterizes the epoch of Christ—with all the correlations and contrasts already gathered round it in 3:24, 4:4 and 16 (see also *Form and Structure*). The aorist subjunctive (βασιλεύσῃ) retains the eschatological note characteristic of the chapter to the end. That the sequence of δικαι- words climaxes in one of the key words of the epistle (δικαιοσύνη) is obviously deliberate. Here again the sense should not be forcibly confined to the sense "status of righteousness" (Cranfield), but must at least include the sense of God's action—δικαιοσύνη as the means by which grace achieves its effect as well as the effect itself (Schlier; see on 1:17; 5:17; and 6:13). So too the ongoing and future dimension of this "righteousness" is indicated in the εἰς ζωὴν αἰώνιον (= εἰς δικαίωσιν ζωῆς, v 18). The ζωή of vv 17–18 is in this climactic conclusion given the fuller description, "eternal life" (see on 2:7), presumably to underscore its eschatological character and to emphasize that in contrast to the epoch which ends in death the epoch

of grace is life unbounded. For Paul's view of salvation-history as implied
here see further Kuss, 275–91.

διὰ Ἰησοῦ Χριστοῦ τοῦ κυρίου ἡμῶν, "through Jesus Christ our Lord." The
piling up of prepositional phrases (διά . . . εἰς . . . διά . . .) and the concluding Christological formula marks the end of this stage of the argument
(Käsemann); see on 6:23 and 8:39. The use of διά as in vv 1 and 11 (see
Form and Structure) maintains to the end the emphasis on Christ's mediatorship
as the decisive factor in effecting the transformation from one epoch to the
other (see on 5:1). The double διά has the effect of reminding readers that
Christ himself is the fullest embodiment and mediator of grace and righteousness.

Explanation

Paul now raises his sight from believers as a group ("we, us") to embrace
humanity as a whole ("man"). Having recalled his earlier indictment of Israel's
pride in chap. 2 (5:11), he now deliberately extends his thought backward
to recall the earlier stage of his argument (1:18ff.). As his opening indictment
focused on humankind as a whole, with clear enough allusions to the figure
of Adam, so now in conclusion to this first major part of his argument he
turns again to view humanity as a whole by reference to Adam. And as it
was Christ who made the difference between an acceptable boasting in God
(5:11) and an unacceptable boasting in God (2:17), so here too it is Christ
who forms the counterpart to Adam, and Christ in whom the history of
humankind takes its decisive turn for the better. In these verses we might
well say that Paul presents the history of humanity as a drama in two parts—
two epochs dominated by the two figures, Adam the tragic hero, and Christ
the redeemer hero.

12   Paul begins with what is in effect a summary of chap. 1, the condition
of the man who has rejected God. At once he introduces the two chief "villains
of the piece"—sin and death. Up to this point they had made only brief
appearances (3:9, 20; 1:32). But now they take up positions center stage. In
dramatic style they are presented as personified powers who exercise a dominant influence upon humanity. "Sin" is not initially defined, but clearly it is
the power which human beings experience drawing them into disobedience
and transgression. "Death" needs no further definition either: it would have
been universally understood as the power which defeats and ends that life
which was the chief effect of creation and indeed its whole point.

The first act unfolds the scope of the tragedy with a few concise phrases.
Sin, the first hostile power, managed to gain entry through one man (Adam);
in its train came its sinister companion death, and death extended its sway
over everyone. They enter upon the world stage from "off-stage"; where
they actually come from Paul does not stop to say; nor, presumably, did he
think it necessary to speculate on the subject. The only pertinent fact is that
they are there, brooding presences whose influence determines the unfolding
of the plot. Nor is the initial relation of the two powers to each other made
any clearer. It is simply assumed that death is the consequence of being
under the power of sin and that no one since the beginning has been exempt
from their twin rule. The implication is that death is not the proper end of

man: death was not part of the original program for humankind; it was the entry of sin, the corrosive effect of man's refusal to live in dependence on God, which ate away his life. Without sin man would not have died.

In all this Paul is obviously thinking in terms of Gen 3 and drawing on a very common understanding of "the fall." Many of his readers would be familiar with the Jewish literature of the time which made use of the Adam and Eve stories in wrestling with the problems of evil and death. And Paul in fact shares the sentiment of wisdom and apocalyptic writers very closely (e.g., Sir 25:24; *2 Apoc. Bar.* 54.15). So Paul could certainly take this widespread understanding as his starting point and draw it into his argument without any elaboration. Indeed his treatment here and elsewhere in Romans (particularly 1:18–32 and 7:7–11) can be regarded as an important part of and contribution to this prominent strand of Jewish theologizing. His distinctive contribution lies not so much in the *analysis* of man's plight—though, as he will shortly remind his readers again, the law plays a very different role in the unfolding plot from the part written for it by other Jewish theologians. The distinctively Christian contribution, however, lies in the *solution*—the disaster of Adam countered and outweighed by the success of Christ.

In introducing the drama in these terms (he does not even need to name "Adam" initially, he speaks simply of "one man") Paul indicates that he wants this figure to be seen not so much as an individual in his own right, but as a more than individual figure, what we might call an "epochal figure"—that is, as the one who initiated the first major phase of human history and thereby determined the character of that phase for those belonging to it. Some of his readers indeed, aware that in Hebrew "Adam" means "man," might have inferred that Paul was using the Adam story simply as a way of speaking about humanity as a whole in timeless terms. But Paul is hardly concerned to make use of the Hebrew meaning of "Adam," and the bulk of his Greek-speaking readership would probably have been unaware of it even if they knew the LXX. Moreover the historical perspective is integral to the point he is making: the two men between them cover the whole of the human story from start to finish. Still less is there any implication of or encouragement to presuppose a more elaborate speculation about the first man (such as the twentieth-century hypothetical construct known as the pre-Christian Gnostic redeemer myth envisaged). All we need to say to make complete sense of Paul's argument here is that the reference to Adam's failure is for Paul a way of characterizing the condition of humankind in the epoch of human history which has extended from the beginning of the human race till now.

At the same time the implication of the argument should not be pushed too far in the opposite direction. In particular, it would not be true to say that Paul's theological point here depends on Adam being a "historical" individual or on his disobedience being a historical event as such. Such an implication does not necessarily follow from the fact that a parallel is drawn with Christ's single act: an act in mythic history can be paralleled to an act in living history without the point of comparison being lost. So long as the story of Adam as the initiator of the sad tale of human failure was well known, which we may assume (the brevity of Paul's presentation presupposes such a knowledge), such a comparison was meaningful. Nor should modern interpretation encour-

age patronizing generalizations about the primitive mind naturally understanding the Adam stories as literally historical. It is sufficiently clear, for
example, from Plutarch's account of the ways in which the Osiris myth was
understood at this period (*De Iside et Oriside* 32 ff.) that such tales told about
the dawn of human history could be and were treated with a considerable
degree of sophistication, with the literal meaning often largely discounted.
Indeed, if anything, we should say that the effect of the comparison between
the two epochal figures, Adam and Christ, is not so much to historicize the
individual Adam as to bring out the more than individual significance of
the historic Christ.

In introducing so many characters in quick succession (one man, sin, death,
all men) Paul evidently felt the need to pause and provide some clarification
of their relationships before proceeding further—even at the cost of leaving
in suspense the first half of a balanced sentence ("just as . . . so also") and
leaving the sentence itself incomplete (the second half does not appear till v
18). Those listeners in Rome familiar with the effect of his enthusiastic disregard for the rules of syntax would no doubt recognize the characteristic of
Paul's style with a smile.

12d   The first clarification (the last four words of v 12) is a vague and
subsequently much disputed clause. The point often missed in exegeting
such ambiguity is that it would probably have been ambiguous to the first
hearers also. From this we may deduce that Paul evidently did not think it
necessary to make his thought any clearer, or even that Paul had not clarified
his own thinking on the point. So it is best to retain the vagueness in our
own translation—"in that all sinned." Certainly the repetition of the "all"
makes the point of emphasis clear: that no one is exempted from the joint
rule of sin and death. And the explanatory clause also seems to reinforce
the point that death is the consequence of sin: all die because all have sinned.
Death continues to dominate humanity not solely because of one primeval
act but because of humankind's continued acts of sin, continued demonstration
that all are under the power of sin, held apart from God, the one life-giving
power which can defeat the power of death. But the relationship between
the one man's initial failure and all men's sin is not an issue to which Paul
addresses himself, and the imprecision of the syntax forbids us to press for
a clear-cut decision on the point. All that Paul seems to want to say is that
this epoch of human history is characterized and determined by the fatal
interplay of sin and death—as evidenced by the fact that everyone sins and
everyone dies—a partnership first established in power at the beginning of
the epoch, through the one man Adam.

13–14   The second clarification seems at first to concern the role of the
law. Those who were familiar with Paul's analysis of man's plight elsewhere
as involving the law as well as sin and death (as in 1 Cor 15:56), would
probably be expecting the law to be brought in. And Paul may have been
aware of an already current tendency in other Jewish theologizing to speak
of Adam's sin as a breach of God's commandments, as his description of
Adam's sin as "transgression" (v 14) and his subsequent treatment in chap.
7 probably implies (cf. 7:7). But here he insists on preserving the historical
time scale: the law did not come in until Moses. This is partly no doubt

because the argument of chap. 4 is still in mind (Abraham received the promise before the law). But partly also because he wants to assert the truly universal character of sin's and death's dominance: sin and death exercise their power independently of the law—that is, over the whole world of humankind without distinction of Jew and Gentile. That the thought stands in some tension with 7:7–11 ("I was once alive apart from the law"—sin cannot extend its dominance apart from the law) suggests that Paul may have been trying to have his cake and eat it. But the suggestion of confusion diminishes as soon as we realize that the main point of the clarification does not concern the law.

In fact the second clarification really concerns sin rather than the law. In v 12 Paul has used the noun "sin" and the verb "sinned," as though sin was synonymous with sinful acts. It is this relation Paul now seeks to clarify. He first distinguishes sin from sin which is "counted" (v 13)—that is, sin as power from sin as act. "Sin" is then understood to be the force which functions as the antecedent to particular acts of sin, that power which man experiences influencing his desires and choices to act against his best interests as a creature of God (the analysis already provided in 1:18–32). Paul then makes a further clarification by distinguishing between sinful acts which count as transgression and those which do not (v 14): all sinned even before the law, but before the law (and apart from the law) such sinful acts do not count as transgression like Adam's, that is, as a deliberate breach of a prohibition known to be a command of God (Gen 3:1–6).

The point Paul is making therefore is that all humankind is under the power of sin, as evidenced by their sinful acts (that is, acts done in disregard for God and his glory as creator—cf. 1:20–23). But not all sinful acts are held by God as transgression, only those committed in deliberate breach of a divine command. Presumably therefore Paul also implies a coordinate distinction between death as a *consequence* of sin and death as a *punishment* for sin. He does see death as a punishment deserved or merited by willful self-seeking (1:32; cf. 6:23), but in the analysis of the human condition here death is primarily a consequence of sin—that is, the inevitable entail of being under the power of sin rather than under the power of God, the inescapable consequence of failure to live in dependence on the one power which can defeat death. In short, Paul could be said to hold a doctrine of *original sin*, in the sense that from the beginning everyone has been under the power of sin with death as the consequence, but not a doctrine of *original guilt*, since individuals are only held responsible for deliberate acts of defiance against God and his law. This in turn implies that Paul's gospel had in view not only those laboring under a sense of guilt but all those subject to sin and death, and that the divine solution he offered was at a fundamental level more redemptive than punitive (cf. 3:25–26).

The historical perspective adopted here does of course to some extent cut across the less time-oriented analysis of chaps. 1 and 2. For here it is the entry of law which turns sin into transgression, while in the earlier analysis the Gentiles in particular were shown to be knowingly guilty of rejecting God without knowledge of the law as such. However, this would only be a problem for those who insisted on a pedantic consistency of hard and fast categories. Paul after all was more than ready to speak of transgression before the law (Adam's transgression was certainly "counted"), so that the more accurate summary should speak of guilt as proportional to knowledge of God, however that knowledge is given (not as proportional to knowledge of the law as such). But what also needs to be remembered is that Paul continually refers to the law because of his concern to demonstrate Israel's false understanding of its position before God. He emphasizes that the law brings knowledge of sin (3:20), that the law turns sin into transgression (4:15), that sin is only accounted in terms of the law (5:13), not because he wants to deny the existence of transgression or guilt apart from the law, but because he wants Israel to recognize that its possession of the law actually increases its need of redemption. Paul does not deny that the law brought benefit to Israel, but because Israel has, in his view, overemphasized that benefit, he is anxious to emphasize the other side of the picture: that is, precisely because the law turns sin into transgression, it makes Israel's sin all the more reprehensible and worthy of condemnation and so Israel's situation much more perilous than that of the Gentiles. This was also the thrust of chap. 2, and will soon become a more explicit theme (5:20; chap. 7), though here it lies below the surface. So too the other chief factor in the analysis of man's plight, the flesh, has also been alluded to earlier (2:28 and 3:20) but will be brought more clearly into play only at a later stage in Paul's argument (particularly 8:3–13).

14c After the clarification of vv 12d–14b, the last clause of v 14 is clearly intended to begin building a bridge back to the theme initially announced in v 12—the comparison and contrast between Adam and Christ. Paul defines the relation of Adam to Christ as that of the "type of the one to come." By this he obviously means that Adam is the exemplar or pattern of Christ in that both are epochal figures: both by one decisive act determine the character of the subsequent epoch for those belonging to that epoch. But the idea of a type is almost certainly also eschatological, denoting a person or event of the past, particularly from the time of the world's or Israel's foundation, which prefigures or demonstrates the character of God's dealings in the new age at the end of history. As Adam by his transgression determined the character of the present age, so Christ has determined the character of the age to come. This same eschatological emphasis is indicated in the description of Christ as "the one to come." That is to say, the verb probably describes Christ not so much as one who was future in relation to Adam, of a coming still within the context of this age, but Christ as the one whose effective role as epochal figure, as the inaugurator of the new age, is always future in relation to this present age. In other words, it is not Christ's birth and ministry which is in view, but his death as the eschatological counterpart to Adam's sin: as Adam's transgression introduced death, so Christ's death introduced life. It is the risen and heavenly Christ who characterizes the age to come, just as it is the fallen Adam who characterizes the present age. Thus the thought is parallel to that of 1 Cor 15:45–49, where the risen Christ is designated "the last Adam," and where the equivalent phrase is "the man from heaven." In neither case is Paul thinking of a particular coming from heaven (the Parousia), more of the new epoch inaugurated by Christ in its character as heavenly and as the age to come.

15–17 With the last clause of v 14 Paul seemed ready to complete the comparison begun in v 12. But once again he pauses, suddenly overwhelmed, or so it must have appeared to Tertius, his scribe, by the realization that a straight comparison was hardly adequate. Like someone about to offer a clear-cut definition, who at the last moment realizes the definition is not quite so clear-cut after all, and who before the definition is complete begins to insert qualifying clauses which complicate the simplicity of the definition as originally conceived. So here Paul, initially struck by the parallel between Adam and Christ as epochal figures, whose single action determined the destiny of the resultant epoch, catches himself and before completing the comparison hastens to emphasize the contrast between the two actions and their results. The comparison remains valid, and indeed is assumed already within the qualifications, but Paul evidently could not bring himself to complete it until he had made clear the very different characters of the single action in each case and particularly their respective effects.

The contrast reemploys the "how much more" form already used in vv 9–10, this time antithetically, to highlight the dissimilarity between the two epochs. No doubt Paul was partly influenced by the apocalyptic perception of the new age as qualitatively superior to the old (soon to be expressed in almost grotesque exaggeration in *2 Apoc. Bar.* 29.5). But in fact the apocalyptic perspective as such only comes to the fore in v 17, where the eschatological reign of the saints following the defeat of death's rule is in view. The stronger influence seems to be his own experience of grace (the dominant motif in these three verses) and his understanding of how that grace came to him through the one man Jesus Christ. This no doubt accounts for the character of the passage, both highly compressed and repetitive; for it is the language of fervent worship rather than that of cool theological reflection. In his sudden exultation at the thought of divine grace in its unlooked-for richness, Paul's concern is to register the fact and character of the contrast rather than to achieve a clear formulation. In consequence it would be unwise to look here for primary definitions of the terms used; for what we have here is language stretched to accommodate the wonder of grace received. Nevertheless the passage is valuable if not for primary definitions at least to show us how broad a range of usage the chosen words could encompass.

15 The contrast is posed initially as between "the trespass" and "the gracious act." The former has already been touched on, and its result: "the many died" (v 12). Paul chose the word "trespass" probably as a variation on the idea of "transgression" (v 14), though it is presumably significant that he sticks with "trespass" throughout the rest of the chapter. The transition may possibly again imply a slight withdrawal from the idea of the basic sin simply as a deliberate breach of a divine command known to be such. For with "trespass" the implication is rather that the fundamental sin has the character of taking a false step, losing one's way, where the trespasser is as much to be pitied for his folly as the transgressor to be condemned for his deliberate rebellion.

The "many" would be recognized as an acceptable variation for the "all men" of v 12, since it is humankind in the mass which Paul clearly has in view in both cases. And his use of the aorist tense ("the many died") would not cause confusion for those who bore in mind that Paul was viewing the epoch of Adam as a whole, from beginning to end; for though the rule of the present age has not yet finished, in that all have not yet died, nevertheless the fact remains that death is the inescapable bottom line for all without exception, as certain for those belonging to this age now or in the future as it was for those already dead. Once again the precise nature of the relation between Adam's trespass and the death of the many is not clarified (even the qualification of v 12d is for the moment not in view). It is the epochal significance of Adam's act as determining both character and end of the epoch as a whole which Paul emphasizes.

The other half of the contrast focuses on the word *grace*. The gracious act, the concrete expression of God's generous outreach, is elaborated as "the grace of God and the gift in grace, that of the one man Jesus Christ." The double phrase and presumably deliberate ambiguity is probably an indication that Paul wanted his readers to think both of the particular manifestation of divine grace in the generous act of Christ (especially his submission to death) *and* of the further particular manifestations of that same grace in their individual lives. They would probably recall the experience of their conversion in these terms (as in 1 Cor 1:4–5) or perhaps with explicit reference to the gift of the Holy Spirit (cf. Acts 2:38; 8:20; 10:45; 11:17). The logic of the contrast required no more than reference to the two actions of the two epochal individuals, but since "grace" in Paul chiefly denotes divine power as experienced, it looks as though Paul's thought spilled over once again from the grace of God in the Christ event to the gracious gift which the one man Jesus Christ made available for those of his epoch. His Roman audiences would take the point that it is the same grace in each instance: Christ's death and resurrection as the actualization of grace *par excellence*; that gracious act as the measure and definition of all grace experienced thereafter. Here too the precise relation between the inaugurating action of the one man and its benefit to all his race is not explained; it is stated simply that the grace actualized in Christ has become available in abundance to the many. For the second time in the verse, Paul uses aorist tense and "the many," to once again underline the epochal significance of Christ's gracious act: it has affected an epochful of humanity, humankind in that age in the mass; and it has determined the character of that epoch from beginning to end as the age of overflowed grace.

The initial contrast therefore sets against each other human failing and the divine initiative of grace. As the age of Adam is characterized by death having the final say, so the age of Christ is characterized by grace actualized and received in plentiful sufficiency. What is sometimes described as Paul's pessimistic assessment of man is actually therefore his realistic appraisal of the human condition and the individual's prospects in the present era (man as having lost his way, with death inescapable). Such realism can be sustained without despair only because it also sees the grace of God as having opened up another chapter beyond that which ends in death.

16 Paul now reexpresses the contrast between the two men and their epochs in different terms. The one who sinned is set directly against the gift which Christ has made available—confirming the clear implication of v

15 that it is not merely an objective display of grace at one point in history which is in view, but also the gift actually received. More striking is the variation of "the one and the many" motif: whereas in v 15 it was the act of one man which determined the destiny of the many (= humankind), now the talk is of the one whose sin resulted in condemnation and of the many trespasses from which the gracious act emerges. With emphasis on judgment and condemnation the human responsibility for sin and trespass is reaffirmed. And the contrasting gift is expressed in language recalling the central imagery of divine vindication, underlining the extent to which for Paul justification and the gift of grace (or Spirit) are simply two sides of the one experience of acceptance by God. Here especially the rhetorical spontaneity of the parallel form of the clauses should inhibit any readiness to look for characteristic or definitive usage here: "judgment from one" is a loose enough formulation, but "gracious gift from many trespasses" is looser still; and the nouns are chosen for their parallel endings rather than because Paul is trying to draw precise distinctions. Once again, it should be noted, Paul sums up the contrast between the epochs in terms of their beginnings and ends: the one man whose sin initiated the present epoch and the condemnation which is its end result; the gracious act which initiated the new epoch and the acquittal which is God's final word in it.

17 Having made his point in the breathless brevity of a theology of awe at grace received, Paul makes one last effort to return to the chief point of comparison between Adam and Christ and to sum up the contrast between them and their epochs at the same time. It was the one man who was responsible for yielding to sin and death: his trespass was in effect a handing over of all humankind to the rule of death. In overwhelming contrast the epoch made possible by Christ is the epoch of life and consists of those "who receive the abundant overflow of grace and of the gift of righteousness"—the present continuous tense presumably reflecting Paul's appreciation of the ongoing character of grace, both as more and more become recipients of it and as those already members of the new age continue to receive it.

The fact that Paul poses the contrast between "death" and "those receiving . . ." ("death reigned"; "those receiving . . . will reign") implies that he is not thinking of the participants of the two epochs as set there without having any say in the matter. If all are subject to death as a consequence of their being born into a race at odds with God, Paul also asserts that the many die as a condemnation for their guilt as trespassers. Whereas the new age is characterized not by the rule of a fate one cannot escape (like death) but by the willing reception of a grace freely offered—inevitably so since, in terms of the analysis of chap. 1, death can only be outwitted for those who yield again their submission as creatures to the creator, in dependence on whom alone life can be sustained despite death.

The double characterization (abundant overflow of grace and of the gift of righteousness) is also striking. Again we should beware of taking the latter phrase as a primary usage of "righteousness," since the flood of language in these verses pulls more than one word out of its more regular setting. But it is clear enough that Paul can think of righteousness as a gift, a potency or status or relationship received from God. The key factor here, however, is the manifest overlap between "grace" and "righteousness" (gift consisting in righteousness): they overlap presumably because both express the outreaching of God to man, and that outreach as experienced in its accepting and sustaining power. At such moments when the heart is full the mind need not insist on careful distinctions between such concepts as grace, Spirit, justification.

Here too the eschatological orientation of Paul's thought is clear: "they shall reign in life." Paul underscores once more that he has in view the whole epoch—death as the final result of one, life of the other. In each case the future end determines the character of the whole. As Paul implies that the old epoch is not yet at an end (death has not yet been experienced by all), so he implies that the new epoch has only begun. By such inferences the careful reader is prepared for one of the central emphases in the next stage of the argument.

One final contrast should not go unnoticed. Adam stands only at the beginning of the epoch, even though his action determines the whole epoch's domination by death (hence the possibility of reading "Adam" as a way of speaking of man/humankind as such). In contrast, the epoch of Christ is not merely initiated by Christ but continues to be determined by Christ throughout its course. Where in the present age it is "the grim reaper" who broods over the offspring of Adam, in the new age it is Christ risen and exalted who enables individuals to receive his grace and to reign in life. All this can be seen as integral to Paul's Adam Christology: Adam as having failed to realize the full purpose of God for man (to reign in life—cf. Ps 8:5–6) by being subjected to death; Christ as having by his resurrection fulfilled that purpose and at the same time made it possible for those who follow him to reign in life with him. So much was fundamental and indeed self-evident to Paul in his conceptualization and understanding of the grace he here rejoices in.

18–19 With v 18 Paul at last feels able to round off the comparison between Adam and Christ left incomplete in v 12. But it is now a more carefully phrased comparison with major elements of the contrast drawn in from vv 15–17. The *correspondence* has already become plain and Paul is in some danger of merely repeating himself. It lies in that fact that the act of *one* man has determined the destiny of *all*, humankind in the mass—a typological correspondence of epochal figures in that the first man introduced the original and present epoch, while the other has introduced the ultimate and future epoch. The *contrast* lies in the nature of the one act and in its effect in each case: Adam's trespass, Christ's righteous deed; the result of the first, condemnation (as in v 16), of the second, acquittal which brings life (a combination of vv 16 and 17). Or in the terms of v 19, the contrast between Adam's disobedience and Christ's obedience, resulting in the many being made sinners in the first case, and being made righteous in the second. Other elements of the contrast (the "how much more," the rule of death in the first epoch, the gift character of the second, the one trespass and the many trespasses) need not be explained again here.

For the first time in these verses the nature of Christ's one act is given some clarification (so far alluded to simply under the heading "the gracious act"). Now it is described as a "righteous deed," and as "the (act of) obedience of the one man." At this point the features of Adam Christology are most sharply drawn, with Christ's work described precisely as an antithesis to Adam's—the deed which accords with God's will set against the trespass which marked humankind's wrong turning, the act defined as obedience precisely because it is the reversal of Adam's disobedience. The inaugurating act of the new epoch is thus presented as a counter to and cancellation of the inaugurating act of the old, Christ's right turn undoing Adam's wrong turn. Paul may well intend to suggest the idea of Christ's role as a retracing that of Adam, a recapitulation or rerunning of the divine program for man in which the first Adam's destructive error was both refused and made good by the last Adam, thus opening the way for the fulfillment of God's purpose for man (cf. Heb 2:6–15). Paul's Jewish readers would also note the significance of his describing Christ's death as a "righteous deed," that is, as an action which meets the law's stipulations, confirming that Paul saw Christ's death as fulfilling the role of the sin offering as laid down by the law (cf 3:25), and so also reminding us that Paul's attitude to the law was not so antipathetic as is sometimes assumed.

Here too the degree to which the two verses have clearly been structured to bring out the parallelism between the two men raises the question of whether Paul has sacrificed precision of language for rhetorical effect. How close is the actual parallel in each case? The question arises with particular reference to the parallelism of the "all men" in v 18 and "the many" in v 19. Does the language of v 18 mean that Paul looked for everyone without exception to share in the life of the new age ("universalism")? Even if Paul had not intended to raise this question, he could hardly deny that it nevertheless arises from the phrasing of his argument. How he would have responded to the question is a good deal less clear. On the one hand, he has already hinted that there is at least an element of human responsibility in the actual receiving of the grace which marks out the members of the new epoch (v 17), with the implication that membership of the new epoch is neither automatic nor conferred without the individual's consent. (It is hard to imagine Paul or his readers envisaging reception of the gift of righteousness apart from the conversion they had all undergone with the concomitant exercise of faith on the part of the convert—as defined for Paul in Hab 2:4 and illustrated by Abraham in Gen 15:6). So Paul may well have meant "all men" in the sense of everyone belonging to that epoch. On the other hand, he could hardly have complained if his Roman (or subsequent) readership took the "all men" as embracing the totality of the human race in each case. Nor should we exclude the possibility that Paul, enthused by the epochal sweep of his vision, cherished the hope of such a universal salvation, however much a more hard-headed analysis may have persuaded him otherwise in another context (2:8–9). How, after all, can grace be "so much more" in its effect if it is less universal than the effect of death? In Paul as in other Christians the logic of love may well have coexisted uneasily with the simpler logic of systematic consistency; according to Jonah it was not otherwise with God!

With v 19 the question is rather whether Paul intended to imply an equal or equivalent element of predeterminedness in each epoch. That is to say, did Paul mean that members of each epoch have a character (sinners, righteous) which is given them prior to any exercise of choice on their part, simply by virtue of their belonging to that epoch (life as inescapable a consequence of Christ's act for the mass of humanity as death was of Adam's)? Or did he simply assume that his readers would understand that a conscious choice of trespass was included in the idea of "sinners" and that a conscious exercise of faith was presupposed by the idea of "righteous" (since he had already argued so persuasively that without faith there is none righteous—1:17; 3:10)? Again Paul leaves his readers in some doubt, and once again the precise cause-and-effect link between the one act and the many's destiny is left unclear. To be sure, the use of a verb to describe the cause-and-effect link for the first time in these verses promises a clearer definition of the link. But the promise is still-born, since the verb chosen ("were made, became") lacks clear definition itself. Indeed it may be that Paul chose it precisely because it left the precise link between the one act and the many's destiny undefined, just as earlier he had used equally ambiguous prepositional phrases ("through one man's sin," etc.), in which case it is the fact of the link which Paul intended to assert rather than to define its precise relation. Here, as elsewhere, Paul refuses to be drawn into a more rigorously defined and consistent systematization of his theology, thus leaving space both for the diversity of opinion and the silence of agnosticism on more than one contentious issue.

If the verb itself proves less than helpful, the tense of its second usage may shed a little more light. For the use of the future in v 19b, as in v 17b, may imply that Paul's perspective is still primarily eschatological, that he sees each epoch from the perspective of its end—according to v 18, condemnation in the one case, acquittal in the other. At that point the character of the members of each epoch will have become established and be recognized as such (sinners in the one case, righteous in the other), without it needing to be explained how these end effects came about (how much predetermined, how much freely chosen; how much consequence of heredity and upbringing, how much willingly embraced). In which case the descriptions chosen (sinners, righteous) function here more as sociological referents than as expressions of blame and praise. Paul's more attentive readers would probably also take the inference that their own standing as righteous is eschatologically incomplete. Probably in deliberate contrast to his kinsfolk's too glib assurance of their covenant righteousness, Paul evidently wants to maintain the believer's quite proper claim to be "righteous" always with the qualification of the eschatological "not yet." To be righteous is not simply to be accepted by God initially, but to be sustained by God through to the final acquittal of life; without the "how much more" of complete (eschatological) salvation, (initial) righteousness and reconciliation remain incomplete (vv 9–10).

20–21 Paul has now drawn out the comparison/contrast between Adam and Christ as far as it will go. The argument which began in chap. 1 with the indictment of man's Adamic willfulness, has now been fittingly completed by the repeated emphasis that this Adamic plight and destiny of man has been more than countered and superseded by the gracious act of Christ and its effect, with the whole of humankind and the whole history of humankind embraced in a simple yet compelling vision of the two men and their two epochs. Paul is now ready to round off the first major section of his treatise. But for one last time he pauses, just as he paused at the beginning of his vision, in v 13, to ensure that the law is not left out of the picture. Why so? For one thing he may have been conscious of the danger of oversimplifying the cause-and-effect link between Adam's trespass and the many's destiny; not simply Adam's sin was involved in the condemnation of v 18 or the being made sinners of v 19, but the multiplied trespasses of the many. For another, his thought may have been prompted by the language he used in vv 18 and 19—condemnation, righteous act, disobedience, sinner, etc.— words which would to a Jew inevitably suggest the law. But if we have followed his train of thought aright, the more probable reason is that the role of the law within the process of sin and within the present epoch lay at the heart of his exposition, at the center of his critique of the understanding of righteousness and salvation which he had been taught as a Jew and had embraced up to the time he was confronted by Christ. He could not round off this fundamental section of his exposition without ensuring that the law was given its proper place within this summary overview.

The role which he actually ascribes to the law must have seemed shocking to most of his Jewish readers. For in a few terse words he turns the role of the law completely on its head. He had already distanced the law with some success from the righteousness of God through faith (3:20–22) as exemplified by Abraham (chap. 4). But now he pulls the gap between law and grace into outright antithesis. Far from being an answer to sin, as his fellow Jews naturally assumed, it increased sin! Far from being an instrument of God in the epoch of grace it is lumped instead with sin and death, a power like them, which like them came in from "off stage" to reinforce the power of sin and death over Adam's race. For Paul to put the law, God's good gift to Israel, so emphatically on the wrong side of the division between the epochs, must have seemed like blackest treachery to many of his countrymen, including Jews at Rome who were hearing his exposition of the gospel for the first time. Nothing he had said so far about the law had prepared them for this.

What Paul means by asserting that the law's function was to *increase* sin is not wholly clear. He may have meant, as in vv 13–14, that the law increases sin by turning sin into transgression—increase in the sense of intensify, by making visible as sin, or make worse by injecting the dimension of guilt. The divine logic in providing the law would then be that only when sin is out in the open can it be dealt with, only when the poison has come to a head can the boil be lanced. He could also think of sin as being increased quantitatively, with the law being seen actually to provoke sin, just as the command of Gen 2:16 could be said to have provoked Adam's transgression by encouraging him to see that which had been forbidden as desirable. This is a contentious line of thought he would develop later on (7:7–12). But more likely here Paul is recalling the actual effect of the law on his own people—their pride in the law which caused them to identify righteousness too much with distinctively Jewish actions, particularly circumcision, and so to lose sight of the deeper, less easily definable righteousness which could be ascribed to Gentile as well as Jew, to the uncircumcised as well as the circumcised, and which therefore could not be defined simply in terms of such "works of the law." By letting their dependence on the law obscure the more direct and fundamental dependence on God they were no better off than the Gentiles (chap. 2); indeed they were much worse off, since having the law should have made them all the more conscious of their condition as sinners than Gentiles who have not the law (cf. 3:20). In this one phrase Paul sums up the whole critique of his people's attitude to the law and gives it a still sharper point.

For Paul the answer to the multiplication and domination of sin is not the law, but grace—and not grace as expressed in the law, but grace apart from the law (3:21). He could state the plight of those belonging to the old epoch in such stark terms because he was so confident that the answer of grace was more than sufficient. The first act of the human drama ends in darkest tragedy—sin reigning with death the final word. The gospel of Christ for Paul is that that power has been broken: God's grace has more than matched the intensification of sin through the law and so given sure promise of life beyond the cold grasp of death. The different tenses used of grace's work ("has become present in greater abundance," "shall reign") would remind his readers that Paul is talking in terms of a whole epoch. As sin and death encompass the whole of the old epoch, so grace encompasses the whole of the new. As grace became present in its overflowing abundance as the gracious act of Christ, so the rule of grace will continue on into the future into life eternal. Once again the perceptive reader would catch the sound of the typical Pauline balance between that which has already been accomplished for and in the believer and the eschatological not-yet. So too he would also recognize that the righteousness through which grace rules is not to be seen as a once for all package (analogous to Israel's election), but as the status of one accepted by God and sustained by God in continuing dependence on his grace, till its final and complete outworking in eternal life.

And always through Jesus Christ as Lord: if the agency of Adam's trespass gave free rein to sin and death, it is precisely the force which continues to come through the one man who defeated sin and death, which sustains the believer against their continuing claims upon him and which will prove finally triumphant. The one man who lost his way condemned those like him to fall short of the destiny intended for man; the one man who refused the wrong turning and completed man's intended destiny thereby made it possible for those who come after him to fulfill that destiny too through the grace which was and is preeminently his.

Thus Paul finally brings the first main stage of his argument to a resounding conclusion, with ringing phrases which both gather up key terms from the preceding chapters and sustain the note of tragedy confounded into a triumphant doxology. But the conclusion is also a coda, which precisely in its shocking character provides an opening for and transition to the next stage of the argument, in which the role of the law for the believer can be further clarified and the condition of the believer, liberated within the new epoch but not yet free from the old, can be elucidated.

IV–V. The Outworking of This Gospel in Relation to the Individual and to the Election of Grace (6:1–11:36)

IV. The Outworking of the Gospel in Relation to the Individual (6:1–8:39)

Introduction

It soon becomes apparent that chaps. 6–8 are dominated by a number of key words and concepts, particularly sin, death, law, and flesh/(body):

	earlier	5:12-21	6:1-23	7:1-25	8:1-13	8:14-39	later
ἁμαρτία	4	6	16	15	5	0	2
θάνατος	2	5	7	5	2	1	0
νόμος	33	3	2	23	5	0	6
σάρξ /(σῶμα)	4/(2)	0/(0)	1/(2)	3/(2)	11/(3)	0/(1)	5/(3)

Simply by looking at these statistics we can draw two conclusions. First, Paul's discussion in 6:1–8:13 is largely directed to the treatment of these key categories: sin, death, law, and flesh. Of the four, only law has appeared with any thematic consistency before these chapters. This immediately implies that Paul's concern in chaps. 6–8 is to clarify what continuing role these factors have for the believer. Since they are all negative factors in one degree or other the implication is that Paul wishes to clarify what effect they continue to have in the life of those who are recipients of God's righteousness.

Second, there is an evident sequence in Paul's treatment of these factors. Sin and death having entered upon the stage of salvation history continue to dominate life in the old age ("sin reigned in death," 5:21) and so dominate most of the discussion, particularly chap. 6 and the first half of chap. 7. Thereafter death falls into the background; but by this point, law has taken center stage, clearly providing the dominant category for chap. 7. With chap. 8 sin and law quickly fade into the background in turn, and the role of chief negative factor is taken by flesh, with "body," qualified by a negative adjective or phrase ("body of sin," "mortal body," "body of death," "dead body," "deeds of the body") providing a near synonym. The implication is that Paul has deliberately chosen to focus attention in turn on each of the negative factors still experienced by the believer. He does so not in any rigid or artificial way: law is not excluded from the discussion of chap. 6, nor flesh from the argument of chap. 7, nor sin and death from the treatment in chap. 8. Indeed, Paul seems deliberately to remind his readers how all three or four factors interact at several points, particularly 5:20–21 (law, sin, death), 7:5 (flesh, sin, law, death), 8:2 (law, sin, death), and 8:3 (law, flesh, sin).

Nevertheless, it is still clear enough that Paul has chosen to focus attention on each negative factor in turn. This should immediately warn us against interpreting these chapters as a description of some progression in the life of the believer, as though Paul thought the believer must somehow pass in spiritual pilgrimage from domination by one negative force to another, or somehow overcome each in turn. The progression is in Paul's presentation, as he passes in review each of the factors which most threaten the life of faith (so also Wilckens, 2:41–42). There is one element of temporal sequence involved, however, as a closer look at the dispersion of these words also reveals. Death, which appeared at the climactic point in 1:32 and 5:21, reappears at the climax of each of chaps. 6–8 (6:23; 7:24; 8:38). Clearly implicit is the understanding of death as "the last enemy" (1 Cor 15:26). Only when it has been overcome will God's grace be able to reign in fullness of life (5:21; 6:9–10).

Word statistics provide us with a further insight, namely, the degree to which Paul sets his key categories in contrasting pairs: sin/grace, death/life, flesh/Spirit:

sin/grace: the crucial antithesis in the transition from chap. 5 to chap. 6 (5:20–6:1)
death/life: 5:10; 5:17; 5:21; (6:2); 6:4; (6:10–11); 6:23; 7:10; 8:2; 8:6; 8:10; 8:13
flesh/Spirit: 1:3–4; 2:28–29; 7:5–6; 8:4–6; 8:9; 8:13

These are not rigid antitheses, of course, as though Paul felt he must always balance each mention of the one by explicit mention of the other. But the negative factors and the corresponding positive factors are in some measure interchangeable, since the negative factors all interact and are interdependent, and since the positive factors are overlapping and to some extent synonymous concepts (cf. particularly 6:4, ἐν καινότητι ζωῆς, with 7:6, ἐν καινότητι πνεύματος). So, for example, Spirit provides the antithesis of sin in 8:2, and law is the antithesis of grace in 6:14–15. Nevertheless it remains a rather striking fact that in chap. 7 in particular law has no answering positive factor. Just as striking, of course, is the total absence of any talk of faith, since it was πίστις which earlier on had provided the chief note in the counterpoint with νόμος (particularly 3:21–22, 27–28, 31; 4:13–16; and later 9:30–32; 10:4–6). The implication is that the role of the law within the life of faith is more ambivalent: it cannot simply be set unequivocally among the negative factors; in some measure at least it crosses the boundary between negative and positive; the antithesis is within the law itself. Hence the argument of 7:7–8:4, with the otherwise puzzling dichotomy in νόμος which is a feature of the final phase of that argument (7:22–23, 25; 8:2).

One further structural feature of chaps. 6–8 calls for attention: the way in which Paul makes an in-principle statement in clear-cut unequivocal terms at the start of each chapter, only to go on immediately to qualify it and to blur the clean-cut lines by showing that the reality of the believer's experience is more ambivalent. The "Already" has to be qualified by the "Not yet"; the indicative of a salvation process begun has to be qualified by the imperative of a salvation process as yet incomplete.

In-principle statement/ *Already / indicative*		*Reality of* *eschatological tension/* *Not yet /imperative*
6:1-11	with reference to sin	6:12-23
7:1-6	with reference to law	7:7-25
8:1-9	with reference to flesh / mortal body	8:10-30

Käsemann's puzzled questions (159) on a number of the topics clarified by the above analysis show that he has failed to grasp the thematic structure and coherence of the section as a whole.

A. Does Grace Encourage Sin? (6:1–23)

1. The Believer Has Died to Sin (6:1–11)

Bibliography

Barth, G. *Die Taufe in frühchristlicher Zeit.* Neukirchen: Neukirchener, 1981. Here 94–103. **Barth, K.** *The Teaching of the Church Regarding Baptism.* London: SCM, 1948. **Barth, M.** *Die Taufe—ein Sakrament?* Zollikon-Zürich: Evangelischer, 1951. Esp. 221–46. **Beasley-Murray, G. R.** *Baptism in the New Testament.* London: Macmillan, 1962. 126–46. **Bianchi, U.** *The Greek Mysteries.* Leiden: Brill, 1976. **Black, C. C.** "Pauline Perspectives on Death in Romans 5–8." *JBL* 103 (1984) 413–33; here 421–24. **Bornkamm, G.** "Baptism and New Life in Paul (Romans 6)." *Experience.* 71–86. **Braumann, G.** *Vorpaulinische christliche Taufverkündigung bei Paulus.* Stuttgart: Kohlhammer, 1962. **Braun, H.** "Das 'Stirb und Werde' in Antike und im Neuen Testament." *Gesammelte Studien.* Tübingen: Mohr, 1962. 136–58. **Cullmann, O.** *Baptism in the New Testament.* London: SCM, 1950. **Dinkler, E.** *Die Taufaussagen des Neuen Testaments.* Sonderdruck aus *Zu Karl Barths Lehre von der Taufe,* ed. K. Viering. Gütersloh: Gütersloher, 1971. 71–78. ———. "Röm 6:1–14 und das Verhältnis von Taufe und Rechtfertigung bei Paulus." In Lorenzi, *Battesimo,* 83–103. **Dunn, J. D. G.** *Baptism.* 139–46. ———. "The Birth of a Metaphor—Baptized in Spirit." *ExpT* 89 (1977–78) 134–38, 173–75. **Eckert, J.** "Die Taufe und das neue Leben: Röm 6:1–11 in Kontext der paulinischen Theologie." *MTZ* 38 (1987) 203–22. **Eichholz, G.** *Theologie.* 202–13. **Fazekas, L.** "Taufe als Tod in Röm 6:3ff." *TZ* 22 (1966) 305–18. **Frankemölle, H.** *Das Taufverständnis des Paulus: Taufe, Tod und Auferstehung nach Röm 6.* SBS 47. Stuttgart: KBW, 1970. **Frid, B.** "Römer 6:4–5." *BZ* 30 (1986) 188–203. **Gäumann, N.** *Taufe und Ethik: Studien zu Römer 6.* Munich: Kaiser, 1967. **Gewiess, J.** "Das Abbild des Todes Christi (Röm 6:5)." *HJ* 77 (1958) 339–46. **Griffiths, J. G.** *Apuleius of Madauros: The Isis-Book (Metamorphoses, Book XI).* Leiden: Brill, 1975. Esp. 294–308. **Gundry, R. H.** *Soma.* 57–58. **Halter, H.** *Taufe.* 35–66. **Jewett, R.** *Anthropological Terms.* 290–94. **Kaye, B. N.** *Chapter 6.*

32–94. **Kearns, C.** "The Interpretation of Romans 6:7." *SPCIC* 1 (1961) 301–7. **Kennedy, H. A. A.** *St. Paul and the Mystery Religions.* London: Hodder & Stoughton, 1914. **Kertelge, K.** *Rechtfertigung.* 233–36, 263–65. **Klaar, E.** "Röm 6:7." *ZNW* 59 (1968) 131–34. **Kuhn, K. G.** "Röm 6:7." *ZNW* 30 (1931) 305–10. **Kuss, O.** "Zu Röm 6:5a." *Auslegung 1.* 151–61. **Lohse, E.** "Taufe und Rechtfertigung bei Paulus." *Einheit.* 228–44. **Meyer, M. W.** *The Ancient Mysteries: A Source Book.* San Francisco: Harper & Row, 1987. **Morgan, F. A.** "Romans 6:5a: United to a Death like Christ's." *ETL* 59 (1983) 267–302. **Mussner, F.** "Zur paulinischen Tauflehre in Röm 6:1–6." *Praesentia Salutis: Gesammelte Studien zu Fragen und Themen des Neuen Testaments.* Düsseldorf: Patmos, 1967. 189–96. **Pelser, G. M. M.** "The Objective Reality of the Renewal of Life in Romans 6:1–11." *Neot* 15 (1981) 101–17. **Petersen, N. R.** "Pauline Baptism and 'Secondary Burial.'" *HTR* 79 (1986) 217–26. = *Christians among Jews and Gentiles,* FS K. Stendahl, ed. G. W. E. Nickelsburg and G. W. MacRae. Philadelphia: Fortress, 1986. 217–26. **Ridderbos, H.** *Paul.* 396–414. **Schlier, H.** "Die Taufe nach dem 6. Kapitel des Römerbriefes." *Zeit.* 47–56. **Schnackenburg, R.** *Baptism in the Thought of St Paul.* ET. Oxford: Blackwell, 1964. Esp. 30–61. ———. "Die Adam-Christus-Typologie (Röm 5:12–21) als Voraussetzung für das Taufverständnis in Röm 6:1–14." In Lorenzi, *Battesimo.* 37–55. **Schnelle, U.** *Gerechtigkeit und Christusgegenwart: Vorpaulinische und paulinische Tauftheologie.* Göttingen: Vandenhoeck & Ruprecht, 1983. Esp. 74–85 **Schrage, W.** "Ist die Kirche das 'Abbild seines Todes'? Zu Röm 6:5." In *Kirche,* FS G. Bornkamm, ed. D. Lührmann and G. Strecker. Tübingen: Mohr, 1980. 205–19. **Schwarzmann, H.** *Die Tauftheologie des heilige Paulus in Röm 6.* Heidelberg: Kerle, 1950. **Scroggs, R.** "Romans 6:7. ὁ γὰρ ἀποθανὼν δεδικαίωται ἀπὸ τῆς ἁμαρτίας." *NTS* 10 (1963–64) 104–8. **Schweizer, E.** "Dying and Rising with Christ." *NTS* 14 (1967–68) 1–14. **Siber, P.** *Mit Christus leben: Eine Studie zur paulinischen Auferstehungshoffnung.* Zürich: TVZ, 1971. 191–249. **Smith, M.** "Transformation by Burial (1 Cor 15:35–49; Rom 6:3–5 and 8:9–11)." *Eranos* 52 (1983) 87–112. **Tannehill, R. C.** *Dying and Rising with Christ.* Berlin: Töpelmann, 1967. **Thüsing, W.** *Per Christum.* 67–93, 134–44. **Thyen, H.** *Studien.* 194–217. **Wagner, G.** *Pauline Baptism and the Pagan Mysteries.* Edinburgh: Oliver & Boyd, 1967. **Warnach, V.** "Die Tauflehre des Römerbriefes in der neueren theologischen Diskussion." *ALW* 5 (1958) 274–332. **Wedderburn, A. J. M.** "Paul and the Hellenistic Mystery-Cults: On Posing the Right Questions." In *La soteriologia dei culti orientali nell' Impero Romano,* ed. U. Bianchi and J. Vermaseren. Leiden: Brill, 1982. 817–33. ———. "Hellenistic Christian Traditions in Romans 6?" *NTS* 29 (1983) 337–55. ———. "Some Observations on Paul's Use of the Phrases 'in Christ' and 'with Christ.'" *JSNT* 25 (1985) 83–97. ———. "The Soteriology of the Mysteries and Pauline Baptismal Theology." *NovT* 29 (1987) 53–72. **Wikenhauser, A.** *Pauline Mysticism: Christ in the Mystical Teaching of St Paul.* Freiburg: Herder; Edinburgh: Nelson, 1960. 109–32. **Windisch, H.** "Das Problem des paulinischen Imperativs." *ZNW* 23 (1924) 265–81.

Translation

[1] *What then shall we say? Are we to persist* [a] *in sin in order that grace might increase?* [2] *Certainly not! Since we have died to sin, how can we still live* [b] *in it?* [3] *Or are you unaware that all we who were baptized into Christ Jesus* [c] *were baptized into his death?* [4] *So then we were buried with him through baptism into death, in order that as Christ was raised from the dead through the glory of the Father,* [d] *so we also should walk in newness of life.* [5] *For if we have become knit together with the very likeness of his death, we shall certainly also be knit together with the very likeness of his resurrection.* [6] *Knowing this, that our old man has been crucified*

with him, in order that the body of sin might be done away with, so that we might no longer serve sin. [7]*For he who has died is declared free from sin.* [8]*But if we have died with Christ, we believe that we shall also live*[e] *with him,* [9]*knowing that Christ having been raised from the dead no longer dies, death no longer exercises lordship over him.* [10]*For the death he died, he died to sin once and for all; but the life he lives, he lives to God.* [11]*So also you must reckon yourselves*[f] *dead indeed to sin and alive to God in Christ Jesus.*[g]

Notes

[a]The unexpected subjunctive has led to different attempts to improve the syntax.

[b]Despite the support of p[46] ζήσωμεν is probably a slip.

[c]B omits Ἰησοῦν.

[d]The six preceding words are omitted by some of the Fathers, presumably because of the unusualness of the formulation.

[e]Again some MSS read συζήσωμεν (see *Note* b)—betraying the tendency to strengthen the ethical thrust.

[f]εἶναι is strongly attested, but may have been added at an early stage to make explicit what was implicit (see Lietzmann).

[g]Some MSS and versions add τῷ κυρίῳ ἡμῶν; but see Metzger.

Form and Structure

The climactic conclusion of 5:20–21, that as a consequence of Christ's act grace has swamped sin, and sin's rule in death has been matched by grace's rule through righteousness to life, naturally raises the question: Has the believer been wholly removed from the realm of sin and death? Have sin and death lost all hold on the believer? The initial answer seems to be clearly in the affirmative (vv 1–11), but the consequent exhortation indicates that the believer is vulnerable to the claims of both lordships and must continually choose between them (vv 12–23).

Initially Paul resumes a modified diatribe style, but now not so much to argue with querulous fellow countrymen, more as a device for exhorting his Roman audiences. This is indicated also by the transition from the third person treatment of 5:12–21, not simply to the first person of 6:1–11, but with the second person of exhortation beginning to come to the fore (vv 3, 11). At the same time the carry-over in thought from 5:20–21 is indicated both by the subject matter, sin and grace, death and life, and by the reappearance of the (ὥσπερ) . . . οὕτως καί format (vv 4, 11) so characteristic of 5:12–21.

The transition point in the argument comes between v 11 and v 12 (so e.g., Lagrange, Bornkamm, Kuss, Black; against the majority, e.g., Gaugler, Nygren, Gäumann, Cranfield, Achtemeier), since vv 1–11 form a coherent unit. (1) V 11 clearly picks up the thematic response of v 2 to the opening question, and so forms an *inclusio* rounding off the initial response to v 1 (Kaye, *Chapter 6*, 64). (2) The structure is clear:

v 1	question posed
v 2	initial answer

vv 3-4   first elaboration using baptismal imagery
vv 5-7, 8-10   second and third elaboration set in parallel (cf. Bornkamm,
                    "Baptism," 75)
v 11   conclusion, restating the initial answer (v 2).

3) Vv 2–11 have more the character of a statement of basic premise; with
vv 12–23 the language of personal address and exhortation ("you") dominates
(with obedience and slavery providing the linking motifs). Thus the eschatological reservation clearly implicit in vv 4, 5, 6, and 8 becomes explicit in the
presentation of a responsibility still to be carried through, with the conclusion
(v 11) once again serving as the launch pad for the next paragraph.

We should also note the Semitisms in v 4, "walk," and v 6, "body of sin"
= "sinful body."

Comment

6:1 τί οὖν ἐροῦμεν; "what then shall we say?" See on 3:5. The phrase is
Paul's way of acknowledging that what he has just said is controversial and
requires further elucidation to avoid possible misinterpretation; cf. particularly
7:7. The question itself does not indicate the introduction of a digression
(see Kaye, *Chapter 6*, 14–23).

ἐπιμένωμεν τῇ ἀμαρτίᾳ; "are we to persist in sin?" The unexpected subjunctive
requires a more forceful translation than the simple future. The verb has
the overtone of stubborn determination, neither good nor bad in itself (cf.
Col 1:23—τῇ πίστει); see BGD, ἐπιμένω. ἀμαρτία here could have the sense
of "sinful action" (see further on 3:9), though the verb can have the force
of "remain in the sphere of," as in 11:22. In the immediate context the
phrase is most likely equivalent to "remain under the lordship of sin" (5:21;
6:14). It is unlikely that the charge here originated in Gal 2:11 ff. (Watson,
Paul, 147), since there Paul disputes the understanding of "sinner," whereas
here he has in view "real" sin.

ἵνα ἡ χάρις πλεονάσῃ, "in order that grace might increase." Here it becomes
evident that the question has been prompted by Paul's immediately preceding
formulation: οὗ δὲ ἐπλεόνασεν ἡ ἀμαρτία, ὑπερεπερίσσευσεν ἡ χάρις (5:20). On
the one hand this should not be taken to imply that Paul is merely indulging
in a rhetorical exercise: his formulation of the gospel had evidently prompted
such rejoinders (as 3:7–8 makes clear [Jones, *Freiheit*, 111, 116–17]). On the
other hand, the fact that the interlocutor goes back behind 5:21 to 5:20 to
formulate his objection is already indication that the question has missed
the point: to remain in (under the rule of) sin means death (5:21).

The fact that the same question emerges both here and in 3:7–8 is significant.
In 3:7–8 it was prompted by Paul's double assertion that his people had
been unfaithful, and yet God remained faithful. Here it is prompted by his
double assertion of the universal rule of sin and death, yet surpassed by the
superabundant provision of grace. This underlies once again that these two
double assertions are equivalent in Paul's mind: Israel's failure is of a piece
with the sin of humankind as a whole; God's faithfulness to Israel is no
different from his grace open to all. The interlocutor is thus not depicted
particularly as a Jew, since in the now universalized statement of the gospel

anyone might fall into the same trap of misunderstanding. But objection from the Jewish or Jewish Christian side is certainly included, for the question arises out of 5:20 and therefore partly as an attempt to show by means of *reductio ad absurdum* the folly of putting the law as the ally of sin (5:20) rather than as the divine answer to sin; "it was the grace of God which was made manifest in the Law" (Montefiore, 31). If "works of the law," *not* in the sense of good works outweighing human transgression (see on 3:20), but rather as the means provided by the law to counter sin (atonement provided for the faithful member of the covenant people), no longer provide that counter (but rather are opposed to grace), then sin has been given free rein, a blank check.

2 μὴ γένοιτο, "certainly not! never!" See on 3:4.

οἵτινες ἀπεθάνομεν τῇ ἁμαρτίᾳ, πῶς ἔτι ζήσομεν ἐν αὐτῇ; "seeing that we have died to sin, how are we still to live in it?" On a possible distinction between ὅς (= "who") and ὅστις (= "who is such that . . ., seeing that he . . .") see Moule, *Idiom Book*, 123–24; Barrett. ἀποθνῄσκω is used here for the first time to describe the death of believers as something which has already happened (so also in different variations in 6:8; 7:6; Gal 2:19; Col 2:20; 3:3). ἁμαρτία is again potentially ambiguous: died, so that the sinful act is no longer possible; but again the context (5:21) implies more strongly that what Paul had in mind is a death which puts the individual beyond the power of sin (as in 6:7, 10), and so unable (because dead!) to live "in" it, that is, in its realm, under its authority. ἀπεθάνομεν/ζήσομεν—here the contrasting pair (see chaps. 6–8 *Introduction*) is in verbal form (as in 6:10), with the contrast heightened by the difference in tenses. For ζάω referring to the conduct of life see BGD, ζάω 3.

In going behind 5:21 to frame his objection to 5:20, the interlocutor has ignored a crucial factor: sin's rule was up to and in death; but death has already occurred, and where death has already occurred sin's rule is past. The aorist should not be forced to render the conclusion that Paul here works with an "ethic of sinlessness" (Windisch, 280). The tense is exhortatively emphatic, to remind his readers that something decisive has happened to them. The language has the same vivid quality and character which we would expect to find in a fundamental life-transforming experience or rite of passage (see below on 6:3). But here, as again the context implies, the transformation is even more fundamental, implying a shift in the ages (5:15–21). As with 5:15; 7:10; and 2 Cor 5:14, the aorist is epochal: death as the only and inevitable end of the epoch: the only way in which the rule of sin can be ended is when it ends in death. As will become clear, it is only possible to speak thus of the believer in the here and now because there is one who has in fact passed from one age and dominion to the other (vv 7–10) and because it is possible for the believer in the here and now to identify with that one (vv 3–5, 11) (cf. particularly Schlatter). This is why Paul can assume that he speaks for all who have believed ("we" Christians as a whole), since their common commitment to Christ has this epochal character of a transferal from one domination to another: believers by definition "have died to sin." Fundamental therefore to the interpretation here is the recognition that Paul's thought is still determined by the Adam/Christ contrast of 5:12–21. The death here spoken of is the death of Adam, and of those in Adam and of the Adamic epoch (Dodd, Tannehill). Cranfield's distinction here of the four different senses in which the believer's death with Christ may be spoken of is helpful (cf. Beasley-Murray, 131–32; Black, "Death," 421–24, distinguishes seven different conceptions of death in 6:1–14), but is in danger of becoming overschematic (cf. his difficulty with v 8) and fails to do sufficient justice to the eschatological or epochal force of the aorist. See further on 6:11.

In view of the important role this passage has played in discussions of baptism, it is important to note that baptism is not the subject of the passage. The theme is one of death to sin and life under grace, which is documented by use of baptismal language in vv 3–4, but then also by different elaborations of the death/life theme (vv 5–6) and by a rationale in which baptism is not mentioned again (vv 7 ff.; Tannehill, 7–10; Dunn, *Baptism*, 139–40; Thyen, 195; Siber, 217, 221–27; Eichholz, *Theologie*, 203; Wedderburn, "Romans 6," 341–43; cf. Frankemölle, 51–52, 55—"salvation-history, not liturgy"; Kaye, *Chapter 6*, 64; acknowledged by Dinkler, 71; but contested by Schnelle, 204 n.386, though without meeting the point). See also on 13:14.

3 ἢ ἀγνοεῖτε; "or do you not know?" The phrase could be simply good teaching style, a polite way of passing on new knowledge (Lietzmann on 7:1; Kuss; Wagner, 278; Dunn, *Baptism*, 144 n.17). But most commentators think that Paul is appealing rather to familiar tradition, at least from the Hellenistic church, if not from the primitive church (see, e.g., Gäumann, 73; Käsemann; Zeller; see further Schnelle, 204 n.389, and on the whole question Siber, 191–213, and particularly Wedderburn, "Romans 6"). The parallel with 7:1, however, suggests that some element of further or fuller teaching is in view—either a point that is obvious (as soon as one thinks about it) rather than a point already familiar, or that Paul deduces an obvious corollary ("baptized into his death") from an already accepted form of speech ("baptized into Christ"), or that he draws attention to an aspect of a familiar teaching which has been overlooked or neglected. Certainly the fact that Paul does not make a careful exposition of the point seems to confirm that he is appealing to something familiar, even if the emphasis he draws from it may be less so for one reason or another. But the precise balance between familiar and unfamiliar cannot be decided by reference to this phrase alone. It depends on what may be deduced from the following phrase. Cf. on 1:13.

Where familiar ideas are in view, the chief debate has been about their source: were they familiar because they were well known in the wider religious world of the time, or because they were specifically Christian ideas familiar to Paul's readers through preaching and catechesis in the Roman congregations? In practice this has become a debate regarding possible influence from the mystery cults either directly or indirectly upon Rom 6:3–4.

This question, as to whether Paul's teaching on Christian initiation was influenced by beliefs and practices of contemporary mystery cults, was introduced at the beginning of the century and continues to be a sensitive and disputed subject. The critique of Wagner in particular has been influential in providing a corrective to the overstatements of earlier history-of-religion hypotheses (for older discussion see, e.g., Kennedy, particularly chaps. 5 and 6; Lagrange, 149–52; Gaugler). But Wagner's response has been criticized in turn for underplaying the closeness of the parallel between 6:3–4 and initiation into the Isis cult as described by Apuleius in *Metamorphoses* 11 (Gäumann, 41–46; Wengst, *Formeln*, 39–40; Käsemann; Griffiths, 52, 258, 298; Schnelle, 77–78; earlier, Lietzmann, 67). It is unfortunate that the discussion has to depend so heavily on that one text, but inevitable in view of the secret nature of the rites of these cults, only tantalizingly illuminated by other evidence, iconographical (Bianchi), epigraphical and archeological (cf. Meyer, 10–12; for full bibliography up to 1977 on the Greco-Roman mystery religions, see B. M. Metzger in *ANRW* II.17.3 [1984] 1259–1423). And though the text is about 100 to 120 years later than Paul, it cannot be denied that it deals with similar themes which were probably deeply rooted in the Isis cult and which were probably typical of other cults as well. A. D. Nock calls Apuleius' account "the high-water mark of the piety which grew out of the mystery religions" (*Conversion* [London: Oxford UP, 1933, 1961] 138).

The key data provided by the Apuleius text are as follows:

(1) the double reference to the devotees as "born again" (*renatus*; 11:16, 21);

(2) the description of the initiation in terms of death (Griffiths' translation):

"the very rite of dedication itself was performed in the manner of a voluntary death and of a life obtained by grace [*precariae salutis celebrari*]" (11:21).

"I approached the boundary of death and treading on Proserpine's threshold, I was carried through all the elements, after which I returned. At dead of night I saw the sun flashing with bright effulgence. I approached close to the gods above and the gods below and worshipped them face to face" (11:23).

"The precise parallel provided by Paul's exposition of Christian baptism in Romans 6:1–11 is very striking" (Griffiths, 52).

This last comment is, however, an overstatement reminiscent of the earlier hypotheses criticized by Wagner. The dissimilarities between Apuleius and Rom 6 should also be given weight.

(3) In Apuleius there is no hint of a water ritual as part of the initiation itself. According to 11:23 "the customary ablution" played only a preparatory role (Wagner, 100–103; Wilckens, 2:57), and took place at the baths, not at the temple itself. This accords with the lack of archeological evidence of water facilities at Greco-Roman Isis-Sarapis sanctuaries (R. A. Wild, *Water in the Cultic Worship of Isis and Sarapis* [Leiden: Brill, 1981] 23–24). In the Eleusinian mysteries the lustrations were also preparatory (Meeks, *Urban Christians*, 152–53).

(4) The initiation rites to the mysteries seem to have been a good deal more complex as a rule, involving "things recited," "things shown" and "things performed" (λεγόμενα, δεικνύμενα, δρώμενα; OCD, "Mysteries"). In other cults, though evidently not the Isis cult, they often included a mystic marriage (Bianchi, 4–5), as presumably is depicted on the frieze of the so-called House of Mysteries at Pompeii, between a bride and Dionysus. The Apuleius description probably included visions (cf. Col 2:18) and seems to describe a visionary journey: the use of lamps to depict "the sun flashing with bright effulgence" is probably implied by the number of pottery lamps discovered in one room of the Pompeian Iseum (Griffiths, 305–6).

(5) The relation of the initiate to Osiris in all this is disputed. Against Wagner, 104–14, Wengst (*Formeln*, 40) and Griffiths (52, 298–99, 301, 304, 307) insist that the thought of the initiate's identification with Osiris in death (and rebirth) is self-evident. Nevertheless the point is unclear.

(i) Although Isis and Osiris were indeed closely associated, the fact remains that Osiris is never mentioned in the key passages. Moreover, in Apuleius the cult of Osiris is separate from, or perhaps more accurately, a second stage on from the Isis initiation, which the hero Lucius undergoes only some time later. "For although the principle of the deity himself (Osiris) and of his faith was associated, and indeed was at one, with that of Isis, yet a very great distinction was made in the rites of initiation" (11:27). This distinction between the cults is borne out by inscriptional evidence (L. Vidman, *Isis und Sarapis bei den Griechen und Römern* [Berlin: de Gruyter, 1970] 15).

(ii) Talk of "identification" with either Isis or Osiris seems questionable. What seems to be envisioned in the central passage (11:23) is a visionary journey which sympathetically repeats or follows the movements of Isis or traverses the extent of her realms, bearing in mind Isis' own initial description of herself as "mother of the universe, the mistress of all the elements . . . the highest of deities, the queen of the dead, foremost of heavenly beings . . ." (11:5). Some merging with the myth of Demeter and Kore (Persephone) is perhaps indicated in the talk of "treading on Proserpine's threshold," the search of Demeter linked with that of Isis. The fact that Lucius worships the gods above and the gods below (11:23) also tells against the idea of identification, since Isis and Osiris would be the chief objects of this worship (as Griffiths, 306–7, recognizes). The same lack of any clear idea of *identification* with the deity is a feature also of the much quoted fragment from Firmicus Maternus 22:1 (see particularly Wedderburn, "Romans 6," 345, and more fully "Soteriology," 57–62; against Schnelle, 77–78).

On the basis of this evidence it can be firmly concluded that a direct influence from any mystery cult or from the Isis cult in particular, on Paul or on the theology of Rom 6:3–4, is most unlikely. Nevertheless, a broad similarity remains. This, however, is better explained against a broader background. For the mystery cults remind us that there was a widespread hunger for assurance of a good life in the future world, and that the imagery of death and life would come naturally to the thought of the ancients when they attempted to describe a reversal in fortune or change in course which would affect their destiny in this life and beyond, prompted as they inevitably were by the annual cycle of the earth's fertility (cf. John 12:24; 1 Cor 15:36); see further Braun, "Stirb." Set against a still broader background, we may cite the almost universal instinct which finds expression in "rites of passage," where an experience of "liminality" seems to be part of the transition and the imagery of "new birth" comes naturally to mind (A. van Gennep, *The Rites of Passage* [Chicago, 1960]; cf. also Smith, "Transformation"). The similarity between Apuleius and Romans at this point, therefore, is best explained by recognizing both as independent expressions of this same broader instinct, where only a small stock of metaphors is adequate to describe this kind of radically transforming experience known to Lucius and Paul. And in the context of the times those familiar with both Christianity and one or more of the mystery cults would be bound to understand the rite and language of Christian initiation as equivalent to that of the mysteries without thereby identifying the two, or calling in question the distinctive claims of each. An initiation which was wholly distinctive and sharply marked off in its significance would not have been open to such questionable interpretations as we find already at Corinth (1 Cor 1:12–15; 10:1–12; 15:29), nor have given rise to the early Fathers' denunciation of these other rites as "spurious imitations" (including Tertullian, *De Baptismo* 5). See further Kuss's judicious assessment (367–76).

All this still leaves unexplained the distinctive Christian features—*baptized into Christ,* and *baptized into his death.* These are best explained not as ad hoc formulations of the deeper instinct just referred to, but more immediately by reference to specific features of the Christian tradition itself.

ὄσοι ἐβαπτίσθημεν εἰς Χριστὸν Ἰησοῦν, "all we who were baptized into Christ Jesus." For ὄσοι used absolutely, in the sense "all those who," see BGD, ὄσος 2. βαπτίζεσθαι has already attained the status of a Christian technical term (though hearers unfamiliar with it would take it in the sense "dip, immerse, plunge into"—BGD; "we have been immersed"—Maillot); Paul can simply assume that all those linked to a Christian congregation will be familiar with it. The word itself, however, does not clarify whether the phrase refers to the ritual act of baptism with all its sacramental significance (so the great majority) or is a metaphor drawn from the rite (so particularly Dunn, *Baptism*), since that in which or with which one is baptized may vary (water, Spirit: Matt 3:11 pars.; Acts 1:5; 11:16; 1 Cor 12:13) and a metaphorical usage is well established in the Christian tradition (at least Mark 10:38 pars.) as well as in wider usage (BGD, βαπτίζω 3) and still more in wider secular usage (LSJ, MM). More evenly divided is the debate as to whether εἰς Χριστὸν Ἰησοῦν is a shorter equivalent of εἰς τὸ ὄνομα Χριστοῦ (as equivalent—see, e.g., Gäumann, 73–74; Cranfield; Schlier; Wilckens; not equivalent—see, e.g., Kuss; Tannehill, 22–24; Fitzmyer; Käsemann; other references in Dunn, *Baptism,* 112, 140 n.4). Certainly the longer phrase refers directly to the ritual act (as 1 Cor 1:13–16 clearly implies). But it is hard to avoid the conclusion that in Paul the εἰς in the shorter phrase was intended to bear a more pregnant sense than "with reference to": the sense of movement into in order to become involved with or part of is certainly implied in the sequence of thought here (vv 3–5), as also in the other nearest parallels (1 Cor 12:13; Gal 3:27; 1 Cor 10:2 being modeled typologically on the "into Christ" formulation—cf. Leenhardt; Thyen, 200–201); and in Paul the aorist passive clearly speaks of something done by God.

In itself the phrase leaves open the question of whether the divine act happens in and through the ritual act (as 6:4 may imply) or is rather imaged by the ritual act (as the metaphorical usage coined by the Baptist suggests—Mark 1:8 pars). I am more persuaded in favor of the latter and may refer simply to *Baptism* and "Birth of a Metaphor" for a fuller treatment (summarized in *Explanation*). With regard to the former, there is nothing in Paul to show that he intended to use the verb in an all-embracing sense—"baptized," either as the inner reality effected in conjunction with or even by means of the human action, or as a description for the whole sacramental reality (there is

some danger of reading the more sophisticated sacramental theology of later
centuries into the language here). As the Baptist's words, which stand uni-
formly at the beginning of the gospel in all four cases, clearly indicate, "baptize"
in reference to the ritual act and "baptize" as metaphor can stand side by
side without conflation or identification (cf. my warning against allowing "baptism" to be used as a "concertina" word—*Baptism*, 5–7); the point is wholly
ignored by Wilckens when he refers Acts 1:5 and 11:16 simply to "Christian
baptism" (2:51), and describes "the experience of baptism . . . (as) the
central 'datum' of the beginning" (2:23), ignoring the stronger evidence that
it was the experience of the Spirit which originally filled this role of primary
datum (see on 8:9). At the same time the continuing vitality of the metaphor
would depend on the continuing significance of the ritual act within the
process of initiation: only if baptism continued to provide focus and occasion
for the divine-human encounter would it serve as a metaphor for the divine
initiative in that encounter.

εἰς τὸν θάνατον αὐτοῦ ἐβαπτίσθημεν, "were baptized into his death." This is
the new or further teaching which Paul presumably wants to draw to their
attention (ἀγνοεῖτε). It is here that the hypothesis of dependence on ideas
from the mysteries becomes increasingly tenuous. For it leaves unexplained
why Paul should assume that the link between the imagery of baptism and
death was or should be obvious. Despite frequent assertions to the contrary
(e.g., Lagrange, Dodd, Barrett), baptism was *not* an obvious symbol for death
(*pace* Moule, *Worship in the New Testament*). The symbolism of cleansing was
much more obvious; and since death did not necessarily mean burial under
the surface of the earth (but typically in tombs and caves) the symbolism of
immersion provided no self-evident link. On the other hand, the practice of
using catacombs for burial may already have become an established practice
of the Jewish community in Rome (Leon, *Jews*, 66), and we cannot exclude
the possibility that Paul was aware of this and had it in mind here. Despite
Ridderbos, *Paul*, 402, it is not "entirely absurd" to see in baptism by immersion
a symbol of burial.

The association of baptism and death is probably distinctively Christian.
Jesus himself was remembered as having made the link (Mark 10:38–39;
Luke 12:50), that is, explicitly using baptism as a metaphor for his own death,
the imagery of death as an overwhelming torrent of destruction (Ps 69:2
[Aq 68:3]; Josephus, *War* 4.137). The ἀγνοεῖτε therefore may refer implicitly
to this tradition as something the Roman believers should know: Paul speaks
of their being baptized to share Jesus' death because Jesus before him had
spoken of his own death as a "baptism" (cf. Cullmann, *Baptism*, 19–20; Robinson, *Wrestling*, 69; other bibliography in Halter, 530 n.25). If the Baptist
had spoken of a baptism which all must undergo, and Jesus was remembered
as having focused that baptism on himself, then Paul here combines the
two: all must be baptized with his baptism (see further Dunn, "Birth of a
Metaphor"). Alternatively, or in addition, the new step Paul takes here is
that of combining two strands of his own teaching which he had not hitherto
linked—baptized into (union with) Christ (as in Gal 3:27 and 1 Cor 12:13),
and dying with Christ (as in Gal 2:20 and 2 Cor 4:10–11). Whatever knowledge
of these traditions Paul could assume on the part of his readers, he certainly

points back to the Adam/Christ contrast of 5:12–21; they have died to sin (v 2) because they have died with Christ and because Christ now lives beyond sin and death, a life which they can share (cf. particularly Schnackenburg, "Voraussetzung").

In all this it is taken for granted, as elsewhere in Paul's "in Christ" and "body of Christ" language, that Christ is personal but somehow more than individual (Moule, *Origin*, 95); it is not so much that they have sympathetically and symbolically reexperienced the decisive epoch-changing event of Christ's death and resurrection as that they have been caught up in the Christ whose death ended the old epoch ruled by sin and death. See also on 6:11.

4 συνετάφημεν αὐτῷ, "we were buried with him." συνθάπτειν is one of about 40 συν- compounds which form a characteristic and distinctive feature of Paul's style and theology (more than half the 40 appear only in Paul in the NT). He uses them both to describe the common privilege, experience and task of believers, usually nouns (συγκοινωνός, συγχαίρειν, σύζυγος, συμπαρακαλεῖσθαι, συναγωνίζεσθαι, συνεργός, etc.), and to describe a sharing in Christ's death and life, usually verbs (συζῆν, συζωοποιεῖν, συμμορφίζεσθαι, σύμμορφος, συμπάσχειν, σύμφυτος, συναποθνῄσκειν, συνδοξάζειν, συνεγείρειν, συνθάπτειν, and συ(ν)σταυροῦν; also συγκληρονόμος; cf. *TDNT* 7:786–87). The two uses were no doubt linked in Paul's mind, to express the communality of believers rooted in a dependence upon their communality in Christ. Note also συμμαρτυρεῖν and συναντιλαμβάνεσθαι with reference to the Spirit, συνεργεῖν with reference to God, and συνωδίνειν and συστενάζειν with reference to creation (all within 8:16–28). The prominence of the death-resurrection motif in the compounds uniting believer to Christ underlines the distinctively Christian (Pauline) character of the teaching. Paul appeals not simply to the wider sense of the appropriateness of death imagery when describing conversion or initiation to a new faith. Fundamental is the eschatological claim that with Christ's death a whole epoch has passed and a new age begun (see also on 6:8). As the συν- compounds later on confirm (8:22), this is not a merely individual experience, but a shared experience which involves creation as well. Since the train of thought from the contrast between the ages and the two individuals who sum up the two ages divided by death (5:12–21) is so clear, it is less likely that Paul derives his συν- language here from the idea of being caught up with the Lord at the final consummation (Käsemann, 162; Schnelle, 79); were that the case the absence of συν- compounds in 1 Thess 4:14–17, which is modeled on older apocalyptic imagery anyway (cf. *1 Enoch* 1.9; Schweizer, "Dying," 2), would be surprising.

διὰ τοῦ βαπτίσματος, "through baptism." Here the ritual act is almost certainly in view (Fazekas, 314; cf. Mark 1:4; 11:30; Luke 7:29; Acts 1:22; 10:37; 13:24; 18:25; 19:3–4; Eph 4:5; Col 2:12; 1 Pet 3:21), though βάπτισμα also appears as a metaphor in Mark 10:38–39. As it stands, the phrase could signify that God acted through the ritual act, though that would run the danger of encouraging the sort of misunderstanding Paul attacks in 1 Cor 10:1–12. Or it could denote baptism as the locus or occasion of God's action (cf. Col 2:12—συνταφέντες ἐν τῷ βαπτισμῷ); but not baptism as acting subject, as, e.g., in Schlier, "Taufe," 55 ("baptism effects . . ."), or Leenhardt ("the rite of baptism makes this grace actual . . ."), or G. Barth 103, ("baptism gives freedom . . . and participation . . ."). Or the "through" phrase could include the idea of baptism as a person's response within and to the action of God (cf. the talk of God accomplishing his purpose "through faith," as in 3:22, 25, 30; and Col 2:12)—baptism as the psychologically climactic expression of commitment to and self-identification with the last Adam. The baptized's faith is, of course, taken for granted (cf. Schlatter; Fazekas, 316; Kertelge, *Rechtfertigung*, 265; Thyen, 203; Ridderbos, *Paul*, 213, 414; Achtemeier, 107), not forgotten, nor denied (cf. particularly 1:17 and the thematic role of πίστις and πιστεύειν in the central argument of chaps. 3–4); the absence of πίστις from this context is more a consequence of Paul's structuring of his argument by focusing in turn on different aspects of the whole (see chaps. 6–8 *Introduction*) than anything else, with βάπτισμα here standing for the already emphasized πίστις. Käsemann rightly notes how little we have to go on here to construct a doctrine of baptism.

εἰς τὸν θάνατον, "into death." The phrase goes with the verb; for the ancients the combination (buried into death) would be neither tautologous nor strange (against Cranfield). "The event of dying, of departure from this world, was first really concluded by burial" (E. Stommel, cited by Schnackenburg, *Baptism*, 34, and Schlier). "θάνατος denotes neither the process of dying, nor the moment in which life is extinguished, but the condition into which someone passes at the end of his life" (Schlatter); cf. NEB: ". . . were buried with him, and lay dead." Petersen notes that the phenomenon of secondary or double burial sheds light on Paul's talk of an event (aorist—[first] burial) which begins a more drawn-out transition. As several have noted, the reference to Jesus' burial as well as to his death probably echoes the kerygmatic formula of 1 Cor 15:3–4 (G. Barth, 100, and Halter, 41, 49, with bibliography).

It is unclear whether in this clause Paul means merely to repeat the final clause of v 3 (the absence of αὐτοῦ in the second clause is hardly significant, despite Frid, 191–94, though in view of v 10 that death can properly be described as a "death to sin"). The superficial attraction of pairing off the most closely related phrases (εἰς τὸν θάνατον/εἰς τὸν θάνατον; ἐβαπτίσθημεν/διὰ τοῦ βαπτίσματος) leaves συνετάφημεν unaccounted for. More likely then in v 4a Paul reorders and elaborates the elements of the preceding thought, splitting up the metaphor βαπτίζεσθαι εἰς τὸν θάνατον into a more direct statement of the epochal reality thus imaged (συνετάφημεν εἰς τὸν θάνατον), and condensing the metaphor back into the ritual act which provided it (διὰ τοῦ βαπτίσματος). Either way baptism here is linked only with Christ's death, with the imbalance of the following clauses (see below and on 6:5; contrast Col 2:12) implying a refusal to extend the association to resurrection (rightly Leenhardt; against, e.g., Bruce). The more closely the imagery of baptism is tied to immersion (LSJ, βαπτίζω, etc.), the less fitted is it to include the thought of reemergence from the water (= resurrection), all the more so since the correlate to immersion "into Christ" would then presumably be reemergence out of Christ? (cf. M. Barth, *Sakrament*, 224–25, 227–29, 243–44). "In this world baptism corresponds to Christ's death, the new περιπατεῖν to Christ's resurrection" (Gäumann, 77; cf. Halter, 50–51) (see also on 13:14). Hence also the inadequacy of equating βαπτισθῆναι with δικαιωθῆναι (as Dinkler, "Verhältnis," does). The metaphors are different, with the latter offering much greater possibilities (including the περιπατεῖν and different tenses).

ἵνα ὥσπερ . . . οὕτως καί, "in order that as . . . so also." The reversion to one of the main structural features of the preceding passage (5:12, 18, 19, and especially 21) is no doubt deliberate. The sweeping comparisons and contrasts between the epochs of Adam and of Christ begin to be particularized and to be qualified. The new epoch of Christ does not mean an end to the old, but neither does its realization in the lives of believers await the complete end of the old. In this age the outworking of the decisive act of Christ is not yet sinless conduct or deathless life, but morally responsible conduct which expresses the life of the Christ beyond death. This ἵνα thus answers to the false and blasphemous ἵνα of v 1 (Wilckens).

ἠγέρθη Χριστὸς ἐκ νεκρῶν, "Christ was raised from the dead," has a formulaic ring (6:4, 9; 7:4; 8:34; 1 Cor 15:12; cf. 15:20; 2 Tim 2:8). The one who effected the resurrection was of course God (cf. the active form of the same formula: Rom 4:24; 8:11; 10:9; 1 Cor 6:14; 15:15; 2 Cor 4:14; Gal 1:1; Eph 1:20; Col 2:12; 1 Thess 1:10; 1 Pet 1:21); see on 4:24 and further Kramer, *Christ*, 19–44.

διὰ τῆς δόξης τοῦ πατρός, "through the glory of the Father." In resurrection formulae the agency used by God is not usually mentioned. Where it is specified elsewhere Paul speaks of God's "Spirit" or his "power" (8:11; 1 Cor 6:14; cf. 2 Cor 13:4); but here he chooses the more unexpected phrase, probably deliberately, to avoid attributing Christ's resurrection to the Spirit (cf. 1:4; 8:11), thus indicating already an awareness that the relation of exalted Christ to Spirit of God was an issue of some theological sensitivity (see further Dunn, *Christology*, 144). In this range of meaning, δόξα usually refers to the visible splendor of heaven, of heavenly beings and of God in particular (in Paul, 1:23; 3:23; 1 Cor 11:7; 15:40–41; 2 Cor 4:6; Eph 1:17), and, more frequently in Paul, of what believers can hope to share in as the climax of God's saving purpose (2:7, 10; 3:23; 5:2; 8:18, 21; 9:23; 1 Cor 2:7; 15:41; Eph 1:18; Phil 3:21; Col 1:27; 3:4; 1 Thess 2:12; 2 Thess 2:14); see further BGD, δόξα, and on 1:21; 3:23; and 9:4. But the more dynamic notion is not unexpected, since there is a relational element in the thought: the divine as perceived by the human, with the thought of the divine as experienced by the human not far away (see references in Cranfield; BGD cites Wisd Sol 9:11 and Philo, *Spec. Leg.* 1.45; in Paul cf. particularly 2 Cor 3:18; Eph 3:16; Phil 4:19; Col 1:11; and 2 Thess 1:9). Black, however, takes the διά as denoting "attendant circumstances, that is, the accompaniment of a manifestation of the glorious power of God."

ἡμεῖς ἐν καινότητι ζωῆς περιπατήσωμεν, "we should walk in newness of life." περιπατέω in the sense of "conduct oneself," used figuratively of the walk of life, is untypical of Greek thought (BGD; *TDNT* 5:941), but characteristically Jewish (e.g., Exod 18:20; Deut 13:4–5; 1 Kgs 9:4; 2 Kgs 22:2; Ps 86:11; Prov 28:18; Isa 33:15). The divergence between Jewish and Greek idiom at this point is indicated by the *in*frequency with which περιπατέω is used to translate the regular הָלַךְ, *hālak* of the OT (only in 2 Kgs 20:3; Prov 8:20; and Eccl 11:9). NT usage therefore reflects knowledge of the Hebrew idiom

rather than of the LXX. So also obviously in its infrequent use outside John
and Paul (Mark 7:5; Acts 21:21; Heb 13:9; Rev 21:24), but also in its more
frequent appearance in John (8:12; 11:9–10; 12:35), and in the predominantly
Pauline usage (Rom 8:4; 13:13; 14:15; 1 Cor 3:3; 7:17; 2 Cor 4:2; 5:7;
10:2–3; 12:18; etc.; not the Pastorals). The aorist (περιπατήσωμεν) presumably
implies that conversion means a decisive transition to a new lifestyle; cf. NEB:
"so also we might set our feet upon the new path of life."

The typical OT metaphor speaks of walking "in the law/statutes/ordi-
nances/ways" of God (e.g., Exod 16:4; Lev 18:3–4; Deut 28:9; Josh 22:5;
Jer 44:23; Ezek 5:6–7; Dan 9:10; Mic 4:2). In writing ἐν καινότητι ζωῆς Paul
clearly intends a contrast. This is implicit both in the καινότης (cf. its only
other NT usage in 7:6: ἐν καινότητι πνεύματος καὶ οὐ παλαιότητι γράμματος;
see further TDNT 3:447–51) and in the ζωή, which in the context is clearly
thought of as derivative from Christ's risen life (ὥσπερ . . . οὕτως . . . ; cf.
BGD, ζωή 2). For Paul the dominion of sin is not broken by the law but
only eschatologically. See also on 6:9 and further on 8:4. The fact that the
second half of the parallel has been suspended (buried with Christ, but not
yet raised with him) also tells against the language being derived from or
framed in parallel to the mysteries, since this "eschatological reservation" is
also distinctively Christian; and an emphasis derived in reaction to a too-
realized (baptismal) eschatology in Corinth (1 Cor 4:8; 10:1 ff.; 15:12) (e.g.,
G. Barth, 94–98; Schnelle, 80) would surely betray more evidence of its polemic
origin.

5 εἰ γὰρ σύμφυτοι γεγόναμεν τῷ ὁμοιώματι τοῦ θανάτου αὐτοῦ, "for if we have
become knit together with the very likeness of his death." εἰ here has the
force of "since" (BGD, εἰ III). γάρ indicates that v 5 provides the reasoning
behind v 4. It is generally agreed that σύμφυτος, which occurs only here in
the NT, derives from συμφύω, "make to grow together, unite (a wound),"
rather than from συμφυτεύω, "plant along with/together." As the verb suggests,
the imagery is probably biological rather than horticultural—the growing
together of the edges of a wound or fusing of the broken ends of a bone
(as in Hippocrates, Aph. 6.24; Art. 14; Soranus 2.57—LSJ, συμφύω; further
Spicq, 845); cf. the discussion in Schnackenburg, Baptism, 47–49; for the
possibility of seeing a botanical metaphor see bibliography in Dunn, Baptism,
141 n.5; also Black and O'Neill. A dative following σύμφυτοι is wholly to be
expected (see LSJ, BGD), so that ὁμοιώματι would be read with σύμφυτοι rather
than instrumentally with the verb. γεγόναμεν: the perfect must be intentional,
to denote an action of the past resulting in a continuing state. Paul, of course,
knew well how to use the distinction between aorist and perfect (cf. particularly
2 Cor 1:19). The emphasis is the same as that likewise denoted by the perfect
in Gal 2:19 (συνεσταύρωμαι) and 6:14 (ἐσταύρωται; Dunn, Jesus, 331).

There has been considerable debate over the meaning of ὁμοίωμα (cf. particularly TDNT 5:192–95; Käsemann). Apart from Rev 9:7 it occurs only in
Paul in the NT—1:23; 5:14; 6:5; 8:3; Phil 2:7. The idea of "likeness" is
fundamental; what remains unclear is the degree of likeness. Souter suggested
that it denotes a concrete likeness in distinction from the more abstract "resem-
blance" denoted by ὁμοιότης (MM, ὁμοίωμα; TDNT 5:191). But the key to
the biblical usage probably lies in the fact that it is regularly used to denote

the form of transcendent reality perceptible to man. So in Plato, *Parmenides* 132D and *Phaedrus* 250B: finite things are ὁμοιώματα in which τὰ παραδείγματα (the heavenly "ideas") are expressed; and in the LXX—Exod 20:4; Deut 4:12, 15; 5:8; Ezek 1:4–5, 16, 22, 26, 28; 8:2–3; etc.; Dan 3:25; so also Philo, *Migr.* 48–49; cf. Sir 34:3; Rev 9:7 (patristic references in Schnackenburg, *Baptism,* 53). The same sense is suggested even in the other most prominent usage in the LXX, in reference to idolatry (Deut 4:16–18, 23, 25; Ps 106:20; Isa 40:18–19; 1 Macc 3:48)—the recognition, in other words, that, however mistakenly, an idol was intended to give concrete representation to spiritual and transcendental realities. Rom 1:23 falls in line with this last category (Haacker, "Probleme," 15–16, compares Acts 17:29). In 5:14 and 6:5 the transcendent realities are the decisive salvation-history events which determined the epochs that followed—Adam's transgression and Christ's death. The ὁμοίωμα is the equivalent concrete reality within the following epoch. A very close likeness seems to be implied in 5:14. In 8:3 and Phil 2:7 the image is of an earthly reality ("sinful flesh," "men"), where the usage may be equivalent to its use in reference to idols—the copy of an inadequate substitute for the Adam of God's creation, with ὁμοίωμα denoting the concrete actuality through which the transcendent reality of Christ's Adamic role or choice came to expression within the terms of Adam's fallen race. The implication of a very close likeness is again present ("like" so as to be fully one with).

What precisely is the equivalent reality to Christ's salvation-history death within the present epoch? It is unlikely that by ὁμοίωμα here Paul means baptism (as, e.g., Schwarzmann, 32–34; Kirk; Warnach, "Tauflehre," 299–311, 317–22; Wikenhauser, 114–15; Barrett; O'Neill; Schnelle, 82–83; cf. Schmidt; others in Gäumann, 51 n.13, and Morgan, 283 n.59): baptism is hardly like Jesus' death; the perfect tense of v 5a indicates a continuing state (still under water!?); and the future tense of v 5b points to something other than a rite already completed (see particularly Tannehill, 32–35) and so rules out also the suggestion that ὁμοίωμα carries the implication of "sacramentally present in baptism" (Schneider, *TDNT* 5:195; Kuss; Mussner, 195; Schlier). Those who discuss the issue under the heading of baptism (e.g., Kuss, 309 ff.; Schnackenburg, 30–44; Dinkler, 73–74; Black) forget that the theme of the passage is "died to sin" (v 2) and that vv 3–4 are only the initial working out of that theme, with baptism providing the first way of speaking about the Christian's union with Christ in his death (see on 6:2; cf. Halter, 54–55). Nor should ὁμοίωμα be referred to Christ's death itself (Bornkamm, "Baptism," 77; Beasley-Murray, 134; Grundmann, *TDNT* 7:791; Frankemölle, 70; Wilckens). If Paul had wanted to say "fused with Christ's death" (cf. "buried with him," "crucified with him") he would not have used ὁμοίωμα at all. Even less convincing is Schrage's suggestion that ὁμοίωμα is to be taken in reference to the *body* of Christ (cf. Mussner, 192; rightly rejected by Schnelle, 211 n.452, and Morgan, 292–93). What the believer has been "fused/knit together with" is the reality of Christ's epoch-ending, sin's-dominion-breaking death, in its outworking in the here and now, Christ's death to the extent that it can be experienced and is effective within the still enduring epoch of Adam (cf. Schlatter; Gewiess; Thüsing, 137–38; Goppelt, *Theology* 2:102; Morgan, 295–98)—death to sin (Frid, 194–97). Thus it also becomes still clearer that an αὐτῷ does not need to be supplied (as most now agree; for the older view see Schnackenburg, 46 n.51; Fitzmyer; the debate is briefly reviewed by Morgan, 272–76): the thought is not simply a repetition of v 4b; the fusion is with the likeness of Christ's death (which is equivalent to fusion with Christ in his death [RSV, NEB, NIV], but *not* to fusion with Christ by means of the likeness of his death [NJB]).

ἀλλὰ καὶ τῆς ἀναστάσεως ἐσόμεθα, "we shall certainly also be knit together with the very likeness of his resurrection." ἀλλά has the sense "certainly" (Lightfoot; cf. BDF, §448.5; BGD, ἀλλά 4), equivalent to the πολλῷ μᾶλλον of 5:9–10. Almost all commentators agree that σύμφυτοι τῷ ὁμοιώματι has to be supplied to complete the balance of the clauses and the sense. There is very little difference between γίνομαι and εἰμί in this case. ἀνάστασις is Christ's resurrection, despite the absence of αὐτοῦ (as in 1:4). In itself the "very likeness of his resurrection" could be the equivalent reality of Christ's resurrection as it may be experienced (like his death) in the here and now (cf. Phil 3:10). But more likely Paul has in mind the full outworking of that epoch-introducing event in the resurrection of the dead (ἀνάστασις νεκρῶν—1:4; 1 Cor 15:21; Phil 3:11)—a resurrection just like his (8:11; 1 Cor 15:47–49; Phil 3:21; Ignatius, *Trall.* 9.2). This is certainly the most obvious implication of the future tense (ἐσόμεθα). In a context where Paul is consistently looking back to the beginnings of the believer's identification with Christ, a logical future (Leenhardt, surprisingly; Schnackenburg, 38; Fitzmyer; Frankemölle, 71–73; cf. Beasley-Murray, 139–40) or current future (Cranfield) could only be misleading. Had he wanted to indicate the thought of a sharing in Christ's resurrection as something which had already taken place or was already in effect, he would have had to use an aorist or perfect or present tense (cf. 2 Cor 4:16; Col 2:12; 3:1). The sequence of thought makes much better sense if ἐσόμεθα is understood as a temporal or eschatological future (so most interpreters); see also 6:8 and the eschatological reservation of 6:4 (Halter 56).

6 τοῦτο γινώσκοντες ὅτι, "knowing this that." γινώσκω has the sense "know, come to know, understand, realize" (BGD). Here the implication is not so much that the particular teaching which follows is already known (though cf. Gal 2:19), or is self-evident from their experience, as that it is an obvious deduction from or reformulation of the preceding argument (cf., e.g., Mark 4:13).

ὁ παλαιὸς ἡμῶν ἄνθρωπος συνεσταυρώθη, "our old man has been crucified with him." παλαιός is used consistently by Paul to denote the condition of life prior to conversion (1 Cor 5:7–8; Col 3:9; also Eph 4:22), explicitly life under the age prior to Christ, the old covenant (2 Cor 3:14; so also Rom 7:6). So here, ὁ παλαιὸς ἄνθρωπος is man belonging to the age of Adam, dominated by sin and death (5:12–21, Wilckens); cf. Eph 2:15: the "new man" is Christ and those "in him" (Barrett; Tannehill, 24–30). The singular (lit., "old man," instead of "old men") is normal style, but does help emphasize the idea of a common humanness worn out by its bondage to sin and death (cf. 8:10). The societal and salvation-history dimension here should not be reduced to the pietistic experience of the individual; but the reference is to Christians ("*our* old man") for whom the domination of sin has been broken by their identification with Christ's death. Nor should "the old man" be taken

as a dispensable part of the Christian: "our old man" (v 6) = the "we" of
vv 2–5, 7. Murray misses the eschatological tension running through these
verses.

συ(ν)σταυρόω: elsewhere in Paul only in Gal 2:19 , but one of several
συν- compound verbs used effectively by Paul (see on 6:4), third in a sequence
of συν- compounds here (συνετάφημεν, σύμφυτος). Following the perfect in v
5 (γεγόναμεν), the aorist is resumed here (but perfect in Gal 2:19), the
aorist denoting (as in vv 3–4) the decisive salvation-history event of Christ's
death whose effect in ending the rule of sin and death enters the experience
of those who are identified and identify themselves with that event in the
commitment of baptism and thereafter (the aorist passive does not exclude
the active imperative; cf. Col 3:9–10; Eph 4:22; and Rom 13:14 with Gal
3:27). The centrality of the cross in Paul's gospel, as the (only) means by
which the rule of sin and death could be broken, is clear here and coherent
with the theology of Christ's death as sin offering outlined in 3:25. For the
horror and degradation of crucifixion in the Greco-Roman world see M.
Hengel, *Crucifixion* (ET; London: SCM, 1977).

ἵνα καταργηθῇ τὸ σῶμα τῆς ἁμαρτίας, "in order that the body of sin might
be done away with, paralyzed" (SH). καταργέω appears in the NT almost
exclusively in the Pauline corpus (25 out of 27 occurrences). In the LXX it
appears only 4 times (all in 2 Esdras = Ezra-Nehemiah). It is little used
elsewhere, though in the papyri it occurs not infrequently in the sense of
"render idle or inactive" (MM). In Paul it is one of the most difficult words
to pin down as to its precise meaning (cf. BGD, *TDNT* 1:452–54). The papyri
sense of "render ineffective" is certainly present in 3:3, 31; 4:14; 1 Cor 1:28
and Gal 3:17. But the much stronger sense "bring to an end, abolish, destroy"
is also clear in 1 Cor 6:13; 15:24, 26; 2 Thess 2:8; also Eph 2:15; 2 Tim
1:10; and Heb 2:14. In between there are a range of uses whose precise
force is difficult to quantify: "released from, taken from the sphere of influence
of" (Rom 7:2, 6); "lose power, pass away, perish" (1 Cor 2:6; 13:8, 10); "set
aside, put away" (1 Cor 13:11); "fade" (2 Cor 3:7, 11, 13); "remove (veil),"
or, better, "end (dispensation)" (2 Cor 3:14); "removed from, estranged from"
(Gal 5:4); "remove, end" (Gal 5:11). The precise location of Rom 6:6 within
this range of meanings cannot be taken for granted. The critical factor seems
to be the eschatological orientation of the particular passage. The verb has
its strongest force when finality of eschatological judgment is in view (1 Cor
15:24, 26; 2 Thess 2:8); but its applicability to earlier conditions and events
is determined by the eschatological thrust of God's purpose as already decisively
effected through Christ and as thus rendering earlier stages passé and thus
serving notice on the powers of this age that their rule is at an end. The
implication of the aorist in v 6 therefore is not of a final judgment already
executed, but of a decisive step taken to "put out of action" (T. W. Manson),
to "render powerless" (NIV) now and to ensure final destruction in the end.
Under the rule of grace sin is powerless and death's power ineffective. See
also on 3:31 and 8:10.

Every time σῶμα appears in Paul modern readers need to be reminded
that it does not denote the physical body as such, rather a fuller reality which
includes the physical but is not reducible to it. It is man embodied in a

particular environment, the body being that which constitutes him a social being, a being who relates to and communicates with his environment. It is as an embodied entity that he can act upon and be acted upon by his environment. So in a physical environment man is embodied as a physical body; but in the resurrection the body is spiritual (1 Cor 15:44). Hence the frequent need to define σῶμα more precisely by means of an adjective or phrase. For example, the phrase θνητὸν σῶμα ("mortal body"—6:12; 8:11; 1 Cor 15:53–54) is not tautologous, but a way of making clear that man in his embodiment in this physical world (or as we would say, this four-dimensional space-time continuum) is subject to corruption, decay, and death. This is all to state that Paul's thought is characteristically Hebraic and only occasionally gives ground, wittingly or unwittingly, to a more typically hellenistic dualism between soul and body, body being separable from the real "me" (so most, e.g., Bultmann, *Theology* 1:194; *TDNT* 7:1060–66; Cranfield; Schlier; NJB—"the self which belonged to sin"; against Gundry, *Soma*, here particularly 57–58; see further on 12:1). Hence in our present case, "body of sin" is not to be designated as a gnostic disparagement of the body (cf. Jewett, *Anthropological Terms*, 292), but denotes man as belonging to the age ruled by sin, "the human existence of the old Weltzeit" (Michel), man under the rule of sin and death (Gaugler). The thought is still controlled by the salvation-history perspective on the whole sweep of universal history (5:12–21). Cf. particularly 7:24 and 8:10; in the LXX Wisd Sol 1:4. It is this belonging to the old age, or, extending the thought, this in-debt dependency (cf. Wisd Sol 1:4) for reality as a person and for social status on the values of this age, which has been brought to an end by the identification with the degradation and humiliation of Christ's death on the cross.

"Sin" has not been mentioned since v 2. The ἵνα clause is thus intended to round off the line of argument begun in v 2 and to show how it meets the problem posed in v 1. It is important to note, however, that there are two purpose clauses (ἵνα, and accusative + infinitive) and two references to ἁμαρτία, and that therefore the response to v 1 has two sides to it.

τοῦ μηκέτι δουλεύειν ἡμᾶς τῇ ἁμαρτίᾳ, "so that we might no longer serve sin." The very formulation, with the μηκέτι and the present tense, implies that the possibility of the believer's *continuing* to serve sin is very real. The aorist identification with Christ in his death therefore provides the enabling to live under the lordship of grace (5:21) but does not prevent the believer from succumbing once again to sin at any particular point. "The imperative is implicit in the indicative" (Halter, 59).

7   ὁ γὰρ ἀποθανὼν δεδικαίωται ἀπὸ τῆς ἁμαρτίας, "for he who has died is declared free from sin." δικαιοῦσθαι ἀπὸ ἁμαρτίας is uncharacteristic of Paul, but is sufficiently well enough attested elsewhere for us to recognize an accepted image (Sir 26:29; *T. Sim.* 6.1; cf. Acts 13:38); though whether "freed from sin" (BGD, δικαιόω 3c) is quite adequate as a translation of these passages is open to question. A better rendering would be "declared free from (responsibility in relation to) sin," "no longer has to answer for sin" (NJB, similarly NEB), where the sinful act rather than the more typically Pauline idea of sin as a power is in view (though see on 3:9). The absolute form of the subject, rather than a σὺν- formulation (as in v 8) also implies that here we do not

have a specifically Christian thought, but something more like a proverb from a larger stock of communal wisdom. This particular version is not attested elsewhere, though reference is usually made to the rabbinic sayings: "When a man is dead he is freed from fulfilling the law" (*Šabb.* 151ᵇ Baraita); "All who die obtain expiation through death" (*Sipre Num.* 112 on 15:31) (Kuhn, "Röm 6:7"; Str-B, 3:232; *TDNT* 2:218). Cranfield disputes any dependence on a proverbial principle like "death pays all debts" (see the more sympathetic treatments of Schlier and Wilckens), though it is a striking fact that the closest parallel to the preceding talk of "the body of sin" uses the imagery of the body in debt to sin (Wisd Sol 1:4: ἐν σώματι κατάχρεῳ ἁμαρτίας), and cf. Sir 18:22 (μὴ μείνῃς ἕως θανάτου δικαιωθῆναι). However, even if the degree to which Paul is dependent on or has adapted a particular proverbial formulation remains unclear, his main thought and its coherence with his own line of thought is clear: death marks the end of sin's rule, in both senses of "end"—climax and cessation; "a dead man can no more be enslaved" (Kuss). What the dead man is freed *for* is not given in the proverb (whether nothingness, or some ill-defined after-life, or other); the image is more of death as a release from a crushing burden (the force of the perfect indicating a complete "wiping clean of the slate"). The saying is, therefore, not Christian in itself (contrast Scroggs, "Romans 6:7"; Kearns, who refers it primarily to Christ, leaving v 10 as somewhat tautologous). The Christian usage comes in what Paul does with it: death is the end of sin's dominion for man (everybody); but only one man (Christ) has died a death which broke the final grip of death (cf. Wilckens).

8 εἰ δὲ ἀπεθάνομεν σὺν Χριστῷ, "but if we have died with Christ." As with v 5 the εἰ here has the force of "since" (BGD, εἰ III). The aorist belongs to the sequence of aorists running from v 2, all of them saying the same thing using varied metaphors—"baptized into his death" (v 3), "buried with him" (v 4), "crucified with him" (v 6). The more explicit resumption of the opening statement of v 2 (ἀπεθάνομεν) underscores the fact, already repeatedly emphasized in vv 3–6, that "we died to sin" only by virtue of the fact that "we died *with Christ*."

The σὺν Χριστῷ (or equivalent formulation) is much less frequent in Paul than the ἐν Χριστῷ, so characteristic of his thought (see on 6:11). But together with the more frequent συν- compounds (see on 6:4) it forms a significant element in his thought. It is less of a technical term than ἐν Χριστῷ (only 4 of the 11 cases where σύν refers to Christ have the full expression σὺν Χριστῷ) and may denote simply "in the company of" rather than a mystic or sacramental or salvation-history participation in the decisive eschatological events of Christ's death and life (for which Paul seems to prefer the συν- compounds: see again on 6:4). So in the predominantly future reference of the phrase: to be with Christ (in heaven)—Phil 1:23, 1 Thess 4:17, 5:10; cf. Col 3:3; to appear with Christ in glory/at the Parousia—Col 3:4, 1 Thess 4:14. Only 2 Cor 4:14 speaks of being raised in the future "with Jesus." And only Col 2:13 (cf. Eph 2:1-10) speaks of believers as *already* having been made alive "with him." Apart from Rom 6:8 only Col 2:20 speaks of believers having died "with Christ"; cf. 8:32 and Col 3:3. Here, however, following in the sequence of συν- compounds (vv 4, 5, 6) it evidently functions as a variation of these and carries the same force as these verbs, of a participation in the salvation-history effects of Christ's death as marking and effecting the end of the rule of sin and death. For a treatment emphasizing the baptismal connections of the phrase, see Kuss, 319–29.

πιστεύομεν ὅτι, "we believe that." This is the only time the verb is used in chaps. 5–8, with the resumptive πίστις in 5:1–2 as the last reference to faith. It is also the first use of πιστεύειν ὅτι to denote the content of belief (as in 10:9 and 1 Thess 4:14) rather than the more pregnant πιστεύειν ἐπί (see on 4:24). Its occurrence here makes clear (1) that the (full) share in Christ's resurrection life is still future, and (2) that however much experience is involved in the preceding aorists, what is in view here is a faith-claim, a conviction rising out of the eschatological significance of Christ's death and resurrection and from the believer's identification with Christ (see also Barrett; Gäumann, 84; Schlier). That a confident rather than tentative trust is in view is indicated by the use of γινώσκειν and εἰδέναι in the parallel verses 6 and 9.

καὶ συζήσομεν αὐτῷ, "we shall also live with him." It is almost impossible to take the future here as merely logical (it follows from the fact that we died with Christ that we have also risen with him); it must refer to a still future sharing in Christ's resurrected life (so most; see particularly Kuss; against Lagrange, Murray, and Cranfield). The saying as a whole seems to have become firmly established in Pauline circles in this sense (despite Col 2:13 and 3:1): 2 Tim 2:11: εἰ γὰρ συναπεθάνομεν, καὶ συζήσομεν (the only other occurrence of this συν- compound in the Pauline corpus or the NT, apart from the not directly relevant 2 Cor 7:3).

9 εἰδότες ὅτι, "knowing that" (see on 5:3): here in the sense of referring to common knowledge, something that is obvious; see on 2:2.

Χριστὸς ἐγερθεὶς ἐκ νεκρῶν οὐκέτι ἀποθνῄσκει, "Christ having been raised from the dead no longer dies." This is the obvious fact which no one would dispute. The premise takes the form of a confessional statement: "Christ was raised (that is, by God) from the dead" (see on 4:24 and 6:4). But it is the logical deduction from that premise to which the εἰδότες refers: if someone has been raised from the dead, death is something past, left behind, no longer having to be experienced as the end point of life. The logic is explicitly Christian, part of Christianity's Jewish heritage. For the "being raised" in view is not simply a recall into this life, which would then still be subject to death (as, e.g., in Mark 5:41); it is eschatological resurrection, the final break-through beyond the reach of death into the new age of a quite different kind of life, ζωὴ αἰώνιος, deathless life (see on 2:7 and 5:21). The οὐκέτι ἀποθνῄσκει does not run counter to the force of the perfect in v 5 (or Gal 2:19). The reference is to Christ in his personal capacity: for himself Christ died, was raised, and will never die again; but as one with Adam, one whose death marks the end of the epoch of Adam, he dies in every death of man and his dying will not be complete till every man has died and the old age ruled by sin and death is completely at an end (cf. 2 Cor 5:14 and Col 1:24).

θάνατος αὐτοῦ οὐκέτι κυριεύει, "death no longer exercises lordship over him." Having been used of Christ's death in vv 3–5 θάνατος reappears as a power, harking back to 5:14, 17 (see on 5:14). The sequence of thought confirms:

that the rule of sin finds its final expression in death (5:21); so the climax of the dying to sin is the dying to death and the dying of death as a power dominating human life; the key to the whole is the death and resurrection of Christ. κυριεύω is used synonymously with βασιλεύω, as the parallel with 5:14, 17 shows; so 6:12/14. In each case it is effective and not merely assertive authority which is in view: death exercises effective lordship—all die! According to *Mekilta* on Exod 20:19, R. Jose (ca. 150) said, "The Israelites stood on Mount Sinai (and accepted the Torah) on condition that the angel of death should not exercise lordship over them" (Str-B, 3:232). If this saying was already current at the time of Paul it would strengthen the contrast Paul is drawing here: the law is not effective to break the rule of death (5:20–21); only Christ's death has done that, and only by walking in the life which comes from the risen Christ can there be a conduct pleasing to God (6:4); see on 6:4.

10 ὃ γὰρ ἀπέθανεν, τῇ ἁμαρτίᾳ ἀπέθανεν ἐφάπαξ, "for the death he died, he died to sin once and for all." For ὃ as accusative in relation to the verb ("that which he died"), see BDF, §154. The parallel in the second phrase in v 2 (ἀπεθάνομεν τῇ ἁμαρτίᾳ) is no doubt deliberate. We should not take it in a different sense (as Michel). What is in view in both cases is the effective power of sin over human life as demonstrated most emphatically in the death which none escape. Jesus, in his oneness with those who belong to this age, shared in that subordination to the power of sin in death. It is because he shared the human condition to the full that his overcoming the death which all die can effectively break the despair and fear of death, and so already break its grip on human life. The ἐφάπαξ underscores the difference between the Christian perspective, based here as always on Jewish eschatology, and the more cyclical view of history, expressed not least in the mystery cults. Christ's death marked an end point of history, of the cosmic age marked out by the entry (5:12) and end of death (cf. the ἐφάπαξ/ἅπαξ in Heb 7:27; 9:12, 26–28; 10:10; and 1 Pet 3:18).

ὃ δὲ ζῇ, ζῇ τῷ θεῷ, "the life he lives, he lives to God." An irreversible transformation has taken place: the circumstances of the new existence are wholly new, with reversion to the old condition no longer possible; death was a single event (aorist), the life has no end (present continuous); in this new age God is the only effective power. Consequently also for the believer, to live in identification with this Christ is to live "for God" and no longer "for sin" (v 2); "the being-in-Christ is already theocentric in that Christ himself lives for God" (Thüsing, 78). In this binding together of Christology and anthropology "we are at the center of the *proprium christianum*" (Halter, 62), quintessential Christianity. See further on 6:11.

11 οὕτως καὶ ὑμεῖς λογίζεσθε ἑαυτούς, "so also you reckon yourselves." The οὕτως καί echoes, no doubt deliberately, the same phrase in 5:15, 18, 19, 21, and 6:4. As the gracious act of obedience of Christ answered the trespass and disobedience of Adam, so the λογίζεσθαι of the believer answers the false reckoning of v 1. λογίζεσθε, here certainly imperative, recalls the prominence of the word in 3:28 and chap. 4 (this is the first use of it since then). The believer's reckoning himself dead to sin and alive to God answers to God's reckoning him righteous. As the context makes clear, it is a strong word, a firm conviction (present tense) expressed in daily conduct (see on 3:28; cf. Käsemann). The admonition confirms that (1) whatever death the believer has died, he is not a merely passive object played upon and manipulated by transcendent forces; (2) the death is not complete, since there is a process of reckoning still involved; (3) the reckoning is itself part of the process of sharing Christ's death. What is in view then is not a fictitious or "pretend" or "merely symbolical" event, but a settled determination to live in the light of Christ's death and in the strength of a power which has already defeated sin's reign in death (cf. particularly Lietzmann, 65–66; Schlier).

νεκροὺς μὲν τῇ ἁμαρτίᾳ, "dead indeed to sin." The phrase harks back to v 2 and with v 10 provides the conclusion to the section. νεκρός (like burial, v 4) is the end result of ἀποθνῄσκειν. The figurative sense is well enough known (BGD, MM) and so would be sufficiently meaningful and realistic—"dead" in the sense of "lost to," "completely out of touch with"; according to Philo the impious understanding dies when it "shrinks into inactivity" (Leg. All. 3.35). The death is not an actual death, nor a mere playing with words, but a living in relation to the power of sin (see on 3:9) as to all intents and purposes dead. See also 6:13; 8:10; Col 2:13; outside Paul, particularly Luke 15:24, 32. That identification with Christ's death is still in view is obvious; cf. particularly 2 Cor 4:10.

ζῶντας δὲ τῷ θεῷ ἐν Χριστῷ Ἰησοῦ, "and alive to God in Christ Jesus." The idea of "living to God" is used in hellenistic Judaism, but of the heroic martyr (4 Macc 7:19; 16:25) or of the few capable of contemplating the higher realities (Philo, Mut. 213—not 13, as BGD has; Heres 111). Paul expects it of all believers since the possibility of so living is dependent not so much on their "reckoning" as on their being "in Christ" and being given to share in his newness of life (6:4). "This participle indicates the whole dynamic of the being-in-Christ . . . and this 'living in Christ' is 'for God'" (Thüsing, 67). See also on 8:13.

This is the first occurrence in Romans of ἐν Χριστῷ Ἰησοῦ in what is often regarded as its most typical Pauline usage: believers as being "in Christ" (8:1; 12:5; 16:3, 7, 9, 10; 1 Cor 1:2, 30; 4:10; 15:18, 19; 2 Cor 5:17; 12:2; Gal 1:22; 2:4; 3:26, 28; etc.), or as doing something "in Christ" (9:1; 15:17; 1 Cor 4:15, 17; 15:31; 16:24; 2 Cor 2:17; 12:19; etc.), both these uses frequently also by means of ἐν κυρίῳ (see on 16:2). To the same effect but slightly different in emphasis is the idea of redemptive power as enacted "in Christ" (3:24; 6:23; 8:2, 39; 1 Cor 1:4; 15:22; 2 Cor 2:14; 3:14; 5:19; Gal 2:17; 3:14; 5:6; etc.). The three usages are clearly interconnected and overlap: it is the meeting of divine power with human commitment "in Christ" which makes possible a quality of life which shares the character of Christ (in however imperfect a manner in this life). The ἐν Χριστῷ of v 11 is the result of the σὺν Χριστῷ of v 8; the death to sin and life to God of v 11 follows from and is dependent upon the death to sin and life to God of v 10. And the whole thought here is still under the influence of 5:12–21: "in Christ" as part of eschatological humanity. Hence the ἐν Χριστῷ denotes not mere location, but something more dynamic in terms of relationship (Goppelt, Theology 2:105); see further Wedderburn's critique of earlier more unitary interpretations of the phrase ("Observations"). See also on 3:24; 6:3c; and 9:1; and for older bibliography see BGD, ἐν I.5.d; Thüsing, 62 ff.; Cranfield, 315 n.6.

Explanation

Paul has now completed the first major section of his exposition of "God's righteousness from faith to faith"—God's action on behalf of man as the manifestation of his faithfulness to which man can only respond in humble and obedient faith. His exposure of man's need of this divine initiative had drawn heavily on the Genesis account of Adam's fall, combining man's refusal to acknowledge God as God, to recognize his own creatureliness, resulting in the diminution of his humanity, his fitness to be a companion of God, a plight embracing not only Gentile idolatry and immorality, but also Jewish presumption of a favored status before God. In a final balanced response to the depressing conclusion of 3:9–20, his declaration of God's saving act in Christ reverted fittingly to the same Adam parallel, climaxing in the antithetical comparison between Adam and Christ in 5:12–21: however serious the consequences of man's disobedience, Christ's act of obedience more than outweighed them; however fearful the combined power of sin, law, and death, grace has proved stronger still.

With this basic statement of the gospel firmly established he can now clarify some of the major corollaries and possible misunderstandings. Above all Paul was probably mindful that there would be those among his Roman correspondents anxious to know how all this worked out in daily living for a Christian. Not that he wanted yet to come down to parenetical specifics: he will first complete his exposition of God's faithfulness to faith in chap. 9–11; the exhortations will follow thereafter. At this point, however, he evidently felt the need to say something about the basic perspective from which believers should see their lives as a whole (and from which they can go on to approach particular ethical issues). Most important of all, in view of his conclusion just reached, how should the believer now view sin, death, and the law? If sin has found its master in grace and death in life (5:20–21), does that mean that sin and death have lost all their power over the believer? And, equally important, does the law still remain on the side of sin, or does the defeat of sin set the law also free to fulfill a more positive role, or has it too been superseded (by the Spirit)? These are the sort of questions Paul evidently has in mind as he begins the next main section of his exposition.

6:1 "What then shall we say? Shall we persist in sin in order that grace might increase?" This question arises for two reasons. The first is the shocking conclusion just drawn: "where sin increased, grace increased all the more" (5:20). If the rising level of sin means that God's gracious power has to be extended all the more in order to counter and overwhelm that sin, then sin is good for God and for the gospel. The logic is obvious and has a certain perverse attraction. Since sin gives God the opportunity to manifest his generosity to man, sin cannot be such a bad thing after all. It was the same logic which Paul's diatribe had forced him to pursue at the beginning of chap. 3: if God remains faithful to Israel, despite Israel's unfaithfulness, if man's lie brings greater glory to God, why is it counted as unrighteousness and as worthy of condemnation (3:3–7)? He had not been able to answer the question then. Now he is in a position to do so.

The second reason for the question is less immediately apparent, but would have been clear enough for those who had been following the main thrust of his argument. In this letter Paul has continually had in view a Jewish mind-set which centers on the intimate correlation of grace and law: God gave the law; law is how the covenant people live by grace. It is this correlation between grace and the (Jewish) law which Paul seeks to break, since in his view it runs counter to the gospel as God's promise to "many nations," Gentile as well as Jew. The point needs to be clearly grasped, since it has often been misunderstood. It is not that anyone said, "Righteousness is by law and not by grace"; no one posed grace and law as alternatives; rather they saw law as the gift of grace. It was *Paul* who posed them as alternatives (hence v 14). In setting grace and sin in sharpest antithesis (5:20–21) Paul had taken the bold step of linking the law with the other side of the antithesis, not with grace, but with sin (5:20). To the loyal Jew's affirmation that the law is the means provided by God for dealing with sins committed within the covenant, Paul's response is sharp: the law in itself does not provide an answer to the power of sin, rather it provides the occasion for sin. By encouraging those "within the law" to rest in the law and to boast in the law (2:17, 23) it encourages a hardness of heart which is impervious to grace and is the antithesis of faith (2:4–5). So the question is inevitable: if you remove the law as the bulwark between grace and sin, in what relation do they stand? Still worse, if you set God's law on the side of sin, have you not turned the whole correlation topsy-turvy, and are you not forced to say that sin promotes grace: no longer that grace gives the law to deal with sin; but rather that God gave his law to provoke sin in order to give greater occasion for grace?!

2 Paul's immediate response is at first puzzling: "Certainly not! We who died to sin, how can we still live in it?" What would he have expected those hearing his letter read out to understand by this talk of "having died to sin"? It could be that such language was well established in the gentile mission, and Paul simply alludes to it as something his readers would be familiar with, although we have no other real evidence of it outside the Pauline correspondence. Or he could have assumed that his own teaching alluded to in earlier correspondence (particularly Gal 2:19 and 2 Cor 5:14) was more widely known, perhaps through teaching and exhortation given in the Roman congregations by individuals closely associated with him (cf. 16:3–16). Be that as it may, he goes on to clarify his meaning by spelling it out in terms of Christ, or more precisely in terms of Christ's death (and resurrection) and their participation therein. In this it becomes clear that, for Paul, the believer has been caught up in the antithesis between Adam and Christ (5:12–21): as Adam represents "the many" under the reign of death because of sin, so Christ stands for "the many" who are recipients of grace (5:15). Christ has become the bulwark between grace and sin: not the law is God's answer to sin, but Christ, specifically Christ in his death.

It is not that Paul would want to argue for a complete discontinuity between the law and Christ. On the contrary, the law's condemnation of sin still stands (3:9–20); the law is there to be fulfilled (2:13, 25–27), and faith is the basis of that desired fulfillment (1:5; 3:27, 31); Christ's death as a sacrificial offering, as an act of obedience, met the just requirement of the law (3:21, 25–26; 5:18–19). The decisive point, however, is that Christ's death and resurrection has brought about a new stage in God's dealings with humanity. The law belongs primarily, with sin, to the era of Adam; but Christ has introduced a new era. As a freely embraced act of obedience, not simply a consequence of man's disobedience (5:19), Christ's death marked the end of the reign of sin and death, and so also of the law as sin's cohort. Consequently the implication is fairly clear, even before we move on from v 2, that the dying to sin here spoken of is not something independent of Christ, but is somehow a sharing in his death, a sharing in his transition from one era to the other. His readers therefore would very likely have heard Paul's opening response as, How can you who identified with Christ live as though Christ never died, as though sin and the law were still dominating factors for present life? For the devout Jew, the logic of grace was the law as God's provision against sin. For the believer in Christ, the logic of grace is identification with one whose life is simply beyond sin.

All this is made clearer by means of the series of vivid metaphors to which Paul devotes the next four verses, each of them highlighting facets of this all-important identification of the believer with the Christ who died and whose death broke the power of sin.

3 "Or do you not know that all of us who were baptized into Christ were baptized into his death?" Whether the opening words assume a ready knowledge of the teaching or are simply the teacher's polite way of imparting new instruction is uncertain. What is more certain is that Paul assumes the idea of being baptized into Christ as something familiar and proceeds to draw out the presumably less familiar corollary: being baptized into Christ means being baptized into his death.

What would the more familiar phrase "baptized into Christ" have meant for Paul's readers? One possibility is that they would have recalled their own baptism, understanding it as an act that united them with Christ. This would be all the more likely if they were familiar with the initiation rites of the mystery cults, which, so it used to be firmly maintained, were thought to achieve a mystical identification with the cult god through some reenactment of his or her fate. Unfortunately, the mystery cults were very good at keeping their rites secret; so much so that we today know very little about them; more to the point, nonparticipants in the first century must have been more or less equally ignorant. From various bits and pieces of evidence we know that in several cults there were ritual washings, but these seem to have been part of the preliminary preparations, and not the act of initiation itself, which was probably a good deal more complicated than a single ritual act in any case. That the idea of a mystical identification between the initiate and the cult god was widespread is equally questionable, often confused as it is with the sympathetic magic of annual fertility rites, or the concept of a holy marriage. The one claim of such cults which would have been widely known was the bare evangelistic assertion that without being initiated into their mysteries there could be no hope of life or light in the future world. But it must remain doubtful whether Paul would have wished his converts to understand Christian initiation as providing that sort of guarantee, not least because he has already polemicized against just such a misunderstanding in the case of the rite of initiation into Judaism (2:25–29; cf. 1 Cor 10:1–13).

The other chief possibility is that Paul is here taking up a metaphorical usage already familiar in Christian tradition. We know that there was a well-established tradition of John the Baptist heralding one who would baptize, not in water as John himself did, but in Spirit and fire (Matt 3:11; Mark 1:8; Luke 3:16; John 1:33). We know too that Jesus himself probably took up and adapted this metaphor by referring it to his own death (Mark 10:38–39; Luke 12:49–50). Luke tells us that it was familiar in the earliest days of the new movement, particularly with reference to Pentecost and similar initiatory experiences of the Spirit (Acts 1:5; 11:16). And the most obvious way of understanding 1 Cor 12:13 is that Paul himself knew and made use of the same metaphor on his own account—"we were all baptized in one Spirit into one body." When such a usage, so closely parallel to Rom 6:3, was so widely known in early Christian tradition, it hardly seems necessary to look further afield for the point of contact with his readers which Paul assumes in 6:3. As Paul clearly implies elsewhere, the initiating experience of the Spirit was usually very vivid, an event often deeply moving and profoundly transforming, which the young Christians would have no difficulty in recalling (e.g., 5:5; 1 Cor 6:9–11; 2 Cor 1:21–22; Gal 3:3, 5; 1 Thess 1:6). Certainly Paul of all people would take it for granted that all believers were bonded together by a common experience of grace (e.g., 5:17; 1 Cor 1:4–5; 15:10; 2 Cor 6:1; Gal 1:6), by a common participation in the one Spirit (cf. 1 Cor 12:13; 2 Cor 13:13; Phil 2:1; Eph 4:3). It is probably his readers' experience of this grace, of this Spirit, to which Paul here refers, using a metaphor whose familiarity he could equally take for granted.

In what sense, however, did Paul intend his readers to understand that they had been "baptized into Christ, into his death"? They presumably were intended not merely to recall their experience of conversion-initiation, but to understand it as somehow identifying them or uniting them with Christ—and not just Christ recognized as alive and present, but Christ in his death. This probably means that Paul is here thinking of Christ in a way we today find hard to grasp, that is, as a "person" who transcends our concept of person as "individual," the person of Jesus Christ no longer a three-dimensional focus of reference. Just as the Wisdom or Word of God, which is the power of God diffused throughout the cosmos, could be conceived in Jewish thought as a personification, in personal terms, so conversely Christ, by his resurrection set free from the constraints of three-dimensional existence, could be conceived as a personal power embodied or manifested in different places at one and the same time. Some such conceptualization seems to be presupposed in Paul's well-known "in Christ" and "body of Christ" language, as also the degree of identification in his mind between the risen Christ and the Spirit of God (8:9–11; 1 Cor 6:17; 15:45); and although he has not yet made any attempt to use such language up to this point in Romans, it is difficult to imagine that he was not thinking in these terms (cf. the parallel passage in Gal 3:27 where he speaks of "putting on Christ"). We do not need to call on the later conceptions of an archetypal man in heaven fragmented in the multiplicity of human beings, or of a mystical absorption into the deity, in order to establish the point that we are dealing here with a more fluid concept of personality. At the least it would mean that Paul understood the power which moved upon and within him and his fellow believers as having a personal character, which was the character of Christ, of Christ crucified and risen; to experience this power was to experience life on the far side of the cross, to share in the life of him who died and rose again.

Moreover, the eschatological significance of Christ as another Adam, as the Adam of the new age, should not be ignored here, as those who were familiar with Paul's wider Adam-Christ parallel (1 Cor 15) would be aware. As Adam "represents" man, generically, so that to speak of Adam is a way of speaking of everyone (5:12–19), so for Paul Christ "represents" a new race of humankind, so that to speak of Christ is a way of speaking also of this new race. The condemnation of all in the present age is that they follow through and reproduce Adam's sin and consequent death, that they must die Adam's death. The gospel is that a similar identity is possible with Christ, that we need not share only in Adam's death, but can share also in Christ's. We may put it this way: Jesus is the *only* one who, having reached the end of this age of Adam, broke through the road-end barrier of death into the age beyond; who, having died Adam's death as an act of obedience, rose to a new life beyond. Christ's death and resurrection thus provide the doorway— for Paul the only doorway—through death to life, from this age under the power of sin to the new age free from sin. To make the transition from old age to new age, from sin through death to life, one must as it were be carried through by Christ, and one must identify oneself unreservedly with the historical event of Christ's death in all its degradation and suffering, as sacrificial offering and act of obedience. Only those who make themselves one with his death can hope to experience the life which is his life in the new age beyond. Now that the righteousness of God has been revealed as his saving act in Christ, the faith which God counts as righteousness, the eschatological faith appropriate to this new state of affairs, is faith in Christ, is the entrusting of oneself to the crucified (3:21–26).

4 V 4 fills out this line of thought a little further: "We were buried with him through baptism into death." Paul reminds his readers that the means by which their identification with Christ's death was achieved was baptism. Paul could be understood to mean that he saw the ritual act as an "effective symbol" which achieved the identification sought, with baptism as an act of immersion seen as mirroring Christ's burial and so as symbolizing the burial of the baptized with Christ. Though burial was by no means always underground, the talk of burial probably arose out of the talk of death as denoting the finality of death, rather than from the mode of baptism (cf. 1 Cor 15:3– 4), and the failure to follow through the symbolism to speak of the emergence from the water as indicative of their having risen with Christ further weakens the association of ideas. Alternatively, "through baptism" could denote the means by which the would-be Christian identified himself or herself with Christ in his death; the surrendering of oneself to the baptizer in immersion could well be seen as symbolizing and expressing the necessary surrender to Christ in death, and as a public act it would often mean a very real renunciation of the ties and friendships of the old life, of the life of the age of Adam. Either way, the event of baptism would usually have been the focus for the most effective meeting of divine grace and human faith. It was the very decisiveness of baptism's breach with the life of this present age (under sin's dominion) which should have showed how impossible it was to agree with the opening question.

The object of being buried with Christ into death is given in the next two clauses of v 4: "in order that as Christ was raised from the dead through the glory of the Father, so we also might walk in newness of life." The object of conversion-initiation is not a better kind of death in the future, but a new quality of life in the here and now. We should note at once how quickly Paul jumps from a deep theological concept (union with Christ in his death) to talk of daily conduct. For Paul, evidently, *the character of daily conduct is actually determined by these deeper realities,* the hidden self-understandings and sources of strength which come to expression in day-to-day living. The proof of such deeper realities is not some profound mystical experience but the daily decisions of everyday relationships and responsibilities. His readers who were familiar with the thought of the Hebrew scriptures would have taken the point that Paul intends here a contrast with the typical Jewish understanding that daily conduct should be determined by the law: Paul refutes the idea that grace makes moral responsibility superfluous. But he also refutes the hidden premise that such conduct means walking "in the law." In the new age and covenant it is the renewed life which is the source and motivation of ethical living.

Some at least of those listening to this letter being read out would no doubt be surprised that Paul does not complete the thought of the first clause of v 4 in the most obvious and most balanced way: "in order that we might also be raised with him into newness of life" (cf. Col 2:12; 3:1). Paul indeed seems to have deliberately avoided speaking of believers' identification with Christ in his resurrection. There is clearly implied a sharing in some degree in Christ's risen life: the possibility of "walking in newness of life" is a consequence of Christ's resurrection; Paul sees the risen Christ as the power source which enables believers to sustain a different motivation, orientation, and lifestyle (cf. 5:10, 21; 7:6; 1 Cor 15:45; 2 Cor 3:6). But by implication the believer is not yet able to share in Christ's resurrection in the same way that he can share in Christ's death (cf. 8:11; 1 Cor 15:51–57). Why this should be so will become clearer in a moment. In the meantime we should note that Paul sets up a tension here, *a tension between the degree of self-identification possible with Christ's death and the degree of self-identification possible with Christ's resurrection.* It is this tension which is at the basis of Christian ethics and conduct, and is the key to understanding the way Paul develops his argument through the next three chapters.

5 Paul goes on to introduce a series of explanations developing and clarifying the assertions of vv 2–4. "For if we have become fused with the very likeness of his death. . . ." The verse is very compressed in form and in imagery and the Roman congregations probably had some difficulty in fixing his meaning. They would recognize the imagery of the broken edges of a wound or ends of a bone knitting together again. But "very likeness" is more ambiguous and its force may not have been immediately apparent. The thought is not of integration with Christ's death as such, as though believers could actually participate in a historical event that took place twenty to twenty-five years earlier; "very likeness" implies at least some distinction from the historical event itself. Nor is the thought of an action having the outward appearance of death (as baptism might be said to have); the idea of being fused with baptism would be very odd, and the second half of the verse looks to a future event, not back to initiation. The thought intended is probably more of the actual equivalent of Christ's death as it comes to expression in conversion and commitment. Evidently, then, Paul does intend to talk of a real dying of the believer, a dying of oneself in belongingness to this age, the era of Adam—dying being understood not so much as the cessation of physical existence as such, but as the severing of all links with this world, as a ceasing to be responsive to the stimuli of this world. His point is that the believer can actually begin to experience this dying and death in the here and now; the opening of oneself in trustful obedience to Christ has the effect of bringing to bear on one's belongingness to and dependency on this world the process of death, that is, the real equivalent of the decisive death of Christ which ended the old epoch ruled by sin and death. Here the importance of the tense of the verb needs to be emphasized: "have become fused" (perfect tense), denoting not a once-for-all event of the past, but an event of the past resulting in a state which lasts through the present. The believer has been and *still is* bonded together with the effect of Christ's death, with the actual outworking of the death which he died in its effect on this present age. As Paul put it in his earlier letter to Galatia, the believer has been crucified with Christ, crucified in relationship to the world, and still hangs there (Gal 2:20; 6:14).

". . . we shall certainly also be fused with the very likeness of his resurrection." Here again Paul's readers would recognize that he is not referring to Christ's resurrection in the past as such, but to believers' resurrection which will be just like his. Here again the tense is significant: it is something that will happen in the future. Here then is the end or goal of the state or process of assimilation to Christ's death—the future resurrection, the redemption of the body (cf. 8:11, 23; Phil 3:10–11). And here the tension already referred to becomes much clearer. *The whole of this life for the believer is suspended between Christ's death and Christ's resurrection,* or more precisely between the very likeness of Christ's death and that of his resurrection, between the conversion-initiation which began the process and the resurrection of the body which will complete it. The very real dying of believers is a lifelong process: they do not sever all links and relationships with this world until the death of the body. How can they? But in the meantime they must let the death of Christ come to increasing effect in their own lives. Only as believers live in the consciousness that they belong to the one who has died completely to this world, only as they identify themselves with Christ in that death, only as they live out of the enabling which comes from the risen life of Christ, only then can they be said to be knit together with the ongoing reality of Christ's death, only then can they hope to show the effect of Christ's death and resurrection in their present lives, only then can they hope to share fully in the completion of the process in the resurrection of the body like Christ's.

6–7 With vv 6–7 the tension in Paul's conception of present Christian existence becomes sharper and likely to cause some confusion. "Knowing this, that our old man was crucified with Christ, in order that the body of sin might be done away with, so that we should no longer be in slavery to

sin; for he who has died has been declared free from sin." It is clear enough
that "our old man" and the "body of sin" both refer to humanity in solidarity
with Adam, our belongingness to the old era, the age dominated by the
power of sin. Does Paul then turn his back on the idea of the believer's
identification with Christ in his death as a lifelong process? Does he mean
his readers to understand that their attachment to the present world was
already completely ended?—that they have been crucified, destroyed, and
have died? And does he therefore mean that the believer as such is in fact
free from sin and so sinless? One answer might be that he did not intend
the two verses to be read quite so abruptly. To nail someone to the cross
was not to kill him there and then but to subject him to a suffering which
inevitably resulted in death after some hours or even days; the verb translated
"might be done away with" could be rendered "might be made ineffective,
powerless," or be taken to describe the end result of the crucifixion, in the
believer's case at the end of this earthly life; and the verb translated "has
been declared free" could mean "has been justified." The difficulty in each
case is that Paul does seem to be looking back to the believer's having died
with Christ as something already accomplished (vv 2, 4, 8); moreover, the
logic of v 6 is that the liberation from sin's slavery is the consequence of the
body-of-sin's destruction and "justified *from* sin" sounds even less like Paul
than "declared free from sin."

8–10 The problem of how to take vv 6–7 is clarified to some degree by
vv 8–10: "But if we died with Christ, we believe that we shall also live with
him, knowing that Christ having been raised from the dead does not die
again—death no longer has authority over him. For he who died, died to
sin once and for all; but he who lives, lives to God." Here it is clear enough
that only Christ has experienced the full effect of death; he has escaped the
power of death, but only by virtue of his being raised from the dead; only
of him is it true that he has died to sin once and for all, that the stimulus of
sin finds no response. It is clear enough also that believers are not yet living
with Christ; from the standpoint of faith, death with Christ lies in the past,
whereas life with Christ lies in the future; however much they share in Christ's
death they do not yet share in Christ's resurrection (v 8).

So the key to vv 6–10 must lie once again in the tension of the believers'
eschatological existence, the tension set up by their being identified with
Christ in death while continuing to be very much part of this world in a
way which is no longer true of Christ, the tension of their experience of the
new life from Christ being necessarily limited so long as they remain embodied
in this world. In an important sense Christ's death and resurrection as obedient
Adam counts for all Adam/humankind: Christ died for all, therefore all died
(2 Cor 5:14); Christ died in the solidarity of sinful flesh, as a sin offering
(8:3), therefore the body of sin has been done away with. Something of
epochal significance has happened in the once-for-allness of Christ's death.
And the point which Paul wishes to get over, even at the risk of overstatement,
is that *believers can share in the epochal once-for-all results of Christ's death.* By
the decisive act of conversion-initiation believers can begin already, even in
this life, to benefit from the decisive act of Christ's death and resurrection.
Their transition from death to life is incomplete, they are suspended as it

were between death and life, they are lying buried with Christ in death (to sin), awaiting the fullness of resurrection, they are still to that extent under the dominion of death till they too have been raised from the dead and death ceases to exercise any rule over them. But the crucial transition has begun; because they already share in the once-for-allness of Christ's death to sin they can be sure their final dying will escape the sting of death (sin— 1 Cor 15:56); because they have already opened themselves in a decisive act of faith to the life-giving power of the risen Christ they can believe with confidence that they will one day share fully in that life.

10–11 Thus the epigram of v 10 summarizing Christ's death and resurrection is stated in such a way that it can serve as a basic principle which determines the believer here and now. "For he that died, died to sin once for all; but he that lives, lives to God. So you also reckon yourselves dead to sin, but living to God in Christ Jesus." In this interim period—epochally between Christ's death and "the resurrection of the dead" (1:4), individually between conversion-initiation and the final resurrection—what is required then is that believers *keep their perspective clear*, that their attitudes to the relationships and attractions of this world be determined in the light of these epochal and decisive events, that they live in this world as those who do indeed share in Christ's death, not yet fully liberated from the power of death, but no longer in bondage to sin, as those who draw their vital energies and motivations from God in Christ Jesus (v 11). It is this basic identification with Christ in his death, accepted in the decisive act of conversion-initiation which provides the starting point for the exhortations that follow.

2. The Believer Should Therefore Live to God (6:12–23)

Bibliography

Bartchy, S. S. ΜΑΛΛΟΝ ΧΡΗΣΑΙ: *First-Century Slavery and The Interpretation of 1 Corinthians 7:21.* SBLDS 11. Missoula: Scholars Press, 1973. **Bornkamm, G.** "Baptism and the New Life in Paul: Romans 6." *Experience.* 79–84. **Beare, F. W.** "On the Interpretation of Romans 6:17." *NTS* 5 (1958–59) 206–10. **Boer, W. P. de.** *The Imitation of Paul: An Exegetical Study.* Kampen: Kok, 1962. 21–23, 50–71. **Borse, U.** "'Abbild der Lehre' (Röm 6:17) im Kontext." *BZ* 12 (1968) 95–103. **Bouttier, M.** "La vie du chrétien en tant que service de la justice pour la sainteté: Romains 6:15–23." In Lorenzi, *Battesimo,* 127–54. **Bultmann, R.** "Das Problem der Ethik bei Paulus." *ZNW* 23 (1924) 123–40. **Byrne, B.** "Living out the Righteousness of God: The Contribution of Rom 6:1–8:13 to an Understanding of Paul's Ethical Presuppositions." *CBQ* 43 (1981) 557–81. **Cambier, J.** "La liberté chrétienne selon saint Paul." *SE* 2:315–53. **Eichholz, G.** *Theologie.* 268–72. **Furnish, V. P.** *Theology.* Esp. 194–98, 224–27. **Gale, H. M.** *Analogy.* 182–89. **Haacker, K.** "Probleme." 9–12. **Hagen, W. H.** "Two Deutero-Pauline Glosses in Romans 6." *ExpT* 92 (1980–81) 364–67. **Halter, H.** *Taufe.* 67–89. **Jones, F. S.** "Freiheit." 110–17. **Kaye, B. N.** *Chapter 6.* 95–133. **Kertelge, K.** *Rechtfertigung.* 263–

75. **Kürzinger, J.** "Τύπος διδαχῆς und der Sinn von Röm 6:17f." *Bib* 39 (1958) 156–76. **Lyall, F.** "Roman Law in the Writings of Paul—the Slave and the Freedman." *NTS* 17 (1970–71) 73–79. **Malan, F. S.** "Bound to Do Right." *Neot* 15 (1981) 118–38. **Merk, O.** *Handeln.* 28–41. **Moffatt, J.** "The Interpretation of Romans 6:17–18." *JBL* 48 (1929) 233–38. **Petersen, N. R.** *Rediscovering Paul.* Philadelphia: Fortress, 1985. 240–57. **Reumann, J.** *Righteousness.* 81–84. **Schotroff, L.** "Die Schreckensherrschaft der Sünde und die Befreiung durch Christus nach dem Römerbrief des Paulus." *EvT* 39 (1979) 497–510. **Schweizer, E.** "Die Sünde in den Gliedern." In *Abraham unser Vater,* FS O. Michel, ed. O. Betz et al. Leiden: Brill, 1963. 437–39. **Toit, A. B. du.** *"Dikaiosyne* in Röm 6: Beobachtungen zur ethischen Dimension der paulinischen Gerechtigkeitsauffassung." *ZTK* 76 (1979) 261–91. **Ziesler, J.** *Righteousness.* 201–3.

Translation

   ¹² *Therefore, do not let sin rule in your mortal body to obey its* ᵃ *desires,* ¹³ *and do not give sin control of what you are or do as weapons of unrighteousness. But give God decisive control of yourselves as being alive from the dead and of what you are and do to God as weapons of righteousness.* ¹⁴ *For sin shall not exercise lordship over you; for you are not under the law but under grace.* ¹⁵ *What then? Should we sin* ᵇ *because we are not under the law but under grace? Certainly not!* ¹⁶ *Do* ᶜ *you not know that when you give control of yourselves as someone's slaves to obey him, you are the slaves of the one you obey, whether of sin resulting in death,* ᵈ *or of obedience resulting in righteousness?* ¹⁷ *But thanks be to God, that when you were slaves of sin you gave your obedience from the* ᵉ *heart to the one to whom you were handed over as a pattern of teaching.* ¹⁸ *Having been set free from sin you became enslaved to righteousness—* ¹⁹ *I speak in human terms on account of the weakness of your flesh. For just as you handed over what you are and do as slaves* ᶠ *to uncleanness and to lawlessness which results in lawlessness,* ᵍ *so now hand over what you are and do as slaves* ᶠ *to righteousness which results in consecration.* ²⁰ *For when you were slaves of sin, you were free in relation to righteousness.* ²¹ *What fruit did you have then? Things of which you are now ashamed, for their end result is death.* ²² *But now having been set free from sin and enslaved to God, you have your fruit which results in consecration, and the end product is eternal life.* ²³ *For the wages of sin is death. But the gracious gift of God is eternal life in Christ Jesus our Lord.*

Notes

   ᵃSome witnesses, including P⁴⁶, read αὐτῇ (referring to sin) in place of αὐτοῦ (referring to the body); but the latter is more strongly attested, and the αὐτῇ was probably inserted on the assumption that a reference to sin's desires was more appropriate (see Metzger).

   ᵇAs with 6:1, the unexpected subjunctive has resulted in different attempts to improve the text, at a relatively late stage of the MS tradition.

   ᶜSome have inserted ἤ ("or") at the beginning of the verse to conform to Paul's formulation in 11:2; 1 Cor 6:2, 9, 16, 19.

   ᵈThe omission of εἰς θάνατον from a few witnesses looks to be an unintentional oversight (Metzger).

   ᵉA adds καθαρᾶς ("from a clean heart"), no doubt with Matt 5:8; 1 Tim 1:5; 2 Tim 2:22; and 1 Pet 1:22 in mind.

   ᶠSome MSS make the would-be-improving alteration of δουλεύειν for δοῦλα.

ᵍ εἰς τὴν ἀνομίαν has been omitted by B and a few others, where it was probably regarded as tautologous.

Form and Structure

The transition from chiefly assertion to exhortation signaled in v 11 characterizes this section, with the contrast heightened by the fact that the second person is used almost exclusively, with the diatribe-style question of v 15 the only exception.

The principal feature of the section is the sustained sequence of antitheses—

13	ὅπλα ἀδικίας τῇ ἁμαρτίᾳ	ὅπλα δικαιοσύνης τῷ θεῷ
14-15	οὐκ ὑπὸ νόμον	ἀλλὰ ὑπὸ χάριν
16	ἤτοι ἁμαρτίας εἰς θάνατον	ἢ ὑπακοῆς εἰς δικαιοσύνην
18	ἐλευθερωθέντες ἀπὸ τῆς ἁμαρτίας	ἐδουλώθητε τῇ δικαιοσύνῃ
19	δοῦλα τῇ ἀκαθαρσίᾳ . . . εἰς τὴν ἀνομίαν	δοῦλα τῇ δικαιοσύνῃ εἰς ἁγιασμόν
20	δοῦλοι τῆς ἁμαρτίας	ἐλεύθεροι τῇ δικαιοσύνῃ
22	ἐλευθερωθέντες ἀπὸ τῆς ἁμαρτίας	δουλωθέντες τῷ θεῷ
21-22	τέλος θάνατος	τέλος ζωὴν αἰώνιον
23	τὰ ὀψώνια τῆς ἁμαρτίας θάνατος	τὸ χάρισμα τοῦ θεοῦ ζωὴ αἰώνιος

The attempt to sustain the antithetical structure without lapsing into mere repetition has two important corollaries:

(a) The variation in the use of the key term δικαιοσύνη: (i) as an antonym to ἁμαρτία (vv 18, 20); as also to ἀδικία (v 13), θάνατος (v 16) and ἀκαθαρσία (v 19); (ii) as a synonym to θεός in antithesis to ἁμαρτία (cf. vv 13 and 19, 18 and 22); cf. also vv 16 and 17 and see on 6:22; (iii) and in the striking phrase ὑπακοὴ εἰς δικαιοσύνην (see on 6:16), functionally equivalent to δικαιοσύνη εἰς ἁγιασμόν (v 19). This flexibility should be sufficient warning against imposing a narrow definition of "righteousness" on Paul's treatment of the theme. For Paul "righteousness" is evidently a summary here for the gracious power of God which claims and sustains the believer and reaches its final expression in eternal life (5:21; 6:23); cf. Reumann, *Righteousness*, 83. Malan offers a more complex analysis.

(b) The maintenance of the already/not yet, before/after tension:

Exhortation	12	13a			16		19	-	21
			15						23
based on indicative		13b	14			17 - 18			22
before/						17	18	19a	20-21	22
after							19b		22

From all this it becomes clear that Paul is attempting to maintain a balanced tension (the eschatological tension; cf. Bornkamm, 80; Kuss, 394–96, 408–14; Halter, 67–69). An important corollary is that since the whole treatment is a series of antitheses and balances it would be a mistake to pick out any one verse and give it undue prominence or dominance in the exegesis of the whole, or, indeed, in the interpretation of a larger Pauline theme. No verse should be exegeted independently of the whole and without reference to the range and variation of the antithetical and balancing statements. Nor is there any real ground for regarding vv 13 and 19 as post-Pauline glosses (against Hagen).

The recall of the main emphases of 5:21 in 6:23 confirms that vv 1–23 is a thematic unit in which the conclusion of 5:12–21 is restated in a way which eliminates the misunderstanding of 6:1. The problem of the continuing relation of the believer to sin and death (since sin has not yet exercised its final say in death) having been thus given a first definitive answer, the way is clear for Paul to focus his attention on the main problem area, the continuing role of the law (chap. 7).

Comment

6:12 μὴ οὖν βασιλευέτω ἡ ἁμαρτία ἐν τῷ θνητῷ ὑμῶν σώματι, "therefore, do not let sin rule in your mortal body." The οὖν indicates the conclusion to be drawn from the preceding argument—not a further reflection, but a practical outworking. This is what the aorist assertions of vv 2 ff. mean in practice. The talk of "sin ruling" recalls 5:21 (see on 3:9 and 5:21). Despite the assertions of vv 2–11, sin's rule is not merely a possibility, but a reality to be resisted all the time (present tense). "Mortal body" is neither simply identical with "the physical organism" (Murray), nor does the exhortation amount to a gnostic disparagement of the material body. Sin would rule over not merely a part of man, but over man as a whole in his belongingness to this world and age, hence as θνητόν, hence as vulnerable to the power of sin playing upon human weaknesses, and hence as "body of sin" (see on 6:6; against Käsemann). On the combination of singular and plural—"your (plural) mortal body (singular)," see on 6:6a ("our old man").

εἰς τὸ ὑπακούειν ταῖς ἐπιθυμίαις αὐτοῦ, "to obey its desires." This is the purpose sin has in seeking to influence and control human beings. "Sin can only rule when one obeys it" (Schlier). The verb ὑπακούειν appears for the first time, but links into the important correlative ὑπακοή; note particularly the intensive use in vv 16–17. Since the Pauline usage outside Romans is relatively sparse (ὑπακοή/ὑπακούω—Rom, 11x; 1 Cor, 0; 2 Cor, 3x; Gal, 0; Phil, 1x; Col, 2x; 1 Thess, 0; 2 Thess, 2x; Philem, 1x; cf. Eph, 2x; Pastoral Epistles, 0; Heb, 3x; 1 Pet, 4x), its thematic importance in Romans is noticeable (see on 1:5). Paul looks for an obedience which answers to the obedience of Christ (see on 5:19); the continuing influence of 5:12–21 is marked. For ἐπιθυμία see on 1:24. Note the parallels, "lusts of heart" (1:24), "lusts of mortal body" (6:12), "lust of flesh" (Gal 5:16), all denoting not merely physical appetites but man's dependency for satisfaction of his needs, including physical needs and also emotional, intellectual, social and religious needs. This dependency provides the means to bring him into slavery, since natural appetite can so easily become overwhelming urge (see on 7:7), with even Christian freedom itself providing opportunity for the same appetites and urges (Gal 5:13, 16–17). It is the possibility and the enabling to control that dependency and to prevent it becoming an overpowering urge which comes from identification with Christ, though never simply as a possibility, and never in independence from that identification. Contrast Epictetus 4.1.170–77: "Freedom is not acquired by satisfying yourself with what you desire, but by destroying your desire" (175).

On the transition from the indicatives dominant in vv 1–11 to the imperatives dominant in vv 12–23 and the proper balance between the two, see especially Furnish, *Theology,* 224–27; Merk, *Handeln,* 28–41; and Käsemann, 172–76. The much-quoted attempt to strike the balance between the two, "Become what you are," does not quite achieve the correct balance. "Become what you are becoming" would better express the eschatological tension, or eschatological reservation, which repeatedly comes to expression in vv 1–11 (vv 4, 5, 6, 8, 11), since it would retain the note of an active cooperation with and living out of the grace which precedes and makes possible all moral effort. "That the defection to sin is a very real possibility for the Christian gives his decision for God the character of freedom, a freedom which conversely he never had under the rule of sin" (Wilckens).

13 μηδὲ παριστάνετε τὰ μέλη ὑμῶν ὅπλα ἀδικίας τῇ ἁμαρτίᾳ, "and do not give sin control of your constituent parts as weapons of unrighteousness." παρίστημι, "put at the disposal of": used repeatedly here—vv 13 (twice), 16, 19 (twice); cf. 12:1. Whether the image is that of slave-owner (vv 16–18), of king (cf. *TDNT* 5:840), or of military force (cf. LSJ, παρίστημι C.II), the effect is the same—acknowledgment of a superior power and authority to whom the only proper response is submission and obedience. Note again the present tense, suggesting a submission to be daily refused (but see also 6:19). μέλος, "part of the body," referring both to limbs and organs, but familiar also in the metaphorical sense of individuals as members of society (*TDNT* 4:555–56); so elsewhere in Paul (12:4–5; 1 Cor 12:12–27; Eph 4:16 [*v.l.*], 25; 5:30; cf. 1 Cor 6:15); otherwise, as here (Rom 6:13, 19; 7:5, 23; Col 3:5). The broader meaning, human "faculties" (Barrett, Black), "capabilities" (Käsemann), "natural capacities" (Cranfield) is wholly appropriate, in view of the larger sense of σῶμα in Paul (see on 6:6). Cranfield notes that ἐν τοῖς μέλεσίν μου in 7:23 is more or less equivalent to the ἐν ἐμοί of 7:17, 20. The plural stands parallel to "your mortal body," emphasizing that the wholeness of a commitment comes to expression in particular concrete acts. The translation at the head of this section ("what you are and do") is an attempt to improve on "members" (unsatisfactory to modern ears) and the rather ponderous "your constituent parts" (used otherwise in this section). ὅπλον, "tool, implement"; in plural, often specifically "implements of war, weapons" (LSJ, ὅπλον III). In Paul it is used only in the plural (6:13; 13:12; 2 Cor 6:7; 10:4; elsewhere in the NT only John 18:3), with the military metaphor very probably in mind (*TDNT* 5:294, and most commentators; cf. particularly 2 Cor 10:4; cf. also 7:11 and on 6:23—ὀψώνια). Paul has no embarrassment in using such military metaphors (cf. 13:12; 1 Thess 5:8; Eph 6:13–17). ἀδικία is again chosen for its breadth, representing all that stands in opposition to God's righteousness (see on 1:18; and further below, v 13c). The personification of the power of sin becomes increasingly vigorous. The alternative is deliberately stark: there is no middle ground, or neutral position; man's desired independence of God is nothing other than a yielding submission and service

on the side of sin in the warfare between unrighteousness and righteousness
(1:18 ff.).

ἀλλὰ παραστήσατε ἑαυτοὺς τῷ θεῷ, "but give God control of yourselves."
The switch to aorist may be partly stylistic, and does not necessarily imply a
once for all surrender (cf. v 16). But it is in some contrast to the present
tense of the preceding clause and presumably indicates deliberate and decisive
commitment, as opposed, perhaps, to the decision by default implied in v
13a (see further on 6:19). The ἑαυτούς stands in parallel to "your constituent
parts," underscoring the Hebraic character of Paul's anthropology (cf. TDNT
7:1064). It is noticeable that with παρίστημι Paul prefers God as the object
(also 12:1), or the personified powers, "uncleanness," "righteousness" (v 19),
whereas with ὑπακούω and ὑπακοή used of the obedience of faith he seems to
prefer to speak of Christ (v 17; 2 Cor 10:5; see on 6:17) or of the gospel as
the one to whom the obedience is offered (as most explicitly in 2 Thess
1:8). This is perhaps suggestive of the theological reservation Paul observes
in speaking of Christ (see on 1:8). Where the former expresses submission
to a sovereign authority and so is more appropriate to the Creator, the latter
allows more a sense of a personal relationship. See also final paragraph of
Comment on 14:3.

ὡσεὶ ἐκ νεκρῶν ζῶντας, "as those alive from the dead," "alive, after being
dead" (Lightfoot). Paul uses ὡσεί only here. Insofar as a distinction is involved
between ὡς and ὡσεί it must be to put a little more weight on the εἰ (ὡς
εἰ)—"as if, as though" (LSJ). The point should not be emphasized as though
Paul would have them pretend to be something which is not true, to live a
charade. The decisive event of Christ's resurrection has happened, making
possible an actual change of the attitude and motivation from which ethical
conduct derives for those identified with Christ in his death and resurrection:
they can live as being sharers in Christ's resurrection life (see on 6:4). At
the same time, the "as though" element prevents us from concluding that
for Paul participation in Christ's resurrection was already past (see again
6:5 and 6:8). So particularly Barrett, Schmidt, and Wilckens, 2:21 n. 76; cf.
Michel: "ὡσεί is not only illustration (Bild) and comparison but also motivation
and determination (Bestimmung)."

καὶ τὰ μέλη ὑμῶν ὅπλα δικαιοσύνης τῷ θεῷ, "and your constituent parts weapons of righteousness to God." In the antithesis with v 13a, the antithetical
opposites are

> instruments of unrighteousness   to sin
> instruments of righteousness   to God

Cf. 5:20–21, where it is "grace" which stands opposite to "sin." Paul does
not envisage an ultimate dualism between sin and God; but sin is such a
power over and in individual and society that only God is sufficient to overcome
it; and he does so as grace and in the power of grace. It is noticeable that
even in this antithesis Paul prefers to speak of the power opposed to God
as "sin" rather than Satan (see on 16:20). In line with the metaphor being
developed, ἀδικία and δικαιοσύνη do not so much denote concrete acts (contrast
ἀδικία in 1:18) as personified superhuman agencies: "unrighteousness," as

the means by which the power of sin effects and exercises its authority over and through the individual; "righteousness," as the power of God to retain the individual (believer) under his sway. Hence the possibility of using δικαιοσύνη alone as the one to whom obedience should be given in the following verses (vv 18–20). "Righteousness" as much as "grace" can be used to describe the manner and mode in which God manifests himself; the gift is inseparable from the giver (Käsemann, "Righteousness," 174; Ziesler, 202). "When believers are exhorted to commit themselves to God as 'instruments' (ὅπλα) of and 'slaves' to righteousness (vv 13, 18), then it is apparent that righteousness is not something under their control. Instead, it is that by which they are to be controlled. Righteousness is not their power to 'do,' but righteousness is the power of God in whose service they stand" (Furnish, *Theology*, 195–96). See also on 5:21.

14 ἁμαρτία γὰρ ὑμῶν οὐ κυριεύσει, "for sin shall not exercise lordship over you." With the future tense here cf. vv 5 and 8; and with the indicative mood cf. the imperative of v 12. Where Paul chooses his tenses so carefully the future must be a temporal future (not hortative, as Moffatt and Fitzmyer; cf. BDF, §362), a promise of what will certainly be for believers when they fully and finally share in Christ's resurrection (cf. Knox). But it is not merely a tantalizing promise; rather it is a promise already being enacted by grace and righteousness, that is, by enabling from God, the possibility of grace to live now as one will live with Christ in the future (v 8)—hence the imperative (v 12). The balance of thought including the salvation-history once-for-all and the eschatological reservation is consistent. Conzelmann's assertion that 6:14 "means that it is impossible to sin" (*Outline*, 229) is a dangerous misstatement of Paul's teaching.

οὐ γάρ ἐστε ὑπὸ νόμον ἀλλὰ ὑπὸ χάριν, "for you are not under law but under grace." Note how once again Paul immediately balances the preceding future by the present tense. The future is a firm promise since they already have a share in the salvation-history transition from an epoch dominated by sin and law to the epoch dominated by grace. Those who put themselves under the lordship of Christ no longer owe allegiance to sin and law, even though the rule of sin has still to have its final say in death (5:21). As usual νόμος means the (Jewish) law, the Torah (against Knox, Murray; see on 2:14). The imagery is still that of a power exercising effective authority over. As in 5:20–21 the law is put together with sin and death as a way of characterizing the dominant powers of the old age, the age of Adam. "Under the law" in particular characterizes the position of the Jewish people as a whole (1 Cor 9:20; Gal 3:23; 4:4–5, 21). By putting themselves so fully under the law as peculiarly theirs they have treated the law in effect as a spiritual power appointed by God to be as it were their national guardian angel (hence the parallel between Gal 4:3 and 4:9). Their being "under the law" therefore characterizes the form of life under the old age as it has been experienced within Judaism (2:1–3:20); see further *Introduction* §5.3 and on 4:14 and 5:20. Consequently in a letter devoted to clarifying the continuities and discontinuities between the covenant given to Abraham and through Israel and its eschatological fulfillment, "under the law" can stand as a general characterization of the old epoch of Adam (but Gaston's thesis, *Paul*, 62–64, followed by Gager, *Origins*, 221–22, that "under the law" actually designates the gentile situation, makes very hard work of the Galatians references). Since a goodly proportion or preponderance of Gentiles are in view as the recipients of the letter (see *Introduction* §2, particularly §2.4.4) the corollary follows once again that they must be mainly Gentiles who had (previously) been attracted to Judaism, that is, attracted by the customs and standards embodied in the law, and so were in danger of thinking they could only participate in the covenant promises by "judaizing," living like the Jews, that is, by putting themselves "under the law." In arguing that Paul does not put law and grace in conflict anywhere in the letter ("law" here being read as an abbreviation for "works of the law"), Kaye again gives too little weight to the ὑπό (as on 3:9) and misses the social function of the law (*Chapter 6*, 110–11). Paul's point then is that in the new epoch ushered in by the death and resurrection of Christ the terms of grace are different from what they had come to be in practice within his own (pre-Christian) Judaism. As so often in Paul's talk of grace the impact of his own experience is evident (see further on 1:5; Dunn, *Jesus*, 202–5). The distinction between epochs is not an absolute before and after Christ, since Abraham accepted the promise and was justified κατὰ χάριν (4:4, 16). But the understanding of the covenant promise characteristic of the Judaism of Paul's day was too much at odds with the free sweep of the one God's grace, so that the antithesis can stand, though not in the overdrawn terms of the classic Lutheran formulation. Neither the latter, expressed in Barrett's note ("Law means the upward striving of human religion and morality . . . and represents man's attempt to scale God's throne"), nor Cranfield's alternative ("under the law" = "under God's disfavor or condemnation"), have grasped the social dimension of the phrase as marking out Israel in its own self-understanding (see again Introduction §5.3).

With 6:14 cf. Gal 5:18:

| Rom 6:14 | οὐκ ἐστε ὑπὸ νόμον | ἀλλὰ ὑπὸ χάριν |
| Gal 5:18 | οὐκ ἐστε ὑπὸ νόμον | εἰ πνεύματι ἄγεσθε |

The parallel between them is a reminder that "grace" and "Spirit" are near synonyms in Paul and that his decision to delay treatment of his theme in terms of the Spirit till chap. 8, with no reference to the Spirit in chap. 6, is of structural rather than theological significance (see chaps. 6–8 *Introduction*).

15 τί οὖν; "what then?"—a quite familiar elliptical expression giving rhetorical flourish, not necessarily marking a break in the argument or a new phase, but designed to keep the argument moving and lively; cf. 11:7 (but not 3:9) and the fuller formula τί οὖν ἐστιν (1 Cor 14:15, 26); elsewhere see BGD, τίς, including Josephus, *War* 2.364. For the fuller formula, τί οὖν ἐροῦμεν see on 3:5.

ἁμαρτήσωμεν ὅτι οὐκ ἐσμεν ὑπὸ νόμον ἀλλὰ ὑπὸ χάριν; μὴ γένοιτο, "should we sin because we are not under law but under grace? Certainly not!" Once again there is the unexpected subjunctive (as in v 1), this time aorist, presumably with the same force as the παραστήσατε of v 13. The verb ἁμαρτάνω occurs only here in chap. 6 and for the last time in the letter. As in its other uses in Romans it denotes a responsible act (2:12; 3:23; 5:12, 14, 16); even without the law such responsible disobedience is possible (2:12; 5:14), and indeed is inevitable from a Jewish perspective (1:18–32). The formulation using the verb is clearly a variant of the preceding formulations using the noun (vv 12–14) and recalls v 1: the responsible sinful act is the inevitable outcome of being under the rule of sin. The question here is not simply a variation on v 1: the ἵνα clause gave the question there an outrageous character; the ὅτι clause here presents the possibility as a somewhat more sober deduction from the emphasis on "already" in the preceding exposition (cf. Kuss; contrast Minear, *Obedience*, 63, who suggests that v 15 alludes to a slogan of "the strong," with Maillot, who sees Paul turning in v 15 to a Jewish-Christian objection). The first person plural breaks the dominance of the second person address of this section (vv 12–23): Paul avoids the impression that this poses a question only for his readers. On μὴ γένοιτο see on 3:4.

16 οὐκ οἴδατε ὅτι; "do you not know that?"—a rhetorical question introducing a well-known or obvious fact (as frequently in 1 Cor—3:16; 5:6; 6:2–3; etc.). Paul prefers the lively diatribe style to the more pedestrian οἴδαμεν γὰρ ὅτι (7:14, 18; 8:22; 2 Cor 5:1). Cf. ἀγνοεῖτε ὅτι in 6:3.

ᾧ παριστάνετε ἑαυτοὺς δούλους εἰς ὑπακοήν, δοῦλοί ἐστε ᾧ ὑπακούετε, "to the one you give control of yourselves as slaves for obedience, you are slaves to the one you obey." The formulation echoes the two halves of v 13—παριστάνετε (present tense) ἑαυτούς (see on 6:13). But the imagery of slavery now appears, to dominate the rest of the chapter. In this context the term of course is not honorific (as in 1:1), but refers to the well known facts about slavery—well known, not least, since large proportions of the population in the chief urban centers round the Mediterranean would be or would have been slaves. "In both Greece and Italy, large numbers of persons . . . sold themselves into slavery" (Bartchy, 46). In first century Corinth, from where Paul was writing, at least one-third of the population would have been slaves, and almost as many again may have been freedmen, freed slaves (Bartchy, 58–59; *OCD*, 995, 996). And the Christian community in Rome was probably made up of a majority of slaves and freedpersons, as both the history of the Jewish community in Rome (see *Introduction* §2.1) and the evidence of chap. 16 strongly suggest (see 16:3–16 *Explanation*).

Although slavery as an institution was taken for granted and as such neither constituted a mark of social degradation nor was clearly marked off in economic terms from other social classes (Bartchy), the distinction between slave and free still remained fundamental in typical Hellenistic self-perception, slavery being antithetical to the Greek idealization of freedom (*TDNT* 2:261–64; Meeks, *Urban Christians*, 20–21). For Paul to call freemen "slaves" could therefore be regarded as insulting, and this may explain the rather labored and tautologous way in which Paul makes his point: if you show by your conduct that you are obeying the mandates of a certain power, then you belong to that power, you are in effect and in reality its slave. The cumbersomeness could, of course, be a case of someone in the course of dictation finding himself caught in an awkward construction (cf. Knox); but it looks too deliberate for that. Many commentators note the parallel in emphasis with Matt 6:24; John 8:34; and 2 Peter 2:19. Kaye suggests Paul's awareness of a Christian tradition, going back to Jesus, using the imagery of slavery for disciples (*Chapter 6*, 120–29). See also on 14:18.

ἤτοι ἁμαρτίας εἰς θάνατον, "whether of sin to death." This is the only instance of ἤτοι in the NT. "Sin" continues to be personified as the power which exercises effective rule over those whose lives are confined within this age, the fifth variation on the same imagery and emphasis in 5 verses (vv 12–16). "Death" reappears in conjunction with sin, completing the same triumvirate of sin, law, death (vv 14–16) which was a feature of 5:20–21. The εἰς has the same force as in 1:16, "with the effect of bringing about"; death as the τέλος (v 21). "Enslavement to sin was, is and continues to be enslavement to death, *also* for Christians" (Halter, 77). As in 5:21 death is the final and most complete expression of sin's power over man; the secret of the gospel is that Christ absorbed sin's worst and turned it into the victory of life (6:7–10). Michel speaks appropriately of the "multilayered" nature of Paul's concept of death (211 n.4).

ἢ ὑπακοῆς εἰς δικαιοσύνην, "or of obedience to righteousness." The use of ὑπακοῆς here is surprising and striking, since θεοῦ or equivalent would seem to be more appropriate. It must be the consequence of the close association between the two ideas, slavery and obedience, which dominate these two verses (vv 16–17—ὑπακοή and ὑπακούω, 4x; δοῦλος, 3x). Slavery and obedience are twin concepts. For the slave, obedience is the only option; as the chattel of his master he has no other function than obedience (cf. particularly Dodd). Conversely, the reality of mastery is indicated by the practical expression of everyday submission. It could of course be that Paul intends a different genitive relation here, slave of obedience = slave marked by obedience. By setting the two genitive phrases in parallel, however, Paul hints at the double causation involved in both: "sin" as a power dominating man, but as also an action for which he is responsible (see on 3:9); "obedience" as man's responsibility, but for which he depends on the enabling or motivating power of whatever or whoever he gives himself to (for ὑπακοή see further on 1:5). Dodd again assumes too quickly "an inadvertence in dictating," failing to realize that "Paul loves nuances" (Käsemann). Schlier, like Dodd, wonders whether Paul still has the obedience of Christ (5:19) in view.

Unusually also, δικαιοσύνη provides the antithetical balance to θάνατος (though cf. 5:18: δικαίωσις ζωῆς). If we press the parallel we would have to understand "obedience which has the effect of bringing about righteousness." The specter of a "works righteousness" should not be raised here, since there is no thought of a self-achieved righteousness, but rather of the obedience of a slave as the obedience which he has no option but to offer. Nevertheless it should not escape notice that Paul here has no misgivings about representing "righteousness" as an "end product," a condition or state or relationship yet to be realized (as elsewhere most clearly in Gal 5:5; see also on 10:10); the flexibility of Paul's concept of "righteousness" should be observed and not squeezed to fit a particular dogmatic scheme (cf. Michel, and further particularly on 1:17 and 5:17). Nor does he seem to have any misgivings about representing righteousness as in some sense the product or result of obedience, even if qualified as obedience enabled by God and righteousness as always God's gift (1:17; 5:17—see Käsemann; and further particularly du Toit and Byrne); here the overlap of the verbal and noun usages should be recognized (see further particularly on 2:13, which in sense is very close to this verse; and cf. Black). All this strengthens the likelihood that Paul's criticism of contemporary Judaism is not aimed in this direction: if the central thrust of his objection was directed against the view that by obedience one could come to or attain righteousness, he would never have expressed himself as he does here (see again 2:17–29; 3:27–31; 4:4).

17 χάρις δὲ τῷ θεῷ, "but thanks be to God"—a regular form, in Christian literature mostly expressing gratitude to God or Christ (see BGD, χάρις 5). The link to the context is not uniform: it can stand on its own (7:25); or be followed by ὅτι (as here) or ἐπί (2 Cor 9:15) or by a relative clause (1 Cor 15:57; 2 Cor 2:14; 8:16).

ἦτε δοῦλοι τῆς ἁμαρτίας ὑπηκούσατε δὲ ἐκ καρδίας, "you were slaves of sin but gave your obedience from the heart." For "slave of sin" and obedience as the only live option for the slave, see on 6:16. ὑπηκούσατε could be translated "you became or have become obedient" (Schlier). The ἐκ καρδίας is important not only as indicating a deeply felt and deeply motivated action from the innermost being, but also as implying a contrast with an obedience which was less deeply rooted, whether coerced (sin's unwilling slave) or superficial. That the Christian reality, whether of grace or response, is at the level of the heart is a characteristic claim of Paul even if this particular prepositional phrase occurs only here (see further on 2:15, 29; 5:5; 10:9–10).

εἰς ὃν παρεδόθητε τύπον διδαχῆς, "to the pattern of teaching to whom you were handed over." The unusual εἰς following ὑπακούω (usually with genitive or dative) is determined by the following παρεδόθητε (BGD, παραδίδωμι 1b end). The clause is awkward but the syntactical meaning clear (Lightfoot compares Acts 21:16); on the unlikelihood of the whole phrase from ὑπηκούσατε being a gloss (Bultmann, "Glossen," 283; O'Neill) see Cranfield, Käsemann and Schlier (with other bibliog.), Haacker. Less certain is the meaning of τύπον διδαχῆς. Most understand the phrase to refer to a fixed catechetical formulation or creed, already so well established and so well known that Paul could refer to it without further detail (e.g., Norden, 270–71; Kürzinger; Beare, 109–10; Kuss; Black; Schlier; Halter, 80; Käsemann with other bibliography; though cf. Spicq, 896); and since the emphasis is on practical outworking of Christian commitment, there is a good deal to be said for this view. On the other hand: (1) τύπος in the Pauline corpus almost always has a personal reference—a particular individual (or individuals) providing a pattern or example of conduct (5:14; Phil 3:17; 1 Thess 1:7; 2 Thess 3:9; 1 Tim 4:12; Tit 2:7; so also 1 Pet 5:3; Ign. *Magn.* 6.2; otherwise only 1 Cor 10:6; see also de Boer, 21–23). Käsemann's suggestion that τύπος διδαχῆς corresponds antithetically to μόρφωσις τῆς γνώσεως καὶ τῆς ἀληθείας ἐν τῷ νόμῳ (2:20) is apposite (cf. Lietzmann) so long as we recall that for Paul ἐν Χριστῷ corresponds to ἐν τῷ νόμῳ: *Christ,* not a creedal or parenetic formulation, has replaced the law (though cf. 10:6–10)—thus rendering unnecessary Schlatter's question, "With the teaching does not the law come back into the community?" (2) The appositional syntax here ("to whom as a pattern") is the same as in Phil 3:17 and 2 Thess 3:9 ("us/ourselves as a pattern"). (3) παραδίδωμι can of course have the technical sense of "hand over, pass on tradition" (so in 1 Cor 11:2, 23; 15:3), but in Paul the more prominent usage is that of handing over to another authority or power (1:24, 26, 28; 1 Cor 5:5; 13:3; 15:24; 2 Cor 4:11; of Jesus' being handed over to death in 4:25; 8:32; 1 Cor 11:23;

Gal 2:20; see also on 4:25). The latter is more obviously appropriate here
since the imagery is of the transfer of a slave's ownership, whereas the idea
of being handed over to a catechetical pattern is rather strained ("an act of
obedience to the baptismal teaching which has mastered ὑς"; so Schlier, TDNT
2:500). Either way NJB's "to which you were introduced" is inadequate.
(4) Although use of common parenetical themes is evident later in the letter
(see 12:9–21; 13:1–7 and 13:11–14 Form and Structure), Romans is too early
for us to be confident that a particular pattern had become already sufficiently
well established to be recognized simply by the phrase τύπος διδαχῆς. Even if
Paul did intend παρεδόθητε to allude to the passing on of tradition the most
immediate parallel would be Col 2:6 ("as you received Christ Jesus as Lord"),
where it is clearly the traditions focusing on Jesus which are in view as providing
pattern and motivation for Christian conduct ("so walk in him"); see further
Dunn, Unity, 144–45; cf. Wilckens and Harrisville. τύπος διδαχῆς in the sense
of Christ as the pattern for Christian parenesis or the model for Christian
conduct is certainly somewhat unexpected here; but Paul makes such limited
use of the word διδαχή (16:17; 1 Cor 14:6, 26) that we cannot draw any
firm conclusions from the word itself. And the emphasis certainly accords
with Paul's parenesis later in Romans and elsewhere (see on 12:14 and 15:5;
and further Dunn, Unity, 68–69, 144–45; cf. T. W. Manson). A reference to
the relationship between Adam and Christ reads too much into the text (against
Borse).

Note the balance of tenses and voices: ἦτε, ὑπηκούσατε, παρεδόθητε. Paul
thus contrives to highlight the interaction of human response and divine
power: the image is of the rebellious slave whose desire to serve another
master results in his being transferred to that master. The aorists, however,
do not imply a long period of rebelliousness but the single act of conversion-
initiation, the transfer of loyalty and lordship which took place in baptism.

18 ἐλευθερωθέντες δὲ ἀπὸ τῆς ἁμαρτίας ἐδουλώθητε τῇ δικαιοσύνῃ, "having
been set free from sin you became enslaved to righteousness." For the first
time in Romans the important theme of Christian freedom is struck (see on
8:2). Here it appears wholly within the metaphor of slavery (vv 18, 20, 22),
Paul thus demonstrating his awareness not only of the fundamental slave/
free antithesis in the society of his time (see on 6:16), but also of the characteristic aspiration of the slave for freedom (see again Meeks, Urban Christians,
20–21). For the possibility and means of manumission see Deissmann, Light,
320–30; OCD, 448; Bartchy, 87–114. The more we recognize the axiomatic
idealization of freedom in hellenistic thought (TDNT 2:261–64), the more
striking we can see Paul's conjunction of the two verbs to be here—"having
been freed . . . you were enslaved." That his readers would think of "sacral
manumission" whereby the slave would be sold to the god in whose temple
the purchase price had been deposited (Deissmann) thus to become the god's
slave is less likely: the god (or the god's temple) functioned more as an intermediary than as a new owner; and the characteristic emphasis of the manumission
contract was the purchase of the slave ἐπ᾽ ἐλευθερίᾳ—for freedom! (Bartchy,
121–25; the eventuality of a captured slave being freed and remaining a slave,
as in m. Git 4.4, is no parallel). The surprising antithesis—freed to be enslaved,

freed by being enslaved—is therefore deliberate and drawn not from a current practice but from the theological insight that man exists only as a creature, only in a relation of dependency on a superior power; his vaunted freedom and independence is illusory. If not enslaved to God, then enslaved to sin; either in Adam or in Christ; *tertium non datur!* The only real freedom for man is as a slave of God, a life lived in recognition of his creaturely dependence. See again 1:18–32 and 5:12–21.

The combination of aorist tense and passive voice is very powerful, recalling the most emphatic statements of vv 2–4 (cf. Schlier). However much Paul wants to emphasize the necessity and importance of human response (the obedience of faith), he never lets slip the even more basic insight that *whatever* is achieved for man's good is achieved by God; obedience begins from that creaturely recognition of complete dependence on the Creator. The point is given added poignancy in this context since the slave was not a "legal person" and so had no choice in the matter as to whether he was freed or refused freedom (Michel, 211 n.1; Bartchy, 98, 106–10). For the idea of slavery to sin see on 6:16. Paul uses δουλόω only here and v 22 in Romans (elsewhere in Paul in this imagery only in Gal 4:3). In a further variation on the use of δικαιοσύνη (see also vv 13, 16) Paul personifies the gracious power of God as characterizing the relation of God to those who render to him creaturely obedience; note the close verbal parallel with v 22, from which it becomes clear that Paul here thinks of "righteousness" as in effect synonymous with "God" (see further *Form and Structure* and on 1:17; 5:17; and 10:6a).

19 ἀνθρώπινον λέγω διὰ τὴν ἀσθένειαν τῆς σαρκὸς ὑμῶν, "I speak in human terms on account of the weakness of your flesh." For similar parenthetical apologies or explanations (Käsemann) see on 3:5. ἀνθρώπινον, "in the language of every day," "as people do in daily life" (BGD). But there is also the implication, strengthened by the use of σάρξ (cf. 8:3), that a contrast between divine and human is also in view (cf. its use in Acts 17:25; 1 Cor 2:13; 4:3–5). Paul was no doubt well aware that the metaphor of slavery, so antithetical to Greek ideals, is an inadequate one for talk of their relation with God (see further Gale; Eichholz, 270; Wilckens). "The weakness of the flesh" characterizes Paul's understanding of the human condition: man as "flesh" is by definition "weak," mortal, corruptible, subject to his all too human desires, blind to the truth of God and of his own creatureliness, etc. A clear disjunction should not be made between moral defect and the inadequacy of human perception (as SH); in Paul's use of σάρξ the two senses run into each other (cf. further particularly Kuss and Schmidt). For ἀσθένεια see further on 8:26. For σάρξ see on 1:3 and 7:5; but this is hardly the first pejorative use of it in Romans (against Harrisville). For the combination of ideas see Mark 14:38 // Matt 26:41; Rom 8:3 and Gal 4:13.

ὥσπερ γὰρ παρεστήσατε τὰ μέλη ὑμῶν δοῦλα τῇ ἀκαθαρσίᾳ καὶ τῇ ἀνομίᾳ εἰς τὴν ἀνομίαν, οὕτως νῦν παραστήσατε τὰ μέλη ὑμῶν δοῦλα τῇ δικαιοσύνῃ εἰς ἁγιασμόν, "for just as you handed over control of your constituent parts as slaves to uncleanness and to lawlessness resulting in lawlessness, so now hand over control of your constituent parts as slaves to righteousness resulting in consecration." Typical of Paul's style is the recall of previous themes (παριστάνειν μέλη—v 13; παριστάνειν . . . δούλους—v 16) in a composite expression which extends the thought still further (ἀκαθαρσία, ἀνομία, ἁγιασμόν). The ὥσπερ . . . οὕτως . . . recalls the frequent use of the same formulation in 5:12, 18, 19, 21, with probably deliberate effect: their previous (preconversion) life belonged within the old epoch of Adam ruled by sin (v 17). The use of the aorist (παρεστήσατε) in reference to their life in the old epoch should not be taken to denote a once-for-all handing over (unless the Adamic motif is stronger than it appears); rather the decisiveness of their submission to sin which characterized their way of life prior to their response to God's righteousness (cf. BDF, §332); "a life deeply and irrevocably committed" (Dodd). Certainly no real contrast can be intended with the imperfect of v 17, and the use of the aorist in both halves of the contrast should prevent too much being made of the difference in tenses in v 13 (see on 6:13). Paul maintains the balance between human responsibility and domination by a stronger power. For μέλος see also on 6:13. The gender of the adjective δοῦλα (neuter, only here in biblical Greek) is, of course, determined by the gender of μέλος, but perhaps helps reinforce the "thing" status of a slave (see on 6:16). The νῦν is eschatological (see on 8:1), the before-and-after of conversion-initiation marking their participation in the transition from old epoch to new.

The Jewish character of the new elements is very marked. ἀκαθαρσία, ἀνομία, and the theme of ἁγιάζειν/ἁγιασμός are all characteristic of and prominent in Jewish thought (see HR and on 15:16) and much less typical of wider Hellenistic concerns. The association of the first two was natural for a Judaism which cherished the memory of Ezra's reforms separating the people of the law from gentile uncleanness (see particularly Ezra 9:10–14 = LXX 2 Esd 9:10–14; 1 Esd 8:69–70). ἀκαθαρσία recalls the Hellenistic Jewish critique of gentile idolatry and sexual standards used by Paul in 1:18–32 (1:24 is the only other time the word is used in Romans). The emphasis on ἀνομία is even more striking (τῇ ἀνομίᾳ εἰς τὴν ἀνομίαν) since this is the only time he uses the word in Romans of his own choice (in 4:7 it stands in an OT quotation); Paul will have wanted to catch its critical assessment of conduct, not least gentile conduct, as outside the law of the covenant (see on 4:7 and *Introduction* §5.3.1); the implication of progressive deterioration, sin begetting sin, also reflects the emphasis of 1:18–32 (Str-B, 3:233, appropriately cites *m. 'Abot* 4.2). ἁγιασμός is not a common word; it is little used in the NT (chiefly Paul— 6:19, 22; 1 Cor 1:30; 1 Thess 4:3, 4, 7; 2 Thess 2:13; elsewhere only in the "Pauline circle"—1 Tim 2:15; Heb 12:14; and 1 Pet 1:2), not well established in the LXX, and hardly to be found outside the Judeo-Christian tradition. But the theme of "consecration" is particularly and distinctively Jewish, and since the ideal of priestly set-apartness and purity was so important within Judaism (cf. Exod 19:6), particularly for Pharisees and Essenes, the language would be very evocative of a Jewish perspective. The force of this multiple allusion would not be much lessened by the fact that in Christian usage ἀκαθαρσία and ἁγιασμός/ἁγιάζειν have already left their earlier cultic context behind and been developed as metaphors of moral force independent of the cult (see on 1:24; 1:7 ἅγιος and 15:16 ἁγιάζειν). To describe ἁγιασμός as "baptismal vocabulary" (Käsemann) runs the danger of reversing that process.

This evocation of the Jewish critique of Gentile morality and the implicit antithesis between Jewish ideals of priestly consecration and gentile lawlessness is therefore undoubtedly deliberate. It strengthens the implication that Paul was writing the letter with Gentiles largely or principally in view (Althaus); the repetition of the definite article with ἀκαθαρσία and ἀνομία (in contrast to ἁγιασμός) reminds them of the uncleanness/lawlessness which they knew well enough from their own experience (Michel). But, more important, it underscores by clear implication that Paul wants to defuse Jewish criticism of his gospel (cf. 6:1) by emphasizing the continuity between his own and characteristic Jewish concerns. The double use of ἀνομία (see *Notes*) is particularly noticeable: it emphasizes the lawlessness of their *previous* state, and so implies the corollary, that their *present* state as believers is a fulfilling of the law. It thus provides further warning against any simplistic description of Paul's position as a complete breach with the law. What Paul looks for in his converts is what the law looked for (cf. particularly Lev 11:44–45; 19:2; 20:26; Deut 7:6; 14:2; 26:19; 28:9)—"holiness," ἁγιασμός, where the word is best understood as the end result of an act (ἁγιάζειν) or process (εἰς ἁγιασμόν), so "consecration," or dedicated state (hence "holy"—see on 1:7 and 15:16), though a firm line between end result and process into cannot be clearly drawn (cf. 6:22; 1 Thess 4:7; 2 Thess 2:13) (cf. Lagrange; Schmidt; Kertelge, *Rechtfertigung*, 272–74); Cranfield thinks ἁγιασμός denotes process rather than state; other bibliography in Käsemann. In the three correlatives, ἁγιάζειν (usually used in the aorist), ἅγιος and ἁγιασμός, the eschatological tension is clearly expressed as the dedication of conversion-initiation and Spirit's anointing, to be lived out with deliberate decision (παραστήσατε) in daily life (which is a reaffirmation in desacralized ethical terms of the Pharisaic ideal of conducting daily life as though a priest in the temple; see on 12:1 and 15:16), with a view to the completed consecration "without which no one will see the Lord" (Heb 12:14). The power by which this end is achieved, Paul is careful to indicate, is δικαιοσύνη, meaning God's gracious, sustaining power (see on 6:18).

20 ὅτε γὰρ δοῦλοι ἦτε τῆς ἁμαρτίας, ἐλεύθεροι ἦτε τῇ δικαιοσύνῃ, "for when you were slaves of sin you were free with regard to righteousness." The verse takes up the language of vv 17–18 in more concise formulation, to drive home the contrast between their present state as believers in Jesus Christ consecrated to God in conversion-initiation and their previous state, with the direct contrast resumed between "sin" and "righteousness" as personified and opposing powers. The metaphor is strained ("free in relation to righteousness" as a dative of respect, BDF, §197), but it follows from v 18 as its converse: to be under the mastery of sin is itself a demonstration that the power of God's gracious enabling and sustaining power is not holding sway or having effective say (see further Jones, 112–14). The eschatological tension keeps the antithesis from being driven through in a completely clear-cut manner. But even so the antithesis cannot be blunted very much: it is not possible to be wholly dominated by sin and at the same time to be under the sway of God's righteousness; in any decision of daily responsible living "sin" and "righteousness" are mutually exclusive alternatives.

21 τίνα οὖν καρπὸν εἴχετε τότε; "what fruit did you have then?" The imagery of "fruit" is slightly odd within the slavery metaphor, but its broader use ("appropriate result or return") is well established and its meaning obvious (see on 1:13).

ἐφ᾽ οἶς νῦν ἐπαισχύνεσθε, "for which you are now ashamed." For the punctuation see Cranfield; older bibliog. in Kuss. The fruit (καρπόν, singular) takes concrete expression in a variety of acts (ἐφ᾽ οἶς—plural) (cf. Gal 5:22). The τότε . . . νῦν . . . antithesis maintains the contrast between the before-and-after of conversion-initiation and of the epochs of Adam and Christ. Here again Paul speaks from a Jewish perspective. A persistent feature of the LXX use of αἰσχύνη is the explicit sexual allusion (1 Sam 20:30; Prov 9:13; Isa 20:4; 47:3; Ezek 16:36, 38; 22:10; 23:10, 18, 29; Nah 3:5; Jud 9:2; 13:16; Harrisville suggests that Ezek 16:61, 63 might have been in Paul's mind); the shame of idolatry is in view in 1 Kings 18:19, 25 and Isa 42:17; 45:16. So, once again, it is the Hellenistic-Jewish critique of gentile religion and morality used in 1:23–27 which is probably in view ("ashamed" therefore of beliefs which they now see to be false and of practices which they now see to be at odds with a life lived to God). Significant also is the number of interlocking themes which are common to this passage and to Ezra's speech in Ezra 9:7–15: shame, uncleanness, lawlessness, slavery, and ἁγίασμα used of the temple (cf. also Ezra 9:15 with Rom 9:27–29). The correlation is too close to be coincidental: consciously or unconsciously Paul echoes the attitude to Gentiles expressed determinatively for post-exilic Judaism in Ezra 9.

τὸ γὰρ τέλος ἐκείνων θάνατος, "for the end result of these things is death." τέλος here clearly in the sense of "outcome," with the strong eschatological emphasis of final outcome or destiny (6:21–22; 2 Cor 11:15; Phil 3:19; cf. 1 Peter 4:17). The eschatological note is distinctively Jewish, but τέλος denoting completion or finality (e.g., τέλος ἔχειν = "to be dead") is equally familiar in wider Greek thought (see LSJ, τέλος II; TDNT 8:49–54). See further on 10:4. That θάνατος is described as "the end result" confirms the force of εἰς θάνατον in v 16 as "resulting in death," and that for Paul death is both the final outcome of sin's rule and the climactic expression of sin's rule (see on 5:21 and 6:16); which is also to say that death is the divinely willed outcome of man's disobedience and turning from God (1:32); for θάνατος see further on 5:12.

22 This verse is a further gathering together of the preceding themes, merging the imagery of vv 18–21 as a way of expressing the richness of the present contrast to their previous state.

νυνὶ δέ, ἐλευθερωθέντες ἀπὸ τῆς ἁμαρτίας δουλωθέντες δὲ τῷ θεῷ, "but now, having been set free from sin, and having become enslaved to God." The wording closely follows v 18 (note again the divine passive), with the eschatological νυνί as in 3:21 heightening the contrast, and τῷ θεῷ replacing τῇ δικαιοσύνῃ, thus confirming that for Paul δικαιοσύνη is essentially the self-manifestation of God in effective power to reclaim and support his sinful people and fallen creation (see further Form and Structure and on 6:18), the equivalent of χάρις in the earlier antitheses of 5:20–6:1; cf. Reumann, Righteousness, 83–84.

ἔχετε τὸν καρπὸν ὑμῶν εἰς ἁγιασμόν, "you have your fruit for consecration." For καρπός see on 1:13; Zeller notes the repeated use of the vision of Israel as a fruitful "plant of righteousness" in Jewish writings (Isa 32:15–17; 60:21;

61:3; *Jub.* 1.16; 16.26; 36.6; *1 Enoch* 10.16; 84.6; 93.2, 5, 10; cf. Jer 32:41; CD 1:7–8); see further on 11:16. For εἰς ἁγιασμόν see on 6:19. Even if what is in view is a final outcome or state (cf. v 19), the present tense (ἔχετε) allows the thought that while the wholly consecrated state is still future, the "fruit" which has that state as its final outcome should already be becoming visible. Alternatively, if the emphasis on the finality of outcome is reserved for the next clause, the εἰς ἁγιασμόν could be taken more closely with καρπός as denoting the actual maturing process itself ("sanctification"). Either way the tension between what is (already) happening and what is (not yet) end result is expressed once more.

τὸ δὲ τέλος ζωὴν αἰώνιον, "and the end result of eternal life." For τέλος see 6:21; for ζωὴ αἰώνιος see on 2:7. The resumption of the climactic antithesis of 5:21 (death/eternal life) is deliberate: Paul has worked his way to a restatement of the conclusion of 5:21 which is so worded as to eliminate the misunderstanding still possible with 5:21 (see further on 6:23).

23 τὰ γὰρ ὀψώνια τῆς ἁμαρτίας θάνατος, "for the wages of sin is death." Paul rings one further change of metaphor: ὀψώνιον, originally denoting a soldier's subsistence pay or ration money, was still largely used of a soldier's pay in particular (as in its LXX use, 1 Esdr 4:56; 1 Macc 3:28; 14:32; and in two of the three other NT uses, Luke 3:14 and 1 Cor 9:7; also Ign. *Pol.* 6.2); but it had broadened beyond that to denote "salary, wages, allowance" in general (cf. 2 Cor 11:8: see MM; Spicq, 637; *NDIEC* 2:93); in view of the thematic importance of slavery in the context we should note that it was possible for slaves to earn a daily wage (Bartchy, 42, 74). Heidland presses the metaphor too hard: that Paul thinks of death as merely subsistence pay, when much greater rewards (presumably) had been promised (cf. Gen 3:4–5); that ὀψώνιον is a continuous and not single payment, so that the thought is of death overshadowing the whole (cf. 5:21); and, more likely, that ὀψώνιον as a legal term stands in contrast with χάρισμα in the second half of the verse (cf. Spicq, 638). "Man has rights only in relation to sin, and these rights become his judgment. When he throws himself on God without claim, salvation comes to him" (*TDNT* 5:592; see also Michel). At all events, the thought is again clearly of death as sin's (final) payoff, that is, not just natural death, but death as the forfeiture of eternal life (Schlatter).

τὸ δὲ χάρισμα τοῦ θεοῦ ζωὴ αἰώνιος, "but the gracious gift of God is eternal life." For χάρισμα see on 1:11; for ζωὴ αἰώνιος see on 2:7. This further recall of a key term of the conclusion in 5:12–21 (χάρισμα—5:15–16), together with the repeated contrast (death, eternal life—5:21) confirms that Paul is deliberately restating that conclusion (see on 6:22).

ἐν Χριστῷ Ἰησοῦ τῷ κυρίῳ ἡμῶν, "in Christ Jesus our Lord." The more typical "in Christ Jesus" formula (see on 6:11) is expanded with liturgical solemnity to bring this section of the argument to its conclusion (as in 5:21; 6:11 *v.l.*; 8:39; cf. 1:4, 7; 15:6). For the titles see on 1:1, 4, 7, 8 and 10:9.

Explanation

6:12 "So do not let sin rule in your mortal body causing you to obey its desires." Only those who have not appreciated the eschatological tension in vv 1–11 would find Paul's turning to moral exhortation at this point surprising. Where the "not yet" of the believers' sharing in Christ's resurrection has not been allowed to qualify the "already" of their identification with Christ in his death, such exhortation can cause only puzzle and confusion: what meaning can such counsel have if the believer is already "dead to sin"? how can a dead person be asked to make moral effort? But those who have recognized the balance in Paul's exposition thus far would have no difficulty in following Paul's train of thought. The point is that the rule of sin belongs to the old epoch (5:21); to be ruled by sin is characteristic of fallen Adam and his race; such self-indulgence and self- (or better national-) righteousness (1:18–2:29) is the mark of "the old man." Without grace such individuals experience their human appetites as a compulsion they cannot resist, an imperative they cannot deny.

For believers who recognize the epochal significance of Christ's death and resurrection, however, that need no longer be the case. Even though their life within this present physical and social environment ("your mortal body") is not yet fully under the power of the risen Christ (cf. 8:11), nevertheless the inescapable urge to satisfy their appetites ("its desires") need no longer be their master. Here the same eschatological tension is clearly implied. For believers the body is still mortal, its appetites still capable of determining their life's character and priorities. But the power of grace, the power of the risen Christ enables them to rise above such merely self-centered concerns. It is this reality which Paul seeks to realize in his readers. Hence the sequence of imperatives. Paul is under no delusion that it will happen automatically, as though conversion-initiation had worked an irreversible transformation which would inevitably manifest itself in daily life. Believers have a *responsibility* in all this, a responsibility to let the power of grace come to expression in their lives. *Moral effort is in no way antithetical to faith*; it is rather the outworking and expression of faith.

13 "Do not give sin control of your constituent parts as instruments of unrighteousness." Paul's thought still focuses on the believers' physicality, since it is their bodily belongingness to this world which is the clearest evidence that the work of grace is not yet complete. If the power of Christ's risen life can manifest itself in the totality of these bodily relationships, then the total victory of grace is all the more assured. But so long as they are in this body there is the very real likelihood that particular deeds and actions will advance the cause of unrighteousness, even that there will be an area of a believer's life which is habitually in the service of sin (the present tense could be translated: "Do not keep giving control . . ."). If the word translated "instruments" is intended to embrace also (or alternatively) the sense "weapons," the implication becomes even clearer that believers must in this life inevitably experience "divided loyalties." Even as believers they may find that one of their actions, even one of their habitual activities, is a tool used by sin to distort their relations with God and with their fellows, and that they must fight with the sustained discipline of a gladiator fighting for his life to avoid that happening.

For believers, however, there is a choice. They can choose to put themselves at God's disposal as those alive from the dead, and their constituent parts as instruments or weapons of righteousness to God. The way to prevent sin's (re)asserting its control is to recall the epochal significance of Christ's righteous act, consciously to view each issue from the perspective of Christ's death and resurrection, to choose and act as though Christ's resurrection had already achieved its complete effect (to act as one would act in the presence of God), or at least as those through whom the risen life of Christ is already flowing. The double aspect of the alternative and the change of tense should not be ignored. The only viable alternative to a constant surrender before sin's power is the decisive committal of the whole person in the central motivation and direction of life, a completeness of committal which has to come to expression in the multitude of individual actions. *Each act involving moral choice is an act of moral commitment, where the decisive commitment of conversion-initiation has to be renewed and realized ever afresh.* Both aspects are necessary. The once for all commitment of conversion-initiation does not *ipso facto* keep individual actions thereafter from being determined by selfish motives. It is only when each act is done for God, as something which God can use to further his purpose for humankind's well-being, that believers can be confident that they are "walking in newness of life."

14 The reason it is possible for believers to avoid a habitual surrender to sin at one point or other in their lives is that sin shall no longer have the dominant say in their lives, because they are not under the law but under grace. Again Paul varies his tenses, no doubt with deliberate intent. The future tense ("sin shall not have mastery over you") is both a statement of fact and a promise; the present tense ("you are . . . under grace") is the basis of the promise. The future tense indicates a state of affairs which is in process of being worked out and is yet to be fully worked out; the present tense, a state of affairs already established by virtue of Christ's death and resurrection and their identification with it. *Grace is the only power which can break the mastery of sin.* It is only as believers live their lives "under grace," in dependence on God's gracious power to sustain and restore, that the power of sin can be defeated, that the enticing voice of self-satisfaction or sectional or national self-interest can be ignored.

The basic perspective from which Paul wants his readers to view their lives is posed by Paul as the alternative of grace over against law. This reintroduction of the law to the discussion might at first have seemed surprising; the exposition thus far in this chapter has been more or less exclusively in terms of sin and death. But evidently the law was never far from Paul's thought as he dictated his exposition, which is a further reminder that Paul all the while is setting his gospel over against the alternative model he learned as a devout Jew and Pharisee, where the law played an integral role in the process of salvation. What is striking is that once again the law is put on what to the great majority of devout Jews would seem to be the wrong side of the antithesis: for Paul being "under the law" is bound up with being under the mastery of sin, with giving control at different points to unrighteousness, with obeying the desires of the mortal body. Such an association would have astonished most of Paul's fellow Jews: for them the law was given by grace precisely to prevent sin, as a bulwark against unrighteousness, as a means of coping with the uncleanness of the body. But for Paul life "under the law" was on the contrary a life bound more closely to sin.

Here for the first time in this letter Paul depicts the law as a power over man. And as his earlier usage indicates, the phrase for him characterizes the people of Israel, the Jews as a nation (Gal 3:23; 4:4–5; 1 Cor 9:20). His point is that far from being a beneficial power for the Jewish people, the law has been a rather baneful influence. What he has in mind presumably is the attitude attacked in chap. 2, namely, the law as a power which encouraged national self-righteous judgment on others, unself-critical presumption of God's favor, and a superficiality which confused outward ritual with the work of the Spirit. Perhaps he has in mind too that to see the relationship with God in terms of law is to open the door to a dominant attitude either of anxious self-scrutiny (cf. 8:15) or of fault-finding scrupulosity (cf. Mark 2:1– 3:6; 7:1–8). In any case we must assume that Paul, in looking back on his life as a Pharisee, had long ago concluded that the law, far from binding individuals closer to God in truthful obedience, actually separated them from God and prevented them from accepting God's grace in its complete gratuitousness ("without works of the law"). Over against the Jewish concept of a national righteousness understood in terms of the law, Paul poses once again the universal offer of righteousness understood in terms of grace from start to finish.

15 "What then? Shall we sin, since we are not under the law but under grace?" For Paul the Pharisee this question is the almost inevitable reflex to the antithesis of v 14. It has the function of picking up once again the question which opened the new stage of the discussion (v 1). But the repetition of the question also echoes the surprise and bewilderment any good Jew would have felt at Paul's disparagement of the law. To set the law over against grace like that was a recipe for moral disaster; to put grace alone in place of the law was to remove God's barrier against sin and means of dealing with sin and to open the floodgates of sin.

16 In his response Paul does not at first say anything about the law; only in chap. 7 does he at last feel able to devote himself to a fuller exposition of the role of the law within his gospel. But first he seeks to squash firmly and finally any suggestion that his gospel encourages sin. The awkward phrasing of v 16 is probably in part at least the result of Paul's trying once again to strike the right balance between the already and the not yet of the eschatological tension: there is a handing of oneself over to a master to be his obedient slave; and there is the daily obedience which must ensue. Conversion-initiation introduced believers into a new relationship; it is this relationship (with God) which must now determine their whole life and all other relationships. It is not a sinless state which would be denied and destroyed by any particular sinful act, but a relationship which can be sustained despite individual acts of disobedience; in a master-slave relationship the master can tolerate and forgive various breaches of discipline, though habitual sin (warned against in v 13) would presumably destroy the relationship itself.

Paul poses two alternatives—slavery of sin, and slavery of God (he actually says, oddly enough, slavery of obedience, but his meaning is clear enough: i.e., slavery as obedience to God; cf. vv 13, 22). His readers would note that he characterizes *both* relationships as that of master and slave. Implicit therefore is the same conviction elaborated in 1:18–32: that man can*not* be *in*dependent;

that the person who refuses God's mastery over him- or herself does not thereby achieve independence, but becomes instead a slave to sin. Evidently for Paul there is no third alternative. The choice confronting everyone is the choice of being ruled by God or being ruled by sin.

The result of being enslaved to sin and of remaining in obedient subservience to the desires of this mortal body (v 12) is death. Death is the end effect of such enslavement to sin (as it is sin which gives death its sting—1 Cor 15:56). By death here Paul means either the end of existence—a life lived exclusively on the level of this mortal body presumably ends with the death of the mortal body; or a state of death, a state characterized by its lack of response to the only power capable of giving and sustaining life beyond death (the life-giving power of God). On the other hand, the result of obedient slavery to God is righteousness, that is, a relationship with God sustained by his gracious power and making for individual wholeness and corporate well-being (evidently for Paul "righteousness," like "wrath," can denote both a continuing process and an eschatological result). Readers who remembered what Paul has already said in chap. 6 would not of course conclude that the obedient believers escape death. What they escape is death as the end, as the final event or state. They still experience death; the "lame duck" presidency of death must run its full course in the dying of the mortal body. But their identification with Christ in his death means that they can look through death to the fuller relation with God only possible beyond death.

Finally on v 16 we should not ignore the point that for Paul righteousness is not some passive or quietist relation with God. It involves obedience. In denying that the believer is under the law (v 15), in implying, indeed, that the law is to be lumped together with sin and death in the either-or of the alternative slaveries, Paul does not by any means exclude the need for obedience on the part of the believer. What Paul objects to is the typical identification of the obedience God looks for with obedience to the law. The obedience God looks for is in Paul's view distinctively different, as he goes on to indicate in v 17.

17 For one thing it is obedience*"from the heart."* Evidently it is this "from the heart" depth or quality of obedience which Paul found lacking in what he has characterized as typical Jewish obedience to the law (2:5, 15, 29). In contrast the risen Christ had drawn from him a heartfelt and wholehearted response which went deeper than anything he recalled experiencing as a Pharisee. Not unnaturally he assumes that his Christian readers have experienced the same sort of fundamental transfer of loyalties which changes the whole life from inside.

For another, it is obedience *to Christ,* "to whom you were handed over as a pattern of teaching." The clause is compressed and open to more than one understanding. But the context invites a personal reference in the relative pronoun ("to whom" rather than "to which"), and with "pattern of teaching" Paul probably also has a person in mind, namely, Christ himself, to whom they rendered obedience and to whom they were handed over. That is to say, Paul is probably still thinking here of Christ in Adamic terms with Christ as the archetypal new man, Christ as the pattern of obedience, particularly in the epochal event of his death (5:19; cf. Phil 2:8), but probably also in the character of his whole life as exemplified in such traditions of his sayings and deeds as were evidently passed on to every new church (cf. e.g., 15:1–6; 1 Cor 11:1; Col 2:6; 1 Thess 4:1–2; 2 Thess 3:6). After all, any new movement calling for a fundamental shift in allegiances is bound to provide new converts with some guidelines regarding lifestyle and behavior. For the first Christians there could be no better exemplar than Christ himself. Whereas the proselyte to Judaism would be directed to the law, for Paul, himself a converted Jew, there is now a different norm and model of obedience—no longer the law, but Christ. Christ's ministry in whole and in part embodied the grace of God (5:15; cf. 2 Cor 8:9) and so provided a clear enough "pattern of teaching" for those who are "not under the law but under grace."

In describing his readers' transfer of ownership Paul uses the passive form of the verb ("to whom you were handed over"), presumably because throughout this paragraph his thought is dominated by the imagery of a slave's being transferred from one master to another. In the actual transaction the slave has no say; his responsibility is simply to obey his master, whoever that may be. At the same time Paul is aware that the real life parallel is not entirely applicable, for he talks of the convert's part in the transfer of ownership: "you yielded wholehearted obedience to the one to whom you were transferred." Indeed Paul may well depict his readers' conversion as an act of defiance to their old master: "you were slaves of sin, but you gave your real allegiance to Christ." Once again the balance between divine initiative and human response, between a faith which simply accepts God's grace and one which exercises itself in moral effort, comes clearly to the surface of Paul's thought.

18 Their conversion-initiation, Paul reminds his readers, was an act of liberation or manumission, for many slaves (though by no means all) in the ancient world, a life's goal. For the Christian slaves and freedmen and freedwomen in the Roman congregations the emotional force of the metaphor must have been very strong. Here once again the thought is of liberation from the domination of self-indulgent desires and selfish habits. Where previously they had lacked real freedom of choice and sin's constraints were too powerful, now that state of affairs no longer pertains. The newly purchased slave who still acts on behalf of his old master is clearly being unfaithful to the new. The new here is depicted as "righteousness"—obviously just a variation on "God" (v 13), "grace" (vv 14, 15), "obedience" (v 16), and Christ (v 17). Like "sin," "righteousness" can be personified, since both are experienced as powers which determine life in a particular direction—"sin" as binding the individual more and more tightly to the process of mortality and corruption which ends in death (vv 12, 16), "righteousness" as transforming the individual more and more to the character of the archetypal new man which ends in the complete sharing in his risen life (vv 5, 8).

19 Paul however was evidently uncomfortable at pressing the metaphor of transfer of slave ownership too far; the idea of being a mere chattel and object before righteousness did not bring out sufficiently the personal character of the relationship with God established by Christ. Hence the disclaimer of v 19b—"I speak in human terms because of the weakness of your flesh." Paul may simply mean that he was conscious of the inadequacy of this all

too human metaphor drawn from daily life. But he may also imply that the
flesh was (by definition) so weak that they were constantly prone to live as
though still slaves of sin, still ruled by the desires of this mortal body. It is
precisely this all too human tendency to give way to the same old selfish
habits and self-centered attitudes which evidently causes Paul to keep repeating
that his readers have an unceasing obligation to live in accordance with their
new relationship to God, in accordance with "the pattern of teaching." Their
conversion-initiation did not accomplish their complete salvation. It opened
them to a new and stronger power source (grace, righteousness), it transferred
them to a new master (God). Now they cannot escape the continuing responsibility to live accordingly.

So once again (v 19b) he urges them: "Just as you gave control of your
constituent parts in slavery to impurity and to lawless deeds which produced
ever more of the same, so now give control of your constituent parts in
slavery to righteousness which produces holiness." The exhortation is in effect
a repetition of vv 13 and 16, but the different wording is not simply a matter
of aesthetic variation of near synonyms. He reminds his readers that before
their conversion-initiation they were willing participants in the sort of impurity
condemned in 1:24. That he is thinking of the predominantly gentile Christians
at Rome is clearly implicit—Christian conversion involving a significant moral
conversion is also attested in 1 Cor 6:9–11. "Lawlessness to lawlessness" would
also recall to his readers the earlier description of the vicious circle of sin
(chap. 1), though Paul's indictment in 1:18–3:20 included Jew as well as
Gentile under the same condemnation.

What is again rather striking is that the antithesis to "lawlessness" is not
obedience to the law, but once again righteousness—righteousness not as
determined by the law, but as determined by grace. Gentile proselytes or
God-worshipers, with the repeated antithesis of vv 14–15 still ringing in their
ears, would be unlikely to miss the point. The significance of this righteousness,
this relation-sustaining and character-transforming power from God, is that
it achieves "holiness," something the protagonists of the law would think of
as a state bound up with, even inseparable from the ritual purity which comes
from proper observance of the law (e.g., Exod 29:1, 21, 33, 36–37, 44; 30:29–
30). Paul in effect is reminding his Gentile addressees, many at least of whom
would previously have been attracted by the moral standards of Judaism,
both that the goal is the same (purity, but inward as well as outward), and
that moral endeavor is necessary, but exercised in terms of the righteousness
of grace, not in terms of the law.

20–22 Paul does not seem to be able to let the metaphor of slavery go.
The contrast between the before and after of conversion-initiation is repeated,
and the tension between the decisiveness of conversion-initiation (as the event
of liberation from the lordship of sin) and the not yet accomplished process
of being made holy is retained. In describing their preconversion state he
points out that being slaves of sin meant also being free with regard to righteousness. The metaphor is still forced, but Paul's message is clear—that
righteousness is the effect of God's lordship over his creatures and cannot
be realized otherwise. Hence too he can treat "God" and "righteousness"
more or less as synonyms (vv 20, 22; cf. 13, 18), since in the event of commit-

ment and of continued obedience he and his converts presumably experienced
God as a constraining and enabling power.

He reminds his readers too that their previous way of life was one of
which they were now ashamed. That he could simply take such a feeling of
revulsion for granted among a largely unknown audience reinforces the impression of v 19 that many Gentiles would have been attracted to both Judaism
and Christianity by the moral standards they shared. Indeed Paul would
regard such a sense of shame as the obverse to the moral effort for which
he has repeatedly called in this section of his letter—both qualities being
signs of the transformation which had taken place in conversion-initiation
and of the psychological impossibility of one so committed readily returning
to the lordship of sin.

The antithesis of end results of the two slaveries is drawn out a little more
sharply than in vv 16 and 19. Paul speaks both of a "fruit/result" and of an
"end": in the one case, impurity (by implication from v 19) and death; in
the other, "holiness/sanctification" and "eternal life." The fact that he refrained
from using "life" in antithesis to "death" in v 16 suggests that he wanted to
reserve talk of "eternal life" for the climax to this section—an impression
confirmed by v 23 which repeats the central antithesis in terms of the contrast
between "wages" (or "compensation") and "free gift."

23 Here it becomes more apparent that Paul's antagonism to impurity
(including sexual irregularity—1:24) is not merely the cultural antipathy to
pagan values of one born and bred a Jew. It is rather a theological insight
or claim that impurity involves such a focusing of vitality on this mortal
body that when death has its say with respect to this same body nothing is
left; the whole person is so reduced to this body that death alone is the
end. This is how the master "sin" rewards his servants; the only payment
"sin" can make is death.

The alternative offered by the gospel is holiness which ends in eternal
life, where "holiness" is probably more clearly conceived as a process (than
in v 19) = "sanctification," that is, the progressive transformation from inside
out (cf. 2:28–29), so that the final rising with Christ is but a continuation
and completion of the whole process (cf. 2 Cor 4:16–5:5). The richer dimension
of Paul's theology which lies behind the thought here (the progressive transformation of the believer into the image of the crucified and risen Christ) might
not be familiar to many of the Roman Christians, though it is part of Paul's
fuller Adam Christology. But at least those who had been following Paul's
train of argument would recognize that the eternal life here spoken of is
nothing other than the life with Christ already spoken of (v 8). For Christ is
the only one who has died and has risen again in his own right and so dies
no more, so that eternal life is simply a sharing in the unending risen life
of Christ. Paul speaks here of "eternal life *in* Christ Jesus our Lord," where
earlier he had spoken of "living *with* Christ." But clearly the idea is the same.
The identification with Christ begun in conversion-initiation will continue
through death to the resurrection beyond. The participation in the powerful
life of the person who is now more than an individual will only reach its
fullest measure in the eternity of his life beyond the tomb.

Paul's characterization of this eternal life as a "free gift" in contrast to the wages of death may be intended to recall the similar contrast in 4:4—the point being that God *owes* man nothing; if the talk is to be of something earned, then only death is in view. The word "free gift" denotes that the eternal life is both an act of grace and itself an embodiment of that same grace. In other words, it is not an object which leaves the possession of the giver and becomes the possession of the believer. It is rather a relationship sustained by God's outflowing power of goodness and embodying that same goodness in its whole character. As such it will still be in terms of Christ (life in Christ, life with Christ) and involve the believer's obedient response to his lordship.

In short, conversion-initiation, the point at which this present train of thought began, is not an isolated and once-and-for-all event in its character of grace meeting obedience. Rather for Paul that first act characterizes the whole of the believer's life as believer. The newness of life there entered upon must be received as a gift of grace ever and again throughout life in this mortal body and beyond in the fullness of resurrection life. The identification with Christ in his death must be reaffirmed ever and again until death plays its last card and the believer can know identification with Christ in his resurrection. The obedience of first commitment must be repeated in every decision of any moral consequence so that it may increasingly be an obedience which results in righteousness, a righteousness which results in sanctification, a sanctification which results in eternal life.

B. What Role Does the Law Play in All This? (7:1–25)

Introduction

The law had been a complicating factor in the conclusion of 5:20–21, not least because it appeared, astonishingly from a Jewish point of view, on the side of sin and death rather than as a means of grace to life. Having gone some way to clarify the continuing role of sin and death in relation to the believer, with only a brief mention of the law (6:14–15), Paul can now turn to the law itself and bring it center stage.

1. The Believer Has Been Released from the Law Which Condemned to Death (7:1–6)

Bibliography

Derrett, J. D. M. "Romans 7:1–4: The Relationship with the Risen Christ." *Law in the New Testament.* London: Darton, 1970. 461–71. **Dulmen, A. van.** *Theologie.* 100–

106. **Gale, H. M.** *Analogy.* 189–98. **Halter, H.** *Taufe.* 90–98. **Jewett, R.** *Anthropological Terms.* 299–301. **Jones, F. S.** *"Freiheit."* 118–22. **Little, J. A.** "Paul's Use of Analogy: A Structural Analysis of Romans 7:1–6." *CBQ* 46 (1984) 82–90. **Lohmeyer, E.** "Sünde, Fleisch und Tod." *Probleme.* 75–156. **Sand, A.** *Der Begriff "Fleisch" in den paulinischen Hauptbriefen.* Regensburg: Pustet, 1967. **Thüsing, W.** *Per Christum.* 93–101.

Translation

¹ *Do you not know, brothers, for I speak to those who know the law, that the law exercises lordship over a man so long as he lives?* ² *For the married woman is bound by the law to her husband while he lives; but if her husband dies she is released from the law of her husband.* ³ *Accordingly she will be named adulteress if, while her husband lives, she becomes another man's. But if her husband dies she is free from the law, so that she is no adulteress if she becomes another man's.*

⁴ *So then, my brothers, you also were put to death in relation to the law through the body of Christ, in order that you might become another's, the one who was raised from the dead, in order that we might bear fruit for God.* ⁵ *For when we were in the flesh the sinful passions which operate through the law were effective in what we are and do so as to bear fruit for death.* ⁶ *But now we have been released from the law, having died* [a] *to that by which we were confined, so that we might serve in newness of Spirit and not in oldness of letter.*

Notes

[a] A Western variant substitutes τοῦ θανάτου for ἀποθανόντες. Both are Pauline (cf. Rom 8:2 and Gal 2:19), but the latter is the harder reading and better attested (see Metzger).

Form and Structure

Vv 1–6 serve structurally: (a) as a gathering up of the main thrust of chap. 6, but now with reference to the law (cf. Luz, "Aufbau," 170), with 7:5–6 functioning as a climax somewhat in the way 2:28–29 serves as a climax to chap. 2; (b) as the equivalent within chap. 7 to 6:1–11; and (c) with 7:5–6 in particular introducing the chief emphases of chaps. 7–8.

(a) The application in v 4 of the principle (v 1) illustrated in vv 2–3 deliberately recalls the terms already used: ἐθανατώθητε τῷ νόμῳ (cf. 6:2) διὰ τοῦ σώματος τοῦ Χριστοῦ (cf. 6:3–6) εἰς τὸ γενέσθαι ὑμᾶς ἑτέρῳ (cf. 6:17–18), τῷ ἐκ νεκρῶν ἐγερθέντι (cf. 6:8–10), ἵνα καρποφορήσωμεν τῷ θεῷ (cf. 6:22). So with v 5, cf. particularly 6:12 and 6:21; and with v 6 cf. particularly 6:4. See also Wilckens and Little, 83.

(b) See chaps. 6–8 *Introduction*; as in chap. 6 the clear-cut lines of 6:1–4/11 become progressively more ambiguous in 6:12–23, so in chap. 7, the clear-cut lines of 7:1–6 become more ambiguous in 7:7–25.

(c) 7:5 in effect traces the course of the discussion in 7:7–25: 7:5a (vv 14–25), 7:5b (vv 7–13), 7:5c (vv 10–11, 13, 24). Likewise 7:6 foreshadows the course of chap. 8: 7:6a (8:1–3); 7:6b (8:4 ff.).

The last two considerations count against Feuillet's thesis ("Plan," 343–44) of a major break at 7:6, to give a rather contrived trinitarian division—1:18–5:11; 5:12–7:6; 7:7–8:39.

Comment

7:1 ἢ ἀγνοεῖτε, ἀδελφοί, γινώσκουσιν γὰρ νόμον λαλῶ, "or do you not know, brothers, for I speak to those who know the law." For the opening phrase see on 6:3. For only the second time in the letter Paul addresses them as ἀδελφοί. The implication is that the subject about to be introduced is a sensitive one in which mutual trust will be all the more important (cf. Schlier). See further on 1:13.

Once again νόμος means the Jewish law, Torah (so most; see on 2:14). The reference can hardly be to "a general principle of all law" (SH; supported with surprising confidence by Käsemann; Lagrange; Knox; also NEB), since Paul goes on (γάρ) to instance a particular legal enactment. A reference to Roman law (Lightfoot, Jülicher, Kühl) is hardly likely: it would be peculiarly condescending for one who had apparently never visited Rome to address residents of the capital city in such terms; the illustration which follows (vv 2–3) presupposes the legislative position in Judaism and is much less applicable to Roman law (see further on 7:2); and "the law" in v 4 is clearly the Torah (Schlier, Wilckens). The fact that Paul could assume a reasonable knowledge of the Torah strengthens the likelihood that the bulk of the gentile converts had previously been adherents to the Jewish synagogues in Rome or elsewhere (God-worshipers). Paul can assume this, either because he has a fair degree of knowledge of the constitution of the congregations in Rome (cf. 16:3–16), or because recruitment of gentile adherents through the synagogue was the almost universal way of establishing the first Christian churches throughout the diaspora (see *Introduction* §2.2.2). Cf. the third-century tomb inscription from Apamea which lays down who may be buried there and concludes, "If anyone acts (contrary to this direction) he knows the law of the Jews" (*CIJ*, 774), implying that the rights of Jewish communities to order their own affairs at least to some extent in conformity with the Mosaic law would be recognized and was quite widely known. Certainly the phrase does not constitute grounds for seeing the bulk of the Roman believers as Jewish Christians, as Zahn argued.

ὅτι ὁ νόμος κυριεύει τοῦ ἀνθρώπου ἐφ' ὅσον χρόνον ζῇ, "that the law exercises lordship over a man so long as he lives." The formulation is surprising, until we realize that the same verb (κυριεύειν) was used in 6:9 and 14 of death and sin. The implication is clear: having recalled in 6:22–23 the thematic statement of the rule of sin and death in 5:21, Paul naturally turns to draw in the third element in that rule, namely, "law." A further implication of the parallel with 6:9 and 14 is that this rule is a baneful thing, a mark of man's state of bondage within the present age. It does not follow that Paul disparaged the necessity for the rule of law in society. But the following metaphor does imply that Paul saw the necessity and character of law's role in ordering social relations as expressive of man's fallen state. For the idiom ἐφ' ὅσον χρόνον cf. Mark 2:19, 1 Cor 7:39 (same metaphor in mind) and Gal 4:1; see BGD, ὅσος 1. For rabbinic parallels to the idea of death freeing from the law, see Wilckens, 2:64 n.241.

2 ἡ γὰρ ὕπανδρος γυνὴ τῷ ζῶντι ἀνδρὶ δέδεται νόμῳ· ἐὰν δὲ ἀποθάνῃ ὁ ἀνήρ, κατήργηται ἀπὸ τοῦ νόμου τοῦ ἀνδρός, "for the married woman is bound by

the law to her husband while he lives [literally, 'the living husband']; but if
the husband dies, she is released from the law of her husband." Here it
becomes evident that Paul is thinking as a Jew in terms of the Jewish law.
In Jewish law the wife was indeed bound to the husband so long as he lived,
since only he had the right of divorce in accordance with Deut 24:1. Paul
would no doubt be aware of the current dispute between the Shammaites
and the Hillelites on the interpretation of that verse, and of the fact that
the dominant view in Jewish society, as reflected also in ben Sira, Philo, and
Josephus, reinforced the husband's rights in the matter (*JPFC* 2:790). Also
indicative of Jewish attitudes is the Mishnah's interest in regulating the transfer
of women from father to husband (Neusner, *Judaism*, 189–90). In Roman
law, on the other hand, marriage could be brought to an end by the free
will of either partner; and indeed by the time of the later republic divorce
by common consent or at the wish of one had become common, "the normal
course in matrimonial affairs" (*OCD*, 650; Carcopino, 95–96, quotation from
96). Moreover, in Roman law a woman was *not* freed from the law of her
husband by his death, since she was obliged to mourn his death and to remain
unmarried for twelve months; otherwise she would forfeit everything which
had come to her from her first husband (P. E. Corbett, *The Roman Law of
Marriage* [Oxford: Clarendon, 1930; repr. 1969] 249; I am grateful to L. K.
Lo for drawing this to my attention). The very use of ὕπανδρος, "under the
power of or subject to a man" (BGD) betokens the more Jewish attitude,
since it hardly appears in nonbiblical literature before this (Polybius 10.26.3),
but is used six times in the LXX (Num 5:20, 29; Prov 6:24, 29; Sir 9:9; 41:21);
see also Str-B, 3:234. On the status of women in more general terms see on
16:2. For καταργέω see on 6:6.

ὁ νόμος τοῦ ἀνδρός, "the law of the husband," is a somewhat tortuous phrase.
Its basic meaning is clear: the law which gives the husband such authority
over his wife (ὕπανδρος); cf. Lietzmann. To take "husband" in apposition
with "law" (Barrett) is unnecessarily forced; see further Cranfield. But perhaps
Paul is already looking to the application of the metaphor—the law which is
on the side of the husband and which holds the wife in subjection; see on
7:4.

3 ἄρα οὖν ζῶντος τοῦ ἀνδρὸς μοιχαλὶς χρηματίσει ἐὰν γένηται ἀνδρὶ ἑτέρῳ,
"so then while the husband lives, she will be named adulteress if she becomes
another man's." μοιχαλίς again betokens a Jewish perspective: the word is
not attested outside the Judeo-Christian tradition prior to this period, but
appears several times in the LXX (Prov 18:22a; 24:55 [MT 30:20]; Ezek
16:38; 23:45; Hos 3:1; Mal 3:5; also *T. Levi* 14.6), and significantly in Matt
12:39; 16:4; James 4:4 (also Mark 8:38; 2 Pet 2:14), but only in this verse
in Paul. Precisely because the husband had such authority over his wife in
Jewish law and society (see on 7:2) the word contains a strong note of shame
and guilt as denoting one who has been particularly disloyal and false. For
χρηματίζω in the sense of "bear a name, be called or named," cf. particularly
Acts 11:26 (BGD); also *hap. leg.* for the Pauline corpus; for the future indicative
as gnomic future, see BDF, §349.1.

ἐὰν δὲ ἀποθάνῃ ὁ ἀνήρ, ἐλευθέρα ἐστὶν ἀπὸ τοῦ νόμου, "but if the husband
dies, she is free from the law"—not "free from the husband." The imagery

of 6:18–22 is still strongly in Paul's mind, with, once again, the clear implication that the law belongs with sin as the power which dominates the age of Adam and from which deliverance is necessary. Jones, 119–22, notes the difference at this point from 1 Cor 7:39 and argues that the addition ("free *from the law*") marks a development in Paul's thinking (despite Gal 4:1–10, 21–31; 5:1) (he thinks 1 Cor was written before Gal).

τοῦ μὴ εἶναι αὐτὴν μοιχαλίδα γενομένην ἀνδρὶ ἑτέρῳ, "so that she is no adulteress in becoming another man's." Paul evidently has the wording of Deut 24:2 in mind (γένηται ἀνδρὶ ἑτέρῳ); see also Cranfield, 333 n.5. Since γίνομαι + dative denotes belonging to someone (cf. Ostraka II 1530—τὸ γινόμενόν μοι = what belongs to me, cited in BGD, γίνομαι II.3), the characteristic Jewish note of husband's authority over wife is sustained to the end of the metaphor.

4 ὥστε, ἀδελφοί μου, "so then, my brothers." For ὥστε as introducing an independent sentence rather than a subordinate clause ("for this reason, therefore"), see BDF, §391, and BGD, 1a. The implication is that Paul intends to draw a conclusion from the principle stated in v 1 and illustrated in vv 2–3, rather than to apply the illustration point by point (see e.g., Nygren, Murray, and Cranfield). The repetition of the personal address ("my brothers") reemphasizes the sensitivity of the subject (v 1); the implication is clear that Paul feels the law to be the most delicate of the issues with which he has to deal.

καὶ ὑμεῖς ἐθανατώθητε τῷ νόμῳ, "you also were put to death in relation to the law." The choice of ἐθανατώθην rather than ἀπέθανον is presumably deliberate. Not that a sharp distinction between them should be inferred, in view of the parallel between v 4 and v 6 and between v 4 and Gal 2:19. But the former is stronger, as 8:13 certainly indicates ("put to death"). In so writing Paul certainly wants to emphasize divine initiative, meaning "put to death by God" (divine passive), an idea fully equivalent to the passives in 6:3–6. What is in view is the same epochal shift in the ages as was outlined in 5:12–21, as an action accomplished by God, and the individual's participation in it as likewise effected by God. Here again we should recall that the metaphorical reality of dying to sin and dying with Christ is larger than baptism (see on 6:2), so that the reference here should not be restricted to baptism (even if it includes baptism), any more than the conclusion of v 4 should be restricted by tying it too tightly to the preceding illustration; contrast, e.g., Gaugler; Käsemann; Schlier; Robinson, *Wrestling*, 77–78; Halter, 93, 96; Zeller.

A second reason why Paul may choose the stronger word is that he wants to indicate some distance between the preceding illustration and the application of the principle of v 1 being made here: a husband's dying in the normal course of nature is *not* the same as the believer's being put to death by God, even though both deaths illustrate in different ways the same point about death ending the lordship of the law. Presumably the καὶ ὑμεῖς is intended to have the same force—"you too" (in addition to vv 2–3) illustrate the point of v 1 (but differently). Thus immediately Paul shows that he envisages this dying of his Roman readers not as an application of vv 2–3 but as a further exposition of v 1. To assume that Paul was unconscious of these differences and inadvertently allowed his exposition to fall into muddle and confusion (Lietzmann; Dodd; Knox; Gale, 192–96; Räisänen, *Law*, 61) is therefore somewhat unfair to Paul; see also particularly Cranfield and Little.

The τῷ νόμῳ is usually taken as a dative of disadvantage (BDF, §188.2). The "with reference to the law" has the same sense as in the preceding verses—the law as wielding authority and domination over man during this life, or (in epochal terms) during the life of this age. It is that plight and condition which Christ's death brought to an end both for himself (6:10) and for those identified with him (6:3–6), so that to live "under the law" (6:14) is to deny the epochal significance of Christ's death. Note once again, however, that "the law" has replaced "sin" (6:2, 10) as the focus of the discussion (see on 7:1), the law in its authority over this age as the ally of sin (cf. Nygren).

διὰ τοῦ σώματος τοῦ Χριστοῦ, "through the body of Christ." In view of the parallelism with the thought of 6:2 ff. it is clear that Paul has in mind the crucified Christ (cf. particularly Col 1:22: ἀποκατήλλαξεν ἐν τῷ σώματι τῆς σαρκὸς αὐτοῦ διὰ τοῦ θανάτου, "he reconciled in the body of his flesh through death"; also Heb 10:5, 10; 1 Pet 2:24); cf. NEB—"by becoming identified with the body of Christ." To see here a eucharistic reference as in 1 Cor 10:16 (cf. Wilckens) or an ecclesiological reference as in 12:5 (e.g., Dodd; Robinson, *Body*, 47; Nygren) runs the risk of broadening the thought too far at this stage and of missing the force of the divine passive as well as of weakening the reference to the once-for-all epochal event of Christ's death. Only by sharing in that (however it be achieved) can the believer be said to have been put to death in reference to the law which dominates life in this age (cf. Lightfoot; Jewett 299–300). We should perhaps give weight to the definite article (*the* Christ) and recognize thereby a more titular force to the name: the crucified one as the Messiah is a claim the first Christians had had to work hard to establish (cf. 8:35; 9:3, 5; 14:18; 15:3, 7, 19; 16:16).

εἰς τὸ γενέσθαι ὑμᾶς ἑτέρῳ, "in order that you might become another's." The εἰς + infinitive here denotes purpose (as already in 1:11; 3:26; 4:11, 16, 18). Although he is not intent to apply the illustration of vv 2–3 in a complete way to believers, Paul is happy to pick up part of its imagery and language since it expresses so well the idea of transfer of lordship (see on 7:3). Cf. particularly 2 Cor 5:15.

τῷ ἐκ νεκρῶν ἐγερθέντι, "him who was raised from the dead." The use of the established formula (see on 6:4) is not simply a reflection of liturgical language but underscores the point that the effectiveness of Christ's epochal act was not only his dying (to sin and law) but also his resurrection. Salvation is effected by the believer's being given to share both in Christ's death and in his resurrection. It should be noted, however, that as in 6:4 the parallel between the believer's sharing in Christ's death and experiencing his risen life is not complete: they were identified with Christ in his death; but they are married to (not yet wholly identified with) the risen Christ. Paul takes some pleasure in the thought of marriage as a metaphor for the intimate relation between Christ and the believer (cf. particularly 1 Cor 6:17; 2 Cor 11:2; cf. Eph 5:25–33), not unnaturally in view of the popularity of its usage by the prophets to describe the relation between Israel and her covenant God (e.g., Isa 54:5–6; 62:4–5; Jer 2:2; Ezek 16:7–8; Hos 1:2; 2:19).

ἵνα καρποφορήσωμεν τῷ θεῷ, "in order that we might bear fruit to God." How little Paul is governed by the preceding illustration (vv 2–3) is indicated by his readiness to recall the further metaphor of 6:21–22, itself caught up in the metaphor of slavery. The metaphor of fruitbearing is sufficiently familiar in the sense "appropriate outcome" (see on 1:13 and 6:21), and so here of moral result (BGD, καρποφορέω; particularly Col 1:10), that it is neither necessary nor appropriate to give it a special sense of childbearing as a way of pressing for more points of contact with vv 2–3 (Denney; Bruce; Gale, 197–98; Cranfield; against SH; Barrett; T. W. Manson; Black, who construes the sense as "married to Christ to bear God's children"[!]; Derrett distorts the obvious sense by taking God as the husband throughout). That the fruit is "for God" underlines the sustained theocentricity of Paul's soteriology (cf. Thüsing, 96–101). For the transition from second person to first, cf. 6:15; but here the thought is also of their (referring to Gentiles in general?) becoming Christians as fruit of Paul's gentile mission (1:13; Phil 1:22; Col 1:6), and possibly too of their mutual interdependence in ministry and daily life (cf. 12:3–8). In this case also Paul sustains the sense of personal involvement through to v 7.

5 ὅτε γὰρ ἦμεν ἐν τῇ σαρκί, "for when we were in the flesh." This is clearly a description of their preChristian position and experience. However, the phrase ἐν (τῇ) σαρκί should not be regarded as a fixed designation of the preconversion state, since Paul can elsewhere speak of his own experience as a believer as ἐν σαρκί (Gal 2:20; Phil 1:22; so also 1 Pet 4:2; *Diogn.* 5.8). Nor is the weight of the negative attaching to it by any means constant, as we can see from the fact that in 8:4–9 ἐν σαρκί is equivalent to κατὰ σάρκα (see on 8:8), while in 2 Cor 10:3 it has a more nearly neutral sense in contrast to the latter. Like σάρξ itself, the phrase ἐν σαρκί in Paul has a range of meaning from the "merely" physical (2 Cor 4:11; Gal 4:14; Col 2:1), through the more explicit sense of human weakness (Rom 7:18; 8:3), to the open connotation of complete contrast and opposition to God (8:8, 9; Philem 16; though to talk of σάρξ even here as "unqualifiedly evil" [Murray], or as a "description of sin itself" [Ridderbos, *Paul*, 103] is unjustified and unwise). One key to proper exegesis, therefore, is to recognize that the physical-moral connotations are all part of a continuum of meaning, not disjunct and distinct meanings, with the precise weighting of physical and moral meaning dependent on the context; and always with some negative overtone—sometimes stronger, sometimes less strong, flesh almost always (cf. Phil 1:24) denoting the weakness and corruptibility of the creature which distances him from the Creator (see further on 1:3 and 7:18; also particularly Sand, *Fleisch*, and *EWNT* 3:549–52). The closest parallels are in DSS: 1QS 11.7, 9, 12; 1QM 4.3; 1QH 4.29–30; 7.17; 9.16; 15.12, 21.

A second key to proper exegesis is to recall that Paul does not think of being "in the flesh" in merely individual terms. On the contrary, "in the flesh" is one of Paul's chief ways of characterizing his own people's failing: they trust "in the flesh" and boast "in the flesh" (Phil 3:3–4; Gal 6:13); they regard the national badge of circumcision "in the flesh" as what marks them off from the Gentiles as God's chosen people (Rom 2:28; also Eph 2:11). That this dimension is also in Paul's mind is indicated by the fact that the law is mentioned as closely involved, and probably too by the use of the first person plural. Paul looks back to his own standing and experience before he encountered the risen Christ and characterizes the typical expression of

Jewish piety as "in the flesh," a misapprehended trust in membership of the covenant people (Käsemann rightly notes that "for Paul the antithesis of letter and Spirit is the same as that of flesh and Spirit"). This whole dimension is completely lost sight of by narrowing translations like "lower nature" (NEB), "sinful nature" (NIV), "natural inclinations" (NJB); as a key theological category in Paul's thought, σάρξ should be given the status of a t.t. and translated "flesh."

Given both ranges of overtone (human weakness; as expressed not least in Israel's boasting), it becomes clear that ἐν σαρκί is not to be defined simply as the mutually exclusive antonym to ἐν Χριστῷ; rather it denotes a condition or attitude which is in contrast to, at odds with, or places restraints upon the ἐν Χριστῷ, and so can describe both the contrast between epochs (Adam/ Christ) and the eschatological tension experienced by the believer, particularly the Jewish believer (see also on 13:14). σάρξ, however, should not be characterized simply as a "power" like sin, death or even law (as by Bultmann, *Theology* 1:201; Schmidt; NIV's "controlled by the sinful nature" is too free), since in contrast to these three, Paul never says ὑπὸ σάρκα (contrast Wilckens). Nor should the antithesis ἐν σαρκί/ἐν Χριστῷ, κατὰ σάρκα/κατὰ πνεῦμα be taken to imply that Christ, Spirit, and flesh are all beings or entities of the same order. On the other hand, if "conditioning context" or "determining condition" would serve as the equivalent to "Machtsphäre," Wilckens would be nearer the mark (see also on 1:4).

τὰ παθήματα τῶν ἁμαρτιῶν, "the sinful passions." Paul's use of πάθημα parallels the broader Greek usage of the time (see LSJ, BGD). Of the 9 occurrences in the Pauline corpus 7 have the sense "suffering, misfortune" (see on 8:18). But here and in Gal 5:24 it is the sense "emotion, feelings, affections" which is clearly in mind, and in a bad sense—so "passions" (as in Plutarch, *Mor.* 1128E); cf. the ambiguity possible in the German "Leidenschaften." Paul does not suspect the emotions per se or wish them suppressed in the Christian life (contrast, after all, Gal 5:22–23); but he is all too aware of their unreliability and volatility in themselves. A life ruled by or lived chiefly on the level of the παθήματα is almost certain to be a tool manipulated by sin (cf. 1:24, ἐπιθυμία). Unusually in Romans ἁμαρτία is used here in the plural, clearly in the sense "sinful acts" (see on 3:9). The genitive is obviously genitive of content ("passions which are sins") or genitive of direction ("passions which come to expression in or as sins"); see BDF, §§166–67.

τὰ διὰ τοῦ νόμου ἐνηργεῖτο ἐν τοῖς μέλεσιν ἡμῶν, "which operate through the law were effective in our constituent parts." The ἐνηργεῖτο must be intended as the verb of the principal clause, leaving τὰ διὰ τοῦ νόμου as a verbless phrase qualifying τὰ παθήματα. "The law" here is once again clearly the Torah (see on 7:1); Paul again evidently regards his experience as a devout Jew, as now perceived by him, as typical of a condition destined for death. διὰ τοῦ νόμου as elsewhere in Romans denotes the divinely intended function of the law, the agency of the law in accordance with God's will (2:12; 3:20, 27; 4:13; 7:7; cf. also Gal 2:19, 21). This astonishing statement is part of a mounting climax in which Paul unfolds his understanding of the law's true role. Having retrieved it from the misunderstanding of his fellow Jews (2:12–29; 3:27–31; 4:13–16), he has at the same time redefined its role with increasing sharpness (3:20; 4:15; 5:13, 20). Now he begins to unfold the most contentious part of his understanding of the law's role. He will safeguard it from misunderstanding (7:7–14), but has still sharper claims to make as he shows how God has allowed the law to be an agent in the service of sin and death (7:21–23; 8:2). Implicit is the assertion that Jewish misunderstanding and abuse of the law was itself an example of how the law served as an agent to produce sinful passions like the boastful presumption which excluded Gentiles as Gentiles from grace. The middle ἐνεργέω, "be at work, operate, be effective," always has an impersonal subject in our literature (BGD). For μέλος see on 6:13.

εἰς τὸ καρποφορῆσαι τῷ θανάτῳ, "so as to bear fruit for death." The εἰς + infinitive here probably denotes purpose and not merely result (Kühl, Schmidt; otherwise Lagrange, Cranfield, Schlier). It is the divine purpose which the law serves in ensuring that sins do not outlast death or that sin should not exercise its power beyond death. The cancer of sin having taken terminal hold on the body of this epoch, God consigns that body to death in order that the life of the resurrection epoch might be wholly free from sin. For καρποφορέω, repeated from 7:4, and elsewhere in Paul only in Col 1:6, 10, see on 7:4. θάνατος here does double service as a power ruling over man in this epoch (in antithesis to God in v 4), and as the fruit itself, the end product of the sinful passions being given unrestricted sway in the bodily existence of this life (as in 6:21, 23). The characteristic note of the inexorable link between sin and death is maintained and reemphasized (5:12, 21; 6:20–23). Michel justifiably compares the sense of disillusion over the failure of the law to prevent sin in *4 Ezra* 3.20–22 and contrasts Paul's conclusion in v 6 with *4 Ezra*'s in 9.36–37: "we who have received the law and sinned will perish. . . .; the law, however, does not perish but remains in its glory."

6 νυνὶ δὲ κατηργήθημεν ἀπὸ τοῦ νόμου, "but now we have been released from the law." Once again the eschatological and conversion-initiation νυνὶ (as in 3:21 and 6:22). The rest of the phrase is repeated from 7:2 (for καταργέω see on 6:6). Paul thus evokes the illustration of vv 2–3 and sums up the point it illustrated—life in the old epoch as life under the law in the double sense: life as regulated by the law at all points (what Paul's Jewish contemporaries would have regarded as a true and *positive* description of covenant status), and life dominated by the sinful passions and headed for death as so determined by the law. To confine the reference to "the law's condemnation" (Cranfield) narrows Paul's point too much; on the other hand, to state that for Paul the Torah itself is done away (Käsemann) is too bold.

ἀποθανόντες ἐν ᾧ κατειχόμεθα, "having died to that in/by which we were confined/restrained." The syntax is awkward, but the meaning is plain enough. To avoid tautology Paul has simply elided the dative following ἀποθανόντες. The ἐν ᾧ obviously refers to the law (as most recognize), not to the "old man" (6:6, SH), or the being "in the flesh" just described (Zahn, Lagrange). Having used θανατόω in v 4 Paul reverts to his more regular ἀποθνῄσκω (as in 6:2, 10); see on 7:4. It is not easy to ascertain the precise connotation of κατέχω, since the root meaning "hold down" (κατὰ ἔχω) can be extended to a wide range of usages—hold back, restrain, arrest; possess, suppress, confine; hold fast, retain, keep in mind; and so on (see LSJ). The sense here is obviously of restraint; what is unclear from the word itself is the severity of the restraint. Since the imagery of the preceding chapter is obviously in mind (including that of slavery) what Paul has in view is most probably the restraint of slavery. A slave is so little his own master that his situation is no different from that of a prisoner (BGD's "by which we were bound" is too strong; similarly NEB, NIV, NJB); those who have not perceived and entered into the epochal effects of Christ's death and resurrection are still locked into the old epoch and its trajectory toward death. In this one phrase Paul synthesizes two of the important emphases of Galatians: conversion-initiation as "dying to the law" and the situation of Israel prior to faith as one of restraint and slavery (Gal 2:19; 3:23–26; 4:1–3).

ὥστε δουλεύειν ἡμᾶς, "so that we might serve." The ὥστε denotes, of course, not fortuitous consequence, but intended result (see further SH). The δουλεύειν recalls the starkness of the emphasis in 6:18 and 22: the liberation from the law's restraint is *not* into an anarchic or self-chosen freedom, but into a different kind of slavery and service—to God. Man is always servant, never more so than when he thinks he is master. The ἡμᾶς reminds us that Paul does not see his experience "under the law" as any different from the slavery from which the gospel had delivered his readers.

ἐν καινότητι πνεύματος καὶ οὐ παλαιότητι γράμματος, "in newness of Spirit and not in oldness of letter." The echo and combination of earlier antitheses is most probably intentional:

>   2:29:   περιτομὴ καρδίας ἐν πνεύματι οὐ γράμματι·
>   6:4, 6: οὕτως καὶ ἡμεῖς ἐν καινότητι ζωῆς περιπατήσωμεν . . .
>   τοῦτο γινώσκοντες ὅτι ὁ παλαιὸς ἡμῶν ἄνθρωπος συνεσταυρώθη.

The double antithesis (γράμμα/πνεῦμα; παλαιότης/καινότης), all the more emphatic for its doubling, expresses a theme which is obviously of considerable importance for Paul: the designation of the period prior to Christ as the *old* epoch (παλαιός —see on 6:6), as the epoch of narrowed and too superficial understanding of God's righteousness—as expressed not least in Jewish Christian insistence that circumcision is inseparable from righteousness (γράμμα —see on 2:29); and the eschatological newness of the epoch introduced by Christ (καινότης —6:4) as marked by the Spirit, that is, by the gift of the Spirit and by life lived in terms of the Spirit (πνεῦμα —see on 5:5 and 8:9). The thought is closely parallel to the argument already developed in 2 Cor 3, where the γράμμα/πνεῦμα antithesis is also central (3:6) to the distinction between old and new covenant (παλαιὰ/καινὴ διαθήκη —3:6, 14) and bound up with the thought of service (2 Cor 3:6–9), with the prophetic promises of Jer 31:31–34 and Ezek 36:26–27 fairly obvious in the background. As the implied contrast of 6:4 also indicated (see on 6:4), Paul evidently has in mind an ethically responsible lifestyle which in its immediacy of direct awareness of what is the ethically responsible conduct stands in sharp contrast to his old pattern of living "by the book." To order one's life by constant reference to the Torah in typically Pharisaic style Paul now sees to be a stifling and destructive experience ("the letter kills!"—2 Cor 3:6); in sharp contrast, to "walk according to the Spirit" (cf. Rom 6:4; 7:6; 8:4) evidently had been and was for him a liberating and vitalizing experience (see further on 8:4; also Dunn, *Baptism*, 146–47). With such an emphasis, there is, of course, a danger of opening the door to the excesses of enthusiasm; it should be noted, therefore, that Paul thinks of the "service" of the Spirit at this point not in terms of spiritual experiences but primarily in ethical terms (as the parallel with 6:4 and the general context makes clear; see also on 12:1–2, and Dunn, *Jesus*, 222–25). On the ambiguity of πνεῦμα meaning (Holy) Spirit or (human) spirit, see on 8:16 (NEB and NJB use lower case). As has long been recognized, the γράμμα/πνεῦμα antithesis should not be taken in the sense "literal (meaning)/spiritual (meaning)" of the OT (see, e.g., SH); that would make too little sense of καινότης, and loses sight of the epochal contrast between the old covenant/age and new so fundamental to Paul.

Explanation

It is important to realize that there is no real break in the flow of argument at this point; the talk of "lordship" in v 1, the continuing treatment of "death," and the metaphors of "fruitbearing" in vv 4–5 and of servitude in v 6, all carry forward themes prominent in the second half of chap. 6. Nevertheless, a new phase in the discussion is clearly introduced in 7:1 by the "Do you not know," signaled particularly by the abrupt reintroduction of talk of "the law." Paul's attempt to explore the ethical corollaries and eschatological tension bound up in his gospel has been fairly straightforward so far, largely because he has posed it simply in terms of sin and death, or, expressed more fully, in terms of the twin antitheses sin and grace, death and life: Christ died to sin and rose again to life; you have already come to share in that death and to experience something of that risen life, although your full participation in Christ's resurrection is not yet; so live in the light of and in the strength of that triple sharing (past, present, future), for so to live is to live by grace.

However, the whole matter is complicated by the third element, which the conclusion to the previous section had lumped together with sin and death, viz., the law. There too, in chap. 5, Paul had developed the sin/grace, death/life antitheses as far as possible without reference to the law (5:15–19), before reintroducing the law to the picture (5:20). So in chap. 6 he has attempted to elaborate the ethical corollaries and eschatological tension implicit in the gospel with as little reference to the law as possible. This was not, we may presume, because he thought the law was irrelevant to these issues; rather, he saw the law as a complicating factor which *confused* these issues, as shown not least by the majority of his Jewish contemporaries, whose spiritual perception had in his view been blunted rather than sharpened by their devotion to the law (chap. 2). When the ethical consequences of faith in Christ were posed in terms of the sharp contrasts between sin and grace, death and life, law had to be counted on the side of sin and death (5:20; 6:14–15). But if the contrasts are not so mutually exclusive as the antitheses seem to imply when taken at face value, if the believer has to reckon with the ongoing reality of the eschatological tension, if sin is still a candidate for the believer's loyalty and life has not yet conquered death in the believer (because he has yet to share fully in Christ's resurrection), then where does the law fit into that more complex picture? Having simplified (perhaps oversim-plified, if some later interpretations of chap. 6 are any indication) the typical moral choice confronting the believer in order to bring out its character as choice, Paul now reintroduces the law and prepares to grapple with the in-creased complexity it brings to the discussion.

7:1 Without striving for a smoother transition, Paul addresses his Roman readership as "those who know the law." Almost certainly they would take him to mean the Jewish law, the Torah, this having been the exclusive reference of the word hitherto. Having "lain low" through the preceding chapter the issue of the law is drawn once again on to center stage.

The basic point of law to which Paul appeals is the fact that a person is subject to the law so long as he lives. The language of "lordship" recalls the use of the same verb ("is master over, controls") in 6:9 and 14—there of the rule of death and of sin. Not surprisingly, in view of 5:20, the same language is now used of the law; for the law is the third member of the fearful triumvirate which strengthens the lordship of the other two, sin and death. The point made is in effect a recapitulation of one side of the exposition as developed in chap. 6: that is, so long as a person has not yet died he is still subject to the rule of sin and death, and now, Paul adds, also of the law. Christ died, once for all, and so is no longer subject to the mastery of sin and death (6:9–10), and so also no longer subject to the mastery of the law. The believer, however, is suspended between Christ's death and resurrection, and so to that extent has not yet escaped from the situation where sin and death can still lay claim to him. What then of the law's claim on him? It is unbroken, "so long as he lives." There is the ground of hope, but also (in the meantime of the "not yet") the somewhat sobering reality. The neat, sharply defined lines of 6:22–23 are already becoming less clear.

2–3 The point of law is illustrated by the case of the married woman. Under Jewish law, once married to her husband she was bound to him, and there was no way provided by the Torah for her to end that relationship prior to his death. Only when he died was she released from that law which bound her to him. The law governing the marriage relationship became inapplicable and so powerless over the wife as soon as the marriage relationship ceased with the husband's death. The authority and power of the law over the wife is shown by the fact that it names her adulteress, with all the oppro-brium, guilt, and liability to the penalty of death which that word then carried, if she consorts with another man while her husband is still alive. Likewise the way in which the power and authority of that law is completely nullified and rendered inoperative by the husband's death is shown by the fact that once her husband is dead the same woman can do precisely the same thing without incurring any name or blame of adultery. There is a death which liberates from the lordship of sin (6:9–10, 18); so there is a death which liberates from the lordship of the law.

4 Paul now applies the principle, that death liberates from the lordship of the law. But since he evidently liked the metaphor of marriage to describe the relation between Christ and the believer, he does not let the illustration go completely. So in developing the basic point he carries forward not only the idea of dying to the law (v 4), but also of union with another, the risen

Christ (v 4), and of being set free from the law which held in check (v 6). However, it is not necessary to push for further points of contact with the illustration (vv 2–3), nor does it follow that Paul intended the illustration to document the changing status of the believer (= the woman freed by the death of her husband). Which is also to say that there is no compulsion in the illustration itself or in Paul's allusion to it to attempt an identification of the believer's former partner—sin, law, the old nature, or whatever. Had Paul intended such an allegorical identification he could easily have made it clear. Such an interpretation tends to be over-fussy and to complicate the basic point. More serious still, such concern about the possible identity of the believer's first partner draws attention away from what might be called the real anomaly, namely, that the only one who has really died is the new partner, Christ! The fact is that the illustration is *not* one of the believer's transition from one state to another, but of the basic principle that death liberates from the law. And the extent, or rather the *limited* extent to which the illustration *is* drawn in to describe the believer shows Paul's consciousness that the reality is much more complex. The paradox thus emerges: it is not by allegorizing the illustration to make it speak of the believer's situation that we hear Paul's teaching most clearly, but by noting where the illustration does *not* fit with the believer's reality.

The real tension in the applicability of the illustration is that it highlights, as the first half of chap. 6 did, only the dying of the believer. "You died to the law through the body of Christ." The phrase would hardly be understood as anything other than a reference to the exposition two or three paragraphs earlier (6:3–6). "The body of Christ" is clearly Christ in his bodily crucifixion, by which he escaped sin and death (6:7, 9), and so also the law. The Roman believers likewise are liberated from "the body of sin" (6:6) and so also from the law, precisely by virtue of their identification with Christ in that death. Any readers tempted to allegorize the illustration would thus see how quickly the allegory is thrown into confusion. For whereas in the illustration the wife does not die, in the reality described in v 4 the believers *have* died. There is no part or aspect of any believer which is remote from the death of Christ (if there was it would still be under the dominion of sin and the law!). On the contrary, it is only by virtue of their complete union with Christ in his death that it is possible for them to be united with the risen Christ.

Moreover, once again there is no reference to the believer as having already risen with Christ. Christ has died and each believer has died through the body of Christ; Christ has been raised from the dead, but not yet the believer (the structure of 7:4 is remarkably like that of 6:4 at this point). It is, we might say, the *dead* believer who is united with Christ; only insofar as he has been and still is (6:5) united with Christ in his death can he be married to the risen Christ. Thus once again the Roman Christians would recognize the clear sense implicit that they are suspended as it were between Christ's death and Christ's resurrection: their identification with Christ is such that union with Christ does not extend to full participation in his resurrection; they can be recipients of Christ's risen life and power in some measure through their union with Christ now risen, but the harsh reality of their present state is that the rule of death is not yet fully broken. And that means that sin and law still threaten, and still exercise control over any dimension of their existence without the liberating power of Christ's death. The principle remains firm: Christ's death liberates the believer from sin and law insofar as he is one with Christ in his death—but only "insofar as."

That all this is not mere theory or an idealized picture of the life of faith is indicated by the easily overlooked switch from second person to first ("that you might become another's . . . in order that we might bear fruit to God"). Paul cannot distance himself from all this talk of sharing Christ's death and experiencing his risen life; it is too much an existential reality for him as well. The fruitbearing, like the walking in newness of life of 6:4, can also be described as "sanctification" (6:22). But in broadening the reference out to include himself at just this point, Paul may also have in mind the fruitbearing which was his as an apostle (cf. 1:13), as he saw Gentile converts draw deep resources from their union with Christ and blossom in lives given to God and in the love of God.

5 Vv 5–6 continue to recapitulate the main thrust of chap. 6 but with the role of the law integrated and clarified. But Paul also takes the opportunity to reintroduce another word whose occasional use earlier gave little enough hint of its importance for Paul's thought (as later in chap. 7 and particularly 8:1–13 will reveal)—"flesh." What he has described at the beginning of the previous section as "our old man" and "the body of sin" (6:6) he now describes as being "in the flesh," as a characterization of his own and his readers' preconversion state or condition: "For when we were in the flesh . . . ." Paul would hardly intend the Roman congregations to think that as believers they were now "*out of* the flesh," certainly not in the most obvious face-value sense of that phrase (= disembodied spirits). Conversion had not involved the shedding or transformation of their mortal bodies (6:12). That was part of the "not yet," to be completed at the still future resurrection (6:5; cf. 8:11, 23). So "in the flesh" clearly has a narrower reference here. But neither could Paul be thinking simply of a moral state from which believers have wholly escaped through conversion. For he does not think of "the flesh" as falling into two clearly distinct compartmentalized meanings (physical and moral). On the contrary, it is precisely the weakness and appetites of "the mortal body" (= the flesh) which are the occasion for sin (= being in the flesh), as he has already reminded them (6:12–13). "When we were in the flesh" therefore must mean "in the flesh" as prior to and exclusive of being "in Christ," "in the flesh" as a kind of living dominated or characterized by the weakness and appetites of this life, exemplified not least in Paul's own people's presumption in their election (2:17–29), as a condition or state now superseded or at least complemented by their also "being in Christ." So the implicit qualification within the phrase "when we were in the flesh" would prevent the reader from thinking that Paul here envisaged (by contrast) a form of Christian existence free from the tension between the old life "in the flesh" and the new life "in Christ." Confusion would only arise when anyone forgot that Paul was here still continuing the clear-cut contrasts of chap. 6 for the sake of sharpening the moral choice when the general exhortations had to be worked out in reference to specific issues.

The description of what characterized their previous life "in the flesh" provides the clearest echoes of the preceding exhortation, with almost every word or phrase paralleled in 6:12–23: "sinful passions" (6:12), "the law" (6:14–15), "in our members" (6:13, 19), "to bear fruit for death" (6:21). One difference is that what 7:5 refers to their preconversion state, 6:12 envisaged as still a possibility for the Roman Christians; but the careful reader would have been unlikely to read the paraenetically sharpened contrasts as ontological antitheses, as we have already seen. The more important difference for Paul's argument is that now in 7:5 the role of the law is integrated into the description of their preconversion state, its role as an active factor in interaction with sin and death given some further clarification—"our sinful passions which are through the law were effective in our members to bear fruit for death." That sin brought forth death would have been clear to all, and Paul's earlier statements to that effect would have raised no eyebrows among an audience so familiar with the Jewish scriptures (5:12; 6:16, 20–21). But that the law had a part in this, rather than opposing sin or deflecting the power of sin through its sacrificial ritual, such a claim must have been shocking even to God-worshipers who had not gone all the way with the cultic requirements of the law to become proselytes. Paul had already spoken of the law in the more passive role of defining sin, as showing sin to be sin, as causing it to be reckoned as sin (3:20; 4:15; 5:13). He had even said that the law caused the transgression (of Adam) to increase, by showing the words and deeds of Adamic man to be transgression, born of sin, by opening the possibility for the covenant people to rest in the law rather than trust in God (5:20). But now he speaks with deceptive simplicity of "passions of sin which come about through the law." What does he mean?

Paul's brevity allows his point to be easily misunderstood. For he does not assign the law to the realm and epoch of sin and death *simpliciter* as though the law was simply one with sin and death. Despite 6:14–15, he evidently does not want the law to be regarded as a negative power from which the believer has escaped (cf. again 3:31). Thus in v 5 he does not simply suggest that the law is the *source* of the sinful passions: their definition as "sinful" may be derived from the law, their character as "sinful" confirmed by the law, but that is not the same thing. Yet at the same time "through the law" must involve more than a passive role of definition for the law. Paul clearly implies that the law played a part in the coming about of these sinful passions. That part will come into clearer focus in the following paragraph where the same "through" phrase occurs repeatedly ("through the law," "through the command": vv 7–13). However, so far as v 5 itself is concerned the answer is probably that Paul intended the phrase to qualify the whole process: it is sinful passions through the law which produce the fruit of death. The implication is not that there are other sinful passions, other than those "which are through the law"; though he may possibly imply that there are other passions which are not "passions of sins" as reckoned by the law. The point seems to be rather that it is sinful passions determined as such by the law which are effective in the production of death. The intended inference seems to be that the law reinforces the connection between sin and death; the law has, as it were, a greenhouse effect, forcing the growth of sin to bring forth the fruit of death (cf. 5:20–21, the law increasing the transgression = sin ruling in death; 1 Cor 15:56, death's sting is sin, but the sting gains its fatal potency from the law). If the law stimulates sinful passions it does so with a view to their work of producing death. The effect of the law is to bind sin to death, to prevent sin's *not* leading to death, either because it is not counted as sin, or gives the illusion that a life lived in terms of the sinful passions can somehow evade the final payment of death (cf. Gen 3:4). If this is what Paul means then it at once becomes clearer how it is that Paul can speak both so positively of the law (as he will again shortly in v 12) and yet so negatively within the same argument. The reason is that the law is God's inside agent, his fifth column within the realm of sin and death, seeming to act with these powers, but in fact working on behalf of salvation history to bring about their ruin and the end of their power.

How much of such deeper ramifications would have been apparent to the bulk of Paul's Roman addressees is something we cannot tell. Perhaps it was little enough for those unfamiliar with the apostle's teaching from other sources. Hence possibly also the speed with which he elaborates the more compressed statement of v 5 in vv 7–13. Nevertheless, it is probably significant that Paul can make this statement in first person plural terms—not so much because he chooses to generalize so casually from his own experience, but rather because he can assume a readership in Rome who were sufficiently familiar with the working of the Jewish law and who also had been sufficiently involved within the synagogue to have experienced at least something of the effects of the law for themselves. That is to say, Paul makes his assertion as a simple statement of fact presumably because he can assume that most believers within the gentile mission churches (Jews and Gentiles) would by now have come to recognize how big a part the law had in fact played in the sins of which they were now ashamed (6:21) and in the nexus of sin and death.

6 "But now we have been released from the law, having died to that by which we were confined. . . ." Paul clearly recalls the language of his illustration (vv 2–3). The state prior to the liberating death (that is, sharing Christ's death) was one in which they had been under the law's constraint, confined by law within the realms of sin and death, haltered by the rope which tied sin to death so firmly. But now Christ has died, the new epoch of the eschatological now has been brought in by Christ's death and resurrection. So the nexus of sin and death is broken, but not in the middle, as though sin no longer produced death (as though this purpose of the law had ceased). It is broken rather at the far end. It has been broken because Christ followed the connection through to the end (death)—and beyond. The sting of death has been drawn by having been used on Christ, absorbed by him, its poison exhausted in the death of Christ (1 Cor 15:56). Consequently those who have identified with Christ in his death (Paul still embraces all his readers within the first person plural) have already begun to experience the other side of the dark doorway of death, and have already begun to share in the life which is beyond sin and death, promising the new relation with Christ apart from the old law and free from the law which condemned them to death.

The consequence is not an irresponsible freedom—that would be a reversion to the old epoch with its sinful passions—but a new service (Paul's language recalls the sustained exhortation of 6:16–22), a service characterized by "newness of Spirit and not oldness of letter." Paul's readers might well recall that both elements of this antithesis had already been used once (2:29—Spirit/letter; 6:4, 6—newness/oldness). The effect of bringing them together is to highlight the contrast between the two epochs which underlies the whole section—the old characterized by law, the new by Spirit.

"The oldness of the letter" is clearly a reference to the law; in the context it could hardly be anything else. But not the law as such. It is not the law as such which Paul sees as characterizing the old epoch before Christ, but the law as "letter" (cf. 2 Cor 3:6). As in 2:27–29, Paul presumably means by this the law observed at what he sees as a superficial level, at indeed the level of the flesh (2:28), with obedience to the law understood in terms of the ritual and cultic acts which mark out the chosen people, the law as the "works" done by devout Jews. The implication of the context is that this is another way of describing the law which binds sin to death and shuts up the "wife" on the wrong side of Christ's death. The reader who recognizes the catchword "letter" therefore is meant to understand that the law understood in terms of "works" (as it was by most of Paul's Jewish contemporaries) does not prevent sin or break the bond of sin and death, but is rather another evidence of that bond. For to understand the law as "letter" is to rest content on this side of death with the nexus unbroken, on the wrong side of Christ's death, in the old epoch, resting on law as national privilege when the promise has already gone to all the nations (cf. 4:13–18).

But those who have identified with Christ in his death have been liberated from the vicious spiral of sin, works, death to serve in "newness of Spirit." The reference is probably to the (Holy) Spirit as the mark of the new epoch and distinguishing feature of those who belong to it (cf. 5:5; 8:9–15; Gal 3:1–14). And though the phrase is sufficiently ambiguous to include the idea of a renewed (human) spirit, Paul probably thought of such renewal primarily as the power of God (the Spirit) moving within and through the believer (cf. Ezek 36:26–27). It is much less likely that he intended "spirit" to mean the deeper meaning of scripture underlying the "letter." One of Paul's main points in making the antithesis is precisely that the service of the new epoch is freed from the law, is not intrinsically dependent on any, or repeated, consultation of the written text. On the contrary, the motivation and direction comes immediately from the Spirit within, that is, the obedience from the heart (6:17), the discernment of the renewed mind (12:2). Paul will certainly have at the back of his mind Christians' claim that in their experience the promise of the new covenant given through Jeremiah had been and was being fulfilled (Jer 31:31–34), that they were experiencing the law written in the heart, and knew the Lord with an immediacy which did not depend on the instruction of another (Jer 31:34). Something of the tremendous sense of liberation and renewal which Paul evidently experienced through his conversion is clearly reflected here (cf. 8:2; 2 Cor 3:3, 17; Gal 5:1), as also the inner dynamism which transformed and transcended anything which might be merely derived from or characterized in terms of a written scroll, however sacred (cf. 8:4, 14–15; Gal 5:18; Phil 3:3). This final antithesis between law and Spirit becomes the heading and synopsis for the next two sections: 7:7–25 on the law, and chap. 8 on the Spirit.

2. But the Law Is Still Exploited by Sin and Death, As Experience Demonstrates   (7:7–25)

Bibliography

Althaus, P. "Zur Auslegung von Röm 7:14ff." *TLZ* 77 (1952) 475–80. **Bader, G.** "Römer 7 als Skopus einer theologischen Handlungstheorie." *ZTK* 78 (1981) 31–56. **Banks, R.** "Romans 7:25a: An Eschatological Thanksgiving." *ABR* 26 (1978) 34–42. **Benoit, P.** "The Law and the Cross according to St Paul." *Jesus* 2:11–39. **Bergmeier, R.** "Röm 7:7–25a (8:2): Der Mensch—des Gesetz—Gott—Paulus—die Exegese im Widerspruch?" *KD* 31 (1985) 162–72. **Blank, J.** "Gesetz und Geist." In *Law of Spirit*, ed. Lorenzi, 73–127. Repr. in *Paulus*, 86–123. **Bornkamm, G.** "Sin, Law and Death (Romans 7)." *Experience.* 87–104. **Braun, H.** "Römer 7:7–25 und das Selbstverständnis des Qumran-Frommen." *ZTK* 56 (1959) 1–18. **Bultmann, R.** "Romans 7 and the Anthropology of Paul" (1932). *Existence and Faith.* London: Hodder & Stoughton, 1960. 173–85. **Cambier, J. M.** "Le 'Moi' dans Rom 7." In *Law of Spirit*, ed. Lorenzi. 13–72. **Dahl, N. A.** *Studies.* 92–94. **Davies, W. D.** *Paul.* 20–27. **Dülmen, A. van.** *Theologie.* 106–119, 138–84. **Dunn, J. D. G.** "Rom 7:14–25 in the Theology of Paul." *TZ* 31 (1975) 257–73. **Eichholz, G.** *Theologie.* 251–60. **Ellwein, E.** "Das Rätsel von Römer 7." *KD* 1 (1955) 147–68. **Espy, J. M.** "Paul's 'Robust Conscience' Re-examined." *NTS* 31 (1985) 161–88. **Fung, R. Y. K.** "The Impotence of the Laws: Towards a Fresh Understanding of Romans 7:14–25." In *Scripture, Tradition and Interpretation*, FS E. F. Harrison, ed. W. W. Gasque and W. S. La Sor. Grand Rapids: Eerdmans, 1978. 34–48. **Gundry, R. H.** "The Moral Frustration of Paul before His Conversion: Sexual Lust in Romans 7:7–25." In *Pauline Studies*, FS F. F. Bruce, ed. D. A. Hagner and M. J. Harris. Exeter: Paternoster, 1980. 80–94. **Hahn, F.** "Gesetzesverständnis" 43–47. **Hofius, O.** "Gesetz." 269–72. **Hommel, H.** "Das 7. Kapitel des Römerbriefs im Licht antiker Überlieferung." *ThViat* 8 (1961–62) 90–116. **Hübner, H.** "Anthropologischer Dualismus in den Hodayoth." *NTS* 18 (1971–72) 268–84. ———. *Law.* 70–78. **Jewett, R.** *Anthropological Terms.* 391–401. **Jonas, H.** "Philosophical Meditation on the Seventh Chapter of Paul's Epistle to the Romans." In *The Future of Our Religious Past*, FS R. Bultmann, ed. J. M. Robinson. London: SCM, 1971. 333–50. **Kertelge, K.** "Exegetische Überlegungen zum Verständnis der paulinischen Anthropologie nach Römer 7." *ZNW* 62 (1971) 105–114. **Keuck, W.** "Dienst des Geistes und des Fleisches: Zur Auslegungsgeschichte und Auslegung von Röm 7:25b." *TQ* 141 (1961) 257–80. **Kümmel, W. G.** *Römer 7 und die Bekehrung des Paulus.* Leipzig: Hinrichs, 1929; reissued Munich: Kaiser, 1974. **Kürzinger, J.** "Der Schlüssel zum Verständnis von Röm 7." *BZ* 7 (1963) 270–74. **Luz, U.** *Geschichtsverständnis.* 158–68. **Lyonnet, S.** "L'histoire du salut selon le ch 7 de l'épître aux Romains." *Bib* 43 (1962) 117–51. ———. " 'Tu ne convoiteras pas' (Rom 7:7)." In *Neotestamentica et Patristica*, FS O. Cullmann. NovTSup

6. Leiden: Brill, 1962. 157–65. **Martin, B. L.** "Some Reflections on the Identity of the *ego* in Rom 7:14–25." *SJT* 34 (1981) 39–47. **Mitton, C. L.** "Romans 7 Reconsidered." *ExpT* 65 (1953–54) 78–81, 99–103, 132–35. **Moo, D. J.** "Israel and Paul in Romans 7:7–12." *NTS* 32 (1986) 122–35. **Müller, F.** "Zwei Marginalien im Brief des Paulus an die Römer." *ZNW* 40 (1941) 249–54. **Osten-Sacken, P. von der.** *Römer 8.* 194–220. **Packer, J. I.** "The 'Wretched Man' of Romans 7." *SE* II (1964) 621–27. **Patte, D.** *Paul's Faith.* 263–77. **Perkins, P.** "Pauline Anthropology in Light of Nag Hammadi." *CBQ* 48 (1986) 512–22. **Philonenko, M.** "Sur l'expression 'vendue au péché' dans l'Épître aux Romains." *RHR* 203 (1986) 41–52. **Räisänen, H.** "Zum Gebrauch von ΕΠΙΘΥΜΙΑ und ΕΠΙΘΥΜΕΙΝ bei Paulus." *ST* 33 (1979) 85–99. Repr. in *Torah.* 148–67. ———. "Sprachliches zum Spiel des Paulus mit ΝΟΜΟΣ" (1983). *Torah.* 119–47. ———. *Law.* 109–113, 141–43. **Ridderbos, H.** *Paul.* 126–30. **Sanders, E. P.** *Law.* 73–81. ———. "Romans 7 and the Purpose of the Law." *PIBA* 7 (1983) 44–59. **Schmithals, W.** *Anthropologie.* 25–83. **Schnackenburg, R.** "Römer 7 in Zusammenhang des Römerbriefes." In *Jesus und Paulus,* FS W. G. Kümmel, ed. E. E. Ellis and E. Grässer. Göttingen: Vandenhoeck & Ruprecht, 1975. 283–300. **Schottroff, L.** "Die Schreckensherrschaft der Sünde und die Befreiung durch Christus nach dem Römerbrief des Paulus." *EvT* 39 (1979) 497–510. **Schrage, W.** *Einzelgebote.* 194–96. **Segal, A. F.** "Romans 7 and Jewish Dietary Law." *SR* 15 (1986) 361–74. **Smith, E. W.** "The Form and Religious Background of Romans 7:24–25a." *NovT* 13 (1971) 127–35. **Snodgrass, K.** "Spheres of Influence." 105–7. **Stalder, K.** *Das Werk des Geistes in der Heiligung bei Paulus.* Zürich: EVZ, 1962. 291–307. **Theissen, G.** *Psychological Aspects of Pauline Theology.* Edinburgh: T. & T. Clark, 1987. 177–265. **Watson, F.** *Paul.* 149–56. **Wenham, D.** "The Christian Life: A Life of Tension? A Consideration of the Nature of Christian Experience in Paul." *Pauline Studies,* FS F. F. Bruce, ed. D. A. Hagner and M. J. Harris. Exeter: Paternoster, 1980. 80–94. **Ziesler, J. A.** "The Role of the Tenth Commandment in Romans 7." *JSNT* 33 (1988) 41–56.

Translation

⁷What then shall we say? That the law is sin? Certainly not! Nevertheless, I would not have experienced sin except through the law; for I would not have known covetousness unless the law had said, "You shall not covet." ⁸But sin, seizing its opportunity through the commandment, stirred up all manner of covetousness in me. For in the absence of the law sin is dead. ⁹And in the absence of the law I was alive once upon a time. But when the commandment came, sin became alive, ¹⁰and I died. The commandment intended for life proved for me a means to death. ¹¹For sin, seizing its opportunity through the commandment, deceived me and through it killed me. ¹²So that the law is holy, and the commandment holy and just and good. ¹³Did that which is good, then, become death to me? Certainly not! But sin, that it might appear as sin, through that which is good producing death for me, in order that sin through the commandment might become utterly sinful.

¹⁴For we know[a] that the law is spiritual; but I am fleshly,[b] sold under sin. ¹⁵For I do not know what I do. For that which I commit is not what I want; but what I hate, that I do. ¹⁶But if that which I do is what I do not want, I agree with the law that it is admirable. ¹⁷But now it is no longer I doing this but sin which dwells[c] within me.

¹⁸For I know that there dwells in me, that is, in my flesh, no good thing; for the willing lies ready to my hand, but not[d] the doing of what is admirable. ¹⁹For I fail to do good as I wish, but evil which I do not wish is what I commit. ²⁰But if what I[e] *do not wish is that which I do, it is no longer I doing it but sin which dwells within me.* [21] *I find then the law, in my case wishing to do the good, to be that for me the evil lies ready to hand.* [22] *For I rejoice in the law of God,*[f] *so far as the inner man is concerned,* [23] *but I see another law in my constituent parts at war with the law of my mind and making me a prisoner to*[g] *the law of sin which is in my constituent parts.* [24] *Wretched man am I! Who will deliver me from the body of this death?* [25] *But thanks be to God*[h] *through Jesus Christ our Lord. So then I myself with my mind serve the law of God and with my flesh the law of sin.*[i]

Notes

[a] The possibility of reading οἶδα μέν instead of οἴδαμεν has occasionally been exploited, most recently by Wilckens.

[b] Some MSS read σαρκικός rather than σάρκινος, an understandable confusion of little significance (see BGD, σαρκικός); the opposite variation occurs in 2 Cor 1:12.

[c] The support for ἐνοικοῦσα rather than οἰκοῦσα includes ℵ and B.

[d] The sentence ends unusually with οὔ, which prompted some copyists to add the unnecessary and less effective εὑρίσκω or γινώσκω (see Metzger).

[e] The ἐγώ does not appear here in many MSS.

[f] B reads νοός instead of θεοῦ, a natural slip or, possibly, deliberate alteration in view of v 23.

[g] The ἐν is slightly awkward here (are three laws in view? [cf. Schlatter, 246]), and is increasingly omitted in the MS tradition.

[h] Some early copyists found the thanksgiving here as awkward as many modern scholars and suggested emendations like ἡ χάρις τοῦ θεοῦ to provide a more direct answer to the question of v 24b (see SH, Lietzmann, Metzger).

[i] Speculative emendation in modern times has wished to omit the whole of the last sentence as a gloss. But see *Comment*.

Form and Structure

With v 7 the crucial issue is posed: has Paul's treatment of the law, particularly in the climactic summary of 5:20, consigned the law to sin, as a power to be redeemed from, and so without positive reference for the believer? The fact that Paul himself poses the question shows that one reading of his treatment of the law thus far could force that question to the fore; but it also implies that Paul regards such a reading as too simplistic. It is clear from the question itself that Paul intends what follows as a defense of the law. A structural analysis helps clarify the line of defense.

vv 7–13   first defense of the law: sin is the real culprit;
vv 14–17   second defense of the law: blame is shifted
              from the law to the self and then again to
              sin;
vv 18–20   an explanation of how sin works (i) through
              the divided "I"
vv 21–23   and (ii) through the divided law.

It should be noted that v 13 does not only conclude vv 7–13, but serves as a transition and introduction to the next section also, in accordance with Paul's usual style (cf. particularly 3:20 and 5:21); the γάρs of vv 14–15 are intended to bring out that connection. V 13b therefore provides a heading

(*Überschrift*) for vv 14–23 (Wilckens, 2:85, 100); see also on 5:20–21 *Form and Structure*.

More important for exegesis, the parallel between vv 14–17 and 18–23 has been given insufficient attention: the analysis in each case is largely the same, with the explanation of the "I" 's failure attributed to sin in both cases (vv 14–17, 18–20), but with the positive affirmation of the law in v 16 answered by the fuller statement of vv 21–23. The effect is to explain the law's role in the same terms as the role of the "I": the divided state of *both* exempts *both* from blame and explains how both are used by the real culprit, sin.

The passage is therefore rightly to be reckoned an apology for the law (e.g., Kümmel, *Römer,* 7; Stendahl, *Paul,* 92; Beker, *Paul,* 105; against Käsemann; Bergmeier; and Watson, *Paul,* 151, 153, 155). It stands as the apology for the law, in fact, which his previous treatment of this major counterpoint theme had made necessary. The usual rendering of νόμος in vv 21, 23 as "general rule" or "principle" (see on 7:21) not only obscures the point but actually distorts and abandons one of Paul's major concerns, namely, to show that there is a function of the law in which it is the tool of sin and death, but that the law as the law of God is exempt from that charge. The clear implication for anyone who has followed this main counterpoint theme throughout is that this abuse of the law by sin and death is the same as, or equivalent in effect to, the abuse of the law indicted in chap. 2 and countered in 3:27–4:25; while "the law of God, the law of the mind" is the law understood in terms of faith, with the obedience of faith, from the heart (1:5; 2:29; 3:31; 6:17). The law as boasted in by "the Jew" is the law functioning within the old age of Adam, as against the law functioning in its properly intended and now eschatological role in the age of Christ.

A psychologizing interest in the "I" (cf. particularly Dodd; Theissen, *Psychological Aspects,* chap. 13) is only of secondary interest, but the logic of the argument and the structure of the three chapters (7:7–25, parallel to 6:12–23 and 8:10–30) are sufficient indication that Paul has in view the eschatological tension of the present stage of salvation history, with both the "I" and the "law" divided between the two ages of Adam and Christ in a period when these two ages overlap. Hence the cry of 7:24 is one of frustration (not of despair) that the process of salvation still has to work through the body of death, and the concluding v 25 is a statement of calm realism that in this interim period the believer's loyalties are bound to be torn between the demands of the two ages to which he belongs. The common view that vv 7–25 is a digressive excursus (e.g., Bornkamm; Barrett; Beker, *Paul,* 83, "a necessary excursus") misses or underplays most of the above considerations. Still less justified is Schmithals's description of 7:17–8:39 as a "foreign body" or "independent tract" in chaps. 1–11 (*Anthropologie,* 18–20). O'Neill's hypothesis that 7:14–25 was not written by Paul derives from a very narrow and lopsided perception of Paul's use of σάρξ. The disagreement among German commentators as to where the passage should be divided (vv 7–12, 13–25—e.g., Michel, Gaugler, Wilckens, so also RSV; or vv 7–13, 14–25, e.g.—Käsemann, Schlier, Zeller, Theissen, 185–86, so also NEB and NJB; ignored by English-language commentators) has only served to obscure the issue.

Note the rhetorical variation achieved by use of κατεργάζομαι, ποιέω, and πράσσω (for possible distinctions see *TDNT* 6:636–37) and of ἀγαθός and καλός. The "I" form is influenced more by Jewish psalm tradition (see on 7:9) than by diatribe style.

Comment

7 τί οὖν ἐροῦμεν, "what then shall we say?" See on 3:5 and 6:1.

ὁ νόμος ἁμαρτία; "that the law is sin?" The spoken or diatribe character of Paul's style is particularly marked here since the phrase reads literally "the law, sin?!" and can only be given effect by inflection of the voice. The fact that Paul can pose the question quite so sharply (the law = sin!) is a clear indication and measure of the extent to which vv 1–6 seem to consign the law solely to the old epoch, equally abhorrent as its partners, sin and death. Some commentators fail to recognize the rhetorically shaped sharpness of Paul's question and overestimate the radicalness of Paul's critique of the law ("radical criticism of the Torah is the inalienable mark of Paul's theology," Käsemann, citing Eichholz, *Theologie,* passim), failing to recognize, among other things, that the parallel between 6:4; 7:6; and 8:4 forbids a polarizing of law and Spirit.

μὴ γένοιτο, "certainly not!" See on 3:4.

ἀλλὰ τὴν ἁμαρτίαν οὐκ ἔγνων εἰ μὴ διὰ νόμου, "nevertheless, I would not have experienced sin except through the law." On ἀλλά see Cranfield. Here once again ἁμαρτία has a fair degree of ambiguity. Clearly it denotes sin as a personified power oppressing human experience in the following verses— so experience/know sin as a force operating on and within the decisions of every day. But hardly to be excluded is the sense of sin as the act (here the act of coveting)—experience/know in the sense of practice as a conscious and all-too-deliberate action (see, e.g., van Dülmen, 107; Hofius, "Gesetz," 269–72; and further on 3:9). Most commentators recognize that with the almost surreptitious transition to the first person singular Paul begins to think in typical terms, once again making increasingly explicit use of the Adam narratives of Gen 2 and 3: "I" = typical man (*homo sapiens*), אָדָם = *'adam* = Adam; that is, Adam is the one whose experience of sin typifies and stamps its character on everyone's experience of sin within the epoch he began (see further on 7:9).

In this and the following clause Paul uses different words meaning "know"— γινώσκω and οἶδα. They overlap in meaning to a large extent and here may be used as synonymous variations. Insofar as they differ, γινώσκω tends to denote the knowledge of personal acquaintance, more experiential in character (cf. 2 Cor 5:21), and so its spectrum of meaning includes the intimacy of the marriage relationship (as in Gen 4:1 LXX and Matt 1:25; BGD, γινώσκω 5); hence the translation above, "experienced," whereas οἶδα tends to denote more rational knowledge about, even though its spectrum of meaning can also include the knowledge of close (but not so close) personal acquaintance (as in Matt 26:72; 2 Cor 5:16; BGD, οἶδα 2). Here both verbs could be translated more explicitly as statements of fact: "I did not experience . . . I did not know" (SH).

εἰ μὴ διὰ νόμου, "except through the law." The absence of the definite article is of no consequence. The reference is just as clearly to the Torah as in the earlier phrase, *with* the definite article, in v 5 which it echoes (see on 7:1). Paul explains the controversial claim of v 5 by reference to the prototypical experience of Adam. That the law had been present in some sense to Adam was probably already a common line of reflection in the different strands of Jewish theology. We certainly cannot be sure when it was that the rabbis began to speak of the Torah as already existing before the creation of the world and of man (e.g., *Tg. Yer.* Gen 3:24; *Pal. Hag.* 2:77c; *Gen. Rab.* 8:2), or of Adam as having been put into the garden to "do service according to the law and keep its commandments" (*Tg. Neof.* Gen 2:15; see further Scroggs, *Adam*, 33, 42–43); but such an assertion was not a difficult or implausible deduction for the rabbis to draw from the identification already made between the Torah and premundane Wisdom (Sir 24:23; Bar 3:36–4:1). Thus the commandment Adam received ("You shall not eat of it," Gen 2:17) could be seen not as an isolated rule but as an expression of the Torah, and in breaking it Adam could be said to have broken the statutes (plural) of God (cf. *4 Ezra* 7.11; *Tg. Neof.* Gen 2:15; *Gen. Rab.* 16:5–6; 24:5; *Deut. Rab.* 2:25; *b. Sanh.* 56b; see further Str-B, 3:37). The oldest form of this teaching may well be as early as Paul: Paul, in his repeated equation of "the commandment" with "(the) law" in vv 8, 9, and 12, quite likely shows his familiarity with it; and in 5:14 he had already described Adam's disobedience as typical of transgression of the law (see also Theissen, *Psychological Aspects*, 203–4). A further consequence of this last observation is that we should not press the different emphases of 5:12–14 and 7:7 into outright inconsistency: even if the law of God was not given formally till Sinai Paul was fully aware that deliberate disregard for and breach of the command of God known to be such was prevalent before Sinai (cf. again 5:14; also 1:32 and 2:12). As already noted on 1:23, Israel's immediate breach of the law given on Sinai in the idolatry of the golden calf was frequently associated with the fall of Adam in Jewish tradition. See further below; cf. also on 2:14.

τήν τε γὰρ ἐπιθυμίαν οὐκ ᾔδειν εἰ μὴ ὁ νόμος ἔλεγεν· οὐκ ἐπιθυμήσεις, "for I would not have known covetousness unless the law had said, 'You shall not covet.'" On the relation of ἔγνων and ᾔδειν see above. ᾔδειν is a pluperfect with imperfect meaning, denoting the beginning of a continuing experience: "I would not have come to that experience of covetousness which I still have." The starkness of Paul's description of how the law actually functions should not be weakened to a "being made aware that he covets" (Kuss, rightly criticized by Schlier). ἐπιθυμέω, like ἐπιθυμία (see on 1:24), does not necessarily denote something wrong ("to desire"—cf., e.g., Ps 119 [LXX 118]:20; Isa 58:2; Phil 1:23; 1 Tim 3:1), and the tenth commandment specifies the kind of "desiring" which is illicit ("your neighbor's wife . . ."). Nevertheless, the influence of the tenth commandment did help establish the sense of "desire" as desire for something forbidden (Exod 20:17; Deut 5:21; *4 Macc* 2.5; cf. Prov 21:26; Mic 2:2), and it is clear from Rom 13:9 that Paul has the tenth commandment in mind. Moreover, particularly where the influence of Stoicism was strong, desire as such tended to be regarded as something sinful because of its impulsive and nonrational character (cf. *4 Macc* 1.3, 31–32; 2.1–6; 3.2, 11–12, 16; Philo, *Leg. All.* 3.15; *Post.* 26). Paul, however, sees it as wrong not because of its irrationality, but because it is desire for self, for self-satisfaction, the characteristic expression of "the mind set on the flesh" (8:6–7) and the inevitable self-expression of the offspring of Adam. It is what sets him against God, and makes him antagonistic to God's authority as Creator (cf. *TDNT* 3:168–71). The equivalent explanation in rabbinic theology centers on the "evil impulse" (*yēṣer hā-rāʿ*, יצר הרע; see Schechter, *Aspects*, chap. 15; Davies, *Paul*, 20–27); and cf. *4 Ezra*'s complaint against the "evil heart" (3:20–26; 4:30–31; etc.).

That wrong desire, lust, or covetousness was the root of all sin was an already established theologoumenon in Jewish thought. The point is already clear in Philo (*Opif.* 152; *Decal.* 142, 150, 153, 173; *Spec. Leg.* 4.84–85). According to the *Apocalypse of Moses* (middle first century A.D.?), a work Paul could have known (cf. particularly 2 Cor 11:4 with *Apoc. Mos.* 17.1–2), Eve attributes her failure to "lust the root and beginning of every sin" (19:3); cf. also *Apoc. Abr.* 24.10. And James makes precisely the same affirmation: "desire/lust (ἐπιθυμία) conceives and gives birth to sin" (1:15). See also Str-B, 3:234–37. In view of the above evidence, Fitzmyer's unwillingness to see here a consistent allusion to Adam and Gen 2–3 is surprising (see also particularly Lyonnet, "Rom 7:7"). But the same evidence indicates that ἐπιθυμία here is broader than "sexual desire" (cf. Ziesler, "Romans 7"; against Gundry, "Romans 7:7–25," 232–33, and Watson, *Paul*, 151–53; but see on 7:11). Still less justified is it to interpret ἐπιθυμία in terms of zeal *for* the law, "striving for achievement" (Bultmann, "Romans 7," 182; Bornkamm, "Sin," 90; Käsemann; Hübner, *Law*, 72–76; Patte, *Paul's Faith*, 266–77) which seriously distorts the line of thought here (see further Wilckens and particularly Räisänen, "ΕΠΙΘΥΜΙΑ").

8 ἀφορμὴν δὲ λαβοῦσα ἡ ἁμαρτία, "but sin, seizing its opportunity." ἀφορμή means literally "the starting point or base of operations for an expedition" and so "occasion or opportunity," with ἀφορμὴν λαμβάνειν a favorite expression, e.g., in Polybius (BGD). The metaphor is military (so we could almost translate "bridgehead") but not exclusively so. This is one of the most vigorous of the personifications of sin as a power, underscoring the human experience of sin as an oppressive force acting upon the individual.

διὰ τῆς ἐντολῆς κατειργάσατο ἐν ἐμοὶ πᾶσαν ἐπιθυμίαν, "through the commandment stirred up all manner of desire in me." The first phrase probably belongs to this clause more than to the preceding words (against Lagrange, Lietzmann, Schlatter, Wilckens; see Schmidt, Cranfield with other bibliography), with the διὰ τῆς ἐντολῆς placed first for emphasis, as in vv 11 and 13, thus marking out the commandment not merely as the occasion for sin but as sin's actual instrument. Throughout this section (vv 8, 9, 12) Paul uses νόμος and ἐντολή as virtual synonyms (Schlier). The commandment in view is "You shall not covet," taken as characterizing the commandment broken by Adam (see on 7:7). κατεργάζομαι is a thematic word in ch 7 (vv 8, 13, 15, 17, 18, 20) and could be translated simply "produce, create" (Schlier). The thought is not of the commandment's being used to create desire as such, but to create the desire the tenth commandment forbade, brought about a desire which was selfish and grasping, thus perverting what was not by nature wrong in itself (ἐπιθυμία—see on 1:24 and 7:7). By giving sin the opportunity of turning man's desire in upon himself (rather than focusing it on God—1:21), the commandment became the means of corrupting what could have been a powerful positive force in his life (cf. Schlatter). Contrast Barrett, who polemicizes too strongly against desire, and religion, as such.

χωρὶς γὰρ νόμου ἁμαρτία νεκρά, "for apart from the law sin is dead." It is unlikely that Paul intends the weak sense, "sin is not perceptible" (BGD, νεκρός 1bβ), with reference to 4:15 and 5:13. At this climactic and focal point of the discussion of the law it is a much more forceful and controversial claim which Paul is making—the law here not as God's agent in making man aware of sin, but as sin's instrument in killing (vv 9–11). νεκρά should therefore be taken in the sense "ineffective, powerless" (Michel; cf. Cranfield), lacking any life force or vitality (cf. James 2:17, 26; also 1 Cor 15:56); οὐ καρποφορεῖ, like an apparently dead branch (Lightfoot). The dramatic pictorial language should not be taken too literally. The words chosen are intended to sharpen the contrast between "sin" and "I" (important in vv 13–25), and their effect depends on readers recognizing (1) the allusion to Gen 2–3, with personified sin taking the part of the serpent and "I" the part of Adam (well expressed by Barrett, despite his too Barthian hostility to "religion"), and (2) the existential experience of a power within, which subverts the life God gives and, if yielded to, destroys it. Paul would certainly be conscious of his earlier use of the phrase χωρὶς νόμου (3:21; note also 3:28 and 4:6) and of its significance as a riposte to the typical Jewish prizing of the law (see on 3:21). The turning of the tables is deliberate: the giving of the law did not provide a realm (Israel with its cult) where the power of sin was broken; on the contrary, as Gen 3 shows, the giving of the commandment simply provides sin with a more effective leverage on man (the devout Jew not excluded). James may be deliberately countering this view by formulating his own (counter-) emphasis in close parallel:

> Romans 7:8: χωρὶς νόμου ἁμαρτία νεκρά·
> James 2:26: ἡ πίστις χωρὶς ἔργων νεκρά ἐστιν·

(See further on 4:1–25 *Form and Structure*.)

9 ἐγὼ δὲ ἔζων χωρὶς νόμου ποτέ, "I was alive once in the absence of the law." For the first time in the letter ἐγώ is used, and it characterizes the rest of the chapter (7 or 8 times: vv 9, 10, 14, 17, 20, 24, 25). For the possible significance of ἐγώ, see Cranfield, 342–44; the range of alternatives for ἔζων is reviewed by Kuss. As most recognize, Paul is almost certainly speaking in typical terms, using the Adam narrative to characterize what is true of man (ʾadam) in general, everyman—somewhat as *2 Apoc. Bar.* 54.19, "Each of us has been the Adam of his own soul"; so already 1:18–32; 3:23; 5:12–19 (see particularly 1:22; 3:23; 5:12–21, passim). The stages marked by ἔζων ποτέ and ἀπέθανον (v 10) clearly reflect the stages of Adam's fall: Gen 2:7, 16–17, "man became a *living* being (ψυχὴν ζῶσαν) . . . And the Lord God *commanded* Adam, 'You may certainly eat of every tree which is in the garden/ paradise, but of the tree of the knowledge of good and evil you shall not eat; for in the day you eat of it you shall certainly die [θανάτῳ ἀποθανεῖσθε]'"; Käsemann, however, may overstate the case a little when he asserts, "There is nothing in our verses which does not fit Adam, and everything only fits Adam" (cf. Schlier).

Most interpreters now also agree that it would be a mistake to treat the passage autobiographically and to look for matching stages in Paul's own experience (see, e.g., Kümmel, *Römer 7*, 76–84, 111–17; Benoit, 14, 27; Leenhardt, 181–85; Achtemeier, 126–28; against Sandmel, *Paul*, 56; Murray). In particular we can hardly refer this clause to his preconversion experience: for though it would be possible to see in it an expression of Paul's confidence as a devout Pharisee prior to his conversion (cf. Gal 1:13–14; Phil 3:4–6), it is hardly possible that he would think of his encounter with the risen Christ as a dying occasioned by the quickening of sin (vv 9–10; against Hendriksen). Nor can we readily identify the stage of being alive with the preteenage experience of the boy Paul (so, e.g., Dodd, Knox, Barrett, Michel, Bruce, Gundry, "Rom 7:7–25"; others in Käsemann, 192–93). It is of course true that in rabbinic teaching a Jewish boy at the age of thirteen becomes "a son of the commandment" (*bar mitzwah;* cf. *m.* ʾ*Abot* 5.24; Davies, *Paul*, 24–27). But we also have statements from the time of Paul which emphasize the effort made by Jewish parents to provide their children with a thorough grounding in the law from earliest years (Philo, *Legat.* 210; Josephus, *Ap.* 2.178; cf. Str-B, 2:144–47); Theissen, *Psychological Aspects*, 251 n.52, notes an inscription from a Jewish gravestone in Rome which describes a child (νήπιος) as "a lover of the law" (φιλόνομος; details in *NDIEC* 1:117). It is most unlikely therefore that a Jewish male of Paul's day could ever think of a period of his life when the law was absent (Kümmel, *Römer 7*, 81). The thought is rather of the childhood of man, the mythical period of the human race's beginnings. Hence we may properly translate the ποτέ as referring to some indeterminate time in the past, or evoke the idea of story telling, the story of Adam (cf. LSJ, ποτέ III.1); that is, "once upon a time," "the time of paradisiacal innocence" (Lietzmann); see particularly Lyonnet, "L'histoire," 130–42.

At the same time, there is an existential character throughout the whole section (vv 7–25), and it is difficult to believe that Paul is not speaking at least to some extent out of his own experience (Dodd, 107; Dahl, *Studies*, 93; Kertelge, "Römer 7," 107–8; Dunn, "Rom 7:14–25," 260–61; Robinson, *Wrestling*, 82; Beker, *Paul*, 240–43; Theissen, *Psychological Aspects*, 190–208— "the I assumes the role of Adam and structures it in the light of personal experience of conflict" [203]; Segal, 362; against Kümmel, *Römer 7*, 85–97). What is true of everyman is true also of him. His own experience of the interplay of sin and law he does not presume to be unique, but typical. We may properly compare the vivid "I" form of Jewish psalm tradition (e.g., Pss 69 and 77; *Pss. Sol.* 5 and 8; 1QH 3.19 ff. and 11:3 ff.), as indeed Paul's own use of first person singular elsewhere (particularly 1 Cor 10:29–30 and Gal 2:18–20). The contrast between Phil 3:4–6 and Rom 7:7–12 should not be discounted, but it is primarily a contrast in perspectives—before and after— Phil 3:4–6 expressing Paul's understanding of the function of the law prior to his conversion ("as to righteousness under the law, blameless"), and Rom 7:7–12 (or 7:7–25) his *Christian* perspective. From his (now) Christian perspective he sees this whole epoch to be under the sway of sin and death (1:18– 3:20; 3:23; 5:12–21), including not least the typical Jewish presumption of blamelessness which he had previously made his own boast (2:1–29). As a Christian he views conversion, including his own, as a deliverance from the rule of sin and death (5:21; 6:2, 13, 20–23; 7:5–6; 8:2; 2 Cor 3:6). Paul would hardly exclude his own conscience-free experience as a Pharisee from the evaluation he now placed on the epoch of Adam as a whole. On the contrary, the presumption of Phil 3:4–6 he saw now to be all too clear evidence of the effectiveness of sin's deception (v 11); in the law, as nowhere else, Paul was confronted with his own past. The typicality of the experience of everyman expressed in the archetypal language of Gen 2–3 presumably therefore should be allowed to embrace a wide and diverse range of particular experiences. See further on 7:7 (ᾔδειν) and below on 7:14–25 passim, particularly 7:14.

The χωρὶς νόμου would again jolt Jewish self-perception: it was in the period χωρὶς νόμου, before the law became a dividing line dividing those having the law from those without (2:12, 14), that man was alive (see further on 7:8 and 7:10). The point as it bears on Paul's attitude to his ancestral faith needs to be made with care: as Wright perceptively notes, the problem addressed by Paul here is not "the hidden Jew in all of us" (Käsemann; an unsavory phrase), but "the hidden Adam in Israel" (*Messiah,* 152); "within the law" is also "in (fallen) Adam." Maillot tries to combine the strengths of all the above considerations by arguing that Paul has in view a legalistic Christianity which Paul must himself have experienced (185; cf. particularly Mitton, Fung, and Segal); but this fits poorly with a pre-Christian stage "without the law," and there is no hint elsewhere that Paul enjoyed what may properly be called a "second conversion."

ἐλθούσης δὲ τῆς ἐντολῆς ἡ ἁμαρτία ἀνέζησεν, "but when the commandment came sin came to life," ". . . sin sprang to life" (NEB, NIV). The reference is clearly to the sequence of Gen 2–3: man created (2:7); given commandment— the coming of the commandment (2:16–17); sin/serpent coming on the scene with the commandment on its tongue (3:2). A reference to the before and after of Sinai (as in Althaus, 75; van Dülmen, 109–10; and particularly Moo, "Israel") is less likely; prior to Sinai sin was far from powerless according to 5:13–14, not to mention Gen 6:1–6 (Luz, *Geschichts,* 165; Zeller; despite Räisänen, *Law,* 147, there is no need to posit a contradiction between the two Romans passages). ἀναζάω would normally mean "come to life again" (BGD); Paul probably used the compound lest his strong language be taken to mean that the law created or gave birth to sin. Paul never speculates on the origin of sin; he simply assumes its reality as a power in human experience (see on 5:12).

10 ἐγὼ δὲ ἀπέθανον, "and I died." This is simply another way of saying what he has already said in 5:12–21: I = Adam = humankind = everyman passed under the sway of death, both as expulsion from the presence of God (and the tree of life) and as its inevitable end in physical and moral corruption to death. Cranfield is unwise to separate this dying so sharply from "the good death of 6:2, 7, 8; 7:4": the death of Christ and with Christ (6:2–11; 7:6) is one outworking of that same sentence of death (Gen 2:16–17); to die one's own death is another (6:16, 21, 23; 7:5).

καὶ εὑρέθη μοι ἡ ἐντολὴ ἡ εἰς ζωήν, αὕτη εἰς θάνατον, "and the commandment which was for life, the very same proved to be for death." In Paul's case εὑρέθη is probably a Semitism, reflecting the Hebrew נִמְצָא, "be found, prove to be" (BDB, אָצָמ Niph.; BGD, εὑρίσκω 2). The force of the εἰς is difficult to quantify (cf. *TDNT* 2:429). Does Paul mean that the commandment was intended to *bring about life*, to lead to life (NEB, NJB), that is, a life not yet possessed, or to *promote* life, to regulate and prosper life already possessed? The parallel phrase, εἰς θάνατον, certainly suggests the former. But Paul elsewhere seems to deny the possibility of a law "making alive" (ζῳοποιῆσαι, Gal 3:21). The most probable solution is that his thought here is still governed by the allusion to Adam: if Adam had lived according to the commandment (Gen 2:16–17) he would have enjoyed free access to the tree of life (cf. Gen 3:22). Whatever the divine intention behind the law, however, the reality for Paul was that it had brought death; "the law triggered off in man a death-bringing process" (Michel). Here in a nutshell is the sharpness of the human dilemma, and the depth of man's tragedy: were it not for sin the law would promote life (lead to and prosper life) in relationship with God; but given the power of sin (origin unknown, but power too well known) the law in actuality provokes man's self-assertion (but note Wilckens's justified rebuttal of a too "Lutheran" interpretation, including Schlier, at this point) and so cuts him off from the life of God. Paul, of course, does not intend to charge God with defective foresight. The contrast is still that between Gen 2 and Gen 3—the law as it would have worked in the absence of sin contrasted with the law as it actually has worked. Not to be ignored once again, however, is the implied sharp reverse to and rebuttal of the traditional Jewish assumption that the law/commandment promoted life (Lev 18:5; Deut 6:24; Prov 6:23; Sir 17:11; 45:5; Bar 3:9; *Pss. Sol.* 14.2; *4 Ezra* 14.30; *m. 'Abot* 2.7; further Str-B, 3:237; according to *Exod. Rab.* 5 [17a] the Torah spells life to the Israelites but death to the Gentiles because they did not accept it [Str-B, 3:238]); the sharpness of the paradox is acknowledged in the αὕτη (Schlier); see also on 4:15 and 10:5.

11 ἡ γὰρ ἁμαρτία ἀφορμὴν λαβοῦσα διὰ τῆς ἐντολῆς ἐξηπάτησέν με καὶ δι' αὐτῆς ἀπέκτεινεν, "for sin seizing its opportunity through the commandment deceived me and through it killed me." The first clause simply repeats the first clause of v 8; as in v 8 the following διὰ τῆς ἐντολῆς goes with the principal verb to provide the first two parallel clauses:

> διὰ τῆς ἐντολῆς   ἐξηπάτησέν με
> καὶ δι' αὐτῆς   ἀπέκτεινεν·

(See on 7:8). The echo of the Genesis account is certainly deliberate:

> Genesis 3:13: ὁ ὄφις ἠπάτησέν με καὶ ἔφαγον,
> "the serpent deceived me and I ate."

The word "deceived" characterizes the Pauline understanding of sin's role in the fall of man:

> 2 Corinthians 11:3: "the serpent deceived [ἐξηπάτησεν] Eve";
> 1 Timothy 2:14: "Adam was not deceived [ἠπατήθη], but the woman was deceived [ἐξαπατηθεῖσα]";

note, however, in contrast to 1 Tim 2:14, that Paul's "I" here includes Eve. Elsewhere the language has more explicit sexual connotations (Herodotus 2.114; Sus 56 Theod.; linked to ἐπιθυμία); cf. the sequence of thought in 1:18–27; hence NEB's translation, "seduced." Cf. also Heb 3:13 and Eph 4:22. Schlier again runs the interpretation too quickly into a typically Lutheran polemic against self-achieved righteousness.

Both the emphasis on the role of the commandment (the agency of the commandment is noted twice) and the ἀπέκτεινεν are likewise derived from the Genesis account. God had attached the warning of death to the commandment (Gen 2:17: ". . . you shall not eat, for in the day that you eat of it you shall die"). The serpent/sin in using the commandment to provoke disobedience to that command thus used it to bring the warning into operation and effect. Paul clearly wishes to press the paradox: it was the command of God which sin has used to bring death into its dominant role on the stage of human life (5:12).

12 ὥστε ὁ μὲν νόμος ἅγιος, καὶ ἡ ἐντολὴ ἁγία καὶ δικαία καὶ ἀγαθή, "so then the law is holy, and the commandment holy and just and good." For ὥστε see on 7:4. The ὁ μὲν νόμος is obviously an anacoluthon, with the contrast clearly implied by the context: the *law* is holy, but *sin* . . . (see BGD, μέν 2a). Paul first uses νόμος and then ἐντολή, no doubt partly for emphasis and partly to make it clear that he was speaking not simply of the single command of Gen 2:16–17 but of the law as a whole, seen archetypally in Gen 2:16–17 (Lagrange; see on 7:7), just as he was speaking of humankind as a whole, seen archetypally in Adam. Others think that by ἐντολή he means to indicate the holiness of every individual commandment (particularly Cranfield).

In describing the law as ἅγιος Paul could hardly use a stronger word to affirm the law as God's law (see on 1:7). Even though manipulated by sin, it has not been removed from the power or purpose of God. This should not be taken as an incoherent and inconsistent attempt on Paul's part to avoid the logic of his own position. Such a judgment would betray a failure to grasp the nature and thrust of Paul's critique of the law as understood within the Judaism of his own day. Paul could only speak as positively of the law as he does here if he thought that his critique was directed against an abuse of the law—by sin, and most manifestly (to his Christian eyes) in the pride and presumption of his own people (see *Introduction* §5.3.2). Thus "the holy," although broadened out from the more restricted sphere of cultic purity (1:7), still embraces the law. Compare and contrast 4 Ezra 9.37, where a similar attempt to exculpate the law from blame for sin and failure remains firmly within the perspective of Jewish self-understanding—that is, the law as Israel's (9:29-37); see further *Introduction* §5.3 and also on 7:24.

The use of δίκαιος for the law likewise indicates a conscious attempt to retain the close correlation of the two words which were axiomatic in Jewish thought (see particularly on 1:17). The commandment can be said to be "just" because it defines the relationships and conduct appropriate to the covenant between Creator and creature (or between God and Israel). Note again the significance of the claim: Paul does not deny this role to the law; his criticism of his own people is not that they were mistaken in regarding the law as norm in this sense, but that they have misunderstood what it was that the law called for (2:1–29). Elsewhere in Romans δίκαιος always refers to people, with the exception of 3:26 where it describes God (see on 3:26).

The third adjective, ἀγαθή, is probably intended to broaden the description to a category universally regarded as positive and desirable (see on 2:7 and 2:10), though Paul may be mindful that he had already put ἀγαθός in some contrast with δίκαιος (5:7): the law deserves universal approbation, not simply from within Judaism. It is also significant that it is this more generally approved feature of the law which he picks up in the next verse (v 13) and which provides the typically desirable category for the "I" of vv 18–19. Watson's suggestion that in calling "the law good Paul is in fact damning it with faint praise" (*Paul*, 156) surprisingly ignores the other two epithets.

Paul clearly cannot think that the misuse of the law by sin (vv 8–11) disqualifies the law as God's, as enactive of his will for his creatures, and as positively beneficial in its outworking. He may even intend to imply that the transgression-provoking and death-bringing functions of the law are ultimately to be included under these heads, that it was not only fair but beneficial to man that his self-seeking and self-assertiveness end in destruction, since only so will the trustful creature be finally delivered from that which is self-destructive; the law's effect in reinforcing sin's power to bring about death thus also brings about escape from sin's power (6:7, 10). See also on 7:5 and 13; and cf. Nygren, 281–82.

13 τὸ οὖν ἀγαθὸν ἐμοὶ ἐγένετο θάνατος; "did that which is good, then, become death to me?" The question is posed as starkly as we would expect from one so immersed in Jewish faith and tradition, both the positive and the negative aspects of the law being sharpened with not merely rhetorical effect. On the one hand, the description of the law as "good" is picked up with a phrase which can be read as identifying the law with that which all see as most praiseworthy, "the good" (cf. particularly 2:10); the rabbis similarly absolutized the same adjective as used particularly in Prov 4:2 (Str-B, 1:809). On the other hand, the use of the law by sin to bring about death is summed up in the harsher phrase, "became death to me"; cf. v 7—"the law, sin?"

μὴ γένοιτο, "certainly not!" See on 3:4.

ἀλλὰ ἡ ἁμαρτία, ἵνα φανῇ ἁμαρτία, διὰ τοῦ ἀγαθοῦ μοι κατεργαζομένη θάνατον, "but sin, that it might appear sin, through that which is good producing death for me." The parallel with v 8 is close, with the progression of the argument from v 8 to v 11 compressed. As in v 8 the διά phrase is attached to κατεργάζεσθαι; see on 7:8. The sentence has no principal verb, thus retaining the colloquial idiom evident in v 7; but the sense is clear. φαίνομαι, which occurs only here in Romans, is widely used in broader Greek usage in the sense "be manifested, be apparent (to sense or mental perception) as, be seen to be" (LSJ, BGD). The idea is that the law unmasks sin, gives it recognizable definition, removes ambiguity from the sinful act; "thereby sin exposed its true character" (NEB); ". . . in order to be identified as sin" (NJB).

ἵνα γένηται καθ᾽ ὑπερβολὴν ἁμαρτωλὸς ἡ ἁμαρτία διὰ τῆς ἐντολῆς, "in order that sin through the commandment might become utterly sinful." καθ᾽ ὑπερβολήν is a familiar idiom to express excess or extraordinary quality: so "to an extraordinary degree, beyond measure, in the extreme" (BGD, ὑπερβολή); in the NT used only by Paul (1 Cor 12:31; 2 Cor 1:8; 4:17; Gal 1:13). ἁμαρτωλός occurs more often as a substantive ("the sinner"—so 3:7; 5:8, 19), but here as an adjective (see BGD). The doubling and reemphasis of the two ἵνα clauses (both final—Kümmel, *Römer* 7, 57; Käsemann) and διά phrases is deliberate. Paul's object may be partly to soften his just sharpened critique of the law, both by appealing to a further or counter function of the law more acceptable to Jewish sensibilities (already referred to twice; see on 3:20 and 4:15), and by giving prominence to the typical Jewish distancing word ἁμαρτωλός (see on 3:7). But his main purpose is rather to emphasize that even the law's being used by sin for death is part of God's fuller and deeper strategy to bring out the character of sin and of its end product and payment—only death (cf. Wilckens).

14 οἴδαμεν γὰρ ὅτι, "for we know that": see on 2:2. Once again we may note in passing that the plural resonates against a background of sympathy toward the law which Paul could presumably assume in congregations largely composed of God-worshipers, proselytes, and Jews.

ὁ νόμος πνευματικός ἐστιν, "the law is spiritual," in the sense, presumably, that it derives from the Spirit (given by inspiration), embodies the Spirit, manifests the Spirit, was intended to address at the level of the Spirit; cf. the use of πνευματικός elsewhere in Paul (in the NT it appears exclusively within the Pauline sphere of influence), particularly 1:11; 1 Cor 2:13; 10:3–4; 12:1; 15:44, 46; Col 1:9; 3:16 (see Dunn, *Jesus*, 207–9). Here too the definition should not be regarded as a lame withdrawal from a more logically polarized conclusion such as can be drawn from the γράμμα/πνεῦμα antithesis of 2:29 and 7:6, not to mention Gal 3 and 2 Cor 3, or as an inconsistent compromise which throws his theology into confusion (Sanders, *Law*, 77–81; Räisänen, *Law*, 142—"a glaring self-contradiction"). Paul is beginning his argument that there is a duality both in the law (law—sin, and law—Spirit), and in himself as a typical believer (flesh—sin, and mind—Spirit; see on 7:21, 22, 23, 25), and that these two dualities are mutually complementary (flesh—law—sin; mind—law—Spirit). In retrieving the law from straightforward identification with sin and death, therefore, Paul does *not* intend to treat it again as he did when a practicing Pharisee. On the contrary, it is the flesh-law tie-up which has brought Israel, in its pride in national identity as the elect people of God, under the power of sin, whereas it is the eschatological outpouring of the Spirit which has liberated Paul and the law from that too narrowing understanding of the law's role. This liberated and liberating tie-up of the law and Spirit Paul expresses more clearly in 8:2–4.

ἐγὼ δὲ σάρκινός εἰμι πεπραμένος ὑπὸ τὴν ἁμαρτίαν, "but I am fleshly, sold under sin." With this verse the reference of the ἐγώ broadens out from that of everyman expressed in terms of the "once upon a time" Adam to that of everyman in the present (εἰμί). With the transition from past to present the note of personal existential involvement immediately becomes sharper (v 15); Theissen interprets the transition as from unconscious to conscious conflict with the law (*Psychological Aspects*, 228–34). The ἐγώ is immediately defined as σάρκινος, that is, the "I" as embodied in flesh, belonging to the realm of flesh, living in and through that which is corruptible and destined to return to dust; σάρκινος presumably having the same range of meaning as σάρξ (see

on 1:3 and 7:5; NJB's "a creature of flesh and blood" restricts the range of
reference too much). On the question of a distinction between σάρκινος and
σαρκικός see Notes; also Denney, Lagrange, and Cranfield. In short, the phrase
speaks of the individual in his belongingness to the epoch of Adam, which
is ruled by sin and death. The careful construction of that last sentence should
be observed. It is not the individual who belongs to the epoch of sin and
death (as though there were some individuals living on earth who did not
belong in any sense to the epoch of Adam, who had already passed beyond
sin and death, and who belonged like those already dead and resurrected
wholly and solely to the new epoch); the "I" as flesh means the individual
in his belongingness to the old epoch. This is not a criticism of the devout
Jew as such, though we should not forget that Paul's criticism of his fellow
Jews does accuse them of a form of fleshliness (see on 2:28). But here the
self-condemnation is of the old epoch "I" in general. In this "I" Paul includes
himself as a believer (see those cited by Wilckens n.344; also on 7:25), not
just in his pre-Christian days (as Schweizer, TDNT 7:144, Beker, Paul, 217–
18, and Martin, "Reflections"; but Osten-Sacken's [218] suggestion that the
"I" of chap. 7 is "a type of the believer, as Adam in Rom 5 is a type of one
to come, Jesus Christ" is too contrived; and Segal's suggestion that Paul's
anguish arises from the fact that he had been forced to compromise his
more radical solution to the problem of food laws for the sake of the more
conservative Christians assumes a link between chap. 7 and chap. 14 which
is otherwise without foundation). The split Paul is about to expound is one
between the epochs of Adam and Christ: the "I" is split and the law is split
in complementary fashion because each belongs to both epochs at the same
time in this period of overlap between the epoch of Adam and the epoch of
Christ, between the era of the flesh and the era of the Spirit. See on 7:9
and further on 7:23, 24. For history of exposition see Kuss, 462–85; Wilckens,
2:101–17. The fact that the "I" is split and can be described as "fleshly"
weakens any parallel which may be drawn with later Gnostic ideas (as in
Perkins).

   With πεπραμένος, from πιπράσκω, the metaphor of slavery so prominent
in 6:16–23 is recalled; though since defeated captives in war were usually
sold as slaves, the imagery of successful surprise attack (vv 8, 11) also naturally
leads into that of slavery. The repeated LXX usage, ἐπράθησαν ποιῆσαι τὸ
πονηρόν, "sold to do evil" (1 Kgs 21 [LXX 20]:25; 2 Kgs 17:17; 1 Macc 1:15)
may be in mind; Philonenko argues for a complex allusion to Isa 50:1. The
perfect tense has its usual force of indicating a condition still in effect from
a past action. In this case the past action refers back to the event(s) of vv 7–
11; what is in view is the consequence of the archetypal "I"'s capture and
subjection to death at the hands of sin, the condition of the "I" within the
epoch of sin and death. The starkness of the description does not exclude
Paul the believer, despite the aorists of vv 4–6. As in chap. 6, the early aorists
(6:1–11) are qualified by what follows (see chaps. 6–8 Introduction). The qualification here is the reminder that the "I" insofar as it is still part of the realm
of flesh, the epoch of Adam, is still "under sin" and under sin's cohort death.
When therefore Käsemann maintains that "what is being said here is already
over for the Christian according to chap. 6 and chap. 8," he is typical of

those who ignore the eschatological qualifications Paul himself provides in these same chapters (still the most popular view among commentators). We find precisely the same self-confession in the Qumran literature, used by those who, very much like Paul, rejoiced in the experience of God's righteousness. The best example is in 1QS 11.9–10: "As for me, I belong to wicked mankind, to the company of ungodly flesh. My iniquities, rebellions, and sins, together with the perversity of my heart, belong to the company of worms and to those who walk in darkness" (Vermes); cf. 1QH passim (e.g., 1.21–27; 4.29–33; 7.16–18; 12.24–31; 13.13–16; further in Braun; cf. Hübner, "Dualismus," and those cited in Dunn, *Jesus,* 445 n.79; see also on 8:5). Such passages should not be dismissed as "the cry of the pious," an expression of human self-assertion (Käsemann); that reduces first-century Judaism to a denigrated stereotype. They should rather be allowed, together with Rom 7:7–25, to serve as a reminder that it is precisely the saint who is most conscious of his sinfulness (cf. Espy, 173–74). Paul's objection to his fellow Jews' attitude to the law is not in view here (as it is in 2:17–29; 3:27–31, and 9:30–10:13). For ὑπὸ τὴν ἁμαρτίαν, see on 3:9.

15 ὃ γὰρ κατεργάζομαι οὐ γινώσκω, "for I do not know what I do." As the γάρ indicates, this verse begins the explanation of what it means to be "sold under sin" (v 14)—that is, not an abject, unquestioning servitude, but a slavery under protest, the frustrated impotence of one who has to live "in newness of Spirit" while still "in the flesh" (see on 7:5). κατεργάζομαι probably has the vaguer sense "do," rather than the more specific "produce, create." If γινώσκω here has the sense of experiential knowledge (see on 7:7) the implication is that Paul existentially disowns his action, even though still admitting that it is his (though see v 17); others take it more in the sense "I do not acknowledge, approve" (e.g., Barrett, NEB, Cranfield; Lightfoot—"I do it in blind obedience. Sin is so imperious a task-master that he does not allow me time to think what I am doing").

οὐ γὰρ ὃ θέλω τοῦτο πράσσω, ἀλλ᾽ ὃ μισῶ τοῦτο ποιῶ, "for that I commit is not what I want, but what I hate that I do." πράσσω, like κατεργάζομαι, is used in an all-embracing sense to cover all action of the "I." The use of μισέω as the antithesis to θέλω is striking: he "hates, abhors, detests" what he does. The disowning is much sharper here: he wholly detests and abhors what he does as one "sold under sin" (v 14).

It is not difficult to parallel such complaints. The most frequently quoted are Epictetus 2.26.4: ὃ θέλει οὐ ποιεῖ καὶ ὃ μὴ θέλει ποιεῖ; and Ovid, *Metamorphoses* 7.20–21: "I see the better and approve it, but I follow the worse" (fuller surveys in Hommel, 106–13, and Theissen, *Psychological Aspects,* 212–19). But there are significant differences. Epictetus finds the answer in the "rational soul" (ψυχὴ λογική): "Point out to the rational governing faculty a contradiction and it will desist" (2.26.7). And Ovid lacks the sharpness of existential frustration which comes to increasingly anguished expression as the passage here continues. This indicates the difference. In Paul we are confronted with the sharpness and frustration of the eschatological tension—that is, a tension which even if present elsewhere is rendered all the sharper and more poignant by the fact that the individual (believer) has already begun to experience the possibilities and promise of a wholly Spirit-directed life (cf. Cranfield).

It is not surprising that the nearest parallels to Rom 7 at this point come in
1QS 11 and 1QH, since they too are an expression of a very similar sense
of eschatological tension and frustration (see on 7:14; Dunn, *Jesus*, 317–18;
Schlier's analysis of the tension in which the "I" is caught as between "man
as creature" and "man in history" [*der geschichtliche Mensch*] does not catch
the eschatological character of the "I"'s plight; cf. also Zeller, 142–44).

16 εἰ δὲ ὃ οὐ θέλω τοῦτο ποιῶ, σύμφημι τῷ νόμῳ ὅτι καλός, "but if that I do
is what I do not want, I agree with the law (and thus bear witness) that it is
admirable" (BGD)—σύμφημι only here in biblical Greek. καλός is if anything
even more general than ἀγαθός (see on 7:12) which it here replaces as a
near synonym, much like the German *schön*, "beautiful, fine, good, splendid"
(see also on 12:17). The verse makes it clear that the major thrust of the
argument is still to defend the law from the false impression which sin's use
of the law gives about the law.

17 νυνὶ δὲ οὐκέτι ἐγὼ κατεργάζομαι αὐτό, "but now it is no longer I doing
this." Although the νυνί and οὐκέτι are primarily logical (so most), the eschatological overtone particularly of the νυνί should not be wholly excluded. The
fact that the "I" can thus disown ὃ οὐ θέλω, ὃ μισῶ, is a consequence of its
eschatological standing in the Already but also the Not yet of eschatological
grace. The language makes clear that the "I" in this passage is not completely
schizoid or split into two, a fleshly "I" (v 14) and a rational "I" (vv 23, 25); it
is the same "I" each time—the "I" "sold under sin" in its fleshliness, and the
"I" as "the inner man" (see on 7:22); there is no disavowal of personal involvement and responsibility here (Murray). For κατεργάζομαι see on 7:15. Gaugler
notes that Paul speaks wholly as a Jew: conviction alone is not enough; the
commandment requires the *act* of obedience.

ἀλλὰ ἡ οἰκοῦσα ἐν ἐμοὶ ἁμαρτία, "but sin dwelling in me." As he did with
the law in vv 7–13, so here, Paul having painted the "I" in blackest terms (v
14) now shows that categories are not so clear-cut; even the "I" in all its
present fleshliness is by no means beyond redemption. Note how Paul rings
the changes in his imagery for the power of sin—up to this point represented
as a military force (vv 8, 11; and again v 23), or slave owner (v 14), sin is
now depicted as a constraining force from within. The ambivalence of the
imagery reflects the ambivalence of the experience of sin—always as a power
exercising great compulsion on the individual, but sometimes more easily
conceptualized as a force bearing upon one from without (social pressures,
constraints of tradition, etc.), at others as a force rising up from within (psychological addiction of ingrained habit, hereditary traits, etc). On οἰκεῖν ἐν see
further 8:9; here too one can speak of a kind of possession (Schmithals,
Anthropologie, 43; Zeller compares Matt 12:43–45 and *T. Naph.* 8.6).

18 οἶδα γὰρ ὅτι οὐκ οἰκεῖ ἐν ἐμοί, τοῦτ᾿ ἔστιν ἐν τῇ σαρκί μου, ἀγαθόν, "for I
know that there dwells in me, that is, in my flesh, no good thing." The echo
of v 14 is marked:

v 14   οἴδαμεν γάρ . . .   ἐγὼ δὲ σάρκινός·
v 18   οἶδα γάρ . . .   ἐν τῇ σαρκί μου·

Likewise the starkness of πεπραμένος ὑπὸ τὴν ἁμαρτίαν (v 14) is matched by
the starkness of οὐκ οἰκεῖ ἐν ἐμοί . . . ἀγαθόν. The dualism is like that of apoca-

lyptic writings, where the contrast with the glory of the age to come highlights negative features of the present age by way of contrast (see, e.g., on 8:18, and Russell, *Method*, 266–68)—the reason being the same, since it is precisely of the "I" as flesh, that is, as belonging to this age, of which Paul says "nothing good" (once again the old epoch "I" in general, not the pious Jew in particular; see on 7:14). Here not least the contrast between σάρξ and σῶμα has to be borne in mind: it is not man's physicality as such which Paul denigrates here ("the I itself is flesh"—Wilckens), for the range of meanings covered by σάρξ and σῶμα overlap precisely where both denote man's embodiment in this three-dimensional time-space complex; yet σῶμα can cross the boundary of the ages, whereas σάρξ belongs firmly to this present age (cf. 1 Cor 15:44–50; 2 Cor 4:7–5:5). The force of σάρξ is precisely that it denotes an unavoidable attachment and tie to this age which must perish before redemption can be complete (Rom 8:11, 23), and which therefore denotes not merely a pre-Christian state (again against Schweizer, *TDNT* 7:133–34). It is precisely this inextricable attachedness to this age concerning which Paul makes the judgment "no good thing." To describe "the flesh" here as "radically evil" (Barrett) is too strong, however; and without the eschatological tension the parallel with the rabbinic יצר הרע ("evil impulse") (Str-B, 4:466–83; Davies, *Paul*, 25–27) is incomplete. For τοῦτ᾽ ἔστιν see on 9:8 and 10:6–8.

The additional echo of vv 12–13 in the repetition of ἀγαθός raises the question whether Paul intends a further allusion to the law—the law "as good" being kept distinct from this attachment to the age of Adam (cf v 14), even though it is manipulated by sin to ensure the fatal outcome to the flesh of its attachment to the age ruled by death (7:5).

τὸ γὰρ θέλειν παράκειταί μοι, τὸ δὲ κατεργάζεσθαι τὸ καλὸν οὔ, "for the willing lies ready to my hand, but not the doing of what is admirable." For παράκειμαι in the sense "lie ready, at disposal" (*TDNT* 3:656), cf. Sir 31 [LXX 34]:16 and P. Oxy. III.530.17 ff. (MM). In early Christian literature it occurs only here and in v 21. The reason for choosing this less than common verb is to stress the *difficulty* of doing good, not that it is impossible (contrast 2:10). The contrast between the willing and the doing is the contrast between on the one hand the renewed heart and enlightened mind (5:5; 6:17; 12:2; contrast 1:21, 28; 2:5), and on the other the yet unredeemed mortal body (8:11, 23). For κατεργάζεσθαι see on 7:15. The near synonymity of ἀγαθός and καλός is in vv 18–19 even clearer than in 7:16; for καλός see on 7:16.

19 οὐ γὰρ ὃ θέλω ποιῶ ἀγαθόν, ἀλλὰ ὃ οὐ θέλω κακὸν τοῦτο πράσσω, "for I fail to do the good which I want, but the evil which I do not want, that I commit." The verse repeats v 15b, but with πράσσω and ποιῶ interchanged (a further reminder of how generalized and unspecific Paul's language is), and with κακόν drawn in as antithesis to ἀγαθόν (see on 2:10). ὃ μισῶ (v 15) = ὃ οὐ θέλω κακόν (here).

20 εἰ δὲ ὃ οὐ θέλω (ἐγώ) τοῦτο ποιῶ, οὐκέτι ἐγὼ κατεργάζομαι αὐτὸ ἀλλὰ ἡ οἰκοῦσα ἐν ἐμοὶ ἁμαρτία, "but if what I do not wish, that I do, it is no longer I doing it but sin which dwells within me." The verse compresses vv 16–17 (see on 7:17). The element squeezed out is the defense of the law in v 16b (see on 7:16). The reason is presumably that this is the element of his argument which he is about to expand with greater definition and qualification, just as he has already clarified and qualified the role of the "I" in vv 14–20 (see further *Form and Structure*); recognition of this point eliminates any justification for seeing vv 19–20 as a gloss (against Leenhardt).

21 εὑρίσκω ἄρα τὸν νόμον, τῷ θέλοντι ἐμοὶ ποιεῖν τὸ καλόν, ὅτι ἐμοὶ τὸ κακὸν παράκειται, "I find then the law, for me who wishes to do the good, that for me the evil lies ready to hand" (literal translation). The individual items of exegesis here can be drawn together to demonstrate the strength of the case for seeing τὸν νόμον as a reference to the Torah. (1) The verse clearly synthesizes and sums up central elements in the preceding analysis. Since one of the main thrusts of 7:7–25 is to defend the law (see *Form and Structure*), the most obvious reference for ὁ νόμος here is "the (Jewish) law." (2) In particular, εὑρίσκω echoes and repeats in variant form what Paul has already said in v 10:

v 10   εὑρέθη μοι ἡ ἐντολὴ . . . εἰς ζωήν . . . εἰς θάνατον·
v 21   εὑρίσκω τὸν νόμον . . .   τὸ καλόν . . . τὸ κακόν·

Where in v 10 thought was only of the frustrated goal of the law, in v 21 the further thought of the relative impotence of the "I" is added. But in both cases what is in view is the harsh discovery through personal experience of how the law, which should be for life and should promote the good, actually helps bring about the opposite. (3) The last two clauses of v 21 are a compressed form of v 18b–19 (cf. on 7:20), with καλόν again providing a variation of ἀγαθόν (as in vv 12–13/16 and 18a/18b/19) in antithesis to κακόν (v 19), and the unusual παράκειμαι (see on 7:18) drawn in again to bring out how easy and convenient Paul finds it (even as a believer) to do evil. Where so many of the themes of the immediately preceding context are thus gathered together, the train of thought cries out for a reference to the law equivalent to that in v 16b. Having explained how the dividedness of the "I" is what exempts it from ultimate blame (vv 17, 20), Paul not unnaturally returns to his main apologetic concern with the law (see *Form and Structure*). (4) In the immediately following sentences it will be the two-sidedness of the law on which Paul focuses (7:22–23, 25; 8:2). The point is, on the one hand, that the two-sidedness of the law reinforces and interacts with the "I" in its own two-dimensional character: as the law of God, reinforcing my desire for good; as the law used by sin, precipitating my action for evil (the point is recognized by Lohse, *Vielfalt*, 135; Hahn, "Gesetzesverständnis," 46; Schmithals, *Anthropologie*, 67; Theissen, *Psychological Aspects*, 188–89, 255–57; Reicke, "Gesetz," 243; and Snodgrass, 105–6; cf. Denney, Barth, Wilckens; half perceived by Blank, "Gesetz" 112–13; see also bibliography on 8:2). And, on the other, that the same apologetic logic works for both: as the dividedness of the "I" shows the fault to be sin's, so too with the two-sidedness of the law. Outwith the rule of sin God's purpose for both the "I" and the law is very positive. See further on 7:22.

Most modern commentators, however, maintain that Paul is using νόμος in the sense of "general rule" or "principle" (e.g., BGD, νόμος 2; *TDNT* 4:107; SH; Lagrange; Lietzmann; van Dülmen, 115–18; Black; Schlier; Zeller; NJB; Bergmeier): "this is regularly what happens, this is generally the rule." Such a meaning is unknown within the NT, though Räisänen has documented it in wider Greek usage (*Law*, 50 n.34, and "NOMOΣ"; against Wilckens). It is difficult, of course, to know what other word than νόμος Paul could have used if that had been his intention, though in that case we might have expected no definite article, or a demonstrative adjective ("this law") (Cranfield and Wilckens, recognizing the problems, resort to referring to v 23 without actually clarifying the meaning here). But the issue depends not so much on wider usage, as on Paul's usage within the flow of his argument. And all Paul's references to the law so far in the letter (3:27 not excluded) have been to the Jewish law, the Torah. Without a clearer indication to the contrary, Paul could hardly expect his Roman readers to give the word a different reference here (since Räisänen cuts out part of the evidence regarding Paul's treatment of the law, it is not so surprising that he finds the rest of Paul's treatment of the law inconsistent; see on 7:14). To be sure, the sentence is framed somewhat awkwardly, but that may be simply because of the note of irony Paul clearly intends (as in v 10): this is what I find the law to be in experience (Gaston, *Paul*, 176, refers to Gen 4:7). And even so, it does in fact make sufficiently good sense as a reference to the Torah: the law as I encounter it in the reality of the situation just described is that evil has a stronger say in my actions. Willing alone is not enough: I still am unable to translate what the law defines as good into practice. Indeed, it is precisely when we recognize v 21 as a reference to the (Jewish) law that we can see what an important conclusion this is for Paul's argument. For this sentence actually gives Paul's reason why the law is ineffectual as a means of grace, unable to provide a secure and continuing basis for man's relation with God (its principal role in Jewish thought). The reason is that the law properly understood (that is, *not* in terms of works) informs the willing but does not enable the doing. Outside the realm of willing, the law is still too much sin's tool to be able to overcome sin in the flesh. This is what the law is found to be in practice, precisely by the man who wills the good which the law requires that whereas good stimulates the will, evil dictates the deed (including the works of the law). See further on 8:2.

22 συνήδομαι γὰρ τῷ νόμῳ τοῦ θεοῦ κατὰ τὸν ἔσω ἄνθρωπον, "for I rejoice in the law of God, so far as the inner person is concerned." συνήδομαι + dative would normally have the sense "rejoice with (someone)" or "rejoice at (something)" (LSJ). It may not be necessary to give it the extended sense of "(joyfully) agree with" here (BGD, Wilckens), since it is the sense of affinity and mutual approbation between the law and the "I" which is in view, rather than the more specific sense of the "I"'s approval of and agreement with the law (though cf. 7:16b). Here beyond question, as most agree, νόμος is the Torah ("the law of God"), not just "God's will in a general sense" (Käsemann). V 22 is an explanation of v 21 (γάρ); so v 22 is best seen as the first part of the explanation of the paradox of Paul's experience of the law expressed in v 21 (see further on 7:21).

The idea of a "person within" (ὁ ἔσω ἄνθρωπος) occurs also in Greek philosophy, initially, it would appear, as a way of speaking about the divine or rational element in man in distinction from his baser, animal and earthly nature, and subsequently in Gnostic thought as the expression of a much

sharper anthropological dualism (see BGD, ἄνθρωπος 2cα; *TDNT* 1:365; Lietzmann; Wilckens 2:93). But someone who calls the "I" "fleshly" (v 14) hardly
belongs to that trajectory of thought (compare and contrast Jewett, *Anthropological Terms*, 391–401, with review of earlier literature). And even if "the inner
person" is not a frequent item in Pauline vocabulary (though cf. 2 Cor 4:16;
Eph 3:16; opposite to "the old man"—Rom 6:6; Col 3:9; Eph 4:22), and
even if his Roman readers were familiar with the more Platonic usage, even
so they would be less than likely to mistake Paul's meaning here. As the
whole context indicates, Paul's is a salvation-history dualism or tension, not
an anthropological dualism: the "I" is split not as a result of creation (or
the fall), but primarily as the result of redemption; the "I" is split because
the "I" of the believer belongs to, is stretched between the old epoch of sin
and death (and law) and the new epoch of grace and life (and Spirit). Nor
can we say that it all amounts to the same thing (Paul seen as describing the
same conflict as that described by Plato in *Republic*, 9.588–92). For integral
to Paul's gospel is death, the death of the "I": "the inner•man" = the "I"
insofar as I am already united with Christ in his death and share in his
resurrection life; the fleshly "I" = the "I" who has not yet died. (All this is
clearer in 2 Cor 4:16 when read within its context of 2 Cor 4:7–5:5; Sanday
and Headlam [SH] are off target in asserting that prior to v 25 there is no
single expression which belongs to Christianity; similarly Leenhardt; contrast
Barrett; Käsemann admits that projecting the pneumatic "inner man" language back "into the life of the unredeemed poses a riddle"). What makes
the difference between the blanket condemnation of 1:18–3:20 and the confession of frustrated resolve in 7:7–25 is all the teaching about Christ's death
which has filled so much of the intervening discussion. For more or less the
same reason it is unlikely that Paul has in mind here the pious Jew (as Michel
and Schmidt argue): he himself had known none of that tension as a law-
abiding Pharisee (Phil 3:4–6; cf. the relative confidence of Deut 30:14 and
Sir 15:15), the reason being, as he now sees, that his law-abiding stayed at
the more superficial level of flesh and works (2:27–29; 3:27); he had not
even reached the stage of frustration! (The illogicality of arguing that the
passage here expresses with Christian hindsight the existential anguish of
the pious Jew—which as a pious Jew he did not actually experience and
which as a Christian he still does not experience!—is not usually appreciated.)
And even if Paul does not exclude the possibility of an inward willing matching
an outward doing on the part of the Gentiles (2:12–16), the point of Paul's
gospel is precisely that it is only by the power of Christ's risen life that that
possibility can be translated into full reality. The gospel not merely liberates
the inner self to a proper appreciation of the law, it also enables an obedience
to that law from the heart (cf. 6:15–18; 7:6). It is the former aspect Paul
has in view here; he will broaden his analysis shortly to embrace the latter
(chap. 8). ·

   23 βλέπω δὲ ἕτερον νόμον ἐν τοῖς μέλεσίν μου ἀντιστρατευόμενον τῷ νόμῳ τοῦ
νοός μου καὶ αἰχμαλωτίζοντά με ἐν τῷ νόμῳ τῆς ἁμαρτίας τῷ ὄντι ἐν τοῖς μέλεσίν
μου, "but I see another law in my constituent parts at war with the law of
my mind and making me prisoner to the law of sin which is in my constituent
parts." The ἕτερον νόμον is clearly the same as ὁ νόμος τῆς ἁμαρτίας ("the law
of sin"), since both phrases are more fully defined in the same words, ἐν

τοῖς μέλεσίν μου ("in my constituent parts"—see on 6:13; NJB's "acting on my body" is too far from the Greek). Here the manner of referring to νόμος gives stronger support than does v 21 to the suggestion that νόμος has a different (ἔτερος) reference than the Torah, "a law of a different kind" (Trench, *Synonyms*, 358). But whether such a distinction between ἔτερος and ἄλλος was intended is far from certain, since the two are often used interchangeably (BGD, ἔτερος 1bγ), and the "difference" could be simply the different way in which the law was experienced when it was used by sin (vv 8, 11, 13), so different from the law acknowledged as good (vv 16, 22). Certainly to speak of "the law of sin" is hardly much of a step beyond speaking of the law used by sin to deceive and kill (v 11); to take "the law of sin" simply as the power exercised over us by sin (Cranfield) ignores this link back to v 11. Under the power of sin the law is experienced as very different from the law of God. See further on 8:2, and cf. particularly Wilckens.

Similarly with ὁ νόμος τοῦ νοός μου, "the law of my mind." It would be hard to dispute that it refers to "the law of God" (vv 22, 25), or to "the law of the Spirit" (8:2). But here too Paul uses a phrase which is susceptible to a different interpretation and thus strengthens the probability that in both phrases he is deliberately choosing provocative language in order to make clear the paradoxical two-sidedness of the law in the epoch of overlap between sin and grace (see further on 8:2). It is quite possible in fact that the phrase here reflects Paul's awareness of the anthropological dualism of Greek thought, where the mind, the rational, is precisely "the inner man" (as in Philo, *Plant.* 42; *Cong.* 97). By so speaking of the mind, indeed, he gives some hostages to fortune by opening up thereby the possibility of interpreting his analysis in terms of Greek thought (as the history of interpretation shows). But in the search for synonyms to provide rhetorical variation in this quite lengthy treatment, "mind" was an obvious variation on the more careful statements about the divided "I" in vv 14–21. And introducing it as he does when his discussion is almost complete, where the salvation-history tension between old epoch and new is already well established, would be enough, he might have thought, to prevent this particular use of "mind" being interpreted other than as a reference to the believer in his belonging to the new epoch; see further on 12:2.

The reemergence of the metaphor of warfare is presumably not merely stylistic or for reasons of aesthetic appeal. Paul has already called upon it in 6:13 (ὅπλα), probably 6:23 (ὀψώνια), and again in 7:8, 11 (ἀφορμή), and it will continue to hover in the background in 8:7 (ἔχθρα) and 8:13 (θανατοῦτε). There is a sharp existential edge to this sustained usage: Paul feels that he is caught up in a warfare with sin, a continuing warfare in which his experience ("I") is typical of believers generally (6:13; 8:13), notwithstanding the aorists of 6:2–4 and 8:2. The same sense of faith under attack (*Anfechtung*) is clearly reflected elsewhere in his letters, particularly 2 Cor 10:3–4 and Gal 5:17.

The metaphor is expressed in its most extreme form here since it speaks not only of warfare but of defeat (αἰχμαλωτίζεσθαι). This is consistent with the other most prominent metaphor in preceding sections, slavery, since defeat in battle usually resulted in the prisoners of war being sold as slaves. The extremeness of the metaphor here therefore matches the starkness of v 14b (see on 7:14). As the warfare is between the two laws, or the law as it lends itself to different usages, so the captivity is to the law, which is to say that man (including the believer) in his belongingness to this age is caught up in and cannot escape the perverse functioning of the law as used by sin. What is in view is not, of course, a final state, any more than in v 14b, but an ongoing experience of warfare and defeat (note the tenses) in which the final outcome of the war in which the individual finds himself is by no means yet settled. The realism which Paul expresses elsewhere about the possibility of the believer failing to reach final (complete) salvation (see on 8:13, 9:3, and 11:21), and which Ignatius expresses using the same imagery in *Eph.* 17.1, is underscored here. Of course, were defeat the only outcome of every battle, or were defeat not experienced and recognized as *defeat*, the speaker could have none of the hope which Paul goes on to express (this crucial point is missed by Wenham). The extremeness of the statement here (and in v 14b) is the proper balance of the earlier over-realized aorists (6:2–4; 7:4–6), which together find their mean in the exhortations of 6:12–23 and 8:12–13 and in the more sober assessments of 7:25b and 8:10–11, 18–24 (see again chaps. 6–8 *Introduction*).

24 ταλαίπωρος ἐγὼ ἄνθρωπος, "wretched man am I." ταλαίπωρος, "miserable, wretched, distressed" (only here and in Rev 3:17 in the NT), could of itself be an expression of despair or condemnation (as in Wisd Sol 3:11; 13:10). But it can also describe the state of a man pulled in two directions. The closest extrabiblical parallel is not the Hermetic *Kore Kosmou* §34–37, or *Jos. Asen.* 6.1–8 (cf. *T. Abr.* B 10) (as Smith, "Background," 128–33, maintains; cf. Schmithals, *Anthropologie*, 75–78), but Epictetus 1.3.5—τί γὰρ εἰμι; ταλαίπωρον ἀνθρωπάριον . . .—where the thought is very similarly of the two-sidedness of everyman: ". . . inasmuch as these two elements were commingled in our begetting, on the one hand the body, which we have in common with the brutes, and, on the other, reason and intelligence, which we have in common with the gods, some of us incline toward the former relationship, which is unblessed by fortune and is mortal, and only a few toward that which is divine and blessed. . . . 'For what am I? A miserable, paltry man,' say they, and 'Lo, my wretched, paltry flesh.' Wretched indeed, but you have also something better than your paltry flesh. Why then abandon that and cleave to this?" (1.3.3–6). In Paul, however, we may assume that it is not so much an anthropological tension which evokes the cry, but the eschatological tension of being caught between the two epochs of Adam and Christ, of death and life; see further Bruce, Zeller, and cf. particularly 2 Cor 4:16–5:4. Elsewhere in early Christian literature this is expressed in terms of the tension of sharing an earthly and heavenly citizenship at the same time (as in Phil 3:20–21; Heb 13:14; *Herm. Sim.* 1.1). The same implication is involved in the association of ταλαίπωρος with δίψυχος, "double-minded," in *Herm. Sim.* 1.3, as also in *1 Clem.* 23.3 = *2 Clem.* 11.2, where the wretchedness is that of unfulfilled hope become oppressive and resulting in the defeat of a hope clouded by doubt (cf. 7:23). The relatively close parallel provided by *4 Ezra* 7.62–69, 116–26, expresses the negative side of the eschatological tension without the positive answer already given in 6:2–11; 7:4–6 and again in 8:2–4; see also on 7:12 and 8:23.

τίς με ῥύσεται ἐκ τοῦ σώματος τοῦ θανάτου τούτου; "who will deliver me from the body of this death?" Where the thought is of spiritual deliverance, rather than deliverance from physical peril, the most characteristic sense of ῥύομαι within the NT writings is eschatological (Matt 6:13 // Luke 11:4; Rom 11:26; 1 Thess 1:10; 2 Tim 4:18). The deliverance in view here therefore is not likely to be conversion, expressed in the decisive acceptance of 5:1 (contrast Kuss), but final deliverance, which is the completion of the good work already begun (Phil 1:6). That is to say, it is not for a deliverance which can be experienced *within* the fleshly constraints of this life, but for deliverance *from* the fleshly constraints of this life. Cf. Michel and Cranfield who refer to Pss 14:7 and 53:6. Barrett's suggestion that the cry arises because "the last hope of mankind, religion, has proved a broken reed" owes more to the early Barth than to Paul. That this *can* be the cry of one who already *has* the Spirit (against e.g., Bornkamm, "Sin," 101; Cambier, "Moi") is sufficiently evident from 8:23 and 2 Cor 5:2–5.

"The body of this death," or "this body of death" (see Käsemann) is obviously a further variation on "body of sin" (6:6), "this mortal body" (6:12), "my flesh" (7:18), "my constituent parts" (7:23); see further on 6:6 and 6:12. Here as in these passages its range of meaning is close to that of σάρξ, precisely because the more neutral σῶμα is qualified as "of death" (see on 7:18, and cf. also 8:13). Once again the clearer and fuller definition provided by the context and by these previous variations would help keep Paul's readers from misunderstanding the phrase in terms of dualistic anthropology. It is equally obvious that "this death" refers back to the death brought about by the machinations of sin (7:10–13); see on 5:12 and 8:10. That physical death is included within the phrase is obvious, even if the idea of a corporate belonging to the age of Adam (5:12–21) is also very much in view. It is the final outworking and end of death's rule over this age, and so defeat of the last enemy (1 Cor 15:26), for which Paul longs here.

25 χάρις δὲ τῷ θεῷ διὰ Ἰησοῦ Χριστοῦ τοῦ κυρίου ἡμῶν, "but thanks be to God through Jesus Christ our Lord." For the first phrase see on 6:17. For διὰ Ἰησοῦ Χριστοῦ see on 1:8. For the full Christological title see on 1:4 and 5:1. The διά may do double service: to stress Christ's mediatorial role in prayer to God; and to imply his mediatorial role as God's agent of the final deliverance (see on 7:24). As Cranfield rightly notes, there is nothing in the formula itself to indicate that it is a deliverance already accomplished which is in view; on the contrary, the closest parallel (1 Cor 15:57) indicates the anticipation of eschatological deliverance (Banks, "Rom 7:25a"). NEB's rendering, "God alone, through Jesus Christ our Lord! Thanks be to God!" (similarly NJB), is far too free.

ἄρα οὖν αὐτὸς ἐγώ, "so then I myself." For ἄρα οὖν see on 5:18. This is the seventh/eighth time that Paul uses ἐγώ in chap. 7, and the last time till 9:3. The αὐτός intensifies and emphasizes the ἐγώ (BGD, αὐτός 1). But it does not follow, as Kuss rightly notes, that we should translate, "I thrown on my own resources" (BGD), "I left to myself" (Moffatt), or "I left on my own," that is, before or without Christ (Lightfoot; SH; Gaugler, 240–44; Mitton, 133–34, followed by Robinson, *Wrestling*, 89–91); that conclusion is determined more by a particular line of interpretation than by the force of the words themselves. The "I" which speaks is both the fleshly "I" (v 14) and the "inner person/man" (v 22). The emphasis is therefore to bring out the fact that it is one and the same "I" on both sides of the warfare and servitude, carefully expressed in the μέν . . . δέ . . . construction that follows.

τῷ μὲν νοΐ δουλεύω νόμῳ θεοῦ, τῇ δὲ σαρκὶ νόμῳ ἀμαρτίας, "on the one hand with my mind I serve the law of God, but on the other with my flesh the law of sin." The clause clearly recalls in its language v 23: "I delight in the law of God" (v 22), "the law of my mind," and "I serve with my mind the law of God," obviously all are variations on the same aspect of the "I"'s existence here expressed; likewise "with my flesh the law of sin" sums up the theme of vv 18–23; see on 7:23, and on σάρξ see on 7:5, 14, 18 (translations like "unspiritual, sinful, disordered nature" [NEB, NIV, NJB] again diminish and distort the breadth of meaning; see on 7:5). The split in the "I" is now more completely fitted to the two-sidedness of the law: the link between the law of God and the mind being already clear (v 22), the link between the law of sin and the flesh, alluded to in v 5, and implied in vv 7–13, is now stated in simple, explicit terms.

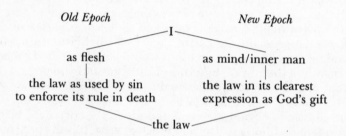

The use of δουλεύω here clarifies its use in and the meaning of 6:6 and 7:6. The purpose of Christ's death and of believers' identification with it is to resolve the double compulsion to service in which believers find themselves, by the destruction of the body of sin/death (6:6; 7:24), that is, by the death of the body and its redemption in resurrection, in the final act of liberation (8:21). The first stage of liberation includes liberation from the law in its misuse as γράμμα (7:6), that is, a recognition that the law of God can be used by sin, including that use which corrupts it into γράμμα; see further on 7:6.

Many commentators fail to appreciate the eschatological tension fundamental to Paul's understanding of the process of salvation. They judge that Paul must be speaking here of life in the old epoch, and therefore life before faith, life under the law as γράμμα, and conclude that since it fits so poorly after v 25a, v 25b must be displaced (e.g., Dodd; Kirk; Müller, "Marginalien"; Eichholz, *Theologie*, 257; Michel has become more cautious in his 5th edition; cf. Dahl, "Missionary Theology," 85—a "delayed conclusion"), or be a gloss (Jülicher; Bultmann, "Glossen," 278–79; and still amazingly popular in German scholarship, as Kuss; Käsemann, who nominates it as "the first Christian interpretation of vv 7–24"; Schlier; Schmithals, *Anthropologie*, 81–82; and Wilckens, with other bibliography in n.399, show; but not Zeller); equally unfounded is Keuck's (279) reading of the phrase as a question (to be answered by an implied "No longer!"); nor does taking 7:25b with 8:1 ff. (as also Kürzinger) resolve the problem. Paul *is* speaking of life in the old epoch of Adam in this section, but since that epoch runs through till death (5:12–21; 1 Cor 15:21–26) believers perforce still belong to it, "in the flesh," "mortal bodies." The balance of v 25b therefore is not an expression of salvation still to begin, but of the process of salvation under way and still to be completed (Dunn, "Romans 7:14–25," here particularly 262–63; Nygren, 284–302; Knox, 499–500; Murray, 257–59, 270–71; Stalder, *Werk*, 291–307; Bruce, 151–53; Packer; Cerfaux, *Christian*, 442; Cranfield; Schnackenburg, 295–300; against most; other bibliography in Hendriksen, 229–30; Käsemann rightly recognizes that the acceptance of v 25b as part of the original undermines his whole interpretation, not just of the context but also of Paul's view of baptism, law, and justification; Theissen's psychological analysis makes better sense once the eschatological tension present in *both* chap. 7 *and* chap. 8 is taken into account). See also on 8:1 and 8:10.

Explanation

7–13 As so often in this letter Paul in making his point has posed it with a sharpness and emphasis which might be misunderstood, or which invited a rejoinder (cf. already 3:1, 9; 4:1; 6:1). In chap. 6 he had already emphasized the discontinuity between the old epoch and the new (6:2–11: the rupture and transition effected in Christ's death and resurrection), but he had qualified it by the subsequent exhortation (6:12–23). Here he has reemphasized that discontinuity in terms of the law, and has characterized the law as both belonging to the old epoch and as an agent involved with sin in binding man closer to death (7:1–6). Such a presentation inevitably poses disturbing questions about the law as Paul sees it. The tension which has lain just under the surface throughout the exposition so far, the tension within Paul's attitude to the law, most clearly visible in chaps. 2–4 and most explicit in 5:20, is now fully exposed and Paul at last turns to address it. For congregations largely composed of either Jews or Gentiles who had been previously attracted to Judaism, there must have been a sense of relief and anticipation; not before time Paul was going to resolve the puzzle he had posed by his surprisingly dismissive treatment of the law.

7 "What shall we say then? Is the law sin?" The question is justified, at least in terms of the rhetorical sharpness of Paul's formulation. He has not actually said so or implied an identification of the law with sin, but he has associated them so closely, with the law as sin's ally and as sin's agent (though implicitly also as God's *agent provocateur*—v 5), that a question along these lines is inevitable.

Paul's first answer to the question ("Is the law sin?") is to refer in effect once again to Adam and the story of Gen 2–3: the relation between the law on the one hand and sin and death on the other as depicted in Gen 2–3 is the vital clue. Initially the reference to Adam is not so clear, but the sudden transition to the first person singular ("I would not have come to know") signals to the readership that what at first might seem simply a generalization from Paul's personal experience is intended also as a statement of typical experience, of (as becomes clear) the prototypical experience of Adam.

Paul asserts as a universal truth that sin is experienced only through the law, and in particular that the desire of covetousness is known only by virtue of the law which forbids coveting. Thus he picks up immediately the key phrase of v 5, "sinful passions which are through the law," and breaks it down into two component parts: the law both provokes the actual experience of sin and makes the coveter aware that his desire is illicit. That this can refer to man as such is hardly clear to modern readers, either man in general (so few have ever heard the tenth commandment given to Israel) or man as represented in Adam (the law was given much later than Adam, at Sinai). But it would have been much more obvious then. For one thing the creation of man and the giving of the law were probably already associated in Jewish thinking, not least the idea that in disobeying "the commandment" of God (Gen 3:1–6) Adam was breaking "the law" of God. Moreover, what was certainly well established at the time of Paul was the view that covetousness or lust is the root of all sin (cf. James 1:15). So Paul's readers would probably have had no difficulty in associating the commandment against the basic sin of lust (desire, covetousness) with the primeval sin of Eve and Adam.

8 V 8 continues to explicate the relation between the law and sin with reference to the fall of Adam. Indeed v 8 amounts in effect to a description of the tactics of the serpent, here personified as "sin." Sin (the serpent) was lurking in the garden prior to man's fall, but had found no opportunity to attack man until the commandment, "You shall not eat of it" (Gen 2:17) had been given. It was precisely through this commandment, by using this commandment, that sin was able to tempt Adam and to produce in him the primary sin of lust. What thus begins to become clear is the nature of the law's agency in all this. The real culprit is sin as a power for evil quite distinct from the law, but taking advantage of the law, perverting the function of the law so that the same commandment ceases to make man conscious that selfish desire is lust and instead provokes the very desire it was designed to warn against. Sin uses the commandment intended as a check on man's inquisitiveness actually to stimulate that inquisitiveness, to transform inquisitiveness into acquisitiveness. All this is the work of sin; the power which provokes man's selfish grasping in all its forms was already active at the beginning, and still dominates the old epoch.

"Apart from the law sin is dead." Paul does not avoid controversial statements. But he obviously does not mean that the purpose of the law was to give life to sin. His thought is entirely controlled by the harking back to the Adam story. Sin (the serpent) was entirely powerless, had no means of "getting at" man, had it not been for the law. It is not impossible, however, that Paul intends a double entendre in passing, for "apart from the law" applies not only to the primeval time of Adam's innocence but also to the eschatological time, the new epoch introduced by Christ (3:21). It is the unholy alliance of the law and sin, or rather the unholy manipulation of the law by sin, which characterizes the intervening epoch and binds them firmly under the lordship of death. As it was the introduction of law which gave sin its chance to make man captive to death, so it is release from the law which ends the rule of both sin and death (7:1–6).

9–10 With v 9 the reference to Adam becomes all but inescapable, and Paul could probably assume by now that most of his readers would have recognized it. For only in the case of Adam is it possible to make such a clear distinction between a before-and-after of the law: before the commandment came, life; after the commandment, sin and death. Some may possibly have thought that Paul had in mind a "golden age" of childhood innocence, before the law entered consciousness and sin became an act of deliberate disobedience. But it is most unlikely that any devout Jew of Paul's day would think that there had ever been a period of his life, at least from circumcision onwards, when the law was absent. Likewise the contrast between life before the law came, and sin and death consequent upon its coming, is too sharp to serve as a description of any period of human (or Israelite) history, whereas it makes clear and good sense as a reference pointing back to man's created state and fall (Gen 2:7, 16–17).

Paul is in some danger at this point of confusing his readers with all the different references to death, particularly the apparent contradiction in thought between v 9 (10, Aland[26]) and v 6: "I died," as a description of man's condition under the old epoch (v 9 [10, Aland[26]]); "we died," as a description of the believer's escape from the old epoch (v 6). The former (v 9), however, is presumably simply an emphatic way of expressing the close connection between sin and death, and the inevitability of death for a life lived under the power of sin: the emphasis reflects the force of the original warning of Gen 2:17 ("In the day you eat of it you shall certainly die"), while the final phrase of v 10 (literally "the same to death") reflects more the idea of death as the final product of sin (as in 6:21, 23; 7:5; cf. James 1:15). Neither of the aorist tenses in question (vv 6, 10) can in fact be taken literally: if "I died" (v 9) denotes man's being caught up, enmeshed in a process whose inevitable end is death, "we died" (v 6) denotes the believer's identification with Christ in his death which will only be fully worked out in the death and resurrection of the body. It is important to recognize that the possibility of confusion arises only because in the last analysis the two deaths are one and the same: the death shared with Christ *is* the end product of sin, but with its sting withdrawn so that it is not in fact the end but the doorway to life with Christ. Sinners do not escape the death which is the fruit of their sin, but they are able to survive it because Christ has endured it with them and for them. It is when we recognize this double aspect of death that we can understand the similar ambivalence in Paul's treatment of the law, and how the law can have both a positive function and a negative function for Paul at one and the same time: negative because it is the glue which binds sin to death; positive because it leaves the sinner no alternative to death other than the death of Christ.

"The commandment which was for life. . . ." There is perhaps just a touch of poignant yearning here for the ideal which might have been, the life of paradise regulated by the commandment of God. Were it not for the intervention of sin the commandment would have promoted life, regulated and produced life. But since sin *has* intervened, the function of the commandment has been to promote death, to enforce death as the consequence of slavery to sin, of the sinful passions (6:20–21; 7:5). The phrase may also deliberately characterize and echo what Paul regards as the typical Jewish attitude to the law (cf. Lev 18:5, cited to similar polemic effect in 10:5). The point is that the latter is a *mistaken* understanding of the law, a function of the law rendered obsolete as early as the fall. To think still of the law as actually bringing about life is to ignore the existential presence and power of sin. Paul's kinsmen still faithful to the law may think that the law acts as a check to sin; they have failed to realize what Paul regards as a firm fact proven by hard experience, Israel's in general but his own included—that the law simply ties the individual more tightly to the sin-death nexus which characterizes the old epoch. The irony of Israel's present condition is that its very pride in the law as proof of their life before God is itself a sign of God's death sentence on all such stirrings of sin (chap. 2).

11 The statement of v 8 is repeated but with an even clearer echo of the Genesis account and with the central sequence (sin, through the commandment, to death) completed with a starkness which emphasizes the law's function as the connecting link between the two. The language deliberately echoes the woman's complaint in Gen 3:13 ("The serpent deceived me and I ate"). Sin seized the opportunity the commandment gave to deceive the primeval pair (Gen 3:1–5: "Did God say, 'You shall not eat of any tree of the garden?'" . . . "You will not die . . ."). By thus using the divine prohibition to provoke disobedience, sin in effect made the commandment a force for death (cf. 5:12). The deception lay not merely in making God a liar ("You shall not die"), but also in misrepresenting God's motives in giving the commandment in the first place. It made the instruction "intended to promote life" sound like the arbitrary command of a dictator fearful of losing his special status and prerogative (Gen 3:4–5: "You will not die. For God knows that when you eat of it your eyes will be opened, and you will be like God, knowing good and evil"). The effectiveness of the deception in the poisoning of human relationships has already been demonstrated in 1:18–32.

12 Paul can now draw a firm conclusion in answer to the earlier question, Is the law sin? He has said enough to substantiate his initial denial of any such equation. Whatever the *link* between sin and the law, however much sin has made *use* of the commandment, the law *itself* is holy, the commandment *itself* holy and just and good. The adjectives are not casually chosen. They might have surprised some of his readers, but in fact nothing that Paul has said about the law has detracted from its character as a gift of God, given to serve his purposes. Sin may have deceived man, but Paul would hardly think that it had caught God unawares or altered his purposes for man. The law is still holy, set apart to God, acceptable to God: the repetition of the adjective gives the point emphasis. The commandment is still just and still defines with all necessary clarity the terms on which the relationship between God and man is based and the consequence of man's disobedience. It is still good, intended to benefit man in the various dimensions of his individual and corporate existence.

13 But how can Paul say this when he has described the law as a means to death (vv 10–11)? If it is not to be *equated* with *sin*, has he not described it nevertheless as a force for *death*? Has he not bound it up so tightly in the nexus of sin and death that to continue calling it "good" is to contradict all that he has just said? Why not go the whole way into an antinomian position and conclude that the law belongs in *character* as well as *function* to the realm of sin and death? Paul, however, cannot allow this; he cannot go off into a dualism which would lead inevitably to a Marcionite antithesis between Jew and Christian, between old covenant and new, between the God of the Jews and the God of the Christians. He is no less convinced as a Christian as well as a Jew that the law *was* given by God, *does* define what God requires, *is* essentially something good. As he rejected the equation between the law and sin so he refuses absolutely to accept that the law is to be blamed for death. The relation between the law on the one hand and sin and death on the other is altogether more subtle. The law may have condemned to death, but the real cause of death is *sin,* sin whose successful deception activated the law as an agent of condemnation.

"But sin, that it might be seen to be sin, producing death for me through what is good. . . ." The point is that the *same* function of the law in linking sin firmly to death can be viewed from another angle. What from one side is sin using the commandment to stimulate the desire which produces death, from another side is the law showing sin for what it really is. The Adam story should not be taken to imply that the law was purely passive, a mere tool wrenched by sin from the hand of God and wholly perverted by sin to its own end. Rather the fact is that the law, *even in being so used,* is actually fulfilling its intended purpose of revealing the true character of sin. Sin seeks to deceive about its connection with death ("You will not die": Gen 3:4), but the law shows that the work and fruit of sin *is* death.

". . . in order that through the commandment sin might become utterly sinful." The agency of the law in the production of death (v 5; "through what is good"—v 13) can now be complemented and integrated with the agency of the law in bringing home the actuality and character of sin (v 7; "through the commandment": v 13). Sin in achieving its end through the law simply shows itself to be a power which kills and which can offer man (in reality as opposed to deception) nothing better than or beyond death. It is the law, even in being manipulated by sin and becoming a power of condemnation, even in that very transition from "for life" to "for death," it is the law which reveals sin's true nature as a power completely outside the realm of God's grace, opposed beyond measure to God's good will and purpose for humankind. Thus even as the power which binds sin to death and determines the consequences of man's disobedience (4:15), the law is still fulfilling its divinely appointed purpose, it is still the measure of good and evil, it still serves man's ultimate benefit by showing what the alternative to humble faith is in all its stark reality.

14–25 What follows is clearly intended by Paul as a clarification and elaboration of this last summary statement exculpating the law from any blame for man's death. Why such a lengthy explanation when he has done what he set out to do—that is, disentangled the role of the law from sin and death so that its involvement with them can be properly appreciated, namely, as God's double agent, used by sin to produce death, but at the same time by God in revealing the deadly effect of sin? Why does Paul not turn at once to the elaboration of the other side of the antithesis of v 6, "newness of Spirit," as some of his readers may have expected? The answer is probably twofold.

First, Paul's last two sentences could be said to have gone too far in reinstating the law, throwing the earlier more negative characterization of the law into possible confusion. If the law is so holy and just and good, is it after all such a bad thing to be "under the law"? How can something good be antithetical to grace (6:14–15)? Indeed, as we noted in chap. 6, Paul's Jewish contemporaries would have thought Paul perverse in failing to take what to them was the obvious step of seeing the law as a vehicle of grace, God's agent in sanctifying his people and effecting his good purpose. To push that line, however, would be to miss Paul's point: the law is holy and just and good precisely in that it effects God's purpose of condemning sin, and of showing sin to be what it is, of binding sin to death. That which is good is still to be set alongside sin and death in characterizing the old epoch (5:20–21). Where Paul's kinsfolk had gone wrong, in terms of the present analysis, is that they thought the law would stop sin bringing forth its fruit of death, and so would break the nexus of sin and death (cf. Lev 18:5). Paul disagrees profoundly: only Christ broke that deadly connection, and precisely by his death. Apart from Christ the law cannot achieve this vital breakthrough, cannot liberate from the dominance of sin and death (but must rather be liberated—7:4–6). It is precisely this inability of the law to bring about man's holiness, righteousness, and good which Paul evidently feels the need to explore further, presumably with his fellow Jews' misunderstanding of the law in mind, though this does not become apparent until 8:3–4.

Second, in integrating the role of the law (7:1–13) into his analysis of how grace has answered the power of sin and death (chap. 6), Paul has once again made his point in clear-cut terms, just as he did in the first half of chap. 6. But just as in 6:12–23 he also went on to qualify the sharpness of the first two indicatives by his sequence of imperatives, so now he proceeds to qualify the clear outlines of the law's double function (7:7–13) to take account of the reality of the eschatological tension. For since sin has not yet produced its complete crop of death (and will not until the death of the mortal body), the reality of the present is that the power of sin and death is still in operation, still holds sway over the old epoch and still holds sway over man so long as he is part of the old epoch. And this means, above all, the believers, who have already identified with Christ in his death but are not yet made wholly one with Christ in his resurrection (and will not be so until their mortal bodies are also made alive—8:11). For it is precisely as believers that they are caught up in the eschatological tension already indicated in 6:12–23. How then is the role of the law affected by this unpalatable fact that sin and death still have a claim and a say over believers insofar as they are not yet wholly one with Christ, how is its more complex relation with sin and death affected by this eschatological tension, by the fact that the believer is suspended (so uncomfortably) between the death and resurrection of Christ? Paul evidently felt the need to explore this tension, and how it is reflected both in the personality of the believer and in the law itself.

14 Throughout this section (vv 7–25) Paul uses the first person singular, "I"/"me." It was clear enough in vv 7–13 that the "I" was Adam, not Paul himself as such or indeed any individual in particular, but man (= *adam*), *every* human being, fallen humanity caught within the realm of sin and death. The sequence of past tenses would have heightened the impression that Paul was describing his *own* past as well, characterizing the universal experience of the old epoch as his own—what he *now* saw, as he looked back from his present position "in Christ," to have been a fatal entrapment in the meshes of sin and death. But the use of the pluperfect in the second half of v 7 ("I would not have known") probably already reflected Paul's awareness that his experience of coveting was not something confined to his pre-Christian period: what he began to experience within the old epoch he still continued to experience. And now in v 14 he switches from the past (vv 7–11) to the present tense: "I am a man of flesh." He makes the transition without fanfare, though no less deliberately (using both "I" and "am"), and perhaps the first listeners would not notice it straightaway. But they could scarcely miss the intensified note of existential anguish and frustration which at once becomes the dominant feature of the following verses. Even if the "I" of vv 7–13 has no specific self-reference to Paul, the expressions which follow are too sharply poignant and intensely personal to be regarded as simply a figure of style, an artist's model decked out in artificially contrived emotions. Paul probably intended the universal "I" of Adam to be kept in mind, but the following verses' character as personal testimony is too firmly impressed upon the language to be ignored. As a statement of what cannot be simply consigned to the past but is still true, Paul's testimony strikes a somewhat chilling and sobering note when compared with vv 4–6. For it says in effect that the Adam of the old epoch is still alive. He dies with the old epoch; that had been said clearly enough in 6:2–11 and 7:1–6. The trouble is, the old epoch itself has not yet run its full course. So long as the resurrection is not yet, the "I" of the old epoch is still alive, still a factor in the believer's experience in this body.

"We know. . . ." The contrast with the otherwise dominant first person singular may well be deliberate. Even though the exposition is moving on from the backward glance to man's fall, the subject matter evidently prevents Paul from reverting completely to the generalizing first person plural. Evidently what Paul has to say he can only say in starkly personal and individual terms. Those whose experience accorded with what follows would recognize its wider reference without needing to have it pointed out. But at least the starkness of the soliloquy can be momentarily relieved by an appeal to the readers' general knowledge of and appreciation for the law.

The description of the law as "spiritual" however is, if anything, even more surprising than the description of it as "holy and just and good" (v 12). For "spiritual" must be intended by Paul to associate the law with the (divine) Spirit, either as to its source or as to its character. And Paul has already indicated clearly enough that the law and the Spirit are more antithetical than complementary, belonging to and indeed characterizing by way of contrast the two epochs, old and new, before Christ and after Christ (7:6; and earlier 2:29; 3:21; 6:14–15). The most probable implication of this surprising juxtaposition therefore is that there is some overlap between the two epochs, that the law is not simply to be confined to the old epoch. The disentangling of the law from the clutches of sin and death (vv 7–13) by no means restores it to the status of an unqualified good, but at least the understanding is thereby liberated to recognize that there is more to the law than its manipulation by sin. But this continued rehabilitation of the law (vv 12–14) only poses the underlying problem more sharply still: if the law is of the Spirit, why can it not after all be a means of grace (if "pneumatic," why not "charismatic"—1:11; 1 Cor 12:1, 4, 31; 14:1)? Why is it that the righteousness of God had to be manifested without the law (3:21)? What is it that keeps the law from fulfilling its spiritual function and aim?

The answer is provided by the second half of the verse, "But I am a man of flesh, sold as a slave to sin." "I" belong to this world, to the old epoch which is to pass; my dependency on the appetites of this mortal body yet continues. As such "I" am still within sin's power, my slavery to sin unbroken; as such "I" am still sin's chattel, sin can have its way with me. The answer is so astounding that many would probably jump to the conclusion that Paul must after all be speaking of his *previous* condition (as many have since). How can he who has died to sin (6:2), who has been liberated from sin (6:18), still be sin's bondslave? But those who appreciated the qualification which the imperatives in 6:12–23 had brought to that chapter's indicatives would also recognize that here too Paul is beginning to sketch in the reality of the eschatological tension. Having outlined the *dis*continuity of the two epochs (7:1–6), now he begins to elaborate the continuity, the continuity in the overlap of the ages of which a redemption begun but not yet completed consists. Having shown that the law in its real nature as good and spiritual cannot therefore be consigned without remainder to the old epoch of Adam, so now he confesses that he himself cannot yet be consigned wholly to the new age of Christ. It is precisely in the overlap of the ages that the law and "I" dance our frustrated fandango, and sin can play cat and mouse with both.

Paul then is evidently reworking the antithesis of 7:6. If that reworking is to be appreciated, attention should not be focused exclusively on the last clause of v 14, as has been so often the case. In Paul's intention the first half of the sentence is equally provocative, and deliberately so. To call the law "spiritual" breaks down the sharp contrast between law and Spirit in 7:6 no less strikingly than calling himself the bondslave of sin. The point is that the initial antithesis was too sharp (as were the indicatives of 6:2–11): the law is not merely sin's cat's-paw, but nor am "I" yet free from sin. In short, the fatal flaw of the old epoch is not the law itself, but the interaction of sin, law and "I" as a man of flesh. How does this work out in the overlap of the epochs?

15 The key to what would otherwise throw his previous exposition into hopeless confusion (v 14) is given by Paul in the explanation that follows. The explanation is, quite simply, that there is a split in the "I," here (v 15) between my willing and my doing: "I don't do what I want, but I do what I hate." Although Paul rings the changes on the terms he uses over the next few verses, in order to give variety and not to press particular distinctions of meaning, the strength of feeling in the opening formulation should not be ignored: there are things he does which he abhors and detests, and yet it is he himself who does them. No wonder he opens his explanation with a confession of confusion or frustration: "I do not understand what I do, I do not even acknowledge my own action."

The point is that, so far as we can tell from Paul's own testimony (Phil 3:4–6), Paul knew no such frustration or self-depreciation in his preconversion days. The existential anguish of v 15 must therefore express or at least include Paul's experience as one who has already been accepted by and through Christ and already received the Spirit. Here precisely is part of the significance of the difference in tenses between vv 7–13 and vv 14–25: where vv 7–13 represent some distancing in time from a past whose character Paul now recognizes, vv 14–25 speak of a present Paul cannot escape, precisely because it is *his* present. It is not Paul the pious Pharisee who speaks here, but Paul the humble believer; and whoever else he speaks of, he certainly speaks of himself. Evidently conversion for Paul meant becoming aware as never before of the power of sin in his own life (cf. Phil 3:7–9), not just as a power now broken insofar as he had died with Christ, but as a power still in play insofar as he was still a man of flesh (cf. Phil 3:10–21).

16–17 The split in the believing "I" matches the "split" in the law. The willing "I" agrees with the law and thus bears witness that it is good. "I" accept the law's definition of God's will, and desire to do it, but still "I" fail. The fault then lies not in the law; in this it is wholly blameless and praiseworthy. But neither does the fault lie in the "I," even in the "I" who am "sold under sin." Rather the fault lies once again with sin; the sin which dwells in me. The careful reader would not fail to note the parallel with v 13: as Paul had there exculpated the law, so now he exculpates himself. This is by no means to say that Paul seeks to escape the responsibility for his wrongdoing; it is still he himself who does what he hates. Rather he confesses his consciousness of sin as a power which can still exercise its lordship over himself as a man of flesh, a constraining power from which he has not yet fully escaped since he is not yet fully redeemed. By thus defining the true nature of his impotence at this point Paul avoids the mistake of allowing self-depreciation to deteriorate into self-detestation.

Paul's strategy is thus beginning to become clear: the split in the believer's "I" corresponds to the double function of the law. There is the willing "I" = the "I" already identified with Christ in his death = the "I" no longer under the law of works but obedient to the law of faith, that is, to the law as spiritual. And there is the impotent "I" = the "I" as a man of flesh = the "I" not yet identified with Christ in his resurrection = the "I" still under the dominion of the law as used by sin to consign me to death. Were it not for sin the double split need never have happened: the "I" who testifies that the law is good and desires to obey it would be able to translate will into action; the law would be a means to life, and death would have no triumph. But sin perverts the law and holds me captive. The liberation of me, not least to a true appreciation of the law, has begun, and begun decisively, but it is not yet complete.

18–20 Vv 18–20 repeat more or less what has just been said (vv 14–17). Paul is conscious that what he writes will be *heard* rather than personally read by most of the letter's recipients. And evidently he wants his point to be clearly understood: he does not exempt the law from blame in order to denigrate humanity as such. "I know"—the singular verb matches the switch from plural to singular in v 14. What Paul says he says of himself. It is the

believing "I" who speaks, so his words have much wider application in intention. But Paul continues to express his analysis as a personal confession; let
all who will acknowledge its truth for themselves.

"In me, that is, my flesh" = "I am a man of flesh" (v 14). Paul does not
take what to many would have been the easy way out; he does not attempt
to distinguish the "I" from "the flesh," to exonerate the willing "I" from
any blame for its impotence by depicting it as imprisoned within the flesh.
He does not, in other words, opt for a dualism which understands the "I"
as an element of a higher world incarcerated within the lower world of matter.
He is confused and frustrated by his powerlessness (v 15), but he understands
well enough that he himself is the subject performing the actions he himself
abhors (vv 15–16). That is why we must speak of a split in the "I" rather
than of a split between the "I" and the flesh. Paul is talking about himself
in his belongingness to the world of flesh, the old epoch. However much he
may also rejoice in his belongingness with Christ to the life beyond the resurrection, the new epoch, he recognizes with all seriousness that he is still
flesh; that is, still inextricably bound up with the fallen world, an attachment
which only death will sever, when the believer's identification with Christ's
death has worked itself out completely.

"No good thing" = "sold under sin" (v 14)—again not an expression of
self-loathing which might become an excuse for a masochistic asceticism or
a license for gluttony. This is Paul's sober evaluation of what it means to be
part of this world with its dependence on the satisfaction of human appetites
and its involvement with people of different views and temperaments. Paul
accepted his being part of this world. He did not seek to escape it into some
wilderness retreat, or to cloak it by spinning some theory of salvation which
refused to acknowledge its reality, or to wallow in it by way of self-indulgence
or self-justification. He simply accepted that there is this dimension of the
believers' existence which remains part of this world, a dimension where
the law's good is constantly perverted, sin's continuing bridgehead or foothold
within believers themselves which the Crucified has not yet conquered.

The main difference between vv 14–17 and vv 18–20 is that the law is
not specifically mentioned in the latter, though its presence is echoed in
Paul's repetition of both variations of the word "good" (vv 18–19; cf. vv 12–
13, 16). The point Paul hopes to make by covering the ground again therefore
may partly be that even when the law is not in focus in an analysis of man
in his belongingness to the old epoch, the situation achieved by sin in its
archetypal attack on man through the commandment (vv 7–13) is still in
force. "I" have the will to do good, the good which the law defines, but not
the strength to translate that willing into action. But the fault is not in the
"I": the "I" is split, suspended between the epochs, divided between my belonging to Christ and my belonging to this age; the blame lies rather with sin.
And it is not the split itself which sin uses, as though sin could manipulate
both "I"s to achieve a kind of schizophrenia. Sin cannot touch me in my
belongingness to Christ, but sin still holds sway over the world to which "I"
still belong as a man of flesh.

All that "I" do, therefore, as a being of flesh bears testimony to the power
of sin. Not that Paul thereby denigrates everything which he does, or denies
that he can do any good prior to the resurrection (cf. 2:7–16). *Both* sides of

the eschatological tension must be observed: what is done in Christ, through the Spirit, bears testimony to the power of God (cf. e.g., 1 Cor 2:4–5). But sin, having achieved its bridgehead in humanity through the law, still sits there and still exercises its influence whether the law is in view or not. The more that any, believers included, live their lives in terms of their attachment to and dependence on this world, the more certain they can be that they are living on sin's terms, whether or not the law has made them aware of it.

21 V 21 is evidently the conclusion to the argument developed and restated in the preceding paragraph (vv 14–20): "So I find the law for me willing to do the good, that evil lies ready to hand." In this way Paul reintroduces talk of the law, now that the impotence of man has been clearly stated and the culpability of sin (without reference to the law, vv 18–20). He does not simply throw up his hands in despair and formulate a further "law," wholly unrelated to the main subject matter of the chapter (the role of the law in relation to sin and death and the believer), a "law of nature"(!) without any clear reference to God or his purpose (an unwelcome loose end for a soteriology as fully thought through as Paul's). Such an interpretation fails to appreciate the sharpness of the tension in Paul's evaluation of the Torah (most clearly evident already in 3:27–31 and 7:12–14). Rather it is the powerlessness of the man of flesh (including the believer) before the continuing power of sin which reveals the powerlessness of the law. Even with a will strengthened by the law, the flesh controlled by sin prevents the translation of the desired good into action.

22–23 Vv 22–23 elaborate the conclusion (v 21) by spelling out explicitly what has already been implicit: that the split in the "I" is mirrored in an equivalent split in the law. In vv 22–23 the double agency of the law (v 13) is matched against and redefined in relation to the believer's divided self. "I delight in the law of God" would most obviously be taken as a reference to the law as holy and just, good and spiritual (vv 12–14), since Paul can hardly mean that he joyfully agrees with the law as characterizing the old epoch in contrast to grace (6:14–15), or that he delights in the law's role as sin's agent in bringing about death (7:10–13). The law thus seen in its true nature as "the law of God" "fits" with "the inner self." Paul's readers could hardly avoid identifying the law in its true nature with the willing "I," the "I" that rejoices in the law from the heart but is frustrated as also a fleshly "I" in the task of translating willing into doing.

In v 23 the matching up of the divided "I" with the divided law is rounded off. The "other law in my constituent parts," more fully defined at the end of the verse as "the law of sin which is in my constituent parts" (= "the law of sin and death," 8:2), can hardly be other than the law used by sin to bring about death, as already explained in vv 11–13. In describing the "other law" as the principal actor, Paul reverts to the portrayal of the law as a power dominating the old epoch (6:14–15): even though the real blame lies with sin (7:7–13), the law can be said to characterize the old epoch, precisely as "the law of sin." "The law of my mind" likewise is hardly to be distinguished from the law recognized by the willing "I" as spiritual and good (vv 14–16), the law of God in which the inner man delights (v 22).

The situation is characterized as one of warfare, with victory going to the

law as used by sin. Here again, and more explicitly than in v 21, the point
is precisely that the law is powerless. That is why the revelation of righteousness
that marks out the new epoch had to be "apart from the law" (3:21), for to
give the law center stage is to revert to the old epoch; the law, even as the
law of God, is not strong enough to defeat the power of sin. That is why
also it would not be enough to characterize the new epoch simply as a deeper
willing to do the law, a fuller appreciation of its nature as spiritual, the law
of God; because that would still leave the "I" powerless. The key is something
else, shortly to be expounded as a new power source (the Spirit, chap. 8).
In the meantime, however, Paul does not mince words in describing the
plight of the human being, including the believer, in membership in the
old epoch. The individual is constantly being taken captive by the law of
sin; moral choice after moral choice proves the extent to which he or she is
still sin's bondslave (v 14). The believer not least insofar as he is still a person
of flesh has to confess defeat repeatedly, precisely because he is still a being
of flesh. The reality of the moral choice, described in 6:13 and perhaps
echoed here, as a *real* choice, where the right choice cannot be taken for
granted (6:2–11 describes the beginning of a new stage but not its completion),
is thus reemphasized with a fearful solemnity, for it is a choice that so often
leads to defeat; indeed, when the options are analyzed solely in terms of sin
and the law, defeat is invariable, for the law is no match for sin.

24 "Wretched man that I am! Who will deliver me from the body of
this death?" The existential anguish of the speaker at his plight just described
bursts forth. Here certainly Paul speaks for himself, and not merely as a
spokesperson for humanity at large; this is not the stylized formulation of
one who is long since removed from the situation in question. The one who
cries for help so piteously cries from *within* the contradiction; he longs for
deliverance *from* the endless war and frequent defeat. "The body of this death"
is Paul in his belonging to this age, and to that extent still under the domination
of sin and death. Sin has not yet brought forth its full fruit of death; or,
alternatively expressed, Paul has not yet been fully conformed to Christ's
death (Phil 3:10). It is for this deliverance that he cries. Once again, not for
escape from the body, as though the problem was materiality; if his readers
were not already aware that Paul looked for a redemption *of* the body (cf. 1
Cor 15), they soon would be (Rom 8:11, 23). For escape, yes; but escape
from the body as bound to death, escape from an age under the dominion
of sin and death, escape from the tension of being suspended between the
two ages, between the death of Christ and his own. This is not a cry of
despair, so much as a cry of frustration; not of despair, because Paul is certainly
confident that the full deliverance will come (cf. 5:9–10; 6:8; 11:26), but of
frustration—the frustration of trying to walk in newness of life (6:4) while
still a man of flesh, the frustration of seeking to serve in newness of Spirit
(7:6) through this body of death.

25 The response to the anguished question of v 24 is rather odd, for it
reads more as a thanksgiving to God than as an answer to his question.
Nevertheless Paul must have intended his readers to understand it as an
answer: either that deliverance will come through Jesus Christ, or that God
will achieve the longed-for deliverance through Christ. In effect it comes to

the same thing, since Paul does not think of Christ acting in any sense independently of God, nor even as merely the agent of God, but rather as the embodiment and expression of God's saving purpose (cf. 10:12–13; 1 Cor 1:24, 30; 8:6; 2 Cor 5:19). In either case the redemption will be achieved through Christ presumably at and/or by means of his Parousia (cf. 11:26; 1 Cor 15:42–57; 1 Thess 1:10). In either case the thanksgiving is directed to God as the effective source of the desired deliverance.

Following the exclamation of confidence in God's purpose through Jesus Christ comes the statement of calm realism about the continuing state of affairs. It is a sober, but fitting conclusion to the exposition of vv 7–25. Until God sets that final deliverance in motion, the condition established epochally through Christ's death and resurrection, and personally through conversion-initiation, still pertains. "I myself serve the law of God with the mind, and the law of sin with the flesh." The "I" is emphatic: the character of the exposition as Paul's personal confession is sustained to the end. There is no attempt to align the "I" solely with the mind: the "I" is equally the "I" of the mind and the "I" of the flesh, Paul himself ever conscious of living in two different dimensions at one and the same time with their conflicting demands and needs. Nor is there anything pejorative about the verb "serve," the same verb used in 7:6. It simply describes the fact of a continuing dependency of the flesh upon appetites and desires that sin manipulates through the law to produce corruption and death; but it also describes a dependency of the mind upon what it perceives as the will of God in and through the Torah. The point is, until the final deliverance is achieved through Jesus Christ, the split continues, epochally between old epoch and new, personally in the believer. The divided "I" continues to experience the divided character of the law: "I" as mind, "I" united with Christ in his death, experience the law as the law of God; "I" as flesh, not yet united with Christ in his resurrection, experience the law as the law of sin.

V 25b is a classic statement of the eschatological tension set up by the death and resurrection of Christ; through his death writing finis to the age of Adam and through his resurrection introducing the age of the last Adam. In Paul's understanding the tension is not one that is natural to man, or one that is consequent upon the fall of man. The fallenness of man is one side of it, but the tension is only set up by the introduction of the eschatological "now" in Christ. And it only becomes personal for Paul with conversion-initiation. The tension then is a tension not simply of redemption delayed, but precisely of a redemption already begun but not yet completed. The very fact that he can envisage a service of the law of God with the mind presupposes a renewed mind (cf. 12:2), a having died with Christ (6:2–11); while the continuing service of the law of sin with the flesh clearly indicates a dimension of the believer's existence not yet caught up in the risen life of Christ (cf. 8:11, 23), a having-not-yet-been-raised with Christ (6:5, 8). The assurance of future deliverance does not itself bring to an end the eschatological tension in which believers find themselves caught.

Contrary to some popular piety, which might have had a following at the time of Paul (cf. 1 Cor 4:8), Paul does not teach that conversion-initiation brings a complete ending of or release from the flesh, or an immediate and lasting victory over the power of sin (as might have been deduced from a shallow reading of 6:1–11 or 7:1–6). On the contrary, it is spiritual warfare which is the sign of life. The eschatological tension is itself a proof that identification with Christ in his death has begun; it is the risen power of Christ which has begun to combat the power of sin. Pastorally this emphasis is of considerable importance, since in it we see Paul accepting with all serious- ness the reality of the human condition in which believers still find themselves— even as Christians still part of this world of flesh and mortality. On the other hand, Paul's teaching here is not intended to provide an easy excuse for persistent moral defeat—only an excuse for defeat experienced as *defeat,* as a wretched captivity and slavery to sin. Paul can and does readily conceive of believers being frequently defeated (v 23) in the continuous sequence of moral choices which confront them (6:12–23), but he cannot conceive of believers treating such defeats as a matter of little consequence, of their ever becoming less earnest in seeking to wage that war, to serve the law of righteous- ness, far less of their justifying and glorying in their subservience to sin. Such a believer has forgotten chap. 6 and has not yet reached chap. 8. In short, 7:7–25 has to be seen within the context of chaps. 6–8, as an exposition of an unavoidable aspect of the believer's life within this world, an aspect impossible to ignore, but never to be viewed in isolation from the preliminary statement and exhortations of chap. 6 or from the complementary exposition of chap. 8.

C. The Eschatological Tension and Fulfillment of God's Purpose through the Spirit (8:1–30)

Introduction

Having dealt in sequence with the continuing impact of the powers of sin and death in the life of the believer (chap. 6) and then with the ambivalent role of the law, whether determined by sin or by God (chap. 7), Paul returns to the conclusion reached in chap. 5 in the same clear-cut terms already used in 6:4 and 7:5, but now with the focus narrowing to the other factor (other than the death and resurrection of Christ), which makes all the differ- ence in the new age: the Spirit (πνεῦμα, 21 times in chap. 8).

The reason Paul left the unfolding of this crucial category till now becomes clear in vv 10 ff. For it is the Spirit which above all else provides the key to understand the eschatological tension in which believers find themselves: the Spirit, whose reception effected sonship to God (vv 14–17), is only the begin- ning ("firstfruits") of a harvest of salvation which remains incomplete until the resurrection of the body (vv 11, 23); and by referring to the Spirit of God the process of individual salvation can be set within a cosmic (vv 18– 28) and salvation-history framework (vv 29–30). Hence in following the pattern of chaps. 6 and 7 (sharp salvation-historical antitheses, followed by a more qualified appraisal; cf. Nygren, 308–9), Paul this time follows through the eschatological qualification to the end, showing how it is the Spirit that brings the eschatological life of believers to complete fruition in the cosmic liberation of the resurrection (vv 11, 19–23), by guaranteeing their hope (vv 24–25; cf. 5:5), by sustaining them in the weakness of their this-ageness (vv 26–27), and by thus confirming their assurance of future glory (vv 17–21, 28–30). "Thus the eschatological theology of Rom 8:18 ff. stands between enthusiasm and realism" (Balz, *Heilsvertrauen*, 125).

1. The Spirit of Life (8:1–11)

Bibliography

Benoit, P. "The Law and the Cross according to St Paul." *Jesus.* 22–32. **Branick, V. P.** "The Sinful Flesh of the Son of God (Rom 8:3): A Key Image of Pauline Theology." *CBQ* 47 (1985) 246–62. **Cranfield, C. E. B.** "The Freedom of the Christian according to Rom 8:2." In *New Testament Christianity for Africa and the World*, FS H. Sawyerr, ed. M. E. Glasswell and E. W. Fasholé-Luke. London: SPCK, 1974. 91–98. **Deidun, T. J.** *Morality.* 69–78, 194–203. **Dibelius**, "Vier Worte." 8–14. **Dülmen, A. van.** *Theologie.* 119–23. **Dunn, J. D. G.** *Baptism.* 147–49. ———. *Jesus.* 315–16. ———. *Christology.* 44–45, 111–12, 144–45. **Fuchs, E.** "Der Anteil des Geistes am Glauben des Paulus: Ein Beitrag zum Verständnis von Römer 8." *ZTK* 72 (1975) 293–302. **Gillman, F. M.** "Another Look at Romans 8:3: 'In the Likeness of Sinful Flesh.'" *CBQ* 49 (1987) 597–604. **Hermann, I.** *Kyrios und Pneuma: Studien zur Christologie der paulinischen Hauptbriefen.* SANT. Munich: Kösel, 1961. 65–66. **Hübner, H.** *Law.* 144–49. **Jones, F. S.** *"Freiheit."* 122–29. **Keck, L. E.** "The Law of 'The Law of Sin and Death' [Rom 8:1–4]: Reflections on the Spirit and Ethics in Paul." In *The Divine Helmsman*, FS L. H. Silberman, ed. J. L. Crenshaw and S. Sandmel. New York: Ktav, 1980. 41–57. **Kuhn, K. G.** "New Light on Temptation, Sin, and Flesh in the New Testament." *The Scrolls and the New Testament.* Ed. K. Stendahl. London: SCM, 1958. 94–113. **Lohse, E.** "ὁ νόμος τοῦ πνεύματος τῆς ζωῆς: Exegetische Anmerkungen zu Röm 8:2." *Vielfalt.* 128–36. ———. "Zur Analyse und Interpretation von Röm 8:1–17." In Lorenzi, *Law of Spirit.* 129–46. **Lyonnet, S.** "Christian Freedom and the Law of the Spirit According to St Paul." In *The Christian Lives by the Spirit*, I. de la Potterie and S. Lyonnet. Tr. John Morris. Staten Island: Alba House, 1971. 145–74. **Moule, C. F. D.** "'Justification' in Its Relation to the Condition κατὰ πνεῦμα (Rom 8:1–11)." In Lorenzi, *Battesimo.* 177–87. **Osten-Sacken, P. von der.** *Römer 8.* 144–56, 226–42. **Paulsen, H.** *Römer 8.* 23–76. **Pfister, W.** *Das Leben im Geist nach Paulus.* Freiburg: Universitätsverlag, 1963. **Räisänen, H.** "Das 'Gesetz des Glaubens' (Röm 3:27) und das 'Gesetz des Geistes' (Röm 8:2)." *NTS* 26 (1979–80) 101–17. Repr. in *Torah*, 95–118. **Schmithals, W.** *Anthropologie.* 83–117. **Schrage, W.** *Einzelgebote.* 71–93. **Schnabel, E. J.** *Law.* 288–90. **Schweizer, E.** "Zum religionsgeschichtlichen Hintergrund der 'Sendungsformel' Gal 4:4 f.; Röm 8:3 f.; Joh. 3:16 f.; 1 Joh. 4:9." *ZNW* 57 (1966) 199 ff. Repr. in *Beiträge zur Theologie des Neuen Testaments.* Zürich: Zwingli, 1970. 83–95. **Stalder, K.** *Das Werk des Geistes in der Heiligung bei Paulus.* Zürich: EVZ, 1962. 387–487. **Stanley, D. M.** *Resurrection.* 189–92. **Thompson, R. W.** "How Is the Law Fulfilled in Us? An Interpretation of Rom 8:4." *Louvain Studies* 11 (1986) 31–40. **Wright, N. T.** "The Meaning of περὶ ἁμαρτίας in Romans 8:3." In *Studia Biblica 1978 III*, ed. E. A. Livingstone. JSNTSup 3. Sheffield: JSOT, 1980. 453–59.

Translation

[1] *So now, there is no condemnation for those in Christ Jesus.*[a] [2] *For the law of the Spirit of life in Christ Jesus has set you*[b] *free from the law of sin and death.* [3] *For what the law was unable to do in that it was weak through the flesh, God sent his own Son in the very likeness of sinful flesh and as a sin offering and condemned sin in the flesh,* [4] *in order that the requirement of the law might be fulfilled in us who walk not in accordance with the flesh but in accordance with the Spirit.* [5] *For those who exist in terms of the flesh take the side of the flesh, whereas those who exist in terms of the Spirit take the side of the Spirit.* [6] *For the flesh's way of thinking is death, whereas the Spirit's way of thinking is life and peace.* [7] *Because the flesh's way of thinking is hostility toward God, for it does not submit itself to the law of God; for it cannot.* [8] *And those who are in the flesh are not able to please God.* [9] *However, you are not in the flesh but in the Spirit, assuming that the Spirit of God does indeed dwell in you—if anyone does not have the Spirit of Christ, he does not belong to him.* [10] *And if Christ is in you, the body is dead because of sin, but the Spirit is life because of righteousness.* [11] *But if the Spirit of him who raised Jesus from the dead dwells in you, he who raised Christ*[c] *from the dead will give life to your mortal bodies as well,*[d] *through*[e] *his Spirit which dwells in you.*

Notes

[a] At the end of v 1 scribes added μὴ κατὰ σάρκα περιπατοῦσιν and later also ἀλλὰ κατὰ πνεῦμα, indicating the practice of clarifying a text by expanding it and the continuing willingness of scribes to follow this practice well into the early centuries. See Metzger.

[b] μέ is read by a number of witnesses and used to be frequently preferred (SH; Lietzmann, in view of strong early Egyptian support, followed by Schmidt); but σέ is now widely preferred as *lectio difficilior* and in view of its MS support (though see Metzger).

[c] Ἰησοῦν appears to have been inserted here and the word order changed at some stage in the transmission of the text, resulting in a variety of combinations. See Metzger.

[d] The καί has been omitted in some MSS as unnecessary.

[e] διά + accusative ("on account of his Spirit . . .") has strong support in the textual tradition, but διά + genitive is almost certainly to be preferred (see especially Cranfield and Metzger; against Schweizer, *TDNT* 6:422).

Form and Structure

As in chap. 7, the opening verses (8:1–4) function as a transition to the main discussion: the answer to sin and death is given (by the death of Christ as sin offering) and the two-sidedness of the law reaffirmed (both "law of . . . death" and "law of . . . life," both weak through the flesh but also fulfilled through the Spirit); and then these much used categories give way to the one other, "flesh," which has appeared episodically before (7:5, 18, 25) but which now comes to dominate the first half of the chapter (σάρξ—13 times in vv 1–13) and to sum up the weakness and corruptibility of man belonging to this age (vv 17 ff). The πνεῦμα/σάρξ antithesis (vv 4–9, 12–13) thus displaces the themes so dominant in chaps. 6 and 7—ἁμαρτία (5 times, but only once after v 3), θάνατος (3 times—vv 2, 6, 38) and νόμος (5 times, but only v 7 after v 4). What has been lacking in chaps. 6–7, namely, a constant category to describe the force which defeats sin and death (and rehabilitates the law) (hitherto only χάρις, δικαιοσύνη, and πνεῦμα episodically), is now given in πνεῦμα. Consequently it is the Spirit who can be described as determinative for Christian belonging and sonship (vv 9, 14).

Stylistic features include the νόμος/νόμος contrast in v 2 and the σάρξ/πνεῦμα antitheses in vv 4–6, 9 (σῶμα/πνεῦμα, vv 10–11), the syntactically inarticulated clause at the beginning of v 3, the epigrammatic terseness particularly of vv 6 and 10, and the sequence of εἰ clauses in vv 9–11 (Paulsen, 38).

Comment

1 οὐδὲν ἄρα νῦν κατάκριμα τοῖς ἐν Χριστῷ Ἰησοῦ, "so now, there is no condemnation for those who are in Christ Jesus." The awkwardness of the transition from 7:25 to 8:1 ("I . . . serve the law of sin. So, now, there is no condemnation . . .") has caused much perplexity and prompted several commentators to resort to the hypothesis that the verse (together with 7:25b) has been displaced, or entered the text as a gloss (see also on 7:25b). Such hypotheses, however, are quite unnecessary. Paul most likely intended a pause between 7:25 and 8:1, an indication of the flow of thought easily signaled both in dictation and in reading the letter to the Roman congregations; once again we must recall that the letter was written more to be *heard* than read. The linking words (ἄρα νῦν) should probably be read with this force. (1) The normal ἄρα phrase used by Paul is ἄρα οὖν (5:18; 7:3, 25; 8:12; 9:16, 18; 14:12, 19). The two particles together strengthen each other and indicate a conclusion or corollary drawn with immediate force from what has just been said. But the ἄρα alone is the weaker linking word of the two and when used thus at the beginning of a new section probably indicates a less direct connection with the immediately preceding context. (2) The νῦν is, as usual, eschatological (as in 3:26; 5:9, 11; 6:19, 21; 8:18, 22; 11:5, 30–31; 13:11; 16:26; as also νυνί in 3:21; 6:22; 7:6, 17). After the exposition of the more confused situation in which the eschatological tension places both the "I" and the law (7:7–25), Paul deliberately recalls the once-for-allness of the eschatological indicative, the opening of the new epoch effected by Christ. (3) κατάκριμα likewise recalls the thought to the great climax of 5:12–21, where the only other NT references occur (see on 5:16). It is the black and white contrast between the epochs (Adam and Christ) marked out so decisively in 5:12–21 to which Paul here reverts, not the grayer area of overlap which characterizes so much of the discussion in the latter halves of chaps. 6 and 7 (but note Bruce's translation, "penal servitude"). If in 8:1 the thought skips back to 7:6 (Barrett, Cranfield, Schlier), it does not stop there. (4) So too the τοῖς ἐν Χριστῷ Ἰησοῦ focuses the thought once again sharply on what it means to belong to the epoch of Christ in distinction to that of Adam. "Those in Christ Jesus" are those who have been identified (and have identified themselves) with Christ in his death (see on 6:11), without complicating the thought (for the moment) that this is not yet a complete and final description of believers in the period before the resurrection of the body.

We may conclude, therefore, that the awkwardness between 7:25 and 8:1 arises only because Paul has followed his usual procedure for each of these chapters (see chaps. 6–8 *Introduction*). That is to say, he states the contrast between the two epochs, and between the before-and-after of conversion-initiation, in simple and sharply antithetical terms, before going on to qualify and soften the antitheses in accordance with the continuing tensions of his (own) experience as a believer. The transition between 7:25 and 8:1 is simply the point at which the more complex analysis of the role of the law in the overlap between the ages has been worked through, at which point Paul pauses and recalls once again the sharply defined terms of his starting point. (The transition between 6:23 and 7:1 was not so awkward: chap. 6 maintained its note of exhortation to the end, whereas chap. 7 ended with its note of calm and sober realism.) 8:1 therefore signals the beginning of a fresh exposition of the reality of the salvation process in the present, this time in terms of the Spirit. Important as it is for Paul to refrain from glossing over the reality of the eschatological tension (7:25b), it is equally and more important to be able also to resort once again to the grand simplicities of faith (8:1).

2 If v 1 is the restatement of the major theme of the composition in the now familiar chord, massively impressive in its solemn simplicity, v 2 is the beginning of yet another variation on it, a third exposition (γάρ), this time in the key of the Spirit. Prominent features of this variation have already been foreshadowed in 2:29; 5:5; and 7:6.

ὁ γὰρ νόμος τοῦ πνεύματος τῆς ζωῆς, "for the law of the Spirit of life." NEB, "the life-giving law of the Spirit," and NJB, "the law of the Spirit which gives life," move too far from the parallelism with "the law of sin and death." Most commentators have found it all but impossible to take this phrase as a reference to the Torah (see, e.g., Dodd, "Law," 37; Nygren; Murray; Leenhardt; Cranfield, who changed his mind from his earlier "Paul and the Law," 166; others in Wilckens, n. 490; most recently Deidun, *Morality*, 194–203; Luz, *Gesetz*, 104; Räisänen, "Gesetz," and *Law*, 50–52; Sanders, *Law*, 15 n.26; Zeller; Harrisville). Above all there is the contrast with 7:6, with its sharp and apparently mutually exclusive antithesis between γράμμα and πνεῦμα; and the even more striking dismissal of any idea that the law could give life in Gal 3:21 (see, e.g., Käsemann, "the irreparably perverted law of Moses"). If νόμος here denotes the Torah it would mean that Paul, who has trampled so heavily on Jewish sensibilities in 5:20; 6:14; and 7:5, has abruptly reverted to more typically Jewish language; Paul here suddenly speaks with the voice of James (James 1:25)!

(1) The problem is eased when we recall that chap. 7 was devoted to explaining the role of νόμος, and, indeed, to defending νόμος. There the link between the law, the Spirit, and life was strongly affirmed: 7:14—ὁ νόμος πνευματικός ἐστιν; 7:10—ἡ ἐντολὴ ἡ εἰς ζωήν. Paul had *already* gone a long way to show that he was not attacking the law, and with the very terms he uses here. "The law of the Spirit of life" is in effect little more than a compact summary of these earlier uses. There is still a tension in the thought, but it is the tension of chap. 7. The phrase here adds nothing to it. (2) So too it must not be forgotten that the immediate sequence of thought begun in v 2 climaxes in v 4 in the assertion that "the requirement of the law" is fulfilled in those "who walk κατὰ πνεῦμα." Paul himself explicitly links the Torah and the Spirit in a wholly positive way in the very next sentence.

(3) These two observations strongly confirm that Paul is able to think of the law in two different ways: the law caught in the nexus of sin and death,

where it is met only by σάρξ, is the law as γράμμα, caught in the old epoch, abused and destructive (see on 2:28–29 and 7:6); but the law rightly understood, and responded to ἐν πνεύματι οὐ γράμματι is pleasing to God (2:29). The twofold law of v 2 therefore simply restates the two-sidedness of the law expounded in 7:7–25 in terms which would already be familiar to his readers. (4) The fact that νόμος is the subject of the sentence should not be given too much weight (as Räisänen, "Gesetz" 115–16): the structuring of the sentence is probably rhetorical—the two laws in the places of emphasis (beginning and end of the sentence); and the emphasis lies on the Spirit ("the law of the *Spirit* of life"), just as in 7:7–25 the chief culprit was not the law, but sin ("the law of *sin* and death"). (5) This correlates completely with Paul's clear assumption that the law is not antagonistic to faith, but is, on the contrary, established through faith (3:31); see further on 3:31; 9:31–32; 10:6–8; and 13:8–10. Since faith and Spirit clearly belong together in Paul's theology, even if for the sake of analysis he hardly brings them together in Romans (but cf. particularly Gal 3:1–14), the most obvious corollary is that "the obedience of faith" (1:5) is another way to describe "walking according to the Spirit" (8:4); only through that coming together of divine power and creative receptivity can the law be met with the response for which God looks.

(6) The eschatological thrust of the context and the phrase should not be overlooked. The law of the Spirit is the eschatological law (cf. Jer 31:31–34; Ezek 36:26–27); 8:1–2 speaks from within the perspective of the new epoch introduced by Christ, whereas 7:23 speaks from within the old epoch of Adam. It is the Spirit which releases "the law of the mind" (7:23) from its impotence. (7) If the inner tensions within Romans are thus resolved, the tension between 8:2 and Gal 3:21 remains. This too may, however, be softened either by positing some development in Paul's thinking on the subject between Gal and Rom (in Galatians more radical, in Romans more compromising in his attitude to the Torah; so Hübner, *Law*), or by arguing that the main thrust of Paul's critique of the law is directed against his own people's too nationalist and presumptuous attitude with regard to the law (see *Introduction* §5.3; 2:17–29; 3:27–4:25; 9:30–10:4), and that this critique dominates Gal while providing only part of the overall presentation of Romans. In fact, v 3 amounts to a repetition of Gal 3:21.

In short, since the second νόμος is still more clearly a reference to the Torah (see further below), it would throw the thought into some confusion to understand the first νόμος differently. The contrast does not lie in the νόμος itself but in the full phrase: "law of *Spirit of life*," "law of *sin and death*" (see further below). The fact that Paul attributes an active role to νόμος here (as in 3:27) is not an effective objection (against Räisänen, *Law*, 51–52); it is the law of *the Spirit of life* which has positive liberating force. In vv 3 and 4 the νόμος is even more clearly a reference to the Torah (see on 8:3); and a very positive role is attributed to this same law in vv 4 and 7. See further on 7:21 and 23; also Schmidt; Moule, "Justification"; Lohse, "Röm 8:2," and "Analyse," 137–40; Hahn, "Gesetzesverständnis," 47–48; Osten-Sacken, 226–34; Hübner, *Law*, 144–49; Wilckens; Schnabel, *Law*, 288–89).

We may note that the two νόμος phrases in v 2 are not constructed in

precise parallel: "Spirit *of* life," "sin *and* death" (against Michel). The reason
may well be that Paul could think of "sin" and "death" as two coordinated
powers whose effective influence could nevertheless be conceived separately
(cf. 5:13–14), whereas "Spirit" and "life" are more closely integrated—different
aspects of the one dynamic outpouring of life from Creator to creature (see
also Schlier). The association of Spirit and life is, of course, deeply rooted
in Jewish thought of man's dependence for the breath/spirit of life wholly
on the Creator (e.g., Gen 6:17; Ps 104:29–30; Ezek 37:5; Tob 3:6; 2 Macc
7:23). The link is equally fundamental to the earliest Christian theology,
particularly of Paul and John (Rom 8:2, 6, 10, 11, 13; 1 Cor 15:45; 2 Cor
3:6; Gal 6:8; John 4:10, 14; 6:63; 7:38–39; 20:22), and brings to expression
the basic Christian claim that God has now (eschatological now) begun through
the Spirit to fulfill his original creative purpose in making man. Cf. also
Gaugler. For πνεῦμα see further on 1:4; 5:5; 8:4 and 9. The ζωή strengthens
the reference back to chap. 5 (vv 10, 17, 18, 21) and the parallel between
6:4 and 8:4.

ἐν Χριστῷ Ἰησοῦ ἠλευθέρωσέν σε, "in Christ Jesus has set you free." The
prepositional phrase should probably be taken with the verb; to take it with
the preceding phrase ("the Spirit of life in Christ Jesus"; cf. Lagrange, Schlatter,
Dodd, Kuss, Schlier) would have very interesting corollaries for Christology
and pneumatology, but the lack of any real parallel elsewhere in Paul (though
cf. 6:23) and its unusualness alongside his other statements on these themes
tell strongly against such a construal (Cranfield); more likely the phrase is
positioned before the verb in order to give it greater emphasis; that is, the
liberation was effected in and through Christ Jesus. The verb recalls 6:18
and 22, where the same decisive aorist tense is used (see on 6:18). Paul thus
evokes once again the sense of liberation which the revelation of Christ Jesus
brought to him in his understanding of the covenant purpose of God (cf.
particularly 2 Cor 3:17, and the frequency of the freedom motif in Galatians
—2:4; 3:28; 4:22–23, 26, 30–31; 5:1, 13). In the light of his exhortations in
chap. 6 and analysis of man's fleshly impotence in chap. 7, we must assume
that Paul saw the act of liberation as decisive, but still qualified or incomplete,
that is, awaiting the final liberation of 8:21 (ἐλευθερωθήσεται). Here as in
chaps. 6 and 7 the opening aorist of chap. 8 should not be taken out of
context or read in isolation from the more circumspect cautions and warnings
which Paul goes on to express (contrast a fairly typical overstatement in Byrne,
Reckoning, 149: "To be 'in Christ' means to have been *radically cut off* . . . from
the old, sin-dominated existence 'in Adam'"; emphasis added). If we are
correct, the sense of being taken prisoner (7:23) *and* of being liberated (8:2)
are both part of the believer's experience in Paul's perception—still imprisoned
as a man of flesh by sin and death, yet at one and the same time already
liberated "in Christ Jesus." The contrast between 7:23 and 8:2 is not the
most extreme expression of the existential contradiction of faith expressed
in and through the condition of human fallenness; cf. Cranfield. The σέ
(see *Notes*) personalizes and individualizes the more general truth (cf. 7:7 ff.;
Gal 2:20).

ἀπὸ τοῦ νόμου τῆς ἁμαρτίας καὶ τοῦ θανάτου, "from the law of sin and death."
Despite reservations on the part of some commentators (see above on νόμος

τοῦ πνεύματος τῆς ζωῆς, and on 7:21) it is most unlikely that νόμος was intended here in some more general sense. Paul has already linked the law, that is, the Torah, too closely with sin and death to allow readily of any other conclusion (5:12–14, 20; 7:5, 9–11, 13, 23–24). The words here simply sum up these earlier descriptions of the interplay of sin, death, and the law in a single forceful phrase.

It is important to remember that it is not the law per se from which Paul speaks of being liberated; it is the law as manipulated by sin and death (especially 7:9–13), the law operating within the context of the age of Adam (5:20–21), the law understood at the level of the flesh and outward definition (γράμμα) (see on 2:28–29 and 7:6); the law binds that manifestation of sin as firmly to death as any other (so the sequence of argument from 1:32 through chap. 2). In the same way, it is not the law *as such* which liberates, but the law in its given purpose for life (7:10), which can only be achieved when it functions truly as an instrument of divine power (rather than of sin), understood and responded to at the level of the πνεῦμα (rather than of σάρξ), all of which itself constitutes a relativizing of all outward norms and so a crucial part of the liberating process. All these contextual points (including the "in Christ Jesus") need to be borne in mind when comparing Stoic and Cynic talk of freedom in relation to the law (in reference to Jones, 124–28, who cites particularly Epictetus 4.1.158 and 4.7.17).

3 τὸ γὰρ ἀδύνατον τοῦ νόμου, "for what the law was unable to do." The γάρ strengthens the conclusion that νόμος throughout these verses means the Torah, since the νόμος here is unquestionably the (Jewish) law (usually taken for granted by commentators), and is introduced as an explanation of the preceding uses of νόμος. The differentiation between the uses of νόμος in vv 2–3 lies not in different senses intended for νόμος itself but in the accompanying phrases which are sufficient to explain the potential for both good and ill in the law (see further on 8:2). ἀδύνατον is used as a substantive— "the powerless, impotent thing." It is difficult to choose between the more active sense ("unable") and more passive ("impossible") (see, e.g., SH and Lagrange), but the effective distinction is not very great (Kuss); either way it does not amount to an attack on the law itself (cf. again 7:9–12). The prepositional phrase, "of the law," leaves unclear what it is of which the powerlessness of the law consists. In such cases it is wiser to leave the translation as vague and as open as the Greek; BDF's "the one thing the law could not do" is too precise and restrictive (§263.2). In its undefined breadth the phrase maintains Paul's challenge to the more characteristic Jewish view that the law provided the necessary resources for the daily walk of the people of God. The phrase as a whole stands without a verb, but most commentators are probably correct in assuming that Paul intended to imply the completion, "what was impossible for the law (God has done)" (BGD, ἀδύνατος 2b); to take it in apposition with τὴν ἁμαρτίαν condemned by God (Cranfield) would have the effect of equating the law with sin, something Paul has clearly set his face against (7:7–23).

ἐν ᾧ ἠσθένει διὰ τῆς σαρκός, "in that it was weak through the flesh." The problem is made plain: the inadequacy of the law lies not in itself but in the conditions in which it has to operate (Wilckens). "Weakness" is not a term of accusation or condemnation in Paul; it is simply descriptive of the human condition (cf. 6:19; 8:26; 14:1–2, 21; 1 Cor 2:3; 8:11–12; 15:43; etc). Israel's failure with regard to the law was their failure to recognize its and their own weakness; they saw the law in terms of ability (δυνατός), not inability (ἀδύνατος). In matters of human salvation, only God is "able" (4:21; 9:22; 11:23). Treating the law as itself an enabling agent is the mistake Paul attacked in 2:17–29. As with all aspects of man's belongingness to this age, so with the law, it is recognition *of* weakness and so of dependence on grace (Spirit) which is the condition and context for God's enabling to come to expression (see particularly 4:19–21; 2 Cor 12:9–10). The διά with genitive ("through") rather than accusative ("because of") is also significant (against BGD, διά A.IV; Lietzmann; Kuss; Käsemann). It is precisely the interaction between the law and the flesh which incapacitates the law—that is, the flesh not only in its grosser manifestations (see on 7:5), but also in its manifestations more characteristic of misconceived piety, such as Paul now saw his earlier faith as a Pharisee to be—the law weakened in its divine purpose by being identified too closely with Israel as a national and physical entity marked out particularly by circumcision (2:28–29; 4:1 ff.; 9:8). It was precisely their engagement with the law too much at the level of the flesh which was Israel's and the law's undoing! For ἐν ᾧ, see BDF §219.2. And on σάρξ, see further on 1:3 and 7:5, 14; Maillot translates σάρξ throughout as "fleshly creature," which is both cumbersome and misleading.

ὁ θεὸς τὸν ἑαυτοῦ υἱὸν πέμψας, "God sent his own Son." Especially since Schweizer's "Hintergrund," the phrase "God sent his Son" has usually been taken as one of the earliest formulations of the Christian understanding of Jesus' life and ministry in terms of incarnation (see, e.g., Paulsen, 42; Ladd, *Theology*, 419; Käsemann; Zeller; Cranfield, "Comments," 270–71, but ignoring the dimension of Adam Christology, without which the verse cannot be understood—see below) This almost unanimous opinion, however, is open to considerable question. (1) The parallel expressions in John 3:16–17 and 1 John 4:9 certainly carry this overtone within the Johannine circle. But the concept of preexistence and incarnation is precisely something which the Fourth Evangelist develops from the earlier Jesus tradition and cannot be presupposed for the earlier formulation. (2) The idea of God's sending someone is well established in Judeo-Christian thought as a way of expressing the messenger's or prophet's authorization, without any reference to his place of origin (e.g., Ps 105:26; Jer 1:7; Mic 6:4; Luke 4:26; 20:13). To be sure, the language is also (naturally) used of sending heavenly messengers—angels (Gen 24:40; Acts 12:11), Spirit (Judg 9:23; Luke 24:49,) and Wisdom (Wisd Sol 9:10). But the Christian usage is more likely drawn from Jesus' own talk of himself as "sent" (that is, in prophetic categories—particularly Mark 9:37 pars.; 12:6 pars.; Matt 15:24). It is significant that the Johannine theology builds so much on and beyond the earlier prophet categories (cf. particularly J. A. Bühner, *Der Gesandte und sein Weg im 4. Evangelium* [Tübingen: Mohr, 1977]). (3) "His own Son" does not necessarily point in a different direction, since the unique intimacy between God and Jesus was initially asserted for Jesus' life without any thought that such intimacy depended on a prior relationship in heaven (cf. Mark 12:6 // Luke 20:13; and the implication of the "Abba" prayer assumed also by Paul—8:15–17); see further on 1:3. Moreover, it is characteristic of Paul elsewhere that he speaks of Jesus as God's Son as a way of increasing the emotional impact of the cross (5:10; 8:32; Gal 2:20; so also here and in Gal 4:4, the closest parallel to 8:3); see Dunn, *Christology*, 38. We constantly need to remind ourselves that these earliest formulations would not have been read in the light of an already established doctrine of incarnation (as we inevitably read them today); Christology was only in process of developing such conceptualizations. To remove them too abruptly from the context of that process may well result in imputing to earliest Christology a kind of polytheism involving two heavenly beings (God and his Son), whereas the process seems rather to have consisted in more careful and subtle redefining of Jewish monotheism. "That God the Father himself is working salvation in that which has happened and will happen through Jesus Christ is what Paul wants to emphasize when he speaks of the Son of God" (Kümmel, *Theology*, 161). See further Dunn, *Christology*, 38–40, 44–45; and "Was Christianity a Monotheistic Faith from the Beginning?" *SJT* 35 (1982) 303–36; also "Let John Be John: A Gospel for Its Time," in *Das Evangelium und die Evangelien*, ed. P. Stuhlmacher (Tübingen: Mohr, 1983) 309–39.

ἐν ὁμοιώματι σαρκὸς ἁμαρτίας, "in the very likeness of sinful flesh." For ὁμοίωμα see on 6:5. There may be deliberate irony here: the concrete form which the divine purpose took was sinful flesh. For σάρξ see on 1:3 and 7:5. In 7:5, 14, and 18 the σάρξ had been more clearly characterized as man in his belongingness to the age of Adam, that is, under the domination of sin, its weaknesses and appetites unscrupulously used by sin to bind man more completely to death. σάρξ ἁμαρτίας is an effective summary statement of Paul's view of the fallen human condition, *not* as a dualistic denunciation of the flesh as in itself sinful, but as a sober recognition that man as flesh can never escape the enticing, perverting power of sin. It was God's purpose that Jesus' ministry should be in this form (so most recently Branick and Gillman). The significance of Paul's use of ὁμοίωμα here is much debated (see, e.g., Käsemann and Cranfield). Probably he used ὁμοίωμα partly because σάρξ ἁμαρτίας is an epochal reality—it was in that form, precisely what all humanity within that reality shared, in which Jesus ministered; and partly because the rule of sin and death did not have its usual final say in his case. His death was itself an epochal event which broke the consequence of sin's hold on the flesh (it is not clear that the sinlessness of Jesus is in view here in the ὁμοίωμα, as is frequently maintained, even though Paul clearly affirms it elsewhere [2 Cor 5:21]); see on 6:5. In other words, this is the language of Adam Christology: another son of God (cf. Luke 3:38) whose entry upon this world had equivalently epochal significance (in effect recalling 5:12–21). Here, however, the fundamental thought is added that God achieved his purpose for man not by scrapping the first effort and starting again, but by working through man in his fallenness, letting sin and death exhaust themselves in this man's flesh, and remaking him beyond death as a progenitor and enabler of a life κατὰ πνεῦμα. Hence whatever the precise force of the ὁμοίωμα, it must include the thought of Jesus' complete identification with "sinful flesh" (cf. NJB: "the same human nature as any sinner"); a docetic interpretation can claim no adequate support in the text (see particularly

Kuss; though cf. also Knox). As at Qumran, the eschatology sharpens the sense of the sinfulness of the current human condition (see on 7:14).

καὶ περὶ ἁμαρτίας, "and as a sin offering" (so NIV), "as a sacrifice for sin" (NEB; so NJB), "as expiatory sacrifice" (Maillot). The phrase περὶ ἁμαρτίας is regularly used in the LXX to translate the Hebrew חַטָּאת(לְ) = "as a sin offering" (e.g., Lev 5:6–7, 11; 16:3, 5, 9; Num 6:16; 7:16; 2 Chron 29:23–24; Neh 10:33 [2 Esd 20:34 LXX]; Ezek 42:13; 43:19). Paul almost certainly intends it in this sense (see particularly Wright and Wilckens, and earlier particularly Denney; Michel has changed his mind in favor of this view). Some commentators prefer to take the phrase in a more general, less specifically sacrificial sense (Lagrange, Lietzmann, Barrett, Murray, Black, Cranfield, Zeller). And there is a strong antipathy to linking Paul's thought to sacrificial categories on the part of some German scholars (most recently Friedrich, Verkündigung, 68–71; but now see also Stuhlmacher's critique of Friedrich, "Sühne oder Versöhnung?"). But such a sacrificial allusion would be wholly natural and unremarkable in a first-century context. Paul can merely allude to it since this way of thinking of Jesus' death was already well established in the Christian congregations (as the pre-Pauline formula in 3:25–26 implies; see 3:21–26 Form and Structure). The theology is fairly clear: the death of the sin offering effects God's condemnation of sin (see below on next clause) by the destruction of the sinful flesh; the only remedy for flesh's incorrigible weakness in the hands of sin is its death (see further on 3:25). Here it functions as part of Paul's Adam Christology: Christ's death, in its identity with sinful flesh, breaks the power of sin by destroying its base in the flesh (the new humanity beyond death is not of flesh, and so also not under sin). "It is the death of sinners which he dies" (Althaus). See further Dunn, "Death of Jesus."

κατέκρινεν τὴν ἁμαρτίαν ἐν τῇ σαρκί, "he condemned sin in the flesh." This can hardly mean that God condemned the operations of sin "in the flesh" but exempted sin's other operations from condemnation. Sin is conceived of by Paul as a power which feeds parasitically upon human weakness and whose effective power in human affairs is limited to the flesh (σάρξ ἁμαρτίας). The phrase must then describe where and how God gave the decisive verdict against sin—"in the flesh." That could suggest a divine strategy whereby the enticingness of the flesh's weakness was used to draw sin to the flesh and so to engage sin's power that the destruction of the flesh became also the destruction of that power. In the most dramatic reversal of all time (quite literally), death is transformed from sin's ally and final triumph (5:21) into sin's own defeat and destruction. At all events the decisive enactment by God (κατέκρινεν—not just sentence pronounced but sentence effected) was clearly the death of Jesus (NIV, "condemned sin in sinful man," is potentially misleading); the death of Christ brought that whole epoch characterized by sin's domination of the flesh to an end (see particularly SH, Fitzmyer and Kuss; against Büchsel, TDNT 3:951–52, who, followed by Cranfield, broadens the reference too much and misses the epochal significance of Christ's death; and the older view of Zahn, Kühl, and Lagrange, referring Paul's argument to the incarnation rather than to Christ's death and resurrection). The corollary has already been indicated in chap. 6: identification with that death ensures that the effect of that condemnation will be liberating rather than destructive.

4 ἵνα τὸ δικαίωμα τοῦ νόμου πληρωθῇ, "in order that the requirement of the law might be fulfilled." The ἵνα should be given full force. It is not that fulfillment of the law's requirement was merely the result (surprising or accidental) of Jesus' mission and death; it was rather God's purpose in sending his Son in the first place. Paul here deliberately and provocatively insists on the continuity of God's purpose in the law and through the Spirit. Against those who can only see that Paul is trying to maintain an untenable both-and at this point—the law at an end (10:4) yet still valid (Räisänen, *Law*, 65; cf. Sanders, *Law*, 99, 104)—we must give Paul the credit for seeing a deeper consistency than his critics allow.

Paul's use of δικαίωμα is interesting since in the two other most closely parallel references (1:32 and 2:26) he uses it in reference to the Gentiles (the only other occurrences in the Pauline corpus are the rhetorically determined 5:16 and 18). In its sense of "requirement" or "claim" (cf. *TDNT* 2:219–20), he has in mind something more or other than the requirements his fellow Jews would normally focus on as part of their distinctive self-definition (circumcision, sabbath, food laws, etc.; see *Introduction* §5.3.3); cf. 2:26, where τὰ δικαιώματα τοῦ νόμου are set in contrast to circumcision in particular. The claim of the law which Paul has in mind is evidently something to which the Gentile can respond *as a Gentile*—closely equivalent, presumably, to τὸ ἔργον (again singular) τοῦ νόμου in 2:15; but a reference specifically to the law of coveting (7:7 ff.: Watson, *Paul*, 157) seems unnecessarily restrictive. See further on 1:32 and 2:15. At all events, it is clear that νόμος here must denote the Torah (against Käsemann, who follows the logic of refusing to identify "the law of the Spirit of life" in v 2 with the Torah, by proposing here the transferred sense of "the rights of the divine will"). On the relation between δικαίωμα and κατάκριμα (v 1) here see Schlatter.

πληρόω in the sense of "fulfill" a commandment is well enough known (BGD, 4b), but still imprecise enough to leave open the question, "Fulfill in what sense?" As with 13:8 and Gal 5:14, the other most closely parallel uses in Paul, πληρωθῇ here cannot mean "fulfill" in a one-to-one sense, an item by item correlation. It must mean "fulfill" in a more profound sense—the essential requirement (note again the singular) which lies behind the individual requirements, the character and purpose which the individual requirements are intended to bring to expression. Paul might well intend to evoke the related sense of fulfillment of prediction or promise (BGD, 4a), since here too the claim to eschatological fulfillment often incorporates a relativizing and subordination of particular details of the original formulation. Paul's claim is certainly precisely that the eschatological situation introduced by Christ and the fulfillment of the promise to the Gentiles have fulfilled the divine purpose in the law, even while relativizing much of its detail as inappropriate to the Gentiles and the age of eschatological fulfillment. This also means that Paul's usage here is not so distant from that of Matt 5:17 as might at first appear (cf. the fuller discussions, e.g., of C. H. Dodd, "Matthew and Paul," *New Testament Studies* [Manchester University, 1953] 53–66; and R. Mohrlang, *Matthew and Paul: A Comparison of Ethical Perspectives*, SNTSMS 48 [Cambridge University, 1984] with bibliography). On the other hand, it does not follow that Paul envisages the possibility of a sinless life here (against

Lietzmann); rather a life in accordance with God's intention in the law, including his provision in the death of Christ as sin offering. At the same time it is obvious that Paul has in mind the role of the law as the standard or yardstick of what God wants, and so of a "doing" or "keeping" ("fulfilling," 13:8–10) of the law in some positive sense (cf. particularly Zeller and Thompson; contrast the rather contrived exegesis of Nygren, and the even more surprising exegesis of Benoit, "Law," 28–32: δικαίωμα = "a verdict of condemnation and punishment whose object is death"). This point stands even if the emphasis is on divine enabling more than on human ability (cf., e.g., Knox: "in this passage Paul speaks not of our fulfilling the just requirement of the law, but of its being fulfilled in us"); but wholly unconvincing is Deidun's argument that the πληρωθῇ indicates "the Law's demand is accomplished (by God) *previous to* any περιπατεῖν on the part of the Christian" (*Morality*, 74; my emphasis).

ἐν ἡμῖν τοῖς μὴ κατὰ σάρκα περιπατοῦσιν ἀλλὰ κατὰ πνεῦμα, "in us who walk not in accordance with the flesh but in accordance with the Spirit." The ἐν ἡμῖν immediately introduces the crucial theological and pastoral assumption that the Spirit is a shared experience which forms their common bond—thus "in us" as an essentially corporate and not merely individual experience; or possibly also "through us" (Schlier). Since περιπατέω, "conduct oneself," would evoke the typical Jewish image of walking in the law(s) of God (see on 6:4), Paul clearly intends to imply that this is only possible as an eschatological reality, as enabled by the Spirit given in the outworking of Jesus' death and resurrection (cf. Osten-Sacken, 242: "the pneumatology of Rom 8 is constitutive for the understanding of the σὺν Χριστῷ in Rom 6"). But note again the parallel with the Qumran sect, which also talks of "walking in the Spirit" (1QS 3.18; 4.6, 12).

The σάρξ/πνεῦμα antithesis reemerges here, to dominate the following verses (see *Form and Structure*). Cf. already 1:3–4; 2:28–29; 7:5–6; and subsequently 8:5–9, 13; (also 1 Cor 5:5; 6:16–17; Gal 3:3; 4:29; 5:16–24; 6:8; Phil 3:3; Col 2:5; 1 Tim 3:16). What is in view here are two alternative and opposed drives which come to expression in the ethical character of everyday decisions and relationships (see further on 1:4). For Paul, the opposition is that between two epochs (see further on 7:5–6); the appropriate ethical walk is the consequence of the Son's mission (8:3), and the enabling factor (the Spirit) has the character of eschatological newness. Paul sees the old epoch as characterized by an inability to live in accordance with God's will (8:3), a dilemma in which his fellow Jews are caught despite their assumption to the contrary (2:28–29; 7:6); hence also the frequency of the contrast in Gal and in Phil 3:3. The exhilaration and vitality of an immediate experience of God's love (5:5) and leading (8:14) is evident behind the formulation. But whereas a not dissimilar experience on the part of the Teacher of Righteousness—or so it would appear (1QH 4.27–33; 7.6–9; 9.14–18; 13.13–20; 14.12–16, 25–26; 16.11–12)—resulted in a stricter application of the Torah, in Paul's case the experience of the Spirit was one of liberation from such an attitude to the law (the Spirit for Paul as both the power *and* the norm of the Christian life—Pfister, 91), bound up as it was with a conviction of God's grace being unconditionally opened to the Gentiles. It was experience of the immediacy of the Spirit which made him aware of the true extent of the "flesh" (cf. Michel). It is true that Paul's attitude here can be described as "enthusiastic" (Käsemann), but while that appropriately describes the motivation and enabling experienced by Paul, the fact that he also describes its end result as "fulfilling the requirement of the law" should warn us against pressing the adjective too hard; see also Schrage's attempt to hold a proper balance between charismatic ethic and commandment (*Einzelgebote*, 71–93). It should also be noted that the initial formulation of the σάρξ/πνεῦμα antithesis is expressed not as mutually exclusive conditions, but more as an exhortation, as contrasting and opposed alternatives (see further on 8:5, 9, and 13). The absence of any explicit mention of "faith" is insignificant: for Paul, to live ἐκ πίστεως = to walk κατὰ πνεῦμα (Lohse, "Analyse," 146); just as to live ἐκ νόμου (or ὑπὸ νόμον) is to walk κατὰ σάρκα (cf. 2:28–29; 7:6).

5 οἱ γὰρ κατὰ σάρκα ὄντες, "for those who exist in terms of the flesh." The γάρ introduces an elaboration of v 4 which runs through to v 11. The οἱ κατὰ . . . ὄντες should not be taken as an ontological classification, as though Paul envisaged two classes of humankind, created differently and forever locked into a particular character and destiny. Even the Qumran sect, whose writings distinguish sharply between the sons of light and the sons of darkness, not least in the famous two spirits passage in 1QS (3.13–23) where the language closely parallels Paul's (1QS 3.18, 20–21; 4.6–18), recognizes that the dividing line cannot be so sharply drawn, that the covenanters themselves belong to *both* groups (1QS 4.23–25; Kuhn, 103–4; other references in Dunn, *Jesus*, 445 n.79); see also on 7:14. The later Gnostic (Valentinian) division of humankind into the three fixed categories of pneumatic, choic, and psychic is, of course, not at all in view (recognized also by Schmithals, *Anthropologie*, 104–5). The closer parallels are in Paul's own use of phrases like οἱ ἐκ νόμου and οἱ ἐκ πίστεως in Rom 4:14, 16, since they describe not so much a given condition as an attitude and orientation (see on 4:14). So here the phrase clearly stands as a variant or at least complement of οἱ κατὰ σάρκα περιπατοῦντες (v 4). Hence to take the phrase as equivalent to the unbaptized (Schlier; cf. Kuss) loses the active force of the phrase and reduces it to a ritually determined distinction such as that to which Paul was objecting. Nor is it quite to the point to see the contrast simply as between the unregenerate and the regenerate (Lietzmann). In modern terms, the sociological category "type" comes closer to Paul's meaning—the type as an abstracted, even idealized model to which individuals conform to greater or less degree, but rarely (if at all) completely. They are κατὰ σάρκα, then, in the sense and to the degree that they are determined by the flesh, its appetites and illusions. "There still exists in them that queer saint who allows himself to be deceived by sin through the Law and for whom the law of sin must ever become the law of death" (Barth, *Shorter*).

τὰ τῆς σαρκὸς φρονοῦσιν, "take the side of the flesh." φρονεῖν means not merely to think, but to have a settled way of understanding, to hold an opinion, to maintain an attitude (elsewhere in Paul cf. particularly 14:6; 1 Cor 13:11; 2 Cor 13:11; Phil 2:2, 5; 3:19; Col 3:2; see also on 11:20 and 12:3). The fuller phrase τά τινος φρονεῖν is well known in the sense, "to be of another's mind, to belong to another's party" (LSJ, φρονέω II.2.c; BGD, 2; Cranfield,

386 n.1). The sense is appropriate here where Paul's thought is of an opposition or warfare between flesh and Spirit. Allowing for the degree of ambiguity in the οἱ . . . ὄντες phrase, Paul presumably has in mind both the willful choosing of the selfish option and a pattern of so choosing which has become so established that the chooser is no longer aware of its selfish character (cf. 1:21–28). His fellow Jews would be unwilling to recognize themselves in this description, though Paul saw the links all too clearly (cf. 2:28; 4:1; 9:3, 5, 8). So today the pious can be the last to recognize when their piety has become a form of self-indulgence.

οἱ δὲ κατὰ πνεῦμα τὰ τοῦ πνεύματος, "whereas those who exist in terms of the Spirit take the side of the Spirit." πνεῦμα of course refers to the Spirit of God (8:9–11), not the human spirit, though nobody in the first century would see the two as wholly disconnected (see further on 8:16). Cf. the contrast between "the works of the flesh" and "the fruit of the Spirit" in Gal 5:19–23.

6 τὸ γὰρ φρόνημα τῆς σαρκὸς θάνατος, "for the flesh's way of thinking is death." φρόνημα occurs only in Rom 8 (vv 6, 7, 27) in the NT; in the LXX only in 2 Macc 7:21 and 13:9. As is usual with -μα suffixes, the resulting noun denotes the result of the action. The result of τὰ τῆς σαρκὸς φρονεῖν is τὸ φρόνημα τῆς σαρκός (Cranfield presses the distinction too pedantically). That it is not a passive framework of thought which is in view is best indicated by Josephus, War 4.358, where φρόνημα ἐλευθερίου has the sense of "determination for freedom." The modern composite "mind-set" probably comes closest to the sense, including both a fixed and resolute way of thinking.

The θάνατος, used here for almost the last time in the analysis of chaps. 6–8, links the description back into the overarching distinction between epochs (see on 5:12 and chaps. 6–8 Introduction). The mind-set of the flesh is characteristic of the epoch under the rule of death and inexorably heading for death. But if death is the hallmark of the mind-set (the epigrammatic structure encourages a breadth of linkage between the two parts of the clause), that also implies that its character will only become finally clear by its outworking; the mind-set of the flesh will not necessarily be recognized in its fatal character before that. As at other points Paul's Christian theology depends on an eschatological validation.

τὸ δὲ φρόνημα τοῦ πνεύματος ζωὴ καὶ εἰρήνη, "but the Spirit's way of thinking is life and peace." As above, φρόνημα indicates a ruling determination without implying that it is necessarily the only factor influencing and determining conduct—the type (in sociological terms) not being fully conformed to by any particular individual. As the parallel in v 6a and the parallel of 2:7 and 10 imply, the ζωή and εἰρήνη are thought of here as primarily future eschatological blessings (ζωή—cf. 5:17, 21; 6:22; 11:15; εἰρήνη—see on 1:7; otherwise SH and Dodd), though once again the ambiguity of the epigrammatic structure allows the inclusion of the idea of a way of thinking determined by the eschatological good which will be its final end.

7 διότι τὸ φρόνημα τῆς σαρκὸς ἔχθρα εἰς θεόν, "because the flesh's way of thinking is hostility toward God." The noun ἔχθρα is found elsewhere in the NT only in Luke 23:12; Gal 5:20; Eph 2:14, 16; and cf. particularly James 4:4. The sense is certainly active here (cf. 5:10). The logic is the same as in

1:18 ff.: the mind-set of the flesh is the same refusal to acknowledge human creatureliness and dependence on God; to make self-satisfaction the highest priority is to reject the self-giving God.

τῷ γὰρ νόμῳ τοῦ θεοῦ οὐχ ὑποτάσσεται, "for it does not submit itself to the law of God." The train of thought continues to parallel 1:18 ff., since ὑποτάσσεσθαι ("be subject to") characterizes the proper state of the creature (Käsemann). It should be noted that once again the attitude to the law (the Torah) is very positive: to be subjected to the law of God is proper to man, is the antithesis of the mind-set of the flesh, and so, by implication, is expressive of the mind-set of the Spirit (cf. v 4). Wilckens (n. 532) rightly protests against the contrived interpretations of Kuss and Lohse at this point. Of course, Paul's Jewish contemporaries would wholly accept what Paul says here, without accepting his judgment that to understand subjection to the law too narrowly as a national (Jewish) privilege is itself a form of flesh (racially) oriented thinking (see further on 10:3; and cf. 1 Clem. 34.5; Herm. Man. 12.5.1). For ὑποτάσσεσθαι as due to God, see Epictetus 3.24.65; 4.12.11; Ps 61:2 LXX [62:1]; 2 Macc 9:12; 1 Cor 15:28 (of Christ!); Heb 12:9; James 4:7; 1 Clem. 20.1; Ign. Eph. 5.3; to Christ, Eph 5:24. See also on 13:1.

οὐδὲ γὰρ δύναται, "for it cannot (do so)." For οὐδὲ γάρ ("for it cannot either") see BDF, §452.3. Again the thought is not ontological (cf. T. Jud. 18.6), but more epochal (note the echo of v 3a: Osten-Sacken, 152). Paul does not have in view an innate incapacity as such, for he has already spoken too clearly of a determined mind-set, an active hostility and the refusal of the creature to submit to its Creator (cf. 9:19–20). At the same time, the same indictment in 1:18 ff. and the continuing blindness of his fellow countrymen to the fleshliness of their mind-set give prominence to the insight that such reactions and attitudes are self-reinforcing and can lock so tightly into a mind-set that it takes a disruptive revelation to shatter the imprisoning mold in which those attitudes have become set.

8 οἱ δὲ ἐν σαρκὶ ὄντες θεῷ ἀρέσαι οὐ δύνανται, "and those who are in the flesh are not able to please God." The clause is a recapitulative summary to reinforce the emphasis; note the repeat of the οὐ δύνανται left to the end of the sentence for added impact. The οἱ ἐν σαρκὶ ὄντες, as a summary of what has been said, is clearly equivalent to οἱ κατὰ σάρκα ὄντες (v 5; so, rightly, Cranfield). As in chap. 5, where Paul deploys a number of δικαι- words for rhetorical variation and effect (so that exegesis of the unusual δικαίωμα in 5:16 must be determined accordingly), so here Paul is not dealing with unitary concepts but with more comprehensive ideas whose particular force in any context must be largely determined by that context. In this case the near equivalence of the κατὰ σάρκα formulation indicates that here too Paul has in mind a type of lifestyle which characterizes life apart from Christ but one to which those "in Christ" can still be drawn (vv 12–13). See also on 7:5.

"To please someone" can be a desirable and fitting objective (Acts 6:5; 1 Cor 10:33; 2 Tim 2:4) except when it becomes a matter of pleasing oneself (Rom 15:1–3), or of merely man-pleasing (Gal 1:10; 1 Thess 2:4; also Col 3:22 and Eph 6:6), or conflicts with the higher duty of pleasing God (1 Cor 7:32–34; 1 Thess 2:4, 15; 4:1). Here again the impossibility is that of being focused in two opposing directions at once: on the flesh, on God (see further on 8:7). The correlative is the praise of God, which in 2:28–29 is again ruled out by an ἐν σαρκί focus.

9 ὑμεῖς δὲ οὐκ ἐστὲ ἐν σαρκὶ ἀλλὰ ἐν πνεύματι, "but you are not in the flesh but in the Spirit." The more generalized description of vv 5–8 is particularized and personalized by the ὑμεῖς. The ἐν σαρκί clearly takes up the ἐν σαρκί of v 8 and recapitulates all that was said about the flesh in vv 5–8. As such the thought is still of mind-sets, of conditioned patterns of thinking and acting— the one determined by belongingness to the world, the other by belongingness to God. What is in view is not ontological transformation but change in orientation and motive centers. Certainly conversion-initiation marked the breaking of the old conditioning and opening to the new power source (Spirit). But it is not a simple before and after conversion which Paul has in mind (as, for example, Schlier; Althaus, 88—"man is wholly 'in the Spirit' or wholly 'in the flesh'"!), as though the σάρξ were no longer a factor for the believer (contrast vv 12–13). The decisive factor is no longer the flesh, but the flesh is still a factor. Of the two types—flesh-man and Spirit-man (see on 8:5 and 6)—Paul naturally assumes that his readers conform more to the latter than to the former.

As is most generally recognized, the ἐν σαρκί cannot be understood as merely locative (they have not been taken out of the flesh), though once again sharp distinctions between "merely" physical and moral connotations of the word should be avoided (see further on 7:5). In the same way, the ἐν πνεύματι cannot be understood merely as denoting an inspired state (cf. 1 Cor 12:3, 9; 14:16; "the linguistic milieu of 'enthusiasm'"—Conzelmann, *Outline*, 209), though the more extensive use as denoting a more established condition (as in 2:29; 14:17; 2 Cor 6:6) should not be taken as sharply distinct from inspiration. Characteristic of the earliest Christian communities was a sense of immediacy in communion with God and of enabling in daily conduct as in worship. Paul's characterization of types (sociologically speaking) in this and the preceding verses is rooted in his own and his churches' experience rather than in dogmatic either-ors of what must be of logical necessity. On the σάρξ/πνεῦμα antithesis see also on 1:3–4 and 8:4.

εἴπερ πνεῦμα θεοῦ οἰκεῖ ἐν ὑμῖν, "assuming that the Spirit of God does indeed dwell in you." The εἴπερ denotes a necessary condition for the validity of the preceding assertion: "if in fact" (RSV), "if only" (NEB). Of itself it does not imply that the condition has been met (cf. 1 Cor 8:5; 15:15; see also on 8:17). We should not therefore take it for granted that Paul naively assumed it was fulfilled in this case (contrast, e.g., NJB, "since"; Cranfield; Harrisville); he would be conscious that many of those hearing his letter read out would be at the inquiry stage, hence the careful definition which follows. See also BDF, §454.2; Dunn, *Baptism*, 148.

This is the first time in Romans that Paul uses the fuller phrase πνεῦμα θεοῦ. The θεοῦ is added for emphasis: it is the Spirit of *God* which achieves the liberation from the conditioning of the flesh. But Paul is also no doubt conscious of the more careful definition of the Spirit he is about to make ("Spirit of Christ"). For πνεῦμα θεοῦ cf. 8:14; 15:19(?); 1 Cor 2:11, 12, 14; 3:16; 6:11; 7:40; 12:3; 2 Cor 3:3; Eph 4:30; Phil 3:3; 1 Thess 4:8.

The οἰκέω is probably chosen to denote a settled relation rather than the more transitory state of possession (though see above on ἐν πνεύματι); cf. 8:11; 1 Cor 3:16; and 2 Cor 6:16. As later rabbinical comment noted, he who dwells in a house is the master of the house, not just a passing guest (Str-B, 3:239); hence perhaps NJB, "the Spirit of God has made a home in you." Zeller notes the parallel in Seneca, *Ep.* 41.2: "there resides within us a divine spirit." But the lack of definition in Seneca, who goes on to quote Virgil ("In each and every good man 'a god [what god we are uncertain] dwells'"), is in sharp contrast to Paul (next clause). Paul perhaps chooses the verb here to mark off the lordship which should characterize the Christian from the lordship of sin (7:17, 20), even though both continue to exert their claim in the lives of believers (see on 8:10). Paulsen, 50, and Zeller note the promise of God's dwelling in/among his people (Lev 26:11–12; Ezek 37:27; Zech 2:11; *Jub.* 1.17; *T. Zeb.* 8.2; *T. Dan.* 5.1; *T. Jos.* 10.2–3; *T. Ben.* 6.4).

εἰ δέ τις πνεῦμα Χριστοῦ οὐκ ἔχει, οὗτος οὐκ ἔστιν αὐτοῦ, "if anyone does not have the Spirit of Christ, that one does not belong to him." The ἔχειν is from the language of possession (elsewhere in the NT usually of demon possession, though often of a long established nature: Matt 11:18; Mark 3:22, 30; 7:25; 9:17; Luke 4:33; 7:33; 13:11; John 7:20; 8:48, 49, 52; 10:10; Acts 8:7; 16:16; 19:13), but in Paul only occasionally, and always of a good possession—Spirit of God, or of faith (1 Cor 7:40; 2 Cor 4:13). Implicit is the understanding of the Spirit as a power which, working from within, manifests itself perceptibly (in word and deed) and determines the whole life of the one so possessed; see further below.

Crucial in understanding this whole realm of Christian spirituality is the recognition that for Paul the Spirit is the Spirit of Christ. This is the end point and climax of a long Judeo-Christian attempt to define the Spirit of God more carefully. Because πνεῦμα is mysterious power, whose most evident effect is in the experience and phenomenon of possession (hence 1 Cor 14:12, "zealous for spirits"), it was important to be able to distinguish the πνεῦμα θεοῦ from other πνεύματα. No firm criteria were ever achieved within Judaism. But the first Christians in effect resolved the issue by making Jesus himself the criterion: the Spirit for them was now to be recognized as the Spirit of Jesus, the Spirit of the Son (Acts 16:7; Gal 4:6; Phil 1:19; 1 Pet 1:11); the πνεῦμα θεοῦ (v 9b) was more clearly defined as the πνεῦμα Χριστοῦ. The Spirit of God may be known now as the Spirit of Christ, that is, by the character of his life and ministry. Cf. Dodd, Käsemann; see further Dunn, *Jesus,* chap. 10.

Equally important for our understanding of Christian beginnings is to recognize that the criterion of belonging to Christ for Paul is possession of the Spirit. Paul's point is not to assert "that every Christian is indwelt by the Spirit" (Cranfield; cf. Althaus, 88, Schmidt, 144). Typical is Ridderbos's reversal of Paul's statement: "To be of Christ, to belong to him, means therefore to 'have' the Spirit" (*Paul,* 221). But Paul's point is rather to remind his readers that only those who have the Spirit can claim to be Christ's; only those whose lives demonstrate by character and conduct that the Spirit is directing them can claim to be under Christ's lordship. Unlike so many of subsequent generations, the key element in Paul's definition of "Christian" (cf. NEB) is not a verbal profession or ritual act (from which possession of the Spirit may be deduced, even if not evident; cf. Gaugler—"this sacramental certainty"), but evidence of the Spirit active in a life as the Spirit of Christ (cf. 1 John 3:24; so rightly Goppelt, *Theology*, 2:120). That evidence could include a variety of manifestations (e.g., love—5:5; joy—1 Thess 1:5; charisms—1 Cor 1:4–7, Gal 3:3, 5; moral transformation—1 Cor 6:9–11; illumination—2 Cor 3:14–17), as well as, in particular, verbal profession (1 Cor 12:3; Rom 10:9–10) and the baptismal act (Rom 6:4). But the crucial element for Paul was evidently the Spirit experienced immediately as the Spirit of Christ (against the either-or of Ridderbos, *Paul*, 221—"not a subjective state of consciousness, but an 'objective' mode of being") (this insight is not to be dismissed by labeling it with the "boo word" "mysticism"—as again Gaugler). So also 8:14. See further Dunn, *Baptism*. For the idea of belonging to Christ cf. 1 Cor 3:23; 15:23; Gal 5:24. The context provides sufficient explanation of the negative form of the statement here (Paul was conscious that living κατὰ πνεῦμα is enabled, not inevitable, for the believer); to see here an excommunication formula (Wilckens, with bibliography) is too formalized and misses the underlying evangelistic and paraenetic thrust of Paul's exposition.

10   εἰ δὲ Χριστὸς ἐν ὑμῖν, "but if Christ is in you." The εἰ is not the same as the εἴπερ of v 9, having here more the force of "since." For the idea of Christ's indwelling see 2 Cor 13:5, Gal 2:20 and Col 1:27; outside Paul cf. particularly John 17:23. The phrase is unusual: Paul prefers to speak of believers' being "in Christ" (as in 8:1); but it matches the unusualness of the ἐν πνεύματι in v 9, whereas Paul thinks of the Spirit's being in believers (M. Bouttier, *En Christ* [Paris: Presses Universitaires de France, 1962] 84 n.65). As is generally recognized, Χριστός is used here synonymously with πνεῦμα θεοῦ = πνεῦμα Χριστοῦ (v 9). It is equally significant for our understanding of earliest Christian theology that whereas the identification of Christ with the other ways of speaking of God's self-manifestation (particularly the Wisdom of God and the Word of God) was complete without remainder (cf. 1 Cor 1:24, 30; 8:6; Col 1:15–17; Heb 1:3–4; John 1:14), the identification with the Spirit of God was made only in terms of the risen and exalted Christ. The astonishing nature of this identification made between a not-long-ago-crucified Galilean and the creative, revelatory, and redemptive power of God should not go unremarked (cf. Ign. *Eph.* 15.3). What it means for Christian theology is that Christ was seen from these very early days as so much an embodiment of this divine power that he had to become himself a factor in their understanding of God, resulting in a redefinition of the one God of Jewish faith (see also on 8:11). What it means for Christian spirituality is that Christ and Spirit are perceived in experience as one—Christ known only in and through the Spirit, the Spirit known only as (the Spirit of) Christ. See further Dunn, *Christology*, 141–48.

τὸ μὲν σῶμα νεκρὸν διὰ ἁμαρτίαν, "the body is dead because of sin." Most commentators take this as a reference to the past event of conversion-initiation ("the death of the body of sin effected in baptism"—Käsemann), since the emphasis of the section is on the freeing of the believer from the power of death and the presence of salvation in the power of the Spirit (see particularly Paulsen, 68–76, with further literature; more recently Osten-Sacken, 239,

Schlier, and Wilckens). But this will not do. (1) As usual, σῶμα does not mean simply physical body but humanity embodied in a particular environment (see on 6:6). As most modern commentators recognize, it should not be individualized ("your bodies," as in RSV); rather, the singular denotes the embodiment which characterizes all human existence in this age. That is to say, it is the σῶμα τῆς ἁμαρτίας (6:6), the σῶμα τοῦ θανάτου (7:24), because this age as such is still under the rule of sin and death, and precisely as σῶμα all humanity is part of this age. This truth of fallen humanity is individualized in v 11. (2) νεκρός denotes a state of deadness (so also with its most frequent use in Paul: οἱ νεκροί = those who have died and are in the state of death, that is, in a state from which they can be made alive again—as in 4:17; 6:13; 14:9). But here it is the state of deadness which results from the coming alive of sin and the resultant death of humankind; sin's coming to life from its state of deadness meant that all who belong to the age of Adam were delivered to the power of death (7:8–11). (3) This makes best sense of the διὰ ἁμαρτίαν, whereas Paul would be unlikely to describe the dying of conversion-initiation as διὰ ἁμαρτίαν, rather as νεκρὸς τῇ ἁμαρτίᾳ (6:11); cf. particularly Zahn, quoted approvingly by Michel; Wilckens's paraphrase, "on the ground that God has condemned sin in the flesh" (v 3), is too forced. Paul simply describes, in a variant formulation, the fact of the joint domination of this age by sin and death.

The weakness of interpreting the phrase as a reference to a death already accomplished at and as the beginning of the Christian life is the basic failure to appreciate the continuing two-sidedness of the believer's existence and experience for Paul. In his view the believer has not been taken out of the body or been wholly removed from the flesh. As body and as flesh believers still belong to this age, and as such are still under their rule. The union with Christ in his death confirms the divine sentence of death on the "sinful flesh," but its final execution awaits the death of the mortal body (see further on 6:6 and 7:24). The Spirit of life has opened believers to a decisively new dimension or age, but the tie to the old age is not yet completely broken. So sin's operations through the body need still to be contested, the sentence of death put into daily effect (v 13); and the rule of death will not be finally ended until the resurrection of the body (v 11); cf. Dibelius, "Vier Worte," 12–13; Schlatter; and particularly Cranfield. We may also compare and contrast Philo, *Leg. All.* 1.108 and 3.72–74, for the equivalent self-understanding within the more sharply dualistic σῶμα—σῆμα schema of Greek thought and without the characteristic eschatological orientation of the first Christians. Whatever parallels with Hellenistic-Gnostic dualism may be drawn to the language, Paul's thought is quite different: the body is dead *because of sin*, and will be resurrected (v 11; Schmithals, *Anthropologie*, 112, 116).

τὸ δὲ πνεῦμα ζωὴ διὰ δικαιοσύνην, "but the Spirit is life because of righteousness." Against the older view that πνεῦμα = human spirit (SH) the strong consensus of modern commentators is that πνεῦμα = Holy Spirit: the context is dominated by πνεῦμα = Spirit of God = Spirit of Christ (vv 9–11); and the link between divine πνεῦμα and ζωή is too firmly established (not least in v 11) to permit any real doubt on the issue (see on 8:2; cf. particularly Murray; but the modern translations have not kept up here—cf. NEB, NIV, NJB; "your spirits"—RSV). δικαιοσυνη is reintroduced after a gap (last time 6:20) in a usage made to appear more unusual than it is by the epigrammatic structure. As denoting the gracious outreach of God in accordance with his role as creator and redeemer (see on 1:17), it could be used almost interchangeably with πνεῦμα and ζωή. Here it denotes particularly the gracious action which inaugurated the new epoch and continues to sustain those in it (cf. particularly 1:17; 3:21–22, 26; 5:17, 21; 6:13, 16–20; the antithesis ἁμαρτία/δικαιοσύνη echoes that characteristic of 6:13–20; Cranfield rightly objects to those who understand δικαιοσύνη here as referring to moral righteousness and the διά as expressing purpose; Kuss reviews the ways in which the phrase has been taken). This is the other side of the eschatological tension, the character of the eschatological age to which the believer also belongs.

11 εἰ δὲ τὸ πνεῦμα τοῦ ἐγείραντος τὸν Ἰησοῦν ἐκ νεκρῶν οἰκεῖ ἐν ὑμῖν, "but if the Spirit of him who raised Jesus from the dead dwells in you." The clause is basically a recapitulation of v 9b: the εἰ has again been substituted for εἴπερ, and has the force of "since"; and the θεοῦ has been elaborated by use once again of one of the most established and best loved formulae (see Paulsen, 51–55, and on 4:24), here using only the most familiar name (Jesus). Talk of the Spirit of God indwelling thus brackets v 10 and confirms that "Christ in you" is a variant and synonymous formulation (v 10). The δέ has more adversative force here, since it contrasts the continuing state of v 10 with what the Christian confidently expects to be its final outcome. The assurance is that the indwelling Spirit is the beginning of a process and guarantee of its completion (see further on 8:23). Note that in this one clause the double foundation of Christian assurance is shown to be interlocked—the resurrection of Christ and the experience of the Spirit (cf. 5:5).

ζῳοποιήσει καὶ τὰ θνητὰ σώματα ὑμῶν, "will give life to your mortal bodies as well"—that is, probably as well as to Jesus in *his* resurrection (Cranfield, Wilckens). As is now agreed (against, e.g., Lietzmann) the ζῳοποιήσει (future tense) clearly refers to the final resurrection (as in 1 Cor 15:22). The new age introduced by Christ is bracketed by the double resurrection—initially of Christ, at the end, of believers—thus completing God's proper work as creator (see on 4:17). As elsewhere this life-giving work of God is characteristically understood as wrought through his Spirit (cf. John 6:63; 1 Cor 15:45; 2 Cor 3:6; see also on 8:2). The θνητὸν σῶμα means not simply the physical body, but humanity's embodiment in this age in its most manifest and characteristic expression, that is, as mortal and corruptible body (see on 6:6), the dimension most vulnerable to the power of sin (see on 6:12). As such it is clearly the same body as in v 10 (though here individualized; see on 8:10); the life-giving power of the Spirit will not extend finally to the body until the resurrection of the body.

διὰ τοῦ ἐνοικοῦντος αὐτοῦ πνεύματος ἐν ὑμῖν, "through his Spirit which dwells in you." For ἐνοικέω see on 8:9. The διά + genitive (see *Notes*) indicates the continuity between the present indwelling Spirit and the future resurrection. This must imply a continuity between the ἔσω ἄνθρωπος (7:22) and the resurrection body—as is strongly suggested also by the line of thought in 2 Cor 4:7–5:5.

Whereas in vv 9–10 Paul is almost casual in the way he freely interchanges phrases, in v 11 he becomes almost coy, caught up in cumbersome repetition, in order to avoid, or so it would appear, expressing the relation of Christ and Spirit with God too casually. The formula "God raised Jesus/Christ from the dead" is used twice; and "God's Spirit dwells in you" is repeated. There is no hint, of course, of Jesus' raising himself to become a divine power equal to or independent of God. But at the same time, the cumbersome repetition seems to be determined by an attempt to avoid attributing the resurrection of Jesus to the Spirit, since it would have been easier simply to say, "If the Spirit that dwells in you gave life to Jesus he will also give life to you." Paul, in other words, seems to avoid describing Jesus' resurrection life as dependent on the Spirit, or absorbed into the divine Spirit—Christ not merely the first of resurrected humanity and certainly not simply a historical figure of lasting importance (the Spirit of Christ in that attenuated sense)— but Christ as still an active force in shaping human destiny, still having a continuing function through the Spirit and as the first resurrected man, but somehow more than either (cf. 1 Cor 15:45; see further Dunn, *Christology*, 144, and on 8:10). Such thoughts seem implicit in Paul's formulation here, and though it would be unwise to press them as examples of his explicit teaching, it can be fairly said that the tensions in conceptuality of the divine which pushed Christian theology in a trinitarian direction are already evident in these verses.

Explanation

Paul has now nearly completed the task he set himself when he posed the conclusion to the first main section of his argument in salvation-history terms (5:12–21). There he had for the first time drawn together the fearful triumvirate who dominate the age of Adam, sin and death, with the law as their unexpected partner (5:20–21). Conscious of the questions this provocative conclusion was bound to raise in the minds of his thoughtful hearers, anxious as they presumably would be for the light his exposition would throw on their faith and its outworking, Paul had moved immediately to clarify the effect of these same dread forces in their continuing relation to the believer. A crucial issue was the role of the law, crucial in view of the heartsearching which Paul's seemingly antinomian assertion must have caused the Jewish members of the Roman congregations and those Gentiles drawn to the new faith through their earlier attraction to the synagogue and the Jewish ethos. But at first he focused primarily on the two chief "villains of the piece," sin and death. Initially he stressed the decisive effects of Christ's death and resurrection on their power, but at the same time he did not forget to complement the indicative of grace with the imperative of obedience, lest his audiences forget even for a moment that the eschatological tension of the life under the cross cannot be escaped (chap. 6).

Believers' attitude and response to the continuing claims of sin and death upon them thus clarified, Paul had then drawn the law back on to the scene, indeed on to center stage, addressing what must have been for many of his Jewish or Jewish-sympathizing audiences the most puzzling aspect of his gospel. Here again, as when it was sin and death primarily to the fore, he had begun by describing the position in bald, uncompromising terms, with the unflattering role of the law, already indicated earlier (5:12–13 and 20–21), now expressed in even sharper, more shocking terms (7:5–6). Then, at last in 7:7–25, he had faced head-on the issue of whether the logic of his exposition did not banish the law wholly to the epoch of Adam, the era of sin and death, to be counted as nothing other than the cat's-paw of sin and death and of no continuing relevance to the believer in the new age introduced by Christ. His answer had been twofold. First, he had pointed out that sin's use of the law proved the law to be a two-edged sword: the law may have allowed sin to entice human beings to their death; but at the same time, and in the same action, it had shown up sin for what it was (7:13), thus conforming to its (other) God-intended purpose (3:20; 4:15). Second, when this two-sided function of the law was matched with the two sides of the inner conflict within the believer, the solution to the problem Paul's gospel caused for a proper understanding of the law became clearer. The law continued to function as God's yardstick which believers would hold ever before themselves as a measure of what God required of man. But at one and the same time the law continued to be used by sin as a snare to trap the very same believers since they still belonged to the race of Adam, to this epoch characterized by man's dependence on the satisfaction of his human appetites and desires.

The problem of the law was thus clarified and at least to some extent resolved by reference to the eschatological tension of the believer's belonging both to the progeny of Adam and to the crucified and risen Christ. Believers should not expect to look to the law for aid in the crisis of temptation, in defeating the claims of sin, for by reason of their still-human weakness, sin was yet able to turn the law's edge into a weapon against them, a chain to bind them. Israel's continuing reliance on the law simply served to demonstrate how successful had been sin's duplicity. To thus clarify the Jekyll and Hyde nature of the law might be sufficient to resolve the problem for the believer's self-understanding, but it also highlighted in sharply poignant terms the frustration and existential agonizing of the believer thus divided between his or her own double identity. So, to redress the balance Paul now begins to describe more fully the outworking of that eschatological tension in the life of the believer. Having resolved the salvation-history tension of the two ages (5:12–21) at the level of the individual believer (chaps. 6–8), he can then complete his arguments by showing how it would work out in relation to his people as a whole (chaps. 9–11).

To round off the picture of the individual caught between the ages, Paul now draws into the center the last two major elements in the overall composition—flesh and Spirit. They had, of course, been already touched on at the earlier stage in the discussion (chaps. 6–8), even when the focus had been primarily on sin, death, and the law (particularly 7:5–6); it would have been hard to avoid all mention of the flesh in describing the enticing power of "the law of sin." But just as the clearer lines of the discussion of sin and death (chap. 6) had been complicated by drawing in the law (chap. 7), so now the focus begins to shift from the law, with flesh and Spirit first being drawn in to accomplish the most rounded and complete statement of all

(8:1–4), and then dominating the subsequent exposition. Paul had already used the contrast flesh/Spirit to characterize Jesus' own move from one epoch to the other (1:3–4) and to distinguish the old epoch of Jewish prerogative, to which his kinsfolk still clung, from the new covenant and its new "Jew" (2:28–29; 7:5–6). Now he evidently felt it most appropriate to use the same terms in bringing his treatment of the individual believer's progress to salvation to its due climax through what remains of this age.

1 Paul would be all too aware of how sobering if not depressing his solution to the problem of the law must be sounding to those hearing it for the first time. He does not pull back from it; he does not waste energy lamenting the tension within the believer's experience or pretending that it could be otherwise; hence the deliberate pathos of the preceding sentence which brought the existential analysis of 7:7–25 to a conclusion (7:25b). But the two-sidedness of the believer's experience is not the end of the story. For though believers belong to the two ages of Adam and Christ at one and the same time, it is their belongingness to Christ which is the more decisive, since Christ is the man who has already conquered sin and death (6:7–10). This fact does not alter or diminish the frustration of the present, rather it increases it; but it also makes it infinitely more bearable. Therefore Paul once more shifts his readers' perspective back again to the crucial indicatives, the decisive salvation-history actions which have already taken place. Just as at the beginning of the two previous phases of this section of his exposition he had focused attention on the decisive effects of their belonging to the Christ whose death and resurrection marked the end of the old epoch and beginning of the new (6:1–11; 7:1–6), so now he once again focuses on the decisive assuredness of what has already happened. His readers, recalling how those clear lines had become a little more blurred when the larger picture came into focus (6:12–23; 7:7–25), would probably realize that a similar enlargement was likely to follow here (8:9–30).

"No condemnation": the harking back to the clear lines of 5:18 is no accident. Because Paul has painted the eschatological tension in such depressingly realistic colors (7:14–25) he evidently felt the need to remind his readers that their continuing captivity to the law of sin as members of this age (7:23) is neither final nor finally determinative. What counts is their being "in Christ Jesus." It is the "in Christ" which makes the difference. To have identified oneself with Christ while still belonging to this age was bound to precipitate or increase existential tension, but that being "in Christ" is what gives the assurance that the end result will be acquittal. The "in Christ" will triumph over the "in Adam"; the tension of living between the two is temporary; the sobering realism of 7:14–25 is matched by the reaffirmed assurance of 8:1.

2 V 2 gives Paul's reason ("for") for such an assurance despite the gloomier picture of 7:14–25. The reason is that one of the two laws mentioned in 7:22–23 is stronger than the other. When looked at from the perspective of salvation history, that is, the perspective of the new age introduced by Christ's death and resurrection, the "I" in bondage is not so depressing as the "I" released by Christ is reassuring. The power of sin is more than matched by the power of the Spirit. The "I" in bondage to sin ends in death; the "I" liberated by the Spirit lives on.

Paul tries to squeeze so much into two compact phrases that he runs some risk of confusing his readers. Does he still mean the law here, the law given to Israel? How could the Paul who warned his Galatian converts so passionately against submitting to the slavery of the law (Gal 4:1–11; 5:1–4) speak of the same law as liberating? Yet readers who had time to reflect on the course of the argument would probably soon find themselves driven to the surprising conclusion that Paul must mean the same law in both phrases, the law given to Israel. "The law of sin and of death" could hardly be other than "the law of sin which is in my constituent parts" (7:23), the very law which sin used so deceitfully to bring man to death (7:11–13). "The law of the Spirit of life" is more surprising, but it is in fact only an extreme expression of the defense of the law already made in describing it as "the commandment which was for life" (7:10) and as "spiritual" (7:14). What we have here is simply a more epigrammatic assertion of the split in the law which matches the split in the "I" of the believer (7:25).

Likewise the idea of liberation as something already accomplished is simply a reversion to the strong indicatives which began chaps. 6 and 7, bearing in mind, as Paul would expect his hearers to do, the qualification of the eschatological tension which he had made in both cases (6:12–23; 7:7–25). The resumption of the indicative does not diminish the qualification, any more than the qualification denies the indicative. Liberation is already accomplished "in Christ." Hence it is as certain in its outworking as the believer's hope of sharing fully in Christ's resurrection, of final acquittal and glory (5:2; 6:5; 8:11, 18, 30). But for the present it is qualified, incomplete, so long as this age lasts. Paul has already given both aspects sufficient emphasis that he might understandably hope his readers would be able to hold even the two most antithetical assertions of 7:23 and 8:2 in proper tension.

Nevertheless, the impression that Paul has caught himself in contradiction is hard to shake off. After all it is the mood of 8:2 which contrasts so sharply with 7:23. It is the exhilarating sense of being liberated which marks out v 2 so clearly; whether it was only in retrospect or not (cf. Phil 3:6), Paul certainly recalled his conversion to faith in Jesus Messiah as an expression of liberation (cf. 2 Cor 3:17) and thought of return to his old lifestyle of obedience to the law as a return to slavery (Gal 4–5). The "Spirit," drawn back into the argument here, he clearly experienced as a power whose transforming effects marked his own ministry in no uncertain manner (cf. 15:18–19; 1 Cor 2:4–5; Gal 3:5), in some distinction from the law (2:28–29; 7:6). How then could he link the law with the Spirit and describe it as that very same liberating power? The contradiction with 7:6 in particular seems blatant.

Yet nothing is to be gained by pushing the tension in Paul's argument into out-and-out contradiction. That Paul could, unusually, choose to speak of "the law of the Spirit" can hardly be denied, since he had already echoed the promise of the new covenant law (Jer 31:33) in terms of the Spirit in an earlier letter (2 Cor 3:3, 6). The point is that for Paul the power of the new covenant is not so different from or discontinuous with the rule of God over Israel exercised through the law; on the contrary, the two are in direct continuity ("my law"). Yet they are different, since the new covenant is a matter of inner power ("upon their hearts"), not of external constraint ("not on tablets of stone"), and consequently it transcends the national and ethnic restrictiveness which inevitably focuses so much and depends so much on the distinctive identity markers of outward ritual which Paul now found so irksome. It is this sense of both continuity and discontinuity with his Jewish heritage to which Paul must cling; otherwise his own self-identity would begin to disintegrate. But it sets up a sometimes agonizing tension which comes to one of its sharpest expressions in this whole section.

That Paul should choose to ascribe such liberation to the law in this exceptional case should not be discounted or ignored. Of course it is the law in its eschatological expression (the law of the Spirit), and to be distinguished from the law in its baneful effect over those belonging to the old age (the law of sin and death), including unbelieving Israel. The point is, however, that Paul could characterize the transformation in himself and his understanding of God's promises in terms of his transformed understanding of the law. It was the law understood, he would say, in its proper function, which had liberated from the law as misunderstood by Israel and shackling the gospel. Here Paul's love-hate relation with the law reaches its most positive expression.

The contradiction, then, is not a contradiction of Paul's logic. It is the contradiction of his experience—his experience as a Jew who believed in Jesus as Messiah, and who, in being called to the Gentiles, found that God's law given to his people had become a cage. It is the contradiction described in the preceding verses (7:7–25), of the law still experienced and delighted in as God's and the law being used by sin to bind his human weakness to death. It is the extremity of that contradiction expressed in the sharply contrasting moods of 7:6 and 7:24 which pushed Paul to the extremity of this paradox: the same law, a force for sin and death in the age without Christ; the same law, a force for life in its eschatological realization through the Spirit.

3–4 That Paul is at this point in fact very positively disposed toward the law (at least the law of the Spirit) is confirmed by his further explanation. For first he reiterates the clarification of the law's role in relation to sin and death already developed in 7:7–25. The law is indeed associated with sin and death and in this company plays a tragic role (7:7–11; 8:2). But nevertheless blame should not be attached to the law; the fault lies in the flesh, in humanity's very human weakness (7:14, 18; 8:3). Then, second, he goes on to describe the purpose of God's action on behalf of individuals: that the just requirement of the law might be fulfilled in them. The liberation of the believer from the law (8:2) takes place in order that the law might be fulfilled by the believer (8:4)! Through Christ's death the law is also liberated, namely, from the power of sin and death—liberated to be a measure once more of what God requires of man. Even if Paul had confused his readers by his too compressed epigram in v 2, the positiveness of his attitude to the law in v 4 could hardly be ignored. Any who might have been tempted to take some of Paul's more extreme statements out of context as an excuse for complete antinomianism (the law only of relevance to the old age) would realize that Paul had no intention of taking that road. On the contrary, he was wholly serious when he claimed that life in Christ was a way of fulfilling the law, and not merely so, but was *the* way of fulfilling the law, *the* fulfillment that

God looked for rather than the kind of obedience Paul had previously offered as a devout Pharisee.

3 What was it that was impossible for the law? Paul is not explicit on the point. Presumably he had in mind the impotence described so graphically in 7:15, 19: the impotence of the man of flesh to meet God's requirements, impotence to measure up to God's purpose for creation because he has forgotten his creatureliness (and in so doing fallen prey to it). But Paul also implies the law's impotence on another front: God in providing his Son as sin offering has done what the law could not do (deal with sin). This would be a yet more provocative challenge to his fellow Jews, since one of the primary functions of the law for Israel was to provide just such a means of dealing with sin—through sacrifice and atonement. Paul seems to include this function within his sweeping "impossible." If so, then Paul here cuts at the very heart of his people's understanding of the law and presses the prophetic critique of the cult to a radical conclusion. And his criticism is once again caught up in the word "flesh." Israel, by treating the law as its own special prerogative, by marking off the covenant people in such clear-cut ethnic terms, by focusing so much on the fleshly rite of circumcision (2:17–29), had made it impossible for the law to function effectively! It was only as the law of faith (3:27), as the law of the Spirit (8:2), that it could function effectively. But by forgetting the logic of faith exemplified by Abraham (chap. 4) and by retaining the fleshly distinction between Jew and Gentile so fundamental to Jewish self-identity, Israel as a whole (through its guardians of the law) had only succeeded in reinforcing the law's impotence.

The full extent of humanity's tragic state is thus summed up again in the same terms used in 7:5—its mortality and animal appetites, with the law prevented by that weakness of the flesh and perverted by sin into a force binding the whole human race to death. And since this is the character of humankind as Adam's progeny, including even Israel, as its emphasis on matters of the flesh confirms, what is clearly required is something with the epochal significance of man's beginning in Adam. As Paul had already argued (chap. 5), the plight of humanity in consequence of one Adamic act could only be retrieved by another and greater Adamic act.

Such is obviously Paul's logic in reminding the Roman congregations of God's answer to the impotence of the law. He sent his own Son, one who was unique in his epochal significance and even closer to God than ever Adam was. Whether the thought of Christ as preexistent was present to Paul is not clear: it does not follow necessarily from the logic of the thought; nor is there any indication that Christians yet thought of Christ as having come from heaven or of his future coming as a *second* coming (cf. 1 Thess 2:19; 3:13; 4:15; 5:23; 2 Thess 2:1, 8). For when Christ is paralleled to Adam (Adam Christology), it is the epochal significance of what he did which is in view; within the terms of the Adam story used by Paul, Christ need be no more preexistent than Adam was. And the language of God sending his Son denotes divine commissioning rather than the origin of the one commissioned. The concern is not speculative but soteriological.

The force of the Adam Christology comes out most clearly in the slightly obscure phrase "in the likeness of sinful flesh." Whatever the precise force of the word translated "likeness," Paul was clearly trying to stress the extent of Christ's identity with sinful flesh: as a man knowing the same mortality, the same human appetites, he fully shared that weakness sin uses so effectively to destroy man; he was completely part of the old epoch of sin and death. But "likeness" denotes both closeness of identity and a degree of distinctiveness. In this case, Paul may have been thinking of Christ precisely in his Adamic capacity, representative of humankind as a whole, not simply as individual in his own right, but sharing the fleshly feebleness before sin of humanity in general. Alternatively he may have had in mind that Christ's Adamic significance lies in the fact that he did not conform wholly to the Adam mold, but smashed it by breaking through the end of death into the life of resurrection. Be that as it may, here it is Christ's oneness with sinful Adam, prior to his death, which Paul most obviously wanted to emphasize.

God sent his Son to deal with sin, or more precisely "sin in the flesh." Since it is through the flesh, through man as he belongs to and is determined by this age, that sin exerts its power (7:5, 14, 17–18), it is in the flesh that that power has to be combatted and broken. Hence the importance of being able to affirm Christ's complete oneness with humankind's sinful flesh. For Paul the breaking of that power was achieved by Christ's death as a sacrifice whereby God condemned that sinful flesh. In the two phrases "for sin" and "condemned" lies the key to Paul's soteriology. The former is frequently used in the LXX in reference to the sin offering, the sacrifice whereby God dealt with sin on a day-to-day basis and which together with the scapegoat provided the centerpiece of the Day of Atonement (Lev 16). Since it is God's dealing with sin which Paul also has in view, he must have intended his readers to recognize the OT terminology (he assumes such a familiarity with the Jewish scriptures throughout the letter). That is to say, it was almost certainly his intention to describe Christ—more specifically, his death—as a sin offering. It was in and by this act that God "condemned sin in the flesh." In this latter phrase Paul's theology of sacrifice achieves a rare degree of explicitness. Sin in the flesh was condemned to destruction by Jesus' death. God's way of dealing with sin in the flesh was by having it put to death, that is, by destroying it, since flesh without life is flesh destroyed.

The logic of Paul's thought here is that sinful flesh could not be healed or redeemed, only destroyed. Man's bodiliness, his nature as an embodied soul, is another matter (8:23). But for his flesh, the degree to which he is wholly one with this age, his weakness and merely human passions, there is no answer except death. That is presumably why God's response to the impotence of the law and the flesh could not be a response simply in terms of forgiveness. Forgiveness dealt only with sinful acts, not with sin itself. Repentance and the sacrificial system did not deal adequately with the root of the problem. The cancer of sin had taken such a firm root on the flesh, on humankind, that the surgery had to be radical; the flesh had to be destroyed, humankind had to die. The old age had to be wound up and a new beginning made. For Paul the good news was that this was just what God had done in Christ: Christ's complete oneness with sinful flesh meant that his death effected the destruction of that sinful flesh, just as his resurrection meant a new beginning for humankind. By identification with Christ in his death individuals could now already share in something of his victory over sin and death, and even though they were still in the flesh, still sin's bondslave in their fleshliness, they could hope in quiet confidence for that complete share in his resurrected life.

It is worth noting that for Paul the decisive act in God's dealing with sin was Christ's death. The act of condemnation presumably refers only to the phrase "for sin, as a sin offering," since the preceding phrase, "in the likeness of sinful flesh," denotes more an affirmation of sinful flesh than its condemnation. In Paul's soteriological perspective at this point, Jesus' life and ministry prior to his death is not in view, except insofar as it documented Jesus' oneness with humanity in its weakness before the power of sin. It is the fact *that* Jesus was a human being so like other human beings, rather than *what* he said or did, that matters at this point. For it was his life in the likeness of sinful flesh which meant that his death constituted the destruction of that sin in the flesh. God did not redeem flesh by an act of incarnation; he destroyed flesh by an act of condemnation.

4 As in the earlier paragraphs of the present section of his exposition, Paul does not dwell on the death of Christ, but goes on to spell out its object. God's purpose did not end in Christ's death, or even in their sharing in it. All that was a means to an end—the primary end of a people "who walk in newness of life" (6:4), who "serve in the new life of the Spirit" (7:4–6), who "walk according to the Spirit" (8:4). God's object was not condemnation, but righteousness. Paul no doubt intended his readers to recognize the implicit middle term between Christ's death as a sin offering and their new life conduct. That such conduct was dependent on Christ's having also been raised, and on their belongingness to the risen Christ, had been clearly enough stated at these earlier points (6:4; 7:4). But now Paul focuses his attention on the other middle term touched on only briefly before—the gift of the Spirit, which was also a consequence of Christ's death and resurrection. The new conduct is made possible not only by identification with Christ in his death but by the power of his resurrection life. To be "in Christ Jesus" (8:1–2) means not simply an ideological decision about the importance of an event in Jerusalem some 20–30 years earlier, but an experience of power—power which released believers from that false perception of the law which made it possible for sin to dominate even the people of the law so completely, power that Paul had found more than sufficient to break the vicious circle of dependence on the satisfaction of merely human desires, the vicious circle of presumption of national prerogative. What Christ's death (and resurrection) achieved was not merely condemnation of sin in the flesh, but the effective possibility of a life lived on a different level from that characterized by the weakness of the flesh. In language so characteristic of his thought Paul asserts once again that the proof of the pudding is in the eating, the proof of his gospel is in the daily conduct enabled by that power of God which they had come to experience in conversion.

Such conduct fulfills the just requirement of the law. It should be noted that Paul does not bring the law in as a concession or afterthought or footnote. It is the purpose of God which he has in view, the purpose of God in sending his Son. God wants the law to be fulfilled, its requirements to be met. That

Paul could express himself in such unequivocal and unqualified terms is important, especially for those who regarded (and regard) his teaching as antinomian. Paul probably had such criticism of his teaching very much in mind at this point. But of course he can speak with such forthrightness because he could assume, or hope, that his earlier teaching was sufficiently clear too. No doubt, then, he would expect his readers to realize that he was talking about the law of the Spirit of life, the law no longer restricted and defined in terms of the flesh. Nor can it be assumed that Paul's Spirit/flesh antithesis can be translated into a distinction between moral and ritual, or between inward and outward, as though he wanted to exclude the whole ritual dimension of the law in principle (as he himself made clear elsewhere—1 Cor 9:20), or looked only for an inward piety (for which the verb "walk" is hardly suitable). But so long as his kinspeople made so much of the law at the level of their own ethnic (that is, fleshly) prerogatives, such requirements of the law (particularly circumcision) belonged to the weakness of the law, to the law as used by sin and death. The law to be fulfilled is the law as it applies to all humanity, Gentile as well as Jew, the law as it speaks to the heart and calls forth the obedience of faith, fulfilled by conduct which expresses inner reliance on God and embodies dependence on his power.

5 In this and the following verses Paul does not hesitate to draw out the antithesis between flesh and Spirit in very sharp, indeed mutually exclusive terms. In doing so it is hardly likely that he intended his audiences to think they themselves had left the flesh behind and that they lived now wholly by the Spirit in a spiritual existence untouched or unaffected by their mortality. That form of perfectionist unrealism would be untypical of Paul. For Paul, the reality was that the "not yet" of the eschatological tension was still in force. Complete salvation awaited the resurrection, the redemption of the body, as he was soon to remind them (8:11, 23). Until that time, with its complete outworking of God's condemnation of the sinful flesh, their continuing fleshliness was an integral element in the continuing eschatological tension (7:25). It is much more likely, then, that Paul sharpened up the antitheses for parenetical reasons because he wanted to make clear to his readers that the choice already made in conversion needs to be reaffirmed and renewed in the religious and ethical decisions of daily life. This is probably implicit in his description of the alternatives (using a familiar phrase) as "taking the side of the flesh" or "espousing the cause of the Spirit." And the very image of "walking" suggests that they are only *in via*. The implication is that walking according to the flesh, taking flesh's side, is still an option for himself and his readers, an implication he will make explicit shortly (vv 12–13). Paul's more immediate concern, however, is to spell out in stark terms the full reality of that option, the character of life according to the flesh and its grim consequences, so that his readers can be in no doubt of the seriousness of the decisions they all must continue to make, of the life-and-death character of the eschatological tension in which they find themselves caught.

The antithesis seems at first to be between two classes of people, indeed between two closed and mutually exclusive groups: one group wholly and only "according to the flesh" and never otherwise; the other wholly and only "according to the Spirit" and never otherwise, with the decision of conversion and gift of the Spirit having settled the matter once and for all. But once again it is highly unlikely that Paul would be so unrealistic (as 7:25 and 8:12–13 again confirm). What Paul has in mind must be opposing patterns of mind-set and lifestyle—two alternative types abstracted from the much greater complexity of humanity, the two basic levels on which individuals can operate, the ultimate options which underlie every moral choice. This is confirmed by the fact that what he describes as classes of people in v 5 he describes as attitudes in v 6. The sharpness of the antithesis therefore does not exclude the likelihood that individuals can and do operate on both levels: on many subjects and in many decisions they walk by the Spirit and take its side; but on others, or at different times, the weakness of the flesh proves too strong for them. The sharpness of the antithesis is the pain of those whose "I" is yet divided between flesh and Spirit.

6 V 6 simply underlines the inevitable end of each mind-set or type or level. Flesh ends in death; it can look forward to nothing beyond decay and corruption, ending in destruction. The fact that Christ in his oneness with sinful flesh died makes the same point: there is no antidote to or escape from the corruptibility of the flesh to death. The whole enterprise of salvation has to operate at and from a different level. Those who live at the level of the perishable and corruptible perish with the perishable. Those whose aspiration and striving does not rise above merely human concerns die with the death of that in which they were alone concerned. But those who live from the Spirit thereby commit themselves to that level which runs through death to life beyond. Those whose motivation and concerns are determined by reference to God thereby open themselves to that power of life and peace which outlasts death.

The echo of 2:7, 10 ("life . . . peace") is probably not accidental, as also his talk of Spirit in terms which permit a broader reference than simply to those who have received the Spirit when they believed in Christ. Paul certainly wants to reaffirm that it is through Christ and the gospel that he and his readers were given access to the Spirit and enabled to live from the level of the Spirit. But he does not express it in such an exclusive way as to deny the possibility of those who had never heard the message of Christ Jesus living according to the Spirit or experiencing life and peace. The main line of God's purpose is clear: Abraham, Israel, Christ, gospel to Jew and Gentile; but it is doubtful whether Paul would have excluded the likelihood of at least some others having learned somehow to live from the Spirit even without the gospel. Where vv 5–6 illuminate that earlier discussion (2:6–16), as they illuminate earlier parts of the main argument, is in providing a further definition of the "patient perseverance in doing good" (2:7), "doing the things of the law" (2:14), in terms of the Spirit, the mind set on the things of the Spirit, life according to the Spirit.

7–8 The impression that Paul intends to recapitulate the earlier stages of his argument and to sum them up in terms of the flesh/Spirit antithesis is strengthened here too. The hostility that climaxed the description of the human plight in 5:10 is now clarified as the mind-set of the flesh, with all the pejorative overtones that word has gathered to itself in the course of the developing exposition. The mind set on the flesh that does not submit to God's law recalls the indictment of Gentile and Jew in chaps. 1 and 2. The inability of those in the flesh to please God reminds one of the vicious circle of sin and sinning in 1:18–32, the awful irony of 2:28–29, and the sweeping condemnation of 3:9–20. In the final analysis there is only one alternative to a life lived out in dependence on God, in the obedience of faith, from the life of the Spirit, and that is the way of the flesh, hostile to God, disobedient to his law, heading for death. Every decision of any moral and religious significance boils down to a choice between these two, and Paul wants his readers to be in no doubt as to the grim reality of that alternative.

The repetition of the phrase "cannot" ("cannot submit to God's law, cannot please God") would be particularly sobering, as it no doubt was intended to be. To live at the level of the flesh, at the level of animal appetites and merely human desires, forgetful of one's creatureliness, is to live where the law is impotent precisely because the mind-set is away from God; it is to live where sin is able to bind closely to death precisely because the one power (of God) which can defeat sin's power has been thrown off. In such a summary passage in a letter so strongly oriented to the question of Jewish privilege, the listening audience of Jew, proselyte, God-worshiper and Gentile, would no doubt recognize an indictment also of Jewish pride in its privilege: the mind-set determined by an assumption of ethnic or national prerogative is hostile to God; obedience to the law which focuses too much on the level of the flesh (as with circumcision) is not obedience to the law; such a mind-set *prevents* the obedience God looks for; its praise is from men, not from God (2:29). Even for an audience who had been closely attentive to Paul's line of argument it was a stunning reversal and shocking claim. At the same time Paul takes care to maintain the vindication of the law achieved in chaps. 7–8: the failure of the flesh is failure to obey the law; submission to the law of God is what pleases God. This distinction, between an obedience at the level of the flesh which is actually disobedience, and conduct determined by the Spirit which fulfills the law's requirements, is the vital link between Paul's indictment of Jewish presumption, his eschatological soteriology and his subsequent parenesis.

9 Lest any should feel unnecessarily threatened by the starkness of what he has just said, Paul switches from generalizing third-person terms and addresses his readers directly: "However, you are not in the flesh but in the Spirit, since, as I assume, the Spirit of God dwells in you." It sounds at first as though he is being highly simplistic in his soteriology or overgenerous in his assumptions, envisaging conversion as a once-for-all and complete transfer from the realm of flesh to that of Spirit. But here too it is hardly likely that Paul intended to congratulate his audiences as enjoying a sinless perfection. And those who recalled how he had begun the two preceding sections of his letter with a similarly sharp contrast between the before and after of conversion-initiation (6:3–7; 7:4–6) would hardly be misled here. Paul means neither that they have left the flesh wholly behind, nor that they are in a constant state of inspiration or permanent ecstasy. The phrases "in flesh" and "in Spirit" are much looser than that, as Paul's usage elsewhere confirms (cf., e.g., 14:17 and Gal 2:20). What Paul assumes is not that the process of salvation is complete but that it has begun, not that their total being has been completely transferred to another realm but that a decisive transfer of allegiance and lordship has already taken place, not that moral effort has been rendered unnecessary but that the inner compulsion of God's Spirit has become the most important factor at the level of primary motivation and enabling.

Paul can make this assumption because belonging to Christ and having the Spirit are for him one and the same thing. Possession of the Spirit is what constitutes a Christian, so naturally he assumes that the members of the Roman congregations have received the Spirit. It is possession of the Spirit which makes the difference; Christ's lordship is realized, documented, and made effective by the presence of the Spirit in a life. In what amounts to the nearest thing to a definition of "Christian" in his writings, Paul defines a Christian, albeit in negative formulation, as one who has the Spirit of Christ.

Implicit in this definition is the clear assumption that reception and possession of the Spirit was something perceptible, something known directly (cf. Acts 19:2) and not merely as the silent corollary of a confession of faith or a ritual act rightly performed. Paul no doubt had in mind a vividness and immediacy of experience such as that already alluded to in 2:29; 5:5; and 7:6. Also implied is that possession of the Spirit is the common denominator of all who belong to Christ, not the special prerogative of some over against the rest. Paul could hardly be clearer: no Spirit of Christ, no belonging to Christ. Although Paul did not know many of his Roman readers personally, the character of the new movement had already become so firmly established as a movement of the Spirit that he could make such an assertion without fear of being controversial.

10 Put in other terms, it is the indwelling power of Christ which makes the difference. Here, as in the earlier chapters (chaps. 6 and 7), Paul begins to blunt the edge of his initial assertions. He has no doubt that Christ is in his readers; their primary loyalty and lordship has already been determined. But equally he is conscious that the "not yet" of the eschatological tension has still to be resolved. And once again he poses it in terms of death and life. Both are still factors for believers. On the one hand, they still experience the reality of a body which is dead, by which Paul must mean what he has previously referred to as "the body of sin" (6:6) and "the body of this death" (7:24). Despite the possible implications of some of his earlier statements, when taken in isolation, the reality of living under the power of death has not yet been left behind. To remind his readers of the full sweep of his analysis in chaps. 6 and 7, he draws sin as the chief culprit back on stage for the last time. It is sin which makes death so effective, and the law an instrument of death (7:9–11; 8:2). Though the effectiveness of sin's strategy through the flesh and the law has been decisively countered by the Spirit, the grip of sin and death on the believer's mortality is still firm. In case of any lingering doubt as to the function of the sharply drawn antitheses in vv 5–9, the echo of 7:24 would surely remove it: even where Christ indwells, sin yet holds sway, a sway of diminishing significance, perhaps, but a sway which cannot be fully escaped so long as this body lasts. Nevertheless, all that being said, the decisive fact which Paul cherishes is the presence of the Spirit in the believer: the Spirit is life by virtue of God's righteousness, the

Spirit as God's acceptance and sustaining power active in those who trust him. The believer escapes neither this body of death nor the death of this body, but God's acceptance, life and power are not subject to sin or death, and when sin plays death as its last card God's Spirit will trump it.

11 Which is just what Paul goes on to say. The eschatological tension between life and death will not last beyond the death of this body, for then even that will be drawn under the power of the Spirit of life in and by resurrection. Paul here clearly indicates to his readers that the dichotomy of chap. 7 and of v 10 should not be pushed. They would no doubt already have appreciated that the body of sin, the body of death, is not to be identified simply as the physical body. Paul would probably not think it necessary to remind them that he was thinking in Hebraic terms of the human body as that dimension of the person whereby his environment, both material and social, is experienced. And he had already indicated that the eschatological tension was not reducible to an antithesis between inward and outward, spirit and matter; it entered into the very "I" of the believer as such (7:14–25). So here, even when he focuses on the "mortal body," Paul's point is precisely that the life-giving work of the Spirit will finally embrace that too; salvation will be completed not by escape from the body but by redemption of the body (v 23).

It is equally important to see that for Paul human bodiliness forms an unbroken continuum, of which the person's physicality is an integral part ("mortal body," "dead body"). It is his weakness as a mere mortal, the appetites and desires of his animal nature, which provide sin with its leverage and domain ("body of sin"). It is precisely here, of course, that human "bodiliness" merges into the more pejorative concept of "fleshliness" ("in flesh"; "according to flesh"); humankind not merely with its appetites and desires but in dependence on their fulfillment, not only mortal but corruptible (the ambiguity of the word "corruptible," both physical and moral, reflecting the similar ambiguity of Paul's word "flesh"). At the same time, however, Paul's gospel is that the life-giving power of the Spirit is active on the same continuum of human bodiliness. The Spirit's life is not confined to a spiritual realm divorced from the material and social; nor is the believer's experience of the Spirit now discontinuous with the experience of final resurrection. On the contrary, the resurrection can be regarded as in a real sense the climax of the bodily outworking of the Spirit's life in the here and now (cf. 2 Cor 4:7–5:5). For it is precisely the power of the Spirit which prevents bodily life from relapsing into merely fleshly existence, life in this age from falling back into solely life in this age, presumably without hope of resurrection.

Thus we can say that in Paul's thinking v 11 is the eschatological outworking of the liberation already experienced in v 2. Insofar as it is their mortality which gives sin and, of course, death their hold over his readers, it is the death and resurrection of these same bodies, of the "I" into a new embodiment (cf. 1 Cor 15:42–49), which will at last bring to an end that dimension where sin and death still exercise their sway, when the *posse non peccare* will at last give way to the *non posse peccare*. Of this Christ's own resurrection from the dead has provided both the pattern and the assurance (cf. 6:7–10).

Readers able to savor Paul's words—and Paul surely did not think of this as a letter to be read only once—would no doubt be struck by the fascinating variation he uses in describing the divine forces operating in Christians' salvation. In these three verses (vv 9–11) Paul speaks in quick succession of "the Spirit of God indwelling," "having the Spirit of Christ," "Christ in you" and "the Spirit of him who raised Jesus indwelling." All of these are evidently equivalent phrases, denoting the same effective power of God as already experienced in significant measure by Paul and his readers; the same inspiring and enabling of leader and prophet which they would have read about in the scriptures, but now, Paul would no doubt affirm, poured out in eschatological fullness for all believers. The interesting point, however, is the way this experience can be described now in terms of Christ as well, with the two terms "Christ" and "Spirit" interdependent. On the one hand, Paul implies that the risen Christ is now experienced in and through the Spirit, indeed as the Spirit of God, the Spirit of creation and of prophecy. It is not that "Christ" and "Spirit" are synonymous, but "Spirit *indwelling*," "Christ *in you*." Christ's effective lordship over his own is coterminous with the Spirit's activity in their lives. On the other hand, Paul implies that the Spirit of God is now to be characterized and identified as the Spirit of Christ, as that power which determined Christ in his ministry and in so doing provided a pattern of life in the Spirit. The life-giving Spirit is not independent of the risen Christ (cf. 1 Cor 15:45).

2. *The Spirit of Sonship* (*8:12–17*)

Bibliography

Bieder, W. "Gebetswirklichkeit und Gebetsmöglichkeit bei Paulus." *TZ* 4 (1948) 22–40. **Byrne, B.** *Sons of God.* **Cambier, J. M.** "La liberté du Spirituel dans Romains 8:12–17." In *Paul and Paulinism,* FS C. K. Barrett, ed. M. D. Hooker and S. G. Wilson. London: SPCK, 1982. 205–20. **Deidun, T. J.** *Morality.* 78–80. **Hester, J. D.** *Paul's Concept of Inheritance.* SJTOP 14 (1968). **Jeremias, J.** *The Prayers of Jesus.* London: SCM, 1967. **Lyall, F.** "Roman Law in the Writings of Paul—Adoption." *JBL* 88 (1969) 458–66. **Osten-Sacken, P. von der.** *Römer 8.* 128–39. **Paulsen, H.** *Römer 8.* 77–106. **Pfister, W.** *Das Leben im Geist nach Paulus.* Freiburg: Universitätsverlag, 1963. 69–87. **Potterie, I. de la.** "Le chrétien conduit par l'Esprit dans son cheminement eschatologique." In *Law of Spirit,* ed. Lorenzi. 209–41. **Rensburg, J. J. J. von.** "The Children of God in Romans 8." *Neot* 15 (1981) 139–79. **Schmithals, W.** *Anthropologie.* 117–37. **Taylor, T. M.** "Abba, Father and Baptism." *SJT* 11 (1958) 62–71. **Vos, J. S.** *Traditionsgeschichtliche Untersuchungen zur paulinischen Pneumatologie.* Assen: van Gorcum, 1973.

Translation

[12] *So then, brothers, we are under no obligation to the flesh to live in accordance with the flesh.* [13] *For if you live in accordance with the flesh, you will certainly die; but if by the Spirit you put to death the deeds of the body,[a] you will live.*

¹⁴*For as many as are led by the Spirit of God, they are sons of God.*ᵇ ¹⁵*For you did not receive a spirit of slavery, falling back into fear; but you received the Spirit of adoption,*ᶜ *by whom we cry, "Abba, Father."* ¹⁶*The*ᵈ *Spirit itself bears witness with our spirit that we are children of God.* ¹⁷*And if children, also heirs— heirs of God and heirs together with Christ, provided that we suffer with him in order that we might also*ᵉ *be glorified with him.*

Notes

ᵃ Some authorities, recognizing that σῶμα is unusually negative here, understandably replaced the phrase with τῆς σαρκός (see Lietzmann).

ᵇ The last three words of v 14 appear in different orders in different traditions, perhaps reflecting recognition that the word order of the text is unusual, though probably deliberate to give added emphasis to the υἱοί (Cranfield).

ᶜ The punctuation at this point has been taken differently, with the ἐν ᾧ unusually treated as the beginning of a new sentence: "When we cry 'Abba! Father!' . . ." (RSV; cf. Barrett); but see Cranfield.

ᵈ D recognizes the awkwardness of the inarticulated syntax at the beginning of v 16 by inserting ὥστε.

ᵉ p⁴⁶ omits the καί.

Form and Structure

This section is held together by the thought of believers as sons or children of God. Apart from anything else, it has the advantage of allowing their relation to Christ, the Son of God, to be filled out in powerful familial imagery— the effect being that vv 14–30 will constitute an elaboration of vv 9–11, with vv 14–17 in effect an exposition of v 9, and vv 18–30 an exposition of vv 10–11. Cranfield's unusual decision to split the paragraph before v 17 rather than after has failed to take account of the way in which Paul so often uses his concluding thought to provide a bridge to the next stage of his reflection (see 5:20–21 *Form and Structure*).

The degree to which vv 15–17 parallel Gal 4:6–7 (see particularly Osten-Sacken, 129–34) suggests the possibility that in both passages Paul is drawing on a sequence of thought more widely familiar in the early churches, as certainly was the case with its central element (Αββα ὁ πατήρ). But the verbal parallel is not close enough to indicate an established form, and it may be simply that it was a favorite sequence of thought for Paul himself, as the parallels between Gal 5:13–24 and Rom 8:2–13 (Paulsen, 67) tend to confirm. See discussion in Wilckens.

The only other features worth noting are the switch back and forth from first person (vv 12, 15b–17) to second person (vv 13–15a), and the piling up of the συν- compounds in v 17 (cf. vv 22, 26, 28–29).

Comment

12 ἄρα οὖν, ἀδελφοί, ὀφειλέται ἐσμὲν οὐ τῇ σαρκὶ τοῦ κατὰ σάρκα ζῆν, "so then, brothers, we are under no obligation to the flesh to live in accordance with the flesh." ἄρα οὖν indicates a compelling conclusion drawn from what has just been said (see on 8:1). Since that conclusion is the exhortation *not* to live in accordance with the flesh, the implication must be that that possibility was in no wise excluded by the preceding exposition. The exhortation here makes nonsense of any interpretation which misconceives the rhetorical sharpness of Paul's antitheses (and aorists). "The boundaries between the realm of the Spirit and the realm of the flesh . . . do not run simply and clearly between the believers on the one side and the nonbelievers, but go right through the believers, through each individual believer" (Kuss, 596–97). See further on 8:4, 8:5, and 8:9. As in chap. 6, the sharper lines drawn in the early part of the chapter provide the basis for the exhortation which follows, not its contradiction (see chaps. 6–8 *Introduction*). For the fourth time in the letter Paul addresses his hearers/readers as ἀδελφοί; see on 1:13. With the first person plural (ἐσμέν) Paul takes care to include himself; since the eschatological tension is no different in his case (7:24!) he needs to exercise the same ethical resolution.

The infrequently used ὀφειλέτης (see on 1:14) is carefully chosen: they belong to the realm of flesh, inescapably (for σάρξ see on 1:3; 7:5, 14); but that belongingness does not constitute an obligation *to* the flesh, as though their being "in the flesh" was reason enough to live solely or predominantly on its terms. The fact that they are σάρκινοι (7:14) may explain and excuse what is done κατὰ σάρκα, but can never justify it. κατὰ σάρκα ζῆν becomes a further variation on κατὰ σάρκα περιπατεῖν, κατὰ σάρκα εἶναι, τὸ φρόνημα τῆς σαρκός, and ἐν σαρκὶ εἶναι. Bornkamm, *Paul*, 156, notes that chap. 8 does not contain a single verb in the imperative; but the imperatival form of the exhortation here is clear enough and not very different from 13:12, 14.

13 εἰ γὰρ κατὰ σάρκα ζῆτε, μέλλετε ἀποθνῄσκειν, "for if you live in accordance with the flesh you will certainly die." The repetition of the final phrase of v 12 shows that Paul has in mind no merely hypothetical or unreal possibility. The danger is real for his hearers: the switch to second person increases the note of warning; and the undiscriminating character of the address indicates that he has in mind not merely inquirers or unbelievers (an evangelistic threat!) but believers as well (see further on 9:3, 11:21, 13:14, and 14:15). The μέλλετε clearly denotes not merely futurity, but the certainty of its happening (see BGD, 1cδ), with the possible overtone of its pressing imminence and therefore urgency (cf. BGD, 1cα); cf. 8:18, and see also on 4:24 and 5:14. As a threat, ἀποθνῄσκειν obviously does not refer simply to the fact of death ending this life. But neither should it be spiritualized and understood as a dying distinct from end-of-life death. The warning is evidently twofold: (1) living κατὰ σάρκα binds the one who so lives more tightly to that which is corruptible and perishable (cf. 8:6 and Gal 6:8, "he who sows to the flesh will from the flesh reap corruption"; φθοράν, "destruction, dissolution"); (2) in consequence he perishes with the destruction of the σάρξ (death is his final state, without life beyond). The μέλλετε presumably means that he hastens the process of corruption in its inevitablity. The goal of God's redemptive purpose is liberation from this slavery of φθορά (v 21). Hultgren, *Gospel*, 99–100, provides an interesting collocation of passages using different "imagery for eschatological peril in Paul's letters." But it is questionable whether passages like 2:8–9; 8:13; 11:21; and 14:15 can be limited to the status of parenesis without doctrinal content, though it remains true that the "doctrinal content" is never spelled out beyond the language of death, destruction, wrath, etc.

εἰ δὲ πνεύματι τὰς πράξεις τοῦ σώματος θανατοῦτε, ζήσεσθε, "but if by the Spirit you put to death the deeds of the body you will live." The parallel with the death-life warning of Deut 30:15 ff. (cf. 11:26 ff.) is probably in Paul's mind, since in each case the thought moves on to inheritance (Deut 11:29, 31; 30:16; Rom 8:17). The parallel is important: Paul expects moral commitment and effort no less than Moses (Str-B compares the rabbinic talk of suppressing the evil impulse, 3:241–42). The difference is that the inheritance is no longer the promised land and the heirs no longer simply those with physical ties to that land (see further on 8:17); and the moral effort is now πνεύματι, by the Spirit (not the human spirit, as SH; alternatives reviewed by Kuss), a realizable possibility only in the eschatological conditions of the Spirit poured out on all the heirs (cf. Gal 4:1–7). The difference from 7:14–25 is that there the Spirit had not yet been brought into the picture.

πρᾶξις does not have a negative force in itself, meaning here simply "acts, actions, deeds" (rightly Kuss; cf. 12:4). The negative connotation which allows a translation like "evil or disgraceful deed" (BGD, 4b; referring to Luke 23:51, Col 3:9, *Herm. Man.* 4.2.1–2), "base pursuits" (NEB), is drawn entirely from the context. Here, however, surprisingly, the negative connotation is provided by σῶμα, where we would have expected σάρξ (cf. Gal 5:19; see also *Notes*). In fact this is about the most negative use of σῶμα in Paul, and clearly the usage here is principally determined by the fact that σῶμα has already been used in this chapter as a stylistic variant for the overloaded σάρξ, with its unusually negative force as the result (the point needs to be more clearly acknowledged by Schmithals, *Anthropologie*, 118–19). Usually denoting man's embodiment in this age (see on 6:6), in a more neutral sense (cf. particularly 12:1, 4–5), here it denotes man's dependency on and degree of identity with this age (Maillot avoids the problems, but also loses the continuity of thought, by using a different paraphrase for each of the σῶμα references in these chapters—except 7:4!). "The deeds of the body" therefore are the actions which express undue dependence on satisfying merely human appetites and ambitions. The present tense (θανατοῦτε) indicates a sustained effort; whatever happened at conversion-initiation (baptism), it evidently was not a once-for-all killing off of "the old man," "the body of sin" (cf. particularly Col 3:5–10). Leenhardt notes the link in thought to 12:1, since "the putting to death the deeds of the body resembles very closely the death of the sacrificial victim." As Zeller notes, the parallels in Philo, *Gig.* 14 and *Ebr.* 70, are too much influenced by Platonic dualism.

ζήσεσθε clearly does not refer to a quality of living during this life, nor does it imply exemption from death; it can only mean eschatological life—that is, life beyond the death which all will die but with which those who live κατὰ σάρκα will end. The switch in sense from ζάω = daily living (8:12–13a) to ζάω = living beyond death (8:13b) seems to invite some confusion (cf. 14:7–9), but Paul presumably sees the two as continuous or at least interconnected, despite the interposition of death (cf. 1:17; 6:10–11, 13). See also on 6:11.

14 The connection of thought between v 13 and v 14 is unclear to many commentators (see particularly Dodd). It is only a problem, however, when we forget that continuity with and fulfillment of the promises to Abraham and Israel is the hidden current which carries Paul's thought forward: the role of the law, the eschatological Spirit, the status of sonship all follow in a natural sequence as topics of an exposition of believers' privileges which is tantamount to the claim that they have entered into the eschatological privileges promised to Israel (this is more explicit in the parallel passage whose argument Paul seems consciously to be echoing in this section [Gal 3–4]; see also *Form and Structure*). Hence, of course, the transition from chap. 8 to chap. 9: the claims made in chap. 8 in particular seem to have transferred Israel's heritage wholly to those who are "of Christ"; what then of Israel? (see further on chaps. 9–11 *Introduction*).

ὅσοι γὰρ πνεύματι θεοῦ ἄγονται, "for as many as are led by the Spirit of God." ὅσοι can have both a restrictive force ("only those who"—Lagrange, Michel) or an inclusive force ("all those who"—Cranfield, Schlier). There may be a deliberate ambiguity. It is the dependence on the Spirit which is decisive and this is an assertion with implications both inclusive (beyond the boundaries of Israel κατὰ σάρκα) and restrictive (as determined by the extent of the Spirit's outpouring). So it is wiser to translate by the more ambiguous "as many as."

ἄγεσθαι πνεύματι is a further variant on περιπατεῖν κατὰ πνεῦμα, κατὰ πνεῦμα εἶναι, τὸ φρόνημα τοῦ πνεύματος, ἐν πνεύματι εἶναι, πνεῦμα ἔχειν, and κατὰ πνεῦμα ζῆν. As such it may simply mean being "led or controlled by the Spirit" (Cranfield, Schlier, Wilckens; "guided"—NJB; de la Potterie, 221–22, notes that in the LXX ἄγειν and its compounds are technical terms in the vocabulary of the Exodus), expressing also "willing devotion and personal obedience" (Pfister, 76–77). At the same time the most natural sense of ἄγεσθαι with such a dative is that of being constrained by a compelling force, of surrendering to an overmastering compulsion (hence NEB's appropriate rendering "moved by the Spirit"); cf. 2 Tim 3:6 with parallels in Aristotle, Plato, etc. (BGD, ἄγω 3). When the dative is πνεύματι the overtones of enthusiastic, even ecstatic behavior are hard to exclude; cf. particularly 1 Cor 12:2, Gal 5:18, and Luke 4:1 (Luke has replaced Mark's ἐκβάλλει by ἤγετο, but Luke's conceptuality of the Spirit is consistently "enthusiastic"; Dunn, *Jesus*, 190; idem, *Unity*, 180–81). Moreover Paul has already drawn in language used elsewhere of possession (πνεῦμα ἔχειν; see on 8:9) and will shortly use the strong verb κράζειν to describe the Spirit's activity in believers (see on 8:15). Käsemann is right therefore to draw attention to the "enthusiastic" character of Paul's vocabulary here: "Paul was not so timid as his expositors . . . a doctrine of the Spirit which is not afraid of the catchword 'being carried off.'" The language is by no means exclusively "enthusiastic" (cf. after all v 13; "v 13a clearly envisages the possibility that the Christian will choose not to comply" [Deidun, 79]); but it is important to note the degree of emotional intensity which Paul assumes in talking of believers' relation to the Spirit (see on 5:5 and 8:9). He evidently understood the Christian life as an integrated balance between moral effort (v 14) and yielding to deeply felt inward compulsions (cf. Gal 5:16, 18, and see further on 12:1–2; cf. Murray). The importance of the context, however, is that he carefully circumscribes this potentially dangerous ethical ideal by identifying the πνεῦμα only as the Spirit of Christ (v 9) and ties the correlated experience of sonship into Christ's sonship (vv 15–17). "To be led by the Spirit" is not a license for uninhibited ecstasy, as Paul would have been the first to remind his readers (1 Cor 12–14; 1 Thess 5:19–22).

οὗτοι υἱοὶ θεοῦ εἰσιν, "they are sons of God." The idea of human beings as "sons of God" would not be strange to Paul's readers. The Stoic talk of Zeus as father of all (since all shared the same divine reason) would no doubt be familiar to many if not all of his audiences (cf. Acts 17:28), as also probably the description of particular individuals as "sons of God" (such as the philosophers Pythagoras and Plato), as a way of asserting that they were specially gifted or favored by (the) god(s) (Dunn, *Christology*, 14–15). Jew and God-worshiper would also be familiar with the equivalent Jewish understanding of Israel as God's son and of individual Israelites as sons of God or children of heaven, particularly the righteous, those whose living and dying was marked by faithfulness to the law (see on 1:3; and further Byrne, *Sons,* chap. 1; note here particularly Deut 14:1 with its usual typical corollary of election as marked out by particular rules; and cf. the eschatological promise of Hos 1:10 which Paul will quote in 9:26). Paul no doubt wrote in full consciousness of this double context of his readers' preunderstanding, and with great deliberateness he takes up the familiar phrase and defines it precisely in terms of the Spirit of God. The divine sonship of individuals is determined by the Spirit of God, the power of God as understood within Jewish tradition, now experienced in eschatological outpouring, but defined in terms of the *Spirit;* not in terms of the law or of faithfulness to the law, as in the wisdom and martyr traditions of Judaism (see again on 1:3; cf. Byrne, *Sons,* 220). Of course these are not to be posed as unyielding either-ors for Paul, as we have seen (8:4), but nevertheless for Paul it is the Spirit which is the primary reference point in defining Christians' sonship, not faithfulness to the law as understood by his Jewish contemporaries.

15 οὐ γὰρ ἐλάβετε πνεῦμα δουλείας πάλιν εἰς φόβον, "for you did not receive a spirit of slavery falling back into fear." The γάρ hardly indicates that v 15 is "a proof of v 14" (Käsemann): being led by the Spirit is already "proof" of sonship (v 14); vv 15–16 fill out the contextual (within the believer's life) rationale of v 14. ἐλάβετε certainly refers to the reception of the Spirit which marked and constituted the beginning of their life as Christians (belonging to Christ) (the phrase is already more or less a t.t. in Christian vocabulary: 2 Cor 11:4; Gal 3:2, 14; John 7:39; 14:17; 20:22; Acts 1:8; 2:33, 38; 8:15, 17, 19; 10:47; 19:2; 1 John 2:27). If "an objective event" is in view to mark the moment of legal transfer to status of sonship (Michel), it does not necessarily follow that the "objective event" is the baptismal act as such, since the impact of the Spirit was at this time generally conceived and recognized in very tangible terms (see on 8:9).

πνεῦμα δουλείας could be simply rhetorical—"the Spirit was not one of slavery" (Barrett, Cranfield, Wilckens). But it could recall such usage as Judg 9:23; 1 Sam 16:14–16; and 1 Kgs 22:19–23, with the implication that in giving them the Spirit, God was not working for their downfall (cf. Rom 11:8). Alternatively the usage may reflect the current way of expressing opposition between God and evil in terms of good and evil spirits, such as we find particularly in the DSS and *T. 12 Patr.* ("spirit of truth" and "spirit of falsehood"—especially 1QS 3.18ff.; spirit of fornication, jealousy, envy, error, etc. and spirit of understanding, holiness, truth, etc.—*T. Reub.* 5.3; *T. Sim.* 2.7; 3.1; 4.7; *T. Levi* 2.3; 9.9; 18.7, 11; *T. Jud.* 13.3; 14.2, 8; 20.1; etc.); cf. 1 Cor 2:12; 2 Cor 11:4; Eph 2:2; 2 Thess 2:2; 2 Tim 1:7. Here, however, the contrast is once again primarily epochal, between the old epoch from whose dominance they have emerged and the new (hence the πάλιν). It is typical of Paul that he should label this epoch as δουλεία; it characterizes creation as a whole (see on 8:21) and the condition of Israel within the old epoch in particular (Gal 4:24; 5:1; Paul sees Israel's condition under the law as equivalent to that of Gentiles under the elemental spirits, hence the equivalent πάλιν of Gal 4:9 and 5:1); cf. particularly Wilckens. The earlier use of the concept of slavery on both sides of the divide (6:16, 18, 20–22; 7:6, 25) was unlikely to confuse (cf. Käsemann).

φόβος is at first sight surprising. Of course it is intended in a negative sense and would be understood so (although φόβος θεοῦ is something very positive—3:18; 2 Cor 5:11; 7:1; Eph 5:21; Phil 2:12). As such it seems to sit oddly with the earlier criticism of Jewish boasting (2:17, 23; 3:27; 4:2), but in fact the two can go together (as Bultmann saw—Theology, 243). The two indeed neatly characterize the sectarian mentality as seen from inside and from outside: the sectarian self-evidently confident that he belongs by virtue of his maintenance of the sect's distinctives as seen within the sect's limited horizons; the same perceived by the critical observer to be motivated by a hidden fear of failing to match up at one or other of the test points by which loyalty to these distinctives is evaluated within the sect. Paul presumably now understood his Pharisaic attitudes in these terms, not as an inadmissible desire to please God by good works (see on 3:20), but as a concern for punctilious exactness in obeying the law (ἀκρίβεια; see Introduction §1.1), which would tend to inject something of a competitive spirit (Gal 1:14; Phil 3:6) and so also of fear, fear of failing to come up to the mark of acceptability to his fellows or of the esteem in which they held him. For a broader interpretation in existentialist terms see Schmithals, Anthropologie, 129–32.

ἀλλὰ ἐλάβετε πνεῦμα υἱοθεσίας, "but you received the Spirit of adoption." As in the antithetical phrase, the genitive may be ambiguous: the spirit which effects adoption, or the spirit which expresses adoption. Either way it is certainly a status which is already real for the believer—"effects sonship, not merely strengthens the consciousness of being a son" (Kuss; against Barrett, "the Spirit which anticipates adoption"; Byrne, Sons, 100, "a spirit that 'goes with' or 'pledges' υἱοθεσία"; but cf. 8:14, 17)—though Paul's use of the same imagery to describe both the already and the not yet within a few verses of each other is certainly striking (see on 8:23). The metaphor of adoption occurs in the NT only in the Pauline literature (8:15, 23; 9:4; Gal 4:5; Eph 1:5) and is drawn from his experience of Greco-Roman law and custom, since it is not a Jewish practice as such (see Cranfield's excellent note). The use of υἱοθεσία rather than υἱός at this point actually increases the contrast with δουλεία since it emphasizes the double gulf between the two: the believer's status has been transformed not only from slave to freedman (see on 6:16) but also from freedman to adopted son (Käsemann's rejection of the sense "adoption," following Zahn, cf. also Gaugler, is both unfounded and misses the point).

ἐν ᾧ κράζομεν, "by whom we cry." The ἐν ᾧ is best taken as referring to the antecedent πνεῦμα rather than as an unarticulated "in that" (see BGD, ἐν 6, for range of uses). The force of κράζομεν is disputed. Pauline usage is little guide. In 9:27 he uses it of a solemn proclamation; on the other hand, 8:15 and Gal 4:6 (the only other occurrences in Paul) both use the same distinctive formula:

Rom 8:15:   πνεῦμα υἱοθεσίας, ἐν ᾧ κράζομεν, Αββα ὁ πατήρ
Gal 4:6:   τὸ πνεῦμα τοῦ υἱοῦ αὐτοῦ . . . κρᾶζον, Αββα ὁ πατήρ.

This fact strongly suggests that Paul is drawing on more widely recognized and used language—in which case the regular usage elsewhere in the NT to denote an intense or loud cry is more relevant. Consequently those commentators are most likely correct who see here a further indication of the deeply emotional (Bieder, "Gebetswirklichkeit," 26) or enthusiastic character of earliest Christian experience and worship, and the degree to which it would be "left to the Spirit" (see particularly Dodd, Kuss; also Wilckens, with others in n.575). Cranfield notes that κράζειν is regularly used in the LXX for "urgent prayer" but does not give enough weight to the "enthusiastic context" (see again on 8:9 and 8:14), and to the fact that a brief ejaculatory utterance seems to be in view rather than a sustained prayer. The sense of inspiration is very strong (even stronger in Gal 4:6, where it is the Spirit who "cries"; "the cry of inspiration"—Schlier, Schmidt)—the consciousness of being moved upon by divine power, of words being given to say (see further Dunn, *Jesus,* 240–41). This is all part of Paul's sense of eschatological newness brought by the Spirit. Str-B note that in rabbinic literature there is no example of the Holy Spirit being brought into connection with the prayer of an Israelite. See further Paulsen, 94–96.

Αββα, ὁ πατήρ, "Abba, Father." The Aramaic (אַבָּא) is translated by the Greek (πατήρ); for use of the nominative to express the vocative see BDF, §147.3. But evidently the ὁ πατήρ is not added by Paul to translate a single-word utterance ("Abba"); the ὁ πατήρ belongs to the utterance as well (so also Gal 4:6; Mark 14:36). This retention of both forms (Aramaic and Greek) is distinctive of this cry (contrast the Greek only: Χριστός passim; κύριος passim). It strengthens the impression that what is in mind is a single dual-form ejaculatory cry (not necessarily "ecstatic"; against Meeks, *Urban Christians,* 88), in which the pray-er delights to be able to address God in the same terms but in different words—an utterance whose rhythm may bear the imprint of frequent repetition in the devotion of worship. This also decreases the likelihood that what Paul has in mind here is the Lord's Prayer as such (a suggestion frequently revived—e.g., *TDNT* 1:6, Lietzmann, Leenhardt, Barrett, Black; others in Wilckens, n.574); it is unlikely that the Lord's Prayer would have begun in two languages (Käsemann; cf. Matt 6:9 // Luke 11:2); and Paul seems to be thinking of a more spontaneous utterance rather than of a fuller liturgical form spoken in unison or of a specifically "baptismal formula" (Taylor) (see further Kuss; Dunn, *Jesus,* 240; Paulsen, 89–91).

It is generally accepted that "Abba" was characteristic and distinctive of Jesus' own prayer life—principally on the basis of Jeremias's work (*Prayers,* 11–65). And although his claims have to be qualified, and oversentimentalizing deductions have too often been drawn from them, it is still justified to assert that Jesus' use of "Abba" most probably implies a sense of intimate sonship on the part of Jesus, expressed as it was in the colloquial language of close family relationship (see Dunn, *Jesus*, §4). The usage here is important. (1) It attests that this language was remembered as that of Jesus: it is precisely because believers found themselves crying to God with the word used by Jesus that they could be so sure that they shared in Jesus' sonship and inheritance (vv 16–17); Wilckens's bold assertion that "an isolated tradition of the mere prayer address of Jesus is hardly conceivable" (n.574) misses the point. (2) The usage is clearly understood as a distinctive badge of Christians (assuring them of their own intimate relation with God). Consequently it could hardly be the case that the prayer address was typical of a wider group, or even of a number of charismatic rabbis (see Dunn, *Christology*, 27). It was rather precisely because it was remembered as so distinctive of Jesus that it could provide a distinctive badge for those who believed in him.

16 αὐτὸ τὸ πνεῦμα συμμαρτυρεῖ τῷ πνεύματι ἡμῶν, "the Spirit itself bears witness with our spirit." The lack of particle or conjunction is surprising—perhaps occasioned by the wonder which moved Paul when he thought both of the experience and of the fact of the Spirit of God so working in him—the Spirit itself! The most obvious way to take the force of the συν- compound is that "the Spirit bears testimony along with our spirit" (see on 2:15; otherwise Cranfield; alternatives reviewed by Kuss); but the lack of a connection leaves it unclear how Paul relates this witness-bearing to the "Abba, Father" cry (contrast NJB—"the spirit of adoption enabling us to cry out, 'Abba, Father!' The Spirit himself . . ." [cf. NIV]; with NEB—"enabling us to cry 'Abba! Father!' In that cry the Spirit . . ." [cf. RSV]). At all events, "the inner witness of the Spirit" is evidently conceived as having more emotional intensity than was conceded even by Wesley (sermon on "The Witness of the Spirit"), and without the more restricted reference to the scriptures which is a feature of Calvin's classic formulation (*Institutes* 1.7.4–5). The semi-legal terminology links the thought with vv 26–27 (see on 8:26).

The second πνεῦμα is clearly the human spirit (so most; otherwise Schweizer, *TDNT* 6:436, Schmidt, Käsemann; Paulsen speaks of "an individuation of the Spirit" [100–101]). Paul does not refer to it very often but often enough for us to recognize that his anthropology recognized a spiritual dimension to man (*not* to be identified with the νοῦς [Wilckens, 2:142–45])—that dimension of his being to which and through which God's Spirit could communicate its revelatory and redemptive power (see on 1:9). Despite the unease of commentators (such as those mentioned above), it is not unimportant to grasp that Paul recognizes an inward conviction which is the believer's own and, though given by the Spirit, is not simply the presence of the Spirit in him (the testimony of two witnesses would be important for Paul in view of Deut 19:15 [Black]): although he evidently has in mind two sides of the same experience (*we* cry; the *Spirit* bears witness), he neither reduces the Spirit to a feeling of sonship, nor absorbs the concept of God's Spirit within his anthropology. This human assent to divine grace is itself an expression of the renewal of "the inner man" (7:22; 2 Cor 4:16).

ὅτι ἐσμὲν τέκνα θεοῦ, "that we are children of God." Paul uses τέκνον (24 times) less frequently than υἱός (36 times) and never for Jesus, whereas υἱός refers to Jesus frequently (1:3, 4, 9; 5:10; 8:3, 29, 32; etc.). Even so, it is evident that Paul makes no clear distinction between the words at this point, since the variation in the context between the two words in reference to Christians (τέκνον—vv 16, 17, 21; υἱός—vv 14, 19) can only be stylistic. In other words "sons" as well as "children" would in Paul's mind include believers, female as well as male. For the concept see further therefore on 8:14. The present tense presumably reflects Paul's assumption that the "Abba, Father" prayer and the walk κατὰ πνεῦμα go together in the believer's life, so that the one is to be identified with the other (against Cranfield, 393).

17 εἰ δὲ τέκνα καὶ κληρονόμοι· κληρονόμοι μὲν θεοῦ, συγκληρονόμοι δὲ Χριστοῦ, "and if children, also heirs—heirs of God and heirs together with Christ." The link is not merely legally logical in terms of Roman law (cf. particularly Hester, 59–61); it is also a characteristic association of ideas in Jewish theology—Israel as God's son(s) (see on 1:3), and as heirs of the promise of the land given to Abraham (see on 4:13); for sonship as itself part of the inheritance see Rev 21:7. The idea of Israel itself as God's inheritance (the lot chosen for himself) is a recurring theme in Jewish literature and was a basic datum of Jewish self-understanding (Deut 32:9; 1 Kgs 8:51, 53; 2 Kgs 21:14; Pss 33:12; 74:2; Isa 63:17; Jer 10:16; Mic 7:18; Jud 13:5; Sir 24:8, 12; *Jub.* 1.19–21; 22.9–10, 15; 33.20; *3 Macc.* 6.3; *2 Apoc. Bar.* 5.1; Ps. Philo 12.9; 21.10; 27.7; 28.2; 39.7; 49.6). It is this hitherto uniquely privileged status which Paul claims with a bold logic born of the correlation of divine promise (to Abraham) with experience of the Spirit (seen as its fulfillment among the Gentiles; cf. particularly Gal 3:1–14, 29; 4:28–29). This link between the Spirit and inheritance is characteristic of Paul's thought (cf. 1 Cor 6:9–11; Gal 4:7; Eph 1:14; Titus 3:5–7). In some ways more striking is the identification of the inheritance as "the kingdom of God," where the thought is consistently of a *future* inheritance yet to be entered into—so consistently, in fact, that it appears to be an already traditional expression taken over by Paul (1 Cor 6:9–10; 15:50; Gal 5:21; Eph 5:5; cf. Matt 25:34; James 2:5), since he seems to make little fresh use of kingdom language elsewhere (see on 14:17); cf. Vos, *Pneumatologie*, 26–33.

The immediate repetition of κληρονόμοι strongly suggests a phrasing provided in dictation and intended for reading. The different ways of understanding the genitives (*of* God, *with* Christ) would cause no difficulty, since the latter stands in a συν- compounded phrase. συγκληρονόμος is attested only in the NT (8:17; Eph 3:6; Heb 11:9; 1 Pet 3:7). Significant for Christology is the fact that Paul here thinks of Christ as also an heir. Since inheritance and kingdom are coterminous for Paul (see above) it coheres with his talk elsewhere of Christ's kingly rule as being given by God and subordinate to God's (1 Cor 15:24–28) and may consciously echo (or influence) therefore the Synoptic tradition of Jesus' assigning to his disciples a share of the kingdom assigned to him by God (Luke 22:29). συγκληρονόμοι Χριστοῦ is the linchpin which holds together all the different strands of Paul's thought which overlap here: the experience of sharing in Christ's Abba-relation to God though the Spirit of Christ, as the basis of the confidence of sharing Christ's inheritance; the idea of Christ as the heir of the promise to Abraham, who in his very act of inheriting (death and resurrection) transformed the inheritance from something merely national to something which transcended national and physical boundaries; and the conviction that the sharing with Christ has to be complete—a sharing in his suffering and death as indispensable for sharing in his risen life—hence the εἴπερ clause below, and the characteristic range of συν- compounds which are such a feature of Paul's theology (see on 6:4) (cf. Hester, 62–67).

εἴπερ συμπάσχομεν, "provided that we suffer with him." Paul takes up the already established link between sonship and suffering in Jewish thought (as in Prov 3:12; Tob 13:4–5; Wisd Sol 3–5; Add Esth 16:14–16; *Pss. Sol.* 13.8–9; Byrne, *Sons*, 63) and adapts it to Christian eschatology. Here again a distinction between εἰ and εἴπερ is evident: in v 17a εἰ denotes a necessary and sufficient condition fulfilled = "since"; but εἴπερ denotes a condition not yet fulfilled and therefore a consequence dependent on the fulfillment of the condition (see also on 8:9). "Seeing that" (Cranfield), "since, as is the case" (Black; so also Lietzmann; Lagrange; Michel; Schmidt; Osten-Sacken, 135 n.18; Harrisville) therefore are inadequate translations; something denoting a hortatory and conditional understanding, as in vv 12–13, is necessary (Kuss, Käsemann). συμπάσχειν, only here and in 1 Cor 12:26 in biblical Greek, means "suffer with, suffer the same thing as," the συν- denoting, as regularly with Paul's favorite συν- compounds, "with Christ" (see on 6:4). It clearly does not denote merely "sympathy with" (cf. LSJ III), or simply that Christ has set them in this suffering (Michaelis, *TDNT* 5:925). Paul has in view an act of identification with Christ (at baptism [6:4], but to describe this simply as "baptismal teaching" [Michel] ignores the fact that it is a much more pervasive theme in Paul's writings [see on 6:2]) and a process of growing conformity to Christ's death in the life of the believer (cf. particularly 2 Cor 4:10; Phil 3:10–11; Althaus)—not as an attempt to glorify or rationalize the experience of suffering, but as the necessary corollary of the view that only Christ's death has ended the old epoch and the rule of sin and death, so that only by participation in that death can the rule of sin and death be broken for others. The εἴπερ therefore preserves the note of eschatological reservation, reminding Paul's readers that the process of sharing in Christ's sufferings and death is a lifelong one (hence the present tense, in distinction from the following aorist), reaching its completion finally only in death (see also on 6:5; and see further Dunn, *Jesus*, 326–88).

ἵνα καὶ συνδοξασθῶμεν, "in order that we might be glorified with him." The final force of the ἵνα should not be weakened. The implication is again clear: suffering with Christ is not an optional extra or a decline or lapse from the saving purpose of God. On the contrary, it is a necessary and indispensable part of that purpose. Without it future glory would not be attained (cf. particularly 2 Tim 2:11–12; 1 Pet 4:13). The basis for a very positive theological response to the age-old problem of suffering is hereby established (cf. also 5:3–5). συνδοξάζω is a uniquely Pauline construction unknown elsewhere in biblical Greek, but attested in a different sense elsewhere (LSJ). That the goal of God's saving purpose is man's experience of and sharing in (God's) glory is frequently asserted (2:7, 10; 5:2; 8:21; 9:23; 1 Cor 2:7; 15:43; 2 Cor 3:18; 4:17; Phil 3:21; Col 1:27; 3:4; 1 Thess 2:12; 2 Thess 2:14; 2 Tim 2:10; Heb 2:10; 1 Pet 1:7; 5:1, 4, 10; 2 Pet 1:3; see also on 8:30). Since δόξα describes the radiance of heaven and of God in particular, in contrast to the duller shades of earth (BGD, δόξα 1; Kuss, 608–18; and see on 1:21), it is natural to describe the hoped-for transformation to heaven in terms of δόξα. In the Judeo-Christian tradition it is seen as part of God's creative purpose in the first place, so that it was natural to express the point in terms of Adam's glory restored and enhanced (see on 3:23). The Christian and particularly Pauline version of the theme is to reexpress this Adam soteriology as an Adam Christology: Christ alone has fulfilled the divine purpose in making man, and man is brought to that divine goal by sharing in or being conformed to Christ's glory (2 Cor 3:18–4:6; Phil 3:21; Col 3:4; 2 Thess 2:14; and, most explicitly outside the Pauline corpus, Heb 2:7–10).

Explanation

12 Paul begins to draw out the consequences of the preceding analysis. His conclusion is not that flesh is no longer a problem for the believer, that the possibility of living in terms of the flesh is no longer open to his hearers, as a careless reading of vv 5–9 might have suggested. On the contrary, living by the flesh is a real possibility for his readers, even though they are "in Christ" and "in the Spirit"; the law of sin and death may still become (again) the determinative factor in their lives rather than the law of the Spirit of life. As in chap. 6, the sharply drawn indicatives are qualified and explained by the following imperatives; God's prior action already accomplished does not absolve them from moral sensitivity and effort. And as in 6:15, the switch back to the first person plural reminds his audiences that they all share a common obligation. The obligation *not* to live by the flesh is, of course, not a recipe for a harsh asceticism or masochism; Paul's thought throughout is of flesh in antithesis to Spirit; that is, of a life dominated by the appetites and ambitions which nurture pride and self-centeredness. The alternative is not expressed, but clearly implied: they are all debtors to God, to Christ, to the Spirit and should live accordingly (as honorable persons in debt would bend all their life's energies to clearing that debt).

13 "For if you live according to the flesh you must die." Paul here puts it beyond dispute that the antitheses of vv 5–9 do not denote the before and after of conversion. On the contrary, his concern (expressed once again in the direct address of second person) is lest his readers fail to exert sufficient moral effort. Their conversion had not settled the issue; their being baptized into Christ's death had not made death a thing of the past. On the contrary, even those whom he has described confidently as "in the Spirit" (v 9) may yet live in and for the flesh. And if they do so, if they let that become the dominant force in their living, they are back on the way to death, the mindset of the flesh. Precisely because believers are still men and women of flesh, still serve the law with the flesh, precisely for that reason the liberation of conversion-initiation is not final or irreversible. This is a warning given to Christians, not to pagans yet unconverted.

What is required of them is responsible moral effort—"putting to death the deeds of the body." The language almost lapses into dualism, as though all bodily functions were by nature evil. But clearly Paul uses the phrase ("deeds of the body") as a somewhat unguarded variant of "living according to the flesh." There is, it is true, a hint of the ascetic and moral prude in Paul (1 Cor 7:1; 9:27), but his thought here is always on the larger issue of dependence on a physical and social indulgence which distances from God.

He describes Christian obligation as a putting to death, an extirpating the deeds of the body. There must be a dying for the person "in the Spirit" as much as for the person "in the flesh." Here too the indicatives in his earlier talk of sharing Christ's death (6:3–4) are not to be pressed, any more than his talk of the deadness of the believer's body (8:10) is to be taken literally. But presumably all these ideas of death are tied up and can be seen together as the outworking of Christ's death (v 17). To put to death the deeds of the body presumably involves both the recognition that the body must die—there is no redemption for belongingness to this age except through death—but also the recognition that moral effort here and now can diminish the effective power of death, by diminishing that area over which sin holds sway in the believer's life—that is, by rooting out and making an end of different expressions of that dependence on physical and social fulfillment which distance from God. It is a determined spiritual discipline Paul sees as essential and calls for, not a masochistic self-abuse.

Thus it becomes clear once again (as in chap. 6) that Paul envisages a balance or tension between divine grace and human effort in the process of salvation. Indeed, the balance Paul strikes does not seem to be so very different from the equivalent balance in Judaism, where a full sharing in the hope of the age to come was usually thought to depend on a disciplined maintaining of one's status within the covenant (by observing the works of the law), or in terms which may already have been current at the time of Paul, on subduing "the evil impulse." And Paul's own insistence that God intended the requirement of the law to be fulfilled in believers (8:4) must have encouraged the comparison. Where Paul's formulation is distinctive, however, is in its emphasis that the necessary discipline can only be maintained in and by the Spirit, by that inner enabling which marked off the new covenant from the old (Jer 31:31–34). Moreover, the object to which the moral effort is to be directed is not defined here in terms of the law, but in terms of the flesh—the point being that for Paul the category of "according to the flesh" was not synonymous with or reducible to "what the law forbids." There is, of course, a large overlap (v 4), but "according to the flesh" is the larger category which cannot be reduced to a series of regulations. Recognition of what is "according to the flesh," "deeds of the body," in any particular instance, cannot be achieved simply by consulting a rule book or written code; on the contrary, even living "in accordance with the law" could also be living "in accordance with the flesh," as Paul's earlier indictment had made clear. To live according to the Spirit, put to death the deeds of the body, evidently meant for Paul a sensitivity to the will of God in each instance to know what was the requirement of the law in that instance (12:2), to distinguish that from what in the end of the day merely promoted selfish pride and presumption (including works of the law).

14 At this point Paul chooses to transpose his exposition from the antithesis between Spirit and flesh to the correlatives Spirit and sonship, both as a way of elaborating the important cautionary exhortation he has just given, while again reassuring his readers of the privileged position they already find themselves in, and as a way of leading into the final qualification of the earlier cut-and-dried language in which the eschatological tension will be set in cosmic context (vv 18–23). It was probably by deliberate plan that Paul delayed the introduction of this image of believers' divine sonship till this point. For, as will quickly become evident, not only does it allow him to unfold the relationship between Christ and Christians with remarkable freshness and vigor at such a developed stage in his argument, but also it provides him the opportunity to bring this stage of his argument (the outworking of God's righteousness for individual believers) to a fitting climax with the elaboration of the eschatological reality of that sonship.

The language Paul uses would be familiar to his audience—"sons of God" as those specially favored by God. They would probably think particularly of those hailed as "sons of God" because of their firm adherence to the laws of clean and unclean food (Deut 14) or because of their loyalty to the covenant (Wisd Sol 2:12–13; etc.). So they would have no difficulty in taking the point of Paul's implied contrast. In defining "sons of God" in terms of the Spirit of God Paul has redefined the terms of God's fatherhood to embrace a potentially much wider circle than Israel "according to the flesh," the covenant promise extended to all the seed of Abraham (chap. 4; Gal 3).

More precisely, "sons of God" are defined as those who are "led by the Spirit of God." Here too the verb evokes an idiom which would be familiar to Greek speakers, that of being led, drawn along by something strongly felt, a desire or passion (cf. 2 Tim 3:6). Paul clearly thinks of the leading of the Spirit in terms of strong inner conviction, of deeply felt compulsion being allowed expression in conduct and lifestyle. The emotional dimension at the heart of Paul's ethical teaching is thus clear. His language, however, cannot be pushed any further in that direction: he does not ask his readers to cultivate a lifestyle which grows out of great surges of emotion or a spirituality dependent on enthusiastic ecstasy. The thought is no different from that of 7:6, and the contrast with a life ruled by selfish passion (7:5) is still implicit here; the righteous demands of the law still provide a looking glass in which sinful passions and fleshly conduct can be recognized (7:13; 8:4). Those familiar with Paul's thought as expressed elsewhere would know well enough that for Paul the leading of the Spirit manifested itself most characteristically in the fruit of the Spirit (Gal 5:18–25). As the Spirit of Christ (8:9), so the measure of the leading of the Spirit is the character of Christ's ministry (cf. Luke 4:1, 14). Nevertheless, the point remains that Paul sees Christian conduct as characteristically expressive of a strong inner motivation, rather than a conduct determined by constant reference to a written code.

Paul's readers would also be unlikely to miss the fact that a further definition of the Christian has been provided, to supplement that in v 9. The one belonging to Christ not only *has* the Spirit, but follows the Spirit's leading. A possession of the Spirit which did not manifest itself in conduct and lifestyle would be a contradiction in terms for Paul. The definition is, no doubt deliberately, framed in open and not restrictive terms: "as many as," not just "only those who." This sonship to God offered by Paul's gospel is not something enjoyed only by a privileged few specially graced by God, nor something

limited to those whose faithfulness to the law marked them out as a class
apart. "As many as respond to the Spirit's leading—they are sons of God."
That Paul is thinking particularly of Christian believers is obvious from the
context, but once again, as in the earlier verses of the chapter, the proposition
is framed in a way that retains the openness of the still earlier discussion of
keeping the law in chap. 2.

15 Verse 15 brings the generalized proposition of v 14 to bear on the
members of the Roman congregations. At your conversion "you did not receive
a spirit of slavery which led you back into fear." By "slavery" Paul almost
certainly has in mind life under the law (cf. Gal 4:24; 5:1), as his largely
Jewish and God-worshiping readership would well realize: concern to place
the law correctly within his new (Christian) perspective is a recurring pattern
in the warp and weft of his argument in Romans, and the closeness of the
parallel between this section and Gal 3–5 (particularly 4:1–7) strongly suggests
that it must have been a recurring pattern in his teaching with which many
of his readers would have been familiar. Of course this was hardly his perception of life under the law when he was still a devout Pharisee, prior to his
encounter with Christ. But as he looks back on that form of life he reckons
it as slavery and marked by fear. He probably has in mind the typically
Pharisaic concern for exactness in obedience to the law, the scrupulous attention to the detailed implementation of the law which we know to have been
characteristic of the Pharisaism of the time. That punctiliousness which had
once been meat and drink to him he now sees as something tremendously
restrictive, as an attitude which stifled and enchained the free-er expression
of love such as Jesus had demonstrated (cf. Mark 2:1–3:6). With insight born
of his conversion Paul sees that attitude to have been motivated (subcon-
sciously) in large part by fear—a fear of failing to match up to a standard
of exact obedience, a fear in other words not so much of God as of what his
fellow Pharisees might think or say of his failure to conform. Paul thus, in
all probability, extrapolates his own experience to that of his readers, confident
that his Jewish and God-worshiping audiences have found in Christianity
the same liberation as he had himself (v 2).

The contrast is posed once again in terms of sonship—in this case of adopted
sonship, though the interchange of terminology (sons, adoption, children
[vv 14–17, 21–23]) implies that Paul hardly wanted to press the distinction,
and in Roman law anyway the rights of an adopted son were no different
from those of a natural son (cf. v 17). The contrast is clearly between the
status of slavery and that of sonship, and all that that meant in terms of
personal freedom and social relationships. Though many slaves could and
did rise to positions of considerable importance and influence within households (including those of state officials), the idea of slavery as such focuses
on the slave's lack of freedom, as one who orders his life at another's behest,
who must live within the terms of a code which restricts him firmly within
servitude, and who as a slave is divided in status from members of the family
by an unbridgeable gulf. Whereas sonship as such, including adoptive sonship,
by contrast speaks of freedom and intimate mutual trust, where filial concern
can be assumed to provide the motivation and direction for living, and conduct
be guided by spontaneous love rather than by law. Here again the contrast

should not be pushed to extreme: Paul hardly envisages a Christian morality totally free of all constraint and restraint; the model presumably is that of the dutiful and devoted son, not of a son careless of his filial obligations. Nevertheless, the greater freedom of sonship is of the essence of the contrast. Paul experienced the Spirit as freedom to express his faith in new and previously impossible ways, freedom to live at the level of person to person rather than of interpreter to written code.

The contrast to the fear of the unliberated Pharisee is the trust expressed in addressing God as "Abba, Father." Paul evidently is able here to assume his readers' familiarity with the phrase. The use of just the same phrase in Gal 4:6 clearly indicates that it was an established formula in the churches known to Paul. The fact that the Aramaic word was thus preserved into the Greek-speaking churches implies that "Abba" had become an established word in the devotions of Aramaic-speaking believers and indicates the character of the devotion inculcated in the newer Greek-speaking congregations. So firmly fixed had the Aramaic word become in Christian spirituality that it was retained in its Aramaic form even when the Greek translation was appended. Paul is thus able to assume that it would also be part of the experience of congregations he had never visited.

The reason why "Abba" had become so firmly established is presumably that it was remembered as a word given its particular resonance by Jesus himself. Attested only once as such in the Jesus tradition (Mark 14:36), it was nevertheless probably a characteristic form and distinctive feature of Jesus' prayer to God. It was evidently taken up by the first followers of Jesus, no doubt in imitation of Jesus, and most likely at his direct instruction (Luke 11:2). Not that Paul here is necessarily thinking of the phrase simply as the beginning of Christian prayer (though no doubt it was), or specifically of the Lord's Prayer. The thought is more general—of Christians as those who echo Jesus' own prayer style and share in his own relation to God. And quite probably he had in mind various occasions in worship marked by single or repeated ejaculation of the phrase (for which the dual form, Aramaic and Greek, would be fitted).

Also implied is the same sort of intimacy as Jesus' own use of the word indicates. Jesus' characteristic prayer address was unusual precisely because "Abba" was so much a family word, expressive of family familiarity and intimacy. For the typical Jewish piety of the period it was almost certainly too bold, overfamiliar, probably considered impudent and irreverent by most. But evidently it was just such familiarity and intimacy the first Christians experienced too; the intimacy of the son rather than the legally determined obedience of the slave. What Paul has in mind cannot, however, be reduced to a merely inner sense, a quiet conviction of sonship. The verb used ("cry out") implies an intensity of feeling or fervor of expression. And its inclusion in the established formula (Gal 4:6) implies that such intensity was a regular feature of the uttered phrase. We cannot exclude the likelihood that for some the cry "Abba, Father" was simply a parroting of what was perceived to be a significant expression of spirituality. But the fact remains that Paul is able to assume such an intensity of spiritual experience as typically Christian, presumably on the basis of his own widespread knowledge of Greek-speaking

congregations. Moreover, since vv 14–15 are explanatory and supportive of
the earlier exhortation to ethical responsibility and moral effort (vv 12–13),
the implication is that such conduct is rooted in and grows out of this fervent
sense of sonship.

16 "The Spirit itself bears witness with our spirit that we are children of
God." It is presumably this same intense consciousness of sonship expressed
in the cry "Abba, Father" which Paul still has in mind—a sense that it is not
just himself praying but his inner being enabled to pray by the enabling of
God (cf. v 26). Here beyond dispute it is an inner confirmation or assurance
that Paul has in mind, not simply the repetition of hallowed phrases, nor a
logical assurance deduced from such repetition, or from a baptism or right
confession made some time in the past. Paul certainly does not reduce assurance to a matter of feeling (as vv 13–14 confirm), but a felt assurance is
what he has in mind here. The continuity of thought from v 14 implies
that for Paul conversion was as much as anything else a liberation of the
emotions. It was certainly his own experience (as the almost unconscious
switch back from second to first person testifies), but he is able to assume
the same to be true of his readers. The emotional quality of his faith and
spirituality thus once again comes clearly to the fore. He would have had
little personal sympathy with a purely rational faith or primarily ritualistic
religion. The inner witness of the Spirit was something not just important
for him but at the heart of what distinguished his faith as a Christian from
what he had known before.

Significant here too is the way in which Paul sees the Spirit as the common
denominator in the train of thought running through these verses. Previously
described in terms of mind-set and lifestyle (vv 5–6, 13–14), the Spirit is
here spoken of in irreducibly emotional and experiential terms. For Paul
the Spirit is the power of God which integrates emotion, thought and conduct
in a life-giving way (there is of course an alternative, pernicious integration
of flesh and sin on the way to death). But it does so precisely as the Spirit
of Christ, the Spirit who brings us to share in the same intimate sonship
which Jesus enjoyed on earth, and does so as the beginning of that process
which ends in the final integration of the body into the wholeness of complete
salvation (vv 9–11, 15–16). To possess the Spirit is to have the Spirit of Christ,
is to share his sonship, is to live as a son led by the Spirit. The extent to
which these different facets of Paul's thinking interlock would probably be
more fully appreciated by the first readers of Paul's letter to Rome than has
been the case in subsequent centuries.

17 Not least of importance in the concept of sonship is the fact that it
links into the theme of inheritance, not unnaturally since the primary purpose
of adoption was to provide a suitable heir. The importance of the inheritance
theme is twofold. As will quickly become apparent it carries a clear implication
of the eschatological "not yet": believers are heirs who have not yet entered
into their full inheritance. But more important is the fact that Paul here
takes up and transforms one of the most emotive themes in Jewish national
self-identity, as most of his readers would be well aware. Central to Jewish
self-understanding was the conviction that Israel was the Lord's inheritance,
the people chosen out of all the nations of the earth to be his own (Deut

32:9). Integral to that national faith was the conviction that God had given Israel the inheritance of Palestine, the promised land. It is this axiom which Paul evokes and refers to the new Christian movement as a whole, Gentiles as well as Jews. *They* are the heirs of God; Israel's special relationship with God has been extended to all in Christ. And the promise of the land has been transformed into the promise of the *kingdom*; the thought of Christian inheritance as inheritance of the kingdom was evidently well enough established in the churches known to Paul so that he has no need to be more explicit. Those familiar with that thought would also draw the corollary of the eschatological "not yet" explicit in the other passages: that inheritance of the kingdom, full citizenship under the rule of God alone, is something still awaited by believers. Paul need not make the allusion any more explicit since he is about to develop an alternative expression of the same point (vv 19–23). The immediately striking point, however, is the casualness with which Paul takes over and extends such a cherished Jewish prerogative. Even more clearly than in his treatment of the law Paul cuts at the heart of his people's covenant faith. Their distinctiveness as God's people is now shared by all who believe in Christ. That this sets up a considerable tension for his understanding of Israel's election within the purpose of God (as had his earlier treatment [3:1–3]) is self-evident. By making the assertion so briefly and bluntly Paul prepares his readers for the next major section of his argument (chaps. 9–11).

For Paul, of course, they are all "heirs of God" because they are all "joint heirs with Christ." These are not merely two loosely connected corollaries of the prior thought of their divine sonship. They are heirs of God by virtue of being fellow heirs with Christ—just as by implication in vv 15–16 they are sons of God by virtue of being given to share in Christ's "Abba" relationship to God. Paul here evidently encapsulates the whole argument of Gal 3–4 (particularly 3:28) in a single phrase. From this we must conclude that he could assume his Roman audiences would be familiar with that line of argument, or that they could be expected to follow the compressed logic of his "in Christ." Either way, the point is that for Paul Christians do not become God's inheritance independently of Christ; that privilege becomes theirs only as a consequence of their belonging to Christ; they are sons as sharing his sonship by adoption. Paul would certainly have resisted any suggestion that God could simply have extended his offer of acceptance to all whether or not Jesus had lived or died. That would have implied a capricious God, arbitrary in his favors. On the contrary, it is Christ who holds together both the continuity and the eschatological enlarging of God's purpose: as Son of David and seed of Abraham he is heir of the original covenant promise; but as Son of God in power in accordance with the Spirit as from the resurrection of the dead (1:3–4) his status as son and heir becomes one which can be shared by those who identify with him.

Yet they will enjoy that full inheritance (in the future) only if their identification with Christ goes all the way, not simply with his lifestyle on earth or in experience of his risen life already, but also in the sharing of his suffering and death. Paul thinks here undoubtedly of the suffering of persecution to which he was no stranger, though included also will be the minor and more petty persecutions which a strange small new sect is always liable to call upon itself. But presumably also he has in mind the more complex train of thought which runs through so much of his previous discussion, summed up in his talk of the "body of death" (7:24) and of "putting to death the deeds of the body" (8:13). Underlying the brief reference here, then, is the thought that such suffering, such corrupting away of the corruptible, is the inevitable consequence of life in this body. If such suffering is to be a stage on the way to a full share in the inheritance of God's kingdom, and not just a full stop, it must be a sharing in *his* suffering; it is suffering accepted and lived through as sharing his suffering which holds the promise of future glory. To be Christ's is to share not just his sonship but his rejection and death; the stark realities of chap. 7 and earlier in chap. 8 are by no means left behind.

With the talk of glory Paul evokes once again the thought of Adam (cf. 1:21, 23; 3:23). For Paul the whole of history reduces to the destinies of two men—Adam and Christ. To be solely a member of Adam is to stay far short of the excellence of God's purpose for humankind, on the way to death. Only Christ has fulfilled that divine purpose. Only he has inherited the glory of God. So only those in Christ will share in that inheritance—but only if they have already shared in his suffering to death. Once again, as in v 13, the sharper lines of v 9 are softened. The full meaning of "having the Spirit of Christ" becomes still clearer: not simply receiving the Spirit, nor simply a sustained quality of conduct and lifestyle (v 14), but a whole life in the course of which the death of Christ achieves full expression.

3. The Spirit as Firstfruits   (8:18–30)

Bibliography

Balz, H. R. *Heilsvertrauen und Welterfahrung: Strukturen der paulinischen Eschatologie nach Römer 8:18–39.* Munich: Kaiser, 1971. **Baumgarten, J.** *Paulus und die Apokalyptik.* WMANT 44. Neukirchen: Neukirchener, 1975. 170–78. **Beker, J. C.** "Suffering and Triumph in Paul's Letter to the Romans." *HBT* 7.2 (1985) 105–19. **Benoit, P.** "'We Too Groan Inwardly . . .' (Romans 8:23)." In *Jesus* 2:40–50. **Bieder, W.** "Gebetswirklichkeit und Gebetsmöglichkeit bei Paulus." *TZ* 4 (1948) 22–40. **Bindemann, W.** *Die Hoffnung der Schöpfung: Römer 8:18–27 und die Frage einer Theologie der Befreiung von Mensch und Natur.* Neukirchen: Neukirchener, 1983. **Black, M.** "The Interpretation of Rom 8:28." In *Neotestamentica et Patristica,* FS O. Cullmann. NovTSup 6. Leiden: Brill, 1962. 166–72. **Brown, R. E.** "The Paraclete in the Fourth Gospel." *NTS* 13 (1966–67) 113–32. **Byrne, B.** *Sons of God.* 103–27. **Cambier, J.** "La liberté chrétienne selon saint Paul." *SE* 2 (1964) 315–53. **Coetzer, W. C.** "The Holy Spirit and the Eschatological View in Romans 8." *Neot* 15 (1981) 180–98. **Cranfield, C. E. B.** "Romans 8:28." *SJT* 19 (1966) 204–15. ———. "The Creation's Promised Liberation: Some Observations on Romans 8:19–21" (1974). In *Bible.* 94–104. **Denton, D. R.** "Ἀποκαραδοκία." *ZNW* 73 (1982) 138–40. **Dietzel, A.** "Beten im Geist: Eine religionsgeschichtliche Parallele aus den Hodajot zum paulinischen Beten in Geist." *TZ* 13 (1957)

12–32. **Dupont, J.** *Gnosis.* 88–104. **Gaugler, E.** "Der Geist und das Gebet der schwachen Gemeinde: Eine Auslegung von Röm 8:26–27." *IKZ* 51 (1961) 67–94. **Gerber, U.** "Röm 8:18ff. als exegetisches Problem der Dogmatik." *NovT* 8 (1966) 58–81. **Grayston, K.** "The Doctrine of Election in Rom 8:28–30." *SE* 2 (1964) 574–83. **Hommel, H.** "Das Harren der Kreatur." *ThViat* 4 (1952) 108–24. **Jones, F. S.** *"Freiheit."* 129–35. **Käsemann, E.** "The Cry for Liberty in the Worship of the Church." In *Perspectives.* 122–37. **Kleinknecht, H.** *Gerechtfertigte.* 333–35, 338–42, 349–54. **Kürzinger, J.** "Συμμόρφους τῆς εἰκόνος τοῦ υἱοῦ αὐτοῦ (Röm 8:29)." *BZ* 2 (1958) 294–99. **Lampe, G. W. H.** "The New Testament Doctrine of Ktisis." *SJT* 17 (1964) 449–62. **Leaney, A. R. C.** "'Conformed to the Image of His Son' (Rom 8:29)." *NTS* 10 (1963–64) 470–79. **Lindars, B.** "The Sound of the Trumpet: Paul and Eschatology." *BJRL* 67 (1984–85) 766–82. **Luz, U.** *Geschichtsverständnis.* 250–55, 369–82. **McCasland, S. V.** "'The Image of God' according to Paul." *JBL* 69 (1950) 85–100. **MacRae, G.** "A Note on Romans 8:26–27." *HTR* 73 (1980) 227–30. **Mayer, B.** *Unter Gottes Heilsratschluss: Prädestinationsaussagen bei Paulus.* Würzburg: Echter, 1974. 136–66. **Montague, G. T.** *The Holy Spirit: Growth of a Biblical Tradition.* New York: Paulist, 1976. 209–13. **Nebe, G.** *"Hoffnung" bei Paulus.* SUNT 16. Göttingen: Vandenhoeck & Ruprecht, 1983. 82–94. **Nickelsburg, G. W. E.** *Resurrection, Immortality, and Eternal Life in Intertestamental Judaism.* HTS 26. Cambridge, MA: Harvard UP, 1972. **Niederwimmer, K.** "Das Gebet des Geistes, Röm 8:26f." *TZ* 20 (1964) 252–65. **Obeng, E. A.** "The Spirit Intercession Motif in Paul." *ExpT* 95 (1983–84) 361–64. ———. "The Origins of the Spirit Intercession Motif in Romans 8:26." *NTS* 32 (1986) 621–32. **Osten-Sacken, P. von der.** *Römer 8.* 60–128, 139–44, 263–309. **Paulsen, H.** *Überlieferung.* 107–32. **Rollins, W. G.** "Greco-Roman Slave Terminology and Pauline Metaphors of Salvation." In *SBL Seminar Papers 1987.* Atlanta: Scholars Press, 1987. 100–110. **Ross, J. M.** "Panta synergei." *TZ* 34 (1978) 82–85. **Schade, H.-H.** *Apokalyptische Christologie bei Paulus.* Göttingen: Vandenhoeck & Ruprecht, 1981. 102–4. **Schlier, H.** "Das, Worauf Alles Wartet: Eine Auslegung von Römer 8:18–30." In *Interpretation der Welt,* FS R. Guardini, ed. H. Kuhn. Würzburg: Echter, 1965. 599–616. **Schmithals, W.** *Anthropologie.* 137–75. **Schniewind, J.** "Das Seufzen des Geistes." In *Nachgelassene Reden und Aufsätze.* Berlin: Töpelmann, 1952. 81–103. **Siber, P.** *Mit Christus Leben. Eine Studie zur paulinischen Auferstehungshoffnung.* Zürich: Theologischer, 1971. 135–68. **Stanley, D. M.** *Resurrection.* 192–95. **Stendahl, K.** "Paul at Prayer." In *Meanings: The Bible as Document and as Guide.* Philadelphia: Fortress, 1984. 151–61. **Swetnam, J.** "On Romans 8:23 and the 'Expectation of Sonship.'" *Bib* 48 (1967) 102–8. **Thüsing, W.** *Per Christum.* 121–25, 272–80. **Vögtle, A.** *Das Neue Testament und die Zukunft des Kosmos.* Düsseldorf: Patmos, 1970. 183–208. **Wischmeyer, O.** "ΘΕΟΝ ΑΓΑΠΑΝ bei Paulus. Eine Traditionsgeschichtliche Miszelle." *ZNW* 78 (1987). 141–44.

Translation

[18] *For I reckon that the sufferings of the present time are not to be compared with the coming glory to be revealed to us.* [19] *For the eager expectation of creation eagerly awaits the revelation of the sons of God.* [20] *For creation was subjected to futility, not willingly, but on account of him who subjected it, in* [a] *hope,* [21] *because* [b] *creation also itself will be set free from the slavery of corruption into the liberty of the glory of the children of God.* [22] *For we know that the whole creation groans and suffers the pains of childbirth together up till now.* [23] *And not only creation, but also we* [c] *ourselves who have the firstfruits of the Spirit, we* [c] *also ourselves groan within ourselves, eagerly awaiting adoption,* [d] *the redemption of our body.* [24] *For in terms of hope, we are saved. But hope which is seen is not hope; for*

who^e *hopes*^f *for what he sees?* ²⁵*But if we hope for what we do not see, we await it eagerly with patience.*

²⁶*In the same way also the Spirit helps us in our weakness.*^g *For we do not know what to pray for as we should, but the Spirit itself intercedes on our behalf*^h *with inarticulate groans.* ²⁷*And he who searches the hearts knows what is the Spirit's way of thinking because he intercedes as God would have it on behalf of the saints.* ²⁸*And we know that for those who love God everything*ⁱ *contributes toward good for those who are called according to his purpose.* ²⁹*For those he knew beforehand he also predetermined to be conformed to the image of his Son, that he should be the firstborn among many brothers.* ³⁰*And those he predetermined, he also called; and those he called, he also justified; and those he justified, he also glorified.*

Notes

^aThe variant reading ἐπ' ἐλπίδι attests some original disagreement, and presumably dialectic variation, as to whether ἐλπίς should be read with a rough breathing or smooth.

^b ὅτι is attested by the best and oldest witnesses (Metzger), but διότι is sometimes preferred as the more difficult reading (Michel, Cranfield).

^cFrom the variety of minor modifications in the textual tradition it is evident that many scribes found the repetition tautologous and unnecessary.

^d"Several witnesses, chiefly Western . . . omit υἱοθεσίαν, a word which copyists doubtless found to be both clumsy in the context and dispensable, as well as seeming to contradict v 15" (Metzger; see also Kuss; against Benoit, "Romans 8:23," and Fitzmyer, who opt for its omission).

^eThe longer version (ὃ γὰρ βλέπει τις, τί καὶ ἐλπίζει) is probably secondary, an understandable attempt to clarify a typically Pauline terseness (see particularly Metzger, Cranfield; otherwise Wilckens, and see *Note* f below). The sense is little affected either way.

^fℵ* and a few other witnesses read ὑπομένει, which as *lectio difficilior* has persuaded some, including Lietzmann, Käsemann, and NEB. But ὑπομένειν used transitively has no parallel within the NT, and the testimony in favor of ἐλπίζει is much weightier. On balance it is more likely that an early editorial decision was made to replace the overworked concept of "hope" with that of patient waiting, otherwise not introduced till v 25.

^gSeveral witnesses by adding τῆς δεήσεως particularize and narrow the reference of weakness to that of weakness in praying; but see on 8:26.

^hThe translation derives from the ὑπερ- prefix to the verb, but there was quite a strong tendency to make the point explicit by introducing the phrase ὑπὲρ ἡμῶν (see Metzger).

ⁱThe reading of ὁ θεός as the subject of συνεργεῖ has some strong support (including P⁴⁶ and B); but the reading without it has more diversified support, and the potential theological awkwardness of reading πάντα as the subject would have been sufficient to encourage an Alexandrian editor to remove the awkwardness by inserting ὁ θεός (Metzger).

Form and Structure

This passage plays a key role in the structure of Paul's argument. (1) It is the climax of the discussion in chap. 8: it picks up the earlier language of liberation from slavery (vv 2, 21), of resurrection (vv 11, 23), of sonship and adoption (vv 14–17, 19, 21, 23), and of the Spirit's part in all this (vv 6, 27; 11, 23; 15, 23; 15–16, 26); and in particular it functions as an elaboration of v 17, as the theme of suffering (vv 17, 18–23, 26) and the δόξα motif indicate (vv 17, 18, 30), serving as a bracket for the whole section (vv 18, 30) and rounding it off with the same climax (cf. Siber, 142–43; Osten-Sacken, 138–42). In the climax the insertion of the Christological parenthesis in v 29 (breaking up the sequence of five aorists) plays the same role as the sequence of συν- compounds in v 17, both serving to focus the central importance of Christ's role in the salvation process.

(2) More important, it is the climax to chaps. 6–8, and indeed of 1:18–8:30. Paul presents this cosmic outworking of salvation in strong Adam terms, as the final reversal of man's failure and climax of his restoration. Hence the verbal links back to 1:18ff.: κτίσις (1:20, 25; 8:20–22), ματαιότης (1:21; 8:20), δοξάζειν (1:21; 8:30), δόξα (1:23; 8:18, 21), εἰκών (1:23; 8:29), σώματα degraded (1:24) and redeemed (8:23). And above all the dominance of the whole Adam motif—with restoration of creation cursed for Adam's sin and dependent on man's own restoration (8:19–23) providing final answer to the dismal analysis of 1:18–32, and the salvation-history sweep of 8:29–30 with its strong Adam-Christology insertion matching the similar sweep of 5:12–21, and bringing the argument back to that point with the issues of chaps. 6–8 having been clarified. (Note also the reworking of the theme of 5:1–5 in 8:18–25; cf. Osten-Sacken, 124–28.)

(3) Equally important is the way in which Paul prepares in this section for the discussion of chaps. 9–11. He deliberately evokes traditional Jewish motifs (present suffering, future vindication [v 18]; final time analogous to primal time [v 21]; the whole Adam theme; divine intercession [v 26]; "he who searches the heart" [v 27]) and language (birth pangs [v 22]; firstfruits [v 23]; hope [vv 24–25]; purpose [v 28]); note particularly the cluster of terms used to describe Israel in vv 27–30—saints, those who love God, the called, firstborn. Paul clearly intends his readers to understand that the blessings they are inheriting are Israel's. Hence the problem: What then of Israel itself?, to which Paul naturally and inevitably turns in chaps. 9–11—with the issue posed not least in terms of adoption, glory (9:4), and divine purpose (9:11) (cf. Berger, "Abraham," *MTZ* 17 (1966) 77–78; Byrne, *Sons*, 127–29; and particularly Wright, *Messiah*, 142–68). This conviction that God's salvation completes both his purpose in creation and his purpose in calling Israel is part of the genius and one of the too little appreciated strengths of Paul's theology. All this tells against Schmithals's claim that vv 18–39 were part of a much earlier Pauline text which he reuses here (*Anthropologie*, 174).

Other literary features of note are the repetition of key words (δόξα/δοξάζειν [vv 18, 21, 30], ἀπεκδέχομαι [vv 19, 23, 25], ἐλπίς/ἐλπίζειν [vv 20, 24–25]), the reappearance of more συν- compounds (vv 22, 26, 29), the threefold sequence of "groaning" (creation, believers, Spirit [vv 22, 23, 26]), and the fivefold οὓς . . . (τούτους) καὶ . . . sequence of vv 29–30. The regularity of the last sequence raises the usual question as to whether Paul was drawing on baptismal or catechetical tradition (Osten-Sacken, 67–73); but the suggestion depends too much on the assumption that such aorists have to be understood as baptismal aorists, and that Paul could not write in an elevated prose style. Some prefer to make the paragraph break between vv 27 and 28 (e.g., Paulsen, 134–35), but little hangs on it.

Comment

18 λογίζομαι ὅτι, "I reckon that." The weight given to λογίζομαι here is not determined by the meaning of the word itself, which can simply denote an opinion or belief (cf. 2:3; BGD, 3), rather by the fact that Paul both opens a new phase of his exposition with it and uses it instead of οἴδαμεν preferred in vv 22, 28. There is a *gravitas* here which can best be brought out with a slightly expanded translation: "I am firmly of the opinion that," "It is my settled conviction that." It should be noted that the conviction is not merely the product of "rational thought on the basis of the gospel" (Cranfield), but even more prominently here of the experience of the Spirit (cf. 5:3–5; 8:23).

οὐκ ἄξια τὰ παθήματα τοῦ νῦν καιροῦ πρός, "the sufferings of the present time are not to be compared with." The idiom in the phrase οὐκ ἄξια . . . πρός would be familiar to Greek speakers—"not of like value, not worth as much as" (LSJ)—though Paul is probably as much or more influenced by semitic usage (Str-B 3:244). πάθημα occurs here in its most regular Pauline sense (see also on 7:5). Since he nowhere else thinks of his Christian suffering without seeing it also as a sharing in the sufferings of Christ (2 Cor 1:5; Phil 3:10; Col 1:24) the thought is probably implied here—the Christological thought being inseparable from the eschatological tension, stretched as it is in this case between vv 17 and 29 (see on 8:17). For the eschatological note of τοῦ νῦν καιροῦ see on 3:26. It is true that it cannot be equated directly with "this evil age" (Käsemann; Gal 1:4), but it does denote the peculiar nature of the "between time," the period between the resurrection of Christ and his coming (again), which has the unique character for believers of being a period of overlap between "this evil age" and the age of resurrection life already shared "in Christ."

τὴν μέλλουσαν δόξαν ἀποκαλυφθῆναι εἰς ἡμᾶς, "the coming glory to be revealed to us." It is natural to hear in the μέλλω the note not only of certainty (see on 8:13) but also of imminence: "on the point of being, about to be revealed" (BGD, BDF, §356, Käsemann; disputed by Lagrange, Wilckens, and Nebe, 84). For δόξα see on 8:17; it indicates a reversal of the mistake of 1:23 (see *Form and Structure*) but otherwise serves a heuristic function here, expressing the confidence that heaven will be a much different quality of existence, an existence fully in the character of heaven, without being able to define it in more detail. ἀποκαλύπτω will have its regular sense of a revelation of a heavenly mystery or reality hitherto secret or unknown (see further Rowland, *Open Heaven*), here, of course, as an eschatological event; that is, the final unveiling (vindication) of a divine strategy and purpose obscured by the harsh reality of events on earth. Cranfield, following Chrysostom in deducing that for Paul the glory was already present and possessed, only concealed, confuses glory with adoption/sonship. The glory is future (see again on 8:17), something hoped for and waited for in hope (5:2; 8:24–25); it belongs to the transition to heaven (hence "*to* us," as well as "*of* us" implied in v 21), the final transformation of this bodily existence into the bodily existence of heaven (Phil 3:21). To understand at this point a present glory distorts and weakens the whole suffering-vindication motif on which Paul is evidently drawing here (cf. Murray). 2 Cor 3:18 is slightly different only because it is a typological elaboration of the midrash on Exod 34:29–35 of which 2 Cor 3:7–18 consists.

The comparison of the suffering of the righteous with the glorious vindication which will be theirs is well established in Jewish thought prior to the time of Paul (see particularly Dan 7:17–27; Wisd Sol 2–5; 2 Macc 7; *1 Enoch* 102–4; see further Nickelsburg, *Resurrection*; Zeller). More difficult is it to document what is regularly described as "the messianic woes" for the period before Paul; Sanders indeed thinks that the "dogma" that suffering must precede the coming of the kingdom is difficult to document before A.D. 135 (*Jesus and Judaism*, 124). It is true that the best parallels come from literature of the post-A.D. 70 period (as cited, e.g., in Str-B, 3:244–45; Wilckens, 2:148–49), and that these would undoubtedly have been shaped in large measure at least by the trauma of the destruction of Jerusalem and the temple in 70. But the idea itself follows directly from Dan 7:21–22, 25–27; 12:1–3, and is already implicit in such passages as *Jub.* 23.22–31; *T. Mos.* 5–10; 1QH 3.28–36, and *Sib. Or.* 3.632–56, not to mention Matt 3:7–12 // Luke 3:7–9, 16–17. And the elements of it are all here—inheritance (= coming kingdom), suffering as a necessary preliminary, and assurance of coming glory which will eclipse all the preceding anguish. Paul draws them together as a statement of conviction in an nonargumentative way, which suggests that he is giving voice to a well-known even if not necessarily widely held view of the future. The absence of an explicit Christological note in the following verses (cf. Nebe, 84), as well as its relative independence as a unit (Michel), confirms that Paul is taking over an earlier eschatological schema which he Christianizes by suspending it from v 17, adding in (probably) the characteristic Christian emphasis on the present experience of the Spirit (vv 23, 26–28), and leading the thought back to its Christological focus (v 29) (cf. Bindemann, 41–42, 69.) Cf. again the sequence of thought in 2 Cor 4:7–5:5, here particularly 4:17. Bindemann's larger thesis that Paul was engaged in a debate with apocalyptic (82–95), however, is too much dependent on the stereotype of apocalyptic as characterized by experience of God as *distant* (86), even though apocalyptic is still more characterized by revelation and the heavenly journey motif. Balz describes the thought structure as "doxological-enthusiastic" insofar as it is not determined by what is immediately present to it but understands the given reality in the light of Christ (130–31).

19 ἡ γὰρ ἀποκαραδοκία τῆς κτίσεως, "for the eager expectation of creation." The noun ἀποκαραδοκία appears only in Christian writers, though the verb occasionally appears earlier (*TDNT* 1:393; BGD). It expresses well the sense of eschatological tension—a straining forward for an eagerly (or anxiously) awaited event (cf. SH, and its only other NT use [Phil 1:20]; Denton denies that the word contains any element of uncertainty or anxiety: "its meaning is eager expectation, confident expectation"). The formulation is slightly awkward (ἀποκαραδοκία . . . ἀπεκδέχεται), but it effectively strengthens the sense (Kuss), and the meaning is clear enough. For the personification of creation see further on 8:22.

What all is included in κτίσις has been the subject of debate for centuries, particularly whether angels or nonbelievers are also in view (see, e.g., Schlatter, Schmidt). It is unlikely that Paul intended a precise definition (cf. v 39) but more than likely that his thought focused primarily on nonhuman creation: the thought is still largely controlled by the Adam motifs (see *Form and Structure*)—the reversal of Adam's fall naturally requires the reversal of the curse on the ground (Gen 3:17–18; so here vv 20–21); and the conviction that the whole created order would be caught in the tribulations introducing the age to come was already a firm part of the end-time scenario which Paul here draws on (see further on 8:22); see particularly the review and discussion in Vögtle, Kuss, Cranfield, and Wilckens.

τὴν ἀποκάλυψιν τῶν υἱῶν τοῦ θεοῦ ἀπεκδέχεται, "eagerly awaits the revelation of the sons of God." As with the verb in v 18 and the nouns in 2:5 and 16:25 (also 1 Cor 1:7; 2 Thess 1:7), ἀποκάλυψις has its full force of "eschatological unveiling from heaven" (see on 1:17). The thought may be paralleled to that of a play in which the final curtain is drawn back to reveal the various actors transformed (back) into their real characters—creation being, as it were, the audience eagerly watching the human actors play their parts on the world stage. If the analogy were pressed we could say that only some of the actors ("the sons of God") will take part in that final curtain call, and that the audience's eagerness is to see who these are and what is this transformation they have undergone (though see also on 5:19 and 11:32). For υἱοὶ θεοῦ see on 8:14: in Paul's thought, of course, those "in Christ" are already "sons of God"; what will be revealed is their status, and it will be revealed by the fact of their sharing in the glory of God. ἀδεκδέχομαι is used six times by Paul (three of them here [vv 19, 23, 25]), always of the eager awaiting of Christian hope (for the ἀποκάλυψις of Christ [1 Cor 1:7, cf. Phil 3:20]; the hope of righteousness [Gal 5:5]; adoption [here v 23])—a distinctive Pauline use reflected also in the only other NT occurrences, Heb 9:28 and 1 Pet 3:20 (TDNT 2:56).

20 τῇ γὰρ ματαιότητι ἡ κτίσις ὑπετάγη, "for creation was subjected to futility." It is not by accident that Paul draws in again the idea of "futility" which he uses elsewhere only in 1:21, since it is precisely his object to show how God's work in and through Christ reverses the plight of man so vividly depicted in 1:18ff. And as in chap. 1, so here, the primary allusion is to the Adam narratives: ματαιότης in the sense of the futility of an object which does not function as it was designed to do (like an expensive satellite which has malfunctioned and now spins uselessly in space), or, more precisely, which has been given a role for which it was not designed and which is unreal or illusory. As man's futility is his assumption that he is an independent creator, the failure to realize that he is but a creature, so the futility of creation is its being seen solely in relation to man (as man's to use or abuse for himself) or as autonomous, an entity in its own right, to be deified in turn (Nature, the Universe), instead of as God's creation to be ordered by God. See further on 1:21 and cf. particularly Schlier and Harrisville. ματαιότης can be regarded as nearly equivalent to φθορά (v 21, as most), so long as the full sweep of *both* words is borne in mind. There is now general agreement that ὑπετάγη is a divine passive (subjected by God) with reference particularly to Gen 3:17–18.

οὐχ ἑκοῦσα ἀλλὰ διὰ τὸν ὑποτάξαντα, ἐφ᾽ ἑλπίδι, "not willingly, but on account of him who did the subjecting, in hope." The phrasing is awkward and suggests a dictation where Paul's thought became slightly tangled but where he decided to press on. οὐχ ἑκοῦσα refers to "creation"—the implication clearly being that creation was not party to Adam's failure but was drawn into it nonetheless (cf. *4 Ezra* 7.11; and further Str-B 3:247–53; Balz, 41–45). More difficult is the διά phrase. (1) διά + accusative suggests that the referent is Adam (Zahn; Robinson, *Wrestling*, 102; Zeller; Byrne, *Reckoning*, 166–67; cf. NJB), and the same verb is used with reference to Adam in the much alluded to Ps 8:7 (1 Cor 15:27; Eph 1:22; Phil 3:21; Heb 2:5–8; 1 Pet 3:22); but in that case we would expect a reference to Adam's failure, not to his God-given function (on account of Adam's transgression), or the phrase would have had to be more complex (on account of him to whom all things were subjected). (2) τὸν ὑποτάξαντα most obviously refers to God, not least in view of Ps 8:7; but then we would expect the preposition to be ὑπό or at least διά + genitive ("through"), and even so the repetition of ὑποτάσσω in reference to God seems unnecessary (see Lagrange and Wilckens; a reference to Christ [Barth, *Shorter*] distorts the thought far too much). The reason for the difficulty is probably that Paul was attempting to convey too briefly a quite complicated point: that God subjected all things to Adam, and that included subjecting creation to fallen Adam, to share in his fallenness; the repetition of the ὑποτάσσω has the further welcome effect of emphasizing that creation's present condition is not the result of chance or fate but deliberately so ordered by God (cf. Michel)—precisely because it is not an end of God's dealings but a stage in his purpose, the means by which the self-destructiveness of sin can be drawn out and destroyed, and creation restored to its proper function as the environment for God's restored children. Hence ἐφ' ἐλπίδι; on the form see BDF, §14, and for ἐλπίς see on 4:18 and 8:24. NEB unwisely weakens the connection of ἐφ' ἐλπίδι to the preceding context, and NJB surprisingly loses the theme of "hope" altogether.

21 As just noted, Paul's thought is clearly that creation itself must be redeemed in order that redeemed man may have a fitting environment. The Adam motif is still strong: Paul's Christological overtone is that redeemed creation will fulfill the role for which it was intended as that which is subjected to (the last) Adam (1 Cor 15:27; Phil 3:21) in concert with his brothers (v 29).

ὅτι καὶ αὐτὴ ἡ κτίσις, "because creation also itself." The use of both καί and αὐτή emphasizes the point: creation is to be redeemed, not redeemed from. Just as the resurrection hope is hope of a resurrection body, so resurrection life is to be part of a complete creation. Paul is certainly picking up here a further facet of the typical Jewish eschatological hope variously expressed: that *Endzeit* would be analogous to *Urzeit* (final time = primal time). In pre-Pauline literature we may refer simply to Isa 11:6–9; 65:17, 25; 66:22; *Jub.* 1.29; 23.26–29; *1 Enoch* 24–25; 91.16–17; Philo, *Praem.* 88–90; *T. Levi* 18.10–11; *Sib. Or.* 3.788–95 (see further Str-B 3:248, 253–55); in other first-century Christian writings cf. particularly Acts 3:21 and Rev 21; but see also on 8:29.

ἐλευθερωθήσεται ἀπὸ τῆς δουλείας τῆς φθορᾶς, "will be set free from the slavery of corruption." The reemergence of the theme of liberty is no doubt deliberate: it recalls the talk of liberation from sin (6:18, 22) and from the law (7:3; 8:2) and ties them all together as mutually reinforcing features of the age of Adam. So here the condition of the environment can be summed up with the same word used in v 15, δουλεία, which loads all the accepted negative connotations of slavery on to the created order as it is now. This slavery is further defined in terms of φθορά—understandably since an inescapable feature of the natural order is decay (see BGD; not just "transitoriness," as Jones, 132). The thought would be familiar to a Greek audience (see on 1:23). But for Paul φθορά is not simply synonymous with materiality: he who lives κατὰ σάρκα will himself suffer φθορά (Gal 6:8; see further on σάρξ on 7:5) (but φθορά should certainly not be taken in the sense of *moral* corruption; see Lagrange); and the point here is that not only believers will be delivered from corruption (1 Cor 15:42, 50) but that creation itself will also be liberated (cf. *4 Ezra* 13.26). Not surprisingly Marcion omitted vv 18–22 (Lietzmann).

εἰς τὴν ἐλευθερίαν τῆς δόξης τῶν τέκνων τοῦ θεοῦ, "into the liberty of the glory of the children of God." The repetition of the note of freedom reemphasizes it as one of the key categories in Paul's soteriology. Clearly in view here is a liberty which is yet future for believers as well as for creation (freedom which consists in sharing in God's glory [Jones, 132]). Consequently its use here is a further example of the eschatological tension of a liberation from the complex hegemony of sin and law, corruption and death, which has begun but is not yet complete—a liberation lived out within the circumstances of decay. Hence vv 22–23. For the last time δόξα appears, emphasizing that God's purpose is incomplete until he has completed his original creative purpose in crowning man with glory (Ps 8:5; cf. particularly *4 Ezra* 7.96–98).

22 οἴδαμεν γὰρ ὅτι, "for we know that"; see on 2:2. The appeal implies a widespread knowledge and use of Jewish apocalyptic traditions within the earliest Christian congregations, including, not least, those of the Diaspora.

πᾶσα ἡ κτίσις συστενάζει καὶ συνωδίνει ἄχρι τοῦ νῦν, "the whole creation groans and suffers the pains of childbirth together up till now." However widely encompassing was Paul's earlier use of κτίσις (see on 8:19), here certainly it is nonhuman, and, as we would say, inanimate creation which is primarily in view. The συν- in the two compound verbs does not refer to Christ (as in v 17); that is a usage which Paul confines to believers—although he does think of all these sufferings as interconnected (v 23). Nor does it refer to a suffering shared with believers; that thought is first introduced in v 23. The thought is not distinctively Christian (see below) and most likely speaks of a suffering in which all creation participates, a groaning "together" rather than "with us" (so most, often quoting Theodore of Mopsuestia: creation does this συμφώνως; quotation in SH). Schmithals notes how *un*dualistic is the thought of sighing *with* rather than to escape *from* creation (*Anthropologie*, 158). Consider also Leenhardt's more wide-ranging reflections.

συστενάζω is very rare, but a not unnatural formation (BGD; should read *T. Iss.* 7.5). Such vivid personification of nature is typical of the more poetic strains of Jewish writing (cf., e.g., Job 31:38; Isa 24:4; Jer 4:28; Hab 3:10; 1QH 3.32–33; Hommel compares Virgil, *Eclogue* 4.50–52). Paul uses "groaning" as a recurring motif in this section; see further on 8:23 and 8:26. συνωδίνω is likewise infrequent, but equally natural (LSJ). The metaphor of birth pains was a natural one to seize on for description of a period of turmoil and anguish likely to end in a new order of things; consequently, it is not surprising that it features quite often in passages where the anguish and prospects were seen to have strong eschatological overtones (Isa 13:8; 21:3; 26:17–18; 66:7–8; Jer 4:31; 22:23; Hos 13:13; Mic 4:9–10; 1QH 3.7–18). Both Christianity

(Mark 13:8 par.; John 16:21; Acts 2:24; 1 Thess 5:3; Rev 12:2) and apocalyptic and rabbinic Judaism (*1 Enoch* 62.4; *4 Ezra* 10.6–16; Str-B 1:950) take the metaphor further (see also Kuss, 630–33). The metaphors are sufficiently common in wider Greek thought (see LSJ, ὠδίνω, ὠδίς; BGD, συνωδίνω; *TDNT* 9:667–68), but seem to lack there the eschatological note characteristic of the Judeo-Christian tradition (cf. Schmidt and see further on 8:18 and 8:23).

In such a strongly eschatological context the νῦν of the final phrase should be given its full eschatological force (see on 3:26)—not merely "this time" of v 18 (Wilckens) but the "now" of eschatological salvation in which the process of salvation is being worked out (cf. 3:21; 7:6; 8:1), with the present labor pains giving promise of the cosmic birth of the new age (cf. Barrett, Käsemann).

23 οὐ μόνον δέ, ἀλλὰ καί, "not only so, but also"; see on 5:3.

αὐτοὶ τὴν ἀπαρχὴν τοῦ πνεύματος ἔχοντες, "we ourselves who have the firstfruits of the Spirit." For πνεῦμα ἔχειν see on 8:9. The ἔχοντες is better taken as causal ("we groan because we have . . .") rather than concessive ("we groan although we have . . .") (Kuss). Most agree that the genitive is epexegetic (the firstfruit which is the Spirit), since this coheres most naturally with what has already been said (vv 9, 11, 15); for less plausible alternatives see Cranfield.

For Paul and his readers ἀπαρχή would certainly speak primarily of the offering of firstlings in sacrifice (LSJ, BGD); Käsemann's rejection of the sacrificial overtone expresses the distaste for the category of cultic sacrifice noted on 8:3; but whereas the metaphor is used to similar effect as ἀρραβών (2 Cor 1:22; 5:5), it is not to be explained simply from ἀρραβών (against also Lietzmann). And though it could be used of all firstlings (e.g., firstborn son—Ps 105 [LXX 104]:36; offspring of sheep and cattle—Deut 12:6; first offerings of goods—Exod 25:2–3; first lump of dough—Rom 11:16; and by extension, first converts—16:5; 1 Cor 16:15; 2 Thess 2:13; cf. James 1:18 and Rev 14:4), the dominant image has reference to the harvest, the firstfruits (literally) of wine press and threshing floor (Exod 22:29 [LXX 28]; 23:19; Lev 2:12; 23:10; Num 15:20; 18:12, 30; Deut 26:2; 2 Chron 31:5; Neh 10:37, 39 [2 Esd 20:38, 40]; Mal 3:8; Jud 11:13). Moreover, the fact that the Spirit is in view here would itself most likely evoke the thought of harvest for Paul and his Jewish readers: Pentecost (the Feast of Weeks) was the principal celebration of the firstfruits of the harvest (Exod 23:16; 34:22; Deut 16:9–12; Philo, *Spec. Leg.* 2.179; R. de Vaux, *Ancient Israel*, 2d ed. [London: Darton, 1965], 490–91); and the association of the first outpouring of the Spirit with Pentecost was probably already established in early Christian memory (Acts 2; Dunn, *Jesus*, 139–42; also *NIDNTT* 2:784–85). Hence NEB: "firstfruits of the harvest to come." The metaphor carries several implications. (1) The firstfruits are the first sheaves of the harvest (or loaves made from them—Num 15:20; Philo, *Spec. Leg.* 2.179); so the harvest has begun. (2) The harvest is the whole of which the firstfruits are a first small part; in this case the whole is the resurrection of the body, the harvest of dead men and women resurrected (1 Cor 15:20, 23). (3) The firstfruits are of a piece with the whole; hence the continuity between the gift of the Spirit, his work in the believer, and the final product of resurrection—σῶμα πνευματικόν (Dunn, *Baptism,* 150). Once again the clear eschatological note cannot be ignored: the final harvest (Isa 27:12; Joel 3:13; Matt 3:12 // Luke 3:17; Gal 6:8) initiated by Christ's resurrection (1 Cor 15:20, 23) is already under way. The sense of ἀπαρχή as "birth certificate" of a free person (suggested as a possibility by LSJ and BGD) has an apparent attractiveness in view of the other birth metaphor in v 22 but in fact would throw the thought in some confusion—a birth certificate already issued while the birth travail is still in progress!

ἡμεῖς καὶ αὐτοὶ ἐν ἑαυτοῖς στενάζομεν, "we also ourselves groan within ourselves." The repeated αὐτοί is "extremely emphatic" (Cranfield), even more so with ἐν ἑαυτοῖς following. There has been a strange unwillingness on the part of some commentators to give the ἐν its most obvious force; hence suggestions of "among ourselves" or "with regard to ourselves," including the idea of a congregation giving free rein to their communal distress once outsiders have been excluded (see particularly Michel, 270 n.22). But the inward sense of frustration of individual believers (as a whole) at the eschatological tension of living in the overlap of the ages seems the most obvious reference, not least in view of the parallel with v 26 and 2 Cor 5:2, 4 (so Murray, Cranfield, Kuss, Schlier)—that is, "in our hearts" (5:5; Schmidt); see further on 8:26. Indeed the groaning here is wholly of a piece with the cry of frustration in 7:24 (cf. Michel); as Käsemann recognizes, the Spirit does *not* exempt from this tension, but he does not follow through the logic of the insight, that the understanding of 8:2's relation to 7:24a needs to take account of 8:23 (as also 8:10). Wilckens, somewhat oddly, describes 8:23 as "the full, eschatological answer to the cry of 7:24"; but while the Spirit certainly provides a positive element lacking in 7:14–25, it expresses its presence in what seems to be the *same* sense of frustration: "we groan because we have the Spirit" (see above on ἔχοντες). See further on 7:24 and 8:10.

The second use of the "groaning" motif (στενάζομεν) of course is deliberately intended to recall creation's groaning in v 22 (συστενάζει), and to emphasize believers' involvement in the eschatological travail of creation. Once again, the point needs to be emphasized that the Spirit does not free from such tension, but actually creates or at least heightens that tension and brings it to more anguished expression; see further on 8:26. The parallels which have been adduced in subsequent Hellenistic thought, particularly the Hermetic writings and the Naasene hymn (see e.g., TDNT 7:602), are more dualistic and less eschatological in character—the sighing of the soul for deliverance *from* the material world and from the prison of the body (Wilckens, 2:150); Philo shows the influence of Greek thought at this point (TDNT 7:600–601). In Paul, in contrast, the split goes through the "I" (not between the "I" and the body/flesh; see on 7:14), and redemption embraces the material creation (including the body) as the climax to a divine purpose, pursued from the beginning of creation, now nearing its fulfillment (see also on 8:22).

υἱοθεσίαν ἀπεκδεχόμενοι, τὴν ἀπολύτρωσιν τοῦ σώματος ἡμῶν, "eagerly awaiting adoption, the redemption of our body." For υἱοθεσία see on 8:15. For ἀπεκδέχομαι, see on 8:19; that Paul would intend the different sense of "infer" here is hardly likely in view of its use in vv 19 and 25 (against Swetnam). The repetition of such key words is obviously intentional (see Form and Structure). Having the Spirit marks off the Christians' "eager awaiting" from that of creation (v 19) (Nebe, 89–90), though it could be said that on this point "the sons of God" within creation play a similar role to that of the Spirit within believers. Paul sees no contradiction in using the metaphor of adoption/ sonship of the Not yet of salvation, when he has already used it of the Already— and in equally emphatic terms (vv 14–17; against Benoit and Fitzmyer [see *Notes*]; Kuss notes how incommoding the legal metaphor is to thought of development and completion, but justifiably compares 1:3–4). Commentators need to take care lest they be misled by the vigor of Paul's language on either emphasis. The fact that υἱοθεσία is related to, dependent upon, the Spirit in both cases should not go unobserved; the Spirit is clearly the key to the Already/Not yet tension in Paul's thought (Dunn, *Jesus*, 310–12). For a somewhat surprisingly similar train of thought see also 1 John 3:1–3. For ἀπολύτρωσις see on 3:24. The specification of the "redemption" as τοῦ σώματος ἡμῶν is a distinctive feature of this occurrence of ἀπολύτρωσις in the Pauline literature (cf. Eph 1:14). Distinctively Judeo-Christian is the whole concept: Lietzmann fails to observe this difference from the more characteristic Greek dualism when he translates "redemption *from* our bodies." Paul's distinction between σῶμα (man's bodily participation in and with his environment) and σάρξ (man's belonging to and dependence on that environment and its society) needs to be kept in mind here (cf. 1 Cor 15:44, 50). This means also that the σῶμα here is not to be sharply distinguished from the σῶμα of 6:6 and 7:24 (rightly Nygren; against Schlier): it is the same embodiment in this age, with all that that involves (including "the slavery of corruption"—v 21; but also "the deeds of the body"—v 13), which can only be transformed when this age itself is transformed with the whole of creation into a new environment in which a different embodiment (σῶμα πνευματικόν—1 Cor 15:44; Phil 3:21) is possible. Rollins (109) notes that σῶμα here may echo the use of σῶμα = slave; cf. particularly 2 Macc 8:11 and Rev 18:13.

24 τῇ γὰρ ἐλπίδι ἐσώθημεν, "for in terms of hope, we are saved." For ἐλπίς see on 4:18. The older view (still, e.g., in Zahn and Schlatter) that the dative should be taken instrumentally (saved *through* hope) gains little or no support now—a modal or associative dative being much preferred (designating accompanying circumstances and manner [BDF, §198]; see Lagrange, Wilckens n.696). For σῴζω see on 5:9. The aorist here is surprising and distinctive within the earlier and main Pauline letters (Schlier finds it unremarkable, but only by referring to Eph 2:5, 8; 2 Tim 1:9; and Titus 3:5). In fact, however, the unusualness of the aorist probably explains the dative's lack of precision, the two being clearly meant to qualify each other: Paul can use the aorist because of the nature of Christian hope, as firm confidence in God's purpose and power (this is no weak statement = "we hope to be saved"; see again on 4:18); but for all the aorist assurance, the complete redemption (v 23) hoped for is still outstanding. So far as hope is concerned we are already saved; but hope itself is not the completion of salvation. The balance achieved here in this one phrase between the Already and Not yet of the eschatological tension is striking. It is likely that Paul directs the assertion against the sort of enthusiastic tendencies which too much emphasis on the experience of the Spirit is always likely to promote, though Käsemann and Schmithals (*Anthropologie*, 150) assume the point too confidently, whereas Wilckens (2:156) finds nothing of it in the text, and Bindemann (30) notes the conspicuous absence of polemic; but see further on 8:26.

ἐλπὶς δὲ βλεπομένη οὐκ ἔστιν ἐλπίς· ὃ γὰρ βλέπει τίς ἐλπίζει; "but hope which is seen is not hope; for who hopes for what he sees?" The character and qualification of the aorist (ἐσώθημεν) is underlined. The distinction between seen and unseen/visible and invisible is characteristic of Greek philosophy (see on 1:20; all that is visible is transitory); but here the thought is not of the invisible world perceptible only at a rational level. The (implied) distinction here is set rather within the framework of Jewish (and Christian) eschatology (Nebe, 91; against Baumgarten, 176, who thinks that Paul's critical interpretation of apocalyptic traditions becomes here "anti-apocalyptic"): that which is unseen is not so much the upper world in perpetual (static) distinction from the lower, as the future world at the far end of the forward movement of history. Cf. particularly 2 Cor 4:18, 5:7, and 1 Pet 1:8–9; also Heb 11:1, since Rom 4:18–22 shows that for Paul "faith" and "hope" are not so clearly distinct as is sometimes suggested. There is probably also an echo here and in the ὑπομονή (v 25) of the contrast in chap. 2 between those who seek with "patience" (Gentile and Jew) and those who put too much trust in what is visible (ἐν τῷ φανερῷ ἐν σαρκί) (2:7, 28). Bultmann, TDNT 2:531, and Gaugler generalize still further: "everything visible belongs to the sphere of the σάρξ in which no hope can be founded."

25 εἰ δὲ ὃ οὐ βλέπομεν ἐλπίζομεν, δι᾿ ὑπομονῆς ἀπεκδεχόμεθα, "but if we hope for what we do not see, we eagerly await it with patience." For ὑπομονή see on 5:3. The reference to "patience" confirms that Paul's thought is moving along the same lines as in 5:3–5 (suffering, hope, Spirit): his theological reflection on "the problem of suffering" had evidently gained a settled outline with firm reference points. ἀπεκδέχομαι appears for the third time in seven verses (vv 19, 23, 25); it characterizes the in-between times not so much as a period of resigned or stoical suffering, nor one (simply) of anguished groaning, nor one of careless enthusiasm, but rather one of eager waiting; patience with a vibrant quality (cf. Beker, "Suffering," 108). The Christian perspective is determined not by the frustrations of the present, but by its future hope; by this it can be seen that the groaning of v 23 (like the cry of 7:24) is of frustration and not of despair. The note of patience, rooted also in the Already of the Spirit, gives the conclusion to this passage, with its sustained apocalyptic character, a surprisingly unapocalyptic (but again not "anti-apocalyptic" —Bindemann, 32) conclusion.

26 ὡσαύτως δὲ καί, "in the same way also"; cf. Mark 14:31; Luke 20:31; 1 Tim 5:25 v.l. (BGD). The reference back is clearly to v 23, πνεῦμα being the immediate link word. The phrase in itself does not specify how closely similar are the phenomena being compared; so to translate with the impreciseness of "similarly, likewise" is quite in order. But at least the construction does imply that in v 23 the groanings are part of the expression of the Spirit's presence (that is, a fundamental feature of the eschatological tension) and not simply a regrettable or accidental byproduct.

τὸ πνεῦμα συναντιλαμβάνεται τῇ ἀσθενείᾳ ἡμῶν, "the Spirit helps us in our weakness." The verb is quite well known in the ancient world in the sense "take part with, assist in supporting, lend a hand, come to the aid of," though "take an interest in" does not seems strong enough (LSJ, BGD, MM, NDIEC 3:68). Two of the three (or four) LXX occurrences refer to the support given to Moses by the appointment of 70 elders (Exod 18:22; Num 11:17; cf. the only other NT reference, Luke 10:40). The sense of taking part in a responsibility or task so that something of its weight or burden is shared or transferred is also bound up with the construction of the word itself; though the συν- is often taken as intensive, rather than in the sense "together with" (e.g., Cranfield, Wilckens). The image of the Spirit shouldering the burden which our weakness imposes on us is quite a vivid one (cf. Ps 89:21 [LXX 88:22]). As with 8:3 the concept ἀσθένεια denotes the condition of man in this age, indeed in his creatureliness, as creature and not creator, with all that that implies for man's need of transcendent support (see on 8:3). Paul has in view not merely the believer's exposure to "external temptations" (Käsemann) or his inability in prayer as such (Cranfield, Kuss; see *Notes*), but the totality of the human condition (the corruptibility of the body, the subvertedness of the flesh) which the believer is still part of and which comes to expression in prayer inability.

τὸ γὰρ τί προσευξώμεθα καθὸ δεῖ οὐκ οἴδαμεν, "for that which we are to pray for as we should we do not know." "The article (τό) makes the whole clause object of οἴδαμεν" (SH, Lagrange; cf. 13:9; Gal 5:14; Eph 4:19; 1 Thess 4:1). The accusative (τί) probably denotes the thing prayed for (cf. Mark 11:24; Phil 1:9; BGD, with bibliog.), rather than the words to be used, which would more naturally be put in the plural ("what things" = words to say in prayer), as in Luke 18:11 (cf. Cranfield; otherwise Wilckens). It is not simply that words fail believers who know all along what they want to pray for but cannot express it. The measure of their confusion and frustration as belonging to both epochs is that they do not know what God's will for them and their social context is. The rendering "we do not know *how* to pray" (as RSV, so NEB, NJB; others in Cranfield) does not catch the full force, though it is nicely ambiguous; but the inability to formulate words is the point more of the second half than of the first half of the verse. It is not insignificant that the main force of the verb "pray" is "to pray for" something; it is not that prayer should be conceived as an exercise in selfish asking; rather is it that prayer characteristically denotes the dependence of the creature on the creator for all good (see particularly Gaugler).

καθὸ δεῖ has a Stoic ring (cf. Epictetus 2.22.20; 3.23.21; *4 Macc.* 7.8) and so could be rendered "as is proper" (BGD, δεῖ 6); but it can serve equally within the strongly monotheistic Judeo-Christian tradition to express the compulsion of the divine ordering of God's will (cf. 2 Macc 6:20; 2 Tim 2:6, 24). The statement stands within the context of Paul's powerful eschatological conviction that God has a purpose for his creation, that it is drawing forward steadily to its (near) climax, and that believers' aspiration in prayer should be to fit their lives into that ongoing purpose. That καθὸ δεῖ here is more or less equivalent to κατὰ θεόν in v 27 is generally recognized.

ἀλλὰ αὐτὸ τὸ πνεῦμα ὑπερεντυγχάνει, "but the Spirit itself intercedes." τὸ πνεῦμα here clearly means the Spirit of God; otherwise the first two clauses of v 27 would be tautologous, and anyway the second clause (of v 27) echoes v 6 (see SH). This is precisely the wonder and poignancy of the eschatological tension: the Spirit does not eliminate or transform believers' total inability to maintain the proper dialogue between God and man; rather the Spirit works in and through that inability. This is the first recorded use of the verb, though the form without the prefix is well enough known (see on 8:27) and the formation a quite natural one. The concept of the Spirit as intercessor seems to be a Christian development of already well-developed motifs within Judaism, particularly that of angelic intercessors (e.g., Job 33:23–26; Tob 12:15; *1 Enoch* 9.3; 15.2; 99.3; 104.1; *T. Levi* 3.5; 5.6–7; *T. Dan* 6.2; see further *TDNT* 5:810–11; Balz, 87–90; Obeng, "Paul," 361). The thought in these cases is of intercession in heaven. But "angel" and "spirit" are near synonyms in the Jewish thought of this time (e.g., *1 Enoch* 15.4, 7; *Jub.* 1.25; 1QH 1.11; Acts 8:26, 29, 39; Heb 1:7, 14), and the idea of the Spirit active on man's behalf from within the human condition is already coming to the surface, whether in the thought of the universal presence of the Spirit (as in Ps 139:7 and Wisd Sol 1:7—notice the parallel logic between Wisd Sol 1:7–8 and Rom 8:26–27), or in the talk of two spirits warring within man (as in 1QS 3.18–4.26; *T. Jud.* 20.1–5; cf. *Jub.* 1.20–23); see also Dietzel, and Brown, "Paraclete," with other literature (Lietzmann unjustifiably ignores this background in suggesting that the closer parallel lies with Gnostic language). However, we will not be far from the truth if we recognize the decisive impulse which led to this more distinctive Christian formulation here in the experience of the first Christians, as they came to the realization that the enabling power of God was sustaining them in the depths of their inability as well as in their higher flights of worship, especially if they could relate it to promises held out by Jesus during his ministry (Mark 13:11 pars.) (Obeng, "Origins," 625–30). This passage surely undermines Beker's claim that "Paul often speaks of the Spirit in an inherently triumphant manner that prevents its integral relation with the weakness and suffering of the crucified Christ" (*Paul*, 244).

στεναγμοῖς ἀλαλήτοις, "with inarticulate groans," "sighs too deep for words" (BGD, RSV). Paul clearly intends with στεναγμοῖς to link the thought back to vv 22 and 23. ἀλάλητος, only here in biblical Greek, is presumably the opposite of λαλητός (= "endowed with speech" in Job 38:14 LXX), that is, without the speech which distinguishes man from animal. The thought is therefore of groans not formulated in words. This means that a specific allusion to glossolalia is unlikely, since Paul evidently thought of glossolalia as spoken language, the language(s) indeed of heaven (1 Cor 12:28, 30; 13:1; 14:2, 10–11; cf. particularly *T. Job* 48.3, 49.2, and 50.1–2; see further Dunn, *Jesus*, 243–44). It is true that there is an overlap in thought of angel and spirit in Jewish thought (see above); so too sharp a line between heavenly intercession (to which Paul will allude shortly in v 34) and the Spirit's intercession on earth should not be drawn. Consequently some have compared the "inarticulate groans" with the "unutterable words" (ἄρρητα ῥήματα) of 2 Cor 12:4 (e.g., Wilckens). The inappropriateness of the suggested parallel lies not in the words themselves but rather in the sense they express: on the one hand, visions of heaven which leave the mind speechless and, on the other, the wordlessness of complete inability in the entanglements and frustration of all too earthly existence; the one focusing on the indescribable character of what has been seen, the other on the inability of believers in this age to put into words the reality of their own condition and relation to God. It is important to recognize here too that for Paul the mark of the Spirit is not necessarily fluency of speech or boldness of prayer (though he knew such experiences too—8:15; 1 Cor 14:14–17; cf. Eph 6:18), but also the inability to use that speech which distinguishes man from animal, the falling back into a more inarticulate mode which expresses more clearly his solidarity with nonhuman creation (v 22), the resort to a kind of primeval dependence in which the creature cannot even boast of articulate speech. Contrast *Philosophensprüche*, 497:7: μόνος ὁ σοφὸς εἰδὼς εὔχεσθαι = "only the wise man knows how to pray" (cited in BGD, προσεύχομαι). The Spirit is here seen as typically active not so much in the heights of spiritual rapture as in the depths of human inability to cope (in "our weakness"—Niederwimmer, 254–59; Luz, *Geschichts*, 382); "only the weak really pray" (Gaugler, "Geist," 93). To that extent Paul may have had in mind the ecstatic excesses of the church in Corinth from where he was writing (see particularly Käsemann; equally confident of a reference to glossolalia are Paulsen, 122–26, and Stendahl, "Prayer," 155); but had he wished his readers to think of glossolalia he would probably have written with greater care (cf., e.g., Schniewind, "Seufzen," 82–84; Montague, 212–13; Obeng, "Paul," 362). And here the thought is more deeply rooted in the context of Paul's reworking of apocalyptic motifs (cf. Bindemann, 76–81), and in the attempt to document the extent of the believer's belonging with fallen creation in its longing for complete eschatological liberty; so that it would be more accurate to see Paul's description here as characterizing *all* prayer (Gaugler). Again it is the measure of Paul's sense of the eschatological tension that he can express the believer's experience in such (humanly) disparaging terms and see just these "inarticulate groans" as the voice of the Spirit. See further on 8:23 and Dunn, *Jesus*, 241–42.

27 ὁ δὲ ἐραυνῶν τὰς καρδίας, "he who searches the hearts." Characteristically Jewish is the description of God as the one who alone knows the hearts of individuals (1 Sam 16:7; 1 Kgs 8:39; Pss 44:21; 139:1–2, 23; Prov 15:11; further references in Zeller), and who tries the (mind and) heart (Pss 17:3, 26:2, Jer 11:20, 12:3, and 17:10, where δοκιμάζειν is a near synonym of the later ἐραυνάω, as Rev 2:23 confirms). Ps 44:21 may have been particularly in Paul's mind, since he goes on to cite the next verse (44:22) in v 36. καρδία here obviously denotes the seat of the inner life, the center (hidden from human eyes) where ambitions and values and motives are rooted; see further on 1:21 and 2:15. The thought is intended here to be one of comfort rather than of warning or caution (as more typically in the passages echoed): Paul assumes an openness and honesty before God expressed in this fumbling and confusion which has not tried to cloak or conceal itself either in strict silence or in idle words, but has confessed its dependence on God in this humbling wordless groaning.

οἶδεν τί τὸ φρόνημα τοῦ πνεύματος, "he knows what is the Spirit's way of thinking." The allusion to v 6 (τὸ φρόνημα τοῦ πνεύματος ζωὴ . . .) is obvious. The conception of God involved here is fascinating. Whereas the Spirit is naturally conceived of as the searching presence of God (as in Ps 139 and Wisd Sol 1:7), or indeed as God's own penetrating self-knowledge (1 Cor 2:10–11), here the thought is of God's outreaching Spirit itself hidden in the heart of man's creaturely inability and known only to God. Such was

the tension within the Jewish concept of God already before Christian reworking of Jewish monotheism—"a kind of movement between God himself and
his Spirit" (Michel). The fact that Jewish monotheism could encompass such
a stretching of its twofold assertion of divine immanence and divine transcen-
dence suggests that it had more room for the Christian reexpression in a
trinitarian direction than is usually recognized. MacRae escapes such inference
by arguing that the subject of ἐραυνῶν is the Spirit (as in 1 Cor 2:10) and
that πνεῦμα = the human spirit. But (1) this breaches the obvious continuity
with v 26, with its use of the familiar motif of the (angelic) Spirit as intercessor,
and (2) results in an effective human prayer needing only the Spirit to search
it out, which again hardly accords with v 26.

ὅτι κατὰ θεὸν ἐντυγχάνει ὑπὲρ ἁγίων, "because he intercedes in accordance
with God on behalf of the saints." The ὅτι could be taken either as causal
("because"—so, e.g., Schmidt, Käsemann, Wilckens) or as explicative ("that"—
so, e.g., SH, Michel, Black, Kuss). Quite how we are to decide what Paul
intended is not clear, since both senses make sense, and nothing much hangs
on the choice. Unfortunately it is not so easy to translate in such a way as
to bring out the ambiguity Paul was evidently content to leave. The phrase
κατὰ θεόν rings slightly oddly in our ears, but was unexceptional at the time;
hence 2 Cor 7:9–11, also Rom 15:5 and 2 Cor 11:17 (see BGD, κατά II.5.a).
God himself can be expressed as the norm for what is best for his people;
or we can translate "in accordance with God's will," since, by implication,
God's will is simply an expression of God, God himself in action. See also
καθὸ δεῖ in v 26. ἐντυγχάνω can have a range of meaning (LSJ), but here the
sense is obviously that of "petition, appeal to," as is appropriate since God
is the one addressed (so also in its other NT usage—8:34; 11:2; Heb 7:25;
cf. Acts 25:24). For ἅγιοι see on 1:7; the absence of the definite article prevents
the thought from becoming too restrictive (cf. Schlier). It is not by accident
that Paul speaks of believers as "saints" for only the second time in the letter,
since in this climax to the elaboration (chaps. 6–8) of his first main conclusion
(chap. 5) he deliberately presents the Christian privileges as both the purposed
end of creation and the fulfillment of God's calling of Israel (see *Form and
Structure*).

28 οἴδαμεν δὲ ὅτι τοῖς ἀγαπῶσιν τὸν θεόν, "and we know that for those who
love God." For οἴδαμεν ὅτι see on 2:2. The knowledge referred to is the common
assumption of faith, referring, as the following phrases make clear, to the
heritage of Jewish conviction (not just Christian tradition [Grayston]) with
which Paul evidently could assume his listeners were familiar. It is the knowledge therefore not so much of personal experience; though some may already
have been able to attest things working out for good in their own personal
circumstances, the thrust of the εἰς ἀγαθόν is eschatological (see below)—as
of the corporate experience of the people of God, where the εἰς ἀγαθόν had
already been tested and proved to some extent at least through Exile, Syrian
crisis, Roman occupation, and the coming and resurrection of Messiah Jesus.

Somewhat surprisingly ἀγαπάω appears for the first time in Romans (though
see also 5:5, 8), though that may be no more than accidental, a result of the
demands of the particular argument of the letter, so that no great theological
point can be made of its infrequency (see Schlatter and on 13:8–9). "Those

who love God" is a characteristic self-designation of Jewish piety (a full listing in Cranfield, 424 n.4), usually following the typically deuteronomistic style, "those who love God and keep his commandments" (Exod 20:6; Deut 5:10; 6:5; 7:9; etc.; Josh 22:5; 1 Kgs 3:3; Neh 1:5; Dan 9:4; CD 19.2; 1QH 16.13); the axiomatic linking of the two elements in Jewish thought is reflected also in Sir 2:15–16, *Pss. Sol.* 14.1–2; *T. Iss.* 5.1–2; *T. Ben.* 3.1, and 1 John 5:2 (see also Mayer, 144–49, 152–54; and Osten-Sacken, 66). It is presumably significant that Paul takes up only the first part of the regular formulation, thereby both evoking Christianity's Jewish inheritance while at the same time separating it from its more distinctively Jewish devotion to the Torah. In view of the following heavy emphasis on divine initiative this phrase is an important reminder that God's purpose works out in personal response and relationship; coerced love is not love.

πάντα συνεργεῖ εἰς ἀγαθόν, "everything contributes toward good." If we take the shorter reading as original (see *Notes*), the most obvious way to read the phrase is with πάντα (rather than with θεός implicit) as the subject (among recent commentators so also Barrett, Käsemann, Mayer [138–42], Hendriksen, Wilckens; but most take θεός as subject—e.g., Denney, Lagrange, Knox, Gaugler, Bruce, Kuss, Paulsen [152–54], Ross, Byrne [*Reckoning*, 173], RSV, NIV, NJB; NEB takes πνεῦμα as the unexpressed subject, approved by Black, "Romans 8:28," and Robinson, *Wrestling*, 104–5; but see particularly the full discussion in Cranfield). Since Paul would mean the same thing in any case, and hence may not have been concerned to remove the ambiguity, little of great moment hangs on the debate (Dodd overreacts to the older AV/KJV translation).

συνεργέω can have the sense "work together with, cooperate in," but the form with εἰς suggests that the alternatives "contribute toward, help to bring about" are closer to Paul's meaning (cf. LSJ, BGD). That Paul is indebted here too (as Michel suggests) to Jewish teaching is shown to be possible by the frequency with which the *T. 12 Patr.* use the verb (*T. Reub.* 3.6; *T. Iss.* 3.7; *T. Dan* 1.7; *T. Gad* 4.5 v.l.; 4.7; *T. Ben.* 4.5); if so the possibility that Paul intended πνεῦμα as the subject greatly increases, since that would echo the most characteristic of the Testaments' formulations. The pious hope that everything will work out for the best for the godly is "a common axiom of antiquity" (Käsemann; Cranfield cites *Hermetica* 9.4 and Plato, *Apol.* 41c-d; see also Balz, 106, Osten-Sacken, 63–64, and Schmithals, *Anthropologie*, 162), but Paul probably has in mind the more characteristic Jewish expressions of it (as in Gen 50:20; Eccl 8:12; Sir 39:27; often cited is the saying attributed to R. Akiba, "Let a man accustom himself to say, 'All the Almighty does, he does for good'"; see further Str-B 3:255–56, and Zeller). In the context here, where Paul has in view the eschatological climax which God has purposed for "all things," the ἀγαθόν will have an eschatological reference (cf. 14:16): the Christian is not dependent on the Micawberish hope that something will "turn up"; his confidence rests rather on the outworking of God's purpose *through* all the contradiction and frustration of the present to its intended end.

τοῖς κατὰ πρόθεσιν κλητοῖς οὖσιν, "for those who are called according to his purpose." πρόθεσις here clearly denotes God's purpose (see again Cranfield); cf. particularly 9:11; Eph 1:11; 3:11; 2 Tim 1:9; and Philo, *Mos.* 2.61 (BGD).

Once again, though the phrase does not lack wider parallels (LSJ, *TDNT*
8:165), Michel is clearly right in seeing here the characteristically Jewish
thought of God's (pretemporal) purpose (עֵצָה = βουλή) moving history and
through history to its intended end as that which Paul has in mind (cf. Ps
33:11; Prov 19:21; Isa 5:19; 19:17; 46:10; Jer 49:20; 50:45; Wisd Sol 6:4;
9:13, 17; 1QS 1.8, 10, 13; 2.23; 3.6; 11.18; 1QH 1.5[?]; 4.13; 6.10–11; 16.8[?];
see also Kleinknecht, 340–41). That Paul's thought is here dominated by
Jewish categories is confirmed by the reappearance of οἱ κλητοί in close conjunction with ἅγιοι (v 27), as in 1:7 (see on 1:7). That his thought is already
moving toward the discussion of chaps. 9–11 is indicated by the parallel
with 9:11 (Michel), where the inside-out inversion of the phrase:

> 8:28:   οἱ κατὰ πρόθεσιν κλητοί·
> 9:11:   ἡ κατ᾽ ἐκλογὴν πρόθεσις

shows that Paul thinks in typically Jewish fashion of God's purpose and divine
calling/election as two sides of the one coin. The point here, however, is
that this can now be said of believers (Gentiles as well as Jews): the inheritance
of Israel has been opened to all in such a way as to put the traditional understanding of God's electing purpose in question. Hence the climax leads naturally into chap. 9. See further *Form and Structure*. "The οὗσιν is probably to
be taken in a pregnant sense. They are called and stand now in and under
this call which has opened and continues to open them to God's encouragement
and claim [*Zuspruch und Anspruch*]" (Schlier). That all hangs on the *extra nos*
of God's purpose is a repeated emphasis here (though Dodd again stands in
some danger of overstating the point).

  29 ὅτι οὓς προέγνω, καὶ προώρισεν, "for those he knew beforehand he also
predetermined"; "God knew his own before ever they were" (NEB). προγινώσκω
obviously means more than simply foreknowledge, knowledge before the
event (as in Acts 26:5 and 2 Pet 3:17; see LSJ). It has in view the more
Hebraic understanding of "knowing" as involving a relationship experienced
and acknowledged (see on 1:21); hence commentators regularly and rightly
refer to such passages as Gen 18:19, Jer 1:5, Hos 13:5, Amos 3:2, and 1QH
9.29–30, whose influence elsewhere in the Pauline correspondence is evident
(1 Cor 8:3; 13:12; Gal 4:9; 2 Tim 2:19) (cf., e.g., Lagrange, Leenhardt).
Together with προώρισεν it is clearly intended to pick up the πρόθεσις of v
28: this acknowledging embrace by God of his own was in hand from the
beginning (cf. particularly Murray). This realization was evidently cherished
in the Pauline and Petrine strands of earliest Christian thought (11:2; 1 Pet
1:2, 20; cf. Acts 2:23 with its similar link between God's foreknowledge and
[pre]determination). Here Paul obviously means to embrace the whole sweep
of time and history, from beginning to end, within the scope of these two
verses (προ- . . . ἐδόξασεν). Since προέγνω has such a full sense, the προώρισεν
adds little to the meaning (cf. NJB). But the association of ideas is natural
(cf. again Acts 2:23), and effectively underscores the προ- emphasis already
given in πρόθεσις (v 28): believers rest in the assurance that their part in the
people of God is not accidental or random, but part of a divine purpose
whose outworking was already clearly envisaged from the beginning. Here

too the thought builds on Jewish precedents (cf. Jer 1:5; *T. Mos.* 1.14) and
was warmly embraced in early Christian theology (Acts 4:28; 1 Cor 2:7; Eph
1:5, 11; Ign. *Eph.* inscr.). See also Dupont, *Gnosis,* 93–104; and Mayer, 155–
59.

συμμόρφους τῆς εἰκόνος τοῦ υἱοῦ αὐτοῦ, "conformed to the image of his Son."
The further συν- compound harks back to the earlier flurry of them in v 17.
Paul has in view the outcome of a process which he describes using the
same terms in Phil 3:21, and using the εἰκών language in 1 Cor 15:49, thus
recalling here the anticipated outcome of the resurrection of the body referred
to in vv 11 and 23. That a process is involved (cf. particularly Phil 3:10
[συμμορφιζόμενος]; 2 Cor 3:18; Cranfield refers to the less directly parallel
Col 3:9–10; but see on 13:14) is not to be denied (Balz, 113–14), but here
and in the most immediately parallel references the thought is directed firmly
to the end result of the process (complete conformity to Christ's death, complete transformation into his likeness) (cf. *TDNT* 7:788, Michel, Siber, 155–
56). It is the sureness of the end as determined from the beginning which
Paul wishes to emphasize. Käsemann's unwillingness to acknowledge this future reference is surprising; a reference to baptism or the language of 6:3–
6 puts more emphasis on the Already of salvation than Paul would wish at
this point. Leaney sets Paul's theme of conformity to God's Son in contrast
to the strongly held idea in the ancient world (including Qumran) of the
need for conformity to the laws of the universe.

ἡ εἰκών τοῦ υἱοῦ αὐτοῦ is of course epexegetic—the image which his Son is;
as the συν- compounds indicate, Paul's thought is of believers becoming like
Christ (in death and resurrection; see below). εἰκών itself can have a range
of meaning similar to that which the English "likeness, image" encompasses
(LSJ), but here the word probably denotes the form which the Son takes,
the concrete representation which his appearance embodies. Almost certainly
Paul has Adam in mind once again, man created in the image (εἰκών) of
God (Gen 1:26–27). The idea of man as the image of God was by no means
exclusively Jewish (See BGD, εἰκών 1b), but in view of the prominence of
the Adam motif earlier in the letter (1:22–24; 3:23; 5:12–19; 7:7–13; 8:20)
it is no doubt the Jewish tradition which influences Paul most here. The
idea of man made in the divine image was a Jewish commonplace of the
period (Sir 17:3; Wisd Sol 2:23; *T. Naph* 2.5; *Apoc. Mos* 10.3; 12.1; 33.5;
35.2; *Adam and Eve* 14.1–2; 37.3; *4 Ezra* 8.44; *2 Enoch* 65.2) which was shared
in early Christianity (1 Cor 11:7; James 3:9). And though there is little or
no thought of the divine image having been lost or defaced, as in later Christian
theologizing, the implication of Paul's language here and elsewhere is of an
image to be formed in Christians by process of transformation (see previous
paragraph); see also Dunn, *Christology,* 105.

The Adam Christology involved is clear: Christ is the image of God which
Adam was intended to be, the Son as the pattern of God's finished product
(cf. Schmidt). In view of confusion and dispute on the point, it should be
noted that Paul has in view the *risen* Christ, the exalted Christ of the last
age, not Jesus as he was on earth; the end of God's creative purposes is
resurrection, not incarnation (so particularly Byrne, *Sons,* 117–18; Zeller).
This is clear from the other parallel passages: 1 Cor 15:49, where the thought

clearly focuses on the *resurrection* state; 2 Cor 3:18—the image an end product of transformation; 2 Cor 4:4—the clear allusion to Paul's own Damascus road experience (4:6) confirms that it is the appearance of the risen Christ which Paul has in mind. The more accurate formulation would be to say that Christ was conformed to the image of sinful flesh (see on 8:3); salvation consists in being conformed to the image of the risen Christ (cf. Schlatter, Lietzmann, Wilckens).

Others argue that εἰκών has in view the other side of the act of creation, the Son as mediator of creation, where it is Wisdom rather than Adam to whom Paul alludes (cf. Wisd Sol 7:26; Philo, *Leg. All.* 1.43; and in Paul, particularly Col 1:15); cf. Cranfield, Käsemann. But while the overlap of usage of εἰκών (Wisdom/Adam) has important implications for a theology of creation, it is the *outcome* (the *eschatological* outcome) of God's creative purpose which seems to be in view here rather than that of Wisdom's agency in creation. (1) The continuity of thought from vv 11 and 15–17 indicates clearly enough that the process of "conforming" must include suffering with Christ; so the context also confirms that the image to which they are to be conformed is that of the resurrected one (as again in 1 Cor 15:49; Phil 3:21)—that is, the working out of the salvation process into the full liberation/redemption of the body (v 23). This is also the significance of πρωτότοκος (see below). (2) Paul's view of history, as has become clear also from the preceding verses, is not cyclical, of an end goal as a *return* to original state (cf. on 8:21), but more of a purpose, formed from the beginning, achieved *through* the process of history, moving toward an intended higher end, not simply returning to the beginning. As Paul has been at some pains to argue, God does not write off the intervening history as a total failure and useless; rather his purpose embraces it, works *through* it, through the travail of a creation subjected to futility, *through* the groaning of believers still beset by sin and under the sway of death, working to achieve not simply a return to pristine purity, but the fuller glory which Adam never attained (see on 3:23), including life *from death*. Again Käsemann ignores the eschatological thrust of the passage in seeing here "an enthusiastic baptismal tradition"; "in baptism the divine image . . . is restored by conformation to the Son" (rightly rejected by Wilckens, n.731).

εἰς τὸ εἶναι αὐτὸν πρωτότοκον ἐν πολλοῖς ἀδελφοῖς, "that he should be firstborn among many brothers." Here too in πρωτότοκος we have a concept which invites disagreement similar to that over εἰκών, since it too can be used of divine Wisdom. But even in these cases the thought is primarily of what God has created (cf. Sir 1:4; 24:9; see further on Col 1:15 in Dunn, *Christology*, 189). And here even more clearly the thought is of the accomplished goal of God's creative action. Hence the more immediate parallels are Col 1:18 and Rev 1:5 (πρωτότοκος τῶν νεκρῶν), and again the thought is of the resurrected Christ as the pattern of the new humanity of the last age, the firstborn (of the dead) of a new race of eschatological people in whom God's design from the beginning of creation is at last fulfilled. The closest parallel indeed is Heb 2:6–10, where Jesus completes the original purpose for Adam (to be crowned with glory) through the suffering of death, in order that he might bring many sons (likewise through suffering and death) to that glory, being thus perfected through suffering (cf. again Wilckens). Since a corporate dimension is in view (Christ as eldest of many brothers) Paul was also probably mindful of the fact that Israel was also called God's "firstborn" (Exod 4:22; Sir 31:9; Pss. Sol. 18.4; other references, including the Torah and the Messiah [cited by Str-B 3:257–58] do not come to clear expression till after Paul's time). The point being, by way of contrast, that in the new epoch, outside the bounds marked by the law, Christ's sonship is the norm and it is shared by all who have received and are led by the Spirit (vv 14–17). Here again it is the Adam motif which predominates (beginning a new family of humankind) rather than the thought of Christ's continuity and identity with the divine (as in Wisdom).

30 οὓς δὲ προώρισεν, τούτους καὶ ἐκάλεσεν, "and those he predestined, he also called." As the two προ- verbs of v 29 take up the πρόθεσις of v 28, so ἐκάλεσεν here takes up the κλητοῖς of v 28. The thought is not of an invitation which might be rejected; God does not leave his purpose to chance but puts it into effect himself. Paul looks at the whole process from the perspective of its successful outcome, where the redeemed gladly affirm that their coming to faith was wholly God's doing; see further on 1:1 and 4:17; and cf. particularly 1 Cor 1:9; 7:17–24; Gal 1:6, 15; 5:8, 13; Eph 4:1, 4; Col 3:15; 1 Thess 2:12; 4:7; 5:24; 2 Thess 2:14. Byrne, Sons, 120, notes the frequent association of "calling" and "sonship" in Jewish thought.

καὶ οὓς ἐκάλεσεν, τούτους καὶ ἐδικαίωσεν, "and those he called, he also justified." For δικαιόω see on 2:13 and 1:17. Since the ἐκάλεσεν denotes divinely accomplished conversion, and the ἐδόξασεν denotes the completion of God's saving purpose (see above), the ἐδικαίωσεν could refer to either of these decisive moments (as, on the one hand, 5:1 and 1 Cor 6:11; or, on the other, 2:13), or indeed to the whole process of salvation linking these two decisive moments—God's saving action in drawing man into the proper relationship with himself and sustaining him therein (through all the anguish and frustration outlined in vv 12–26) until the final acquittal and glorious conclusion—the whole process seen again from its end point. In querying the absence of any mention of sanctification Cranfield misses this potential breadth of δικαιόω and works with a too dogmatically determined distinction between justification and sanctification.

οὓς δὲ ἐδικαίωσεν, τούτους καὶ ἐδόξασεν, "and those he justified, he also glorified." For δοξάζω and the thought of sharing in God's glory as the final goal of God's creative and redemptive purpose see on 3:23 and 8:17. Paul naturally brings the whole analysis of vv 18–30 to a climax with the same concept he used in v 17. Equally significant is the fact that the only previous use of δοξάζειν as such was 1:21. The two uses therefore bracket the beginning and end of the whole process of salvation. It is a finely conceived reversal that the δοξάζειν which man failed to give to his Creator in the beginning is finally resolved in God's δοξάζειν of man. In terms of Adam theology, this is the δόξα which God intended for man when he created him in the first place (Ps 8:5; cf. again Heb 2:8–10). The aorist should not be required to yield the idea of a glorification already accomplished now, in baptism or wherever (cf. particularly Käsemann, Paulsen, 159, and Schlier): if a process of glorification is at all in view here (Jülicher; Schlatter—"sanctification is also glorification"; cf. 2 Cor 3:18), it is the process seen from its end point and completion (aorist; "the certainty of completed salvation" [Mayer, 163–65])—hence, presumably the somewhat hymnic style (Wilckens compares 1 Tim 3:16). Here again it is important to recognize that in vv 29–30 Paul deliberately sets the whole process of cosmic and human history between its two poles, pretemporal purpose and final glorification as the completion of that purpose. Only within this context should the issue of predestination be raised (with reference, e.g., to SH, Dodd, and Kuss), since Paul is not inviting reflection on the classic problems of determinism and free will, or thinking in terms of a decree which excludes as well as one which includes (see also on 9:18 and 22). His thought is simply that from the perspective of the end it will be evident that history has been the stage for the unfolding of God's purpose, the purpose of the Creator fulfilling his original intention in creating.

Explanation

The thought of the last sentence was highly compressed. In effect it serves as a summary statement of what Paul has still to say to round off his exposition of God's righteousness being revealed apart from the law and what that means in the here and now for those who have believed, Gentile as well as Jew. In the elaboration which follows, the "with Christ" is left to one side for the moment, and it is the other implication bound up in the idea of inheritance on which attention is focused, namely, the eschatological not yet of an inheritance still outstanding.

In the elaboration Paul quickly indicates that the broadening out of God's saving purpose beyond Israel as such has not only Gentile believers in view, but the whole of creation. The inheritance of the redeemed people of God is no longer simply the promised land (Palestine) but the whole world (cf. 4:13). Thus the Adam motif reemerges with still greater strength. What God has in view, always had in view from the first with Abraham, is the reversal of Adam's fall and of its consequences. The analysis of the human condition which began in chap. 1 in terms of Adam is shown to climax in the restoration not only of the sons of God to the glory God intended for man from the first, but also of the cosmos. Creation and salvation are in no sense in antithesis. Redemption is not so much an escape from creation as simply the completion of God's original purpose in and for creation.

18 The elaboration of v 17 begins with a statement of firm conviction, that the present suffering bears no comparison with and will be greatly outweighed by the future glory they will enjoy. As in the earlier climactic statement of 5:1–5, the hope of glory is not held apart from or without relation to the far from glorious present. And as in that earlier passage, there is no sense that the present sufferings undermine or contradict the hope of glory. On the contrary, suffering is part of the process (of sharing Christ's death), itself a sign of the wasting away of the present age which must precede and accompany the emergence of the new. The language is thoroughly apocalyptic— the contrast between the present and the future ages, the talk of revelation, and the sense of the imminence of the eschatological denouement. But implied is the more distinctively Christian conviction that the ages already overlap, that believers can be confident in the certainty (and imminence) of the eschatological climax because the work of eschatological liberation and renewal has already begun. As Paul had indicated more clearly in an earlier exposition of the same train of thought, the unveiling of eschatological glory in part at least is to be seen as the outworking of what is already happening within believers (2 Cor 4:7–5:5). It is precisely this assurance given by the "already" of the "Abba"-crying Spirit and the frustration of the "not yet" of the suffering body which constitute the eschatological tension.

19 Verse 19 extends the thought to creation. Paul's vision of God's saving purpose drives him beyond any idea of a merely personal or human redemption. What is at stake in all this is creation as a whole and the fulfillment of God's original intention in creating the cosmos. However much Paul's dualism of decision (flesh versus Spirit) seems to invite a cosmic dualism (matter and spirit, creation and heaven), Paul has no doubts whatsoever that creation is involved in that eschatological glory to which he and his readers look forward. As implied in his opening exposition (1:18–23) and elsewhere in his argument (particularly 4:17), Paul's faith is in God as creator. By "creation" he presumably means the whole created order into which God set man, the context of man's present embodiment. This is implied by the clear allusion to the narratives of creation and of man's/Adam's fall (Gen 1–3, particularly in the next sentence [v 20])—creation understood in distinction from humankind (and from the creator), as also in 1:25. As (the rest of) creation in the beginning had its role in relation to man, the crown and steward of creation (Gen 1:26–30; 2:19), so creation's rediscovery of its role depends on the restoration of man to his intended glory as the image of God.

Paul's vision is vivid: creation personified, full of wistful eager longing (like a supporters' club craning their necks forward to see whether their favorite son has crossed the finish line and their common celebration is assured), all too acutely aware that its own fulfillment is bound up with the entry of God's sons upon their full inheritance—a transformed creation being part of that inheritance (v 21). The language of apocalyptic is sustained: what creation awaits so impetuously is the revelation of the sons of God in their completed redemption—an unveiling presumably from heaven (cf. 2 Cor 5:1–5). Implicit is thought of the Parousia (as in 1 Thess 4:16–17 and 1 Cor 15:42–52), but because of creation's subservient position its redemption can be described simply as a consequence of man's.

20 The reason why the created order awaits so longingly man's redemption is because creation itself is caught up in man's fallen state. Paul assumes that his Roman readers would recognize the allusion once again to the narrative of Adam's creation and fall (Gen 1–3). In particular, the talk of God "subjecting" creation may well have evoked the psalmist's description of creation subordinated to man (Ps 8:6); while in describing the restriction imposed on creation Paul would almost certainly expect his readers to think initially of Gen 3:17–18. Creation was subjected to the same futility as man found to be the result of his overweening ambition (Rom 1:21). The point Paul is presumably making, through somewhat obscure language, is that God followed the logic of his purposed subjecting of creation to man by subjecting it yet further in consequence of man's fall, so that it might serve as an appropriate context for fallen man: a futile world to engage the futile mind of man. By describing creation's subjection as "unwilling" Paul maintains the personification of the previous verse. There is an out-of-sortness, a disjointedness about the created order which makes it a suitable habitation for man at odds with his creator.

By "futility" Paul probably has in mind the same sense of futility of life which found expression in Jewish thought most clearly in Ecclesiastes—that weariness and despair of spirit which cannot see beyond the stultifying repetitiveness of life, the endless cycle of decay and corruption, the worthlessness of a lifelong effort which may be swept away overnight by a storm or be parched to nothingness in a drought, the complete insignificance of the individual in the tides of time and the currents of human affairs—all indeed that, had man but realized it, was going to make it impossible for him to be "as god," made it inevitable that he would become subservient to useless idols and mere things. Yet for Paul, of course, that is not, could not be the last word. The same character of creation-bound existence which causes some to despair, seen from another angle becomes a ground for hope. Looked at in terms of man's vaunted independence from God the future for the world is bleak. But seen in terms of the creator's purpose, the present state of affairs is not all there is to look forward to; the goal of the created order will be determined by God, not by the puny mind of man. As the suffering of believers becomes a ground of hope because it is experienced as the formation of character and renewal of the inner man (5:3–4; 2 Cor 4:16), so the out-of-jointness of creation itself is testimony that it was not always intended to be thus. From the beginning the primal-time subjection to futility had the final-time fulfillment of God's original purpose for man and his habitation in view. Even in its futility creation is still God's.

21 The end God has in view for his creation is eschatological liberation, liberation from the slavery of corruption. Paul deliberately picks up the theme of liberation and slavery once again, thereby tying the thought here into the earlier expression of the same theme (vv 2, 15). The slavery of the law as used by sin they had already been liberated from—the restrictiveness of Israel's too narrow understanding of the law, the slavery of a concern for scrupulous obedience "to the letter" which sin was able to turn to its own advantage so effectively. They were already rejoicing in that liberty. But there is also a slavery to corruption, the complete inability to escape from the physical deterioration and dissolution which characterizes the created order (and on which sin has capitalized). And believers are still part of that created order; like creation as a whole, they have not yet been liberated from that slavery. Paul's confidence, however, is that those in Christ will assuredly enter into that fuller liberty—the liberty of the splendor God always had in view for man when he created him; confidence too that creation will share that liberty. As man fallen into futility required a world given over to corruption and decay as his appropriate setting, so man liberated from both sin and the flesh will require an incorruptible setting for his resurrected embodiment (cf. 1 Cor 15:42–50).

22 To win greater acceptance for his visionary confidence Paul appeals to his readers' common knowledge. The picture he sketches would not be strange to anyone with poetic imagination: the contortion of the earth in an earthquake, the devastation of flood and fire, the desolation caused by warfare or famine, could all be evoked by the image of the earth in pain; even more familiar would be the image of mother earth in childbirth at each new springtime. But Paul's vision is the grander sweep of Jewish apocalyptic, where such images are used not to depict the annual cycle of the seasons or occasional disasters, but to evoke the climactic transition from this age and created order to the new age of God's final purpose. It is an all-embracing process involving the total cosmos, "the whole creation" joining "together" in fractured chorus. Paul evidently can assume his readers' acquaintance with this Jewish belief in such a period of fearful tribulation and anguish, "the birth pangs of the Messiah," as they came to be known, whether because such apocalyptic imagery was familiar throughout the diaspora, or because it had already become part of Christian thought too (cf. Mark 13:8). What a disinterested observer might regard merely as a geological phenomenon, or as the unfortunate effect of changing weather systems, Paul sees as the slow animal-like writhing of creation's discomfort at the present alienation from and distortion of what might have been and will yet become. This is how the course of creation's history can be characterized "up to the present." The implication of the metaphor of labor pains, however, as of the eschatological "now," is that the time for groaning will soon be past, the delivery of the new creation from the womb of the old is imminent—though Paul's thought cherishes as much the certain hope of that deliverance as of its nearness.

23 The implication that this travail of creation is of a piece with the eschatological tension experienced by believers is already clear. The suffering of the saints is part of a cosmic drama into which all creation, inanimate as well as animate, is drawn. But lest the point be insufficiently clear Paul spells it out. We ourselves are caught up in the same cosmic unease too deep for words. He claims an empathy between Christian suffering and the hidden forces working in nature—not the cycle of the seasons or nature's amazing fertility, which so motivated the religious fervor typical of the ancient world, but the deeper movements of history, including natural history—and not simply as an endless repetition of the same phenomena, but history moving to an end, a final climax. For the spokesman of a small movement still in its infancy the vision is audacious. But of course for Paul it was not a new movement, rather the climax of a purpose begun in Adam, picked up again in Abraham and Israel, and now through Jesus Christ already broadened out to embrace the Gentiles. Paul does not thereby seek to glorify his own mission; his work is simply a small part in a cosmic plan from the beginning of time; but it was that vision which drove him on and which made his work so successful and of such lasting influence.

In thus setting Christian self-understanding against a cosmic background Paul also provides a clear outline of the salvation process as he saw it working out in believers' experience. The two decisive moments are reception of the Spirit and redemption of the body, with the intervening period characterized by eschatological tension—the strain between what has already become and what is yet to become, the strain of a relationship with God already established but not yet matured.

The first decisive moment which integrates the individual into the plan of cosmic redemption is the gift of the Spirit, God's effective power reaching out to man and welcomed by him as the chief directive force in his life. Paul here of course simply picks up his earlier definition of the Christian as one who "has the Spirit" (v 9). But here he enlarges the definition to "having the firstfruits of the Spirit." Thereby he characterizes the gift of the Spirit (or the work of the Spirit in a believer's life) as the beginning of a larger process. The image it would most probably evoke in his audiences was that of the harvest, a typical and effective Jewish and now also Christian image for the final ingathering at the end of history. By the harvest Paul almost certainly had in mind the resurrection, the ingathering of resurrected bodies (1 Cor 15:20, 23). The gift of the Spirit is but the beginning of that process which will end with the resurrection, the redemption of the body. Also implied in the metaphor is the thought that this final end is of a piece with the beginning (the first sheaf is not different from the many sheaves of the complete harvest, the first lump of dough no different from the dough of the whole batch; cf. 11:16); the believer already experiences the life of the age to come in however incomplete and restricted a manner. To respond to the prompting of a loving Spirit is to breathe the air of heaven. Paul's audience would no doubt recognize a second implication, that the final ingathering would not be long delayed; the firstfruit is the beginning of a harvest already being reaped.

The time between the two chief moments (Spirit and resurrection) Paul characterizes as a time of groaning. His thought here is clearly the same as in 2 Cor 5:3–4 and little different from the agonized cry of 7:24. The groaning is of frustration that the life of the Spirit cannot yet achieve full expression in the believer's present embodiment. Like the groaning of creation (v 22), it is the frustration that one's own human weakness causes so many of one's highest endeavors still to end in futility, a groaning at salvation begun but not yet complete. Such is not the only perspective from which Paul expects believers to view their bodily relation to creation, as he shows elsewhere (1 Cor 11:25–26) and will remind his readers later (Rom 14:14a, 20b). But Paul the Christian not only rejoices in the bounty of the earth, he also resonates with its contradictions and tragedies, because he finds therein mirrored his own sense of eschatological dis-ease. The implication, as in chap. 7, is that this sense of frustration should not be seen as something negative or alarming. On the contrary, it is the person who senses nothing of this alienation in nature, content to live only in and for this world, as Paul would say, at the level of the flesh, who stands in greater peril. For it is the claim of God on a person which sets up this tension, the Spirit of God active in a life which causes the frustration. The groaning is a sign of the Spirit's presence (v 26), the Spirit of God drawing the believer into harmony with the deeper rhythms of a creation longing for its own eschatological fruition.

The second and final moment in the process of individual (and corporate) salvation is "the redemption of the body," by which Paul obviously means the resurrection of the body (v 11; 2 Cor 5:1–5). Implicit here is its nature as "spiritual body" (1 Cor 15:44–46)—a body activated by the Spirit as the present body is activated by the soul. The promise is that the firstfruits of the Spirit in motivating and directing, so often frustrated in the present body by its dependence on the satisfaction of all too human desires, will achieve fulfillment in a new embodiment energized wholly by the Spirit. By using the word "redemption" in reference to the "not yet" of the resurrection body Paul reemphasizes to his readers that redemption is not complete with the gift of the Spirit, and cannot be complete within this body, within the present mode of creation. By describing that final moment also as "adoption" Paul even more clearly indicates that the sonship presently enjoyed by the believer is incomplete. The choice of terms is obviously deliberate to underline the continuity of thought from v 14. In being given to share in Christ's sonship the believer shares its two-stage character—both sonship while yet in the flesh, and sonship "according to the Spirit as from the resurrection of the dead" (1:3–4), with the in-between time marked by suffering "with him" (8:17).

24–25 The not-yetness of the salvation process at present means that Christian faith is characterized as hope. Paul makes something of the point, quite likely because he feared that there were some in the Roman congregations who, like others at Corinth from where he was writing, overemphasized the "already" aspect of salvation, who took a too enthusiastic delight in the experience of the Spirit already given. Such an emphasis could only achieve coherent expression in a dualistic disregard for believers' bodily involvement in this present world and its contradictions. Paul has no room for such spiritualistic disengagement from the real world. The believer's bodily engagement with creation in its present mode is itself part of the process of salvation, is itself part of the believer's experience of salvation as an experience of hope.

His logic is straightforward: if we "hope" for something, that must mean by definition that we do not see it within our grasp, we do not yet have it. We exercise hope in relation to that which lies ahead of us, in the still invisible future. Paul the Christian will not allow his attention to become wholly absorbed in the present, whether its responsibilities or its frustrations. His gaze repeatedly lifts to the far horizon, and the hope of what lies beyond it is what sustains his faith despite the contradictions of the present. He would probably have no need to remind his readers of the positive character of this "hope" (unlike the weaker modern version which merges into mere wishful thinking). And the no doubt deliberate use of the aorist ("we are saved," rather than "we are being saved") makes the same point. Salvation is something certain for those who have the Spirit and are led by the Spirit. Christian hope is a confident hope, as he already affirmed in 5:1–5, because it is based on the experience of the Spirit already given, and because the resurrection of Christ also has the nature of "firstfruits," ensuring the participation of others in the resurrection of the dead (8:11; 1 Cor 15:23). These two factors are sufficient, Paul suggests firmly, to sustain believers' hope and to enable them to endure the contradictions and frustrations of the present bodily existence with the patience which matures their sonship.

26 If Paul does not allow his attention to be wholly focused on the present (vv 22–23), neither does he allow his hope for the future (vv 24–25) to distract him from the harsh reality of the interim period, between the firstfruits of Christ's resurrection and the liberation of the whole cosmos, between the firstfruits of the Spirit and the redemption of the body. The Spirit, the same experience of (assurance as to) God's fatherly acceptance (8:15–16), of God's overflowing love (5:5), which gives him confidence regarding the future, also sustains in the weakness of the present. Hope and weakness are in no way contradictory for Paul—as though hope could only be something irrational and speculative in the face of the depressing reality of sin's continuing power and flesh's continuing weakness. On the contrary they are bound into one experience for the believer—the experience of the Spirit as an experience of being sustained and helped forward in and through what would otherwise be a crippling weakness. Whereas the law remained impotent in this situation (8:3), because it remained too much a force over against the individual in the weakness of his flesh, enticing and condemning at one and the same time, the Spirit is a power which comes to the aid of the individual in that same weakness. And not as a distant intercessor in heaven (Paul's readers would know of several heavenly angelic spirit intercessors in Jewish thought), but as a very present help within. In Paul's understanding and experience, the Spirit does not wholly overcome the weakness of the flesh and leave it behind; the believer as believer, as having the Spirit, still remains of the flesh. But it does sustain in that weakness and keep that weakness from determining the believer's future: salvation in the present works through human weakness; God's power is most effective in the locus of man's powerlessness (2 Cor 12:9–10). So here: throughout this section his talk of future glory is counterpointed by repeated reminders of present suffering and corruption (vv 17–23); and the climax to his expressed hope of glory is his confession of the human weakness which still besets the believer.

This divine enabling comes to expression in the believer's prayer—not in inspiring particular requests which anticipate the will of God with prophetic foresight, nor in enabling a fluency and eloquence of utterance which might provoke some of the great Roman poets and orators to envy—but in the inarticulate groans of persons who do not know what to say and who can express their need before God only in the anguished frustration of eschatological tension. This, with 7:24, is one of the most striking expressions of the character of the eschatological tension for Paul; an inability still afflicting believers which is not just a physical weakness, but which affects their whole relation to God at the level of basic communication. The tension with his earlier talk of the Spirit's praying is particularly sharp: of course believers know to cry "Abba! Father!" and can fall back on the Lord's Prayer (8:15); but nevertheless, at the same time and equally typical, is their sense of ignorance and helplessness before God.

Paul presupposes that there is a right form of prayer, a form that presumably expresses the proper relation of creature to Creator: a proper honoring and thanking, acknowledging and worshiping (1:21, 25, 28), a proper tuning in to God's will which knows what God wants. But the believers' present is still so far from a complete restoration to that paradisaical ideal (and eschatological intent) that they do not know what to pray for (Paul assumes that his Roman audiences have shared the same frustrating experiences in prayer). Such a plight, however, Paul would not see as any reason to desist from prayer, to abandon so hopelessly inadequate an exercise. On the contrary, it is that very inarticulate groaning which is itself an effective form of prayer—the point presumably being that what is fundamental in prayer is not the saying of words, but the expression of dependence on God. And nowhere does man express more clearly his abandoning of the primeval pride which brought about his downfall than in a prayer which is so inadequate and humbling. That Paul is thinking here of glossolalia as such is unlikely, especially since the glossolalia which he heard at every meeting for worship in Corinth (1 Cor 14) seems to have been regarded by some Corinthian believers as a mark of spirituality, something to be proud of (cf. 1 Cor 14:12). But glossolalia recognized as something undignifying, something beneath man's self-respect as a rational being (cf. 1 Cor 14:20), would be of a similar order to the wordless groaning Paul has in mind here. It is the expression of human helplessness, ignorance and inarticulateness, especially for man who sacrificed his relation to God for the fruit of knowledge, which Paul has in view, since it is that which makes it possible for God to reclaim man for himself. The paradox which Paul delights to embrace is that such acknowledgment of human weakness is not only the precondition of salvation but is itself the assurance that salvation is in process. It is precisely the *believers'* expression of agonized frustration and impotence which is also, at one and the same time, the *Spirit's* intercession on their behalf (cf. vv 15–16).

27 The assurance Paul feels able to give is that God, who looks beyond outward appearance and mere words, recognizes full well what the inarticulate groans signify—namely, that basic orientation to and dependence on God which still looks to God even when it has nothing to say. He knows what is "the mind-set of the Spirit." Paul picks up again, no doubt deliberately, the phrase used in v 6. He thus confirms once again that the mind-set of the Spirit, while antithetical to "the mind-set of the flesh" (v 6), is not something wholly divorced from the flesh; on the contrary, it expresses itself through the weakness of the flesh. He confirms too that what he means by the phrase is a basic orientation of attitude, a primary direction of life, rather than a life which expresses only that orientation and direction; the mind-set of the Spirit is sustained in and through the eschatological tension of a flesh still captivated by sin and a body still dominated by death. Not least, Paul confirms that the mind-set of the Spirit is not a humanly achieved attitude, but an attitude enabled by the grace of God and sustained by God's power in and through the confession of dependence on God in and through human weakness. It is not that human weakness is in and of itself a sign of God's grace; on the contrary, human weakness unacknowledged is the very mind-set which gives sin its hold over a person. Rather it is the acknowledgment of dependence on God's enabling which constitutes effective prayer, precisely because it is in and through such creaturely dependence on God that God can work to accomplish his will.

28 Paul assumes that his readers will have in mind the continuity of
thought from the previous verses in which human suffering and creation's
travail have been integrated. The assurance that he offers his readers here
then is that the experience of human contradiction in which they share as
believers is no cause for despair, because God is also God of creation; his
purpose for believers is also his purpose for creation and works through
creation. His people therefore can be confident that their place within God's
purpose is basically in harmony with the unfolding history of creation. Those
who love God are those who have acknowledged their creatureliness and let
that fact shape their living. Their confidence is in God who is both Creator
and Father. Just as believers can still pray even when their prayer is marked
by complaint and irritation or the complete frustration of speechlessness, so
they can still trust even when their sense of alienation and contradiction is
at its sharpest, the sense of complete helplessness in the face of nameless
forces. They can draw on the assurance that the Spirit who is active in these
very frustrations and groanings is active also in these dark providences to
bring about good—that is, presumably, for Paul, in helping forward the maturing of the believer (cf. 5:4) and the mortification of the deeds of the body
(8:13).

The thought as expressed here has a certain triteness—the final consolation
of the decent man who finds that circumstances continually conspire against
his best endeavors. Similar sentiments were already current in both Jewish
and Greco-Roman thought, and Paul's Roman audiences would probably be
familiar with the sentiment as a fairly commonplace religious maxim. Somewhat surprisingly Paul seems to invite such comparison by expressing himself
in the vaguer language which would fit more than one religious system:
that the providence behind events, however hidden and unknown it may
be, is ultimately good. And by offering it as a hope "to those who love God"
(the first time he has used such a phrase in the letter), he may at first seem
to be commending merely the indomitableness of a piety which clings defi-
antly to its faith, come what may. But in fact, the idea of *loving* God
is untypical of Greco-Roman religiosity, while being characteristically Jewish. Paul therefore draws the vaguer hope of all religious piety within the
circle of the more distinctive Jewish faith in the one God. The vaguer, more
speculative piety of Greco-Roman religiosity is given clearer definition
and more substantial foundation in the Jewish trust in God as Creator and
Father.

This imposition of a Jewish perspective on a more widely familiar theologoumenon is reinforced by Paul's description of the beneficiaries of the consolation not only as "those who love God," but also as "saints" (v 27) and "called."
In so writing Paul not only echoes his opening greeting (1:7) but, as there,
probably also intends to imply that those who belong to Christ stand in continuity with Israel. The balance of human response is present in the place given
to "loving God," but the dominant emphasis is on God's action in calling
and setting apart (not of Jew from Gentile, or of priest from people, but of
those having the Spirit from the mind-set of the flesh, Jew as well as Gentile).
And this note increases in intensity as he moves to the climax of this stage
of his exposition. This divine initiative is no sudden decision by God; his

calling of Gentiles in particular was not simply occasioned by Israel's rejection; it was all part of God's purpose from the first. It is, again, precisely the conviction that God is creator and not only savior which assures Paul that the divine intention embraced Gentile as well as Jew long before Abraham became the archetypal "called" (whereas his people's attempt to retain their special prerogatives forgets that the God of Israel is also creator of all things and of all beings).

29–30 Having hidden nothing of the contradiction and temptation in which believers find themselves, Paul rounds off his discussion of what God's righteousness means for believers in the harsh reality of daily existence, by voicing his firm certainty that God's will stands over all, in control of all, and that his purpose to bring his creation and creatures to their full intended potential is undefeatable. The goal he purposed for his people was formulated in the mists of time, effected by his own summons, to bring his human creation back into fullness of relation with himself, owned by him and sustained by him and given to share in his splendor. In the full assurance of faith Paul sets aside all the "ifs" and "buts," the qualifications and warnings of the previous three chapters, and affirms the certainty of God fulfilling his purpose of creation and salvation in the tense of action already completed.

The goal of the creator-savior is expressed in terms of the original creation transposed into eschatological mode, as Paul could expect his readers to recognize. It is a transforming of believing man back into the image of God which disobedient man lost. It is the sharing of his glory with the man he had made and into which man never fully entered (3:23). And it has become possible because in one man, Jesus Christ, that image of God has come to full expression, not for himself alone but as a relationship he can share with others. At this climactic point Paul picks up again the emphasis of vv 15–17—that this divine goal is achieved only in and through Christ. Since the language of shared sonship ("eldest of many brothers") so clearly echoes that earlier statement, Paul would no doubt expect his readers to understand the Christological assertion in similar terms. That is to say, that what he has in view is Christ as eschatological Adam, the risen Christ who in his resurrection was crowned with glory and honor and given the dominion over all things originally intended for Adam (cf. Ps 8:4–6 and 1 Cor 15:20–27)—a power and privilege to be shared with an ever-widening circle as eldest brother, firstborn from the dead (cf. Col 1:18; Rev 1:5). Also that salvation is a process of being conformed to this image of the eschatological Adam, precisely through suffering with him and sharing his death to the final dying of the mortal body in sure and certain hope of sharing his risen life to the full (v 17; cf. Phil 3:10, 21; 2 Cor 3:18). In this way Paul recalls the great sweep of his earlier conclusion (5:15–19): as Adam by his disobedience brought many to death, so Christ has brought many to life. But now also the continuing hegemony of sin and death and their manipulation of the law through the weakness of the flesh, which still darkened that earlier conclusion (5:20–21), is shown to be short lived, the darkness sure to be expelled in the triumph of God's purpose. In this way Paul brings his exposition full circle, from the somber analysis of Adam's failing and self-destructiveness to the climax of the second Adam's success and life-productiveness.

D. Second Conclusion: The Triumph of God—His Faithfulness and the Assurance of Faith (8:31–39)

Bibliography

Balz, H. R. *Heilsvertrauen und Welterfahrung.* Munich: Kaiser, 1971. 116–23. **Caird, G. B.** *Principalities and Powers: A Study in Pauline Theology.* Oxford: Clarendon, 1956. **Dahl, N. A.** "The Atonement—An Adequate Reward for the Akedah? (Rom 8:32)." In *Neotestamentica et Semitica,* FS M. Black, ed. E. E. Ellis and M. Wilcox. Edinburgh: T. & T. Clark, 1969. 15–29. **Davies, P. R.** and **Chilton, B. D.** "The Aqedah: A Revised Tradition History." *CBQ* 40 (1978) 514–46. **Déaut, R. le.** "La presentation targumique du sacrifice d'Isaac et la soteriologie paulinienne." *SPCIC* 2:563–74. **Dibelius, M.** *Die Geisterwelt im Glauben des Paulus.* Göttingen: Vandenhoeck & Ruprecht, 1909. 110–13. **Fiedler, P.** "Röm 8:31–39 als Brennpunkt paulinischer Frohbotschaft." *ZNW* 68 (1977) 23–34. **Hay, D. M.** *Glory at the Right Hand: Psalm 110 in Early Christianity.* SBLMS 18. Abingdon: Nashville, 1973. **Hayward, R.** "The Present State of Research into the Targumic Account of the Sacrifice of Isaac." *JSS* 32 (1981) 127–50. **Hodgson, R.** "Paul the Apostle and First Century Tribulation Lists." *ZNW* 74 (1983) 59–80. **Kleinknecht, H.** *Gerechtfertigte.* 335–37, 342–47, 354–56. **Luz, U.** *Geschichtsverständnis.* 370–76. **Müller, C.** *Gottes Gerechtigkeit.* 57–72. **Münderlein, G.** "Interpretation einer Tradition. Bemerkungen zu Röm 8:35f." *KD* 11 (1965) 136–42. **Osten-Sacken, P. von der.** *Römer 8.* 14–60, 309–19. **Paulsen, H.** *Römer 8.* 133–77. **Roetzel, C.** "The Judgment Form in Paul's Letters." *JBL* 88 (1969) 305–12. **Schille, G.** "Die Liebe Gottes in Christus. Beobachtungen zu Röm 8:31–39." *ZNW* 59 (1968) 230–44. **Schlier, H.** *Principalities and Powers in the New Testament.* Freiburg: Herder, 1961. **Schoeps, H. J.** "The Sacrifice of Isaac in Paul's Theology." *JBL* 65 (1946) 385–92. **Schrage, W.** "Leid, Kreuz und Eschaton. Die Peristasenkataloge als Merkmale paulinischer theologia crucis und Eschatologie." *EvT* 34 (1974) 141–75. **Schwartz, D. R.** "Two Pauline Allusions to the Redemptive Mechanism of the Crucifixion." *JBL* 102 (1983) 259–68. **Segal, A. F.** "'He Who Did Not Spare His Own Son . . .': Jesus, Paul and the Akedah." In *From Jesus to Paul,* FS F. W. Beare, ed. P. Richardson and J. C. Hurd. Waterloo, Ontario: Wilfrid Laurier University, 1984. 169–84. **Swetnam, J.** *Jesus and Isaac.* AnBib 94. Rome: Biblical Institute, 1981. **Synofzik, E.** *Vergeltungsaussagen.* 101–4. **Thüsing, W.** *Per Christum.* 219–22. **Wengst, K.** *Formeln.* 55–56, 61. **Wink, W.** *Naming the Powers.* Philadelphia: Fortress, 1984. Esp. 47–50.

Translation

[31] *What therefore shall we say in view of these things? If God is for us, who is against us?* [32] *He who indeed did not spare his own Son but gave him up for us all, how shall he not also with him give us all things?* [33] *Who will bring charges against the elect of God? It is God who justifies.*[a] [34] *Who is there to condemn? It is Christ (Jesus)*[b] *who died, rather was raised,*[c] *who also is at the right hand of God, who also intercedes on our behalf.* [35] *Who will separate us from the love of Christ?*[d] *Affliction, or distress, or persecution, or hunger, or nakedness, or danger, or sword?* [36] *As it is written,*

For your sake we are being killed all the day;
we are reckoned as sheep for slaughter.

[37] *But in all these things we prevail completely through* [c] *him who loved us.* [38] *For I am convinced that neither death nor life, nor angels nor* [f] *rulers, neither things present nor things to come nor powers,* [g] [39] *neither height nor depth, nor any other creature will be able to separate us from the love of God which is in Christ Jesus our Lord.*

Notes

[a] It would be possible to punctuate all the phrases as questions (Lietzmann, Barrett, Fitzmyer, Achtemeier). The great majority punctuate as above (see, e.g., Cranfield).

[b] Textual traditions are more or less equally divided on whether Ἰησοῦς was original or was added.

[c] In some traditions, including ℵ*, ἐκ νεκρῶν has been added to ἐγερθείς, presumably since the fuller phrase is the more common (4:24; 6:4, 9; 7:4; 8:11; 10:9), but here it disturbs the parallel with ἀποθανών.

[d] ℵ reads θεοῦ (instead of Χριστοῦ), and B reads θεοῦ τῆς ἐν Χριστῷ Ἰησοῦ. The latter is almost certainly a harmonization with v 39, and the former also (see Lietzmann, Metzger), though perhaps it also reflects a certain monotheistic scrupulousness; but see *Comment*.

[e] D F G read διά + accusative = "on account of . . ."—thus narrowing the reference to a look back to the past event of Christ's death rather than maintaining the sense of a continuing flow of sustaining love.

[f] ἐξουσίαι has been added by some traditions in view of the usual association between it and ἀρχή (see *Form and Structure*).

[g] There was an understandable tendency in some traditions to move δυνάμεις back before ἐνεστῶτα to link it with its more natural associate ἀρχαί (see Metzger).

Form and Structure

The third main section (chaps. 6–8), having climaxed on a note of high and confident assurance (vv 26–30), sustains the crescendo in a purple passage of praise that what God has already done in and through Christ has established a bond of love which cannot be broken. "In this victory song of salvation assurance the whole letter has its center" (Schmidt). The rhythmic structure is probably the product of intense feeling rather than of artifice. The sense of exultation would no doubt be conveyed in the reading, with the pattern of question and answer determined by the flow of thought as voiced by the reader. The natural divisions, or longer pauses, would come between vv 31–32, 33–34, 35–37, and 38–39. V 32 may be regarded as an elaboration of v 31b, and vv 33–34 of 31c (Wilckens). Schmithals, *Anthropologie*, 178–80, suggests a diatribe format where vv 31b–32 function as basic statement, vv 33–37 as discussion, and vv 38–39 as resume. Typical of the exalted style is the echo of cherished formulae and the catching up of snatches of teaching material.

Whether we have to go further and see behind these verses an already structured hymnic form is much more debatable. In particular, Osten-Sacken's (24–25) reconstruction of a pre-Pauline form consisting of vv 31b–32a, 33–35a, 38–39 is open to the usual criticism of such reconstructions, in that it has to invert two clauses (vv 31b and 31c), and is somewhat arbitrary in cutting out vv 35b–37, including the *peristasis* (tribulation) catalog of v 35b, which on the face of it answers well to the question of v 35a. It is probably the case that vv 32 and 34 incorporate or at least echo already established confessional material (see on 8:32 and 8:34); but Paulsen (137–51) pushes too hard in arguing that vv 31–34 are drawn from a pre-Pauline hymn, since the two suggested strophes are quite unbalanced, thus undermining the grounds for seeing a preformed hymn in the first place.

As to the rest of the paragraph, the *peristasis* catalog in v 35 has several partial parallels elsewhere in Paul:

θλῖψις	Rom 2:9	2 Cor 6:4		2 Thess 1:4
στενοχωρία	Rom 2:9	2 Cor 6:4	2 Cor 12:10	
διωγμός			2 Cor 12:10	2 Thess 1:4
λιμός		2 Cor 11:27		
γυμνότης		2 Cor 11:27		
κίνδυνος		2 Cor 11:26		
μάχαιρα				

So too the sequence of ten items in vv 38–39 has several partial parallels in the Pauline corpus:

θάνατος	1 Cor 3:22		Phil 1:20			
ζωή	1 Cor 3:22		Phil 1:20			
ἄγγελοι						1 Pet 3:22
ἀρχαί		1 Cor 15:24	Col 1:16; 2:10, 15	Eph 1:21	3:10; 6:12	
ἐνεστῶτα	1 Cor 3:22			cf. Eph 1:21		
μέλλοντα	1 Cor 3:22			cf. Eph 1:21		
δυνάμεις		1 Cor 15:24		Eph 1:21		1 Pet 3:22
ὕψωμα				cf. 3:18		
βάθος				cf. 3:18		
κτίσις			cf. Col 1:16			

It is evident at a glance: (1) Paul's dictation, particularly of the second list, falls naturally into pairs—θάνατος/ζωή, ἐνεστῶτα/μέλλοντα, ὕψωμα/βάθος, and unusually ἄγγελοι/ἀρχαί (the normal pairing is ἀρχή/ἐξουσία—1 Cor 15:24; Eph 1:21; 3:10; 6:12; Col 1:16; 2:10, 15; cf. 1 Pet 3:22). The δυνάμεις disrupts the pairings, but there is no need to hypothesize any textual disturbance (cf. SH; Dibelius, *Geisterwelt*, 110); in the context of spontaneous dictation the finished form is likely to be less smooth than a piece polished for aesthetic effect (as Dibelius, 111, also noted; cf. Wilckens). Schille's suggestion ("Liebe," 238) that Paul inserted ἐνεστῶτα and μέλλοντα into traditional material is also unnecessary. (2) There is no evidence that Paul is drawing on established formulae or lists. On the contrary, the sequences here are marked both by the inclusion of unusual elements (cf. Col 1:16—θρόνος; Eph 6:12—κοσμοκράτωρ) and by the exclusion of more regular elements (cf., e.g., v 35 with the fuller lists of 2 Cor 6:4 and 11:27, and vv 38–39 with Col 1:16 and Eph 1:21). The most obvious conclusion is that this is Paul's own composition, drawing on familiar elements and naturally contrasting pairs, without any attempt at an exhaustive listing. "Nevertheless, one can see how close Paul's prose can come to hymnic style" (Käsemann).

The passage clearly functions as a conclusion to chap. 8 (Osten-Sacken, 53–57): vv 31–32 take up from the divine initiative of v 3, the assurance of no κατάκριμα in v 34 echoing that of v 1, the σὺν αὐτῷ of v 32 gathering up the συν- compounds of v 17 in particular, the ἐντυγχάνω of v 34 linking back to vv 26–27, and the climactic theme of complete victory in vv 35–39 dispelling any misgivings which might still linger from vv 17–28. But not just of chap. 8: the mood and theme is strongly reminiscent of 5:1–11 (cf. Dahl, *Studies,* 88–89; Osten-Sacken, 59–60; Kleinknecht, 337), and though sin and law are not mentioned (implied in vv 33–34), it is no accident that the first item of the final list (v 38) is death, the final threat left hanging over the believer at the end of chap. 5 and prominent thereafter, but mentioned for the last time in the letter at v 38. More striking still is the way 8:31–39 serves to sum up the whole argument to this point. It is not simply that there are a number of echoes and verbal allusions to the earlier chapters (παρέδωκεν—v 32; 1:24, 26, 28; δικαιόω—v 33; 2:13 etc.; κατακρίνω—v 34; 2:1; θλῖψις and στενοχωρία—v 35; 2:9; κτίσις—v 39; 1:25), but vv 31–34 in effect bring us back to the point reached at the beginning of chap. 3: there the heavenly trial scene with God's faithfulness to Israel having to be defended; here the same trial scene with God's faithfulness to his own being celebrated— a fitting climax to the exposition of God's faithfulness to faith (1:17).

This last observation points to another important feature of the passage— its strongly Jewish character: the allusion to Isaac in v 32 (meshed into an allusion to Isa 53:6—Kleinknecht, 344–45), "the elect of God" (v 33), the Christ (v 35), the use of Ps 44:22 (v 36), and the emphasis on the love of God (vv 37, 39); in addition Osten-Sacken, 30–34, cites a number of Jewish parallels to the question and answer sequence. Above all is the transformation of the theme of 3:1–8: God's faithful love endures through and surmounts all. As much here as anywhere Paul has taken over cherished themes of Israel's self-consciousness as the people of God and applied them without restriction to Gentile as well as Jew. Inevitably therefore his very formulation of this climactic statement of his gospel, here as well as in vv 18–30, forces his discerning reader to ask, If so, what then of God's people the Jews? In other words, as so often in his exposition, Paul uses the concluding statement of one argument to provide a lead into the next (see 5:20–21 *Form and Structure*).

Comment

31 τί οὖν ἐροῦμεν πρὸς ταῦτα; "what therefore shall we say in view of these things?" See on 3:5. For πρός in a transferred sense meaning "in reference to, concerning," see Moule, *Idiom Book,* 53. The question obviously introduces a conclusion, certainly to the final section 8:18–30; but since 8:18–30 is itself the climactic conclusion of the whole sequence of chap. 6–8 (matching the role of 5:12–21 in the section 1:18–5:21; see 8:18–30 *Form and Structure*), the ταῦτα can be taken to refer to the whole developed line of argument in chaps. 6–8; and since 8:18–30 effectively rounds off the whole argument so far (1:18–8:30; see again 8:18–30 *Form and Structure*) it is not going too far (despite Wilckens, n.767) to refer the ταῦτα to the whole (cf. Cranfield). NEB catches the mood well, "With all this in mind, what are we to say?"

εἰ ὁ θεὸς ὑπὲρ ἡμῶν, τίς καθ᾿ ἡμῶν; "if God is for us, who is against us?" The note of exuberance and joyous elation is unmistakable; cf. BDF §496.2. εἰ obviously means "if" in the sense "since it is so." For the ὑπέρ/κατά ("on our side/against") cf. particularly Mark 9:40 and 2 Cor 13:8. The strongly

Jewish character of the question should not be underplayed: (1) Its force derives from Jewish monotheism. The confidence is rooted not simply in *some* god being "for us," but the *one* God. This is why the answer to the question itself can be left open, and does not depend on the answer "No one." There may be many "against us" (cf. vv 38–39), but in relation to the one God, they are as nothing. The confidence is that of Isa 40 ff. (2) The phrase echoes similar expressions of confidence in the Psalms and strikes a basic chord in the theme of the suffering righteous (Kleinknecht, 342). Cranfield quite properly cites Pss 23:4; 56:9 (not LXX), 12; and 118:6–7; Wilckens's objection that the psalmist's formulation is μεθ᾽ ἡμῶν rather than ὑπὲρ ἡμῶν is not decisive since the two prepositions are so nearly synonymous at this point (cf. Mark 9:40 with Matt 12:30). (3) Since Paul is obviously looking forward to the consummation of God's purpose (vv 29–30), the thought is probably already on the final judgment at the end of history (cf. Michel), as the following verses seem to confirm. The point then is that in the final judgment God's purpose will prevail and be seen to have done so through the preceding more ambiguous history. As such, the verse and what follows takes up and provides a part answer to the issue raised in 3:1–8. As in 3:3–6 the issue is the faithfulness of God; so here it is in effect the triumph of God's faithfulness to his own which is asserted so boldly (God "for us," not merely for himself). But now the beneficiaries of that faithfulness have been redefined as those who are κατὰ πνεῦμα.

Once again, therefore, the extent to which Paul sees his mission and its outcome as the fulfillment of *Jewish* hope is underlined. The more clearly this is seen, of course, the sharper becomes the yet unanswered part of 3:1–8: given this confident assurance of faith in respect of Christ, what of God's faithfulness to those originally elected as God's people? When the extent to which Paul here understands Christian assurance in terms of Jewish heritage is thus grasped, the transition between the end of chap. 8 and the beginning of chap. 9 ceases to be a problem. So too when the depth of the Jewish context of Paul's thought is grasped here the suggestion that Paul is drawing on Stoic parallels, in any more than an incidental way, is undermined (cf. Cranfield; parallel in Bultmann, *Stil,* 19). The more the phrase "God for us" is understood as a summary of Paul's gospel, the more important becomes the Jewish character and continuity implicit in it.

32 ὃς γε τοῦ ἰδίου υἱοῦ οὐκ ἐφείσατο ἀλλὰ ὑπὲρ ἡμῶν πάντων παρέδωκεν αὐτόν, "he who indeed did not spare his own son but gave him up for us all." The γέ is probably intensive, emphasizing either the following phrase—"even his own Son" (BGD)—or the preceding—"he who indeed" (cf. BDF, §439.3). The ἰδίου matches the ἑαυτοῦ of v 3. οὐ φείδεσθαι here as in 11:21 and 2 Cor 13:2 has the note of judgment executed, the same judgment as fallen man's conduct calls forth (1:32); see on 8:3. The παρέδωκεν clause certainly echoes a well-established Christian theological understanding of Christ's death (see further on 4:25). The active form of the verb differs from the passive in 4:25, and though the active is the more regular Christian formulation, at this point it serves to answer the triple παρέδωκεν of 1:24, 26, 28, thus strengthening the impression that 8:31–39 is intended to round off the whole argument thus far (1:18–8:30; see *Form and Structure*): God's handing over his Son in grace answers his handing over his creatures in wrath. ὑπέρ can mean simply "for the benefit of" (8:27, 31, 34; 9:27; 10:1; 15:30; 16:4; etc.), but in this context it signifies the vicariously representative death of sacrifice (14:15; 1 Cor 1:13; 11:24; 15:3; etc.) or martyr (cf. 5:6–8; 9:3). The addition of πάντων to the usual formula is also clearly deliberate—*all*, including Gentile as well as Jew—thus in line with Paul's consistent use of the same word in Romans (cf. particularly 1:5, 16; 2:9–10; 3:4, 9, 20, 22, 23; 4:11, 16; 5:12, 18), which reemerges explicitly in 10:4, 11, 12, 13; 11:26, 32, and again in 15:11, 33 and 16:26. The "us" therefore is "the new humanity" (Michel) who constitute the brothers and sisters of the risen Christ, the eschatological Adam (v 29).

It is difficult to avoid seeing in the first clause an allusion to Gen 22:16 (so most who raise the issue; see, e.g., Schoeps, le Déaut, and others cited in Swetnam, 80 n.459; to which add particularly Wilckens; against particularly Kuss and Schlier):

Rom 8:32:	τοῦ ἰδίου υἱοῦ οὐκ ἐφείσατο
Gen 22:16 LXX:	οὐκ ἐφείσω τοῦ υἱοῦ σου τοῦ ἀγαπητοῦ
Gen 22:16 MT:	וְלֹא חָשַׂכְתָּ אֶת־בִּנְךָ אֶת־יְחִידְךָ

Paul uses ἰδίου rather than ἀγαπητοῦ, but the difference is not great, and Paul may have wanted to avoid any confusion of his assertion of Christ's elder brotherhood (vv 14–17, 29) which ἀγαπητός = יָחִיד ("only one") might cause (he wanted to assert that his readers are ἀγαπητοί—1:7; cf. 11:28 and 12:19). Even so, a Jew as familiar with OT language as was Paul could hardly have been unaware that he was echoing Gen 22:16 (an echo of 2 Sam 21:1–14 is more remote, despite Schwarz, 265–66).

The more crucial question is whether Paul was simply adapting a familiar phrase without intending to make any theological capital out of it, or used it deliberately with theological (and polemical) intent. The issue is complicated by the still-continuing dispute regarding the extent to which there was already a tradition of Jewish reflection about the binding of Isaac. In particular there is some doubt as to how far Jewish thought had already before A.D. 70 attributed vicarious significance to the event (Davies and Chilton; but see also Hayward and Segal; the debate turns on such points as the significance of Philo, *Abr.* 172, and the dating of Ps. Philo [NB 18.5; 32.2–4; 40.2], as well as the targumic traditions). However, we do know that Abraham's offering of Isaac was a matter of considerable importance in pre-Pauline Judaism, as a demonstration of Abraham's faithfulness (see on 4:2). If Paul is making a particular point here, therefore, it is not in terms of the atonement being an adequate reward for the Akedah (= binding or sacrifice of Isaac) (against Dahl, "Atonement," who pays too little attention to the context of 8:32 within Romans). The point being made rather comes out in the contrast between chap. 4 and 8:32: Paul has excluded or ignored any reference to the offering of Isaac in chap. 4, where his Jewish interlocutor would have expected it; and instead he has introduced his allusion at the climax of his argument, and referred it to God. In what must be accounted a very neat turning of the tables, Paul indicates that Abraham's offering of his son serves as a type not of the faithfulness of the devout Jew, but rather of the faithfulness of God.

πῶς οὐχὶ καὶ σὺν αὐτῷ τὰ πάντα ἡμῖν χαρίσεται; "how shall he not also with him give us all things?" The πῶς plays the same role as πολλῷ μᾶλλον in 5:9, 10, 15, 17, underlining the same exultant note of confidence typical of both these concluding sections (5:1–21 and 8:31–39). The σὺν αὐτῷ must take up the παρέδωκεν: God has given his Son; in addition he will give "all things." Though whether the thought is simply of Christ's death as guarantee of what is yet to come (Kuss) or of the giving of Christ as involving his solidarity in sinful flesh (v 3) and the fellowship of his sufferings and glorification (v 17) (so Michel) is less clear. In view of the prominence of Adam Christology motifs in the preceding context, the latter is more likely.

Most take τὰ πάντα as referring to "the fullness of salvation" (Cranfield; cf. 5:10). While it can obviously denote "everything" just referred to (as in 2 Cor 4:15; 5:18; 12:19; Phil 3:8; Col 3:8), it probably refers here to "the all" = creation (Wilckens): τὰ πάντα most often has this sense in Paul (11:36; 1 Cor 8:6; 11:12; 15:27–28; Phil 3:21; Col 1:16–17, 20; Eph 1:10–11, 23; 3:9; 4:10); and it fits best with the Adam Christology which has lain behind vv 18–30 in particular (cf. again 1 Cor 15:27; Phil 3:21; Eph 1:22). In other words what seems to be envisaged is a sharing in Christ's lordship (Ps 110:1 alluded to in v 34) over "the all" (Ps 8:6 being regularly merged with Ps 110:1 in earliest Christian thought—Dunn, *Christology*, 108–10); Christ again being understood as the one who fulfills God's mandate for man (Ps 8:6), but precisely as the head of a new humanity who share his sonship and his devolved authority. The χαρίσεται is therefore a genuine future, looking to the final completion of God's original purpose in making man. The sense of "give graciously, freely, as a favor" (BGD; see also Cranfield) is obviously of deliberate intent: it not merely reinforces in this rounding off conclusion the emphasis on grace (χάρις) so characteristic of Paul's gospel (1:5; 3:24; 4:4, 16; 5:2, 15, 17, 20, 21; 6:1, 14, 15); it also underscores the basic point that man's lordship over creation *is* a gift from God, and only to be exercised as such in dependence on him. Once again the triumph of God's creative purpose answers the slavery to things which man's failure to acknowledge this dependence on God had brought him to (1:21–25).

33 τίς ἐγκαλέσει κατὰ ἐκλεκτῶν θεοῦ; "who will bring charges against the elect of God?" ἐγκαλέω is a legal t.t. referring to the formal process of laying charges against someone—so also "accuse, prosecute, take proceedings against" (LSJ, MM; in biblical Greek Prov 19:5; Wisd Sol 12:12; Sir 46:19; Acts 19:38; 23:28; cf. ἔγκλημα). Clearly envisaged is the final judgment scene at the close of history (see further on 2:2). Though the rhetorical form renders it unnecessary to seek a reference to a particular accuser, a Jewish reader would think naturally of (the) Satan (in view of Job 1–2 and Zech 3:1–2), even though the role of Satan had become much elaborated in Jewish thought in the meantime (*IDB* 4:224–28; see further on 16:20).

With the phrase ἐκλεκτοὶ θεοῦ Paul once again takes over a central element in Jewish self-understanding (1 Chron 16:13; Pss 89:3 [LXX 88:4]; 105 [LXX 104]:6; Isa 42:1 LXX; 43:20; 45:4; 65:9, 15, 22 [LXX 22–23]; Sir 46:1; 47:22; Wisd Sol 3:9; 4:15; *Jub.* 1.29; *1 Enoch* 1.3, 8; 5.7–8; 25.5; 93.2; intensified in the *Similitudes* [40.5; 41.2; 48.1; 51.5; etc.]; 1QS 8.6; CD 4.3–4; 1QM 12.1, 4 [?]; 1QH 2.13; 1QpHab 10.13; *Sib. Or.* 3.69); see also *TDNT* 4:182–84. It is one of Paul's major concerns to demonstrate the continuity between the Israel of old and the eschatological people of God (see *Form and Structure*), and one he shares with other NT writers (cf. Mark 13:20, 22, 27 par.; Luke 18:7; Col 3:12; Titus 1:1; 1 Pet 1:1; Rev 17:14).

θεὸς ὁ δικαιῶν, "it is God who justifies." The immediate repetition of θεός increases the emphasis on it. For δικαιόω see on 2:13 and 8:30, the present tense once again reminding us that God's justifying action is not a once-for-all event (at conversion or whenever), but an ongoing sustaining. And with the thought so clearly on the final judgment, the idea of δικαιοῦν as God's final vindication and acquittal is certainly present. As is generally agreed, it must be regarded as highly likely that Paul here echoes, deliberately or unconsciously, Isa 50:8: ἐγγίζει ὁ δικαιώσας με· τίς ὁ κρινόμενός μοι; (in more detail, Osten-Sacken, 43–45). In the picture of God's servant in Isa 50 Paul sees not Christ but Christians (Wilckens).

34 τίς ὁ κατακρινῶν; "who is there to condemn?" This translation helps bring out the ambiguity of the Greek since the verb could be punctuated either as a present or a future; but it is almost certainly eschatological in intent, again referring to the final judgment (Michel; Synofzik, 103). Since it is the judge (= God) who alone can give sentence of condemnation, the question has already been answered in the previous phrase (NJB follows an ancient tradition of the Greek Fathers [see Lagrange] in running vv 33b and 34a together: "When God grants saving justice who can condemn?"); however, Paul's answer serves to underline the degree to which already Christ was seen as having been given share in *God's* role as judge (cf. particularly 2:16 and 2 Cor 5:10 with Rom 14:10; and see below).

Χριστὸς (Ἰησοῦς) ὁ ἀποθανών, μᾶλλον δὲ ἐγερθείς, "it is Christ (Jesus) who died, rather was raised." The "died . . . was raised" has a formulaic ring (cf. particularly 1 Cor 15:3–4; 2 Cor 5:15; 1 Thess 4:14), but it is the balanced form of the statement which is more established than the particular wording (cf. especially elsewhere in Romans—5:10; 6:4, 9–10; 7:4; 14:9). The μᾶλλον supplements and thereby clarifies or indeed corrects what has preceded (cf. 1 Cor 14:1, 5; Gal 4:9; BGD 3d), and so has the same effect as the πολλῷ μᾶλλον of 5:9–10. It is important for Paul's soteriology to remember that Jesus' death was not decisive for salvation on its own. Paul is still thinking in terms of Adam soteriology, of Jesus' death as an end of Adam (see on 8:3), opening the way for the new Adam to appear in resurrection (1 Cor 15:20–22).

ὃς καί ἐστιν ἐν δεξιᾷ τοῦ θεοῦ, "who also is at the right hand of God." The echo of Ps 110 [LXX 109]:1 (εἶπεν ὁ κύριος τῷ κυρίῳ μου, Κάθου ἐκ δεξιῶν μου) is obviously deliberate: the frequency with which the passage is cited in the NT shows clearly that it was a passage much loved and used in earliest Christology (Mark 12:36 pars.; 14:62 pars.; Acts 2:34–35; Heb 1:13; and with ἐν as the preposition, as above—Eph 1:20; Col 3:1; Heb 1:3; 8:1; 10:12; 12:2; 1 Pet 3:22; see also Hay, and on 10:9). "The right hand" denotes power (see, e.g., Exod 15:6, 12; Deut 33:2; Job 40:9; Pss 17:7; 18:35; etc.; BGD fittingly cites *Pss. Sol.* 13.1; Josephus, *War* 1.378); hence a seat at the right hand is the seat of special honor (1 Kgs 2:19; Ps 45:9; in the NT particularly Acts 2:33; 5:31; and 7:55–56).

To appreciate the significance of Ps 110:1 being used of Jesus we must note two points. (1) The force of the original psalm would presumably have been a highly honorific way of asserting that Israel's king was appointed by God as, in effect, God's vice-regent over his people. (2) In the period around and following Paul there seems to have been a fair degree of speculation regarding heroes of the faith having been exalted to a glorious throne in heaven—a speculation probably stimulated by the plural "thrones" in Dan 7:9; so particularly Adam (*T. Abr.* 11.4–18), Enoch (*Sim. Enoch = 1 Enoch* 45.3; 51.3; 55.4; 61.8; 69.27–29; 71.14), Melchizedek (11QMelch), Job (*T. Job* 33.3), the Messiah (R. Akiba, according to *b. Sanh.* 38b). The striking feature of the earliest Christian use of Ps 110:1 then is not the claim itself, but the fact that it was made of one whose life was of very recent memory (rather than of a hero from the dim mists of Israel's ancient past). Those who see here simply a case of "cognitive dissonance" (a failed prophecy being met by its vigorous reassertion as a way of coping with the failure) should ask themselves why the Teacher of Righteousness at Qumran or the failed messianic prophets of the time (Theudas, the Egyptian, etc.; Josephus, *Ant.* 20.97–98, 169–72) did not come to be spoken of in the same way.

ὃς καὶ ἐντυγχάνει ὑπὲρ ἡμῶν, "who also intercedes on our behalf." For ἐντυγχάνω see on 8:27. The imagery is of heavenly intercession such as was attributed to angels already within Jewish thought (see on 8:26; cf. Enoch in *1 Enoch* 13.4, but 14.4–7). We have here therefore another example of earliest Christology taking over various categories used to describe the reality of heaven and focusing them in an exclusive and exhaustive way on Christ. The thought was very important for Hebrews (particularly 7:25; cf. 1 John 2:1), but here may be as much an outworking of Paul's Adam Christology (the last Adam interceding for his race, somewhat like *T. Abr.* 11), as of a latent high-priest Christology. Kleinknecht (345) notes that the theme of intercession can also be tied into that of the suffering righteous (Job 42:8–10; Isa 53:12; *T. Ben.* 3.6–8). On the relation to the intercession of the Spirit in v 26 see Wilckens.

35 τίς ἡμᾶς χωρίσει ἀπὸ τῆς ἀγάπης τοῦ Χριστοῦ; "who will separate us from the love of Christ?" The word order gives some emphasis to the ἡμᾶς. The rhetorical denial of the possibility of such separation is in effect a restatement of the strong συν- emphasis stemming from v 17, the point being that such sufferings as are about to be listed should be seen as evidence of union with the crucified one, not a cause for doubting his love. The free interchange in the Paulines between the phrases ἀγάπη τοῦ θεοῦ (5:5; 8:39; 2 Cor 13:13; 2 Thess 3:5) and ἀγάπη τοῦ Χριστοῦ (8:35—see *Form and Structure*; 2 Cor 5:14; Eph 3:19) is striking (elsewhere in the NT only the former—Luke 11:42; John 5:42; 1 John 2:5; 3:17; 4:9; 5:3; Jude 21), as also perhaps the presence of the definite article with Χριστός reflecting once again the degree to which Paul was thinking in Jewish terms—Jesus as the Messiah who has fulfilled the Jewish expectation and hope, not least by expressing and embodying the (covenant) love of God for his people (see also on 7:4 and 9:3, 5).

θλῖψις ἢ στενοχωρία ἢ διωγμὸς ἢ λιμὸς ἢ γυμνότης ἢ κίνδυνος ἢ μάχαιρα, "affliction or distress or persecution or hunger or nakedness or danger or sword." With θλῖψις and στενοχωρία the fearsome tribulation of the end time is in view;

see further on 8:18; for the words themselves see on 2:9. In our literature διωγμός always means persecution for religious reasons; with the listing here, cf. particularly Mark 4:17 par.; 2 Cor 12:10; and 2 Thess 1:4. λιμός, "hunger, famine," is also a feature of "the last days" in Mark 13:8 pars.; Rev 6:8; and 18:8. In this context γυμνότης, "nakedness," naturally has a negative connotation = lack of clothing necessary to bodily health and normal relationships; hunger and lack of proper clothing are natural associates in a description of human deprivation (cf., e.g., *T. Zeb.* 7.1; Matt 25:35–36; 2 Cor 11:27; James 2:15). κίνδυνος, "danger, risk"; elsewhere in the NT only in 2 Cor 11:26. μάχαιρα, "sword," is an obvious metonomy for violent death or war (cf. Gen 31:26; *Sib. Or.* 8.120; Matt 10:34; BGD). NJB translates the last two items, "threats or violence." It may be no accident that Paul brings the list to a climax in just these two words, including the unusual μάχαιρα, since he may have suspected that these might very well prove to be final hurdles in his own case (cf. 15:31).

Similar lists are well known elsewhere, particularly in Stoic literature; *Peristasenkatalog* = catalog of difficult circumstances (περιστάσεις); see, e.g., Epictetus' discourse on the subject, with particular reference to nakedness (1.24) and his catalog in 3.24.28–29 (see further Bultmann, *Stil*, 19; Lagrange, 218). Other not dissimilar lists of opposing circumstances or tribulations naturally appear in Jewish literature, particularly in eschatological contexts (cf., e.g., *Jub.* 23.13; *1 Enoch* 103.9–15; *Pss. Sol.* 15.7; see further Schrage, "Leid," 143–46; Hodgson shows that the net can be cast still wider, citing examples from Josephus, Nag Hammadi, the Mishnah, and Plutarch). Paul uses the form regularly in 2 Cor (4:7–12; 6:4–10; 11:23–27; 12:10); see further V. P. Furnish, *2 Corinthians* AB (1984) ad loc. with literature. The list here contains several elements in common with 2 Cor 11 (κίνδυνος, λιμός, γυμνότης) and 2 Cor 12 (διωγμός, στενοχωρία). Like the 2 Cor 11 list, it focuses exclusively on outward tribulation, without evincing the consciousness of an inner dimension which elsewhere is so typical of Paul's sense of eschatological tension. To that extent the list here is nearer to the Stoic parallels in its immediate form; but, of course, the thought of Christian suffering continues to be controlled by v 17, echoed in v 35a. The parallel with 2 Cor 11:23–27 also makes clear that such a list is not a mere literary form but is a firsthand expression of Paul's own experience. Since he regarded his own experience as the outworking of the eschatological tension between the ages (of Adam and of Christ), he naturally saw his experience as typical for all his fellow believers (Michel, Käsemann).

36 καθὼς γέγραπται ὅτι, "as it is written"; see on 1:17.

> Ἕνεκεν σοῦ θανατούμεθα ὅλην τὴν ἡμέραν,
> ἐλογίσθημεν ὡς πρόβατα σφαγῆς.
> For your sake we are being killed the whole day
> we are reckoned as sheep for slaughter.

The quotation is verbatim from Ps 44:22 [LXX 43:23]. Subsequently it was used by the rabbis in reference to the martyrs of the Maccabean and Hadrian times (Str-B 3:259–60), but there may already be an echo in Zech 11:4, 7 (πρόβατα τῆς σφαγῆς); cf. also Isa 53:7. This should not be taken as an indication that Jews generally expected persecution or as proof of an anti-Semitism deeply rooted in the ancient world. Jews as such were by no means unpopular or disliked as a rule (see *Introduction* §2.2.2). Where they were held in disdain, it was not necessarily on grounds of race but because of their peculiar practices (refusal to eat pork, etc.) and unwillingness to recognize any god but their own (see also *Introduction* §2.3.1). The persecution referred to in such passages as Zech 11 and Wisd Sol 5 included internal strife, persecution of righteous (Jew) by unrighteous (Jew). For tribulation as the necessary precursor to the new age see on 8:18; cf. *1 Enoch* 103.9–15.

Given the parallel with the Maccabean martyrs, it is not insignificant that whereas the Maccabean martyrs died "for the sake of God's laws" (2 Macc 7:9, 11; similarly *4 Ezra* 7.89), in Paul's thought Christ has become the decisive expression of the special relation between God and his people (vv 35, 39); cf. Matt 5:11; Mark 8:35; Rev 1:9. ὅλην τὴν ἡμέραν, "all the day," is semitic, indicating no escape; cf. 1 Cor 15:31 and 2 Cor 4:10–11 (Michel).

37 ἀλλ' ἐν τούτοις πᾶσιν ὑπερνικῶμεν διὰ τοῦ ἀγαπήσαντος ἡμᾶς, "but in all these things we prevail completely through him who loved us." For ἐν τούτοις πᾶσιν, "in (the midst of) all these things" is probably to be preferred to "in spite of all these things" (Cranfield, against Bruce). ὑπερνικάω is a heightened form of νικάω, hence something like "win a glorious victory, win more than a victory"; hence AV/KJV, RSV, and NIV, "we are more than conquerors"; NEB, "overwhelming victory is ours." Note again the parallel from Stoicism in Epictetus 1.18.22 (*TDNT* 4:942, 944). The Christian addition is noteworthy: both the exhilaration of the ὑπερ- compound, and the διὰ τοῦ ἀγαπήσαντος ἡμᾶς, "through him who loved us"; the aorist referring to God's love expressed in the gift of his Son (vv 31–32). Paul is fond of ὑπερ- compounds (Schlier): ὑπεραυξάνω (2 Thess 1:3), ὑπερβαλλόντως (2 Cor 11:23), ὑπερβάλλω (2 Cor 3:10; 9:14; cf. Eph 1:19; 2:7; 3:19), ὑπερβολή (Rom 7:13; 1 Cor 12:31; 2 Cor 1:8; etc.), ὑπερεκπερισσοῦ (1 Thess 3:10; 5:13; cf. Eph 3:20), ὑπερεκπερισσῶς (1 Thess 5:13), ὑπερεντυγχάνω (Rom 8:26), ὑπερέχω (Phil 2:3; 3:8; 4:7), ὑπερλίαν (2 Cor 11:5; 12:11), ὑπερπερισσεύω (Rom 5:20; 2 Cor 7:4), ὑπερυψόω (Phil 2:9), ὑπερφρονέω (Rom 12:3). Between them, the συν- (see on 6:4) and the ὑπερ- compounds characterize the distinctive and central emphases of Paul's soteriology.

38 πέπεισμαι γὰρ ὅτι οὔτε . . . οὔτε . . . , "for I am convinced that neither . . . neither. . . ." The force of the perfect passive is to underline Paul's complete certainty ("I have been convinced and continue to be so; nothing has shaken that assurance"); cf. particularly 14:14; 15:14; 2 Tim 1:5, 12, Heb 6:9, Pol. *Phil.* 9.2 (BGD, πείθω 4). The forcefulness of the assertion is strengthened by the sequence of οὔτε (rather than ἤ, as in v 35). The conviction of course is based primarily on God's love in Christ (vv 35, 39) as displayed especially on the cross (v 32) and subsequent triumph (v 34; cf. particularly 14:9; 1 Cor 15:25–27; Col 2:15); not simply as a matter of rational persuasion, but also as something experienced (5:5).

οὔτε θάνατος οὔτε ζωή, "neither death nor life." θάνατος appropriately heads the list, not simply because of v 36, but primarily because death has loomed throughout chaps. 5–8 as the great hostile power (see chaps. 6–8 *Introduction*), the fullest measure of sin's power over this age (cf. 1 Cor 15:26; see on

5:12, 21). Vv 38–39 therefore pick up the conclusion of 5:21 with the problem posed in it of sin's continuing rule over this age now answered as fully as it can be (chaps. 6–8). See also Cranfield. In view of the repeated contrast between death and life throughout the preceding chapters (see again chaps. 6–8 *Introduction*), the fact that the two are here linked in negative conjunction is somewhat surprising. It is not necessary to suppose that Paul is now thinking of "life" as a personified or angelic being or hostile power. The contrast clearly narrows the thought to "this life" and reflects Paul's understanding of life in this age as one of suffering (vv 17ff.) and not-yet-achieved salvation (cf. 2 Cor 5:8; Phil 1:23). That apart, the death/life pairing is simply a way of embracing every conceivable condition of humankind (cf. 14:7–9; 1 Cor 3:22; Phil 1:20).

οὔτε ἄγγελοι οὔτε ἀρχαί, "neither angels nor rulers." Both words occur for the only time in Romans. ἄγγελοι is simply a name for the beings who people heaven (in distinction from those who people earth; cf. 1 Cor 4:9; 13:1), usually conceived as agents of heaven or intermediaries between heaven and earth (cf. Gal 1:8; 4:14). As such it can be used of "good" angels ("angels of the presence," etc.; see on 8:26; cf. 2 Cor 11:14; 2 Thess 1:7), but just as readily for hostile angels, regularly related to Gen 6:1–4 (see, e.g., *1 Enoch* 6–8; *Jub.* 5.1; *T. Reub.* 5.6; further BGD, ἄγγελος). A more negative note frequently attaching to the word is a somewhat surprising feature of Paul's usage, as here (1 Cor 6:3; 11:10; 2 Cor 12:7; Gal 3:19; Col 2:18). Paul probably has in mind particularly the idea of angels as inhabiting the lower reaches of heaven (or lower heavens; cf. 2 Cor 12:2; Eph 6:12), and therefore as a potential barrier between God and his people on earth; but also perhaps the idea of angels as rulers of the nations (Deut 32:8; Dan 10:13; Sir 17:17; *Jub.* 15.31–32) and therefore potential opponents to God's extending his direct rule over the Gentiles as well as the Jewish nation. The lack of specification is probably intentional—the whole range of heavenly beings, however conceived. ἀρχαί is the most frequently used name for angelic and demonic powers in the different listings of the Pauline corpus (see *Form and Structure*); "demons" (NIV) is too limiting a translation. The fact that it also denotes civil or political officials implies that the heavenly community was conceived as similarly structured. See further on 13:1.

οὔτε ἐνεστῶτα οὔτε μέλλοντα, "neither things present nor things to come." The perfect participle of ἐνίστημι forms a natural antithesis with the present participle of μέλλω (as in Sextus Empiricus 2.193; Plato, *Plant.* 114; *PGM* 5.295; in Christian literature 1 Cor 3:22; *Barn.* 1.7; 4.1; 5.3); on μέλλοντα cf. Col 2:17. It is not necessary to assume that hostile beings are in mind (Wilckens), particularly in view of vv 18–23, 28, 35, even if Paul would naturally think of heavenly agency in the adverse occurrences of life (cf. 2 Cor 12:7). Whether deliberate or not the inclusion of the time dimension in the list substantially heightens the note of assurance.

οὔτε δυνάμεις, "neither powers"—another title for supernatural beings, quite familiar in extrabiblical Greek as well as Judeo-Christian literature (see BGD, δύναμις 5, 6). It was natural to conceive of heavenly beings as characterized by power (e.g., 2 Kgs 17:16 LXX; *4 Macc* 5.13; Philo, *Conf.* 171; Matt 24:29; Mark 14:62; Acts 8:10). See also *Form and Structure*.

39 οὔτε ὕψωμα οὔτε βάθος, "neither height nor depth." The contrast most

likely uses astronomical terms: ὕψωμα as the apogee of the planets, the highest
point in the heavens reached by the heavenly body (Knox, *Gentiles*, 106–7;
TDNT 8:613). The more usual antithetical partner is ταπείνωμα = the lowest
point in the planet's course (see LSJ). βάθος is also used as the opposite (Vettius
Valens 241.26), but usually of the celestial space below the horizon from
which the stars arise (Lietzmann; BGD). The fact that the list runs on to
"any other creature" could suggest that Paul has in mind celestial powers
(Schlatter, Lietzmann, Black, Käsemann), but in view of the impersonal character of ἐνεστῶτα and μέλλοντα it may be that he meant only the full extent of
space above (visible) and below (SH; *TDNT* 8:614; and especially Cranfield,
referring to Ps 139:8, followed by Zeller; Wink, 49, refers particularly to *1
Enoch* 18.11). At the very least his thought and assurance embrace all that is
or can be imagined as belonging to the full sweep of space as well as of
time.

οὔτε τις κτίσις ἐτέρα, "nor any other creature." Since God alone is creator,
nothing else is omitted in κτίσις. The status of the preceding members of the
list is likewise relativized: powers etc. they may be, but only creatures. The
phrase not only ties up the thread of vv 19–22 but also provides the appropriate
answer to 1:25: the role of the creature as creature is reaffirmed; God's act
in Christ corrects the false and futile condition of creation in this age.

δυνήσεται ἡμᾶς χωρίσαι ἀπὸ τῆς ἀγάπης τοῦ θεοῦ τῆς ἐν Χριστῷ Ἰησοῦ τῷ κυρίῳ
ἡμῶν, "shall be able to separate us from the love of God which is in Christ
Jesus our Lord." The final emphasis on the love of God is not accidental in
view of vv 28, 35, 37. As Michel rightly notes: in Jewish thought "love" is
bound up with election (see on 1:7 and 8:28). Here again it is no accident
that Paul sums up his gospel as a whole and the argument of chaps. 6–8 in
particular in this way, since it is precisely his claim that God's covenanted
love in Christ embraces *all* who believe, the "us" who own Christ Jesus as
Lord, Gentile as well as Jew. Not only so, but these final words sum up in
most emphatic tone Paul's confidence in the *faithfulness* of God to those whom
his love has thus embraced and sustains. Both points (the faithfulness of his
love for Gentile as well as Jew) provide the natural bridge forward into chaps.
9–11.

As in 5:21 and 6:23 (also 7:25a) the final phrase rounds off the argument
with fitting solemnity. The variation of preposition in these final formulations
(ἐν—6:23; 8:39; διά—5:21; 7:25) indicates that the thought of Jesus as embodying God's gift/love and as mediating his grace and our thanks are closely
interconnected and overlapping ideas for Paul. Certainly we can take it as
central to Paul's understanding of God and of God's relation to Jesus, that
it is *God's* love which Jesus expresses. See also on 5:21 and 6:23.

Explanation

31 Paul has now said all that needs saying to show that his understanding
of the gospel as bringing the righteousness of God to all through faith apart
from the law does not discourage moral effort (chap. 6), or abandon the
law to sin and death (chap. 7), or ignore the reality of the believer's still
being subject to the weakness of the flesh (chap. 8). With mounting assurance
of faith he lets slip the halter of the eschatological qualification a further

notch and gives free rein to his confidence in God. The thought flows directly from the preceding line of argument—the gift of the Spirit as God's commitment to them, and despite continuing suffering and the shared weakness of the present order, the assurance of God's purpose over all. But Paul lifts his eyes still higher in an expression of trust which looks beyond individual believers, and even the cosmic character of the present age, to embrace all reality and time. As such his paean of praise provides a fitting conclusion to the whole argument from 1:18 onwards—a praise of God as creator, the ultimate power behind, beyond, above the universe. With the one God, creator of all things, and all things being "for us," the opposition of anything else or of any other beings is the opposition of infinitely lesser forces, whose power, however terrible it may appear to those still within this age, is still as nothing beside the power of God. In thus giving God the glory and thanksgiving due him as creator, Paul shows how faith in Christ restores man to that position of trustful dependence, the abandonment of which has been his downfall (1:21). As such too all his arguments about man's "faith" have been transposed into a celebration of God's faithfulness. So that vv 31–39 become also a conclusion to the exposition of 1:16–17—or, more precisely, a partial conclusion, since such a triumphant assertion of God's faithfulness inevitably forces the reader back to the still suspended question, What then of God's faithfulness to Israel? (chaps. 9–11).

32 The ground of Paul's assurance as to God's faithfulness to his own is preeminently Christ. In the preceding section the experience of the Spirit in his own and his fellow believers' lives had largely filled the horizon of Paul's thought. But that was the climax of the particular line of argument he had developed through the preceding chapters. Now he steps back a little, and in the larger picture, embracing the whole of time and space, it is the Christ event which is the mid-point of time, the fulcrum point of all. Not that the importance of the considerations adduced from the presence of the Spirit is lessened, simply that the derivative character of the Spirit's work in salvation is underlined, as reproducing the sonship of Christ both now and in the resurrection (8:15–23).

In particular, the ground of assurance is the death of Christ, God's not sparing his own Son, but handing him over "for us all." The richness of the allusion, picking up elements of already traditional formulation, would probably not be lost on his readers, not least the echo of Abraham's offering of Isaac (Gen 22:12, 16), the talk of Christ's death as a handing over (cf. Rom 4:25), and the evocation of Paul's earlier description of Jesus' death as a sacrifice provided by God (3:25; 8:3). But what the language emphasizes here is less the idea of Jesus' death as sacrifice, and more the thought of God's commitment to his own in and through Christ (God for us). The extent of God's commitment to his flawed creation is his giving of his own Son to death in oneness with and on behalf of that creation. In a way which even the metaphor of sonship can only express imperfectly Paul sees Christ as the commitment of God.

As in 5:9–10, Paul's faith surges forth from that central point. If God has already committed himself so far, given so much of himself, then of a surety with Christ "he will graciously give us all things." Paul may have had in mind simply those things necessary for salvation. But in a context where the thought has already been transposed to a cosmic perspective it is more likely that he had in mind the "all things" of creation, the "all things" which God intended to put under man's feet from the first (Ps 8:6). This goal of creation has been achieved in Christ the new man, firstborn from the dead and eldest brother of a new family (v 29). As he has been given lordship over all things at God's right hand (v 34—Ps 110:1), so those who are Christ's will "with him" share that dominion over the rest of creation, thus fulfilling the original purpose of the creator for man made in his image. As the Spirit is the first installment and guarantee of God's redemptive purpose at the individual level (8:23), so Christ's death, resurrection, and exaltation is the first installment and guarantee of the fulfillment of God's creative purpose at the salvation-historical and cosmic level.

33 In a manner reminiscent of (Second) Isaiah, in whom the tension between exultant hope and harsh reality is equally poignant, Paul evokes a picture of the heavenly court (with Isa 50:8 providing a close echo). It need not be the final judgment only which is in view, since, as in Second Isaiah, the heavenly court can be regarded as in continual session as it were, the court to which appeal can be made against the judgments of men at any time. Though since Paul's perspective has already enlarged to include creation as a whole (vv 19ff.) and the whole sweep of time (vv 29–30), the finality of the court's judgment is certainly in view. Like a court officer seeking out witnesses for the prosecution, Paul challenges the whole galaxy of created beings of all ages: "Who will bring a charge against God's elect?" The question is loaded, of course. For "the elect of God" are those chosen by God. As in vv 29–30, the fact that the initiative in heavenly vindication lies wholly with God is stressed. By taking over the thought of divine election, so fundamental to Israel's self-identity, Paul implies that those he is addressing stand in full continuity with and completion of God's purpose for Israel. But that is not his primary concern at this point; he merely provides a half-conscious pointer toward the next phase of the argument (chaps. 9–11). What is at stake here in any accusation against God's elect is the continuity and completion of God's purpose from the beginning of time.

The answer then is inevitably, "No one!" For the verdict of acquittal is God's vindication of his own purpose in creating man in the beginning. In these three words, "God who justifies," Paul sums up so much of what he has been trying to say throughout. That the righteousness God looks for is simply man's acceptance of and living out his creatureliness before the creator, sustained by God, and that the final acquittal will be God's perfecting his creative and redemptive purpose in man, with the corollary that it is impossible to reduce "justification" to a one-tense doctrine. More important, it is *God* who justifies, where the decisive factor has nothing to do with works of law but turns completely on the two ringing declarations of vv 31 and 32—God for us, as proved and given effect by the handing over of his son—with the corollary that only in and through Christ is God's original and final purpose fulfilled.

34 The implicit train of thought becomes explicit in the further question and answer. Who is to condemn? the Satan, or any other of the hostile angelic

or spiritual forces who have chosen to stand out against God? No! The verdict
of acquittal or condemnation lies wholly with God alone. God's commitment
to his own in Christ is how his acquittal comes to effect. How that happens
on the earthly plane Paul has already indicated clearly enough in chaps.
6–8. Here in the conclusion he envisages the heavenly counterpart to that
life-death, Spirit-flesh struggle on earth—viz., the risen Christ interceding
effectively (it is implied) for his own.

Even though he runs the risk of confusing his imagery (not for the first
time), Paul follows through the courtroom metaphor: the Judge's "right-hand
man" is on our side, a more powerful, and more favored advocate than *any*
who might plead against him. Here Paul takes up, unusually for him, the
idea of Jesus as heavenly intercessor, perhaps again echoing an already familiar
Christian formula. The idea was popular elsewhere in earliest Christian faith,
and had obviously been adapted from the older Jewish belief in the role of
archangels as heavenly intercessors. Paul's point would then be that the decisive
factor for believers is Christ's exaltation to a position of special favor and
authority beside God (his right hand—Ps 110:1), above that of any (other)
angelic being (including the Satan). The success of his advocacy over that of
any challenge is assured, since his resurrection and exaltation to God's right
hand was God's own doing, the mark of God's own authorization and approval
of those he represents.

Quite how Paul intended the different strands of thought in vv 31–32
and 33–34 to hang together is not clear. If he meant the extended metaphor
of the courtroom to be understood in close continuity from vv 31–32, the
implication would be that the risen Christ pleads his sacrificial death before
the Judge on behalf of those who have died with him. And this conjunction
of sacrifice and intercessor in one person may have been already well enough
established in Christian thought for Paul simply to leave the idea merely
juxtaposed rather than integrated (cf. Heb 7:25; 1 John 2:1–2). It may, however, be significant that he places some emphasis on Christ's resurrection
and exaltation—"who died, but still more was raised . . ."—by which Paul
may indicate that he was consciously operating with a different metaphor
where it was Christ's resurrection and exaltation rather than his death which
mattered. Either way it would probably be a mistake to boil down the range
of Paul's imagery into a single theological statement, as though logical consistency was a higher prize to be grasped than the richness of diverse evocative
metaphors.

35 Paul is convinced, moreover, that Christ's role in heaven is not merely
as representative of his people on earth before the eternal Judge. He is also
able to reach out and sustain his people still on earth. His love enfolds them
as a power which hostile and untoward circumstances cannot disrupt or prevent. For Paul, of course, Christ's love is nothing other than God's love (v
39). The exalted Christ no less than Christ handed over to death is "God
for us" (v 31). This uniquely mediatorial role, representing man to God and
God to man, within a monotheistic faith, has only incomplete parallels within
the Judaism of Paul's day (Wisdom as God's representative, angelic intercession, an exalted saint like Enoch). That Paul could speak thus of an older
contemporary, crucified only 25 years or so previously, is a further reminder

of the revolutionary impact of the Christ event on Paul and the first Jewish-Christians. And since Christ's love is the love of the Creator, even the worst that can happen within creation and to man embodied therein holds no terrors for the believer—neither the final death throes of this age, nor the situations of distress where every exit seems blocked, nor the fierce persecution to which Paul was no stranger, nor the cruelly recurring phases known to every community when food supplies and personal resources fail completely, nor the daily risks which lurked round every corner even under the Pax Romana, nor the final sword thrust of bandit or enemy soldier or executioner. As Christ himself passed through such suffering to the bitterest end and beyond, so his love reaches back to those still enmeshed within these tribulations, able to sustain them and bring them through to where he is.

36 Paul underscores the thought of the suffering of this age by citing a passage (Ps 44:22) that quite probably had already been used of martyrs and of the persecuted righteous. In times of great natural or humanly contrived disasters, the affliction can become so sustained and all-oppressive that there seems no end to it ("all the day") and death an everyday commonplace ("as sheep for slaughter"). Even so, Paul implies, can the strain of "the thousand natural shocks that flesh is heir to" be added to the groaning of the man who belongs to Christ and who seeks still to walk by the Spirit through it all. The eschatological tension remains to the last breath of this mortal body.

37 Yet Paul does not allow this last reminder of the all too human condition of the believer to throw the reader back into the somber mood of 7:21–25. For the theme is now that God's commitment to his own outlasts all that, his righteousness sustains through it and eventuates in final vindication, Christ's love enables the believer to transcend it even when toiling in the thick of it. In all these eventualities and circumstances, even in the midst of them (and Paul knew all about that), Paul and his readers were conscious of a love which enabled them to rise above and triumph over them all. The use of the heightened form of the verb marks the swelling note of a supreme confidence that in the last analysis God's love outweighs and is more than a match for the worst that can happen. The life of the Spirit, though under perpetual threat from the believer's own attractedness to the life of the flesh, need fear nothing from merely outward circumstances, however horrendous. The minor key of 7:24–25 is still part of the symphony's final movement (8:36), but this last transition from minor to major in the majestic chords of the finale (vv 36–37), makes the assurance of triumph all the more moving and convincing. The use of the past tense ("him who loved us") is presumably meant to take the reader back once again to the cross: it is the fact that Christ shared these "thousand natural shocks" to their final expression and overcame the last enemy, death, in glorious resurrection, which provides believers again and again with the base point of their confidence, the one firm ground when all else trembles and quakes and collapses in ruin.

38–39 Then ringing above even the crescendo of the final chorus comes the voice of the soloist once more in the soaring note of faith. Paul evidently felt the need to reach beyond the formulas and corporate utterances to state his faith in God in Christ as something intensely personal, as a matter of deepest personal conviction. The sweep of his faith is truly majestic. No longer simply situations of stress and suffering within life, but the boundary situations of life and beyond life, the powers that determine eternal destiny, all fall under his gaze, with no different result: *nothing* can loose the embrace of God's love in Christ. "Neither death"—he chooses this word first to recall and sum up all his argumentation and exhortation of the last three chapters: for those in Christ, who share Christ's death, their own dying holds no fears. "Nor life"—not now the tribulations of this life (v 35), but life itself, somewhat surprisingly now posed as a possible threat (instead of the usual contrast between life and death), but presumably because life in this age constitutes something of a threat so long as sin rules in the flesh. "Nor angels, nor rulers, . . . nor powers"—Paul uses terms which would embrace the complete range of spiritual forces, however conceived—good or evil, every possibility and eventuality is included (as with death and life). What Paul actually believed about heavenly beings and their power over events and individuals on earth is never clear; the existential realities about which he was most concerned were primarily sin and death. His concern here, however, is pastoral rather than speculative: whatever names his readers give to the nameless forces which threaten the Creator's work and purpose, they are in the end impotent before him who is God over all. "Nor things present nor things to come"— Paul is conscious of the fourth dimension as well, time itself, and the inexorable march of temporal processes of change and decay; however fearful they may be to those caught within time, they are of ephemeral moment to him who is from the beginning, is now and will be in the end, Creator, Sustainer, and Judge.

"Neither height nor depth"—Paul deliberately draws on current astronomical terms to denote the full sweep of the heavens visible and invisible to the human eye, and thus all astrological powers known and unknown which could be thought to determine and control the fate and destiny of human beings. Whatever force they might bring to bear on believers, and again Paul's concern is primarily a pastoral *ad hominem,* the love of God is greater still. "Nor any other creature"—lest any thing or power within reality could be said to have been omitted from the above list, Paul rounds it off with an all-embracing addendum. Since God alone is Creator and since God is one, "any other creature" means "every thing else." Nothing, but nothing, can separate from "God's love in Christ Jesus our Lord." In this mystery—God for us in Christ, Jesus the crucified as Lord—lies the heart of Paul's assurance. This towering confidence rests foursquare on Christ, on God's commitment to his own in Christ and on their commitment to this Christ as Lord, master and determiner of all. With this much said, no more need be said, and both chorus and soloist fall silent.